Lecture Notes in Computer Science 9117

Commenced Publication in 1973
Founding and Former Series Editors:
Gerhard Goos, Juris Hartmanis, and Jan van Leeuwen

Roberto Paredes · Jaime S. Cardoso
Xosé M. Pardo (Eds.)

Pattern Recognition and Image Analysis

7th Iberian Conference, IbPRIA 2015
Santiago de Compostela, Spain, June 17–19, 2015
Proceedings

Editors
Roberto Paredes
Universitat Politècnica de València
València
Spain

Xosé M. Pardo
Universidade de Santiago de Compostela
Santiago de Compostela
Spain

Jaime S. Cardoso
Universidade do Porto
Porto
Portugal

ISSN 0302-9743   ISSN 1611-3349 (electronic)
Lecture Notes in Computer Science
ISBN 978-3-319-19389-2   ISBN 978-3-319-19390-8 (eBook)
DOI 10.1007/978-3-319-19390-8

Library of Congress Control Number: 2015939810

LNCS Sublibrary: SL6 – Image Processing, Computer Vision, Pattern Recognition, and Graphics

Springer International Publishing AG Switzerland is part of Springer Science+Business Media
(www.springer.com)

Preface

It is our pleasure to present the proceedings of the 7th Iberian Conference on Pattern Recognition and Image Analysis, IbPRIA 2015. The conference was held in Santiago de Compostela, Spain, following in the footsteps of previous successful meetings in Andraxt (2003), Estoril (2005), Girona (2007), Póvoa de Varzim (2009), Las Palmas de Gran Canaria (2011), and Madeira (2013).

IbPRIA is an international conference co-organized every two years by the Portuguese (APRP - Associação Portuguesa de Reconhecimento de Padrões) and Spanish (AERFAI - Asociación Española de Reconocimiento de Formas y Análisis de Imágenes) chapters of the IAPR International Association for Pattern Recognition. IbPRIA is a single-track conference consisting of high-quality, previously unpublished papers, presented either orally or as a poster, intended to act as a forum for research groups, engineers, and practitioners to present recent results, algorithmic improvements, and promising future directions in pattern recognition and image analysis.

This year's IbPRIA was held during June 17–19, 2015, in Santiago de Compostela, Spain and was hosted by the University of Santiago de Compostela, with the support of CITIUS (Centro Singular de Investigación en Tecnoloxías da Información).

There was a very positive response to the Call for Papers for IbPRIA 2015. We received 141 full papers from 36 countries and 83 were accepted (35 as oral and 48 as poster) for presentation at the conference, where each paper was reviewed by at least two reviewers. The high quality of the scientific program of IbPRIA 2015 was due first to the authors who submitted excellent contributions and second to the dedicated collaboration of the international Program Committee and the other researchers who reviewed the papers. We would like to thank all the authors for submitting their contributions and for sharing their research activities. We are particularly indebted to the Program Committee members and to all the reviewers for their precious evaluations, which permitted us to produce this publication.

We were also very pleased to benefit from the participation of the invited speakers Raquel Urtasun, University of Toronto, Jesús Malo, Universitat de València, and Professor Daniel Cremers, Technical University of Munich. We would like to express our sincere gratitude to these world-renowned experts.

The work of the seven co-chairs was also very valuable. Furthermore, we are also grateful to all members of the local Organizing Committee. Their work was essential to the success of IbPRIA 2015.

Finally, we look forward to meeting you at the next edition of IbPRIA, in Portugal in 2017.

April 2015

Roberto Paredes
Jaime S. Cardoso
Xosé M. Pardo

Organization

General Chairs

General Co-chair AERFAI:

Roberto Paredes   Universidad Politécnica de Valencia, Spain

General Co-chair APRP:

Jaime S. Cardoso   Faculdade de Engenharia da Universidade do Porto (FEUP), Portugal

Local Chair

Xose M. Pardo   Universidade de Santiago de Compostela, Spain

Local Organizing Committee

Maria J. Carreira   Universidade de Santiago de Compostela, Spain
Xose R. Fdez-Vidal   Universidade de Santiago de Compostela, Spain
Roberto Iglesias   Universidade de Santiago de Compostela, Spain
David L. Vilariño   Universidade de Santiago de Compostela, Spain
Pablo G. Tahoces   Universidade de Santiago de Compostela, Spain
David Vazquez   CVC, Universitat Autònoma de Barcelona, Spain

Tutorial Chairs

Luis Alexandre   Universidade da Beira Interior, Portugal
Maria Vanrell   CVC Campus UAB, Spain

Workshop Chairs

João M. Sanches   Instituto Superior Técnico Lisboa, Portugal
Joan Martí   Universitat de Girona, Spain

Contest Chairs

Luis F. Teixeira   Universidade do Porto, Portugal
Carlos Orrite   Universidade de Zaragoza, Spain

Program Committee

Ajay Kumar	The Hong Kong Polytechnic University, Hong Kong, SAR China
Alexandre Xavier Falcão	University of Campinas, Brazil
Ana Maria Mendonça	Faculty of Engineering of University of Porto, Portugal
António J.R. Neves	University of Aveiro, Portugal
Bernardete Ribeiro	Universidade de Coimbra, Portugal
Colin de la Higuera	Nantes University, France
Constantine Kotropoulos	University of Thessaloniki, Greece
Costantino Grana	Univertità degli studi di Modena e Reggio Emilia, Italy
Edwin Hancock	University of York, UK
Enrique Vidal	Universidad Politécnica de Valencia, Spain
Filiberto Pla	Universitat Jaume I, Spain
Francisco Casacuerta	Universidad Politécnica de Valencia, Spain
Gilson A. Giraldi	National Laboratory for Scientific Computing, Brazil
Giorgio Giacinto	Università degli Studi di Cagliari, Italy
Gustavo Carneiro	University of Adelaide, Australia
Henning Müller	University of Applied Sciences Western Switzerland, Switzerland
Hermann Ney	RWTH Aachen, Germany
Jorge S. Marques	Universidade Tecnica de Lisboa, Portugal
Jose Luis Alba	Universidad de Vigo, Spain
João M. Sanches	Universidade Tecnica de Lisboa, Portugal
Luis Alexandre	Universidade da Beira Interior, Portugal
Manuel Montes	INAOEP, Mexico
Marcello Pelillo	University of Venice, Italy
Margarita Chli	University of Edinburgh, UK
Margarita Kotti	Imperial College London, UK
Max Viergever	University of Utrecht, The Netherlands
Nicolas Perez de la Blanca	Universidad de Granada, Spain
Nicu Sebe	University of Trento, Italy
Paolo Rosso	Universidad Politécnica de Valencia, Spain
Petra Perner	Institute of Computer Vision and Applied Computer Sciences, Germany
Ricardo Torres	University of Campinas, Brazil

Contents

Image and Signal Processing

Image and Signal Processing

Applications

Oral Sessions: Pattern Recognition and Machine Learning

Spatiotemporal Stacked Sequential Learning for Pedestrian Detection

Alejandro González[1,2]([✉]), David Vázquez[1,2], Sebastian Ramos[2],
Antonio M. López[1,2], and Jaume Amores[3]

[1] Autonomus University of Barcelona, Barcelona, Spain
[2] Computer Vision Center, Barcelona, Spain
{agalzate,dvazquez,sramosp,antonio}@cvc.uab.es
[3] United Technologies Research Center, Cork, Ireland
AmoresJ@utrc.utc.com

Abstract. Pedestrian classifiers decide which image windows contain
a pedestrian. In practice, such classifiers provide a relatively high response at neighbor windows overlapping a pedestrian, while the responses
around potential false positives are expected to be lower. An analogous
reasoning applies for image sequences. If there is a pedestrian located
within a frame, the same pedestrian is expected to appear close to the
same location in neighbor frames. Therefore, such a location has chances
of receiving high classification scores during several frames, while false
positives are expected to be more spurious. In this paper we propose to
exploit such correlations for improving the accuracy of base pedestrian
classifiers. In particular, we propose to use two-stage classifiers which
not only rely on the image descriptors required by the base classifiers
but also on the response of such base classifiers in a given spatiotemporal neighborhood. More specifically, we train pedestrian classifiers using
a stacked sequential learning (SSL) paradigm. We use a new pedestrian
dataset we have acquired from a car to evaluate our proposal at different
frame rates. We also test on well known dataset, Caltech. The obtained
results show that our SSL proposal boosts detection accuracy significantly with a minimal impact on the computational cost. Interestingly,
SSL improves more the accuracy at the most dangerous situations, *i.e.*
when a pedestrian is close to the camera.

1 Introduction

Localizing humans in images is key for applications such as video surveillance,
avoiding pedestrian-to-vehicle collisions, etc. Developing a reliable vision-based
pedestrian detector is a very challenging task with more than a decade of history by now. As a result, a plethora of features, models, and learning algorithms, have been proposed to develop the pedestrian classifiers which are at
the core of pedestrian detectors [10]. The research for boosting the accuracy of
pedestrian classifiers has followed different lines. Some authors have researched
image descriptors well-suited for pedestrians (*e.g.*, HOG [4], HOG+LBP [21],

© Springer International Publishing Switzerland 2015
R. Paredes et al. (Eds.): IbPRIA 2015, LNCS 9117, pp. 3–12, 2015.
DOI: 10.1007/978-3-319-19390-8_1

Haar+EOH [11], others have researched different image modalities (*e.g.*, appearance+depth+motion [8,22]), others have focused on the pedestrian model (*e.g.*, DPM [9,14,17]. The outcome of each of the above mentioned proposals is a pedestrian classifier, termed here as *base classifier*, which provides a relatively high response at neighbor windows overlapping a pedestrian. In fact, non-maximum suppression (NMS) is usually performed as last detection stage in order to merge overlapped detections to a single one. An analogous reasoning applies for image sequences. If there is a pedestrian located within a frame, the same pedestrian is expected to appear close to the same location in neighbor frames, while false positives are expected to be more spurious. In fact, this may allow removing such undesired spurious by the use of a tracker. In this paper we propose to exploit such expected *response correlations* for improving the accuracy of the classification stage itself. We propose to use a two-stage classification strategy which not only rely on the image descriptors required by the base classifiers, but also on the response of the own base classifiers in a given spatiotemporal neighborhood. More specifically, we train pedestrian classifiers using a stacked sequential learning (SSL) paradigm [2].

Temporal SSL involves the analysis of window volumes, these volumes may change depending on the application, the target conditions and camera movement. In this paper, we are specially interested in on-board pedestrian detection within urban scenarios. Therefore, camera and targets are in movement. Accordingly, in this paper we test our SSL approach for a fixed neighborhood (*i.e.*, fixed spatial window coordinates across frames) and for an scheme relying on an egomotion compensation approximation (*i.e.*, varying spatial window coordinates across frames). Moreover, in order to assess the dependency of the results with respect to the frame rate, we acquired our own pedestrian dataset at 30 fps by normal driving in an urban scenario. This new dataset is used as main guide for our experiments, but we also complement our study with other challenging dataset publicly available, Caltech. In this paper we start by using a competitive baseline in pedestrian detection [7], namely a holistic base classifier based on HOG+LBP features and linear SVM. Note that HOG+LBP/linear-SVM is base of different more sophisticated detectors: deformable models (DPM) [9], occlusion handling [15,21], node experts in random forest [16] and domain adaptation [18]. Altogether, we think that HOG+LBP/linear-SVM is a proper baseline to start assessing our proposal. Moreover we have extended this baseline with the HOF [20] motion descriptor that complements the appearance and texture features of the baseline. Overall, the obtained results show that our spatiotemporal SSL proposal boosts detection accuracy significantly. Especially, when the pedestrians are close to the camera, *i.e.* in the most critical situations. Therefore, encouraging to augment the study for other pedestrian base classifiers as well as other object categories.

The rest of the paper is organized as follows. In Sect. 2 we review some works related to our proposal. Section 3 briefly introduces the SSL. In Sect. 4 we develop our proposal. Section 5 presents the experiments carried out to assess our spatiotemporal SSL, and discuss the obtained results. Finally, Sect. 6 draws our main conclusions.

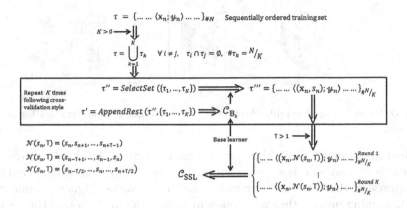

Fig. 1. SSL learning. See main text in Sect. 3 for details.

2 Related Work

The use of motion patterns as image descriptors was already proposed as an extension of spatial Haar-like filters for video surveillance applications [3,12,19] and for detecting human visual events [13]. In these cases, original spatial Haar-like filters were extended with a temporal dimension. Popular HOG descriptor was also extended using optical flow [5,20]. In all cases motion information was complemented with appearance information (*i.e.*, Haar/HOG for luminance and/or color channels). In contrast with these approaches, our proposal does not involve to compute new temporal image descriptors as new features for the classification process. As we will see, we use the responses of a given base classifier in neighbor frames as new features for our SSL classifier. In fact, our proposal can also be applied to base classifiers that already incorporate motion features. Therefore, the reviewed literature and our proposal are complementary strategies. Focusing on single frames, it has been recently shown how pedestrian detection accuracy can be boosted by analyzing the image area surrounding potential pedestrian detections. In particular, [1,6] follow an iterative process that uses contextual features of several orders for progressively enhancing the response for true pedestrians and lowering it for hallucinatory ones. Our SSL proposal does not require new image descriptors and is not iterative, which makes it inherently faster. Moreover, we treat equally spatial and temporal response correlations.

Finally, we would like to clarify that our SSL proposal is not a substitute for NMS and tracking post-classification stages. What we expect is to allow these stages to produce more accurate results by increasing the accuracy of the classification stage.

3 Stacked Sequential Learning (SSL)

Stacked sequential learning (SSL) was introduced by Cohen *et al.* [2] with the aim of improving base classifiers when the data to be processed has some sort

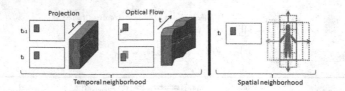

Fig. 2. Different types of neighborhood for SSL. See main text in Sect. 4.1 for details.

of sequential order. In particular, given a data sample to be classified, the core intuition is to consider not only the features describing the sample but also the response of the base classifier in its neighbor samples. Figure 1 summarizes the SSL learning process that we explain in more detail in the rest of this section.

Let τ be an ordered training sequence of cardinality N. The SSL approach involves to select a sub-sequence for training a base classifier, $\mathscr{C}_B$, and the rest to apply $\mathscr{C}_B$ and so training the SSL classifier, $\mathscr{C}_{SSL}$. If this is done once, then the final classifier $\mathscr{C}_{SSL}$ would be trained with less than N samples. Thus, to avoid this, it is followed a cross-validation style were τ is divided in $K > 0$ disjoint sub-sequences, $\tau = \cup_{k=1}^{K} \tau_k \wedge i \neq j \Rightarrow \tau_i \cap \tau_j = \emptyset$, and K rounds are performed by using a different subset each round to test the $\mathscr{C}_{B_k}$ and the rest of sub-sets for training this $\mathscr{C}_{B_k}$. At the end of the process, joining the K sub-sequences processed by the corresponding $\mathscr{C}_{B_k}$, we can have N *augmented* training samples for learning $\mathscr{C}_{SSL}$. $k = 1$ means to train the C_B and C_{SSL} on the same training set, without actually doing partitions.

Let us explain what means *augmented* training samples. The elements of τ, *i.e.*, the initial training samples, are of the form $< \mathbf{x_n}; y_n >$, where $\mathbf{x_n}$ is a vector of features with label y_n. Therefore, the elements of each sub-sequence τ_k are of the same form. As we have mentioned before, during each round k of the process, a sub-sequence τ'' is selected among $\{\tau_1, \ldots, \tau_K\}$, while the rest are appended together to form a sub-sequence τ'. From τ' it is learned $\mathscr{C}_{B_k}$ and applied to τ'' to obtain a new τ'''. The elements of τ''' are of the form $< (\mathbf{x_n}, s_n); y_n >$, where we have augmented the feature $\mathbf{x_n}$ with the classifier score $s_n = \mathscr{C}_{B_k}(\mathbf{x_n})$. Therefore, after the K rounds, we have a training set of N samples of the form $< (\mathbf{x_n}, s_n); y_n >$. It is at this point when we can introduce the concept of neighbor scores into the learning process. In particular, the final training samples are of the form $< (\mathbf{x_n}, \mathscr{N}(s_n, T)); y_n >$, where $\mathscr{N}(s_n, T)$ denotes a neighborhood of size $T > 1$ anchored to the sample n.

4   SSL for Pedestrian Detection

In this section, without loosing generality, we will assume the use of the *past neighborhood* (Sect. 3) to illustrate and explain our SSL approach (use previous images to do detection in the current one). Actually there is no need to save the previous images, saving the already computed scores is enough to compute the current SSL descriptor making the computation of SSL very computational efficient.

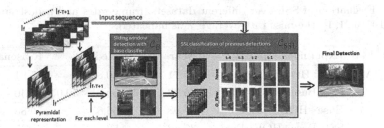

Fig. 3. Two-stage pedestrian detection based on SSL. See main text in Sect. 4.3 for details.

4.1   Spatiotemporal Neighborhoods for SSL

For object detection in general and for pedestrian detection in particular, applying SSL starts by defining which are the neighbors of a given window under analysis. In learning time, such a window will correspond either to the bounding box of a labeled pedestrian or to a rectangular chunk of the background. In operation time (*i.e.*, testing), such a window will correspond to a candidate generated by a pyramidal sliding window scheme or any other candidate selection method. In this paper we assume the processing of image sequences and, consequently, we propose the use of a spatiotemporal neighborhood.

Temporal SSL involves the analysis of window volumes. Therefore, there are several possibilities to consider (see Fig. 2). Let us term as W_f the set of coordinates defining an image window in frame f, and $\mathbf{V}_f = \mathrm{vol}(\cup_{l=0}^{T-1} W_{f-t})$ the window volume defined by a temporal neighbor of T frames. The simplest volume is obtained by assuming fixed locations across frames, which we term as *projection* approach. In other words, $W_f = W_{f-1} = \ldots = W_{f-(T-1)}$. Another possibility consists in building volumes taking into account motion information. For instance, $W_f = W_{f-1} + t_{OF(W_{f-1})}$, where $t_{OF(W_{f-1})}$ is a 2D translation defined by considering the *optical flow* contained in W_{f-1}, and $'+'$ stands for summation to all coordinates defining W_{f-1}.

Spatial SSL involves the analysis of windows spatially overlapping the window of interest (see Fig. 2). For instance, we can fix a 2D displacement $\Delta = (\delta_x, \delta_y)$ and n_x displacements in the x axis, to the left and to the right, an analogously for the y axis given a n_y number of up and down displacements.

Our proposal combines both ideas, the temporal volumes and the spatial overlapping windows, in order to define the spatiotemporal neighborhood required by SSL (Sect. 3).

4.2   SSL Training

As usual, we assume an image sequence with labeled pedestrians (*i.e.*, using bounding boxes) for training. Negative samples for training are obtained by random sampling of the same images, of course, these samples cannot highly overlap labeled pedestrians. The cross-validation-style rounds of SSL (Sect. 3)

Table 1. Evaluation of SSL over different datasets, frame rates and pedestrian sizes. For FPPI $\in [0.01, 1]$, the miss rate average % is indicated.

Dataset	FPS	Experiment	Near	Medium	Reasonable
CVC08	Any	Base: HOG+LBP	39.71	50.83	45.91
	3	SSL(Base) Proj. - OptFl.	36.03 - 36.72	50.01 - 50.04	44.40 - 44.02
		Base+HOF	47.98	56.65	50.88
		SSL(Base+HOF) Proj.	37.62	52.21	45.47
	10	SSL(Base) Proj. - OptFl.	35.49 - 34.79	50.22 - 49.42	43.56 - 42.10
		Base+HOF	39.24	52.37	42.43
		SSL(Base+HOF) Proj.	29.42	44.62	37.13
	30	SSL(Base) Proj. - OptFl.	34.18 - 34.01	49.84 - 48.04	42.90 - 41.73
		Base+HOF	37.81	53.39	38.78
		SSL(Base+HOF) Proj.	27.37	46.53	35.85
Caltech	25	Base	45.4	82.3	59.4
		SSL(Base) Proj. - OptFl.	40.6 - 38.9	81.2 - 80.4	59.4 - 57.6
		Base+HOF	33.8	78.4	52.9
		SSL(Base+HOF) Proj	32.0	77.1	51.6

are performer with respect to the images of the sequence, not with respected to the set of labeled pedestrians and negative samples as it may suggest the straightforward application of SSL (note that pedestrian/negative labels are for individual windows not for full images). Moreover, as we have seen in Sect. 4.1, the neighborhood relationship is not only temporal but spatial too. The training process is divided in two stages. First, we train the auxiliary classifiers ($\mathscr{C}_{B_k}$) as usual using three bootstraping rounds. Then we train the SSL classifier (using final $\mathscr{C}_{B_k}$ as auxiliary), again we run three bootstrapping rounds for obtaining the final classifier ($\mathscr{C}_{SSL}$). Using the full training dataset, we also assume the training of a base classifier $\mathscr{C}_B$. Another possibility is to understand the different $\mathscr{C}_{B_k}$ as the result of a bagging procedure and ensemble them to obtain $\mathscr{C}_B$. Without loosing generality, in this paper we have focused on the former approach.

4.3   SSL Detector

The proposed pedestrian detection pipeline is shown in Fig. 3. As we can see there are two main stages. The first stage basically consists in a classical pedestrian detection method relying on the learned base classifier $\mathscr{C}_B$. In Fig. 3 we have illustrated the idea for a pyramidal sliding window approach, but using other candidate selection approaches is also possible. Detections at this stage are just considered as potential ones. Then, the second stage applies the spatiotemporal SSL classifier, $\mathscr{C}_{SSL}$, to such potential detections in order to reject or keep them as final detections.

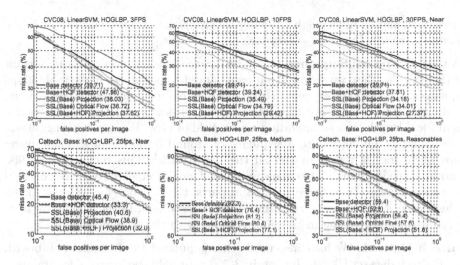

Fig. 4. Results for CVC08 and Caltech datasets. At the top row there are the 30 fps, 10 fps and 3 fps cases of CVC08 using the *near* testing subset. The last two cases are obtained by sub-sampling the video sequence, but always keeping the same training and testing pedestrians. At the bottom row there are the experiments over the *near*, *medium* and *reasonable* testing of Caltech dataset.

There are some details worth to mention. First, the usual non-maximum suppression (NMS) is only done for the output of the second stage. Second, for ensuring that true pedestrians reach the second stage, we apply a threshold on $\mathscr{C}_B$ such that it guarantees a very high detection rate even having a very high rate of false positives. In our experiments this usually implies that while the $\mathscr{C}_B$ processes hundred of thousands windows (for pyramidal sliding window), $\mathscr{C}_{SSL}$ only process a few thousands. Third, although in Fig. 3 we show pyramids of images for a temporal neighborhood of T frames, what we actually keep from frame to frame are the already computed features, so that we compute them only once. However, this depends on the type of temporal neighborhood we use (Sect. 4.1). For instance, using projection style no feature are needed to keep (*i.e.*, keeping the classification scores is enough). However, if we use optical flow we may need to compute features in previous frames if the window under consideration does not map to a location where they were already computed.

5 Experimental Results

Protocol. As evaluation methodology we follow the de-facto Caltech standard for pedestrian detection [7], *i.e.*, we plot curves of false positives per image (FPPI) *vs* miss rate. The miss rate average in the range of 10^{-2} to 10^0 FPPI is taken as indicative of each detector accuracy, *i.e.*, the lower the better. Moreover, during testing we consider three different subset: *Near* subset include pedestrians with height equal or higher than 75 pixels, *medium* subset include pedestrian between 50 and 75 pixel height. Finally we group the two previous subset in the *reasonable* subset (height $>= 50$ pixels).

CVC08 On-board Sequence (CVC08). Since the temporal axis is important for the SSL classifier, we acquired our own dataset to be sure we have stable 30 fps sequences. The sequences were acquired on-board under normal urban driving conditions. The images are monochrome and of 480×960 pixels. We used a 4 mm focal length lens, so providing a wide field of view. We drove during 30 min approximately, giving rise to a sequence of around 60,000 frames. Then, using steps of 10 frames we annotated all the pedestrians[1]. This turns out in 7,900 annotated pedestrians, 5,400 reasonable and non occluded. We have divided the video sequence into three sequential parts, the first one for training (3,600 pedestrians), the last one for testing (1300 pedestrians), in the middle we have leaved a gap for avoiding testing and training with the same persons.

Caltech Dataset. We have also used other popular dataset acquired on-board. The Caltech dataset [7], which contain 3,700 reasonable pedestrians for training. It is worth to mention that the images were acquired at 25 fps.

Base Detectors. For the experiments presented in this section we use our own implementation of HOG and LBP features, using TV-L1 [23] for computing optical flow, we obtain HOF features [20] as well. We call Base to the HOG+LBP/ Linear-SVM and Base+HOF to the HOG+LBP+HOF/Linear-SVM.

Experiments. Experiments are based on the ST-SSL with $(\Delta x, \Delta y, \Delta f) = (3, 3, 5)$. In preliminary experiments we tested several values of K (Fig. 1), obtaining very similar results, thus we set $K = 1$ for speed up the training. In Table 1 we show the results for the SSL experiments. As baseline detectors we use the Base and Base+HOF. The experiments are run over the different datasets, and frame rates (CVC08). We tested them for different ranges of pedestrian sizes. We observe significant accuracy improvements for all the tested datasets comparing the baseline detector and its SSL counterpart. For instance, in CVC08 near with SSL(Base+HOF) we obtain an accuracy improvement of ten points approximately. Also, significant accuracy improvements are obtained for all the tested frame rates (30 fps, 10 fps, 3 fps) of CVC08 dataset. Besides, we observe an improvement due to the optical flow in the volume generation at high frame rates. However, no significant difference is observed at low frame rates. The SSL accuracy improvement is more clear for the near pedestrians. In Fig. 4 we plot the accuracy curves obtained for some representative experiments.

Discussion. SSL approach outperforms its baseline in almost all the tested configurations. However, the improvement is more clear for near pedestrians at high frame rates. If we generate the *past neighborhood* over the far away pedestrians, we should expect a *past neighborhood* with pedestrians smaller than the minimum pedestrian size that the base detector can detect. That is why the SSL improvement is not so clear for the medium subset. However, in near pedestrians *past neighborhood* is more probable to find a history of confident responses. This is a

---

[1] Publicly available in: http://www.cvc.uab.es/adas/site/?q=node/7.

very relevant improvement since for close pedestrians the detection system has less time to take decisions like braking or doing any other manoeuvre. Regarding the neighborhood generation approaches, the optical flow slightly improves the projection one as it captures the movement of the pedestrians in the temporal neighborhood.

6   Conclusion

In this paper we have presented a new method for improving pedestrian detection based on spatiotemporal SSL. We have shown how even simple projection windows can boost the detection accuracy in different datasets acquired on-board. We have shown that our approach is effective for different frame rates. In this paper we have focused on HOG+LBP/Linear-SVM and HOG+LBP+HOF/ Linear-SVM pedestrian base classifiers, thus, our immediate future work will focus on testing the same approach for other base classifiers of the pedestrian detection state-of-the-art. Regarding the improvement obtained using optical flow neighborhood, we want to further explore different approaches for dealing with the neighborhood generation for moving pedestrians.

Acknowledgments. This work is supported by the Spanish MICINN projects TRA2011-29454-C03-01 and TIN2011-29494-C03-02.

References

1. Chen, G., Ding, Y., Xiao, J., Han, T.: Detection evolution with multi-order contextual co-occurrence. In: CVPR, Portland, Oregon, USA (2013)
2. Cohen, W., de Carvalho, V.: Stacked sequential learning. In: IJCAI, Scotland (2005)
3. Cui, X., Liu, Y., Shan, S., Chen, X., Gao, W.: 3d Haar-like features for pedestrian detection. In: ICME, Bejing, China (2007)
4. Dalal, N., Triggs, B.: Histograms of oriented gradients for human detection. In: CVPR, San Diego, CA, USA (2005)
5. Dalal, N., Triggs, B., Schmid, C.: Human detection using oriented histograms of flow and appearance. In: Leonardis, A., Bischof, H., Pinz, A. (eds.) ECCV 2006. LNCS, vol. 3952, pp. 428–441. Springer, Heidelberg (2006)
6. Ding, Y., Xiao, J.: Contextual boost for pedestrian detection. In: CVPR, USA (2012)
7. Dollár, P., Wojek, C., Schiele, B., Perona, P.: Pedestrian detection: an evaluation of the state of the art. T-PAMI **34**(4), 743–761 (2012)
8. Enzweiler, M., Gavrila, D.M.: A multi-level mixture-of-experts framework for pedestrian classification. T-IP **20**(10), 2967–2979 (2011)
9. Felzenszwalb, P., Girshick, R., McAllester, D., Ramanan, D.: Object detection with discriminatively trained part based models. T-PAMI **32**(9), 1627–1645 (2010)
10. Gerónimo, D., López, A.: Vision-Based Pedestrian Protection Systems for Intelligent Vehicles. Springer, New York (2013)
11. Gerónimo, D., Sappa, A., Ponsa, D., López, A.: 2D-3D based on-board pedestrian detection system. CVIU **114**(5), 583–595 (2010)

12. Jones, M., Snow, D.: Pedestrian detection using boosted features over many frames. In: CVPR, Anchorage, AK, USA (2008)
13. Ke, Y., Sukthankar, R., Hebert, M.: Efficient visual event detection using volumetric features. In: ICCV, Beijing, China (2005)
14. Lafferty, J., McCallum, A., Pereira, F.: Real-time pedestrian detection with deformable part models. In: IV, Madrid, Spain (2012)
15. Marin, J., Vázquez, D., López, A., Amores, J., Kuncheva, L.: Occlusion handling via random subspace classifiers for human detection. Cyber (2013)
16. Marin, J., Vázquez, D., López, A., Amores, J., Leibe, B.: Random forests of local experts for pedestrian detection. In: ICCV, Sydney, Australia (2013)
17. Ramanan, D.: Part-based models for finding people and estimating their pose (2009)
18. Vázquez, D., López, A., Marín, J., Ponsa, D., Gerónimo, D.: Virtual and real world adaptation for pedestrian detection. T-PAMI 36(4), 797–809 (2013)
19. Viola, P., Jones, M., Snow, D.: Detecting pedestrians using patterns of motion and appearance. In: ICCV, Nice, France (2003)
20. Walk, S., Majer, N., Schindler, K., Schiele, B.: New features and insights for pedestrian detection. In: CVPR, San Francisco, CA, USA (2010)
21. Wang, X., Han, T.X., Yan, S.: An HOG-LBP human detector with partial occlusion handling. In: ICCV, Kyoto, Japan (2009)
22. Wojek, C., Walk, S., Schiele, B.: Multi-cue onboard pedestrian detection. In: CVPR, Miami Beach, FL, USA (2009)
23. Zach, C., Pock, T., Bischof, H.: A duality based approach for realtime TV-l1 optical flow. In: DAGM, Heidelberg, Germany (2007)

Social Signaling Descriptor for Group Behaviour Analysis

Eduardo M. Pereira[1,2](✉), Lucian Ciobanu[1], and Jaime S. Cardoso[1,2]

[1] INESC TEC, Porto, Portugal
[2] Faculty of Engineering of the University of Porto, Rua Dr. Roberto Frias, 378,
4200 - 465 Porto, Portugal
ejmp@inescporto.pt

Abstract. Group behaviour characterisation is a topic not so well studied in the video surveillance community due to its difficulty and large variety of topics involved, but mainly because the lack of valid semantic concepts that relate collective activity to social context. In this work, our proposal is three-fold: a new definition of semantic concepts for social group analysis considering environment context, a novel video surveillance dataset that conveys a sociological perspective, and a descriptor that emphasises social interactions cues within a group. Promising results were revealed in order to deal with such complex problem.

1 Introduction

Increasing research in video surveillance has been demanding the monitoring of complex human activities related to group of individuals. Such complexification has lead to higher levels of semantic abstraction that translate relational connections among people in groups. Collective structure varies depending on context, but common attention and position-based cues could be used as basis for further mid-level representations that encode relations involving social interaction between individuals within a group. Modelling collective activity within a sociological principled way has an undeniable value for both low-level problems such as pedestrian tracking, and high-level applications such as anomaly detection in security and human behaviour prediction for marketing purposes.

Assuming that the group discovery problem is solved, we focus on group behaviour characterisation. Our proposal build on trajectory data a multi-scale histogram descriptor that combines and accumulates relational position-based and attention-based features. The powerful and effectiveness of such representation was stated on our previous work [1] for the classification of individual profiles. In this work, we extend our study to a more complex problem, the analysis of collective behaviour of small groups in a very specific context, namely shopping-mall. Under the proposed descriptor we inspect the relevance of social signaling features that explore interaction among humans, a topic not so well studied in the video surveillance community.

We validate our approach on a novel video surveillance dataset entirely annotated taking in consideration social-psychological principles. We extend recent

© Springer International Publishing Switzerland 2015
R. Paredes et al. (Eds.): IbPRIA 2015, LNCS 9117, pp. 13–22, 2015.
DOI: 10.1007/978-3-319-19390-8_2

evidence on group activity, which state that individual actions guide recognition of collective activities [2], to a higher semantic perception of group behaviour within social context. Therefore, this work presents the following contributions: (i) a new definition of semantic concepts for social group analysis considering environmental context; (ii) a complete social annotation of a very rich dataset for human activity analysis to detect and classify *individual profiles (I.P.)* and *group behaviours (G.B.)*, that will be publicly released for the research community; (iii) a descriptor that identify meaningful social interactions cues within a group, and aggregates them dynamically over time through a trajectory sampling scheme to robustly discriminate among several collective behaviours.

2 Related Work

Analysing the group structure and extracting its behaviour has important practical applications and has attracted the attention of the research community in surveillance settings. Under computer vision field such problem involves many research topics such as object detection, tracking, action discovery, human-to-human and human-to-object interactions recognition. Such tasks are complex and mutually dependent. Knowing how individuals are related to each other considering space structure and social context could give us the insight of how actions and reactions define social group behaviour [3].

In the literature, collective behaviour analysis tend to fit into two types of taxonomy: the one that considers groups as a collective and homogeneous block where individual is transformed by the group, the so-called macroscopic studies [4], and the one that analyse groups as the composition of individual agents that interact with each other and with the environment, the microscopic approaches [5]. For our specific scenario, microscopic studies are more suitable but their formulation is not enough to derive social semantic behaviour. Such approaches follow different models such as social force [5], virtual agents [6], and cellular automata [7]. In particular, Chang et al. [8] adopted a probabilistic grouping strategy which accounts with a pairwise spatiotemporal measure between people. A connectivity graph was built for further segmentation of groups and derivation of individual probabilistic models. However, no object-scene relation was considered, and they did not use relational context to describe individual behaviour. Floor fields models [7] effectively aid tracking in crowd scenes, but local attractive and repulsive forces have only physical meaning. Generalisation of discrete choice models (DCM) to obtain different group structures was presented in [9] through the inclusion of relational matrices, but they just presented simulations over synthetic data without inferring any type of semantic behaviour.

The work of [2] considered the composition of a crowd by small groups and incorporated a hierarchical clustering technique based on social psychological models. Their results were correlated with a ground truth collected by two sources, namely interviews and real-time observers. To the best of our knowledge this is the closest study that brings together computer vision and sociological fields. However, they not made publicly available the dataset, and they also lack to assign semantic collective behaviour into social environment. In [10], it was demonstrated the importance of attention-based cues on video-surveillance scenario that normally were used in other domains such as meeting analysis. However, their approach accounts with many features and they did not evaluate the discriminative value and social meaning of each one. We got inspiration from both works and embed social analysis into a robust descriptor formulation.

3 Semantic Concepts and Annotation

Our aim is to add and explore semantics in group behaviours, a topic not so well explored on the literature. We look for a real-life surveillance dataset with large duration, intense activity, and high diversity of semantics in terms of individual and collective activity, in order to extend it for new human activity analysis challenges. We found the IIT (Israel Institute of Technology) dataset and grant permissions from the authors [11]. It is composed by several urban scenarios such as shopping, subway, and street. We chose the shopping-mall since its social context provides more well-defined behaviours. This scenario comprises three videos, but until this moment, due to the intensive manual labor involved, only one video is annotated (83155 frames with resolution 512×384 @25 fps).

We were advised by the lab of social-psychology of the University of Porto[1] during the annotation process. They help us to analyse and identify individual profiles and group behaviours. We follow the definition of group dynamics presented in [12] that explains the interdependence degree among individuals and their influence over the group behaviour they belong to. The complete validation of this work in the field of social-psychology would require an intense and continuous observation process of the same space. However, we validate the annotation process considering the sociological objective measure proposed in [13]. This effort represents a complete new methodology for social annotation of datasets in the field of computer vision.

The annotation was subdivided into two levels: (i) *low-level features*, related to human detection and tracking, trajectories are acquired from bounding box of enclosing person's annotation on each frame. Re-identification was not considered. When a person is partially or fully occluded, his bounding box was not marked. Also, a full-oriented gaze-direction $[0°, 360°]$ was annotated over the person's head; (ii) *high-level semantics*, labels related to I.P.s and G.B.s, where a trajectory and a group could reveal different profiles and behaviours, respectively. There are the following I.P.s: (i) *distracted (Dist.)*, (ii) *exploring (Exp.)*, (iii) *interested (Int.)*, (iv) *disoriented (Dis.)*; and the following G.B.s: (i) *equally interested (E.I.)*, (ii) *balance interests (B.I.)*, (iii) *unbalance interests (U.I.)*, (iv) *chatting (CHAT.)*. Objects of interest in the scene were marked, namely candy box, toy cars, and electric stairs. Table 1 summarises some relevant statistics about the annotation. Please refer to [1] for a more detailed explanation about I.P.s.

---

[1] Faculdade de Psicologia e de Ciências da Educação da Universidade do Porto - http://sigarra.up.pt/fpceup.

Table 1. Dataset statisticis.

Frames Annotated	Annotation duration	Elapsed Time (I.P.)	Elapsed Time (G.B.)	I.P.s distribution	G.B.s distribution	Average Individuals per frame	Average Individuals per group
80894	02:22:49	203.5 (s) Dist	30.7 (s) E.I	869 total	255 total	3.5	1.8
(97.3)%	(hh:mm:ss)	35.3 (s) Exp	23 (s) B.I	45 Dist	193 E.I		(max: 9)
		12.8 (s) Int	100.3 (s) U.I	776 Exp	27 B.I		
		4.2 (s) Dis	83.7 (s) CHAT	41 Int	28 U.I		
				7 Dis	7 CHAT		

The I.P.s and G.B.s are defined considering the environment as social context. For instance, an individual is considered *distracted* if he is not aware of the environment in that moment. The G.B. concepts are described as:

– *Equally Interested (E.I.)*, when a group presents a coherent behaviour, i.e. one of the following conditions are satisfied: (i) individuals show interest for the same object, therefore all I.P.s should be *interested*; (ii) individuals explore the environment in a similar perspective and in a close position, therefore all I.P.s should be *exploring*, their gaze should be similar, and they should be close to each others.
– *Balance Interests (B.I.)*, when individuals within a group do not reveal the same level of interest but maintain the same behaviour, i.e. the following condition is verified: (i) individuals explore the environment in a similar perspective but not so close to each other, therefore all I.P.s should be *exploring*, their gaze should be relatively similar, and they can be a bit far away from each other.
– *Unbalance Interests (U.I.)*, when a group reveals different types of behaviour in the scene at the same time, i.e. the following condition is satisfied: (i) individuals show different individual profiles and the distance among them, as well as their gaze, can vary.
– *Chatting (CHAT.)*, when a group can be considered a free-standing conversational group (FCG), i.e. the following condition is verified: (i) individuals should be fixed in a position talking with each other (movable individuals while chatting are not considered). By default, all the I.P.s are considered as *distracted*.

4   Proposed Framework

Following our previous work [1], we extended the key-point sampling strategy with multi-scale histogram representation to group behaviour analysis. For this purpose, several attention-based and position-based features were explored in order to obtain discriminative power in terms of classification and meaningful value in terms of social context. The same Bag-of-Features (BoF) approach was considered but we investigated new forms of sampling, pooling and feature matching techniques. For the classification process, we kept the same nonparametric discriminative approach using SVM, while testing different settings.

4.1   Social-Based Descriptor

Our descriptor collects information from key-point trajectory sampling where different features are encoded into a multi-scale histogram controlled by R, the number of granularity levels where the number of bins are given by 2^R, and concatenated to form the final descriptor's histogram. The descriptor also considers different timescales to smooth the gathered information from trajectory' steps. We verified that temporal smoothing did not carried significant difference under our settings probably due to the low spatial complexity and noise associated to the annotated data.

We model group behaviour in terms of space layout, social environment and nonverbal behavioural interactions. Such social signaling constraints involve attention and position-based cues. Inspired by the feature-based study of [10], our aim is to simplify feature identification and collection while keeping global discriminative value. This process is translated by the number of features considered as well as the number of measurements required to acquire a complete feature. For instance, in [10] they identified 4 attention-based cues and 5 position-based cues, and all features measurements, except one, were collected over pair-wise individual relations. In our case, we just considered 5 features, and just 2 of them involve pair-wise measurements. Another difference is that in [10] for each feature they account with each single pair-wise relation per sampling step, while in our case we compute a single global contribution for each feature per sampling step. The proposed social descriptor is composed by the concatenation of the following features:

- *average velocity*, $\bar{v}_g$, is the average velocity taken from all the individuals within a group.
- *average distance*, $\tilde{p}_g$, is the average distance between a pair of individuals, considering all the pair-wise relations within a group.
- *velocity variance*, $\mathrm{Var}[v_g]$, is the variance of the velocity from all the individuals within a group.
- *looking at each other*, $laeo_g$, is a pair-wise relationship and expresses the minimum angle difference between the individual's gaze and the displacement vector between both individual's positions. For each individual, we just considered individuals which fall inside his field of view. This measurement is determined as the mean square error (MSE) of all the differences in order to augment discrepancies.
- *profiles*, P_p, it reflects the occurrence of I.P.s within a group. In this case, no global measure per sampling step is compute. All profiles contributions are considered individually.

4.2   Group Behaviour Classification

The descriptor is fixed-length to be embedded into a BoF classification approach. The codebook was build by running k-means over a subset of the annotated data. The obtained clusters form the vocabulary to be used on further training and classification processes.

(a)   (b)

Fig. 1. (a) Detected chessboard points for camera calibration; (b) Horizontal vanishing line (blue), ground plane's projection area (green), ground points (red) to calculate scale factors and reprojection errors, and objects of interest (purple) (Color figure online).

We trained a multi-class classifier to identify the different G.B.s. Each sample is a sequential number of frames with I.P.s and G.B.s labels, individual trajectories and gaze orientations. Each sequence is treated as a bag. On each bag a temporal sampling, τ, is assumed to acquire feature information from key-point trajectory sampling and form a descriptor. The final descriptor vector for each behaviour is a histogram obtained by nearest cluster counting, which is used as input for the SVM classifier.

Under the classification framework we investigate two problems: (i) feature matching, related to the coding step whose importance relies on a correct cluster histogram matching between descriptor and obtained vocabulary, as well as a proper distance measure; (ii) pooling strategy, related to the way of how the encoded features are summarised to form the final descriptor representation, and its relevance pass through the discriminative power of the descriptor. For the former one, we normalize individual feature's histograms and global descriptor histogram. After that we compute histogram matching independently, and combine distances on final descriptor by either the average or the maximum value. For the latter, we subdivide a bag into temporal gaps, Γ, and considered two pooling configurations, average and max, of such sequences for the entire bag.

We took advantage of our backward feature selection technique proposed in [1] to inspect feature discriminative importance on final descriptor and formulate conclusions about the social meaning of each one.

5   Experimental Results

The manual trajectories and gazes were projected onto the ground plane to correctly estimate distances and angles of interest. We follow the camera calibration and ground-plane projection described in [1]. Figure 1 illustrates some information from calibration, ground plane estimation and manual annotation.

To evaluate our descriptor performance, we compare the classification results with a baseline descriptor and a competitive descriptor, referred here as Chamveha, that builds over our descriptor formulation but uses the features presented in [10]. The baseline is composed by the same features enumerated on Sect. 4.1, but instead of considering a multiscale histogram based on keypoint trajectories, it simply considers the mean (μ) and standard deviation (σ) of each feature, except for the P_p feature. Under our experiments, $R = 3$ showed a good trade-off between accuracy and dimensionality length, which leads to a 116-dimensional feature vector for our descriptor.

For exhaustive classification evaluation, we adopted a 2-fold cross-validation repeated over 100 random iterations. In order to obtain fair results we kept classes proportions from the original dataset for each fold. The evaluation considers three standard parameters: accuracy (A), recall (R), and precision (P). We investigated classification performance over different kernels, namely linear, RBF and intersection, without optimisation of parameters. Apart from performance, we want to analyse feature matching method, distance function, and pooling strategy. We ran experiments over all possible combinations and compare results over an overall F-score of all classes. For sake of simplicity and lack of space we only report in this work the most significant to support our conclusions. In this way, we verified that the intersection kernel SVM and the histogram intersection measure are the best performing alternatives, which corroborates that the combination of both generate better visual codebooks under unsupervised learning [14]. Table 2 summarises the global measure that sustain our conclusions about feature matching and pooling strategy problems.

Table 2. F-score results (%) for the combination of both histogram matching techniques and both pooling configurations

Matching	Average		Maximum	
Pooling	Avg.	Max.	Avg.	Max.
Baseline	*45.1*	44.8	44.6	44.3
Chamveha	*45.5*	45.3	31.8	32.5
Our	**54.4**	***55.7***	**50.8**	**53.2**

5.1 Feature Matching

For this problem we compare average histogram matching with max histogram matching computed from individual feature's histogram on final descriptor. In this way, the distances from all cluster centers are stored and a decision is made taking one of both techniques. For evaluation we considered the F-score measure over both pooling strategies fixing each matching technique.

Overall evaluation shows supremacy performance of our descriptor and average histogram matching reveals better results. Inspecting individual classification of each G.B. we can take the following conclusions: (i) in general E.I. presents the highest results for all descriptors, which is expected since it has a large number of samples and it is a well-defined behaviour; (ii) the baseline and Chamveha descriptors reveal problems in recognising the CHAT behaviour (R $\simeq 5\,\%$), while our descriptor attains a much higher performance (R $\simeq$ 75 %); (iii) maximum matching largely affect our descriptor performance on B.I. behaviour, while average matching brings a minor decrease on U.I. behaviour. This makes sense since B.I. and U.I. are nearly related and are the most difficult ones to recognise and distinguish, therefore an average matching could incorporate contributions from all features; (iv) for the Chamveha descriptor the opposite from the previous conclusion holds. Since this descriptor aggregates more features, there could be redundant information that could confuse the classifier if an average matching is taken. Also CHAT behaviour manifest the same performance decrease, which corroborates our conclusion.

5.2   Pooling Strategy

The objective of pooling strategy is to achieve invariance over possible transformations, provide compact representations and achieve higher performance removing irrelevant information. Indeed pooling strategy could modify the BoF representation. In this way, we investigate if the temporal subdivision of bags and their mode of aggregation affect final performance.

   Overall evaluation confirms our expectation. Under our settings, since we are using annotated data, background noise is reduced and features are acquired with high level of confidence. Therefore, we state negligible difference among both pooling techniques. However, we adopted the max pooling technique for further analysis, since it presents a slightly large difference among all descriptors.

5.3   Classification Results

Considering the metrics presented on Table 3, in special the importance of accuracy for classification tasks and the relevance of recall rate for surveillance systems, we highlight conclusions that state the value of our descriptor formulation as well as the pertinence of the selected features to translate social interactions.

Table 3. Classification results (%) for all G.B.s.

	E.I.			B.I.			U.I.			CHAT.			Avg.		
	P	R	A	P	R	A	P	R	A	P	R	A	P	R	A
Baseline	**90.9**	87.6	**82.9**	39.5	**46.7**	**90.1**	32.4	36.4	86.9	14.6	11.3	94.4	44.4	45.5	88.6
Chamveha	88.4	86.1	79.8	17.4	16.6	87.9	**36.2**	**43.4**	87.8	36.2	38.5	95.3	44.6	46.1	87.7
Our	87.0	**88.1**	79.9	23.9	22.9	88.6	34.6	25.1	**88.3**	**81.5**	**90.4**	**98.8**	**56.8**	**56.6**	**88.9**

   At first glance, the Chamveha descriptor superimposes the remaining descriptors in U.I. behaviour, the most complex one. This reveals that some of its features improve its performance over our descriptor. However, it also sustains the importance of our descriptor sampling strategy as an effective representation over time. E.I. and CHAT behaviours are the most well-defined. It is expectable that for the E.I. behaviour the baseline performs at the same level of remaining descriptors. Low performance on CHAT behaviour for the baseline descriptor is explained by the lack of information about the individual profiles, which is a feature that our descriptor includes. The high performance of baseline on B.I. probably is due to its simplicity, since the mean and standard deviation of each feature might encompass and describe such behaviour composed by individuals that share common behaviour but present few differences of space interests. Indeed, the high performance of the baseline in E.I. and B.I. behaviours proves that our descriptor covers a good selection of discriminative features to describe individual interactions within a group, and that a global measurement that account with single occurrences could be representative enough to identify a collective behaviour. The high performance of our descriptor on CHAT behaviour proves its versatility over a wide range of collective behaviours. We should emphasise the hight contrast between the number of samples per G.B.

The feature importance inspection, illustrated in Fig. 2, clearly shows that all selected features contribute in a balance way for the discriminative power of our descriptor (refer to [1] for a more detailed explanation about this technique).

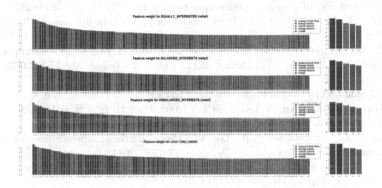

Fig. 2. Features' importance analysis.

6   Conclusions

In this work we addressed the characterisation of collective behaviour within a social context. For this purpose, we elaborated semantic concepts sustained on social-psychology principles and embedded them into the annotation of a novel video surveillance dataset for human activity recognition. Such process was advised by experts on sociological field.

We obtained promising recognition rates for such a complex problem, and validated the scalability of our trajectory-based descriptor to gather meaningful information over time. We also presented a preliminary approach towards the inspection of real sociological meaning of each feature. However, further work should be done over this direction. We are also embedding our framework into a more complete system to account with automatic trajectories and semi-supervised multi-label classification in order to understand better the limitations of our approach.

Acknowledgment. This work is financed by National Funds through the FCT -
Fundação para a Ciência e Tecnologia (Portuguese Foundation for Science and Technology) within PhD grant reference SFRH/BD/51430/2011, and post-doctoral grant
SFRH/BPD/85225/2012. The authors would like to thank Amit Adam for supplying
the video sequences, Kelly Rodrigues and the Social Psychology Research Group of the
University of Porto for their scientific advice.

References

1. Pereira, E.M., Ciobanu, L., Cardoso, J.S.: Context-based trajectory descriptor for human activity profiling. In: Proceedings of IEEE International Conference System, Man, Cybernetics, San Diego, CA, USA (2014)
2. Ge, W., Collins, R.T., Ruback, B.: Vision-based analysis of small groups in pedestrian crowds. IEEE Trans. Pattern Anal. Mach. Intel. **34**, 1003–1016 (2012)
3. Rummel, R.J.: Understanding Conflict and War: The Conflict Helix, vol. 2. Sage Publications, Beverly Hills (1976)
4. Zhou, B., Wang, X., Tang, X.: Understanding collective crowd behaviors: learning a mixture model of dynamic pedestrian-agents. In: CVPR, pp. 2871–2878 (2012)
5. Helbing, D., Molnár, P.: Social force model for pedestrian dynamics. Phys. Rev. E **51**, 4282–4286 (1995)
6. Klügl, F., Rindsfüser, G.: Large-scale agent-based pedestrian simulation. In: Georgeff, M., Klusch, M., Müller, J.P., Petta, P. (eds.) MATES 2007. LNCS (LNAI), vol. 4687, pp. 145–156. Springer, Heidelberg (2007)
7. Ali, S., Shah, M.: Floor fields for tracking in high density crowd scenes. In: Forsyth, D., Torr, P., Zisserman, A. (eds.) ECCV 2008, Part II. LNCS, vol. 5303, pp. 1–14. Springer, Heidelberg (2008)
8. Chang, M.C., Krahnstoever, N., Ge, W.: Probabilistic group-level motion analysis and scenario recognition. In: ICCV, pp. 747–754 (2011)
9. Qiu, F., Hu, X.: Modeling group structures in pedestrian crowd simulation. Simul. Model. Pract. Theor. **18**, 190–205 (2010)
10. Chamveha, I., Sugano, Y., Sato, Y., Sugimoto, A.: Social group discovery from surveillance videos: a data-driven approach with attention-based cues. In: Proceedings of the British Machine Vision Conference, BMVA Press (2013)
11. Adam, A., Rivlin, E., Shimshoni, I., Reinitz, D.: Robust real-time unusual event detection using multiple fixed-location monitors. IEEE Trans. Pattern Anal. Mach. Intel. **30**(3), 555–560 (2008)
12. Cartwright, D., Zander, A.: Group Dynamics: Research and Theory. Harper & Row, New York (1968)
13. McPhail, C., Wohlstein, R.T.: Using film to analyze pedestrian behavior. Sociol. Methods Res. **10**, 347–375 (1982)
14. Wu, J., Rehg, J.M.: Beyond the euclidean distance: Creating effective visual codebooks using the histogram intersection kernel (2009)

A New Smoothing Method for Lexicon-Based Handwritten Text Keyword Spotting

Joan Puigcerver[✉], Alejandro H. Toselli, and Enrique Vidal

Pattern Recognition and Human Language Technology Research Center,
Universitat Politècnica de València, Camí de Vera s/n, 46022 València, Spain
{joapuipe,ahector,evidal}@prhlt.upv.es

Abstract. Lexicon-based handwritten text keyword spotting (KWS) has proven to be a very fast and accurate alternative to lexicon-free methods. Nevertheless, since lexicon-based KWS methods rely on a predefined vocabulary, fixed in the training phase, they perform poorly for any query keyword that was not included in it (i.e. out-of-vocabulary keywords). This turns the KWS system useless for that particular type of queries. In this paper, we present a new way of smoothing the scores of OOV keywords, and we compare it with previously published alternatives on different data sets.

Keywords: Keyword spotting · Lexicon-based · Word-graph · Smoothing · Handwritten text recognition

1 Introduction

The aim of handwritten text keyword spotting (KWS) is to determine, given a predefined confidence level, in which documents or image regions, a given keyword is present. This work, focuses on the case where queries are presented to the system as strings typed by the user (known as Query-by-String) [8].

In the recent past, word-graphs (WG) have been proposed for KWS in handwritten text images [11]. This approach takes the statistical morphological, lexical and language models, previously trained for a handwriting text recognition task, and uses an extension of Viterbi algorithm to generate a word-graph for each text-line, containing a set of possible transcriptions of that particular line and its likelihood. From these WG, line-level confidence scores are computed for each keyword and indexed line, to allow for a fast lookup, with a confidence threshold given by the user.

This method provides much faster searches than traditional lexicon-agnostic methods, such as the HMM-filler method [1], or KWS methods based on bi-directional recurrent neural networks (BLSTM) [2]. Moreover, the Precision–Recall performance provided by the lexicon-based method gives better results than the traditional HMM-filler and comparable with that based on BLSTM.

Unfortunately, an important problem of lexicon-based methods is how to deal with out-of-vocabulary (OOV) queries: since this methods rely on a fixed

© Springer International Publishing Switzerland 2015
R. Paredes et al. (Eds.): IbPRIA 2015, LNCS 9117, pp. 23–30, 2015.
DOI: 10.1007/978-3-319-19390-8_3

vocabulary, determined during the training phase of the system, they will give a null score for any keyword not included in this training lexicon. In order to cope with this problem, this paper presents a new technique for smoothing the scores given by a lexicon-based system, and we compare it with previous publications.

We will show that our proposal improves the ones presented in [6]. In both cases, a similarity metric between an OOV keyword and the indexed ones is used to approximate the score of the OOV events. We also compare our method with [5], which is a combination of lexicon-based and HMM-filler systems, which gives excellent performance results. However the use of the HMM-filler significantly dampers the speed of the system, even when fast search approaches are used [10], as we show in the experiments.

The paper is organized as follows: Sect. 2 introduces basic concepts of the KWS framework used in this work, Sect. 3 briefly describes the existing smoothing methods and presents the proposed method in detail, Sect. 4 presents the experiments conducted to evaluate this work and compare it to previously published works, and final conclusions are drawn in Sect. 5.

2 Keyword Spotting Framework Review

The KWS method used in this work was originally presented in [11]. For each query keyword v and each text line, represented by $\mathbf{x}$, the system tries to model a score $S(\mathbf{x}, v)$ which measures how likely is the event "keyword v is written in $\mathbf{x}$", or re-phrased as "text line $\mathbf{x}$ is relevant for keyword v". Following [11], we define the score as:

$$S(\mathbf{x}, v) \stackrel{\text{def}}{=} \max_{1 \leq i \leq n} P(v \mid \mathbf{x}, i) \tag{1}$$

$P(v \mid \mathbf{x}, i)$ is known as the *frame-level word posterior*, which is the probability that the word v is present in the line image $\mathbf{x}$ at position i. As shown in [11], this posterior can be directly approximated from the WG of the line image obtained as a byproduct of recognizing the image with a HTR system based on optical models such as HMMs and n-gram language models.

Observe that the previous score is equivalent to the probability of a Bernoulli distribution over a random variable R, measuring how likely is the event "text line $\mathbf{x}$ is relevant for keyword v".

$$P(R \mid \mathbf{x}, v) \stackrel{\text{def}}{=} \begin{cases} S(\mathbf{x}, v) & R = 1 \\ 1 - S(\mathbf{x}, v) & R = 0 \end{cases} \tag{2}$$

3 Out-of-Vocabulary Queries

In the introduction we briefly explained one drawback of the lexicon-based KWS method, related to the out-of-vocabulary keywords. Since this KWS approach uses a n-gram LM which assigns a null probability to any keyword not seen during its training, the frame-level word posterior $P(u \mid \mathbf{x}, i) = 0$, for all keyword $u \notin V$, on any line image $\mathbf{x}$.

In this section, we will briefly explain some of the solutions that have recently been introduced in the literature to mitigate this problem, along with our contribution.

3.1   Line-Level Smoothing with Levenshtein Distance

In [6], a first attempt to solve this problem is presented. Here the score of an OOV keyword u is smoothed using the scores of the indexed keywords $v \in V$ and the Levenshtein distance $d(u, v)$ between both strings, using:

$$S(\mathbf{x}, u) \overset{\text{def}}{=} \max_{v \in V} S(\mathbf{x}, v)^{1-\alpha} \cdot e^{-\alpha d(u,v)} \tag{3}$$

The parameter α is tuned using a validation set and is intended to balance the contribution of the Levenshtein distance on the score of the OOV event.

3.2   Frame-Level Word Posterior Smoothing

In the previous work [6], a frame-level smoothing is also presented. This method, first smooths the frame-level word posterior $P(u \mid \mathbf{x}, i)$ of a keyword $u \notin V$, following:

$$\tilde{P}(u \mid \mathbf{x}, i) = \frac{\sum_{v \in V} P(v \mid \mathbf{x}, i) \cdot f(u, v)^\alpha}{1 + \sum_{v \in V} P(v \mid \mathbf{x}, i) \cdot f(u, v)^\alpha} \tag{4}$$

The parameter α is tuned again using a validation partition and the function $f(u, v)$ is a similarity measure based on a stochastic error correcting approach, indicating how similar are the keywords $u \notin V$ and $v \in V$. Finally, the score $S(\mathbf{x}, u)$ is computed as in Eq. 1, but using $\tilde{P}(u \mid \mathbf{x}, i)$ instead.

3.3   Lexicon-Based and HMM-Filler Combination

This approach, presented in [5], is actually a combination of two different systems, each of them with different strengths and issues. When a query keyword v is indexed (i.e. not an OOV), it can be immediately honored using the precomputed scores given by the lexicon-based approach. Otherwise, a lexicon-free HMM-filler model is used to serve the query. The resulting score is obtained using:

$$S(\mathbf{x}, v) = \begin{cases} S_G(\mathbf{x}, v) & v \in V \\ \exp(S_F(\mathbf{x}, v))^\eta & v \notin V \end{cases} \tag{5}$$

Here, $S_G(\mathbf{x}, v)$ are the scores given by the lexicon-based system and $S_F(\mathbf{x}, v)$ are the scores given by the HMM-filler. The exponentiation of the HMM-filler scores and the parameter η are required because this model does not give properly normalized scores, which have to be be scaled to an appropriate range.

3.4 New Proposed Line-Level Smoothing

The proposed line-level score smoothing is based on the probabilistic interpretation of the scores obtained from the lexicon-based KWS approach. As we mentioned before, the score $S(\mathbf{x}, v)$, given by this approach, can be interpreted as $P(R \mid \mathbf{x}, v)$. Then, we can marginalize this distribution for a particular $u \notin V$, with all $v \in V$, resulting in:

$$P(R \mid \mathbf{x}, u) = \sum_{v \in V} P(R, v \mid \mathbf{x}, u) = \sum_{v \in V} P(R \mid \mathbf{x}, u, v) \cdot P(v \mid \mathbf{x}, u) \qquad (6)$$

Then, we make two independence assumptions: First, assume that v is conditionally independent of $\mathbf{x}$, given u, i.e. $P(v \mid \mathbf{x}, u) \approx P(v \mid u)$. Then, we assume that $P(R \mid \mathbf{x}, u, v) \approx P(R \mid \mathbf{x}, v)$, which implies that the fact that a line $\mathbf{x}$ is relevant for a pair of keywords $u \notin V$ and $v \in V$, actually depends only on the keyword $v \in V$. After these assumptions, Eq. 6 is approximated as:

$$P(R \mid \mathbf{x}, u) \approx \sum_{v \in V} P(R \mid \mathbf{x}, v) \cdot P(v \mid u) \qquad (7)$$

$P(v \mid u)$ is a similarity probability distribution which has to be normalized across all $v \in V$, which differs from the one introduced in [6], which had to be normalized across all $u \in \Sigma^*$. Since the distribution is over a finite set of elements, it can be defined in arbitrary ways that do not exhibit the problems of [6] (it was affected by the length of the keywords and had estimation issues). Particularly, we choose a distribution based on the Levenshtein distance $d(u, v)$:

$$P(v \mid u) \overset{\text{def}}{=} \frac{\exp(-\alpha \, d(u, v))}{\sum_{v' \in V} \exp(-\alpha \, d(u, v'))} \qquad (8)$$

In the same way that the previous smoothing methods did, we introduce a parameter α to tune the contribution of the similarity measure.

4 Experiments

In order to compare the proposed method with previous works, several experiments were conducted on different corpora. Performance assessment, corpora, experimental setup and results are explained below.

4.1 Performance Assessment

Assessment is measured using the average precision (AP) metric [7], based on the recall and precision measures. As is usually done, we use the interpolated precision in order to smooth plain precision [4]. AP is a scalar summary of the precision and recall, which are functions of a threshold used to determine whether the score $S(\mathbf{x}, v)$ is high enough to assume that v is relevant in $\mathbf{x}$. Additionally, we report the mean average precision (mAP), which is also widely adopted in the literature. It is computed by averaging the AP of each keyword. We decided to optimize our parameters based on the AP metric.

Finally, we also compared the number of seconds required to compute the scores of an OOV query, in each corpus. We only considered the OOV keywords for this comparison, since the scores of in-vocabulary keywords can be precomputed and the lookup speed becomes asymptotically constant.

4.2 Corpora

The "Cristo-Salvador" (CS) dataset is a small XIX century single-writer Spanish manuscript. We used exactly the same partitioning as [6,10]. Since the CS corpus is quite small, we ignored capitalization and diacritics to build the lexicon and the LM, and performed cross-validation to tune all parameters.

Regarding IAM, it consists of English handwritten texts from many writers. We used the same data partitions used in previous KWS experiments [1,2,5,10]. In addition to the text in the line images, we used three external text corpora (LOB, Brown and Wellington), which were used to build a 20K-word lexicon and train a LM (test lines were excluded from LOB).

In both cases, we used the lexicon of the test lines as the query set. In the case of IAM, we subtracted from the query set all stop words, as in [5]. Table 1 summarizes the most important information of the corpora.

Table 1. Tables summarizing the corpora used for experimentation.

(a) Basic statistics of the selected databases.

	CS		IAM		
	Train	Test	Train	Valid.	Test
Running Chars	35 863	26 353	269 270	39 318	39 130
Running Words	6 223	4 637	47 615	7 291	7 197
# Lines	675	497	6 161	920	929
Char Lex. Size	78	78	72	69	65
Word Lex. Size	2 236	1 671	7 778	2 442	2 488
OOV Lex. Size	—	1 051	—	435	437

(b) Details of the selected query sets for the test partition in each dataset.

	CS	IAM
# Line images: N	497	929
# Query words: M	1 671	2 209
# Line-query events: $M \cdot N$	830 487	2 052 161
# OOV Line-query events	522 347	405 973
# Relevant line-query events	4,346	3 446
# Relevant OOV line-query events	1,341	496

4.3   Experimental Setup

In each corpus, we trained a a left-to-right HMM model with GMM distributions on the states, for each character included in the training set. The standard embedded Baum-Welch training algorithm was used [12]. Details about preprocessing, feature extraction, number of states and mixtures in the GMM, etc. can be found in [11] for the CS dataset, and [1] for IAM.

A bi-gram LM was used to build the lexicon-based system. In the case of CS, the transcripts of the training set were used, converting lowercase characters to uppercase. For IAM, the LM was trained using the external LBW corpus, restricted to the 20 K most frequent words. Finally, the standard Kneser-Ney back-off was used to smooth the probabilities of unseen bi-grams [3].

The approach described in [11] was used, in order to speedup the search using the HMM-filler. In a *preparatory phase*, character-lattices (CL) are obtained using the "filler", for each of the test lines. The maximum node input degree (NID) of these was set to 30. Then, during the *search phase*, the scores of each query are computed using the CL. For the lexicon-based method, WG were generated using the standard HTK software, with the described language models, with a maximum NID value equal to 40, and not using any pruning technique during the decoding. Further details about the lexicon-based method can be found in [5,6].

Concerning the tuning of parameters, we used the same values as the reference papers [5,6], for the existing methods. As for our method (Sect. 3.4), we used the IAM validation set and performed cross-validation on CS. We finally set α to 4, for both corpora.

Experiments were conducted on a Intel Core 2 Quad Q9550 CPU at 2.83 GHz, running Ubuntu Linux 14.04. All custom software was implemented in C++.

4.4   Results

Table 2 summarizes the main results obtained on the test set of each corpora.

Table 2. Line-level Average Precision (AP) and Mean Average Precision (mAP) provided by each smoothing method on the test set of the corpora. Results tagged with † and ‡ were presented in [5,6], respectively. Query time (Qtime) is the average time required to serve the OOV queries, expressed seconds.

Method	CS			IAM		
	AP	mAP	Qtime	AP	mAP	Qtime
No smoothing	55.6	29.0	—	69.1	68.8	—
Line Max. (sec. 3.1)	†57.8	†45.0	0.44	69.8	76.0	8.78
Posteriorgram (sec. 3.2)	†58.8	†46.7	27.21	70.2	76.1	42.48
WG + HMM-Filler (sec. 3.3)	72.5	76.6	177.10	‡76.9	‡82.2	58.16
This work (sec. 3.4)	59.5	46.0	0.52	71.3	76.0	9.96

Compared to the method described in Sect. 3.1, for both datasets, our proposal improves the previous AP results (about 1.7 points of absolute improvement), while maintaining similar computational costs. This is because the asymptotic running time of both algorithms is the same and the new method successfully uses more information from the index: the contribution of all in-vocabulary keywords is considered, instead of a maximum.

Moreover, the proposed work slightly improves the AP of the method described in Sect. 3.2 (about 0.9 points of absolute improvement), and is able to obtain the smoothed scores in much faster times (about 50 times faster in CS and 4 times faster in IAM). It is important to notice that the running time of method Sect. 3.2 depends both on the size of V, and the average number of edges per node in the line WG, which can be interpreted as the *perplexity* of the WG. In the CS case, the perplexity of the WG is much higher than in the IAM case (35.8 vs 23.6), since fewer training data was available for both the HMM and LM. However, the size of the vocabulary is much higher for IAM. On the other hand, the perplexity of the WG does not affect the speed of our method, which works directly with the index scores. The interaction between these two factors explains why method Sect. 3.2 is slower in IAM than in CS, but is faster in IAM than in CS when it is *relatively* compared to our proposal.

It is worth pointing out that the computation of the Levenshtein distances has been done naively in this work, with an asymptotic cost of $O(|q| \cdot L \cdot |V|)$, where q is the query string, $L = \max_{v \in V} |v|$, and $|s|$ gives the length of string s. Nevertheless, this computation can enormously reduced by using *tries* for indexing the vocabulary, or limiting the maximum number of errors allowed [9].

Finally, we show that the combination of the Lexicon-based and the HMM-filler methods gives better AP results than any of the proposed methods, but at a much higher computational cost: our method is 340 times faster in CS and 6 times faster in IAM, when compared to Sect. 3.3. The reason explaining the differences in the speedup is the same as explained above.

5   Conclusions

We presented a new method for smoothing the scores given by the lexicon-based system, based on the similarity between the OOV keyword and the indexed vocabulary. Futhermore, we performed a detailed comparison of different alternatives that try to alleviate the problem caused by OOV queries when using a lexicon-based KWS system for handwritten text images.

The presented smoothing method gives better results than most of the compared alternatives, and it is comparable in speed to the fastest of the previous methods, also based on similarity measures.

Only the combination of a lexicon-based system and a HMM-filler surpasses our proposal, among the studied methods. Nevertheless, it comes with a time cost several orders of magnitude bigger than our proposal, specially when the CL are big or have a high average number of edges per node, which may result impractical in some real scenarios (i.e. Cristo-Salvador corpus).

In the future, we are planning to investigate ways of effectively indexing open-lexicon systems and combine them with lexicon-based approaches, thus allowing for faster and more accurate searches for both in-vocabulary and out-of-vocabulary queries.

Acknowledgments. This work was partially supported by the Spanish MEC under FPU grant FPU13/06281 and under the STraDA research project (TIN2012-37475-C02-01), by the Generalitat Valenciana under the grant Prometeo/2009/014, and through the EU 7th Framework Programme grant tranScriptorium (Ref: 600707).

References

1. Fischer, A., Keller, A., Frinken, V., Bunke, H.: Lexicon-free handwritten word spotting using character HMMs. Pattern Recogn. Lett. **33**(7), 934–942 (2012). special Issue on Awards from ICPR 2010
2. Frinken, V., Fischer, A., Manmatha, R., Bunke, H.: A novel word spotting method based on recurrent neural networks. IEEE Trans. Pattern Anal. Mach. Intell. **34**(2), 211–224 (2012)
3. Kneser, R., Ney, H.: Improved backing-off for N-gram language modeling. In: International Conference on Acoustics. Speech and Signal Processing (ICASSP 1995), vol. 1, pp. 181–184. IEEE Computer Society, Los Alamitos (1995)
4. Manning, C.D., Raghavan, P., Schtze, H.: Introduction to Information Retrieval. Cambridge University Press, New York (2008)
5. Puigcerver, J., Toselli, A.H., Vidal, E.: Word-graph and character-lattice combination for KWS in handwritten documents. In: 14th International Conference on Frontiers in Handwriting Recognition (ICFHR), pp. 181–186 (2014)
6. Puigcerver, J., Toselli, A.H., Vidal, E.: Word-graph-based handwriting keyword spotting of out-of-vocabulary queries. In: 22nd International Conference on Pattern Recognition (ICPR), pp. 2035–2040 (2014)
7. Robertson, S.: A new interpretation of average precision. In: Proceedings of the International ACM SIGIR Conference on Research and Development in Information Retrieval (SIGIR 2008), pp. 689–690. ACM, New York (2008)
8. Rodriguez-Serrano, J.A., Perronnin, F.: Handwritten word-spotting using hidden markov models and universal vocabularies. Pattern Recogn. **42**(9), 2106–2116 (2009). http://www.sciencedirect.com/science/article/pii/S0031320309000673
9. Shang, H., Merrettal, T.: Tries for approximate string matching. IEEE Transac. Knowl. Data Eng. **8**(4), 540–547 (1996)
10. Toselli, A.H., Vidal, E.: Fast HMM-filler approach for key word spotting in handwritten documents. In: Proceedings of the 12th International Conference on Document Analysis and Recognition (ICDAR), pp. 501–505 (2013)
11. Toselli, A.H., Vidal, E., Romero, V., Frinken, V.: Word-graph based keyword spotting and indexing of handwritten document images. Universitat Politcnica de Valncia, Technical report (2013)
12. Woodland, P., Leggetter, C., Odell, J., Valtchev, V., Young, S.: The 1994 HTK large vocabulary speech recognition system. In: International Conference on Acoustics, Speech, and Signal Processing (ICASSP 1995), vol. 1, pp. 73–76, May 1995

Empirical Evaluation of Different Feature Representations for Social Circles Detection

Jesús Alonso[✉], Roberto Paredes, and Paolo Rosso

Pattern Recognition and Human Language Technologies Research Center,
Universitat Politècnica de València, Valencia, Spain
jealnan@posgrado.upv.es
https://www.prhlt.upv.es/

Abstract. Social circles detection is a special case of community detection in social network that is currently attracting a growing interest in the research community. We propose in this paper an empirical evaluation of the multi-assignment clustering method using different feature representation models. We define different vectorial representations from both structural egonet information and user profile features. We study and compare the performance on the available labelled Facebook data from the Kaggle competition on learning social circles in networks. We compare our results with several different baselines.

Keywords: Social circles detection · Community detection · Feature representations

1 Introduction

Nowadays, users in social networks tend to organize the contacts in their personal networks by means of social circles, a tool already implemented by the major companies, like for instance Facebook lists or Google+ circles. However, this labelling is still mostly done manually and therefore a growing interest has risen in the automatic detection of these circles. In addition, this problem is related to the more general task of community detection in graphs, or the identification of subnetworks in a given network. The main difference between both problems is the use of information from users' profiles, apart from information from the network structure itself.

Despite the lack of a precise and well-accepted definition of community, there is a wide variety of methods and techniques designed to cope with community detection [3,10]. Moreover, some techniques specifically designed for social circles detection are being developed currently [6,7]. In this article, we present our approach based on multi-assignment clustering (MAC) [4,13], originally a clustering technique for Boolean vectorial data not necessarily related to networks or graphs. The advantage of this technique is the possibility to assign the same object into several different clusters, different social circles. MAC has already been tried for social circles detection [6,7] but only using a very simple feature representation, considering only user profile features, ignoring the network

© Springer International Publishing Switzerland 2015
R. Paredes et al. (Eds.): IbPRIA 2015, LNCS 9117, pp. 31–38, 2015.
DOI: 10.1007/978-3-319-19390-8_4

structure. In our work we propose different and novel approaches by considering different representations of both network structure and user profile features.

The rest of the paper is structured as follows. In section two, we present previous works on community detection and social circles detection. In section three, we describe thoroughly our methodology, including the different data representations proposed and the baseline methods to compare with. In section four, we present the dataset and the evaluation measure of our experiments. In section five, we discuss the obtained results. Finally, we draw some conclusions.

2   Previous Work

2.1   Community Detection in Networks

From an abstract point of view, a network is equivalent to a graph, defined by a set of nodes connected by edges. Nevertheless, from the point of view of researchers devoted to a diversity of fields, the concept of network has additional connotations. Networks can represent real structures such as social networks, biological networks (neural synaptic networks, metabolical networks), technological networks (the Internet, the World Wide Web), logistic networks (distribution networks), etc. There is no well-accepted formal definition of community in general networks. However, there is a consensus on the fact that it consists of a group of nodes that are more densely connected to each other than to the nodes outside. The relation of membership in a community usually has an extra meaning, and the vertices in a community will probably share common properties or play similar roles within the graph.

Community detection is the task of automated identification of the communities of a network. A considerable number of methods have been developed to solve this problem [3, 10].

In real networks nodes are often shared among different communities. The most popular technique to detect overlapping communities is the clique percolation method [8]. Given a graph, a k-clique is defined as a complete subgraph of size k. Clique percolation consists in the identification of k-clique communities, defined as the union of all k-cliques that can be reached from each other through a series of adjacent k-cliques. Despite of the good performance of this technique, clique percolation remains a hard computational problem, new and improved implementations still scale worse than some other overlapping community finding algorithms.

2.2   Application to Social Networks and Social Circles Detection

The study of social networks is a research topic with a history of decades and it has been recently revitalized by the appearance of new information and communication technologies which have opened new ways of interacting. Clustering of this social content has been studied designing several procedures. Some approaches base the clustering on the network links [10], while others consider the semantic content of social interactions [15]. In between both methodologies, there has also been work on combining the links and the content for doing the clustering [9,12]. Very recently, a new technique studied the characteristics of community structures formed around topical discussion clusters, using modularity maximization algorithms [2].

Social circles detection is a special case of this framework. Within a social network, an ego network or egonet is defined as the subgraph of the contacts of a particular user (called the ego). Thus, it includes all the contacts of the ego and the contact relationship between every pair of them. Then, the social circles of an ego can be considered as clusters of the egonet. Social circles may overlap (share nodes), for example university friends who were high school friends as well; and they may also present hierarchical inclusion (the nodes of a circle totally included into another), for example university friends into a generic friends category. Apart from the links of the egonet, user profile information is also normally considered in this task. The latest works on social circles detection define a generative model that considers circle memberships and a circle-specific profile similarity metric [6,7].

3 Methodology

3.1 Multi-Assignment Clustering

Multi-Assignment Clustering (MAC) [4,13] is a clustering method, originally developed for Boolean vectorial data, which allows for the possibility to assign the same object into several different clusters. It provides a decomposition of the data matrix $\mathbf{x}$ into a matrix containing the clusters prototypes $\mathbf{z}$ and a matrix representing the degree to which a particular data vector belongs to the different clusters $\mathbf{y}$. Finding optimal matrices $\mathbf{z}$ and $\mathbf{y}$ is NP-hard [14], but a probabilistic representation allows to drastically simplify the optimization problem. In [13] the authors propose to model the probability of x_{ij} under the signal model as:

$$p(x_{ij}|\mathbf{z},\beta) = \left[1 - \prod_{k=1}^{K} \beta_{kj}^{z_{ik}}\right]^{x_{ij}} \left[\prod_{k=1}^{K} \beta_{kj}^{z_{ik}}\right]^{1-x_{ij}} , \text{ where } \beta_{kj} := p(y_{kj} = 0) \quad (1)$$

In addition to the signal model, there is a noise model for the difference between the original data and the reconstruction made from $\mathbf{z}$ and $\mathbf{y}$. The model parameters are inferred by deterministic annealing [1,11]. When MAC is applied to social circles detection, $\mathbf{y}$ is the matrix indicating which users belong to the different clusters, social circles.

In [6,7] MAC was already employed and considered as a baseline method for social circles detection, although using only user profile information. This piece of evidence that MAC is a state-of-the-art technique, having recent and influential publications, helped us making the choice over alternative soft-clustering strategies. In this work, we propose to explore further its possibilities for this task, investigating novel representations. We defend the fact that this technique still has potential and better results can be obtained. Furthemore, MAC is more adequate for large networks than other methods with a very high computational cost, like clique percolation.

As a novelty, we model the structural information of the egonets into diverse vectorial representations ready to be supplied to the algorithm. Several vectorial representations for user profile features were developed as well. Unlike the original MAC, we allow the input to be real data in $[0, 1]^n$ as a way to model a hierarchy of link levels in the case of structural information, or an aggregation of the number of feature values shared by two users profiles in the case of user profile information.

In all the experiments, the input data matrix $\mathbf{x}$ is a horizontal concatenation of a matrix $\mathbf{s}$, containing structural network information, and a matrix $\mathbf{p}$, containing profile features information: $\mathbf{x} = [\mathbf{s} \,|\, \mathbf{p}]$. Rows represent users of the egonet and therefore for every user u there is a row vector of structural network information, $\mathbf{s}_u$, and a row vector of profile features information, $\mathbf{p}_u$. Therefore, the number of rows of the matrix $\mathbf{x}$ is the number of users in the ego-network $|\,u\,|$, and the number of columns of the matrix $\mathbf{x}$ is the total number of features used to represent structural and profile information of each user.

3.2 Structural Network Representation

In this subsection, we present the different representations of the structural network information that have been considered. All of them transform graph links into the matrices $\mathbf{s}$. We use the following concepts:

- *Friendship Ranks:* when there is a link between two users, we say they are direct friends or rank 1 friends. When two users are not direct friends but have a common direct friend, we say they are rank 2 friends. Friendship ranks of greater levels can be further defined. In this study we consider up to rank 3 friends. There is a column in $\mathbf{s}$ for every friendship rank and user in the egonet. An element of $\mathbf{s}$ is 1 if the row user and the column user are friends of such rank, and 0 otherwise. Obtaining in total $3 \times |\,u\,|$ structural features for each user.
- *Weighting:* the data is weighted depending on the friendship rank it represents. Rank 1 friendship is left with 1, whereas rank 2 friendship is weighted to 0.5 and rank 3 friendship is weighted to 0.25. Like in the previous case, obtaining in total $3 \times |\,u\,|$ structural features for each user.
- *Aggregation:* for every user, the different friendship ranks are aggregated into just one value. This is obtained by calculating the maximum weighted friendship rank. Reducing the number of structural features to $|\,u\,|$.

From these concepts we define the representations shown in Table 1.

3.3 User Profile Representation

There are up to 57 profile features for every user in the data corpus we used for the experiments. Nevertheless, some of them are very seldom informed whereas

Table 1. Representations of structural network information

Representation	Definition
r1	Rank 1
r12	Ranks 1 and 2
r123	Ranks 1, 2 and 3
r12w	Ranks 1 and 2, weighted
r123w	Ranks 1, 2 and 3, weighted
r12a	Ranks 1 and 2, aggregated
r123a	Ranks 1, 2 and 3, aggregated

others are redundant or not relevant for the task. As a consequence, we have selected the 3 most informative features and we use only these. The selected features are: *hometown*, *schools* and *employers*. Each of these features can take different discrete values from a finite set.

We define as $\mid f \mid$ the number of features considered, and as $\mid v \mid$ the total number of values of the considered features that are taken by at least one user in the egonet. We encode the profile features information in the matrices $\mathbf{p}$, for which the following representations have been defined:

- *Explicit:* There is a column of $\mathbf{p}$ for every different value of the considered features. An element of $\mathbf{p}$ is 1 if the row user takes the column value for the respective feature, and 0 otherwise. Obtaining in total $\mid v \mid$ profile features for each user.
- *Intersection:* There is one column of $\mathbf{p}$ for every user in the egonet and every considered profile feature. An element of $\mathbf{p}$ is 1 if the sets of values of the row user and the column user, for that particular feature, intersect. It is 0 otherwise. In this case, obtaining $\mid f \mid \times \mid u \mid$ profile features for each user.
- *Weighted:* There is just one column of $\mathbf{p}$ for every user in the egonet. An element of $\mathbf{p}$ represents the proportion of features for which the row user and the column user share at least one value. It is calculated as $\frac{|s|}{|f|}$, where $\mid s \mid$ is the number of features shared between both users. Reducing the number of profile features to $\mid u \mid$.

4   Experiments

The corpus we use for the experiments is the one published for the Kaggle competition on learning social circles in networks [5]. The data consist of hand-labelled friendship egonets from Facebook and a set of 57 profile features for every node in those networks. We discarded every egonet for which the ground truth is not available. Out of the 60 egonets we finally considered, the smallest one contains 45 users and the largest one contains 670 users. The 60 egonets altogether comprise 14,519 users.

The degree of a given user is defined as the number of different circles which it belongs to. MAC takes as a parameter the range of possible degrees of the users of an egonet. In all our experiments the minimum degree is set to 0 and we try several values for the maximum degree, up to 3. In this regard, unlike previous studies, we do not include any prediction technique for the number of circles within the egonets, using the number of circles of the ground-truth instead. In future works, that would be easily incorporated with methods such as the bayesian information criterion employed in [6,7].

The evaluation measure of our experiments, and proposed in Kaggle, is calculated as follows:

An evaluation measure for every egonet e is computed as an edit distance between the ground truth circles (g_e) and the predicted circles (p_e): $\mathrm{EDM}_e = \mathrm{d}(g_e, p_e)$. Four basic edit operations are considered: adding a user to an existing circle, creating a circle with one user, removing a user from a circle and deleting a circle with one user; every one of them at cost 1.

The evaluation measure of the whole dataset is the sum of the edit distances obtained for all the egonets.

$$\mathrm{EDM} = \sum_{e \in E} \mathrm{EDM}_e, \qquad (2)$$

being E the set of the egonets in the corpus.

The smaller EDM is, the better the performance of the prediction.

5   Results

We compare our results to several different baselines. First of all, we consider MAC when it receives only structural information, using an r1 representation. MAC with only profile features, in this case, we use an explicit representation of the features. The use of both baselines has the aim to show to what degree the combination of structural network and profile information improves either of these sources of information when taken independently.

Empty circles is the third baseline we employ. This baseline relies on the fact that the evaluation measure used in this study heavily penalizes the misclassification of users into circles. Thus, defining no circle at all performs better than other possible simple baselines like connected components or classifying all the friends of an ego into just one circle.

Finally, we have considered a very high-performing baseline by using a 5-clique percolation algorithm. However, this cannot be done for every egonet due to its exponential computational complexity. Therefore, we replace the clique percolation predictions by empty circles in those cases.

It would be interesting to report results of the participants of the Kaggle competition from which we borrowed the data, as well. Unfortunately, there are only publicly available rankings for the test dataset, for which the ground truth is not available. Thus, there is no possibility to make this comparison.

The evaluation measures obtained by the baselines and our experiments are shown in Table 2. Only results obtained from weighted and aggregated structural egonet representations are presented, as non-weighting has always performed worse.

Table 2. Baselines and results of the experiments

Baseline	EDM		
MAC only structure	18679		
MAC only profile	20271		
Empty circles	17101		
Clique percolation	15350		

Data representation		EDM		
Structural	Profile	deg. 1	deg. 2	deg. 3
r12w	Explicit	16962	16803	16827
r12w	Intersection	16032	16360	15927
r12w	Weighted	17001	16955	16920
r123w	Explicit	17106	17053	17082
r123w	Intersection	16520	16504	16518
r123w	Weighted	16994	17065	17075
r12a	Explicit	15797	15619	**15570**
r12a	Intersection	16433	16840	16694
r12a	Weighted	15725	15751	15625
r123a	Explicit	16804	16770	16703
r123a	Intersection	16960	17000	17383
r123a	Weighted	16634	16542	16558

The best results have been produced when considering friendship of ranks 1 and 2, aggregated; and an explicit representation of the profile features information, allowing MAC for a maximum degree of 3. This representation has provided a value of EDM close to that obtained from the clique percolation baseline. All the experiments using the structural network representation r12a have given low values of EDM, outperforming the empty circles baseline in all the cases and most of the other representations as well. The combination of (weighted) structural network information and profile features has always performed better than structure or profile separately.

6   Conclusions

Network structure and profile features are complementary sources of information for social circles detection. In addition, weighting of structural network information with respect to friendship levels is crucial to improve the results and get close to the ones provided by methods such as clique percolation. This work opens the door to new research in the topic, being possible future experiments the use of a greater set of profile features or better retrieved ones and the adoption of other prediction techniques or even a more in-depth study of MAC.

Acknowledgement. This work was developed in the framework of the W911NF-14-1-0254 research project Social Copying Community Detection (SOCOCODE), funded by the US Army Research Office (ARO).

References

1. Buhmann, J., Kühnel, H.: Vector quantization with complexity costs. IEEE Trans. Inf. Theor. **39**(4), 1133–1145 (1993)
2. Dey, K., Bandyopadhyay, S.: An empirical investigation of like-mindedness of topically related social communities on microblogging platforms. In: International Conference on Natural Languages (2013)
3. Fortunato, S.: Community detection in graphs. Phys. Rep. **486**(3), 75–174 (2010)
4. Frank, M., Streich, A.P., Basin, D., Buhmann, J.M.: Multi-assignment clustering for boolean data. J. Mach. Learn. Res. **13**(1), 459–489 (2012)
5. Kaggle: Learning social circles in networks. http://www.kaggle.com/c/learning-social-circles
6. McAuley, J., Leskovec, J.: Learning to discover social circles in ego networks. Adv. Neural Inf. Process. Syst. **25**, 539–547 (2012)
7. McAuley, J., Leskovec, J.: Discovering social circles in ego networks. ACM Trans. Knowl. Discov. Data (TKDD) **8**(1), 4 (2014)
8. Palla, G., Dernyi, I., Farkas, I., Vicsek, T.: Uncovering the overlapping community structure of complex networks in nature and society. Nature **435**(7043), 814–818 (2005)
9. Pathak, N., DeLong, C., Banerjee, A., Erickson, K.: Social topic models for community extraction. In: The 2nd SNA-KDD Workshop (2008)
10. Porter, M.A., Onnela, J.P., Mucha, P.J.: Communities in networks. Not. Amer. Math. Soc. **56**(9), 1082–1097 (2009)
11. Rose, K., Gurewitz, E., Fox, G.C.: Vector quantization by deterministic annealing. IEEE Transactions on Information Theory **38**(4), 1249–1257 (1992)
12. Sachan, M., Contractor, D., Faruquie, T.A., Subramaniam, L.V.: Using content and interactions for discovering communities in social networks. In: Proceedings of the 21st International Conference on World Wide Web, pp. 331–340 (2012)
13. Streich, A.P., Frank, M., Basin, D., Buhmann, J.M.: Multi-assignment clustering for Boolean data. In: Proceedings of the 26th Annual International Conference on Machine Learning, pp. 969–976 (2009)
14. Vaidya, J., Atluri, V., Guo, Q.: The role mining problem: finding a minimal descriptive set of roles. In: Proceedings of the 12th ACM Symposium on Access Control Models and Technologies, pp. 175–184 (2007)
15. Zhou, D., Councill, I., Zha, H., Giles, C.L.: Discovering temporal communities from social network documents. In: Seventh IEEE International Conference on Data Mining, PP. 745–750 (2007)

Source-Target-Source Classification
Using Stacked Denoising Autoencoders

Chetak Kandaswamy[1,2,3]([✉]), Luís M. Silva[2,4], and Jaime S. Cardoso[3]

[1] Instituto de Investigação e Inovação em Saúde, Universidade do Porto,
Porto, Portugal
chetak.kand@gmail.com
[2] INEB - Instituto de Engenharia Biomédica, Porto, Portugal
[3] INESC TEC and Faculdade de Engenharia, Universidade do Porto, Porto, Portugal
[4] Departamento de Matemática, Universidade de Aveiro, Porto, Portugal

Abstract. Deep Transfer Learning (DTL) emerged as a new paradigm
in machine learning in which a deep model is trained on a source task
and the knowledge acquired is then totally or partially transferred to
help in solving a target task. Even though DTL offers a greater flexibility in extracting high-level features and enabling feature transference
from a source to a target task, the DTL solution might get stuck at
local minima leading to performance degradation-negative transference-,
similar to what happens in the classical machine learning approach. In
this paper, we propose the Source-Target-Source (STS) methodology
to reduce the impact of negative transference, by iteratively switching
between source and target tasks in the training process. The results show
the effectiveness of such approach.

Keywords: Deep neural network · Transfer learning · Optimization

1 Introduction

Transfer learning is an approach in which the knowledge acquired by a machine
trained to solve a task is applied with minor modifications to solve a new target
task without having to follow the whole training procedure. It is anticipated that
new tasks and concepts are learned more quickly and accurately by exploiting
past knowledge. In the past, a variety of transfer learning tasks have been investigated, including lifelong learning [1], multi-task learning [2], cross-domain learning [3], self-taught learning [4], and *deep transfer learning* (DTL) [5,8] to name a
few. We investigate the DTL approach proven to be successful in object recognition and image recognition problems using a layer-by-layer feature transference
on large-scale data in either a supervised [5] or a unsupervised [6] setting.

C. Kandaswamy—This work was financed by FEDER funds through the *Programa
Operacional Factores de Competitividade* COMPETE and by Portuguese funds
through FCT Fundação para a Ciência e a Tecnologia in the framework of the
project PTDC/EIA-EIA/119004/2010. We thank Faculdade de Engenharia, Universidade do Porto.

© Springer International Publishing Switzerland 2015
R. Paredes et al. (Eds.): IbPRIA 2015, LNCS 9117, pp. 39–47, 2015.
DOI: 10.1007/978-3-319-19390-8_5

All these methods have shown that there is a limitation on choosing the source problem that would offer good features to solve the new target problem. Even though the problem existed for more than a decade, very few viable solutions have appeared to deal with the problem of negative transference, that is when the knowledge leads to a lower performance on the target problem than the no-transference approach. In the case of neural networks, negative transference occurs due to two reasons: (1) specialization of higher layer neurons to the source problem [7] and (2) fragile co-adaptation of neurons is broken by splitting of transferred layer and randomly initialized layer leads to difficulty in optimization [8]. It is observed either of these two reasons may dominate, depending on whether features are transferred from the bottom, middle, or top of the network. It is observed that the bottom-layer features are standard [7,8] regardless of the cost function or dataset used, called as *general*, similarly the top-layer features depend greatly on the chosen dataset and task, called as *specific*. We may therefore pose the following questions:

- If feature transference is performed, should we transfer general or specific features?
- If feature transference is performed, can we avoid or minimize negative feature transference?

Generally problems change with environment, thus providing only a few training observations to solve the problem. In this paper, we analyse such questions and propose the Source-Target-Source (STS) approach and study the performance STS for two cases: (1) using a few number of examples, and (2) using complete data. As we will see, STS not only effectively reduces the issue of negative transference as well as improves performance over the positive transference situations.

2 Baseline, Transfer Learning and STS Approaches

Let's represent a dataset by a set of tuples $D = (x_n, y_n) \in X \times Y$, where X is the input space and Y is a set of labels. Assume that the n instances are drawn by a sampling process from the input space X with a certain probability distribution $P(X)$. The dataset is split into subsets of training, validation and test sets, $D = \{(x_n, y_n), (x_v, y_v), (x_m, y_m)\}$ drawn from the same distribution $P(X)$. We assume that the "source" dataset D_S with input space X_S and a set of labels Y_S is drawn from a distribution $P_S(X)$ and "target" dataset D_T with input space X_T and a set of labels Y_T is drawn from a distribution $P_T(X)$. Such $P_S(X)$ and $P_T(X)$ may be equal or different.

Baseline (BL): Stacked Denoising Autoencoders (SDA) are multiple layer networks where each one is trained as a denoising autoencoders (dA) (see Fig. 1-BL). SDA training comprises of two stages: an unsupervised pre-training stage followed by a supervised fine-tuning stage. During pre-training (PT), the network is generated by stacking multiple dA one on top of each other thus learning *unsupervised features*, represented as a vector $U(w)$ of optimal weights and

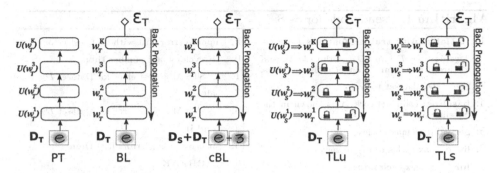

Fig. 1. A pictorial representation of approaches: Pre-training (PT), Baseline (BL), Combined Baseline (cBL), TL unsupervised (TLu),and TL supervised (TLs).

biases. Then a logistic regression layer is added on top and the whole network is fine-tuned (FT) in a supervised way. Thus learning *supervised features* $\mathbf{w} = (w^1, ..., w^K)$, where K is the number of layers.

Combine Baseline (cBL): Given D_S and D_T, a cBL classifier is any function $g(x)$ that is trained from a random combination of instances from $x_S \in X_S$ and $x_T \in X_T$ and then training the SDA to solve for target task Y_T.

Transfer Learning (TL): We first train the source network with source data D_S and Y_S and then copy its hidden layers to the target network. In case $Y_S \neq Y_T$, then we add a classifier layer randomly initialized. The network is trained towards the target task Y_T. We have a choice to fine tune this entire network $\mathbf{w}_T$ as a multi-layer perceptron using back-propagation or *lock* a layer, meaning the transferred feature from source network $\mathbf{w}_S^1 \Rightarrow \mathbf{w}_T^1$ do not change during the error propagation for the target task. This opens up several possible approaches to solve a problem as shown in the Fig. 1 TLu and TLs, where the layers are optionally locked or unlocked. This causes fragile co-adaptation of neurons between layers leading to optimization difficulties. The choice of whether or not to fine-tune the first layer of the target network or not depends on the size of the target dataset and number of parameters [6]. When the performance of the newly trained target network exceeds the performance of the baseline approach we have positive transference; otherwise we have negative transference.

Transfer Learning Unsupervised (TLu): We transfer the unsupervised features of the SDA model from the source to the target network, i.e., $U(\mathbf{w}_S) \Rightarrow \mathbf{w}_T$ as depicted in Fig. 1 TLu. Once the features are transferred to the target network, we add a logistic regression layer for the target task Y_T. Then we fine-tune the entire classifier like a regular multi-layer perceptron with back-propagation choosing to lock or unlock certain layer to solve the target task.

Transfer Learning Supervised (TLs): This is same as supervised layer based approach (SSDA) [7] where we train on the network with BL approach and then we transfer features from source to target network. By selecting to lock or unlock certain layer to solve the target task as illustrated in Fig. 1 TLs.

Algorithm 1. Pseudocode for STS

1: **Initialize with trained features** D_T:

2: Two datasets D_S and D_T, with tasks Y_S and Y_T are drawn from P_S and P_T distributions.

3: Select D_S dataset to train

4: **baseline:** train network A as shown in the baseline approach

5: Set value to max cycles

6: list of max cycles errors to zero

7: **for** M in max cycles **do**

8:     **transfer:** transfer features from network A to new network B as shown in the transfer learning approach

9:     update errors list with best test error

10:     **if** cycle = odd number **then**

11:         STS M = test error for Dataset D_S

12:     **else**

13:         STS M = test error for Dataset D_T

14:     **end if**

15:     **if** error < avg(errors list) **then**

16:         **BREAK**

17:     **end if**

18:     Switch between dataset D_S and D_T

19: **end for**

2.1 Source-Target-Source Framework

In this paper we propose a STS approach[1]. The main idea of transfer learning is that the knowledge (features) learnt in a source domain provide a good initialization for the learning task in a target problem, better than starting the learning in the target domain at random (likely to get stuck in a poor local optimum). In here we propose to iterate the learning between both domains. The intuition is that, like in typical metaheuristics in optimization (i.e. tabu search and simulated annealing), moving the learning from one domain to the other will 'shake' the current local optimal solution, allowing us to keep exploring the space of solutions (ideally, allowing us to reach a better solution in the process). Likewise the metaheuristics in optimization, we keep track of the solutions reached in each iteration, and the outputted solution is the best of all. The pseudo-code for the STS process is listed in Algorithm 1.

Evaluation: We are interested in measuring the improvement using the transferred features over random initialization. We use relative improvement as a measure for comparing the performance of baseline over transfer approach.

$$relative\ improvement = \frac{Baseline\ Avg.\ error\ rate - compared\ method\ Avg.\ error\ rate}{Baseline\ Avg.\ error\ rate}$$

3 Experimental Setup and Results

We evaluate the framework in two different settings for the character recognition task: We use the *MNIST* dataset P_L which has 60,000 training and 10,000 testing instances with labeled hand-written digits from 0 to 9. Additionally, the Chars74k dataset was modified to obtain *Lowercase* dataset P_{LC} labelled lowercase letters from a-to-z and, the *Uppercase* dataset P_{UC} labelled uppercase letters from A-to-Z. Both lowercase and uppercase dataset have 19,812 training and 6,604 testing instances.

---

[1] The naming 'source' and 'target' is some what misleading in our learning framework.

For object recognition tasks: We generated three shapes datasets each with 6,000 training and 14,000 testing instances. First, the *canonical* dataset P_{Sh1} have canonical objects, i.e., equilateral triangle, circle and square. Second, the *non-canonical* dataset P_{Sh2} have non-canonical objects, i.e., triangle, ellipse and rectangles. Finally, the *curve Vs. corner* dataset P_{Sh3} have objects shapes with a curved surface or a corner. All the datasets[2] used in our experiments have images with 28 x 28 pixels and a sample of each dataset are shown in Fig. 2.

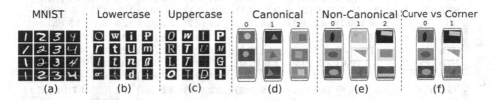

Fig. 2. Samples from character recognition tasks: (a) digits P_L, (b) lowercase P_{LC} and, (c) uppercase P_{UC}; Samples from shape recognition tasks: (d) Canonical P_{sh1}, (e) Non-Canonical P_{sh2} and (f) curve vs. corner P_{sh3}

Training Deep Neural Network: The network we used in character recognition experiments had three hidden layers with [576, 400, 256] units i.e., and the networks used in object recognition experiments also had three hidden layers with [100, 200, 300] units, in order of [bottom, middle, top] respectively. Both networks have an output layer appropriate to the number of classes being considered. All hidden layers were pre-trained as denoising autoencoders via gradient descent, using the cross-entropy cost and a learning rate of 0.001. Pre-training ran for a minimum of 50 epochs in the case of character recognition tasks, and for a minimum of 60 epoch when using object recognition tasks. The complete networks were fine-tuned via gradient descent, using the cross-entropy cost and a learning rate of 0.1. The fine-tuning ran until the validation error did not decrease below 0.1 % or until 1000 epochs for all tasks. Our code for experiments was based on the Theano library 6 and ran with the help of a GTX 770 GPU.

3.1 Transferring Specific Vs. Generic for STS Approach

In this experiment, we intentionally set adverse configurations for feature transference, to study the two main causes of negative feature transference. First, by transferring specific features on tasks that are different, $Y_S \neq Y_T$ we focus on feature specialization in tasks 1 to 4 as listed in Table 1. Second, by transferring generic features on distribution that are similar, we focus on splitting of

---

[2] We would like to acknowledge researchers making available their datasets, Center for Neural Science, New York University for MNIST; Microsoft Research India for Chars74k; and LISA labs, University of Montreal, Canada for BabyAI shapes.

Table 1. Comparison of percentage average error rate ($\bar{\varepsilon}$) for BL, cBL, TLu, TLs and STS approach for different ratios of target data (P_T) reusing source (P_S) distribution. Tasks 1 to 4 study *specific* feature transfer on character recognition problem and tasks 5 & 6 study *generic* feature transfer on object recognition problem.

Approach			Ratio of total number of training samples							#
	P_T	P_S	0.05	0.1	0.2	0.3	0.4	0.5	1	
BL	P_L		6.4 (0.1)	4.7 (0.1)	3.3 (0.1)	2.7 (0.2)	2.3 (0.0)	2.3 (0.4)	1.5 (0.1)	
TLu	P_L	P_{LC}	7.4 (0.2)	5.3 (0.1)	3.8 (0.2)	3.5 (0.7)	2.7 (0.2)	2.5 (0.2)	2.3 (0.0)	①
TLs	P_L	P_{LC}	7.4 (0.1)	5.8 (0.2)	4.6 (0.2)	3.7 (0.0)	3.2 (0.2)	2.9 (0.1)	2.1 (0.1)	
STS	P_L	P_{LC}	**2.6 (0.1)**	**2.1 (0.0)**	**2.0 (0.1)**	**1.9 (0.1)**	**1.8 (0.0)**	**1.7 (0.1)**	**1.5 (0.0)**	
BL	P_L		6.4 (0.1)	4.7 (0.1)	3.3 (0.1)	2.7 (0.2)	2.3 (0.0)	2.3 (0.4)	1.5 (0.1)	
TLu	P_L	P_{UC}	7.4 (0.3)	5.6 (0.6)	4.0 (0.2)	3.1 (0.1)	2.8 (0.2)	3.0 (0.5)	2.1 (0.3)	②
TLs	P_L	P_{UC}	7.6 (0.3)	5.8 (0.2)	4.4 (0.2)	3.5 (0.0)	3.1 (0.0)	2.7 (0.0)	2.0 (0.1)	
STS	P_L	P_{UC}	**2.4 (0.0)**	**2.2 (0.2)**	**1.9 (0.0)**	**1.7 (0.1)**	**1.7 (0.1)**	**1.6 (0.1)**	**1.5 (0.0)**	
BL	P_{LC}		17.1 (0.1)	13.3 (0.2)	10.8 (0.1)	9.5 (0.1)	8.4 (0.1)	7.7 (0.6)	4.8 (0.1)	
TLu	P_{LC}	P_L	17.1 (0.6)	13.8 (0.6)	10.9 (0.2)	9.2 (0.4)	8.2 (0.4)	7.2 (0.2)	**4.7 (0.2)**	③
TLs	P_{LC}	P_L	18.9 (0.2)	14.6 (0.8)	11.3 (0.2)	9.6 (0.2)	8.7 (0.4)	7.5 (0.2)	5.3 (0.3)	
STS	P_{LC}	P_L	**12.3 (0.3)**	**9.7 (0.0)**	**8.5 (0.6)**	**7.2 (0.4)**	**6.7 (0.2)**	**6.0 (0.1)**	5.0 (0.2)	
BL	P_{UC}		16.2 (0.2)	12.9 (0.2)	10.4 (0.2)	9.1 (0.1)	8.5 (0.7)	7.3 (0.5)	4.9 (0.2)	
TLu	P_{UC}	P_L	15.9 (0.3)	13.2 (0.4)	10.8 (0.3)	9.1 (0.3)	8.0 (0.1)	7.4 (0.3)	**4.6 (0.1)**	④
TLs	P_{UC}	P_L	16.5 (0.3)	13.6 (0.5)	10.8 (0.2)	9.2 (0.2)	8.5 (0.2)	7.4 (0.1)	5.0 (0.2)	
STS	P_{UC}	P_L	**10.8 (0.4)**	**9.1 (0.1)**	**7.8 (0.2)**	**6.8 (0.1)**	**6.6 (0.1)**	**6.1 (0.1)**	4.7 (0.1)	
BL	P_{Sh2}		37.9 (10.2)	36.6 (4.8)	25.1 (3.6)	16.9 (9.6)	14.7 (7.8)	11.9 (7.1)	**4.2 (2.3)**	
cBL	P_{Sh2}	P_{Sh1}	28.7 (6.3)	13.6 (2.2)	12.6 (10.4)	9.9 (8.0)	6.6 (3.0)	13.0 (8.4)	10.6 (6.7)	⑤
TLs	P_{Sh2}	P_{Sh1}	32.3 (2.3)	32.0 (3.3)	30.7 (4.1)	26.9 (1.7)	26.4 (1.9)	27.0 (1.3)	24.0 (0.3)	
STS	P_{Sh2}	P_{Sh1}	**7.7 (2.6)**	**6.2 (2.4)**	**5.9 (3.5)**	**5.4 (3.1)**	**5.3 (2.6)**	**5.0 (3.0)**	5.2 (2.2)	
BL	P_{Sh2}		37.9 (10.2)	36.6 (4.8)	25.1 (3.6)	16.9 (9.6)	14.7 (7.8)	11.9 (7.1)	**4.2 (2.3)**	
cBL	P_{Sh2}	P_{Sh3}	31.0 (1.8)	30.5 (8.8)	18.4 (11.3)	20.0 (11.2)	5.6 (1.7)	12.4 (7.6)	8.9 (6.6)	⑥
TLs	P_{Sh2}	P_{Sh3}	25.0 (3.3)	20.7 (1.8)	18.4 (2.0)	18.4 (1.1)	16.8 (1.8)	17.2 (1.7)	15.5 (2.5)	
STS	P_{Sh2}	P_{Sh3}	**6.1 (2.3)**	**5.9 (2.7)**	**5.8 (2.6)**	**4.9 (2.1)**	**5.0 (2.2)**	5.7 (3.0)	5.6 (2.6)	

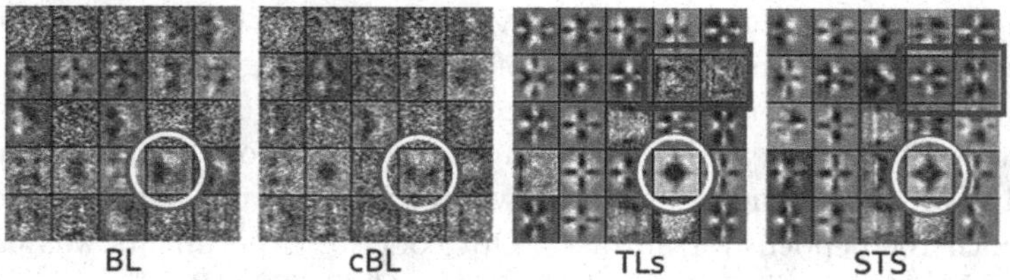

Left margin labels: Characters — Tasks are different (groups 1–4); Objects — Tasks are similar (groups 5–6).

BL   cBL   TLs   STS

Fig. 3. Feature samples from first layer of non-canonical object recognition task. We observe the transition of same features becoming more distinct, from BL towards STS approach are marked in red circle and from TLs towards STS marked in blue box (Color figure online).

co-adapted neurons between layers in tasks 5 & 6 in Table 1. Here we study the effects of negative feature transference problems with few training samples.

First, we study the effects of transferring *specific features* on character recognition problem. In Table 1 for TLu and TLs approach, tasks 1 & 2 shown negative transference for classifying handwritten digits P_L by reusing source network P_{LC} and P_{UC}. Tasks 3 & 4 show positive transference for classifying either P_{LC} and

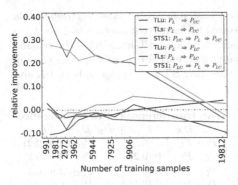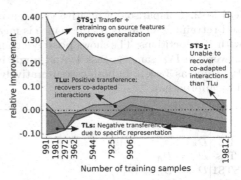

Fig. 4. (**Left:**) Relative improvement over baseline approach for character recognition tasks 3 & 4 as listed in Table 1; (**Right:**) Relative improvement for the tasks on the left, the regions are enclosed to observe relative improvement between two different approaches. We observe negative transference for **TLs** (supervised) approach as it gets stuck at local solution space of specialized features. **TLu** (unsupervised) approach easily recovers the fragile co-adapted neurons as the unsupervised features are not target specific. Also TLu improves over the baseline for complete training data. **STS** approach as intended shake the current local optimal solution, thus overcoming the specialized features of source network unlike TLs approach. The STS shows performance improvement, but unable to recover the fragile co-adapted neurons thus using complete target data, had lower performance than TLu and baseline.

P_{UC} by reusing source network P_L training on complete data. Using STS we observe for tasks 1 to 4 outperforms other approaches for few target samples. In tasks 1 & 2 on STS outperforms BL approaches with a relative improvement of $\approx 59\%$ and in tasks 3 & 4 on STS shows $\approx 30\%$ improvement for 0.05 % of target data. Figure 4. illustrates the relative improvement performance of BL, TLu, TLs and STS approaches for the tasks 1 & 2.

Second, tasks 5 & 6 analyse the effects of transferring *generic features* on object recognition problem as shown in Table 1. Intuitively canonical objects belong to a subset of non-canonical objects (equilateral triangles belong to a subset of triangles), thus $P_{Sh1} \in P_{Sh2}$ and also number of categories to classify in source and target tasks are equal $Y_S = Y_T$. Thus the only change are due to splitting of co-adapted neurons between the layers while fine-tuning. As we have forced to *lock* the bottom layer, making the optimization harder. cBL, TLu and TLs approaches show negative transference as intended. As solving non-canonical objects is more difficult than solving canonical objects [7]. Using STS approach we observe a relative improvement of $\approx 81\%$ for the same task using 0.05 % of total training data, and baseline approach performs better when using complete training data. Figure 3 shows the non-canonical task features for BL, cBL, TL and STS approach using 0.05 % of total training data.

To solve for complete target data using STS, we implement repeating several cycles of STS (see Algorithm 1) till a certain stop criteria is reached. we observe significant improvements using STS over both positive and negative transferred features using TLs as listed in Table 2.

Table 2. Comparison of positive vs. negative transference using *complete target data* and retraining all layers; Performance is measured using percent average test error ($\bar{\varepsilon}$) with 10 repetitions; TLs shows **positive** transference for classifying MNIST P_L reusing Lowercase P_{LC} same as Task 1. And **negative** transference for classifying P_{LC} reusing P_L, same as Task 3. In both cases iteratively repeating **STS** outperforms both BL and TLs approaches.

	Iterative STS	-ve transference			+ve transference		
		D_B	D_A	$\bar{\varepsilon}$	D_B	D_A	$\bar{\varepsilon}$
BL	D_A	P_{LC}	P_L	1.7 (0.3)	P_L	P_{LC}	4.9 (0.2)
TLs	$D_B \Rightarrow D_A$	P_{LC}	P_L	1.9 (0.2)	P_L	P_{LC}	4.5 (0.2)
STS1	$D_A \Rightarrow D_B \Rightarrow D_A$	P_{LC}	P_L	$\overline{1.6}$ (0.1)	P_L	P_{LC}	$\overline{4.9}$ (0.1)
STS2	$D_B \Rightarrow D_A \Rightarrow D_B \Rightarrow D_A$	P_{LC}	P_L	1.9 (0.1)	P_L	P_{LC}	**4.4 (0.2)**
STS3	$D_A \Rightarrow D_B \Rightarrow D_A \Rightarrow D_B \Rightarrow D_A$	P_{LC}	P_L	1.6 (0.1)	P_L	P_{LC}	4.9 (0.1)
STS4	$D_B \Rightarrow D_A \Rightarrow D_B \Rightarrow D_A \Rightarrow D_B \Rightarrow D_A$	P_{LC}	P_L	1.9 (0.1)	P_L	P_{LC}	4.5 (0.2)
STS5	$D_A \Rightarrow D_B \Rightarrow D_A \Rightarrow D_B \Rightarrow D_A \Rightarrow D_B \Rightarrow D_A$	P_{LC}	P_L	**1.5 (0.1)**	P_L	P_{LC}	5.0 (0.1)

4   Conclusions and Discussion

Our experiments with the character and object recognition tasks show a deep neural network learns new task more quickly and accurately using transfer learning approach. Unfortunately, they are unreliable for different source and target distribution, because sometime they lead to negative feature transference. The STS algorithm was designed to avoid negative transfer, by recovering fragile co-adapted interactions of neurons between the layers. We make several contributions as listed: 1. The STS approach outperform both baseline and transfer learning approaches. 2. We observe TLu and TLs approach for transferring generic features on distribution that are similar and transferring specific features on tasks that are different to study the impact of splitting of co-adapted neurons. 3. Finally, using the cyclic STS approach reduced the transferability gap between the source and the target tasks. We summarize that the STS outperforms both the baseline and the transfer learning approaches.

Even though the cyclic STS reduced the transferability gap between the source and the target tasks. A pattern is observed when the initial transference was negative. In negative transference case of cyclic STS, we observe odd cycles perform better than even cycles. Iteratively switching the training between the source and the target did not sufficiently perturb the solution out of local minima to a new solution space. We would like to explore this issue by repeating the transference several times and train the network to jump to a new solution space to obtain good generalization. Also exploring the possibility of using multiple source problem to obtain diverse and generic features.

References

1. Thrun, S.: Learning to learn: introduction. In: Learning To Learn (1996)
2. Caruana, R.: Multitask learning. Mach. Learn. **28**(1), 41–75 (1997)

3. Daumé III, H., Marcu, D.: Domain adaptation for statistical classifiers. J. Artif. Intell. Res. (JAIR) **26**, 101–126 (2006)
4. Raina, R., Battle, A., Lee, H., Packer, B., Ng, A.Y.: Self-taught learning: transfer learning from unlabeled data. In: ACM Conference on Proceedings (ICML) (2007)
5. Ciresan, D., Meier, U., Schmidhuber, J.: Multi-column deep neural networks for image classification. In: IEEE Conference on Computer Vision and Pattern Recognition (CVPR). IEEE (2012)
6. Kandaswamy, C., Silva, L.M., Alexandre, L.A., de Sá, J.M.: Improving deep neural network performance by reusing features trained with transductive transference. In: Wermter, S., Weber, C., Duch, W., Honkela, T., Koprinkova-Hristova, P., Magg, S., Palm, G., Villa, A.E.P. (eds.) ICANN 2014. LNCS, vol. 8681, pp. 265–272. Springer, Heidelberg (2014)
7. Kandaswamy, C., Silva, L.M., Alexandre, L.A., Sousa, R. Santos, J.M., de Sá, J.M.: Improving transfer learning accuracy by reusing stacked denoising autoencoders. In: IEEE Conference on SMC. IEEE (2014)
8. Yosinski, J., et al.: How transferable are features in deep neural networks? In: Advances in Neural Information Processing Systems (2014)

On the Impact of Distance Metrics
in Instance-Based Learning Algorithms

Noel Lopes[1,2]([✉]) and Bernardete Ribeiro[2]

[1] UDI, Polytechnic of Guarda, Guarda, Portugal
[2] Department of Informatics Engineering, CISUC, University of Coimbra,
Coimbra, Portugal
noel@ipg.pt, bribeiro@dei.uc.pt

Abstract. In this paper we analyze the impact of distinct distance metrics in instance-based learning algorithms. In particular, we look at the well-known 1-Nearest Neighbor (NN) algorithm and the Incremental Hypersphere Classifier (IHC) algorithm, which proved to be efficient in large-scale recognition problems and online learning. We provide a detailed empirical evaluation on fifteen datasets with several sizes and dimensionality. We then statistically show that the Euclidean and Manhattan metrics significantly yield good results in a wide range of problems. However, grid-search like methods are often desirable to determine the best matching metric depending on the problem and algorithm.

Keywords: Distance metrics · Instance-based learning · Incremental learning · Nearest Neighbor · Incremental Hypersphere Classifier (IHC)

1 Introduction

Incremental learning algorithms embody the potential to deal with large scale datasets and data streams. Rather than requiring access to the complete dataset, they adjust their models continuously with upcoming data. One of such algorithms, recently proposed, is the Incremental Hypersphere Classifier (IHC), which possesses desirable characteristics in terms of multi-class support, complexity, scalability, interpretability and potential to handle concept drifts [8,9]. Moreover, it has been successfully used as an instance selection method for choosing a representative subset of the data that was later used to derive improved batch models [7].

Despite these advantages, IHC is a distance based learning method and naturally it is sensitive to the choice of the distance metric. In this context, in this paper, we analyze the impact of distinct distance metrics in both the 1-NN and the IHC algorithms. The reason to analyze the effects of the distance metrics also in the 1-NN is because we can look at IHC as a generalization of the former.

The remainder of this paper is organized as follows. The next section details the IHC algorithm and Sect. 3 describes the metrics that were analyzed in this study. Section 4 presents the experimental results and finally, in Sect. 5 the conclusions and future work are delineated.

© Springer International Publishing Switzerland 2015
R. Paredes et al. (Eds.): IbPRIA 2015, LNCS 9117, pp. 48–56, 2015.
DOI: 10.1007/978-3-319-19390-8_6

2 Incremental Hypersphere Classifier (IHC) Algorithm

Let us consider a training dataset, $\{(\mathbf{x_i}, y_i) : i = 1, \ldots, N\}$, composed by N samples, each encompassing an input vector, $\mathbf{x_i} \in \mathbb{R}^D$, with D features, and the associated class label, $y_i \in \{1, \ldots, C\}$, where C is the number of classes.

For each training sample, i, IHC defines an hypersphere with center $\mathbf{x_i}$ and radius ρ_i as follows:

$$\rho_i = \frac{\min(d(\mathbf{x_i}, \mathbf{x_j}))}{2}, \text{ for all } j \text{ where } y_j \neq y_i \qquad (1)$$

where $d(\mathbf{x_i}, \mathbf{x_j})$ is the distance between $\mathbf{x_i}$ and $\mathbf{x_j}$ input vectors (see Sect. 3). The hypersphere's delineate the regions of influence of the associated samples and are used to classify new instances. Basically, given a new data point, $\mathbf{x_k}$, it is classified with the class associated to the nearest hypersphere (not the nearest sample). More precisely, $\mathbf{x_k}$ is associated to class y_i (i.e. $y_k = y_i$) provided that:

$$d(\mathbf{x_i}, \mathbf{x_k}) - ga_i\rho_i \leq d(\mathbf{x_j}, \mathbf{x_k}) - ga_j\rho_j, \text{ for all } j \neq i \qquad (2)$$

where g (gravity) controls the extension of the zones of influence, increasing or shrinking them and a_i is the accuracy of sample i when classifying itself and the forgotten training samples for which i was the nearest sample in memory. A forgotten sample is one that either has been removed from memory or did not qualify to enter the memory in the first place. Hence, the accuracy is only updated when the memory is full. In such a scenario, at each iteration, the accuracy of a single (nearest) sample is updated, while the accuracy of all the others remains unchanged. The accuracy is the first mechanism of defense against outliers, reducing effectively their influence in the model.

Notice that for $g = 0$ the decision rule of the IHC is exactly the same as the one of the 1-NN (see Eq. 2). Hence, by fine-tuning g, IHC will always yield better or equal performance than 1-NN. This is important because Cover and Hart [3] demonstrated, in the limit $N \to \infty$, that the 1-NN error rate is never more than twice the minimum achievable error rate of an optimal classifier [2].

A major advantage of the IHC algorithm relies on the possibility of building models incrementally on a sample-by-sample basis. Figure 1 presents the hypersphere's generated by IHC and the resulting decision surface, (a) prior to and (b) after the addition of a new sample, for a toy problem. Notice that the samples near the decision border have smaller radius than those furthest, providing a simple method for determining the relevance of each sample. Hence, when the memory is full, the samples with smaller radius are kept, while those with bigger radius are discarded. By doing so, we keep the samples that play the most significant role in the construction of the decision surface (given the available memory) while removing those that have less or no impact in the model.

Unfortunately, outliers will most likely have a small radius and end-up occupying our limited memory resources. Thus, although their impact is diminished by the use of the accuracy in Eq. 2, it is still important to identify and remove them from memory. To address this problem IHC mimics the process used by the

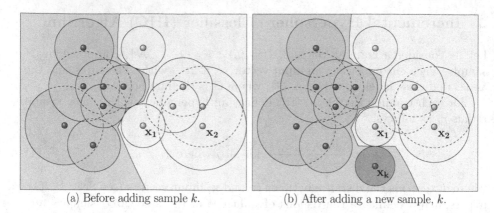

(a) Before adding sample k.   (b) After adding a new sample, k.

Fig. 1. Hypersphere's and decision surface generated by IHC ($g = 1$) for a toy problem.

IB3 algorithm [1,11], which consists of removing all samples that are believed to be noisy by employing a significance test.

A more detailed description of the IHC can be found elsewhere [8,9] and a working version of the algorithm, including its source code, can be found at http://sourceforge.net/projects/ihclassifier/.

3   Distance Metrics

A distance metric is a function that measures the similarity between two vectors, $\mathbf{x_i} = [x_{i1}, x_{i2}, \ldots, x_{iD}]$ and $\mathbf{x_j} = [x_{j1}, x_{j2}, \ldots, x_{jD}]$, yielding a non-negative real number, representing the degree of discrepancy between the two data points.

Although a large number of distance metrics have been proposed in the literature, the most widely used and well known metric is still the Euclidean distance, stated by Euclid more than two thousand years ago. Another extensively used metric, is the Manhattan, also known as the city-block distance [6].

Table 1 presents the distance metrics used in this study. For the Minkowsky metric, p was set to the number of features, D, in order to give more weight to the individual distance components as the space dimensionality increases [5].

4   Experimental Results

Our goal consists of analyzing the impact of distinct distance metrics in both the 1-NN and the IHC algorithms. With that purpose in mind, we carried out extensive experiments on fifteen UCI databases [4] with distinct characteristics (number of samples, features and classes). For statistical significance, each experiment was executed using repeated 5-fold stratified cross-validation. Altogether 30 different random cross-validation partitions were created, accounting for a total of 150 runs per benchmark and algorithm settings. The experiments were conducted using the 1-NN and the IHC algorithm with both $g = 1$ and $g = 2$

Table 1. Distance metrics' formulas.

Metric	Formula
Euclidean	$d(\mathbf{x_i}, \mathbf{x_j}) = \left(\sum_{k=1}^{D} (x_{ik} - x_{jk})^2 \right)^{\frac{1}{2}}$
Manhattan	$d(\mathbf{x_i}, \mathbf{x_j}) = \sum_{k=1}^{D} |x_{ik} - x_{jk}|$
Canberra	$d(\mathbf{x_i}, \mathbf{x_j}) = \sum_{k=1}^{D} \frac{|x_{ik} - x_{jk}|}{|x_{ik}| + |x_{jk}|}$
Chebychev	$d(\mathbf{x_i}, \mathbf{x_j}) = \max(|x_{ik} - x_{jk}|)$
Minkowsky	$d(\mathbf{x_i}, \mathbf{x_j}) = \left(\sum_{k=1}^{D} |x_{ik} - x_{jk}|^p \right)^{\frac{1}{p}}$

Table 2. Best distance metric depending on the database and chosen algorithm.

Database	Samples	Inputs	Classes	1-NN	IHC ($g = 1$)	IHC ($g = 2$)
Balance	500	4	3	Chebychev	Chebychev	Canberra
Breast cancer	569	30	2	Manhattan	Manhattan	Euclidean
Ecoli	336	7	8	Euclidean	Minkowsky	Minkowsky
German	1000	59	2	Euclidean	Canberra	Manhattan
Glass	214	9	6	Manhattan	Manhattan	Manhattan
Haberman	306	3	2	Minkowsky	Euclidean	Euclidean
Heart-statlog	270	20	2	Canberra	Canberra	Canberra
Ionosphere	351	34	2	Manhattan	Chebychev	Chebychev
Iris	150	4	3	Chebychev	Minkowsky	Chebychev
Pima	768	8	2	Euclidean	Minkowsky	Euclidean
Sonar	208	60	2	Manhattan	Manhattan	Euclidean
Tic-tac-toe	958	9	2	Canberra	Euclidean	Minkowsky
Vehicle	946	18	4	Euclidean	Euclidean	Euclidean
Wine	178	13	3	Manhattan	Manhattan	Manhattan
Yeast	1484	8	10	Manhattan	Euclidean	Euclidean

settings. Table 2 presents the main characteristics of the experimental databases as well as the best distance metric for each algorithm. Moreover, Fig. 2 presents the results for the 1-NN and Figs. 3 and 4 the results for the IHC algorithm, using respectively $g = 1$ and $g = 2$ settings. In addition, Fig. 5 reports the average F-score results for each distance metric. Note that, with the exception of the Iris problem, the best results were obtained with the IHC algorithm.

Using the Wilcoxon signed rank test, the null hypothesis of the 1-NN having an equal or better F-score than the IHC (considering $g = 1$) is rejected at a significance level of 0.005 for the Euclidean, Manhattan, Canberra and Minkowsky distance metrics and rejected at a significance level of 0.01 for the Chebychev

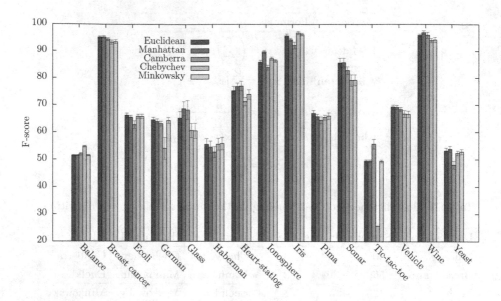

Fig. 2. Benchmark results for the 1-NN, according to the distance metric used.

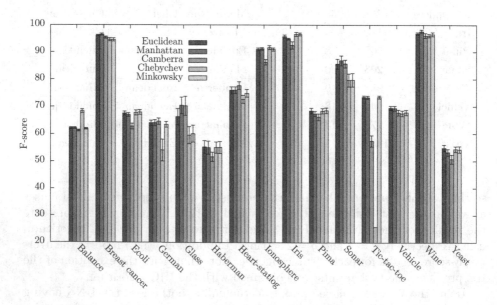

Fig. 3. Benchmark results for the IHC ($g = 1$), according to the distance metric used.

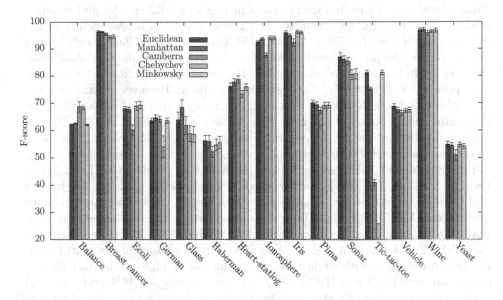

Fig. 4. Benchmark results for the IHC ($g = 2$), according to the distance metric used.

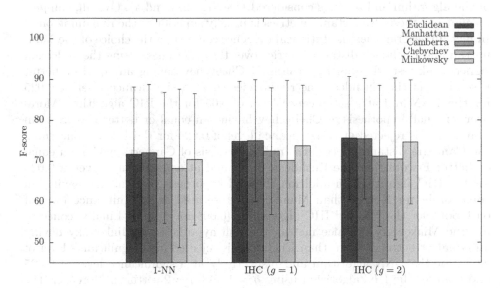

Fig. 5. Average performance for the 1-NN and IHC algorithms, according to the distance metric used.

metric. The same holds true when setting $g = 2$, except for the Canberra metric. Thus, these results corroborate the ones in Lopes and Ribeiro [8] and strongly evidence that the IHC significantly outperforms the 1-NN independently of the distance metric used (see Figs. 2, 3, 4 and 5). On average the Chebychev distance metric yielded the poorest results, both for the 1-NN and for the IHC algorithms (see Fig. 5). In particular, concerning the Tic-tac-toe problem, its performance is very poor (25.74 %) for all of the algorithms analyzed. However, considering the Ionosphere and Iris databases, this metric actually performed better than the remaining ones in most of the cases (see Table 2 and Figs. 2, 3 and 4). Excluding the Chebychev metric, in general Canberra yielded, on average, the worst results as compared to the remaining metrics (see Fig. 5). Nevertheless, it consistently yielded the best results for the Heart-statlog problem (see Table 2, and Figs. 2, 3 and 4). Minkowsky performs, on average, better than the Chebychev and Canberra and therefore it appears to be a better choice than these distance metrics (see Fig. 5), although there is no compelling statistical evidence to support this decision. This metric performed particularly well on the Ecoli problem (see Table 2 and Figs. 2, 3 and 4). The average performance of Manhattan and Euclidean is similar, with slightly advantage for the Manhattan distance metric, concerning the 1-NN and IHC with $g = 2$ (respectively +0.37 % and +0.16 %) and slightly advantage for the Euclidean metric, considering the IHC algorithm with $g = 1$. In the case of the NN algorithm, the results confirm the findings of Salzberg [10], which suggested that the differences between these two metrics were not significant, from the point of view of the NN algorithm. Notwithstanding, the Manhattan performs particularly well on the Glass problem regardless of the algorithm and settings considered (see Figs. 2, 3 and 4). Overall, the performance of these two distance metrics is usually superior to the remaining ones. In fact, in general, there is statistical evidence compelling the choice of the Manhattan and Euclidean distance metrics over the other ones. Using the Wilcoxon signed rank test, the null hypothesis of Chebychev having an equal or better F-score than the Euclidean metric is rejected at a significance level of 0.025 for the 1-NN and at a significance level of 0.05 for the IHC algorithm. Moreover, the null hypothesis of Chebychev having an equal or better F-score than Manhattan is rejected at a significance level of 0.025 for the 1-NN. Concerning the Canberra distance metric, the null hypothesis of Canberra having an equal or better F-score than the Euclidean is rejected at a significance level of 0.025 for the IHC algorithm. In addition the null hypothesis of Canberra having an equal or better F-score than Manhattan is rejected at a significance level of 0.01 both for the NN and IHC algorithms (0.005 for $g = 1$). Finally, concerning the Minkowsky distance metric, the null hypothesis of Minkowsky having an equal or better F-score than Euclidean is rejected at a significance level of 0.025 for the 1-NN algorithm and respectively at a significance level of 0.025 and 0.05 for the IHC algorithm using $g = 1$ and $g = 2$ settings. Moreover, the null hypothesis of Minkowsky having an equal or better F-score than Manhattan is rejected at a significance level of 0.05 for the 1-NN algorithm. Nevertheless, the No-Free-Lunch theorem [12] still applies and using the appropriate distance metric is fundamental for improving the generalization capabilities of distance based Machine Learning (ML) algorithms. Therefore, performing a grid search with the distance metric and g parameters (in the case of the IHC), using the training data, is vital to enhance the algorithms' generalization capabilities.

5 Conclusions and Future Work

The distance metric is a pivotal parameter of distance based ML algorithms and models. The empirical results, obtained in this paper, evidence that the best metric depends on the problems' data distribution (see Table 2) and therefore grid-search like methods are crucial to potentially determine the most-advantageous metric for a given problem and algorithm. This study also demonstrates that the Euclidean and Manhattan, two of the most commonly used distance metrics, which consistently yield good results over a wide range of problems (see Figs. 2, 3 and 4), are probably the best choices for distance based learning methods when performing a grid-search method is not a viable option. In this scenario, the Manhattan distance is preferred, in particular for large datasets, since it is computationally less demanding. Future work will analyze combining different distance metrics as well as building ensembles using distinct distance metrics.

Acknowledgments. This work is partly funded by iCIS (CENTRO-07-ST24-FEDER-002003).

References

1. Aha, D., Kibler, D., Albert, M.: Instance-based learning algorithms. Mach. Learn. **6**(1), 37–66 (1991)
2. Bishop, C.M.: Pattern Recognition and Machine Learning. Springer, New York (2006)
3. Cover, T.M., Hart, P.E.: Nearest neighbor pattern classification. IEEE Trans. Inf. Theor. **13**(1), 21–27 (1967)
4. Frank, A., Asuncion, A.: UCI machine learning repository. http://archive.ics.uci.edu/ml
5. de Geer, J.P.V.: Some aspects of Minkowski distance. Department of Data Theory, Leiden University (1995)
6. Hassanat, A.B.A.: Dimensionality invariant similarity measure. J. Am. Sci. **10**(8), 221–226 (2014)
7. Lopes, N., Correia, D., Pereira, C., Ribeiro, B., Dourado, A.: An incremental hypersphere learning framework for protein membership prediction. In: Corchado, E., Snášel, V., Abraham, A., Woźniak, M., Graña, M., Cho, S.-B. (eds.) HAIS 2012, Part III. LNCS, vol. 7208, pp. 429–439. Springer, Heidelberg (2012)
8. Lopes, N., Ribeiro, B.: An incremental class boundary preserving hypersphere classifier. In: Lu, B.-L., Zhang, L., Kwok, J. (eds.) ICONIP 2011, Part II. LNCS, vol. 7063, pp. 690–699. Springer, Heidelberg (2011)
9. Lopes, N., Ribeiro, B.: Adaptive many-core machines. In: Lopes, N., Ribeiro, B. (eds.) Machine Learning for Adaptive Many-Core Machines – A Practical Approach. SBD, vol. 7, pp. 189–200. Springer, Heidelberg (2015)

10. Salzberg, S.: Distance metrics for instance-based learning. In: Ras, Z., Zemankova, M. (eds.) Methodologies for Intelligent Systems. LNCS, vol. 542, pp. 399–408. Springer, Heidelberg (1991)
11. Wilson, D., Martinez, T.: Reduction techniques for instance-based learning algorithms. Mach. Learn. 38(3), 257–286 (2000)
12. Wolpert, D.H.: The lack of a priori distinctions between learning algorithms. Neural Comput. 8(7), 1341–1390 (1996)

Multi-class Boosting for Imbalanced Data

Antonio Fernández-Baldera[1], José M. Buenaposada[2], and Luis Baumela[1(✉)]

[1] Dept. de Inteligencia Artificial, Universidad Politécnica de Madrid, Madrid, Spain
antonio.fbaldera@upm.es, lbaumela@fi.upm.es
[2] ETSII, Universidad Rey Juan Carlos, Madrid, Spain
josemiguel.buenaposada@urjc.es

Abstract. We consider the problem of multi-class classification with imbalanced data-sets. To this end, we introduce a cost-sensitive multi-class Boosting algorithm (*BAdaCost*) based on a generalization of the Boosting margin, termed *multi-class cost-sensitive margin*. To address the class imbalance we introduce a cost matrix that weighs more hevily the costs of confused classes and a procedure to estimate these costs from the confusion matrix of a standard 0|1-loss classifier. Finally, we evaluate the performance of the approach with synthetic and real data-sets and compare our results with the AdaC2.M1 algorithm.

Keywords: Boosting · Multi-class classification · Imbalanced data

1 Introduction

Imbalanced classification problems are characterized for having large differences in the number of samples in each class. This frequently occurs in complex data-sets, such as those involving class overlap, small sample size, or within-class imbalance. In this situation, standard classifiers perform poorly since they minimize the number of misclassified training samples disregarding minority classes [1]. Solutions to the class imbalance problem may be coarsely organized into data-based, that re-sample the data space to balance the classes, and algorithm-based approaches, that introduce new algorithms that bias the learning towards the minority class [1]. Boosting methods have been extensively used to address the problem of classification with imbalanced data-sets [1,2] and cost-sensitive classification for two-class problems [3–5]. However, with the exception of AdaC2.M1 [2], no previous work has addressed the problem of multi-class Boosting in presence of imbalanced data.

In our proposal we merge both multi-class and cost-sensitive perspectives into a new Boosting algorithm, BAdaCost, that stands for *Boosting Adapted for Cost-matrix*. We introduce the concept of *Multi-class Cost-sensitive Margin*, which serves as link between multi-class margins and the values of the cost matrix, both of them considered as argument of a loss function. We also present a procedure to estimate this matrix from the confusion matrix of a standard 0|1-loss classifier. We justify BAdaCost's good properties in a set of experiments.

© Springer International Publishing Switzerland 2015
R. Paredes et al. (Eds.): IbPRIA 2015, LNCS 9117, pp. 57–64, 2015.
DOI: 10.1007/978-3-319-19390-8_7

2   Background

In this section we briefly review some Boosting results related to our proposal. We start by introducing AdaBoost [6]. Given N training data instances $\{(\mathbf{x}_i, l_i)\}$, where $\mathbf{x}_i \in X$ encodes the object to be classified and $l_i \in L = \{+1, -1\}$ is the class label, the goal of AdaBoost is learning a strong classifier $\text{sign}(\mathbf{H}(\mathbf{x})) = \text{sign}(\sum_{m=1}^{M} \beta_m G_m(\mathbf{x}))$ based on a linear combination of weak classifiers, $G_m :$ $X \to L$. At each round m, a *direction* for classification, $G_m(\mathbf{x}) = \pm 1$, and a *step size*, β_m are added to an additive model whose goal is to minimize the empirical risk of the *Exponential Loss Function* [7], $\mathcal{L}(l, G_m(\mathbf{x})) = \exp(-l\, G_m(\mathbf{x}))$, defined over $z = l\, G_m(\mathbf{x})$, usually known as the *margin* [8].

2.1   Multi-class Boosting with Vectorial Encoding

A successful way to generalize the symmetry of class-label representation in the binary case to the multi-class case is using a set of vector-valued codes that represent the correspondence between the multi-class label set $L = \{1, \dots, K\}$ and a collection of vectors $Y = \{\mathbf{y}_1, \dots, \mathbf{y}_K\}$, where $\mathbf{y}_k$ has a value 1 in the kth coordinate and $\frac{-1}{K-1}$ elsewhere. It is immediate to see the equivalence between classifiers G defined over L and classifiers $\mathbf{g}$ defined over Y, $G(\mathbf{x}) = l \in L \Leftrightarrow \mathbf{g}(\mathbf{x}) = \mathbf{y}_l \in Y$. Zou, Zhu and Hastie [8] used this codification to generalize the concept of binary margin to the multi-class case using a related vectorial codification in which a K-vector $\mathbf{y} = (y_1, \dots, y_K)^\top$ is said to be a *margin vector* if it satisfies the *sum-to-zero* condition, $\sum_{i=1}^{K} y_i = 0$. The SAMME algorithm generalizes the binary AdaBoost to the multi-class case [9]. It uses the above codification and an exponential loss whose risk is minimized using a stage-wise additive gradient descent approach. In this loss function the binary margin, $z = lG(\mathbf{x})$, is replaced by the multi-class vectorial margin defined with a scalar product, $z = \mathbf{y}^\top \mathbf{g}(\mathbf{x})$, producing the *Multi-class Exponential Loss Function* (MELF), $\mathcal{L}(\mathbf{y}, \mathbf{g}(\mathbf{x})) = \exp\left(-\frac{\mathbf{y}^\top \mathbf{g}(\mathbf{x})}{K}\right)$.

In this paper we generalize the class-label representation here described so that our Boosting algorithm can model the asymmetries arising when training on an unbalanced data set.

2.2   Cost-Sensitive Binary Boosting

Classifiers that weigh certain types of errors more heavily than others are called cost-sensitive. They are used for example in medical diagnosis and object detection problems. Optimal cost-sensitive Boosting in two-class problems has been already studied in the literature [3–5]. The solution in [3] is based on minimizing the *Cost-sensitive Binary Exponential Loss Function* (CBELF) $\mathcal{L}(l, f(\mathbf{x})) = I(l = 1)\exp\left(-lC_1 f(\mathbf{x})\right) + I(l = -1)\exp\left(-lC_2 f(\mathbf{x})\right)$, where $I(\cdot)$ is the indicator function and C_j are the costs of the two possible errors. Classification with imbalanced data-sets is a typical cost-sensitive problem. To counter balance the bias in the data we want the classifier's loss function to under-weigh errors from the majority class. In this paper we generalize the Cost-sensitive AdaBoost [3] to the multiple-class case and use it to solve imbalanced problems.

3 Multi-class Cost-Sensitive Margin

In this section we introduce the multi-class cost sensitive margin, based on which we derive the BAdaCost algorithm. Let us suppose the misclassification costs for our multi-class problem are encoded using a $K \times K$-matrix $\mathbf{C}$, where each value $C(i, j)$ represents the cost of misclassifying an instance with real label i as j. We can assume without loss of generality [10] that $C(i, i) = 0, \forall i \in L$, i.e. the cost of correct classifications is null. We introduce an essential change in the MELF to handle this kind of problems. Firstly, let $\mathbf{C}^*$ be a $K \times K$-matrix defined in the following way

$$C^*(i, j) = \begin{cases} C(i, j) & \text{if } i \neq j \\ -\sum_{h=1}^{K} C(j, h) & \text{if } i = j \end{cases}, \ \forall i, j \in L. \tag{1}$$

For our cost-sensitive classification problem each value $C^*(j, j)$ will represent a "negative cost" associated to a correct classification, i.e. a "reward".

The jth row in $\mathbf{C}^*$, denoted as $\mathbf{C}(j, -)$, is a margin vector that encodes the cost structure associated to the jth label. By using it we can define the *multi-class cost-sensitive margin value* for an instance $(\mathbf{x}, l)$ with respect to the multi-class vectorial classifier $\mathbf{g}(\cdot)$ as $z_C := \mathbf{C}^*(l, -) \cdot \mathbf{g}(\mathbf{x})$. It is easy to verify that if $\mathbf{g}(\mathbf{x}) = \mathbf{y}_i \in Y$, for a certain $i \in L$, then $\mathbf{C}^*(l, -) \cdot \mathbf{g}(\mathbf{x}) = \frac{K}{K-1}\mathbf{C}^*(l, i)$. Hence, multi-class cost-sensitive margins obtained from a discrete classifier $\mathbf{g} : \mathbf{x} \to Y$ can be computed using the "label valued" analogous of $\mathbf{g}$, $G : \mathbf{x} \to L$, $z_C = \mathbf{C}^*(l, -) \cdot \mathbf{g}(\mathbf{x}) = \frac{K}{K-1}\mathbf{C}^*(l, G(\mathbf{x}))$. We use this generalized margin as argument for the MELF in order to obtain the *Cost-sensitive Multi-Class Exponential Loss Function (CMELF)*, $\mathcal{L}_C(l, \mathbf{g}(\mathbf{x})) := \exp(z_C) = \exp(\mathbf{C}^*(l, -) \cdot \mathbf{g}(\mathbf{x}))$, as the loss function for our problem. Although any other margin-based loss functions could have been used, we use the exponential loss to maintain the similarity with the original AdaBoost algorithm. The new margin, z_C, yields negative values when classifications are correct under the cost-sensitive point of view, and positive values for from costly (wrong) assignments. Moreover, the range of margin values of z_C is much broader than the $z = \pm 1$ values of AdaBoost.

The CMELF is a generalization of the MELF and CBELF. Let $\mathbf{C}_{0|1}$ be the cost matrix with zeros in the diagonal and ones elsewhere. This matrix encodes a multi-class problem free of costs. Further, it is well known that any matrix $\lambda\mathbf{C}_{0|1}$, with $\lambda > 0$, represents the same problem [10]. If we take into account that $\mathbf{y}^\top\mathbf{g}(\mathbf{x})$ has two possible values ($\frac{K}{K-1}$ when correct and $\frac{-K}{(K-1)^2}$ for errors) it is straightforward to prove that $\frac{1}{K(K-1)}\mathbf{C}_{0|1}$ will lead exactly to the same values of MELF when applied over the CMELF. In other words, the MELF is a particular case of the CMELF. On the other hand, it is also immediate to see that for a binary classification problem the values of $\mathbf{C}^*$ lead to the CBELF. Hence, it is a special case of CMELF as well.

Vectorial classifiers, $\mathbf{f}(\mathbf{x}) = (f_1(\mathbf{x}), \ldots, f_K(\mathbf{x}))^\top$, provides us with a *degree of confidence* for classifying sample $\mathbf{x}$ into every class. Hence, they use the max rule, $\arg\max_{k=1,\ldots,K} f_k(\mathbf{x})$, for label assignment [9,11]. It is immediate to see that this criterion is equivalent to assigning the label that maximizes the multi-class margin, $\arg\max_{k=1,\ldots,K} \mathbf{y}_k^\top \mathbf{f}(\mathbf{x}) = \arg\min_{k=1,\ldots,K} -\mathbf{y}_k^\top \mathbf{f}(\mathbf{x})$. Since $-\mathbf{y}_k^\top \mathbf{f}(\mathbf{x})$ is proportional to $\mathbf{C}_{0|1}^*(k,-)^\top \mathbf{f}(\mathbf{x})$, we can extend the decision rule to the cost-sensitive field just by assigning $\arg\min_{k=1,\ldots,K} \mathbf{C}^*(k,-)\mathbf{f}(\mathbf{x})$.

4 BAdaCost: Boosting Adapted for Cost-Matrix

In this section we present the BAdaCost, a multi-class cost-sensitive Boosting algorithm. As we have defined the CMELF and given a training sample $\{(\mathbf{x}_i, l_i)\}$ we minimize the empirical expected loss, $\sum_{n=1}^N \mathcal{L}_C(l_n, \mathbf{f}(\mathbf{x}_n))$. The minimization is carried out by fitting an additive model, $\mathbf{f}(\mathbf{x}) = \sum_{m=1}^M \beta_m \mathbf{g}_m(\mathbf{x})$. The weak learner selected at each iteration m will consists of an optimal step of size β_m along the direction $\mathbf{g}_m$ of the largest descent of the expected CMELF. In *Lemma 1* we show how to compute them.

Lemma 1. *Under the above assumptions, both β_m and $\mathbf{g}_m$ are given by minimizing:*

$$(\beta_m, \mathbf{g}_m(\mathbf{x})) = \arg\min_{\beta, \mathbf{g}(\cdot)} \sum_{j=1}^K \left(S_j \exp\left(\beta C^*(j,j)\right) + \sum_{k \neq j} E_{j,k} \exp\left(\beta C^*(j,k)\right) \right), \quad (2)$$

where the values of $S_j = \sum_{\{n:G(\mathbf{x}_n)=l_n=j\}} w_n$, $E_{j,k} = \sum_{\{n:l_n=j,G(\mathbf{x}_n)=k\}} w_n$ and $w_n = w_n exp\left(\beta_m \mathbf{C}^*(l_n,-)\mathbf{g}_m(\mathbf{x}_n)\right)$. Given a known direction $\mathbf{g}$, the optimal step $\beta(\mathbf{g})$ can be obtained as the solution to

$$\sum_{j=1}^K \sum_{k \neq j} E_{j,k} C^*(j,k) A(j,k)^\beta = -\sum_{j=1}^K S_j C^*(j,j) A(j,j)^\beta, \quad (3)$$

being $A(j,k) = \exp(C^*(j,k))$, $\forall i,j$. Finally, given a value of β, the optimal descent direction $\mathbf{g}$, equivalently $G(\cdot)$, is

$$\arg\min_{G(\cdot)} \sum_{n=1}^N w_n \left(A(l_n,l_n)^\beta I\left[G(\mathbf{x}_n)=l_n\right] + \sum_{k \neq l_n} A(l_n,k)^\beta I\left[G(\mathbf{x}_n)=k\right] \right). \quad (4)$$

The BAdaCost pseudo-code is shown in Algorithm 1. At each iteration, we add a new multi-class weak learner $\mathbf{g}_m : X \to Y$ to the additive model weighted by β_m, a measure of the confidence in the prediction of $\mathbf{g}_m$. The optimal weak learner that minimizes (Eq. 4) is a cost-sensitive multi-class classifier trained using the data weights, w_i, and a modified cost matrix, $\mathbf{C}_{wl}$, with $C_{wl}(i,j) = A(i,j)^\beta, \forall i,j$.

Algorithm 1. BAdaCost

1: **Input:** Cost matrix $\mathbf{C}$, N labeled training instances $(\mathbf{X}, \mathbf{Y})$ and number of iterations M

2: **Output:** The trained weak learners and weights (G_m, β_m), $m = 1, \ldots, M$

3:

4: Initialize weight vector $\mathbf{w} \in \mathbb{R}^N$, with $w_i = 1/N$; $\forall i = 1, \ldots, N$.

5: $\mathbf{C}^* := \text{computeFullCostMatrix}(\mathbf{C})$ { *Using equation (1)* }

6: **for** $m = 1, \ldots, M$ **do**

7:      $\beta := 1$; $c := \infty$; $\Delta c := \infty$.

8:      **while** $\Delta c \geq \gamma$ **do**

9:          $\mathbf{C}_{wl} := \text{computeWLCostMatrix}(\mathbf{C}^*, \beta)$.

10:          $G := \text{trainMulticlassCostSensitiveWL}(\mathbf{X}, \mathbf{Y}, \mathbf{w}, \mathbf{C}_{wl})$.

11:          $\beta := \text{computeBeta}(\mathbf{C}^*, G, \mathbf{w}, \mathbf{Y})$ { *Solving equation (3)* }

12:          $c_{new} := \text{computeCost}(\mathbf{C}^*, G, \mathbf{w}, \mathbf{Y}, \beta)$ { *Using β and G in equation (2)* }

13:          $\Delta c := c - c_{new}$; $c := c_{new}$.

14:      **end while**

15:      $G_m := G$; $\beta_m := \beta$.

16:      Translate G_m into $\mathbf{g}_m : X \to Y$.

17:      Update weights $w_i = w_i \exp(\beta_m \mathbf{C}^*(l_i, -) \mathbf{g}_m(\mathbf{x}_i))$ for $i = 1, \ldots, N$, and re-normalize vector $\mathbf{w}$.

18: **end for**

19: Output Classifier: $\mathbf{H}(\mathbf{x}) = \arg\min_k \mathbf{C}^*(k, -)\mathbf{f}(\mathbf{x})$, where $\mathbf{f}(\mathbf{x}) = \sum_{m=1}^M \beta_m \mathbf{g}_m(\mathbf{x})$.

---

5   Experiments

In this section we experimentally evaluate BAdaCost's accuracy on imbalanced data-sets. In our experiments we use CART weak-learners and regularize our Boosting algorithm using shrinkage and re-sampling.

5.1   Cost Matrix Construction

A preliminary issue when using a cost-sensitive algorithm for solving an imbalance problem is establishing the cost matrix, $\mathbf{C}$. A straightforward solution would be to set the costs inversely proportional to the class imbalance ratios. However, this solution does not take into account the complexity of the classification problem. i.e. the amount of class overlap, within-class imbalance, etc. Here we introduce an alternative solution that considers the problem complexity. To this end we introduce a cost matrix that weighs more hevily the errors of poorly classified classes, hence the classifier will concentrate on the difficult minority classes.

Let $\mathbf{F}$ be the confusion matrix and $\mathbf{F}^*$ the matrix obtained when dividing each row i, $\mathbf{F}(i, -)$, by $\mathbf{F}(i, \cdot) = \sum_j F(i, j)$, i.e. the number of samples in class i. Then $F^*(i, j)$ is the proportion of data in class i classified as j. In a complex and imbalanced data-set, a 0|1-loss classifier (e.g. BAdaCost with 0|1-losses) will tend to over-fit the majority classes. So, off-diagonal elements in rows $\mathbf{F}^*(i, -)$ for majority (alt. minority) classes will have low (high) scores. Hence, the resulting matrix after setting $F^*(i, i) = 0, \forall i = 1 \ldots K$ is already a cost matrix. Finally, to improve numerical conditioning, we set $\mathbf{C} = \lambda \mathbf{F}^*$, for a small $\lambda > 0$.

5.2   Synthetic Datasets

The aim of this synthetic experiment is to visually analyze the performance of BAdaCost. We sample data from 2D Mixtures of Gaussian (MoG) probability distributions (see Fig. 1a) that represent a typical multi-class computer vision object detection problem. Two minority classes represent the target objects (colored areas in Fig. 1a) and a majority class that represents the background (black area in Fig. 1a). For training we sample 500 data for each class 1 (red) and 2 (green), and 5000 samples for class 3 (black). We also sample 1000 data from each class for testing. We run BAdaCost twice, firstly using a 0|1 cost matrix (see results in Fig. 1b) and in second place using a cost matrix built as described in Sect. 5.1 (see results in Fig. 1d).

In Fig. 1c we can see that, for 0|1 costs, training error evolves close to zero, whereas the testing error rate in a balanced data set levels-off above 0.4. This is an expected behavior, since this classifier optimizes the number of misclassified training samples, which come mostly from the background class, thus overfitting. Note here that, altough the classes are imbalanced, the error rate is a meaningful classification measure because the testing data set is balanced. When using a cost matrix, see Fig. 1e, we get a much better testing error rate of 0.2. The training error rate in this case is higher than that for the 0|1 cost matrix. This is also as expected, since the cost matrix has effectively moved the class boundary towards the majority class.

To visually appreciate the effect produced when training with an unbalanced data-set and the benefits of BAdaCost, in Fig. 1b and d we show respectively the result of classifying all points on a grid in the feature space of this problem with the 0|1 and the imbalanced cost matrix. We can see a much better reconstruction using the imbalanced cost matrix.

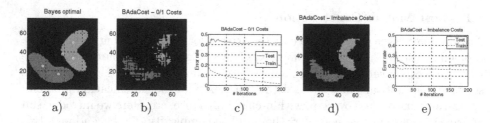

Fig. 1. Synthetic experiment 1. Simulated computer vision object detection problem with majority background class (black) (Color figure online).

5.3   Real Data-set: Synapse and Mitochondria Segmentation

In the last years we have seen advances in the automated acquisition of large series of images of brain tissue. The complexity of these images and the high number of neurons in a small section of the brain, makes the automated analysis of these images the only practical solution. Mitochondria and synapses are two interesting cell structures that will be the object of detection. Unfortunately, the proportion of them w.r.t. the background is quite small, which makes the problem highly skewed. In our experiment we used an image stack obtained from the somatosensory cortex of a rat, with a resolution of $3.686\,\mu m$ per pixel. The thickness of each layer is $20\,\mu m$ [12]. From this data set we collected a training set composed of 10,000 background, 4000 mitochondria and 1000 synapse data and a testing set with 20,000 data per class.

In this section we use the BAdaCost algorithm to label pixels in these images as mitochondria, synapse and background, and compare the results with those achieved by the AdaC2.M1 algorithm. Following [12], we apply to each image in the stack a set of linear Gaussian filters at different scales to compute zero, first and second order derivatives. For each pixel we get a vector of responses $S = (s_{00}, s_{10}, s_{01}, s_{02}, s_{11}, s_{02})$ that are respectively obtained applying the filters $G_{\sigma*}, \sigma \cdot G_\sigma * \frac{\partial}{\partial x}, \sigma \cdot G_\sigma * \frac{\partial}{\partial y}, \sigma^2 \cdot G_\sigma * \frac{\partial^2}{\partial x^2}, \sigma^2 \cdot G_\sigma * \frac{\partial^2}{\partial xy}, \sigma^2 \cdot G_\sigma * \frac{\partial^2}{\partial y^2}$ where G_σ is a zero mean Gaussian with σ standard deviation. For a given σ the pixel feature vector is given by $f(\sigma) = (s_{00}, \sqrt{s_{10}^2 + s_{01}^2}, \lambda_1, \lambda_2)$ where λ_1 and λ_2 are the eigenvalues of the Hessian matrix of the pixel, that depend on s_{20}, s_{02} and s_{11}. The final 16 dimensional feature vector for each pixel is given by the concatenation of the $f(\sigma)$ vector at 4 scales (values of σ).

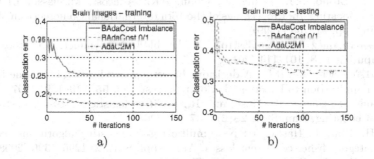

Fig. 2. Brain images experiment with a heavily imbalanced data-set.

In this experiment we compare BAdaCost (with 0|1 costs), AdaC2.M1 and BAdaCost (with the imbalanced cost matrix described in Sect. 5.1). In Fig. 2 we show the training and testing classification errors of the three algorithms. The behavior of BAdaCost in the real experiment is similar to those obtained with synthetic data. The 0|1-cost classifier has lower training error and higher testing error, whereas the the classifier with imbalanced cost matrix achieves the best generalization on the test set. The AdaC2.M1 classifier with imbalanced matrix achieve marginally better results than the 0|1-cost BAdaCost, but clearly worse than the imbalanced BAdaCost.

6 Conclusions

In this paper we have addressed the problem of multi-class classification with imbalanced data-sets. By extending the notion of multi-class margin to the cost-sensitive margin we introduced the *BAdaCost* algorithm and a procedure to estimate the cost matrix from the 0|1-loss confusion matrix. We have shown experimentally that BAdaCost performs as expected from a cost-sensitive algorithm and outperforms the AdaC2.M1 when dealing with imbalanced data.

Acknowledgments. This research was funded by the spanish *Ministerio de Economía y Competitividad*, project number TIN2013-47630-C2-2-R.

References

1. He, H., Garcia, E.A.: Learning from imbalanced data. IEEE Trans. Knowl. Data Eng. **21**(9), 1263–1284 (2009)
2. Sun, Y., Kamel, M.S., Wang, Y.: Boosting for learning multiple classes with imbalanced class distribution. In: Proceedings of the International Conference on Data Mining. ICDM '06, pp. 592–602 (2006)
3. Masnadi-Shirazi, Hamed, Vasconcelos, N.: Cost-sensitive boosting. Trans. Pattern Anal. Mach. Intell. **33**, 294–309 (2011)
4. Fan, W., Stolfo, S.J., Zhang, J., Chan, P.K.: Adacost: Misclassification cost-sensitive boosting. In: Proceedings of the 16th International Conference on Machine Learning, pp. 97–105 (1999)
5. Landesa-Vazquez, I., Alba-Castro, J.L.: Double-base asymmetric adaboost. Neurocomputing **118**, 101–114 (2013)
6. Freund, Y., Schapire, R.E.: A decision theoretic generalization of on-line learning and an application to boosting. J. Comput. Syst. Sci. **55**, 119–139 (1997)
7. Friedman, J., Hastie, T., Tibshirani, R.: Additive logistic regression: a statistical view of boosting. Ann. Stat. **28**(2), 337–407 (2000)
8. Zou, H., Zhu, J., Hastie, T.: New multicategory boosting algorithms based on multicategory fisher-consistent losses. Ann. Appl. Stat. **2**, 1290–1306 (2008)
9. Zhu, J., Zou, H., Rosset, S., Hastie, T.: Multi-class AdaBoost. Stat. Interface **2**, 349–360 (2009)
10. O'Brien, D.B., Gupta, M.R., Gray, R.M.: Cost-sensitive multi-class classification from probability estimates. In: Proceedings of the 25th International Conference on Machine Learning, pp. 712–719 (2008)
11. Fernandez-Baldera, A., Baumela, L.: Multi-class boosting with asymmetric weak-learners. Patt. Recogn. **47**(5), 2080–2090 (2014)
12. Cetina, K., Márquez-Neila, P., Baumela, L.: A comparative study of feature descriptors for mitochondria and synapse segmentation. In: Proceedings of the International Conference on Pattern Recognition (2014)

Computer Vision

Object Discovery Using CNN Features
in Egocentric Videos

Marc Bolaños[1]([✉]), Maite Garolera[2], and Petia Radeva[1,3]

[1] Universitat de Barcelona, Barcelona, Spain
{marc.bolanos,petia.ivanova}@ub.edu
[2] Hospital de Terrassa-Consorci Sanitari de Terrassa, Terrassa, Spain
mgarolera@cst.cat
[3] Computer Vision Center of Barcelona, Bellaterra, Spain

Abstract. Lifelogging devices based on photo/video are spreading faster everyday. This growth can represent great benefits to develop methods for extraction of meaningful information about the user wearing the device and his/her environment. In this paper, we propose a semi-supervised strategy for easily discovering objects relevant to the person wearing a first-person camera. The egocentric video sequence acquired by the camera, uses both the appearance extracted by means of a deep convolutional neural network and an object refill methodology that allow to discover objects even in case of small amount of object appearance in the collection of images. We validate our method on a sequence of 1000 egocentric daily images and obtain results with an F-measure of 0.5, 0.17 better than the state of the art approach.

Keywords: Object discovery · Egocentric videos · Lifelogging · CNN

1 Introduction

Ubiquitous computing is more present everyday in our lifes, and with it: life-logging devices [1,2] are increasing their popularity and spread. By wearing life-logging cameras, we can build applications that convert huge amounts of data into meaningful information about the persons and their environment. Wearable cameras offer an easy manner to acquire information about our daily life tasks, and extract information about our typical activities and habits.

In this paper, we address the problem of discovering which are the usual objects that form the environment of a person wearing the camera from a life-logging sequence by means of an Object Discovery (OD) method. Using this technique, as we can see in Fig. 1, we want to find the objects and environments that are able to distinguish the users of the wearable camera. Several works have been previously done in the OD field, some using segmentation techniques [3,4], others extracting objects relying on visual words [4–6], and combining clustering techniques with context information [7,8].

On the other hand, recently the use of Deep Neural Networks, and more precisely, Convolutional Neural Networks (CNN) is proving its huge potential to

© Springer International Publishing Switzerland 2015
R. Paredes et al. (Eds.): IbPRIA 2015, LNCS 9117, pp. 67–74, 2015.
DOI: 10.1007/978-3-319-19390-8_8

Fig. 1. Subset of frames from 3 different lifelogging sets. The first and third belonging to the same person, and the second to another one.

address different problems in the field of computer vision ([9–11], just to mention a few). Lately, a new method for egocentric activity recognition [12] using CNN data has been proposed for activity recognition. However, no methods on object discovery using these features exist yet.

Our proposal mainly relies on combining an object discovery method inspired by the work of Lee and Grauman [13]. However, we use both an appearance mode based on a feature extraction provided by a CNN pre-trained on ImageNet [14, 15], and a refill methodology on already discovered instances. This strategy allows to construct classes of categories even with a low number of instances and also to discover in an iterative and semi-supervised way the important objects present in lifelogging videos (Fig. 2) according to their importance and frequency of appearance.

Fig. 2. Images acquired by a lifelogging device, where objects of interest appear like: mobile phone, person, or TV monitor.

2   The Object Discovery Approach

Our algorithm is based on several steps: it extracts image regions representing object candidates from each image, similar to [13] separates a part of them to the initial pool of discovered samples (40 %), assesses the "easiness" for the remaining, and applies an iterative process by clustering, labeling the best cluster and applying a supervised expansion to find harder instances of the discovered object (see Fig. 3). It uses both appearance and local context features about each object. Appearance are extracted with a CNN [15], and context is provided by the refill procedure, very suitable for lifelogging.

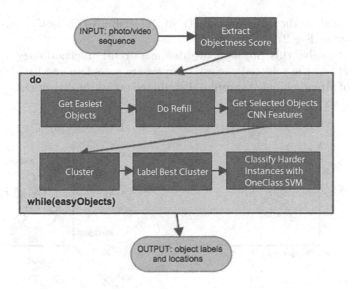

Fig. 3. Object discovery algorithm scheme.

2.1 Objectness and Easiness

The object sampling and candidates extraction, we used, rely on the objectness score proposed by Ferrari et al. [16], which combines 3 different methods and obtains an $objScore \in [0,1]$ proportional to the probability of a window being an object. The $easyScore$ measure is defined as:

$$easyScore(\omega) = objScore(\omega). \tag{1}$$

A subset of samples is selected at each iteration filtering by their easyScore so that:

$$easyScore(\omega) > \mu + 1.25\sigma - 0.1t, \tag{2}$$

where μ and σ are respectively, the mean and the standard deviation of all scores. Hence, the number of easy samples increases at each iteration.

2.2 Refill Strategy

The objectness measure seems a promising method for obtaining object candidates, in general. However, this technique does not obtain the same results in lifelogging datasets due to the fact that images are not captured by a person looking on objects of the world, but are acquired while person is wearing the camera. Due to the inherent low frequency of appearance of different objects of the real world, to the limited image quality of the wearable lifelogging devices and to the constant moving of the user, wide part of the photos are unclear, dark, blurry, or deformed by the fisheye camera (see Fig. 1). All this causes lower precision of object candidates extraction leading to a very high number of image regions obtained by the objectness method [16] with "No Object" instances (see the 7th image in Fig. 2).

In order to solve this problem, we define a "refill" methodology as follows: at each iteration, the selected easiest samples are complemented with a certain percentage of already labeled samples distributed on all the object classes (except the "No Object" class).

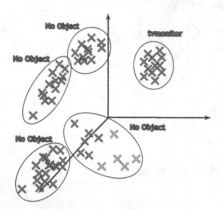

Fig. 4. Example of clusters formed only using the easiest samples

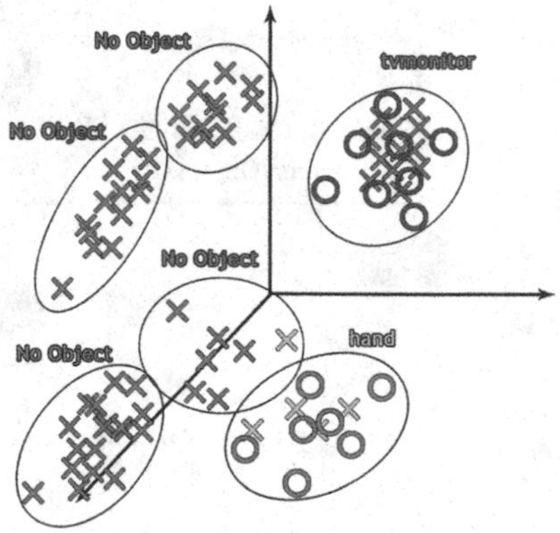

Fig. 5. Example of clusters formed adding the refill samples

In this way, we aid to address two problems: (1) difficulty to form a cluster from a very small set of class instances, and (2) difficulty to link samples of the same class that were blurry and unclear[1] (see Figs. 4 and 5).

2.3 Features for Object Discovery

As features, we used a pre-trained CNN, which captures information about millions of images in a succession of convolutional and pooling layers [14]. We deleted the last layer, which offers a supervised classification in 1,000 ImageNet classes, and used the output of the penultimate layer as our features (4096 variables). Note that our approach is different to the one of [13] that used: LAB histograms for extracting colour information, Pyramid HOG for extracting shape information, and Spatial Pyramid Matching [17] for extracting texture information.

2.4 Clustering and Hard Instancess Classification

After the features are extracted for the easiest and the refilled instances on each iteration, we apply an agglomerative Ward clustering. We use as cutoff criterion (similarly to the easiness filtering) 2 times the standard deviation plus

---

[1] Refilling the space with more samples of the same class can form a more compact and clear cluster.

the mean of the distances between clusters in the resulting hierarchy. Moreover, once the clusters are formed, we get the Silhouette Coefficient [18] on each of the clusters for selecting the most reliable one and label it with a majority voting strategy w.r.t the ground truth. This coefficient is only calculated on the unlabeled samples, never using the refilled ones. At the end of each iteration, an OneClass-SVM (with $\nu = 0.1$) is built with the new cluster and the rest of the easy samples are classified[2] with it for searching for harder instances.

3   Results

In this section, we discuss the lifelogging dataset, we used, and expose the different types of tests applied to illustrate the performance of the method proposed.

3.1   Lifelogging Dataset and Test Settings

Our dataset is a subset of the one used in [19,20], consisting of 1.000 images from a person's work day, from which 50.000 object candidates were extracted. To validate our method, we used the labels of the most frequent objects appearing, that are: "tvmonitor", "mobilephone", "hand" and "person" (Fig. 6).

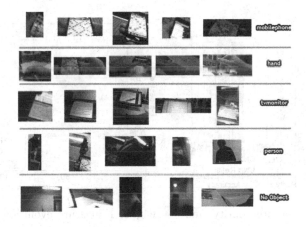

Fig. 6. Image samples of each object class

Using the objectness measure provided by [16], and after previously labeling all the objects present in the image, we assigned the corresponding true labels to each object candidate, considering only valid matches when their Overlapping Score (OS) was greater or equal than 0.4:

$$OS = \frac{|GT \cap \omega|}{|GT \cup \omega|}, \tag{3}$$

---

[2] On any case, the refilled samples, which were already labeled, can only get their labels changed if they did not belong to the initial selection set (40 %).

where GT stands for ground-truth and ω for the window detected by the method. Due to the challenging images (Subsect. 2.2 Refill Method) presented to the objectness measure, a very high percentage of samples (more than 76 %) could not be considered objects, and were labeled as "No Objects".

We performed three different test settings to evaluate our proposal:

1. CNN Features.
2. CNN Features with Refill.
3. Features of [13].

3.2   Tests Comparison

To evaluate our approach, we first calculated the general accuracy of the clustering methodology, giving the same weight to any sample from any class. The associated purity is defined as exactly the same as the accuracy, but without taking into account the "No Object" samples. The average per-class precision and recall defined by Sokolova et al. [21], allows to obtain the average F-measure. All measures were averaged by 5 executions per setting. Using these different measures, we compared all settings at the end of the easiest samples discovery (Fig. 7) and the F-measure for all settings on each iteration (Fig. 8).

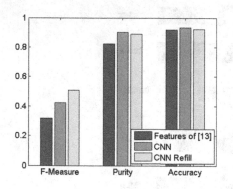
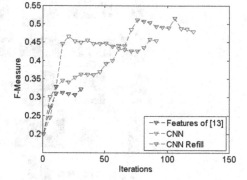

Fig. 7. Final F-measure, purity and accuracy for each setting

Fig. 8. F-measure evolution for each different setting

Looking at the first figure (Fig. 7), we can see that there is no change for any method on the accuracy, which is clearly due to the high number of "No Object" samples available, which are very easy to find everywhere and make the greater percentage of it. About the purity, we can observe changes on any setting using the CNN features, indicating that they can form more pure clusters for their best representation. Although there is a subtle purity decrease when using Refill, it is caused by the random initialization of the pool of discovered samples which, furthermore, is not statistically different. And finally, comparing the F-measure obtained, we can see more clearly that using CNN outperforms the features of [13], and that our complete method of CNN and Refill outperforms simply using the CNN features.

Comparing the evolution of the F-measure through the iterations (Fig. 8), first we have to consider that although in all the settings the amount of discovered samples at the end of the iterative process is similar, using CNN features (compared to those in [13]) produces smaller clusters because they are more distinguishable from the rest, and this makes the discovery process longer. And a similar phenomen happens when using the refill strategy, but in this case it is due to the fact that we add more samples at each iteration appart from the easiest ones.

Hence, using the CNN features combined with the refill strategy, the results clearly improved. This is caused by the discovery of different classes of samples. While when using the features of [13], we are only able to discover the two classes with more samples ("No Object" and "tvmonitor"), getting about 0.3 of F-measure, with CNN and the refill strategy, we can discover instances of each of the classes, getting about 0.5 of F-measure. On average, the approximate amount of image samples discovered using the best method (CNN Refill) are: "No Object" - 5000, "tvmonitor" - 500, "hand" - 50, "mobilephone" - 50 and "person" - 20. The total number of clusters labeled on average were about 120.

4 Conclusions

In this paper, we proposed a new object discovery algorithm that relies on features extracted from a pre-trained CNN, adapted for lifelogging photo/video sequences, and using a refill strategy for finding easily the classes with less samples. We proved that both the CNN features and the refill strategy can produce much better F-measure results and can discover a greater number of unfrequent classes than the state of the art approach. Furthermore, it has been proved that this combined strategy also works better than the previous ones for very noisy, blurry images and those with no objects.

As a future work, we plan to improve the objectness measure by training it on lifelogging images, to extend our object discovery including a context-awareness term similar to [13], and to use the discovered objects to characterize the environment of the persons wearing the camera.

References

1. Hodges, S., Williams, L., Berry, E., Izadi, S., Srinivasan, J., Butler, A., Smyth, G., Kapur, N., Wood, K.: SenseCam: a retrospective memory aid. In: Dourish, P., Friday, A. (eds.) UbiComp 2006. LNCS, vol. 4206, pp. 177–193. Springer, Heidelberg (2006)
2. Michael, K.: Wearable computers challenge human rights. ABC Science (2013)
3. Schulter, S., Leistner, C., Roth, P., Bischof, H.: Unsupervised object discovery and segmentation in videos. In: Proceedings of the British Machine Vision Conference, pp. 53.1–53.12. BMVA Press (2013)
4. Russell, B.C., Freeman, W.T., Efros, A.A., Sivic, J., Zisserman, A.: Using multiple segmentations to discover objects and their extent in image collections. In: IEEE Computer Society Conference on Computer Vision and Pattern Recognition, vol. 2, pp. 1605–1614. IEEE (2006)

5. Sivic, J., Russell, B.C., Efros, A.A., Zisserman, A., Freeman, W.T.: Discovering objects and their location in images In: Tenth International Conference on Computer Vision, ICCV, vol. 1, pp. 370–377. IEEE (2005)
6. Liu, D., Chen, T.: Unsupervised image categorization and object localization using topic models and correspondences between images. In: 11th International Conference on Computer Vision, ICCV, pp. 1–7. IEEE (2007)
7. Lee, Y.J., Ghosh, J., Grauman, K.: Discovering important people and objects for egocentric video summarization. In: Conference on CVPR, pp. 1346–1353. IEEE (2012)
8. Lee, Y.J., Grauman, K.: Object-graphs for context-aware visual category discovery. IEEE Trans. Pattern Anal. Mach. Intell. **34**(2), 346–358 (2012)
9. Honglak, L., Roger, G., Rajesh, R., Ng, A.Y.: Convolutional deep belief networks for scalable unsupervised learning of hierarchical representations. Computer Science Department, Stanford University, Stanford (2009)
10. Honglak, L., Yan, L., Rajesh, R., Peter, P., Ng, A.Y.: Unsupervised feature learning for audio classification using convolutional deep belief networks. Computer Science Department, Stanford University, Stanford (2009)
11. Goodfellow, I.J., Bulatov, Y., Ibarz, J., Arnoud, S.: Vinay Shet: Multi-digit Number Recognition from Street View Imagery Using Deep Convolutional Neural Networks. Google Inc., Mountain View (2014)
12. Moghimi, M., Azagra, P., Montesano, L., Murillo, A.C., Belongie, S.: Experiments on an RGB-D wearable vision system for egocentric activity recognition. In: 3rd Workshop on Egocentric (First-person) Vision, CVPR (2014)
13. Lee, Y.J., Grauman, K.: Learning the easy things first: self-paced visual category discovery. In: Conference on Computer Vision and Pattern Recognition (CVPR), pp. 1721–1728. IEEE (2011)
14. Krizhevsky, A., Sutskever, I., Hinton, G.E.: Imagenet classification with deep convolutional neural networks. In: Advances in Neural Information Processing Systems, pp. 1097–1105 (2012)
15. Jia, Y.: Caffe: an open source convolutional architecture for fast feature embedding (2013). http://caffe.berkeleyvision.org/
16. Alexe, B., Deselaers, T., Ferrari, V.: What is an object? In: Conference on Computer Vision and Pattern Recognition (CVPR), pp. 73–80. IEEE (2010)
17. Lazebnik, S., Schmid, C., Ponce, J.: Beyond bags of features: spatial pyramid matching for recognizing natural scene categories. In: IEEE Computer Society Conference on Computer Vision and Pattern Recognition, vol. 2, pp. 2169–2178. IEEE (2006)
18. Tu, Z.: Auto-context and its application to high-level vision tasks. In: IEEE Conference on Computer Vision and Pattern Recognition, CVPR, pp. 1–8. IEEE (2008)
19. Bolaños, M., Garolera, M., Radeva, P.: Active labeling application applied to food-related object recognition. In: Proceedings of the 5th International Workshop on Multimedia for Cooking & Eating Activities, ACM Multiedia International Conference, pp. 45–50 (2013)
20. Bolaños, M., Garolera, M., Radeva, P.: Video segmentation of life-logging videos. In: Perales, F.J., Santos-Victor, J. (eds.) AMDO 2014. LNCS, vol. 8563, pp. 1–9. Springer, Heidelberg (2014)
21. Sokolova, M., Lapalme, G.: A systematic analysis of performance measures for classification tasks. Inf. Process. Manage. **45**(4), 427–437 (2009)

Prototype Generation on Structural Data Using Dissimilarity Space Representation: A Case of Study

Jorge Calvo-Zaragoza[✉], Jose J. Valero-Mas, and Juan R. Rico-Juan

Departamento de Lenguajes y Sistemas Informáticos,
Universidad de Alicante, Alicante, Spain
{jcalvo,jjvalero,juanra}@dlsi.ua.es

Abstract. Data Reduction techniques are commonly applied in instance-based classification tasks to lower the amount of data to be processed. Prototype Selection (PS) and Prototype Generation (PG) constitute the most representative approaches. These two families differ in the way of obtaining the reduced set out of the initial one: while the former aims at selecting the most representative elements from the set, the latter creates new data out of it. Although PG is considered to better delimit decision boundaries, operations required are not so well defined in scenarios involving structural data such as strings, trees or graphs. This work proposes a case of study with the use of the common RandomC algorithm for mapping the initial structural data to a Dissimilarity Space (DS) representation, thereby allowing the use of PG methods. A comparative experiment over string data is carried out in which our proposal is faced to PS methods on the original space. Results show that PG combined with RandomC mapping achieves a very competitive performance, although the obtained accuracy seems to be bounded by the representativity of the DS method.

1 Introduction

In the Pattern Recognition (PR) field, two fundamental approaches can be found depending on the model used for representing the data [6]: a first one, usually known as structural or syntactical, in which data is represented as symbolic data structures such as strings, trees or graphs; and a second one, known as statistical methods or feature representations, in which the representation is based on numerical feature vectors.

The election of one of these approaches has some noticeable consequences: structural methods offer a wide range of powerful and flexible high-level representations, but only few PR algorithms and techniques are capable of processing them; feature methods, although less flexible in terms of representation, depict a larger collection of PR techniques for classification tasks [3].

Independently of whether we use a structural or a feature representation, instance-based PR methods, as for instance the k-Nearest Neighbor rule (kNN), may be applied. These methods, instead of obtaining a set of classification rules

© Springer International Publishing Switzerland 2015
R. Paredes et al. (Eds.): IbPRIA 2015, LNCS 9117, pp. 75–82, 2015.
DOI: 10.1007/978-3-319-19390-8_9

out of the available information, need to examine all the training data each time a new element has to be classified. As a consequence, these methods not only depict considerable memory requirements in order to store all the data, which in some cases might be a very large number of elements, but also show a low computational efficiency as all training information must be checked at each classification task [14].

Data Reduction (DR) techniques, a particular subfamily of the Data Preprocessing (DP) methods, try to solve these limitations by means of selecting a representative subset of the training data [11]. Two of the most common approaches for performing this task are Prototype Generation (PG) and Prototype Selection (PS) [13]. Both methods focus on reducing the size of the initial training set for lowering the computational requirements and removing noisy instances while keeping, if not increasing, the classification accuracy. The former method creates new artificial data to replace the initial set while the latter one simply selects certain elements from that set. Moreover, PG methods usually show a superior reduction and accuracy than the PS ones.

It must be pointed out that the two aforementioned DR techniques show a high dependency on the data representation used. PS algorithms have been widely used in both structural and feature representations as the elements are not transformed but simply selected. On the other hand, PG methods do require to modify the data in order to create new elements and, while this process can be easily performed in feature representations, it becomes remarkably difficult for structured data.

In this paper we shall study the possibility of applying PG methods to structured representations by means of using Dissimilarity Space (DS) methods so as to solve the aforementioned difficulty. DS techniques map structured data to feature representations, thereby allowing the use of statistical PR techniques not available for structured representations.

The rest of the paper is structured as it follows: Sect. 2 introduces the issue of Prototype Generation in structured data as well as the proposed approach; Sect. 3 presents the experimentation scheme implemented, the different data sets used and the results obtained; finally, Sect. 4 shows the general remarks obtained out of the study and proposes some possible future work.

2   Prototype Generation for Structural Data

The use of PS in instance-based classification assumes that the decision boundaries can be perfectly delimited by a subset of the prototypes in the training set, which may not always be true. PG methods, on the other hand, create new prototypes merging or evolving, when necessary, elements of the initial set to better define the decision boundaries [19].

As aforementioned, generating new prototypes in structural data is not a trivial matter. Some examples of works addressing this issue are [1] in which the median of a strings set is calculated using edit operations or [9] in which an iterative algorithms for the computation of the median operation on graphs is exposed. Nevertheless, all of them take advantage of the knowledge of the specific structural data to create these new prototypes. Therefore, generalization to other structural representation cannot be assumed.

A possible solution to this issue is to use DS methods to map the structural data into a feature representation where these merging operations can be easily applied. Broadly, DS representations are obtained by computing pairwise dissimilarities between the elements of a representation set, which actually constitutes a subset of the initial structural training data selected following a given criterion.

In this paper we focus on the particular DS representation called RandomC, which shall be explained in the following section, for a proof-of-concept experience. The election of this method is motivated by its large application in the DS field as well as by the fact that the sampling process is performed equally for all clases in the set. Only one DS method is considered as the main aim of the paper resides in the DR techniques.

Using this method, the classification results obtained after applying a set of PG techniques to the feature representation will be compared to the results obtained when using PS techniques in both the initial structural space and the feature one so as to check whether PG can be useful in these situations.

2.1 Dissimilarity Space Transformation: RandomC

Let $\mathcal{X}$ denote a structural space in which a dissimilarity function $d : \mathcal{X} \times \mathcal{X} \to \mathbb{R}^+$ is defined. Let Y represent the set of labels or classes of our classification task. Let T be a labeled set of prototypes such that $T = \{(x_i, y_i) : x_i \in \mathcal{X}, y_i \in Y\}_{i=1}^{|T|}$.

In order to map the prototypes of T onto a feature space $\mathcal{F}$, we resort to RandomC algorithm [15]. This algorithm selects a random subset of prototypes $R \subseteq T$, in which the number of prototypes of each class is exactly c (tuning parameter), that is, $|R| = c|Y|$. The elements of R are noted r_i with $1 \leq i \leq |R|$. Then, a prototype $x \in \mathcal{X}$ can be represented in $\mathcal{F}$ as a set of features $(v_1, v_2, v_3, \ldots, v_{|R|})$ such that $v_i = d(x, r_i)$. This way, a $|R|$-dimensional real-valued vector can be obtained for each point in the space $\mathcal{X}$.

In order to compare the influence of parameter c in the feature representation, some different values will be considered at experimentation stage.

3 Experimentation

Figure 1 shows the implemented set-up for performing the experimentation. As it can be checked, out of the initial structural elements, a feature representation is obtained using the DS algorithm RandomC. In this experimental scheme, we fix its c parameter to retrieve 5, 10 or 15 prototypes per class.

DR techniques are then applied to both data representations but, while PS methods are applied to structural and feature representations, PG is only performed on the latter. The techniques used are listed in the following section.

In terms of the data used, two different isolated symbol datasets have been selected: the NIST SPECIAL DATABASE 3 (NIST3) of the National Institute

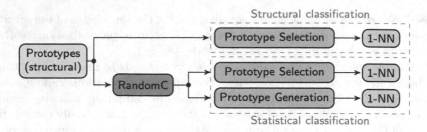

Fig. 1. Experimental set-up tested. RandomC is used as DS method. PS is applied to both structural and feature data while PG is only performed on the latter. 1-NN is used for the classification in all cases.

of Standards and Technology, from which a subset of the upper case characters was randomly chosen (26 classes, 6500 images) and the United States Postal Office (USPS) handwritten digit dataset [12] (10 classes, 9298 samples). In both cases, contour descriptions with Freeman Chain Codes [10] are extracted.

Nearest Neighbor (NN) algorithm, parameterized with k = 1, is used for the classification. Edit distance is considered as the dissimilarity measure for structural data whereas Euclidean distance is applied in the DS representation.

3.1 Data Reduction Strategies

A representative set of PS algorithms covering a wide range of selection variants was used for the experimentation. However, in order to perform a fair comparison between the two DR strategies, we are only showing the results for the PS algorithms retrieving similar size reductions to the PG algorithms. These DR techniques are now briefly introduced:

Prototype Selection (PS) Algorithms

- Fast Condensing Nearest Neighbor (FCNN) [2]: computes a fast, order-independent condensing strategy based on seeking the centroids of each label.
- Farther Neighbor (FN) [16]: gives a probability mass value to each prototype following a voting heuristic based on neighborhood. Prototypes are selected according to a parameter (fixed to 0.3 in our case) that indicates the probability mass desired for each class in the reduced set.
- Cross-generational elitist selection, Heterogeneous recombination and Cataclysmic mutation algorithm (CHC) [7]: evolutionary algorithm commonly used as a representative of Genetic Algorithms in PS. The configuration of this algorithm has been the same as in [4].

Prototype Generation (PG) Algorithms

- Reduction by Space Partitioning 3 (RSP3) [18]: divides the whole space until a number of class-homogeneous subsets are obtained; a prototype is then generated from the centroid of each subset.

- Evolutionary Nearest Prototype Classifier (ENPC) [8]: performs an evolutionary search using a set of prototypes that can improve their local quality by means of genetic operators.
- Mean Squared Error (MSE) [5]: generates new prototypes using gradient descent and simulated annealing. Mean squared error is used as cost function.

The parameters of these algorithms have been established following [19].

3.2 Results

Results obtained for the different datasets proposed can be found in Tables 1 and 2 respectively. The performance metrics considered are the accuracy of the classification task and the size of the reduced set obtained (in % with respect to the whole dataset). ALL refers to results obtained when using the whole training set (no DR algorithm is applied).

Table 1. Results obtained with the NIST dataset for the proposed DS algorithm RandomC configurations. No DS depicts results obtained in the initial structural space. Selection and generation techniques are regarded as PS and PG respectively. ALL stands for the case in which no selection or generation is performed. Size normalization (%) is obtained with respect to the ALL case.

Type	Algorithm	RandomC (5)		RandomC (10)		RandomC (15)		No DS	
		Acc	Size	Acc	Size	Acc	Size	Acc	Size
–	ALL	86.1	100.0	86.7	100.0	87.0	100.0	91.0	100.0
PS	FCNN	82.0	30.9	82.0	30.4	82.3	29.9	87.8	21.1
	1-FN(0.3)	79.7	16.8	81.5	16.9	81.2	16.9	87.9	15.8
	CHC	74.5	3.0	73.1	3.2	73.1	3.2	83.9	3.0
PG	RSP3	86.2	38.6	86.2	39.4	86.1	38.4	–	–
	ENPC	84.7	18.6	84.7	17.7	84.8	15.7	–	–
	MSE	82.8	7.0	83.2	5.6	83.1	5.7	–	–

A first initial remark is that, in general, the DS process carries a reduction in the classification accuracy. For a given algorithm, when comparing the No DS accuracy results with any of the corresponding RandomC cases, there is a significant decrease in these figures. In the NIST set this effect is more noticeable: for instance, in the 1-FN(0.3) case of the NIST dataset, roughly a 10 % is missed between the original space and the RandomC (10) one. In the USPS, however, this effect is less accused, getting even to the point that the results obtained for the PS algorithms in the feature representation are similar, and in some cases better, than the corresponding ones in the initial space.

A second important point to comment is that for both structural and feature representations, PS techniques depict a decrease in the classification accuracy

Table 2. Results obtained with the USPS dataset for the proposed DS algorithm RandomC configurations. No DS depicts results obtained in the initial structural space. Selection and generation techniques are regarded as PS and PG respectively. ALL stands for the case in which no selection or generation is performed. Size normalization (%) is obtained with respect to the ALL case.

Type	Algorithm	RandomC (5)		RandomC (10)		RandomC (15)		No DS	
		Acc	Size	Acc	Size	Acc	Size	Acc	Size
–	ALL	91.3	100.0	91.7	100.0	91.7	100.0	91.8	100.0
PS	FCNN	87.7	21.1	88.4	20.1	88.2	20.1	87.6	20.2
	1-FN(0.3)	89.3	15.0	89.8	15.0	89.6	15.0	89.6	10.1
	CHC	87.4	0.9	88.0	0.9	88.4	0.9	89.2	0.8
PG	RSP3	91.4	18.7	91.7	17.7	91.7	18.3	–	–
	ENPC	89.8	5.7	90.7	5.0	90.6	5.5	–	–
	MSE	88.9	1.1	89.8	1.2	89.4	1.2	–	–

when compared to the ALL case. This effect is a consequence of the reduction in the set size. PG, on the other hand, is capable of both achieving a remarkable size reduction, just as PS, and retrieving classification results close to the ALL case, showing the robustness of these methods. Especially interesting is the RSP3 algorithm which gets the same accuracy as the corresponding ALL scenario with barely a third of the initial set size.

Nevertheless, the main outcome out of the results obtained by the PG algorithms is that the scores they obtain in the feature domain are similar, when not higher, than the ones obtained by PS schemes in the initial structural space. This proves the proposed strategy as a clear competitor of PS in structural data, especially considering the simplicity of the RandomC DS algorithm employed.

Computation times were also measured for the classification schemes. Results proved DS strategies as much faster than structural ones because of the complexity reduction achieved by using Euclidean distance instead of Edit distance. For instance, classification times for the ALL case in the structural space for NIST and USPS span for 1127 and 216 s respectively while, for the RandomC (15) case, these tasks are accomplished in 102 and 6 s respectively.

Experiments show that the performance of PG seems to be limited by the results achieved by the ALL case in the feature space, then limiting the application of these techniques in situations where performance is a must. However, as the maximum achievable score is given by the ALL case, not PG algorithm but the DS technique are actually limiting the performance. In sight of this, performance might be boosted with the use of more robust DS algorithms.

Finally, the different c values for RandomC do not seem to have a remarkable effect on the results. For a given PS or PG technique, neither accuracies nor sizes do significantly change as this parameter is varied. As a consequence, low c values may be considered.

4   Conclusions

Prototype Generation techniques for Data Reduction in instance-based classification aim at creating new data out of the elements of a given set so as to lower the memory requirements while precisely defining the decision boundaries. Although these methods are commonly used in statistical Pattern Recognition, they turn out to be quite challenging for structural data as the merging operations required cannot be as clearly defined as in the former approach. It has been proposed the use of Dissimilarity Space representations, which allow us to map structural data representations into feature ones, so as to benefit from the advantages Prototype Generation methods depict.

The experimentation performed shows some important outcomes. PG approaches applied to structural data using a DS representation are capable of competing with PS methods in the original space even though the mapping process implies information losses. However, PG methods are not capable of achieving accuracies reached in the non-reduced structural space as the mapping process does always carry a decrease in the overall performance, thus bounding the maximum achievable accuracy in the target space. Finally, classification using DS representations has been proved as a faster option than the one performed in the structural space as costly distance functions like Edit Distance are replaced by low-dimensional Euclidean distance. This evinces the proposed approach as an interesting trade-off option between precision and time consumption.

Furthermore, work developed here opens several avenues for future work and extensions. For instance, a more comprehensive experimental setup could be addressed with datasets of other complex structures (such as trees or graphs), including a larger set of PS and PG algorithms. Moreover, experimentation with more advanced methods to map structured data into feature vectors, such those reported in [15,17], would be of great interest since accuracy achieved in our results seems to be bounded by the DS method applied. Finally, the inclusion of artificial noise in the data as well as the use of different parameters for the Nearest Neighbor classifier could be considered so as to assess the robustness of the system in adverse scenarios.

Acknowledgements. This work was partially supported by the Spanish Ministerio de Educación, Cultura y Deporte through a FPU fellowship (AP2012–0939), the Spanish Ministerio de Economía y Competitividad through Project TIMuL (No. TIN2013-48152-C2-1-R supported by EU FEDER funds), Consejería de Educación de la Comunidad Valenciana through project PROMETEO/2012/017 and Vicerrectorado de Investigación, Desarrollo e Innovación de la Universidad de Alicante through FPU program (UAFPU2014–5883).

References

1. Abreu, J., Rico-Juan, J.R.: A new iterative algorithm for computing a quality approximated median of strings based on edit operations. Pattern Recogn. Lett. **36**, 74–80 (2014)

2. Angiulli, F.: Fast nearest neighbor condensation for large data sets classification. IEEE Trans. Knowl. Data Eng. **19**(11), 1450–1464 (2007)
3. Bunke, H., Riesen, K.: Towards the unification of structural and statistical pattern recognition. Pattern Recogn. Lett. **33**(7), 811–825 (2012)
4. Cano, J.R., Herrera, F., Lozano, M.: On the combination of evolutionary algorithms and stratified strategies for training set selection in data mining. Appl. Soft Comput. **6**(3), 323–332 (2006)
5. Decaestecker, C.: Finding prototypes for nearest neighbour classification by means of gradient descent and deterministic annealing. Pattern Recogn. **30**(2), 281–288 (1997)
6. Duda, R.O., Hart, P.E., Stork, D.G.: Pattern Classification. Wiley, New York (2001)
7. Eshelman, L.J.: The CHC adaptive search algorithm: how to have safe search when engaging in nontraditional genetic recombination. In: Proceedings of the First Workshop on Foundations of Genetic Algorithms. Indiana, USA, pp. 265–283 (1990)
8. Fernández, F., Isasi, P.: Evolutionary design of nearest prototype classifiers. J. Heuristics **10**(4), 431–454 (2004)
9. Ferrer, M., Bunke, H.: An iterative algorithm for approximate median graph computation. In: 20th International Conference on Pattern Recognition (ICPR), pp. 1562–1565 (2010)
10. Freeman, H.: On the encoding of arbitrary geometric configurations. IRE Trans. Electron. Comput. **EC–10**(2), 260–268 (1961)
11. García, S., Luengo, J., Herrera, F.: Data Preprocessing in Data Mining. Springer, Switzerland (2015)
12. Hull, J.: A database for handwritten text recognition research. IEEE Trans. Pattern Anal. **16**(5), 550–554 (1994)
13. Li, Y., Huang, J., Zhang, W., Zhang, X.: New prototype selection rule integrated condensing with editing process for the nearest neighbor rules. In: IEEE International Conference on Industrial Technology ICIT, pp. 950–954 (2005)
14. Mitchell, T.M.: Machine Learning. McGraw-Hill Inc., New York (1997)
15. Pekalska, E., Duin, R.P.W.: The Dissimilarity Representation for Pattern Recognition: Foundations And Applications (Machine Perception and Artificial Intelligence). World Scientific Publishing Co., Inc, USA (2005)
16. Rico-Juan, J.R., Iñesta, J.M.: New rank methods for reducing the size of the training set using the nearest neighbor rule. Pattern Recogn. Lett. **33**(5), 654–660 (2012)
17. Riesen, K., Neuhaus, M., Bunke, H.: Graph embedding in vector spaces by means of prototype selection. In: Escolano, F., Vento, M. (eds.) GbRPR. LNCS, vol. 4538, pp. 383–393. Springer, Heidelberg (2007)
18. Sánchez, J.: High training set size reduction by space partitioning and prototype abstraction. Pattern Recogn. **37**(7), 1561–1564 (2004)
19. Triguero, I., Derrac, J., García, S., Herrera, F.: A taxonomy and experimental study on prototype generation for nearest neighbor classification. IEEE Trans. Syst. Man Cybern. C **42**(1), 86–100 (2012)

Estimation and Tracking of Partial Planar Templates to Improve VSLAM

Abdelsalam Masoud$^{(\boxtimes)}$ and William Hoff

Colorado School of Mines, Golden, CO, USA
{amasoud,whoff}@mines.edu

Abstract. We present an algorithm that can segment and track partial planar templates, from a sequence of images taken from a moving camera. By "partial planar template", we mean that the template is the projection of a surface patch that is only partially planar; some of the points may correspond to other surfaces. The algorithm segments each image template to identify the pixels that belong to the dominant plane, and determines the three dimensional structure of that plane. We show that our algorithm improves the accuracy of visual simultaneous localization and mapping (VSLAM), especially in scenes where surface discontinuities are common.

Keywords: Tracking · Visual SLAM · Structure from motion

1 Introduction

For mobile robot applications, it is important to perform Simultaneous Localization and Mapping (SLAM). Visual sensors (*i.e.*, cameras) are attractive for SLAM due to their low cost and low power. Much research has been performed on VSLAM (visual SLAM), including approaches using a single camera, which we focus on here. Most approaches detect feature points in the environment, using an interest point operator (*e.g.*, [1]) that looks for small textured image templates. These templates are then tracked through subsequent images, and their 3D locations, along with the camera motion, are estimated.

In order to track image templates, most existing algorithms assume (either implicitly or explicitly) that each image template is the projection of a single planar surface patch (e.g., [2,3]). The Lucas-Kanade algorithm and its variants [4] is a good example of methods to track planar templates. These algorithms compute the image deformation of reference template $T(\mathbf{x})$, so as to minimize the sum of squared differences between $T(\mathbf{x})$ and a region of the current image $I(\mathbf{x})$. If the patch is planar, then its appearance can be accurately predicted in subsequent images.

For example, a homography (projective) transformation can accurately model the deformation of the image template from the reference image to the current image. Even if a surface is curved, it can appear to be locally planar if the patch size is small enough. However, as the distance between the reference camera

© Springer International Publishing Switzerland 2015
R. Paredes et al. (Eds.): IbPRIA 2015, LNCS 9117, pp. 83–92, 2015.
DOI: 10.1007/978-3-319-19390-8_10

Fig. 1. Interest points detected in a scene. Templates that appear to encompass more than one surface are shown as green; the others are shown as red (Color figure online).

and the current camera increases, the prediction error of a curved patch also increases. Tracking will eventually fail when the camera has moved far enough.

A more difficult problem occurs when the template encompasses two disjoint surfaces, which may be widely separated in depth. Unfortunately, such templates often are detected by interest point operators, because the boundary between the surfaces often yields good image texture. However, even small camera motion will cause tracking to fail in such cases.

Some environments have many nonplanar surfaces. Figure 1 shows the top 64 points that were automatically detected by an interest point operator [1], using a template window size of 15×15 pixels. By visual inspection, 36 of these templates encompass more than one surface. Tracking of these templates will fail after a short time, using tracking algorithms that make the single-plane assumption.

If we can model the true 3D structure of a patch, then we can more accurately predict its appearance, and potentially track it over a longer distance. When a feature is visible over a large visual angle, the error in its estimated 3D location is reduced. This also improves the accuracy of the derived camera poses.

In this work, we present such an algorithm that estimates the 3D structure of a patch, as it is tracked through a sequence of images. We assume that the image template is the projection of a planar surface, but some of the points in the template may not belong to that surface (*i.e.*, they may belong to other surfaces). We automatically identify the points belonging to the "dominant" plane of the patch, and the parameters of that plane. This allows us to accurately predict the appearance of the pixels belonging to the dominant plane, and ignore the others. As a result, the algorithm is better able to track templates that encompass surface discontinuities. A preliminary version of this work was published in [5].

The contribution of this paper is that we have incorporated the new partial plane tracking algorithm into a standard VSLAM algorithm. We show that the new approach achieves significantly better accuracy, as compared to a VSLAM algorithm that uses the standard whole plane tracking method.

Note that we make no assumptions about the color distributions of the regions (*e.g.*, that one region is lighter than another). As a result, methods such as mean-shift [6] that segment and track based on color differences are not applicable.

The remainder of this paper is organized as follows: Sect. 2 describes the new template tracking method, and Sect. 3 describes the overall VSLAM algorithm. Section 4 presents experimental results, and Sect. 5 provides conclusions.

2 Modeling and Tracking of Partial Planar Templates

Each template to be tracked is represented by a small square subimage (we use size 15×15 pixels) from the image where the template was first detected. We use a standard interest point operator [1] to detect points to track. Let $\mathbf{X}_0$ be the 3D point location at the center of the template, and $\mathbf{x}_{ref}$ be the corresponding image point.

We assume that a template is the image projection of a planar surface patch in the scene, which we call the "dominant plane". However, only some of the points in the template are projections of the dominant plane; hence we use the name "partial planar template". The other points may be projected from other surfaces (we do not try to model these other surfaces; only the dominant plane). Let $p_{ref}(\mathbf{x})$ represent the probability that image point $\mathbf{x}$ in the reference image belongs to the dominant plane for the template. Initially, $p_{ref}(\mathbf{x}) = 0.5$ for all points in the template. Note that for conventional algorithms, $p_{ref}(\mathbf{x})$ is always equal to 1.0, because they assume that the template is the projection of a single planar surface.

Initially, we have no 3D information on new templates, and so we use a 2D method (normalized cross correlation) to track new templates to subsequent images. After the camera has translated sufficiently far, we can perform triangulation to estimate the 3D position of the center of the template (we use a threshold of 2.0 degrees of visual angle between the first and last observations). We also initialize the surface normal vector of the template to point away from the camera, as done by [2] and others.

As each new image is acquired, three steps are performed on each template: (1) matching, (2) updating the surface normal, and (3) updating the probability mask. These are described in the subsections below.

2.1 Matching

To match a template to a new image, we warp the template from the reference image to the current image in order to predict its appearance. A plane is represented by the equation $\mathbf{n}^T \mathbf{X} = d$, where $\mathbf{n}$ is the normal vector, d is the perpendicular distance to the origin, and $\mathbf{X}$ is any point on the plane. We can transform a planar surface from one image to the other using the homography matrix given by

$$\mathbf{H} = \mathbf{K}(\mathbf{R} + \mathbf{t}\mathbf{n}^T/d)\mathbf{K}^{-1} \tag{1}$$

where $\mathbf{K}$ is the camera intrinsic parameter matrix, $\mathbf{n}$ is the surface normal, and $\mathbf{R}$ and $\mathbf{t}$ are estimated rotation and translation between the cameras, respectively [2].

Let $\mathbf{w}(\mathbf{x}; \mathbf{P})$ denote the warping function that implements the homography transformation as described above, where $\mathbf{P}$ is a vector of parameters, consisting of the set $\mathbf{R}, \mathbf{t}, \mathbf{n}, d$. Note that d can be found from the location of the template center using $d = \mathbf{n}^T \mathbf{X}_0$. The warp $\mathbf{w}(\mathbf{x}; \mathbf{P})$ takes the pixel $\mathbf{x}_1$ in the first image and maps it to location $\mathbf{x}_2 = \mathbf{w}(\mathbf{x}_1; \mathbf{P})$ in the second image. We warp the template to the current image using

$$T_{curr}^{(\mathbf{P})}(\mathbf{x}) = T_{ref}(\mathbf{w}(\mathbf{x}; \mathbf{P})) \tag{2}$$

The superscript $\mathbf{P}$ is used to emphasize that the result depends on the parameters $\mathbf{P}$. Similarly, let $p_{curr}^{(\mathbf{P})}(\mathbf{x})$ be the probability mask for the template, warped from the reference to the current image.

To match the template to the current image, we search a 2D region around the predicted location to minimize the sum of squared differences, weighted by the probability at each pixel:

$$\triangle \mathbf{x} = \operatorname*{argmin}_{\triangle \mathbf{x}} \sum_{\mathbf{x} \in N(\mathbf{x}_c)} |T_{curr}^{(\mathbf{P})}(\mathbf{x}) - I_{curr}(\mathbf{x} + \triangle \mathbf{x})|^2 p_{curr}^{(\mathbf{P})}(\mathbf{x}) \tag{3}$$

where $N(\mathbf{x}_c)$ is the $H \times W$ neighborhood surrounding the predicted location of the template center. The size of the search neighborhood is determined by the uncertainty of the camera pose and the uncertainty of the 3D location of the point. Since the size is usually relatively small, an exhaustive search is performed.

If the sum of squared differences, weighted by the probability is below an empirically derived threshold (we used a value of 40.0 in this work), we consider the template to be successfully matched to the location $\mathbf{x}_0 = \mathbf{x}_c + \triangle \mathbf{x}$ in the current image.

2.2 Updating the Surface Normal

After a template has been matched, we update its surface normal, which is parameterized by the two direction angles (θ, ϕ). We search for the angles that minimize the sum of square differences weighted by the probability:

$$(\theta, \phi) = \operatorname*{argmin}_{\theta, \phi} \sum_{\mathbf{x} \in N(\mathbf{x}_c)} |T_{curr}^{(\mathbf{P})}(\mathbf{x}) - I_{curr}(\mathbf{x} + \triangle \mathbf{x})|^2 p_{curr}^{(\mathbf{P})}(\mathbf{x}) \tag{4}$$

A non-linear optimization algorithm [7] is used for the search. Since we usually have a fairly good estimate of the surface normal from the previous images, there is usually a fairly small correction to the angles. However, in the case of highly slanted patches, the correction from the initial orientation can be larger.

2.3   Updating the Probability Mask

We next the probability mask $p_{ref}(\mathbf{x})$. We first take the region of the current image where the template matched, and map it back to the reference image.

$$T^{(\mathbf{P})}_{match}(\mathbf{x}) = I_{curr}(\mathbf{w}^{-1}(\mathbf{x}; \mathbf{P})) \tag{5}$$

The residual error between the template in the reference image and the corresponding region in the current image is:

$$r(\mathbf{x}) = T_{ref}(\mathbf{x}) - T^{(\mathbf{P})}_{match}(\mathbf{x}) \tag{6}$$

If the point $\mathbf{x}$ belongs to the dominant plane, then the magnitude of the residual $r(\mathbf{x})$ should be small. We assume that the residuals are normally distributed, so that the probability of measuring residual r, given that the point is on the dominant plane, is $p(r|\mathbf{x} \in D) = N(0, \sigma^2 D)$, where σ_D is the standard deviation of residuals for points on the dominant plane.

Similarly, if the point $\mathbf{x}$ does not belong to the dominant plane (*i.e.*, it belongs to the "background"), then the probability of the residuals is is $p(r|\mathbf{x} \in B) = N(0, \sigma^2 B)$, where σ_B is the standard deviation of residuals for points in the background.

The probability mask is estimated recursively. Given the probability mask estimated from the residuals at times 1 through $t - 1$, we can estimate the probability at time t using the discrete Bayes filter [8]:

$$p(\mathbf{x} \in D|r_{1:t}) = \eta p(r_t|\mathbf{x} \in D)p(\mathbf{x} \in D|r_{1:t-1}) \tag{7}$$

$$p(\mathbf{x} \in B|r_{1:t}) = \eta p(r_t|\mathbf{x} \in B)p(\mathbf{x} \in B|r_{1:t-1}) \tag{8}$$

We choose η so that $p(\mathbf{x} \in D|r_{1:t}) + p(\mathbf{x} \in B|r_{1:t}) = 1$. Then the updated probability mask is $p_{ref}(\mathbf{x}) = p(\mathbf{x} \in D|r_{1:t})$.

2.4   Example of Synthetic Image

To illustrate our method, we show results on a synthetic image. Two planar surfaces were created in a checkerboard pattern (Fig. 2, left). Both planes were perpendicular to the camera's line of sight. The two surfaces were textured with random noise using the same parameters. Next, interest points were detected in the synthetic image (Fig. 2, right), using 15×15 templates.

The camera was then translated to the right. The result of tracking one of the templates (the template outlined in red in Fig. 2) is shown in Fig. 3. This template encompasses two planar regions, because it is located at one of the corners of the checkerboard pattern. The evolution of the probability mask over time is shown in the bottom row. By the end of the sequence, the algorithm appeared to correctly segment the template and identify the pixels belonging to the dominant (foreground) plane, with only a few errors.

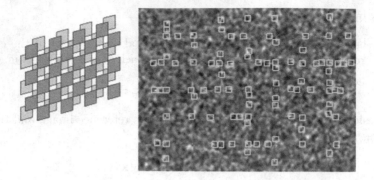

Fig. 2. Synthetic image. (Left) 3D structure. (Right) Interest points (Color figure online).

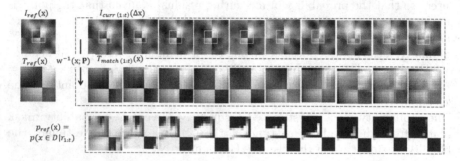

Fig. 3. The reference template (left column) is tracked for 50 frames. The results for every 5th frame are shown. (Top row) Image region surrounding the tracked point. (Middle row) The matched template, warped back to the reference image. (Bottom row) Probability mask, where white indicates a high probability of the point to belong to the dominant plane.

3   Integration of Tracking Method with VSLAM

We integrated the tracking method with a conventional VSLAM algorithm similar to [3]. The algorithm determines the poses of the cameras and the 3D positions of tracked points from images (Fig. 4). Some images are designated as "keyframes", and these poses are refined using bundle adjustment over a sliding window.

The "pose estimation" step is performed using the points which have 3D information. A standard PnP ("Perspective-n-Point") algorithm is used, with a RANSAC [9] approach to eliminate outliers. We next initialize new 3D points from 2D points by performing triangulation if there is sufficient visual angle between observations.

An image is designated as a "keyframe" if the camera has moved sufficiently far from the previous keyframe. Bundle adjustment is performed over the last $N = 3$ keyframes. We collect all points that were observed in the N keyframes,

```
While input data is available do
  Get next image
  Track existing points to the new image
  Estimate pose from 2D to 3D point correspondences
  Initialize new 3D points using triangulation
  Update surface normal and probability masks
  If this pose is a keyframe
    Do bundle adjustment over last N keyframes
    Acquire new points to track
  End If
End While
```

Fig. 4. VSLAM algorithm pseudocode.

and optimize their 3D locations as well as the poses of the N keyframes, to minimize the reprojection error of the points. We acquire new points if the number of points being tracked in the current image falls below a threshold (we used a threshold of 200 points).

As with all VSLAM algorithms that use a single moving camera, there is a scale ambiguity in the results if only image measurements are used. Some additional information must be used to resolve the ambiguity. In this work we resolve the ambiguity by physically measuring the pose of the second keyframe (the first keyframe is considered to be at the origin). This defines a true metric scale for all results.

4 Experimental Results

We compared the performance of the VSLAM algorithm using the "partial plane" tracking method to the same algorithm using the "whole plane" tracking method. The whole plane method is identical to the partial plane method, except that the probability mask $p_{ref}(\mathbf{x})$ is always equal to 1.0, and we skip the step of updating the probability mask. Therefore, any improvement in performance can be attributed to the use of the new partial plane tracking method.

Three datasets were used to test the algorithm. The first two are image sequences that we collected (called "CSM Indoor" and "CSM Outdoor"), shown in Fig. 5.

The "CSM Indoor" dataset consists of 40 images, in which the camera translates in the XZ plane and simultaneously rotates. The estimated camera poses and 3D point positions are shown in Fig. 6.

Figure 7 (left) shows the estimated camera trajectories for the two methods, as well as the ground truth. As can be seen, the whole plane method tracks well in the beginning, but then the positional error starts to increase significantly. This is due to the fact that the number of tracked points starts to decline, because the whole plane tracking method cannot track partial planar templates for very

Fig. 5. Sample images from "CSM Indoor" and "CSM Outdoor" datasets.

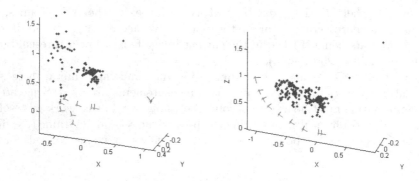

Fig. 6. Estimated camera poses and structure, for "CSM Indoor" dataset. (Left) Results using whole plane method. (Right) Results using partial plane method.

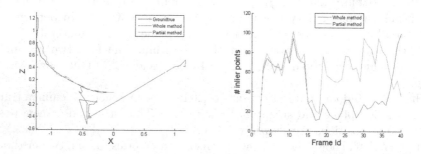

Fig. 7. "CSM Indoor" scene. (Left) camera trajectories. (Right) number of tracked points.

 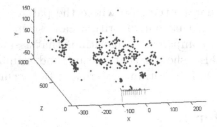

Fig. 8. "ACTS Road" scene. (Left) Sample image from dataset. (Right) Reconstructed scene, showing 3D point locations and camera poses at keyframes for the partial planar method.

Table 1. Experimental results comparing whole plane and partial plane methods. RMSE (root mean squared error) of camera translation (in meters) and orientation (in radians) is shown with respect to ground truth. We did not have ground truth camera orientations for the CSM sequences, so RMSE of orientation is unknown for those.

Sequence	Tracking plane method	Mean # frames tracked	Mean # inlier 3D points	RMSE translation	RMSE orientation
CSM indoor	Whole plane	4.6	41.4	1.18	-
	Partial plane	5.7	60.9	0.2	-
CSM outdoor	Whole plane	7.5	34.1	2.51	-
	Partial plane	8.3	54.8	1.23	-
ACTS road	Whole plane	18.0	51.3	24.97	0.394
	Partial plane	30.9	85.8	2.15	0.035

long. Figure 7 (right) shows the number of inlier 3D points being tracked at each frame.

The remaining dataset is from the Computer Vision Group at Zhejiang University, and has been used by the research community to evaluate structure-from-motion algorithms [10]. A sample image and the estimated camera poses and 3D point positions are shown in Fig. 8.

Table 1 summarizes the results from the three datasets. As can be seen, features can be tracked for a greater number of frames using the partial plane method than with the whole plane method. The average number of inlier 3D points being tracked in each frame is greater using the partial plane method. The partial plane method also yields significantly more accurate camera poses.

5 Conclusions

We have presented a novel algorithm to segment and track partial planar templates, using a sequence of images from a moving camera. Unlike existing algorithms that assume a feature arises from a single planar patch, our algorithm can handle the case where the patch encompasses more than one surface. We showed that our algorithm can estimate and track such features over a longer time, compared to algorithms that assume a patch contains only a single plane. We also showed that the method significantly improves the performance of a VSLAM algorithm, in terms of the accuracy of motion and structure estimates.

References

1. Shi, J., Tomasi, C.: Good features to track. In: Proceedings of CVPR, pp. 593–600 (1994)
2. Davison, A., Reid, I., Molton, N., Stasse, O.: MonoSLAM: real-time single camera SLAM. IEEE Trans. PAMI **29**(6), 1052–1067 (2007)
3. Klein, G., Murray, D.: Parallel tracking and mapping for small AR workspaces. In: Proceedings of ISMAR 2007, pp. 1–10 (2007)
4. Baker, S., Matthews, I.: Lucas-Kanade 20 years on: a unifying framework. Intl J. Comput. Vision **56**, 221–255 (2004)
5. Masoud, A., Hoff, W.: Segmentation and tracking of partial planar templates. In: Proceedings of Winter Conference on Applications of Computer Vision, pp. 1128–1133 (2014)
6. Comaniciu, D., Meer, P.: Mean shift: a robust approach toward feature space analysis. IEEE Trans. PAMI **24**(5), 603–619 (2002)
7. Lagarias, J., et al.: Convergence properties of the nelder-mead simplex method in low dimensions. SIAM J. Optim. **9**(1), 112–147 (1998)
8. Thrun, S., Burgard, W., Fox, D.: Probabilistic Robotics. MIT Press, Cambridge (2005)
9. Fischler, M., Bolles, R.: Random sample consensus: a paradigm for model fitting with applications to image analysis and automated cartography. Comm. ACM **24**(6), 381–395 (1981)
10. Zhang, G., Jia, J., Wong, T., Bao, H.: Consistent depth maps recovery from a video sequence. IEEE Trans. PAMI **31**(6), 974–988 (2009)

Human Centered Scene Understanding Based on 3D Long-Term Tracking Data

Rainer Planinc(✉) and Martin Kampel

Computer Vision Laboratory, Vienna University of Technology,
Favoritenstr. 9-11/183-2, 1040 Vienna, Austria
rainer.planinc@tuwien.ac.at

Abstract. Scene understanding approaches are mainly based on geometric information, not considering the behavior of humans. The proposed approach introduces a novel human-centric scene understanding approach, based on long-term tracking information. Long-term tracking information is filtered, clustered and areas offering meaningful functionalities for humans are modeled using a kernel density estimation. This approach allows to model walking and sitting areas within an indoor scene without considering any geometric information. Thus, it solely uses continuous and noisy tracking data, acquired from a 3D sensor, monitoring the scene from a bird's eye view. The proposed approach is evaluated on three different datasets from two application domains (home and office environment), containing more than 180 days of tracking data.

Keywords: Long-term tracking · Human-centric · Scene understanding

1 Introduction

Traditional scene understanding is object centered (e.g. [3,6,9]) rather than human centered. Human centered scene understanding focuses on functional aspects based on information not provided by the scene and objects itself, but on information how persons interact with the scene and which functionality the scene offers for a human [5]. The use of long-term tracking of humans in order to describe object functions within a room is introduced by Delaitre et al. [2]. Due to the combination of pose analysis (standing, sitting and reaching) and object appearance (geometrical information), the interaction between human actions and objects are modeled. The use of pose estimation is still challenging, since the pose estimation does not work robustly when being applied in practice and introduces wrong pose estimations [2]. However, based on performing long-term tracking, this effect can be minimized by enhancing the amount of tracking data and thus enhancing the accuracy of the pose estimation at a specific location. Although Delaitre et al. [2] use long-term tracking to model person-object interactions, their analysis is based on time-lapse videos, only offering discrete but not continuous information (snapshots).

While Delaitre et al. [2] recognize the objects, Fouhey et al. [4] extends their approach by not only recognizing objects, but modeling the scene in 3D, based on

© Springer International Publishing Switzerland 2015
R. Paredes et al. (Eds.): IbPRIA 2015, LNCS 9117, pp. 93–100, 2015.
DOI: 10.1007/978-3-319-19390-8_11

the object functionality. Again, time-lapse videos are analyzed to detect the pose and combined with a 3D room geometry hypothesis in order to model the room based on the functionality it is offering. Similar to [2], the authors focuses on the poses standing, sitting and reaching in order to classify surfaces into walkable, suitable and reachable surfaces. Based on the pose information, estimates of the functional surfaces are generated and combined with the geometric information obtained by the room hypothesis.

In contrast, a human-centric scene modeling approach based on depth videos is introduced by Lu and Wang [8]. For this proof of concept, a background model is learned from the depth data and used to obtain the human silhouette. In combination with pose estimation performed on the silhouette of the person, objects are modeled as 3D boxes within the scene. Together with geometric knowledge (estimation of vanishing points) of the scene, a room hypotheses including supporting surfaces for human actions is created and walkable areas are estimated. However, analysis and evaluation of the algorithm is performed on only several minutes of data and only deals with a few depth frames, but not a long-term analysis. Moreover, the authors [8] state that skeleton data could theoretically be used as well, but is not stable enough to obtain reasonable results, since skeleton data is noisy and defective.

Long-term human centered scene understanding is either performed by the use of time-lapse videos [2], is based on still-image pose estimation [4] or is a proof of concept [8]. Hence, the contribution of this paper is twofold: first, a novel human-centric scene understanding approach based on continuous long-term tracking data of humans is introduced. Second, the proposed scene understanding approach does not incorporate geometric information and thus is solely based on long-term tracking data (position and pose). With the proposed approach, a scene can be modeled according to the functions being used by the human. The proposed approach is evaluated during a long-term evaluation over the duration of more than 180 days of tracking data. The rest of this paper is structured as follows: Sect. 2 describes the proposed approach, an evaluation is presented in Sect. 3. Finally, a conclusion is drawn in Sect. 4.

2 Methodology

The proposed approach combines the advantages of 3D depth data together with long term tracking and introduces a novel approach for human-centric scene understanding, solely based on noisy tracking information. Depth data is obtained by the use of an Asus Xtion pro live, the detection and tracking of the person is performed using the OpenNI SDK [1][1]. The 3D position of a person within a frame is obtained from long-term tracking data, where filtering mechanisms to reject unreliable tracking data are applied. The filtered long-term

---

[1] Since Primesense is not supporting the OpenNI project any longer, the authors would like to stress that the proposed approach is fully independent from third party companies. Hence, other depth cameras and tracking algorithms can be used in order to obtain the long-term tracking data.

tracking data is clustered according to the height (distance to the ground floor) into walking and sitting clusters. Kernel density estimation together with non maxima suppression and the calculation of a convex hull yields in "hotspots" of each activity region, representing areas being commonly used by humans. In the following sections, detailed information about the proposed filtering, clustering and modeling of the regions are provided.

2.1 Filtering

Long-term tracking data contains noise and tracking errors (e.g. furniture is wrongly tracked as a person), influencing the results of the proposed approach. Hence, tracking data is filtered according to plausibility rules in order to ensure robust results. Although the filtering step removes a high amount of tracking information (i.e. all other activities and tracking information except walking and sitting), this does not influence the overall performance since the approach focuses on long-term tracking, thus ensuring a sufficient number of reliable information is available. Filtering is based on the following three features: (1) it can be assumed that a person being either walking or sitting is in an upright pose (body orientation), (2) the tracked Center of Mass (CoM) is within a plausible range of height (i.e. lower than 1.6 m) and (3) the confidence values of OpenNI are used to eliminate "unreliable" CoM values in order to ensure correct tracking data. During the initial filtering step the skeleton data is used in order to detect the orientation of the body, based on the idea of Planinc and Kampel [10].

2.2 Clustering

Interesting functional areas within indoor environments are sitting and walking areas, and thus are in the focus of research (e.g. [2,4,5]). Hence, tracking data (CoM) is clustered into sitting and walking areas using the k-means algorithm. In a first step, the ground floor parameters are calculated using OpenNI and the height of the CoM for each tracking position is calculated. Tracking data is clustered for each frame according to its distance to the ground floor (=height), using the k-means algorithm, resulting in two cluster: sitting and walking. K-means is chosen since it is fast and the number of cluster is known in advance. However, this approach assumes that both, a sitting and walking area are within the field of view. If only one type of area is within the field of view (i.e. either sitting or walking), the obtained clusters need to be merged (e.g. by analyzing the distance of the cluster centers).

2.3 Kernel Density Estimation

A kernel density estimation with a bi-variate Gaussian kernel is performed in order to estimate the probability density function of the clustered data. The estimation is performed on both classes (sitting and walking) separately in order to model the probability density function of both classes. This step is performed

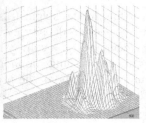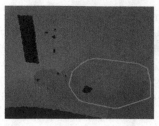

Fig. 1. Example of the workflow: unfiltered tracking data (left), kernel density estimation (middle) and contour of sitting area (right)

to detect "hotspots" within the clustered data, i.e. areas being relevant for this class. Non maxima suppression is applied to suppress irrelevant areas and allows to focus on the main areas, being representative for each class. The relevant area is obtained by applying a fixed threshold to the probability density function, where the resulting contour describes the functional areas within the scene. In order to aggregate smaller but similar areas, the convex hull of all contours is calculated to ensure a coherent area. Figure 1 illustrates an example of the proposed workflow: unfiltered tracking points of the sitting class (left) are filtered and a kernel density estimation as well as non-maxima suppression is performed (middle). The corresponding contour plot visualizes the sitting area (right).

3   Results

Publicly available datasets containing depth information focus on the detection of human activities, e.g. the UTKinect-Action Dataset [14], the Cornell Activity Dataset [12] or the DailyActivity3D [13]. The aim of these datasets is to detect human actions and activities and hence, different activities and actions are recorded in short sequences, while the person is standing in front of the sensor. On the other hand, scene understanding datasets (e.g. NYU Depth Dataset v2 [11], Berkeley 3-D Object Dataset [7]) does not contain tracking information since traditional scene understanding approaches are based on geometric information.

Our proposed approach neither focuses on the detection of actions within short sequences, nor on the incorporation of geometric information. In contrast, the introduced approach focuses on human behavior on the long-term and thus, no datasets are available. Hence, three different datasets (monitoring of a kitchen, living room and office environment) were recorded from a bird's eye view and is publicly available[2] in order to allow comparisons in the future. All scenes contain a sitting area as well as a walking area to be detected by the proposed approach. The evaluation of the proposed approach is performed on 90 days tracking data of the living room, 74 days of tracking data in the kitchen and 20 days of tracking inside the office.

---

[2] http://tracking-dataset.planinc.eu.

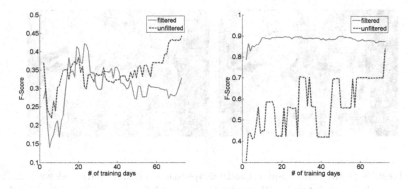

Fig. 2. F-score of the sitting (left) and walking area (right) in the kitchen dataset depending on the number of training samples (average of 6 runs)

Repeated sub-sampling validation is performed by randomly choosing the training set 6 times and averaging the results of all 6 runs. Figure 2 depicts the dependency of the f-score on the size of the training set (number of training days), where the sitting area of the kitchen is shown in the left picture and the walking area of the kitchen is shown in the right picture. The red dotted curve depicts the result of the unfiltered data, whereas the blue curve depicts the result if applying the filtering step as introduced in Sect. 2. The walking area is modeled with a resulting f-score of 0,87 for the filtered data and 0,84 for unfiltered data. However, the f-score for the sitting area achieved only 0,44 (unfiltered) respectively 0,33 (filtered).

In order to perform further analysis on these quantitative results, qualitative evaluation of the results is shown in Fig. 3: during the 6 runs, two different models are obtained - the correct one is obtained four times (depicted on the left side) and a wrong one is obtained two times (depicted on the right side). The wrong model is generated due to wrong tracking data and thus, the sitting area is modeled much bigger than it actually is. This strong influence of the wrong tracking data is a result of much less training data, hence when using more training data, the influence of each training day is minimized. However, the low f-score is also a result of the ground truth labeling - as can be seen in the left image of Fig. 3, the detected sitting area considers only one bench while the other bench is ignored since the second bench is already outside the tracking range. Moreover, the table is considered as sitting area in the ground truth and thus an f-score of 1 can not be achieved. Hence, ground truth annotation need to be adopted according to the range limits of the tracking algorithm and the table need to be excluded from the ground truth. However, qualitative analysis of the walking area in the kitchen dataset shows that the walking area is modeled very well in both cases and thus result in an f-score of greater than 0,8. Moreover it is shown, especially in the walking area of the kitchen, that the filtering step is able to enhance the robustness of the proposed approach, since a more stable and higher f-score is achieved.

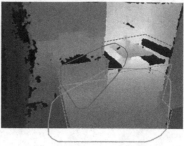

Fig. 3. Results of the scene understanding approach: sitting (red) and walking areas (blue) in the kitchen dataset with respective ground truth marked with dotted lines (Color figure online)

The quantitative results of the living room and office dataset are depicted in Figs. 4 and 5: in contrast to the kitchen dataset, higher f-scores are achieved. The f-score for the sitting and walking area in the living room is 0,75 respectively 0,73, both for the filtered dataset. On the office dataset, f-scores of 0,68 for the sitting area and 0,88 for the walking area are achieved by using the maximum number of training data. The office dataset only consists 20 days of monitoring, hence the influence of increasing the training set can be seen since the f-score raises with adding additional training data. Moreover, the office dataset is not as challenging as the kitchen and living room training set since almost no tracking errors are present and thus, applying the filtering does not dramatically change the result. This is due the fact that the most common tracking errors experienced with the living room and kitchen dataset are the fitting of the skeleton to doors and other objects. In the office scene, no doors are within the field of view and thus enhancing the robustness of the tracker, yielding in better results already with little training data.

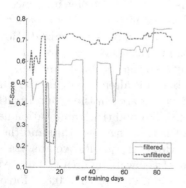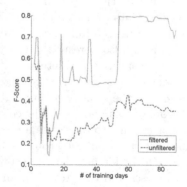

Fig. 4. F-score of the sitting (left) and walking area (right) in the living room dataset depending on the number of training samples (average of 6 runs)

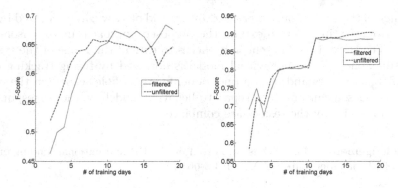

Fig. 5. F-score of the sitting (left) and walking area (right) in the office dataset depending on the number of training samples (average of 6 runs)

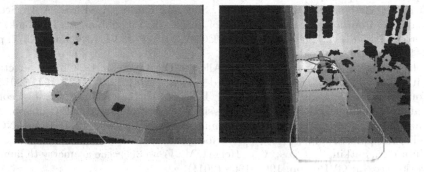

Fig. 6. Results of the scene understanding approach: living room (left) and office dataset (right) with respective ground truth marked with dotted lines (Color figure online)

Qualitative analysis of the results show that the regions are modeled accurately and confirm the quantitative results: Fig. 6 depicts the detected sitting (red) and walking area (blue) of the living room (left) and office dataset (right). The corresponding ground truth is shown with dotted lines. Similarly to the kitchen dataset, also in the office dataset the ground truth of the sitting area is larger since all possible positions to sit are considered within the ground truth annotation - however, this does not mean that all possible positions to sit are actually used by the person, since people tend to usually sit on the same spots and do not change these spots often.

4   Conclusion

This paper introduced a novel method for human centered scene understanding, based on continuous tracking data obtained from a depth sensor. Quantitative and qualitative evaluation showed that the proposed approach is able to accurately model functional areas and thus showed that a human-centric approach is feasible for scene understanding. Due to possible occlusions, the limited field of view range of the sensor, only areas within the field of view can be covered by the system. However, in order to extend the proposed approach, more sensors can be used. Therefore, two different approaches to extend the range of the system are feasible: one generic behavioral model is obtained by fusing tracking data from different sensors and obtain one model for the whole scene. On the other hand, each sensor can obtain a separate behavior model for the corresponding field of view and only the results are combined.

Acknowledgement. This work is supported by the EU and national funding organisations of EU member states (AAL 2013-6-063).

References

1. OpenNI (2011). http://www.openni.org. Accessed 10 April 2014
2. Delaitre, V., Fouhey, D.F., Laptev, I., Sivic, J., Gupta, A., Efros, A.A.: Scene semantics from long-term observation of people. In: Fitzgibbon, A., Lazebnik, S., Perona, P., Sato, Y., Schmid, C. (eds.) ECCV 2012, Part VI. LNCS, vol. 7577, pp. 284–298. Springer, Heidelberg (2012)
3. Felzenszwalb, P.F., Girshick, R.B., McAllester, D., Ramanan, D.: Object detection with discriminatively trained part-based models. PAMI **32**(9), 1627–1645 (2010)
4. Fouhey, D.F., Delaitre, V., Gupta, A., Efros, A.A., Laptev, I., Sivic, J.: People watching: human actions as a cue for single view geometry. In: Fitzgibbon, A., Lazebnik, S., Perona, P., Sato, Y., Schmid, C. (eds.) ECCV 2012, Part V. LNCS, vol. 7576, pp. 732–745. Springer, Heidelberg (2012)
5. Gupta, A., Satkin, S., Efros, A.A., Hebert, M.: From 3D scene geometry to human workspace. In: CVPR, pp. 1961–1968 (2011)
6. Gupta, S., Arbelaez, P., Malik, J.: Perceptual organization and recognition of indoor scenes from RGB-D images. In: CVPR, pp. 564–571 (2013)
7. Janoch, A., Karayev, S., Jia, Y., Barron, J., Fritz, M., Saenko, K., Darrell, T.: A category-level 3-d object dataset: putting the kinect to work. In: ICCV Workshop on Consumer Depth Cameras for Computer Vision, pp. 141–165 (2013)
8. Lu, J., Wang, G.: Human-Centric Indoor Environment Modeling from Depth Videos. In: Fusiello, A., Murino, V., Cucchiara, R. (eds.) ECCV 2012 Ws/Demos, Part II. LNCS, vol. 7584, pp. 42–51. Springer, Heidelberg (2012)
9. Mutch, J., Lowe, D.G.: Multiclass Object Recognition with Sparse, Localized Features. In: CVPR, vol. 1, 11–18 (2006)
10. Planinc, R., Kampel, M.: Robust fall detection by combining 3D data and fuzzy logic. In: Park, J.-I., Kim, J. (eds.) ACCV Workshops 2012, Part II. LNCS, vol. 7729, pp. 121–132. Springer, Heidelberg (2013)
11. Silberman, N., Hoiem, D., Kohli, P., Fergus, R.: Indoor Segmentation and Support Inference from RGBD Images. In: Fitzgibbon, A., Lazebnik, S., Perona, P., Sato, Y., Schmid, C. (eds.) ECCV 2012, Part V. LNCS, vol. 7576, pp. 746–760. Springer, Heidelberg (2012)
12. Sung, J., Ponce, C., Selman, B., Saxena, A.: Human activity detection from rgbd images. In: PAIR, pp. 842–849 (2011)
13. Wang, J., Liu, Z., Wu, Y., Yuan, J.: Mining actionlet ensemble for action recognition with depth cameras. In: CVPR, pp. 1290–1297 (2012)
14. Xia, L., Chen, C., Aggarwal, J.: View invariant human action recognition using histograms of 3d joints. In: CVPR-Workshop, pp. 20–27 (2012)

Fast Head Pose Estimation
for Human-Computer Interaction

Mario García-Montero[1], Carolina Redondo-Cabrera[1],
Roberto López-Sastre[1(✉)], and Tinne Tuytelaars[2]

[1] GRAM, University of Alcalá, Alcalá de Henares, Spain
robertoj.lopez@uah.es
[2] ESAT - PSI, iMinds, KU Leuven, Leuven, Belgium

Abstract. This paper describes a Hough Forest based approach for fast head pose estimation in RGB images. The system has been designed for Human-Computer Interaction (HCI), in a way that with just a simple web-cam, our solution is able to detect the head and simultaneously estimate its pose. We leverage the Hough Forest with Probabilistic Locally Enhanced Voting model, and integrate it into a system with a skin detection step and a tracking filter for the head orientation. Our implementation drastically speeds up the head pose estimations, improving their accuracy with respect to the original model. We present extensive experiments on a publicly available and challenging dataset, where our approach outperforms the state-of-the-art.

Keywords: Head pose estimation · Hough Forest · Tracking · Detection

1 Introduction

Human-Computer interaction (HCI) is gradually getting more and more attention. As people interact by means of many different channels, including body posture and head pose, an important step towards more natural interfaces is the visual analysis of the user movements by the machine. Besides the interpretation of full body movements, as done by systems like the Kinect for gaming, new interfaces would highly benefit from an automatic and fast estimation of the head pose, as the one presented in this work.

Recent state-of-the-art methods based on the principle of Hough Forests (HFs) [14] have proved to be very successful detecting and estimating the pose of the head (*e.g.* [11,12,18,19]). All these methods train a Random Forest (RF) [13] for a joint classification and regression. For inference, patches are densely sampled from the image and the model determines for each patch whether it belongs to the face or the background. Additionally, for head patches, the model performs a regression to localize the center of the head and to estimate its pose. However, while the methods presented in [11,18,19] require depth images, the HF with Probabilistic Locally Enhanced Voting (PLEV) described in [12] has achieved state-of-the-art results using only 2D imagery.

© Springer International Publishing Switzerland 2015
R. Paredes et al. (Eds.): IbPRIA 2015, LNCS 9117, pp. 101–110, 2015.
DOI: 10.1007/978-3-319-19390-8_12

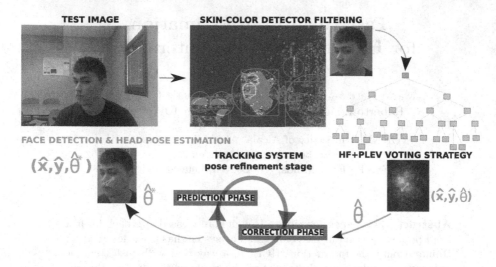

Fig. 1. Our approach is able to jointly estimate the localization and the continuous pose of the head. We start performing a skin-color filtering, and then we follow a HF + PLEV regression voting [12], in conjunction with a tracking step to consolidate the final head orientation estimations (Color figure online).

Here we leverage the HF with PLEV model [12], and design an approach to get a fast head pose estimation (see Fig. 1). Our solution is able to perform the detection and estimation using a simple web-cam. We incorporate into the system a skin-color filtering and a tracking stage to refine the pose estimations. Our implementation has been completely developed in C++, which makes our model dramatically faster than the original approach of [12]. Furthermore, our experimental validation shows that the proposed solution is able to outperform the state-of-the-art results in the *Biwi Kinect Head Pose Database* (Biwi) [11] using only RGB images.

The rest of the paper is organized as follows. In the next section, a review of related work is given. Section 3 introduces the proposed system. Section 4 presents the experimental evaluation. We conclude in Sect. 5.

2   Related Work

The literature contains several works on head pose estimation [20], which can be conveniently divided depending on whether they use RGB images, depth data or both.

In general, approaches that use RGB images are sensitive to illumination and the lack of distinctive features. Therefore, some of the recent works use depth as the primary cue. Breitenstein *et al.* [8], first compute hypotheses of nose locations from high-resolution depth images, and then minimize an error function between these hypotheses and the reference pose images. Lately, some works propose to use a RF combined with a Hough voting strategy to solve the problem [11,12,18,19].

Fanelli *et al.* [19] introduce the use of RF for real time head pose estimation from high quality range scans. The approach was later adapted to depth data from consumer depth cameras [11,18]. In [12], the authors propose to extend the HF voting with the concept of *Probabilistic Locally Enhanced Voting* (PLEV), a regression strategy which consists in modulating the regression with a kernel density estimation to consolidate the votes in a local region near the maxima detected in the Hough space. Schulter *et al.* [1] have improved the RF proposing the novel Alternating Regression Forest, which are able to minimize a global loss to obtain better generalization, in contrast to the local minimization process employed during the learning of traditional RF. Finally, Riegler *et al.* [16] describe a method that combines convolutional neural networks with the idea of Hough Forests for a continuous head pose estimation.

Within the 2D image-based algorithms, we focus here on appearance-based methods. In contrast to our model, a common appearance-based approach is to discretize the head poses and learn a *separate* detector for each of them, *e.g.* [2,3, 9,17]. Several works rely on statistical models of the face shape and appearance, *e.g.*, Active Appearance Models [4] and their extensions [5–7], but their focus is usually on detection and tracking of facial features. These methods rely on coarse quantizations of the poses for multi-view face detection, instead of considering that the pose estimation is ultimately a continuous problem. Recently, Demirkus *et al.* [21] have proposed a hierarchical temporal graphical model to estimate a continuous head pose angle from real-world videos. The introduced methodology provides a probability density function (PDF) of head poses for each video frame, rather than a single decision. However, only the yaw angle is considered, while our solution performs estimations simultaneously for the pitch, yaw and roll angles.

We build our approach on the work described in [12]. So, ours is also a HF based strategy. However, unlike [1,11,18,19], we present a model which does not need depth information but RGB images. Specifically, we have developed a compact implementation of the HF+PLEV [12] using C++. In order to get a fast system for HCI, we have extended the HF+PLEV [12] to work with a preprocessing filter for selecting face candidate regions, implementing a skin-color detection step. This preprocessing speeds up the pose estimations. Finally, we feed a tracking model *only* with the pose estimations of the face candidate regions to improve the predictions. We evaluate the use of two tracking solutions: a Kalman Filter [22] and the Condensation algorithm [23]. All these extensions let us build a final model which is faster than the original HF+PLEV [12], and also more precise – our results show that our implementation improves the results reported in [12].

3   The Model

3.1   Learning a HF for Head Pose Estimation

A typical RF [13] is an ensemble classifier consisting of a set of randomized decision trees. During training, a binary weak classifier is learned for each non-leaf node. At runtime, test samples are passed through the trees, and the output is computed by averaging the distributions learned at the reached leaf-nodes. HF [14] are a generalization of the Hough transform within the RF framework. The randomized trees are trained to learn a mapping from sampled d-dimensional features to their corresponding votes in a Hough space $\mathcal{H} \in \mathbb{R}^H$.

We build on the approach of Redondo-Cabrera et $al.$ [12]. As it is described in [12], in the HF $\mathcal{F}$, we aggregate a set of T binary decision trees $T_t(\mathcal{P}) : \mathcal{P} \to \mathcal{H}$, where $\mathcal{P} \subseteq \mathbb{R}^d$ is the d-dimensional feature space and $\mathcal{H} \subseteq \mathbb{R}^h$ describes the Hough space where the hypotheses are encoded. This Hough space lets us recover hypotheses for the location and the continuous pose of the head at multiple scales. Each head hypothesis $\mathbf{h} \in \mathcal{H}$ can be defined as $\mathbf{h} = (x_h, y_h, \theta_h, s_h)$, where x_h and y_h encode the face center (in our case, the tip of the nose), $\theta_h \in \mathbb{R}^p$ represents the continuous pose, and s_h identifies the scale.

Each of the decision trees T_t is built using a set of sampled patches $P_i = \{(\mathcal{I}_i, c_i, d_i, \theta_i)\}$, where $\mathcal{I}_i = \{I_i^1, I_i^2, ..., I_i^N\}$ defines the appearance of the training image, I_i^j is the jth appearance channel, $c_i \in \mathcal{C} : \{0, 1\}$ is a class label (0 for a background sample and 1 for a head sample), $d_i = (x_i, y_i)$ encodes the relative 2D location of the face center to the sampled patch. And θ_i defines the continuous pose of the head. Training a single decision tree involves recursively splitting each node such that the training data in newly created child nodes is pure according to class label, relative 2D location and pose.

In our case, as in [12], the split function $f(\mathcal{I}_i; \tau_1, \tau_2, \{R_i\}_{i=1}^4)$ is characterized by the following parameters: the appearance channel specified by $\tau_1 \in \{1, 2, ..., N\}$, four asymmetric rectangles defined within the patch $\{R_i\}_{i=1}^4$, and a threshold $\tau_2 \in \mathbb{R}$ for the difference of average values of the rectangular areas. We then define

$$f(\mathcal{I}_i; \tau_1, \tau_2, \{R_r\}_{r=1}^4) = \begin{cases} 0 \text{ if } f_a(\mathcal{I}_i; \tau_1, \{R_r\}_{r=1}^4) < \tau_2, \\ 1 \text{ otherwise.} \end{cases} \tag{1}$$

with $f_a(\mathcal{I}_i; \tau_1, \{R_r\}_{r=1}^4) = |R_1|^{-1} \sum_{q \in R_1} I_i^{\tau_1}(q) - \sum_{r=2}^4 \left(|R_r|^{-1} \sum_{q \in R_r} I_i^{\tau_1}(q) \right)$.

Each node chooses the best splitting function by optimizing one of the following three impurity measures, $\mathcal{M}_*(\mathcal{S})$, which are chosen randomly during training. The class label impurity is measured as in [15] by

$$\mathcal{M}_c(S) = H(S) - \sum_{child \in (left, right)} \frac{S^{child}}{S} H(S^{child}), \tag{2}$$

where $H(S)$ is the entropy given by $H(S) = - \sum_{c=0}^1 p(c|S) \log(p(c|S))$, and $p(c|S)$ indicates the empirical distribution over classes within the set S.

The impurity of the relative 2D patch location, as in [14], is defined by

$$\mathcal{M}_d(S) = \sum_{child \in (left, right)} \sum_{j:c_j=1} \| d_j - \frac{1}{|S^{child}|} \sum_{k:c_k=1} d_k \|^2. \tag{3}$$

And the impurity of the head pose is computed as in [12]:

$$M_p(S) = \sum_{child \in (left,right)} \sum_{j:c_j=1} \left(\frac{min\left\{(\|\theta_j - \boldsymbol{\theta}_A\|), 360° - (\|\theta_j - \boldsymbol{\theta}_A\|)\right\}}{180°} \right)^2,$$

(4)

where $\boldsymbol{\theta}_A$ is the viewpoint angle average over all foreground patches in the set S^{child} and it is computed taking the cyclic nature of pose angles into account.

3.2 Fast Head Detection and Pose Estimation for HCI

Given a test image, see Fig. 1, we start performing a *pixel-based* skin detection method. This can be considered a preprocessing step to find candidate face regions.

Our pixel-based skin detector uses a thresholding method to classify skin and non-skin pixels [10]. This kind of skin detector defines the boundaries of the skin cluster in certain color spaces using a set of fixed skin thresholds.

After the skin detection step, image patches are sampled only from the candidate regions identified. We also incorporate a stride parameter, which controls how densely patches are extracted, thus easily steering speed and accuracy of the regression.

These patches traverse the learned trees and cast votes to the multidimensional Hough voting space $\mathcal{H} \subset \mathbb{R}^{2+p}$ based on the location and pose distributions stored in the leaves. Note that p is the number of angles that defined the continuous pose of the face. The forest-based estimate is then computed by aggregating votes from different patches at different scales $\{s_1, s_2, \ldots, s_S\}$. Following a standard HF regression approach [14], votes are accumulated in an additive way into the corresponding Hough voting spaces $\{\mathcal{H}^1, \mathcal{H}^2, \ldots, \mathcal{H}^S\}$, where $\mathcal{H}^i \in \mathbb{R}^{2+p}$. Then, these Hough spaces are stacked and scaled, so the maxima can be jointly localized at multiple scales. For finding these maxima, we use the procedure described in [12] named PLEV, where a local Hough region ($H_r^{\hat{h}} \subset \mathcal{H}^i$), rather than a single Hough maximum, is considered for the regression of the pose. PLEV aggregates all *pose* votes received in $H_r^{\hat{h}}$, obtaining a global distribution $g_r^{\hat{h}}$ in the Hough region, which can be computed as,

$$g_r^{\hat{h}} = \sum_{v_i \in H_r^{\hat{h}}} \left(\sum_{L_j \to v_i} \frac{p(c = 1|L_j)}{|L_j|} p(\theta|L_j, v_i) \right),$$

(5)

where $p(c = 1|L_j)$ and $|L_j|$ encode the foreground likelihood and the number of patches in leaf L_j, respectively. $p(\theta|L_j, v_i)$ is the distribution of poses associated to the patches in leaf L_j which cast a vote in $H_r^{\hat{h}}$, which we denote as $L_j \to v_i$.

We finally perform a Gaussian KDE on $g_r^{\hat{h}}$ distribution in order to obtain a smooth probability density function for the pose estimation,

$$f_{g_r^{\hat{h}}}(\theta) = \frac{1}{|g_r^{\hat{h}}|} \sum_{\forall g_r^{\hat{h}}(i)} \frac{1}{\sqrt{2\pi}} \exp(\frac{(\theta - g_r^{\hat{h}}(i))^2}{2h^2}),$$

(6)

with h the bandwidth and $|g_r^{\hat{h}}|$ the total number of voting positions considered. At last, our final hypothesis for the pose $\hat{\theta}$ is obtained as $\arg\max_{\hat{\theta}} = f_{g_r^{\hat{h}}}(\theta)$.

3.3 Head Pose Estimation Tracking

The approach in [12] works on each frame independently. Here we propose to *refine the pose estimation* with a tracking solution (see Fig. 1). Our aim is to improve the accuracy of the predictions for head pose values $\hat{\theta}$, avoiding noisy results. For doing so, we integrate into the system a tracking approach to obtain the refined estimations $\hat{\theta}^*$. In our model, the tracking is done for each of the angles of the face (pitch, yaw and roll) independently. We experimentally validate the use of two off-the-shelf trackers: a Kalman filter (KF) [22] and a Particle filter (PF) [23].

We perform a validation process which affects to the initialization and configuration parameters of each of the tracking filters. This validation phase is based on a triple tuning process, one for each angle to estimate in $\hat{\theta}$, as they are tracked with separated filters.

We first take the trained HF+PLEV $\mathcal{F}$, and choose a set of training images to tune the tracking parameters. With the PF, we have performed the validation to tune the following parameters: (a) the number of samples generated by the filter (N), (b) the number of iterations, and (c) the characteristic parameters of the dynamical model $(A, \bar{x}, B)$, which is of the following form:

$$x_t - \bar{x} = A(x_{t-1} - \bar{x}) + Bw_t, \tag{7}$$

where w_t are independent vectors of independent standard normal variables, x_t is the state-vector, $\bar{x}$ is the mean value of the state, and A and B area matrices representing the deterministic and stochastic components of the dynamical model, respectively.

For the KF, the validation step consists in adjusting the initialization for the following matrices: (a) process noise covariance (Q), (b) measurement noise covariance (R), (c) posteriori error estimate covariance (P) and (d) measurement (H) [22]. We initialize the first predicted state of the KF according to $\hat{\theta}$.

4 Experiments

4.1 Experimental Setup

Data Set. We report the performance of our model using only the RGB images provided in the dataset *Biwi Kinect Head Pose Database* (Biwi) [11]. It contains over 15 K images of 20 people. The head pose range covers about ±75 degrees yaw and ±60 degrees pitch. Ground truth is provided in the form of the 3D location of the head and its rotation. Following [11], we split the database into two sets: a testing and training set of respectively 2 (subjects 1 and 12) and 18 subjects. We use the training subject 24 for validation.

Implementation Details. We have developed the complete system in C++, porting all the Matlab functions of the original HF+PLEV [12].

During training, the positive examples are cropped and rescaled to the same size, chosen so that the largest bounding box dimension is equal to 100 pixels. 20 positive and 20 negative patches, with size of 32×32 pixels, are randomly extracted from each training image. Our forests have 15 trees with a maximum depth of 20. In each node, 20.000 binary tests are considered during learning. For the PLEV we consider a neighborhood size of 11×11 pixels. We use the 32 feature channels used in [14].

For the skin-color detector, we apply an image conversion to the YCrCb color space. The color filter restrictions allow to recognize as skin pixels those complying: $Y \in [15, 235]$,$Cb \in [60, 122]$,$Cr \in [135, 170]$. A filtering of all the candidate regions is performed, discarding regions whose area in pixels is out of the interval $[4000, 40000]$, or whose aspect ratio ($\frac{height}{width}$) does not belong to the interval $[0.5, 3]$. Following the validation process described for the tracking filter parameters, these are values chosen. For the PF: $N = 1300$, $N_{iterations} = 500$, $\bar{x}_{yaw} = 0.1$, $\bar{x}_{pitch} = 0.15$, $\bar{x}_{roll} = 0.15$, $A_{yaw} = 0.5$, $A_{pitch} = 7$, $A_{roll} = 0.5$, $B_{yaw} = 0.079$, $B_{pitch} = 0.3$, $B_{roll} = 0.079$. For the KF: $H = I$, $Q = I10^{-4}$, $R_{yaw} = I10^{-1}$, $R_{pitch} = I10^4$, $R_{roll} = I10^3$, $P_{yaw} = I10^1$, $P_{pitch} = I10^8$, $P_{roll} = I10^5$. I denotes the identity matrix.

4.2   Face Detection and Head Pose Estimation Results

Results are reported in Table 1, offering a comparison between the state-of-the-art using depth and RGB images.

First, it is worth mentioning that our estimations for the pitch, yaw and roll reduce the error with respect to [12], even for a lower missed frames ratio (1.4 %). Moreover, our model, using the same trained forest than in [12], and considering that the tracking is only done for the pose estimations (not for the face localizations), achieves a face detection performance slightly higher than in [12]. Results show that the KF is able to mainly reduce the pitch and roll errors. The PF lets us reduce all the pose errors, and especially those associated to the roll. We experimentally observe that the PF casts a slightly superior accuracy than the KF. In conclusion, our approach outperforms both the face detection and head pose estimation state-of-the-art results reported in [12] when only RGB images are used.

Note that our model, using simply RGB data, outperforms the results of methods which need depth images, such as [1,16,18]. It is relevant that our error for the roll estimation is the lowest reported using this dataset. Regarding to the yaw and pitch errors, the increment of our errors is 1.5° and 1.7°, respectively, compared to the winning methods using depth. For the nose direction error, our method is far from [18], but note that their missed frames ratio is higher. For a comparable missed frames ratio, $i.e.$ [16], our method offers a slightly better nose direction estimation. As a conclusion, we can claim that our model is able to improve the state-of-the-art-results for the problem of head pose estimation from RGB images, which is an important contribution. Qualitative results are provided in Fig. 3.

Table 1. Results using the Biwi Kinect Head Pose Database.

Images	Model	Position error (mm)	Direction error (°)	Yaw (°)	Pitch (°)	Roll (°)	Missed (%)
Depth	[16]	8.1 ± 5.3	9.8 ± 8	$\mathbf{3.8 \pm 3.7}$	6.7 ± 6.6	4.3 ± 4.9	**1**
	[1]	10.8 ± 6.1	12.2 ± 9	$5.5° \pm 5.8°$	$7.8° \pm 7.9°$	$5° \pm 4.4°$	3
	[12]	$\mathbf{7.2 \pm 12.1}$	7.3 ± 5.9	$4.1° \pm 6.9°$	$3.9° \pm 4°$	$3.2° \pm 3°$	5
	[11]	12.2 ± 22.8	$\mathbf{5.9 \pm 8.1}$	$3.8 \pm 6.5°$	$\mathbf{3.5 \pm 5.8°}$	$5.4 \pm 6.0°$	6.6
	[18]	14.7 ± 22.5	–	$9.2 \pm 13.7°$	$8.5 \pm 10.1°$	$8 \pm 8.3°$	1
Images	Model	Position error (pixels)	Direction error (°)	Yaw (°)	Pitch (°)	Roll (°)	Missed (%)
RGB	[12]	3.2 ± 1.4	9.8 ± 6.8	5.8 ± 5.9	5.8 ± 4.8	3.5 ± 3.4	2.4
	Ours + KF	$\mathbf{3 \pm 1.4}$	9.4 ± 7.5	5.8 ± 6.4	5.1 ± 4.6	3.1 ± 3.3	1.4
	Ours + PF	$\mathbf{3 \pm 1.4}$	9.1 ± 6.9	5.3 ± 6.3	5.2 ± 4.4	$\mathbf{2.8 \pm 2.9}$	1.4

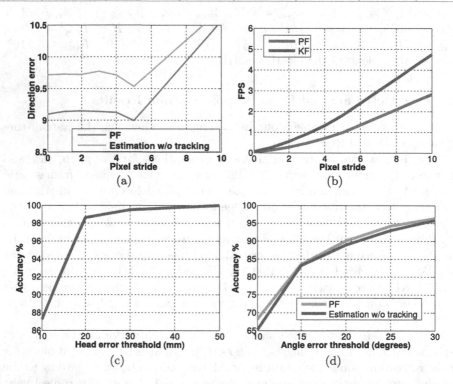

Fig. 2. (a) and (b) quantitative results as a function of the stride pixel parameter. (a) Errors for nose direction. (b) Frames per second (FPS). Frame accuracy of our method for different success thresholds of (c) the head position in mm and (d) the head pose in degrees.

Our model has been designed to perform a fast estimation for HCI, while the accuracy does not degrade. In the following experiment, we evaluate the performance of our approach as a function of the stride parameter. Recall this parameter

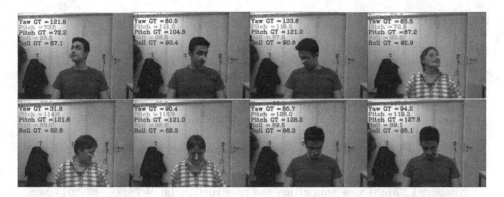

Fig. 3. Qualitative results. Ground truth in blue, good estimations in green and wrong estimations in red (Color figure online).

controls the spatial sampling of the patches to be extracted within an input candidate region identified by the skin detection step. It can be tuned to find the desired trade-off between accuracy and runtime of the process. Figure 2(a) shows how the direction error varies with respect to the stride. We can observe that our model with PF systematically reports better results than our implementation without the tracking. This reveals that the tracking solution implemented really improves the performance of the system. Figure 2(b) shows the frames per second of our implementation for different stride values. It is relevant to note that our approach is able to process up to 3 frames per second, using the PF, reporting a direction error lower than 11^{0}.

Finally, we report the accuracy as a function of the success threshold for the head localization error and for the pose estimation error in Figs. 2(c) and (d), respectively. We can observe (see Fig. 2(c)) that our model gives a good performance for all success thresholds in the head position regression. It achieves a 87.24 % for the most restrictive threshold of 10 mm. With respect to the angle error threshold used to evaluate the pose estimation, Fig. 2(d) shows that the tracking with PF improves the accuracy of the model. It is worth to mention that for a restrictive threshold of $10°$, our implementation with tracking reports a 68.2 % of accuracy, compared to the 65 % of our approach without the tracking stage.

5 Conclusion

We have proposed a fast HCI solution to estimate the location and continuous pose of the head. We combine the HF+PLEV model with a preprocessing step for the skin detection. Then the pose estimations are refined employing a tracking methodology. Our model simply needs RGB images, and it is able to report state-of-the-art results, while not relying on the availability of depth information.

Acknowledgements. This work is supported by projects CCG2013/EXP-047, CCG2014/EXP-054, TEC2013-45183-R, SPIP2014-1468, ERC Starting Grant COGNIMUND and the MECD Collaboration Grants 2014/15.

References

1. Schulter, S., Leistner, C., Wohlhart, P., Roth, P.M., Bischof, H.: Alternating regression forests for object detection and pose estimation. In: CVPR (2013)
2. Jones, M., Viola, P.: Fast multi-view face detection. Technical report (2003)
3. Morency, L.P., Sundberg, P., Darrell, T.: Pose estimation using 3D view-based eigenspaces. In: AMFG (2003)
4. Cootes, T.F., Edwards, G.J., Taylor, C.J.: Active appearance models. PAMI **23**(6), 681–685 (2001)
5. Cootes, T.F., Wheeler, G.V., Walker, K.N., Taylor, C.J.: View-based active appearance models. In: AMFG (2000)
6. Ramnath, K., Koterba, S., Xiao, J., Hu, C., Matthews, I., Baker, S., Cohn, J., Kanade, T.: Multi-view aam fitting and construction. IJCV **76**(2), 183–204 (2008)
7. Storer, M., Urschler, M., Bischof, H.: 3d-mam: 3d morphable appearance model for efficient fine head pose estimation from still images. In: Workshop on Subspace Methods (2009)
8. Breitenstein, M.D., Kuettel, D., Weise, T., Van Gool, L.J., Pfister, H.: Real-time face pose estimation from single range images. In: CVPR (2008)
9. Ding, H.X., Fang, C.: Head pose estimation based on random forests for multiclass classification. In: ICPR (2010)
10. Vezhnevets, V., Sazonov, V., Andreeva, A.: A survey on Pixel-Based skin color detection techniques. In: GraphiCon (2003)
11. Fanelli, G., Dantone, M., Gall, J., Fossati, A., Van Gool, L.: Random forests for real time 3D face analysis. IJCV **101**(3), 437–458 (2013)
12. Redondo-Cabrera, C., Lopez-Sastre, R., Tuytelaars, T.: All together now: simultaneous object detection and continuous pose estimation using a hough forest with probabilistic locally enhanced voting. In: BMVC (2014)
13. Breiman, L.: Random forests. Mach. Learn. **45**(1), 5–32 (2001)
14. Gall, J., Yao, A., Razavi, N., van Gool, L., Lempitsky, V.: Hough forests for object detection, tracking, and action recognition. PAMI **33**(11), 2188–2202 (2011)
15. Criminisi, A., Shotton, J., Konukoglu, E.: Decision forests: a unified framework for classification, regression, density estimation, manifold learning and semi-supervised learning. FTCGV **7**(2–3), 81–227 (2012)
16. Riegler, G., Ruther, M., Bischof, B.: Hough networks for head pose estimation and facial feature localization. In: BMVC (2014)
17. Ghodrati, A., Pedersoli, M., Tuytelaars, T.: Is 2D information enough for viewpoint estimation? In: BMVC (2014)
18. Fanelli, G., Weise, T., Gall, J., Van Gool, L.J.: Real time head pose estimation from consumer depth cameras. In: GAPR (2011)
19. Fanelli, G., Gall, J., Van Gool, L.J.: Real time head pose estimation with random regression forests. In: CVPR (2011)
20. Murphy-Chutorian, E., Trivedi, M.M.: Head pose estimation in computer vision: a survey. PAMI **31**, 607–626 (2009)
21. Demirkus, M., Precup, D., Clark, J.J., Arbel, T.: Probabilistic temporal head pose estimation using a hierarchical graphical model. In: Fleet, D., Pajdla, T., Schiele, B., Tuytelaars, T. (eds.) ECCV 2014, Part I. LNCS, vol. 8689, pp. 328–344. Springer, Heidelberg (2014)
22. Welch, G., Bishop, G.: An Introduction to the Kalman Filter. Technical report (2006)
23. Isard, M., Blake, A.: CONDENSATION - conditional density propagation for visual tracking. IJCV **29**(1), 5–28 (1998)

Structured Light System Calibration for Perception in Underwater Tanks

Flávio Lopes[✉], Hugo Silva, José Miguel Almeida, and Eduardo Silva

INESC TEC Technology and Science, Instituto Superior de Engenharia do Porto,
Rua Dr. António Bernardino de Almeida 431, 4200-072 Porto, Portugal
{flavio.m.lopes,hugo.m.silva,jose.m.almeida,eduardo.silva}@inesctec.pt

Abstract. The process of visually exploring underwater environments is still a complex problem. Underwater vision systems require complementary means of sensor information to help overcome water disturbances. This work proposes the development of calibration methods for a structured light based system consisting on a camera and a laser with a line beam. Two different calibration procedures that require only two images from different viewpoints were developed and tested in dry and underwater environments. Results obtained show, an accurate calibration for the camera/projector pair with errors close to 1 mm even in the presence of a small stereos baseline.

1 Introduction

The process of visual exploring underwater environments is an important research challenge. The range of unmanned vehicles that require underwater perception capabilities is rapidly growing due to the more frequent use of this vehicles in inhospitable places such as oil and gas platforms and deep sea underwater mining.

In this paper, we propose to develop a structured light system (SLS) for conducting perception tasks in underwater infrastructures. Normally, pure visual methods struggle in underwater environments due to phenomenons such as: poor scene illumination, lack of image texture and water disturbances like high turbidity, absorption and scattering [1]. Therefore, conventional computer vision approaches using stereo vision suffer from the difficulty of obtaining correspondences between image points. One way of overcoming such limitation is by using laser based techniques [2], or laser techniques combined with photometric stereo [3]. In [4] structured light systems are used to perform bathymetric operations using Remotely Operational Vehicles and discoverer diffuse flow on the seafloor.

To perform such operations in an accurate manner, an efficient calibration procedure that allows to calibrate the camera and the laser must be developed. Therefore, our main work was to develop, experiment and evaluate calibration methods that allow to perform all necessary SLS calibration.

The problem of calibrating a triangulation system between a laser (projector) and a camera has already been addressed by many authors, but the underlying

© Springer International Publishing Switzerland 2015
R. Paredes et al. (Eds.): IbPRIA 2015, LNCS 9117, pp. 111–120, 2015.
DOI: 10.1007/978-3-319-19390-8_13

idea is still subject of ongoing research specially when trying to apply it for underwater operations. In [5] a calibration rig consisting of lines with known parameters is used. The intersection of the laser plane with each line gives an image point to world line correspondence. Having enough correspondences a 4 × 3 transformation matrix which maps a 2D image point to its 3D coordinate on the laser plane can be recovered. Reid et al. [6] uses a similar solution, using a calibration rig consisting of planes with known parameters. Projecting the line laser onto the known planes gives an image point to world plane correspondence, and then the 8-point algorithm [7] is used to find the transformation matrix.

One of the methods used in our experiments was a modified version on the method developed by Huynh [8]. The method uses a calibration rig consisting of two planes with 12 points (control points) with known 3D coordinates. The points form 4 straight lines, and by using the cross-ratio invariance [7], the 3D coordinates of the point of intersection of the laser plane with these 4 lines can be determined, allowing to obtain 2D image point to 3D world point correspondences that are used to recover the transformation matrix.

Some of these methods are complex and so other simpler methods that require just a few measurements to a known planar target from different viewpoints can also be used to compute the camera and projector calibration [9,10]. An image of the calibration board is captured, along with the line of its intersection with the laser plane. Then by correspondences between board points and their image coordinates, the pose of the calibration board with respect to the camera center can be determined, resulting in a known world plane. The image of the laser line is then back-projected to the world plane. Performing this operations with the calibration board at different orientations results in a 3D point cloud spanning the laser plane, from which the parameters that define the laser plane can be recovered.

2   Geometric Model

Our proposed structured light system is composed of a camera and a single projector equipped with a line beam. The main objective is to be able to obtain accurate 3D points information from objects that are illuminated by the projector, see Fig. 1.

2.1   Camera Model

The camera model follows a classic pinhole model of perspective projection divided into intrinsic (1) and extrinsic parameters.

$$K = \begin{bmatrix} f_x & s & c_x \\ 0 & f_y & c_y \\ 0 & 0 & 1 \end{bmatrix} \tag{1}$$

where K is the intrinsic parameter matrix, that contains the focal length $\mathbf{f}$ (f_x, f_y), the skew s, and the principal point $\mathbf{c}$ (c_x, c_y) information. There is still one

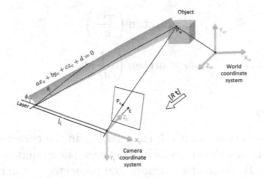

Fig. 1. Geometric model of the SLS system

parameter missing which is the lenses distortion that needs to be compensated when calibrating the camera [11].

For the extrinsic parameters, the projection of a 3D world point $\mathbf{P}_w$ represented in the world coordinate system to a 2D image point $\mathbf{p}$ (x,y), in the image plane is given by:

$$\tilde{\mathbf{p}} \simeq K[R|\mathbf{t}]\tilde{\mathbf{P}}_\mathbf{w} \tag{2}$$

where R is the rotation matrix, K the intrinsic parameters and $\mathbf{t}$ the translation vector that allows to translate a point between the world reference frame and the camera reference frame. While $\tilde{\mathbf{p}}$ is a 2D image point and $\tilde{\mathbf{P}}_\mathbf{w}$ is the same point in the 3D world point reference frame, both in homogeneous coordinates representation.

2.2 Projector Model

For the projector calibration, the perspective projection does not hold since the light stripe is not directly illuminated from the optical center of the projector. Therefore, most applications do not use the projection of the light stripe, and instead prefer to represent the projector by applying the equation of a plane. The light stripe that appears in 3D space can be expressed in the camera coordinate frame by the plane equation, described by:

$$a_i x_c + b_i y_c + c_i z_c + d = 0 \tag{3}$$

where i is the light stripe number, a_i, b_i, c_i, and d_i are its coefficients. From here, it is possible to define the baseline l_i i.e. the distance between the camera and the projector, and also the projection angle θ_i i.e. the angle between the light stripe and the Z_c axis, and the tilt angle ϕ_i i.e. the angle between the Y_c axis and the light stripe. The parameters can be obtained by the following expressions:

$$l_i = \left(\frac{d_i}{a_i}\right) \tag{4}$$

$$\theta_i = \arctan\left(\frac{-ci}{a_i}\right) \tag{5}$$

$$\phi_i = \arctan\left(\frac{-b_i}{a_i}\right) \tag{6}$$

2.3   Triangulation

For obtaining the 3D world point information $\mathbf{P_w}$ in the camera reference frame as $\mathbf{P_c}$ (x_c, y_c, z_c), a triangulation principle between the camera viewpoint and the light stripe is used. To do so, the camera and projector parameters are derived from (2) and (3), as given by:

$$\begin{bmatrix} f_x & s & 0 \\ 0 & f_y & 0 \\ a_i & b_i & d_i \end{bmatrix} \begin{bmatrix} \frac{x_c}{z_c} \\ \frac{y_c}{z_c} \\ \frac{1}{z_c} \end{bmatrix} = \begin{bmatrix} x - c_x \\ y - c_y \\ -c_i \end{bmatrix} \tag{7}$$

So, we can estimate $\mathbf{P_c}$ coordinates as:

$$x_c = \frac{x - c_x}{f_x} z_c \tag{8}$$

$$y_c = \frac{y - c_y}{f_y} z_c \tag{9}$$

$$z_c = \frac{l_i}{-\frac{c_i}{a_i} - \left(\frac{x-c_x}{f_x}\right) - \frac{b_i}{a_i}\left(\frac{y-c_y}{f_y}\right)} \tag{10}$$

The triangulation principle is used to compute the depth coordinate z_c (10). Afterwards, x_c, y_c coordinates are obtained based on the scaling relation with the camera (8), (9), we consider skew $s = 0$.

3   Calibration

Prior to be able to use the structured light system for obtaining accurate 3D underwater measurements, there is the need to perform a global system calibration. Not only we need to calibrate the camera (intrinsic and extrinsic parameters), but also to relate the projector position with respect to the image plane.

3.1   Camera Calibration

The first step to obtain a global system calibration is to recover all camera parameters. Therefore, we start by obtaining the camera intrinsic parameters by using an offline toolbox procedure.

For the camera extrinsic parameters, they are obtained by taking at least two images of a plain chessboard in different viewpoints. Afterwards, all chessboard corners present in each image are detected using the Harris corners detector [12].

The extrinsic parameters (rotation matrix R, translation vector $\mathbf{t}$) are recovered based on homography decomposition method [7].

We establish that 3D world points in the world reference frame have null component in Z_w axis, i.e., so for all the selected points z_W value is zero. These points can be represented in homogeneous coordinates by Eq. (11). The 2D points in image plane without distortion, can be represented in homogeneous coordinates by Eq. (12).

$$\tilde{\mathbf{P}}_{\mathbf{w}} = \begin{bmatrix} x_w \\ y_w \\ 0 \\ 1 \end{bmatrix} \tag{11}$$

$$\tilde{\mathbf{P}}_{\mathbf{u}} = \begin{bmatrix} u \\ v \\ 1 \end{bmatrix} \tag{12}$$

To define the set of points, $\tilde{\mathbf{P}}_{\mathbf{u}}$ and $\tilde{\mathbf{P}}_{\mathbf{w}}$, all corners of the chessboard are used. So, we can relate a world point $\tilde{\mathbf{P}}_{\mathbf{w}}$ and its image correspondent $\tilde{\mathbf{P}}_{\mathbf{u}}$ up to a unknown scale λ by means of homography H as given by:

$$\lambda \tilde{\mathbf{P}}_{\mathbf{u}} = H \tilde{\mathbf{P}}_{\mathbf{w}} \tag{13}$$

To calculate the rotation matrix and translation vector is necessary to perform homography H decomposition by:

$$H = K \begin{bmatrix} \mathbf{r_1} \ \mathbf{r_2} \ \mathbf{t} \end{bmatrix} = \begin{bmatrix} \mathbf{h_1} \ \mathbf{h_2} \ \mathbf{h_3} \end{bmatrix} \tag{14}$$

With the intrinsic parameters known, the transformation from world coordinates to the camera coordinate frame can be obtained by:

$$\begin{cases} \mathbf{r_1} = \lambda_1 K^{-1} \mathbf{h_1} \\ \mathbf{r_2} = \lambda_2 K^{-1} \mathbf{h_2} \\ \mathbf{r_3} = \mathbf{r_1} \times \mathbf{r_2} \\ \mathbf{t} = \lambda_3 K^{-1} \mathbf{h_3} \end{cases} \tag{15}$$

$$\begin{cases} \lambda_1 = \frac{1}{||A^{-1}h_1||} \\ \lambda_2 = \frac{1}{||A^{-1}h_2||} \\ \lambda_3 = \frac{\lambda_1 + \lambda_2}{2} \end{cases} \tag{16}$$

Thus, the rotation matrix relating the world coordinate system to the camera coordinate system is described by:

$$R_{\text{temp}} = \begin{bmatrix} \mathbf{r_1} \ \mathbf{r_2} \ \mathbf{r_3} \end{bmatrix} \tag{17}$$

Since the matrix R_{temp} does not satisfy the orthonormality constraint of a standard rotation matrix. It is necessary to normalize and orthonormalize the matrix, using the SVD (Singular Value Decomposition) by:

$$R = U W' V^T \tag{18}$$

where the matrix W' is:

$$W' = \begin{bmatrix} 1 & 0 & 0 \\ 0 & 1 & 0 \\ 0 & 0 & ||UV'|| \end{bmatrix} \tag{19}$$

With the calculation of the matrix R and the translation vector $\mathbf{t}$ is possible define the position of the optical center of the camera relative the world's reference, thus completing the calibration process of extrinsic parameters.

3.2   Projector Calibration

For the projector calibration we implemented two different methods that are describe in detail in the following sections. The first method denoted as **SLSC-CR** method is based on the cross-ratio invariance principle. While the second denoted as **SLSC-LP** is based on the robust fitting of the laser line projection.

The methods allows us to obtain control points belonging to the light stripe. Afterwards, by non-linear least squares fitting is possible to define the equation of the plane in the camera coordinate frame using control points of two different images taken in different viewpoints. Thus, by Eq. (20) is possible to determine each axis component (a, b, c, d):

$$d_i = \frac{|ax_c + by_c + cz_c + d|}{(a^2 + b^2 + c^2)^{\frac{1}{2}}} \tag{20}$$

where x_c, y_c, z_c are the control points coordinates is the camera reference frame.

3.3   SLSC-CR Method

The objective for the projector calibration is to discover the equation of the plane that describes the projector light stripe in the camera reference frame.

Our first implementation is denoted as SLSC-CR (Structured Light System Calibration - Cross-Ratio). The cross-ratio allows to calculate the relationship between a set of a collinear points belonging to the same line. This relationship is invariant under projective transformation, and can helps us relate known laser points in the image reference frame with the laser points correspondences in the world reference frame.

The relationship used to establish the cross-ratio is displayed in Fig. 2. It contains the 3D camera coordinate frame with four collinear points (a, q, c, d) and 3D world coordinate frame defined on the calibration target with points (A, Q, C, D). The plane π_C defines the camera plane, plane π_W is the calibration target plane and π_l is the projector plane.

We start by calculating the cross-ratio using a set of points in image coordinates for each horizontal line of the planar chessboard. The following procedure was defined:

- a_i and d_i - corners of the right and left side of the chessboard.

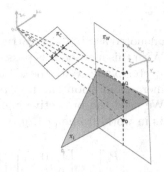

Fig. 2. Control points used to calculate the cross-ratio.

Fig. 3. Point selection based on light stripe chessboard position.

b_i or c_i - middle corner of the chessboard (the definition of this point depends of the q_i point position)

- q_i - intersection point between the projector plane and target horizontal line.

For computing the cross-ratio is necessary to preserve the correct order of selected points. Therefore, we considered two different situations for the projector line points, i.e., when the projector focus on the right side or left side of the calibration plane. In Fig. 3 is possible to see control points selection in both cases.

Afterwards, the value of the cross-ratios using 4 collinear points in image plane, can be defined as CR_i. As the value of cross-ratio is invariant, the value of CR_i in world plane is the same. So, we can calculate the Eq. (21) in order to control point Q, as given by (when the projector focus on the left side):

$$CR_i = \frac{(A_i - C_i)(Q_i - D_i)}{(A_i - D_i)(Q_i - C_i)} \iff Q_i = \frac{-A_iD_i + C_iD_i + A_iC_iCR_i - C_iD_iCR_i}{A_iCR_i - D_iCR_i - A_i + C_i}$$

(21)

When the projector focus in the right side, a similar procedure can be used.

For this procedure was considered, for each image, at least six control points. The control points in world coordinates can be computed from their corresponding camera coordinates.

3.4   SLSC-LP Method

Our second implementation denoted as SLSC-LP (Structured Light System Calibration - Line Projection). With this method it is possible to increase the control points that defining the projector plane. With the 2D image points belonging to the light stripe and the camera calibration parameters is possible obtain these points in 3D coordinates. We used the projective equation and assuming that $z_w=0$ to calculate the points in world frame (x_w, y_w):

$$\begin{bmatrix} P_u \\ P_v \\ 1 \end{bmatrix} = K\begin{bmatrix} R & | & t \end{bmatrix}\begin{bmatrix} x_w \\ y_w \\ z_w \\ 1 \end{bmatrix} \iff \begin{bmatrix} P_u \\ P_v \\ 1 \end{bmatrix} = \begin{bmatrix} f_x & 0 & c_x \\ 0 & f_y & c_y \\ 0 & 0 & 1 \end{bmatrix}\begin{bmatrix} R_{11} & R_{12} & R_{13} & t_x \\ R_{21} & R_{22} & R_{23} & t_y \\ R_{31} & R_{32} & R_{33} & t_z \end{bmatrix}\begin{bmatrix} x_w \\ y_w \\ z_w \\ 1 \end{bmatrix}$$

$$(22)$$

$$\begin{cases} x_w\underbrace{(P_{x'}R_{31} - R_{11})}_{a1} + y_w\underbrace{(P_{x'}R_{32} - R_{12})}_{b1} = \underbrace{(P_{x'}t_z + t_x)}_{c1} \\ x_w\underbrace{(P_{y'}R_{31} - R_{21})}_{a2} + y_w\underbrace{(P_{y'}R_{32} - R_{22})}_{b2} = \underbrace{(P_{y'}t_z + t_y)}_{c2} \end{cases}$$

$$(23)$$

$$\begin{cases} (b_2a_1 - b_1a_2)x_w = (b_2c_1 - b_1c_2) \iff x_w = \dfrac{(b_2c_1 - b_1c_2)}{(b_2a_1 - b_1a_2)} \\ (a_2b_1 - a_1b_2)y_w = (a_2c_1 - a_1c_2) \iff y_w = \dfrac{(a_2c_1 - a_1c_2)}{(a_2b_1 - a_1b_2)} \end{cases}$$

$$(24)$$

$$P_{x'} = \frac{P_u - c_x}{f_x} \qquad P_{y'} = \frac{P_v - c_y}{f_y}$$

$$(25)$$

4   Experimental Results

In this section results for both methods implemented with experiments in dry and underwater environments are presented.

4.1   Experimental Setup

Our experimental setup consists of a red 635 nm wavelength line laser beam, and a camera with SXGA resolution both contained in a water proof casing with a 10 cm baseline, see Fig. 4. The procedures were implemented in MATLAB as a proof concept. As for the processing time it is mainly dependent on the number of images that are used for calibrating the SLS system.

In order to validate the proposed solutions, we compare the methods solution with the results obtained using known 6 points 3D information (world coordinates) obtained using the camera sensor model with 2D image information by applying the cross-ratio invariance. Then, both method results are compared against these obtained points. This can be considered a weak ground-truth system. In future work, we plan to use a LIDAR system that can map the real position of the planar chessboard and compare the results of both implementations with the 3D LIDAR information.

Fig. 4. Structured light system underwater experimental setup

Table 1. RMS Error Comparison between **SLSC-CR** and **SLSC-LP** in dry environments

Methods	x (mm)	y (mm)	z (mm)	xyz (mm)
SLSC-CR	0.3207	0.3346	1.2340	1.8893
SLSC-LP	0.2134	0.3473	0.6491	1.0579

Table 2. RMS Error Comparison between **SLSC-CR** and **SLSC-LP** in underwater environments

Methods	x (mm)	y (mm)	z (mm)	xyz (mm)
SLSC-CR	0.1068	0.4215	1.8795	2.4078
SLSC-LP	0.1192	0.3642	1.7798	2.2632

4.2   Results

The results presented in Table 1, clearly show that the line projection method performs more accurately than the demonstrated by the cross-ratio method, with over 40 % improvement. For obtaining this results we used 96 points (6 control points over 16 images). The same experiment was performed in underwater environment, see Table 2. The line projection also outperforms the cross-ratio projection method. It is important to mention that both methods accumulate 2x more error in the underwater environment.

5   Conclusions and Future Work

In this work we present two methods for performing the calibration of a structured light system for perception in underwater tanks. The first implementation was based on the cross-ratio invariance principle, while the second implementation was based on finding the line projection in the camera reference frame. The results comparison of both methods in dry and underwater experiments shows that the line projection method has lower root mean square error both in dry and underwater calibration scenario. The system will be in future work used for underwater inspection operations of ship hulls and harbor walls, and a new version for mapping in industrial indoor underwater tanks is also being currently develop.

References

1. Schechner, Y.Y., Karpel, N.: Clear underwater vision. In: Proceedings of the 2004 IEEE Computer Society Conference on Computer Vision and Pattern Recognition, 2004, CVPR 2004, 27 June–2 July 2004, vol. 1, pp. I-536–I-543 (2004)
2. Bruno, F., Bianco, G., Muzzupappa, M., Barone, S., Razionale, A.V.: Experimentation of structured light and stereo vision for underwater 3D reconstruction. ISPRS J. Photogrammetry Remote Sens. **66**(4), 508–518 (2011). ISSN: 0924–2716
3. Srinivasa, Narasimhan, S.G., Nayar, S.K.: Structured light methods for underwater imaging: light stripe scanning and photometric stereo. In: Proceedings of 2005 MTS/IEEE OCEANS, pp. 2610–2617, September 2005
4. Inglis, G., Smart, C., Roman, C., Carey, S.: Detection of diffuse sea floor venting using structured light imaging. Poster OS11B-1473 presented at 2011 Fall Meeting, AGU, San Francisco, Calif., 5–9 December 2011
5. Chen, C., Kak, A.: Modeling and calibration of a structured light scanner for 3-d robot vision. In: IEEE International Conference on Robotics and Automation, vol. 4, pp. 807–815 (1987)
6. Reid, I.D.: Projective calibration of a laser-stripe range finder. Image Vis. Comput. **14**(9), 659–666 (1996)
7. Hartley, R., Zisserman, A.: Multiple View Geometry in Computer Vision. Cambridge University Press, New York (2003)
8. Huynh, D.Q., Owens, R.A., Hartmann, P.E.: Calibrating a structured light stripe system: a novel approach. Int. J. Comput. Vision **33**, 73–86 (1999)
9. Yamauchi, K., Saito, H., Sato, Y.: Calibration of a structured light system by observing planar object from unknown viewpoints. In: 19th International Conference on Pattern Recognition, ICPR 2008, pp. 1–4, 8–11 December 2008
10. Zhou, F., Zhang, G.: Complete calibration of a structured light stripe vision sensor through planar target of unknown orientations. Image Vis. Comput. **23**(1), 59–67 (2005). ISSN: 0262–8856
11. Zhang, Z.: Flexible camera calibration by viewing a plane from unknown orientations. In: International Conference on Computer Vision, ICCV 2009, pp. 666–673 (2009)
12. Harris, C., Stephens, M.: A combined corner and edge detector. In: Proceedings of the 4th Alvey Vision Conference, pp. 147–151 (1988)

Dense 3D SLAM in Dynamic Scenes Using Kinect

Mohamed Chafik Bakkay$^{(\boxtimes)}$, Majdi Arafa, and Ezzeddine Zagrouba

Research Team on Intelligent Systems in Imaging and Artificial Vision
(SIIVA)-RIADI Laboratory, Institut Supérieur D'Informatique,
Université de Tunis El Manar, Rue Abou Rayhane Barouni, 2080 Ariana, Tunisia
mohamedchafik.bakkay@isi.rnu.tn, arafamajdi@gmail.com,
ezzeddine.zagrouba@fsm.rnu.tn

Abstract. In this paper, we present a dense 3D SLAM method for dynamic scenes consisting on building, in real-time, a 3D map of the scene using Kinect. The method starts by segmenting and removing moving objects from the scene in order to avoid mismatches in the alignment step, then, calculates the scene current camera pose for each new acquisition. This method has the advantage of producing a dense map through the use of all pixels of the RGBD camera in order to achieve higher pose accuracy. The method also includes a loop closure detection thread to detect and merge duplicate regions. Quantitative evaluations using a various sets of scenes and benchmark datasets show that the proposed method produces a real-time 3D reconstruction with higher accuracy and lower trajectory error compared to the state-of-the-art methods.

Keywords: 3D SLAM · Dynamic scene · Kinect · Scene flow · ICP

1 Introduction

3D perception is one of the most important abilities for an autonomous moving robot. In fact, it provides a lot of information supporting machine navigation. Such systems, commonly called SLAM (Simultaneous Location And Mapping), contain three main steps: data acquisition, data alignment and 3D maps fusion. A 3D acquisition is particularly more relevant than a 2D acquisition, since providing the information of the scene depth, facilitates the robot localisation and the recognition tasks, especially when operating in unstructured environments and under real-world conditions. For this kind of acquisition, RGBD cameras such as Microsoft Kinect proved to be efficient yet low-cost devices that provide high quality depth and color maps in real-time. However, Kinect has significant drawbacks influencing the 3D acquisition task. First, it fails to capture transparent, specular and reflective objects [2]. Second, due to the distance between the projector and the IR camera, some parts of background objects are shaded by foreground ones in depth map and depths could not be estimated in these regions [1]. Finally, there are unstable depth values in region contours [2]. Besides the device's limitations, the presence of dynamic objects in a scene is one of the most challenging problems that the navigation system should achieve. In fact, the presence of moving objects in the scene may causes mismatches in the alignment step. Therefore, dynamic components in the scene should be inspected and removed.

© Springer International Publishing Switzerland 2015
R. Paredes et al. (Eds.): IbPRIA 2015, LNCS 9117, pp. 121–129, 2015.
DOI: 10.1007/978-3-319-19390-8_14

In this paper, we propose a dense 3D SLAM method that builds in real-time an accurate 3D map of the scene by accumulating Kinect RGBD maps into a single, continuously refined model. (1) The method proceeds as follows: it inspects and removes moving objects, using a fast and accurate scene flow estimation. This step avoids mismatches in the alignment step in order to build accurate model. (2) It computes simultaneously an accurate trajectory of the camera. (3) It corrects accumulated errors by involving a global map optimization step while using a loop closures detection thread to recognize and merge duplicate regions.

The remaining part of this paper is structured as follows: Sect. 2 is devoted to a brief synthesis of the most relevant works on SLAM methods. In Sect. 3, we detail the proposed method for 3D SLAM in dynamic environments. Then, experimental results and an objective comparative study are shown in Sect. 4 in order to demonstrate the effectiveness of the proposed work. Section 5 concludes the paper and presents some directions for future works.

2 Related Works

Considerable number of approaches has been proposed to improve different aspects of the SLAM technique (accuracy and computational time) depending on its diverse application fields [6, 7]. These approaches differ by the nature of the scene (static or dynamic). Most SLAM approaches, whether dense [11] or feature-based [4], assume a static scene or treat dynamic content as outlier. However, in the most cases, the environment of the robot contains moving objects which cannot be robustly handled by these static methods. The dynamic environment, which is more challenging and difficult to control, is less studied in the literature. Few methods for SLAM in dynamic environments [6, 12] are proposed. Most of them use 2D acquisition which is fast but not suitable for complicated scene. Thus, methods for SLAM in dynamic environments, based on 3D acquisition, are proposed to achieve more accuracy. They generally used RGBD sensors to achieve real-time performance. However, they do not treat the noise of these devices. Moreover, the object detection is generally done using optical flow which is not very accurate compared to scene flow [2, 5]. Kinectfusion method [12] is able to reconstruct moving object in a dynamic scene. However, a static pre scan of the background is first acquired. In [6], Keller et al. initially indicate dynamic objects as outliers in point matching during the alignement step made by ICP algorithm. However, this operation badly affects the algorithm's convergence because moving objects should be removed from the scene before starting the alignment step. Typically, the steps of SLAM method are: data acquisition, detection of dynamic objects, images alignment and fusion. For the acquisition step, most of the methods used active devices [11] which are faster than the passive ones [3]. These devices such as Kinect capture RGB images along with per-pixel depth information. However, they do not provide a complete model and require a fusion step to reconstruct the full scene. The object detection is typically based on visual information which is not sufficient to discriminate objects and is very sensitive to lighting changes. Therefore, it is interesting to involve additional data sources such as geometric information [11]. Jens et al. [8] proposed a relevant approach that uses optical flow and depth Information to detect moving objects. Some methods use a machine learning model to achieve high quality segmentation [10]. However, many optimizations should be made to reduce the complexity of treatments and to minimize the very high computational time cost. The alignment step is required to estimate the robot ego-motion between the consecutive positions. Different variants of ICP [6] and Extended Kalman Filter are used [7]. Finally, a fusion step is performed to obtain a global model. Some methods use volumetric techniques [14] which achieve high quality models. However, they need high computational cost due to the transition between data representations. On the other hand, point based representation [6], commonly used for larger sized reconstructions, reduces computational complexity and have lower memory overhead than volumetric techniques. However, it may fail to represent complex environments. Thus, a trade-off between speed and quality using both point-based and volumetric representation could be performed such as surfel representation [9].

3   Proposed Method

First, we used a Kinect camera since it offers a compromise between performance and price. As mentioned in the first section, such device cannot work properly with all kinds of objects. Thus, the depth map is first improved by applying a spatio-temporal filter [2]. Second, we opted to remove moving objects from depth maps in order to avoid mismatches in the alignment step. We performed a fast and accurate region growing segmentation method based on scene flow estimation [2]. Then, a dense alignment step, using all pixels of the RGBD images, is done to achieve higher pose accuracy while a parallel loop-closure detection thread is called. Finally, a fusion step is performed to obtain a global model using an efficient surfel map representation.

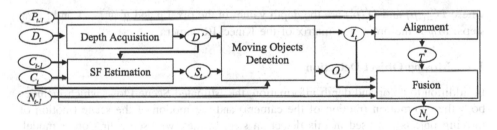

Fig. 1. Outline of the proposed method

Figure 1 shows the schematic overview of the proposed scheme. A depth map filtering is performed to improve the quality of Kinect's input depth D_t. Then, an accurate output scene flow (SF) S_t is computed using the Filtered depth D'_t and the two consecutive Kinect's input color frames C_{t-1} and C_t. A segmentation step is used to detect moving objects O_t based on D'_t and S_t. It generates a segmented RGBD image I_t that contains only the background of the current acquisition. An alignment step estimates transformation T^* between the consecutive positions using I_t and the 3D previous images P_{t-1}. Finally, the fusion step merges the aligned clouds N_{t-1} into a global consistent 3D model N_t. All these steps of the proposed approach represented in Fig. 1 is detailed in following subsections.

3.1 Depth Acquisition

Before using the Kinect's depth map, a stereo-calibration step between IR and RGB cameras is required. It consists in computing extrinsic and intrinsic parameters of the two cameras [2] in order to put them in the same plan. This implies that the color and depth images at a certain location will belong to the same object point in the scene. Moreover, a depth filtering step is performed to fill the holes in the registered depth map, while using adaptive median filter as described in Eq. (1).

$$D'(p) = median\{D(q)/q \in \Omega_p\}.(1 - \psi(p)) + median\{D(q)/q \in \Omega_p^b\}.\psi(p), \quad (1)$$

where $D'(.)$ is the Kinect input depth. $\psi(p)$ is a Heaviside step function that will decide if the hole is caused by transparent object ($\psi(p) = 0$) or shaded object ($\psi(p) = 1$). Ω_p is the neighborhood of pixel p and Ω_p^b is its background neighborhood.

3.2 Scene Flow Estimation

The perception of the motion is very useful in the segmentation step. Thus, we proposed a dense real-time Scene Flow estimation described in Eq. (2). It is fast and avoids over-smoothing objects boundaries, occlusion problem and Kinect noise without hardware modification. Indeed, it improves simultaneously the quality of the device depth map and the estimated optical flow by applying an adaptive spatial filter combined with 3D Kalman filter to add temporal smoothness at the object edges [2].

$$\left(\dot{X} \quad \dot{Y} \quad \dot{Z}\right)^T = \begin{bmatrix} M_{IR} \\ 0_3^T & 1 \end{bmatrix}^{-1} .(p' - p, D_t'(p') - D_{t-1}'(p), 1)^T, \quad (2)$$

where $D_{t-1}'(p)$ and $D_t'(p')$ are the depth values of the pixel p and p' at $t-1$ and t time steps. M_{IR} is the projection matrix of the Kinect IR camera.

3.3 Moving Object Detection

In addition to color and depth information, the estimated Scene Flow, which includes both the ego-motion (motion of the camera) and the motion of the scene (motion of moving objects), is used in this detection step. In fact, we used a first order model, given by Eq. (3), to describe the propagation of each 3D point P in the scene.

$$P_{t+1} = \begin{pmatrix} R_f & \Delta t.R_f \\ 0 & R_f \end{pmatrix} P_t + \begin{pmatrix} T_f \\ 0 \end{pmatrix}, \quad (3)$$

where P_t is the 3D coordinate vector of the point P at time step t. R_f and T_f are the rotation and the translation of the camera between two consecutive frames C_{t-1} and C_t. In this model, we assume a constant motion during the time interval Δ_t between time steps t and $t+1$. Then, pixels that have absolute velocity upper than a threshold [8] are chosen to seed segmentation as they probably belong to moving objects. Starting from these areas, we perform a region growing procedure based on visual information, depth and absolute velocity to identify dynamic regions.

3.4 Alignment Step

We propose to match the current frame only with a subset of key-frames based on sparse visual features. We involve RANSAC algorithm to compute the optimal transformation between the feature points in pixel space. Then, a dense alignment step is performed to refine the rigid transformation. For that, we use an iterative point-to-point registration algorithm (ICP) which is initialized by the rigid transformation. Then, for each point in the source cloud p_s, it determines the nearest one in the target cloud p_t. For more accuracy, we employ the squared re-projection distance error along each target point's normal n_j^i as described in Eq. (4).

$$T^* = \arg\min_T \left[\left(\frac{1}{|A_f|} \sum_{i \in A_f} |Proj(T(f_s^i)) - Proj(f_t^i)|^2 \right) + \left(\frac{1}{|A_d|} \sum_{j \in A_d} w_j |(T(p_s^j) - p_t^j).n_t^j|^2 \right) \right], \quad (4)$$

where the first part measures average squared distances for the visually associated feature points by minimizing the re-projection error. The matrix A_f contains the associations between feature points in the two frames. Each term in the summation measures the squared distance between a feature point in the target frame f_t^i and the transformed pose of the associated feature point f_s^i in the source frame. The second part is the ICP optimization between source cloud p_s and the target cloud p_t. The set A_d contains the associations between the points in the dense point cloud. The loop exits when the transformation no longer changes above a small threshold θ or when the maximum number of iterations is reached. Otherwise, the dense data associations are recomputed using the most recent transformation.

3.5 Fusion Step

The fusion step is required to join all available scans into a single non-redundant model. In our method we proposed to use a mesh surfel representation to faithfully incorporate all input data into an efficient and concise model. A surfel consists of a location, a surface orientation, a patch size and a color [9]. The use of surfels has the advantage of working well for the most type of object surfaces. Also, they are well suited to model dynamic geometry. Finally, the reconstructed model can be easily updated by live measurements while keeping the global model very consistent.

4 Experimental Study

We proposed to evaluate the segmentation method using two benchmark datasets as depicted in Fig. 2. In the first row, we used "wave" dataset.[1] In the second row, we used "tomato" dataset.[2] We compared segmentation results based on color (d), depth (e) and proposed method (f) (color + depth + scene flow). As we can see in Fig. 2, the best segmentation is given by our method because the moving object is detected properly.

---

[1] http://personal.ee.surrey.ac.uk/Personal/S.Hadfield/sceneparticles.html.

[2] http://www.umiacs.umd.edu/research/POETICON/telluride_dataset.

Moreover, we propose to evaluate the geometric correctness of our 3D models before and after removing dynamic objects from the scene. We measure the dimensions of objects from the obtained model and compare them with the real dimensions measured from the physical world. Figure 3 shows that the quality of the obtained model in (a) is poor and involves distorted objects in dynamic areas. This is mainly due to the failure of the alignment step because it considers the outliers. This problem is highlighted by quantitative evaluation (c) which shows that measurements in the 3D model after the removing moving object (b) are more accurate than (a).

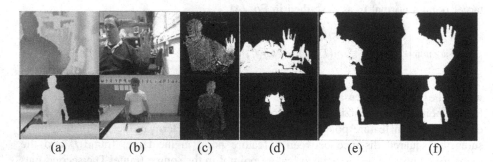

(a)   (b)   (c)   (d)   (e)   (f)

Fig. 2. Moving object segmentation results. (a) depth (b) color (c) scene flow (d) segmentation based on depth (e) segmentation based on color (f) proposed segmentation.

Table 1. RMSE of absolute trajectory error (m) for our SLAM system in comparison to three state-of-art systems.

	"fr1/360" dataset	*"fr1/room" dataset*	*"fr1/xyz" dataset*
Visual SLAM [7]	0.083	**0.053**	0.011
MRSMap [13]	0.069	0.069	0.013
Kinectfusion [12]	0.913	0.313	0.026
Proposed method	**0.061**	0.062	**0.009**

To evaluate the accuracy of the proposed SLAM system, we compared the RMSE of the absolute camera trajectory error with three state-of-art systems, namely the Dense visual SLAM system [7], the multi-resolution surfel maps (MRSMap) [13] and the PCL implementation of KinectFusion [12]. We used three datasets from the freiburg1s. As shown in Table 1, our system gives better results on "fr1/360" and "fr1/xyz" datasets.[3] In contrast, on "fr1/room" dataset which contains a long and complex trajectory, our method's accuracy is less than [7] since the scene doesn't contain moving objects. As shown in Fig. 4b, we notice that the error between ground truth trajectory and the proposed one is low.

---

[3] http://vision.in.tum.de/data/datasets/rgbd-dataset.

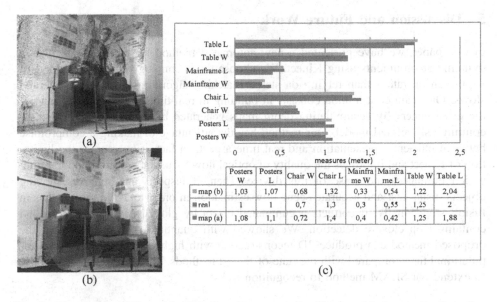

Fig. 3. Reconstructed 3D model. (a) before object removing (b) after object removing from the scene (c) measures of virtual dimensions comparing those in the physical world.

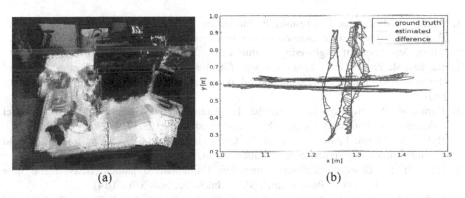

Fig. 4. Proposed method results using "fr1/xyz" dataset. (a) reconstructed 3D map (b) camera trajectory compared to the ground truth one.

As the computational time cost widely varies from a method to another when including all treatments, then, for each method, we propose to compare only the critical steps time cost (alignment + segmentation + fusion). We see in Table 2 that our contribution preserve the real-time aspect while improving the quality of results.

Table 2. Computational time cost of some recent SLAM methods.

Methods	Kerl et al. [7]	Newcombe et al. [12]	Keller et al. [6]	Proposed method
Cost per frame(ms)	32	**25**	38.04	34

5　Discussion and Future Work

In this paper, we have presented a new automated method for dense 3D SLAM in dynamic environments using Kinect. We choose this technology since it is a modern depth sensor, rather than relying on stereo matching algorithms which are generally slows. Our main contribution consists in building in real-time an accurate 3D map of the environment by accumulating depth maps generated by the Kinect into a single continuously refined model. Our method has the advantage of making a compromise between efficient representation and real-time aspect. In fact, it overcomes the limitation of Kinect and improves the quality of optical flow by using a spatio-temporal filter which eliminates the noise of this device. Then, it inspects and removes moving objects, using fast and accurate scene flow estimation in order to avoid mismatches in fusion step. Finally, it corrects accumulated errors by global map optimization and contains loop closure detection. We showed with quantitative evaluations that the proposed method can produce 3D reconstruction with higher accuracy and low computational time compared with the state-of-the-art methods. In future work, we propose to extend our SLAM method to recognition tasks.

References

1. Andersen, M., Jensen, T., Lisouski, P., Mortensen, A., Hansen, M., Gregersen, T., Ahrendt, P.: Kinect depth sensor evaluation for computer vision applications. Technical report ECE-TR-6, Department of Engineering, Aarhus University, Denmark (2012)
2. Bakkay, M., Zagrouba, E.: Spatio-temporal filter for dense real-time scene flow estimation of dynamic environment using a mobile rgb-d camera. Pattern Recogn. Lett. J. (Submitted) (2014)
3. Barhoumi, W., Bakkay, M., Zargouba, E.: Automated photo-consistency test for voxel colouring based on fuzzy adaptive hysteresis thresholding. IET 7, 713–724 (2013)
4. Bylow, E., Sturm, J., Kerl, C., Kahl, F., Cremers, D.: Real-time camera tracking and 3d reconstruction using signed distance functions. In: RSS Conference (2013)
5. Hadfield, S., Bowden, R.: Scene particles: Unregularized particle based scene flow estimation. IEEE Trans. Pattern Anal. Mach. Intell. 36, 564–576 (2014)
6. Keller, M., Lefloch, D., Lambers, M., Izadi, S., Weyrich, T., and Kolb, A.: Real-time 3d reconstruction in dynamic scenes using point-based fusion. 3DV (2013)
7. Kerl, C., Sturm, J., Cremers, D.: Dense visual slam for rgb-d cameras. In: Proceeding of the International Conference on Intelligent Robot Systems (IROS) (2013)
8. Klappstein, J., Vaudrey, T., Rabe, C., Wedel, A., Klette, R.: Moving object segmentation using optical flow and depth information. In: Proceedings of the 3rd Pacific Rim Symposium on Advances in Image and Video Technology (PSIVT) (2009)
9. Krainin, M., Henry, P., Ren, X., Fox, D.: Manipulator and object tracking for in-hand 3d object modeling. Int. J. Rob. Res. 30(11), 1311–1327 (2011)
10. Li, T., Putchakayala, P., Wilson, M.: Scholarly Project, CS 4758 - Robot Learning, Departement Of Computer Science. Cornell University (2011)
11. Majdi, A., Bakkay, M., Zagrouba, E.: 3D modeling of indoor environments using kinect sensor. In: IEEE Conference on International Image Information Processing (2013)

12. Newcombe, R.A., Izadi, S., Hilliges, O., Molyneaux, D., Kim, D., Davison, A.J., Kohli, P., Shotton, J., Hodges, S., Fitzgibbon, A.: Kinectfusion: Real-time dense surface mapping and tracking. In: Proceedings of the 10th IEEE International Symposium on Mixed and Augmented Reality (ISMAR) (2011)
13. Stückler, J., Behnke, S.: Integrating depth and color cues for dense multi-resolution scene mapping using rgb-d cameras. In: Proceedings of the IEEE International Conference on Multisensor Fusion and Information Integration (MFI) (2012)
14. Zeng, M., Zhao, F., Zheng, J., Liu, X.: Octree-based fusion for realtime 3d reconstruction. Transaction of Graphical Models **75**, 126–136 (2013)

Scene Recognition Invariant to Symmetrical Reflections and Illumination Conditions in Robotics

D. Santos-Saavedra$^{(\boxtimes)}$, X.M. Pardo, R. Iglesias, A. Canedo-Rodríguez, and V. Álvarez-Santos

CITIUS, University of Santiago de Compostela, A Coruña, Spain
{david.santos,xose.pardo}@usc.es

Abstract. Scene understanding is still an important challenge in robotics. In this paper we analyse the impact of several global and local image representations to solve the task of scene recognition. The performance of the different alternatives were compared using a two benchmarks of images: (a) the public database KTH_IDOL and, (b) a base of images taken in the Centro Singular de Investigacion en Tecnoloxias da Informacion (CITIUS), at the University of Santiago de Compostela. The results are promising not only regarding the accuracy achieved, but mostly because we have found a combination of an holistic representation and local information that allows a correct classification of images robust to specular reflections, illumination conditions, changes of viewpoint, etc.

Keywords: Scene recognition · Holistic representations · Local representations · Invariance to symmetries · CENTRIST · GIST · SURF · Spatial pyramid · Local difference binary patterns

1 Introduction

One of the limitations of today's robots is *scene understanding*. Knowing "where am I" has always being an important research topic in robotics and computer vision [1]. There are many approaches that use different sensor modalities (Sonar, Laser, Compass, Wi-Fi, etc.) [2–4] to determine the topological localization of the robot, i.e., its position in a map. Nevertheless, robots are still unable to understand their environments, they are not aware if they are moving in a room that is similar to another one where they have been moving previously. In this paper we describe the work that we have done to get a robot being able to recognize the scene. In this case we assume that the robot will take one observation at some location and it will use a classifier to identify this observation. The different classes represent general categories of places and not particular instances. That means that the robot assigns the same label to different places that pertain to the same category. We have tested the performance of different SVM classifiers which use different image descriptors to solve the task of scene recognition, these image descriptors work at different abstraction levels.

© Springer International Publishing Switzerland 2015
R. Paredes et al. (Eds.): IbPRIA 2015, LNCS 9117, pp. 130–137, 2015.
DOI: 10.1007/978-3-319-19390-8_15

2   Feature Extraction

In this work we have carried out a detailed analysis of the performance of scene recognition in different scenarios using local and global features, as well as a combination of both of them.

2.1   Global Representations

One of the first descriptors we have considered is the CENsus Transform hIS-Togram (CENTRIST) [5]. This representation captures properties, such as, rough geometry and generalizability by modeling the distribution of local structures. CENTRIST is easy to implement, has nearly no parameters to tune, and is invariant to uniform illumination variations. Besides, it is extremely fast (from the computational point of view), what is a very important characteristic in robotics.

The Census Transform (CT) is a non-parametric local transform based on the comparison amongst the intensity value of each pixel of the image with its eight neighboring pixels, as illustrated in Fig. 1. As we can see in this figure, if the center pixel is bigger than (or equal to) one of its neighbors, a bit 1 is set in the corresponding location. Otherwise a bit 0 is set. The eight bits generated after all the comparisons have to be put together following always the same order, and then they are converted to a base-10 number in the interval $[0, 255]$. This process maps a 3×3 image patch to one of 256 cases, each corresponding to a special type of local structure, and it is repeated for every pixel of the original image. The Census Transform (CT) is also referred to as the *Local Difference Sign Binary Pattern* (LSBP).

Obviously the information about the magnitude of the intensities is lost in the *LSBP*. This is the reason why X. Meng et al. [6] suggested the use of the so-called *Local Difference Magnitude Binary Pattern* (LMBP) as a further piece of information to complete the representation of the image. In this case, the LMBP is computed as the intensity difference between the center pixel and its neighboring pixels. If the difference in intensity amongst the center pixel and one of its neighbors is higher than a threshold T, a bit 1 is set, otherwise a bit 0 is set. Like in the case of the Census Transform, the eight bits generated after all the comparisons have to be put together following always the same order, and then they are converted to a base-10 number.

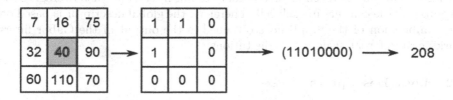

Fig. 1. Illustration of the Census Transform Process on a 3×3 image patch

Thus, for every image we can compute the holistic representation given by the combination of the *LMBP* and the *LSBP*. Once this process is over, we can compute the histogram of LSBP and LMBP as a feature representation. Both the LSBP and the LMBP histograms are 256 dimensions (the bins of the histograms are each one of the values that the LMBP and LSBP can take), therefore, the new feature representation is 512 dimensional (256×2). It is a common practice to suppress the first and the last bins of these histograms, due to noise cancellation and the removal of not significant information, that is the reason why the dimension that appears in Fig. 2 is 508. We will call *LDBP* (local difference binary pattern) to the combination of the LSBP and LMBP histograms.

Lazebnik et al. [7] suggested the use of *spatial pyramids* when holistic approaches are used for image categorization. This technique works by partitioning the image into increasingly fine sub-regions and computing histograms of features inside each region. Due to the different size of the blocks obtained in the different partitions, the number of features in each one of them would be different. This makes necessary the normalization of all histograms by the total weight of the number of features. An efficient way of doing it is by enforcing the total number of features in all images to be the same, i.e., resizing the image between different levels so that all blocks contain the same number of pixels. Finally, the feature representations obtained for all blocks are concatenated to form an overall feature vector for each image (Fig. 2). This means that at each level the size of the image descriptor is ($508 \times number\_of\_blocks$) (where 508 is the number of dimensions of the vector with the concatenated LSBP and LMPB histograms). If we consider that this size would now be multiplied by the number of levels of the spatial pyramid, it is easy to understand that we would end with a very high dimensional descriptor. Because of this, and considering the fact that the histogram representation of LSBP and LMBP are correlated with each other [6], it is possible to use principal component analysis (PCA) to reduce their size. In our case, we have carried out this principal component analysis (using a set of images taken in the environment where the robot moves), and as a result of it, we could project each 508 descriptor to a new space of 80 dimensions (Fig. 2).

Another global representation that we have considered is the gist of scene [8]. The *gist* of a scene represents all that information that an observer can comprehend after a single glimpse of an image, and it is most commonly associated with low-level global features such as color, spatial frequencies and spatial organization. The Gist descriptor is a global representation that divides the image into a 4×4 grid, filtering each cell using a bank of Gabor filters, and then averaging the responses of these filters in each cell. Therefore, the global descriptor is based on the combination of the amplitudes obtained in the output of the Gabor filters working at different scales and orientations.

2.2 Local Descriptors

Finally, we also have considered the use of local descriptors, i.e., the discovering of salient points in the image. In particular, we used a bag-of-visual-words

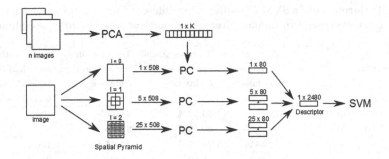

Fig. 2. Schematic representation of the combined use of the global features described in section II and the Spatial Pyramid Splitting. To classify any image the spatial pyramid partitions the image into different blocks, being necessary to get the feature description (CT, or the combination LSBP+LMBP) for every block. The vector that describes every block is projected into a new space with less dimensions (using the results of a principal component analysis). Finally, the transformed vectors are combined together and used as input to a SVM that classifies the image.

model, which works on three stages: (i) Obtaining of the local descriptors; (ii) Quantization of the descriptors into a codebook; (iii) description of the image as a collection of words. We have used SURF [9] to detect the interest points and their description. Regarding the second stage, quantization of the descriptors, we have used k-means to cluster them. In this case the cluster centers act as our dictionary of visual words. Finally, an image is represented by the histogram of the visual words, i.e. this histogram is treated as the feature vector of the image that is going to be used by the classifier.

3   Experimental Results

3.1   First Set of Experiments

We have created an image set obtained in the Centro Singular de Investigacion en Tecnologias de la Informacion (CITIUS), at the University of Santiago de Compostela, to analyse the performance of a classifier that categorizes each image using the different representations described in the previous sections. We have divided our images in 11 different classes: *Office, Entrepreneurship Laboratory, Staircase, Common staff areas (first and second floors), Assembly Hall, Common staff areas (S1 floor), Kitchen, laboratories 1,2 and 3, Common staff areas (ground floor), instrumentation laboratory, robotics laboratory.* These images were taken different days and at different hours, therefore with different illumination conditions: daylight (natural illumination), artificial illumination only, and half-light (penumbra or semidarkness), i.e. natural illumination but at the end of the day or with the blinds off.

We have analysed the performance of a Support Vector Machine (SVM), using different image descriptors (Table 1). In this table we can see the perfor-

Table 1. Performance of a SVM Classifier using different feature representations. These results are the average performance after using four test sets (4-fold cross-validation)

Feature representation	Performance all images 11 classes	Train=artificial test=artificial 5 classes	Train=artificial test=natural 5 classes	Train=artificial test=half-light train (5 classes) test (1 class)
Census Transform (LSBP)	78.75 %	84.52 %	33.63 %	100 %
LDBP(LSBP+LMBP)	**80.78**%	**83.33**%	**32.73** %	100 %
LMBP	59.54 %	78.57 %	**34.55** %	100 %
Gist	77.35 %	75.00 %	24.36 %	0 %
SURF	77.48 %	83.33 %	42.73 %	95.24 %
LMBP+SURF	79.07 %	89.29 %	**41.82**%	100.00 %
LBP(LSBP+LMBP)+SURF	**87.71**%	**89.29**%	**40.00**%	100.00 %

mance of the classifier when it was trained using only the images taken under certain illumination conditions and then tested using different conditions (columns 2,3 and 4 of Table 1). In this case, we can notice that the number of classes has been reduced because some rooms or laboratories have no windows and therefore it is not possible to get images with natural illumination. In the last column of the table we can see even a situation in which the SVM classifier was trained using only the images taken under artificial illumination, but then the performance of the classifier was analysed considering the images corresponding to only one of the classes, but under half-light conditions. This kind of analyses allow us to determine the performance and robustness of the classifier when the illumination conditions vary very significantly. According to the results, we can notice that when only a holistic representation is used the best result is achieved with the Local difference binary patterns (LDBP), only one of the results is slightly better using the LMBP. Nevertheless, this performance is surpassed clearly when the holistic representation (either LDBP or LMBP) is combined with the visual bag of words model (local representation). In this case the best combination is achieved with the LDBP and the visual bag of words (SURF).

3.2   Second Set of Experiments: Robustness to Symmetries

We have analysed the robustness of the SVM classifier on recognizing mirror images. Using the same set of images described before obtained in the Centro Singular de Investigacion en Tecnologias de la Informacion (CITIUS), we have doubled the size of the test set, by adding images that are got from the original ones by specular reflection. Obviously we have analysed the performance of the SVM classifier when the training and validation data set are still the same, but the test set has been altered by including the extra images obtained from the original ones by specular reflection. Table 2 shows the experimental results we got in this case.

Table 2. Performance of a SVM Classifier with different feature representations and using augmented test sets with symmetrical images

Feature representation	Performance Train 11 classes test (augmented with symmetrical images)
Census Transform (LSBP)	72.12 %
LDBP(LSBP+LMBP)	**73.62%**
LMBP	53.80 %
LDBP(LSBP+LMBP)+SURF	**81.89%**

Table 3. Performance of a SVM Classifier with different feature representations, using the KTH_IDOL benchmark

	LSBP			LMBP			LDBP			GIST		
	cloudy	night	sunny	cloudy	night	sunny	cloudy	night	sunny	cloudy	night	sunny
cloudy	95.16	89.99	92.62	80.50	71.57	76.09	96.66	90.09	94.51	93.64	89.67	94.23
night	89.32	95.48	84.86	70.89	72.58	68.11	89.00	96.32	81.14	90.30	95.80	82.31
sunny	93.01	81.43	93.95	79.35	68.07	78.66	93.71	81.90	94.61	88.89	85.50	95.60

	Robot Minnie			
	LSBP	**LMBP**	**LDBP**	**GIST**
Dumbo	59.32	45.09	61.39	56.66

Table 4. Performance of a SVM Classifier with different feature representations, using the KTH_IDOL benchmark

	SURF			Combined: LDBP + SURF			Combined: LMBP + SURF		
	cloudy	night	sunny	cloudy	night	sunny	cloudy	night	sunny
cloudy	92.03	81.12	84.19	97.52	92.59	95.12	95.47	87.90	90.46
night	82.17	90.86	72.55	91.11	96.85	86.08	87.21	92.44	79.15
sunny	82.11	65.78	89.22	94.63	87.27	96.81	91.92	82.47	94.17

	Robot Minnie		
	SURF	Combined: LDBP + SURF	Combined: LMBP + SURF
Dumbo	58.05	67.82	62.45

4   Third Set of Experiments: Use of Public Benchmark

We have also used a public benchmark of images to analyse the performance of a classifier using the different image descriptors: KTH_IDOL1 data base (Image Database for rObot Localization [10]). In this case we have carried out two analyses: in the first one, we analysed the performance of the classifiers using different image representations and their robustness to illumination conditions. In particular we have used an image sequence recorded using a mobile robot platform called Dumbo (a PowerBot equipped with a pan-tilt Canon VC-C4 camera at 36 cm from the floor level and tilted approximately 13°). The acquisition was conducted within a five room office environment under three different illumination and weather conditions: in cloudy weather (natural and artificial light), in sunny weather (direct natural light dominates) and at night (only artificial light). In the experiments we have carried out, we train the classifier using the images captured under a particular weather condition, but the performance was analysed separately for each of the three weather conditions (Tables 3 and 4). On a second analysis, we have observed the robustness of the classifiers to a change of the viewpoint, in this case we used the images obtained from the environment with the robot Dumbo mentioned before, but to analyse the performance of the classifiers we used a sequence of images taken from another robot (Minnie), equipped with a camera that was 98 cm above the floor (in the case of the robot Dumbo it was at 36 cm).

5   Conclusions and Future Work

This paper describes an analysis of different image descriptors both, holistic and local, to represent appearance and identify the scene. We have built different classifiers using these image descriptors and tested their performance using two data sets: (i) images collected at the CITIUS research centre, University of Santiago de Compostela, and a public database (KTH_IDOL). From the experimental results we can conclude that working with a representation that combines global and local features is the best option. Regarding the holistic information, we determined that the use of the Local Difference Binary Pattern (LDBP=LMBP+LSBP) allows the achievement of performance that is better than using the Census Transform, LMBP, or GIST. On the other hand, the use of this representation ($LDBP = LMBP + LSBP$), together with the Spatial Pyramid Splitting, allows a further improvement in the performance of the classifier. Finally, the combination of the $LDBP$ with the interest point detection and description provided by the use of SURF and the Bags of Word, allows a significant improvement of the performance of the classifier. We also plan to test the performance of these descriptors in new public databases [11,12].

Acknowledgment. This work was supported by grants: GPC2013/040 (FEDER), TIN2012-32262.

References

1. Wu, J., Christensen, H.I., Rehg, J.M.: Visual Place Categorization: Problem, Dataset, and Algorithm. In: The 2009 IEEE/RSJ International Conference on Intelligent Robots and Systems, pp. 4763–4770 (2009)
2. Canedo-Rodriguez, A., Alvarez-Santos, V., Santos-Saavedra, D., Gamallo, C., Fernandez-Delgado, M., Iglesias, R., Regueiro, C.V.: Robust multi-sensor system for mobile robot localization. In: Ferrández Vicente, J.M., Álvarez Sánchez, J.R., de la Paz López, F., Toledo Moreo, F.J. (eds.) IWINAC 2013, Part II. LNCS, vol. 7931, pp. 92–101. Springer, Heidelberg (2013)

3. Drumheller, M.: Mobile robot localization using sonar. IEEE Trans. Pattern Anal. Mach. Intell. **2**, 325–332 (1987)
4. Hahnel, D., Burgard, W., Fox, D., Fishkin, K., Philipose, M.: Mapping and localization with RFID technology. In: Proceedings of the 2004 IEEE International Conference on Robotics and Automation, ICRA 2004. vol. 1, pp. 1015–1020. IEEE, April 2004
5. Wu, J., Rehg, J.M.: CENTRIST: a visual descriptor for scene categorization. IEEE Trans. Pattern Anal. Mach. Intell. **33**(8), 1489–1501 (2011)
6. Meng, X., Wang, Z., Wu, L.: Building global image features for scene recognition. Pattern Recogn. **45**(1), 373–380 (2012)
7. Lazebnik, S., Schmid, C., Ponce, J.: Beyond Bags of Features: Spatial Pyramid Matching for Recognizing Natural Scene Categories. In: Proceedings of the 2006 IEEE Computer Society Conference on Computer Vision and Pattern Recognition (CVPR 2006), pp. 2169–2178 (2006)
8. Oliva, A.: Gist of the scene. In: Itti, L., Rees, G., Tsotsos, J.K. (eds.) Encyclopedia of Neurobiology of Attention, pp. 251–256. Elsevier, San Diego (2005)
9. Bay, H., Ess, A., Tuytelaars, T., Van Gool, L.: Speeded-up robust features (SURF). Comput. Vis. Image Underst. **110**(3), 346–359 (2008)
10. Luo, J., Pronobis, A., Caputo, B., Jensfelt, P.: The KTH-IDOL2 database. Technical report CVAP304, Kungliga Tekniska Hgskolan, CVAP/CAS, October 2006. http://cogvis.nada.kth.se/IDOL/
11. Martinez-Gomez, J., Garcia-Varea, I., Caputo, B.: Overview of the imageCLEF 2012 robot vision task. In: CLEF 2012 Evaluation Labs and Workshop, Online Working Notes, Rome, Italy, 17–20 September 2012. ISBN: 978-88-904810-3-1
12. Caputo, B., Müller, H., Martinez-Gomez, J., Villegas, M., Acar, B., Patricia, N., Marvasti, N., Üsküdarlı, S., Paredes, R., Cazorla, M., Garcia-Varea, I., Morell, V · ImageCLEF 2014: overview and analysis of the results. In: Kanoulas, E., Lupu, M., Clough, P., Sanderson, M., Hall, M., Hanbury, A., Toms, E. (eds.) CLEF 2014. LNCS, vol. 8685, pp. 192–211. Springer, Heidelberg (2014)

System for Medical Mask Detection
in the Operating Room Through
Facial Attributes

A. Nieto-Rodríguez, M. Mucientes$^{(\boxtimes)}$, and V.M. Brea

Center for Research in Information Technologies (CiTIUS),
University of Santiago de Compostela, Santiago de Compostela, Spain
{adrian.nietorodriguez,manuel.mucientes,victor.brea}@usc.es

Abstract. This paper introduces a system that detects the presence or absence of the mandatory medical mask in the operating room. The overall objective is to have as few false positive face detections as possible without losing mask detections in order to trigger alarms only for healthcare personnel who do not wear the surgical mask. The medical mask detection is performed with two face detectors; one of them for the face itself, and the other one for the medical mask. Both detectors run color processing in order to enhance the true positives to false positives ratio. The proposed system renders a recall above 95 % with a false positive rate below 5 % for the detection of faces and surgical masks. The system provides real-time image processing, reaching 10 fps on VGA resolution when processing the whole image. The Mixture of Gaussians technique for background subtraction increases the performance up to 20 fps on VGA images. VGA resolution allows for face or mask detection up to 5 m from the camera.

Keywords: Face detection · Facial attributes · AdaBoost

1 Introduction

This paper introduces a system that triggers an alarm when the healthcare personnel do not wear the mandatory mask in the operating room. As apparent, the utility of the system is the detection of a breach in the medical protocol. The overall objective is to provide the least possible rate of false alarms in order not to disrupt the normal activity in the operating room, while keeping a high recall in the detection of faces with masks.

The faces classification system detects the presence of faces in an image and classifies them into two categories: (i) faces with surgical mask and (ii) faces without surgical mask. The Viola-Jones face detector is the base of this work [10].

Actual conditions in the operating room oblige to yield real-time image processing with a low false positive rate and a high recall. Figure 1 collects different challenges to the face classification system. Garment foldings and shades are

© Springer International Publishing Switzerland 2015
R. Paredes et al. (Eds.): IbPRIA 2015, LNCS 9117, pp. 138–145, 2015.
DOI: 10.1007/978-3-319-19390-8_16

the most common source of false face detections, which in turn are very difficult to dismiss as actual detections without further postprocessing, and thus a lower frame rate. Mask detection poses similar challenges. Portions of clothing next to skin areas might also give false mask detections. A worse situation occurs when a mask prompts a false alarm of a maskless face. As will be seen throughout the paper, this happens when its tone in the HSV color space is similar to that of the skin. A less critical situation comes with healthcare personnel wearing surgical mask and glasses, which makes it hard to give a detection, as either a face or a mask. Finally, it is also difficult not to miss rotated and/or leaning faces or masks. In this work, the former is met with synthetic rotations in the training phase [7]. The latter is tackled with a high enough frame rate to detect the face in a frontal position; before the person is leaned. Tackling all the above conditions leads to a robust system, making its actual deployment in the operating room acceptable by the medical staff.

This work lies within the framework of facial attributes identifiers [9], or more generally within the context of short-term person recognition or soft biometrics techniques [1,2]. The Viola-Jones detector is the starting point in most of the facial attribute identifiers to find the region of interest where the trait is analyzed. Several approaches are possible for facial attributes, namely, (i) to detect the presence of a given attribute, e.g. beard or mustache, (ii) to provide the value of the trait with a certain probability, e.g. hair color or facial measurements, or (iii) to sort people, e.g. by ethnicity, age or gender. Our work classifies faces into two categories, namely, faces with and without surgical mask. Even though this is not the first paper on facial attributes identifiers, the lack of specific surgical mask detectors in the literature, as well as the constraints imposed by the conditions of the operating room causes us to introduce specific detectors incorporating color as a property during the training phase in order to enhance the true to false positives ratio.

The paper is organized as follows. Section 2 addresses the faces classification system. Experimental results are given in Sect. 3. Finally, the conclusions are outlined.

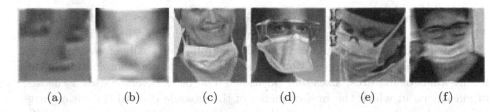

(a)   (b)   (c)   (d)   (e)   (f)

Fig. 1. Challenges to the face classification system. (a) and (b) are false faces from shades and garment foldings, (c) portions of clothing next to skin might give false positives of mask detection, (d) is a mask with a tone similar to that of skin, (e) is a leaning mask face with glasses, and (f) shows a face with the mask below the nose (wrong position).

2 Faces Classification System

The faces classification system detects the presence of faces in an image and classifies them into two categories: (i) faces with surgical mask and (ii) faces without surgical mask. The final goal of the system is to generate an event whenever a person without a surgical mask enters an area in which the use of the mask is required. Figure 2 shows the components of the faces classification system. The system consists of four components: the faces detector, the faces with mask detector, and two color filters —one for each detector.

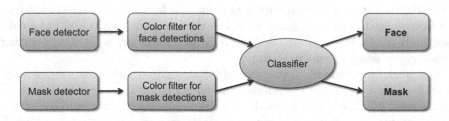

Fig. 2. Faces classification system.

The operation mode of the faces classification system is as follows. When a new image enters the system, both the faces detector and faces with mask detector generate a list of candidate detections represented with a bounding box and a score proportional to the confidence in the detection. Then, each of the lists is filtered by the corresponding color filter, eliminating false positives of the detection stage. Finally, as both lists can share detections (complete or partial overlapping), the final decision on the detected class is taken based on the confidence scores of the overlapping regions. All these steps are described in detail in the following sections.

2.1 Faces Detector

The faces detector is based on the well-known Viola and Jones faces detector [10]. This detector uses very simple rectangular features which evaluate the difference of intensity among rectangular regions. The number of possible features is huge —160,000 for a detector resolution of 24×24— due to the combination of different kinds of features, sizes and positions. The faces detector uses a cascade of classifiers, in which the first elements of the cascade discard the easiest negatives and, as it moves forward in the cascade, the classifiers are more specific and discriminate the most difficult cases. In [10], each classifier of the cascade was learned with AdaBoost.

In this paper we have used a variant of AdaBoost, called LogitBoost [4], which fits an additive logistic regression model by stagewise optimization of the log-likelihood. Moreover, we introduce random rotations in the positive training examples (faces) in order to make the learned classifier robust to small rotations of the faces. The masks detector follows the same strategy, but we use Gentle AdaBoost [4] instead of LogitBoost. Gentle Adaboost exhibits a good generalization ability, as it prevents large updates in pure regions. This characteristic is specially important for the mask detector, as overfitting would lead the system to identify as mask other clothes of the surgical team.

Both detectors work at different image scales. This means that a face will usually be detected several times and, therefore, the number of detections can be used as a confidence in the detection. This detection threshold (ϵ_d) allows the designer to manage the balance between precision and recall (sensitivity). At this stage we look for classifiers with a high recall (we look for a low false negatives rate), as the number of false positives will be reduced by the color filters.

2.2   Color Filter for Faces

Both the faces detector and the faces with mask detector work on gray images. Nevertheless, color information is very relevant in order to identify faces and, also, to distinguish between faces with and without surgical mask. The objective of the color filters stage is to reduce the number of false positives, but trying to avoid an increase in the number of false negatives. Both filters — for faces and faces with mask— use the skin tone on the HSV color space, as HSV codifies the tone in one channel —hue channel. We have determined the skin tone range using all the faces —without mask— in the training set. The process is as follows:

1. For each face in the training set, we build its individual hue histogram.
2. The dominant hue value for each face is calculated summing up the elements of the individual histogram inside a sliding window, and selecting the highest value along the histogram. This helps to prevent the selection of isolated peaks in the histogram.
3. Each face in the training set contributes to the global histogram adding one element in the position of its selected highest value.
4. The skin tone range is the minimum interval of the global histogram to which all the values over a threshold belong.

The idea behind the faces color filter is that most of the pixels in the detection area must have a skin tone. For the faces with mask color filter, the pixels with skin tone should be in the upper part of the image, while the pixels in the lower part should have quite a different tone. Therefore, for each of the color filters, the faces classification system has to learn the features —position and size of the area in which the hue of the pixels has to be analyzed— and the threshold.

The faces color filter uses just one feature, which is the percentage of pixels inside a rectangular area with a hue value within the skin tone range. To select the position and size of the rectangular area, and the percentage of pixels — threshold—, the system uses the average class entropy [3]:

$$E(A, T; S) = \frac{|S_1|}{|S|} Ent(S_1) + \frac{|S_2|}{|S|} Ent(S_2) \qquad (1)$$

$$Ent(S) = -\sum_{i=1}^{k} P(C_i, S) log_2(P(C_i, S)) \tag{2}$$

where A is the attribute —or feature— used to classify the examples set S, and T is the threshold. Thus, for a given value of T, the examples set is divided into two sets, with S_1 being the set of examples with A values $\leq T$, and S_2 the set of examples with A values $> T$. Therefore, the classification system will look for the value of T that minimizes the average class entropy (Eq. 1), as that threshold corresponds to the value that better separates both categories (faces and non faces).

The faces with mask color filter is based on a similar approach. However, the faces with mask have two meaningful areas: (i) the upper area, which should have pixels with skin tone, and (ii) the lower area, which corresponds with the mask and should have pixels outside the skin tone range. Taken this into account, we have defined four different features:

- The quotient of the number of pixels within the skin tone range between the upper and lower part of the image.
- The percentage of pixels within the skin tone range in the two parts of the image.
- The percentage of pixels within the skin tone range in the upper part of the image.
- The percentage of pixels within the skin tone range in the lower part of the image.

This color filter is, in fact, a cascade of filters, where each stage of the cascade uses one of the described features. The cascade has the following characteristics:

- Each stage uses a single feature, and a feature can only be used in one stage.
- For each feature, the system learns the position and size of the rectangular areas —one or two areas, depending on the feature—, and a threshold —the quotient of the number of pixels or the percentage of pixels.
- For each stage, the training examples are those which passed the previous stages.
- At each stage, all the selectable features compete among each other. The classification system will pick the feature —and the positions, sizes, and threshold— that minimizes the average class entropy (Eq. 1).

2.3 Classification

All those candidate detections —generated by the detectors— that passed the color filters are classified in the corresponding category. However, there are many detections with complete or partial overlap and belonging to both classes. In order to classify these cases, the system uses the score of each detection, which corresponds with the number of detections at the different image scales. Thus, the system will select the category with the highest score.

3 Results

3.1 Face Detector

The face detector comprises two stages; one of them on gray-scale images, and a subsequent one with color. The training phase for the gray-scale case has been performed with the LFW image dataset [6]. The test phase has been run on CMU Frontal Face Test Set [8]. We have used 10,000 positive and 5,000 negative images during the training phase. In order to enhance robustness, the faces of the training phase have been subject to rotations up to $\pm 15°$. The face detector contains a cascade of 20 classifiers. Each one of them is a decision tree with two depth levels with 0.999 and 0.5 as detection and false positive thresholds, respectively. During the test the scale of the face detection goes from 20×20 up to whole size of the image with 1.2 as scaling factor between successive scales.

The color face filter has been built on the histogram of the tone in the HSV color space for more than 13,000 images from LFW [6]. The resultant histogram shows that the skin tone of faces lies within the $[340°, 50°]$ range. The training phase has been made with 4,000 positive and negative images. The test has been run on the image dataset BAO [5]. The training phase yields the most adequate position and size of the feature within a window of 20×20 pixels, and 67% as the best skin percentage within the feature subwindow. These values have been found by minimizing entropy (Eq. 1). Figure 3a shows the ROC curve of the face detector with and without the color filter —the ROC of the Viola-Jones detector from OpenCV is included as a reference.

3.2 Mask Detector

As in the case of face detection, the mask detector comprises two stages; one of them on gray-scale images, and a subsequent one with color. The training phase for the mask detector on gray-scale images has 4,000 positive and 15,000 negative images. A forth of the positive images have been extracted from image search engines from the Internet. The remaining percentage of positive images are the result of the same synthetic transformations used for the maskless face detector. Half of the negative set are background images. The other half comprises maskless faces.

The mask color filter finds the definitions —position, size and threshold— of the features. Four conditions have to be met in order to classify a face as a face with surgical mask, namely: (i) the skin pixels ratio between the upper and lower part is over one; (ii) an overall percentage of pixels with skin tone above 7% of the pixels of the upper and lower parts of the feature; (iii) a minimum percentage of 9% of the pixels in the upper part; and (iv) less than 50% of pixels in the lower part with skin tone. All the above numbers have been found by minimizing entropy (Eq. 1) over a set of 4,000 positive cases, 2,000 maskless faces, and 2,000 background images. The results of the mask detector with and without color are shown in Fig. 3b.

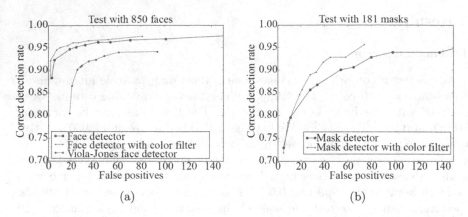

Fig. 3. ROC curves of the face classification system for (a) face and (b) mask detectors.

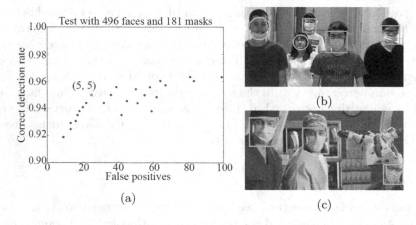

Fig. 4. Face and mask detectors combined: (a) results, (b) and (c) examples of masks (in rectangles) and faces (in circles).

3.3   Face and Mask Detectors Combined

The face classifier combines the face and the mask detector. Figure shows the results with both detectors combined. The test has been run on images with maskless faces from BAO [5] and images of our own image dataset with masks. The test contains 99 images with 496 faces and 181 maskless faces. We set a minimum number of detections across all the scales for the face and the mask detector. The case with a threshold of 5 detections for both face and mask has been chosen. This results in a true positive ratio of around 95 % with less than 40 false positives. Figures 4b and c show the results with this classifier in two different scenarios. Figure 4b shows how the system works with faces and masks. Figure 4c displays an example in the operating room.

4 Conclusions

This paper has introduced a system that triggers an alarm when the healthcare personnel do not wear the mandatory medical mask in the operating room. The system combines a face and a mask detector which use the tone in the HSV color space. The positive and false positive rates are above 95 % and below 5 % on 496 faces and 181 masks from the BAO database and an own image dataset for faces with masks. The system works in real-time on a conventional PC, and it will be deployed in the operating room in the near future.

Acknowledgment. This work was supported by the Galician Ministry of Education under grant EM2014/012, MINECO (Spain) under project TEC2012-38921-C02-02 (European Regional Development Fund (ERDF/FEDER)), and the ERDF/FEDER under the project CN2012/151 of the Galician Ministry of Education.

References

1. Anguelov, D., Kuang-Chih, L., Gokturk, S., Sumengen, B.: Contextual identity recognition in personal photo albums. In: IEEE Conference on Computer Vision and Pattern Recognition (CVPR) (2007)
2. Dantcheva, A., Velardo, C., D'Angelo, A., Dugelay, J.L.: Bag of soft biometrics for person identification. Multimedia Tools Appl. **51**(2), 739–777 (2011)
3. Fayyad, U., Irani, K.: Multi-interval discretization of continuous valued attributes for classification learning. In: Proceedings of the 13th International Joint Conference on Artificial Intelligence (IJCAI), Chambery, France, pp. 1022–1029 (1993)
4. Friedman, J., Hastie, T., Tibshirani, R.: Additive logistic regression: a statistical view of boosting (with discussion and a rejoinder by the authors). Ann. stat. **28**(2), 337–407 (2000)
5. Frischholz, R.: Bao face database at the face detection homepage (2012)
6. Huang, G., Mattar, M., Berg, T., Learned-Miller, E.: Labeled faces in the wild: a database for studying face recognition in unconstrained environments. Technical report, University of Massachusetts (2007)
7. Lienhart, R., Kuranov, A., Pisarevsky, V.: Empirical analysis of detection cascades of boosted classifiers for rapid object detection. In: Michaelis, B., Krell, G. (eds.) DAGM 2003. LNCS, vol. 2781, pp. 297–304. Springer, Heidelberg (2003)
8. Rowley, H.A., Baluja, S., Kanade, T.: Neural network-based face detection. IEEE Trans. Pattern Anal. Mach. Intell. **20**(1), 23–38 (1998)
9. Vaquero, D., Feris, R., Duan, T., Brown, L., Hampapur, A., Turk, M.: Attribute-based people search in surveillance environments. In: Workshop on Applications of Computer Vision (WACV) (2009)
10. Viola, P., Jones, M.: Robust real-time face detection. Int. J. Comput. Vision **57**(2), 137–154 (2004)

Image and Signal Processing

New Method for Obtaining Optimal Polygonal Approximations

Angel Carmona-Poyato[✉], Eusebio J. Aguilera-Aguilera,
Francisco J. Madrid-Cuevas, and D. López-Fernandez

Departamento de Informática Y Análisis Numérico, Universidad de Córdoba,
Córdoba, Spain
ma1capoa@uco.es

Abstract. In this work a new method for obtaining optimal polygonal approximations is presented. The new method is iterative and uses a improved version of the method proposed by Salotti. In the first iteration, the Perez method is used with a random starting point for obtaining a suboptimal polygonal approximation. In the rest of iterations, the improved Salotti method is used. The best error value obtained in the previous iterations is used as a value of pruning for the next iterations. The farthest point from the starting point, in the obtained polygonal approximation, is used as starting point in the next iteration. Tests have shown that in a small number of iterations, global optimal polygonal approximation is obtained. The results show that the computation time is significantly reduced, compared with existing methods.

Keywords: Digital planar curve · Optimal polygonal approximations · Salotti's method · Perez's method

1 Introduction

Polygonal approximations of digital planar curves is an important problem in image processing, pattern recognition and computer graphics. The problem can be defined as follows: given a digital planar curve C with N points, approximate it by an other digital planar curve C_a with a prefixed number of points M so that the obtained error in this approximation is minimized. This problem is known as min-ϵ problem. To solve this problem, many methods have been proposed:

- Using graph theory [1,2].
- Using dynamic programming [3,4].
- Using A*-algorithm [5,6].

These methods solve this problem in $O(N^2)$-$O(MN^2)$ time when an starting points is prefixed. The main drawback of the cited methods is due to the solution depends on the starting point. For this reason, all the points of the contour

---

This work has been developed with the support of the Research Projects called TIN2012-32952 and BROCA both financed by Science and Technology Ministry of Spain and FEDE.

R. Paredes et al. (Eds.): IbPRIA 2015, LNCS 9117, pp. 149–156, 2015.
DOI: 10.1007/978-3-319-19390-8_17

should be tested as starting point for obtaining the optimal polygonal approximation. Thus, the computational complexity increases one level of complexity and becomes $O(N^3)$-$O(MN^3)$.

In this work, a method based on the Salotti method [5,6] is proposed to solve the min-ϵ problem. Its computational complexity is close to $O(N^2)$ and between $O(N^2)$-$O(MN^2)$. Therefore the computational complexity of the cited methods is reduced one level.

In Sect. 2 the main related methods are described. The proposed method is explained in Sect. 3. The experimental results are shown in Sect. 4 and, finally, the main conclusions are summarized in Sect. 5.

2   Related Methods

2.1   Perez's Method

Perez et al. [3] proposed a method, based on dynamic programming, to solve the min-ϵ problem, when the considered error is the integral square error (ISE). The value of ISE for a polygonal approximation is defined as

$$ISE = \sum_{i=1}^{N} e_i^2 \tag{1}$$

where e_i is the orthogonal distance from P_i to the approximated line segment, and P_i depicts any point of the digital curve. Dynamic programming is an optimization method which makes a decision based on all possible previous states with a proper recurrence relation. Perez et al. used the next recursive function to solve the min-*epsilon* problem:

$$E(N, M) = \min_{M-1 \leq i \leq N-1} \{E(i, M-1) + e(P_i, P_N)\}$$

where $E(N, M)$ depicts the minimum error of approximate the first N points by using M points, $E(i, M-1)$ depicts the minimum error of approximate the first i points by using $M-1$ points, and $E(P_i, P_j)$ depicts the error of approximate the curve segment between P_i and P_N by a single edge.

If the values of $e(P_i, P_N)$ are calculated in an incremental way, the computational complexity of this method is $O(MN^2)$ in open planar curves or closed curves when the starting point is prefixed. However, in closed curves, when all the points should be considered as starting point, the computational complexity is $O(MN^3)$.

2.2   Salotti's Method

Salotti [5,6] proposed a method, based on the search of the shortest path in a graph using A^*-algorithm, to solve this problem. If the A^*-algorithm is applied to solve this problem, it is slower than Perez method because there a cost for the management of the graph and the sort of the nodes. In order to reduce the search, Salotti [5] proposed two improvements:

- Obtain a first rough polygonal approximation to estimate the value of a threshold on the maximum global error. Thus, nodes which cannot lead to optimal solutions are pruned. This rough polygonal approximation is obtained by using a suboptimal method with low computational complexity.
- Stop the exploration of successors of the shortest path in the graph as soon as possible. For this reason, Salotti proposed a simple solution to stop the exploration using a lower-bound. This lower-bound is calculated using the linear regressions y/x and x/y to estimate least-square errors. So, he obtains the next expression for the lower-bound:

$$E_{low}^{P_i \to P_j} = \frac{1}{2} Min(E_{reg1}^{P_i \to P_j}, E_{reg2}^{P_i \to P_j})$$

where E_{reg1} and E_{reg2} are the errors calculated using the the linear regressions y/x and x/y.

Using these improvements, Salotti managed to reduce the time complexity of the A^*−algorithm. In this case the computational complexity is close to $O(N^2)$. However, in this method the starting point is prefixed. Therefore, all the points should be considered as starting point. In this case the computational complexity is close to $O(N^3)$.

2.3 Horng's Method

Horng et al. [4] used three techniques to reduce the time complexity of the dynamic programming algorithm proposed by Perez [3]

- Incremental error measure to estimate $e(P_i, P_j)$ in a constant time [3].
- Error measure reuse when the starting point changes. So, unnecessary repeated computations are avoided, because each error measure is computed only once, although the starting point changes [7].
- Initial point determination. He proposed to apply dynamic programming using a random starting point, and then applied dynamic programming using as starting point the vertex farthest from the starting point of the first iteration and separated from its nearest vertex by more than a given threshold [4].

Horng's method has an overall computational complexity of $O(MN^2)$. However it does not guarantee the optimal solution, because may be that the starting point in the second iteration does not belong to the optimal polygonal approximation.

3   Proposed Method

3.1   Improved Salotti's Method

The proposed method is relied on an improvement of the Salotti method [6]. To improve the Salotti method, we propose to calculate the lower-bound using the minimum error of the best line segment approximating a set S of consecutive points $(P_i, \ldots, P_j)$ instead of using the linear regressions y/x and x/y to estimate least-square errors. Thus, the time taken to calculate the lower-bound is halved. To calculate the best line segment approximating, total least squares has been used:

- Calculate

$$\bar{x} = \sum_{i=1,n} \frac{x_i}{n}$$

$$\bar{y} = \sum_{i=1,n} \frac{y_i}{n}.$$

- Calculate the covariance matrix.
- Calculate the maximum eigenvalue of the covariance matrix.
- Calculate the eigenvector corresponding to the maximum eigenvalue.
- The best line segment approximation has this eigenvector as direction vector and passing through the point $P(\bar{x}, \bar{y})$.

3.2   Optimal Polygonal Approximation

Our proposal is based on the following statement:

If we obtain the global optimal polygonal approximation of M points for a planar digital curve of N points, any optimal polygonal approximation that uses any of these M points as prefixed starting point will be a global optimal polygonal approximation.

Demonstration: *The demonstration is obvious. If we obtain the optimal polygonal approximation of M points for a planar digital curve of N points, using a prefixed starting point; any optimal polygonal approximation of M points obtained using any of the M points of the previous polygonal approximation will be equal or better than the previous optimal polygonal approximation. Therefore if we use any of the M points of the global optimal polygonal approximation, as starting point to obtain an optimal polygonal approximation, this approximation will be equal to the global optimal polygonal approximation (it can no be better).*

Our method can be summarized in the following steps:

1. Select a random starting point.
2. Obtain the optimal polygonal approximation for this starting point using the Perez method, because in this iteration no value of pruning is used and in this case the Perez method is faster. Obviously, this is not the global optimum.
3. Select the farthest point to the starting point of the polygonal approximation obtained in the previous step.
4. Obtain the polygonal approximation, with the improved Salotti method, using the farthest point of the previous step as starting point. Thus, the influence of a bad choice of the starting point is minimized. In this case, the value of ISE corresponding to the first polygonal approximation is used as value of pruning in the second polygonal approximation, so the computation time is greatly decremented.

5. Repeat steps 3 and 4, using the best obtained value of ISE in the previous iterations as value of pruning, until the global optimal approximation is obtained.

This method has the next advantages:

- The Perez method is the fastest method to obtain an optimal polygonal approximation when a starting point is prefixed and no value of pruning is used.
- From the second iteration, the lowest value obtained of ISE is used as value of pruning for the next iterations. Thus, the time is highly reduced.
- When the farthest point of the previous iteration is selected in the next iteration, the influence of a bad choice of the starting point is minimized.
- The value of ISE in each iteration is always less or equal than than to the value of ISE of previous iterations. Due to this, the global optimal polygonal approximation is quickly reached.

Though the Perez method [3] is used in the first iteration, because in this iteration there is not value of pruning and it is faster than improved Salotti method, in the remaining iterations is better to use the improved Salotti method because:

- Improved Salotti method use the best value of ISE of the previous iterations, as value of pruning and therefore is faster.
- In each iteration, the value of ISE is less or equal than to the value of ISE of the previous iterations, so the value of pruning is getting smaller and therefore the computation time in each iteration is getting smaller.

4   Experimental Results

Our method has been tested using 25 closed planar digital curves corresponding to 25 digital contours. The number of points of these contours ranging from 553 to 1913. All the global optimal polygonal approximations between 15 and 50 points has been calculated. In total, 900 global optimal polygonal approximations have been obtained. We use values between 15 and 50 because produce optimal polygonal approximations similar to the original contours and their number of points are appropriate (they are neither too high nor too low).

Figure 1 shows some of the digital contours used in this experiment and their global optimal polygonal approximations for 30 points.

In order to test the accuracy of our method, the global optimal polygonal approximation has been obtained using improved Salotti method for all possible starting points.

Table 1 shows the percentage of global optimal polygonal approximations obtained depending on the number of iterations.

Table 1 shows that by using only two iterations we obtain the global polygonal approximation more than 95 percent of cases. Using 4 iterations we obtain more than 99 percent of cases and using 5 iterations we obtain 100 percent.

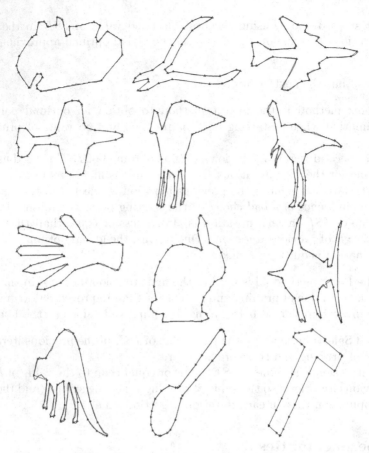

Fig. 1. Some of the digital contours used in this experiment and their global optimal polygonal approximations for 30 points

In order to evaluate the computation time of each iteration for the proposed method and the compared methods, Fig. 2 shows the computation time used to obtain the global optimal polygonal approximation of 15 points for the contour of the *plane*7. In this case we need 5 iterations to obtain the global optimal.

The obtained results from this experiment can be summarized as follows:

– The computation time when the Perez method is used is the same in all iterations.
– The computation time is gradually decreased from the second iteration, when the Salotti method or the proposed method are used, because the best value of *ISE* is used as value of pruning.
– The computation time of the proposed method, relied on the improved Salotti method, is less than the Salotti method. In this case the computation time is reduced about 16 percent.

Table 1. Summary of the percentage of global optimal polygonal approximations obtained depending on the number of iterations

Iterations	% of global optimal obtained
2	95.78
3	98.07
4	99.27
5	100

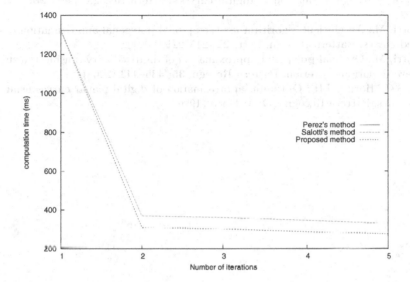

Fig. 2. Computation time in each iteration using the Perez method, the Salotti method and the proposed method to obtain global optimal polygonal approximation for plane7 with 15 points

5   Conclusions

The conclusions of this work can be summarized as follows:

- A new iterative method to obtain global optimal polygonal approximations is presented.
- This method is relied on an improvement of the Salotti method.
- This improvement reduces the computation time about 16 percent.
- The experimental results show that by using only two iterations the global polygonal approximation is obtained more than 95 percent of cases, using 4 iterations is obtained more than 99 percent of cases and using 5 iterations we obtain 100 percent.
- Since the computational complexity of the method Salotti is close to $O(N^2)$, it can be considered that the computational complexity of the proposed method is also close to $O(N^2)$ and between $O(N^2)$-$O(MN^2)$.

References

1. Pikaz, A., Dinstein, I.: Optimal polygonal approximation of digital curves. Pattern Recogn. **28**, 371–379 (1995)
2. Chen, D.Z., Daescu, O.: Space-efficient algorithms for approximating polygonal curves in two-dimensional space. Int. J. Comput. Geom. Appl. **13**, 95–111 (2003)
3. Perez, J.C., Vidal, E.: Optimum polygonal approximation of digitized curves. Pattern Recogn. Lett. **15**, 743–750 (1994)
4. Horng, J.H., Li, J.T.: An automatic and efficient dynamic programming algorithm for polygonal approximation of digital curves. Pattern Recogn. Lett. **23**, 171–182 (2002)
5. Salotti, M.: An efficient algorithm for the optimal polygonal approximation of digitized curves. Pattern Recogn. Lett. **22**, 215–221 (2001)
6. Salotti, M.: Optimal polygonal approximation of digitized curves using the sum of square deviations criterion. Pattern Recogn. **35**, 435–443 (2002)
7. Pei, S.C., Horng, J.H.: Optimum approximation of digital planar curves using circular arcs. Pattern Recogn. **29**, 383–388 (1996)

Noise Decomposition Using Polynomial Approximation

Manya Afonso[✉] and J. Miguel Sanches

Instituto de Sistemas e Robótica, Instituto Superior Técnico, Lisbon, Portugal
{mafonso,jmrs}@isr.ist.utl.pt

Abstract. In some imaging modalities based on coherent radiation, the noise contaminating an image may contain useful information, thereby necessitating the separation of the noise field rather than just denoising. When the algebraic operation that relates the image and noise is known, the noise component can be estimated in a straightforward manner after denoising. However, for some statistical models such as Poisson noise, this algebraic relation is not known. In this paper, we propose a method for simultaneously estimating the image and separating the noise field, when we do not know the algebraic relation between them. It is assumed that the image is sparse and the noise field is not, and appropriate regularizers are used on them. We use a polynomial representation to relate the image and noise with the observed image, and iteratively estimate the polynomial coefficients, the image, and noise component. Experimental results show that the method correctly estimates the model coefficients and the estimated noise components follow their respective statistical distributions.

Keywords: Speckle · Denoising · Poisson noise · Polynomial fitting · Fluorescence microscopy

1 Introduction

Speckle noise is present in a multitude of different coherent imaging modalities such as Ultrasound (US), *Synthetic Aperture Radar* (SAR), *Optical Coherence Tomography*, LASER, and fluorescence microscopy images. In some of these modalities, the noise contaminating the image may hold information such as texture, that may be useful. For example, ultrasound (US) images are corrupted with multiplicative speckle noise which some authors argue is not truly noise because it is dependent of the intrinsic acoustic properties of tissues, and therefore, its texture often carries useful information for characterization of tissues and/or pathologies (see [14] and references therein). A recent study uses the statistical distribution of fluorescence microscopy images of proteins in cells for the detection of cancer [12].

There are several methods proposed in literature for image denoising, for non-additive noise with their respective statistical models appropriate for the

© Springer International Publishing Switzerland 2015
R. Paredes et al. (Eds.): IbPRIA 2015, LNCS 9117, pp. 157–164, 2015.
DOI: 10.1007/978-3-319-19390-8_18

particular modality. Their goal is noise removal in order to make their morphological features more visible and well defined, and therefore discard noise patterns which can contain useful information.

When the noise is known to be additive, after obtaining an estimate of the image $\widehat{\mathbf{x}}$ by using a denoising algorithm on the noisy image $\mathbf{y}$, it is trivial to compute the estimate of the noise field as $\widehat{\boldsymbol{\eta}} = \mathbf{y} - \widehat{\mathbf{x}}$. For Ultrasound images, it has been shown that the multiplicative model $\mathbf{y} = \mathbf{x}\boldsymbol{\eta}$ is a reasonable although inexact approximation modeling the image formation process [9]. The decomposition assuming a multiplicative algebraic model was also used in tissue characterization and diagnosis from B-Mode and *Intra-Vascular US* (IVUS) images [13]. Noise field estimation has been reported for Rician noise in MRI [1,4].

However, without knowing the algebraic model, it is not possible to compute the noise. For example, in the case of Poisson noise which is the model for fluorescence microscopy imaging, the noise that corrupts the images is related to the photon-counting process at the detectors.

In this paper, we address the problem of estimating the noise component when the algebraic relation between the image and the noise is unknown. We assume that the noisy image is the result of a polynomial function in two variables, relating the image and noise field. Polynomial approximation for image decomposition into the cartoon and texture components was used in [15,16], assuming additive Gaussian noise. We assume that the image has a coherent structure and is piecewise smooth, whereas the noise term is non-sparse. A sparse regularizer is used on the image, and one which *discourages* sparsity is used on the noise component. The resulting formulation is solved iteratively using alternating minimization, leading to simultaneous estimation of the denoised image, noise field, and polynomial coefficients. Experimental results for additive and multiplicative noise show that our method is able to correctly estimate the algebraic model, and the distribution of the estimated noise component matches the respective statistics. We also present experiments with Poisson noise, a synthetic example and one with a real fluorescence microscopy image, in which it was found that the histogram of the separated noise field resembles a Poisson distribution with unit parameter.

2   Proposed Method

Without knowledge of the algebraic observation model, we use a polynomial representation to relate the image $\mathbf{x}$, noise $\boldsymbol{\eta}$, and noisy image $\mathbf{y}$,

$$\mathbf{y} = f(\mathbf{x}, \boldsymbol{\eta}, \mathbf{a}) = a_0 + a_1\mathbf{x} + a_2\boldsymbol{\eta} + a_3\mathbf{x}.\boldsymbol{\eta}, \tag{1}$$

where the vector of coefficients $\mathbf{a} = [a_0, a_1, a_2, a_3]^T$ would also have to be estimated in the estimation process. The order used in (1) is sufficient to account for the additive $\mathbf{y} = \mathbf{x} + \boldsymbol{\eta}$, ($\mathbf{a} = [0, 1, 1, 0]^T$) and multiplicative $\mathbf{y} = \mathbf{x}.\boldsymbol{\eta}$, ($\mathbf{a} = [0, 0, 0, 1]^T$) models, but will have to be higher to account for higher order terms, such as the squared amplitudes of Rician noise, which is the model for MRI.

We define the discrepancy term for the model from (1) as the squared ℓ_2-norm of the difference,

$$J(\mathbf{y}, \hat{\mathbf{x}}, \hat{\boldsymbol{\eta}}, \hat{\mathbf{a}}) = 0.5\|\mathbf{y} - f(\hat{\mathbf{x}}, \hat{\boldsymbol{\eta}}, \hat{\mathbf{a}})\|_2^2, \tag{2}$$

where $\hat{\mathbf{x}}, \hat{\boldsymbol{\eta}}, \hat{\mathbf{a}}$ are the respective estimated values. We assume that the image $\mathbf{x}$ is sparse, and therefore use a total variation (TV) [11] regularizer on $\mathbf{x}$ to promote piece-wise smoothness. The only assumption we make about the noise $\boldsymbol{\eta}$ is that it is non-sparse. Therefore we use an ℓ_p norm regularizer with $p \geq 2$, to obtain a non-sparse solution [5]. For computational simplicity, we use the ℓ_2 norm in this work. Indicator functions which restrict $\boldsymbol{\eta}$ to be statistically close to a certain distribution are also possible but will not be considered in this paper.

The optimization problem with this regularization is therefore,

$$\min_{\mathbf{x}, \boldsymbol{\eta}, \mathbf{a}} J(\mathbf{x}, \boldsymbol{\eta}, \mathbf{a}) + \frac{\lambda_x}{2}\mathrm{TV}(\mathbf{x}) + \frac{\lambda_\eta}{2}\|\boldsymbol{\eta}\|_2^2, \tag{3}$$

where $\lambda_x, \lambda_\eta > 0$ are the regularization parameters and $\mathrm{TV}(.)$ is the isotropic TV function.

We solve (3) using the Augmented Lagrangian(AL)/Alternating Direction Method of Multipliers (ADMM) method [6,7,17], because of its mathematical elegance and computational simplicity. This leads to a Gauss-Seidel process in which at each iteration we estimate each variable from $\mathbf{x}, \boldsymbol{\eta}, \mathbf{a}$, keeping the other two fixed. Applying AL/ADMM to (3) leads to the following iterative process where $\mathbf{u}$ and θ are the respective auxilliary variables for $\mathbf{x}$, and $\boldsymbol{\eta}$,

$$\mathbf{u}^{(l+1)} = \arg\min_{\mathbf{u}} \frac{\mu_u}{2}\|\mathbf{x}^{(t)} - \mathbf{u} - \mathbf{d_u}^{(t)}\|^2 + \frac{\lambda_x}{2}\mathrm{TV}(\mathbf{u}), \tag{4}$$

$$\mathbf{x}^{(t+1)} = \arg\min_{\mathbf{x}} J(\mathbf{y}, \mathbf{x}, \boldsymbol{\eta}^{(t)}, \mathbf{a}^{(t)}) + \frac{\mu_x}{2}\|\mathbf{x} - \mathbf{u}^{(t)} - \mathbf{d_u}^{(t)}\|^2, \tag{5}$$

$$\theta^{(t+1)} = \arg\min_{\theta} \frac{\mu_\eta}{2}\|\boldsymbol{\eta}^{(t)} - \theta - \mathbf{d}_\theta^{(t)}\|^2 + \frac{\lambda_\eta}{2}\|\theta\|_2^2, \tag{6}$$

$$\mathbf{a} \leftarrow \text{Polynomial fitting}(\mathbf{y}, [\mathbf{x}^{(t+1)}, \boldsymbol{\eta}^{(t+1)}]), \tag{7}$$

$$\boldsymbol{\eta}^{(t+1)} = \arg\min_{\boldsymbol{\eta}} J(\mathbf{y}, \mathbf{x}^{(t)}, \boldsymbol{\eta}, \mathbf{a}^{(t)}) + \frac{\mu_\eta}{2}\|\boldsymbol{\eta} - \theta^{(t)} - \mathbf{d}_\theta^{(t)}\|^2, \tag{8}$$

$$\mathbf{d_u}^{(t+1)} = \mathbf{d_u}^{(t)} - \mathbf{x}^{(t+1)} + \mathbf{u}^{(t+1)}, \tag{9}$$

$$\mathbf{d}_\theta^{(t+1)} = \mathbf{d}_\theta^{(t)} - \boldsymbol{\eta}^{(t+1)} + \theta^{(t+1)}. \tag{10}$$

The variables $\mathbf{d_u}, \mathbf{d}_\theta$ are the so-called Bregman weight vectors [17], and $\mu_x, \mu_\eta > 0$ are the weight terms for the constrained optimization (see [2] for details). The step (4) is computed using a few iterations of Chambolle's algorithm [3]. Steps (6), (5), and (8) are least squares minimization problems and have linear closed form solutions.

Notice that at each iteration, we update the vector of coefficients $\mathbf{a}$ using a polynomial fitting in two variables [8,10], using the values $(\mathbf{x}^{(t+1)}, \boldsymbol{\eta}^{(t+1)})$. We are not updating $\mathbf{a}$ strictly in the AL framework. We initialize $\mathbf{a}$ with a vector of ones. Since we deal with a polynomial of a relatively small order in this work, we do not make any assumption about its nature and consequently do not introduce any further parameter controlling its level of sparsity. This kind of approach for updating **a** will be addressed in a future paper.

3   Experimental Results

All experiments were performed in MATLAB, on an Ubuntu Linux server with 64 GB of RAM. The iterative process was run until the relative difference between successive iterates of the denoised image fell below the tolerance of 10^{-3}. We first validate the proposed method with the additive Gaussian and Multiplicative Rayleigh noise models, for which we know the algebraic models. We then apply the method to a synthetic example with Poisson noise, and to a real fluorescence microscopy image.

3.1   Known Algebraic Models

For the additive and Gaussian noise model, we add Gaussian noise with zero mean and standard deviation $\sigma = 15$, which corresponds to an SNR of 10 dB. The observed noisy image is shown in Fig. 1(a), the estimate of the image is shown in Fig. 1(b), and the estimated noise field is shown in Fig. 1(c). We see from the entry in Table 1 that the estimated polynomial is close to the expected one. The offset in the constant term of the polynomial doesn't change the relation between $\widehat{\mathbf{x}}$ and $\widehat{\boldsymbol{\eta}}$. The slight offset to the right in the noise histogram as shown in Fig. 1(d) can be attributed to this offset. The analytically computed probability density function (PDF) for Gaussian noise with $N(0, \sigma)$ is shown as a red curve, and the Kullback-Leibler divergence is presented in the Table 1.

Figure 2 illustrates the results for the Lena image multiplied by Rayleigh distributed noise with parameter equal to one. We again see from the Table 1 that the estimated polynomial describes correctly the relation, but has an offset only in the constant term.

Table 1. Estimation of polynomial coefficients approximating the model, and statistical validation of estimated noise field.

Image	Model	Polynomial		KL div.
		Known	Estimated	
Lena	Additive, Gaussian (SNR 10 dB)	$[0, 1, 1, 0]$	$[-0.33, 1.0, 0.95, -0.0]$	0.15
Lena	Multiplicative, Rayleigh	$[0, 0, 0, 1]$	$[2.02, 0.081, -0.028, 0.97]$	0.0052
Lena	Poisson	—	$[1.01, 1.0, 0.99, 1.0]$	0.85
Fluorescence microscopy	Poisson	—	$[1.0, 1.0, 0.99, 1.001]$	0.55

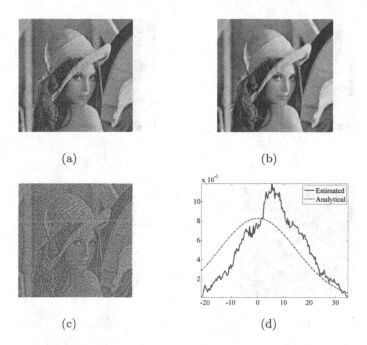

(a)

(b)

(c)

(d)

Fig. 1. Lena image with Gaussian noise (SNR 10 dB). (a) noisy image, (b) denoised estimate, (c) estimated noise field, (d) histogram of noise field.

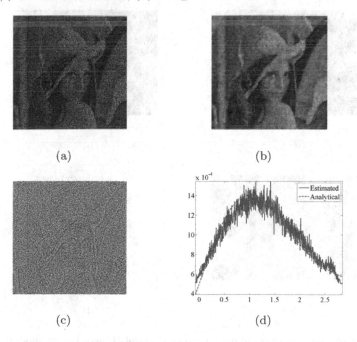

(a)

(b)

(c)

(d)

Fig. 2. Lena image with Rayleigh noise. (a) noisy image, (b) denoised estimate, (c) estimated noise field, (d) histogram of noise field.

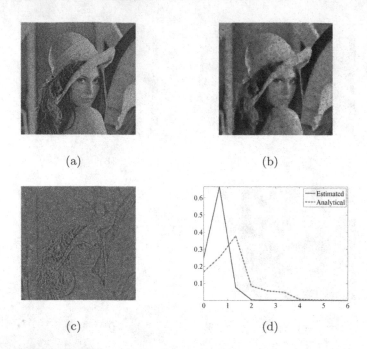

Fig. 3. Lena image with Poisson noise. (a) noisy image, (b) denoised estimate, (c) estimated noise field, (d) histogram of noise field.

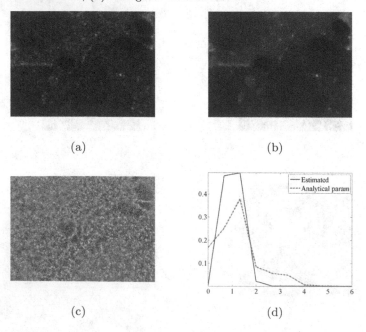

Fig. 4. Fluorescence microscopy image, green channel (Poisson noise model). (a) noisy image, (b) denoised estimate, (c) estimated noise field, (d) histogram of noise field (Color figure online).

3.2   Unknown Algebraic Model

For Poisson noise, the results of applying the proposed method on the Lena image corrupted with Poisson noise are shown in Fig. 3. We can see from Table 1 that all four polynomial coefficients are close to one. A difficulty in characterizing the estimated noise is that the shape of the PDF curve is different for the parameter of the Poisson distribution $\Lambda = 1$ and $\Lambda > 1$. In this work, the plots of the PDFs presented in Fig. 3(d), and the KL distance from the estimated noise histogram in Table 1 were assuming that $\Lambda = 1$. The corresponding results for the fluorescence microscopy image are presented in Fig. 4. Only the green channel is shown, since it is the component of interest for the protein E-cadherin.

4   Conclusions

We have proposed a method for separating the noise component from a noisy image for observation models for which the algebraic operation that relates the noise free image and the noise component is not known. The method models the interaction between the image and noise using a polynomial approximation, and iteratively estimates the polynomial coefficients, along with the two components. Experimental results on synthetic experiments showed that the method was able to correctly estimate the coefficients for the additive Gaussian and multiplicative and Rayleigh models, as well as succeed in separating a statistically valid noise component for the Poisson model. Current and future work includes extending the proposed method to the case when some pixel values are missing or statistical outliers. A higher order polynomial may also be useful for distributions such as Rician noise. Another direction of future work would be refining the stopping criterion for a tradeoff between the quality of the denoised image and the KL divergence of the noise field.

Acknowledgements. This work was supported by the **Fundação para a Ciência e Tecnologia** (FCT), Portuguese Ministry of Science and Higher Education, through a Post-doctoral fellowship (contract no. **SFRH/BPD/79011/2011**) and FCT project **PEst-OE/EEI/LA0009/2013**.

References

1. Aelterman, J., Goossens, B., Pizurica, A., Philips, W.: Removal of correlated rician noise in magnetic resonance imaging. In: Proceedings of EUSIPCO, vol. 2008 (2008)
2. Afonso, M., Bioucas-Dias, J., Figueiredo, M.: Fast image recovery using variable splitting and constrained optimization. IEEE Trans. Im. Proc. **19**(9), 2345–2356 (2010)
3. Chambolle, A.: An algorithm for total variation minimization and applications. J. Math. Imaging Vis. **20**(1), 89–97 (2004)
4. Coupé, P., Manjón, J.V., Gedamu, E., Arnold, D., Robles, M., Collins, D.L.: Robust Rician noise estimation for MR images. Med. Image Anal. **14**(4), 93–483 (2010)
5. Donoho, D.: Compressed sensing. IEEE Trans. Inf. Theor. **52**(4), 1289–1306 (2006)

6. Eckstein, J., Bertsekas, D.: On the DouglasRachford splitting method and the proximal point algorithm for maximal monotone operators. Math. Program. **55**(3), 293–318 (1992)
7. Goldstein, T., Osher, S.: The split Bregman method for ℓ_1 regularized problems. SIAM J. Imaging Sci. **2**(2), 323–343 (2009)
8. Hastie, T., Tibshirani, R., Friedman, J., Franklin, J.: The elements of statistical learning: data mining, inference and prediction. Math. Intelligencer **27**(2), 83–85 (2005)
9. Michailovich, O., Tannenbaum, A.: Despeckling of medical ultrasound images. IEEE Trans. Ultrason. Ferroelectr. Freq. Control **53**(1), 64–78 (2006)
10. Nocedal, J., Wright, S.: Numerical Optimization, 2nd edn. Springer, Heidelberg (2006)
11. Rudin, L., Osher, S., Fatemi, E.: Nonlinear total variation based noise removal algorithms. Phys. D **60**, 259–268 (1992)
12. Sanches, J.M., Figueiredo, J., Fonseca, M., Durães, C., Melo, S., Esménio, S., Seruca, R.: Quantification of mutant e-cadherin using bioimaging analysis of in situ fluorescence microscopy a new approach to cdh1 missense variants. Eur. J. Hum. Genet. (2014)
13. Seabra, J., Sanches, J.: Ultrasound speckle/despeckle image decomposition for tissue analysis. In: Sanches, J.M., Laine, A.F., Suri, J.S. (eds.) Ultrasound Imaging: Advances and Applications. Springer, New York (2012)
14. Seabra, J.C.R.: Medical ultrasound b-mode modeling, de-speckling and tissue characterization assessing the atherosclerotic disease, Ph.D. Dissertation, Instituto Superior Técnico, May 2011
15. Selesnick, I., Arnold, S., Dantham, V.: Polynomial smoothing of time series with additive step discontinuities. IEEE Trans. Sig. Process. **60**(12), 6305–6318 (2012)
16. Selesnick, I.W.: Simultaneous polynomial approximation and total variation denoising. In: 2013 IEEE International Conference on Acoustics, Speech and Signal Processing (ICASSP). IEEE (2013)
17. Radu, V., Yin, W., Osher, S., Goldfarb, D.: Bregman iterative algorithms for ℓ_1 minimization with applications to compressed sensing. SIAM J. Imaging Sci. **1**(1), 143–168 (2008)

Color Correction for Image Stitching by Monotone Cubic Spline Interpolation

Fabio Bellavia$^{(\boxtimes)}$ and Carlo Colombo

Computational Vision Group, University of Florence, Firenze, Italy
{fabio.bellavia,carlo.colombo}@unifi.it

Abstract. This paper proposes a novel color correction scheme for image stitching where the color map transfer is modelled by a monotone Hermite cubic spline and smoothly propagated into the target image. A three-segments monotone cubic spline minimizing color distribution statistics and gradient differences with respect to both the source and target images is used. While the spline model can handle non-linear color maps, the minimization over the gradient differences limits strong alterations on the image structure. Adaptive heuristics are introduced to reduce the minimization search space and thus computational time. Experimental comparisons with respect to the state-of-the-art linear mapping models show the validity of the proposed method.

Keywords: Color transfer · Image stitching · Photometric blending

1 Introduction

Color correction is an essential step nowadays in image and video stitching pipelines [8]. After the spatial image registration, colors between corresponding pixels can have strong inconsistencies, due to different acquisition light conditions, such as varying exposure levels and viewpoints, which cannot be eliminated by image blending techniques alone [1]. Different color correction methods have been proposed across the years. In particular, worth to be mentioned are the gain compensation [1] and the Reinhard's method [5], both modelling linear color map functions.

The gain or exposure compensation was introduced to address color balancing in panoramic mosaicing by a least-square minimization approach, in order to get a symmetric blending across the overlapping area across multiple images. On the other hand, the Reinhard's method proposes a linear transformation to make the mean and the standard deviation of color distribution of the target image corresponding to those of the source image. Extensions of both methods have been proposed [7,8].

Beyond model-based parametric approaches as those described above, modeless non-parametric approaches exist [4], but according to a recent evaluation work [10] the two cited methods are preferable in the general case of image stitching due to their output quality, stability and speed. This paper introduces

© Springer International Publishing Switzerland 2015
R. Paredes et al. (Eds.): IbPRIA 2015, LNCS 9117, pp. 165–172, 2015.
DOI: 10.1007/978-3-319-19390-8_19

a novel color correction algorithm using a monotone spline model as mapping function to better handle non-linear maps. The proposed model, described in Sect. 2, is obtained by exhaustively searching the knots defining the spline which minimizes an error function based on the intensity values and the gradients of the source and target images. Due to the complexity of the minimization function, not analytically manageable, to speed-up the computation and provide the results in reasonable time, adaptive heuristics have been introduced to reduce the minimization search space. Details are presented in Sect. 2.1.

In order to better handle local image properties, overlapping areas between the source and target images are divided into blocks and the corresponding local color maps are computed. Local color maps are then propagated smoothly with morphological operators and Gaussian blur to provide a smooth color change across non-overlapped areas. This last step is described in Sect. 2.2.

Finally, in Sect. 3 a quantitative experimental evaluation has been carried out on real images. The new spline method is compared against the Reinhard's method and an asymmetric version of the gain compensation, according to quantitative measures, in a similar way to the approach of [10], in Sect. 3.1. As shown in Sect. 3.2, according to the evaluation, the proposed spline method achieves better and robust results in terms of image quality, while maintaining reasonable computational times.

Conclusions and future work are discussed in the end of the paper (Sect. 4).

2   Method Description

2.1   Spline Color Mapping

Given a source image I_1 and a target image I_2, the proposed method aims to obtain a color corrected source image $\tilde{I}_1$ which looks similar to image I_2 by a transformation f between color intensity values, i.e. for a pixel $\mathbf{p}$ in the overlapping areas between the two images it holds

$$\tilde{I}_1(\mathbf{p}) = f(I_1(\mathbf{p})) \approx I_2(\mathbf{p}) \tag{1}$$

In addition, a smooth transition between overlapping and non-overlapping areas of the target image is required to not alter the corrected source image. The Reinhard's method [5] defines a linear color map function f_R so that the mean and standard deviation of the intensity values between the corrected source image $\tilde{I}_1$ and target image I_2 are equal by imposing

$$f_R(x) = \frac{\sigma_2}{\sigma_1}(x - \mu_1) + \mu_2 \tag{2}$$

where μ_k, σ_k are respectively the mean and standard deviation for a generic image I_k, here assumed to be computed only in the common area $I_1 \cap I_2$. On the other hand, with the gain compensation method, the gains g_k defined as

$$\tilde{I}_k(\mathbf{p}) = g_k\, I_k(\mathbf{p}) \tag{3}$$

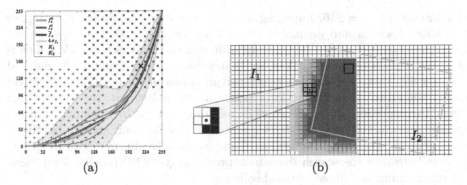

Fig. 1. (a) An example of the search space of the two spline knots K_1 and K_2 for the minimization of the error E_s, bigger marks underline the selected knots, see text for more details. (b) An example of the color map propagation, see text for more details (Color figure online).

are chosen to minimize a quadratic error between the intensity values of the source and target images (see [1] for more details).

In this paper, we propose a more general color mapping function f_s using a monotone Hermite cubic spline [3] with 4 knots. Two of the knots are fixed to the extremal mapping values to preserve the bijective property. Taking into account the monotonic constraint, this implies that $f_s(0) = 0$ and $f_s(255) = 255$, assuming a single channel 8-bit integer color range. The choice of the other two non-fixed knots $K_m = (x_m, y_m) = (x_m, f_s(x_m))$, with $m \in \{1, 2\}$ and $x_1 < x_2$ and $y_1 < y_2$, gives rise to different color mapping functions, from linear to sigmoid-like and exponential models (see Fig. 1(a), green and red lines). In particular, we look for the model that minimizes the following weighted error function E_s:

$$E_s = w_\mu \, e_\mu + w_\sigma \, e_\sigma + \sum_{d \in \{x,y\}} \sum_{n=1,2} w_{d,I_n} \, e_{d,I_n} \tag{4}$$

where the w_k are given weight values (according to our experiments, we set $w_\mu = 0.5$ and all the others to $w_k = 0.1$). The errors $e_\mu = |\mu_s - \mu_2|$ and $e_\sigma = |\sigma_s - \sigma_2|$ are respectively the absolute differences between mean values and the standard deviations of the color intensities of the corrected source image and the target image, in a way similar to the Reinhard's method. Here, μ_s, σ_s are the corresponding statistics for the corrected source image. To improve structure similarity with the target image but also to constrain the image structure to the source image, the average derivative absolute differences e_{d,I_n} in the direction d are taken into account in the minimization thus defining

$$e_{d,I_n} = \frac{1}{|I_1 \cap I_2|} \sum_{\mathbf{p} \in (I_1 \cap I_2)} \left| \frac{\partial \tilde{I}_1}{\partial d}(\mathbf{p}) - \frac{\partial I_n}{\partial d}(\mathbf{p}) \right| \tag{5}$$

Since an analytical solution for minimizing the proposed error e_s is not trivial, an exhaustive search for the two knots can be done instead. In the case of

8-bit integer, i.e. $n = 256$, imposing only the monotonic condition, this implies that knot abscissas and ordinates count both for $n(n-1)/2$ so that we get $t = (n(n-1)/2)^2 = n^2(n-1)^2/4 \approx 10^9$ different error values to check, which is infeasible in practice. Nevertheless, the search space can be dramatically reduced by observing that, for a given knot, perturbations of its position only slight change the error e_s and some knot positions are redundant, see Fig. 1(a) for a visual explanation. In our case, still referring to Fig. 1(a), defining uniform squared grids in the range of $[0, 144]$ and $[111, 255]$ for each knot respectively, with a step of 8 (i.e., a 19×19 grid size) and a chess-like alternate grid sampling, drastically reduces the search space to approximately 3×10^4 possible knot pairs, still maintaining an almost optimal solution.

The process can still be optimized further by pre-computing the possible splines associated to each knot pair and it can take advantage of parallel CPU processing, reducing to about 4000 error evaluations per thread on a 8 core CPU. Furthermore, according to our experiments, the error on the mean intensity color e_μ is predominant, while other error measures just refine the solution. We then define a double step check: if the error e_μ for the current solution is greater than $e_\mu + 15$ of the best solution so far, we discard the current solution avoiding to compute the full error E_s, thus saving computation.

Finally, if more local color maps have to be computed, as described in the next section, one can take advantage of the already computed neighbourhood color maps, since close color maps change smoothly. Assuming 8-connectivity image blocks, given the color map f_s^0 (green line in Fig. 1(a)) and at least b already optimized of its adjacent block color maps f_s^i (red lines) with $i = 1, \ldots, b$ and $3 \leq b \leq 8$, an "average" spline can be computed on which to sample the knots (yellow area). In particular for a given $0 \leq x_m \leq 255$ we constrain y_m to

$$\overline{f}_s(x_m) - 4\,\sigma_{f_s(x_m)} \leq y_m = f_s^0(x_m) \leq \overline{f}_s(x_m) + 4\,\sigma_{f_s(x_m)} \qquad (6)$$

where $\overline{f}_s(x_m)$ and $\sigma_{f_s(x_m)}$ are respectively the mean and standard deviation of the neighbourhood spline mapping values f_s^i already computed (purple and yellow lines respectively).

2.2   Color Map Propagation

Due to the general inability of a single color map to cover correctly all the color transformations in the overlapped image area, the source and target images are aligned and the area divided in blocks of size 32×32 px as shown in Fig. 1(b), to reflect the color locality property. Color maps are computed for each block with at least 50 % of overlap between the two images (red blocks). A wider area of size 64×64 px centered in the block (black square on the red block) is used for the color map computation to avoid abrupt color changes.

In order to achieve a smooth change towards non-overlapping areas of the corrected source image $\overline{I}_1$, color maps of the boundary blocks of the overlapping area are propagated as follows. Considering the block-like versions of the source and target images I_1 and I_2, boundaries of the overlapping region are expanded over non-overlapping blocks of I_1 using the dilation morphology operator [6] with a square 3×3 block kernel.

An increasing label $l = 0, 1, \ldots, u$ is assigned accordingly to the iteration, stopping to grow when a number of blocks equal twice the number of the overlapping blocks has been incorporated or no more blocks can be included (see Fig. 1(b), blue gradient blocks). Since boundary blocks are labelled $l = 0$, starting from the blocks with $l = 1$, a smoothed color map is obtained for these blocks by applying a convolution with a normalized 3×3 Laplacian pyramid kernel [2] on the adjacent blocks with a lower label value. Kernel weights corresponding to equal or higher label values are set to 0 and the kernel is re-normalized (see zoomed grid image); convolution is performed between corresponding map values, i.e. between the $f_s(x)$ for a same x of the adjacent blocks. Finally, we linearly blend the propagated color values with the effective values in the non-overlapping area of the source image. Explicitly

$$\tilde{I}_1(\mathbf{p}) = \frac{l^\star}{u} I_1(\mathbf{p}) + \left(1 - \frac{l^\star}{u}\right) f_s^\star(I_1(\mathbf{p})) \tag{7}$$

where $l^\star$ and $f_s^\star$ are the interpolated values of l and f_s in the color map corresponding to the block containing $\mathbf{p}$ after a Gaussian expansion [2] is used to avoid block-like effects, see Fig. 2(e) for an output example.

3   Experimental Results

3.1   Evaluation Setup

The proposed method was evaluated on a novel dataset of 52 registered color image pairs belonging to 6 real planar scenes, obtained by varying the image exposition. Images and code for the evaluation are freely available[1]. We compare the proposed spline method against Reinhard's method and an asymmetric version of the gain compensation (see the additional material[2] for more details). The color map propagation described in Sect. 2.2 was applied to all methods in order to achieve a fair comparison, thus only varying the color map function computation.

For each image pair we run two different tests to evaluate the methods. In the first test T_1, we just considered the error with respect to the target image as ground-truth in the overlapping area $R = I_1 \cap I_2$ between the two aligned images. To evaluate the color propagation, in test T_2, a random chosen connected subset of 40% of the overlap area $R^\star \subset R$ was considered as the effective overlapping area to obtain the color map, while color propagation was made in the remaining overlapping area $R^c = R \setminus R^\star$ (see Fig. 2).

In both setups we considered the results obtained on grayscale images (luminance channel) and color images. In the latter case the methods were applied to each of the RGB channels independently. Using the ground-truth target image

---

[1] http://cvg.dsi.unifi.it/download/spline/spline.zip.
[2] http://cvg.dsi.unifi.it/download/spline/spline_additional_material.zip.

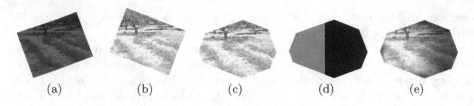

(a)   (b)   (c)   (d)   (e)

Fig. 2. Source image (a), target image (b), overlapping area $R = I_1 \cap I_2$ (c), $R^\star$ (gray) and R^c (black) regions (d) and spline method output (e) for an example T_2 test setup (Color figure online).

I_2, we evaluated the color corrected source image $\tilde{I}_1$ according to *Structural SIMilarity (SSIM)* index [9] and error measures defined on the intensity values and gradient, denoted respectively as E_c and E_d. The $SSIM$ index is an image quality index that measures the structure coherence of one image with another. It was already used in color transfer evaluations [10] and works on grayscale images only. Assuming the RGB colorspace, the error E_c on the image intensities is defined instead as the average *root mean square* (RMS) error for each considered pixel $\mathbf{p}$, which reduces to the average absolute error in the case of grayscale images

$$E_c = \frac{1}{|A|} \sum_{\mathbf{p} \in A} RMS \left(G_{\sigma_e} * \tilde{I}_1(\mathbf{p}) - G_{\sigma_e} * I_2(\mathbf{p}) \right) \tag{8}$$

where A is the image region among $\{R, R^\star, R^c\}$ on which to evaluate the error. Convolution with a Gaussian kernel G_{σ_e} with standard deviation $\sigma_e = 8$ has been applied to both the corrected source and target images in order to cope with small image misalignment errors. The gradient error E_d is defined in similar way.

In order to rank the methods, since the dataset contains image pairs going from small color variations to challenging ones, we promote strong error differences between the methods with respect to small ones. For a given image pair and evaluation criterion, we define the *normalized smooth rank* $r(m)$ for the value m associate to a method as

$$r(m) = \frac{|m - m_b| + \delta}{\sum_{n \in \{m\}} (|n - m_b| + \delta)} \tag{9}$$

where m_b is the best value among those of the compared methods (the maximum for the $SSIM$ index, the minimum for the E_c and E_d errors), and δ is a tolerance factor to avoid strong rank variations in the case of small measure differences, set to $\delta = 1$ in the case of the $SSIM$ index and E_c and to $\delta = 0.1$ for E_d.

3.2   Results

Table 1 shows the average smooth ranks for each method in the case of color and grayscale images for the different tests and evaluation criteria, while in

Table 1. Average smooth rank (%) for the difference evaluation measures, best values are in bold.

	T_1			T_2								
	R			R^*			R^c			R		
	Spline	Reinhard's	A. Gain	Spline	Reinhard's	A. Gain	Spline	Reinhard's	A. Gain	Spline	Reinhard's	A. Gain
$SSIM$ index	**12.9**	32.0	55.0	**13.1**	30.8	56.0	**18.3**	22.1	59.4	**14.8**	27.4	57.7
E_c (RGB)	**05.2**	12.9	81.7	**06.0**	12.4	81.4	14.0	**10.8**	75.0	**08.5**	10.8	80.5
E_c (gray)	**07.8**	12.6	79.5	**08.4**	12.3	79.1	16.8	**12.6**	70.4	**11.5**	11.8	76.6
E_d (RGB)	**14.7**	44.8	40.4	**15.3**	42.7	41.9	29.3	**27.9**	42.6	**29.4**	39.8	30.7
E_d (gray)	**21.0**	44.9	33.9	**21.2**	43.6	35.0	**33.2**	33.3	33.3	32.0	38.1	**29.7**

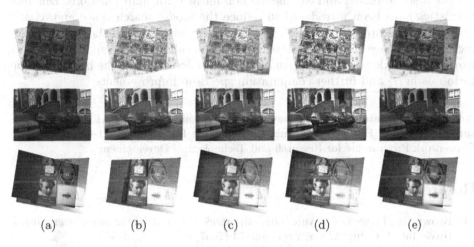

(a)   (b)   (c)   (d)   (e)

Fig. 3. Source images (a), target images (b), spline (c), Reinhard's (d) and asymmetric gain compensation (e) outputs for some image pairs used in the evaluation (Color figure online).

Fig. 3 some challenging examples are shown. Corrected source images are overimposed on the target image, without applying any blending to better appreciate the outputs. For detailed results on each image pair, see the additional material (See footnote 2). According to the results, the proposed spline method provides in general the best outputs, followed by Reinhard's method, while the asymmetric gain compensation gives the worst results. This holds for the $SSIM$ index and the E_c and E_d errors in both the color and grayscale cases. As an additional observation, it can be noted that color images give higher errors, since some information is lost by handling the color channels independently.

About the computing time, the average time per block are 550 ms, 2 ms and 2 ms respectively for the spline, Reinhard's and asymmetric gain compensation methods. Furthermore, the average time for block in the case of the spline method double from 550 ms to 1200 ms when the adaptive search space according to adjacent color maps is not implemented (see 6). The computing time of the spline method is reasonable (about 5 min for a color image pair) and feasible for off-line tasks, also considering the better visual output quality of the method with respect to the second ranked Reinhard's method in the case of challenging image pairs. In this cases, the Reinhard's method look more unrealistically contrasted or with wrong colors due to strong exposure variations (see Fig. 3, top and middle rows) or misalignment issues (bottom row).

4   Conclusions

This paper describes a novel color correction method for image stitching, which adopts a spline model and can handle non-linear color map functions. Different heuristics have been introduced to reduce the model search space and, consequently, the computation time. The comparison with state-of-the-art color correction algorithms shows the robustness and the validity of the approach. Future work will include to test adaptive block shapes according to the image segmentation as in [7] and further computation speed-up improvements.

Acknowledgement. This work has been carried out during the ARROWS project, supported by the European Commission under the Environment Theme of the "7th Framework Programme for Research and Technological Development".

References

1. Brown, M., Lowe, D.G.: Automatic panoramic image stitching using invariant features. Int. J. Comput. Vis. **74**(1), 59–73 (2007)
2. Burt, P.J., Adelson, E.H.: A multiresolution spline with application to image mosaics. ACM Trans. Graph. **2**(4), 217–236 (1983)
3. Fritsch, F.N., Carlson, R.E.: Monotone piecewise cubic interpolation. SIAM J. Numer. Anal. **17**(2), 238–246 (1980)
4. Jia, J., Tang, C.: Tensor voting for image correction by global and local intensity alignment. IEEE Trans. Pattern Anal. Mach. Intell. **27**(1), 36–50 (2005)
5. Reinhard, E., Ashikhmin, M., Gooch, B., Shirley, P.: Color transfer between images. IEEE Comput. Graph. Appl. **21**(5), 34–41 (2001)
6. Soille, P.: Morphological Image Analysis. Principles and Applications, 2nd edn. Springer, Heidelberg (2003)
7. Taiand, Y., Jia, J., Tang, C.: Local color transfer via probabilistic segmentation by expectation-maximization. In: Computer Vision and Pattern Recognition, pp. 747–754 (2005)
8. Uyttendaele, M., Eden, A., Szeliski, R.: Eliminating ghosting and exposure artifacts in image mosaics. In: Computer Vision and Pattern Recognition, pp. 509–516 (2001)
9. Wang, Z., Bovik, A.C., Sheikh, H.R., Simoncelli, E.P.: Image quality assessment: from error visibility to structural similarity. IEEE Trans. Image Process. **13**(4), 600–612 (2004)
10. Xu, W., Mulligan, J.: Performance evaluation of color correction approaches for automatic multi-view image and video stitching. In: Computer Vision and Pattern Recognition, pp. 263–270 (2010)

Structured Output Prediction with Hierarchical Loss Functions for Seafloor Imagery Taxonomic Categorization

Navid Nourani-Vatani[1], Roberto López-Sastre[2(✉)], and Stefan Williams[3]

[1] ERED, MAN Truck and Bus AG, Munich, Germany
[2] GRAM, University of Alcalá, Alcalá de Henares, Spain
robertoj.lopez@uah.es
[3] ACFR, University of Sydney, Sydney, NSW 2006, Australia

Abstract. In this paper we study the challenging problem of seafloor imagery taxonomic categorization. Our contribution is threefold. First, we demonstrate that this task can be elegantly translated into a Structured SVM learning framework. Second, we introduce a taxonomic loss function in the structured output classification objective during learning that is shown to improve the performance over other loss functions. And third, we show how the Structured SVM can naturally deal with the problem of learning from data imbalance by scaling the cost of misclassification during the optimization. We present a thorough experimental evaluation using the challenging and publicly available *Tasmania Coral Point Count* dataset, where our models drastically outperform the state-of-the-art-results reported.

Keywords: Seafloor imagery · Categorization · Recognition · Structured prediction

1 Introduction

Autonomous Underwater Vehicle (AUV) systems have recently been shown to be effective tools for rapidly and cost-effectively delivering a vast amount of high-resolution, accurately geo-referenced, and precisely targeted optical and acoustic imagery of the seafloor [1]. Processing of this vast amount of collected imagery to label content is difficult, expensive and time consuming. Because of this, typically only a small subset of images are labeled, and only at a small number of points. In order to make full use of the raw data returned from the AUV, this process needs to be automated.

There are, however, many challenges associated with processing images captured underwater. Natural scene illumination may be very poor, and there is often little regular structure with which to delineate objects.

Despite these challenges, there have been many recent advances in the processing of imagery from underwater scenes (e.g. [2,3]). These advances have

© Springer International Publishing Switzerland 2015
R. Paredes et al. (Eds.): IbPRIA 2015, LNCS 9117, pp. 173–183, 2015.
DOI: 10.1007/978-3-319-19390-8_20

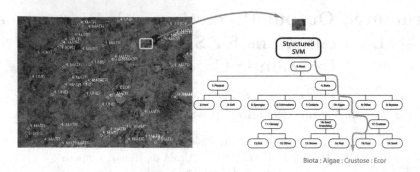

Biota : Algae : Crustose : Ecor

Fig. 1. Overview of our approach. Given a taxonomy, our objective is to classify the image patches according to this. We demonstrate this task can be elegantly translated into the Structured SVM learning framework.

implications in a diverse range of application areas, including marine ecology, archeology, geology as well as industrial and defense applications.

In this paper, we address the task of studying ecosystems and populations from seafloor images. To facilitate this task, we propose an approach to provide marine scientists quantitative data on bottom-dwelling organisms and physical morphology derived from large image archives collected by AUV systems.

For such applications, the state-of-the-art consists of taking a small subset of images, manually labeling the content, and extrapolating to assess distribution and coverage over wider geographical areas, as it has been described in [4]. Essentially, this is a imagery taxonomic categorization problem, see Fig. 1, where we are given a pre-determined taxonomy, and the objective is to classify the image patches adhering to this taxonomy.

In this study, we show that this problem can be elegantly translated into a structured learning framework [5], paying special attention to the design of the loss function and potential imbalance in the data set. The main contributions of this paper are: (a) We propose a Structured SVM (SSVM) based approach to seafloor imagery classification, and perform a thorough experimental evaluation of a set of taxonomic loss functions; (b) We formulate the novel Weighted Hierarchical Difference (WHD) loss, which is able to report the best classification results; (c) We show how the Structured SVM can naturally deal with the problem of learning from data imbalance by scaling the cost of misclassification during the optimization; (d) We demonstrate that taxonomy-based learning using SSVM yields improved results when hierarchical losses are used, outperforming both standard multi-class SVMs and other hierarchical SVM ensembles [6]; (e) A thorough experimental evaluation is reported, using the challenging and publicly available *Tasmania Coral Point Count* dataset [4], where our models drastically outperform the state-of-the-art-results.

The rest of the paper is organized as follows. In the next section, a review of related work, within the context of seafloor image categorization, is given. Section 3 introduces the proposed solution. Section 4 presents the results. Our conclusion is given in Sect. 5.

2 Related Work

There has been substantial research on classification of seafloor species. In [7], starfish detection results from underwater imagery are reported. Approaches for classification of kelp have been also described, e.g. [4]. Multi-class classification has also been attempted, focused mainly on the categorization of different coral species [3,8].

Common for all these approaches is a choice of one or more image-based descriptors and a (collection of) flat classifier(s). More recently, [6] have taken advantage of the taxonomical hierarchy of the species for classification. In a hierarchy with 19 classes, a large framework of 19 binary classifiers, one per node, is employed. The authors presented an in-depth analysis of various training and testing methodologies and have shown state-of-the-art results on their data set.

In this paper we propose the use of an SSVM formulation for the task of taxonomical hierarchical classification. Our approach differs with the approach of [6] in several ways. Firstly, since we are employing a single linear classifier, in the form of an SSVM, it is a much leaner setup with a simplified training and testing strategy. This also signifies, that the amount of training data (and time) is considerably reduced. Secondly, in [6] the hierarchical taxonomy is used *outside* of the classifier through a decision tree. However, we incorporate the taxonomical hierarchy *inside* the loss function of the structured classifier.

Within the same context, i.e. taxonomic categorization, other learning methods have been already proposed to make use of specialist-imposed taxonomies [9–11]. Interestingly, in [11], the authors show that the performance of an SSVM [5] based approach can be improved by using an ensemble of local SVMs in some data sets. In our work, we claim that a SSVM with an appropriate hierarchical loss function can efficiently solve the problem, even improving complex ensembles of SVMs [6]. Several hierarchical loss functions are proposed in [9,10], but they differ from the novel Weighted Hierarchical Difference (WHD) loss proposed in this work. In particular, the hierarchical loss in [10] only considers a penalization based on the common ancestor, while our WHD accumulates a loss through the whole hierarchy.

3 Seafloor Imagery Taxonomic Categorization

We formulate the problem of seafloor imagery taxonomic categorization as a structured output prediction problem. We first describe our model, which we propose for solving the taxonomic classification of benthic images using an SSVM [5]. Then, we describe the learning algorithm and introduce the taxonomic loss functions to be evaluated. In order to further improve the performance of the prediction, we propose the novel Weighted Hierarchical Difference (WHD) loss function. Finally, to deal with the problem of learning from data imbalance, we describe a learning strategy, that consists of scaling the misclassified structured predictions during the optimization.

3.1 Model Formulation

Using SSVMs, we are able to generalize the SVM to the case of the complex interdependent output space defined by the problem of seafloor imagery taxonomic categorization. Let us assume we are given a collection of N training image patches $\mathcal{I} = \{(x_1, y_1), \ldots, (x_N, y_N)\} \in \mathcal{X} \times \mathcal{Y}$, where $x_i \in \mathbb{R}^d$ encodes the image appearance, and y_i represents the ground truth label of the image in the corresponding taxonomy with a total of C nodes, i.e. $y_i \in \{1, 2, \ldots, C\}$.

With an SSVM we are able to learn a model w associated to a *score* function

$$f(x_i, \hat{y}) = < w, \phi(x_i, \hat{y}) >, \qquad (1)$$

which is able to assign a scalar value that indicates how the structured prediction $\hat{y}$ fits the appearance encoded in x_i. Note that during training the objective is to find the classifying hyperplane w for the combined feature representation $\phi(x_i, \hat{y})$ [5].

The specific form of $\phi(,)$ depends on the nature of the problem. Similar to [9], when $\mathcal{Y}$ is taxonomically structured, $\phi(x_i, \hat{y})$ decomposes as $\phi(x_i, y) = \lambda(y) \otimes x_i$, where $\lambda(y)$ is a binary vector that encodes the hierarchical relationship between classes, and $\otimes$ is the Kronecker product, thus $\phi(x_i, y) \in \mathbb{R}^{C \times d}$. In particular, the taxonomy is defined to be an arbitrary lattice (e.g. the tree in Fig. 2a), where *all* its elements correspond to categories. It is important to note, that in other taxonomic approaches [9, 11] only the minimal elements, i.e. the leaves in the tree, correspond to the categories. In our approach, however, we allow the prediction to be cast at any level of the tree structure. We assume one unique root node, and for every node y in the taxonomy, we define the set of nodes on the path from the root to the node y by $\Omega(y)$. For instance, for the class 10:`Algae`, in the taxonomy shown in Fig. 2a, $\Omega(10) = \{0, 4, 10\}$. We then encode this information in a binary vector $\lambda(y)$ for each node y, where the ith element is given by

$$\lambda_i(y) = \begin{cases} 1 \text{ if } i \in \Omega(y) \\ 0 \text{ otherwise.} \end{cases} \qquad (2)$$

The corresponding binary vector for class 10:`Algae` in the taxonomy is

$$\lambda(10) = \{1, 0, 0, 0, 1, 0, 0, 0, 0, 0, 1, 0, 0, 0, 0, 0, 0, 0, 0, 0\}.$$

3.2 Learning

Our objective is to learn a mapping from sampled features x_i to their corresponding output in the structured output space $\mathcal{Y}$, i.e. the taxonomy. That is, for a set of training images $\mathcal{I} = \{(x_1, y_1), \ldots, (x_N, y_N)\}$, we want to train a *linear* model w that given an image x_i, tends to cast the true structured output for the taxonomy $\hat{y} = y_i$. We formulate this as the following regularized learning problem:

$$\underset{w, \xi}{\arg\min} \frac{1}{2} w^\top w + \frac{C}{n} \sum_{i=1}^{n} \xi_i \text{ s.t. } \forall i, \xi_i > 0, \qquad (3)$$

$$\forall i, \forall y \in \mathcal{Y} \backslash y_i : \ \phi(x_i, y_i) - \phi(x_i, y) \geq \Delta(y_i, y) - \xi_i, \tag{4}$$

where $\Delta(,)$ is the loss function. The constraint from (4) specifies the following. Consider the ith training image x_i and its corresponding true structured label y_i. We want the true label to score higher than all other hypothesized labellings y.

Intuitively, violating a margin constraint involving a $y \neq y_i$ with high $\Delta(y_i, y)$ should be penalized more severely than a violation involving an output value with smaller loss. This can be accomplished by re-scaling the margin accordingly, as it is shown in Eq. (4). The formulation in Eqs. (3) and (4) is often called margin re-scaling [5]. The optimization for the training problem outlined is solved following the cutting plane algorithm in the SVMStruct software package [12].

3.3 Taxonomic Loss Functions

In the formulated structured output taxonomic prediction, different loss functions $\Delta(,)$ can be considered. In this section, we describe all the loss functions that are evaluated in this work. We also introduce the novel Weighted Hierarchical Difference (WHD) loss.

Standard Taxonomic Loss Functions. Given the ground truth label y and the corresponding prediction $\hat{y}$, and considering that $\mathcal{Y}$ is taxonomically structured, we can define the following standard hierarchical loss functions.

We consider three distinct loss functions: 1) the distance to the nearest ancestor in the tree $\Delta_n(\hat{y}, y)$; 2) the classical distance through the tree $\Delta_t(\hat{y}, y)$ [13]; 3) and the hamming distance $\Delta_h(\hat{y}, y) = \sum_i |\lambda_i(\hat{y}) - \lambda_i(y)|$ [11], which counts the number of non-shared nodes on the path between the true class y and the prediction $\hat{y}$.

We also consider it important to analyze the performance of taxonomic loss functions, that explicitly incorporate the hierarchical statistics for true positives (tp), false positives (fp), false negatives (fn) and true negatives (tn). These can be efficiently obtained from the taxonomy and with y and $\hat{y}$. Once these hierarchical statistics are computed, we proceed to define the following taxonomic loss functions: $\Delta_{precision}(\hat{y}, y) = tp/(tp + fp)$, $\Delta_{recall}(\hat{y}, y) = tp/(tp + fn)$, $\Delta_{accuracy}(\hat{y}, y) = tp/(tp + fp + fn)$, $\Delta_{hier.hamming}(\hat{y}, y) = (tp + tn)/(tp + fp + fn + tn)$ and $\Delta_{f_1}(\hat{y}, y) = (2 \cdot tp)/(2 \cdot tp + fp + fn)$.

Finally, one simple loss, which can be incorporated to our approach, is the standard 0/1 loss function

$$\Delta_0(\hat{y}, y) = \begin{cases} 0 \text{ if } \hat{y} = y \\ 1 \text{ otherwise.} \end{cases} \tag{5}$$

Note that $\Delta_0(\hat{y}, y)$ transforms our taxonomic classification problem into a standard multi-class prediction problem (with each node of the taxonomy representing a different, and unrelated, class).

Weighted Hierarchical Difference. One of the main limitations of the hamming distance $\Delta_h(\hat{y}, y)$ [11], is that it does not penalize an error higher up the hierarchy more severely; an aspect we consider fundamental for taxonomic categorization problems. Consider a classifier mistaking a Yellow Labrador (*Canis lupus familiaris*) to a Persian Cat (*Felis catus*) or mistaking the Yellow Labrador with a Golden Retriever. The former is obviously a bigger mistake and should incur a greater penalty.

To highlight this difference, in this paper, we propose the following loss, which we call the Weighted Hierarchical Difference (WHD) loss,

$$\Delta_{\text{WHD}}(\hat{y}, y) = \sum_i |\Psi(\lambda_i(\hat{y})) - \Psi(\lambda_i(y))|. \tag{6}$$

Essentially, this WHD computes the L^1-norm of the difference of vectors $\Psi(\lambda(\hat{y}))$ and $\Psi(\lambda(y))$. We define $\Psi()$ as a weighting function, which divides each component i of the binary vector $\lambda(y)$ by the level it belongs to. For instance, in the taxonomy shown in Fig. 2a, for the class 10:`Algae`, we have that $\Psi(\lambda(10)) = (1, 0, 0, 0, 1/2, 0, 0, 0, 0, 0, 1/3, 0, 0, 0, 0, 0, 0, 0, 0, 0, 0)$.

We have incorporated all these loss functions to the SVMStruct package [12]. A reference implementation of the code has been made publicly available[1].

3.4   Dealing with Imbalanced Taxonomies

Data imbalance is a typical problem of taxonomic data sets. The larger the number of classes in the hierarchy, the more difficult it is to guarantee that all classes are assigned a similar number of samples when collecting the data. In this section, we show that learning from highly imbalanced data is a problem that can be naturally addressed employing a weighting strategy for the cost of a misclassification during learning of the SSVM.

Learning from imbalanced data is problematic. As it is shown in [14], an SVM learned with an imbalanced data set can be skewed and become unfavorable to the minority class. Different techniques have been proposed to deal with this problem.

Oversampling is a data preprocessing technique, that balances the data set before training [15]. Basically, the minority classes are oversampled in order to get a data set where all classes have similar number of samples. However, both the training time and the memory requirements of the algorithm naturally increase. Furthermore, if non-linear kernels are used, the test time might increase too.

In order to solve these oversampling problems, we formulate an SSVM approach where, we propose to dynamically weight the taxonomic loss function during the optimization according to the number of samples per class. This weighting is chosen such that a misclassification of a small class is penalized more.

We proceed to define different error costs for the different classes in our taxonomy. In a standard binary SVM classifier, this is accomplished by adjusting the cost parameter to $C^+ = \alpha^+ \times C$ and $C^- = \alpha^- \times C$, where C is the original cost parameter and α^+/α^- are weight constants for the large and small classes, respectively. These weight constants are often set to the inverse of the class size ratios.

---

[1] https://github.com/nourani/Seafloor_SSVM.

In our SSVM formulation, the cost of a misclassification can be adjusted by adding a weight penalty α_i to the loss, i.e. $\Delta(y_i, y)/\alpha_i$. So, (4) is transformed as follows,

$$\forall i, \forall y \in \mathcal{Y}\backslash y_i : \ \phi(x_i, y_i) - \phi(x_i, y) \geq (\Delta(y_i, y)/\alpha_i) - \xi_i. \tag{7}$$

We define α_i as the penalty for an incorrect classification of label y_i. In our experiments we follow the standard procedure of setting the penalty to the inverse of the class instance ratios: $\alpha_i = n_i/N$, where n_i is the number of instances in class i and N is the total number of training instances in the taxonomy. For small classes, α_i will be small and the loss for misclassification will become larger, compensating for the lack in training instances.

The experimental validation shows that our weighting strategy outperforms the oversampling method, both in classification accuracy and runtime.

4   Results

4.1   Experimental Setup

For our experimental validation, we use the publicly available *Tasmania Coral Point Count* data set, introduced in [4], which consists of 1258 images labeled by expert marine scientists, with each image containing 50 labels at 50 randomly selected pixels, adhering to the taxonomical hierarchy shown in Fig. 2(a). There are more than 130 different species labels in the data set, which have been collapsed to 19 classes (c.f. Figure 2(b)) with the guidance of marine scientists.

From Fig. 2(b) it can be seen that the data set is extremely unbalanced. Some of the parent nodes contain no instances, while other parent nodes do contain labels. What this signifies is that not all labels go to the leaf nodes. It is necessary to formulate a classification strategy, that both takes into account the unevenness and the labeling philosophy of the data set.

For all the experiments, the data set is divided into 80 % training samples and 20 % test samples following the experimental setup in [4]. Exponential grid search in the range $10^{-2} - 10^2$ is used to find the cost parameter, C, for the SSVM classifier proposed, by training on 2/3 of the training samples and validating on the last 1/3. For the visual features, we follow [6] and for each image patch (of 31×31 pixels) we compute the Histogram Fourier Local Binary Patterns [16] (LBP-HF) descriptor. We evaluate the performance of our solutions using the modified hierarchical F1-score introduced in [6].

4.2   Seafloor Imagery Taxonomic Categorization

We start the experimental validation assessing the performance of the different taxonomic loss functions proposed. We compare our results with the baseline methodology, which consists of a multi-class SSVM [5] employing a 0/1-loss, i.e. Δ_0. We have used the code available for multi-class classification at [12].

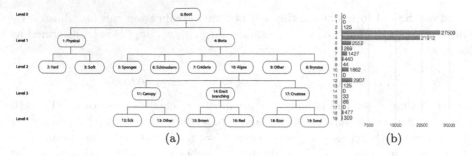

(a)   (b)

Fig. 2. (a) The hierarchy, and (b) number of instances per class in the *Tasmania Coral Point Count* data set.

Table 1. Performance of the 10 loss functions
on the *Tasmania* data set.

Loss	H-F1$_{mod}$	Accuracy	Precision	Recall
Δ_0	88.67	**67.58**	16.41	17.99
Δ_{WHD}	**89.06**	**67.58**	17.19	**22.66**
Δ_{f_1}	**89.06**	**67.58**	16.40	15.23
$\Delta_{precision}$	88.28	66.02	13.28	15.63
Δ_{recall}	87.50	62.89	17.58	16.02
$\Delta_{accuracy}$	**89.06**	**67.58**	16.79	17.19
$\Delta_{hier.ham}$	**89.06**	67.19	16.02	22.27
Δ_n	77.73	50.00	**18.36**	17.97
Δ_t	84.38	67.19	15.63	15.63
Δ_h	84.38	**67.58**	15.23	15.63

Table 2. Comparison with a flat
multi-class SVM classifier scheme
and the state-of-the-art.

Method	H-F1$_{mod}$ %
Flat multi-class	66.67
MPS$_{0.5}$ [6]	80.24
Δ_{WHD} (Ours)	**89.06**

Table 1 shows the performances of the loss functions in terms of the hierarchical F1-score, accuracy, precision and recall. We observe that the new WHD loss function is performing the best. We also compare our method to a flat multi-class SVM classifier and the state-of-the-art reported on the same data set by [6] (see Table 2). The authors of [6] presented a one-classifier-per-node hierarchical approach employing max probability switching with thresholding, MPS$_{0.5}$. For the flat SVM classification scheme, we have trained a standard multi-class linear SVM, using the LibSVM [17] package. Table 2 shows that our SSVM approach significantly improves both the baseline and the state-of-the-art MPS$_{0.5}$.

The results reported illustrate some important outcomes. Firstly, employment of SSVM has greatly improved the performance over the one-node-per-classifier approach of [6] from 80.24 % to 89.06 %. Secondly, this large improvement of 8 % has come in addition to a considerably simplified methodology and setup. We can conclude that taxonomy-based learning using SSVM yields improved results when hierarchical losses are used, outperforming both standard multi-class SVMs and other hierarchical SVM ensembles [6]. Finally, Fig. 3 shows some qualitative results.

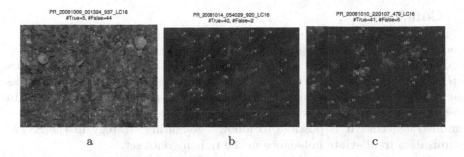

Fig. 3. Qualitative results. The location of the ground truth label is shown with a ○ marker and green text. Red marker indicates incorrect classification. (a) One of the worst results on the test set. (b-c) Two of the best classification results.

Table 3. Main results analyzing the data imbalance on the sampled test set.

Method	Prec	Rec	H-F1$_{mod}$	Samples [n]	Time [s]	Mem [GB]
Std. SSVM	16.41	7.42	69.53	48,181	544	**0.5**
Std. SSVM + Oversampling	15.39	**13.00**	72.27	305,474	3259	5.2
Weighted SSVM	**18.48**	9.13	**73.05**	48,181	**228**	**0.5**
Weighted flat SVM (LibSVM)	7.27	3.30	51.32	48,181	11887	1.0

4.3 Learning from Imbalanced Data

Here we propose an experimental validation to analyze the influence of the data imbalance on the described solutions. We start evaluating the performance of a standard SSVM with and without oversampling. We also evaluate the proposed approach, described in Sect. 3.4, named Weighted SSVM. For the sake of comparison, we also report the performance of a weighted flat multi-class SVM. Note that, to ensure a proper evaluation, we oversample the test data and draw an equal number (847) of instances for each class, while maintaining the overall total number of test samples (11854). When an SSVM is used, we report the performance obtained using our novel WHD loss function.

Table 3 shows the main results. All times reported are on a 2.3 GHz i7 processor. We observe that the proposed Weighted SSVM obtains the best results in terms of the H-F1 score and precision. This has been accomplished by increasing both the precision and the recall by ~ 2 % compared to the Std. SSVM. Our Weighted SSVM also finishes the training in almost half the time of the Std. SSVM. The SSVM with oversampling does not outperform our Weighted SVM even though it uses 5× as much training data, resulting in a ten-fold increase in both processing time and memory usage compared to the proposed Weighted SSVM. Our weighted approach is clearly the best approach for dealing with imbalance in the training data.

5 Conclusion

A novel approach to seafloor imagery taxonomic categorization has been developed. We have evaluated the incorporation of the taxonomy inside the loss function of an SSVM formulation. We have also introduced the novel WHD loss function, whose results show a significantly better performance compared to the state-of-the-art on a new challenging underwater data set. We have further demonstrated that it is possible to follow a weighting strategy in the SSVM optimization to alleviate imbalance in the training data set.

Acknowledgements. The authors acknowledge the Australian National Research Program (NERP) Marine Biodiversity Hub for the taxonomical labeling and the Australian Centre for Field Robotics for gathering the image data.

References

1. Williams, S., Pizarro, O., Jakuba, M., Johnson, C., Barrett, N., Babcock, R., Kendrick, G., Steinberg, P., Heyward, A., Doherty, P., et al.: Monitoring of benthic reference sites: using an autonomous underwater vehicle. IEEE Robot. Autom. Mag. **19**(1), 73–84 (2012)
2. Johnson-Roberson, M., Kumar, S., Williams, S.: Segmentation and classification of coral for oceanographic surveys: a semi-supervised machine learning approach. In: IEEE OCEANS, pp. 1–6 (2006)
3. Beijbom, O., Edmunds, P.J., Kline, D., Mitchell, B., Kriegman, D.: Automated annotation of coral reef survey images. In: IEEE CVPR, pp. 1170–1177 (2012)
4. Bewley, M., Douillard, B., Nourani-Vatani, N., Friedman, A., Pizarro, O., Williams, S.: Automated species detection: an experimental approach to kelp detection from sea-floor AUV images. In: ACRA (2012)
5. Tsochantaridis, I., Hofmann, T., Joachims, T., Altun, Y.: Support vector machine learning for interdependent and structured output spaces. In: ICML, p. 104 (2004)
6. Bewley, M., Nourani-Vatani, N., Rao, D., Douillard, B., Pizarro, O., Williams, S.: Hierarchical classification in AUV imagery. In: Mejias, L., Corke, P., Roberts, J. (eds.) Field and Service Robotics. Springer, Switzerland (2015)
7. Smith, D., Dunbabin, M.: Automated counting of the northern pacific sea star in the derwent using shape recognition. In: DICTA, pp. 500–507, September 2007
8. Soriano, M., Marcos, S., Saloma, C., Quibilan, M., Alino, P.: Image classification of coral reef components from underwater color video. In: MTS/IEEE Conference and Exhibition OCEANS, pp. 1008–1013 (2001)
9. Cai, L., Hofmann, T.: Hierarchical document categorization with support vector machines. In: ACM CIKM, pp. 78–87 (2004)
10. Tuia, D., Muñoz-Marí, J., Kanevski, M., Camps-Valls, G.: Structured output SVM for remote sensing image classification. J. Signal Process. Syst. **65**(3), 301–310 (2011)
11. Binder, A., Müller, K., Kawanabe, M.: On taxonomies for multi-class image categorization. Int. J. Comput. Vision (IJCV) **99**, 281–301 (2012)
12. Joachims, T.: Multi-class support vector machine (2008). http://www.cs.cornell.edu/people/tj/svm_light/svm_multiclass.html

13. Wang, K., Zhou, S., Liew, S.: Building hierarchical classifiers using class proximity. In: International Conference on Very Large Data Bases (VLDB) (1999)
14. Veropoulos, K., Campbell, C., Cristianini, N.: Controlling the sensitivity of support vector machines. In: IJCAI, vol. 1999, pp. 55–60 (1999)
15. Japkowicz, N., Stephen, S.: The class imbalance problem: a systematic study. Intell. Data Anal. **6**(5), 429–449 (2002)
16. Ahonen, T., Matas, J., He, C., Pietikäinen, M.: Rotation invariant image description with local binary pattern histogram fourier features. In: Salberg, A.-B., Hardeberg, J.Y., Jenssen, R. (eds.) SCIA 2009. LNCS, vol. 5575, pp. 61–70. Springer, Heidelberg (2009)
17. Chang, C., Lin, C.: LIBSVM: a library for support vector machines. ACM Trans. Intell. Syst. Technol. **2**, 27:1–27:27 (2011)

Escaping Path Approach with Extended Neighborhood for Speckle Noise Reduction

Marek Szczepanski[✉], Krystian Radlak, and Adam Popowicz

Faculty of Automatic Control, Electronics and Computer Science,
Silesian University of Technology, Akademicka 16, 44-100 Gliwice, Poland
Marek.Szczepanski@polsl.pl

Abstract. This paper presents a new approach to multiplicative noise removal in ultrasound images. The proposed algorithm utilizes concept of digital paths created on the image grid presented in [14] adapted to the needs of multiplicative noise reduction. Digital Paths are used to determine the filter weights taking into account the structures present in the image. Method of creating path is crucial for the efficiency and speed of the filter. The new approach uses special type of digital paths based on so called Escaping Path Model created with extended neighborhood system. The experiments confirmed that the proposed algorithm achieves a comparable results with the existing state of the art denoising schemes in suppressing multiplicative noise in ultrasound images.

Keywords: Image filtering · Multiplicative noise · Digital paths · Ultrasound imaging · Extended neighborhood

1 Introduction

Ultrasound imaging is widespread in diagnosing ailments or assessing the state of the soft tissues in organs. The ultrasound imaging is non invasive, relatively inexpensive and is performed in real time. However, the images are degraded by speckle noise [9], which affects their quality reducing the contrast and concealing the details. Consequently, a proper interpretation of the results and a correct diagnosis can be difficult. Therefore, image denoising and enhancement is strongly needed and many approaches has been proposed. A survey on speckle noise reduction methods can be found in [10].

Speckle noise is a kind of multiplicative distortion appearing due to signal multiplication by a noise process, and is quite difficult to remove [1]. This kind of noise is common to laser, sonar and synthetic aperture radar (SAR) imagery and depends on the structure of imaged tissue and various imaging parameters [6]. According to the literature, speckle noise can be approximated by the Gamma distribution [15], the Rayleigh distribution [17] or the Fisher-Tippett distribution [13]. A simplified speckle noise model can be defined as

$$u(x) = v(x) + v(x)^\gamma \cdot \eta(x; 0, \sigma^2), \tag{1}$$

© Springer International Publishing Switzerland 2015
R. Paredes et al. (Eds.): IbPRIA 2015, LNCS 9117, pp. 184–191, 2015.
DOI: 10.1007/978-3-319-19390-8_21

where $u(x)$ is the observed image, $v(x)$ is the original image and $\eta(x) \sim N(0, \sigma^2)$ is a zero-mean Gaussian noise. The factor γ depends on the kind of an ultrasound device and additional processing related to image formation. In [11] Loupas et al. have shown that the model described by Eq. (1) with $\gamma = 0.5$ fits better to data than the simple multiplicative model with $\gamma = 1$ or the Rayleigh model. This model has been employed in our work, since it has been used successfully in many studies [3,6,8].

The main aim of this research is to create efficient technique capable of multiplicative noise suppression and compare it to existing state of the art denoising schemes. The proposed approach uses the concept of digital paths exploring spatial pixel neighborhood to determine the filter weights. The original algorithm presented in [14] perfectly removes Gaussian noise and after some modifications impulsive noise, but cannot cope with multiplicative interferences. The new approach uses special type of digital paths so called *Escaping Path* and modified path length calculation based on topological as well as gray-scale distances. Additionally to increase filter strength, modified neighborhood relation domain will be used. The new approach is inspired by extended von Neumann neighborhood [12] originally defined for cellular automata.

This work is organized as follows. The next Section provides a short description of digital paths approach and introduced modification. In Sect. 3 we perform a comparison with existing state of the art solutions and finally we conclude the paper.

2 Escaping Path Filter (EPF)

General form of the fuzzy adaptive filters proposed in this work is defined as weighted average of inputs inside the spatial window W that are in neighborhood relation $\mathcal{N}$ with center pixel x:

$$\hat{v}(x) = \sum_{x_i \in \mathcal{N}(x)} w_i u(x_i) = \frac{\sum_{x_i \in \mathcal{N}(x)} \mu(x, x_i) u(x_i)}{\sum_{x_i \in \mathcal{N}(x)} \mu(x, x_i)}, \tag{2}$$

where $u(x_i)$ and $\hat{v}(x)$ denote filter inputs and output respectively, μ_i is a similarity function calculated over digital paths originating from window center x, associated with point x_i and bounded by the processing window W.

Let us to define a digital path $P = \{p_i\}_{i=0}^{n}$ as a sequence of neighboring points $(p_i, p_{i+1}) \in \mathcal{N}$. The length $L(P)$ of the digital path $P \{p_i\}_{i=0}^{n}$ is simply $\sum_{i=1}^{n} \rho(p_0, p_{i+1})$, where ρ denotes the distance between two adjacent points of the path.

So we can define the connection cost over digital path $P = \{p_i\}_{i=0}^{n}$ as a measure of dissimilarity between image pixels $p_0, p_1, \ldots, p_n$ forming a specific path linking p_0 and p_n [4,16].

The connection cost between adjacent points of digital paths $\Lambda^{W,1}$ can be represented as a combination of topological distance and the difference of gray levels:

$$\Lambda^{W,1}\{p_i, p_{i+1}\} = |F(p_{i+1}) - F(p_i)| \cdot \rho^W(p_i, p_{i+1}), \tag{3}$$

where $\rho^W(p_{i-1}, p_i)$ is the topological length of a path segment. Thus, the connection cost for the entire path $\Lambda^{W,n}$ can be calculated as the sum of its consecutive segments:

$$\Lambda^{W,n}\{p_0, p_1, p_2, \ldots, p_n\} = \sum_{i=0}^{n-1}\left[|F(p_{i+1}) - F(p_i)| \cdot \rho^W(p_i, p_{i+1})\right]. \tag{4}$$

Let us now define a similarity function μ_i, analogous to a membership function used in fuzzy systems, between the center point $x = p_0$ and its ith neighbor $x_i = p_1$ crossed by the digital path connecting pixel p_0, its neighbor p_1 with all possible points p_n which can be reached in n steps from p_0.

The aim of taking into account the points p_2, ..., p_n when calculating the similarity between p_0 and p_1 is to explore not only the direct neighborhood of p_0 but also to use the information on the local image structure. This can be done by acquiring the information on the local image features investigating the connection costs of digital paths originating at p_0, passing p_1 and then visiting successive points, till the path reaches length n. This approach will be further denoted as DPA$_{1st}$ to distinguish it from two-dimensional DPA$_{last}$ algorithm proposed in the work [14]. In this case the similarity function takes the form:

$$\mu^{W,n}(x, x_i) = \mu^{W,n}(p_0, p_1) = \sum_{m=1}^{\omega} \exp\left[-\beta \cdot \Lambda^{W,n}\{p_0, p_1, p_2^m, \ldots, p_n^m\}\right], \tag{5}$$

where ω denotes number of all possible paths $P = \{p_0, p_1, p_2^m, \ldots, p_n^m\}$ with n steps, originating at $x = p_0$, crossing $x_i = p_1$ and totally included in processing window W, m is the number of a specific path and β is the filter design parameter.

Next step is a normalization of the similarity function - normalized similarity function can be be defined as follows:

$$\psi^{W,n}(x, x_i) = \psi^{W,n}(p_0, p_1) = \frac{\mu^{W,n}(x, x_i)}{\sum_{p_j \in \mathcal{N}(x)} \mu^{W,n}(x, x_j)}. \tag{6}$$

Assuming that the pixel $x = p_0$ is the pixel under consideration, with $u(x_i)$ representing the pixel $x_i = p_1$, the filter output $\hat{v}(x)$ is given as follows:

$$\hat{v}(x) = \sum_{x_i \in \mathcal{N}(x)} \psi^{W,n}(x, x_i) \cdot u(x_i). \tag{7}$$

In the case of highly distorted images we have two possibilities to increase the efficiency of the filter, increase the area of its operation through the use of longer paths, or apply it iteratively. The second method is faster and more efficient, and

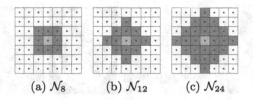

(a) $\mathcal{N}_8$ (b) $\mathcal{N}_{12}$ (c) $\mathcal{N}_{24}$

Fig. 1. Neigborhood systems used in our approach: (a) Standard 8 neighborhood, (b) and (c) extended von Neuman Neigborhood of range 2 and 3.

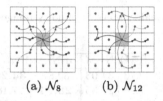

(a) $\mathcal{N}_8$ (b) $\mathcal{N}_{12}$

Fig. 2. Escaping Path Model illustration for path with two steps and 5×5 processing window with different neighborhood systems

in addition we can change the filter strength control parameter β in subsequent iterations. In particular, β could be modified as follows:

$$\beta(\kappa) = \beta(\kappa - 1) \cdot \alpha, \quad \kappa = 1, \ldots, m. \tag{8}$$

The performance of the new filters strongly depends on the type of digital paths selected. Different models of paths result to application-specific filters. For most of the image filtering tasks best results are obtained for the *Self Avoiding Path* model (SAP), but our experiments show that in the case of ultrasound images best results are obtained for so called *Escaping Path Model* (EPM), so the new filter will be called *Escaping Path Filter* (EPF). In this model the topological distance from the starting point in the following steps must be increased.

This approach using the 8 neighborhood relationship is highly effective, but for heavily distorted images may not be sufficient. Thus, in the new filter we introduced extended von Neumann neighborhood [12] originally defined for cellular automata. Different neighborhood systems used in our approach are presented in Fig. 1. Figure 2 shows selected escaping paths with two steps in 5×5 processing window created with different neighborhood systems.

3   Experiments

The standard test images *Goldhill*, *Boat* and artificially generated *Phantom* were chosen to compare the standard synthetic tests. Additionally more realistic model of USG introduced in work [7] was used for modeling *Fetus* image with artifacts based on real acquisition process. Virtually noise free reference image was obtained by averaging of 500 simulated images (see Fig. 3). The evaluation of the proposed filter performance was made using a set of state of the art

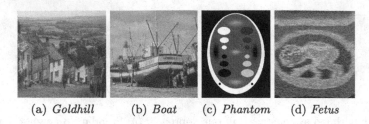

(a) *Goldhill*   (b) *Boat*   (c) *Phantom*   (d) *Fetus*

Fig. 3. Test images.

Table 1. Comparison of the quality metrics of noisy images restored by the new filter and competitive techniques.

Image		Noise σ	WF	SRAD	NLM	OBNLM	PNLM	PPBF	DPA$_{last}$	EPF
GOLDHILL		0.2	30.76	30.73	34.03	30.87	**34.20**	32.80	32.83	33.63
		0.4	27.09	27.26	27.35	**28.24**	27.18	27.11	27.77	27.98
		0.6	22.24	23.69	16.49	24.43	22.75	18.56	24.96	**25.24**
BOAT		0.2	31.01	32.06	**35.40**	32.61	34.52	32.64	32.61	33.48
	PSNR	0.4	26.69	26.96	27.68	**28.06**	27.34	26.91	27.10	27.49
		0.6	21.90	23.98	15.54	24.13	22.13	20.00	24.20	**24.21**
PHANTOM		0.2	37.36	42.52	43.07	38.64	42.21	37.01	44.98	**48.57**
		0.4	28.57	30.82	30.31	30.34	30.43	29.50	34.65	**37.60**
		0.6	21.19	24.14	20.15	23.76	23.00	21.15	26.63	**27.32**
FETUS			24.73	18.62	27.27	18.78	26.77	25.93	26.69	**27.34**
GOLDHILL		0.2	0.77	0.88	0.88	**0.90**	**0.90**	0.86	0.87	**0.90**
		0.4	0.64	0.67	0.65	0.69	0.64	0.69	0.69	**0.70**
		0.6	0.43	0.54	0.20	0.56	0.42	0.35	**0.59**	**0.59**
BOAT		0.2	0.84	0.92	**0.93**	**0.93**	0.92	0.88	0.89	0.90
	SSIM	0.4	0.67	0.72	0.69	0.69	0.67	**0.74**	0.73	**0.74**
		0.6	0.43	**0.65**	0.25	0.63	0.39	0.53	0.59	0.61
PHANTOM		0.2	0.98	0.99	0.99	**1.00**	0.98	0.95	0.99	**1.00**
		0.4	0.91	**0.96**	0.95	0.93	0.91	0.89	0.95	0.94
		0.6	0.67	0.89	0.56	0.79	0.80	0.68	0.88	**0.93**
FETUS			0.66	0.86	**0.90**	0.84	0.76	0.87	0.852	**0.90**

filtering designs capable of suppressing a speckle noise using source codes provided by authors of respective papers. Followed filters were used for comparison: Wiener Filter [10], Speckle Reducing Anisotropic Diffusion (SRAD) [20], Non-Local Means (NLM) [2], Optimized Bayesian Non-Local Means (OBNLM) [3], Probabilistic Non-Local Means (PNLM) [19], Probabilistic Patch-Based Weights (PPBW) [5] and Digital Paths Approach (DPA$_{last}$) [14].

Filter parameters are optimized in accordance with the recommendations of their authors and tuned to achieve the best possible PSNR ratio. The control parameters α and β for the proposed technique were selected experimentally to obtain optimal results in terms of the PSNR quality coefficient. The images were contaminated by the multiplicative noise described in Eq. (1) with mean

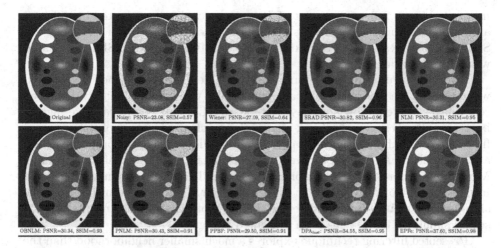

Fig. 4. Illustrative examples of the filtering efficiency of PHANTOM test image contaminated by multiplicative noise with $\sigma = 0.4$.

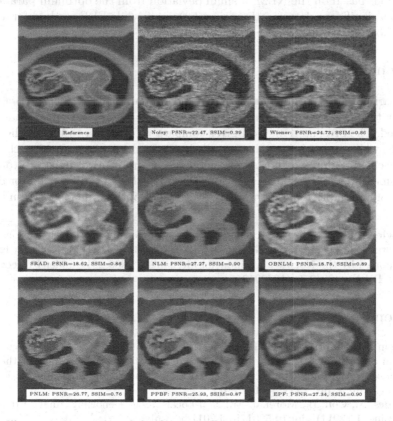

Fig. 5. Illustrative examples of the filtering efficiency evaluated on *Fetus* image simulated by the *Field II* application.

$\mu = 0$ and $\sigma = 0.2, 0.4, 0.6$ except of *Fetus* image which is corrupted by different artifacts during modeling process. The effectiveness is assessed in terms of Peak Signal to Noise Ratio (PSNR) and Structural SIMilarity index (SSIM) calculated with default parameters [18].

The numerical results are summarized in Table 1. Analyzing the PSNR index, we noticed that a new EPF approach particularly well cope with highly disturbed real images, while for low noise levels standard NLM and PNLM can give slightly better results. Tests on synthetic images show a clear advantage of the proposed filter. Figure 4 exhibits the restoration quality achieved using the proposed design and other filters. As can be observed, any of tested filters gives satisfactory results. Most filters suppressed speckle noise, but the small details were blurred. The most important part of work seems to be provided for the images resulting from the simulation of actual ultrasound device. The exemplary restoration results of ultrasound simulated images has been presented in Fig. 5.

Presented filtering technique explores a much smaller neighborhood than the non-local means based methods therefore this method is much faster and less aggressively blurs homogenous parts of the image. It should be noted that for all methods based on the NLM, a small deviation from the optimum parameters leads to a significant deterioration in performance while EPF method for a wide range of parameters gives acceptable results.

4   Conclusions

A comparison of algorithms based on the Non-Local Means concept and a novel filter for the suppression of multiplicative noise in ultrasound images has been presented. The presented method gives comparable or better results to the other methods, while maintaining substantially lower sensitivity to parameter changes. The presented technique shows very good results in terms of image restoration quality measures and visual inspection. However, there is still a need for development of an adaptive algorithm capable to yield optimal denoising results.

Acknowledgments. Marek Szczepanski was supported by the Polish National Science Center (NCN) under the Grant: DEC-2012/05/B/ST6/03428. Krystian Radlak was supported by the Norwegian Financial Mechanism 2009-2014 under Project Contract No. Pol-Nor/204256 /16/2013.

References

1. Achim, A., Bezerianos, A., Tsakalides, P.: Ultrasound image denoising via maximum a posteriori estimation of wavelet coefficients. In: Proceedings of the 23rd Annual International Conference of the IEEE Engineering in Medicine and Biology Society, vol. 3, pp. 2553–2556 (2001)
2. Buades, A., Coll, B., Morel, J.-M.: Non-Local Means Denoising. Image Processing On Line, **1** (2011). doi:10.5201/ipol.2011.bcm_nlm
3. Coupe, P., Hellier, P., Kervrann, C., Barillot, C.: Nonlocal means-based speckle filtering for ultrasound images. IEEE Trans. Image Proc. **18**(10), 2221–2229 (2009)

4. Cuisenaire, O.: Distance transformations: fast algorithms and applications to medical image processing. Ph.D. Thesis, Universite Catholique de Louvain, October 1999

5. Deledalle, C.-A., Denis, L., Tupin, F.: Iterative weighted maximum likelihood denoising with probabilistic patch-based weights. IEEE Trans. Image Proc. **18**(12), 2661–2672 (2009)

6. Hacini, M., Hachouf, F., Djemal, K.: A new speckle filtering method for ultrasound images based on a weighted multiplicative total variation. Sig. Process. **103**, 214–229 (2013)

7. Jensen, J.A., Svendsen, N.B.: Calculation of pressure fields from arbitrarily shaped, apodized, and excited ultrasound transducers. IEEE Trans. Ultrason. Ferroelectr. Freq. Control. **39**(2), 262–267 (1992)

8. Krissian, K., Kikinis, R., Westin, C. F., Vosburgh, K.: Speckle-constrained filtering of ultrasound images. In: IEEE Computer Society Conference on Computer Vision and Pattern Recognition, vol. 2, pp. 547–552 (2005)

9. Latifoglu, F.: A novel approach to speckle noise filtering based on artificial bee colony algorithm: An ultrasound image application. Comput. Methods Programs Biomed. **111**(3), 561–569 (2013)

10. Loizou, C.P., Theofanous, C., Pantziaris, M., Kasparis, T.: Despeckle filtering software toolbox for ultrasound imaging of the common carotid artery. Comput. Methods Programs Biomed. **114**(1), 109–124 (2014)

11. Loupas, T., McDicken, W.N., Allan, P.L.: An adaptive weighted median filter for speckle suppression in medical ultrasonic images. IEEE Trans. Circuits Syst. **36**(1), 129–135 (1989)

12. Von Neumann, J.: Theory of Self-Reproducing Automata. University of Illinois Press, Champaign (1966)

13. Slabaugh, G., Unal, G., Fang, T., Wels, M.: Ultrasound-specific segmentation via decorrelation and statistical region-based active contours. In: IEEE Computer Society Conference on Computer Vision and Pattern Recognition, vol. 1, pp. 45–53 (2006)

14. Szczepanski, M., Smolka, B., Plataniotis, K.N., Venetsanopoulos, A.N.: On the geodesic paths approach to color image filtering. Sig. Process. **83**(6), 1309–1342 (2003)

15. Tao, Z., Tagare, H.D., Beaty, J.D.: Evaluation of four probability distribution models for speckle in clinical cardiac ultrasound images. IEEE Trans. Med. Imaging **25**(11), 1483–1491 (2006)

16. Toivanen, P.J.: New geodesic distance transforms for gray scale images. Pattern Recogn. Lett. **17**, 437–450 (1996)

17. Wagner, R.F., Smith, S.W., Sandrik, J.M., Lopez, H.: Statistics of speckle in ultrasound b-scans. IEEE Trans. on Sonics and Ultrasonics **30**(3), 156–163 (1983)

18. Wang, Z., Bovik, A.C., Sheikh, H.R., Simoncelli, E.P.: Image quality assessment: from error visibility to structural similarity. IEEE Trans. on Image Proc. **13**(4), 600–612 (2004)

19. Yue, W., Tracey, B., Natarajan, P., Noonan, J.P.: Probabilistic non-local means. IEEE Signal Process. Lett. **20**(8), 763–766 (2013)

20. Yu, Y., Acton, S.T.: Speckle reducing anisotropic diffusion. IEEE Trans. on Image Proc. **11**(11), 1260–1270 (2002)

Adaptive Line Matching for Low-Textured Images

Roi Santos$^{(\boxtimes)}$, Xosé R. Fdez-Vidal, and Xosé M. Pardo

Centro de Investigación en Tecnoloxías da Información (CITIUS),
Universidade de Santiago de Compostela,
Campus Vida S/n, 15782 Santiago de Compostela, Spain
{roi.santos,xose.vidal,xose.pardo}@usc.es

Abstract. A novel approach for line matching is proposed, aimed at achieving good performance with low-textured scenes, under uncontrolled illumination conditions. Line matching is performed by an iterative process that uses structural information collected through the use of different line neighbourhoods, making the set of matched lines grows robustly at each iteration. Results show that this approach is suitable to deal with low-textured scenes, and also robust under a wide variety of image transformations.

Keywords: Line matching · Low texture images · Man-made environments

1 Introduction

One of the key steps to obtain three-dimensional representation of points from multiple images is to identify homologous features among pairs of images, such as points or lines, across different views. In recent years several feature-based methods, such as Moment Invariants [1], Steerable Filters [2], Differential Invariants [3] or SIFT [4], have been proven useful for achieving reliable correspondences among images. However, these methods have difficulties when dealing with low-textured objects and homogeneous surfaces, which are typical in man-made environments. Therefore, it is essential to use line segments as matching features due to their abundance on man-made objects, and also because they bring us greater structural information. However, automatic line matching presents many difficulties such as inaccurate locations of line segment endpoints, object occlusions leading to missing line counterparts, or the fragmentation of lines, often causing the loss of topological connections among line segments.

In Wang et al. [5], line segments are grouped based on the line spatial proximity and relative saliency, and then these groups are matched by using the geometric configuration of their segments, and appearance information. This strategy is useful to deal with large viewpoint changes, and non-planar scenes.

This paper presents a novel approach for line matching aimed at achieving good performance with low-textured image pairs, using information from the lines local appearance and their geometric properties. It also takes into account

R. Paredes et al. (Eds.): IbPRIA 2015, LNCS 9117, pp. 192–199, 2015.
DOI: 10.1007/978-3-319-19390-8_22

the geometrical arrangement among several kinds of neighbouring segments, which has been shown to be profitable to deal with low-textured scenes, and robust for a wide variety of image transformations.

2 Line Matching

We used the line detection approach described in [6], that is robust to different illumination conditions, and gives good location and low fragmentation of straight contours in images. Once a set of line segments is extracted for each view, they are introduced into the line matching module (Fig. 1).

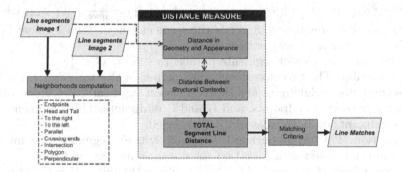

Fig. 1. Flowchart for the iterative matching process.

Each line matching iteration is executed in four steps. Firstly, the distance is computed between each pair of line segments by taking into account their local structure (neighbouring lines), their geometric properties and also their local appearance. After that, the strongest correspondences are added to the set of matched lines on the basis of a matching criterion. Thirdly, the weakest correspondences are broken, for the sake of robustness. The loop ends when all the matched lines remain paired with the same partner for at least T iterations. Results are obtained with $T = 5$, which is found to be a balanced choice between the stability of line matches and time consumption.

A pair of segments (i, j) is matched based on a NNDR (nearest/next distance ratio) criterion. Results were obtained with a distance ratio $\lambda = 1.5$ for the first stage of the algorithm, and $\lambda = 1.2$ for the second one. Besides, for the first iteration, only the $N = 10$ lines with the best distance ratio are matched, even without satisfying the thresholds, ensuring that the algorithm starts with an initial seed of a suitable size.

The weakest correspondences are selected by means of an affine-regular voting method, in which each pair of matched lines votes to the other pairs. A matched pair (u, v) gives a positive vote $(p_i+ = 1)$ to the pair (i, j) when the line pairs $P^{(i)} = \{i, u\}$ and $P^{(j)} = \{j, v\}$ are related by a local affine transformation $(c(P^{(i)}, P^{(j)}) < c_{TH})$, and gives a null vote otherwise. At end of each loop iteration, the match of any segment i with a low number of votes $(\sum_{N-1} p_i < 0.4N)$ is broken in order to remove the most dubious matches.

For each line i, several neighbourhoods $\{N_k^{(i)}, k = 1 \dots 9\}$ are considered in order to make the method robust to differences in occlusions, perspective, fragmentation of lines and misdetections between views, at a low cost. They are also useful in situations where multiple lines have an identical local structure (repetitive patterns).

1. Endpoints: This neighbourhood is formed by the three closest segments to i based on the minimum distance between endpoints.
2. Head and tail: The two neighbours are the closest segments to each endpoint of the line i.
3. On one side: Neighbourhood is formed by three segments i_1, i_2 and i_3. The segment i_1 is the closest to i that has their endpoints on the same side of i, fulfilling $d_\theta(i, i_1) = \frac{2}{\pi} \cdot |(\theta_i - \theta_{i_1})| < \frac{1}{4}$ and $d_l(i, i_1) = \frac{|l_i - l_{i_1}|}{\max(l_i, l_{i_1})} < \frac{1}{2}$, where θ is the segment orientation, and l is the segment length. The segment i_2 (i_3) is chosen in the same way with respect to i_1 (i_2).
4. Parallel: The two closest segments parallel to i: $d_\theta(i, i_k) < \frac{1}{4}$.
5. Perpendicular: The two closest segments perpendicular to i: $d_\theta(i, i_k) > \frac{3}{4}$.
6. Crossing ends: Neighbours are the two closest segments to i based on the distance between i endpoints, and i_1 and i_2 midpoints. Those segments that have endpoints on both sides of i are preferred.
7. Intersection: This neighbourhood is formed by three segments that intersect i and are the closest to it based on the distance between midpoints.
8. Polygon: Chain of segments, $\{i_1, \dots, i_n\}$, where the tail of i_1 is the closest to the head of i, the tail of i_2 is the closest to the head of i_1, and so on. The neighbourhood is only considered if the tail of i is the closest to the head of i_n ($n < 4$), closed chain, and it is the same when exchanging head/tail.

Distance in Geometry and Appearance Features. Line segment geometry is described by properties such as orientation, length, and location of endpoints, while appearance is described by samples and average of gray level intensity on both sides of the segment, and average phase congruency. A vector $\boldsymbol{d} = (d_{cr}, d_{cl}, d_{PC}, d_\rho, d_\theta, d_l, d_x, d_y)$ is built for each pair of segments to be compared. Its components are in $[0, 1]$, and all of them vanish if a segment is compared with itself. The components of the vector $\boldsymbol{d}(i, j)$ are:

1. Contrast, $d_{cr}(i, j) = (I_i^r - I_j^r)/\max(I_i^r, I_j^r)$, where I^r is the ratio of the average intensity on the right side of the segment to the average intensity of the image. The component d_{cl} is defined analogously on the left side.
2. Normalized difference in phase congruency, $d_{PC}(i, j) = \frac{|PC_i - PC_j|}{\max(PC_i, PC_j)}$, where PC is the phase congruency averages of the pixels of a segment.
3. Intensity correlation, $d_\rho(i, j) = 1 - \rho^2(R_i, R_j)$. Where R is a set of gray levels of pixels sampled around a segment, and $\rho(R_i, R_j)$ is the correlation coefficient between the samples around the two segments. It is invariant to global illumination changes.
4. Angular distance, $d_\theta(i, j) = \frac{2}{\pi} \cdot |(\theta_i - \theta_j)|$, where $\theta \in [-\frac{\pi}{2}, \frac{\pi}{2}]$ is segment orientation.

5. Difference in length: $d_1(i,j) = \frac{|l_i - l_j|}{\max(l_i, l_j)}$.

6. Difference between midpoints x-coordinates, $d_x(i,j) = |m_x^i - m_x^j| / \max(m_x^i, m_x^j)$. Analogously for $d_y(i,j)$.

The distance measure is computed as: $z(i,j) = \sum_{k=1}^{8} w_k \cdot d_k(i,j)$, where d_k are the components of d, and w_k are normalized weights. These weights are adaptively computed at the beginning of the algorithm for each pair of views by using a Principal Component Analysis (PCA).

To compute the weights w_k, components of d are calculated for each possible line pairing to give a matrix $X^{P \times 8}$:

$$X = [d_{cl}(i_n, j_m) \,|\, d_{cr}(i_n, j_m) \,|\, d_{PC}(i_n, j_m) \,|\, \ldots \,|\, d_y(i_n, j_m)], \tag{1}$$

where (i_n, j_m) represents all possible segment pairs between views ($n = 1 \cdots N$, $m = 1 \cdots M$ and $P = N \cdot M$)

Then, PCA is performed over X, obtaining a linear transformation that let us write each element of the data matrix $d_k^{(i)}$ in the new coordinate system as a linear combination of the principal components pc^t.

$$d_k^{(i)} = \sum_{t=1}^{8} \alpha_{kt}^{(i)} \cdot pc_k^t, \sum_t (\alpha_{kt}^{(i)})^2 = 1, k = 1 \ldots 8 \tag{2}$$

Since matching is made between all possible line pairs, most of them will be wrong, so most of the components of d should have a value close to 1, the highest dissimilarity. Those d_k that contribute less to the variability of the data are able to discern that almost all matches are wrong, consequently weights w_k are assigned as follows:

$$w_k = \frac{1}{\sum_{t=1}^{8} \alpha_{kt}^2 \cdot S_t}, k = 1 \ldots 8 \tag{3}$$

where S_t is the total percentage of variance associated with pc_t^1. Thus, vector components whose projection on the pc^1-direction (the direction of maximum variance) are large will be assigned to small weights.

Distances between geometric and appearance features of matched lines are used to estimate whether the images are related by a global transformation in illumination or affine geometry.

Distance Between Structural Contexts. The distance between structural contexts resembles the likelihood that the neighbourhoods of two lines are the same under a local affine transformation. To obtain the set of affine invariants, the convex hull of each line neighbourhood is constructed as the smallest convex polygon containing all the vertices of the neighbours and the line segment itself (Fig. 2). Then, by making use of the area invariance property associated with the affine transformation, a set of convex hull affine invariants are constructed by taking ratios between the areas of the polygons formed by connecting consecutive vertices on the convex hull [7]. Thus, for a line i with a neighbourhood

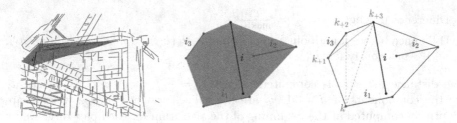

Fig. 2. From left to right: Convex hull (shaded region) of a line neighbourhood for a real image. Convex hull of a line i neighbourhood $N^{(i)} = \{i_1, i_2, i_3\}$. Triangles $\{k, k_{+1}, k_{+2}\}$, $\{k_{+1}, k_{+2}, k_{+3}\}$, $\{k_{+2}, k_{+3}, k\}$, $\{k_{+3}, k, k_{+1}\}$ and quadrangle $\{k, k_{+1}, k_{+2}, k_{+3}\}$ involved in the construction of vector Ω_k^N.

$N^{(i)} = \{i_1, i_2, \ldots, i_n\}$, the set of affine invariants $\Omega^{N^{(i)}} = \{\Omega_1^{N^{(i)}}, \ldots, \Omega_n^{N^{(i)}}\}$, stores the ratios of the areas of every possible triangle in the quadrangle to the area of the quadrangle itself, see Fig. 2. To establish the correspondence between two neighbourhoods $N^{(i)}$ and $N^{(j)}$, the following measure is used:

$$c(N^{(i)}, N^{(j)}) = \min_{l=1,\ldots,n} \min_{k=1,\ldots,m} \|\Omega_l^{N^{(i)}} - \Omega_k^{N^{(j)}}\|^2, \tag{4}$$

where $\Omega^{N^{(i)}}$ and $\Omega^{N^{(j)}}$ are the set of the affine invariants of the two neighbourhoods, n and m are the number of vertices of their convex hulls respectively. $c(N^{(i)}, N^{(j)})$ vanishes for two neighbourhoods whose convex hulls are affine-regular polygons. A threshold $c_{TH} = 0.02$ is set to decide whether the transformation is affine or not.

The final neighbourhood measure $Z(N^{(i)}, N^{(j)})$ for two neighbourhoods $N^{(i)} = \{i_1, \ldots, i_N\}$ and $N^{(j)} = \{j_1, \ldots, j_P\}$, is computed as:

$$Z(N^{(i)}, N^{(j)}) = \begin{cases} 1 & , c(N^{(i)}, N^{(j)}) > c_{TH} \quad \| \quad N \neq P \\ \frac{1}{(N+1)\tau} \sqrt{z^2(i,j) + \min_{\sigma \in S_N} \sum_{k=1}^{N} z\prime^2 \left(i_k, j_{\sigma(k)}\right)}, & \text{otherwise} \end{cases} \tag{5}$$

where $z(\cdot, \cdot)$ is the measure defined previously, S_N is the symmetric group including all permutations among neighbouring segments, aimed to achieve invariance against the order they were taken. τ is the number of elapsed iterations when all the neighbourhoods $N^{(i)}$ and $N^{(j)}$ are matched, or $\tau = 1$ otherwise, and $z\prime(\cdot, \cdot)$ is a refinement of $z(\cdot, \cdot)$ defined as:

$$z\prime(i,j) = \begin{cases} 0 & , (i,j) \text{ match with each other} \\ 1 & , i \text{ matches } k \neq j, \text{ or vice versa} \\ z(i,j) & , \text{otherwise} \end{cases} \tag{6}$$

Total Segment Line Distance. The distance measure between two lines $D(i,j) \in [0,1]$ is given as:

$$D(i,j) = \frac{\sum_{k=1}^{9} W_k \cdot Z(N_k^{(i)}, N_k^{(j)})}{\sum_{k=1}^{9} W_k} \tag{7}$$

where $N_k^{(i)}$ and $N_k^{(j)}$ are the neighbourhoods of the matching lines and W_k a set of weights. These weights are initiated to 1 and are updated at each iteration by using PCA, in a similar way to that described in eq. (3) for weights w_k, but now we are interested on correct matches. Now, the data matrix is obtained from $Z(N_k^{(i)}, N_k^{(j)})$ for each neighbourhood of the matched lines. We should now get distances close to 0 for most of the neighbourhoods, and therefore we should assign a higher weight to those neighbourhoods that have so far contributed less to the variability of the data, since they are able to discern that almost all matches are correct. Consequently, weights W_k are updated as follows:

$$W_k = \frac{1}{1 - \sum_{t=1}^{9} \alpha_{kt}^2 \cdot S_t}, k = 1 \ldots 9 \tag{8}$$

where α_{kt} are a set of coefficients obtained directly from the analysis, and $S_t \in [0,1]$ is the total percentage of variance associated with each principal component.

3 Results

In this section, our approach is evaluated on man-made environments. We will test the ability of our line matching method to tackle scenes with low texture and repetitive patterns. Moreover, we want to test its accuracy under a wide range of differences in perspective between pairs of views. To tests the method a set of images taken from public databases [8,9] were used, see Fig. 3. These are images of buildings exhibiting repetitive patterns, small to moderate viewpoint changes, different scales, and occlusions.

Our method was compared with two state-of-the-art line matching approaches: Line Signatures (LS) [5], and the method proposed by Zhang et al. (AG) [10]. Both implementations were supplied by their authors.

In order to objectively compare the methods, both the number of correct matchings and precision are significant. Besides, line matchings between several fragmented or overlapping segments corresponding to the same perceived line are less significant than matches between the whole perceived line segments, since the latter provide a higher and non-redundant information. The measure that we use to compare line matching methods takes into account not only the ratio of correct to total matchings, but also the relative importance of each one. A lower weight is assigned to those matches that provide redundant or confusing information. For a perceived line l, with N_l extracted segments related to it, either because they are fragments of l, or because they are overlapping, the corresponding weight s_l is defined as:

$$s_l = \frac{1}{N_l} \sum_{n=1}^{N_l} c_n, \qquad c_n = \begin{cases} \frac{1}{N_l} & \text{, segment } i_n \text{ correctly matched} \\ 0 & \text{, otherwise} \end{cases} \tag{9}$$

where $\frac{1}{N_l}$ is the probability of correct detection of the perceived line, and $\sum_{n=1}^{N_l} c_n$ is the probability of the correct matching. Finally, the total matching measure S between two images is defined as the average of the scores s_l for

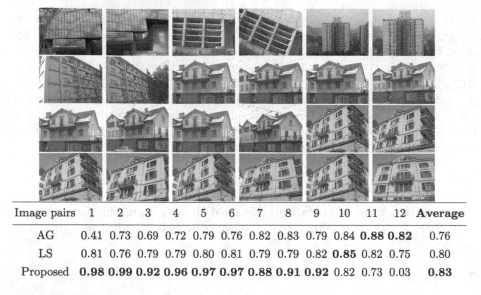

Image pairs	1	2	3	4	5	6	7	8	9	10	11	12	**Average**
AG	0.41	0.73	0.69	0.72	0.79	0.76	0.82	0.83	0.79	0.84	**0.88**	**0.82**	0.76
LS	0.81	0.76	0.79	0.79	0.80	0.81	0.79	0.79	0.82	**0.85**	0.82	0.75	0.80
Proposed	**0.98**	**0.99**	**0.92**	**0.96**	**0.97**	**0.97**	**0.88**	**0.91**	**0.92**	0.82	0.73	0.03	**0.83**

Fig. 3. Sample images 1 to 12 (ordered left to right and top to bottom) from public databases [8, 9]. Table with the matching scores obtained by the three methods.

Fig. 4. Pair of views number 5 and its matching results (left to right) for: our approach, AG and LS . Black lines are correct matches and red lines are wrong matches.

each one of the perceived lines: $S = \frac{1}{P} \sum_{l=1}^{P} s_l$, where P is the number of the matched lines.

As Fig. 3 shows, our method achieves the highest score for most of the image pairs. Note that a high score S means not only a high number of correct matches, but also a small number of redundant pairings between fragmented or overlapping lines. A visual comparison of these matching results is given in Fig. 4. This image pair shows two views of a building related by a moderate change of viewpoint. AG and LS return a large number of overlapping lines, giving more confusing results than the proposed method. The proposed method outperforms the rest for this image pair ($S_{proposed} = 0.97$, $S_{AG} = 0.79$, $S_{LS} = 0.80$), but also for those image pairs related by moderate changes of viewpoint. However, it can be seen in Fig. 3 that the performance of the proposed method decayed in pairs with large changes in perspective. In the last case, the fixed parameters used in all the tests were too strict to propagate a reliable matching between views. LS and AG are laxer in that sense at the expense of reliability.

4   Conclusions

This paper reports a novel method for line matching specifically designed to achieve good performance in man-made environments, characterised by low-textured objects, under uncontrolled illumination conditions. Our approach achieves a good performance over a wide range of images. It has been shown that it is suitable to deal with a variety of images of buildings covering a wide range of transformations, including scale, rotation, and viewpoint changes. It seems that the proposed iterative adaptive process and the use of different kinds of neighbourhoods to provide structural information around each line are suitable to obtain a high accuracy. The future work will focus on making the whole method more robust to strong differences in perspective between views.

References

1. Mindru, F., Tuytelaars, T., Van Gool, L., Moons, T.: Moment invariants for recognition under changing viewpoint and illumination. Comput. Vis. Image Underst. **94**, 3–27 (2004)
2. Freeman, W.T., Adelson, E.H.: The design and use of steerable filters. IEEE Trans. Pattern Anal. Mach. Intell. **13**, 891–906 (1991)
3. Montesinos, P., Gouet, V., Deriche, R.: Differential invariants for color images. In: Proceedings of ICPR 1998, Recognition, pp. 838–840 (1998)
4. Lowe, D.G.: Distinctive image features from scale-invariant keypoints. Int. J. Comput. Vis. **60**, 91–110 (2004)
5. Wang, L., Neumann, U., You, S.: Wide-baseline image matching using Line Signatures. In: Proceedings of ICCV 2009, pp. 1311–1318 (2009)
6. López, J., Fuciños, M., Fdez-Vidal, X.R., Pardo, X.M.: Detection and matching of lines for close-range photogrammetry. In: Sanches, J.M., Micó, L., Cardoso, J.S. (eds.) IbPRIA 2013. LNCS, vol. 7887, pp. 732–739. Springer, Heidelberg (2013)
7. Yang, Z., Cohen, S.: Image registration and object recognition using affine invariants and convex hulls. IEEE Trans. Image Process. **8**, 934–946 (1999)
8. Fan, B., Wu, F., Hu, Z.: Line matching leveraged by point correspondences. In: Proceedings of CVPR2010, pp. 390–397 (2010)
9. Shao, H., Svoboda, T., Van Gool, L.: HPAT indexing for fast object/scene recognition based on local appearance. In: Bakker, Erwin M., Lew, Michael, Huang, Thomas S., Sebe, Nicu, Zhou, Xiang Sean (eds.) CIVR 2003. LNCS, vol. 2728. Springer, Heidelberg (2003)
10. Zhang, D.-H., Liang, J., Guo, C.: Photogrammetric 3D measurement method applying to automobile panel. In: Proceedings of the 2nd International Conference on Computer and Automation Engineering (ICCAE), Singapore, February 2010, pp. 70–74

Unsupervised Approximation of Digital Planar Curves

Eusebio J. Aguilera-Aguilera$^{(\boxtimes)}$, Angel Carmona-Poyato,
Francisco J. Madrid-Cuevas, and Rafael Medina-Carnicer

Department of Computing and Numerical Analysis, Maimonides Institute for
Biomedical Research (IMIBIC), University of Cordoba, Cordoba, Spain
i22agage@uco.es
http://www.uco.es/

Abstract. In this work we face the problem of determining how many line segments are sufficient to represent a shape. In order to solve this problem we use a method that analyzes the length of the polygonal approximations. This method is used to determine the number of segments that a polygonal approximation needs to represent a shape.

Our proposal has been tested using a dataset of real shapes, obtaining good results. The present method has several advantages over previous solutions.

Keywords: Computational geometry · Digital planar curve · Polygonal approximation

1 Introduction

Polygonal approximations of digital planar curves are widely used in computer vision for a variety of applications like image analysis [1], shape analysis [2] and digital cartography [3].

The problem of obtaining a polygonal approximation can be formulated into two separated ways, depending on the objective function that we want to optimize:

- min-#: Minimize the number of line segments M that forms a polygonal approximation, such that, the distortion error does not excess a threshold ε_0.
- min-ε: Given a number of line segments M, minimize the distortion error associated to the polygonal approximation.

Before the polygonal approximation is obtained we must determine the most suitable value for the parameter M or ε_0, depending on the problem we are solving. Therefore, a method to obtain a convenient parameter value is needed.

This work has been developed with the support of the Research Projects called TIN2012-32952 and BROCA both financed by Science and Technology Ministry of Spain and FEDER.

R. Paredes et al. (Eds.): IbPRIA 2015, LNCS 9117, pp. 200–207, 2015.
DOI: 10.1007/978-3-319-19390-8_23

Several alternatives can be found in the literature. Gribov et al. [4] proposed to find a solution with the best balance between the number of segments M and the distortion (Integral Squared Error, ISE). This is done by creating an objective function, $C = \text{ISE} + \lambda \cdot M$, which includes the number of segments and the distortion value. This objective function is solved by using the Lagrange Multiplier method which minimizes the objective function.

Carmona-Poyato et al. [5] proposed a method that obtains the number of segments that represent a shape. This process is driven by an objective function which must to be minimized. This function, $F_n = \frac{\text{ISE}}{\text{CR}^n}$, was introduced by Marji et al. [6], and is used to compare different methods to obtain polygonal approximations. The method proposed by Carmona-Poyato et al. finds a threshold value for the objective function $F_2 = \frac{\text{ISE}}{\text{CR}^2}$, and uses this value as the number of segments M for the polygonal approximation.

Another proposal was introduced by Kolesnikov et al. [7]. The authors proposed a method to determine the number of segments that represent a shape. This is done by computing the distortion error for all possible values of M using an optimal method. Then, the authors obtains the value a for the parametrized Figure of Merit pFOM $= \text{ISE} \cdot M^a$, fitting a log-linear model. The method obtains the minimum value of the criterion pFOM $= \text{ISE} \cdot M^a$ and this value is the number of segments that represents a shape. The value of the parameter a depends on the selection of values M_1 and M_2 which define the lower and upper bounds of the error values used for fitting the model.

2   Our Proposal

Previous proposals appearing in the literature use some distortion measure related to the Integral Squared Error (ISE). This distortion value measures the euclidean distance between the approximated segments and the points of the original contour. Let's suppose that we approximate a curve S between points i and j using the segment $\overline{s_i s_j}$, then the distortion $\Delta(i,j)$ associated to this approximation can be defined as follows:

$$\Delta(i,j) = \sum_{k=i}^{j} d(s_k, \overline{s_i s_j})^2 \tag{1}$$

where $d(s_k, \overline{s_i s_j})$ is the euclidean distance from the point s_k of S to the segment $\overline{s_i s_j}$. The ISE associated to a polygonal approximation is the summation of the distortion $\Delta(i,j)$ associated to every segment $\overline{s_i s_j}$ which forms the polygonal approximation.

Therefore, the ISE distortion measure is similar to the difference between the discrete areas of the polygonal approximation and the original contour. The minimum number of points, that form a polygonal approximation with a value of distortion (ISE) of zero, are named as breakpoints in the literature. The number of breakpoints are usually high, because these points include the noise introduced in the contour. Using this measure for obtaining a good polygonal approximation, and therefore, select a suitable value for parameter M, has proven to be a hard task.

Previous works (see [5,7]) have analyzed the function that they used to select the number of segments that is suitable for approximate a digital planar curve. This function, F_2 for Carmona-Poyato et al. [5] and pFOM$_p$ for Kolesnikov et al. [7], presents a Region Of Interest (ROI), where the number of segments for a suitable polygonal approximation is located. This function and its ROI is shown in Fig. 1(a). The problem for this function is to find the ROI because is located in a local minimum. Furthermore, the function FOM is hard to model, therefore, we need to compute all values of the function, instead of computing some values and fitting using a model.

We propose to face this problem using a different approach. Instead of using the ISE distortion measure, we use length (perimeter) of the curve and the polygonal approximation. Using the length of the polygonal approximation as a distortion measure has some advantages. For example, we know the original value for the length of the curve we want to approximate.

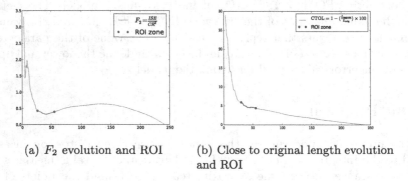

(a) F_2 evolution and ROI   (b) Close to original length evolution and ROI

Fig. 1. Evolution for functions F_2 and CTOL for contour named tinopener. The Regions Of Interest (ROI) are highlighted.

We define a distortion function which indicates how close is the polygonal approximation to the digital planar curve that is been approximated. We define the function Close To Original Length function as follows:

$$\text{CTOL} = (1 - \frac{L_{\text{approx}}}{L_{\text{orig}}}) \times 100 \qquad (2)$$

where L_{approx} is the length of the polygonal approximation and L_{orig} is the length of the original digital planar curve. This function is expected to decrease as new segments are added to the polygonal approximation. An example of this function is shown in Fig. 1(b). This figure also shows the same ROI that is highlighted in the F_2 function. The evolution of the CTOL function has a sharp fall and then the value decreases smoothly until the minimum value is reached. We follow the next procedure in order to obtain a value for the parameter M:

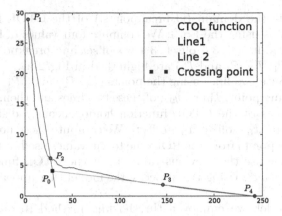

(a) Lines and original CTOL function for contour tinopener

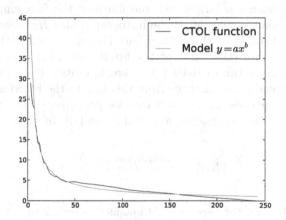

(b) Fitted model and original CTOL function for contour tinopener

Fig. 2. We compute the values of the CTOL function for the two lines. We also compute several values near of the crossing point of the two lines. Then, we use these values to estimate the CTOL function using the model $y = ax^b$.

1. The CTOL function can be fitted using a model in order to avoid the computation of the entire function. We have tried several models to fit this function, and the best model found is $y = ax^b$, because we have obtained the best coefficient of determination for this model. In order to fit the CTOL function with the model $y = ax^b$, we compute the values for several polygonal approximations with different values of M, using the method proposed by Perez and Vidal [8].

(a) We divide the domain ($[3, \text{breakpoints}]$) of the CTOL function in ten subdomains using the Eq. 3. We compute four values of function CTOL using the values 3, $3 + \text{offset}$, $3 + 6 \times \text{offset}$ and breakpoints. These four points (P_1, P_2, P_3 and P_4) are highlithed in Fig. 2(a).

(b) We compute two lines using the points (P_1, P_2) and (P_3, P_4). We obtain the crossing point, $P_0(x_0, y_0)$, of these two lines and then, compute three more values of the CTOL function homogeneously distributed in the subdomain $[x_0 - \text{offset}, x_0 + \text{offset}]$. We compute these points in order to add more points from the ROI zone to the values used to fit the function.

(c) Finally, we use the previous values to fit the CTOL function using the model $y = ax^b$. Using this process, the model that appear in Fig. 2(b) is obtained.

2. Using this model, we employ a thresholding method to obtain a suitable value of M for the polygonal approximation that faithfully represent the curve. Rosin [9] proposed a thresholding method for unimodal distributions. This method is based on finding a corner in the histogram plot. We first draw a straight line from the largest bin and finish at the first empty bin. Then, the threshold point is selected as the histogram index H_i that maximizes the perpendicular distance to the defined line. Therefore, we use the straight line from the largest bin (the value of the fitted model for $x = 3$) to the first empty bin (value of the model for $x = \text{breakpoints}$). Then we compute the maximum perpendicular distance from this line to the fitted model $y = ax^b$. This procedure give us a value of x that we propose as the optimal value of line segments for approximating a digital curve faithfully.

$$\text{offset} = \frac{(\text{breakpoints} - 3)}{10} \tag{3}$$

Table 1. Values for the parameter M obtained using the proposed method

Contour	M	Carmona's merit	Contour	M	Carmona's merit
Dino1	32	90.8644	Plane3	60	95.1343
Dino2	28	95.0222	Plane4	51	95.5333
Dino3	35	99.3780	Plane5	68	96.9134
Dino4	37	83.7387	Plane6	52	94.5385
Dino5	35	82.7739	Plane7	53	92.0972
Dino6	39	83.5618	Plane8	46	92.0660
Dino7	34	90.8322	Pliers	26	43.9221
Fish	40	94.6493	Rabbit	43	70.3785
Hand	33	88.3519	Screwdriver	19	99.3879
Hammer	14	99.8897	Spoon	12	89.6461
Plane1	53	93.3996	Tinopener	31	88.6354
Plane2	56	83.6908			

3   Experimental Results and Discussion

We have used this procedure to obtain a suitable polygonal approximation for a set contours commonly used in the literature. Then, the method proposed by Perez and Vidal [8] was used to obtain the optimal polygonal approximation using the value of the parameter M obtained by the proposed method. The values obtained using this procedure appear in Table 1. We have also used the proposed merit function by Carmona-Poyato et al. [10]. This merit measure, that is a derivation of the merit function proposed by Rosin [11], takes into account the number of segments M of the polygonal approximation.

The results obtained by the proposed unsupervised method provides adequate shape representation with a number of segments that faithfully represents

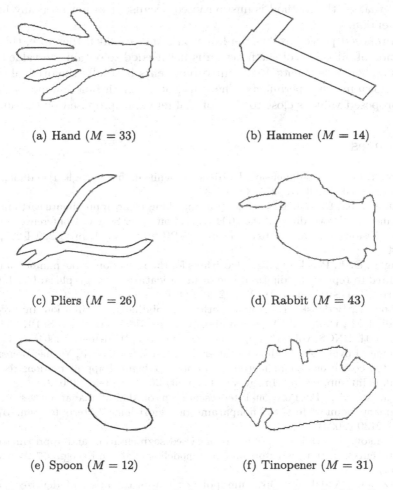

(a) Hand ($M = 33$)   (b) Hammer ($M = 14$)

(c) Pliers ($M = 26$)   (d) Rabbit ($M = 43$)

(e) Spoon ($M = 12$)   (f) Tinopener ($M = 31$)

Fig. 3. Polygonal approximation obtained using the optimal method by Perez-Vidal and the value of M supplied by the proposed method.

the original digital planar curve, as is shown in Table 1. The values of merit are high (mean value is 87.8484), and does not vary significantly (standard deviation is ±11.9180). The values of merit indicate that the number of segments selected represent faithfully the original shape. Some examples of the results obtained by the proposed method are shown in Fig. 3.

4   Conclusions

We have presented a method to select a suitable value for the parameter M for a polygonal approximation that represents faithfully the original digital planar curve. This procedure presents some advantages over previous proposals:

- The method does not need any parameter to be set in order to find the value of M, that is, the method is unsupervised because does not need any human intervention.
- The proposed procedure fits the function using a model, therefore, the computation of all values of the function is not needed to obtain the value of M.
- The number of segments M obtained represents faithfully the original shape, as is shown in the experiments. The values of the merit function indicates that the proposed value is close to the optimal reference proposed by the authors.

References

1. Lowe, D.G.: Three-dimensional object recognition from single two-dimensional images. Artif. Intell. **31**, 355–395 (1987)
2. Grauman, K., Darrell, T.: Fast contour matching using approximate earth mover's distance. In: Proceedings of the 2004 IEEE Computer Society Conference on Computer Vision and Pattern Recognition, CVPR 2004, vol. 1, pp. I-220–I-227, June 2004
3. Douglas, D.H., Peucker, T.K.: Algorithms for the reduction of the number of points required to represent a digitized line or its caricature. Cartographica: Int. J. Geog. Inform. Geovisualization **10**(2), 112–122 (1973)
4. Gribov, A., Bodansky, E.: A new method of polyline approximation. In: Fred, A., Caelli, T.M., Duin, R.P.W., Campilho, A.C., de Ridder, D. (eds.) SSPR 2004 and SPR 2004. LNCS, vol. 3138, pp. 504–511. Springer, Heidelberg (2004)
5. Carmona-Poyato, A., Medina-Carnicer, R., Muñoz Salinas, R., Yeguas-Bolivar, E.: On stop conditions about methods to obtain polygonal approximations relied on break point suppression. Image Vis. Comput. **30**(8), 513–523 (2012)
6. Marji, M., Siy, P.: Polygonal representation of digital planar curves through dominant point detectiona nonparametric algorithm. Pattern Recogn. **37**(11), 2113–2130 (2004)
7. Kolesnikov, A., Kauranne, T.: Unsupervised segmentation and approximation of digital curves with rate-distortion curve modeling. Pattern Recogn. **47**(2), 623–633 (2014)
8. Perez, J.C., Vidal, E.: Optimum polygonal approximation of digitized curves. Pattern Recogn. Lett. **15**(8), 743–750 (1994)
9. Rosin, P.L.: Unimodal thresholding. Pattern Recogn. 34, 2083–2096 (2001)

10. Carmona-Poyato, A., Medina-Carnicer, R., Madrid-Cuevas, F.J., Muñoz Salinas, R., Fernández-García, N.L.: A new measurement for assessing polygonal approximation of curves. Pattern Recogn. **44**(1), 45–54 (2011)

11. Rosin, P.: Techniques for assessing polygonal approximations of curves. IEEE Trans. Pattern Anal. Mach. Intell. **19**(6), 659–666 (1997)

On the Modification of Binarization Algorithms to Retain Grayscale Information for Handwritten Text Recognition

Mauricio Villegas[✉], Verónica Romero,
and Joan Andreu Sánchez

PRHLT, Universitat Politècnica de València,
Camí de Vera s/n, 46022 València, Spain
{mauvilsa,vromero,jandreu}@prhlt.upv.es

Abstract. The amount of digitized legacy documents has been rising over the last years due mainly to the increasing number of on-line digital libraries publishing this kind of documents. The vast majority of them remain waiting to be transcribed to provide historians and other researchers new ways of indexing, consulting and querying them. However, the performance accuracy of state-of-the-art Handwritten Text Recognition techniques decreases dramatically when they are applied to these historical documents. This is mainly due to the typical paper degradation problems. Therefore, robust pre-processing techniques is an important step for helping further recognition steps. This paper proposes to take existing binarization techniques, in order to retain their advantages, and modify them in such a way that some of the original grayscale information is preserved and be considered by the subsequent recognizer. Results are reported with the publicly available ESPOSALLES database.

1   Introduction

In the last years, large amounts of handwritten historical documents residing in libraries, museums, archives and other institutions have been digitized both to preserve them and to make them available to the general public. The automatic transcription of these historical documents is a challenging problem related to Document Image Analysis and Natural Language Processing. The advances in these fields have made possible in recent years to start exploring this problem.

Available OCR technologies are not applicable to historical documents, since characters can not be isolated automatically in these images. Therefore, holistic, segmentation-free text recognition techniques are required. This technology is generally referred to as *"off-line Handwritten Text Recognition"* (HTR) [6]. Several approaches have been proposed in the literature for HTR based on hidden Markov models (HMM) [6,12], recurrent neural networks [2], or hybrid systems using HMM and neural networks [9]. These systems have proven to be useful in a restricted setting for simple tasks. However, in the context of historical documents, their performance decreases dramatically, mainly due to paper degradation problems encountered in this kind of documents, such as presence of

R. Paredes et al. (Eds.): IbPRIA 2015, LNCS 9117, pp. 208–215, 2015.
DOI: 10.1007/978-3-319-19390-8_24

smear, significant background variation, uneven illumination, and dark spots, require specialized image-cleaning and enhancement algorithms. In addition, show-through and bleed-through problems can render the distinction between background and foreground difficult [1]. The combination of these and other problems make the pre-processing of these documents a difficult task.

In this paper we present a new technique to extract handwritten text from noisy backgrounds and improve the quality of the image, making it more legible. It is based on the well known Sauvola binarization method [10], with the main difference that it produces a grayscale image, a feature that we show that is more adequate for an HMM-based HTR system. The following section gives a brief overview of the complete HTR system considered in this paper. Then in Sect. 3, the proposed pre-processing method is described in detail. The corpus and the experimental results are presented in Sects. 4 and 5. Finally, conclusions are drawn in Sect. 6.

2   Handwritten Text Recognition

The HTR system used in this paper followed the classical architecture composed of three main modules: document image pre-processing, line image feature extraction and HMM and language model training/decoding [12].

In the pre-processing module, the pages are first divided into line images as explained in [8]. Given that it is quite common for handwritten documents to suffer from degradation problems it is necessary to first apply appropriate filtering methods to remove the background, noise, improve the quality of the image and to make the documents more legible. This part of the pre-processing is the main focus of this paper. Three different methods have been tested. The first one is the background estimation and subtraction method used in [8], the second one is the classical Sauvola thresholding [10], and the final one is the proposed method described in Sect. 3. In Sect. 5 we can see the different results obtained with the three methods. Continuing with the other pre-processing steps, after filtering, the skew and slant of each line are corrected. Finally the size is normalized separately for each line. A more detailed description of this process is found in [8]. Then, each pre-processed line image is represented as a sequence of feature vectors representing gray levels and gradients [12].

Given a handwritten sentence image represented by a feature vector sequence ($\mathbf{x}$), the HTR problem can now be formulated as the problem of finding a most likely word sequence, $\mathbf{w}$, i.e., $\mathbf{w} = \arg\max_{\mathbf{w}} P(\mathbf{w} \mid \mathbf{x})$. Using the Bayes' rule we can decompose this probability into two probabilities:

$$\hat{\mathbf{w}} = \arg\max_{\mathbf{w}} P(\mathbf{w} \mid \mathbf{x}) = \arg\max_{\mathbf{w}} P(\mathbf{x} \mid \mathbf{w})P(\mathbf{w}) \qquad (1)$$

$P(\mathbf{x} \mid \mathbf{w})$ is typically approximated by concatenated character models, usually HMMs [3], while $P(\mathbf{w})$ is approximated by a word language model, usually n-grams [3].

In this work, the characters were modeled by continuous density left-to-right HMMs with 6 states and 64 Gaussian mixture components per state. These models were estimated from training text images represented as feature vector sequences using the Baum-Welch algorithm. On the other hand, each lexical word was modeled by a stochastic finite-state automaton and the concatenation of words into text line sentences was modeled by bi-grams models, with Kneser-Ney back-off smoothing [5].

All these finite-state (character, word and sentence) models were *integrated* into a single *global* model on which a search process is performed for decoding the feature vectors sequence **x** into the words sequence **w**. This search is optimally carried out by using the Viterbi algorithm [3].

3   Proposed Approach

In the context of ancient texts, it can be observed that the writing strokes vary greatly in width and darkness, not only between different pages or lines, but also within single words. Because of this, when applying thresholding techniques, there is always a risk that parts of the strokes are lost due to the hard black or white decision. Since the thresholding methods cannot be expected to work perfectly, this problem could be addressed somehow in order to improve recognition results.

To this end, instead of thresholding, i.e., assigning pixels to be either black or white depending on whether a pixel value is below or above a certain threshold, we relax the method such that values in a band near the threshold are mapped to a transition between black and white. The intuition behind this is that instead of a thresholded image, our aim is to use the probability that each pixel is above or below the threshold. In general this probability can't be estimated explicitly since many popular thresholding techniques are not derived from probabilistic principles. Nevertheless, pixels for which the thresholding technique is very certain should be assigned values very close to or equal to black or white, thus retaining the strength of the technique in question, and only for the least certain pixels the resulting image will be assigned a shade of gray. Little can be assumed about the distribution of the pixels in these transitions, so we opt for a simple linear mapping function, symmetric with respect to the threshold value. The only parameter to decide is how wide is the transition from black to white, or in other words the slope of the line. For this, we can note that ink strokes tend to have similar transitions from ink color to background throughout a document which means that the amount of pixels in the transitions should be more or less constant for any region of text.

Due to the good performance of local based thresholding methods, in this work we have taken as reference Sauvola's method [10], and we have modified it following the previously mentioned idea. In Sauvola's, given an input image, for every pixel a threshold is computed based on the pixel's neighborhood. Like the original Niblack's method [7], Sauvola's method computes the threshold based on the neighborhood's mean and standard deviation values. The threshold $T(x, y)$

for a pixel position (x, y) is given as follows

$$T(x, y) = \mu(x, y) \left[1 + k \left(\frac{\sigma(x, y)}{R} - 1 \right) \right], \tag{2}$$

where $\mu(x, y)$ and $\sigma(x, y)$ are the neighborhood's mean and standard deviation, respectively, R is the dynamic range of the standard deviation, and k is a parameter that needs to be adjusted. The neighborhood is a square region of W pixels wide, centered at the corresponding pixel. This algorithm is very fast, since it is well known that the mean and standard deviation of any sub-window of an image can be efficiently computed by using integral images [11].

Now to obtain the function for the linear transition, the mapping should be symmetric with respect to the threshold value, which means that for an input value equal to the threshold T the output should be $\frac{G}{2}$ being G the maximum grayscale value. From this we can deduce that the y-axis intercept is $\frac{G}{2} - mT$, where m is the slope of the line. As mentioned before, the slope of the line m should be set such that the expected number of pixels that fall in the transition is constant. To achieve this approximately without requiring more computations, the same standard deviation σ of the Sauvola sub-window can be used by setting the transition to be a fixed factor s of σ, in which case the slope becomes $m = \frac{G}{2 \cdot s \cdot \sigma}$ (the 2 is just to simplify a bit the final equation). After a few manipulations it can be shown that the pixel values of the resulting output image $O(x, y)$ for a given input $I(x, y)$ should be assigned as follows:

$$O(x, y) = \text{limit\_gray} \left(\frac{G}{2} \left| \frac{I(x, y) - T(x, y)}{s \cdot \sigma} + 1 \right| \right). \tag{3}$$

The factor s must be adjusted empirically, although in our experimentation it was observed that a good value is $s = 1$. In Eq. 3, limit_gray has been introduced so that the function is defined for all input range, not just for the transition, and it is defined as $\text{limit\_gray}(v) = \{ 0 \text{ if } v < 0, G \text{ if } v > G, v \text{ otherwise} \}$.

Figure 1 compares the results obtained for a couple of examples. Note that the proposed technique produces a very similar result to the binarized, important so that it is useful for text recognition, but can be observed how grayscale information is preserved.

4   The ESPOSALLES Corpus

In this paper the experiments have been carried out on the publicly available ESPOSALLES[1] database [8]. Most specifically, we used the LICENSES part, which was compiled from a handwritten marriage license book conserved at the Archives of the Cathedral of Barcelona.

The book was written by only one person between the years 1617 and 1619 in old Catalan. It has 173 pages in total. Figure 2 presents an example page.

---

[1] The corpus is publicly available at: http://www.cvc.uab.es/5cofm/groundtruth.

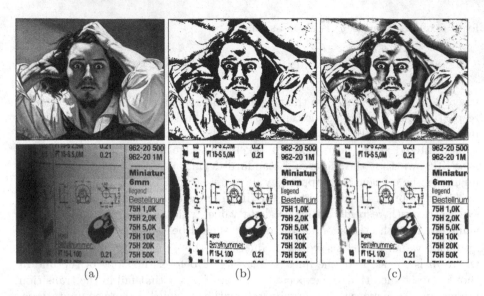

(a)   (b)   (c)

Fig. 1. Example images that illustrate the difference obtained by the Sauvola thresholding and the proposed technique. Columns: (a) original image, (b) binarized and (c) proposed. Top row: Gustave Courbet's portrait. Bottom row: example from [11].

Fig. 2. Example of an ESPOSALLES marriage license page.

These pages contain 5,447 lines grouped in 1,747 licenses. The whole manuscript was transcribed line by line by an expert palaeographer. The complete annotation of LICENSES contains around 60,000 running words from a lexicon of around 3,500 different words. More information can be found at [8].

5   Experimental Results

The objective of the experimentation was to compare the different methods for the image filtering pre-processing step (as described in Sect. 2), while keeping the rest of the HTR system fixed. The parameters for both the Sauvola thresholding and the proposed algorithm were chosen by manually analyzing the resultant images for a few examples. With this visual inspection it was verified that for the selected parameters that when the thresholding discarded parts of the strokes, the proposed algorithm was capable of keeping part of that lost information. The final parameters were $W = 30$ pixels, $R = 128$, and $k = 0.2$, which are common to both algorithms, and for the proposed algorithm the slope parameter of the linear transition was set to $s = 1$. With these parameters the performance of the complete handwriting recognition system was estimated by a 7-fold cross-validation procedure using the partitions proposed in [8]. The rest of the processing steps and training of the models was exactly the same as the ones from [8].

Table 1. Word error rate results for the LICENSES of the ESPOSALLES corpus comparing the proposed technique with the baseline and previously published results.

Approach	WER (%)	95 % Conf. int.[a]
Previously published [8]	16.1	15.8–16.4
with Sauvola thresholding	13.4[b]	13.1–13.7
with proposed technique	13.1[b]	12.8–13.4

[a] Wilson interval estimation.
[b] Proposed method better than Sauvola for a confidence level of 90 % using a two-proportion z-test.

The quality of the transcription is given by the well known *Word Error Rate* (WER). It is defined as the minimum number of words that need to be substituted, deleted or inserted to convert the sentences recognized by the system into the reference transcriptions, divided by the total number of words in these transcriptions. Table 1 shows the WERs obtained for the three different methods studied. First the result from [8], then replacing the background removal by a Sauvola thresholding, and then again replacing the background removal by the proposed technique. The first thing to note in the table is that for this corpus, the previously used background removal technique performs considerably worse than local thresholding, obtaining a relative improvement of about 16.8 %. Then comparing the results of the proposed technique and the thresholding, there is a smaller, although still significant improvement. From this we can observe that the hard decision that a thresholding technique imposes, definitely discards useful information that benefits a recognizer based on HMMs and Gaussian mixtures.

In Fig. 3 a few example images are presented comparing the original, and the result after applying the thresholding or the proposed technique. In these images it can be observed that strokes that are locally lighter than other neighboring strokes, with thresholding there is a risk that these are discarded. On the other hand, with the proposed technique there is a much lower chance that locally light strokes be completely removed, instead these are mapped to a shade of

Fig. 3. Example images from the ESPOSALLES corpus comparing (a) the original image with (b) the thresholded image and (c) the proposed approach.

gray. Furthermore, the handwritten text looks smoother and more natural since all of the boundaries between background and strokes have a softer transition.

6   Conclusions

In this paper we have presented a new image pre-processing technique designed for extracting handwritten text from noisy backgrounds and improving the quality of the image making it more legible. The method is based on the well known Sauvola thresholding technique [10], although with the key difference that the objective is to obtain a grayscale image instead of simply a bitmap. This diminishes the risk that a relatively light writing stroke be completely removed due to a hard black or white decision of thresholding. In the experiments performed, the first finding was that a local thresholding technique performs much better than previously used methods based on background estimation and subtraction on the ESPOSALLES corpus. The second finding was that as expected, avoiding the conversion of the images to bitmaps, more information from the original image is preserved, which does result in an improvement in recognition performance for an HMM Gaussian mixture-based HTR system. Presented here is only a small experiment, thus in future works a more extensive experimentation should be carried out trying out several corpora and analyzing the effect of the parameters of the algorithm. Also similar modifications could be proposed for other thresholding methods that have been more recently proposed in the literature such as the ones mentioned in [4].

Acknowledgments. The research leading to these results has received funding from the European Union's Seventh Framework Programme (FP7/2007-2013) under grant agreement No. 600707 - tranScriptorium and the Spanish MEC under the STraDA project (TIN2012-37475-C02-01).

References

1. Drida, F.: Towards restoring historic documents degraded over time. In: Proceedings of 2nd IEEE International Conference on Document Image Analysis for Libraries (DIAL 2006), Lyon, France, pp. 350–357 (2006)
2. Graves, A., Liwicki, M., Fernandez, S., Bertolami, R., Bunke, H., Schmidhuber, J.: A novel connectionist system for unconstrained handwriting recognition. IEEE Trans. Pattern Anal. Mach. Intell. **31**(5), 855–868 (2009)
3. Jelinek, F.: Statistical Methods for Speech Recognition. MIT Press, Cambridge (1998)
4. Khurshid, K., Siddiqi, I., Faure, C., Vincent, N.: Comparison of niblack inspired binarization methods for ancient documents. In: Berkner, K., Likforman-Sulem, L. (eds.) 16th Document Recognition and Retrieval Conference, DRR 2009, SPIE Proceedings, vol. 7247, pp. 1–10. SPIE, San Jose (18–22 January 2009). doi:10.1117/12.805827
5. Kneser, R., Ney, H.: Improved backing-off for m-gram language modeling, Detroit, USA, vol. 1, pp. 181–184 (1995)
6. Marti, U., Bunke, H.: Using a statistical language model to improve the preformance of an HMM-based cursive handwriting recognition system. IJPRAI **15**(1), 65–90 (2001)
7. Niblack, W.: An Introduction to Digital Image Processing, pp. 115–116. Prentice-Hall, Englewood Cliffs (1986)
8. Romero, V., Fornés, A., Serrano, N., Sánchez, J., Toselli, A., Frinken, V., Vidal, E., Lladós, J.: The ESPOSALLES database: An ancient marriage license corpus for off-line handwriting recognition. Pattern Recogn. **46**, 1658–1669 (2013). doi:10.1016/j.patcog.2012.11.024
9. España-Boquera, S., Castro-Bleda, M.J., Gorbe-Moya, J., Zamora-Martínez, F.: Improving offline handwriting text recognition with hybrid hmm/ann models. IEEE Trans. Pattern Anal. Mach. Intell. **33**(4), 767–779 (2011)
10. Sauvola, J., Pietikäinen, M.: Adaptive document image binarization. Pattern Recog. **33**(2), 225–236 (2000). doi:10.1016/S0031-3203(99)00055-2
11. Shafait, F., Keysers, D., Breuel, T.M.: Efficient implementation of local adaptive thresholding techniques using integral images. In: Proceedings of the SPIE 6815, Document Recognition and Retrieval XV, 681510, pp. 1–6, January 2008. doi:10.1117/12.767755
12. Toselli, A.H., Juan, A., Keysers, D., González, J., Salvador, I., Ney, H., Vidal, E., Casacuberta, F.: Integrated handwriting recognition and interpretation using finite-state models. Int. J. Pattern Recog. Artif. Intell. **18**(4), 519–539 (2004). doi:10.1142/S0218001404003344

Applications

Improving the Minimum Description Length Inference of Phrase-Based Translation Models

Jesús González-Rubio[✉] and Francisco Casacuberta

Pattern Recognition and Human Language Technology Center,
Universitat Politècnica de València, Camino de Vera s/n, 46021 Valencia, Spain
{jegonzalez,fcn}@prhlt.upv.es

Abstract. We study the application of minimum description length (MDL) inference to estimate pattern recognition models for machine translation. MDL is a theoretically-sound approach whose empirical results are however below those of the state-of-the-art pipeline of training heuristics. We identify potential limitations of current MDL procedures and provide a practical approach to overcome them. Empirical results support the soundness of the proposed approach.

1 Introduction

Since their introduction, phrase-based (PB) models [1] have become the state-of-the-art pattern recognition approach to machine translation. However, despite their empirical success, their inference procedures still rely on a long decoupled pipeline of heuristics. Stages in the pipeline cannot recover errors made in earlier stages which forces each individual step to massively over-generate hypotheses. As a result, inferred phrasal lexicons [2] suffer of a huge degree of redundancy that penalizes the efficiency of PB systems. A clear indicator of these deficiencies [3] is, for example, the fact that PB models usually cannot generate the sentence pairs in which they have been trained in.

The *minimum description length* (MDL) principle [4] is a theoretically-sound alternative for PB inference. MDL, formally described in Sect. 3, is a general inference procedure that "learns" by "finding regularities" in the data. It embodies a form of Occam's Razor in which the best model for a given data is the one that provides a better trade-off between goodness-of-fit on training data and "expressiveness" of the model.

We build on the work by González-Rubio et al. [5] who described a practical MDL inference approach for PB models. Such approach, described in Sect. 4, is based on a greedy iterative procedure that generalizes an initial model that perfectly describes training data. The generalization procedure reduces the complexity of the initial model by segmenting sentences and merging common phrase pairs according to an MDL objective. Despite being theoretically-sound, these MDL PB models provide poor translation quality in comparison to state-of-the-art PB models. In Sect. 5, we study the potential reasons behind such poor

---

J. González-Rubio—This author is now at Unbabel Lda. 1000-201 Lisboa, Portugal.

R. Paredes et al. (Eds.): IbPRIA 2015, LNCS 9117, pp. 219–227, 2015.
DOI: 10.1007/978-3-319-19390-8_25

empirical performance and propose an extended segmentation process to address this practical challenge.

Finally, the experiments in Sect. 6 compare the proposed approach against the MDL PB estimation proposed in [5], and a state-of-the-art PB estimation [2]. Results show that the proposed approach was able to boost the performance MDL PB models while inferring significantly smaller phrasal lexicons than conventional PB models.

2   Related Work

Different authors have proposed formal approaches to infer PB models, e.g. [6,7]. In contrast to these approaches, MDL inference is automatically protected against overfitting and, despite being closely related to Bayesian inference, it does not suffer from its interpretation difficulties. In fact, MDL has a clear interpretation independently of whether or not there exists some underlying "true" distribution.

In [8], an MDL objective is used to prune out a phrasal lexicon previously estimated. In contrast, we use the MDL principle to directly estimate a PB model from a parallel corpora. Regarding [5], we expand their ideas by proposing an extended segmentation procedure that boosts the translation quality of MDL PB models.

Finally, our iterative segmentation process is similar to the recursive alignment model (MAR) [9]. Our method, however, learns a complete phrasal lexicon, whereas MAR only learns a word alignments as part of a larger pipeline.

3   The Minimum Description Length Principle

Given a set of data $\mathcal{D}$, the objective of statistical inference is to obtain the most probable model Φ given the data. Such posterior probability can be decomposed as follows:

$$\Pr(\Phi \mid \mathcal{D}) = \frac{\Pr(\Phi) \cdot \Pr(\mathcal{D} \mid \Phi)}{\Pr(\mathcal{D})} \propto \Pr(\Phi) \cdot \Pr(\mathcal{D} \mid \Phi) \qquad (1)$$

According to information theory [10], the negative logarithm of the probability of an event measures its description length. Therefore, searching for a MDL is equivalent to searching for a good probability distribution; which allows us to re-write Eq. (1):

$$\mathrm{DL}(\Phi \mid \mathcal{D}) = -\log \Pr(\Phi \mid \mathcal{D}) \propto \mathrm{DL}(\Phi) + \mathrm{DL}(\mathcal{D} \mid \Phi) \qquad (2)$$

where function $\mathrm{DL}(\Phi) = -\log \Pr(\Phi)$ measures the description length of model Φ, and $\mathrm{DL}(\mathcal{D} \mid \Phi) = -\log \Pr(\mathcal{D} \mid \Phi)$ denotes the description length of the data given the model.

Given these considerations, the goal of MDL inference [4] is to obtain the model $\widehat{\Phi}$ with a shorter description length for a given data set $\mathcal{D}$:

$$\widehat{\Phi} = \underset{\Phi}{\mathrm{argmin}}\, \mathrm{DL}(\Phi \mid \mathcal{D}) = \underset{\Phi}{\mathrm{argmin}}\, \mathrm{DL}(\Phi) + \mathrm{DL}(\mathcal{D} \mid \Phi) \qquad (3)$$

According to the MDL principle, the best model $\widehat{\Phi}$ is thus the one that reaches an optimal trade-off between model complexity and accuracy in the description of the data. A more detailed description of the MDL principles and methods can be found in [11].

4   MDL Phrase-Based Models

PB models translate following a generative process with three steps [1]: (1) the source sentence is divided into segments known as phrases, (2) each source phrase is translated into a target phrase, and (3) target phrases are reordered to conform the final translation. The main probability distribution is thus a phrase lexicon that describes the translation probability between source and target language phrases. Next sections describe how to estimate such phrase lexicons following an MDL objective [5].

Algorithm 1. Iterative inference procedure for MDL PB model estimation.

---

    input   : Φ (initial PB model)
    output : $\widehat{\Phi}$ (generalized PB model)
    auxiliary: collect(Φ) (Returns the set of possible segmentations of model Φ)
            ΔDL(s, Φ) (Returns variation in DL when segmenting Φ according to s)
            sort($\mathcal{S}$) (Sorts segmentation set $\mathcal{S}$ by variation in DL)
            commit($\mathcal{S}$, Φ) (Apply segmentations in $\mathcal{S}$ to Φ, returns variation in DL)

1 **repeat**
2      $\mathcal{S} \leftarrow$ collect(Φ);
3   candidates $\leftarrow$ [];
4   **for** s $\in \mathcal{S}$ **do**
5          $\Delta' \leftarrow \Delta$DL(s, Φ);
6   **if** $\Delta' \leq 0$ **then**
7   candidates .append($\{\Delta', s\}$);

8   sort(candidates);
9      $\Delta \leftarrow$ commit(candidates, Φ);
10 **until** $\Delta > 0$;
11 **return** Φ;

4.1   Description Length Functions

Let us start with the description length $DL(\mathcal{D} \mid \Phi)$ of a data set $\mathcal{D}$ given a model Φ. Following information theory [10], the natural approach to compute such description length (in bits) is to use its lower bound given by $DL(\mathcal{D} \mid \Phi) = -\log_2(\Pr(\mathcal{D} \mid \Phi))$.

The description length $DL(\Phi)$ can be measured as the number of bits required to send model Φ over a channel. This can be computed by serializing Φ into a sequence of symbols and then computing the length of the optimal encoding of such sequence. To serialize a PB model, we require one symbol for each word in the source and target vocabularies, another symbol to separate the source and target sides in a phrase pair, and one additional symbol to distinguish between the different pairs in the phrase lexicon.

The example toy PB model {La|||The, casa|||house, azul|||blue} will be serialized as "La|The•casa|house•azul|blue", where symbol • separates the phrase pairs, and | separates the two sides of each pair. To compute the description length of the model, we assume a uniform distribution so that each of K different symbols is encoded using $-\log_2(\frac{1}{K})$ bits. In the example, we require 3 bits for each symbol[1], and 33 bits to encode the whole serialized PB model (11 symbols). This uniform code is obviously not optimal. Still, using a common encoding, we can fairly compare different models.

4.2 Inference Procedure

The minimization in Eq. (3) requires to a search for an optimal phrase lexicon. Obviously, an exhaustive search over all possible sets of phrase pairs is unfeasible in practice. We follow the ideas in [9] and implement the search as an iterative generalization procedure. Let $\mathcal{D} = \{\mathbf{f}_n, \mathbf{e}_n\}_{n=1}^{N}$ be a data set with N sentence pairs, The initial PB model would be a "sentence-based" model that we generalize by identifying parts of the phrase pairs that could be used in isolation. From a probabilistic point of view, this process moves some of the probability mass which is concentrated in the training data out to other data still unseen. Consider this initial "sentence-based" PB model:

La casa azul|||The blue house   Esta casa azul|||This blue house

Esta casa verde|||This green house

it can be segmented to obtain a new PB model:

La|||The   Esta|||This   casa azul|||blue house   casa verde|||green house

which explains a new translation (La casa verde→The green house) and has a shorter length (19 symbols vs. 23 original symbols). In [5], only segmentations that bisect the phrases are considered. In Sect. 5 we propose an extended segmentation approach.

Algorithm 1 describes the MDL PB inference by iterative generalization. First, we collect the potential segmentations of the current PB model (line 2). Then, we estimate the variation in description length due to the application of each segmentation (lines 3–7). Finally, we sort the segmentations (line 8) and apply the one with largest length reduction to obtain a new PB model (line 9). The algorithm stops when no reduction is achievable [5,12]. The number of segmentations under consideration (bisections) is bounded by $O(N \cdot L \cdot M)$, where N is the number of training sentences, and L and M are the maximum length, in words, among the source and target sentences respectively.

4.3 Estimating the Impact of a Segmentation

The key component of Algorithm 1 is function $\Delta\mathrm{DL}(\mathrm{s}, \Phi)$ that evaluates the impact of a candidate segmentation s on the description length of PB model Φ. That is,

---

[1] We have 8 different symbols: one symbol for each of the six words, plus • and |.

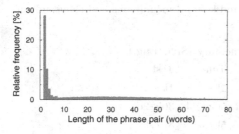
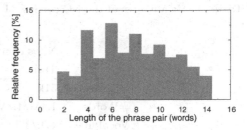

Fig. 1. Histogram of lengths (source plus target words) for two PB models: a conventional MDL model (left) and the same model after further segmenting long phrase pairs (right).

$\Delta DL(s, \Phi)$ computes the difference in description length between the current model Φ and the model Φ' that would result from committing to s:

$$\Delta DL(s, \Phi) = DL(\Phi') - DL(\Phi) + DL(\mathcal{D} \mid \Phi') - DL(\mathcal{D} \mid \Phi) \qquad (4)$$

The length difference between phrase lexicons $(DL(\Phi') - DL(\Phi))$ is given by the difference between the lengths of the phrase pairs added and removed. The difference for the data is given by $-\log_2\left(\frac{\Pr(\mathcal{D}|\Phi')}{\Pr(\mathcal{D}|\Phi)}\right)$. These probabilities can be computed by translating the training data. However, this is a prohibitively expensive approach. Instead, we estimate the data description length in closed form.

The probability of a phrase pair $\{\tilde{f}, \tilde{e}\}$ in a PB model is computed as the number of occurrences of the pair divided by the number of occurrences of the source (or target) phrase [1]. We thus estimate the probabilities in the segmented model Φ' by counting the occurrences of the replaced phrase pairs as occurrences of the new segmented pairs. Let $\{\tilde{f}_0, \tilde{e}_0\}$ be a phrase pair bisected into $\{\tilde{f}_1, \tilde{e}_1\}$ and $\{\tilde{f}_2, \tilde{e}_2\}$. The direct phrase probabilities in Φ' will be identical to those in Φ except that:

$$P_{\Phi'}(\tilde{e}_0 \mid \tilde{f}_0) = 0$$

$$P_{\Phi'}(\tilde{e}_1 \mid \tilde{f}_1) = \frac{N_{\mathcal{D}}(\{\tilde{f}_1, \tilde{e}_1\}) + N_{\mathcal{D}}(\{\tilde{f}_0, \tilde{e}_0\})}{N_{\mathcal{D}}(\tilde{f}_1) + N_{\mathcal{D}}(\{\tilde{f}_0, \tilde{e}_0\})} \quad P_{\Phi'}(\tilde{e}_2 \mid \tilde{f}_2) = \frac{N_{\mathcal{D}}(\{\tilde{f}_2, \tilde{e}_2\}) + N_{\mathcal{D}}(\{\tilde{f}_0, \tilde{e}_0\})}{N_{\mathcal{D}}(\tilde{f}_2) + N_{\mathcal{D}}(\{\tilde{f}_0, \tilde{c}_0\})}$$

where $N_{\mathcal{D}}(\cdot)$ are counts in $\mathcal{D}$. Inverse probabilities are computed similarly.

Finally, the variation in data description length is given by the ratio between the estimated probability of the new pairs in Φ' and that of the pairs replaced from Φ:

$$\frac{\Pr(\mathcal{D} \mid \Phi')}{\Pr(\mathcal{D} \mid \Phi)} \approx \frac{P_{\Phi'}(\tilde{e}_1 \mid \tilde{f}_1) \cdot P_{\Phi'}(\tilde{e}_2 \mid \tilde{f}_2)}{P_{\Phi}(\tilde{e}_0 \mid \tilde{f}_0)} \cdot \frac{P_{\Phi'}(\tilde{f}_1 \mid \tilde{e}_1) \cdot P_{\Phi'}(\tilde{f}_2 \mid \tilde{e}_2)}{P_{\Phi}(\tilde{f}_0 \mid \tilde{e}_0)} \qquad (5)$$

where the two factors account for the direct and inverse phrase probabilities.

Note that we only consider the direct and inverse phrase probability distributions. A similar approach can be followed to estimate the change in direct and inverse lexical probabilities [2] but we left this extension for future developments.

5   Improving MDL Inference

MDL provides a simple and theoretically-sound approach to perform statistical inference. However, its application to natural language tasks, such as machine translation,

Table 1. Main figures of the NC corpus. M and k stand for millions and thousands of elements.

	News commentary (Spa./Eng.)		
	Train	Tune	Test
#Sentences	51k	2k	1k
#Words	1.4M/1.2M	56k/50k	30k/26k
Vocabulary	47k/35k	5k/5k	8k/7k

presents diverse practical challenges due to the intrinsic sparsity of human language. Frequencies of words in natural language follow a power law [13]. Thus, many of the words (or sequences of words) in a parallel corpus will appear only once. Since MDL "learns" by "finding regularities", this fact imposes a fundamental limitation to the MDL generalization procedure. Consider the following example toy PB model:

La casa azul|||The blue house   Este coche verde|||This green car

Tu bicicleta rosa|||Your pink bike

Obviously, there is a clear correspondence between parts of the source and target phrases, e.g. La↔The or coche verde↔green car. However, no bisection provides a reduction in description length. A consequence of this is that MDL tend to estimate phrase lexicons with long phrase pairs, see Fig. 1 (left). There, long phrase pairs (more than 15 words[2]) account for almost half the pairs and 91 % of the words in the model. This is an important limitation since long phrase pairs generalize poorly.

To address this limitation, we extend the process in Sect. 4.2 with a subsequent segmentation step to split the remaining long phrase pairs into more general units. Specifically, we implement the state-of-the-art phrase extraction procedure [2]. Figure 1 (right) shows the phrase lengths resulting after such extended segmentation process. Long phrase pairs have been replaced by shorter, more general bilingual phrases.

6   Experiments

We conducted experiments on the Spanish-to-English News Commentary (NC) translation task [14], see Table 1. All sentences were tokenized and lowercased.

We inferred MDL PB models with the training partitions as described in Sects. 4 and 5. Then, we included them in a log-linear PB model [1] and generated translations for the test partitions [2]. Since we only estimate the direct and inverse phrase probabilities, see Sect. 4.3, we did not use lexical probabilities [2] in our experiments. Translation quality was measured with BLEU [15] and TER [16]. BLEU measures the accuracy of the automatic translations while TER measures their distance to a reference.

Table 2 shows size (number of phrase pairs) of the inferred MDL PB models, and BLEU and TER scores of their translations. As a comparison, we display results for a state-of-the-art PB system [2]. Results show that the proposed MDL inference obtained

---

[2] 14 is the maximum phrase pair length usually considered by conventional PB systems.

much more concise models (less than one tenth the number of phrases) than the standard inference pipeline. However, these smaller models were not able to deliver translations of similar quality which is consistent with previous results reported in [5]. The extended segmentation approach proposed in Sect. 5 dramatically improved the quality of the generated translations at the cost of an increase in the size of the PB model.

Table 2. Size (number of phrase pairs) of the inferred MDL PB models, and quality (tune/test) of the generated translations. M and k stand for millions and thousands of elements respectively.

	BLEU [%]($\uparrow$)	TER [%]($\downarrow$)	Size
State-of-the-art	31.4/30.7	48.0/47.2	2.2M
$MDL : DL(\Phi)$	24.0/23.7	58.3/56.8	79.5k
$+ DL(\mathcal{D} \mid \Phi)$	24.0/23.8	57.5/56.0	79.1k
$+$ Further segmentation	29.1/28.1	50.6/49.4	1.4M

Results obtained considering only the description length of the PB model (DL(Φ)) and considering the total description length (DL(Φ)+DL($\mathcal{D} \mid \Phi$)) were virtually the same. This fact, consistent with previous work [17], indicates that, for PB models, the structure (set of phrase pairs) has the greater impact in translation quality, with only scarce improvements due to the actual probabilities assigned to the phrase pairs.

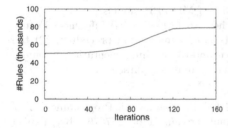 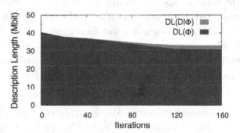

Fig. 2. Changes in the PB model during MDL inference. Left plot displays the number of rules of the model while the plot in the right displays its total description length broken down into model description length (bottom) and data description length given the model (top).

We also measured the changes of the model and the translation quality during the inference process. Figure 2 displays the number of phrase pairs (left) and the total description length (right) of the intermediate PB models generated during the MDL inference procedure. The total description length is broken down into description length of the model (DL(Φ), bottom) and description length of the data given the model (DL($\mathcal{D} \mid \Phi$), top). We can observe that although the number of phrase pairs of the intermediate models increased over time, their description length actually went down.

This indicates that we are inferring more general models with a looser fit on the training data. Moreover, the improvements in model description length made up for the loss in data description length which indicates that we were indeed generalizing successfully.

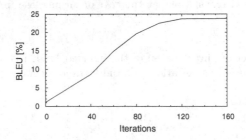

Fig. 3. Variation in test BLEU over iterations.

Finally, Fig. 3 displays the BLEU for the translations of the test partition over time. Translation quality increased with the iterations reaching its maximum at the end of the inference process. This again came to confirm the soundness of MDL inference.

7   Conclusions and Future Developments

We have studied a simple, unsupervised inference procedure for PB models based on the MDL principle. We have also identified a potential practical limitation of MDL and have proposed an approach to overcome it. Empirical results have shown that the proposed approach was able to boost the quality of MDL PB models.

MDL provides a solid foundation from where to formalize PB inference. Future developments may include (1) a more sophisticated segmentation procedure, (2) the inclusion of lexical models in the MDL inference, and (3) the implementation of a more parsimonious segmentation approach for the long remaining phrase pairs.

Acknowledgments. Work supported by the EU 7th Framework Programme (FP7/ 2007–2013) under the CasMaCat project (grant agreement nᵒ 287576), by Spanish MICINN under grant TIN2012-31723, and by the Generalitat Valenciana under grant ALMPR (Prometeo/2009/014).

References

1. Koehn, P., Och, F.J., Marcu, D.: Statistical phrase-based translation. In: Proceedings of the North American Chapter of the Association for Computational Linguistics on Human Language Technology, pp. 48–54 (2003)
2. Koehn, P., Hoang, H., Birch, A., Callison-Burch, C., Federico, M., Bertoldi, N., Cowan, B., Shen, W., Moran, C., Zens, R., Dyer, C., Bojar, O., Constantin, A., Herbst, E.: Moses: open source toolkit for statistical machine translation. In: Proceedings of the Association for Computational Linguistics, Demonstration Session (2007)

3. Sanchis-Trilles, G., Ortiz-Martínez, D., González-Rubio, J., González, J., Casacuberta, F.: Bilingual segmentation for phrasetable pruning in statistical machine translation. In: Proceedings of the Conference of the European Association for Machine Translation (2011)
4. Rissanen, J.: Modeling by shortest data description. Automatica **14**(5), 465–471 (1978)
5. González-Rubio, J., Casacuberta, F.: Inference of phrase-based translation models via minimum description length. In: Proceedings of the Conference of the European Chapter of the Association for Computational Linguistics, pp. 90–94 (2014)
6. Marcu, D., Wong, W.: A phrase-based, joint probability model for statistical machine translation. In: Proceedings of the Conference on Empirical Methods in Natural Language Processing, pp. 133–139 (2002)
7. DeNero, J., Bouchard-Côté, A., Klein, D.: Sampling alignment structure under a bayesian translation model. In: Proceedings of the Conference on Empirical Methods in Natural Language Processing, pp. 314–323 (2008)
8. Zhang, J.: Model-based search for statistical machine translation. Master's thesis, Edinburgh University, United Kingdom (2005)
9. Vilar, J.M., Vidal, E.: A recursive statistical translation model. In: Proceedings of the ACL Workshop on Building and Using Parallel Texts, pp. 199–207 (2005)
10. Shannon, C.: A mathematical theory of communication. Bell Syst. Techn. J. **27**, 379–423/623–656 (1948)
11. Grünwald, P.: A tutorial introduction to the minimum description length principle (2004). http://arxiv.org/abs/math/0406077
12. Saers, M., Addanki, K., Wu, D.: Iterative rule segmentation under minimum description length for unsupervised transduction grammar induction. In: Dediu, A.-H., Martín-Vide, C., Mitkov, R., Truthe, B. (eds.) SLSP 2013. LNCS, vol. 7978, pp. 224–235. Springer, Heidelberg (2013)
13. Zipf, G.K.: The Psychobiology of Language. Houghton-Mifflin, Boston (1935)
14. Callison-Burch, C., Fordyce, C., Koehn, P., Monz, C., Schroeder, J.: (Meta-) evaluation of machine translation. In: Proceedings of the Workshop on Statistical Machine Translation, pp. 136–158 (2007)
15. Papineni, K., Roukos, S., Ward, T., Zhu, W.J.: Bleu: A method for automatic evaluation of machine translation. In: Proceedings of the Meeting on Association for Computational Linguistics, Association for Computational Linguistics, pp. 311–318 (2002)
16. Snover, M., Dorr, B., Schwartz, R., Micciulla, L., Makhoul, J.: A study of translation edit rate with targeted human annotation. In: Proceedings of Association for Machine Translation in the Americas, pp. 223–231 (2006)
17. Turchi, M., De Bie, T., Cristianini, N.: Learning to translate: a statistical and computational analysis. Technical report, University of Bristol (2009)

A Kinect-Based System to Assess Lymphedema Impairments in Breast Cancer Patients

Rita Moreira[1], André Magalhães[2], and Hélder P. Oliveira[1](✉)

[1] INESC TEC, Faculdade de Engenharia, Universidade do Porto, Porto, Portugal
helder.f.oliveira@inescporto.pt
[2] Faculdade de Medicina, Universidade do Porto, Porto, Portugal

Abstract. Common breast cancer treatments, as the removal of axillary lymph nodes, cause severe impairments in women's upper-body function. As a result, several daily activities are affected which contributes to a decreased QOL. Thus, the assessment of functional restrictions after treatment is essential to avoid further complications. This paper presents a pioneer work, which aims to develop an upper-body function evaluation method, traduced by the identification of lymphedema. Using the Kinect, features of the upper-limbs motion are extracted and supervised learning algorithms are used to construct a predictive classification model. Very promising results are obtained, with high classification accuracy.

1 Introduction

About 25 % of women diagnosed with breast cancer present cancer cells in the axillary lymph node system [6]. In these cases, treatments comprise the removal of axillary nodes, as well as radiotherapy to the axilla. Both these procedures cause serious damage in the lymphatic system of the upper-limb, as the interruption of the lymphatic drainage, resulting in the accumulation of lymph fluid in the arm subcutaneous tissue and, as consequence, decreased distensibility of the joints and increased limb weight. Therefore, severe upper-limb problems are normally verified in these patients, as traduced by the appearance of lymphedema. Lymphedema is regarded as incurable, progressive, disfiguring and disabling disorder highly correlated with a decreased Quality Of Life (QOL) [7]. Also, it can be considered as an aesthetic problem [3,12].

An objective evaluation of upper-body motion restrictions can be an helpful tool in the determination of the sequel related to cancer treatment. With an early identification of impairments, therapeutic interventions can lead to greater success in managing upper-limb morbidity, with improved outcomes for survivors [1]. However, there is no clinical standard for diagnosis and the methods currently used have problems of objectivity or inaccuracy [14].

The present work proposes an objective method for lymphedema assessment, an important indicator of the Upper-Body Function (UBF) status in breast cancer patients. For this purpose, a low-cost sensor is used, the Microsoft Kinect, which provides RGB and depth data and allows a simplified skeleton tracking.

© Springer International Publishing Switzerland 2015
R. Paredes et al. (Eds.): IbPRIA 2015, LNCS 9117, pp. 228–236, 2015.
DOI: 10.1007/978-3-319-19390-8_26

Features of the patients' upper-limbs motion are extracted and a predictive classification model is built using supervised classification algorithms. The results obtained were very promising, which validates the methodology proposed.

2 Related Work

2.1 Upper-Limb Volume Measurements

Currently methodologies used to assess limb edema include water displacement, circumference measurements, bioelectrical impedance spectroscopy (BIS) or imaging techniques [14]. When performed properly, water displacement is accurate, still, it is time-consuming, non portable and nonhygienic. Regarding the multiple circumferential measurements, sources of error arise from the assumption of circular cross-section of the limb. Imaging techniques, such as computed tomography, require equipment that is not commonly available in clinics. On the other hand, BIS involve the use of several electrodes placed along the arm, which leads to a high lifetime operational cost.

To overcome the limitations of traditional methods, research is been done for the application of the arising Three-Dimensional (3D) technologies on body volume estimation [17]. Non-invasive 3D body-surface scanners are transforming the ability to accurately measure the body size, shape, and skin-surface area, since they combine precision and reproducibility. These features make them appealing for widespread clinical applications. Nonetheless, they are very expensive devices and are quite difficult to be handled by non-professionals. On the other hand, Lu *et al.* [11] explored the use of the low-cost sensor Kinect for arm modeling and volume measurement. However, the proposed method is quite complex since it depends on gyroscopes and accelerometers attached to the sensor.

2.2 Upper-Limb Motion Evaluation

The assessment of functional status after breast cancer treatment should also have in attention activity limitations traduced by limited shoulder ROM. Normally, UBF evaluation rely on subjective measurements of patients experiences and function limitation [2]. Thus, several generic self-report questionnaires have been developed to capture the effects of injury in the upper-body function (see Table 1). Although easy-to-use and useful to provide reference data, subjective methods are generally not accurate and have problems related to impartiality and poor reproducibility.

On the other hand, tests of flexibility, strength and endurance are also reported in the assessment of limbs functional limitations. The most common used in breast cancer patients is the goniometry [8], which assesses active and passive shoulder ROM in all planes. Other approaches can include the use of isometric and isokinetic dynamometry and/or maximal performance of a set of tasks/exercises using the repetition maximum method [8].

In conclusion, methods currently available to assess UBF status are non-practical for clinical settings, non reproducible and non accurate. Nonetheless, recent 3D scanners are an attractive tool with potential applications in this field.

Table 1. Self-report scales used for upper-body function assessment. Adapted from [2].

Scale	Measure	Description	Comments
PSFS [15]	Clinical measure of function	3 items; 11-point scale	Measures change in function specific to the individual survivor
DASH [9]	Pain-related disability	30 items; 5-point scale	Has not been validated in the breast cancer patients
UEFI [16]	Upper-body function	20 items; 5-point scale	Valid and sensitive in breast cancer patients
KAPS [10]	Upper-body symptoms and function	13-items; 5-point scale	Identify shoulder and arm problems during breast cancer treatment

3   An Upper-Body Function Evaluation System

This paper addresses the development of a Kinect-based system for the evaluation of UBF, traduced by the identification of lymphedema, an important indicator of upper-limbs functional status, including the acquisition of a breast cancer patients database. The database comprises color, depth and skeleton data of the patients performing adduction and abduction movements of the upper-limbs. The complete medical information is available for each patient, such as lymphedema diagnosis and treatments used.

The proposed system can be implemented as a sequence of a few high-level operations (see Fig. 1). Firstly, an effective segmentation of the patient was accomplished. Further, the arm contour is detected and movements' features are extracted. Thereafter, a predictive model is built, using a machine learning methodology, to evaluate the upper-body functional status.

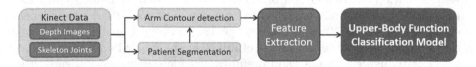

Fig. 1. System flowchart of the proposed method.

3.1   Patient Segmentation

Ideally, the data acquisition would be carried out in a uniform background but, occasionally, there is also the presence of non-desirable objects (see Figs. 2(a) and (b)). Therefore, global thresholding methods, such as Otsu's, are not effective in this case, as previously verified [13]. In this manner, the skeleton joints are used to identify pixels where the body of the patient is positioned: a double threshold is defined using the maximum and minimum values of intensity at these pixels.

A margin of 5% above and below the maximum and minimum, respectively, is used (see Fig. 2(b)) to guarantee the segmentation of all body. Further, to remove small holes, a fill holes filter is applied and to smooth the body shape, a median filter (11×11) is used.

3.2 Arm Contour Detection

The upper-arm is bounded superiorly by the shoulder, inferiorly by the elbow and communicates medially with the axilla [4]. In this fashion, to define the arm contour, a set of points should be found (see Fig. 2(c)): the armpit (A_1), the medial (E_1) and lateral (E_2) elbow point, the medial (S_2) and lateral shoulder point (S_1). With this in mind, we start by the detection of the patient contour, which can be iteratively assessed to find the points of interest: The armpit (A_1) will correspond to the pixel closer and beneath the Kinect shoulder joint S. Further, the medial elbow point (E_1), will be the pixel closer to the elbow joint E and medially positioned in relation to the line segment $\overline{SE}$. On the other hand, to detect E_2, is selected the pixel closer to the joint E and laterally positioned in relation to the line segment $\overline{SE}$. To find S_2, we search the pixel that forms with the shoulder S a line parallel to $\overline{E_1E_2}$. Finally, S_1 will be the point of intersection between $\overline{E_1A_1}$ and $\overline{S_2S}$. This process is done for the right and left arm, and repeated each frame available for each patient.

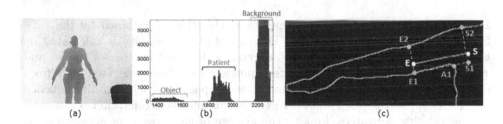

Fig. 2. (a) Normalized depth image and (b) correspondent histogram, where is possible to identify the double threshold used for segmentation (vertical lines). (c) Kinect Shoulder and Elbow joints (red dots) and upper-arm detected points (green dots) (Color figure online).

3.3 Feature Extraction

After the initial data processing, a selection of features was performed, in order to evaluate the upper-body mobility. It is important to refer that the methods described bellow are performed in all frames available for each patient.

Range of Motion. ROM is obtained measuring the angle between the upper-limb and the patient body. On other words, it is computed the angle θ between the line segment $\overline{A_1E_1}$, and the line $\overline{H_1H_2}$, defined by the head and hip points of the Kinect skeleton (see Fig. 3(b)). Therefore, the ROM of the right and left shoulder is obtained and their ratio is computed. From this data, two features are selected: the ROM at the maximum height achieved by the hand ($maxROM$) and the average of the ROM ratio along all movement (μROM).

Volume. In this case, the depth data is used to quantify the volume ratio between the upper-arms. First, a plan of reference is defined as the maximum depth value on the arm (the most distant point), represented by a red block in Fig. 3(a). Further, the volume is defined as the sum of unit values between the estimated plan and the arm surface. An average value of each arm volume is obtained, and their ratio is computed (μVOL).

Hand Height and Width. To evaluated the hand height and width reached during the abduction movement, the x and y coordinates of the hands joints are analyzed, and the Shoulder Center (SC) joint is used as a reference point. This means that, for all the frames, it is computed the difference between the hand coordinates and the SC point (see Fig. 3(c)). Thereafter, the ratio of the y values of both hands is computed, as well as the ratio of x values. The following features are then obtained: ratio of the maximum height achieved by the hand ($maxH$); width at the maximum height point ($maxW$); average of the height ratio (μH) and average of the width ratio along all movement (μW).

Hand Acceleration. The movement's acceleration is obtained by the variation of hand position over time. The instantaneous velocity is calculated by the Eq. 1, where T is the sampling interval, n the total number of frames and x, y, z represent the hand coordinates (meters). To reduce generated noise from environment and small body movements, a low-pass filter with cutoff frequency of 2 Hz is applied to $u_{inst}[n]$. Then, the instantaneous acceleration is obtained by the velocity derivative. Finally, the average of the movement acceleration is computed for each hand and their ratio is extracted as a feature (μAcc).

$$u_{inst}[n] = \frac{dx, y, z}{dt}\Big|_{t=nT} \quad (m/s) \qquad (1)$$

Elbow Flexion. Using the shoulder, elbow and wrist joints, it is possible to calculate the angle between the elbow-wrist and elbow-shoulder lines (see Fig. 3(d)) and, therefore, assess the elbow flexion. This angle is obtained for the right and left elbow, their ratio is computed and the average is used as a feature ($\mu ElbF$).

3.4   Classification Models

A total of 9 features were extracted, which allowed the use of machine learning techniques to build a predictive classification model. The development of the model calls for a ground truth (GT) for result comparison. For this purpose, the patients were divided in two classes: patients diagnosed with lymphedema,

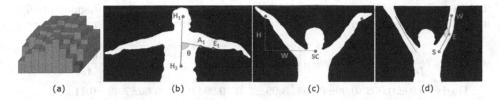

Fig. 3. (a) Volume quantification based on voxels, (b) shoulder ROM θ, (c) hand height (H) and width (W) measures and (d) angle computed to detected elbow flexion (Color figure online).

which will present reduced upper-limb motion, and without lymphedema. Different supervised learning algorithms were tested: the Fisher Linear Discriminant Analysis (LDA), the Naive Bayes Classifier and Support Vector Machines (SVMs). In order to explore all the possibilities and compare performances, the models were trained and tested for all the possible combinations of features, which leads to 2^9 different subsets, by means of a Leave One Out (LOO) scheme [5].

4 Results

4.1 Database

The present research depends on the availability of training and testing examples for the development of models. Therefore, this research included the collection of training data with the Microsoft Kinect. An acquisition application was developed, using the Microsoft SDK 1.8, to acquire RGB and depth frames (640×480) each 15 frames per second, as well as the available skeleton joints. During the acquisition protocol, patients were placed at 2 m from the sensor to perform simple movements of abduction and adduction with the upper-limbs. Currently, the database includes 48 patients, from which 24 present lymphedema.

4.2 Patient Segmentation

For validation of the automatic method used, a manual segmentation of the patient was performed to use as GT. Two similarity indexes were computed, the Dice coefficient and Jaccard Index, in order to compare the automatic and the manual segmentation. Moreover, the similarity between contours were evaluated by the Hausdorff distance and the average distance. The results (Table 2) demonstrate an high similarity and overlap between the proposed method and the GT. The average distance is relatively low and the Hausdorff distance, which represents the worst case scenario, has an mean around 4 pixels. Thus, the method used appears to be valid for the patient segmentation in depth images.

4.3 Arm Contour Detection

In this case, the Dice coefficient and the Jaccard Index, as well as the average and Hausdorff distances, were also computed to evaluate the method used

Table 2. Dice coefficient and Jaccard Index results for body and arm segmentation, and contour detection error (pixels) evaluated by the Hausdorff and average distance.

	D	J	Detected$\Rightarrow$GT		GT$\Rightarrow$Detected	
			h	Avg	h	Avg
Body	0.99±0.003	0.99±0.005	3.99±7.31	0.09±0.21	3.60±7.42	0.11±0.33
Arm	0.78±0.048	0.65±0.066	12.9±2.80	4.82±1.03	12.71±4.25	4.91±1.18

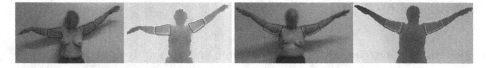

Fig. 4. Examples of arm detected contour (red/black) and ground truth (green/gray) (Color figure online).

for upper-arm segmentation. The results obtained (see Table 2) show that this method is more error prone, when compared with the body segmentation, but still quite satisfactory (see Fig. 4). Those errors can be explained by the manual segmentation carried out, since it is harder to control and operator-dependent. Furthermore, the automatic detection of the arm points is done based on the Kinect skeleton, which can also be a source of errors.

4.4 Upper-Body Functional Evaluation

The classification models were designed considering all possible subsets of features, by a LOO scheme, testing different supervised learning classifiers: LDA, Naive Bayes and SVMs. Models considering binary classes were trained, classifying the patients with and without lymphedema. SVMs training was performed with linear, polynomial and radial basis function (RBF) kernels. For all these cases, exponentially growing sequences of C were tested, from $C = 2^{-2}$ until $C = 2^6$. For the polynomial kernel the order varied from 2 to 6, while γ, for the RBF kernel, was tested with: $\gamma = 0.25, 0.5, 0.75, 1$. For each classifier, it is presented the parameters and the set of features that lead to lower miss-classification errors (see Table 3). In some of the tests, more than one subset of features obtained the same miss-classification error. For those cases, the ones with less complexity are chosen.

The best performance was verified for the SVM classifier, either with the polynomial and RBF kernel, with a miss-classification error of 0.19. For this case, the confusion matrix is also presented (see Table 4), as well as the precision and recall. In this manner, it is possible to verify how many of the positive predictions are actually correct (precision), and how many of the positive labeled instances were actually been matched (recall). High precision values were obtained, which is traduced in a big proportion of cases that are correctly assigned. Although, it can also be noted that the most common miss-classification cases are lymphedema

Table 3. Classification results for the different classifiers tested.

Classifier	Kernel	C	Order	γ	MER	Feature Set
LDA	–	–	–	–	0.29	$[maxROM, maxWidth]$
NaiveBayes	–	–	–	–	0.27	$[\mu ElbF, \mu Acc, \mu ROM]$
SVM	Linear	2^{-1}	–	–	0.25	$[maxROM, \mu ElbF, \mu Acc]$
SVM	Polynomial	2^3	4	–	0.19	$[maxWidth, \mu ROM]$
SVM	RBF	2^4	–	0.75	0.19	$[\mu VOL, maxWidth, \mu ROM]$

Table 4. Confusion matrix for the SVM model for a polynomial and RBF kernel.

Predict / True	No lymph	Lymph	Precision	Recall
No lymph	21	3	0.86	0.75
Lymph	6	18		

patients that are not considered, traduced by a lower recall value. Either way, the results are still very promising, since the model have proved to be capable of performing a correct classification, overlooking only 6 cases. As a result, the method developed appears to be a suitable solution for the evaluation of the UBF in breast cancer patients. Notwithstanding, it would be important to increase the recall of the model to reduce false negative classifications. The most common features used in almost all the selected models are the $maxW$ and the μROM, as well as the $maxROM$, the $\mu ElbF$ and the μAcc. Therefore, these features are probably the ones that have greater influence in the functional assessment.

5   Conclusion

The main goal of this research was the study of a Kinect-based method for the diagnosis of the UBF impairments, suitable for breast cancer patients. The work included the collection of a data set, using the Kinect device, composed by patients with and without lymphedema, since this disease is an accurate indicator of the upper-body motion status. Using the depth and skeleton data available, features of the movements performed by each patient were extracted and several supervised learning algorithms were tested, in order to build a predictive classification model. The best performance was obtained using the SVM classifier, with a miss-classification error of 0.19. Therefore, these findings suggest that the methodology proposed is efficient in the evaluation of the upper-body function. It is important to have in attention that there is no similar work in literature, so it is not possible to compare the results with other methods. Henceforward, more research is needed in order to progress in this direction and validate results.

Acknowledgments. This work is financed by the FCT Fundação para a Ciência e a Tecnologia (Portuguese Foundation for Science and Technology) within project UID/EEA/50014/2013

References

1. Bulley, C., Coutts, F., Blyth, C., Jack, W., Chetty, M., Barber, M., Tan, C.: Prevalence and impacts of upper limb morbidity after treatment for breast cancer: a cross-sectional study of lymphedema and function. Cancer Oncol. Res. **1**, 30–39 (2013)
2. Campbell, K., Pusic, A., Zucker, D., McNeely, M., Binkley, J., Cheville, A., Harwood, K.: A prospective model of care for breast cancer rehabilitation: function. Cancer **118**, 2300–2311 (2012)
3. Cardoso, M.J., Oliveira, H.P., Cardoso, J.S.: Assessing cosmetic results after breast conserving surgery. J. Surg. Oncol. **110**(1), 37–44 (2014)
4. Drake, R., Vogl, A., Mitchell, A.: Gray's Anatomy for Students. Elsevier Health Sciences, London (2009)
5. Duda, R.O., Hart, P.E., Stork, D.G.: Pattern Classification, 2nd edn. Wiley Interscience, New York (2000)
6. Goyal, A., Newcombe, R., Chhabra, A., Mansel, R.: Morbidity in breast cancer patients with sentinel node metastases undergoing delayed axillary lymph node dissection (ALND) compared with immediate ALND. Ann. Surg. Oncol. **15**, 262–267 (2008)
7. Hayes, S., Janda, M., Cornish, B., Battistutta, D., Newman, B.: Lymphedema after breast cancer: incidence, risk factors, and effect on upper body function. J. Clin. Oncol. **26**(21), 3536–3542 (2008)
8. Hayes, S., Rye, S., Battistutta, D., DiSipio, T., Newman, B.: Upper-body morbidity following breast cancer treatment is common, may persist longer-term and adversely influences quality of life. Health Qual Life Outcomes **8**(1), 92 (2010)
9. Hudak, P., Amadio, P., Bombardier, C., Beaton, D., Cole, D., Davis, A., Hawker, G., et al.: Development of an upper extremity outcome measure: the DASH (disabilities of the arm, shoulder, and head). Am. J. Ind. Med. **29**, 602–608 (1996)
10. Kwan, W., Jackson, J., Weir, L., Dingee, C., McGregor, G., Olivotto, I.: Chronic arm morbidity after curative breast cancer treatment: prevalence and impact on quality of life. J. Clin. Oncol. **20**(20), 4242–4248 (2002)
11. Lu, G., DeSouza, G., Armer, J., Anderson, B., Shyu, C.: A system for limb-volume measurement using 3D models from an infrared depth sensor. In: IEEE Symposium on Computational Intelligence in Healthcare and e-health, pp. 64–69 (2013)
12. Oliveira, H.P., Cardoso, J.S., Magalhaes, A., Cardoso, M.J.: Methods for the aesthetic evaluation of breast cancer conservation treatment: a technological review. Curr. Med. Imaging Rev. **9**(1), 32–46 (2013)
13. Oliveira, H., Cardoso, J., Magalhaes, A., Cardoso, M.: A 3D low-cost solution for the aesthetic evaluation of breast cancer conservative treatment. Comput. Methods Biomech. Biomed. Eng. Imaging Vis. **2**, 90–106 (2014)
14. Stanton, A., Badger, C., Sitzia, J.: Non-invasive assessment of the lymphedematous limb. Lymphology **33**, 122–135 (2000)
15. Stratford, P.: Assessing disability and change on individual patients: a report of a patient specific measure. Physiotherapy Can. **47**, 258–263 (1995)
16. Stratford, P., Binkley, J., Stratford, D.: Development and initial validation of the upper extremity functional index. Physiotherapy Canada **53**(4), 259–267 (2001)
17. Trombetta, C., Abundo, P., Felici, A., Ljoka, C., Di Cori, S., Rosato, N., Foti, C.: Computer aided measurement laser (CAML): technique to quantify post-mastectomy lymphoedema. J. Phys. Conf. Ser. **383**, 012018 (2012)

Arabic Writer Identification Using Local Binary Patterns (LBP) of Handwritten Fragments

Yaâcoub Hannad[1]([⊠]), Imran Siddiqi[2],
and Mohamed El Youssfi El Kettani[1]

[1] ACIRS Laboratory, Ibn Tofail University, Kenitra, Morocco
y.hannad@gmail.com, elkettani@univ-ibntofail.ac.ma
[2] Department of Computer Science, Bahria University,
Islamabad, Pakistan
imran.siddiqi@bahria.edu.pk

Abstract. This paper presents a novel approach for off-line text-independent writer identification using Arabic handwritten images. Exploiting the idea that graphical fragments of handwriting characterize the writer, we propose a local approach based on texture analysis of small writing fragments where each fragment is represented by its Local Binary Pattern (LBP) histogram. The proposed method benefits from the efficiency of the LBP as a texture descriptor and the high discriminative power of handwritten fragments to improve the performance of writer identification. The proposed technique evaluated on a database of 130 writers realizes promising identification rates with reduced execution time.

Keywords: Writer identification · Arabic handwriting · Local binary patterns (LBP) · Handwritten fragments

1 Introduction

Identification of individuals from handwritten document images is an active area of research which finds applications in a number of interesting problems including forensic document analysis, verification of signatures and classification of historical archives [1]. A number of studies have validated the hypothesis that handwriting is individualistic and can be used as an effective biometric modality [2]. A variety of features, global or local, can be extracted from a given handwritten text to characterize its writer. During the last decade, significant research has been carried out on writer identification and related tasks but a major proportion of these contributions are based on text in the Latin script. Writer identification from handwritten text in other scripts (like Arabic and other Asian scripts) remains a relatively less investigated area [3]. In some cases, systems primarily developed for Latin scripts have been directly evaluated on writings in other scripts with varying degrees of success [9].

As a function of handwriting acquisition mechanism, writer identification is categorized into online and offline techniques. In online writer identification, recognition is

© Springer International Publishing Switzerland 2015
R. Paredes et al. (Eds.): IbPRIA 2015, LNCS 9117, pp. 237–244, 2015.
DOI: 10.1007/978-3-319-19390-8_27

performed at the time of writing which is provided on specialized handwriting acquisition devices. Offline writer identification predicts the identity of the writer using scanned images of handwriting. From the view point of textual content, writer identification is distinguished into text-dependent and text-independent modes. In text-dependent writer identification, a writer is required to produce the same text in training and evaluation modes. Text-independent methods do not impose any constraints on the textual content of the training and test samples and are more close to the real world identification scenarios.

In our study, we are interested in identification of writers form offline Arabic handwritten texts. The proposed technique relies on segmenting the handwriting into small fragments and characterizing each fragment by the histogram of local binary patterns. Two writing samples are then compared by computing the dissimilarity between their fragments.

The existing approaches for off-line Arabic writer identification are mainly based on two major groups of features, structural and textural. The structural features [5–7] computed at local or global levels, are aimed to capture the structural properties of writing like average line height, inter and intra-word distances and inclination etc. Texture analysis of handwriting considers each writing as a different texture and comprises in extracting a set of features from different regions of interest (blocks) or complete image [4, 8, 14]. In some cases, structural and textural features have been combined to enhance the identification performance [9, 10].

Among different Arabic writer identification systems proposed in the literature, the techniques presented in [6] and [9] demonstrate the effectiveness of features based on local writing fragments in characterizing the writer. The main drawback of these methods is the high computational complexity of the comparison between writing fragments. Inspired by the high discriminative power of small writing fragments and to overcome the bottleneck of high computational power, we propose a novel approach for offline Arabic wrier identification. The originality of the proposed technique lies in representing the texture of small fragments of writing using LBP histograms allowing an efficient as well as effective comparison between fragments of two writings. The details on the proposed methodology are presented in the next section while Sect. 3 summarizes the results of the experimental evaluations carried out to validate the ideas developed in this study. Finally, we conclude the paper with a discussion on some interesting future research directions on this problem.

2 Proposed Methodology

As discussed earlier, a number of studies have demonstrated the usefulness of exploiting small writing fragments in characterizing the writer [6, 9, 15, 16]. The major issue with these local approaches is the considerable execution time they require in order to compare the writing fragments of two samples. We propose an effective representation of writing fragments allowing an efficient comparison.

Like most of the pattern classification problems, our proposed framework comprises three main modules, pre-processing, feature extraction and identification (classification).

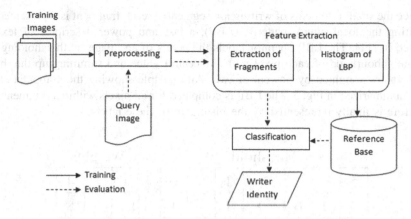

Fig. 1. An overview of the proposed system

An overview of the proposed system is illustrated in Fig. 1 while each of the three modules is discussed in the following sub-sections.

2.1 Pre-processing

Pre-processing generally comprises a series of operations to bring the images into a form that is appropriate for subsequent processing. Since we work on contemporary Arabic texts and the images are already binarized, the pre-processing in our case simply comprises extraction of connected components which are fed to the next step of feature extraction.

2.2 Feature Extraction

Feature extraction relies on representing a given writing by a set of features. We have chosen small fragments of writing as the basic unit for feature extraction and sub-sequent comparison of two writings. These fragments are obtained by dividing each component into small windows (blocks) of size $N \times N$ from left to right and top to bottom. The window size N is chosen empirically and the windows containing a very low proportion of text pixels are eliminated considering them noise. Figure 2 shows an example of the fragments extracted from a connected component.

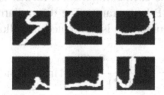

Fig. 2. Writing fragments extracted from a component

Once the small fragments of writing are segmented, each fragment is represented by computing the local binary patterns (LBP), a fast and power descriptor of texture proposed in [11]. The LBP operator labels the pixels of an image by thresholding the 3 × 3 neighbourhood of each pixel with the central value and summing up the thresholded values weighted by powers of two. An example showing the computation of LBP is summarized in Fig. 3. The LBP is computed for all pixels within a fragment and the texture is finally represented by the histogram of these labels.

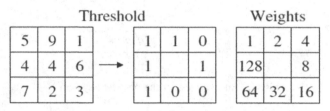

LBP code: 1+2+8+64+128=203

Fig. 3. Example of LBP code calculation

It should be noted that local binary patterns have been applied to writer identification in [12] and realized appreciable identification rates. The technique in [12], however, computes local binary patterns from the complete (normalized) images of handwriting. We, on the other hand, characterize the small fragments of writing using LBP histograms. This representation not only allows exploitation of the high discriminative power of these fragments but the fast computation of LBP histograms also results in an efficient matching of two writing samples. Other techniques based on local fragments [6], [15, 16] rely on direct matching of pixels to compare these fragments which is not only very inefficient but is also sensitive to noise and other image variations.

Each handwritten document image D in the training set is represented by the set of LBP histograms computed from the small writing fragments. A reference base of known writers is produced which is used in the identification (classification) step discussed in the next section.

2.3 Classification (Identification)

To identify the author of a query document Q, the writing in question is compared with all the samples in the database. Similar to the training phase, the query image is divided into connected components and each component is further divided into small fragments which are represented by LBP histograms. The dissimilarity between the query document Q and a reference document D is computed as follows.

$$\mathrm{DIS}(Q, D) = \frac{1}{\mathrm{Card}(Q)} \sum_{i=1}^{\mathrm{Card}(Q)} \underset{h_j \in D}{\mathrm{Min}} \left(\mathrm{distance}\left(q_i, h_j \right) \right) \tag{1}$$

where q_i and h_j are the LBP histograms of fragments i and j of documents Q and D respectively. The distance between the histograms is given by the Hamming distance.

$$\text{distance}(q_i, h_j) = \sum_{n=1}^{N \dim} |q_{in} - h_{jn}|$$ (2)

where "$N \dim$" is the length of the LBP histogram.

Finally, the writer of query document is identified as the writer of the document in the reference base which reports the minimum dissimilarity.

$$\text{Writer } (Q) = \text{ArgMin}\left(\underset{Di \,\in\, Base}{\text{DIS}(Q, D_i)} \right)$$ (3)

In the next section, we present the results of the experiments carried out to evaluate the proposed methodology.

3 Experiments and Results

This section details the experiments and the corresponding results along with a comparison and discussion. We first present the database used in our study followed by the experimental results and discussion.

3.1 Database

In our study, we have employed the most widely used Arabic handwritten database – the IFN/ENIT database [13]. It comprises 2,200 forms with more than 26,000 handwritten Arabic Tunisian town/village names collected from 411 different writers. All forms are scanned at a resolution of 300 dpi and are available as binary images. The database was mainly developed for training and evaluation of Arabic handwriting recognition systems but has also been widely used for evaluation of writer identification systems [8–10].

3.2 Results

To evaluate the performance of the proposed identification scheme, we selected a random sample of 130 writers from the database. For each of the writers, 30 word images are used in the training set and 20 as test set.

As discussed earlier, each writing is characterized by the set of LBP histograms computed from small writing fragments obtained by dividing the text into windows. The identification rates are naturally sensitive to the window size used for division of writing. We, therefore, present the identification rates as a function of window size as summarized in Fig. 4. It can be seen that the identification rates are low for smaller window sizes and begin to stabilize from a size of 80 × 80 onwards. An identification rate of 83 % is realized on a window size of 100 × 100. In comparison to other similar studies which work on small fragments [6, 9, 15], this window size is relatively larger. This large window size, however, is justified as we treat each fragment as a texture and a significant part of handwritten text is required for a better characterization of the writer.

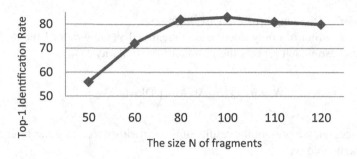

Fig. 4. Writer identification rates as a function of window size N

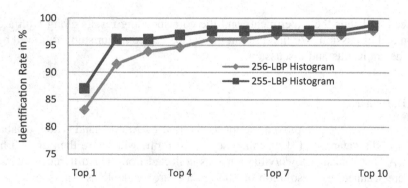

Fig. 5. Comparison of writer identification rates on 256 and 255 bin LBP histograms

An interesting aspect of LBP histogram is that the LBP code of the white (text) pixels inside the fragment (all 1 s) and the black pixels in the background (all 0 s) result in the same value (255) and are counted in the same bin (index = 256) of the histogram. This last bin of the histogram, therefore, may not be very informative. Hence, to study the identification rates ignoring this non-discriminative bin, we represent each fragment by a 255 bin histogram eliminating the last bin and compute the corresponding identification rates. This results in an improved identification rate of 87 % as compared to 83 % when using all 256 bins. The detailed comparative identification rates (Top K) using 255 and 256 bins are summarized in Fig. 5 where the 255 bin histograms realize better identification rates as discussed.

3.3 Comparison and Discussion

Since the IFN/ENIT database has been previously employed for evaluation of Arabic writer identification techniques, we present a comparison of the proposed approach with these methods. The comparison is carried out with two state-of-the-art methods presented in [8] and [9]. Table 1 summarizes the identification rates of the aforementioned systems along with the number of writers used in each study. The GLCM and GLRL based textural features proposed in [8] realize an identification rate of 82 % on 130 writers while the combination of features proposed in [9] achieves an identification rate of 88 % on 350 writers. Our proposed scheme based on representing writing fragments by LBP histograms outperforms the texture descriptors employed in [8]. The performance of the method in [9] is naturally better than our technique as this scheme, in addition to a codebook of writing fragments, also rests on a number of other probability distributions which are used as features leading to a very high dimensional feature vector.

Furthermore, our approach based on the LBP histograms allows an efficient comparison of writing fragments as opposed to the direct comparison using correlation measure employed in other similar studies [1, 16]. Table 2 shows the average times to compare two fragments of size 100 × 100 using LBP histograms and the correlation measure defined in [1]. It can be seen that the comparison using LBP features is approximately 5 times faster than the pixel based comparison leading to an overall efficient identification system.

Table 1. Comparison of writer identification performance on IFN/ENIT database

Systems	Database	Number of writer	Identification rate (Top1)
Chawki et al. [8]	IFN/ENIT	130	82 %
Bulacu et al. [9]	IFN/ENIT	350	88 %
Proposed approach	**IFN/ENIT**	**130**	**87 %**

Table 2. Execution times to compare 100 × 100 fragments

	Correlation measure defined in [1]	Proposed dissimilarity measure
Execution time	0.063 s	**0.012 s**

4 Conclusion

In this paper, we presented a novel approach for off-line, text-independent writer identification using Arabic handwritings. The approach mainly relies on local analysis of writing fragments using LBP histograms as feature. The proposed technique evaluated on 130 writers from the IFN/ENIT database not only realized a promising identification rate of 87 % but also resulted in reduced execution time for comparison of writing fragments. In our further study on the subject, we intend to use extended LBP codes to improve the identification rates. Combining the histograms extracted from different fragment sizes can also be explored. The ideas put forward in this paper can also be evaluated on writings in other scripts.

References

1. Bensefia, A., Nosary, A., Paquet, T., Heutte, L.: Writer identification by writer's invariants. In: Proceedings of the Eighth International Workshop on Frontiers in Handwriting Recognition (IWFHR 2002) (2002)
2. Srihari, Cha, S., Arora, H., Lee, S.: Individuality of Handwriting. J. Forensic Sci. **47**(4), 1–17 (2002)
3. Awaida, S., Mahmoud, S.A.: State of the art in off-line writer identification of handwritten text and survey of writer identification of arabic text. Educ. Res. Rev. **7**(20), 445–463 (2012)
4. Said, H.E.S., Tan, T.N., Baker, K.D.: Personal identification based on handwriting. Pattern Recogn. **33**, 149–160 (2000)
5. Gazzah, S., Amara, N.B.: Neural networks and support vector machines classifiers for writer identification using arabic script. In: The Second International Conference on Machine Intelligence (ACIDCA-ICMI 2005), pp. 1001–1005. Tozeur, Tunisia (2005)
6. Chawki, D., Labiba, S.: Une approche locale en mode indépendant du texte pour l'identification de scripteurs: Application à l'écriture arabe. In: CIFED 2008, pp. 151–156. Rouen, France October 2008
7. Awaida, S.M., Mahmoud, S.A.: Writer identification of arabic text using statistical and structural features. Cybern. Syst. **44**(1), 57–76 (2013)
8. Chawki, D., Labiba, S.: A texture based approach for arabic writer identification and verification. In: IEEE International Conference on Machine and Web Intelligence, pp. 115–120 (2010)
9. Bulacu, M., Schomaker, L., Brink, A.: Text-independent writer identification and verification on offline arabic handwriting. In: Proceedings of 9th International Conference on Document Analysis and Recognition (ICDAR 2007), vol. II, pp. 769–773. IEEE Computer Society Curitiba, Brazil, 23-26 September 2007
10. Abdi, N., Khemakhem, M., Ben-Abdallah, H.: An effective combination of MPP contour-based features for off-line text-independent arabic writer identification. In: Ślęzak, D., Pal, S.K., Kang, B.-H., Gu, J., Kuroda, H., Kim, T.-H. (eds.) Communications in Computer and Information Science, vol. 61, pp. 209-220, ISBN 978-3-642-10545-6. Springer-Verlag, Heidelberg (2009)
11. Ojala, T., Pietikäinen, M., Mäenpää, T.: Multiresolution gray-scale and rotation invariant texture classification with local binary patterns. IEEE Trans. Pattern Mach. Intell. **24**(7), 971–987 (2002)
12. Bertolini, D., Oliveira, L.S., Justino, E., Sabourin, R.: Texture-based descriptors for writer identification and verification. Expert Syst. Appl. **40**, 2069–2080 (2013)
13. Pechwitz, M., Maddouri, S., Märgner, V., Ellouze, N., Amiri, H.: IFN/ENIT – Database of handwritten arabic words. In: The 7th Colloque International Francophone sur l'Ecrit et le Document (CIFED 2002). Hammamet, Tunis, 21-23 Oct. 2002
14. Shahabi, F., Rahmati, M.: Comparison of Gabor-based features for writer identification of Farsi/Arabic handwriting. In: Tenth International Workshop on Frontiers in Handwriting Recognition (2006)
15. Siddiqi, I., Vincent, N.: Writer identification in handwritten documents. In; Proceedings of the 9th International Conference on Document Analysis and Recognition (2007)
16. Bensefia, A., Paquet, T., Heutte, L.: A writer identification and verification system. Pattern Recogn. Lett. **26**(13), 2080–2092 (2005)

A Fuzzy C-Means Algorithm for Fingerprint Segmentation

Pedro M. Ferreira$^{(\boxtimes)}$, Ana F. Sequeira, and Ana Rebelo

INESC TEC, Porto, Portugal
{pmmf,afps,arebelo}@inesctec.pt

Abstract. Fingerprint segmentation is a crucial step of an automatic fingerprint identification system, since an accurate segmentation promote both the elimination of spurious minutiae close to the foreground boundaries and the reduction of the computation time of the following steps. In this paper, a new, and more robust fingerprint segmentation algorithm is proposed. The main novelty is the introduction of a more robust binarization process in the framework, mainly based on the fuzzy C-means clustering algorithm. Experimental results demonstrate significant benchmark progress on three existing FVC datasets.

Keywords: Fingerprint segmentation · Fuzzy C-means clustering · Morphological processing

1 Introduction

Fingerprint recognition systems have been developed to be used in a wide range of personal identification domains, such as civil identification, access control and forensics. A fingerprint recognition system is composed by several processing steps: from fingerprint segmentation to minutiae extraction and matching [1]. A fingerprint image is usually composed by two distinct regions: the foreground and the background. The foreground area, which contains effective ridge information, is originated from the contact of a fingertip with the sensor. The noisy area at the border of the image, with no effective information, corresponds to the background. The separation of the content into these two groups allows to: (1) remove spurious minutiae located at the boundary of the foreground; and (2) speed up the following tasks by restricting the processing to the foreground area, making the fingerprint segmentation one of the most relevant steps of an automatic fingerprint recognition system [1].

Several fingerprint segmentation methods have been proposed. Bazen *et al.* [2] suggested a pixel-wise method, in which three features (coherence, mean and variance) are computed for each pixel and then a linear classifier associates the pixel with the foreground or the background. The method presented by Chen *et al.* [3] uses a block cluster degree along with a linear classifier. Wu *et al.* [4] proposed a fingerprint segmentation method based on the Harris corner detector. The image points with the strongest Harris response are considered as

© Springer International Publishing Switzerland 2015
R. Paredes et al. (Eds.): IbPRIA 2015, LNCS 9117, pp. 245–252, 2015.
DOI: 10.1007/978-3-319-19390-8_28

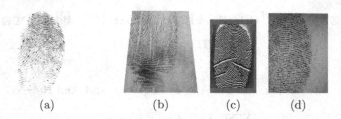

(a)   (b)   (c)   (d)

Fig. 1. Sample images of FVC2004 database. The sensors used in (a), (b), (c), and (d) are low-cost optical sensor, low-cost capacitive sensor, optical sensor, and synthetic generator, respectively.

foreground points and the final segmentation is obtained as their convex hull. Liu *et al.* [5] suggested a classification using the AdaBoost classifier with two novel features (block entropy and block gradient entropy) and several commonly used features (coherence, mean, variance and Gabor features). More recently, Fahmy *et al.* [6] proposed a fingerprint segmentation method based on morphological operations. A range filter is applied to the fingerprint image followed by an adaptive thresholding binarization. A final morphological post-processing step is performed in order to remove holes in both foreground and background.

Fingerprints acquired by different sensors display different background noise as may be observed in Fig. 1. Most of the available segmentation algorithms demonstrate lack of adaptability to this variability of noise, which increases errors in the fingerprint recognition process.

In this paper, we proposed an extension of the algorithm presented by Fahmy *et al.* [6] by introducing a new binarization process in the framework. Our segmentation method overcomes the problems inherent to the image capture with various sensors. The effectiveness of the proposed algorithm is validated by experiments performed on all available databases of the Fingerprint Verification Competition (FVC)[1]. The satisfatory results of this method will make possible to address a challenge posed by the Portuguese Mint and Official Printing Office (INCM), that often uses and promotes the R&D of the country.

The paper is organized in four sections including the Introduction (Sect. 1). In Sect. 2, the proposed fingerprint segmentation method is fully described. Section 3 reports the experimental results. Finally, conclusions and topics for future work are presented in Sect. 4.

2   Proposed Fingerprint Segmentation Method

As already mentioned, the baseline for the methodology proposed in this paper follows the morphological fingerprint segmentation algorithm presented by Fahmy *et al.* [6]; throughout this paper the algorithm of Fahmy *et al.* [6] will be referred as the baseline method. The main novelty of the proposed method is related to the involved binarization process. While in the baseline method [6] a simple

---

[1] https://biolab.csr.unibo.it.

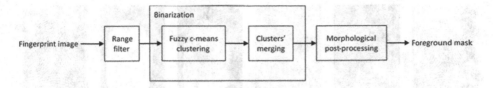

Fig. 2. Architecture of our proposed framework for fingerprint segmentation.

adaptative thresholding binarization is used, we suggest a more robust binarization method by using a Fuzzy C-means (FCM) approach. Since fingerprint images are frequently contaminated by noise (e.g., produced by the sensors) our approach is capable of coping with noise based on the clusters association of the FCM algorithm.

The high-level operations that compose our algorithm are presented in Fig. 2. First, a block-wise range filter is applied to the grey-scale fingerprint image in order to enhance the ridges. Afterwards, the resulting range image is binarized using the FCM algorithm along with a clusters' merging procedure. Finally, a set of morphological operations is applied to the binary image in order to compute the final foreground mask. Next, the several steps will be explained in more detail.

2.1 Range Filter

The problem of fingerprint segmentation is tightly coupled with the extraction of features, especially when it comes to the development of segmentation methods with sensor interoperability. The proposed methodology uses the range image as a feature. As demonstrated by Fahmy et al. [6], the range image provides better performance and interoperability capabilities than entropy and entropy-gradient features.

The range filter is a non-linear filtering method that replaces the original grey level of a pixel by the range value of the grey levels of the pixels in a specified neighbourhood:

$$R(i,j) = \max\{I(m,n)|(m,n) \in w(i,j)\} - \min\{I(m,n)|(m,n) \in w(i,j)\} \quad (1)$$

where I is the input image, R is the output image, and w represents the neighbourhood centred at image coordinates (i,j). The resulting range image is illustrated in Fig. 3b, in which the boundaries of the ridges are clearly enhanced.

2.2 Binarization

The binarization process is composed by two main steps: (1) the range image is clustered using the FCM algorithm and then (2) a clusters' merging procedure is applied in order to build up the final foreground mask.

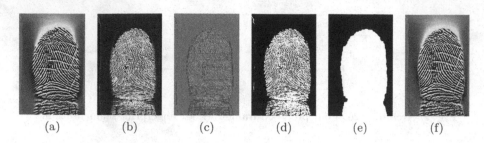

(a)   (b)   (c)   (d)   (e)   (f)

Fig. 3. Outputs of the proposed fingerprint segmentation method: (a) Original image, (b) Range filter response, (c) FCM clustering of image (b) for $C = 3$, (d) Binary image, (d) Final foreground mask, and (d) Foreground boundary superimposed on the original image.

FCM Clustering. FCM is a clustering algorithm in which a sample can be associated into more than one cluster with different degrees of similarity [7]. Let $X = (x_1, x_2, ..., x_N)$ denotes an image with N pixels to be partitioned into C clusters, where x_j represents the data samples, with $j = 1, \ldots, N$. The goal is to find an optimal fuzzy C-partition that minimizes the following objective function:

$$J(U, V; X) = \sum_{j=1}^{N} \sum_{i=1}^{C} u_{ij}^m \|x_j - v_i\|^2 \tag{2}$$

where v_i is the centroid of the ith cluster, u_{ij} is the membership function of pixel x_j, $\|\cdot\|$ represents the Euclidean distance, and m is a weighting exponential parameter on each fuzzy membership with $1 \leq m < \infty$.

Although the fingerprint area is essentially composed by two distinct objects, namely the ridges (dark pixels) and the valleys (bright pixels), the FCM algorithm is used in order to cluster the range image into three clusters ($C = 3$). The underlying assumption is that one of the clusters will be composed by pixels with high probability of being foreground, another one by pixels with high probability of being background, and a third one by pixels where the decision is not sufficiently reliable. The advantage of partitioning the range image into three clusters rather than just two is to avoid misclassified pixels especially in low quality fingerprint images. Hence, after this, a clusters' merging procedure is used in order to classify each cluster as foreground or background.

Clusters' Merging Procedure. Given the resulting clusters $C_i, i = 1, ..., 3$, and the mean $\overline{C_i}$ intensity of each cluster in the range image R, the clusters C_i are classified as foreground and background as follows:

- the cluster with the highest mean intensity is considered as foreground. Intuitively, pixels with higher range filter response belong to ridges and, hence, should be considered as foreground (green pixels of Fig. 3c).
- the cluster with the lowest mean intensity is considered as background. The assumption is that pixels with lower range filter response belong to valleys or noise and, hence, should be classified as background (red pixels of Fig. 3c).

– the remaining cluster (blue pixels of Fig. 3c) is selected for further analysis.

The remaining cluster is composed by pixels of both foreground and backgound classes. To find the resultant classification it is important to know the relation among the pixels. In doing so, a connected component analysis is performed. Each connected region is considered as foreground or background according to two criteria:

Let R_i be the ith connected region and R_{d_i} be its dilated region.

1. The neighbourhood-based criterion is defined by:

$$\frac{A(R_{d_i} \cap foreground)}{A(R_{d_i})} > T_1 \tag{3}$$

where A denotes the area in pixels and T_1 is a threshold experimentally obtained. In this manner, a connected region R_i is classified as foreground if it is in the neighbourhood of pixels already classified as foreground.
2. The variance-based criterion is defined by:

$$\frac{|\sigma^2(R_i) - \sigma^2(R_{d_i})|}{max(\sigma^2(R_i), \sigma^2(R_{d_i}))} > T_2 \tag{4}$$

where $\sigma^2(\cdot)$ denotes de variance of the grey-levels within the specified region and T_2 is a threshold experimentally obtained. This condition guarantee that connected regions with high grey level differences to their neighbouring-pixels are not excluded.

Afterwards, the foreground region is computed as the union of all the connected components R_i which met at least one of the conditions previously described. The final result of this step is illustrated in Fig. 3d.

2.3 Morphological Post-processing

At this stage the binary foreground mask is composed by several disjoint binary regions with ragged boundaries. Therefore, a post-processing is required in order to obtain the final foreground mask. The post-processing operations include: (1) a morphological closing filter in order to join small adjacent regions; (2) a region filling algorithm to fill interior holes of the binary objects; (3) a morphological opening filter to eliminate thin protrusions and, generally, smooth the contours; and (4) the largest binary component of the image is selected and assumed as the final foreground mask. The result of the morphological post-processing is illustrated in Fig. 3e.

3 Experimental Results

The main goal of fingerprint segmentation is to remove the noisy background from the images and, hence, increase the overall accuracy of an automatic fingerprint recognition system. In this regard, the quantitative evaluation of the

Table 1. The comparison of the 4 segmentation methods in terms of Err.

	Average $Err(\%)$
Proposed	**6.50**
Fahmy *et al.* [6] (baseline)	7.47
NBIS [8]	11.50
Kovesi [9]	15.05

proposed fingerprint segmentation algorithm was made in two steps: (i) a comparison of the automatic segmentation results with ground-truth data (obtained by manually segmenting fingerprint images); and (ii) a goal-directed performance evaluation, in order to assess the overall accuracy of a fingerprint recognition system that integrates the proposed segmentation method.

In both evaluations, the proposed fingerprint segmentation algorithm was directly compared with other three state-of-the-art algorithms: (1) the baseline segmentation algorithm [6]; (2) the fingerprint segmentation method of the MINDTCT module from NBIS [8]; and (3) a well known variance-based method presented by Kovesi [9].

Experiments were conducted using the public FVC databases: FVC2000, FVC2002 and FVC2004. These databases include fingerprint images acquired with several sensor types (i.e. optical, capacitive and thermal sweeping sensors). Each of them contains four databases, namely DB1_A, DB2_A, DB3_A and DB4_A, composed by 800 fingerprint images acquired from 100 persons with 8 fingerprints per person. The parameters used by the proposed segmentation method were the same in all the experiments. The FCM algorithm used $m = 2$ and the thresholds of the clusters merging procedure were fixed as $T_1 = 0.8$ and $T_2 = 0.2$.

3.1   Ground-Truth Based Evaluation

In this experiment 240 images from the three FVC databases were randomly selected. It includes 20 images of each subset in order to guarantee the evaluation in images acquired from different sensor types.

The manual segmentation of the fingerprint images was performed by three specialists in fingerprint recognition. The segmentation error rate (Err) used to quantify the boundary differences, between the manual segmentation (GT) and the automatic segmentation (AS), is defined as:

$$Err = \frac{\#(GT \oplus AS)}{\#GT} \times 100 \tag{5}$$

where $\oplus$ represents the exclusive-OR operation. Err is a measure of the misclassified pixels in the foreground and the background. Table 1 presents the average Err of the three specialists for each segmentation method involved in the comparison. The proposed segmentation method outperformed the three state-of-art segmentation methods. Figure 4 shows the segmentation of some images using the proposed technique.

Fig. 4. Results of the proposed fingerprint segmentation algorithm in images of the FVC databases aquied from different sensors types.

Table 2. The comparison of the segmentation methods in terms of $EER(\%)$. Numbers in boldface are the best results.

	FVC2000				FVC2002				FVC2004				Average	Stdev
	DB1	DB2	DB3	DB4	DB1	DB2	DB3	DB4	DB1	DB2	DB3	DB4		
Proposed	2.64	**1.18**	**4.61**	**3.14**	1.72	**0.71**	**5.29**	2.11	5.71	**5.71**	**5.50**	4.47	**3.57**	**1.87**
Fahmy *et al.* [6] (baseline)	4.64	1.27	4.79	3.29	1.61	0.82	5.36	2.18	5.90	7.75	5.61	4.64	3.84	1.98
Kovesi [9]	2.07	1.29	11.03	3.24	**1.47**	0.91	7.43	**1.96**	5.74	5.79	7.84	**4.39**	4.43	3.19
NBIS [8]	**2.04**	1.33	11.07	3.29	1.52	1.01	7.60	2.07	**5.46**	6.43	11.29	4.54	4.80	3.65

3.2   Goal-Directed Performance Evaluation

In this section, a goal-directed performance evaluation that assesses the overall improvement in the system performance that incorporates the proposed segmentation method is presented. Such evaluation is capable of providing a more reliable assessment of the performance benchmark and is directly associated with the ultimate goal of the system. In this regard, an in-house robust fingerprint verification system was built up and the proposed fingerprint segmentation method was compared with other three state-of-the-art methods by replacing the segmentation module of their system.

Table 2 summarizes the results in 9600 images of the FVC databases in terms of EER (equal-error rate). A first observation is that the in-house fingerprint verification system achieves, in general, better results when it uses the proposed segmentation algorithm rather than the other three state-of-the-art methods. More concretely, the performance of the fingerprint verification system is improved in 7 of the 12 FVC databases when our segmentation method is integrated in the system. Likewise, the proposed fingerprint segmentation method promotes the lowest average EER (3.57 %) and the lowest standard deviation (1.87 %). These results indicate that the proposed segmentation algorithm outperforms the existing methods and can handle better with the sensor interoperability problem. When compared with the baseline algorithm, the proposed segmentation method promoted an overall improvement in the system performance.

4   Conclusions

The purposes of segmentation in the fingerprint recognition context are both the reduction of the computation time of the following processing steps and, most importantly, the exclusion of many spurious minutiae located at foreground boundaries. In this paper, a new fingerprint segmentation algorithm was proposed taking as baseline the method presented by [6]. The main contribution was the introduction of a more robust binarization process in the framework. The binarization process comprises two steps: (1) a FCM clustering, followed by (2) a clusters' merging procedure in order to build up the final foreground mask.

Experimental results suggest that the proposed segmentation method outperforms other existing methods in both segmentation error rate and overall improvement in the fingerprint system recognition performance.

Acknowledgements. This work is financed by the FCT Fundação para a Ciência e Tecnologia (Portuguese Foundation for Science and Technology) within project UID/ EEA/50014/2013. The second author thanks to FCT for the PhD grant SFRH/BD/ 74263/2010.

References

1. Maltoni, D., Maio, D., Jain, A.K., Prabhakar, S.: Handbook of Fingerprint Recognition, 2nd edn. Springer Professional Computing, London (2009)
2. Bazen, A.M., Gerez, S.H.: Segmentation of fingerprint images. In: ProRISC 2001 Workshop on Circuits, Systems and Signal Processing. pp. 276–280 (2001)
3. Chen, X., Tian, J., Cheng, J., Yang, X.: Segmentation of fingerprint images using linear classifier. EURASIP J. Appl. Signal Process. **2004**, 480–494 (2004)
4. Wu, C., Tulyakov, S., Govindaraju, V.: Robust point-based feature fingerprint segmentation algorithm. In: Lee, S.-W., Li, S.Z. (eds.) ICB 2007. LNCS, vol. 4642, pp. 1095–1103. Springer, Heidelberg (2007)
5. Liu, E., Zhao, H., Guo, F., Liang, J., Tian, J.: Fingerprint segmentation based on an adaboost classifier. Front. Comput. Sci. China 5(2), 148–157 (2011)
6. Fahmy, M., Thabet, M.: A fingerprint segmentation technique based on morphological processing. In: 2013 IEEE International Symposium on Signal Processing and Information Technology(ISSPIT), December 2013
7. Suri, J.S., Wilson, D.L., Laxminarayan, S.: Handbook of Biomedical Image Analysis - Volume II:Segmentation Models Part B. Kluwer Academic/Plenum Publishers, London/New York (2005)
8. Watson, C.I., Garris, M.D., Tabassi, E., Wilson, C.L., Mccabe, R.M., Janet, S., Ko, K.: User's guide to NIST biometric image software (NBIS) (2007)
9. Kovesi, P.: Matlab and octave functions for computer vision and image processing. http://www.csse.uwa.edu.au/~pk/Research/MatlabFns/#fingerprints

Word-Graph Based Applications
for Handwriting Documents: Impact
of Word-Graph Size on Their Performances

Alejandro H. Toselli[✉], Verónica Romero, and Enrique Vidal

PRHLT Research Centre, Universitat Politècnica de València,
Camino de Vera, S/n, 46022 Valencia, Spain
{ahector,vromero,evidal}@prhlt.upv.es

Abstract. Computer Assisted Transcription of Text Images (CATTI) and Key-Word Spotting (KWS) applications aim at transcribing and indexing handwritten documents respectively. They both are approached by means of Word Graphs (WG) obtained using segmentation-free handwritten text recognition technology based on N-gram Language Models and Hidden Markov Models. A large WG contains most of the relevant information of the original text (line) image needed for CATTI and KWS but, if it is too large, the computational cost of generating and using it can become unaffordable. Conversely, if it is too small, relevant information may be lost, leading to a reduction of CATTI/KWS in performance accuracy. We study the trade-off between WG size and CATTI &KWS performance in terms of effectiveness and efficiency. Results show that small, computationally cheap WGs can be used without loosing the excellent CATTI/KWS performance achieved with huge WGs.

1 Introduction

In recent years, large quantities of historical handwritten documents are being scanned into digital images, which are then made available through web sites of libraries and archives all over the world. Despite this, the wealth of information conveyed by the text captured in these images remains largely inaccessible (no plain text, difficult to read even for researchers). Given the amount of text, automated methods are needed to allow the users to transcribe and/or search, and also to add value to mass-digitisation and preservation efforts of Culture Heritage institutions. To this end, the *tranScriptorium*[1] project aims at fulfil these requirements with the development of two different applications: the *Computer Assisted Transcription for Test Images* (CATTI) [1], intended to speed up transcription process, and the *KeyWord Spotting* [2] for automatic indexing of untranscribed handwritten material under the so called *Precision-Recall trade-off model*. Actually, both applications rely on what is called *word lattice* or *Word Graph* (WG), which are previously produced by a standard HMM-based handwritten text recognition system. It is worth noting that in their own

---

[1] http://www.transcriptorium.eu.

© Springer International Publishing Switzerland 2015
R. Paredes et al. (Eds.): IbPRIA 2015, LNCS 9117, pp. 253–261, 2015.
DOI: 10.1007/978-3-319-19390-8_29

conception, CATTI and KWS approaches do not require the use of WGs for performing corresponding tasks. However, usually large response times due to running CATTI and KWS without WGs would rather affect their usabilities.

A WG is a data structure proposed by several authors some decades ago during the development of Automatic Speech Recognition (ASR) technology [3]. They are generated through a natural extension of the standard dynamic programming Viterbi decoding algorithm, which determines the single best HTR hypothesis. An important shortcoming of WGs is the large computing cost entailed by their generation, often very much larger than the cost of the basic Viterbi decoding process itself. WG generation cost depends on many factors, including the input sequence length and decoding vocabulary size. But a major factor is, by far, a parameter known as *maximum node input degree* (IDG), which specifies the amount of information retained at each node during the WG generation process. In addition to reducing IDG, other pruning techniques, such as *beam-search, histogram pruning*, etc. can also be used to accelerate the WG generation process at the expense some loss of the information retained in the resulting WGs [3].

This paper studies how different sizes of WGs pruned by different IDG values impact on the effectiveness/efficiency performance of both CATTI and KWS applications. This study will serve as a reference for making good enough estimations of required space-time resources for tasks entailing the processing of massive handwritten material using CATTI and WG-based KWS.

2   Overview of HTR and WGs Technology

This section is devoted to introduce the basics of the *handwritten text recognition system* (HTR) used to generate WGs required by both CATTI and WG-based KWS.

2.1   HTR Based on HMMs and N-Grams

The employed HTR technology is based on *Hidden Markov Models* (HMMs) and N-grams, and follows the fundamentals presented in [4]. This recognizer accepts a handwritten text line image, represented as a sequence of feature vectors $\mathbf{x}$, and find a most likely word sequence $\widehat{\mathbf{w}}$ according to: $\widehat{\mathbf{w}} = \arg\max_{\mathbf{w}} p(\mathbf{x} \mid \mathbf{w}) \cdot P(\mathbf{w})$. The conditional density $p(\mathbf{x} \mid \mathbf{w})$ is approximated by morphological word models, built by concatenating character HMMs [5], and the prior $P(\mathbf{w})$ is approximated by an N-gram language model [5].

The search (or decoding) of $\widehat{\mathbf{w}}$ is optimally carried out by using the Viterbi algorithm [5]. Moreover, rather than obtaining just a single best solution (i.e. $\widehat{\mathbf{w}}$) a huge set of best solutions can be obtained in the form of a WG as a byproduct of this decoding process. For a more detailed description of this HTR system, including text line processing, model training and decoding, refers to [1].

2.2 Word-Graphs

A WG represents very efficiently a huge number word sequence hypotheses whose posterior probabilities are large enough, according to morphological character likelihood and prior (language) models, used to decode a text line image, represented as a sequence of feature vectors. WGs also store additional important data about these hypotheses; namely, alternative word segmentations and word decoding likelihoods.

Formally, a WG is represented as a weighted directed acyclic graph whose edges are labelled with words and weighted with scores derived from the HMM (likelihood) and N-gram (prior) probabilities. It is defined as a finite set of nodes Q and edges E, including an initial node $\nu_I \in Q$ and a set of final nodes $F \subseteq (Q - \nu_I)$. Each node ν is associated with a horizontal position of $\mathbf{x}$, given by $l(\nu) \in [0, n]$, where n is the length of $\mathbf{x}$. For an edge $(\nu', \nu) \in E$ $(\nu' \neq \nu, \nu' \notin F, \nu \neq \nu_I)$, $v = \omega(\nu', \nu)$ is its associated word and $s(\nu', \nu)$ is its score, corresponding to the likelihood that the word v appears in the *image segment* delimited by frames $t(\nu') + 1$ and $t(\nu)$.

A *complete path* of a WG is a sequence of nodes starting with node ν_I and ending with a node in F. Complete paths correspond to whole line decoding hypotheses. WGs considered in this work are unambiguous; that is, no two complete paths exist in a WG which correspond to the same sequence of words.

2.3 Complexity Cost

It is well known that the computational complexity of the Viterbi algorithm is linear with the length of $\mathbf{x}$ and the cost can be made largely independent of the lexicon size and the overall size of the models used by means of well known pruning techniques such as *beam-search* [5]. However, when the decoding process includes WG generation, the overall computing cost is observed to grow very fast with the WG size (exponentially with the WG size, according to [6]).

On the other hand, *error correcting parsing* carried out by CATTI on a WG (see [1]) as well as the WG normalization process required by KWS, entails an extra computational cost which mainly depends on the total number of WG edges. However, according to [7], as well as to our own observations, this cost is negligible; typically less than 1 % of the total cost required for generating a large WG.

3   Outline of WG-Based CATTI and KWS Applications

3.1   WG-Based CATTI Application

The CATTI system is presented in detail in [1]. In the CATTI framework, the human transcriber is directly involved in the transcription process since he/she is responsible of validating and/or correcting the HTR output.

The interactive transcription process starts when the HTR system proposes a full transcript of a feature vector sequence $\mathbf{x}$, extracted from a handwritten text line image. In each interaction step the user validates a prefix of the transcript which is error free and introduces some amendment to correct the erroneous text that follows the validated prefix, producing a new prefix **p**. At this point, the system takes into account the new prefix and tries to complete it by searching for a most likely suffix, $\hat{\mathbf{s}}$, according to:

$$\hat{\mathbf{s}} = \arg\max_{s} P(\mathbf{s} \mid \mathbf{x}, \mathbf{p}) \approx \arg\max_{s} p(\mathbf{x} \mid \mathbf{p}, \mathbf{s}) \cdot P(\mathbf{s} \mid \mathbf{p}) \tag{1}$$

As in conventional HTR, $p(\mathbf{x} \mid \mathbf{p}, \mathbf{s})$ can be approximated by HMMs and $P(\mathbf{s} \mid \mathbf{p})$ by and n-gram model conditioned by **p**. The main difference is that now **p** is given. Therefore, the search must be performed over all possible suffixes **s** of **p**. This search is carried out using the WGs obtained during the recognition process, achieving a very efficient, linear cost search [1]. This process is repeated until a complete and correct transcript of the input signal **x** is reached.

3.2 WG-based Handwritten Image KWS

The WG-based KWS approach presented here is *line-based*. The goal is to determine whether a given keyword is or is not in each text line image, no matter how many occurrences of the word may appear in the line. According to [2], an adequate global line-level measure $S(v, \mathbf{x})$ to score the degree of presence of a keyword v in a text line (represented by its feature vector sequence **x**), without considering any specific position within the line image, is given by:

$$S(v, \mathbf{x}) \stackrel{\text{def}}{=} \max_{i} P(v \mid i, \mathbf{x}) \tag{2}$$

where the frame-level word posterior, $P(v \mid i, \mathbf{x})$, is the probability that the word v is present in the line image at position i (the index of a feature vector **x**). In [2] it is shown how this probability can be directly and efficiently computed by using WGs. Specifically, it can be obtained by considering the contribution of all the WG edges labelled with v, which correspond to segmentation hypotheses that include the frame i; that is:

$$P(v \mid i, \mathbf{x}) \approx \sum_{\substack{(\nu', \nu) \in E: \\ v = \omega(\nu', \nu), \\ t(\nu') < i \leq t(\nu)}} \frac{\alpha(\nu') \cdot s(\nu', \nu) \cdot \beta(\nu)}{\beta(\nu_I)} \tag{3}$$

where $\alpha(.)$ is the *forward* and $\beta(.)$ *backward* accumulated path scores which can be efficiently computed on the WGs by dynamic programming [2,8].

4 Experiments

To compare the performance of both the CATTI and WG-based KWS approaches for different WG sizes, several experiments were carried out. The evaluation measures, corpora, experimental setup and the results are presented next.

4.1   Evaluation Measures

WG sizes effect on CATTI and KWS performances are assessed in terms of effectiveness (accuracy) and efficiency (time and space requirements).

To asses the effectiveness of the CATTI system we use the *word stroke ratio* (WSR). It can be defined as the number of word level user interactions necessary to achieve the reference transcription of the text image considered, divided by the total number of reference words. The WSR gives an estimation of the needed human effort to produce correct transcriptions using the CATTI system.

For effectiveness assessment of the KWS approach, we employed the popular scalar measure called *average precision* (AP) [9]. The AP is based on the standard *recall* and *interpolated precision* [10] measures, which are functions of a threshold used to decide whether a score $S(v, \mathbf{x})$ (see (2)) is high enough to assume that a word v is in $\mathbf{x}$. Actually, the AP is defined as the area under the Recall-Precision curve.

On the other hand, computing times required for efficiency assessment are reported in terms of total *elapsed* times needed using a dedicated single core of a 64-bit Intel Core Quad computer running at 2.83 GHz.

4.2   Corpora Description

Experiments were carried out on two different corpora: "Cristo-Salvador" (CS) [11] and Parzival database (PAR) [12][2].

CS is a XIX century Spanish manuscript which was kindly provided by the *Biblioteca Valenciana Digital* (BiVaLDi). It is composed of 50 color images text pages, written by a single writer and scanned at 300 dpi.

Table 1. Basic statistics of the partition of the CS and PAR databases. OOV stands for Out-Of-Vocabulary words.

	CS			PAR			
	Training	Test	Total	Training	Valid	Test	Total
Running chars	35 863	26 353	62 216	64 436	26 211	38 339	128 986
Running words	6 223	4 637	10 860	14 042	5 671	8 407	28 120
Running OOV(%)	0	29.03	–	0	14.58	12.40	–
# Lines	675	497	1 172	2 237	912	1 328	4 477
Char lex. size	78	78	78	90	80	82	96
Word lex. size	2 236	1 671	3 287	3 221	1 753	2 305	4 936

On the other hand, PAR is a medieval manuscript from the XIII century referred to as *St. Gall, collegiate library, cod. 857.* It is composed by 45 pages,

---

[2] CS and PAR are publicly available for research purposes from http://www.prhlt.iti.upv.es/page/data and www.iam.unibe.ch/fki/databases, respectively.

written by multiple authors in the Middle High German language. Table 1 summarizes statistical information of data partitioning used for each corpus.

4.3   System Setup

The line images of both the CS and PAR training partitions were used to train corresponding character HMM models using the standard embedded Baum-Welch training algorithm [5]. A left-to-right HMM was trained for each of the elements appearing in the training text images (78 for CS and 82 for PAR), such as lowercase and uppercase letters, symbols, special abbreviations, possible spacing between words and characters, crossed-words, etc. Meta-parameters of the HTR feature extraction modules for CS [1] and PAR [13], as well as corresponding HMM models, were optimized through cross-validation on the CS training data and on the PAR validation data, respectively. The optimal number of states per HMM for CS was 14 with 16 Gaussian densities per state, and 8 states with 16 Gaussians per state for PAR.

The training set transcripts of both corpora were also used to train the respective 2-grams with Kneser-Ney back-off smoothing (for the PAR final evaluation, the language model training includes also the validation data).

For each line image of the test partition, five WGs were obtained for the following input degree values: 3, 5, 10, 20 and 40. All these WGs were generated using the HTR system [1] with the previously trained models (HMMs and 2-grams). Table 2 shows some statistics of the resulting WGs for different maximum input degrees (IDG), along with the *minimum word error rates* $(W(\%))$ [14] and their average computing time generation (T_{gen}).

Table 2. Statistics of the CS and PAR WGs obtained for different IDG values. All the figures are numbers of elements, averaged over all the generated WGs, with exception of the *minimum word error rates* $(W(\%))$ values. T_{gen} stands for the average WG generation time (minutes). Standard deviation for Nodes, Edges and Words are below $\pm 25\%$ and $\pm 35\%$ of their average values for CS and PAR respectively.

| | CS | | | | | PAR | | | | |
IDG	Nodes	Edges	Words	$W(\%)$	T_{gen}	Nodes	Edges	Words	$W(\%)$	T_{gen}
3	66	182	31	40.9	3.2	38	102	22	18.8	1.5
5	175	796	57	38.7	4.2	80	346	38	16.3	2.0
10	670	6 008	128	36.7	7.1	224	1 831	77	15.1	3.8
20	2 416	42 990	279	34.9	15.0	618	9 751	153	14.3	6.8
40	7 600	272 850	530	33.6	36.3	1 643	51 951	297	13.6	16.5

The $W(\%)$ is a *goodness* property of WGs. For each WG, it has been computed measuring, by dynamic programming [14], the minimum edit distance from the reference to a word sequence hypothesis in the WG.

For CATTI, once the WGs were generated, the system used them directly to complete the prefixes accepted by the user. For each interaction, the decoder parsed the validated prefix **p** over the WG and then continued searching for the suffix **s** that maximizes the posterior probability according to Eq. (1).

For KWS, the WGs were normalized and the frame-level word posterior probabilities $P(v \mid i, \mathbf{x})$ were computed according to Eq. (3). Finally, word confidence scores, $S(v, \mathbf{x})$, were computed from these probabilities as described in Eq. (2).

4.4   Results and Discussion

Experiments with the WG-based application approaches described in Sect. 3 were carried out for the increasingly large WGs described in Sect. 4.3. For CATTI application, in each of these five trials, the respective *word stroke ratio* (WSR) along with the average time required to load the WG in the system and the average interaction time (T_{wld} and T_{int} in seconds) are reported in Table 3. In addition, for the KWS application are shown the *Average Precision* (AP) and the average indexing time (T_{ind} in seconds).

Table 3. Left: CATTI WSR for different IDG values along with the average WG load time and word interaction times: T_{wld} and T_{int} (seconds). Right: KWS figure AP along with the average indexing time: T_{ind} (seconds). 95 % confidence intervals are below ±1 % in PAR and ±3 % in CS for WSR, and below ±0.01 in PAR and ±0.03 in CS for AP.

	CATTI CS			CATTI PAR			KWS CS		KWS PAR	
IDG	WSR	T_{wld}	T_{int}	WSR	T_{wld}	T_{int}	AP	T_{ind}	AP	T_{ind}
3	44.3	$2\,10^{-3}$	$4\,10^{-4}$	20.05	$2\,10^{-3}$	$3\,10^{-4}$	0.699	10^{-5}	0.878	10^{-5}
5	43.7	0.007	10^{-3}	19.7	0.005	$8\,10^{-4}$	0.715	$8.7\,10^{-4}$	0.888	$2.2\,10^{-4}$
10	43.4	0.046	10^{-2}	19.3	0.02	0.005	0.720	$3.9\,10^{-2}$	0.893	$2.1\,10^{-2}$
20	43.3	0.338	0.067	18.9	0.104	0.029	0.722	$3.1\,10^{-1}$	0.894	$1.9\,10^{-1}$
40	43.3	2.228	0.459	18.9	0.565	0.169	0.722	2.1	0.895	1.05

From the results, we observe that for WG input degree values larger than 10, the WSR (43.4/19.3 CS/PAR) of CATTI and the AP (0.720/0.893 CS/PAR) of KWS do not improve significantly. On the other hand, the WSR/AP only rises/drops about less than 2 % by using very much smaller WGs (corresponding to an input degree of 5, with around less than 6 times the number of WG edges on average. As a result, the overall WG generation costs required using these WGs become orders of magnitude lower than the costs incurred using the WGs with largest input degree (see Tables 2 and 3).

Therefore, we conclude that an *Indeg* of 5 constitutes a very good trade-off between CATTI and KWS accuracy and computing cost.

5   Remarks and Conclusions

Performance of two applications, CATTI and KWS, for handwritten document images based on word graphs is studied in this paper. In these applications respectively, interaction process and confidence scores are driven/computed using word graphs generated during a decoding process of text line images using optical HMMs and N-Gram language models. The specific work presented in this paper focuses on how the performance of both applications is affected by using WGs of different sizes, where WG size is controlled by limiting the node maximum input degree during WG generation.

From the reported WSR and AP figures, no significant differences are observed for WG input degrees equal to or larger than 5. For this input degree, the word graphs are really small, in the order of hundred of nodes and edges on the average. Such word graphs not only allow extremely fast computing of the CATTI interactive process and the required line-level KWS word confidence scores, but also can themselves be generated with low extra computing cost with respect to the standard Viterbi decoding computing cost.

These estimates can be used to gauge the computational resources that will be needed for performing CATTI and WG-based KWS on massive collections of handwritten document images.

Acknowledgments. Work partially supported by the Spanish MICINN projects *STraDA* (TIN2012-37475-C02-01) and by the EU 7th FP *tranScriptorium* project (Ref: 600707).

References

1. Romero, V., Toselli, A.H., Vidal, E.: Multimodal Interactive Handwritten Text Transcription. Series in Machine Perception and Artificial Intelligence (MPAI). World Scientific Publishing, Singapore (2012)
2. Toselli, A.H., Vidal, E., Romero, V., Frinken, V.: Word-graph based keyword spotting and indexing of handwritten document images. Technical report, Universitat Politècnica de València (2013)
3. Oerder, M., Ney, H.: Word graphs: an efficient interface between continuous-speech recognition and language understanding. In: IEEE International Conference on Acoustics, Speech, and Signal Processing, vol. 2, pp. 119–122, April 1993
4. Bazzi, I., Schwartz, R., Makhoul, J.: An omnifont open-vocabulary OCR system for English and Arabic. IEEE Trans. Pattern Anal. Mach. Intell. **21**(6), 495–504 (1999)
5. Jelinek, F.: Statistical Methods for Speech Recognition. MIT Press, Cambridge (1998)
6. Ström, N.: Generation and minimization of word graphs in continuous speech recognition. In: Proceedings of IEEE Workshop on ASR 1995, Snowbird, Utah, pp. 125–126 (1995)
7. Ortmanns, S., Ney, H., Aubert, X.: A word graph algorithm for large vocabulary continuous speech recognition. Comput. Speech Lang. **11**(1), 43–72 (1997)

8. Wessel, F., Schluter, R., Macherey, K., Ney, H.: Confidence measures for large vocabulary continuous speech recognition. IEEE Trans. Speech Audio Process. **9**(3), 288–298 (2001)

9. Robertson, S.: A new interpretation of average precision. In: Proceedings of the International ACM SIGIR Conference on Research and Development in Information Retrieval (SIGIR 2008), pp. 689–690. ACM, USA (2008)

10. Manning, C.D., Raghavan, P., Schutze, H.: Introduction to Information Retrieval. Cambridge University Press, USA (2008)

11. Romero, V., Toselli, A.H., Rodríguez, L., Vidal, E.: Computer assisted transcription for ancient text images. In: Kamel, M.S., Campilho, A. (eds.) ICIAR 2007. LNCS, vol. 4633, pp. 1182–1193. Springer, Heidelberg (2007)

12. Fischer, A., Wuthrich, M., Liwicki, M., Frinken, V., Bunke, H., Viehhauser, G., Stolz, M.: Automatic transcription of handwritten medieval documents. In: 15th International Conference on Virtual Systems and Multimedia, VSMM 2009, pp. 137–142 (2009)

13. Pesch, H., Hamdani, M., Forster, J., Ney, H.: Analysis of preprocessing techniques for latin handwriting recognition. In: ICFHR, pp. 280–284 (2012)

14. Evermann, G.: Minimum Word Error Rate Decoding. Ph.D. thesis, Churchill College, University of Cambridge (1999)

Temporal Segmentation of Digital Colposcopies

Kelwin Fernandes[1,2](✉), Jaime S. Cardoso[1,2],
and Jessica Fernandes[3]

[1] INESC TEC, Porto, Portugal
[2] Universidade do Porto, Porto, Portugal
kafc@inesctec.pt
[3] Universidad Central de Venezuela, Caracas, Venezuela

Abstract. Cervical cancer remains a significant cause of mortality in low-income countries. Digital colposcopy is a promising and inexpensive technology for the detection of cervical intraepithelial neoplasia. However, diagnostic sensitivity varies widely depending on the doctor expertise. Therefore, automation of this process is needed in both, detection and visualization. Colposcopies cover four steps: macroscopic view with magnifier white light, observation under green light, Hinselmann and Schiller. Also, there are transition intervals where the specialist manipulates the observed area. In this paper, we focus on the temporal segmentation of the video in these steps. Using our solution, physicians may focus on the step of interest and lesion detection tools can determine the interval to diagnose. We solved the temporal segmentation problem using Weighted Automata. Images were described by their chromacity histograms and labeled using a KNN classifier with a precision of 97 %. Transition frames were recognized with a precision of 91 %.

Keywords: Cervical cancer · Colposcopic images · Histogram distances · Temporal segmentation · Weighted finite automata

1 Introduction

Despite the possibility of prevention with regular cytological screening, cervical cancer remains a significant cause of mortality in low-income countries. This being the cause of more than half a million cases for year, and killing more than a quarter of a million in the same period [1].

Digital colposcopy is a promising and inexpensive technology for the detection of cervical intraepithelial neoplasia. The diagnostic sensitivity with these resources ranges between 67 to 98 %, depending on the expertise of the doctor [1]. The resection of lesions in the first visit could reduce the costs involved in a scheme of successive visits. Also, it would ensure the appropriate care of patients with poor adherence to treatment.

According to the protocol proposed by the World Health Organization (WHO) [1], detection of preinvasive cervical lesions during a colposcopic screening covers the following steps (see Fig. 1): macroscopic view with magnifier white light, followed by observation under green light for diagnosis of aberrant vascularization

© Springer International Publishing Switzerland 2015
R. Paredes et al. (Eds.): IbPRIA 2015, LNCS 9117, pp. 262–271, 2015.
DOI: 10.1007/978-3-319-19390-8_30

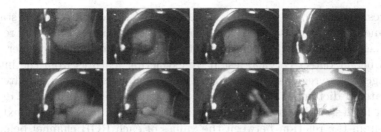

Fig. 1. **Top:** Diagnosis steps. From left to right: macroscopic observation, green filter, Hinselmann and Schiller. **Bottom:** Transition frames. The first three frames have occlusions of the cervix area and the last one presents a strong illumination difference after removing the green filter (Color figure online).

and then evaluate the cervical characteristics after exposure to acetic acid solution (Hinselmann) and potassium iodine (Schiller) [1]. Although Hinselmann and macroscopic observation cannot be differentiated on healthy patients, these two steps can be distinguished using contextual information. Throughout the procedure, the expert disturbs the cervix area to achieve better focus, to move from one step to the next, to clean the cervix area, etc. Figure 1 shows four transition frames. These scenes do not bring useful information for the diagnosis and should not be considered in the detection of lesions.

The goal of the project is to provide a more effective tool for the diagnosis of pre-invasive lesions, for environments with different resource availability and with different training staff. Our aim is to develop a diagnostic tool that can automatically identify neoplastic tissue from digital images. During the first phase of the study, we aim to achieve automatic recognition of each of the phases mentioned in the colposcopic study of a patient, in order to fine tune the diagnosis of cervical lesions. The temporal segmentation generated by our tool can be used by further techniques to detect lesions.

2   State-of-the-art

Colposcopic image processing has been a topic of interest in the last decade among computer vision researchers [2–7]. These works cover different topics from preprocessing and region segmentation [2,4], specularity removal [2,4] to computer-aided diagnosis systems that partially handle the WHO protocol [5–7].

Das *et al.* proposed a specular reflection (SR) detection algorithm based on the intensity level of the three RGB channels and reconstruct these areas using a smooth interpolant that fills the damaged area [2]. Then, they segment the cervix area using the K-means clustering algorithm. Gordon *et al.* segment the cervix region using unsupervised clustering via Gaussian Mixture Modeling [4]. They use as features the *a* channel of the *CIE - Lab* color space and the distance of a pixel to the center of the image. Then, they apply ad hoc rules to detect the clusters that represent the ROI. Roubakhsh *et al.* [3] extracted a set of features obtained by correspondence analysis (CA), color gradient, statistics measurements of the color histograms (e.g. skewness, energy) and the red level of the image. Then, they fed these features into a Neuro-Fuzzy classifier. Alush and Goldberger detect cervical lesion by extracting features from the intensity of the edges of the regions obtained by the Watershed transform [5]. After that, they created a dictionary of instances using a clustering algorithm. A different approach for lesion detection was carried out by Park *et al.* [6] who extracted features from the relation between the values of each RGB channel before and after the application of acetic acid. In the classification stage, they used an ensemble of classifiers. Finally, Acosta *et al.* built time series using the intensity change after the application of acetic acid [7]. They fitted a parabola to the time series and, using a Naive Bayes classifier, determined the lesions according their severity degree.

Although these works report good results in the lesion detection, they focus only in the Hinselmann step of the WHO protocol. To the best of our knowledge, there is no previous work on the development of a platform that covers the whole protocol. Given that our final goal is to detect lesions in any stage of the protocol, this work focuses on the temporal segmentation of the different aforementioned steps.

3   System Overview

An automated system is proposed in this paper to segment the different steps of the colposcopic assessment. Our system can be splitted in three stages: transition removal, diagnosis-step classification (frame labeling) and temporal segmentation. Figure 2 illustrates this process.

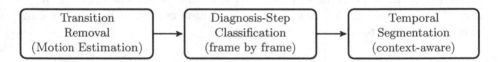

Fig. 2. Flow chart describing the proposed framework.

In general, the temporal segmentation problem implies finding simultaneously the segments and the labels. It is a hard problem which can be addressed sequentially. In this work, we take advantage of the knowledge domain by labeling the frames without considering the context and then, minimizing the temporal inconsistencies using the WHO protocol definition. The labeling is done by classification using templates from previous colposcopies and the temporal segmentation is done by translating the colposcopic procedure to a non-deterministic weighted automaton, which can be implemented using Dynamic Programming (DP). The temporal boundaries optimization tries to reach maximal consistency with the preassigned labels. The remainder of this section details the proposed system.

3.1   Transition Removal

In order to remove transition scenes, we adopted a motion-based approach. We assume that transitions correspond to frames with high motion. First, we apply a Gaussian blur to atenuate noisy pixels. Then, motion is estimated using the Euclidean pixel-wise distance between a frame and its neighborhood (W frames before and after the given frame). Finally, we apply a thresholding operator to differentiate between transition and non-transition frames. Equation (1) shows the formula that determines if a given frame belongs to a transition. Therein, I_i stands for the $i-th$ frame of the sequence I. Although more advanced approaches could be implemented, this standard procedure attained already a very good performance.

$$ Transition(i) = \left(\frac{1}{2W} \sum_{w \in [-W..W]} \| \mathcal{G}(I_{i+w}) - \mathcal{G}(I_i) \|_2 > \; threshold \right) \quad (1) $$

3.2   Diagnosis Step Classification

Each colposcopic image is represented by its one-dimensional hue histogram and saturation histogram. In order to efficiently reduce the presence of noisy objects in the boundaries of the image, we masked the region of interest by removing everything outside a image-centered circle (with diameter equal to 0.75 of the image side). This approach considers that the cervix region occupies more than half of the cervigram image [2] and that it is approximately centered.

The diagnosis step classification is done in a per-frame basis. We propose a classification method based on K-Nearest Neighbors (KNN). The similarity between two images is defined by the average distance between their histograms. We compared three histogram distances. The bin-to-bin Minkowski distance of order 1 (L_1), which is equivalent to the Histogram Intersection distance [8] and the cross-bin distances: Earth Mover's distance (EMD) [8] and Circular Earth Mover's distance ($CEMD$) [9]. Given the huge amount of images and the low intra-variance between image within the same video, we indexed an equally spaced subset of images in the KNN knowledge base. Each video contains the same number of images per phase in order to avoid oversampling and bias. We smooth the labels by selecting the mode of a local window.

3.3   Temporal Segmentation

Finally, we have to decide the temporal boundaries between the diagnosis steps. For this purpose, let's generalize the problem of temporal segmentation as the problem of *universality* in a Weighted Finite Automaton (WFA) [10], whereby we aim to accept a word (sequence of predicted labels) with minimal accumulated value. The WFA is derived from the domain-dependant protocol. Furthermore, the transition weights are related to the presence of mislabeling. Although

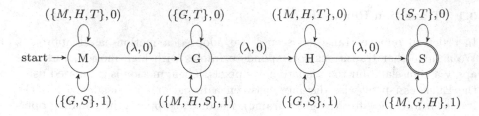

Fig. 3. Weighted Finite Automaton that recognizes the temporal segmentation of colposcopies (Transition - T, Macroscopic view - M, Green - G, Hinselmann - H and Schiller - S).

the problem of universality is PSPACE-complete [10], if any transition in our policy either consumes an input character or moves "forward" to another state in a directed acyclic graph, the recognition problem holds the conditions to formulate a DP implementation. Figure 3 shows a graphical representation of the automaton. We denote each phase by its first letter. The automaton represented in Fig. 3 is formally defined as $A =< \Sigma, Q, \Delta, c, \{M\}, \{S\}, 0, v >$, where

- $\Sigma = \{T, M, G, H, S, \lambda\}$.
- $Q = \{M, G, H, S\}$.
- $\Delta \subseteq Q \times \Sigma \times Q$ is the transition relation defined below, together with the cost function $c : \Delta \longrightarrow \{0, 1\}$. The accepted labels of each state are defined by the top-loop transitions shown in Fig. 3.
  - $(s, q, s) \longrightarrow 0$, if $q \in accepted\_labels(s)$.
  - $(s, q, s) \longrightarrow 1$, if $q \notin accepted\_labels(s)$.
  - $(s, \lambda, s') \longrightarrow 0$, if $s' \neq s$ and s' follows s in the protocol.
  - $v \in \mathbb{N}$, the minimal threshold that accepts the word.

Using the same reasoning we could instantiate any other policy in a straightforward manner. As we said before, given that after each transition the recognition problem is smaller, we can implement this automaton using the DP function defined in the Eq. (2), where seq stands for the sequence of labels predicted by the step classifier, next(s) returns the protocol step that follows s and has_next(s) $\equiv (s \neq S)$. It is assumed that the preconditions are evaluated in the same order they are shown. The optimal boundaries can be retrieved from the DP matrix. Since the number of steps in the colposcopic procedure is constant, the performance of the algorithm is linear in the length of the sequence.

$$B[i, s] = \begin{cases} 0, & \text{if } i = length(seq) \\ B[i+1, s], & \text{if } seq[i] \in \{\text{transition}, s\} \\ min(B[i+1, M], B[i, H]), & \text{if } s = M \wedge seq[i] = H \\ B[i+1, H], & \text{if } s = H \wedge seq[i] = M \\ min(B[i, next(s)], 1 + B[i+1, s]), & \text{if has\_next(s)} \\ 1 + B[i+1, s]), & \text{otherwise} \end{cases} \quad (2)$$

4   Experiments

In this section we describe the experiments that we performed in this work. We gathered a dataset of 56 colposcopies from different patients that cover a total of 143640 colposcopic images, with every image resized to 64 × 64 pixels. Sequences were manually annotated by a specialist. The videos and annotations are public on request. Table 1 shows the number of frames per video in each phase. In order to avoid biased results due to differences in the length of the procedures, every patient was equally weighted in the compilation of the results.

Table 1. Statistics of the class distribution per video

Class	Number of frames			Percentage	
	Min	Max	Avg.	Max	Avg.
Transition	0	6488	1071	59.76	39.53
Macroscopic	66	1380	313	100.00	13.88
Green	0	767	187	31.32	7.72
Hinselmann	0	2104	688	52.60	28.45
Schiller	0	2752	304	32.33	10.42
Video	200	11998	2565	–	–

For the assessment of every step of the proposed framework we used a *leave-one-patient-out cross-validation* approach (LOOCV). In this sense, each colposcopy is entirely new for the system at the evaluation stage.

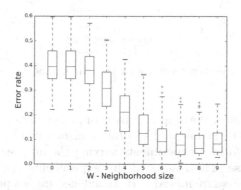

Fig. 4. Error rate of the transition removal method using different neighborhood sizes

For the classification of the transition frames we performed several experiments varying the number of neighbors. This parameter is internally learned using LOOCV. Figure 4 shows the performance of the algorithm at different

Table 2. Transition classifier results

Class	Precision	Recall	F-measure
Non-transition	0.9325	0.9129	0.9206
Transition	0.8610	0.8820	0.8672
Weighted Avg.	0.9146	0.9087	0.9087

values of W. Table 2 shows the classification results for this stage. The average accuracy of the transition recognition is 90.86 %. Furthermore, 93.25 % of the frames that pass to the next stage (colposcopic-step classification) belong to non-transition interval. There is room for human error in the decision of the boundaries of the transition intervals, i.e., it is difficult for a trained human to decide where is the beginning of a transition interval and where it ends. This artifact is also common between the different steps of the colposcopic evaluation. Therefore, the errors shown in these experiments are prone to small human inaccuracies.

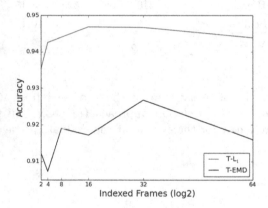

Fig. 5. Colposcopic step accuracy varying the number of indexed frames

For the assessment of the step classification, the number of neighbors in the KNN was set to 5 and the hue and saturation histograms had 180 and 256 bins respectively. We performed experiments varying the number of indexed frames in the KNN database. The results of this experiments can be seen in Fig. 5. The highest accuracy was achieved with 16 indexed frames per phase per video. These results include the temporal segmentation.

Table 3 shows the classification metrics for each colposcopic step using two distance functions: L_1 (equivalent to Histogram Intersection) and EMD. We compare each distance before and after temporal segmentation. Contrary to what we thought, $CEMD$ did not improve the accuracy but a obtained a significant performance impact. Therefore, we only show the results related to the first two

Table 3. Average classification metrics per class: Macroscopic, Green, Hinselmann and Schiller. Results with 16 indexed frames per video. The results denoted by T-d, where d is the similarity distance, include the temporal segmentation step.

Phase	Distance	Transition				Non-transition			
		Acc.	Prec.	Rec.	F	Acc.	Prec.	Rec.	F
Macro	L₁	0.82	0.36	0.28	0.52	0.70	0.38	0.31	0.52
	T-L₁	**0.96**	**0.99**	**0.78**	**0.84**	**0.98**	**1.00**	**0.95**	**0.95**
	EMD	0.80	0.32	0.28	0.48	0.65	0.33	0.31	0.49
	T-EMD	0.95	**0.99**	0.74	0.80	0.96	**1.00**	0.89	0.89
Green	L₁	**0.97**	0.97	**0.67**	**0.75**	**1.00**	**1.00**	**0.98**	**0.98**
	T-L₁	**0.97**	**0.98**	0.66	0.74	0.99	**1.00**	0.96	0.96
	EMD	**0.97**	0.96	**0.67**	**0.75**	**1.00**	**1.00**	**0.98**	**0.98**
	T-EMD	**0.97**	0.97	0.63	0.70	0.99	0.99	0.91	0.90
Hins	L₁	0.80	0.75	0.55	0.56	0.67	0.76	0.62	0.60
	T-L₁	**0.92**	**0.96**	**0.79**	**0.81**	**0.92**	**0.98**	**0.89**	**0.88**
	EMD	0.80	0.76	0.47	0.54	0.65	0.76	0.53	0.58
	T-EMD	0.91	0.93	0.76	0.77	0.89	0.95	0.86	0.83
Sch	L₁	0.90	0.74	0.60	0.60	0.88	0.79	**0.93**	0.79
	T-L₁	**0.91**	**0.83**	**0.61**	**0.65**	**0.89**	**0.89**	**0.93**	**0.82**
	EMD	0.88	0.67	0.54	0.52	0.82	0.70	0.82	0.62
	T-EMD	0.89	0.77	0.55	0.55	0.84	0.84	0.83	0.71
Avg.	L₁	0.87	0.70	0.52	0.61	0.81	0.73	0.71	0.72
	T-L₁	**0.94**	**0.94**	**0.71**	**0.76**	**0.95**	**0.97**	**0.93**	**0.90**
	EMD	0.86	0.68	0.49	0.57	0.78	0.70	0.66	0.67
	T-EMD	0.93	0.91	0.67	0.70	0.92	0.94	0.87	0.83

distances. As can be seen in the results, the selection of the decision boundaries using the proposed DP algorithm improves the detection of almost every stage. On average, the temporal segmentation algorithm improved the accuracy in 14 % and 28 % in the Macroscopic view phase. In general, the L_1 distance achieved better performance than the *EMD*. Figure 6 shows an example of the step detection results before and after the temporal decision.

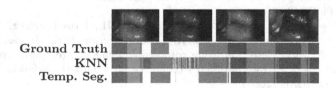

Fig. 6. Timeline with the steps represented by colors: Transition (gray), Macroscopic View (red), Green (green), Hinselmann (white) and Schiller (brown) (Color figure online).

5   Conclusions

In this work we provided a framework to temporarily segment a colposcopic assessment according to its different steps. To assess the quality of the proposed framework we gathered and annotated an open dataset of 56 colposcopies. The proposed framework achieved a precision of 91.46 % in the transition detection using an efficient threshold on motion estimation. Using chromacity information (hue and saturation histograms), we achieved a precision of 96.65 % in the step classification. As we observed in the experiments, for this problem the L_1 distance behaved better than the *EMD*, because histograms from different stages are near, and noisy pixels have a high weight in the resulting *EMD*. Contextual information provided valuable information to smooth and improve the classification results obtained by the per-frame KNN classifier.

Acknowledgement. This work is financed by the FCT - Fundação para a Ciência e a Tecnologia (Portuguese Foundation for Science and Technology) within project UID/EEA/50014/2013.

References

1. Guía global para la prevención y control del cáncer cervicouterino. Technical report, International Federation of Gynecology and Obstetrics, October 2009
2. Das, A., Kar, A., Bhattacharyya, D.: Elimination of specular reflection and identification of ROI: the first step in automated detection of cervical cancer using digital colposcopy. In: 2011 IEEE International Conference on Imaging Systems and Techniques (IST), pp. 237–241. IEEE (2011)
3. Rouhbakhsh, F., Farokhi, F., Kangarloo, K.: Effective feature selection for pre-cancerous cervix lesions using artificial neural networks (2012)
4. Gordon, S., Zimmerman, G., Long, R., Antani, S., Jeronimo, J., Greenspan, H.: Content analysis of uterine cervix images: initial steps towards content based indexing and retrieval of cervigrams. In: Medical Imaging, International Society for Optics and Photonics, 61444U–61444U (2006)
5. Alush, A., Greenspan, H., Goldberger, J.: Lesion detection and segmentation in uterine cervix images using an arc-level MRF. In: 2009 IEEE International Symposium on Biomedical Imaging: From Nano to Macro, ISBI 2009, pp. 474–477. IEEE (2009)
6. Park, S.Y., Follen, M., Milbourne, A., Malpica, A., MacKinnon, N., Markey, M.K., Richards-Kortum, R., MacAulay, C., Rhodes, H.: Automated image analysis of digital colposcopy for the detection of cervical neoplasia. J. Biomed. Opt. **13**(1), 014029–014029 (2008)
7. Acosta-Mesa, H.G., Zitova, B., Rios-Figueroa, H., Cruz-Ramirez, N., Marin-Hernandez, A., Hernandez-Jimenez, R., Cocotle-Ronzon, B.E., Hernandez-Galicia, E.: Cervical cancer detection using colposcopic images: a temporal approach. In: 2005 Sixth Mexican International Conference on Computer Science, ENC 2005, pp. 158–164. IEEE (2005)
8. Rubner, Y., Tomasi, C., Guibas, L.J.: The earth mover's distance as a metric for image retrieval. Int. J. Comput. Vis. **40**(2), 99–121 (2000)

9. Rabin, J., Delon, J., Gousseau, Y.: Circular earth mover's distance for the comparison of local features. In: 2008 19th International Conference on Pattern Recognition, ICPR 2008, pp. 1–4. IEEE (2008)

10. Almagor, S., Boker, U., Kupferman, O.: What's decidable about weighted automata? In: Bultan, T., Hsiung, P.-A. (eds.) ATVA 2011. LNCS, vol. 6996, pp. 482–491. Springer, Heidelberg (2011)

Goal-Driven Phenotyping Through Spectral Imaging for Grape Aromatic Ripeness Assessment

Marcos X. Álvarez-Cid[1]([✉]), Antón García-Díaz[1], Jorge Rodríguez-Araújo[1],
Alberto Asensio-Campazas[1], and Mar Vilanova de la Torre[2]

[1] AIMEN Technology Center, R/ Relva 27A, 36410 O Porriño, Spain
marcos.xose.alvarez@aimen.es
http://www.aimen.es
[2] Biological Mission of Galicia (CSIC), P.O. Box 28, 36080 Pontevedra, Spain
http://www.mbg.csic.es

Abstract. In this paper, we describe a systematic approach to the design of an active spectral imaging system for *in vivo* phenotyping. Our approach takes into account two major factors: spectral sensitivity of the sensor and spectral composition of the illuminant. Similarly to previous works, we adopt a scheme consisting on dimensionality reduction and SVR regression of target chemical parameters from spectral datacubes. We find that high prediction accuracies may be achieved for different sets of parameters depending on the illuminant. Furthermore, in most cases the combination of a single monochromatic illuminant with a dichromatic image sensor (passband and stopband) suffices, which paves the way for the design of tailored low cost imagers. Besides, we demonstrate *in vivo* estimation of aromatically relevant compounds of white and red grape varieties, not addressed before to our knowledge.

Keywords: Hiperspectral imaging · Grape harvest · Aromatic maturity · Chemometrics

1 Introduction

Wine quality is conditioned by a number of diverse factors that determine grape maturity and therefore the time to start grape harvest. Consequently, the wine industry demands novel techniques and instruments to assess grape maturity in function of specific enological goals (e.g. targeted bouquet).

Grape ripeness encompasses a multi-faceted concept, as it is determined by the weather conditions, the terroir, the grape cultivar and even the style of wine to be produced. Depending on the enological aspect under consideration, bibliography refers to different types of grape ripeness, such as phenolic, physiological, aromatic, industrial or technological.

The relation between sweetness and acidity present in the grape pulp is a typical indicator used by wineries to determine maturity. However, there is a shift towards differentiation and microzonification [10] that drives an increasing

© Springer International Publishing Switzerland 2015
R. Paredes et al. (Eds.): IbPRIA 2015, LNCS 9117, pp. 272–280, 2015.
DOI: 10.1007/978-3-319-19390-8_31

interest on *in vivo* estimation of aromatic compounds. This trend is even more pronounced in areas where ancient and minority cultivars have been preserved, like Galicia, in NW Spain.

The state-of-the-art approach to the measurement of aromatic compounds implies sampling bunches or berries in the vineyard and performing expensive Gas Chromatography-Mass Spectrometry (GC-MS) analysis. This is an industrious task that takes a long time to deliver the results and requires trained personnel.

On the contrary, hyperspectral imaging is a non-destructive technique that has shown its feasibility in remote sensing and precision agriculture applications [3]. In this work we demonstrate the suitability of this technology for *in vivo* phenotyping. A case study aimed at predicting the content of aromatic compounds in 4 Galician grape cultivars from hyperspectral cubes was developed. After applying a classical PCA dimensionality reduction scheme on the hypercubes and PLS and SVR regression models referred to the targeted chemical compounds, we found that the prediction results for each chemical strongly depend on the used illuminant. This suggests that using image sensors adapted to the spectral response of the best performing illuminants for each compound is a feasible approach to get tailored low cost multispectral imagers. The proposed methodology is easily extendable to other grape cultivars or plants, taking into account that the relevant compounds and illuminations to be applied will differ in every case.

The remainder of the paper is organised as follows. Section 2 provides a general overview of the basics of hyperspectral imaging applied to precision agriculture and food control quality processes. Section 3 describes our proposal for the assessment of aromatic ripeness of several Galician red and white grape cultivars through hyperspectral imaging, presenting the experimental results in Sect. 4. Finally, Sect. 5 collects the main conclusions that can be extracted from this work.

2   Hyperspectral Imaging in Viticulture

In recent years spectral vision has turned into one of the cutting-edge technologies within the fields of precision agriculture [2, 4] and food quality control [8]. To this extent, viticulture is one of the industries that is attracting a bigger research effort [1], quite probably due to the economic and cultural significance, and the low degree of technification achieved by the sector until now.

Spectral imaging introduces a number of benefits over other mature spectral technologies used in viticulture, such as near-infrared spectroscopy (NIRS) [7, 9]. For instance, while NIRS can only obtain one spectrum per sample, imaging adds spatial information, since a data cube with several spectra is delivered in a single measurement.

If only the spectral resolution is considered, imaging systems can be categorized into two groups, depending on the amount of bands the spectrum is split in. Multispectral imaging can handle a few bands, whereas hyperspectral imaging can provide information of hundreds or even thousands of bands.

Nowadays, close-range sensors are becoming more popular [6]. The higher spectral and spatial resolution enable the measurement *in vivo* of several parameters of interest from the enological point of view, such as extractable polyphenols in red grape skins, anthocyanins or technological ripeness, to cite some. Anyway, to the best of our knowledge, multi or hyperspectral imaging has not been applied yet to the estimation of aromatic ripeness.

3   Methodology

3.1   Sample Acquisition

Three traditional *Vitis vinifera* red cultivars (*Pedral, Sousón* and *Mencía*) and one white (*Albariño*) grown in Galicia (NW Spain) during the 2013 vintage were considered in this study. Up to 32 samples of grapes were analysed (14 white and 18 red). The grapes were harvested by hand at different dates during September and October 2013, then transported to the laboratory of *Misión Biológica de Galicia - CSIC.* These samples were kept frozen until February 2014.

3.2   Analysis of Grape Volatile Composition

Once the samples thawed at ambient temperature, grapes were pressed using a Thermomix V4-15S kitchen appliance and the musts centrifuged at 5000 rpm for 20 min. Afterwards, musts were frozen at −20 °C. The analysis of aromatic composition was carried out by solid-phase extraction (SPE) and the subsequent extract quantification by gas chromatography (GC-MS), following the methodology described by Vilanova et al. [11].

3.3   Hyperspectral System

The hyperspectral cubes were acquired just before pressing the samples, using a self-built testbench. It is a stand made of 35 mm aluminium frames that can bear, together or separately, the weight of both a multi and a hiperspectral camera, as well as the illumination system. The whole ensemble was covered with a quasi-lambertian fabric to avoid luminic reflections, noises and interferences and to get a lighting as scattered as possible over the sample.

The spectrograph used in this experiment is a Specim Imspector V10E and the Vis/NIR sensor is a Photonfocus MV1-D1312-C020-160 camera. Both devices work in the 400–1000 nm spectral range, that can be sliced into up to 776 sub-bands. To minimize the storage requirements without affecting the predictive performance of the system, an 8X spectral binning factor was applied on all the datasets, finally resulting in a total of 97 sub-bands per cube. Figure 1 shows a 3D representation of one of the acquired cubes.

Fig. 1. 3D representation of a grape sample hypercube (Color figure online)

The grapes were lit up with different wavelengths in order to extract more information about their aromatic composition. Five different illuminants were considered in this study: 4 monocromatic in the UV-A, red, green and blue regions and one polycromatic that blends the light from a halogen spotlight and a white LED panel. These illuminants were used both separately and combining the polychromatic illuminant with every single monochromatic panel. During the preprocessing stage, the hyperspectral cubes were calibrated against a diffuse 99 % reflectance PTFE standard, aiming to avoid any undesirable lighting effect.

4   Experimental Results and Discussion

In order to demonstrate the potential of hyperspectral imaging for plant phenotyping and characterization, we have developed an experiment aiming to set up a procedure for the *in vivo* prediction of the concentration of aromatic compounds in 4 Galician grape cultivars. PLS and SVR models were developed using the Python scikit-learn implementation of these algorithms. In both cases the results showed a satisfactory behaviour but, as PLS slightly outperformed SVR, our discussion will only refer to the latter. An exhaustive search was conducted to find the optimal SVR parameters for each problem.

Principal Component Analysis (PCA) was implemented to reduce the problem dimensionality. The number of components found to deliver the best throughput was 4, accounting the first one around 96 % of the variance. A further analysis of the principal components enables the determination of two key aspects in any tailored system for plant phenotyping based on spectral imaging: the effective spectral sub-bands of the sensors and the wavelength of the active illumination to be used. Both parameters can be tuned jointly to detect the presence of a certain compound. As Fig. 2 suggests, monocromatic lighting is likely

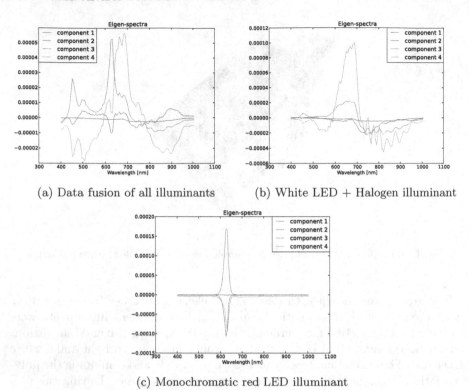

(a) Data fusion of all illuminants   (b) White LED + Halogen illuminant

(c) Monochromatic red LED illuminant

Fig. 2. Spectral plot of the first four principal components eigenvectors for white grape samples using different illumination arrangements (Color figure online)

to enhance the detection of compounds which spectral response lies within the illumination band, while the combination of illuminants blurs the discrimination among chemicals.

The statement above is confirmed by the results shown in Table 1, which gathers the figures of merit of the SVR model for the compounds that show the best predictive response in white and red grapes respectively. The bolded values represent the illuminant that provided a higher coefficient of determination for each compound. It can be checked that, in general, monochromatic illuminations allow better predictions. Moreover, there is a *prevailing illumination* that hits a higher number of chemicals at the same time, namely green in the case of white grapes, and UV in the case of red ones.

Finally, Figs. 3 and 4 display the predicted concentrations *vs.* the chemical analysis results for the cases bolded in Table 1. These graphs exhibit that the proposed approach turns specially interesting in the case of Albariño (white) grapes, as the most important aromatic compounds for this variety are correctly characterized [5].

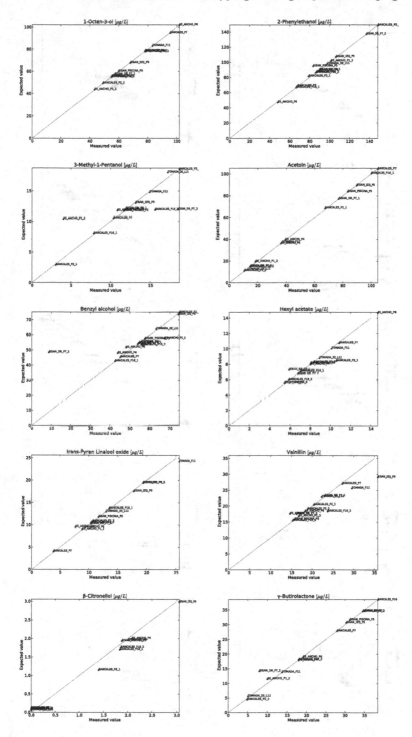

Fig. 3. Regression plots representing the chemical compounds that show a better predicting score for white cultivars

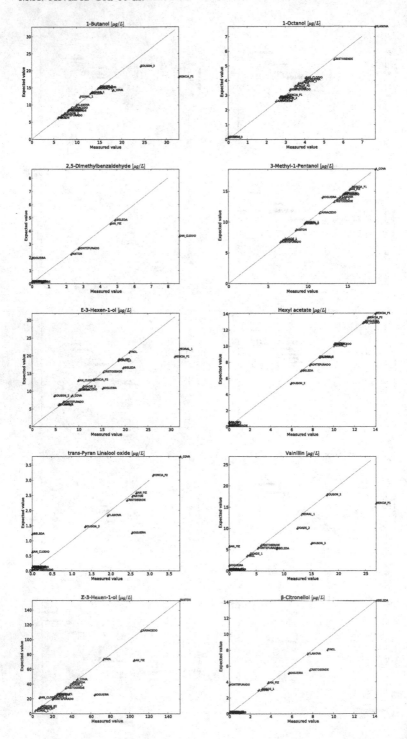

Fig. 4. Regression plots representing the chemical compounds that show a better predicting score for red cultivars (Color figure online)

Table 1. Coefficients of determination (r^2) and mean squared errors (MSE) of the SVR model for the chemicals that reached a better performance.

(a) White cultivars

Illuminant / Compound	White		UV		Blue		Green		Red		All	
	r^2	MSE	r^2	MSE	r^2	MSE	r^2	MSE	r^2	MSE	r^2	MSE
1-Octen-3-ol	0,299	203,9	**0,999**	0,067	0,613	112,6	0,671	95,74	0,585	120,8	0,147	248,0
2-Phenylethanol	0,114	577,6	0,333	434,9	0,391	397,2	0,376	407,2	**0,985**	9,538	0,106	582,8
2,5-Dimethylbenzaldehyde	0,993	0,008	0,829	0,209	0,807	0,229	0,992	0,010	0,819	0,214	**0,994**	0,007
3-Methyl-1-Pentanol	0,359	13,83	0,501	10,77	**0,673**	7,060	0,547	9,768	0,473	11,37	0,598	8,669
Acetoin	0,922	89,98	0,786	246,1	0,667	383,6	0,982	20,72	**0,999**	0,251	0,899	115,9
Benzyl alcohol	0,175	209,0	0,260	187,3	**0,518**	122,0	0,284	181,2	0,417	147,7	0,199	202,8
Hexyl acetate	0,218	4,948	0,772	1,441	0,238	4,826	**0,925**	0,476	0,289	4,498	0,063	5,931
HO-Trienol	0,894	0,473	0,454	2,443	0,984	0,072	**0,984**	0,071	0,903	0,435	0,237	3,414
trans-Pyran Linalol ox.	0,743	7,874	0,911	2,717	**0,987**	0,395	0,822	5,456	0,109	27,29	0,087	27,97
Vainillin	0,224	27,83	0,142	30,79	0,796	7,312	**0,967**	1,193	0,178	29,48	0,168	29,83
β-Citronellol	0,956	0,050	0,789	0,238	0,961	0,044	0,810	0,214	**0,990**	0,011	0,681	0,359
γ-Butyrolactone	**0,977**	2,906	0,704	38,22	0,945	7,121	0,821	23,04	0,967	4,294	**0,977**	2,992
Mean r^2	0,573		0,623		0,715		0,765		0,643		0,430	
Median r^2	0,551		0,738		0,734		0,821		0,702		0,218	

(b) Red cultivars

Illuminant / Compound	White		UV		Blue		Green		Red		All	
	r^2	MSE	r^2	MSE	r^2	MSE	r^2	MSE	r^2	MSE	r^2	MSE
1-Butanol	0,174	38,04	0,016	45,31	**0,703**	13,69	0,699	13,86	0,108	41,06	0,566	19,98
1-Octanol	0,274	2,026	0,130	2,426	-0,01	2,798	-0,01	2,798	**0,996**	0,011	0,323	1,889
2,5-Dimethylbenzaldehyde	0,514	2,790	**0,711**	1,660	0,162	4,809	0,161	4,815	0,270	4,188	0,470	3,040
3-Methyl-1-Pentanol	0,551	5,104	**0,979**	0,240	0,463	6,108	0,460	6,141	0,393	6,907	0,891	1,245
E-2-Hexanal	0,493	8475	0,640	6015	0,315	11449	0,315	11455	**0,696**	5088	0,033	16165
E-3-Hexen-1-ol	0,224	47,05	**0,737**	15,94	0,071	56,32	0,071	56,32	0,492	30,78	0,070	56,41
Ethyl lactate	-0,10	15,91	**0,999**	0,008	0,710	4,185	0,705	4,256	0,462	7,772	0,022	14,12
Hexyl acetate	0,176	22,43	0,216	21,35	**0,998**	0,052	0,997	0,077	-0,08	29,34	-0,07	29,34
trans-Pyran Linalol ox.	0,550	0,810	**0,888**	0,201	0,153	1,523	0,153	1,524	0,226	1,392	0,146	1,536
Vainillin	0,561	26,01	**0,761**	14,16	0,513	28,82	0,517	28,58	0,604	23,42	0,339	39,17
Z-3-Hexen-1-ol	0,303	1175	**0,908**	154,8	0,616	647,7	0,616	648,0	0,048	1606	0,132	1463
β-Citronellol	0,696	5,199	0,256	12,73	**0,932**	1,158	0,031	1,186	0,108	15,25	0,559	7,543
Mean r^2	0,368		0,603		0,469		0,468		0,360		0,290	
Median r^2	0,398		0,724		0,488		0,489		0,332		0,234	

5   Conclusions

Spectral imaging has shown its suitability for phenotyping. More specifically, this approach was tested on 3 Galician red and 1 white grape cultivars to predict the content of aromatic compounds, delivering a faithful characterization of some of the most significant chemicals, specially in the case of Albariño grapes.

Active illumination is key to maximize the success rate of such system, similarly to solutions based on punctual sensors, like Multiplex® [6], which is just able to assess the anthocyanin content for a reduced set of red cultivars. The advantages that our approach introduces are a wider scope, as a higher number of chemicals can be accurately predicted at the same time, and its flexibility, as it can be tuned depending on the application. This opens the door for the development of low cost bespoke multispectral systems providing a similar performance to dearer hyperspectral cameras.

In the future we aim to assess the robustness and stability of the procedure by analysing longer time series and by refining the definition of the parameters that can affect the choice of the proper illumination or effective spectral sub-bands.

Acknowledgements.. This work was financed by the Spanish Ministry of Economy and Competitiveness through the Spanish Centre for Technological and Industrial Development CDTI, and the Galician Regional Government, within the FEDER-INNTERCONECTA programme, Galicia 2013 Call (Grant No. ITC-20133114). The authors would also like to thank the wineries Pazo de Señoráns and Señorío de Rubiós for providing the grape samples and SAEC DATA for supporting the regression software development.

References

1. Arnó, J., Martínez-Casasnovas, J.A., Ribes-Dasi, M., Rosell, J.R.: Review. precision viticulture. research topics, challenges and opportunities in site-specific vineyard management. Span. J. Agric. Res. **7**(4), 779–790 (2009)
2. Chen, Y.-R., Chao, K., Kim, M.S.: Machine vision technology for agricultural applications. Comput. Electron. Agric. **36**(2–3), 173–191 (2002)
3. Dale, L.M., Thewis, A., Boudry, C., Rotar, I., Dardenne, P., Baeten, V., Pierna, J.A.F.: Hyperspectral imaging applications in agriculture and agro-food product quality and safety control: a review. Appl. Spectrosc. Rev. **48**(2), 142–159 (2013)
4. Davies, E.R.: The application of machine vision to food and agriculture: a review. Imaging Sci. J. **57**(4), 197–217 (2009)
5. Diéguez, S.C., Lois, L.C., Gómez, E.F., De La Peña, M.L.G.: Aromatic composition of the vitis vinifera grape Albariño. LWT - Food Sci. Technol. **36**(6), 585–590 (2003)
6. Ghozlen, N.B., Cerovic, Z.G., Germain, C., Toutain, S., Latouche, G.: Non-destructive optical monitoring of grape maturation by proximal sensing. Sens. **10**(11), 10040–10068 (2010)
7. González-Caballero, V., Sánchez, M.-T., López, M.-I., Pérez-Marín, D.: First steps towards the development of a non-destructive technique for the quality control of wine grapes during on-vine ripening and on arrival at the winery. J. Food Eng. **101**(2), 158–165 (2010)
8. Gowen, A.A., O'Donnell, C.P., Cullen, P.J., Downey, G., Frías, J.M.: Hyperspectral imaging - an emerging process analytical tool for food quality and safety control. Trends Food Sci. Technol. **18**(12), 590–598 (2007)
9. Guggenbichler, W., Huck, C.W., Kobler, A., Popp, M., Bonn, G.K.: Near infrared spectroscopy, cluster and multivariate analysis - contributions to wine analysis. J. Food Agric. Environ. **4**(2), 98–106 (2006)
10. Morais, R., Fernandes, M.A., Matos, S.G., Serôdio, C., Ferreira, P.J.S.G., Reis, M.J.C.S.: A ZigBee multi-powered wireless acquisition device for remote sensing applications in precision viticulture. Comput. Electron. Agric. **62**(2), 94–106 (2008)
11. Vilanova, M., Genisheva, Z., Graña, M., Oliveira, J.M.: Determination of odorants of young wines from different international grape varieties (Vitis vinifera) using GC-MS. South Afr. J. Enol. Vitic. **34**(3), 212–222 (2013)

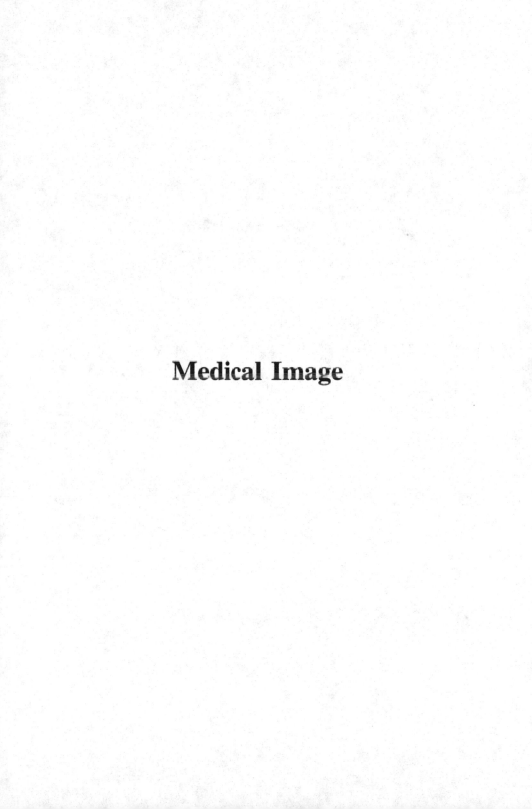

Robust 3D Active Shape Model for the Segmentation of the Left Ventricle in MRI

Carlos Santiago$^{(\boxtimes)}$, Jacinto C. Nascimento, and Jorge S. Marques

Institute for Systems and Robotics, Instituto Superior Técnico, Lisboa, Portugal
carlos.santiago@ist.utl.pt

Abstract. 3D Active shape models use a set of annotated volumes to learn a shape model. The shape model is defined by a fixed number of landmarks at specific locations and takes shape constraints into account in the segmentation process. A relevant problem in which these models can be used is the segmentation of the left ventricle in 3D MRI volumes. In this problem, the annotations correspond to a set of contours that define the LV border at each volume slice. However, each volume has a different number of slices (i.e., a different number of landmarks), which makes model learning difficult. Furthermore, motion artifacts and the large distance between slices make interpolation of voxel intensities a bad choice when applying the learned model to a test volume. These two problems raise the following questions: (1) *how can we learn a shape model from volumes with a variable number of slices?* and (2) *how can we segment a test volume without interpolating voxel intensities between slices?* This paper provides an answer to these questions and proposes a 3D active shape model that can be used to segment the left ventricle in cardiac MRI.

Keywords: Active shape model · 3D segmentation · Cardiac MRI · Interpolation

1 Introduction

Active shape models (ASMs) are commonly used to segment medical images because they lead to robust shape estimates [1]. The ASM approach uses the concept of Point Distribution Model (PDM) to learn the shape statistics from a set of annotated volumes (training set), which defines the surface of the object using a set of labeled landmarks. However, this strategy assumes that all the surface models have the same landmarks.

This assumption is not always true. For example, in the segmentation of the left ventricle (LV), in MRI volumes, the number of slices associated to the LV is subject dependent. This means that the number of landmarks used to define the

C. Santiago—This work was supported by FCT [UID/EEA/5009/2013] and [SFRH/BD/87347/2012].

© Springer International Publishing Switzerland 2015
R. Paredes et al. (Eds.): IbPRIA 2015, LNCS 9117, pp. 283–290, 2015.
DOI: 10.1007/978-3-319-19390-8_32

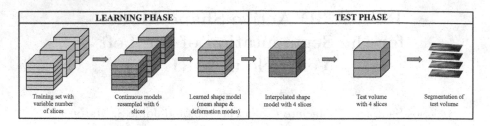

Fig. 1. Diagram of the proposed approach: (1) Learning phase - learning an ASM from volumes with a variable number of slices; and (2) Test phase - applying the learned model to a test volume.

LV surface is different. This leads to the following question: *how can we learn the shape statistics of the LV surface from volumes with a variable number of slices?*

This paper answers this question. Before learning the shape statistics, the surface models in the training set are normalized with respect to the number of slices. The normalization is done by modeling the position of each landmark (surface point) along the LV axis through interpolation. This allows the LV surfaces to be resampled at different positions (i.e., to determine the number of slices in the surface model), which allows the shape model for each slice to be learned. A schematic illustration of the proposed approach is depicted in Fig. 1 (learning phase).

After learning the shape model, we use it to segment new volumes (test phase), which may have a different number of slices. This means that the 2D contours of the learned model may not match the slices of the test volumes. Interpolation is a feasible solution [2–4], but causes the loss of contrast along the LV border (see Sect. 3). This leads to the second question: *how can we segment a test volume without interpolating voxel intensities between slices?*. We propose an alternative approach that consists in interpolating the learned model statistics, i.e., mean shape and modes of deformation.

The remainder of this paper is organized as follows. Section 2 describes the proposed shape representation and how it is used to resample the training surface models. Section 3 explains how the learned model is applied to segment a test volume. Section 4 describes the experimental setup and the results obtained using the proposed approach, and final conclusions are presented in Sect. 5.

2 Learning Phase - Interpolating the Training Surface Models

In order to learn the shape model, we resample the surface models in the training set using an interpolated model of landmarks' position along the LV axis. Under the assumption that, for any training volume v, the first (basal) slice is located at the $s_1 = 0$ and the last (apical) slice at $s_{S^v} = 1$, the axial position of the slices is given by

$$s_m = \frac{m-1}{S^v - 1}, \tag{1}$$

where $m = 1, \ldots, S^v$, and S^v is the number of slices in volume v. Let $\boldsymbol{x}_v(s_m) \in \mathbb{R}^{2N \times 1}$ be the LV contour on the m-th slice, defined by N points,

$$\boldsymbol{x}_v(s_m) = \left[\boldsymbol{x}^{1\top}(s_m), \boldsymbol{x}^{2\top}(s_m), \ldots, \boldsymbol{x}^{N\top}(s_m) \right]^\top, \tag{2}$$

where $\boldsymbol{x}^i(s_m) = \left[x_1^i, x_2^i \right]^\top \in \mathbb{R}^{2 \times 1}$ is the position of the i-th point. We assume that all the contours are sampled with N points and that there is a correspondence between the i-th point of one contour and the i-th point of another contour, i.e., they represent the same landmark. We wish to model the slice contour as a function of the axial position, $\widehat{\boldsymbol{x}}_v(s)$, for any $s \in [0, 1]$.

2.1 Interpolated Surface Model

The proposed approach aims to describe the position of the contour points of a specific volume v, $\widehat{\boldsymbol{x}}_v(s)$, along the LV axis by using a combination of K polynomial basis functions, $\boldsymbol{\psi}(s) \in \mathbb{R}^{K \times 1}$,

$$\widehat{\boldsymbol{x}}_v(s) = \boldsymbol{C}_v \boldsymbol{\psi}(s), \tag{3}$$

where $\boldsymbol{C}_v \in \mathbb{R}^{2N \times K}$ is the coefficient matrix associated to volume v. The coefficient matrix is specific of volume v and each line in the matrix is associated to a coordinate of a specific contour point. On the other hand, the polynomial basis, $\boldsymbol{\psi}(s) = \left[1, s, \ldots, s^{K-1} \right]^\top$, depend only on the slice position, s.

This representation provides an estimate of the LV contour for any position $s \in [0, 1]$. This will be used to resample the surface models in the training set. However, first, the coefficient matrix $\boldsymbol{C}_v$ associated to the surface model, v, has to be estimated from the corresponding annotations. This is addressed in the following subsection.

2.2 Resampling the Surface Models in the Training Set

In order to resample a specific surface model of volume v in the training set, the corresponding coefficient matrix $\boldsymbol{C}_v$ has to be computed, based on the available annotations. First, let us denote $\boldsymbol{X}_v^i \in \mathbb{R}^{2 \times S^v}$ as the position (trajectory) of the i-th point in the contour along the axial position s,

$$\boldsymbol{X}_v^i = \begin{bmatrix} \boldsymbol{X}_{1v}^i \\ \boldsymbol{X}_{2v}^i \end{bmatrix} = \begin{bmatrix} x_1^i(s_1), \ldots, x_1^i(s_{S^v}) \\ x_2^i(s_1), \ldots, x_2^i(s_{S^v}) \end{bmatrix} = \left[\boldsymbol{x}^i(s_1), \ldots, \boldsymbol{x}^i(s_{S^v}) \right]. \tag{4}$$

The coefficient $\boldsymbol{c}_j^i \in \mathbb{R}^{1 \times K}$, which is the line from matrix $\boldsymbol{C}_v$ associated with the trajectory points $\boldsymbol{X}_{jv}^i$, is computed by finding

$$\boldsymbol{c}_j^i = \arg\min_{\boldsymbol{c}} \| \boldsymbol{X}_{jv}^i{}^\top - \boldsymbol{\Psi} \boldsymbol{c}^\top \|^2 + \gamma \| \boldsymbol{c} \|^2, \tag{5}$$

where $\boldsymbol{\Psi} = [\boldsymbol{\psi}(s_1), \ldots, \boldsymbol{\psi}(s_{S^v})]^{\top} \in \mathbb{R}^{S^v \times K}$ is the concatenation of the polynomial basis $\boldsymbol{\psi}(s_m)$ for $m = 1 \ldots, S^v$, and γ is a regularization constant. This is a ridge regression formulation [5] that has the following solution

$$c_j^i = X_{jv}^i \boldsymbol{\Psi} \left(\boldsymbol{\Psi}^{\top} \boldsymbol{\Psi} + \gamma \boldsymbol{I} \right)^{-1}, \tag{6}$$

where $\boldsymbol{I}$ is the $K \times K$ identity matrix. This approach differs from the ordinary least squares due to the regularization term, which constrains the solution and allows the estimation of c_j^i not only for $K \leq S^v$, but also when $K > S^v$.

The solution (6) can be computed for all the lines in C_v, leading to

$$C_v = X_v \boldsymbol{\Psi} \left(\boldsymbol{\Psi}^{\top} \boldsymbol{\Psi} + \gamma \boldsymbol{I} \right)^{-1}, \tag{7}$$

where $X_v = [\boldsymbol{x}_v(s_1), \ldots, \boldsymbol{x}_v(s_{S^v})] \in \mathbb{R}^{2N \times S^v}$. Now, the contour, $\widehat{\boldsymbol{x}}_v(s)$, can be obtained for any position $s \in [0, 1]$ using (3).

This approach is used to resample all the surface models in the training set at $s_m = \frac{m-1}{S^r - 1}$, $m = 1, \ldots, S^r$, where S^r is the desired number of slices. This guarantees that all volumes have the same number of landmarks.

2.3   Learning the Shape Statistics

Once all the surface models in the training set have been resampled, it is possible to learn a shape model. We assume a surface model results from deforming the mean shape and applying a transformation associated to the pose of the LV. Therefore, before computing the shape statistics, all the surface models have to be aligned. This is done by finding, for each surface, a global (pose) transformation T_θ that minimizes the following sum of squared errors

$$E(\theta) = \sum_{m=1}^{S^r} \sum_{i=1}^{N} \left\| T_\theta \left(\widehat{\boldsymbol{x}}^i \left(\frac{m-1}{S^r - 1} \right) \right) - \boldsymbol{x}_{\text{ref}}^i \left(\frac{m-1}{S^r - 1} \right) \right\|^2, \tag{8}$$

where $\boldsymbol{x}_{\text{ref}}$ is a reference shape (for instance, one of the training shapes randomly selected), and $T_\theta(\cdot)$ is a 2D similarity transformation with parameters $\theta = \{\boldsymbol{a}, \boldsymbol{t}\}$, applied to all slices, such that

$$T_\theta \left(\widehat{\boldsymbol{x}}^i(s) \right) = \widehat{\boldsymbol{X}}^i(s) \boldsymbol{a} + \boldsymbol{t}, \tag{9}$$

where

$$\widehat{\boldsymbol{X}}^i(s) = \begin{bmatrix} \widehat{x}_1^i(s) & -\widehat{x}_2^i(s) \\ \widehat{x}_2^i(s) & \widehat{x}_1^i(s) \end{bmatrix}, \boldsymbol{a} = \begin{bmatrix} a_1 \\ a_2 \end{bmatrix}, \boldsymbol{t} = \begin{bmatrix} t_1 \\ t_2 \end{bmatrix}.$$

We are only interested in the translation, rotation and scaling within the axial (slice) plane to guarantee that the slice contours remain orthogonal to the LV axis. The minimization of (8) leads to a standard least squares solution similar to [6].

After the training surfaces have been aligned, the mean shape of each slice, $\overline{x}(s)$, is computed as the average slice contour over all the volumes in the training set. The first L main modes of deformation, $D(s) = [d_1(s), \ldots, d_L(s)] \in \mathbb{R}^{2N \times L}$, and the corresponding eigenvalues, $\lambda_l(s)$, are obtained by Principal Component Analysis (PCA), where $d_l(s) \in \mathbb{R}^{2N \times 1}$ is the l-th main mode of deformation at the axial position s, and $L \leq 2N$ is the number of main deformation modes that are used.

3   Robust 3D ASM - Segmenting a Test Volume

The shape model learned by the previous methods is used to segment other cardiac MR volumes. As before, the number of slices in a test volume, which we denote as S^t, may not be the same as the learned shape model, S^r. In case $S^t \neq S^r$, one possible approach would be to interpolate the volume to determine the intensity values at the same axial positions as the shape model contours. However, the spatial resolution of MRI between axial slices is very low (approximately 10 mm spacing between slices), and motion artifacts can cause significant displacements in the location of the LV contour in consecutive slices. Consequently, the location of the LV border may become hard to determine in interpolated images, as shown in Fig. 2

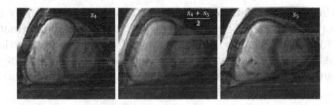

Fig. 2. Example of an interpolated image, at $s = \frac{s_4 + s_5}{2}$, obtained by linear interpolation between two consecutive slices, s_4 and s_5.

We propose a different approach that consists in resampling the shape model (mean shape and deformation modes) to have the same number of slices as the test volume. The mean shape can be easily interpolated using the strategy in Sect. 2. We compute the corresponding coefficient matrix, $\overline{C}$, using (7), and resample the mean shape at S^t slices, $s = \frac{m-1}{S^t-1}$, with $m = 1, \ldots, S^t$, using (3).

On the other hand, computing the main modes of deformation for intermediate slices is not straightforward. The reason is that the modes of deformation are sorted according to the value of the corresponding eigenvalues. Since eigenvalues are learned independently for each slice, it is not possible to find corresponding deformation modes in different slices. Therefore, we use a simpler approach, that consists in finding the correspondences between deformation modes in consecutive slices and use them to perform a linear interpolation, as follows. Consider a slice position, $s \in [s_m, s_{m+1}]$, located between slices s_m and s_{m+1}. The deformation modes at this slice, $D(s) = [d_1(s), \ldots, d_L(s)]$, are determined using linear interpolation between corresponding deformation modes in s_m and s_{m+1}. Let $\alpha \in [0, 1]$ be the relative distance of slice $s \in [s_m, s_{m+1}]$ to s_m,

$$\alpha = \frac{s - s_m}{s_{m+1} - s_m}. \tag{10}$$

Without loss of generality, we assume that s_m is the closest slice (i.e., $\alpha \leq 0.5$). The l-th deformation mode and corresponding eigenvalue are given by

$$d_l(s) = (1 - \alpha)d_l(s_m) + \alpha d_{F(l)}(s_{m+1}) \tag{11}$$
$$\lambda_l(s) = (1 - \alpha)\lambda_l(s_m) + \alpha\lambda_{F(l)}(s_{m+1}), \tag{12}$$

where $F(\cdot)$ maps the correspondences between the deformation modes in s_m to s_{m+1},

$$F(l) = \arg \min_n \|d_l(s_m) - d_n(s_{m+1})\|. \tag{13}$$

This interpolation process is repeated for all the deformation modes at all the required slices, i.e., for $l = 1, \ldots, L$ and for $s = \frac{m-1}{S^t-1}$, with $m = 1, \ldots, S^t$.

Once all the deformation modes and eigenvalues have been computed, we define the LV surface as

$$x(s) = T_\theta\left(\overline{x}(s) + D(s)b(s)\right). \tag{14}$$

This means that the segmentation of the test volume is obtained by finding the parameters for the pose transformation, $\theta = \{a, t\}$, and the deformation coefficients, $b(s)$. In this work, this is achieved using the robust estimation method called EM-RASM, which is able to compute the shape model parameters in the presence of outliers. See [7] for an in-depth description of this methodology.

4   Results

The proposed method was evaluated on a set of 20 volumes extracted from the publicly available dataset provided by Andreopoulos and Tsotsos [4]. This database provides the endocardial contour of the LV that will be considered as ground truth.

The results were obtained using a leave-one-out scheme, where the shape model was trained using 19 volumes and then applied to the remaining (test) volume. In all the tests, each slice contour was resampled, in arc-length, at $N = 40$ points, and the surface models were resampled at $S^r = 8$ slices, using $K = 6$ and $\gamma = 10^{-5}$. Therefore, the total number of points in the surface models was $N \times S^r = 320$. In the test phase, the total number of points in the resampled shape model was $N \times S^t$ (it depended on the test volume). The segmentation was quantitatively evaluated using the average Dice similarity coefficient [8], d_{Dice}, and the average minimum distance between the surface model points and the ground truth, d_{AV}, measured in mm.

Some examples of the segmentations are shown in Fig. 3. It is possible to see that the obtained segmentations are similar to the ground truth, although the algorithm performs better in the basal slices than in the apical slices. This is due to the fact that the LV chamber is very small in apical slices, and its borders are often irregular. The overall results, according to the Dice coefficient and the average minimum distance, were $d_{\text{Dice}} = 0.88 \pm 0.07$ and $d_{\text{AV}} = 1.3 \pm 0.7$ mm.

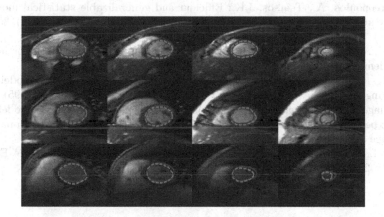

Fig. 3. Examples of the obtained segmentations. Each line shows a different volume and each row a different slice, starting at the basal slice (left) and ending at the apex (right). The red and dashed green lines are the output of the proposed algorithm and the ground truth, respectively (Color figure online).

5   Conclusion

This paper proposes a 3D Active Shape Model (ASM) for the segmentation of the left ventricle in cardiac MRI. Although ASMs based approaches are commonly used to segment medical images, they cannot be directly used in cardiac MRI the volumes have the variable number of slices.

We propose to deal with this issue by using a continuous representation for the surface model, which allows the surface model to be resampled to a predefined number of slices. By resampling all the surface models in the training set, we establish a correspondence for the landmarks (surface points) between all the surface models. Furthermore, the same problem arises in the test phase, because the learned model may have a different number of slices. The proposed approach interpolates the learned model, i.e., the mean shape and the main modes of deformation, to avoid interpolating intensity values between the volume slices.

The results show that the proposed method is able to accurately segment the LV.

References

1. Heimann, T., Meinzer, H.: Statistical shape models for 3d medical image segmentation: a review. Med. Image Anal. **13**(4), 543–563 (2009)

2. Mitchell, S.C., Bosch, J.G., Lelieveldt, B.P., van der Geest, R.J., Reiber, J.H., Sonka, M.: 3-d active appearance models: segmentation of cardiac mr and ultrasound images. IEEE Trans. Med. Imaging **21**(9), 1167–1178 (2002)
3. Kaus, M.R., von Berg, J., Weese, J., Niessen, W., Pekar, V.: Automated segmentation of the left ventricle in cardiac mri. Med. Image Anal. **8**(3), 245–254 (2004)
4. Andreopoulos, A., Tsotsos, J.K.: Efficient and generalizable statistical models of shape and appearance for analysis of cardiac mri. Med. Image Anal. **12**(3), 335–357 (2008)
5. Hoerl, A.E., Kennard, R.W.: Ridge regression: biased estimation for nonorthogonal problems. Technometrics **12**(1), 55–67 (1970)
6. Cootes, T.F., Taylor, C.J., Cooper, D.H., Graham, J.: Active shape models-their training and application. Comput. Vis. Image Unders. **61**(1), 38–59 (1995)
7. Santiago, C., Nascimento, J.C., Marques, J.S.: A robust active shape model using an expectation-maximization framework, In: 2014 21th IEEE International Conference on Image Processing (ICIP), pp. 6076–6080. IEEE (2014)
8. Dice, L.R.: Measures of the amount of ecologic association between species. Ecology **26**(3), 297–302 (1945)

Kernel-Based Feature Relevance Analysis for ECG Beat Classification

D.F. Collazos-Huertas[1](✉), A.M. Álvarez-Meza[1], N. Gaviria-Gómez[2], and G. Castellanos-Dominguez[1]

[1] Signal Processing and Recognition Group, Universidad Nacional de Colombia, Manizales, Colombia
dfcollazosh@unal.edu.co
[2] Grupo Telecomunicaciones Aplicadas (GITA), Universidad de Antioquia, Medellín, Colombia

Abstract. The analysis of Electrocardiogram (ECG) records for arrhythmia classification favors the developing of aid diagnosis systems. However, current devices provide large amounts of data being necessary the development of signal processing methodologies to reveal relevant information. Here, a kernel-based feature relevance analysis approach is introduced to highlight discriminative attributes in ECG-based arrhythmia classification tasks. For such purpose, morphological and spectral-based features are extracted from each provided heartbeat. Then, a linear mapping is learned by using a Kernel Centered Alignment-based scheme to highlight the most relevant features when estimating nonlinear dependencies among samples. The proposed approach is performed as a cascade classification scheme to avoid biased results due to unbalance issue of the studied phenomenon. The results yield a performance rate of 86.52% (sensitivity), 97.57% (specificity), and 92.57% (accuracy) in a well-known database, which validate the reliability of the proposed algorithm in comparison to the state-of-art.

Keywords: Kernel functions · ECG feature extraction · Relevance analysis

1 Introduction

The Electrocardiogram (ECG) is a non-invasive clinical tool that provides useful information to support analysis of heart diseases, including detection of heart arrhythmias from ECG recordings [1]. Overall, a suitable ECG classification system usually involves the following stages: feature extraction, feature selection/reduction, and classifier building. To date, several strategies have been proposed to extract features from ECG recordings, describing morphology in time, frequency content domain, high order statistics, etc. [2]. Provides a thorough list of approaches that have been proposed for cardiac arrhythmia classification [3]. However, classifier system performance strongly depends on the quality of the

© Springer International Publishing Switzerland 2015
R. Paredes et al. (Eds.): IbPRIA 2015, LNCS 9117, pp. 291–299, 2015.
DOI: 10.1007/978-3-319-19390-8_33

extracted feature set, which must be salient in terms of distinguishing different arrhythmias [4].

In order to accomplish feature relevance analysis, there are several works taking into account the specifics of diverse heart arrhythmias. To illustrate, authors in [5] introduce a quality feature selection scheme based on the Range-Overlaps Method (ROM) that assigns, for each type of heartbeat, a range of previously defined relevance values. However, ROM faces difficulties for automatic calculation of these values that are only provided from a set of time quality characteristics. In another approach, called Phase Space Reconstruction (RSP) [6], features containing salient information about the signal variability are computed using Gaussian Mixture Models (GMM) that may behave poorly in modeling classes with very few samples (unbalanced datasets). The conventional reduction dimension using Principal Component Analysis (PCA) is also widely used, e.g., projection of the embedding space as a linear combination of input attributes is considered in [4,7]. Nonetheless, relevant data patterns can be hidden in the input space if linear descriptors are used to extract discriminative information [8]. In addition, the obtained mappings can be biased since they assume a uniform data class distribution, that is, the unbalance class issue is not considered [9].

In this work, a feature relevance analysis approach based on kernel representations is proposed for supporting ECG beat classification tasks. For this purpose, morphological and spectral-based features are extracted to represent obtained heartbeats from an ECG record. Then, in order to reveal relevant features a linear mapping is learned using a Kernel Centered Alignment (KCA)-based scheme, which estimates nonlinear relationships among samples by favoring discriminative attributes. Particularly, the proposed approach is carried out as a cascade framework to avoid biased results when analyzing unbalance classes. The results were obtained testing the approach in a well-known dataset we show that our approach outperforms, in most of the cases, the state-of-the-art techniques related to heartbeat classification tasks in terms of sensitivity, specificity, and accuracy measures.

This paper is organize as follows: in Sect. 2 the feature relevance analysis method is described in detail. The experimental set-up is presented in Sect. 3. The results and discussion are presented in Sect. 4. Finally, conclusions are presented in Sect. 5.

2   Feature Relevance Analysis Based on Kernel Alignment

Heartbeat feature extraction: Let $\{\nu \in \mathbb{R}^L\}$ be a collection of recorded Electrocardiograms (ECG) holding each one L samples, $X \in \{x_i : i = 1, \ldots, N\}$ be a heartbeat matrix with dimension $\mathbb{R}^{N \times T}$ and extracted from the ECG collection, where each row vector $x_i \in \mathbb{R}^T$ is a single beat extracted by means of an R peak-based beat segmentation within a temporal interval lasting $T \in \mathbb{R}$. Let $Z \in \mathbb{R}^{N \times D}$ be a feature matrix holding row vectors $\{z_i \in \mathbb{R}^D\}$, which are extracted in accordance to the following principles [10]:

Morphological features: Based on the Heart Rate Variability (HRV), three features are computed, namely: the R to R interval $z_{i1} = r_i - r_{i-1}$, being $r_i \in \mathbb{R}$ the

R-peak location at the i-th beat, the previous R to R interval $z_{i2} = r_{i-1} - r_{i-2}$, and the following R to R interval $z_{i3} = r_{i+1} - r_i$. The previous and posterior R to R difference are extracted: $z_{i4} = z_{i1} - z_{i2}$ and $z_{i5} = z_{i3} - z_{i1}$. The Atrial P wave morphology index is calculated as [9]: $z_{i6} = (z_{i3}/z_{i1})^2 + (z_{i2}/z_{i1})^2 + (1/3 \sum_{a=1}^{3} z_{ia}^2 \log(z_{ia})^2)$. The morphological dissimilarity z_{i7} between the current QRS-complex $q_i \in \mathbb{R}^{T'}$ at heartbeat x_i, $T' < T$, and the linearly averaged QRS-complex over the last 10 QRS is computed through the Dynamic Time Warping (DTW). The polarity z_{i8}, energy z_{i9}, and variance z_{i10} of q_i are considered.

Spectral-based features: Features $\{z_{i11}, \ldots, z_{i15}\}$ are the first five Fourier-based decomposition coefficients. Features $\{z_{i16}, \ldots, z_{i26}\}$ are the Hermite coefficients of the QRS complex spectra. The DWT coefficients are calculated through the second order Daubechies wavelet (DB2): the subset of features $\{z_{i26}, \ldots, z_{i252}\}$ are both the approximation and the detail coefficients of the employed wavelet-based decomposition, subset $\{z_{i253}, \ldots, z_{i266}\}$ are the minimum to maximum ratio and the variance of each decomposition level. Also, the following parameters of the cosine modulated Gaussian atom reconstructing the ECG signal are calculated: amplitude z_{i267}, frequency z_{i268}, phase z_{i269}, delay z_{i270}, and duration z_{i271}.

Therefore, the input training set holds N_T heartbeat feature vectors $\{z_i : i = 1, \ldots, N_T\}$ extracted from a set of ECG recordings.

Feature relevance analysis: In order to get the most relevant feature vectors in terms of heartbeat discrimination, we compute their pairwise relationships through the introduced heartbeat similarity kernel $K \in \mathbb{R}^{N_T \times N_T}$ with elements:

$$k_{ij} = \kappa_z (d_{ZA} (z_i, z_j)), \forall i, j \in \{1, \ldots, N_T\} \tag{1}$$

where $d_{ZA} : \mathbb{R}^D \times \mathbb{R}^D \to \mathbb{R}$ is a distance operator implementing the positive definite kernel function $\kappa_z(\cdot)$. Here, we rely on the Mahalanobis distance defined in D-dimensional space with inverse covariance matrix $AA^\top$ as: $d_{ZA}^2(z_i, z_j) = (z_i - z_j) AA^\top (z_i - z_j)^\top$ where matrix $A \in \mathbb{R}^{D \times D'}$ holds the linear projection $y_i = z_i A$, with $y_i \in \mathbb{R}^{D'}$, $D' \leq D$.

Based on the already estimated heartbeat feature similarities, we propose to learn the matrix A by adding prior knowledge about heartbeat membership (e.g., normal or pathological beats) enclosed in the matrix $B \in \mathbb{R}^{N_T \times N_T}$. Thus, we measure the dependence between the matrices K and B through the following kernel target centered alignment function [8]:

$$\rho(K, B) = \frac{\langle HKH, HBH \rangle_F}{\|HKH\|_F \|HBH\|_F}, \rho \in [0, 1] \tag{2}$$

where $H = I - N_T^{-1} 11^\top$, with $H \in \mathbb{R}^{N_T \times N_T}$, is a centering matrix, $1 \in \mathbb{R}_T^N$ is an all-ones vector, and notations $\langle \cdot, \cdot \rangle_F$ and $\|\cdot, \cdot\|_F$ stand for the Frobenius inner product and norm, respectively. Generally, the centered version of the alignment coefficient in Eq. (2) results in a better correlation estimation than its uncentered version [11]. Therefore, we propose to learn beat similarities taking advantage of the Kernel Center Alignment (KCA) cost function described by Eq. (2). Indeed, the prior knowledge about the beats can be employed to highlight relevant features by learning the matrix A that parameterizes a Mahalanobis distance between pairwise samples. Therefore, a KCA-based function can be formulated to compute the projection matrix A as follows:

$$A^* = \underset{A}{\mathrm{argmax}}\, \rho\,(K_A, B), \tag{3}$$

where K_A is the resulting heartbeat kernel matrix for a provided A projection as given in Eq. (1). Given the matrix A^*, a relevant feature matrix $Y \in \mathbb{R}^{N_T \times D'}$ holding row vectors y_i can be estimated, which encodes a linear combination of heartbeat discriminative features according to the prior knowledge considered in B. Finally, a feature relevance vector $\varrho \in \mathbb{R}^D$ index can be estimated by analyzing the contribution of each input feature for building the projection matrix A^* as: $\varrho_d = \sum_{j=1}^{D'} |a_{dd'}|; \forall d \in D, \forall d' \in D'$, with $a_{dd'} \in A$. The main assumption behind the introduced relevance index is that the largest values of ϱ_d should point out to better input attributes since they exhibit higher overall dependencies to the estimated embedding.

3   Experimental Set-Up

Database: We used MIT-BIH arrhythmia dataset[1], which contains labeled ECG recordings, that were acquired through two channels with a sampling frequency of 360 Hz, 11 bits of resolution, and amplitude range of 10 mV. For concrete testing, 6537 beats are randomly chosen with their labels, namely six classes are considered: Normal (normal beat), LBBB (left bundle branch block beat), RBBB (Right bundle branch block beat), APC (atrial premature beat), VESC (ventricular escape beat), and PACE (paced beat). In order to test the capability of the proposed kernel-based feature relevance analysis approach, 3103 heartbeats are used as the training set and the remaining 3434 as the testing set [4]. Table 1 describes in detail the employed ECG recordings.

Preprocessing and feature estimation: Given an ECG record, a R peak position-based segmentation is employed to extract its heartbeats. Particularly, each heartbeat x is segmented with a fixed window size value $T = 200$, namely 100 samples before and after the detected R. Moreover, a Z-score-based approach is used to normalize each heartbeat [4]. In addition, heartbeat feature extraction is performed as discussed in Sect. 2. Regarding this, the first five Fourier coefficients are chosen ranging from 1 to 20 Hz. Moreover, since the ECG representative frequency bands are contained in the range from 0.1 to 30 Hz the DB2 wavelet-based decomposition is carried out using a central frequency value of $fc = 0.67$ Hz.

With regards to the proposed KCA-based feature relevance analysis, a cascade scheme is performed aiming to avoid the unbalance issue of the studied dataset. First, all the samples are split into two representative groups: Normal

---

[1] http://www.physionet.org/physiobank/database/html/mitdbdir/mitdbdir.htm.

Table 1. Distribution of the studied ECG beats

Dataset	Type	File number	Number of each file	Total
Training subset	Normal	100, 101, 103, 105, 108, 112, 113, 114, 115	100	1800
		117, 121, 122, 123, 202, 205, 219, 230, 234		
	PACE	102, 104, 107, 217		300
	RBBB	118, 124, 212, 231		300
	LBBB	109, 111, 207, 214		300
	APC	209, 222, 232, 220, 223		300
	VESC	207	103	103
Testing subset	Normal	100, 101, 103, 105, 108, 112, 113, 114, 115	100	1800
		117, 121, 122, 123, 202, 205, 219, 230, 234		
	PACE	102, 104, 107, 217	100	400
	RBBB	118, 124, 212, 231	100	400
	LBBB	109, 111, 207, 214	100	400
	APC	209, 222, 232	100	382
		220	47	
		223	35	
	VESC	207	52	52
Total				6537

and Pathological. Then, the rotation matrix $\boldsymbol{A}^\dagger \in \mathbb{R}^{D \times D'}$ is estimated to learn the embedding space $\boldsymbol{Y}^\dagger \in \mathbb{R}^{N_T \times D'}$. For this purpose, given the class membership value $l_i^\dagger = \{1, 2\}$ for each heartbeat, a target kernel matrix $\boldsymbol{B}^\dagger \in \mathbb{R}^{N_T \times N_T}$ is computed as: $b_{ij}^\dagger = \delta(l_i^\dagger - l_j^\dagger)$, being $\delta(\cdot)$ the delta function. Second, only the pathological samples are considered, that is, those within the following groups: LBBB, RBBB, APC, VESC, and PACE. Hence, the projection matrix $\boldsymbol{A}^\ddagger \in \mathbb{R}^{D \times D'}$ and the embedding space $\boldsymbol{Y}^\ddagger$ is learned using the introduced KCA-based approach, based on the pathological kernel matrix $\boldsymbol{B}^\ddagger \in \mathbb{R}^{N_P \times N_P}$ with elements $b_{ij}^\ddagger = \delta(l_i^\ddagger - l_j^\ddagger)$, being N_P the number of pathological samples and with $l_i^\ddagger = \{3, 4, 5, 6\}$. Moreover, the KCA optimization in Eq. (3) is solved by a gradient descent based algorithm using a learning rate value of $5e^{-3}$, a convergence tolerance of $1e^{-5}$, and a maximum iteration value of 400 [8]. The embedding space size is experimentally fixed as $D' = 5$ and the optimization is initialized with a Principal Component Analysis-based projection. Besides, a Gaussian kernel is employed in Eq. (1) to extract all pairwise similarities between heartbeat feature vectors as:

$$\kappa_z \left(\mathrm{d}_{\mathrm{ZA}} \left(\boldsymbol{z}_i, \boldsymbol{z}_j \right) \right) = \exp \left(-\mathrm{d}_{\mathrm{ZA}}^2 \left(\boldsymbol{z}_i, \boldsymbol{z}_j \right) / (2\sigma^2) \right), \tag{4}$$

where $\sigma \in \mathbb{R}^+$ is the kernel bandwidth. Here, the σ value is estimated by maximizing the information potential variability among samples [12].

Regarding the classification stage, a soft margin Support Vector Machine (SVM)-based classifier is employed. Particularly, two SVMs are trained, one for each provided embedding space, $Y^\dagger$ and $Y^\ddagger$. Additionally, both classifiers are trained using a Gaussian kernel. The SVM regularization parameters are tuned by heuristic search of the set $[0.1, 1, 10, 100, 1000]$, and the kernel bandwidths are calculated by maximizing the information potential variability among samples. Note that the proposed feature relevance analysis and the SVMs classifiers are trained using the training subset while the testing subset is employed for measuring the system performance, as described in Table 1. Three performance metrics are computed: sensitivity $S_e = T_P / T_P + F_N$, specificity $S_p = T_N / T_N + F_P$, and accuracy $\epsilon = T_P + T_N / N_{TS}$, where T_N and T_P are the true negatives and the true positives, F_N and F_P are the false negatives and the false positives, and N_{TS} is the number of samples of the testing set.

4   Results and Discussion

In Fig. 1(a) the 2D embedding spaces and the learned kernels are show for both normal vs pathological and pathological classes. Moreover, in Fig. 1(b) the obtained relevance vectors are presented. As seen, the proposed approach

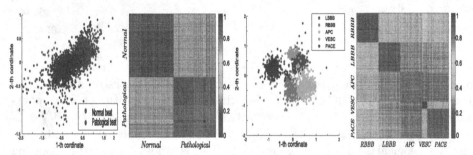

(a) Embedding space and similarity matrix. Left: Normal/Patological. Right: Pathological beats types.

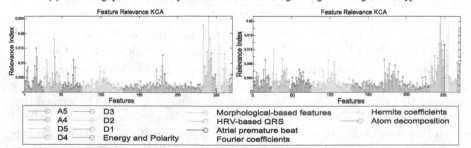

(b) Relevance index results: Left) normal vs pathological. Right) pathological classes.

Fig. 1. Embedding results and data analysis

Table 2. Classification results (N/A: not provided)

Autor	Measure	NORMAL	LBBB	RBBB	APC	VESC	PACE
[7]	Se%	N/A	N/A	N/A	N/A	N/A	N/A
	Sp%	N/A	N/A	N/A	N/A	N/A	N/A
	Acc%	97.44	94.5	93.7	83.3	N/A	98.63
[6]	Se%	66.67	78.33	72.88	N/A	N/A	98.33
	Sp%	94.64	95.98	95.67	N/A	N/A	98.70
	Acc%	N/A	N/A	NA	N/A	N/A	N/A
[5]	Se%	65.84	51.93	52.2	54.02	N/A	N/A
	Sp%	92.43	95.05	94.98	84.77	N/A	N/A
	Acc%	N/A	N/A	N/A	N/A	N/A	N/A
[4]	Se%	99.56	98.75	99.25	97.91	94.23	100.00
	Sp%	99.39	99.89	100.00	99.91	99.00	100.00
	Acc%	99.45	99.80	99.94	99.76	99.44	100.00
This study	Se%	95.00	88.65	89.51	78.55	78.78	88.67
	Sp%	88.87	99.17	99.47	97.79	100.00	99.20
	Acc%	89.22	93.75	96.00	82.46	100.00	94.00

is able to estimate a linear projection of the input samples highlighting dis criminative patterns according to the class membership prior knowledge. In fact, the computed projection matrix $A^\dagger$ reveals that the morphological features, the Fourier and the Hermite coefficients, and some DWT-based detail and approximation coefficients encode mainly discriminative information to separate between normal and pathological beats. In turn, heartbeat features based on atom decomposition, HRV, and atrial premature are the most relevant for separating pathological classes from the attained projection matrix $A^\ddagger$.

Moreover, the proposed approach is compared against some state-of-the-art algorithms as shown in Table 2. Overall, our proposed method outperforms, in most of the cases, the state-of-the-art techniques in terms of the studied performance measures. Hence, both the estimated embeddings and the introduced cascade classification facilitates the heartbeat discrimination. Although the heartbeat discrimination proposals presented in [5–7] aim to reveal relevant features by performing linear and/or probabilistic-based embeddings, e.g., PCA, Linear Discriminant Analysis, Independent Component Analysis, nonlinear relationships are not suitable encoded during the mapping leading to unsuitable classification results for some of the studied classes. With respect to the heartbeat classification approach presented in [4], using the PCA and the LDA methods as feature extraction techniques with a Probabilistic Neural Network (PNN)-based classifier attains suitable results.

5   Conclusions

A concrete approach of kernel-based feature relevance analysis is introduced to support ECG beat classification tasks. The proposed relevance analysis aims at highlighting the most relevant features based on the estimation of the existing nonlinear dependencies among samples. However, dependencies among samples are computed using the conventional KCA-based scheme to infer the linear mapping from the input feature space. Besides, heartbeat class membership prior knowledge is employed to point out discriminative input attributes. Due to the unbalance of the considered arrhythmia classes that may seriously bias classification performance, we introduce a cascade training scheme that splits the classification task in two stages: first, pathological or normal labels are determined, further, in case of pathological label, the particular type of arrhythmia is classified. Validation of the proposed kernel-based feature relevance analysis is carried out on well-known databases, where several morphological and spectral-based features are extracted to represent each segmented heartbeat. Carried out experiments show that our approach outperforms, in most of the cases, the state-of-the-art techniques related to heartbeat classification. Additionally, the proposed feature relevance analysis scheme facilitates the identification of discriminative features by the introduced relevance index value. As future work, authors plan to extent the proposed approach using an unsupervised formulation for supporting heartbeat clustering tasks. Moreover, some information theory-based cost functions will be incorporated to measure the similarity between kernel functions to enhance the system performance.

Acknowledgments. This work is supported by *Programa Nacional de Formación de Investigadores "Generación del Bicentenario"*, 2011/2012 funded by COLCIENCIAS and the project *"Plataforma tecnológica para los servicios de teleasistencia, emergencias médicas, seguimiento y monitoreo permanente de pacientes y apoyo a los programas de prevención"* Eje 3 - ARTICA.

References

1. Kutlu, Y., Kuntalp, D.: Feature extraction for ecg heartbeats using higher order statistics of wpd coefficients. Comput. Methods Programs Biomed. **105**(3), 257–267 (2012)
2. Karpagachelvi, S., Arthanari, M., Sivakumar, M.: Ecg feature extraction techniques-a survey approach. arXiv preprint arXiv:1005.0957 (2010)
3. da S. Luz, E.J., Nunes, T.M., De Albuquerque, V.H.C., Papa, J.P., Menotti, D.: Ecg arrhythmia classification based on optimum-path forest. Expert Syst. Appl. **40**(9), 3561–3573 (2013)
4. Wang, J.S., Chiang, W.C., Hsu, Y.L., Yang, Y.T.C.: Ecg arrhythmia classification using a probabilistic neural network with a feature reduction method. Neurocomputing **116**, 38–45 (2013)
5. Yeh, Y.C., Chiou, C.W., Lin, H.J.: Analyzing ecg for cardiac arrhythmia using cluster analysis. Expert Syst. Appl. **39**(1), 1000–1010 (2012)
6. Nejadgholi, I., Moradi, M.H., Abdolali, F.: Using phase space reconstruction for patient independent heartbeat classification in comparison with some benchmark methods. Comput. Biol. Med. **41**(6), 411–419 (2011)

7. Zhang, L., Peng, H., Yu, C.: An approach for ecg classification based on wavelet feature extraction and decision tree. In: 2010 International Conference on Wireless Communications and Signal Processing (WCSP), pp. 1–4. IEEE (2010)
8. Brockmeier, A., Choi, J., Kriminger, E., Francis, J., Principe, J.: Neural decoding with kernel-based metric learning. Neural Comput. **26**, 1080–1107 (2014)
9. Rodríguez-Sotelo, J.L., Peluffo-Ordoñez, D., Cuesta-Frau, D., Castellanos-Domínguez, G.: Unsupervised feature relevance analysis applied to improve ecg heartbeat clustering. Comput. Methods Programs Biomed. **108**(1), 250–261 (2012)
10. Castro Hoyos, C., Peluffo Ordonez, D.H., Rodríguez-Sotelo, J.L., Dominguez, G.C.: Effectiveness of morphological and spectral heartbeat characterization on arrhythmia clustering for holter recordings. In: SIPAIM (2014)
11. Cortes, C., Mohri, M., Rostamizadeh, A.: Algorithms for learning kernels based on centered alignment. J. Mach. Learn. Res. **13**, 795–828 (2012)
12. Álvarez-Meza, A.M., Cárdenas-Peña, D., Castellanos-Domínguez, G.: Unsupervised kernel function building using maximization of information potential variability. In: Bayro-Corrochano, E., Hancock, E. (eds.) CIARP 2014. LNCS, vol. 8827, pp. 335–342. Springer, Heidelberg (2014)

Spatial-Dependent Similarity Metric Supporting Multi-atlas MRI Segmentation

M. Orbes-Arteaga[1], D. Cárdenas-Peña[1]([✉]), Mauricio A. Álvarez[2],
A.A. Orozco[2], and G. Castellanos-Dominguez[1]

[1] Universidad Nacional de Colombia, Manizales, Colombia
{hmorbesa,dcardenasp}@unal.edu.co
[2] Universidad Tecnológica de Pereira, Pereira, Colombia

Abstract. A locally weighted normalized mutual information (wNMI) metric is proposed to highlight spatial correspondences in an image pair. Aiming to account for local similarities, our proposal computes the normalized mutual information on local regions and linearly weights them depending on their information. Additionally, we introduce a criterion for tuning the number of regions based on the variability maximization of the metric values in a given dataset. To assess our proposal, we compare wNMI to means squares (MS), cross correlation (CC) and global normalized mutual information (NMI) to select the closest atlases on a multi-atlas segmentation scheme for labeling ganglia basal structures. Obtained results show that our proposed measure provides a more robust atlas selection.

Keywords: Magnetic resonance imaging · Normalized mutual information · Multi-atlas segmentation · Template selection

1 Introduction

Brain magnetic resonance images (MRI) have been widely used on several medical applications: quantification of the neuropathology progression like Alzheimer's disease, building realistic head conductivity models for brain mapping algorithms, and building population atlases for understanding the natural brain MRI distributions, among others. Usually, these applications perform volumetric and/or shape-based analyses on the structures of interest, which must be identified. Nevertheless, there are complex structures having poor contrast and high anatomical variability, making hard to perform accurate segmentation of tissues. To cope with this drawback, atlas-based preprocessing algorithms have been proposed allowing to incorporate relevant *a priori* spatial information about the brain structures. In these approaches, pre-segmented images (termed atlases) are non-linearly mapped to a query subject and the labels are propagated to enhance the further segmentation. However, atlas effectiveness is highly dependent on the selected image metric.

© Springer International Publishing Switzerland 2015
R. Paredes et al. (Eds.): IbPRIA 2015, LNCS 9117, pp. 300–308, 2015.
DOI: 10.1007/978-3-319-19390-8_34

The image metric allows to measure the similarity between atlas and query images for assessing the registration and to select the most informative images in a multi-atlas scheme. A variety of image metric measures have been introduced for image registration tasks. Intensity-based ones, as Mean Squared Difference and Correlation Coefficient, can be used only in mono-modal registration, and usually assume a linear correlation between image intensities, independence and stationarity. On the other hand, information-based measures do not require any assumption about the intensity model. Normalized mutual information (NMI), being the most employed, measures the amount of information shared by an image pair, and it is computed from the joint image histogram holding the whole image intensity values. Nevertheless, the metrics computed over the whole coordinate space are not robust to inherent MRI artifacts as the spatially varying bias fields, since it leads to different intensity relations at different locations.

To overcome the aforementioned problems, authors in [1] proposed to estimate a second-order mutual information by taking into account intensity co-occurrences between neighboring voxels. However, a four dimensional histogram is tremendously sparse as there is not enough data in a typical brain image pair to fill all the bins [2]. In [3], adaptive sampling of the image was carried out using octrees, from which an information-based measure is computed. The main drawbacks of the octree-based sampling are its high sensitivity to noise and its bias to structure alignment. A linearly weighted combination of local NMIs is introduced in [4] to achieve a single metric value. In the approach, weights are dependent only on the region size, not on the amount of information on it. Therefore, regions such as borders and corners, usually belonging to background, bias the metric.

Hence, we propose to compute a locally weighted normalized mutual information (wNMI) metric. Local NMIs, from regular partitions, are linearly combined using weights depending on each partition information. Additionally, a criterion for tuning the number of partitions regarding a variability function is introduced. As any metric is biased towards its registration accuracy, we evaluate the wNMI at template selection in a multi-atlas segmentation task. The proposed metric is compared against state-of-the-art metrics on three different MRI datasets. Obtained results show that our measure provides a more suitable selection, being the most robust among all considered metrics.

2 Materials and Methods

Let $\mathcal{X} = \{\boldsymbol{X}^n, \boldsymbol{L}^n : n = 1, \ldots, N\}$ be a labeled MRI dataset holdig N image-segmentation pairs, where $\boldsymbol{X}^n = \{x_r^n \in \mathbb{R} : r \in \Omega\}$ is the n-th MR image, the value r indexes the spatial elements, and the matrix $\boldsymbol{L}^n = \{l_r^n \in [1, C] : r \in \Omega\}$ is the provided image segmentation into $C \in \mathbb{N}$ classes, which for 3D volumes holds dimension $\Omega = \mathbb{R}^{T_a \times T_s \times T_c}$, with $\{T_a, T_s, T_c\}$ as the Axial, Sagittal and Coronal sizes, respectively.

2.1   Global Image Similarity Metrics

In order to compare globally a given image pair $\{\boldsymbol{X}^n, \boldsymbol{X}^m\}$, the following image similarity metrics are widely used:

- *Mean-Squares (MS):* This metric is the average square difference along the space:

$$d\{\boldsymbol{X}^n, \boldsymbol{X}^m\} = \mathbb{E}\left\{(x_r^n - x_r^m)^2 : \forall r \in \Omega\right\} \qquad (1)$$

  where notation $\mathbb{E}\{\cdot\}$ stands for the expectation operator.
- *Correlation Coefficient Histogram (CCH):*

$$d\{\boldsymbol{X}^n, \boldsymbol{X}^m\} = \frac{\mathbb{E}\left\{h(x_r^n, x_s^m)(x_r^n x_s^m - \bar{x}^n \bar{x}^m) : \forall r, s \in \Omega\right\}}{\mathbb{E}\left\{h(x_r^n)(x_r^n - \bar{x}^n)^2\right\} \mathbb{E}\left\{h(x_r^m)(x_r^m - \bar{x}^m)^2\right\}} \qquad (2)$$

  where $h(x^n, x^m) \in \mathbb{R}^+$ is the joint histogram function between input images, and $\bar{x}^v \in \mathbb{R}$, with $v \in \{m, n\}$, is the average intensity of the respective image $\boldsymbol{X}^v$.
- *Normalized Mutual Information (NMI):*

$$d\{\boldsymbol{X}^n, \boldsymbol{X}^m\} = \frac{\mathbb{H}\{\boldsymbol{X}^n\} + \mathbb{H}\{\boldsymbol{X}^m\}}{\mathbb{H}\{\boldsymbol{X}^n, \boldsymbol{X}^m\}} \qquad (3)$$

  where notation $\mathbb{H}\{\boldsymbol{X}^n, \boldsymbol{X}^m\}$ stands for the joint entropy between $\boldsymbol{X}^n$ and $\boldsymbol{X}^m$.

Nevertheless, all the above described metrics are computed over the whole image and do not account for the knowledge about identified pre-existing localities. Furthermore, features extracted from these regions usually allow a better representation for content discrimination. Also, these metrics are far from being robust to most of the artifacts (like bias field) since the image intensity distribution changes along the space [5].

2.2   Spatial-Dependent Similarity Metric

The most common approach to extract local information from the image $\boldsymbol{X}$ consists in separating the P different regions or blocks, $\boldsymbol{\Xi}_p$, from which appropriate features are computed describing each particular block. For 3D volumes, $P = P_a \times P_s \times P_c$ being $\{P_a, P_s, P_c\}$ the number of partitions along each axis, respectively. Therefore, the image is represented as a set of separated blocks $\{\boldsymbol{\Xi}_p \in \mathbb{R}^{\rho_a \times \rho_s \times \rho_c} : p \in [1, P]\}$, s.t., $\boldsymbol{\Xi}_p \cap \boldsymbol{\Xi}_q = \emptyset : \forall p, q \in [1, P]$, and $\rho_v = T_v/P_v$, where $v \in \{a, s, c\}$.

The introduction of image similarity metrics that are computed block-wise over the space domain, termed *spatial-dependent similarity metrics*, results in the block distance set $\{d\{\boldsymbol{\Xi}_p^n, \boldsymbol{\Xi}_p^m\}\}$. In order to obtain an scalar spatial-dependent similarity metric, $\Delta^{n,m} \in \mathbb{R}^+$, the weighted sum of local distances is widely used as follows:

$$\Delta^{n,m} = \sum_{p \in P} \omega_p d\{\boldsymbol{\Xi}_p^n, \boldsymbol{\Xi}_p^m\}$$

where $\omega_p \in \mathbb{R}^+$ is the combination weight of the p-th block so that $\sum_{p \in P} \omega_p = 1$.

Generally, each combination weight is assumed to determine the influence of the corresponding block in the metric $\Delta^{n,m}$. Bearing this in mind, a straightforward estimation of each weight is to assume its contribution to be proportional to the partition size. Thus, in case of the equally-sized blocks, the p-th weight is computed as [4]:

$$\omega_p = \rho_a \times \rho_s \times \rho_c / |\Omega| = const, \forall p \subseteq P \tag{4}$$

As a result of the uniform space partitioning, the estimated weights in Eq. (4) lead to the plain averaged block distance, that is, $\Delta^{n,m} = \mathbb{E}\left\{d\{\boldsymbol{\Xi}_p^n, \boldsymbol{\Xi}_p^m\} : \forall p \in P\right\}$.

Due to the fact that in practice blocks hold different uncertainty, a more elaborate combination weight rule is proposed taking into account the contribution of each block in terms of information, that is:

$$\omega_p = \left(- \log\left(\mathbb{E}\left\{d\{\boldsymbol{\Xi}_p^n, \boldsymbol{\Xi}_p^m\} : \forall n, m \in [1, n]\right\}\right)\right)^{\alpha} / \omega^* \tag{5}$$

where $\alpha \in \mathbb{R}^+$ spans the combination weight distribution and $\omega^* \in \mathbb{R}^+$ is a normalization factor. Accordingly, the resulting spatial-dependent similarity metric becomes the following bounded weighted average:

$$\Delta^{n,m} = (\omega^*)^{-1} \sum_{p \in P} \left(- \log\left(\mathbb{E}\left\{d\{\boldsymbol{\Xi}_p^n, \boldsymbol{\Xi}_p^m\} : \forall n, m \in [1, n]\right\}\right)\right)^{\alpha} d\{\boldsymbol{\Xi}_p^n, \boldsymbol{\Xi}_p^m\} \tag{6}$$

Since we are looking for a measure highlighting the spatial similarities between image pairs, the number of partitions and the gain factor of mixing weights have to wide spread the distribution of δ for a given dataset. Hence, as proposed by [6], the variability of the set of pair-wise image metric values, $\{\Delta^{n,m}\}$, is chosen as tuning criterion for parameters $\{P, \alpha\}$:

$$\max_{P, \alpha} \mathrm{var}\left\{\Delta^{n,m} : \forall n, m \in [1, N]\right\} \tag{7}$$

3   Experimental Set-Up

Aiming to evaluate the metric performance, the three datasets are considered for subcortical structure segmentation in a multi-atlas scheme (see Table 1). The following structures presenting interest in Parkinson surgery are considered (see Fig. 1): *hypothalamus* (HYPO), *amygdala* (AMYG), *putamen* (PUT), *caudate nucleus* (CAUD), *thalamus* (THAL), and *pallidum* (PAL).

IBSR18: Holding 18 T1-weight scans of normal subjects from the Internet Brain Segmentation Repository[1]. Provided scans are bias field corrected using Autoseg routines from the Center for Morphometric Analysis and supplied with two separate segmentations, a tissue classification and a 34-structure labeled volume.

---

[1] http://www.cma.mgh.harvard.edu/ibsr.

Table 1. Summary of the testing dataset characteristics.

Database	No. subjects	Males	Age (years)	Volume size	Voxel size (mm)
IBSR18	18	14	7 to 71	$256 \times 256 \times 128$	$0.8 \times 0.8 \times 1.5$ to $1.0 \times 1.0 \times 1.5$
MICCAI12	35	13	18 to 90	$256 \times 256 \times 287$	$1.0 \times 1.0 \times 1.0$
NSE	30	15	20 to 54	$192 \times 256 \times 124$	$0.93 \times 0.93 \times 1.5$

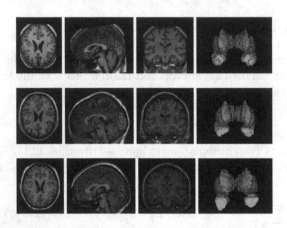

Fig. 1. Exemplary of MRI databases. Top to bottom: IBSR18, MICCAI12, and NSE dataset samples. Left to right: axial, sagittal, coronal views, and ground-truth segmented structures.

MICCAI12: This dataset that was used for the MICCAI 2012 *Multi-Atlas Labeling and Statistical Fusion* challenge (https://masi.vuse.vanderbilt.edu/workshop2012) is a subset of the Open Accces Series of Imaging Studies (OASIS) database. All images were expertly labeled with 26 structures.

NSE: This data (at www.brain-development.org) contains 30 MRI scans recorded on the 1.5 Tesla GE Signa Echospeed scanner. Provided de-faced and anonymized volumes corresponding to coronal T1 weighted 3D scans. Also, each subject contains a volume with 83 manually labeled structures following the protocols in [7].

3.1 Image Preprocessing and Tuning of Metric Parameters

For the sake of comparison within a single common space, all images are spatially normalized into the Talairach space where each image is rigidly aligned to the ICBM atlas (MNI305-template), allowing to properly extract the morphological feature set from each considered image. To this end, the Advanced Normalization Tool (ANTS) is employed with a quaternion-based mapping and MI metric as parameters.

For the label propagation, every pre-labelled dataset image has to be spatially mapped into the query image spatial coordinates (*target space*) with a non-linear

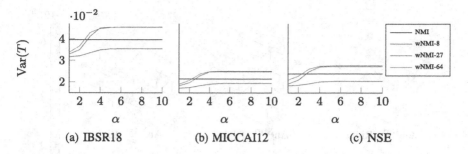

Fig. 2. Power gain factor (α) and number of partitions (P) tuning for all considered databases.

transformation, so that query and atlas images match the best. The registration procedure is performed using the ANTS tool under default parameters: elastic deformation as the mapping function (**Elast**), MI as the similarity metric, and 32-bins histograms for estimating the probability density functions. To get a finer alignment, the registration is performed at three sequential resolution levels: *(i)* the coarsest alignment with a resolution of $1/8 \times Original\ space$, and 100 iterations, *(ii)* the middle resolution $1/4 \times Original\ space$ and 50 iterations, and *(iii)* the finest deformation with a resolution of $1/2 \times Original\ space$ parameter and 25 iterations, the Gaussian regularization method is employed ($\sigma = 3$).

The proposed approach lies on the hypothesis that regularly partitioned blocks provide enough information about localities. To this end, the number of blocks P as wells as the gain factor α for the mixing weights should be tuned up. Particularly, we tune these parameters by carrying out step-wise incremental search within the intervals: from 1 to 4 partitions along each axis, i.e. $P = [1, 8, 27, 64]$, and $\alpha = [1, \cdots, 10]$. The optimal parameter set is assumed as the one maximizing the objective function in Eq. (7). Figure 2 shows the tuning curves estimated for all tested parameter sets. It is important to note that $P = 1$ corresponds to the regular global NMI metric. Therefore, it does not require to tune any mixing weight $\{\omega_p\}$ nor the gain factor α. As seen, our proposal achieves a larger variance of image similarities than the regular global NMI, spreading wider the metric value distribution, and highlighting the local features.

Regarding the selected configuration, two considerations are taken into account. Firstly, the exponent gain factor maximizes the cost function at $\alpha = 4$ for all datasets and image partitions, so it can be taken as the optimal value for all latter experiments. Secondly, it is observed that the larger the number of partitions - the larger the cost function. Nevertheless, when the number of partitions is increased, the cost function improvement decreases and the number of exponents to tune growths exponentially. Therefore, the number of partitions is chosen as $P = 27$, even though it is suboptimal.

Figure 3 shows the 3D scatter plotting all resulting exponents for the selected parameters ($\alpha = 4, P = 27$). The spatial location of each element corresponds to the spatial location of the image partition, while the color and size are directly

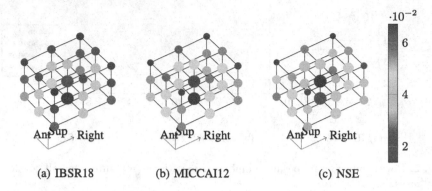

(a) IBSR18   (b) MICCAI12   (c) NSE

Fig. 3. Resulting weight distribution for the three datasets. Markers are located at the center of each partition. Color and size are directly proportional to metric parameter value.

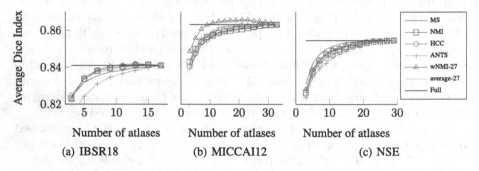

Fig. 4. Average dice index similarities for different number of atlases and considered metrics.

proportional to the value. As shown, image regions corresponding to corners provide the least information to the similarity metric, as they use to correspond to image background. Also, the exponents are symmetrically distributed along the coronal axis, i.e., from left to right, implying that both brain hemispheres are equally relevant for the metric. Lastly, the inferior brain region has the largest exponent, which can be due to the subcortical structures contained on it, allowing to enhance the image discrimination.

3.2   Similarity Metric Comparison

All considered structures are segmented using the atlas-voting label propagation approach in the target image space on each database. To assess the metric performance on the atlas selection task, the Dice Index similarity, $\varrho = 2\langle \boldsymbol{L}_c, \boldsymbol{O}_c\rangle/(\|\boldsymbol{L}_c\|_1 + \|\boldsymbol{O}_c\|_1) \in \mathbb{R}+$, is employed comparing the c-th labeling class on the resulting segmentation, $\boldsymbol{O}$, against the one on the provided ground-truth, $\boldsymbol{L}$, being $\|\cdot\|_1$ to the 1-norm. The results for multi-atlas segmentation with all templates selected in the common space are shown in Fig. 4. It is worth noting that there is no consistency on the global metrics, since the performance varies from database to database. Regarding the straightforward block averaging, although its results are consistent, it only achieves the best selection when all atlases are used. On the other hand, the proposed wNMI performs the best for IBSR18 and MICCAI12 databases and achieves the second best selection curve for the NSE database. Moreover, it is important to highlight that proposed measure provides a subset of templates outperforming the whole atlas subset.

4   Concluding Remarks

We propose a metric based on weighted local mutual information for computing image similarity. Our method outperforms the global mutual information in atlas selection and enhances the accuracy segmentation in multi-atlas scheme. Regarding the metric parameters, our proposed tuning criterion exhibits the same behavior for the three considered databases, proving that the approach strategy is robust. According to Fig. 2, it must be noted the variance raises as the number of partition is increased. However, the larger the number of partitions, the more the parameters to tune. Therefore, there should be a compromise between computational burden and the cost function value. Additionally, we propose to compute a weight for each partition depending on its information. To accentuate the difference between the weights, a gain factor α is estimated. As shown in Fig. 2, we found that $\alpha = 4$ is the optimal value that maximizes the variance in the similarity matrices for all databases.

From resulting metric parameters, shown in Fig. 3, it is clear that each partition provides different information to the resulting metric. Being the borders and corners the least informative, while the central partition the most one. Such a fact is due to shape dispersion in ganglia basal structures in human brains. Aiming to test our metric, an atlas selection task is carried out in a multi-atlas segmentation scheme. Other similarity measures in the state of the art are also compared. According to results in Fig. 4, the performance for benchmark metrics is not consistent along the tested databases. This can be due to the different imaging protocols and subject demographics. Moreover, intensity-based measures underperform when image intensity difference is large or there are inherent MRI artifacts. On the other hand, information-based measures are robust to noise and intensity changes, but the global ones do not capture spatial information. As a result, our metric overcomes all the above mentioned problems, proving to be robust on the tested databases. As future work, other information-based metrics can be tested as the combination core. Also, as the number of partitions and the gain factor were compute using a cost function, the optimal weights can be stated as an optimization problem. Finally, aiming to enhance the image spatial dependencies, new metrics taking into account neighboring block similarities can be proposed.

Acknowledgments. This work was supported by *Programa Nacional de Formación de Investigadores "Generación del Bicentenario"*, 2011/2012, the research project 111056934461, both funded by COLCIENCIAS, and the research project 22506 founded by Dirección de Investigación Sede Manizales (DIMA).

References

1. Rueckert, M., Clarkson, M,J., Hill D,L., Hawkes, D,J.: Non-rigid registration using higher-order mutual information. In: Proceedings of SPIE Medical Imaging, vol. 2, pp. 438–447 (2000)
2. Razlighi, Q.R., Kehtarnavaz, N., Yousefi, S.: Evaluating similarity measures for brain image registration. J. Vis. Commun. Image Represent. **24**(7), 977–987 (2013)
3. Sundar, H., Shen, D., Biros, G., Xu, C., Davatzikos, C.: Robust computation of mutual information using spatially adaptive meshes. In: Ayache, N., Ourselin, S., Maeder, A. (eds.) MICCAI 2007, Part I. LNCS, vol. 4791, pp. 950–958. Springer, Heidelberg (2007)
4. Studholme, C., Drapaca, C., Iordanova, B., Cardenas, V.: Deformation-based mapping of volume change from serial brain mri in the presence of local tissue contrast change. IEEE Trans. Med. Imaging **25**(5), 626–639 (2006)
5. Rivaz, H., Karimaghaloo, Z., Collins, D.L.: Self-similarity weighted mutual information: a new nonrigid image registration metric. Med. Image Anal. **18**(2), 343–358 (2014)
6. Álvarez-Meza, A.M., Cárdenas-Peña, D., Castellanos-Dominguez, G.: Unsupervised kernel function building using maximization of information potential variability. In: Bayro-Corrochano, E., Hancock, E. (eds.) CIARP 2014. LNCS, vol. 8827, pp. 335–342. Springer, Heidelberg (2014)
7. Gousias, I.S., Rueckert, D., Heckemann, R., Dyet, L.E., Boardman, J.P., Edwards, D., Hammers, A.: Automatic segmentation of brain mris of 2-year-olds into 83 regions of interest. NeuroImage **40**(2), 672–684 (2008)

Color Detection in Dermoscopy Images Based on Scarce Annotations

Catarina Barata[1]([✉]), M. Emre Celebi[2],
and Jorge S. Marques[1]

[1] Institute for Systems and Robotics, Instituto Superior Técnico, Lisboa, Portugal
ana.c.fidalgo.barata@ist.utl.pt
[2] Department of Computer Science, Louisiana State University, Shreveport, LA, USA

Abstract. Dermatologists often prefer clinically oriented Computer Aided Diagnosis (CAD) Systems. However, the development of such systems is not straightforward due to lack of detailed image annotations (medical labels and segmentation of their corresponding regions). Most of the times we only have access to medical labels that are not sufficient to learn proper models. In this study, we address this issue using the Correspondence-LDA algorithm. The algorithm is applied with success to the identification identification of relevant colors in dermoscopy images, obtaining a precision of 82.1 % and a recall of 90.4 %.

Keywords: Melanoma diagnosis · Correspondence-LDA · Image annotation · Color detection

1 Introduction

Computer Aided Diagnosis (CAD) systems for the analysis of dermoscopy images must fulfill a set of requirements, in order to be accepted by the medical community. For a system to be included in routine clinical practice it must be able to: (i) help dermatologists (instead of replacing them) and (ii) provide comprehensive information that justifies the diagnosis [1]. A way to solve the previous issues is to develop clinically oriented CAD systems [2] that are inspired by medical procedures [3]. These systems try to detect and characterize dermoscopic criteria (e.g., key colors or dermoscopic structures) [3], which are then used to diagnose the lesions.

One of the main problems of clinically oriented CAD systems it that they require detailed image annotations (i.e., medical labels and segmentation of relevant structures and colors) performed by experts. A dermatologist can easily provide medical labels stating whether or not a dermoscopic criterion is present or absent, but the segmentation of the corresponding regions is more difficult to obtain since this is a time consuming and highly subjective task. The absence of segmentations might result in incomplete systems. To prevent such issues, it is necessary to design systems that are capable of dealing with weakly annotated images (i.e., images for which there is only a medical label), and still provide

© Springer International Publishing Switzerland 2015
R. Paredes et al. (Eds.): IbPRIA 2015, LNCS 9117, pp. 309–316, 2015.
DOI: 10.1007/978-3-319-19390-8_35

information about the presence/absence of dermoscopic criteria as well as their location within the lesion.

This paper explores an approach to develop clinically oriented CAD systems, in which it is possible to learn a probabilistic representation of the dermoscopic criteria using only medical text labels. The probabilistic model used to learn the correlation between medical labels and image regions is a topical model called Correspondence-Latent Dirichlet Allocation (corr-LDA) [4]. This model is applied with success to the problem of color detection and to the best of our knowledge, this is the first time that such a model is applied to dermoscopy images. The remaining of the paper is organized as follows. Section 2 gives an overview of the investigated problem and identifies the main variables. Section 3 describes the general framework of the corr-LDA model and Sect. 4 describes the application of the model to dermoscopy images. Finally, Sect. 5 presents the experimental results and Sect. 6 concludes the paper.

2   Problem Statement

Dermatologists consider six clinically relevant colors (dark and light brown, blue-gray, black, red, and white [3]) that can be found in skin lesions. Some of these colors are more common in melanomas and the presence of 3 or more colors usually signals a suspicious lesion. A possible strategy to address the automatic detection of colors is to learn color models based on color region segmentations performed by dermatologists, as proposed in different works (e.g., [5,6]). Then, the learned models are applied to new images in order to identify the existing colors and their locations. These approaches can only be applied when color segmentations performed by experts are available, which is a considerable drawback. In this work, we do not have this information. Therefore, we investigate an alternative strategy that does not require medical segmentations.

Our dataset contains D dermoscopy images in which the lesions were divided into small patches, each patch being characterized by a feature vector r_n^d, $n = 1, ..., N^d$, where N^d is the number of patches of image d. Besides the patches, we have for each image a set of global texts labels provided by a group

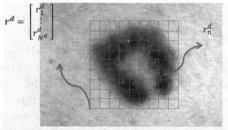

Medical Text Labels (w^d) : Blue-Gray (w_1^d), Black (w_2^d), Dark Brown (w_3^d), Light Brown (w_4^d), White (w_5^d)

Fig. 1. Available information given image d: r_n^d is the feature vector of the $n-th$ patch, $\mathbf{r}^d$ is the set of feature vectors, w_m^d is one of the text labels, and $\mathbf{w}^d$ is the set of labels.

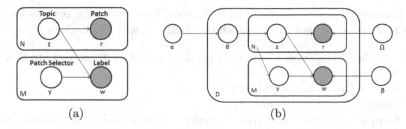

(a)   (b)

Fig. 2. Graphical representations of Corr-LDA: simplified (left) and complete representation (right). Each of the boxes represents an image, a patch or a label replication. The filled circles represent the variables observed in the training set.

of dermatologists w_m^d $m = 1, ..., M^d$, stating which are the M^d colors that can be found in the lesion d. Figure 1 exemplifies the used notation. Our goal is to be able to estimate a probabilistic model to represent the data, such that is not only possible to predict global labels for the lesion but also to be able to associate a color to each of the patches. An algorithm that suits this kind of formulation is corr-LDA [7]. This method allows the estimation of two important probabilities: (i) the label distribution given the image information $p(w_m^d|\mathbf{r}^d)$ and (ii) the distribution of the label given a single patch $p(w_m^d|r_n^d)$. The first probability can be used to predict global labels for the lesion, while the second probability can be used to fulfill the goal of associating a label to each patch. In the following section we address the main characteristics of corr-LDA and show how to compute the relevant probabilities.

3   Corr-LDA

corr-LDA is a probabilistic topic models that generates images using latent variables called topics [4]. This model is an extension of the popular LDA [4], which was proposed for text analysis and retrieval and later used with success in image analysis tasks such as scene recognition [8]. Without modifications, LDA can not be used for image annotation. Thus Blei and Jordan proposed the altered version corr-LDA that is capable of estimating a joint distribution between an image ($\mathbf{r}$) and its labels ($\mathbf{w}$), using the topics as hidden variables.

In order to obtain a better understanding of how the observed and latent variables relate to each other, take a look at Fig. 2(a). This figure depicts the generative process of corr-LDA, which can be summarized as follows. First, each of the N patch feature vectors (r_n) is generated conditioned on a topic z_n. This allows the creation of an image $\mathbf{r} = \{r_1, ..., r_N\}$ characterized by a set of latent topics $\mathbf{z} = \{z_1, ..z_N\}$. Then, each of the M labels w_m is generated. To generate a label it is necessary to first select an image patch and then condition the choice of the label on the topic that was used to create the patch. The selection of the image patches to be used in the labeling process is performed using the latent indexing variable y_m that takes values between 1 and N.

Each of these variables is generated by parametric distribution depending on a set of parameters. Figure 2(b) shows the parameters involved in this model, as well as the generative process for a set of D images. The generative process involved in the creation of the pair image patches/labels $(\mathbf{r}^d, \mathbf{w}^d)$ is as follows [7]

1. For each image d, from a set of D images, sample a topic distribution $\theta \sim$ Dirichlet(α).
2. For each of the N image patches r_n
   (a) Sample $z_n \sim$ Multinomial(θ).
   (b) Sample $r_n \sim p(r|z_n, \Omega)$ from a multivariate Gaussian distribution conditioned on z_n.
3. For each of the M labels w_m
   (a) Sample $y_m \sim$ Uniform$(1, ..., N)$.
   (b) Sample $w_m \sim p(w|y_m, \mathbf{z}, \beta)$ from a multinomial distribution conditioned on the z_{y_m} topic.

α is the Dirichlet parameter and has the same size as the number of topics (K). Ω is the set of parameters of one of the $k = 1, ..., K$ multivariate Gaussian distributions that characterize the image patches, and β is the distribution of the possible labels over each of the k topics. These are model parameters, while θ is an image specific parameter of size K that is sampled once per image.

The application of corr-LDA can be divided into two phases. The first one is the learning phase, where the parameters of the model are estimated. In the second phase, the estimated parameters and distribution are applied to new images (test phase). Let us now focus on the learning stage. This phase depends on the estimation of the posterior distribution of the latent variables $(\theta, \mathbf{z}, \mathbf{y})$ given the patches' features and the global labels

$$p(\theta, \mathbf{z}, \mathbf{y}|\mathbf{w}, \mathbf{r}, \alpha, \beta, \Omega) = \frac{p(\theta, \mathbf{z}, \mathbf{r}, \mathbf{y}, \mathbf{w}|\alpha, \beta, \Omega)}{p(\mathbf{r}, \mathbf{w}|\alpha, \beta, \Omega)}. \tag{1}$$

However, the exact computation of the posterior distribution is intractable. To tackle this issue, Variational Inference is used to compute an approximation for the posterior [4,7]. This approach consists of using Jensen's inequality to obtain a family of bounds of the log-likelihood [9]. The lower bounds are defined using a set of variational parameters (γ, ϕ, λ). Based on this, it is possible to formulate a factorized distribution of the latent variables as follows

$$q(\theta, \mathbf{z}, \mathbf{y}) = q(\theta|\gamma) \left(\prod_{n=1}^{N} q(z_n|\phi_n) \right) \cdot \left(\prod_{m=1}^{M} q(y_m|\lambda_m) \right), \tag{2}$$

where γ is a K-dimensional Dirichlet parameter, ϕ_n are N K-dimensional multinomial parameters and λ_m are M N-dimensional multinomial parameters. These parameters are chosen during an optimization process that tries to compute the tightest possible lower bound (for details refer to [4,7]). The estimation of the parameters is performed using a variational EM. This method consists of iteratively applying the following two steps until convergence

- **E-Step:** The variational parameters $(\gamma^d, \phi^d, \lambda^d)$ are estimated for each image in the dataset and the lower bound is computed.

– **M-Step:** The model parameters α, β, and Ω are estimated by maximizing the lower bound obtained in the E-step.

The update equations for all the parameters will be introduced in the following section. Given an approximation for the posterior, it is also possible to compute the conditional distributions of interest $p(w|\mathbf{r})$ and $p(w|r_n)$ (please refer to [7]). After parameter estimation, corr-LDA can be applied to new images. First, the E-step must be applied to all the images using the estimated model parameters (α, β, Ω) in order to obtain the image specific variational parameters and distributions. Then, the joint probabilities $p(w|\mathbf{r})$ and $p(w|r_n)$ are computed in order to obtain global and patch labels.

4 Application to Dermoscopy Images

This section describes the application of corr-LDA to dermoscopy images as well as some modifications introduced to the original algorithm.

In order to apply corr-LDA, we divide the dermoscopy images into small non-overlapping patches of size 12×12 (same sized used in [6]) and characterize each of them using the mean color vector in the HSV color space. Patches which area is more than 50 % outside the lesion are discarded. Then, the features extracted from the training set were used to estimate the parameters of a corr-LDA model. Finally, the estimated parameters were applied to the test images as described in the previous section. To label the image patches we apply $p(w|r_n)$ to compute the probability of the six colors and then label the patch according to the color that has the highest probability. Global labeling is performed as follows. First, we compute $p(w|\mathbf{r})$ for each of the six colors and then we compare the outputs with an empirically determined threshold. Each color is considered present if $p(w|\mathbf{r})$ is above the threshold.

4.1 Inclusion of von-Mises Distribution

The HSV color space is a mixture of angular (Hue) and linear (Saturation and Value) information. The original corr-LDA assumes that the observations are modeled using Gaussian distributions. This is not appropriate in the case of the Hue channel, since this is a periodic angular measure. In order to describe the HSV color content, we modified the patch distribution $p(r_n|z_n, \Omega)$. In our approach, the H channel is modeled by a von-Mises distribution, while S and V channels are modeled using a multivariate Gaussian [7], as before. The von-Mises distribution is periodic, so it can be used to describe angular data such as H. Assuming independence between H and the remaining channels it is possible to obtain the following formulation

$$p(r_n|z_n, \Omega) = \nu(\mathrm{H}_n|z_n, \tau, \varepsilon). \; G(\mathrm{S}_n, \mathrm{V}_n|z_n, \mu, \Sigma), \tag{3}$$

where G is 2-dimensional Gaussian and ν is a von-Mises distribution

$$\nu(\mathrm{H}_n|z_n, \tau, \varepsilon) = \frac{1}{2\pi I_0(\varepsilon)} e^{\varepsilon \cos(\mathrm{H}_n - \tau)}, \tag{4}$$

where I_0 is the modified zero-order Bessel function of the first kind and $\varepsilon \geq 0$ denotes the concentration of the distribution around the mean τ.

Considering the new formulation of $p(r|z_n, \Omega)$ it is now possible to define the update equations for all the parameters. These equations are obtained by taking derivatives of the lower bound with respect to each of the parameters (refer to [4,7] for more details). The update equations are as follows

- **E-step** (performed for each lesion d)

$$\gamma_k^d = \alpha_k + \sum_{n=1}^{N_d} \phi_{nk}^d, \quad \lambda_{mn}^d \propto \exp\{\sum_{k=1}^{K} \phi_{nk}^d \log p(w_m|y_m = n, z_m = i, \beta)\}, \quad (5)$$

$$\phi_{nk}^d \propto p(r_n|z_n = k, \tau, \varepsilon, \theta, \Sigma) \exp\{E_q[\log q(\theta_k|\gamma^d)]\}.$$
$$\cdot \exp\{\sum_{m=1}^{M_d} \lambda_{mn}^d \log p(w_m|y_m = n, z_m = i, \beta)\}, \quad (6)$$

- **M-step** (performed using all the training set)

$$\alpha \text{ - use the Newton Raphson method } [4], \beta \propto \sum_{d=1}^{D} \sum_{l=1}^{M_d} w_{lm}^d \sum_{n=1}^{N_d} \phi_{nk}^d \lambda_{ln}^d, \quad (7)$$

$$\mu_k = \frac{\sum_{d=1}^{D} \sum_{n=1}^{N_d} \phi_{nk}^d [S,V]_n^d}{\sum_{d=1}^{D} \sum_{n=1}^{N_d} \phi_{nk}^d}, \tau_k = \tan^{-1}\left(\frac{\sum_{d=1}^{D} \sum_{n=1}^{N_d} \phi_{nk}^d \sin H_n^d}{\sum_{d=1}^{D} \sum_{n=1}^{N_d} \phi_{nk}^d \cos H_n^d}\right), \quad (8)$$

$$\varepsilon_k = \frac{\bar{R} - \bar{R}^3}{1 - \bar{R}^2}, \quad \text{where} \quad \bar{R} = \frac{\sum_{d=1}^{D} \sum_{n=1}^{N_d} \phi_{nk}^d \cos([H]_n^d - \tau_k)}{\sum_{d=1}^{D} \sum_{n=1}^{N_d} \phi_{nk}^d}, [10] \quad (9)$$

$$\Sigma_k = \frac{\sum_{d=1}^{D} \sum_{n=1}^{N_d} \phi_{nk}^d ([S,V]_n^d - \mu_k)([S,V]_n^d - \mu_k)^T}{\sum_{d=1}^{D} \sum_{n=1}^{N_d} \phi_{nk}^d}. \quad (10)$$

5   Results

The proposed approach was evaluated on a set of 142 images randomly selected from the EDRA database [3]. This is a multisource dataset that contains dermoscopy images form three different university hospitals: University Federico II of Naples (Italy), University of Graz (Austria), and University of Florence (Italy). Each of the images was analyzed by a group of dermatologists who provided text labels regarding the presence or absence of the six clinically relevant colors (dark and light browns, blue-gray, black, red, and white).

To evaluate the performance of corr-LDA in the color detection problem we compute two metrics for each color: precision and recall. Precision corresponds to the proportion of images where a specific color was correctly identified among all the images where that color was detected. Recall is the percentage of images where the color was correctly identified. Both of these metrics are computed using a leave-one-out approach, where one of the images is kept for testing and the remaining 141 are used to estimate the parameters of corr-LDA. This is procedure is repeated for the 142 images and the final scores are the average of the individual scores.

Figure 3 shows some examples of the output of corr-LDA as well as the labels provided by the experts. Table 1 shows the performance scores for each of the colors and the average performance of the model. Color identification is a challenging problem, especially if one is using only text labels, but corr-LDA achieves good results. The worse scores are obtained for the red and white colors, although good recall scores are obtained. This performance was expected since the num-

Table 1. Color detection results.

	Precision	Recall	#Images
Blue-Gray	91.7%	86.4%	103
Dark-Brown	96.3%	98.5%	134
Light-Brown	91.6%	91.3%	115
Black	84.3%	100%	100
Red	68.4%	76.5%	17
White	61.3%	90.0%	10
Average	82.1%	90.4%	-

Dark and light browns, blue, black   Dark and light browns, blue, black

Dark brown, red, blue, white, black   Dark and light browns, red, blue, white, black.

Fig. 3. Original image medical labels (left) and output of corr-LDA (right).

ber of examples for each of these colors is significantly smaller than those of the remaining colors. We plan to address this problem by including more examples of these two colors.

6 Conclusions

This paper describes a methodology to detect relevant colors in dermoscopy images using weakly annotated data, i.e., we only have access to medical text labels. In order to tackle this issue, we use corr-LDA to obtain a probabilistic model that relates text labels and image features. This allows us to not only obtain global image labels but also to label image patches. The original corr-LDA was altered in order to include a von-Mises-Gaussian distribution, which was more suitable to describe the Hue data.

The obtained results were promising, with an average precision of 82.1 % and a recall of 90.4 %.

Acknowledgments. This work was funded by grant SFRH/BD/84658/2012 and by the FCT project FCT [UID/EEA/50009/2013].

References

1. Dreiseitl, S., Binder, M.: Do physicians value decision support? a look at the effect of decision support systems on physician opinion. Artif. Intel. Med. **33**(1), 25–30 (2005)
2. Korotkov, K., Garcia, R.: Computerized analysis of pigmented skin lesions: a review. Artif. Intel. Med. **56**(2), 69–90 (2012)
3. Argenziano, G., Soyer, H.P., De Giorgi, V., et al.: Interactive atlas of dermoscopy. In: EDRA (2000)
4. Blei, D., Ng, A., Jordan, M.: Latent dirichlet allocation. J. Mach. Learn. Res. **3**, 993–1022 (2003)
5. Seidenari, S., Pellacani, G., Grana, C.: Computer description of colours in dermoscopic melanocytic lesion images reproducing clinical assessment. Br. J. Dermatol. **149**(3), 523–529 (2003)
6. Barata, C., Figueiredo, M.A.T., Celebi, M.E., Marques, J.S.: Color identification in dermoscopy images using gaussian mixture models. In: ICASSP 2014, pp. 3611–3615 (2014)
7. Blei, D., Jordan, M.: Modeling annotated data. In: 26th ACM SIGIR, pp. 127–134. ACM (2003)
8. Fei-Fei, L., Perona, P.: A bayesian hierarchical model for learning natural scene categories. In: CVPR 2005, vol. 2, pp. 524–531. IEEE (2005)
9. Jordan, M.I., Ghahramani, Z., Jaakkola, T.S., Saul, L.K.: An introduction to variational methods for graphical models. Mach. Learn. **37**(2), 183–233 (1999)
10. Sra, S.: A short note on parameter approximation for von mises-fisher distributions: and a fast implementation of $I_s(x)$. Comput. Stat. **27**(1), 177–190 (2012)

Poster Sessions: Pattern Recognition and Machine Learning

Spectral Clustering Using Friendship Path Similarity

Mario Rodriguez[(✉)], Carlos Medrano, Elias Herrero, and Carlos Orrite

University of Zaragoza, I3A, Zaragoza, Spain
mrodrigo@unizar.es

Abstract. As an important task in machine learning and computer vision, the clustering analysis has been well studied and solved using different approaches such as k-means, Spectral Clustering, Support Vector Machine, and Maximum Margin Clustering. Some of these approaches are specific solutions to the Graph Clustering problem which needs a similarity measure between samples to create the graph. We propose a novel similarity matrix based on human being perception which introduces information of the dataset density and geodesic connections, with the interesting property of parameter independence. We have tested the novel approach in some synthetic as well as real world datasets giving a better average performance in relation to the current state of the art.

Keywords: Graph Clustering · Spectral Clustering · Similarity matrix

1 Introduction

Clustering is a challenging task very useful in many machine learning applications such as image segmentation, intelligent grouping, or data mining. The organization of a dataset into meaningful groups may have different valid solutions depending on the underlying criteria, leading to different valid clustering algorithms. Two of the most common ones are Mixture of Gaussians, usually optimized with an Expectation Maximization process, and k-means, which creates a Voronoi Tessellation. However, they only find hyperellipsoidal clusters and the optimization processes find local optima [1]. An approach with promising results solving these problems is the use of Graph Clustering algorithms [2].

Graph Clustering (GC). The core of any GC algorithm comprises two steps: (i) generation of a graph $G = (V, E)$ from an affinity matrix $S \in \Re^{n \times n}$ and (ii) minimization of an objective function. There are several possible objective functions, being $NCut$ the most commonly adopted, which is an NP-hard problem [3]. However, it is possible to find an approximate solution by solving a relaxed version of the optimization process by means of Spectral Clustering (SC), which derives the solution from the leading eigenvectors of the Laplacian matrix. A non-linear transformation is performed over the original points using these eigenvectors, and the new points obtained are clustered, usually by k-means [4].

© Springer International Publishing Switzerland 2015
R. Paredes et al. (Eds.): IbPRIA 2015, LNCS 9117, pp. 319–326, 2015.
DOI: 10.1007/978-3-319-19390-8_36

Recent researches have been carried out to improve SC or more generally GC, but just a few of them have addressed the similarity measure used to construct the graph [2,5,6]. Depending on the goal or the data nature itself, the needed graph may differ, and so its construction process. The most popular measures are ε-neighbourhood, k-nearest neighbour and Fully Connected graph [7].

This paper introduces a novel generation process of the similarity matrix with the goal of partitioning point sets into groups motivated by the human being perception. As an example, let us consider the goal of modelling groups of friends within a social network. The model should reflect the fact that two subjects are more likely to belong to the same group of friends if they share friends and not in every group friends are equally close, so the model should manage different levels of friendship. In order to obtain a better understanding of the goal with the help of Fig. 3a we observe two dense rings and a sparse Gaussian distribution easily separable for a human being but impossible using only a direct distance.

As shown following, our approach not only outperforms in average the results of some state of the art methods, but also avoids any parameter estimation. In Sect. 2 we overview previous baseline methods. Then, we detail our algorithm in Sect. 3. Section 4 analyses the performance of our proposal in relation to existing algorithms. Finally, we provide some discussions in Sect. 5.

2 Baseline Approaches for Similarity Matrix Generation

When transforming a dataset, $X = \{x_i\}$, into a graph for clustering, the goal is to model the relationship between data points with a similarity graph $G = (V, E)$. The graph is composed by the vertices set $V = \{v_i\}$ representing the data points, $x_i = v_i$, and the edges matrix $E = \{e_{ij}\}$ representing the adjacency matrix, $E = S = \{s_{ij}\}$. There are several approaches for creating S, being the traditionally more used: (i) ε-neighbourhood graph (εG), (ii) k-nearest neighbour graph (kG), and (iii) fully connected graph (FG) [7], represented in Fig. 1 (a, b and c). εG and kG obtain an unweighted graph with connected vertices depending on distance or nearest neighbours respectively. FG has all vertices mutually connected usually weighted with the Gaussian function $s_{ij} = exp(-\|x_i - x_j\|^2/(2\sigma^2))$, where σ controls the width of the neighbourhood. These popular approaches have been modified in subsequent studies in order to include different characteristics of data structure as the methods we explain next.

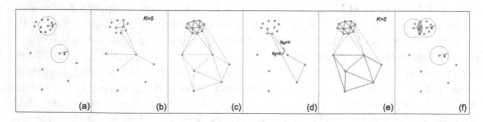

Fig. 1. Representation of similarity construction methods: εG, kG, FG, PB, LS, LD

Path-Based Similarity (PB) [8]. This approach considers the similarity of two points based on the connection trough a set of successive points. The set of points is considered a path and the minimum similarity along this given path determines the similarity between points. Then, the best path is selected using the following equation:

$$s'_{ij} = \max_{p \in \wp_{ij}} \{\min\{s_{ik}, s_{kt}, \dots, s_{rj}\}\} \tag{1}$$

where $\wp_{ij}$ denotes the set of all paths from x_i to x_j.

Robust Path-Based Similarity (RPB) [9]. As Path-Based approach is not robust enough towards noise and outliers, this modification introduces a confidence weight for each point so as to improve the performance.

$$c'_j = \sum_{x_i \in \aleph_j} s_{ij} \tag{2}$$

where $\aleph_j$ represents the neighbourhood of x_j, being the results high dependent of its definition. Finally, the pairwise connections inside a path s_{kt} are replaced with the weighted ones $c'_k s_{kt} c'_t$.

Local Scaling (LS) [10]. Instead of selecting a single scaling parameter σ, like in FG, Local Scaling uses a parameter σ_i for each data point x_i. $\sigma_i = \|x_i - x_K\|$, where x_K is the K'th neighbour of x_i. The final expression is:

$$s'_{ij} = exp^{\frac{\|x_i - x_j\|^2}{(\sigma_i \sigma_j)}} \tag{3}$$

This similarity measure is adaptable to different scales being able to deal with multi-scale clusters and background clutter.

Local Density Adaptive (LD) [11]. Two points belong to the same cluster if they share a dense neighbourhood. The *Common-Near-Neighbour* $(CNN(x_i, x_j))$ measure is defined as the number of points in the join region of the ε -neighbourhoods around x_i and x_j, where the ε -neighbourhood of one point represents the hypersphere-like region, of hyperradius ε, around that point.

$$CNN(x_i, x_j) = \left| \{x_k \mid \|x_i - x_k\| \leq \varepsilon, \|x_j - x_k\| \leq \varepsilon\} \right| \tag{4}$$

where x_k is a point in the intersection of x_i and x_j surrounding regions. Following this measure the similarity between two points becomes:

$$s'_{ij} = exp^{-\frac{\|x_i - x_j\|^2}{2\sigma^2(CNN(x_i, x_j)+1)}} \tag{5}$$

In Fig. 1(d, e, f) we find a graph description of PB, LS and LD approaches.

3   Friendship Path Similarity (FP)

The clustering criteria of (i) the distribution density around the samples and (ii) the manifold structures, have been addressed separately in previous works however, as far as we are concerned, none of them combine both. Our novel proposal performs these objectives through consecutive stages (Fig. 2): (a) initial similarity matrix using the inverse of the Euclidean distance, (b) modification in such a way that the similarity between two samples depends on the density of the dataset, and (c) connection of every two samples through a geodesic path.

3.1   Friendship Matrix

Given the dataset X with $x_i \in \Re^d$, we compute the Euclidean distance matrix D^E, we use the notation d_{ij}^E for their members. Samples should be all different in order to avoid the singularity of $d_{ij}^E = 0$. Using this distance we obtain a similarity matrix S where $s_{ij} = 1/d_{ij}^E$. As the graphs we are working with have no self loops, the diagonal of S is zero. This initial similarity selection has the advantage of avoiding any parameter estimation in contrast to the Gaussian approximation used in previous algorithms. However, it lacks the property of a sudden fall in the similarity when a specific distance is reached, useful for decreasing intra-cluster similarities. Nevertheless, we are able to obtain a sudden fall in the similarity related to the local density using the following process.

To generate the Friendship Matrix we start by obtaining the diagonal degree matrix D with diagonal elements $d_{ii} = \sum_{j=1}^{n} s_{ij}$. As $d_{ii} > 0 \forall i$, D is invertible. A low degree in S means that the point belongs to a low density distribution in comparison to higher degrees in the matrix. But as we want every cluster to have a similar density, we normalize these values as follows:

$$\widehat{F} = D^{-1}S \tag{6}$$

From a Random Walks point of view, the matrix $\widehat{F}$ is the transition matrix where the row i represents the transition probability of jumping in one step from vertex v_i to any other vertex [7]. In contrast to this view, we describe each row as the friendship a vertex assign to the others based on their similarity. This transformation leads to a non symmetric matrix where every row corresponds to a simplex $\Delta = \{\mathbf{r} \in \Re^n : r \geq 0 : \mathbf{e}^T\mathbf{r} = 1\}$, $\mathbf{e}$ being a vector of unit elements.

Fig. 2. Sketch of our approach and its similarity matrix evolution

According to the graph theory, $\widehat{F}$ represents a directed graph with edge values dependent on the neighbourhoods density. The vertex v_i is located in a region with density d_i and v_j with density d_j. If $d_i \approx d_j$ then $\widehat{f}_{ij} \approx \widehat{f}_{ji}$ but if $d_i \gg d_j$ then $\widehat{f}_{ij} \ll \widehat{f}_{ji}$. By selecting the smallest value of pairwise edges we obtain a low value on edges connecting different dense regions, which we consider to belong to different clusters.

$$f_{ij} = \min \{\widehat{f}_{ij}, \widehat{f}_{ji}\} \tag{7}$$

3.2   Friendship Path

This last step improves the Friendship Matrix by connecting points across a geodesic path through the new dense manifold structures obtained in the previous stage. Based on [8] we applied the following formulation to the Friendship Matrix obtaining the new similarity matrix $S' = \{s'_{ij}\}$:

$$s'_{ij} = \max_{p \in \wp_{ij}} \{\min\{f_{ik}, f_{kt}, \ldots, f_{rj}\}\} \tag{8}$$

where $\wp_{ij}$ denotes the set of all paths from x_i to x_j.

4   Experiments

In order to test our proposal we have conducted several experiments dealing with synthetic as well as real world datasets. We compare the similarity matrices denoted as FG, PB, RPB, LS and LD with the proposed FP. After their computation we obtain k clusters using the normalized Spectral Clustering [4].

Our proposal FP is free of any parameter, while the remaining methods under analysis need to tune some of them. In this sense, authors provide some guidelines about how to estimate them. In FG , PB, RPB and LD approaches σ is provided by searching over values from 10 to 20 percent of the total range of the Euclidean distances and the one giving the tightest clusters is picked, as suggested in [4]. For RPB [9] defines the neighbourhood as large enough to include at least two neighbours in each neighbourhood. The authors of LS propose empirically the use of $K = 7$ neighbours. Finally, LD uses a neighbourhood distance ε obtained by searching the tightest clusters inside a range. In this experiments we have not used the proposed formula given in [11] since we found it may give a negative value if the distribution has outliers, it uses a negative factor proportional to the maximum distance which is not offset by any other one.

Throughout the experiments we utilize the Normalized Mutual Information (NMI) between provided ground truth clustering and each algorithm output, as it is a common measure for determining the quality of the clusters [12].

4.1   Synthetic Dataset

Figure 3 draws 9 labelled synthetic datasets included in the public repository [13]. These datasets have been chosen because of the non-linearities, combined

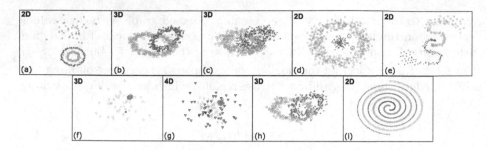

Fig. 3. Synthetic datasets from [13]: (a) RG, (b) 2R3D.1, (c) 2R3D.2, (d) RD, (e) 2S, (f) 4G, (g) 5G, (h) 2R, (i) 2Spi. Up-left corner indicates the dataset dimensionality

with noise in the distribution, they exhibit. NMI scores over these datasets are displayed in Table 1, where we can verify how FP outperforms or at least draws previous methods for all datasets under analysis. Moreover, the errors in some of the datasets like 2R3D.2 can be explained, partially, by the increase of noise, but also by an inconsistent ground truth assignation in the clusters intersections. For instance, in Fig. 1d, where the RD dataset is represented, we have enhanced with circles two points which, although being generated from the Gaussian distribution, are better clustered in the ring distribution. In RD, and probably in 4G and 5G datasets, this problem leads to a small decrease of the NMI rate, but the high noise in 2R3D.2 increases its significance.

Figure 4 displays the behaviour of FG and PB with five different sigma values and LS with five k neighbours Each group of five bars represents the different results for the same dataset and approach but modifying the parameter. The graphics reflect how important is the parameter selection, showing sudden falls in the results when a bad selection is done.

Table 1. NMI for 9 synthetic datasets [13]. *Dim*: dimensionality. k: clusters

Dataset	Dim	k	FG[4]	PB[8]	RPB[9]	LS[10]	LD[11]	FP
RG	2	3	.371	.826	.746	.311	.58	**1**
2R3D.1	3	2	.121	**1**	.886	0.453	.122	**1**
2R3D.2	3	2	.147	.529	.543	.187	.141	**.708**
RD	2	2	.086	**.957**	.624	.176	.036	**.957**
2S	2	2	.546	.963	.117	.368	.598	**1**
4G	3	4	**.982**	.964	.805	**.982**	.361	**.982**
5G	4	5	.091	.866	.742	.926	.091	**.938**
2R	3	2	.124	**1**	.777	.186	.105	**1**
2Spi	2	2	0	**1**	.119	.001	0	**1**
Mean			.27	.90	.59	.39	.22	**.95**

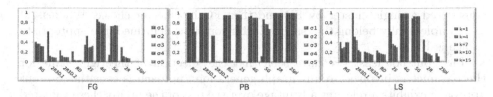

Fig. 4. NMI in synthetic datasets using FG, PB and LS with 5 different parameter values

Table 2. NMI for 5 UCI datasets [14], USPS dataset [15] and COIL-20 dataset [16]. *Dim*: dimensionality. *k*: clusters

Dataset	*Dim*	*k*	FG[4]	PB[8]	RPB[9]	LS[10]	LD[11]	FP
Iris	4	3	.766	.822	.416	.766	.742	**.841**
Wine	13	3	**.928**	.475	.152	**.928**	.893	.788
Ionosphere	34	2	.129	.192	.196	**.204**	.136	.187
Glass	10	7	.659	.683	.646	.673	.669	**.799**
Breast Cancer	9	2	.785	.747	.764	.09	**.802**	.685
USPS	256	10	**.529**	.382	.212	.42	.264	.418
Coil20	16384	20	.791	**.925**	.546	.685	.504	.921
Mean			.65	.60	.42	.53	.57	**.66**

4.2 Real World Dataset

In this section we run some experiments with real world dataset in order to obtain a better overview. Table 2 displays the results over five examples taken from the UCI repository, the USPS dataset and the COIL-20 dataset. In order to evaluate the USPS dataset we have used the 2007 instances available in the test set with samples of hand written numbers. It can be noticed how FP slightly wins in NMI average even though it only has the best results in two of the seven examples. In addition, we are also able to observe how PB exhibits worse results than FG in these experiments in contrast with the ones obtained in the synthetic datasets.

5   Conclusions

The experiments carried out on synthetic datasets show that our FP approach obtains the best scores, which is easily explainable because of the topological structure of the data, well captured by the FP algorithm. Additionally, we have run some experiments dealing with real world datasets. FP obtains, in average, the best result however, the simple FG algorithm obtains a similar average, being the best in 2 of the 7 datasets. This performance is explained by the kind of clusters each method finds. Same density clusters somehow overlapped are considered a single cluster by FP and then FG is a better choice. Whereas, if the samples really belong to a single cluster somehow deformed, the appropriate choice is FP.

Last but not least, we have seen that the selection of the right value for the parameters involved in any graph generation approach is essential. So, our approach exhibits a relevant advantage over the rest of the approaches evaluated because no parameter is needed at any step of the algorithm.

Acknowledgments. This work was partially supported by Spanish Grant TIN2013-45312-R (MINECO) and FEDER. Mario Rodriguez was sponsored by Spanish FPI Grant BES-2011-043752 and EEBB-I-14-08410.

References

1. Jain, A.K.: Data clustering: 50 years beyond k-means. Pattern Recogn. Lett. **31**(8), 651–666 (2010)
2. Schaeffer, S.E.: Graph clustering. Comput. Sci. Rev. **1**(1), 27–64 (2007)
3. Shi, J., Malik, J.: Normalized cuts and image segmentation. IEEE Trans. Pattern Anal. Mach. Intell. **22**(8), 888–905 (2000)
4. Ng, A.Y., Jordan, M.I., Weiss, Y.: On spectral clustering: analysis and an algorithm. Advances in Neural Information Processing Systems (NIPS), pp. 849–856. MIT Press, Cambridge (2001)
5. Nie, F., Wang, H., Huang, H., Ding, C.: Unsupervised and semi-supervised learning via l1-norm graph. In: IEEE Intenational Conference on Computer Vision (ICCV), pp. 2268–2273 (2011)
6. Kim, T.H., Lee, K.M., Lee, S.U.: Learning full pairwise affinities for spectral segmentation. In: IEEE Conference on Computer Vision and Pattern Recognition (CVPR), pp. 2101–2108. IEEE (2010)
7. Ulrike Von Luxburg. A tutorial on spectral clustering (2007)
8. Fischer, B., Buhmann, J.M.: Path-based clustering for grouping of smooth curves and texture segmentation. IEEE Trans. Pattern Anal. Mach. Intell. **25**(4), 513–518 (2003)
9. Chang, H., Yeung, D.-Y.: Robust path-based spectral clustering. Pattern Recogn. **41**(1), 191–203 (2008)
10. Zelnik-Manor, L., Perona, P.: Self-tuning spectral clustering. Advances in Neural Information Processing Systems (NIPS), pp. 1601–1608. MIT Press, Cambridge (2004)
11. Zhang, X., Li, J., Hong, Y.: Local density adaptive similarity measurement for spectral clustering. Pattern Recogn. Lett. **32**(2), 352–358 (2011)
12. Strehl, A., Ghosh, J.: Cluster ensembles – a knowledge reuse framework for combining multiple partitions. J. Mach. Learn. Res. **3**, 583–617 (2003)
13. Fischer, I., Poland, J.: Data sets used. In: Amplifying the Block Matrix Structure for Spectral Clustering (2005). http://www.dr-fischer.org/pub/blockamp/index.html
14. Frank, A., Asuncion, A.: UCI machine learning repository (2010). http://archive.ics.uci.edu/ml
15. Keysers, D.: U.S.P.S. dataset (1989). http://www-i6.informatik.rwth-aachen.de/keysers/usps.html
16. Nayar, S.K., Nene, S.A., Murase, H.: Columbia object image library (coil-20) (1996). http://www.cs.columbia.edu/CAVE/software/softlib/coil-20.php

R-Clustering for Egocentric Video Segmentation

Estefania Talavera[1,2]([✉]), Mariella Dimiccoli[1,3], Marc Bolaños[1],
Maedeh Aghaei[1], and Petia Radeva[1,3]

[1] Universitat de Barcelona, Barcelona, Spain
{etalavera,marc.bolanos,maghaeigavari,petia.ivanova}@ub.edu
[2] University of Groningen, Groningen, The Netherlands
[3] Computer Vision Center, Barcelona, Bellaterra, Spain
mariella.dimiccoli@cvc.uab.es

Abstract. In this paper, we present a new method for egocentric
video temporal segmentation based on integrating a statistical mean
change detector and agglomerative clustering(AC) within an energy-
minimization framework. Given the tendency of most AC methods to
oversegment video sequences when clustering their frames, we combine
the clustering with a concept drift detection technique (ADWIN) that
has rigorous guarantee of performances. ADWIN serves as a statistical upper bound for the clustering-based video segmentation. We integrate both techniques in an energy-minimization framework that serves
to disambiguate the decision of both techniques and to complete the segmentation taking into account the temporal continuity of video frames
descriptors. We present experiments over egocentric sets of more than
13.000 images acquired with different wearable cameras, showing that
our method outperforms state-of-the-art clustering methods.

Keywords: Temporal video segmentation · Egocentric videos · Clustering

1 Introduction

Lifestyle behaviour is closely related with health outcomes, in particular, to non-
communicable diseases such as obesity and depression, that represent a major
burden in developed countries. A promising way towards studying one's lifestyle
is through the use of wearable cameras, able to digitally capture a person's
everyday activities into the so called lifelogging. However, the automatic recognition of daily routines using wearable devices is very challenging due to the
huge amount of collected data (up to 3.000 images per day). Moreover, daily
routines are typically composed of many complex events, with a large variability
depending on factors such as time, location and individual. This work proposes
an algorithm for grouping similar temporally adjacent images into segments,
providing a structure to egocentric videos, that is important for further analysis
such as video summarization and analysis. Considering the environment as a
strong characteristic of an event, these segments are supposed to characterize
different environments in which the camera wearer acts (Fig. 1).

© Springer International Publishing Switzerland 2015
R. Paredes et al. (Eds.): IbPRIA 2015, LNCS 9117, pp. 327–336, 2015.
DOI: 10.1007/978-3-319-19390-8_37

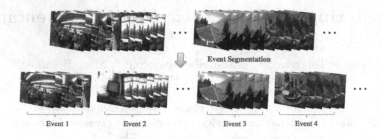

Fig. 1. Example of temporal segmentation of a SenseCam sequence.

Previous methods for egocentric temporal segmentation can be classified into two broad classes, depending on whether they rely on low-level or high-level features. Basically, the former class has as focus what the *wearer sees* and uses as image representation features that are able to capture the characteristics of the environment around the wearer, such as color and texture; the latter class focuses on what the *wearer does* and thus uses as image representation high-level concepts such as objects and activities.

Early works based on low-level features include the one of Doherty et al. [5], which is based on the use of MPEG-7 descriptors for image representation that are available from the sensor, and the one of [16], that uses a time-constrained k-means algorithm based on color descriptors. Recent methods focus on motion-based features. Usually, optical flow is used to distinguish between static, moving the head/camera and *in-transit* frames [3,17]. This classification offers a segmentation that focuses in the activities and movements performed by the user, but is prone to fail when the environment changes while performing the same activity (e.g. the user is in transit but, first gets out of their workplace, then is walking on the street and finally enters to the underground). To focus on long-term activities, Poleg et al. [21] proposed the use of integral motion, which is closely related to wearers' activity. By integrating the instantaneous displacements at fixed image patches, the variations due to head rotation are eliminated, since their mean is practically zero, leaving only the consistent displacement caused by forward motion. Methods based on motion analysis assume high temporal resolution, but the temporal resolution of many lifelogging devices, such those considered in this paper, is very low.

Works based on high-level features are generally more recent. In [14], first important people and objects are discovered by measuring their interaction with the camera wearer and then the frames which reflect the key objects happening are selected. In [20], the authors propose a summarization tool based on analysis of video structures and video highlights. By emphasizing on both the content balance and the perceptual quality of the summary, the authors employ a normalized cut algorithm to globally and optimally partition a video into clusters. Furthermore, in [13], the authors present a video segmentation approach based on the study of spatio-temporal activities within the video, that leads to a visual activity estimation by measuring the number of interest points, jointly obtained in the spatial and temporal domains.

In this paper, we rely on low-level features. Our approach is a *Graph-Cut (GC) extension* technique [3,4] that takes advantage of two methods having complementary properties: ADWIN [2] - a concept drift technique for mean change detection that is highly precise, but usually leads to temporal under-segmentation; and agglomerative clustering (AC), which usually has a high recall, but leads to temporal over-segmentation. Our approach, that we call **R-Clustering**, *regularizes* the over-segmentation of the AC through the upper bound provided by ADWIN. Based on the excellent accuracy achieved recently for classification in a variety of computer vision tasks [8,12], we use Convolutional Neural Network (CNN) vector activation over the entire image as a global image feature descriptor. CNN features are able to focus just in the environment appearance and do not need to rely on a motion information that, would be unfeasible to estimate reliably taking into account the very low temporal resolution of the wearable devices we considered (up to 3fpm). As an example of application, we illustrate the utility of the proposed method for the detection of social events. In the next section, we detail the proposed approach. In Sect. 3, we discuss experimental results and, finally, in Sect. 4 we draw some conclusions.

2 The R-Clustering Approach for Temporal Video Segmentation

Due to the low-temporal resolution of egocentric videos, as well as to the camera wearer's motion, temporally adjacent egocentric images may be very dissimilar between them. Hence, we need robust techniques to group them and extract meaningful video segments. In the following, we detail each step of our approach that relies on an AC regularized by a robust change detector within a GC framework.

Clustering Methods. The AC method follows a general bottom-up clustering procedure, where the criterion for choosing the pair of clusters to be merged in each step is based on the distances among the image features. The inconsistency between clusters is defined through the *cut* parameter. In each iteration, the most similar pair of clusters are merged and the similarity matrix is updated until no more consistent clustering are possible. We chose the Cosine Similarity to measure the distance between frames features, since it is a widely used measure of cohesion within clusters, specially in high-dimensional positive spaces [23]. However, due to the lack of incidence for determining the clustering parameters, the final result is usually over-segmented.

Statistical Bound for the Clustering. To bound the over-segmentation produced by AC, we propose to model the video as a multivariate data stream and detect changes in the mean distribution through an online learning method called Adaptative Windowing (**ADWIN**) [2]. ADWIN works by analyzing the content of a sliding window, whose size is adaptively recomputed according to its rate of change: when the data is stationary the window increases, whereas when the data is statistically changing, the window shrinks. According to ADWIN, whenever two large enough temporally adjacent (sub)windows of the data, say W_1 and W_2, exhibit distinct enough means, the algorithm concludes that the expected values within those windows are different, and the older (sub)window is dropped. *Large enough* and *distinct enough* are defined by the Hoeffding's inequality [9], testing if the difference between the averages on W_1 and W_2 is larger than a threshold, which only depends on a pre-determined confidence parameter δ. The Hoeffding's inequality guarantees rigorously the performance of the algorithm in terms of false positive rate.

This method has been recently generalized in [6] to handle k−dimensional data streams by using the mean of the norms. In this case, the bound has been shown to be:

$$\epsilon_{cut} = k^{1/p}\sqrt{\frac{1}{2m}\ln\frac{4}{k\delta'}}$$

where p indicates the p−norm, $|W| = |W0|+|W1|$ is the length of $W = W_1 \cup W_2$, $\delta' = \frac{\delta}{|W|}$, and m is the harmonic mean of $|W0|$ and $|W1|$. Given a confidence value δ, the higher the dimension k is, the more samples $|W|$ the bound needs to reach assuming the same value of ϵ_{cut}. The higher the norm is used, the less important is the dimensionality k. Since we model the video as a high dimensional multivariate data stream, ADWIN is unable to predict changes involving a small number of samples, which often characterizes life-logging data, leading to under-segmentation. Moreover, since it considers only the mean change, it is enable to detect changes due to other statistics such as the variance. The ADWIN under-segmentation represents a statistical bound for the AC (see Fig. 2 (right)). We use GC as a framework to integrate both approaches and to regularize the over-segmentation of AC by the statistical bound provided by ADWIN.

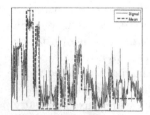 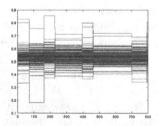 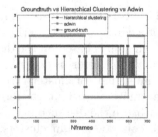

Fig. 2. Left: change detection by ADWIN on a $1 - D$ data stream, where the red line represents the estimated mean of the signal by ADWIN; Center: change detection by ADWIN on a 500-D data stream, where, in each stationary interva, the mean is depicted with a different color in each dimension; Right: results of the temporal segmentation by ADWIN (green) vs AC over-segmentation (blue) vs ground-truth shots (red) along the temporal axis (the abscissa)(Color figure online).

Graph-Cut Regularization of Egocentric Videos. GC is an energy-minimization technique that minimizes the energy resulting from a weighted sum of two terms: the *unary energy* $U(\_)$, that describes the relationship of the variables to a possible class and the *binary energy* $V(\_,\_)$, that describes the relationship between two neighbouring samples (temporally close video frames) according to their feature similarity. GC has the goal to smooth boundaries between similar frames, while attempts to keep the cluster membership of each video frame according to its likelihood. We define the unary energy as a sum of 2 parts ($U_{ac}(f_i)$ and $U_{adw}(f_i)$) according to the likelihood of a frame to belong to segments coming from the AC and ADWIN. The GC energy to minimize is as follows:

$$E(f) = \sum_i ((1 - \omega_1)U_{ac}(f_i) + \omega_1 U_{adw}(f_i)) + \omega_2 \sum_{i,n \in N_i} \frac{1}{N_i} V_{i,n}(f_i, f_n)$$

where $f_i, i = \{1, ..., m\}$ are the set of image features, N_i are the temporal frame neighbours of image i, ω_1 and ω_2 ($\omega_1, \omega 2 \in [0, 1]$) are the unary and the binary weighting terms respectively. Defining how much weight do we give to the likelihood of each unary term (AC and Adwin, always combining the events split of both methods), and balancing the trade-off between the unary and the pairwise energies, respectively. The minimization is achieved through the max-cut algorithm, leading to a temporal video segmentation with similar frames having as large likelihood as possible to belong to the same event, while maintaining video segment boundaries in neighbouring frames with high feature dissimilarity.

Features. As image representation for both segmentation techniques, we used the CNN features [10]. The CNN features trained on ImageNet [12] have demonstrated to be successfully transferred to other visual recognition tasks such as scene classification and retrieval. In this work, we extracted the 4096-D CNN vectors by using the Caffe [10] implementation trained on ImageNet. Since each CNN feature has a large variation distribution in its value, and this could be problematic when computing distances between vectors, we used a signed root normalization to produce more uniformly distributed data [24]. First, we apply the function $f(x) = sign(x)|x|^\alpha$ on each dimension and then we l_2-normalize the feature vector. In all the experiments, we take $\alpha = 0.5$. Following we apply a PCA dimensionality reduction keeping 95 % of the data variance. Only in the GC pair-wise term we use a different feature pre-processing, where we simply apply a 0–1 data normalization.

3   Results and Validation

In this section, we discuss the datasets, the statistical validation measurements, tests and comparison to other methods as well as a possible application of the R-Clustering.

Data. To evaluate the performance of our method, we used 2 datasets (one public [11] and one made by us), composed of 10 days with a total of 13324 images, acquired by two different wearable devices: SenseCam [22] and Narrative (http://getnarrative.com/). The main differences between the two kind of devices are the frame rate (3 fpm vs 2 fpm) and the lens (fisheye vs normal). The data adquired by the SenseCam contain a larger number of frames per day with a larger field of view and significant deformation and blurring. Both datasets include 5 days each, containing a mix of indoor and outdoor scenes with numerous foreground and background objects. All data has been manually annotated to provide ground-truth segmentation.

Statistical Measurements. As evaluation criterion (following [15]), we used the F-Measure (FM): $FM = 2(RP)/(R + P)$, where P is the precision ($P = TP/(TP+FP)$), R is the recall ($R = TP/(TP+FN)$) and TP, FP and FN are the number of true positives, false positives and false negatives.

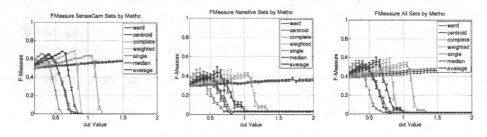

Fig. 3. F-Measure evolution for the two kind of datasets, applying different clustering methods and cut value. The abscissa (X) defines the cut value and the ordinate (Y) - the F-Measure.

Tests on Different Agglomerative Clustering methods. We performed several tests on different AC, namely: single, centroid, average, weighted, complete, ward, and median, that basically vary in the way the distance between cluster elements is estimated [19]. Figure 3 (left) represents the F-Measure of the different clusterings on the SenseCam data, Fig. 3 (center) - on the Narrative data and Fig. 3 (right) on all data. We can observe that the clustering follows the same behaviour for the two types of data sets, although for the SenseCam the methods are achieving better results than for the Narrative sets. That is reasonable due to the significant difference in image appearance. Despite for the SenseCam sets the complete is achieving the same results as the average methods, the third figure shows how for the whole data the average method is achieving the best results (FM=0.56), followed by the complete (FM=0.55) and the single (FM=0.54). The cut value seems to be very influential for the results since there is a point from which, for each method, clusters all data in one single cluster, leading to FM=0.

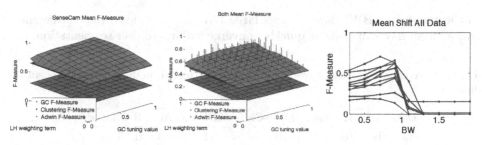

Fig. 4. Average F-Measure of R-Clustering with the best parameters for the Sense-Cam data (left), and on all datasets (center). The abscissa (X) defines the pair-wise term, the ordinate (Y) the ADWIN vs. AC trade-off and the applicate (Z) shows the corresponding FM. The red surface represents the F-measure of AC and the orange one of ADWIN. MeanShift performance for video segmentation (right). The abscissa (X) defines the bandwith. The blue line represents the average FM, whereas the red lines are the FM per each dataset (Color figure online).

Tests on R-Clustering Using Graph-Cuts. We tested the R-Clustering performances according to the parameters ω_1 and ω_2. Figure 4 (left) shows the average measure on the Sensecam data as a function of both parameters. The optimal F-Measure on all datasets is achieved when $\omega_1 = 1$ and $\omega_2 = 0.5$ (Fig. 4 (center)). Despite the average AC achieves the best performance on our data sets (FM=0.56), the R-Clustering based on this AC method just achieves a FM=0.63. Whereas when it is based on the single clustering, the one that was achieving in AC the second best results (FM=0.54), it achieves the highest FM=0.66 with R-Clustering. Table 1 shows the optimal F-measure for AC, ADWIN and R-Clustering, where the application of R-Clustering method clearly outperforms the F-Measure obtained by the AC and ADWIN technique. Thus, by having $\omega_1 = 1$ as unary energy parameter proves that the combination of ADWIN (by using its resulting likelihoods and labels initialization) and AC (by using its clusters split in the GC labels initialization) helps to obtain better results by the R-Clustering. In Fig. 4 (center), the lines depict the standard deviation on each combination of parameters, hence the standard deviation of the best peak results is very low (std=0.17, short line) compared to the higher deviation (longer lines) in the center, meaning that our method is robust and stable. Final video segments can be seen in Fig. 5 that shows three segments corresponding to metro, office and street environments, extracted from a Narrative set.

Tests on Other Clustering Methods. We compare R-Clustering to K-Means [18] and MeanShift (MS) [7] (see Fig. 4 (right) and Table 1) that achieved FM=0.52 and FM=0.49, respectively. The worse performance can be explained by several facts. The k-Means algorithm requires the number of clusters to be specified and it is not a robust method due to its local minima problem. Considering MeanShift (MS), it is based on density estimation which can deal with arbitrarily shaped data distributions, but its problem is that it is very sensitive

334   E. Talavera et al.

to the bandwith (BW) parameter: a large BW can slow down the convergence and a small BW can make it quickly converge leading to over-segmentation.

Table 1. Average F-Measure result for each of the tested methods on our egocentric datasets.

Datasets	K-Means	Mean-Shift	ADWIN	AC	R-Clustering
Narrative	0.32	0.38	0.32	0.45	**0.55**
SenseCam	0.65	0.60	0.31	0.68	**0.79**
All	0.52	0.49	0.31	0.56	**0.66**

Fig. 5. Illustration of our R-Clustering segmentation results for 3 events from a Narrative set.

Fig. 6. Illustration of detecting social events in temporally segmented videos.

Application to Human Tracking for Social Events characterization. Temporal segmentation is very useful to detect social events, which are characterized by the presence of people with whom the camera's wearer communicates. Since the presence of people in a specific event likely last from the beginning of the event to its end, social events can be extracted by relying on temporal segmentation. As outlined in [1], due to the substantial difference in frame rate between videos captured by a SenseCam and classical videos, state-of-the-art tracking methods are not directly applicable to lifelogging videos. In

[1], the authors introduced a novel approach, called bag-of-tracklets, that allows to extract robust tracklet prototypes from video segments containing trackable people. While in this work temporal segments are defined manually, we use our detected segments as a pre-processing step for extracting tracklets of people in egocentric videos (Fig. 6).

4   Conclusions

In this work, we proposed a novel methodology for automatic egocentric video segmentation that is able to segment low temporal resolution data by global low-level processing. R-Clustering is a robust segmentation approach based on a GC extension technique, that integrates a statistical bound by the concept drift method ADWIN and AC, two methods with complementary properties for temporal video segmentation. We evaluated the performance of R-Clustering on different clustering techniques and on 10 datasets acquired through different wearable devices, and we showed the improvement of the proposed method with respect to the state-of-the-art.

Acknowledgments. This work was partially founded by TIN2012-38187-C03-01 and SGR 1219.

References

1. Aghaei, M., Radeva, P.: Bag-of-tracklets for person tracking in life-logging data. In: CCIA 2014, pp. 35–44, Barcelona, Spain, October 2014
2. Bifet, A., Gavalda, R.: Learning from time-changing data with adaptive windowing. In: SDM, vol. 7. SIAM (2007)
3. Bolaños, M., Garolera, M., Radeva, P.: Video segmentation of life-logging videos. In: Perales, F.J., Santos-Victor, J. (eds.) AMDO 2014. LNCS, vol. 8563, pp. 1–9. Springer, Heidelberg (2014)
4. Boykov, Y., Veksler, O., Zabih, R.: Fast approximate energy minimization via graph cuts. IEEE Trans. Pattern Anal. Mach. Intell. **23**(11), 1222–1239 (2001)
5. Doherty, A.R., Smeaton, A.F.: Automatically segmenting lifelog data into events. In: Proceedings of WIAMIS 2008, pp. 20–23. IEEE Computer Society, Washington, DC (2008)
6. Drozdzal, M., Vitria, J., Segui, S., Malagelada, C., Azpiroz, F., Radeva, P.: Intestinal event segmentation for endoluminal video analysis. In: ICIP (2014)
7. Fukunaga, K., Hostetler, L.: The estimation of the gradient of a density function, with applications in pattern recognition. IEEE Trans. Inf. Theor. **21**(1), 32–40 (2006)
8. Goodfellow, I.J., Ibarz, J., Bulatov, Y., Arnoud, S., Shet, V.: Multi-digit Number Recognition from Street View Imagery Using Deep Convolutional Neural Networks. Google Inc., Mountain View (2014)
9. Hoeffding, W.: Probability inequalities for sums of bounded random variables. J. Am. Stat. Assoc. **58**(301), 13–30 (1963)
10. Jia, Y. : Caffe: An open source convolutional architecture for fast feature embedding (2013). http://caffe.berkeleyvision.org/

11. Jojic, N., Perina, A., Murino, V.: Structural epitome: a way to summarize one's visual experience. In: NIPS, pp. 1027–1035 (2010)
12. Krizhevsky, A., Sutskever, I., Hinton, G.E.: Imagenet classification with deep convolutional neural networks. In: Pereira, F., Burges, C., Bottou, L., Weinberger, K. (eds.) NIPS 25, pp. 1097–1105. Curran Associates Inc., Red Hook (2012)
13. Laganire, R., Bacco, R., Hocevar, A., Lambert, P., Pas, G., Ionescu, B.: Video summarization from spatio-temporal features. In: TVS, pp. 144–148. ACM (2008)
14. Lee, Y.J., Ghosh, J., Grauman, K.: Discovering important people and objects for egocentric video summarization. In: CVPR, pp. 1346–1353. IEEE (2012)
15. Li, Z., Wei, Z., Jia, W., Sun, M.: Daily life event segmentation for lifestyle evaluation based on multi-sensor data recorded by a wearable device. In: EMBC 2013, pp. 2858–2861. IEEE (2013)
16. Lin, W.-H., Hauptmann, A.: Structuring continuous video recording of everyday life using time-constrained clustering. Computer Science Department 959 (2006)
17. Lu, Z., Grauman, K.: Story-driven summarization for egocentric video. In: CVPR, pp. 2714–2721. IEEE (2013)
18. MacQueen, J.B.: Some methods for classification and analysis of multivariate observations. In: Le Cam, L.M., Neyman, J. (eds.) Proceedings of the 5th Berkeley Symposium on Mathematical Statistics and Probability, vol. 1, pp. 281–297 (1967)
19. Murtagh, F., Contreras, P.: Methods of hierarchical clustering. CoRR, abs/1105.0121 (2011)
20. Ngo, C.-W., Ma, Y.-F., Zhang, H..: Automatic video summarization by graph modeling. pages 104–109. IEEE Computer Society (2003)
21. Poleg, Y., Arora, C., Peleg, S.: Temporal segmentation of egocentric videos. In: IEEE Conference On Computer Vision and Pattern Recognition (CVPR) (2014)
22. SenseCam. Sensecam overview (2013)
23. Tan, P.N., Steinbach, M., Kumar, V.: Introduction to Data Mining, 1st edn. Addison-Wesley Longman Publishing Co., Boston (2005)
24. Zheng, L., Wang, S., He, F., Tian, Q.: Seeing the big picture: Deep embedding with contextual evidences. CoRR, abs/1406.0132 (2014)

Applying Basic Features from Sentiment Analysis for Automatic Irony Detection

Irazú Hernández-Farías$^{(\boxtimes)}$, José-Miguel Benedí, and Paolo Rosso

Pattern Recognition and Human Language Technology, Universitat Politècnica de València, Valencia, Spain
{dhernandez1,prosso}@dsic.upv.es,jmbenedi@prhlt.upv.es
https://www.prhlt.upv.es/

Abstract. People use social media to express their opinions. Often linguistic devices such as irony are used. From the sentiment analysis perspective such utterances represent a challenge being a polarity reversor (usually from positive to negative). This paper presents an approach to address irony detection from a machine learning perspective. Our model considers structural features as well as, for the first time, sentiment analysis features such as the overall sentiment of a tweet and a score of its polarity. The approach has been evaluated over a set classifiers such as: Naïve Bayes, Decision Tree, Maximum Entropy, Support Vector Machine, and for the first time in irony detection task: Multilayer Perceptron. The results obtained showed the ability of our model to distinguish between potentially ironic and non-ironic sentences.

Keywords: Automatic irony detection · Figurative language processing · Sentiment analysis

1 Introduction

The ability to recognize ironic intent in utterances is performed by humans in a relatively easy way although not always. We develop this ability since childhood and, over years with social interaction we increase it. In many cases we are able both to understand and to produce such utterances without a strict definition of what is or may be considered an ironic expression. Irony is a sophisticated, complex and prized mode of communication; it is intemately connected with the expression of feelings, attitudes or evaluations [2]. Moreover, irony can be considered as a strategy, which is intented to criticise or to praise. Sometimes but not always, it means the opposite of the literal meanings; generally irony shows or express some kind of contradiction [1].

Recently interest for discover information in social media has been growing. Twitter, offers a face-saving ability that allows users to express themselves employing linguistic devices such as irony. User-generated content is difficult to analyse: Internet language is hard to analyze due to the lack of paralinguistic cues; in addition one needs to have a good understanding of the context of the

© Springer International Publishing Switzerland 2015
R. Paredes et al. (Eds.): IbPRIA 2015, LNCS 9117, pp. 337–344, 2015.
DOI: 10.1007/978-3-319-19390-8_38

situation, the culture in question, and the people involved [8]. For research areas such sentiment analysis (SA), irony detection is important to avoid misinterpreting ironic statement as literal [11].

For computational linguistic purposes, most of the time irony and sarcasm are often viewed as the same figurative language device. Irony is often considered as an umbrella term that covers also sarcasm [12]. Previous works are mainly based on the classification of tweets as ironic or sarcastic and rely solely on text analysis.

This paper presents an approach for irony detection using a set of features that combine both surface text properties and information exploited from sentiment analysis lexicons. The main contribution of this paper is to take advantage of the classification of utterances according to their polarity. We consider in order to detect irony it is important to take into account the sentiment expressed in a tweet. Our model improves state-of-the-art results. The rest of this article is organized as follows: previous works on automatic irony detection are introduced in Sect. 2. In Sect. 3 we describe the set of features used. In Sect. 4, dataset, classifiers, experimental setting and evaluation of our approach are presented. Finally, in Sect. 5 we draw some conclusions and discuss future work.

2 Related Work

Recently automatic irony detection has attracted the attention of researchers from both machine learning and natural language processing [11]. A shared task on figurative language processing has been organized at SemEval 2015[6][1].

A survey that includes both philosophical and literary works investigating ironic communication and some computational efforts to operationalize irony detection is presented by Wallace in [11]. Reyes et al. [10] address the problem of irony detection as a classification task; the authors proposed a model employing to four types of conceptual features: signatures, unexpectedness, style and emotional scenarios. Bosco et al. in [4] present a study that investigates sentiment and irony in online political discussion social media in Italian. Buschmeier et al. [5] present an analysis of 29 features (such as punctuation marks, emoticons, interjections and bag-of-words); the authors' main goal is to investigate the impact of features removal on the performance of their approach. Barbieri and Saggion [3] used six groups of lexical features (frequency, written-spoken, intensity, structure, sentiments, synonyms, ambiguity), in order to classify ironic tweets (the same dataset of [10] was used).

3 Proposed Features

We address irony detection as a classification problem, considering different types of features. In our model, we consider some features previously applied

---

[1] Given a set of tweets the task consist in determining whether the user has expressed a positive, negative or neutral sentiment; more information is available at: http://alt.qcri.org/semeval2015/task11/.

in irony detection. Moreover, we propose two sentiment analisys features (*Sentiment Score* and *Polarity Value*) in order to take advantage of resources that allow to measure the overall sentiment expressed in each tweet. We can distinguish the set of features into *Statistical-based* and *Lexical-based*. *Statistical-based* are surface patterns that can be obtained taking into account the frequency of some words or characters in the tweet. *Lexical-based* are obtained by using information beyond the textual content of the tweet, i.e. applying external resources.

The first set, **Statistical-based** features is composed of four dimensions: a) *Textual Markers (TM)*, features widely used in this task, which include frequency of visual cues as: lenght of tweet, capitalization, punctuation marks, and emoticons[2]; b) *Counter-Factuality (CF)*[3], the frequency of discursive terms that hint at opposition or contradiction in a text such as "nevertheless"[4]; c) *Temporal Compression (TC)*[3], the frequency of terms that identify elements related to opposition in time, i.e. terms that indicate an abrupt change in a narrative; and d) *POS-based features (POS)*, where each tweet has been processed using a POS-tagger developed for this kind of texts called ARK[5]; we take into account frequency of verbs, nouns, adjectives and adverbs.

Our second set of features, **Lexicon-based**, exploits different knowledge bases to represent each tweet: a) *Semantic Similarity (SIM)*[3], consists in obtaining the degree of inconsistency measuring the relationship between the concepts contained in each tweet using the WordNet::Similarity[6] module; b) *Emotional Value (EV)*[3], where the emotional value is calculated taking into account the categories described by Whissel [13], in her Dictionary of Affect in Language (DAL)[7], c) *Sentiment Score(SS)*, in order to catch the overall sentiment (positive, negative or neutral) expressed in a tweet. We applied a lexicon developed by Hu-Lui in [7][8]; and d) *Polarity Value(PV)*, this feature allows to identify the rate of evaluation, either to criticize (negative) or to praise (positive). We use

---

[2] Using emoticons, with few characters is possible to display one's true feeling; sometimes they are virtually required under certain circumstances in text-based communication, where the absence of some kind of cues can hide what was originally intended to be humorous, sarcastic, ironic, and often negative [14].

[3] Feature previously applied by Reyes et al. [10].

[4] The complete list of words can be downloaded from http://users.dsic.upv.es/grupos/nle.

[5] http://www.ark.cs.cmu.edu/TweetNLP/.

[6] https://codegoogle.com/p/ws4j/. This module allows to calculate a set of seven different similarity measures.

[7] DAL is composed by 8,000 English words, distributed in three categories: *Activation*, refers to the degree of response, either passive or active, that humans exhibit in an emotional state; *Imagery*, quantifies how easy or difficult is to form a mental picture for a given word; and *Pleasantness*, quantifies the degree of pleasure suggested by a word.

[8] http://ww.cs.uic.edu/~liub/FBS/.

AFINN[9] lexicon, which contains a list of words labelled with a polarity valence value between minus five (negative) and plus five (positive) for each word.

The last two features in this set (*Sentiment Score(SS)* and *Polarity Value(PV)*) have not been previously used in irony detection. Our main motivation to use sentiment analysis features is that an ironic utterance is subjective, hence contains a positive or negative opinion. On the other hand, we taking into account a feature that allows us obtaining a polarity value from each tweet, so we have both the "overall"sentiment and a score of the polarity. In sentiment analysis, there are several resources that could help to improve the detection of ironic tweets.

4   Experiments and Results

The dataset used in this work was compiled by Reyes et al. [10] and consists of a total of 40,000 tweets written in English, distributed in four different classes: Irony, Education, Humor and Politics. The corpus was built retrieving 10,000 tweets that contain one of the following hashtags: #irony, #education, #humor and #politics. These hashtags allow to have tweets in which users explicitly declare their ironic attempt, and a large sample of non-ironic tweets. In order to perform classification process, we apply a set of classifiers widely used in text classification tasks. Some of them has been used in irony identification. The set of classifiers[10] is composed by: Decision Tree (*DT*), Maximum Entropy (*ME*), Naïve Bayes (*NB*), Random Forest (*RF*) and Support Vector Machine (SVM, with a RBF kernel)[11] and Multilayer Perceptron (*MLP*, we used a backpropagation based multilayer perceptron, with sigmoid functions, a learning rate of 0.3 and 500 epochs in each run; we did not perform any parameter tuning.). In this paper we propose to apply *MLP*, that has never been used for irony detection.

As in [3] and [10], we perform a set of binary classifications between Irony and Education/Humor/Politics. Each experiment has been performed in a 10-fold-cross-validation setting. We run experiments for one baseline: *Bag Of Words (BOW)*. We exploit only most frequent unigrams per class (1,000) in order to represent each tweet. This baseline relies on standard text classification features. According to [11], words counts alone offer an insufficient representation for verbal irony detection.

We apply two different vector representation approaches for experimental purposes. Each tweet was converted to a vector composed by 16 features. No feature selection technique was performed. In the first approach the features belonging to *Statistical-based* were taking into account the frequency of each one; while *Lexicon-based* are represented in different ways: the semantic similarity is the value obtained using the above-mentioned module; emotional value is

---

[9] http://github.com/abromberg/sentiment_analysis/blob/master/AFINN/ AFINN-111.txt.

[10] We used Weka toolkit's version of each classifier available at http://www.cs.waikato. ac.nz/ml/weka/downloading.html.

[11] Default parameters for each algorithm were used.

calculated taking into account values in DAL over words that compose each tweet; the sentiment score can be *positive* (more positive than negative terms), *negative* (more negative than positive terms) or neutral (same amount of positive and negative terms); finally, the polarity value is assigned by calculating the difference between the positive and the negative polarity of each tweet according to AFINN lexicon.

In the second approach we applied the representativeness criterion presented by Reyes et al. [10] in order to assign a value for *Statistical-based* features; the representativeness of a given document d_k (e.g. a tweet) is computed according to:

$$\delta_{i,j}(d_k) = \frac{f_{ij}}{|d_k|} \tag{1}$$

where i is the i-th feature; j is the j-th dimension; f is the feature dimension frequency; and $|d_k|$ is the lenght of the k-th document d_k. If $\delta_{i,j}(d_k)$ is ≥ 0.5, a value of 1 is assigned; otherwise, a representativeness value of 0 (not representative at all) is assigned; and the *Lexicon-based* features were represented as the same way above described for the first approach.

Three experiments were carried out using the classification algorithms mentioned above. Each experiment are constructed under different criteria. Two of them (**Lesk** and **Wu-Palmer**) are based in the first representation approach while the third (**Rep, Representativeness**) takes into account the second approach. The difference between *Lesk* and *Wu-Palmer* is the semantic similarity[12], that take into account, using Lesk and Wu-Palmer measures respectively.

In Table 1, we report F-measure results of our classification experiments. It can be observed that all results overcome the baseline. The bold values are used to highlight those F-measures greater than state-of-the-art (See Table 3). The best result is achieved by *SVM* in the three sub-tasks (binary classification Irony vs. Education, Irony vs. Humor and Irony vs. Politics). As reported by [3] and [10], higher results in F-measure are achieved by *ironic-vs-politics* classification, while lower F-measure lie in *ironic-vs-humor*. We carried out the t-test (with a 95 % confidence level) in order to see if the best results are statistically significant.

Moreover, we calculated the *Classification Error Rate (CER)*. In Table 2 CER values for each binary classification (*Iro-Edu, Iro-Hum* and *Iro-Pol*) are presented. As can be seen, our model obtains satisfactory CER rates. The best results(bold values in Table 2) are obtained by: SVM, MLP and RF.

As mentioned above, the dataset has been used before ([3] and [10]). The results reported by their authors are shown in Table 3. In both works a Decision Tree classifier was used. The last two rows in the table correspond to our results using the Decision Tree classifier.

As Table 2 shows, our approach improves the F-measure obtained previously by state-of-the-art approches. In order to determine which features are more rel-

---

[12] We performed experiments using each similarity measure of the WordNet::Similarity module. Due to lack of space, we report only the results with highest classification rates. The similarity measures are described in detail in [9].

Table 1. Results in F-measure for the baseline and each representation approach corresponding to binary classification. The underlined values are statistically significant.

	Irony-Education				Irony-Humor				Irony-Politics			
	BOW	Lesk	Wu-Palmer	Rep	BOW	Lesk	Wu-Palmer	Rep	BOW	Lesk	Wu-Palmer	Rep
DT	0.34	**0.78**	**0.78**	0.68	0.34	0.75	0.74	0.70	0.34	**0.79**	**0.79**	0.63
ME	0.37	**0.75**	**0.75**	0.66	0.37	0.74	0.74	0.69	0.36	**0.76**	**0.76**	0.59
MLP	0.50	**0.78**	**0.78**	0.67	0.50	0.75	0.76	0.70	0.50	**0.79**	**0.79**	0.61
NB	0.44	0.70	0.70	0.66	0.46	0.69	0.70	0.65	0.45	0.70	0.71	0.57
RF	0.16	**0.79**	**0.79**	0.68	0.16	0.76	0.76	0.70	0.16	**0.81**	**0.81**	0.63
SVM	0.63	**0.80**	**0.80**	0.68	0.59	**0.77**	**0.78**	0.69	0.64	**0.81**	**0.80**	0.63

Table 2. Results in terms of CER

	Irony-Education				Irony-Humor				Irony-Politics			
	BOW	Lesk	Wu-Palmer	Rep	BOW	Lesk	Wu-Palmer	Rep	BOW	Lesk	Wu-Palmer	Rep
DT	66.01	43.65	43.75	63.12	65.1	49.67	51.72	59.58	65.41	41.05	41.36	72.22
ME	62.58	49.88	49.93	67.46	62.48	50.51	50.64	60.17	63.13	46.82	46.59	79.24
MLP	50	43.8	42.87	64.76	50	48.25	**42.87**	60.07	50	40.82	40.96	76.53
NB	55.18	59.62	59.31	66.31	53.68	60.43	59.27	68.82	54.91	53.36	57.46	77.55
RF	84.11	40.5	40.71	63.22	84.31	46.19	45.97	59.71	84.2	**37.09**	**36.88**	72.59
SVM	55.18	**40.1**	**40.15**	63.65	55.08	**44.17**	44.07	60.7	54.46	37.93	37.88	73.82

evant in our model, Information Gain[11] was calculated. There are some features that seem to contribute more than others in our model to discriminate between classes (see Fig. 1). As can be seen, the textual markers (TM) features are a good indicator of this kind of utterances. Moreover, also the sentiment analysis features (SS and PV) showed to have an important impact on irony detection. This strenght the idea that irony detection is strongly related to sentiment analysis.

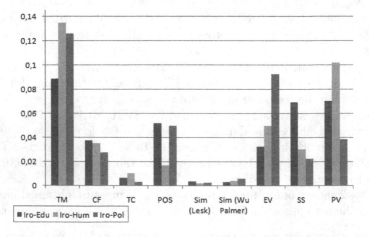

Fig. 1. Information gain for our set of features

Table 3. Results in F-measure of our model against state-of-the-art

	Irony vs.		
	Education	Humor	Politics
Reyes et al.	0.70	0.76	0.73
Barbieri and Saggion	0.73	0.75	0.75
Our approach Lesk	**0.78**	0.75	**0.79**
Our approach Wu-Palmer	**0.78**	**0.79**	**0.79**

According to Fig. 1, features related to SA seem to be quite important to identify ironic from non-ironic tweets. From this we may say that using features and resources for SA could improve performance of models for irony detection.

5 Conclusions

Given the growing interest in exploiting knowledge generated in social media, irony detection has attracted the attention of different research areas. Different approaches have been proposed to tackle this task. In this paper we proposed a model for ironic tweets classification, taking advantage for the first time of sentiment analysis features. The proposed model obtained higher values in terms of f-measure than those reported in the state-of-the-art using the same dataset. One of the best results was obtained by *MLP*, a method has not been previously used for irony detection. Also in terms of CER, our model showed good performance in classification rates of ironic tweets in the experiments we carried out. As future work an in-depth analysis of the impact of the proposed features is needed. We plan to exploit further features and resources from sentiment analysis.

Acknowledgments. The National Council for Science and Technology (CONACyT Mexico) has funded the research work of the first author (Grant No. 218109/313683, CVU-369616). The research work of third author was carried out in the framework of WIQ-EI IRSES (Grant No. 269180) within the FP 7 Marie Curie, DIANA-APPLI CATIONS (TIN2012-38603-C02-01) projects and the VLC/CAMPUS Microcluster on Multimodal Interaction in Intelligent Systems.

References

1. Alba-Juez, L.: Irony and the other off record strategies within politeness theory. J. Engl. Am. Stud. **16**, 13–24 (1995)
2. Attardo, S.: Irony markers and functions: towards a goal-oriented theory of irony and its processing. Rask **12**, 3–20 (2000)
3. Barbieri, F., Saggion, H.: Modelling Irony in Twitter, pp. 56–64. Association for Computational Linguistics (2014)
4. Bosco, C., Patti, V., Bolioli, A.: Developing corpora for sentiment analysis: the case of irony and senti-tut. IEEE Intell. Syst. **28**(2), 55–63 (2013)

5. Buschmeier, K., Cimiano, P., Klinger, R.: An impact analysis of features in a classification approach to irony detection in product reviews. In: Proceedings of the 5th Workshop on Computational Approaches to Subjectivity, Sentiment and Social Media Analysis, pp. 42–49. Association for Computational Linguistics (2014)
6. Ghosh, A., Li, G., Veale, T., Rosso, P., Shutova, E., Reyes, A., Barnden, J.: Sentiment analysis of figurative language in twitter. In: Proceedings of the International Workshop on Semantic Evaluation (SemEval-2015), Co-located with NAACL and *SEM (2015)
7. Hu, M., Liu, B.: Mining and summarizing customer reviews. In: Proceedings of the Tenth ACM SIGKDD International Conference on Knowledge Discovery and Data Mining, KDD 2004, pp. 168–177(2004)
8. Maynard, D., Greenwood, M.: Who cares about sarcastic tweets? investigating the impact of sarcasm on sentiment analysis. In: Proceedings of the Ninth International Conference on Language Resources and Evaluation (LREC-2014), European Language Resources Association (ELRA) (2014)
9. Pedersen, T., Patwardhan, S., Michelizzi, J.: Wordnet::similarity: measuring the relatedness of concepts. In: Proceedings of the 9th National Conference on Artificial Intelligence, pp. 1024–1025. Association for Computational Linguistics
10. Reyes, A., Rosso, P., Veale, T.: A multidimensional approach for detecting irony in twitter. Lang. Resour. Eval. **47**(1), 239–268 (2013)
11. Wallace, B.C.: Computational irony: a survey and new perspectives. Artif. Intell. Rev. **43**, 467–483 (2013)
12. Wang, A.P.: #irony or #sarcasm – a quantitative and qualitative study based on twitter. In: Proceedings of the PACLIC: the 27th Pacific Asia Conference on Language, Information, and Computation, pp. 349–356. Department of English, National Chengchi University (2013)
13. Whissell, C.: Using the revised dictionary of affect in language to quantify the emotional undertones of samples of natural languages. Psychol. Rep. **2**, 509–521 (2009)
14. Wolf, A.: Emotional expression online: gender differences in emoticon use. CyberPsychology Behavior **3**, 827–833 (2000)

Exploiting the Bin-Class Histograms for Feature Selection on Discrete Data

Artur J. Ferreira[1,3]([✉]) and Mário A.T. Figueiredo[2,3]

[1] Instituto Superior de Engenharia de Lisboa, Lisboa, Portugal
arturj@isel.pt
[2] Instituto Superior Técnico, Universidade de Lisboa, Lisboa, Portugal
[3] Instituto de Telecomunicações, Lisboa, Portugal
mario.figueiredo@lx.it.pt

Abstract. In machine learning and pattern recognition tasks, the use of feature discretization techniques may have several advantages. The discretized features may hold enough information for the learning task at hand, while ignoring minor fluctuations that are irrelevant or harmful for that task. The discretized features have more compact representations that may yield both better accuracy and lower training time, as compared to the use of the original features. However, in many cases, mainly with medium and high-dimensional data, the large number of features usually implies that there is some redundancy among them. Thus, we may further apply feature selection (FS) techniques on the discrete data, keeping the most relevant features, while discarding the irrelevant and redundant ones. In this paper, we propose relevance and redundancy criteria for supervised feature selection techniques on discrete data. These criteria are applied to the bin-class histograms of the discrete features. The experimental results, on public benchmark data, show that the proposed criteria can achieve better accuracy than widely used relevance and redundancy criteria, such as mutual information and the Fisher ratio.

Keywords: Feature selection · Feature discretization · Discrete features · Bin-class histogram · Matrix norm · Supervised learning · Classification

1 Introduction

High-dimensional (HD) datasets (*i.e.*, with a large number of features) are becoming increasingly common in many different application domains of machine learning and pattern recognition. For instance, we can find them in different areas, such as genomics, bioinformatics, computer vision, satellite image analysis, and multimodal audio-visual processing. When dealing with HD data, one often resorts to *feature discretization* (FD) [1] and *feature selection* (FS) [2] procedures. FS methods aim at finding an adequate subset of the original features,

© Springer International Publishing Switzerland 2015
R. Paredes et al. (Eds.): IbPRIA 2015, LNCS 9117, pp. 345–353, 2015.
DOI: 10.1007/978-3-319-19390-8_39

whereas FD looks for compact data representations, desirably ignoring irrelevant fluctuations on the data for the task at hand, and leading to more robust classifiers, and lower training time.

The literature on FD and FS is vast, with many unsupervised and supervised techniques. A comprehensive list of FS techniques can be found in [2]. Regarding FD, there are several comprehensive reviews, such as the recent survey in [3].

FS methods can be grouped into four classes [2]: wrappers, embedded methods, filters, and hybrid methods. A filter retains some of the features and discards others, based on a criterion that is independent of any subsequent learning algorithm. Although filters are the simplest and fastest approaches, thus expected to perform worse than the other types of methods, it is often the case that they are the only applicable option on HD datasets, where the other approaches can be computationally too expensive.

Regarding FD methods, the dynamic techniques that take into account feature interdependencies are usually preferable to their static counterparts, which discretize each feature individually. However, when dealing with HD data, dynamic FD methods have a prohibitive computational cost, and one has to resort to suboptimal static methods. Thus, when learning from HD data, it is useful to apply some FS filter after data discretization, in order to remove the remaining feature interdependencies. As a consequence, we can combine FD and FS techniques, yielding joint discretization and selection.

1.1 Our Contribution

In this paper, we propose four criteria for relevance and redundancy assessment for FS purposes, on discrete features. After running some FD technique, we apply one of our criteria in order to select and keep an adequate subset of features. After the FD process is carried out, the *bin-class histogram* (BCH) of each feature is computed. In a nutshell, the BCH for one feature holds the number of times that each discretization bin occurs among each class, considering all the available data patterns (see Sect. 3 for details).

The remainder of the paper is organized as follows. Section 2 briefly reviews some existing supervised FD and FS techniques. Section 3 details the proposed criteria for relevance and redundancy assessment. The experimental evaluation of our methods, compared against standard methods on public benchmark datasets is reported in Sect. 4. Finally, Sect. 5 ends the paper with some concluding remarks and directions for future work.

2 Short Review of Feature Discretization and Selection

2.1 Feature Discretization

Many datasets have continuous features (formally, real-valued, but in practice stored with a floating point representation). Some classification algorithms can only deal with discrete features; in this case, a discretization procedure is needed as a pre-processing stage. Regardless of the type of classifier used, discretized features may lead to better results, as compared to their original version [1].

The *information entropy maximization* (IEM) method [4] is a well-known supervised FD technique. It relies on the principle that the most informative features to discretize are the most compressible ones. IEM adopts an entropy minimization heuristic for discretization into multiple intervals; it operates in a recursive, incremental, top-down fashion, computing the discretization bins that minimize the number of bits per feature.

The *class-attribute interdependence maximization* (CAIM) [5] algorithm aims at maximizing the class-attribute interdependence and to generate a (possibly) minimal number of discrete intervals. Similarly to IEM, CAIM does not require a predefined number of bins, being an incremental top-down approach. The experimental reported in [5], comparing CAIM with six other FD algorithms, show that the discrete features generated by CAIM almost always have the lowest number of bins and yield the highest classification accuracy.

2.2   Feature Selection

This section briefly reviews two well-known relevance criteria widely used as supervised FS filters (and in hybrid methods). Consider a supervised dataset, with d features and n instances (each known to belong to one of C classes, $\{1, 2, ..., C\}$), stored in $d \times n$ matrix X (*i.e.*, X_{ij} is the i-th feature of the j-th instance). The class labels are given in a $C \times n$ binary matrix Y, where $Y_{cj} = 1$, if and only if the j-th instance belongs to class c.

In the multi-class case ($C > 2$, assuming class labels in $\{1, 2, ..., C\}$), the Fisher ratio (FiR) for the i-th feature (see, *e.g.*, [6]) is given by

$$\text{FiR}_i = \sum_{c=1}^{C} n_c (\mu_{ci} - \eta_i)^2 \left(\sum_{j=1}^{c} n_c \sigma_{ci}^2 \right)^{-1}, \tag{1}$$

where $n_c = \sum_{j=1}^{n} Y_{cj}$ is the number of instances in class c,

- $\mu_{ci} = \frac{1}{n_c} \sum_{j=1}^{n} X_{ij} Y_{cj}$ is the sample mean of feature i in class c;

- $\eta_i = \frac{1}{n} \sum_{j=1}^{n} X_{ij}$ is the global sample mean of the i−th feature;

- $\sigma_{ci}^2 = \frac{1}{n_c} \sum_{j=1}^{n} Y_{cj} (X_{ij} - \mu_{ci})^2$ is the sample variance of feature i in class c;

Another widely used measure of feature relevance is (the sample-based estimate of) the *mutual information* (MI) [7] between each feature and the class label. The MI is non-negative, being zero if and only if the two involved variables are statistically independent [7].

When using either the FiR or the MI for relevance-based FS on a d-dimensional dataset, we simply keep the $m \leq d$ top-ranked features, according to the adopted

Feature 1

$$\begin{bmatrix} 12 & 4 & 0 \\ 2 & 5 & 9 \\ 5 & 0 & 8 \\ 6 & 16 & 8 \end{bmatrix}$$

Feature 2

$$\begin{bmatrix} 16 & 0 & 0 \\ 2 & 0 & 9 \\ 1 & 0 & 16 \\ 6 & 25 & 0 \end{bmatrix}$$

b=4, c=3, n=75 (25 per class)

Fig. 1. The *bin-class histogram* (BCH) matrix for two discrete features with four bins in a three-class problem, with 25 instances per class.

relevance measure. Both the FiR and the MI are *global* ranking measures, in the sense that they assign a number (a relevance value) to each feature. However, when dealing with discrete data, one can further analyze the distribution of the discretization bins among patterns of all classes, thus having some *local* insight on the discriminative power of each feature. Despite its popularity [8], when dealing with HD data, MI may not be the best relevance criteria [9].

With HD data, it is often the case that we have redundant features, which convey the same information. Keeping all these features may have harmful consequences for the learning task, thus they should be discarded. In this context, some FS filters follow the *relevance-redundancy* (RR) approach, such as the *relevance-redundancy feature selection* (RRFS) method [10], which finds the most relevant subset of features, and then efficiently searches for redundancy in this subset, selecting only highly relevant features with low redundancy.

3 Proposed Relevance and Redundancy Criteria

In this Section, we describe the proposed relevance and redundancy criteria for discrete data and its usage for FS filters. The relevance of the discrete feature is computed by checking the histogram of each discretization interval, across the different classes. The proposed method works as follows:

1. (independently) discretize all the d features in the dataset, with some FD method (e.g. one of the techniques mentioned in Sect. 2.1);
2. obtain the $b_i \times C$ *bin-class histogram* (BCH) matrix $\mathbf{B}^{(i)}$ for each feature i, where b_i is the number of discretization bins of the i-th feature (specifically, $B_{ac}^{(i)}$ is the number of times that feature i takes values in the a-th bin and the class label is c; Fig. 1 illustrates the BCH matrices for two discrete features with four bins ($b_1 = b_2 = 4$) in a three-class problem ($C = 3$), for a dataset with $n = 75$ patterns, 25 per class);
3. apply one of the criteria r_1, r_2, r_3, or r_4 (see below), to assess the relevance (and/or the redundancy) of each feature and keep the most relevant ones.

The key idea of this proposal is to use the local information provided by the BCH, in order to identify the most discriminative features. The rationale is that this local information may be more meaningful for this task, as compared to global indicators such as the FiR and the MI.

The relevance of a discrete feature is proportional to the non-uniformity of its histogram across the discretization bins and classes. For instance, if a given row (discretization bin) of the BCH matrix has an (almost) uniform distribution, this shows that particular discretization level does not contribute to distinguishing among the classes. A special and interesting case is the occurrence of zeros in this matrix, which implies that a given discretization level never occured in the patterns of a given class.

We propose four criteria to assess the relevance of feature i based on its BCH matrix. The first two aim at assessing the non-uniformity of the BCH matrix:

- $r_1^{(i)}$: the number of zero entries in matrix $\mathbf{B}^{(i)}$;
- $r_2^{(i)}$: the sum of the absolute differences between all pairs of columns of $\mathbf{B}^{(i)}$:

$$r_2^{(i)} = \sum_{k=1}^{C-1} \sum_{m=k+1}^{C} \left\| \mathbf{B}_k^{(i)} - \mathbf{B}_m^{(i)} \right\|_1, \tag{2}$$

where $\mathbf{B}_k^{(i)}$ and $\mathbf{B}_m^{(i)}$ denote the k-th and the m-th columns of $\mathbf{B}^{(i)}$.

The other two criteria are based on *matrix norms* and *matrix similarity* measures [11,12]. The key idea is that an ideal BCH matrix (after normalizing each column to sum to one) is a "rectangular identity matrix" (*i.e.*, an identity with possibly several additional rows of zeros). In detail,

- $r_3^{(i)} = \mathrm{trace}(\bar{\mathbf{B}}^{(i)}(\bar{\mathbf{B}}^{(i)})^T)$, where $\bar{\mathbf{B}}^{(i)}$ is the the normalized version of $\mathbf{B}^{(i)}$, such that its columns sum up to one. The maximum value of the trace of $\bar{\mathbf{B}}^{(i)}(\bar{\mathbf{B}}^{(i)})^T$ is C, which is achieved by the ideal matrix (as explained above).
- $r_4^{(i)} = \mathrm{trace}\left(\sqrt{(\bar{\mathbf{B}}^{(i)})^T \bar{\mathbf{B}}^{(i)}}\right)$, called the trace (or nuclear) norm, which is also equal to the sum of the singular values of $\bar{\mathbf{B}}^{(i)}$. The relevance of a feature is proportional to this value.

These criteria can be applied to both binary or multi-class problems. For the example in Fig. 1, these relevance values are: i) for feature 1, $r_1=2$, $r_2=74$, $r_3=1.14$, and $r_4=1.67$; ii) for feature 2, $r_1=5$, $r_2=132$, $r_3=2.01$, and $r_4=2.39$. Thus, feature 2 will be considered more relevant than feature 1, which is in accordance with the above considerations about the $\mathbf{B}^{(i)}$ matrix.

4   Experimental Evaluation

We report an experimental evaluation, carried out on public domain standard benchmark datasets, from the UCI [13] and the *gene expression model selector* (GEMS)[1] repositories. We perform a supervised classification task with the linear

---

[1] www.gems-system.org.

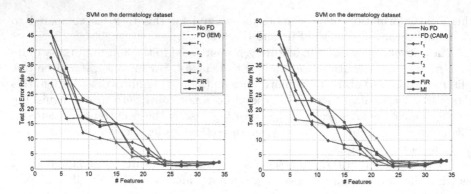

Fig. 2. SVM test set error rate (%), 10-fold CV, for the Dermatology dataset, as functions of the number of features for different FS relevance-only criteria: IEM discretization (left); CAIM discretization (right).

support vector machines (SVM) classifier from Weka[2], with its default parameters. The classification accuracy is assessed using 10-fold *cross validation* (CV). For each CV fold, the IEM and CAIM FD methods (see Sect. 2.1) are applied to the training partition to learn a quantizer, which is then applied to the test partition. We perform FS with relevance-only FS filters and relevance-redundancy filters, comparing our criteria against the FiR and the MI.

Figure 2 shows the test set error rate as functions of the number of features for the relevance-based FS filters with our relevance measures: r_1, r_2, r_3, r_4, the FiR and the MI, after IEM and CAIM discretization. We use the Dermatology dataset, a skin disease diagnosis problem, with $d = 34$ features, $C = 6$ classes, and $n = 358$ instances. The horizontal lines refer to the baseline error without FS; one of these lines corresponds to the absence of FD whereas the other corresponds to FD by the corresponding discretization method (IEM or CAIM). The error rates reported by our four relevance criteria are competitive with those attained by FiR and MI. Regarding the impact of the FD method on the final results, we find no appreciable differences between these methods.

Figure 3 shows the results of the test set error rate as functions of the number of features for the relevance-based FS filters, on the Hepatitis and Dexter datasets with IEM discretization. On the Hepatitis dataset, r_3 and r_4 achieve the best results, with error rates below the baseline values. On the Dexter dataset (with sparse data), r_2 is clearly more adequate than the other three criteria.

Table 1 reports the test set error rate attained by the same methods of Fig. 2, using IEM discretization, for several datasets, with quite different types of data. We rank the features according to the relevance criteria and we keep the $m < d$ top-ranked features. These results show that the proposed relevance measures attain results similar or better to those of FiR and MI, in different problems. Altough none of the relevance criteria outperforms all the others, we can observe

---

[2] www.cs.waikato.ac.nz/ml/weka.

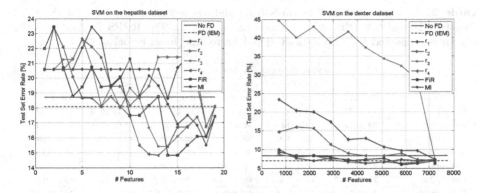

Fig. 3. SVM test set error rate (%), 10-fold CV, for the Hepatitis (left) and Dexter (right) datasets, as functions of the number of features, for different FS relevance-only criteria with IEM discretization.

Table 1. Test set error rate (%), for the SVM classifier, 10-fold CV, for datasets with c classes, n instances, with dimensionality d. We perform FS to select subsets with $m < d$ features. The best results (lower error) are in bold face.

Dataset $(d; c; n)$	m	FD (IEM)	Relevance-Only Feature Selection					
			r_1	r_2	r_3	r_4	FiR	MI
Wine (13;3;178)	8	2.25	**1.11**	2.22	3.48	2.22	2.75	2.22
Hepatitis (19;2;155)	12	18.08	20.58	19.45	16.66	**14.90**	18.15	20.15
Ionosphere (33;2;331)	30	11.42	11.71	**10.86**	12.29	12.00	12.26	11.97
Dermatology (34;6;358)	24	2.52	2.27	3.34	1.98	**1.11**	1.96	1.98
Sonar (60;2;208)	24	21.19	36.09	33.66	21.13	**20.18**	21.63	21.68
M-Libras (90;15;360)	63	**23.89**	26.11	27.44	28.00	29.44	29.67	30.11
Colon (2000;2;62)	800	18.81	19.05	19.05	**15.48**	17.14	17.14	17.38
Example1 (9947;2;50)	4370	**2.78**	3.11	**2.78**	3.11	**2.78**	**2.78**	**2.78**
Prost.-Tumor (10510;2;102)	2100	8.82	6.82	6.82	8.82	8.82	8.82	**5.73**
Leukemia1(5327;3;72)	2128	4.29	**2.86**	**2.86**	4.29	4.29	4.29	**2.86**
ORL10P (10304;10;100)	3090	2.0	**0.0**	**0.0**	3.0	1.0	1.0	**0.0**
Brain-Tumor2 (10367;4;90)	4144	20.00	24.00	24.00	**18.00**	**18.00**	**18.00**	24.00
Dexter (20000;2;2600)	2936	7.33	17.33	**6.67**	40.67	9.67	8.33	8.00

that despite their simplicity r_1 and r_2 achieve good results; in fact, r_2 is the best for the sparse data of the Dexter dataset. The relevance criteria r_3 and r_4 also achieve results which are usually equal or better than those of FiR and MI.

We now assess the results of the filter RRFS method (see Sect. 2.2), using the same relevance criteria as in the previous experiments, for the same datasets as in Table 1. The results reported in Table 2 suggest that the proposed relevance criteria are also useful for relevance-redundancy FS filters. In many datasets, the proposed criteria yield the lowest test set error rate.

Table 2. Average number of features (m_*) and test set error rate (%), for the SVM classifier, 10-fold CV (the same datasets as in Table 1). The RRFS method uses the M_S values reported for each dataset. The best results (lower error) are in bold face.

Dataset; M_S	RRFS - Relevance-Redundancy Feature Selection					
	$m_1; r_1$	$m_2; r_2$	$m_3; r_3$	$m_4; r_4$	$m_f; FiR$	$m_m; MI$
Wine; 0.95	7.9; **2.2**	7.2; **2.2**	8.9; 3.9	8.9; 3.9	8.6; 3.3	9.6; 2.7
Hepatitis; 0.95	13.7; 21.2	15.3; 22.6	16.2; 23.1	16.2; 23.1	16.7; **17.9**	16.2; 20.5
Ionosphere; 0.95	32.0; 12.8	32.0; 12.8	32.0; **10.8**	32.0; **10.8**	32.0; 11.0	32.0; 11.9
Dermatology; 0.95	32.9; 2.2	33.0; **1.6**	33.0; 2.2	33.0; 2.2	32.9; 2.2	32.8; **1.6**
Sonar; 0.95	56.6; 22.1	56.3; 20.7	56.8; 20.2	56.8; 20.2	57.4; **19.7**	55.2; 21.2
M-Libras; 0.95	44.1; 30.2	52.6; **26.6**	62.1; **26.6**	62.1; **26.6**	33.3; 42.7	37.2; 35.0
Colon; 0.6	73.1; **14.7**	73.3; **14.7**	48.9; 17.8	48.9; 17.8	73.9; 22.8	66.3; 27.3
Example1; 0.6	4392.0; **3.5**	4387.8; 3.6	4371.6; 3.7	4371.6; 3.7	4257.9; 3.7	4402.1; 4.2
Prost.-Tumor; 0.6	6950.1; 8.6	6959.6; 8.6	6933.5; **7.6**	6933.5; **7.6**	7053.7; 9.6	7160.0; **7.6**
Leukemia1; 0.6	2740.4; 4.3	2774.3; **2.9**	2685.7; **2.9**	2685.7; **2.9**	2848.8; **2.9**	2774.9; **2.9**
ORL10P; 0.9	2924.4; 2.0	2596.0; **0.0**	2561.2; **0.0**	2561.2; **0.0**	3416.3; 1.0	3436.8; 2.0
Brain-Tumor2; 0.6	4767.7; **20.0**	4773.0; **20.0**	4527.6; 22.0	4527.6; 22.0	4316.4; 28.0	4585.5; 24.0
Dexter; 0.6	7287.0; 7.7	7288.4; 7.7	7285.5; 7.7	7285.5; 7.7	7197.5; 8.0	7289.9; **7.3**

5   Conclusions

We have proposed new criteria for supervised selection of discrete features, based on their bin-class histograms. Our experiments suggest that all the proposed criteria are useful for both relevance-only and relevance-redundancy FS filters. The classifiers learned on the features selected by our methods usually attain equal or better accuracy than those learned on the original discretized or non-discretized features. The proposed criteria attain equal or better results than two widely used FS criteria, on different types of data. We conclude that the proposed criteria deserve further study.

References

1. Witten, I., Frank, E.: Data Mining: Practical Machine Learning Tools and Techniques. Elsevier, Morgan Kauffmann, Amsterdam (2005)
2. Guyon, I., Gunn, S., Nikravesh, M., Zadeh, L. (eds.): Feature Extraction, Foundations and Applications. Springer, Heidelberg (2006)
3. Garcia, S., Luengo, J., Saez, J., Lopez, V., Herrera, F.: A survey of discretization techniques: taxonomy and empirical analysis in supervised learning. IEEE Trans. Knowl. Data Eng. **25**(4), 734–750 (2013)
4. Fayyad, U., Irani, K.: Multi-interval discretization of continuous-valued attributes for classification Learning. In: International Joint Conference on Artificial Intelligence (IJCAI), pp. 1022–1027 (1993)
5. Kurgan, L., Cios, K.: CAIM discretization algorithm. IEEE Trans. Know. Data Eng. **16**(2), 145–153 (2004)
6. Duda, R., Hart, P., Stork, D.: Pattern Classification, 2nd edn. Wiley, New York (2001)
7. Cover, T., Thomas, J.: Elements of Information Theory. Wiley, New York (1991)

8. Brown, G., Pocock, A., Zhao, M., Luján, M.: Conditional likelihood maximisation: a unifying framework for information theoretic feature selection. J. Mach. Learn. Res. **13**, 27–66 (2012)
9. Franay, B., Doquire, G., Verleysen, M.: Theoretical and empirical study on the potential inadequacy of mutual information for feature selection in classification. Neurocomputing **112**, 64–78 (2013)
10. Ferreira, A., Figueiredo, M.: Efficient feature selection filters for high-dimensional data. Pattern Recogn. Lett. **33**(13), 1794–1804 (2012)
11. Srebro, N., Shraibman, A.: Rank, trace-norm and max-norm. In: Auer, P., Meir, R. (eds.) COLT 2005. LNCS (LNAI), vol. 3559, pp. 545–560. Springer, Heidelberg (2005)
12. Strang, G., Borre, K.: Linear Algebra, Geodesy, and GPS. Cambridge Press, Wellesley (1997)
13. Frank, A., Asuncion, A.: UCI machine learning repository (2010). http.//archive. ics.uci.edu/ml

Time-Series Prediction Based on Kernel Adaptive Filtering with Cyclostationary Codebooks

S. García-Vega$^{(\boxtimes)}$, A.M. Álvarez-Meza, and G. Castellanos-Dominguez

Signal Processing and Recognition Group, Universidad Nacional de Colombia,
Bogotá, Colombia
{segarciave,amalvarezme,cgcastellanosd}@unal.edu.co

Abstract. A kernel adaptive filtering approach called Kernel Adaptive Filtering with Cyclostationary Codebooks (KAFCC) to support one-dimensional time-series prediction is proposed. KAFCC builds multiple codebooks to encode relevant interleaved random processes to obtain an estimation from an input-output nonlinear mapping. The proposed methodology creates a competition among different codebooks at every time instant to highlight the relations among the current input and previously detected cyclostationary dynamics. Namely, a kernel-based quantization function is introduced to build a new codebook if the current dynamic was not properly learned in the past. The proposed methodology is tested on one-dimensional time-series and compared against state-of-the-art techniques in terms of prediction accuracy. Attained results show that KAFCC provides an effective way to predict time-series.

Keywords: Adaptive filtering · Kernel function · Cyclostationarity

1 Introduction

An interesting topic that has become of great interest today for scientific community on machine learning are the applications based on adaptive filtering. Particularly, adaptive filtering approaches are used in fields where statistical characteristics vary periodically with time (cyclostationary processes), e.g., telecommunications, telemetry, radar, sonar applications, weather forecasting, etc [1]. Broadly, adaptive filtering approaches adjust its coefficients according to the amount of the correction error that is calculated within a given optimization framework. So, the *Least-mean-square* (LMS) is the baseline adaptive filtering rule that minimizes an Euclidean metric-based cost function. There are some adaptive LMS-based methods that have developed, such as: *recursive least-square, extended recursive least-squares*, and *exponentially weighted recursive least-squares* [2]. However, due to knowledge of the input time-series cycles are practically not assured, accuracy on these L2-based algorithms is not enough, especially, under highly non-stationary conditions. Hence, generalized filtering methods appear as an alternative to include testing for cyclostationarity,

© Springer International Publishing Switzerland 2015
R. Paredes et al. (Eds.): IbPRIA 2015, LNCS 9117, pp. 354–361, 2015.
DOI: 10.1007/978-3-319-19390-8_40

nevertheless, achieved computational cost is high and the filter accuracy is still not good enough [3,4].

In this regard, Kernel Adaptive Filtering (KAF) techniques appear as an alternative to perform better estimations by applying input-output nonlinear mappings via a Reproducing Kernel Hilbert Space (RKHS). So, KAF techniques minimizes a given instantaneous cost function, so that their adaptive ability relies on the correction of error prediction at every iteration to build incrementally the filter output. These algorithms include different kernel LMS-based versions, and kernel affine projections. For supporting prediction tasks of one-dimensional time-series, KAF provides the following advantages: they have no local minima with the squared error cost function, they have moderate complexity in terms of computation and memory, and they belong to online learning methods and have good tracking ability to handle non-stationary conditions. Additionally, some KAF-based alternatives, like Quantized-Kernel-Least-Mean-Square (QKLMS), store the input samples into a single quantization vector (codebook), which is updated at every time instant. Hence, this memoryless codebook can not take advantage of learned information from cyclically interleaved processes. Furthermore, the KAF must learn each cyclic random structure as it were a new process, thereby riding of salient information and reducing performed accuracy.

We propose an adaptive filtering approach called KAF using Cyclostationary Codebooks (KAFCC) to support one-dimensional time-series prediction tasks. As online kernel learning method, we select the QKLMS that has shown to perform high accuracy under nonstationary conditions while providing a moderate computational cost. However, our method estimates multiple codebooks along time to encode relevant interleaved random processes. Thus, cyclostationary dynamics are highlighted by means of a kernel-based quantization function that allows building a new codebook if the current dynamic was not properly learned in the past. In addition, provided codebooks are employed to estimate the current output as linear combination of KAF-based predictions where the combination weights are fixed based on a non-linear gating function [5]. Obtained results of KAFCC testing, carried out on real one-dimensional data, show an improved time-series prediction accuracy with the benefit of better data interpretability.

2   KAF Using Cyclostationary Codebooks - KAFCC

Let $u \in \mathbb{R}^m$ be a m-dimensional input vector related to the output signal $d \in \mathbb{R}$ through a continuous nonlinear input-output mapping $f : \mathbb{R}^m \to \mathbb{R}$. So, given a sequence of input-output pairs $\{u_t, d_t : t = 1, 2, \dots\}$, a Kernel Adaptive filter (KAF) is a kernel-based sequential estimator of f such that f_t is updated on the basis of the last estimate f_{t-1} and current example [6]. Overall, KAF approaches employs an unique estimator f_t based on a set of previously analyzed samples $C_{t-1} = \{c_{t-1}^i \in \mathbb{R}^m : i = 1, \dots, t-1\}$, termed the codebook. Thus, the estimation $\hat{d}_t \in \mathbb{R}$ is calculated as: $\hat{d}_t = f(u_t) = \sum_{i=1}^{t-1} \alpha_{t-1}^i \kappa(u_t, c_{t-1}^i)$, where $\alpha_{t-1}^i \in \mathbb{R}$ is the weight associated to the codeword c_{t-1}^i, and $\kappa : \mathbb{R}^m \times \mathbb{R}^m \to \mathbb{R}$ is a positive definite kernel function that allows computing pairwise similarities in $\mathbb{R}^m$. Here, due to its mathematical tractability and its advantages for finding Hilbert spaces with universal approximating capability, the Gaussian kernel is used to find pairwise similarities as: $\kappa_{\sigma_q}\left(\boldsymbol{u}_t, \boldsymbol{c}_{t-1}^i\right) = \exp\left(\frac{-\|\boldsymbol{u}_t - \boldsymbol{c}_{t-1}^i\|_2^2}{2\sigma_q^2}\right)$, where $\sigma_q \in \mathbb{R}^+$ is the kernel bandwidth and $\|\cdot\|$ stands for the 2-norm. The KAF approaches employ a linear least mean square algorithm in the Reproducing Kernel Hilbert Space (RKHS) created by κ to update f_t, yielding:

$$\begin{cases} f_1 = 0 \\ e_t = d_t - f_{t-1}(\boldsymbol{u}_t) \\ f_t = f_{t-1} + \eta e_t \kappa(\boldsymbol{u}_t, \cdot) \end{cases}, \tag{1}$$

where $e_t \in \mathbb{R}$ is the instantaneous error.

Here, we propose to predict the t-th output as a linear combination of P_t KAF-based estimators by learning cyclostationary codebooks as:

$$\hat{d}_t = \sum_{p=1}^{P_t} w_t^p \hat{d}_t^p(\boldsymbol{u}_t), \tag{2}$$

where $w_t^p \in \mathbb{R}^+$ is the weight associated to the p-th estimation of d_t, $\hat{d}_t^p \in \mathbb{R}$. Regarding this, each $\hat{d}_t^p$ is calculated by applying an KAF using the p-th codebook as follows: $\hat{d}_{t-1}^p = \sum_{j=1}^{N_{t-1}^p} \alpha_{t-1}^{p,j} \kappa\left(\boldsymbol{u}_t, \boldsymbol{c}_{t-1}^{p,j}\right)$, where $\boldsymbol{c}_{t-1}^p \in \mathbb{R}^m$ is the j-th codeword in codebook $\boldsymbol{C}_{t-1}^p = \{\boldsymbol{c}_{t-1}^{p,j} : j = 1, \ldots, N_{t-1}^p\}$, N_{t-1}^p is the number of codewords in $\boldsymbol{C}_{t-1}^p$, and $\alpha_{t-1}^{p,j} \in \mathbb{R}$ is the weight associated to $\boldsymbol{c}_{t-1}^{p,j}$. In turn, the non-negative weights w_t^p are learned using a non-linear gating function as $w_t^p = \frac{\exp(v_t^p)}{\sum_{p=1}^{P_t} \exp(v_t^p)}$, where the gate parameter $v_t^p \in \mathbb{R}$ is the intermediate weight at the t-th iteration that is obtained by a gradient descend based approach [7]:

$$v_t^p = v_{t-1}^p + \mu\left(2e_t\left[\hat{y}_t^p - \sum_{l=1, l \neq p}^{P_t} \hat{y}_t^l\right] w_t^p\left[1 - w_t^p\right]\right), \tag{3}$$

being $\mu \in \mathbb{R}^+$ the learning rate. In this sense, the gating function allows preserving convexity in w_t^p and creates a competition among the different codebooks [8]. Thus, the higher the p-th weight value the higher the relevance of codebook p for estimating the current output. In addition, the proposed methodology employs a vector quantization approach to check whether is necessary to build a new codebook with the current sample $\boldsymbol{u}_t$. Therefore, a codebook will be created if the current sample encodes new information according to the previously detected time-series dynamics. Cyclostationary dynamics are identified by analyzing the similarity among $\boldsymbol{u}_t$ and the set $\{\boldsymbol{C}_{t-1}^p : p = 1, \ldots, P_t\}$ as

$$s_p = \max_{1 \leq j \leq |\boldsymbol{C}_{t-1}^p|} \kappa_\sigma\left(\boldsymbol{u}_t, \boldsymbol{c}_{t-1}^{p,j}\right),$$ where $s_p \in \mathbb{R}$. Then, the nearest codebook to current sample is found as the maximum value s_p^* in s_p. If s_p^* is higher than a given

threshold $U_{ac} \in [0, 1]$, u_t can be represented by the cyclosatationary dynamic encoded in codebook $c_{t-1}^{p^*}$ using a quantized KAF technique [9]. Otherwise, the current sample is used to build a new codebook. Algorithm 1 describes the proposed KAFCC.

Algorithm 1. – KAFCC

Inputs: $\{u_t, d_t\}$, U_{ac}, ϵ_U, η, $C_0 = \{c_1, \ldots, c_{P_0}\}$, $\alpha_0 = \{\alpha_1 \ldots, \alpha_{P_0}\}$
Computation:
  while $\{u_t, d_t\}$ available **do**
    1) Compute the weights of each *codebook* using Eq. (??)
    2) Compute the adaptive filter output using Eq. (2)
    3) Compute the prediction error: $c_t = d_t - \hat{d}_t$
    4) Build a new *codebook*?
$$s_p = \max_{1 \leq j \leq |C_{t-1}^p|} \kappa_\sigma \left(u_t, c_{t-1}^{p,j} \right)$$
$$s_p^* = \max_p s_p$$
    if $s_p^* > U_{ac}$ % Do not build a new *codebook*
      if $s_p^* > \epsilon_U$
$$C_{t-1}^{p^*, j_p^*} = C_{t-1}^{p^*, j_p^*}; \ \alpha_{t-1}^{p^*, j_p^*} = \alpha_{t-1}^{p^*, j_p^*} + \eta c_t$$
      else
$$C_{t-1}^{p^*} = \left\{ C_{t-1}^{p^*}, u_t \right\}; \ \alpha_{t-1}^{p^*} = \left\{ \alpha_{t-1}^{p^*}, \eta c_t \right\}$$
      end
    else % a new *codebook* is built
$$C_{t-1}^{P+1} = \{C_{t-1}, u_t\}; \ \alpha_{t-1}^{P+1} = \eta c_t$$
    end
  end while

---

3 Experimental Set-up and Results

3.1 Databases

The proposed KAFCC is tested as tool to support prediction tasks under nonstationary conditions. In this sense, two time-series are used. The first one is the *Santa Fe*[1] time-series, which is an univariate time record of a single observed quantity, measured in a physics laboratory experiment and the second one is the well-known *Lorenz* system, which is a dynamical system of a chaotic flow, noted for its butterfly shape, described by the following set of differential equations: $\dot{x} = \sigma(y - x)$, $\dot{y} = -xz + \gamma x - y$, $\dot{z} = xy - Bz$. These time-series are used in this work, because are good examples of complicated behavior in terms of stationarity, that is, the time-series are very predictable on the shortest time, but has global events that can be harder to predict. The proposed methodology is validated in terms of system accuracy as well as sensitivity to free parameters, using as baseline the QKLMS method. Figure 1 shows the employed databases.

---

[1] http://www-psych.stanford.edu/~andreas/Time-Series/SantaFe.html.

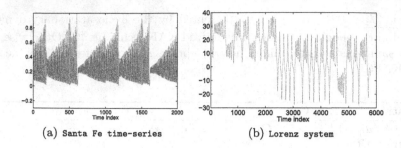

(a) Santa Fe time-series   (b) Lorenz system

Fig. 1. Employed databases

3.2   Results and Discussion

In our experiments, the previous 40 points $u_t = [d(t-40), \ldots, d(t-1)]$ are used as input vector to predict the current value d_t. Additionally, the parameter settings are as follow: $\eta = 0.9$, $\epsilon_U = 0.5$, and $U_{ac} = 0.3$. Figure 2 shows the system accuracy for both QKLMS and KAFCC. The aim is to predict the *Santa Fe* time-series shown in Fig. 2(a). The system accuracy is computed over the last 30 % of the predicted signal using the relative error. It is important to point out some significant differences between both approaches, i.e., QKLMS uses only one *codebook* to predict all the time-series, while KAFCC uses multiple *codebooks* to predict the time-series and at the same time adjusts the weight associated to each *codebook*. Another important difference is the sensibility to the free parameters, e.g., *quantization size* (Fig. 4(a)), which is a parameter that allows to both approaches decide if a sample is updated or stored into the *codebook* as a new *codeword*. Figures 2(a) and (b) show the reconstructed signal using QKLMS and KAFCC, respectively. Obtained results in Fig. 2(b) confirm that our algorithm is robust against non-stationary conditions, i.e., reconstructed signal using KAFCC seems to follow more closely the original signal. This fact is supported by the obtained relative error which is 7.8 % against the 12.4 % obtained in QKLMS . In this figure, the sequence of colors is a clear indication that linear combination used by KAFCC improves the system accuracy, because each

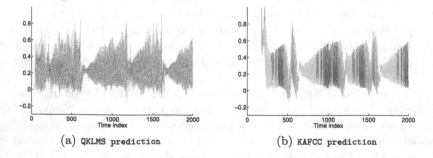

(a) QKLMS prediction   (b) KAFCC prediction

Fig. 2. Santa Fe time-series prediction.

color is associated to a different *codebook*. The original Santa fe time-series has a length of 1000 points. So, the santa fe time-series in Fig. 1 is simply the same signal concatenated two times, that is, the first one is between iteration 1 and 1000, and the another is between iteration 1001 and 2000. Note that KAFCC identify exactly the same *codebook* sequence on each segment, e.g., on the last segment (900 – 1000 and 1900 – 2000), when the sample number 900 arrives, the algorithm does not known this dynamic and therefore a new *codebook* is created (red color). Then, when the same segment appears again at iteration 1900, the algorithm does not create a new *codebook* because such a dynamic was previously learned at iteration 900, and therefore the *codebook* represented by the red color is employed once again, which means that KAFCC take advantage of the stored information on previous *codebooks*, while QKLMS under non-stationary conditions forgets the previous learning results and re-learning the input-output mapping when system switch to a new state, and consequently the prediction error in QKLMS is higher than KAFCC. The attained results with KAFCC are promising, however, the computational burden in KAFCC is higher than QKLMS, because it employs a cost function considering all the previous relevant states to obtain a better prediction. Also, to evaluate system robustness against different testing noise conditions, the *Lorenz* time-series in Fig. 1(b) is corrupted with additive white Gaussian noise to get different Signal to Noise Ratio conditions, $SNR = \{1, \ldots, 10\}$[dB]. In Fig. 3, some results in terms of prediction accuracy are shown. The performance of both compared algorithms is measured according to the relative error. Note that, each box represents the general behavior on each SNR level, where the red line is the median performance. As seen from this figure, KAFCC outperforms QKLMS, which is a clear indication of robustness against noisy and non-stationary conditions.

Furthermore, there are some parameters in KAFCC such as the step size (η), kernel band-width (σ), and the *codebook* threshold (U_{ac}). Namely, both KAF approaches (QKLMS and KAFCC) has identical behavior when some of these parameters are changed. However, the quantization size (ϵ_U) is a parameter

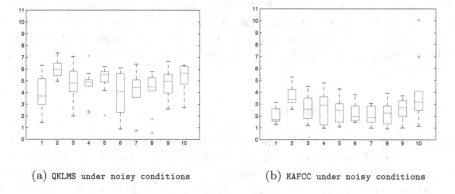

(a) QKLMS under noisy conditions   (b) KAFCC under noisy conditions

Fig. 3. Lorenz time-series prediction

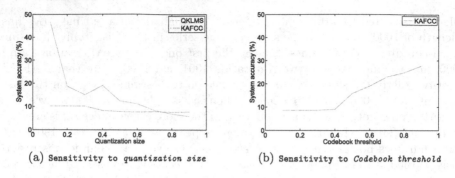

(a) Sensitivity to *quantization size*   (b) Sensitivity to *Codebook threshold*

Fig. 4. Sensitivity to free parameters (Color figure online).

that modifies significantly the behavior in terms of system accuracy. Hence, the sensitivity to free parameter is analyzed based on the behavior induced by quantization size variations. To this end, all the other parameters are fixed, that is, σ is automatically computed as in [10], $\eta = 0.9$ and $U_{ac} = 0.3$. Figure 4(a) shows how the system accuracy is affected by quantization size variations. Here, QKLMS is represented by the red line, while KAFCC is represented by the blue line. On the other hand, the proposed KAFCC has an additional parameter that we call *codebook* thershold (U_{ac}). This parameter controls the amount of *codebooks* that are created. Figure 4(b) shows the system accuracy in KAFTC for different values of U_{ac} when $\eta = 0.9$ and $\epsilon_U = 0.5$.

According to Fig. 4(a), the system accuracy in KAFCC is constant for different values of ϵ_U, while QKLMS shows to be sensitive to this parameter. The consistency in KAFCC can be attributed to the linear combination of *codebooks* with its respective weights that are updated along the time, allowing smooth changes in the final prediction. Additionally, it is necessary to study how the *codebook* threshold modifies the system accuracy in KAFCC. In this sense, Fig. 4(b) shows that the system accuracy has an inverse relation with U_{ac}, in other words, the higher the U_{ac} value the lower the system accuracy. This fact can be attributed to the amount of created *codebooks*, because when the parameter U_{ac} is low, less *codebooks* will be created, and therefore, the prediction, only considers the most compact *codebooks* in terms of similarity to the current sample. So, the success on the system accuracy for KAFCC is highly sensitive to the distance among *codebooks*.

4   Concluding Remarks

A methodology based on KAF which uses a linear combination of multiple *codebooks* to support prediction tasks in one-dimensional time-series is proposed. That is, KAFCC builds multiple *codebooks* encoding relevant interleaved random processes. Thus, cyclostationary dynamics are highlighted by means of a kernel-based quantization function that allows building a new codebook if the current dynamic was not properly learned in the past. Besides, the current output in KAFCC is calculated as a linear combination of KAF-based estimators using a non-linear gating function to obtain the each filter weight. Our KAF approach is compared with QKLMS in terms of sensitivity to free parameters and system accuracy. The results, show that our algorithm is robust under non-stationary conditions, and is a suitable tool to predict one-dimensional time-series. The attained results in terms of system accuracy show how KAFCC is a suitable tool for supporting one-dimensional time series under non-stationary conditions. Particularly, obtained results over a well-known real-world dataset, e.g., Santa Fe time-series, exhibits how KAFCC take advantage of the information learned on previous detected cyclostationary dynamics. The above demonstrates that using multiple codebooks with particular statistical properties, improves the prediction tasks in comparison with state-of-the-art techniques. As future work, proposed KAFCC should be extended for multi-dimensional time-series prediction problems.

Acknowledgements. This work is supported by *Programa Doctoral Becas COL-CIENCIAS - Formación de alto nivel para la ciencia, la tecnología y la innovación año 2014.*, and *Programa Nacional de Formación de Investigadores "Generación del Bicentenario" 2011/2012* funded by COLCIENCIAS. As well as by the research project 16882 funded by Universidad Nacional de Colombia and Universidad de Caldas.

References

1. Gardner, W.A., Napolitano, A., Paura, L.: Cyclostationarity: half a century of research. Signal Process. **86**(4), 639–697 (2006)
2. Liu, W., Príncipe, J.C., Haykin, S.: Kernel Adaptive Filtering: A Comprehensive Introduction. John Wiley & Sons Inc, New York (2010)
3. Lundén, J., Koivunen, V., Huttunen, A., Poor, H.V.: Collaborative cyclostationary spectrum sensing for cognitive radio systems. IEEE Trans. Signal Process. **57**(11), 4182–4195 (2009)
4. Madisetti, V.: Digital Signal Processing Fundamentals, 2nd edn. CRC Press Inc, Boca Raton (2009)
5. Pokharel, R., Seth, S., Principe, J.C.: Quantized mixture kernel least mean square. In: IJCNN (2014)
6. Liu, W., Principe, J.C., Haykin, S.: Kernel Adaptive Filtering: A Comprehensive Introduction, 1st edn. Wiley Publishing, New York (2010)
7. Pokharel, R., Seth, S., Principe, J.C.: Mixture kernel least mean square. In: IJCNN (2013)
8. Sutton, R.S., Barto, A.G.: Introduction to Reinforcement Learning, 1st edn. MIT Press, Cambridge (1998)
9. Zhao, S., Zhu, P., Jose, P.: Quantized kernel least mean square algorithm. IEEE Trans. Neural Netw. Learn. Syst. **23**, 22–32 (2012)
10. Cardenas-Pena, D., Orbes-Arteaga, M., Castro-Ospina, A., Alvarez-Meza, A., Castellanos-Dominguez, G.: A kernel-based representation to support 3d MRI unsupervised clustering. In: ICPR (2014)

Latent Topic Encoding for Content-Based Retrieval

Ruben Fernandez-Beltran[✉] and Filiberto Pla

Institute of New Imaging Technologies, Universitat Jaume I, Castellón, Spain
{rufernan,pla}@uji.es

Abstract. This work presents a new encoding approach based on latent topics which is specially designed to Content-Based Retrieval tasks. The novelty of the proposed Latent Topic Encoding (LTE) lies in two points: (1) defining the visual vocabulary according to the hidden patterns discovered from the local descriptors; and (2) encoding each sample by accumulating the proportion of its local features over topics. Several retrieval simulations using two different databases have been carried out to test the performance of the proposed approach with respect to the standard visual Bag of Words (BoW). Results show that LTE encoding is able to outperform the traditional visual BoW when the retrieval task is performed in the latent topic space.

Keywords: Encoding · Visual Bag-of-Words · Topic modelling · Content-based retrieval

1 Introduction

The evolution of technology is leading to bigger multimedia databases and this fact makes the task of retrieving relevant data more complex. Content-Based Retrieval (CBR) is concerned about providing users with those images or videos which satisfy their queries, that is, semantic concepts that users have in their minds and they are looking for. Over the last years, CBR has been widely addressed by the research community and many approaches have been developed [1,2]. Despite all this research, the semantic gap [3] between computable low-level features and high-level concepts makes the CBR field still a challenge especially for huge and complex databases.

In general, a CBR system has three main components involved in the retrieval process: (1) a query, represented by a few examples of the concept the user is interested in; (2) a database, which is used to extract samples related to the query concept; and (3) a ranking function, which sorts the database according to the relevance to the query. These three components are usually integrated

This work was partially supported by FPU-AP-2009–4435 from the Spanish Ministry of Education, PROMETEOII/2014/062 project from Generalitat Valenciana and Project ESP2013–48458-C4-3-P from Ministerio de Economia y Competitividad.

R. Paredes et al. (Eds.): IbPRIA 2015, LNCS 9117, pp. 362–369, 2015.
DOI: 10.1007/978-3-319-19390-8_41

together with the user in an relevance feedback scheme [4] to provide the most relevant samples through several iterations.

The ranking function can be considered the kernel of the retrieval system because it is in charge of scoring the samples to perform the ranking, however there are more factors which affect to the retrieval performance. One of the most important ones is the encoding technique. The ranking function requires the query as well as the database encoded in feature vectors, that is, samples have to be represented in a specific space in which the ranking function works. The typical pipeline to obtain this space is made up of two steps: (1) extraction of local features (e.g. SIFT [5]); and (2) encoding the local features of each sample in a vector (e.g. histogram of quantized local features). In this work, we are going to focus just on the second step, the encoding techniques specially applied to the CBR problem.

In computer vision, the standard encoding procedure is the visual Bag of Words (BoW) [6]. This encoding approach starts by learning a visual vocabulary composed from the clustering of the local features of the training set. Then, each sample is represented in a single histogram of visual words by accumulating the number of local features into their closest clusters. The main drawback of this approach is the hard assignment of words, i.e. it selects the best representing visual word ignoring the relevance and relationship with other clusters. This fact generates an information loss which may be critical to deal with the semantic gap challenge in CBR. More recent advances replace the hard quantization of features with alternative encodings which are able to retain more information about the original features. There are mainly two trends in this field: (1) expressing features as combination of visual words (co-occurrence models [7], soft quantization [8], local linear encoding [9]); and (2) recording the differences between the features and the visual words (Fisher encoding [10], super-vector encoding [11]).

Despite the fact that some of these methods have shown to obtain good results in classification challenges, the CBR problem has an utterly different nature. In a typical classification problem, we have a training set which is supposed to provide enough information about the classes we want to classify. However, in a retrieval problem the class to retrieve is a priori unknown, it is up to the user's query, and besides we only have few examples of this class, the user initialization and feedback is very limited. As a result, we have to deal with complex classes having very little information about the target. The vast majority of encoding methods obtain the visual vocabulary by clustering the local features and doing that each visual word represents a visible pattern of the data. Nevertheless, in an application like CBR the visible patterns of the data may not be enough to distinguish among unconstrained classes with little information about their structure. At this point, it may be useful to consider other kind of representation techniques beyond the traditional clustering processes are able to provide for the visual vocabulary. Specifically, one of the most suitable techniques for this purpose may be latent topics.

Topic models have been successfully used in many areas (e.g. video classification [12] or even CBR [13]) because they are able to extract hidden patterns from the data distribution and represent the data according these patterns as well. The typical way they have been used is based on reducing the dimensionality of the initial representation space commonly obtained by the standard visual BoW. This paper presents a novel encoding method completely based on latent topics, which defines the visual vocabulary by means of hidden patterns and performs the quantization by accumulating the contribution of each topic to each local feature. We argue that our proposal provides a more suitable codification for CBR than the standard visual BoW, especially when the retrieval task is performed in the latent topic space.

The rest of the paper is organized as follows. Section 2 presents the Latent Topic Encoding (LTE) method. In Sect. 3, the experimental setting is described as well as the retrieval results obtained by LTE and BoW over two different databases. Finally, Sect. 4 draws the main conclusions arisen from this work and highlights some points as a future work.

2   Latent Topic Encoding

The characterization of image or video samples is based on: (1) a local descriptor; and (2) an encoding function. The most common local descriptor methods provide a different number of feature points per sample. Besides, the dimensionality of these feature points is usually very limited to represent the wide variety of features in the visual domain. As a result, the encoding function is in charge of increasing the dimensionality of the descriptor space and representing the whole database using the same visual vocabulary.

In the case of the standard visual BoW, the visual vocabulary is obtained by a clustering process, typically K-Means. Each visual word represents a group of feature points which are spatially close in the descriptor space. However, a distance function is not the best discriminative criteria in applications with a huge semantic gap [3], like in CBR. In those cases, the topology of the space is often not well defined according to the semantics of the data, in other words, samples related to the same query concept may not be close in the descriptor space. At the same time, the hard-assignment of feature points to visual words generates an information loss which might lead to a retrieval precision drop. The proposed LTE encoding method tries to cope with these problems by using latent topics.

Topic models are a suite of statistical algorithms which are able to uncover the hidden structure in document collections. Starting from a specific data matrix $P(\mathcal{W}|\mathcal{C})$ which describes a corpus of documents $\mathcal{C}$ in a particular space $\mathcal{W} \subset \mathbb{N}^n$, latent topic algorithms are able to obtain two matrices: (1) the description of topics in words $P(\mathcal{W}|\mathcal{Z})$ (2) and the description of documents in topics $P(\mathcal{Z}|\mathcal{C})$. The number of extracted topics (Z) is a parameter which has to be established in advance for the most common algorithms. Let us show how the proposed LTE encoding method takes advantage of topic models to define the visual vocabulary as well as to assign feature points to visual words in the CBR context.

In a CBR system, we start with a set of D image or video samples $\mathcal{D} = \{d_1, d_2, \ldots, d_D\}$ in the database, Q query examples $\mathcal{Q} = \{q_1, \ldots, q_Q\}$ to represent the concept the user wants to retrieve and a specific ranking function $\mathcal{R}$ which obtains a ranking $\mathcal{D}'$ of the database $\mathcal{D}$ given the query $\mathcal{Q}$. For this work, we are going to assume that $\mathcal{Q} \subset \mathcal{D}$, that is, queries are selected from the own database, nevertheless further improvements can be aimed at allowing the use of external queries. For each sample $d_i, 1 <= i <= D$, a local descriptor algorithm (e.g. SIFT [5]) is applied to obtain a set of P_i feature points $\mathcal{P}_i = \{p_{i1}, p_{i2}, \ldots, p_{iP_i}\}$ for that specific sample d_i. We assume that $p_{ij} \in \mathbb{N}^n, 1 <= i <= D, 1 <= j <= P_i$. Note that, some local descriptors characterize directly the feature points in $\mathbb{N}^n$ (e.g. counting orientations of gradient) but for other descriptors which characterize the points in $\mathbb{R}^n$ a truncating process must be done.

The proposed LTE method is based on considering each feature point $p_{ij} \in \mathbb{N}^n, 1 <= i <= D, 1 <= j <= P_i$, a document of a topic model algorithm, specifically LDA [14] has been used for this work but any other topic model algorithm could be used instead. The visual vocabulary is defined as the set of topics extracted from the corpus containing all the feature points, therefore each visual word represents a hidden pattern in the descriptor space instead of a group of points such as in the BoW approach. The assignment of feature points to visual words is made by accumulating the topic proportion of the points of each sample, that is, the feature points expressed in topics are used to weight the contribution of each point to each visual word. In particular, the LTE method is made up of the following steps:

1. Build a corpus $\mathcal{C}$ with all the feature points, $\mathcal{C} = \bigcup_{i=1}^{D} \mathcal{P}_i$
2. Apply a latent topic algorithm (LDA) over $\mathcal{C}$ in order to discover Z topics.
3. Define the visual vocabulary as the extracted topics, $P(\mathcal{W}|z_k), 1 <= k <= Z$
4. Represent each sample in a single histogram as the accumulation of its topic vectors, $h'_i = \sum_{j=1}^{P_i} P(\mathcal{Z}|p_{ij})$
5. Normalize each histogram to obtain the final encoding, $h_i = h'_i/|h'_i|$

Note that, the number of topics Z has the same meaning than the number of clusters in the BoW case, therefore it has to be a number much higher than the dimensionality n of the local feature space obtained by the descriptor. In fact, one of the novelties of LTE is to use topic models to increase the dimensionality of a space rather than decreasing it.

3   Experiments

The experiments aim at comparing the proposed LTE encoding method with respect to the classical BoW for CBR tasks. Section 3.1 describes the two used databases, Sect. 3.2 presents the performed retrieval simulations and Sect. 3.3 shows the obtained results.

3.1   Datasets

– **Abnormal Object Dataset (AOD):** The AOD dataset [15] is a balanced image collection with 617 challenging objects over 6 categories (Aeroplane,

Boat, Car, Motorbike, Sofa and Chair). A sofa with the appearance of a car or a motorbike which looks like a plane are some instances of AOD. These unusual images have been selected to make confusion among categories in order to increase the semantic gap between low-level features and concepts. To extract the local features, we have used the SIFT [5] descriptor and over these features both BoW and LTE encoding methods have been applied.

- **Columbia Consumer Video Database (CCV):** The CCV databse [16] contains 9317 YouTube videos over 20 semantic categories, most of which are complex events, along with several objects and scenes. For the experiments, we have considered a subset (sCCV) with 6 random classes (Playground, Wedding Ceremony, Swimming, Skiing, Bird and IceSkating) and for each one we have selected 100 random samples. Regarding to the description method, the SIFT [5] algorithm has been applied to the middle frame to obtain the local features of the videos. As in the former dataset, BoW and LTE encoding functions have been used over these features.

3.2   Retrieval Simulations

For the experiments, we have used the retrieval scheme proposed in [13] which is based on Relevance Feedback (RF). In this RF scheme, a simulation has four main parameters: Q the number of samples of the initial query, S the number of top items examined by the user in each feedback iteration, I the number of feedback iterations and R the number of times that the random initialization of the query is repeated per class. According to these parameters, we propose four different retrieval scenarios using in all of them $I = 5$ and $R = 100$: (1) $Q = 1$ $S = 20$, (2) $Q = 2$ $S = 20$, (3) $Q = 1$ $S = 40$ and (4) $Q = 2$ $S = 40$.

The target of each simulation is directed to retrieve samples of a specific class of the dataset, but without using any class label information. The initial query is initialized with Q random samples of a single class c and then the simulation process has to retrieve samples of that class through I feedback iterations using three different ranking functions: (1) euclidean distance (EC); (2) cosine similarity (CS); (3) and the ranking function proposed in [13] called Latent Topic Rank (LTR). In a nut shell, EC ranks the database according the minimum average euclidean distance to the query, CS according the minimum angle and LTR according to the maximum probability following the expression presented in [13]. At each iteration, the S top ranked items are inspected by a simulated user who marks the samples of the class c. These positive samples are computed as correctly retrieved samples and they are used to expand the query. Finally, this expanded query is triggered as a new query for the next iteration.

In the case of the BoW approach, we have used the K-Means clustering to build the visual vocabulary whereas the LDA topic model [14] has been applied for the LTE encoding. Our objective is to compare the retrieval performance of the proposed LTE encoding with the traditional visual BoW using the retrieval scheme presented in [13] and three different ranking functions: EC, CS and LTR. In addition, we are interested in testing how both BoW and LTE encoding methods perform in the latent topic space. That is, we are going to use BoW and LTE representations as a base to apply LDA in order to analyse the retrieval performance in the latent space depending on the used encoding method.

3.3 Results and Discussion

Figure 1 shows the results in six graphics organized in a 3×2 matrix. Each row is related to a different ranking function (EC, CS and LTR) and each column contains the retrieval results for a specific dataset (AOD and sCCV). Inside each graphic, we can see the average precision for each one of the 4 simulations using 8 different representations of the data. That is, each bar represents a retrieval experiment using a particular characterization of the database. Specifically, *vBoW_500* relates to the standard visual BoW with 500 clusters by k-means, *LTE_500* indicates the proposed LTE encoding method with 500 topics by LDA, *vBoW_1000* is the visual BoW with 1000 clusters and *LTE_1000* the LTE with 1000 topics. Besides, we have applied LDA with 200 topics over these

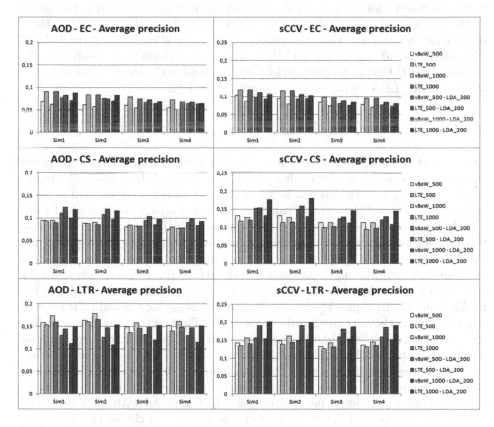

Fig. 1. Average precision for the retrieval simulations. Ranking functions by rows: (1) euclidean distance (EC), (2) cosine similarity (CS) and (3) latent topic rank (LTR). Datasets by columns: (1) AOD and (2) sCCV.

4 characterizations to test how the encoding method affects the retrieval performance in the topic space. Note that we have added the text *LDA_200* to the four last captions to indicate that these simulations are performed in the topic space obtained by LDA with 200 topics. In order to make clearer the comparison between LTE and BoW, we show the results grouped in pairs of bars, one for the visual BoW approach blue (odd bars) and another for the LTE method (even bars) using in both cases the same vocabulary size. For each pair of bars, if the second bar is higher than the first one, the LTE encoding is outperforming the visual BoW codification in terms of average precision.

Having a look at Fig. 1, the first noticeably point is the general low precision values obtained in the experiments. This fact shows how important the semantic gap is for these collections. Regarding to the ranking functions, the best average precision has been obtained by LTR and the worse by EC. In the case of the EC ranking, the LTE encoding outperforms the visual BoW approach in all the simulations. However, for the CS and LTR we observe a different pattern. For these two ranking functions, LTE is slightly worse than visual BoW in the initial representation space (*vBoW_500* and *vBoW_1000*) but noticeable better in the latent topic space (*vBoW_500* - *LDA_200* and *vBoW_1000* - *LDA_200*). In general, we can see that the proposed LTE encoding function provides a competitive advantage over visual BoW when the retrieval task is performed in the topic space, that is, the retrieval function is used in the latent space obtained after applying LDA to the encoding produced by LTE.

4   Conclusions and Future Work

In this work, we have presented a new encoding method which defines the visual vocabulary according to the hidden patterns of the local descriptors and represents each sample as the accumulation of its local features represented in these topics. The novelty of the proposal lies on defining an encoding method completely based on latent topics, i.e. topics are used to define vocabulary as well as to make a soft encoding of the local features over topics. For the experiments, we have used the LDA model and SIFT descriptors but any other topic model or descriptor could be used. According to the retrieval results, we can highlight two main points: (1) LTE encoding is more effective than visual BoW for EC ranking and (2) LTE provides a competitive advantage for CS and LTR ranking functions when they are used in the topic space. That is, the proposed encoding method is more suitable than BoW approach in applications to manage samples in the topic space. LTE could be interpreted as extracting the topic structure twice from the descriptor space. The first topic extraction to encode the data and the second one to bring this encoding to a higher semantic level. Future work is focused on comparing the proposed LTE method with more advanced encoding functions and defining an automatic strategy to choose the size of the vocabulary.

References

1. Lew, M.S., Sebe, N., Djeraba, C., Jain, R.: Content-based multimedia information retrieval: state of the art and challenges. ACM TMCCA **2**(1), 1–19 (2006)
2. Ren, W., Singh, S., Singh, M., Zhu, Y.S.: State-of-the-art on spatio-temporal information-based video retrieval. Pattern Recogn. **42**(2), 267–282 (2009)
3. Smeulders, A., Worring, M., Santini, S., Gupta, A., Jain, R.: Content-based image retrieval at the end of the early years. IEEE TPAMI **22**(12), 1349–1380 (2000)
4. Zhou, X., Huang, T.: Relevance feedback in image retrieval: a comprehensive review. Multimedia Syst. **8**(6), 536–544 (2003)
5. Lowe, D.: Distinctive image features from scale-invariant keypoints. Int. J. Comput. Vis. **60**(2), 91–110 (2004)
6. Sivic, J., Zisserman, A.: Video google: a text retrieval approach to object matching in videos. In: ICCV, vol. 2, pp. 1470–1477 (2003)
7. Li, F., Perona, P.: A Bayesian hierarchical model for learning natural scene categories. In: CVPR, pp. 524–531 (2005)
8. Philbin, J., Isard, M., Sivic, J., Zisserman, A.: Lost in quantization: improving particular object retrieval in large scale image databases. In: CVPR (2008)
9. Wang, J., Yang, J., Yu, K., Lv, F., Huang, T., Gong. Y.: Locality-constrained linear coding for image classification. In: CVPR (2010)
10. Perronnin, F., Sánchez, J., Mensink, T.: Improving the fisher kernel for large-scale image classification. In: Daniilidis, K., Maragos, P., Paragios, N. (eds.) ECCV 2010, Part IV. LNCS, vol. 6314, pp. 143–156. Springer, Heidelberg (2010)
11. Zhou, X., Yu, K., Zhang, T., Huang, T.S.: Image classification using super-vector coding of local image descriptors. In: Daniilidis, K., Maragos, P., Paragios, N. (eds.) ECCV 2010, Part V. LNCS, vol. 6315, pp. 141–154. Springer, Heidelberg (2010)
12. Bosch, A., Zisserman, A., Muñoz, X.: Scene classificationv via pLSA. In: Leonardis, A., Bischof, H., Pinz, A. (eds.) ECCV 2006. LNCS, vol. 3954, pp. 517–530. Springer, Heidelberg (2006)
13. Fernández-Beltran, R., Pla, F.: An interactive video retrieval approach based on latent topics. In: Petrosino, A. (ed.) ICIAP 2013, Part I. LNCS, vol. 8156, pp. 290–299. Springer, Heidelberg (2013)
14. Blei, D., Ng, A., Jordan, M.: Latent dirichlet allocation. J. Mach. Learn. Res. **3**(4–5), 993–1022 (2003)
15. Saleh,B., Farhadi, A., Elgammal. A.: Object-centric anomaly detection by attribute-based reasoning. In: CVPR, pp. 787–794 (2013)
16. Jiang, Y.G.,Ye, G., Chang, S.F., Ellis, D., Loui, A.C.: Consumer video understanding: a benchmark database and an evaluation of human and machine performance. In: ACM ICMR (2011)

Dissimilarity-Based Learning from Imbalanced Data with Small Disjuncts and Noise

V. García[1], J.S. Sánchez[2](✉), H.J. Ochoa Domínguez[3], and L. Cleofas-Sánchez[2]

[1] Multidisciplinary University Division, Universidad Autónoma de Ciudad Juárez,
Ciudad Juárez, Chihuahua, Mexico
[2] Department of Computer Languages and Systems,
Institute of New Imaging Technologies, Universitat Jaume I,
Castelló de la Plana, Spain
sanchez@uji.es
[3] Department of Electrical and Computer Engineering,
Universidad Autónoma de Ciudad Juárez,
Ciudad Juárez, Chihuahua, Mexico

Abstract. This papers compares the behavior of three linear classifiers modeled on both the feature space and the dissimilarity space when the class imbalance of data sets interweaves with small disjuncts and noise. To this end, experiments are carried out over three synthetic databases with different imbalance ratios, levels of noise and complexity of the small disjuncts. Results suggest that small disjuncts can be much better overcome on the dissimilarity space than on the feature space, which means that the learning models will be only affected by imbalance and noise if the samples have firstly been mapped into the dissimilarity space.

Keywords: Dissimilarity space · Imbalance · Small disjuncts · Noise

1 Introduction

A complex problem in many supervised learning applications is associated with significant disparities between the prior probabilities of different classes, which is usually known as the class imbalance problem [16]. A data set is said to be imbalanced when the samples of one class largely outnumber the samples of the other classes. For a binary problem, the minority class is also referred to as positive because it is often the most interesting one from the point of view of the learning task, whereas the majority class is generally quoted as negative.

The main dilemma in imbalanced data is that the majority class distorts the decision boundaries to the detriment of the minority class, which leads to very low accuracies in classifying positive samples [6]. However, several studies have pointed out that class distributions do not hinder the learning task by itself, but there usually exist other difficulties related with this problem that contribute to the loss of performance [5]. Among others, small disjuncts and noisy data represent two practical examples of data complexities that should be addressed in detail so that the classification models can achieve better performance results [7].

© Springer International Publishing Switzerland 2015
R. Paredes et al. (Eds.): IbPRIA 2015, LNCS 9117, pp. 370–378, 2015.
DOI: 10.1007/978-3-319-19390-8_42

The reasons of focusing this study on small disjuncts and noisy data are twofold: the existence of class imbalance is closely linked to the problem of small disjuncts and noise, and learning from imbalanced data with these two complexities has been shown to heavily degrade the classification performance of most machine learning models [9,14,15,18].

Briefly, the problem of small disjuncts corresponds to the situation in which several small clusters cover very few samples from one class and are surrounded by samples from the other class [4]. On the other hand, noise refers to data imperfections, anomalies and errors introduced during the data gathering and preprocessing phases, which leads to the presence of a number of samples from one class located in some region of the other class [2, Chap. 5].

In the literature, one can find a plethora of works aimed at analyzing the effect of these two complexities on feature-based classification. However, the implications of using other alternative spaces have not received the attention they deserve. In particular, this paper concentrates on the dissimilarity space because it has been reported to be truly effective on a number of real-life applications.

In the dissimilarity-based classification approach [10], samples to be classified are encoded using pairwise dissimilarities (distances from other samples in the data set). The justification for constructing classifiers in a dissimilarity space is that a dissimilarity measure should be small for similar samples and large for distinct samples, thus allowing for efficient and reliable discrimination of classes. Another important characteristic is that the dimensions of a dissimilarity space symbolize homogeneous types of information and therefore all dimensions can be considered as equally relevant. On the other hand, for a complex problem, a simple linear classification model in a dissimilarity space could separate the classes more easily than the same classifier in a feature space [13].

The question we try to answer with the present study is what happens in the dissimilarity space when the classifier is modeled from imbalanced data with small disjuncts and noise. More specifically, this work aims at discovering whether and how linear classifiers built on the dissimilarity space suffer from those data complexities as they indeed do on the feature space.

2   Classification in the Dissimilarity Space

Traditional learning and classification methods rely on the description of samples by means of set of observable features. An alternative to the feature space is the dissimilarity space proposed by Pękalska and Duin [10], in which the dimensions are defined by vectors measuring pairwise dissimilarities between examples and individual prototypes from an initial representation set $R = \{p_1, \ldots, p_r\}$. This can be chosen as the complete training set $T = \{x_1, \ldots, x_n\}$, a set of generated prototypes, a subset of T that covers all classes, or even an arbitrary set of labeled or unlabeled samples [12].

Given a dissimilarity measure $d(\cdot, \cdot)$, which is required to be nonnegative and to obey the reflexive condition $(d(x_i, x_i) = 0)$ but it might be non-metric, a dissimilarity representation is defined as a data-dependent mapping function

$D(\cdot, R)$ from T to the dissimilarity space. This means that every example $x_i \in T$ is represented by an r-dimensional vector in the dissimilarity space, $D(x_i, R) = \{d(x_i, p_1), \ldots, d(x_i, p_r)\}$, that is, each dimension corresponds to a dissimilarity to a prototype from R. Therefore, dissimilarities between all examples in T to R are represented by a matrix $D(T, R)$ of size $n \times r$, which corresponds to the dissimilarity representation we want to learn from [11].

$$D(T, R) = \begin{bmatrix} d(x_1, p_1) & d(x_1, p_2) & \cdots & d(x_1, p_r) \\ d(x_2, p_1) & d(x_2, p_2) & \cdots & d(x_2, p_r) \\ \vdots & \vdots & \ddots & \vdots \\ d(x_n, p_1) & d(x_n, p_2) & \cdots & d(x_n, p_r) \end{bmatrix}$$

When a new instance $\mathbf{x}$ has to be classified, the sample is mapped into the dissimilarity space by calculating the dissimilarity between $\mathbf{x}$ and all prototypes in the representation set R, resulting in a one-dimensional matrix (vector) $D(\mathbf{x}, R) = [d(\mathbf{x}, p_1), d(\mathbf{x}, p_2), \ldots, d(\mathbf{x}, p_r)]$. This dissimilarity vector $D(\mathbf{x}, R)$ is passed through the classifier for yielding a class label to the new instance $\mathbf{x}$.

In a general classification scenario, a drawback related to the use of features is that different samples may have the same representation, thus resulting in class overlap (i.e. some samples of different classes are represented by the same feature vectors). In the dissimilarity space, however, only identical samples (with the same class label) have a zero-distance, which means that there does not exist class overlap.

3   Experimental Databases

The databases used in this paper correspond to three synthetic imbalanced data sets [9] that have already been employed in previous research studies on small disjuncts and class overlapping. The databases represent binary classification problems with samples randomly and uniformly distributed in the two-dimensional real-valued space. Each of the three databases was designed according to two different configurations: data sets with 600 samples and an imbalance ratio of 1:5 and data sets with 800 samples and an imbalance ratio of 1:7.

The three different shapes of the minority class surrounded uniformly by the majority class are subcluster, clover and paw. In subcluster, the samples from the minority class are located inside five rectangles. Clover represents a nonlinear setting, where the minority class resembles a flower with elliptic petals (five subregions). In paw, the minority class is decomposed into three elliptic subregions of varying cardinalities, where two subregions are located close to each other, and the remaining smaller subregion is separated.

In addition, noise was simulated by disturbing the borders of the subregions, considering five different levels of borderline samples from the minority class subregions: 0 %, 30 %, 50 %, 60 % and 70 %. Two examples of this are plotted in Fig. 1, which correspond to the cases with 0 % and 70 % of borderline samples in the databases with 600 samples and an imbalance ratio of 1:5, thus allowing the reader to visualize the areas with small disjuncts. Therefore, the experiments were carried out over a total of 30 databases: 3 shapes × 2 set sizes/imbalance ratios × 5 noise levels.

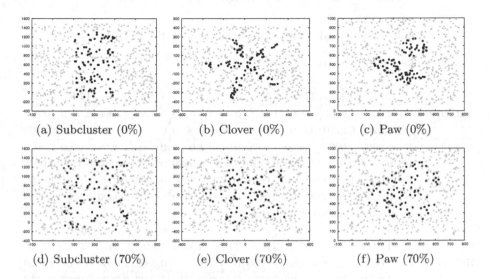

(a) Subcluster (0%)   (b) Clover (0%)   (c) Paw (0%)

(d) Subcluster (70%)   (e) Clover (70%)   (f) Paw (70%)

Fig. 1. Experimental databases with 0 % (upper row) and 70 % (lower row) of border-line samples from the minority class subregions

4   Experiments and Results

We focused our study on three linear classification models, the Fisher's linear discriminant (FLD), the support vector machine (SVM) and the logistic linear classifier (LOG), comparing their behavior on the feature space (FS) and on the dissimilarity space (DS). The SVM models were constructed using a linear kernel function with the soft-margin constant $C = 1.0$. On the other hand, due to the small size of the training data sets, we chose the representation set R to be equal to the training set T (that is, $r = n$), which means that the mapping function from T to the dissimilarity space results in a square matrix of size $n \times n$.

The 5-fold cross-validation method was adopted for the experimental design because it appears to be the best estimator of classification performance compared to other methods, such as bootstrap with a high computational cost or re-substitution with a biased behavior [1]. Each original data set was randomly divided into five stratified parts of equal (or approximately equal) size; for each fold, four blocks were pooled as the training set, and the remaining part was used as an independent test set.

The performance of the classifiers was analyzed by means of the true positive rate $TPR = TP/(TP + FN)$, which is the proportion of positive samples that are correctly classified, and the true negative rate $TNR = TN/(TN + FP)$, which is the proportion of negative cases that are correctly classified. Here TP and TN denote the number of positive and negative examples correctly classified respectively, whereas FP and FN represent the number of misclassifications on negative and positive examples respectively.

Table 1. TPR and TNR results achieved with the FLD classifier

No. Examples = 600, Imbalance ratio = 1:5

		0 %		30 %		50 %		60 %		70 %	
		TPR	TNR	TPR	TNR	TPR	TNR	TPR	TNR	TPR	TNR
Subcluster	FS	0.0000	1.0000	0.0000	1.0000	0.0000	1.0000	0.0000	1.0000	0.0000	1.0000
	DS	0.8200	0.9760	0.5700	0.9460	0.4400	0.9040	0.4700	0.8860	0.4600	0.9020
Clover	FS	0.0000	1.0000	0.0000	1.0000	0.0000	1.0000	0.0000	1.0000	0.0000	1.0000
	DS	0.8700	0.9700	0.6500	0.9320	0.5600	0.9280	0.5300	0.8980	0.4200	0.9020
Paw	FS	0.0000	1.0000	0.0000	1.0000	0.0000	1.0000	0.0000	1.0000	0.0000	1.0000
	DS	0.9200	0.9820	0.7100	0.9480	0.6100	0.9320	0.5700	0.9300	0.5300	0.9040

No. Examples = 800, Imbalance ratio = 1:7

		0 %		30 %		50 %		60 %		70 %	
		TPR	TNR	TPR	TNR	TPR	TNR	TPR	TNR	TPR	TNR
Subcluster	FS	0.0000	1.0000	0.0000	1.0000	0.0000	1.0000	0.0000	1.0000	0.0000	1.0000
	DS	0.8300	0.9871	0.5200	0.9514	0.4200	0.9314	0.3900	0.9429	0.3000	0.9157
Clover	FS	0.0000	1.0000	0.0000	1.0000	0.0000	1.0000	0.0000	1.0000	0.0000	1.0000
	DS	0.8600	0.9814	0.6100	0.9571	0.4800	0.9471	0.4200	0.9343	0.3300	0.9300
Paw	FS	0.0000	1.0000	0.0000	1.0000	0.0000	1.0000	0.0000	1.0000	0.0000	1.0000
	DS	0.9200	0.9943	0.6900	0.9600	0.5500	0.9557	0.5100	0.9486	0.3900	0.9371

Tables 1–3 report the FLD, SVM and LOG performance results applied on the feature space and the dissimilarity space. The most relevant observation is that the classifiers on the feature space assign all test samples to the majority class, which means that all positive samples have been misclassified (TPR = 0) irrespective of the noise level. However, when the models run on the dissimilarity space, the results suggest a certain trade-off between TPR and TNR, that is, the accuracy on the majority class decreases slightly but with a very significant increase of the accuracy on the minority class, especially with low levels of borderline samples.

It is also interesting to remark that the performance of the dissimilarity-based classifiers on the minority class degrades progressively as the level of borderline samples increases. This can be explained by the fact that noise seems to increase the number of small disjuncts, which in turn leads to a decrease in accuracy of the models because of a larger number of errors produced by these small disjuncts. In fact, this effect has already been showed empirically in the case of learning on the feature space [17].

From the results here reported, it appears that small disjuncts in imbalanced databases can be handled better on the dissimilarity space than on the feature

Table 2. TPR and TNR results achieved with the SVM classifier

No. Examples = 600, Imbalance ratio = 1:5

		0 %		30 %		50 %		60 %		70 %	
		TPR	TNR	TPR	TNR	TPR	TNR	TPR	TNR	TPR	TNR
Subcluster	FS	0.0000	1.0000	0.0000	1.0000	0.0000	1.0000	0.0000	1.0000	0.0000	1.0000
	DS	0.8400	0.9700	0.6000	0.9380	0.4600	0.8980	0.5400	0.8800	0.4700	0.8880
Clover	FS	0.0000	1.0000	0.0000	1.0000	0.0000	1.0000	0.0000	1.0000	0.0000	1.0000
	DS	0.8800	0.9720	0.6800	0.9260	0.5600	0.9180	0.5600	0.8940	0.4300	0.8920
Paw	FS	0.0000	1.0000	0.0000	1.0000	0.0000	1.0000	0.0000	1.0000	0.0000	1.0000
	DS	0.9600	0.9900	0.7100	0.9380	0.6500	0.9260	0.5900	0.9280	0.5400	0.9000

No. Examples = 800, Imbalance ratio = 1:7

		0 %		30 %		50 %		60 %		70 %	
		TPR	TNR	TPR	TNR	TPR	TNR	TPR	TNR	TPR	TNR
Subcluster	FS	0.0000	1.0000	0.0000	1.0000	0.0000	1.0000	0.0000	1.0000	0.0000	1.0000
	DS	0.8800	0.9829	0.5700	0.9486	0.4200	0.9186	0.4700	0.9314	0.3800	0.9114
Clover	FS	0.0000	1.0000	0.0000	1.0000	0.0000	1.0000	0.0000	1.0000	0.0000	1.0000
	DS	0.8700	0.9771	0.6100	0.9514	0.5100	0.9457	0.4600	0.9286	0.3700	0.9257
Paw	FS	0.0000	1.0000	0.0000	1.0000	0.0000	1.0000	0.0000	1.0000	0.0000	1.0000
	DS	0.9500	0.9943	0.7100	0.9557	0.6100	0.9500	0.5200	0.9500	0.4600	0.9300

Table 3. TPR and TNR results achieved with the logistic linear classifier

No. Examples = 600, Imbalance ratio = 1:5

		0 %		30 %		50 %		60 %		70 %	
		TPR	TNR	TPR	TNR	TPR	TNR	TPR	TNR	TPR	TNR
Subcluster	FS	0.0000	1.0000	0.0000	1.0000	0.0000	1.0000	0.0000	1.0000	0.0000	1.0000
	DS	0.8200	0.9760	0.5700	0.9460	0.4400	0.9040	0.4700	0.8860	0.4600	0.9020
Clover	FS	0.0000	1.0000	0.0000	1.0000	0.0000	1.0000	0.0000	1.0000	0.0000	1.0000
	DS	0.8700	0.9700	0.6500	0.9320	0.5600	0.9280	0.5300	0.8980	0.4200	0.9020
Paw	FS	0.0000	1.0000	0.0000	1.0000	0.0000	1.0000	0.0000	1.0000	0.0000	1.0000
	DS	0.9200	0.9820	0.7100	0.9480	0.6100	0.9320	0.5700	0.9300	0.5300	0.9040

No. Examples = 800, Imbalance ratio = 1:7

		0 %		30 %		50 %		60 %		70 %	
		TPR	TNR	TPR	TNR	TPR	TNR	TPR	TNR	TPR	TNR
Subcluster	FS	0.0000	1.0000	0.0000	1.0000	0.0000	1.0000	0.0000	1.0000	0.0000	1.0000
	DS	0.8300	0.9871	0.5200	0.9514	0.4200	0.9314	0.3900	0.9429	0.3000	0.9157
Clover	FS	0.0000	1.0000	0.0000	1.0000	0.0000	1.0000	0.0000	1.0000	0.0000	1.0000
	DS	0.8600	0.9814	0.6100	0.9571	0.4800	0.9471	0.4200	0.9343	0.3300	0.9300
Paw	FS	0.0000	1.0000	0.0000	1.0000	0.0000	1.0000	0.0000	1.0000	0.0000	1.0000
	DS	0.9200	0.9943	0.6900	0.9600	0.5500	0.9557	0.5100	0.9486	0.3900	0.9371

space. When class noise is injected into the data sets, the TPR achieved with the dissimilarity-based classifiers decreases, but it is still superior to that produced by the feature-based linear models. Finally, we have also observed that the classes seem to be better clustered when the samples are mapped into the dissimilarity space, which gives rise to higher performance rates.

In order to analyze the inter-class separability in both spaces, we then calculated the F1 and F2 measures as defined by Ho and Basu [3]. F1 corresponds to the maximum Fisher's discriminant ratio, which quantifies how separated are two classes according to a given feature. F2 computes, for each feature, the length of the overlap range normalized by the length of the total range in which all values of both classes are distributed; the volume of the overlap region for two classes is the product of normalized lengths of overlapping ranges for all features.

Figure 2 shows the bar charts of F1 and F2 scores in both spaces for all levels of noise and for each database. Note that the higher the F1 value, the more separable the data set and conversely, the lower the F2, the higher the inter-class separability. Examination of this figure reveals that, irrespective of the percentage of borderline samples from the minority class subregions, the classes are more separable on the dissimilarity space than on the feature space, which explains the superiority of the performance on the dissimilarity space.

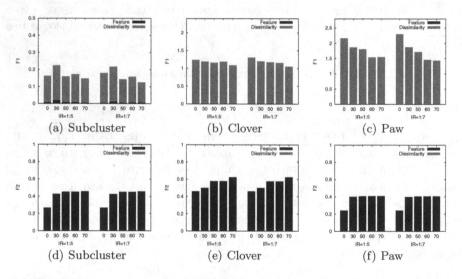

Fig. 2. Bar charts of F1 (upper row) and F2 (lower row) scores for each database on the feature and the dissimilarity spaces

5   Concluding Remarks and Future Research

The present paper has analyzed the performance of three linear classifiers that have been modeled both on the feature space and on the dissimilarity space when the databases are not only characterized by class imbalance but also by the presence of small disjuncts and noisy samples.

The experimental results over artificial databases have suggested that small disjuncts are not implicitly error prone in the dissimilarity space, which is in deep contrast with their effect on feature-based classification. This means that classifiers should concern only with imbalance and noise when samples are mapped into the dissimilarity space, but not with the potential impact of small disjuncts.

Noise in imbalanced databases cannot be completely solved by means of the dissimilarity-based representation, but its effect on the minority class seems to be alleviated a lot. This has been observed with the computation of F1 and F2 measures and demonstrated with the fact that the huge differences between the true positive and true negative rates in the feature space disappear in the dissimilarity space, with a slight decrease of the performance on the majority class and a considerable increase of the performance on the minority class.

Considering that there exists an increasing demand for the development of effective and efficient methods to handle massive databases, an avenue for future research refers to the use of active and incremental learning strategies [8] in order to improve both the accuracy and the required training time by choosing the most informative samples for training the classification model.

Acknowledgment. This work has partially been supported by the Mexican Science and Technology Council (CONACYT-Mexico) through the Postdoctoral Fellowship Program [223351 and 232167], the Spanish Ministry of Economy [TIN2013-46522-P] and the Generalitat Valenciana [PROMETEOII/2014/062].

References

1. Alpaydin, E.: Introduction to Machine Learning. MIT Press, Cambridge (2010)
2. García, S., Luengo, J., Herrera, F.: Data Preprocessing in Data Mining. Springer, Heidelberg (2015)
3. Ho, T.K., Basu, M.: Complexity measures of supervised classification problems. IEEE Trans. Pattern Anal. Mach. Intell. **24**(3), 289–300 (2002)
4. Holte, R.C., Acker, L.E., Porter, B.W.: Concept learning and the problem of small disjuncts. In: Proceedings of 11th International Joint Conference on Artificial Intelligence, vol. 1, pp. 813–818, Detroit (1989)
5. Japkowicz, N., Stephen, S.: The class imbalance problem: a systematic study. Intell. Data Anal. **6**(5), 429–449 (2002)
6. Jo, T., Japkowicz, N.: Class imbalances versus small disjuncts. SIGKDD Explor. Newsl. **6**(1), 40–49 (2004)
7. López, V., Fernández, A., García, S., Palade, V., Herrera, F.: An insight into classification with imbalanced data: empirical results and current trends on using data intrinsic characteristics. Inf. Sci. **250**, 113–141 (2013)
8. Lughofer, E.: Single-pass active learning with conflict and ignorance. Evol. Syst. **3**(4), 251–271 (2012)
9. Napierała, K., Stefanowski, J., Wilk, S.: Learning from imbalanced data in presence of noisy and borderline examples. In: Szczuka, M., Kryszkiewicz, M., Ramanna, S., Jensen, R., Hu, Q. (eds.) RSCTC 2010. LNCS, vol. 6086, pp. 158–167. Springer, Heidelberg (2010)

10. Pękalska, E., Duin, R.P.W.: Dissimilarity representations allow for building good classifiers. Pattern Recogn. Lett. **23**(8), 943–956 (2002)
11. Pękalska, E., Duin, R.P.W.: The Dissimilarity Representation for Pattern Recognition: Foundations and Applications. World Scientific, Singapore (2005)
12. Pękalska, E., Duin, R.P.W., Paclík, P.: Prototype selection for dissimilarity-based classifiers. Pattern Recogn. **39**(2), 189–208 (2006)
13. Pękalska, E., Paclik, P., Duin, R.P.W.: A generalized kernel approach to dissimilarity-based classification. J. Mach. Learn. Res. **2**, 175–211 (2002)
14. Prati, R.C., Batista, G.E.A.P.A., Monard, M.C.: Learning with class skews and small disjuncts. In: Bazzan, A.L.C., Labidi, S. (eds.) SBIA 2004. LNCS (LNAI), vol. 3171, pp. 296–306. Springer, Heidelberg (2004)
15. Seiffert, C., Khoshgoftaar, T.M., Van Hulse, J., Folleco, A.: An empirical study of the classification performance of learners on imbalanced and noisy software quality data. Inf. Sci. **259**, 571–595 (2014)
16. Sun, Y., Wong, A.K.C., Kamel, M.S.: Classification of imbalanced data: a review. Int. J. Pattern Recogn. Artif. Intell. **23**(4), 687–719 (2009)
17. Weiss, G.M., Hirsh, H.: The problem with noise and small disjuncts. In: Proceedings of 15th International Conference on Machine Learning, pp. 574–578, Madison (1998)
18. Weiss, G.M.: The effect of small disjuncts and class distribution on decision tree learning. Ph.D. thesis, Rutgers University, New Brunswick (2003)

Binary and Multi-class Parkinsonian Disorders Classification Using Support Vector Machines

Rita Morisi[1]([✉]), Giorgio Gnecco[1], Nico Lanconelli[2], Stefano Zanigni[3],
David Neil Manners[3], Claudia Testa[3], Stefania Evangelisti[3],
Laura Ludovica Gramegna[3], Claudio Bianchini[3], Pietro Cortelli[3],
Caterina Tonon[3], and Raffaele Lodi[3]

[1] IMT Institute for Advanced Studies, Piazza S. Ponziano 6, 55100 Lucca, Italy
rita.morisi@imtlucca.it
[2] Dipartimento di Fisica e Astronomia, Alma Mater Studiorum,
University of Bologna, Viale Berti-Pichat 6/2, 40127 Bologna, Italy
[3] Functional MR Unit, Policlinico S.Orsola-Malpighi,
Department of Biomedical and NeuroMotor Sciences,
University of Bologna, Bologna, Italy

Abstract. This paper presents a method for an automated Parkinsonian disorders classification using Support Vector Machines (SVMs). Magnetic Resonance quantitative markers are used as features to train SVMs with the aim of automatically diagnosing patients with different Parkinsonian disorders. Binary and multi–class classification problems are investigated and applied with the aim of automatically distinguishing the subjects with different forms of disorders. A ranking feature selection method is also used as a preprocessing step in order to asses the significance of the different features in diagnosing Parkinsonian disorders. In particular, it turns out that the features selected as the most meaningful ones reflect the opinions of the clinicians as the most important markers in the diagnosis of these disorders. Concerning the results achieved in the classification phase, they are promising; in the two multi–class classification problems investigated, an average accuracy of 81 % and 90 % is obtained, while in the binary scenarios taken in consideration, the accuracy is never less than 88 %.

Keywords: Support Vector Machines · Feature selection · Binary classification · Multi–class classification · Parkinsonian disorders classification

1 Introduction

In this study we investigate the application of Support Vector Machines (SMVs) for the automatic diagnosis of patients with different Parkinsonian disorders using features obtained from Diffusion Tensor Imaging (DTI), proton Magnetic Resonance Spectroscopy (^{1}H-MRS) and morphometric-volumetric analysis. In the medical context, machine learning methods represent a useful tool to help the clinicians in the diagnosis of different diseases. The application of a suitable machine learning technique is, in fact, able to provide a first quick and automatic diagnosis,

© Springer International Publishing Switzerland 2015
R. Paredes et al. (Eds.): IbPRIA 2015, LNCS 9117, pp. 379–386, 2015.
DOI: 10.1007/978-3-319-19390-8_43

helping the experts for its successive refinement. At the same time, also feature selection techniques can be extremely useful to automatically determine and provide the clinicians information about the most important and informative set of markers collected from the patients study to diagnose a disorder. In this work, the potentiality and utility of these methods are studied and applied to data collected from patients affected by degenerative Parkinsonisms, such as Idiopathic Parkinson's Disease (PD), Progressive Supranuclear Palsy (PSP) and Multiple System Atrophy (MSA), with the cerebellar (MSA-C) and Parkinsonian (MSA-P) variants. Although these disorders are characterized by different clinical features, response to pharmacological treatment and prognosis, their in vivo differential diagnosis is often challenging. In order to improve the accuracy of clinical diagnostic criteria, various promising biomarkers have been identified [1]. These biomarkers can be provided to an automatic machine learning method, such as SVMs, in order to improve the diagnostic accuracy and to help the clinicians to discriminate Parkinsonian syndromes at an individual level. Recently, SVMs have been applied in binary classification scenarios to distinguish, indeed, patients with PD from those with PSP [2], for the automatic classification of PD patients from normal volunteers [3], and the automatic discrimination of PD from atypical forms of Parkinsonism [4].

In this work we aim at studying not only an automatic approach to distinguish subjects with two different Parkinsonian disorders among the four forms of Parkinsonism (PD, PSP, MSA–C, and MSA–P), whose data we are provided of, but also at investigating the application of a multi-class classification method in order to automatically distinguish the subjects with the four different forms of disorders. In particular, we investigate the potentiality of SVMs in a four class classification scenario, when each single disorder is treated as a single class, and in a three class classification scenario, considering MSA–C and MSA–P as a single class. A similar study, but with a different multi-class classification approach, is described in [5], where a statistical approach is used. Our method consists in a different approach, in particular it combines 1-vs all SVMs with probabilistic output to distinguish patients with different forms of Parkinsonism. We also investigate the applicability of a ranking procedure as a feature selection technique, to assess the significance of every "clinical marker" we have from each single patient study in distinguishing the different disorders. This kind of preprocessing phase is important to keep the dimension of the problem small, thus making easier the computation of the classifier; but also to provide the clinicians a useful tool to understand the most informative parameters for the diagnosis of these disorders. Finally, to evaluate the capability of the features selected in discriminating the different disorders, an approach based on a comparison of Receiver Operating Characteristic (ROC) curves is also used.

2   Methods

2.1   Dataset and Preprocessing

We include in the study 8 MSA-C, 7 MSA-P, 17 PSP and 26 PD consecutive patients who underwent brain MR at the Functional MR Unit of the Policlinico

S. Orsola Malpighi, in Bologna, Italy, as part of the diagnostic work-up. Clinical diagnosis were performed according to current criteria [6]. Thus, the dataset X we are provided of, consists of $l = 58$ sample–labeled pairs (x_i, y_i) $i = 1, \ldots, l$, where $x_i \in \mathbb{R}^d$ and $y_i \in \{1, 2, 3, 4\}$. $l_1 = 8$ samples belong to class 1, $l_2 = 7$ belong to class 2, $l_3 = 17$ to class 3, while $l_4 = 26$ samples are from class 4. x_i represents the i–th patient, with his corresponding label y_i that refers to his particular disorder. $d = 152$ features are collected for each sample; they are obtained from DTI, proton spectroscopy and morphometric-volumetric analysis. All participants underwent the same brain MR protocol with a 1.5 T GE scanner. Some of the d features, such as mean DTI parameters (Fractional Anisotropy, FA, and Mean Diffusivity, MD) were computed by using a Region of Interest (ROI) method, while others derive from an histogram–analysis method [7]. In addition, semi-automated volumetric features and DTI parameters were obtained by using FSL tools (http://fsl.fmrib. ox.ac.uk/fsl/fslwiki/). After having computed the $d = 152$ features, each one is re–scaled inside the interval $[-1, 1]$ in order to give them the same importance a–priori.

2.2   Classification Model

An SVM with linear kernel is used, since by running some preliminary comparison tests with other kernels (e.g., polynomial, radial basis function), it turned out that the linear SVM performed better than the others. Indeed, it is not unusual that in high-dimensional datasets with a small number of samples, radial basis function and polynomial kernels lead to overfitting, while the linear kernel provides the best result [8]. In the following, we first consider a classical binary classification problem, with l samples x_i, $i = 1, \ldots, l$, and the corresponding labels $y_i \in \{-1, 1\}$. In this context, the formulation of the binary linear SVM is described by the following optimization problem:

$$\text{minimize}_{w,b,\xi} \quad (\frac{1}{2} w^T w + C \sum\nolimits_{i=1}^{l} \xi_i)$$
$$\text{subject to} \quad y_i f(x_i) \geq 1 - \xi_i, \text{ for } i = 1, \ldots, l, \tag{1}$$
$$\xi_i \geq 0, \text{ for } i = 1, \ldots, l,$$

where $C > 0$ is a penalty term and $f(x_i) = w^T x_i + b$ is an affine function of x_i. Beside the model described by (1) which assigns a sample x_i to one of the two classes according to the sign of $f(x_i)$, a probabilistic output can also be used [9]. More precisely, given a sample x_i and the corresponding value of $f(x_i)$, the a-posteriori probability of x_i to belong to one of the two classes $y_i \in \{-1, 1\}$ can be estimated by a sigmoid function in the following way:

$$P(y_i = j | x_i) = \frac{1}{1 + \exp(Af + B)}, \tag{2}$$

where j is either equal to -1 or 1. Then, x_i is automatically assigned to the class y_i with the highest posterior probability between the two. The parameters

A and B in formula (2) are estimated by solving a regularized maximum likelihood problem, following the procedure described in [10]. A probabilistic output is also used in the multi–class classification scenario. In that case, to automatically classify the samples according to the different classes, we use a combination of K two-classes 1–vs all classifiers, where K represents the number of classes presented, i.e., $K = 4$ in the four–class classification study, while $K = 3$ when MSA–C and MSA–P are considered as a single class. More specifically, K binary 1–vs all linear SVMs with probabilistic output $P_k(x)$ $(k = 1, \ldots, K)$ are trained, i.e., for each class the training is realized by labeling the samples belonging to the class chosen as samples from the "positive" class, while all the others are grouped together in the "negative" class. Once the K classifiers are trained, a new input x is tested by presenting it to all the K classifiers, then it is assigned to the class with the highest a-posteriori probability, i.e., the one that maximizes $P_k(x)$. We run a leave-one-out cross-validation procedure (LOOCV) to determine the penalty C value (see (1)) that leads to the best accuracy, computed as the percentage of samples correctly classified on an independent evaluation set. This process is repeated for each classification scenario, when both the entire set and only a subset of features (see the next section) is considered. Note that, for each classification problem taken into consideration, the C value that leads to the best accuracy may depend on the classification problem itself. In other terms, different classification problems may have different optimal C's.

2.3   Feature Selection

A feature selection method is also applied to the dataset as a preprocessing step in all the problems treated, in order to understand if some features are more meaningful and useful than others for diagnosis purposes. Thus, the clinicians can be provided of more information about the importance of some parameters used for the diagnosis. In addition, it is interesting to see if the features automatically selected, agree with the ones considered as the most useful ones by the experts opinions. We apply a ranking criterion to the d features in the dataset X which orders the features according to their capability of assigning each sample to the correct class. In particular, for each binary classification problem, an independent evaluation criterion is used, i.e., the features are considered individually in determining their capability to discriminate the two classes, when each feature is used alone. We choose the relative entropy criterion [11] as the method to assess the significance of every feature in separating the two labeled classes. First, its value is computed for each of the d features. Then, the features are ranked decreasingly with respect to their relative entropies, following the procedure described in [12]. Depending on the subsequent classification problem one is interested in, the $\tilde{d} < d$ features corresponding to the $\tilde{d}$ best values of the ranking can be subsequently selected, to form a reduced dataset $\tilde{X} \in \mathbb{R}^{l \times \tilde{d}}$ (this procedure is repeated for several choices of $\tilde{d}$). Then, in each binary classification scenario, we evaluate the outcome of the feature selection method by means of Receiver Operating Characteristic (ROC) curves. By comparing the ROC curve obtained with only $\tilde{d}$ features corresponding to the $\tilde{d}$ best values of the ranking, and the one for the entire set of d features, an estimate of the goodness of the feature selection method can be done. We propose to build the ROC curve by changing the value of the threshold on the probabilistic output of the SVM. All the described methods are implemented using MATLAB and, specifically for the classification part, we use the codes described and implemented in [9].

3   Results

We first investigate two binary classification scenarios, where the first one considers all the combinations between pairs of different disorders, i.e., PSP vs. PD, MSA–C vs. MSA–P and so on, while the second one consists in classifying each disorder versus the other three, grouped in a single class. Subsequently, we consider two multi–class classification problems: a 4–class problem (i.e., the number of classes is equal to the number of disorders), and a 3–class one (the classes MSA–C and MSA–P are here grouped into one single class, as being variants of the same disorder). Also for the binary classification problems, we perform some tests by considering MSA–C and MSA–P as a single class, named as MSA. From now on, we will indicate with $A_{i,j} = \frac{\#\text{samples correctly classified}}{l_i + l_j}$ the accuracy achieved in the first binary classification scenario, whereas $A_{i,\text{all}}$ indicates the accuracy achieved in the second one. Finally, we denote by A_3 and A_4 the accuracies obtained for the two multi-class problems. The last three accuracies are computed as $\frac{\#\text{samples correctly classified}}{l}$. For both the binary and the multi–class situations we compare the performances of the linear SVM obtained with the entire set of features and with only a small subset extracted by the ranking procedure described in Subsect. 2.3. A LOOCV procedure is performed in both the situations (i.e., a dataset with either d or $\tilde{d}$ features), to determine the best C value for each kind of problem. In particular, in the reduced-dimension scenario, we compute the accuracy of the SVM by considering a reduced dataset made of the first $\tilde{d} = 10$, $\tilde{d} = 20$, $\tilde{d} = 30$ and $\tilde{d} = 40$ ranked features. Note that, since the number of samples at our disposal is small, all the results reported are the average of the correctly classified samples obtained by the LOOCV procedure, without considering an independent test set for the final evaluation.

Figure 1a shows two comparisons, in terms of ROC curves, between the outcomes obtained with the entire set of features and a reduced set ($\tilde{d} = 10$), for two binary problems: "PD vs all", and "PD vs PSP". In the default case of the value $\frac{1}{2}$ for the threshold, the accuracy achieved in the "PD vs all" situation is $A_{4,\text{all}} = 83\%$ with $d = 152$ features, and $A_{4,\text{all}} = 84\%$ with $\tilde{d} = 10$ features. Concerning the "PD vs PSP" scenario, the accuracy achieved in both the situations is $A_{3,4} = 98\%$. Regarding the optimal value for C, in the "PD vs PSP" scenario, one of the values that lead to the highest accuracy is the same for both the situations and it is equal to $C = 0.1$. In the "PD vs all" scenario, instead, there is not a best C value in common: $C = 0.01$ when $d = 152$ features are considered, and $C = 1$ with $\tilde{d} = 10$ features. Note that, by an inspection of the ROC curves, it is possible to set a value of the threshold different from the one considered by default by the SVM (i.e., $\frac{1}{2}$), that leads to a higher accuracy.

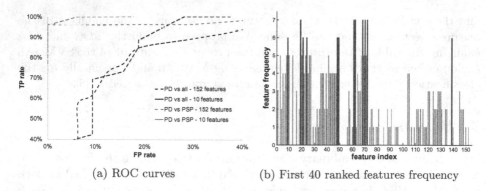

(a) ROC curves   (b) First 40 ranked features frequency

Fig. 1. For two of the binary classification problems considered in the paper: (a) comparison between the ROC curves obtained with the entire set of features ($d = 152$), and the first $\tilde{d} = 10$ ranked features; (b) frequency of the first 40 ranked features in the 8 binary classification problems "one disorder vs another".

Table 1. Best accuracy achieved by the SVM with the corresponding optimal C value and the optimal number of features used in the "one disorder versus another" problem.

	PD vs				PSP vs			MSA–C vs MSA–P
	PSP	MSA–C	MSA–P	MSA	MSA–C	MSA–P	MSA	
Accuracy	98 %	100 %	88 %	90 %	100 %	96 %	97 %	93 %
# features	10	152	10	30	10	152	10	20
Optimal C	0.1	0.001	0.12	1	0.001	0.18	1	0.04

Nevertheless, since we are interested in an automatic classification procedure, we prefer to maintain the threshold equal to $\frac{1}{2}$ for the computation of the final accuracy. In this way, the method is as general and as automatic as possible. Figure 1b shows the frequency of the first 40 features extracted by the ranking procedure in the 8 binary problems "one disorder versus another" (whose results are reported in Table 1). In dark are highlighted the most used features, i.e., those appearing among the first 40 ranked features in at least 6 binary problems over the 8 total. Specifically, they are: Magnetic Resonance Parkinsonism Index (MRPI), MD Middle Cerebellar Peduncle (MCP) right (R), MD MCP R+left(L), MD cerebellar White Matter (WM), MD pre-frontal WM L, MD pre-frontal WM, MD Posterior Fossa (PF) (25° percentile), MD Posterior Fossa (PF) (50° percentile), MD cerebellar hemisphere R (50° percentile), MD cerebellar hemisphere L (50° percentile) and MD cerebellar hemispheres R+L. Note that, 48 features over a total of 152 are never listed in the first 40 features, suggesting a negligible contribution of them to the performance of the classifier.

Tables 1 and 2 show the classification results in the binary cases. Each type of scenario has been studied by considering the entire set of features, then also the dataset made of only the first $\tilde{d} = 10$, 20, 30 or 40 first ranked features. We decided not to consider datasets with a number of features more than 40 because we consider at most 40 features to be a good compromise between keeping the dimension of the problem relatively small and obtaining a good accuracy.

Table 2. Best accuracy achieved by the SVM and the corresponding optimal C value and number of features for the "1–class vs all" binary problem.

	PD vs all	PSP vs all	MSA–C vs all	MSA–P vs all	MSA vs all
Accuracy	90 %	95 %	95 %	88 %	93 %
# features	40	10	10	10	152
Optimal C	1	1	0.9	1	0.02

Table 3. Confusion matrices in the multi-class scenario. The results shown are the best achieved in terms of features used and optimal C value. "Actual" and "Predicted" stand for actual label and predicted label, respectively.

	Predicted			
Actual	MSA–C	MSA–P	PSP	PD
MSA–C	7	0	0	1
MSA–P	1	0	0	6
PSP	1	0	14	2
PD	0	0	0	26

(a) # classes $K = 4$

	Predicted		
Actual	MSA	PSP	PD
MSA	11	0	4
PSP	0	16	1
PD	0	1	25

(b) # classes $K = 3$

The results reported are the best among all these possibilities, according to the LOOCV procedure described above. Concerning the multi-class situation, we report the results achieved in Table 3; subtable (a) refers to the 4 class classification problem, while subtable (b) reports the 3-class classification results. The predicted and actual labels are reported by means of a confusion matrix; for instance, subtable (a) shows that 8 patients have MSA–C (sum over the first row) and 7 of them are correctly classified, while one is erroneously classified as a PD patient. The corresponding accuracy is $A_4 = 81\%$, and is obtained by using the first 10 features and the value 0.8 for C. Finally, the best accuracy achieved by the linear SVM in the 3-class problem (MSA–C and MSA–P are grouped in a single class) is $A_3 = 90\%$, and is obtained with 40 features and $C = 0.5$. The corresponding predicted and actual labels are reported in subtable (b).

4 Conclusions

In this study, we employed a linear SVM to distinguish among patients with different Parkinsonian disorders. The results achieved are promising; in particular, in the multi–class scenario an accuracy $A_3 = 90\%$ is obtained in the 3–class problem, while in the binary scenarios the accuracy is never less than 88 %. In both the binary and multi–class classification results, as Tables 1, 2 and 3 show, it is clear that MSA–P is the most critical disorder to be distinguished. The feature selection analysis revealed that the most important and meaningful information in distinguishing patients with different disorders resides in a small subset of features, which is in line with the features most used by the experts in this kind of classification problem. From Tables 1 and 2, it is clear that only 3 case-studies need the entire set of features to achieve the best accuracy, while in most of the other problems the best result is achieved with only the first 10 ranked features. Indeed, as pointed out in [13], in many medical applications, where usually a large number of disease markers is provided while a small number of data records is available, a feature selection preprocessing often leads to an improvement of the results achieved and also helps in the interpretation of the results. As possible future improvements, we first intend to better validate our approach by evaluating and testing this learning technique on an independent test set; secondly an application of other classification models, such as the one proposed by [5], will be taken in consideration in order to investigate the capability of SVMs in this particular context. Finally, we intend to use additional methods, such as graph-based techniques, to extract additional information about the structure of the data, and use them to improve our results.

References

1. Sharma, S., et al.: Biomarkers in Parkinson's disease (recent update). Neurochem. Int. **63**(3), 201–229 (2013)
2. Cherubini, A., et al.: Magnetic resonance support vector machine discriminates between parkinson disease and progressive supranuclear palsy. Mov. Disord. **29**(2), 266–269 (2014)
3. Long, D., et al.: Automatic classification of early Parkinson's disease with multimodal MR imaging. PloS one **7**(11), e47714 (2012)
4. Haller, S., et al.: Individual detection of patients with Parkinson disease using support vector machine analysis of diffusion tensor imaging data: initial results. Am. J. Neuroradiol. **33**(11), 2123–2128 (2012)
5. Marquand, A.F., et al.: Automated, high accuracy classification of Parkinsonian disorders: a pattern recognition approach. PloS one **8**(7), e69237 (2013)
6. Gelb, D.J., Oliver, E., Gilman, S.: Diagnostic criteria for Parkinson disease. Arch. Neurol. **56**(1), 33–39 (1999)
7. Rizzo, G., et al.: Diffusion-weighted brain imaging study of patients with clinical diagnosis of corticobasal degeneration, progressive supranuclear palsy and parkinson's disease. Brain **131**(10), 2690–2700 (2008)
8. Ben-Hur, A., Jason, W.: A user's guide to support vector machines. In: Carugo, O., Eisenhaber, F. (eds.) Data Mining Techniques for the Life Sciences, pp. 223–239. Humana Press, New York (2010)
9. Chang, C.C., Lin, C.J.: LIBSVM: a library for support vector machines. ACM Trans. Intell. Syst. Technol. **2**(3), 27:1–27:27 (2011)
10. Platt, J.C.: Probabilistic outputs for support vector machines and comparisons to regularized likelihood methods. In: Smola, A.J., Bartlett, P.L., Scholkopf, B., Schurmans, D. (eds.) Advances in Large Margin Classifiers, pp. 61–74. MIT Press, Cambridge (1999)
11. Battiti, R.: Using mutual information for selecting features in supervised neural net learning. IEEE Trans. Neural Netw. **5**(4), 537–550 (1994)
12. Theodoridis, S., Koutroumbas, K.: Pattern Recognition, 4th edn. Academic Press, New York (2009)
13. Abdel-Aal, R.E.: GMDH-based feature ranking and selection for improved classification of medical data. J. Biomed. Inform. **38**(6), 456–468 (2005)

Peripheral Nerve Segmentation Using Speckle Removal and Bayesian Shape Models

Hernán F. García[1]($^{\boxtimes}$), Juan J. Giraldo[1], Mauricio A. Álvarez[1],
Álvaro A. Orozco[1], and Diego Salazar[2]

[1] Grupo de Investigación en Automática, Universidad Tecnológica de Pereira,
La Julita, Pereira, Colombia
{hernan.garcia,juanjogg1987,malvarez,aaog}@utp.edu.co
[2] Hospital Santa Mónica, Risaralda, Colombia
diegosalazar@anestecoop.com

Abstract. In the field of medicine, ultrasound images have become a useful tool for visualizing nerve structures in the process of anesthesiology. Although, these images are commonly used in medical procedures such as peripheral nerve blocks. Their poor intelligibility makes it difficult for the anesthesiologists to perform this process accurately. Therefore, an automated segmentation methodology of the peripheral nerves can assist the experts in improving accuracy. This paper proposes a peripheral nerve segmentation method in medical ultrasound images, based on Speckle removal and Bayesian shape models. The method allows segmenting efficiently a given nerve by performing a Bayesian shape fitting. The experimental results show that performing a speckle removal before fitting the model, improves the accuracy due to the enhancement of the image to segment.

Keywords: Peripheral nerve segmentaion · Speckle removal · Bayesian shape models

1 Introduction

Medical image segmentation is a very important but difficult step in image processing; this issue has gained relevant importance in biomedical applications in recent years [1]. Ultrasound (US) images for diagnosis and analysis in a human body are used everywhere in the field of medicine. Particularly, ultrasound images are used to locate nerve structures with the purpose of practicing regional anesthesia. The regional anesthesia consists on injecting an anesthetic in the proximity of nerve structures to block sensibility in medical patients. Although, these images are an important tool in medicine, the non-uniformities of texture derived by the acquisition process, makes the correct location of the nerve structures a difficult process to the medical specialist. Mainly, due to the fact that different artifacts are introduced in the capture process and a noise known as speckle degrades the image quality [2].

© Springer International Publishing Switzerland 2015
R. Paredes et al. (Eds.): IbPRIA 2015, LNCS 9117, pp. 387–394, 2015.
DOI: 10.1007/978-3-319-19390-8_44

Automatic image segmentation has been applied on intravascular images [3], tumors and trans-cranial reconstructions and fetal images [4]. Several techniques have been developed for segmenting these type of ultrasound images including Markov random field methods [5], fuzzy cluster methods and unsupervised clustering methods [6]. The main problem of these methods, is that the texture information is modeled without considering the variability of shapes corresponding to the anatomical structures to be analyzed. That is why we need to introduce some prior information related to the shapes to be modeled [7].

The model-based approaches make use of a prior knowledge of given shape (i.e. peripheral nerve contour) in an input image and finds a matching between the model and a new image [8]. The main reason is that the model deforms a given shape by using Bayesian inference. Bayesian shape models (BSM) use the prior distribution of shape objects (nerve contour) for modeling the variability of shapes, over a set of manual landmarks that represent the shape contours of a given object [7]. The segmentation process from ultrasound images has to consider the speckle noise as a main issue that makes the segmentation task more difficult [4]. This is due, to the non-uniformities of texture that are added by the noise itself. Therefore, the segmentation process might be corrupted with shape outliers that do not represent a nerve structure [2]. Due to the prior knowledge used to segment a shape contour by the BSM model, our contribution is based on the speckle removal process that combined with a BSM model can improve the segmentation accurately of the given shape contour related to a nerve structure, in comparison with common methods such as active shape models [9]. Furthermore, to the best of our knowledge, there are not relevant works focusing on the segmentation of peripheral nerves with the purpose of assisting the process of anesthesiology. Consequently, this paper contributes to the study of automatic segmentation for this type of nerve structures.

In this paper, we propose a Bayesian shape model with speckle removal for peripheral nerve segmentation. Here, we use a Bayesian framework to derive a non-local (NL) means filter adapted to a relevant ultrasound noise model with the aim to remove the speckle noise and preserve the contour information of the ultrasound image. Then, a Bayesian shape model is introduced to match a nerve structure contour in a given ultrasound image using the shape prior information provided for the training process of the model. The paper proceeds as follows, Sect. 2 depicts the materials and methods. Sections 3 and 4 show the experimental results, conclusions and some future works.

2   Materials and Methods

2.1   Database

The database used in this work comes from Universidad Tecnológica de Pereira (UltraDB-UTP) and Santa Monica Hospital of Pereira-Colombia. This database contains recordings of ultrasound images from ten patients of surgical anesthesia in which peripheral nerve blocks was performed. The database was labeled by a specialist in anesthesiology from the Santa Monica Hospital with a Sonosite

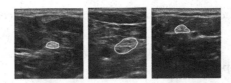

Fig. 1. An example of ultrasound images for median nerve (left), peroneal nerve (middle) and ulnar nerve (right) with manual segmentation in the region of interest (ROI).

NanoMaxx device[1]. The location of the nerve structures in the patients corresponds to the forearm (ulnar and median nerves), and the backside of the knee (peroneal nerve). The database was built with 30 images corresponding to the ulnar nerve, 15 images for peroneal nerve, and 30 images for median nerve respectively. All database images were recorded in DICOM format with a 640×480 pixel-size. Figure 1 shows the types of images belonging to the database.

2.2   Nonlocal Means-Based Speckle Filtering

In ultrasound image segmentation, restoration is expected to improve the qualitative inspection of the image and the performance of quantitative image analysis techniques. We use the adaptation of the Non Local (NL) means filter proposed by Coupé *et al.* in [10] for speckle reduction in ultrasound (US) images. We use a Bayesian framework to derive a NL-means filter adapted to a relevant ultrasound noise model [11]. Let us consider a gray-scale noisy image $u = (u\,(x_i))$, $x_i \in \Omega^{\dim}$ defined over a bounded domain $\Omega^{\dim} \subset \mathbb{R}^{\dim}$ and $u\,(x_i) \in \mathbb{R}_+$ is the noisy intensity observed at pixel $x_i \in \Omega^{\dim}$.[2] Equivalent to the conditional mean estimator proposed in [11], the estimator $\hat{\mathbf{v}}(B_{i_k})$ of a block B_{i_k} can be defined as

$$\hat{\mathbf{v}}(B_{i_k}) = \frac{\sum_{j=1}^{|\Delta_{i_k}|} \mathbf{u}(B_j) p\,(\mathbf{u}(B_{i_k})|\mathbf{u}(B_j))}{\sum_{j=1}^{|\Delta_{i_k}|} p\,(\mathbf{u}(B_{i_k})|\mathbf{u}(B_j))}, \tag{1}$$

where $p\,(\mathbf{u}(B_{i_k})|\mathbf{u}(B_j))$ denotes the probability density function of $\mathbf{u}(B_{i_k})$ given the noise free and unknown patches $\mathbf{u}(B_j)$ with B_i as a square block centered at x_i of size $|B_i| = (2\alpha + 1)^{\dim}$ and Δ_i as a square search volume centered at pixel x_i of size $|\Delta_i| = (2M + 1)^{\dim}$ (M is the search area size and α is the patch size). In the case of an additive white Gaussian noise, the likelihood $p\,(\mathbf{u}(B_{i_k})|\mathbf{u}(B_j))$ will be proportional to $e^{-\|\mathbf{u}(\mathbf{B}_{i_k}) - \mathbf{u}(\mathbf{B_j})\|^2 / h^2}$ and the speckle model is given by

$$u(x) = v(x) + v^{\gamma}(x)\eta(x), \tag{2}$$

where $v(x)$ is the original image, $u(x)$ is the observed image and $\eta(x) \sim \mathcal{N}(0, \sigma^2)$ is a zero-mean Gaussian noise. This model is able to capture reliably image

---

[1] http://www.sonosite.com/products/nanomaxx.

[2] Dim denotes the image grid dimension. In this work, we used dim = 2 for 2D images.

statistics since the factor γ depends on ultrasound devices related to image formation [2].

2.3   Bayesian Shape Model

We use a probabilistic formulation for the shape segmentation. The problem is carried out in two models: one related to the prior shape distribution in tangent shape space (variability of the peripheral nerve contour) and the other is a likelihood model in image shape space [7]. Assuming that a 2D shape is described by N landmark points in the ultrasound image (peripheral nerve), we define $\mathbf{s}_i$ as a shape instance of the training set $\{\mathbf{s}_i\}_{i=1}^{L}$ where L is the number of training shapes (peripheral nerves labeled). The vector $\mathbf{s}_i$ can be transformed into the tangent space $\mathbb{C}_\mu$ by aligning $\mathbf{s}_i$ with $\boldsymbol{\mu}$ (mean shape of the training set) as $\{\mathbf{x}_i \in \mathbb{C}_\mu : \mathbf{x}_i = T_i(\mathbf{s}_i)\}_{i=1}^{L}$ [7]. The covariance matrix of tangent shape is estimated as,

$$\Sigma = \frac{1}{L-1} \sum_{i=1}^{L} (\mathbf{x}_i - \boldsymbol{\mu})(\mathbf{x}_i - \boldsymbol{\mu})^\top. \tag{3}$$

Prior Shape Model. We used a Probabilistic Principal Component Analysis (PPCA) to model the shape variations of the nerve structures [12]. The model is defined as,

$$\mathbf{x} = \boldsymbol{\mu} + \boldsymbol{\Phi}_r \mathbf{b} + \boldsymbol{\Phi}\boldsymbol{\varepsilon}, \tag{4}$$

where $\boldsymbol{\Phi}^\top$ is the tangent projection matrix whose row vectors are the eigenvectors of Σ; $\boldsymbol{\Phi}_r$ consists the first r columns of $\boldsymbol{\Phi}$; $\mathbf{b}$, the shape parameter, is a $r-$dimensional vector distributed as a multivariate Gaussian $\mathcal{N}(0, \Lambda)$, where $\Lambda = \mathrm{diag}(\lambda_1, \cdots, \lambda_r)$; λ_i is the ith eigenvalue and r is the number of modes (variance) to retain in PCA; $\boldsymbol{\varepsilon}$ denotes an isotropic noise in the tangent space and it is a random vector, which is independent of $\mathbf{b}$ and it is distributed as

$$p(\boldsymbol{\varepsilon}) \sim \exp\left\{-\|\boldsymbol{\varepsilon}\|^2/(2\sigma^2)\right\} \text{ with } \sigma^2 = \frac{1}{2N-4} \sum_{i=4+1}^{2N-4} \lambda_i.$$

We implemented the expectation maximization algorithm (EM) to compute the posterior of the model parameters such as shape b, scale s, translation c and pose θ given the observed shape vector y.

$$p(b, c, s, \theta | y) \propto \exp\left\{-\frac{1}{2}\left[\left(\sigma^2 + s^{-2}\rho^2\right)^{-1}\left(\left\|\boldsymbol{\Phi}_r^\top T_\theta^{-1}(y) - b\right\|^2\right.\right.\right.$$
$$\left.\left.\left. + \left\|\boldsymbol{\Phi}_r^\top T_\theta^{-1}(y)\right\|^2\right) + \frac{s^2}{\rho^2}\left\|\Lambda^\top T_\theta^{-1}(y)\right\|^2 + b^\top \Lambda^{-1} b\right]\right\}$$
$$\cdot \frac{cte}{\left(\sigma^2 + s^{-2}\rho^2\right)^{(N-2)} s^{-4}\rho^4}, \tag{5}$$

where the cte does not vary with (b, c, s, θ), and $\boldsymbol{\Phi}_r$ is the sub-matrix of $\boldsymbol{\Phi}$ obtained by removing the first r columns, and $T_\theta^{-1}(y)$ is a transform over θ parameter.

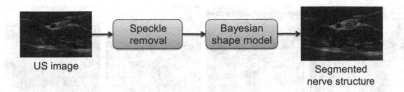

US image

Segmented
nerve structure

Fig. 2. Peripheral nerve segmentation pipeline. First the speckle noise is removed from all database images and then the BSM model deforms the shape contour to match a given nerve structure.

2.4 Peripheral Nerve Segmentation Method

Due to the non-uniformities introduced by the speckle noise in the ultrasound images, we propose a preprocessing step before performing the BSM training, to remove the speckle noise and preserve the nerve structures. We use the NL-means filter implementation proposed by Coupé et al. in [10], with MATLAB in a Core $i3$ with 2.1 GHz and $4\,GB$ RAM.

After the NL-means filter removes the speckle noise, we use the Bayesian shape model to segment the nerve contour in the US image. This model was trained from a set of manually labeled landmarks (58 for each nerve image) of peripheral nerve structures (ulnar, peroneal and median nerves). For the Bayesian shape model implementation, we used the *asmlib-opencv*[3] library compiled on $C++$ using the MinGW platform. Figure 2 shows the peripheral nerve segmentation pipeline proposed in this work. We train three models, one for each nerve structure to segment.

3 Results

3.1 NL-means Filter

The experimental setup it is based on segmentation of the peripheral nerve structures of the UltraDB-UTP database. This process was carried out for each of the three peripheral nerves of the database. To perform this task, we first filter all images from database to remove the speckle noise. In this work we use for the filter parameters $M = 7$ as search area size $\alpha = 3$ for the patch filter size and $h = 0.7$ as smoothing parameter [10]. The results shown in Fig. 3, indicate that the filter efficiently removes the speckle component while enhancing the edges and preserving the peripheral nerve structures.

3.2 Peripheral Nerve Segmentation

To measure quantitatively the segmentation accuracy, we computed the mean squared error (MSE) of the euclidean distance between the shape fitted by the

---

[3] We use the BSM implementation available on https://code.google.com/p/asmlib-opencv/.

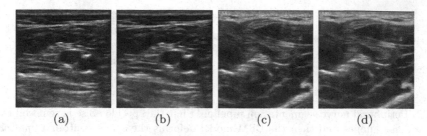

| (a) | (b) | (c) | (d) |

Fig. 3. Results obtained with the NL-means filter for peripheral nerves structures. Figures (a) and (b) show the filtering process for the peroneal nerve (unfiltered image left and filtered image right respectively). Figures (c) and (d) show the filtering process for the median nerve (same case as (a) and (b)). The filter efficiently removes the speckle while enhancing the edges and preserving the image structures.

model and the manual landmarks (ground truth) for the ultrasound images. Figure 4 shows the segmentation accuracy of the proposed method. We train one model for each peripheral nerve. The results show that the BSM model segments a peripheral nerve accurately. Furthermore, the results show that adding the NL-means filter improves the performance of the BSM model in the segmentation of the nerve structures. Additionally we report the segmentation accuracy using common shape segmentation techniques such as active shape models (ASM) [8]. The results show a better performance when the proposed scheme was used, obtaining MSE values between 1.353 ± 0.317 pixels for BSM+NL-means scheme and 1.808 ± 0.266 pixels for the BSM model without the speckle removal. Furthermore, the results show that the proposed scheme using BSM+NL-means, outperforms conventional segmentation methods such as ASM.

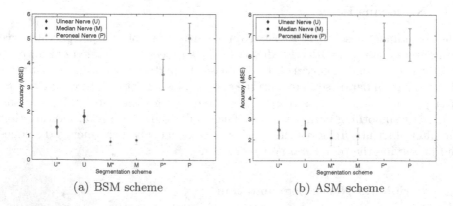

| (a) BSM scheme | (b) ASM scheme |

Fig. 4. Segmentation accuracy for the three peripheral nerves (Ulnar (U), Median (M) and Peroneal (P)). The figure shows the segmentation scheme using BSM and ASM models. Also, the $*$ symbol in the x-axis means that the segmentation scheme with speckle removal was used.

Finally, Fig. 5 shows the segmentation process starting from the initial shape to be deformed by the model, until the nerve structure has been segmented. The result shows that the model needs few iterations to converge, with a low computational cost in performing a segmentation process.

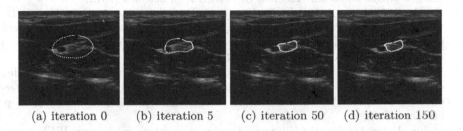

(a) iteration 0   (b) iteration 5   (c) iteration 50   (d) iteration 150

Fig. 5. Peripheral nerve segmentation process for the cubital nerve. Figure shows the shape deformation process starting from the initial shape (mean shape of the dataset) to the segmented shape.

4 Conclusions

In this paper, we introduced a new method for peripheral nerve segmentation in ultrasound images based on speckle removal and Bayesian shape models. The proposed approach can efficiently remove the speckle noise present in the ultrasound image by performing a NL-mean filter over the ultrasound image. The experimental results show that using a non-local search performed to remove speckle noise, enhances the image information while preserving edges of nerve structures and removing the noise present. Here, a Bayesian shape model was built to capture the shape variations from the peripheral nerve structures. Additionally, results showed an accurate segmentation in comparison with common segmentation techniques such as active shape models.

Two main tasks are left as future work: Firstly, the Bayesian shape model can be trained to segments 3D structures from ultrasound volumes. Secondly, it would be interesting to propose an automatic shape prior model that can be used to initialize the nerve contour for shape segmentation.

Acknowledgments. This research was developed under the project financed by the Pereira Technological University with code CIE 6-13-6. H.F. García is funded by Colciencias under the program: *formación de alto nivel para la ciencia, la tecnología y la innovación - Convocatoria 617 de 2013.*

References

1. Dougherty, G.: Medical Image Processing: Techniques and Applications. Biological and Medical Physics, Biomedical Engineering. Springer, New York (2011)

2. Tao, Z., Tagare, H.D., Beaty, J.D.: Evaluation of four probability distribution models for speckle in clinical cardiac ultrasound images. IEEE Trans. Med. Imaging **25**(11), 1483–1491 (2006)

3. Katouzian, A., Angelini, E., Carlier, S., Suri, J., Navab, N., Laine, A.: A state-of-the-art review on segmentation algorithms in intravascular ultrasound (ivus) images. IEEE Trans. Inf. Technol. Biomed. **16**(5), 823–834 (2012)

4. Rueda, S., Fathima, S., Knight, C., Yaqub, M., Papageorghiou, A., Rahmatullah, B., Foi, A., Maggioni, M., Pepe, A., Tohka, J.: Evaluation and comparison of current fetal ultrasound image segmentation methods for biometric measurements: a grand challenge. IEEE Trans. Med. Imaging **33**, 797–813 (2013)

5. Peng, Z., Wee, W., Lee, J.H.: Automatic segmentation of mr brain images using spatial-varying gaussian mixture and markov random field approach. In: Conference on Computer Vision and Pattern Recognition Workshop, CVPRW 2006, p. 80, June 2006

6. Noble, J., Boukerroui, D.: Ultrasound image segmentation: a survey. IEEE Trans. Med. Imaging **25**(8), 987–1010 (2006)

7. Zhou, Y., Gu, L., Zhang, H.J.: Bayesian tangent shape model: estimating shape and pose parameters via bayesian inference. In: Proceedings of the 2003 IEEE Computer Society Conference on Computer Vision and Pattern Recognition, CVPR 2003, pp. 109–116 (2003)

8. Xue, Z., Li, S.Z., Teoh, E.K.: Bayesian shape model for facial feature extraction and recognition. Pattern Recogn. **36**, 2819–2833 (2004)

9. Cootes, T.F., Taylor, C.J.: Statistical models of appearance for computer vision (2004)

10. Coupe, P., Hellier, P., Kervrann, C., Barillot, C.: Nonlocal means-based speckle filtering for ultrasound images. IEEE Trans. Image Process. **18**(10), 2221–2229 (2009)

11. Kervrann, C., Boulanger, J., Coupé, P.: Bayesian non-local means filter, image redundancy and adaptive dictionaries for noise removal. In: Sgallari, F., Murli, A., Paragios, N. (eds.) SSVM 2007. LNCS, vol. 4485, pp. 520–532. Springer, Heidelberg (2007)

12. Tipping, M.E., Bishop, C.M.: Probabilistic principal component analysis. J. Roy. Stat. Soc. Ser. B **61**, 611–622 (1999)

Measuring Scene Detection Performance

Lorenzo Baraldi[✉], Costantino Grana, and Rita Cucchiara

Dipartimento di Ingegneria "Enzo Ferrari", Università degli Studi di Modena e
Reggio Emilia, Via Vivarelli 10, 41125 Modena, MO, Italy
lorenzo.baraldi@unimore.it

Abstract. In this paper we evaluate the performance of scene detection
techniques, starting from the classic precision/recall approach, moving
to the better designed coverage/overflow measures, and finally proposing an improved metric, in order to solve frequently observed cases in
which the numeric interpretation is different from the expected results.
Numerical evaluation is performed on two recent proposals for automatic
scene detection, and comparing them with a simple but effective novel
approach. Experimental results are conducted to show how different measures may lead to different interpretations.

Keywords: Scene detection · Measures · Clustering

1 Introduction

The large availability of videos on the Internet has led to great interest in fields
different from simple entertainment or news broadcasting, such as education
(Massive Open Online Courses). This also led to a strong interest in the re-use
of video content coming from major broadcasting networks, which have been
producing high quality edited videos for popular science purposes.

Unfortunately, re-using videos in ones own presentations or video aided lectures is not an easy task, and requires video editing skills and tools. There is a
growing need for managing video content, but the basic unit for this task cannot
be the single frame: higher level groupings are needed, such as DVD chapters.
The problem is that most of the on-line reusable content is not provided with
editor defined video sub units. Scene detection may help in this situation, going
beyond frames and even beyond simple editing units, such as shots [3]. The task
is to identify coherent sequences (scenes) in videos, without any help from the
editor or publisher. As it is common in newer research areas, evaluating the
performance of automatic systems is not an easy task [2]: techniques previously
employed for different purposes are applied to newer problems, even if they do
not perfectly match with the objective at hand, but are easily understood from
previous experience. Often this approach leads to erroneous interpretations of
the experimental evaluations.

In this paper we try to tackle the problem of evaluating scene detection
techniques, starting from the classic precision/recall approach, moving to the

© Springer International Publishing Switzerland 2015
R. Paredes et al. (Eds.): IbPRIA 2015, LNCS 9117, pp. 395–403, 2015.
DOI: 10.1007/978-3-319-19390-8_45

better designed coverage/overflow measures, and finally propose an improved definition of the latter ones, which solve frequently observed cases in which the numeric interpretation would be quite different from the expected results. Numerical evaluation is performed on two recent proposals for automatic scene detection, which are compared with the different measures, together with our simple approach. The experimental results will show the different aspects which may be wrongly evaluated with unsuitable measures.

2   Recent Scene Detection Techniques

Video decomposition techniques aim to partition a video into sequences, like shots or scenes. Shots are elementary structural segments that are defined as sequences of images taken without interruption by a single camera. Scenes, on the contrary, are often defined as series of temporally contiguous shots characterized by overlapping links that connect shots with similar content [5]. Most of the existing works can be roughly categorized into three categories: *rule-based methods*, that consider the way a scene is structured in professional movie production, *graph-based methods*, where shots are arranged in a graph representation, and *clustering-based methods*. They can rely on visual, audio, and textual features.

We focus our evaluation on three different scene detection algorithms. We propose a clustering approach, where we modify the standard spectral clustering algorithm in order to produce temporally consistent clusters; we evaluate the method in [4], where scene boundaries are detected from the alignment score of symbolic sequences, and the multimodal approach presented in [7].

A Spectral Clustering Approach. Our scene detection method generates scenes by grouping adjacent shots. Shots are described by means of color histograms, hence relying on visual features only: given a video, we compute a three-dimensional histogram for each frame, by quantizing each RGB channel in eight bins, for a total of 512 bins. Then, we sum histograms from frames belonging to the same shot, thus obtaining a single L_1-normalized histogram for each shot.

In contrast to other approaches that used spectral clustering for scene detection, we build a similarity matrix that jointly describes appearance similarity and temporal proximity. Its generic element κ_{ij} defines the similarity between shots $\mathbf{x}_i$ and $\mathbf{x}_j$ as

$$\kappa_{ij} = \exp\left(-\frac{d_1^2(\psi(\mathbf{x}_i), \psi(\mathbf{x}_j)) + \alpha \cdot d_2^2(\mathbf{x}_i, \mathbf{x}_j)}{2\sigma^2} \right) \qquad (1)$$

where $\psi(\mathbf{x}_i)$ is the normalized histogram of shot $\mathbf{x}_i$, d_1^2 is the Bhattacharyya distance and $d_2^2(\mathbf{x}_i, \mathbf{x}_j)$ is the normalized temporal distance between shot $\mathbf{x}_i$ and shot $\mathbf{x}_j$, while the parameter α tunes the relative importance of color similarity and temporal distance. To describe temporal distance between frames, $d_2^2(\mathbf{x}_i, \mathbf{x}_j)$ is defined as

$$d_2^2(\mathbf{x}_i, \mathbf{x}_j) = \frac{|m_i - m_j|}{l} \qquad (2)$$

where m_i is the index of the central frame of shot $\mathbf{x}_i$, and l is the total number of frames in the video. The spectral clustering algorithm is then applied to the similarity matrix, using the Normalized Laplacian and the maximum eigen-gap criterion to select k, that therefore is equal to $\arg\max |\lambda_i - \lambda_{i-1}|$, where λ_i is the i-th eigenvalue of the Normalized Laplacian.

Fig. 1. Effect of α (from left to right 0, 0.5 and 1) on similarity matrix κ_{ij}. Higher values of α enforce connections between near shots and increase the quality of the detected scenes (best viewed in color).

As shown in Fig. 1, the effect of applying increasing values of α to the similarity matrix is to raise the similarities of adjacent shots, therefore boosting the temporal consistency of the resulting groups. Of course, this does not guarantee a completely temporal consistent clustering (i.e. some clusters may still contain non-adjacent shots); at the same time, too high values of α would lead to a segmentation that ignores color dissimilarity. The final scene boundaries are created between adjacent shots that do not belong to the same cluster.

A Sequence Alignment Approach. The method presented in [4], unlike the previous one, represents shots by means of key-frames. The first step of this method, therefore, is to extract several key-frames from each shot: frames from a shot are clustered using the spectral clustering algorithm, color histograms as features, and the euclidean distance to compute the similarity matrix. The number of clusters is selected by applying a threshold Th on the eigenvalues of the Normalized Laplacian.

The distance between a pair of shots is defined as the maximum similarity between key-frames belonging to the two shots, computed using histogram intersection. Shots are clustered using again spectral clustering and the aforesaid distance measure, and then labeled according to the clusters they belong to. The same threshold Th is used to select the number of clusters at this step.

Finally, to create scene boundaries, they compare successive non-overlapping windows of shot labels using a modified version of the Needleman-Wunsh algorithm, that considers the visual similarity of shot clusters and the frequency of sequential labels in the video.

A Multimodal Technique. The method in [7] extends the Shot Transition Graph (STG) using multimodal low-level and high-level features. To this aim, multiple STGs are constructed, one for each kind of feature, and then a probabilistic merging process is used to combine their results.

The used features include visual features, such as HSV histograms, outputs of visual concept detectors trained using the Bag of Words approach, and audio features, like background conditions, speaker histogram, and model vectors constructed from the responses of a number of audio event detectors.

3 Measures for Evaluating Scene Segmentation

To evaluate the results of the aforementioned approaches, we organize evaluation measures in three categories: *boundary-level measures*, that consider the problem of scene detection as a boundary detection problem, and therefore evaluate correctly and wrongly detected boundaries; *shot-level measures* that, on the contrary, compare the number of corresponding or overlapping shots between the ground truth and the detected segmentation, and *frame-level measures*, that consider the number of frames instead of the number of shots.

Boundary Level. The first level to assess the quality of a scene segmentation is to count correctly and wrongly detected boundaries, without considering the temporal distance between a ground truth cut and the nearest detected cut. The most used measures in this context are precision and recall, together with the F-Score measure, that summarizes both. Precision is the ratio of the number of correctly identified scenes boundaries to the total number of scenes detected by the algorithm. Recall is the ratio of the number of correctly identified boundaries to the total number of scenes in the ground truth.

Of course this kind of evaluation does not discern the seriousness of an error: if a boundary is detected one shot before or after its ground truth position, an error is counted in recall as if the boundary was not detected at all, and in precision as if the boundary was put far away. This issue appears to be felt also by other authors, with the result that sometimes a tolerance factor is used. For example, [6] uses a *best match* method with a sliding window of 30 s, so that a detected boundary is considered correct if it matches a ground truth boundary in the sliding window.

Fig. 2. Samples results on our dataset. Row (a) shows the ground-truth segmentation, (b) the individual shots boundaries, row (c) shows the results of our method, (d) those of [7] and (e) those of [4] (best viewed in color).

Shot Level. On an different level, detected scene can be evaluated with regards to their compliance to the ground truth in terms of overlap. Vendrig *et al.* [8], for example, proposed the Coverage and Overflow measures. Coverage C measures the quantity of shots belonging to the same scene correctly grouped together, while Overflow $\mathcal{O}$ evaluates to what extent shots not belonging to the same scene are erroneously grouped together. Formally, given the set of automatically detected scenes $\mathbf{s} = [\mathbf{s}_1, \mathbf{s}_2, ..., \mathbf{s}_m]$, and the ground truth $\tilde{\mathbf{s}} = [\tilde{\mathbf{s}}_1, \tilde{\mathbf{s}}_2, ..., \tilde{\mathbf{s}}_n]$, where each element of $\mathbf{s}$ and $\tilde{\mathbf{s}}$ is a set of shot indexes, the coverage C_t of scene $\tilde{\mathbf{s}}_t$ is proportional to the longest overlap between $\mathbf{s}_i$ and $\tilde{\mathbf{s}}_t$:

$$C_t = \frac{\max_{i=1...,m} \#(\mathbf{s}_i \cap \tilde{\mathbf{s}}_t)}{\#(\tilde{\mathbf{s}}_t)} \tag{3}$$

where $\#(\mathbf{s}_i)$ is the number of shots in scene $\mathbf{s}_i$. The overflow of a scene $\tilde{\mathbf{s}}_t$, $\mathcal{O}_t$, is the amount of overlap of every $\mathbf{s}_i$ corresponding to $\tilde{\mathbf{s}}_t$ with the two surrounding scenes $\tilde{\mathbf{s}}_{t-1}$ and $\tilde{\mathbf{s}}_{t+1}$:

$$\mathcal{O}_t = \frac{\sum_{i=1}^{m} \#(\mathbf{s}_i \setminus \tilde{\mathbf{s}}_t) \cdot \min(1, \#(\mathbf{s}_i \cap \tilde{\mathbf{s}}_t))}{\#(\tilde{\mathbf{s}}_{t-1}) + \#(\tilde{\mathbf{s}}_{t+1})} \tag{4}$$

The computed per-scene measures can then be aggregated into values for an entire video as follows:

$$C = \sum_{t=1}^{n} C_t \cdot \frac{\#(\tilde{\mathbf{s}}_t)}{\sum \#(\tilde{\mathbf{s}}_i)}, \quad \mathcal{O} = \sum_{t=1}^{n} \mathcal{O}_t \cdot \frac{\#(\tilde{\mathbf{s}}_t)}{\sum \#(\tilde{\mathbf{s}}_i)} \tag{5}$$

finally, an F-Score measure can be defined to combine Coverage and Overflow, by taking the harmonic mean of C and $1 - \mathcal{O}$.

Frame Level. We identify two drawbacks of Vendrig's measures, hence propose an improved definition of these. The first one is that, being computed at the shot level, an error on a short shot is given the same importance of an error on a very long shot. On the other hand, we propose to normalize $\mathcal{O}_t$ with respect to the length of $\tilde{\mathbf{s}}_t$ instead of that of $\tilde{\mathbf{s}}_{t-1}$ and $\tilde{\mathbf{s}}_{t+1}$, since we believe that the amount of error due to overflowing should be related to the current scene length, instead of its two neighbors. As an example, consider a ground truth segmentation where a long scene is surrounded by two short scenes: if the detected scene is the union of all three, the actual amount of overflow for the middle scene is quite small, while the usage of shot-level measures would result in a 100 % overflow.

Therefore, we propose the Coverage* and Overflow* metrics, where the cardinality operator $\#$ is replaced with the number of frames of a scene, $l(\mathbf{s}_i)$, and overflow is redefined as follows:

$$\mathcal{O}_t^* = \min \left(1, \frac{\sum_{i=1}^{m} l(\mathbf{s}_i \setminus \tilde{\mathbf{s}}_t) \cdot \min(1, l(\mathbf{s}_i \cap \tilde{\mathbf{s}}_t))}{l(\tilde{\mathbf{s}}_t)} \right) \tag{6}$$

Note that we limit the amount of overflow to one. The corresponding C^* and $\mathcal{O}^*$ for an entire video can be obtained in the same way of Eq. 5, using the newly defined cardinality operator.

4   Evaluation

We evaluate the aforesaid measures and algorithms on a collection of ten challenging broadcasting videos from the Rai Scuola video archive[1], mainly doc-
umentaries and talk shows. Shots have been obtained running the state of
the art shot detector of [1] and manually grouped into scenes by a set of
human experts to define the ground truth. Our dataset and the corresponding annotations are available for download at http://imagelab.ing.unimore.it/
files/RaiSceneDetection.zip. We reimplemented the approach in [4] and used the
executable of [7] provided by the authors. The threshold Th of [4] was selected
to maximize the performance on our dataset, and α was set to 0.05 in all our
experiments.

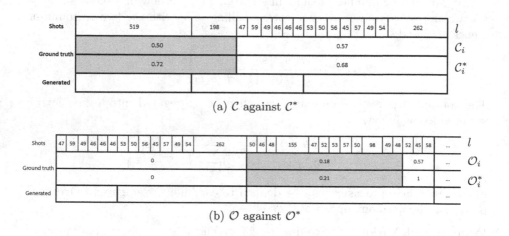

(a) $\mathcal{C}$ against $\mathcal{C}^*$

(b) $\mathcal{O}$ against $\mathcal{O}^*$

Fig. 3. Comparison of shot level and frame level measures.

Tables 1, 2 and 3 compare the three different approaches using Boundary
level, Shot level and Frame level metrics. As show in Table 1, detected boundaries
rarely correspond to ground truth boundaries exactly, therefore leading to poor
results in terms of precision and recall, even when considering a recent and state-
of-the-art approach like [7]. The difference between the results obtained with shot
and frame level measures, on the other hand, are produced by the alteration of
the cardinality operator and by the change of normalization in Overfow*.

To visualize the effect of our improved definition of coverage, consider Fig. 3a,
where we compare the two definitions of coverage on a frame sequences from our
dataset. First row shows the detected shots and their corresponding length in
frames, while the second and the third rows show the ground truth and generated scene segmentation. The first ground truth scene, according to Vendrig's
definition, gets a 0.5 coverage, since the generated scene covers one shot out of

---
[1] http://www.scuola.rai.it.

Table 1. Performance comparison using Boundary level metrics.

Video	Spectral clustering			Chasanis et al. [4]			Sidiropoulos et al. [7]		
	F-Score	Precision	Recall	F-Score	Precision	Recall	F-Score	Precision	Recall
V_1	0.12	0.09	0.17	0.25	0.20	0.33	**0.29**	0.25	0.33
V_2	**0.36**	0.27	0.55	0.00	0.00	0.00	0.30	0.33	0.27
V_3	**0.37**	0.29	0.53	0.13	0.13	0.13	0.31	0.36	0.27
V_4	**0.30**	0.23	0.43	0.10	0.10	0.10	0.22	0.50	0.14
V_5	**0.44**	0.31	0.75	0.00	0.00	0.00	0.36	0.31	0.42
V_6	0.18	0.10	0.75	0.00	0.00	0.00	**0.36**	0.29	0.50
V_7	**0.18**	0.33	0.13	0.00	0.00	0.00	0.13	0.13	0.13
V_8	0.10	0.06	0.27	0.13	0.10	0.18	**0.21**	0.25	0.18
V_9	**0.25**	0.16	0.62	0.00	0.00	0.00	0.21	0.33	0.15
V_{10}	0.23	0.15	0.60	**0.26**	0.38	0.20	0.19	0.33	0.13
Average	0.25	0.20	0.48	0.09	0.09	0.09	**0.26**	0.31	0.25

Table 2. Performance comparison using Shot level metrics.

Video	Spectral clustering			Chasanis et al. [4]			Sidiropoulos et al. [7]		
	F-Score	$\mathcal{C}$	$\mathcal{O}$	F-Score	$\mathcal{C}$	$\mathcal{O}$	F-Score	$\mathcal{C}$	$\mathcal{O}$
V_1	0.64	0.81	0.48	0.70	0.64	0.24	**0.72**	0.84	0.37
V_2	**0.68**	0.61	0.22	0.36	0.80	0.77	0.59	0.85	0.55
V_3	**0.65**	0.68	0.38	0.58	0.73	0.52	0.58	0.90	0.57
V_4	**0.74**	0.69	0.22	0.50	0.65	0.60	0.33	0.94	0.80
V_5	**0.77**	0.68	0.11	0.25	0.93	0.86	0.66	0.76	0.41
V_6	0.51	0.37	0.17	0.18	0.89	0.90	**0.71**	0.77	0.34
V_7	0.30	0.97	0.82	0.37	0.70	0.75	**0.51**	0.78	0.62
V_8	0.59	0.53	0.33	**0.62**	0.57	0.32	0.45	0.88	0.70
V_9	**0.67**	0.55	0.15	0.27	0.87	0.84	0.43	0.92	0.72
V_{10}	**0.57**	0.42	0.12	0.54	0.91	0.62	0.44	0.94	0.71
Average	**0.61**	0.63	0.30	0.44	0.77	0.64	0.54	0.86	0.58

two. Our definition, on the contrary, considers the number of frames inside a shot, and therefore accounts for the fact the first shot is longer than the second. This results in a 0.72 coverage, which is surely a more realistic numerical result.

In Fig. 3b, instead, we compare Overflow and Overflow*. As it can be seen, the overflow of the first ground truth scene is zero according to both measures, since the corresponding generated scenes don't overlap with others ground truth scenes, while the numerical results for the second ground truth scenes are quite similar, even if Overflow* considers the number of frames and has a different kind of normalization. The difference between our definition and Vendrig's one becomes clear in the third ground truth scene, where our measure reports a 100 % overflow, since the third generated scene overlaps the ground truth one

Table 3. Performance comparison using the Frame level metrics.

Video	Spectral clustering			Chasanis *et al.* [4]			Sidiropoulos *et al.* [7]		
	F-Score*	C^*	O^*	F-Score*	C^*	O^*	F-Score*	C^*	O^*
V_1	0.69	0.82	0.40	**0.70**	0.65	0.24	**0.70**	0.63	0.20
V_2	**0.76**	0.77	0.24	0.60	0.91	0.55	0.61	0.73	0.47
V_3	**0.69**	0.77	0.37	0.51	0.87	0.64	0.51	0.89	0.64
V_4	**0.68**	0.70	0.34	0.54	0.70	0.56	0.22	0.95	0.88
V_5	**0.77**	0.68	0.13	0.34	0.92	0.79	0.57	0.66	0.50
V_6	0.58	0.42	0.06	0.20	0.89	0.88	**0.74**	0.72	0.24
V_7	0.39	0.95	0.76	0.37	0.75	0.76	**0.56**	0.69	0.53
V_8	**0.63**	0.66	0.40	0.59	0.65	0.47	0.15	0.89	0.92
V_9	**0.77**	0.70	0.14	0.07	0.83	0.96	0.15	0.94	0.92
V_{10}	**0.65**	0.53	0.15	0.50	0.93	0.66	0.11	0.93	0.94
Average	**0.66**	0.70	0.30	0.44	0.81	0.65	0.43	0.80	0.63

by more than its length, while Vendrig's definition only reports a 0.57 overflow, since the next scene, which has no intersection with the detected one, is 9 shots long.

Finally, we note that the three metrics behave differently and there is not a complete agreement among them: [4] performs worse than the other two methods according to all the three measures, while [7] performs equal or slightly worse than our spectral clustering approach according to Boundary level and Shot level metrics. When shot duration is taken into account, using Frame level metrics, our spectral clustering approach considerably outperforms all the others approaches.

5 Conclusions

We have investigated the problem of evaluating scene detection algorithms and suggested metrics that try to reduce the gap between the numerical evaluation and the expected qualitative results. Experiments have been conducted on three different groups of metrics and on three different and recent approaches to scene segmentation. Results shows that the problem of scene detection is still far from being solved, and that simple approaches like our spectral clustering technique can sometimes achieve better or equivalent results than more complex methods.

Acknowledgments. This work was carried out within the project "Città educante" (CTN01_00034_393801) of the National Technological Cluster on Smart Communities co funded by the Italian Ministry of Education, University and Research - MIUR.

References

1. Apostolidis, E., Mezaris, V.: Fast shot segmentation combining global and local visual descriptors. In: IEEE International Conference on Acoustics, Speech and Signal Process, pp. 6583–6587 (2014)
2. Baraldi, L., Paci, F., Serra, G., Benini, L., Cucchiara, R.: Gesture recognition in ego-centric videos using dense trajectories and hand segmentation. In: Proceedings of 10th IEEE Embedded Vision Workshop (EVW), Columbus, Ohio, June 2014
3. Bertini, M., Del Bimbo, A., Serra, G., Torniai, C., Cucchiara, R., Grana, C., Vezzani, R.: Dynamic pictorially enriched ontologies for video digital libraries. IEEE MultiMedia 16(2), 41–51 (2009)
4. Chasanis, V.T., Likas, C., Galatsanos, N.P.: Scene detection in videos using shot clustering and sequence alignment. IEEE Trans. Multimedia 11(1), 89–100 (2009)
5. Hanjalic, A., Lagendijk, R.L., Biemond, J.: Automated high-level movie segmentation for advanced video-retrieval systems. IEEE Trans. Circuits Syst. Video Technol. 9(4), 580–588 (1999)
6. Rasheed, Z., Shah, M.: Detection and representation of scenes in videos. IEEE Trans. Multimedia 7(6), 1097–1105 (2005)
7. Sidiropoulos, P., Mezaris, V., Kompatsiaris, I., Meinedo, H., Bugalho, M., Trancoso, I.: Temporal video segmentation to scenes using high-level audiovisual features. IEEE Trans. Circuits Syst. Video Technol. 21(8), 1163–1177 (2011)
8. Vendrig, J., Worring, M.: Systematic evaluation of logical story unit segmentation. IEEE Trans. Multimedia 4(4), 492–499 (2002)

Threshold of Graph-Based Volumetric Segmentation

Dumitru Dan Burdescu[1(✉)], Liana Stanescu[1], Marius Brezovan[1],
Cosmin Stoica Spahiu[1], and Florin Slabu[2]

[1] Computers and Information Technology Department, Faculty of Automatics,
Computers and Electronics, University of Craiova,
Bvd. Decebal, Nr. 107, 200440 Craiova, Dolj, Romania
{dburdescu,lia_stanescu}@yahoo.com,
{mbrezovan,stoica_cosmin}@software.ucv.ro
[2] Departament of Computer Science, University of Craiova,
A.I Cuza Street, Nr. 13, 200585 Craiova, Dolj, Romania
f.slabu@yahoo.com

Abstract. Among the many approaches in performing image segmentation, graph based approach is gaining popularity primarily due to its ability in reflecting global image properties. Volumetric image segmentation can simply result an image partition composed by relevant regions, but the most fundamental challenge in segmentation algorithm is to precisely define the spatial extent of some object, which may be represented by the union of multiple regions. The aim in this paper is to present a new and efficient method as complexity to detect visual objects from color volumetric images and efficient threshold. We present a unified framework for original volumetric segmentation that uses a tree-hexagonal structure defined on the set of the voxels. The advantage of using a tree-hexagonal network superposed over the initial image voxels is that it reduces the execution time and the memory space used, without losing the initial resolution of the image.

Keywords: Volumetric segmentation · Graph-based segmentation · Dissimilarity · Threshold

1 Introduction and Related Work

Segmentation is the process of partitioning an image into non-intersecting regions such that each region is homogeneous and the union of no two adjacent regions is homogeneous.

Volumetric Segmentation can be formulated as a spatial graph partitioning and optimization problem [1, 2].

The graph theoretic formulation of digital image segmentation is as follows:

1. The set of points in an arbitrary feature space are represented as a weighted undirected spatial graph G = (V, E), where the nodes of the graph are the points in the feature space.

© Springer International Publishing Switzerland 2015
R. Paredes et al. (Eds.): IbPRIA 2015, LNCS 9117, pp. 404–414, 2015.
DOI: 10.1007/978-3-319-19390-8_46

2. An edge is formed between every pair of nodes yielding a dense or complete graph.
3. The weight on each edge, $w(i,j)$ is a function of the similarity between nodes 'i'and 'j'.
4. Partition the set of vertices into disjoint sets $V_1, V_2, \ldots, V_K$ where by some measure the similarity among the vertices in a set V_i is high and, across different sets V_i, V_j is low.

In the digital image segmentation and data clustering community, there has been much previous work using variations of the minimal spanning tree or limited neighborhood set approaches [3]. Although those use efficient computational methods, the segmentation criteria used in most of them are based on local properties of the spatial graph.

To overcome the problem of fixed threshold in [4] ones determine the normalized weight of an edge by using the smallest weight incident on the vertices touching that edge. Other methods [5, 6] use an adaptive criterion that depends on local properties rather than global ones. In contrast with the simple graph-based methods, cut-criterion methods capture the non-local cuts in a graph are designed to minimize the similarity between pixels that are being split [7, 8]. The normalized cut criterion [8] takes into consideration self similarity of regions. An alternative to the graph cut approach is to look for cycles in a graph embedded in the image plane. In [9] the quality of each cycle is normalized in a way that is closely related to the normalized cuts approach. Other approaches to planar image segmentation consist of splitting and merging regions according to how well each region fulfills some uniformity criterion. Such methods [10] use a measure of uniformity of a region. In contrast [5, 6] use a pair-wise region comparison rather than applying a uniformity criterion to each individual region. Complex grouping phenomena can emerge from simple computation on these local cues [11]. A number of approaches to segmentation are based on finding compact clusters in some feature space [12].

Our previous works for planar images [13, 14, 15, 16] are related to the works in [5, 6] in the sense of pair-wise comparison of region similarity. In these papers we extend our previous work for planar images [17, 18] by adding new steps in the volumetric segmentation algorithm that allows us to determine regions closer to it.

2 Constructing a Virtual Tree-Hexagonal Structure

The *segmentation module* creates Tree-Hexagonal Structure (prism cells) defined on the set of the image voxels of the input volumetric image and a spatial grid graph having tree-hexagons as cells of vertices. In order to allow a unitary processing for the multi-level system at this level we store, for each determined component C, the set of the tree-hexagons contained in the region associated to C and the set of tree-hexagons located at the boundary of the component. In addition for each component the dominant color of the region is extracted. This implies that there will be less ambiguity in defining boundaries and regions [18]. As a consequence we construct atree-hexagonal structure (prism cells) over the voxels of an input volumetric image, as presented in Fig. 1.

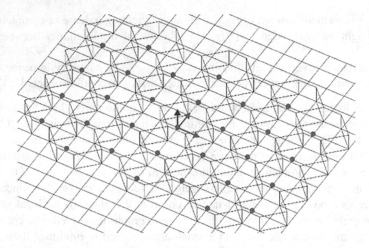

Fig. 1. Virtual tree-hexagonal structure constructed on the spatial image voxels

Let I be an initial volumetric image having the three dimensions h × w × z (e.g. a matrix having 'h' rows, 'w' columns and 'z' deep of matrix voxels). In order to construct a tree-hexagonal grid (prism cells) on these voxels we retain an eventually smaller image with:

$$h' = h - (h - 1) \bmod 2$$

$$w' = w - w \bmod 4$$

$$z' = z \tag{1}$$

In the reduced image at most the last line of voxels and at most the last three columns and deep of matrix of voxels are lost, assuming that for the initial image h > 3 and w > 4 and z ≥ 1, that is a convenient restriction for input images.

Each tree-hexagon (prism cell) from the tree-hexagonal grid contains sixteen voxels: - such twelve voxels from the frontier and four interior frontiers of voxels. Because tree-hexagons voxels from an image have integer values as coordinates we select always the left up voxel from the four interior voxels to represent with approximation the gravity center of the tree-hexagon, denoted by the pseudo-gravity center. We use a simple scheme of addressing for the tree-hexagons of the tree-hexagonal grid that encodes the volumetric location of the pseudo-gravity centers of the tree-hexagons as presented in Fig. 1.

Each tree-hexagon (prism cell) represents an elementary item and the entire virtual tree-hexagonal structure represents a spatial grid graph, $G = (V; E)$, where each tree-hexagon H in this structure has a corresponding vertex v ∈ V. The set E of edges is constructed by connecting tree-hexagons that are neighbors in 8-connected sense.

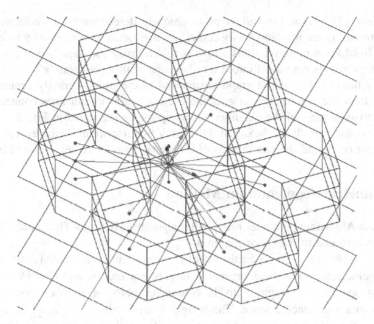

Fig. 2. The grid graph constructed on the pseudo-gravity centers of the tree-hexagonal grid

The vertices of this graph correspond to the pseudo-gravity centers of the hexagons from the tree-hexagonal grid and the edges are straight lines connecting the pseudo gravity centers of the neighboring hexagons, as presented in Fig. 2.

Let $h \times w \times z$ the three dimension of the initial volumetric image verifying the previous restriction. Given the coordinates $\langle 1 ; c ; d \rangle$ of a voxel 'p' from the input volumetric image, we use the linear function,

$$ip_{h;w;z} = (1-1) \times w \times z(c-1)z + d \qquad (2)$$

in order to determine an unique index for the voxel.

It is easy to verify that the function 'ip' defined by the Eq. (2) is bijective.Its inverse function is given by:

$$ip_{h;w;z}^{-1} = \langle 1 ; c ; d \rangle \qquad (3)$$

where:

$$l = k/(w \times z) \qquad (4)$$

$$c = (k - (l-1) \times w \times z)/z \qquad (5)$$

$$d = k - (l-1) \times w \times z + (c-1) \times z \qquad (6)$$

Relations (4), (5), and (6) allow us to uniquely determine the coordinates of the voxel representing the pseudo-gravity center of a tree-hexagon specified by its index(its address). In addition these relations allow us to determine the sequence of coordinates of all sixteen voxels contained into a tree-hexagon with an address 'k'.

The vertices of this spatial graph correspond to the pseudo-gravity centers of the hexagons from the tree-hexagonal grid and the edges are straight lines connecting the pseudo-gravity centers of the neighboring hexagons, as presented in Fig. 2.

We associate to each tree-hexagon 'H' from V two important attributes representing its dominant color and the coordinates of its pseudo-gravity center, denoted by g(h).

3 Volumetric Segmentation Method

The beneath Algorithm1 includes many other algorithms but only Threshold Algorithm is presents here due to the space required.

Let $V = \{h_1, h_2, \ldots, h_{|V|}\}$ be the set of tree-hexagons (prism cells) constructed on the volumetric image voxels as presented in previous section and $G = (V, E)$ be the undirected spatial grid-graph, with E containing pairs of tree-hexagons that are neighbors in a 8-connected sense. The weight of each edge $e = (h_i, h_j)$ is denote by $w(e)$, or similarly by $w(h_i, h_j)$, and it represents the dissimilarity between neighboring elements 'h_i' and 'h_j' in a some feature space. Components of an image represent compact regions containing voxels with similar properties. Thus the set V of vertices of the spatial graph G is partitioned into disjoint sets, each subset representing a distinct visual object of the initial spatial image.

A segmentation, S, of V is a partition of V such that each component $C \in S$ corresponds to a connected component in a spanning sub-graph

$$GS = (V, ES) \text{ of } G, \text{ with } ES \subseteq E \tag{7}$$

The set of edges E–ES that are eliminated connect vertices from distinct components. The common boundary between two connected components $C', C'' \in S$ represents the set of edges connecting vertices from the two components:

$$cb(C', C'') = \{(h_i, h_j) \in E \mid h_i C', h_j \in C''\} \tag{8}$$

The set of edges E−ES represents the boundary between all components in S. This set is denoted by *bound(S)* and it is defined as follows:

$$bound(S) = \cup_{C', C'' \in S} cb(C', C'') \tag{9}$$

In order to simplify notations throughout the paper we use C_i to denote the component of a segmentation S that contains the vertex $h_i \in V$. The key element in this definition *is the evidence for a boundary between two components.*

Definition 1. Let $G = (V; E)$ be the undirected spatial graph constructed on the tree-hexagonal structure of an input digital image, with $V = \{h_1, h_2, \ldots, h_{|V|}\}$. A proper segmentation of V, is a partition S of V such that there exists a sequence $\langle S_i, S_{i+1}, \ldots, S_{f-1}, S_f \rangle$ of segmentations of V for which:

- $S = S_f$ is the final segmentation and S_i, is the initial segmentation,
- S_j is a proper refinement of S_{j+1}, (i.e., $S_j \subset S_{j+1}$) for each $j = i, \ldots, f - 1$,
- segmentation S_j is too fine, for each $j = i, \ldots, f - 1$,
- any segmentation S_1 such that $S_f \subset S_1$, is too coarse,
- segmentation S_f is neither too coarse no too fine.

The volumetric segmentation algorithm starts with the most refined segmentation, $S_0 = \{\{h_1\}, \{h_2\}, \ldots, \{h_{|V|}\}\}$ and it constructs a sequence of segmentations until a proper segmentation is achieved. Each segmentation S_j is obtained from the segmentation S_{j-1} by merging two or more connected components for there is no evidence for a boundary between them [18]. The evidence for a boundary between two components is determined taking into consideration some features in some model of the digital image. When starting, for a certain number of segmentation components the only considered feature is the color of the volumes associated to the components and in this case we use a *color based region* model. When the components became complex and contain too much tree-hexagons, the color model is not sufficient and geometric features together with color information are considered. In this case we use a *syntactic based region* with a color-based region model for volumes. In addition syntactic features bring supplementary information for merging similar volumes in order determine objects.

Definition 2. Let $G = (V; E)$ be the undirected spatial graph constructed on the tree-hexagonal structure of a volumetric input image and S a color-based segmentation of V . The segmentation S is too fine in the color-based region model if there is a pair of components $C'; C'' \in S$ for which adjacent$(C', C'') = $ true and ExtVar$(C'; C'') = $ IntVar$(C'; C'') + $ tresh $(C'; C'')$ where the adaptive and efficient threshold tresh $(C'; C'')$ is given by

$$\text{tresh } (C'; C'') = {}^{tresh}/\min(|C'|; |C''|); \tag{10}$$

where $|C|$ denotes the size of the component C and the threshold '*tresh*' is a global adaptive value defined by using a statistical model in Algorithm 1.

The maximum internal contrast between two components $C'; C'' \in S$ is defined as follows: IntVar$(C'; C'') = \max\{\text{IntVar}(C'); \text{IntVar}(C'')\}$

Let $G = (V, E)$ be the initial spatial graph constructed on the tree-hexagonal structure of a volumetric input image. The proposed segmentation algorithm will produce a proper segmentation of V according to the Definition 1. We start our method with Volumetric Segmentation Algorithm which calls other procedures and functions.

Algorithm 1. Volumetric Segmentation Algorithm

1: **procedure** SEGMENTATION(l, c, d,P, H, Comp)
2: **Input** l, c, d, P
3: **Output** H, Comp
4: $H\leftarrow$*CREATEHEXAGONALSTRUCTURE(l, c, d, P)
5: $G\leftarrow$*CREATEINITIALGRAPH(l, c, d, P,H)
6: *CREATECOLORPARTITION(G,H,Bound)
7: G' $\leftarrow$*EXTRACTGRAPH(G,Bound, $th^k g$)
8: *CREATESYNTACTICPARTITION(G,G', $th^k g$)
9: Comp$\leftarrow$*EXTRACTFINALCOMPONENTS(G')
10: **end procedure**

The input parameters represent the volumetric image resulted after the pre-processing operation: the array P of the spatial image voxels structured in '1' lines and 'c' columns and 'd' depths. The output parameters of the volumetric segmentation procedure will be used by the contour extraction procedure: the tree-hexagonal grid stored in the array of tree-hexagons H, and the array *Comp* representing the set of determined components associated to the objects in the input spatial image. The global parameter $th^k g$ is the thresholds and it is calculated by (10).

The color-based segmentation and the syntactic-based segmentation are determined by the procedures CREATECOLORPARTITION and CREATESYNTACTICPAR-TITION respectively.

The color-based and syntactic-based segmentation algorithms use the tree-hexagonal structure H created by the function CREATEHEXAGONALSTRUCTURE over the voxels of the initial spatial image, and the initial triangular grid graph G created by the function CREATEINITIALGRAPH. Because the syntactic-based segmentation algorithm uses a graph contraction procedure, CREATESYNTACTICPARTITION uses a different graph, G', extracted by the procedure EXTRACT GRAPH after the color-based segmentation finishes.

Both algorithms for determining the color-based and syntactic based segmentation use and modify a global variable (denoted by CC).The variable CC is an array having the same dimension as the array of hexagons 'H'.

The procedure EXTRACTFINALCOMPONENTS determines for each determined component C of Comp, the set $sa(C)$ of tree-hexagons belonging to the component, the set $sp(C)$ of tree-hexagons belonging to the frontier, and the dominant color $c(C)$ of the component.

4   Threshold Algorithm

The global parameter threshold '$th^k g$' is determinate by using Algorithm 1 which calls other algorithms. This threshold value is better used at the Algorithm 2, where the expression tresh(t_i, t_j) is given by the relation (10), where 't_i' and 't_j' representing the components Ct_i and Ct_j respectively.

Algorithm 2. The Threshold Algorithm

1: **function** DETERMINETHRESHOLD(G)
2: **Input** $G = (V,E)$
3: **Output** $\text{th}^k g$
4: *Determine the histogram $\mathbf{g} = [g_1, ..., g_k]^T$
5: $T \leftarrow Tmax \leftarrow 500$; eps$\leftarrow 0.95$; $Iter \leftarrow 10$
6: Init$\leftarrow$*INITIALESTIMATE()
7: Beta$max \leftarrow 1/Tmax$
8: $tmax \leftarrow \lceil \log(Betamax)/\log(eps) \rceil$
9: **for all** $t \leftarrow 0$, $tmax-1$ **do**
10: Beta$\leftarrow 1/T$
11: Teta(0) $\leftarrow$ Teta
12: **for all** $l \leftarrow 1$, $Iter$ **do**
13: **for all** $i \leftarrow 1$, k and $j \leftarrow 1,2$ **do**
14: *Compute $w_{i,j,beta}$
15: **end for**
16: **for** $j \leftarrow 1,2$ **do**
17: *Compute $alfa^{(t+1)}{}_j$, $a^{(t+1)}{}_j$, and $b^{(t+1)}{}_j$
18: **end for**
19: **end for**
20: $T \leftarrow T \times$ eps
21: Teta$\leftarrow$Teta(t)
22: **end for**
23: $\text{th}^k g \leftarrow$*DISTRIBINTERSECTION(Teta)
24: **return** $\text{th}^k g$
25: **end function**

We used a fixed number of iterations for the algorithm for two reasons:

(a) we reduce the computational complexity of the entire algorithm, and
(b) the schedule of the algorithm assure sufficiently good estimation of the vector of parameters Teta.

The function DISTRIBINTERSECTION calculates the threshold '$th^k g$' at the intersection of the two determined Gaussian distributions, as presented in Fig. 3.

The computational complexity of this function is $O(k)$, because it implements a linear searching by traversing in parallel two vectors of dimension 'k', where 'k' is the dimension of the histogram $k(x)$.

The computational complexity of the function INITIALESTIMATE is also $O(k)$. The computational complexity of the histogram generation is $O(m)$, where 'm' represents the cardinal of the set E, because this operation involves a traversal of the list representing the set of the edges E.

The computational complexity of the algorithm is given by the running time for estimating the values $w_{i,j,Beta}$, $alfa_j$, a_j and b_j.

1. The estimation value for $w_{i,j,Beta}$ can be determinate in constant time, because it involves the estimation of the Gamma function, and this estimation can be done in constant time [19].

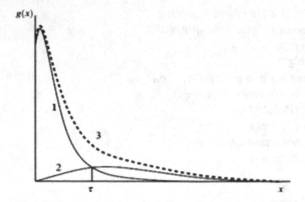

Fig. 3. A typical histogram of color distances (3) with the estimated densities of the non-boundary (1) and boundary distances (2)

2. The running time for estimating $alfa_j$ and b_j is $t1 = O(k)$.
3. The running time for estimating a_j is also $t2 = O(k)$, by the fact that the *trigamma* function, $Psi - 1(x)$, can be estimated by using a Newton method in maximum 5 iterations with an approximation of 15 digits [19].

It follows that the running time for a iteration of the inner loop of the Algorithm 2 related to the algorithm is $t3 = O(k)$, and the running time for a iteration of the external loop is also $t4 = O(k)$, because *Iter* is a constant. In conclusion the running time for algorithm is $t5 = O(k)$, because *tmax*, the length of the sequence of values associated to the schedule of the algorithm, is also a constant in the algorithm.

We conclude that the computational complexity of Algorithm 2 is linear and

$$T(DETERMINETHRESHOLD) = O(m), \tag{11}$$

because the number of the bins of the histogram is less than the number of the edges of the graph, $k < m$.

The pair-wise comparison predicate can be defined as a weighted sum of the dissimilarity functions. The weights associated to the dissimilarity functions are determined also in an adaptive way.

5 Conclusions

The problems of segmentation algorithms are well-studied one in literature and there are a wide variety of approaches that are used. We propose a novel volumetric image segmentation algorithm that is based on graph-based segmentation method and then we introduced an efficient threshold as complexity of volumetric segmentation algorithm. The key to the whole algorithm of volumetric segmentation is the structure of prism cells. The algorithm runs in time linear in the number of spatial graph edges and is also fast in practice.

Enhancement and generalization of this method is possible in several further directions. First, it could be modified to handle open curves for the purpose of medical diagnosis. Second, research direction is the using of composed shape indexing for both semantic and geometric image reasoning. Incorporation of the fuzzy set theory into graph based frameworks can achieve enhanced segmentation performances.

References

1. Silberman, N., Hoiem, D., Kohli, P., Fergus, R.: Indoor segmentation and support inference from RGBD images. In: Fitzgibbon, A., Lazebnik, S., Perona, P., Sato, Y., Schmid, C. (eds.) ECCV 2012, Part V. LNCS, vol. 7576, pp. 746–760. Springer, Heidelberg (2012)
2. All'ene, C., Audibert, J.-Y., Couprie, M., Keriven, R.: Some links between extremum spanning forests, watersheds and min-cuts. Image Vis. Comput. **8**(10), 1460–1471 (2010)
3. Grundmann, M., Kwatra, V., Han, M., Essa, I.: Efficient hierarchical graph-based video segmentation. In: Proceedings of IEEE Computer Vision and Pattern Recognition (CVPR), pp. 2141–2148 (2010)
4. Weinlanda, D., Ronfardb, R., Boyerc, E.: A survey of vision-based methods for action representation, segmentation and recognition. Comput. Vis. Image Underst. **115**(2), 224–241 (2011)
5. Felzenszwalb, P., Huttenlocher, W.: Efficient graph-based image segmentation. Int. J. Comput. Vis. **59**(2), 167–181 (2004)
6. Guigues, L., Herve, L., Cocquerez, L.P.: The hierarchy of the cocoons of a graph and its application to image segmentation. Pattern Recogn. Lett. **24**(8), 1059–1066 (2003)
7. Gdalyahu, Y., Weinshall, D., Werman, M.: Self organization in vision: stochastic clustering for image segmentation, perceptual grouping, and image database organization. IEEE Trans. Pattern Anal. Mach. Intell. **23**(10), 1053–1074 (2001)
8. Shi, J., Malik, J.: Normalized cuts and image segmentation. IEEE Trans. Pattern Anal. Mach. Intell. **22**(8), 885–905 (2000)
9. Jermyn, I., Ishikawa, H.: Globally optimal regions and boundaries as minimum ratio weight cycles. IEEE Trans. Pattern Anal. Mach. Intell. **23**(8), 1075–1088 (2001)
10. Cooper, M.: The tractibility of segmentation and scene analysis. Int. J. Comput. Vis. **30**(1), 27–42 (1998)
11. Malik, J., Belongie, S., Leung, T., Shi, J.: Contour and texture analysis for image segmentation. Int. J. Comput. Vis. **43**(1), 7–27 (2001)
12. Comaniciu, D., Meer, P.: Robust analysis of feature spaces: color image segmentation. IEEE Trans. Pattern Anal. Mach. Intell. **24**(5), 603–619 (2002)
13. Stanescu, L., Burdescu, D., Brezovan, M.: A comparative study of some methods for color medical images segmentation. EURASIP J. Adv. Signal Process. **128**(1), 5–23 (2011)
14. Brezovan, M., Burdescu, D., Ganea, E., Stanescu, L.: An adaptive method for efficient detection of salient visual object from color images. In: Proceedings of the 20th International Conference on Pattern Recognition, Istanbul, Turkey, pp. 2346–2349 (2010)
15. Burdescu, D., Brezovan, M., Ganea, E., Stanescu, L.: A new method for segmentation of images represented in a HSV color space. In: Fitzgibbon, J., Blanc-Talon, S., Philips, D., Sato, Y., Popescu, C., Scheunders, P. (eds.) Advanced Concepts for Intelligent Vision Systems. LNCS, vol. 5807, pp. 606–760. Springer, Heidelberg (2009)
16. Stanescu, L., Burdescu, D., Brezovan, M., Mihai, C.R.G.: Creating New Medical Ontologies for Image Annotation. Springer, New York (2011). ISBN 13: 9781461419082, 10: 1461419085

17. Burdescu, D., Stanescu, L., Brezovan, M., StoicaSpahiu, C.: Computational complexity analysis of the graph extraction algorithm for 3D segmentation. In: IEEE Tenth World Congress on Services-SERVICES 2014, pp. 462–470 (2014). ISBN-13: 978-1-4799-5069-0
18. Burdescu, D.D., Brezovan, M., Stanescu, L., Stoica-Spahiu, C.: A spatial segmentation method. Int. J. Comput. Sci. Appl. **11**(1), 75–100 (2014). ©Technomathematics Research Foundation
19. Cormen, T., Leiserson, C., Rivest, R.: Introduction to Algorithms. MIT Press, Cambridge (1990)

Brain Neural Data Analysis with Feature Space Defined by Descriptive Statistics

Lachezar Bozhkov[1]([⊠]) and Petia Georgieva[2]

[1] Computer Systems Department, Technical University of Sofia,
8 St.Kliment Ohridski Boulevard, 1756 Sofia, Bulgaria
lachezar.bozhkov@gmail.com
[2] DETI/IEETA, University of Aveiro, 3810-193 Aveiro, Portugal
petia@ua.pt

Abstract. We consider learning to discriminate emotional states of human subjects, based on their brain activity observed via Electroencephalogram (EEG). EEG signals are collected while subjects were viewing high arousal images with positive or negative emotional content. This problem is important because such classifiers constitute "virtual sensors" of hidden emotional states, which are useful in psychology science research and clinical applications. The feature selection has a major role.

Recently we have proposed a sequential feature selection (SFS) procedure that reduced the inherent data variability among subjects and led to a high inter-subject emotion recognition accuracy (98 %). However the SFS is a computationally intensive approach that is difficult to apply to any classification model. In this paper we extend that line of research and propose a computationally less involved feature selection technique based on descriptive statistics (mean and standard deviation) of the neural signatures across subjects. This approach reveals to be a good compromise between prediction accuracy and numerical complexity.

Keywords: Affective computing · Emotion valence recognition · Feature reduction · Event related potentials (ERPs)

1 Introduction

Automatic detection and recognition of human emotions is the focus of the research field Affective Computing (AC). Different AC modalities have been investigated such as facial expression, voice, text, body language, posture and more recently also physiological signals such as Galvanic Skin Response (GSR) Electrocardiogram (ECG) or Electroencephalogram (EEG) [1].

Since emotions are known to fluctuate due to internal (brain-driven) or external (stimulus-driven) events, affective neuroscience (AN) emerged as a new AC approach that attempts to find the neural signatures of emotional states [2]. Among various brain imaging modalities [3] (EEG, Magneto Encephalography, functional Magneto Resonance Images, Positron Emission Tomography), the EEG is by far the most studied due to its noninvasiveness, cheap and simple technology. In [4] a comprehensive review of

© Springer International Publishing Switzerland 2015
R. Paredes et al. (Eds.): IbPRIA 2015, LNCS 9117, pp. 415–422, 2015.
DOI: 10.1007/978-3-319-19390-8_47

the EEG-based emotion recognition systems is provided, however only few of them deal with inter subject classification models.

In fact, the major challenge in AC is the attempt to generalize the results across many subjects due to the high brain data variability and the ambiguity in the most relevant features for the decision making. The feature construction is crucial for achieving robust decoding and predictions of emotional states across subjects.

The objective of this paper is to identify the common neural signatures of positive and negative emotional states across various subjects based on Event Related Potentials (ERPs). ERPs are transient components in the EEG generated in response to a stimulus (high arousal images with positive and negative valence in the present study).

Recently, we have proposed a recursive procedure, termed Sequential Feature Selection (SFS), to identify the most relevant features [5]. The inter-subject classification based on the SFS extracted features achieved the record cross validation of 98 %, which outperforms previous results [4]. However, SFS has a quadratic O (n^2) computational complexity that hampers its application to more sophisticated discrimination models. In this paper we propose a linear complexity approach to identify the representative inter-subject features based on descriptive statistics of the initial set of features.

The paper is organized as follows. In Sect. 2 we briefly describe the data set. The proposed statistical feature space reduction is discussed in Sect. 3. The results of the hierarchical voting classification model based on the selected features are presented in Sect. 4. Finally, in Sect. 5 our conclusions are drawn.

2   Data Set

A total of 26 female volunteers participated in the study. The signals were recorded while the volunteers were viewing high arousal images with positive and negative valence. For each image, signals from 21 EEG channels, positioned according to the 10–20 system, and 2 EOG channels (vertical and horizontal) were sampled at 1000 Hz and stored. The signals were recorded while the volunteers were viewing pictures selected from the International Affective Picture System (IAPS) picture repository. A total of 24 high arousal (IAPS rating > 6) images with positive valence (M = 7.29 ± 0.65) and negative valence (M = 1.47 ± 0.24) were selected. Each image was presented 3 times in a pseudo-random order and each trial lasted 3500 ms: during the first 750 ms, a fixation cross was presented, then one of the images was presented during 500 ms and at last a black screen appeared during 2250 ms. The raw EEG signals were first filtered (band-pass filter between 0.1 and 30 Hz.), eye-movement corrected, baseline compensated and segmented into epochs using NeuroScan software. The single-trial signal length is 950 ms with 150 ms before the stimulus onset. The ensemble average for each condition (positive/negative valence) was also computed and filtered using a Butterworth filter of 4th order with passband [0.5–15] Hz. Thus, the filtered ensemble average signals cover the frequency band ranges corresponding to Delta ([0.5–4] Hz), Theta ([4–8] Hz) and Alpha neural activity ([8–12] Hz).

3   Feature Selection

Most of the ERP-based affective state detection systems rely on the frequency content of the signals [4]. The features are measures of the ERP energy in certain frequency bands, as Power Spectral Density (PSD) or Spectral Power Asymmetry.

However, recent findings report evidence about temporal correlates between emotional stimuli processing and the occurrence of subsequent positive and negative potentials, known as waves C1, P1, P2, P3, when the stimulus is loaded with intensive emotions [3]. These waves are associated with specific time of occurrence (early/late waves). Therefore, in the present study, temporal features (amplitudes and latencies) are extracted from the filtered, segmented and ensemble averaged ERP data. Starting by the localization of the first minimum after time = 0 s, the features are defined as a sequence of the local positive and negative picks, and their respective latencies (time of occurrence). Twelve temporal features are stored (Table 1) corresponding to the amplitudes of the first three local minimums (Amin1, Amin2, Amin3), the first three local maximums (Amax1, Amax2, Amax3), and their associated latencies (Lmin1, Lmin2, Lmin3, Lmax1, Lmax2, Lmax3).

Table 1. Temporal features

#	Feature name	Mean & sdv (s)	#	Feature name	Mean & sdv (s)
1	A_{min1}	-0.275 ± 0.145	7	L_{min1}	0.077 ± 0.031
2	A_{max1}	0.066 ± 0.165	8	L_{max1}	0.155 ± 0.054
3	A_{min2}	-0.121 ± 0.148	9	L_{min2}	0.220 ± 0.08
4	A_{max2}	0.124 ± 0.142	10	L_{max2}	0.311 ± 0.099
5	A_{min3}	-0.042 ± 0.121	11	L_{min3}	0.398 ± 0.123
6	A_{max3}	0.119 ± 0.130	12	L_{max3}	0.486 ± 0.130

As a result, in this inter-subject setting, the starting feature set is a wide matrix X with dimension of 252 columns (21 channels × 12 features) and 52 lines (the ensemble averaged positive and negative labeled trials of 26 subjects). Due to the low number of training examples, cross validation with leave-one-out subject is adopted. The emotion valence is predicted based on hierarchical classification in the normalized feature space, Xnorm = (X − Xmean)/Std(X). Five standard classifiers are first trained, namely Linear Discriminant Analysis (LDA), k-Nearest Neighbors (kNN), Naïve Bayes (NB), Support Vector Machines (SVM), Decision Trees (DT, and the final decision is made with the majority votes of the classifiers (VOTE). In our previous work [5] we have applied the VOTE approach on (i) the complete feature space (252 features), (ii) PCA selected features and (iii) the Sequential Feature Selection (SFS) subset. The results are summarized in Table 2.

Starting from an empty set, SFS increments sequentially a new feature that best predicts the class at the current iteration. The process stops when there is no more improvement in the prediction. SFS is a very effective way to identify the dominant neural signatures across subjects. However it is a computational heavy and time

Table 2. Inter-subject cross validation accuracy of the hierarchical classifier VOTE

All features (252)	PCA (16 features)	SFS (max 10 features)
75 %	69,23	98.08

consuming procedure, which was the main motivation to look for a computationally less intensive alternative.

Inter-subject Feature Space Reduction Based on Descriptive Statistics. We propose to reduce the feature space based on the central tendency (arithmetic mean) and dispersion (standard deviation) of the inter-subject temporal feature distribution.

Each subplot of Figs. 1 and 2 represents one temporal feature over all EEG channels. 21 columns of points are the distribution of the respective feature across the participating 26 subjects. The red and the blue lines incorporate the mean of the positive and negative labeled trials. Note that, there are features with almost identical means or standard deviation for both classes, and features as the latency 4 (Lmax2), latency 6 (Lmax3), amp 3 (Amin2), amp 6 (Amax3) with statistically well discriminable positive and negative class distribution. Further to that, we observe that channels (5, 6, 7, 9, 10, 11, and 20) are overall consistent with respect to the statistical discriminability of the latency ± labels and channels (5, 6, 7, 9, 10, 11, and 12) with respect to the amplitude ± labels.

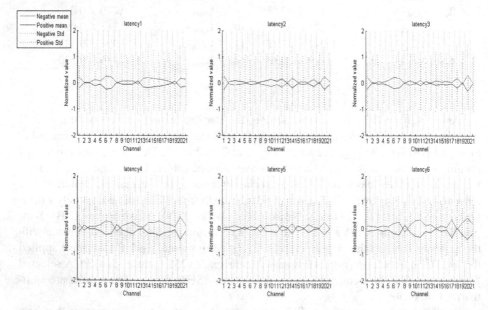

Fig. 1. Means and standard deviation of the latency feature distribution across subjects and channels. Positive class (red line) and negative class (blue line) distribution (Color figure online).

4   Results and Discussion

4.1   Classification Based on Single Features

The inter-subject feature distribution represented on Figs. 1 and 2 suggests that the classification may be favored, by subtracting features with statistically identical inter-subject class distribution. In order to test this hypothesis we run VOTE classifier with each channel related temporal feature (252 runs). The dots on Fig. 3 correspond to the runs. Most of the features have relatively small distance between the positive and negative class means and the cross validation accuracy is in the range of 35–65 %. The classifier accuracy increases for features with bigger distance, and for example the few features with difference of their class means above 0.6 achieve 75 % accuracy.

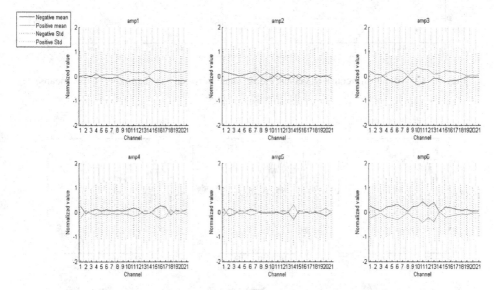

Fig. 2. Means and standard deviation of the amplitude feature distribution across subjects and channels. Positive class (red line) and negative class (blue line) distribution (Color figure online).

4.2   Combining Features with the Best Discriminative Capacity

Now the goal is to combine the N features with the best discriminative capacity. It is hard to estimate N in advance, therefore the classification starts with the best feature (the one with the highest absolute difference between its class distribution means or dispersion). The next classification run adds the second best feature and so on, up to the complete set of features. The results for the individual classifiers (LD, kNN, NB, SVM, and DT) and the hierarchical classifier VOTE are summarized in Figs. 4 and 5. As it was expected, for each classification model there is an optimal combination of features that maximize the accuracy. After that, the performance of the classifiers degrades. Note that the distance between the class distribution means is more reliable measure for the feature discriminative capacity than the difference between its class distribution

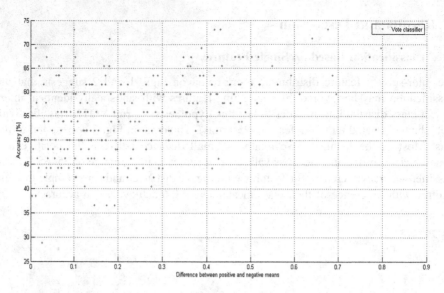

Fig. 3. Classification accuracy versus the distance between the feature +/- class means.

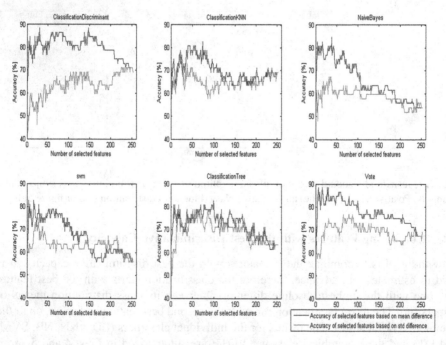

Fig. 4. Classification accuracy versus sequentially incremented best features. Features are ranked by the distance between their class distribution means (blue) or the difference between their class distribution dispersion (red). Classifiers LD, kNN, NB, SVM, DT, VOTE (Color figure online).

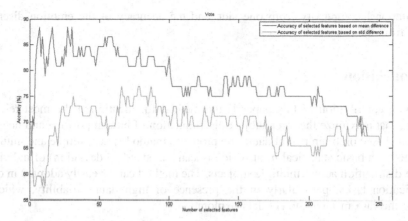

Fig. 5. VOTE classification accuracy versus sequentially incremented best features. Features are ranked by the distance between their class distribution means (blue) or the difference between their class distribution dispersion (red) (Color figure online).

dispersions. Table 3 resumes the classification accuracy of the six studied classifiers over the first 17 iterations of best incremented features. Features are ranked by the distance between their class distribution means. Though the maximum reached VOTE accuracy of 88.46 % is lower than the SFS-based VOTE classification (Table 2), they are in the same range. These results reflect the compromise between simplicity and

Table 3. Classification accuracy for the best features selected by the distance between their class distribution means. Classifiers LD, kNN, NB, SVM, DT, VOTE.

# of features	Feature Added	VOTE	LDA	KNN	NB	SVM	DT
1	Ch 11 amp6	63,46	65,38	57,69	65,38	65,38	63,46
2	Ch 20 latency4	71,15	69,23	65,38	75,00	65,38	67,31
3	Ch 20 latency6	69,23	73,08	69,23	75,00	71,15	67,31
4	Ch 13 amp6	80,77	82,69	69,23	82,69	82,69	69,23
5	Ch 17 latency6	84,62	78,85	73,08	76,92	75,00	73,08
6	Ch 10 amp3	86,54	78,85	73,08	80,77	78,85	73,08
7	Ch 11 latency6	**88,46**	84,62	75,00	80,77	80,77	80,77
8	Ch 6 amp6	82,69	76,92	71,15	76,92	75,00	75,00
9	Ch 20 latency3	86,54	80,77	69,23	80,77	78,85	80,77
10	Ch 14 amp5	82,69	78,85	63,46	80,77	76,92	76,92
11	Ch 10 latency6	78,85	75,00	65,38	78,85	71,15	76,92
12	Ch 11 amp3	82,69	76,92	65,38	76,92	73,08	75,00
13	Ch 16 latency4	80,77	73,08	63,46	80,77	71,15	73,08
14	Ch 12 amp3	84,62	76,92	67,31	80,77	75,00	76,92
15	Ch 6 amp3	86,54	76,92	71,15	78,85	75,00	73,08
16	Ch 16 amp4	**88,46**	80,77	73,08	82,69	82,69	78,85
17	Ch 1 latency2	84,62	75,00	73,08	78,85	78,85	75,00

computational complexity from one side and the accuracy of the emotion discrimination from the other side.

5 Conclusion

The main contribution of this paper is the method for identifying the most relevant features that maximize the inter subject discrimination of human positive and negative emotions based on brain neural data. The proposed method is fast, simple and intuitive. It counts with basic statistical information (mean and standard deviation) of individual feature distribution across multiple subjects. The method can be easily adopted in other classification tasks, particularly in the presence of high data variability, which is usually the case in inter-subject data exploration.

References

1. Calvo, R.A., D'Mello, S.K.: Affect detection: an interdisciplinary review of models, methods, and their applications. IEEE Trans. Affect. Comput. 1(1), 18–37 (2010)
2. Dalgleish, T., Dunn, B., Mobbs, D.: Affective neuroscience: past, present, and future. Emot. Rev. 1, 355–368 (2009)
3. Olofsson, J.K., Nordin, S., Sequeira, H., Polich, J.: Affective picture processing: an integrative review of erp findings. Biol. Psychol. 77, 247–265 (2008)
4. Jatupaiboon, N., Panngum, S., Israsena, P.: Real-time EEG-based happiness detection system. Sci. World J. 2013, 12 p (Article ID 618649)
5. Bozhkov, Lachezar, Georgieva, Petia, Trifonov, Roumen: Brain neural data analysis using machine learning feature selection and classification methods. In: Mladenov, Valeri, Jaync, Chrisina, Iliadis, Lazaros (eds.) EANN 2014. CCIS, vol. 459, pp. 123–132. Springer, Heidelberg (2014)

Extremely Overlapping Vehicle Counting

Ricardo Guerrero-Gómez-Olmedo, Beatriz Torre-Jiménez,
Roberto López-Sastre$^{(\boxtimes)}$, Saturnino Maldonado-Bascón,
and Daniel Oñoro-Rubio

GRAM, University of Alcalá, Alcalá de Henares, Spain
robertoj.lopez@uah.es

Abstract. The challenging problem that we explore in this paper is to precisely estimate the number of vehicles in an image of a traffic congestion situation. We start introducing TRANCOS, a novel database for extremely overlapping vehicle counting. It provides more than 1200 images where the number of vehicles and their locations have been annotated. We establish a clear experimental setup which will let others evaluate their own vehicle counting approaches. We also propose a novel evaluation metric, the Grid Average Mean absolute Error (GAME), which overcomes the limitations of previously proposed metrics for object counting. Finally, we perform an experimental validation, using the proposed TRANCOS dataset, for two types of vehicle counting strategies: counting by detection; and counting by regression. Our results show that counting by regression strategies are more precise localizing and estimating the number of vehicles. The TRANCOS database and the source code for reproducing the results are available at http://agamenon.tsc.uah.es/ Personales/rlopez/data/trancos.

1 Introduction

Extremely overlapping vehicle counting is a very challenging problem. See Fig. 1, where we show different traffic congestion images. To precisely estimate the number of vehicles present in this type of scenes is not an easy task, even for a human. Building automatic counting solutions able to deal with this problem would allow the development of systems that precisely monitor the evolution of a traffic jam. This information would result invaluable for the public authorities in charge of the maintenance and planning of road infrastructures.

To the best of our knowledge, this work presents the first attempt to provide a dataset, and an associated benchmark, to experimentally evaluate the performance of different approaches dealing with the problem of extremely overlapping vehicle counting. There are other datasets which have been previously used to evaluate the precision of vehicle detection approaches, e.g. [1–4], but none of them contain traffic congestion images where the overlap between the vehicles is considerable.

For instance, the car detection task in the PASCAL VOC [1] benchmark has reached an Average Precision above 50 %. Most of the winner methods in this

© Springer International Publishing Switzerland 2015
R. Paredes et al. (Eds.): IbPRIA 2015, LNCS 9117, pp. 423–431, 2015.
DOI: 10.1007/978-3-319-19390-8_48

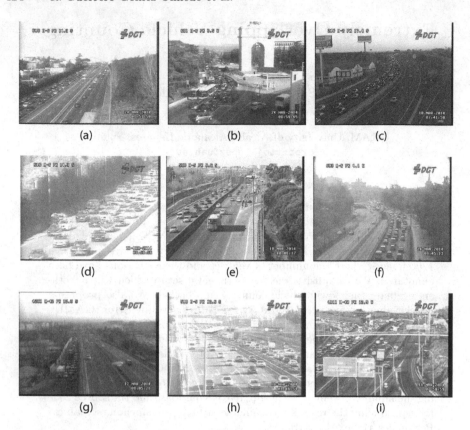

Fig. 1. TRaffic ANd COngestionS (TRANCOS) database images. These pictures show how challenging the proposed problem of extremely overlapping vehicle counting is, even for a human.

dataset are based on detectors using Histogram of Oriented Gradients (HOG) features [5] and sliding window strategies. Figure 2a depicts the results of a HOG based detector [6] in one of our images. It seems clear that novel solutions need to be explored. We show in this paper that this type of strategy, named counting by detection, does not improve the precision reported by counting by regression techniques, e.g. [7,8].

But also some additional problems have to be considered within this novel context. Typically, public authorities deploy a big net of cameras for the traffic surveillance. This fact implies that the network bandwidth must be controlled, hence the images delivered have a low resolution. This aspect directly affects the performance of gradient based features object detectors (e.g. [5]). Furthermore, in these images the vehicles normally occupy a few pixels and the context becomes fundamental to actually recognize the objects. See Fig. 2b, where a car can be easily confused with a black couch. In summary, the proposed scenario presents an interesting object counting problem which has not been previously explored.

Fig. 2. (a) Results of the HOG detector [6] in a traffic congestion image. (b) In these images the vehicles typically occupy a few pixels, and it becomes difficult to identify the typical cues that we use for finding cars (e.g. wheels, license plates). Instead, note that the context results fundamental to determine whether a blob represents a car or a black couch, for example.

The key contributions of our work can be summarized as follows. First, we release the novel TRaffic ANd COngestionS (TRANCOS) dataset, which has been specifically designed to evaluate the performance of extremely overlapping vehicle counting solutions. With more than 1200 traffic jam images and 46700 annotated vehicles, TRANCOS comes with the clear experimental setup detailed in this paper, in order to set a new benchmark. Second, we propose a novel evaluation metric, the Grid Average Mean absolute Error (GAME) metric. We show that the GAME metric overcomes some of the limitations of previously proposed metrics for object counting, such as the Mean Absolute Error (MAE) [9]. And third, we complete the paper with an experimental validation, using the TRANCOS dataset, for three state-of-the-art methods for object counting: a counting by detection approach based on the HOG detector described in [6]; and the two counting by regression approaches [7,8], which have previously reported the best results for the problem of crowd counting. The experimental results confirm that the counting by regression strategies are more precise localizing and estimating the count of the vehicles. Our aim with this work is to offer to the computer vision community a novel benchmark for the problem of extremely overlapping vehicle counting.

The rest of the paper is organized as follows. Section 2 reports on related work. Section 3 includes a detailed description of the TRANCOS dataset and the proposed GAME metric. In Sect. 4 we show the experimental validation, and Sect. 5 concludes the paper.

2   Related Work

To the best of our knowledge, the vehicle counting problem in traffic congestion images has not been previously systematically studied. There are works for vehicle detection in conditions of relatively high traffic in highways, such as the models in [10–12]. But the problem proposed in this paper is completely different. First, all these previous works offer solutions adapted to video, and

we simply provide still (low resolution) images, obtained from real traffic surveillance cameras. They all incorporate a background subtraction step to their
system pipelines, but with the TRANCOS dataset this is not possible. Moreover, our images cover a variety of viewpoints and scenarios, and not simply
two or three fixed scenes. This implies that the parameterization of the scene
cannot be considered. Finally, the grade of overlap between the vehicles that
the TRANCOS dataset offers is considerable, in sharp contrast to the rest of
datasets.

We understand the extremely overlapping vehicle counting problem as a
variant of the problem of crowd counting [7–9,13–15]. In this paper we consider two families of solutions. First, we have the popular counting by detection
approaches, which count instances of objects through scanning the image space
using a detector trained with local image features (e.g. [5]). Second, we have
the counting by regression solutions (e.g. [7]), which count objects by learning a
direct mapping from low-level imagery features to objects density. The approach
in [8] follows this idea too, but, instead of a linear transformation, the model uses
a Regression Forest combined with a spatial average of the estimated densities
to make smoother predictions. In this paper we evaluate the performance of all
these state-of-the-art approaches using the novel TRANCOS dataset.

3   TRANCOS Dataset

We introduce in this section the TRANCOS dataset. Although there are several datasets for assessing the performance of vehicle detection approaches (e.g.
[1–4]), TRANCOS is the first one focused on the problem of vehicle counting
in traffic jam images, captured using *real* traffic surveillance cameras. Figure 1
shows a sample of the images provided by TRANCOS, which illustrates how
challenging the proposed problem is. Note that all the collected images contain
traffic congestions, covering a variety of different scenes and viewpoints, with
changes in the lighting conditions, and considerable different levels of overlap
and crowdedness, even within the same image.

Specifically, the database consists of 1244 images. They have been acquired
from a selection of public traffic surveillance cameras provided by the Directorate
General of Traffic (DGT) of the Government of Spain. The cameras selected
monitor different highways located in the area of Madrid, which typically present
heavy traffic congestions.

Each image has been manually annotated. For this purpose, we follow a dot-
ting annotation strategy, as in [7], and provide for each image the exact number
of vehicles and their locations. In total, 46796 vehicles have been annotated.
A Region of Interest (ROI) to identify the road region, is also provided for each
image.

The main goal of TRANCOS is to evaluate vehicle counting approaches,
especially under extremely overlapping conditions. So, any method using this
dataset has to predict, for each test image, the number of vehicles, and their
locations in the images. We propose the following experimental setup which has

to be followed by any method using the dataset. The acquisition of the images has been done during three different weeks, which lets us distribute the images in three separate sets: training (403 images), validation (420) and test (421). We define two types of training strategies: (1) methods which are trained using only the provided training and validation data; (2) methods built using any data except the provided test data. In both cases, the test set must be used strictly for reporting of results alone - it must not be used in any way to train or tune systems, for example by running multiple parameter choices and reporting the best results obtained. This has to be done using the validation images, for instance.

With TRANCOS[1] we provide a set of tools for accessing the dataset and annotations described. For the evaluation metric, we introduce the novel GAME metric, which is detailed in Sect. 3.1.

3.1   The GAME Metric

In datasets for crowd counting, such as the UCSD Pedestrian Dataset [9], the metric chosen to evaluate the performance is the Mean Absolute Error (MAE), which is defined as follows,

$$\text{MAE} = \frac{1}{N} \cdot \sum_{n=1}^{N} |e_n - gt_n|, \qquad (1)$$

where e_n corresponds to the estimated objects count for image n, and gt_n is the ground truth provided for image n, being N the total number of images considered.

While this metric seems fair for establishing a comparative, we have observed in our experiments that it often leads to mask mistaken estimations. The reason is that the MAE does not take into account *where* the estimations have been done in the images.

In order to provide a more accurate evaluation, we introduce here the Grid Average Mean absolute Error (GAME) metric. Our objective is clear: to offer an evaluation metric which simultaneously considers the object count, and the location estimated for the objects. With the GAME metric, we proceed to subdivide the image in 4^L non-overlapping regions, and compute the MAE in each of these subregions. We formulate the GAME as follows,

$$\text{GAME}(L) = \frac{1}{N} \cdot \sum_{n=1}^{N} \left(\sum_{l=1}^{4^L} |e_n^l - gt_n^l| \right), \qquad (2)$$

where, e_n^l is the estimated count in a region l of image n, and gt_n^l is the ground truth for the same region in the same image. The higher L, the more restrictive the GAME metric will be. Note that the MAE can be obtained as a particularization of the GAME when $L = 0$.

---

[1] http://agamenon.tsc.uah.es/Personales/rlopez/data/trancos.

As it can be seen in Fig. 3, our GAME metric is able to penalize those predictions with a good MAE but a wrong localization of the objects.

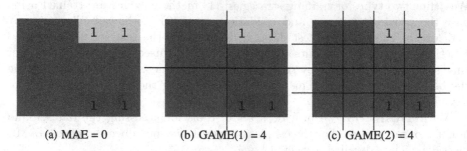

(a) MAE = 0   (b) GAME(1) = 4   (c) GAME(2) = 4

Fig. 3. Toy example for the GAME and MAE metrics. We see in green the estimation and in red the ground truth, representing the count of the vehicles and their location in the image. The MAE in (a) is of 0, even when the objects have not been correctly located. In (b) and (c) we show how the GAME is able to penalize the count when the localization is wrong (Color figure online).

4   Results

4.1   Experimental Setup

Our main objective is to establish a novel benchmark for the problem of vehicle counting in traffic congestion situations. For doing so, we offer here the experimental validation for three different state-of-the-art methods using the described TRANCOS dataset.

The first method we implement is a counting by detection approach using the de facto standard detector based on HOG features [5]. Explicitly, we build our approach using the implementation of [6]. We design two different strategies to train this detector. The first one (HOG-1), consists in collecting positive and negative examples using the PASCAL VOC 2007 Dataset [1]. This HOG-1 lets us evaluate how challenging are the images provided in the novel TRANCOS dataset, when a well known dataset is used for learning the vehicle counting solutions.

Our second approach, HOG-2, uses the training data provided with the TRANCOS dataset, but the negatives are extracted using the PASCAL VOC 2007 and the GRAM-RTM [2] datasets. Note that with the TRANCOS dataset we do not provide bounding boxes annotations, but dots. Therefore, to collect positive examples for training the HOG-2, we proceed as follows. For each training image, we apply the detector HOG-1 at multiple scales and collect detections which later are manually filtered to identify those that contain correct positive examples. These positives are used to train the HOG-2 detector. This way, we are able to train the detector using data generated from the same distribution provided with the TRANCOS dataset.

We also analyze the performance of two counting by regression models, using only the TRANCOS data. First, we follow the approach in [7] to learn a linear regression model to predict vehicle densities in the images. For the visual features, we compute dense SIFT [16] descriptors, which are then quantified using a K-means clustering to build the visual codebook. We call this approach [7] + SIFT. We assign to each pixel the code of the cluster in the visual codebook of its corresponding SIFT descriptor. We use a visual vocabulary size of 2000, and the parameter C of the regressor is fixed to $C = 1000$ using the validation set.

Second, we learn a Random Forest regression model for the vehicle densities following the model described by Fiaschi et al. in [8]. In this case, we integrate in our approach different features. We start using a simple feature: the normalized RGB values of the pixels ([8] + RGB Norm). The second feature we use is the Local Binary Pattern (LBP), using the VLFeat implementation [17] ([8] + LBP). The third feature type consists in a concatenation of the following filter responses ([8] + Filters): the gray-scale value of the pixel, the Laplacian of Gaussian filter response, the Gaussian gradient magnitude and the eigenvalues of the structure tensor of the image.

4.2 Vehicle Counting Evaluation

We start reporting the performance of the model HOG-1, which casts a MAE of 34.01. This confirms that: (a) training in the PASCAL VOC is not adequate, due to the different nature of data distribution of the two datasets; (b) the problem proposed by the TRANCOS dataset is very challenging.

Table 1 shows the results obtained for the rest of methods. We include both the MAE and GAME (for $L = \{1, 2, 3\}$) metrics. Let us start analyzing the MAE results. One first observes that the counting by detection HOG-2 drastically reduces the MAE of the HOG-1 to 13.29. This error can be considered equivalent to the one reported by the counting by regression model [7] + SIFT. With respect to the approaches following [8], we observe that the best results are obtained using normalized RGB features and the filter responses ([8] + RGB Norm + Filters). Another interesting conclusion is that the MAE of these state-of-the-art models is significantly higher than the previously reported performances of the same models addressing the crowd counting problem in other datasets. Again, this reveals that the problem proposed by the TRANCOS dataset is really challenging.

We can conclude that the best approach in terms of MAE is the HOG-2. However, the GAME metric shows that this is not true. We have observed that the HOG-2 approach casts multiple wrong detections, which contribute to improve the count of the objects, but they are actually false positives. The GAME metric is able to overcome this limitation, because it penalizes the wrong localizations of the object counts.

Observe Table 1 GAME columns for a clear comparison of the different methods. First, as it was expected, the higher L the higher the error of the models.

The best performance is now systematically obtained by [7] + SIFT. Furthermore, in Fig. 4 we can see that it is the HOG-2 the one suffering the biggest increment of the error. Also, for $L > 2$ all the counting by regression models improve the results of HOG-2. Our results show that [7] + SIFT is the best approach counting and localizing the vehicles in the images.

Table 1. Vehicle Counting Results. We report the MAE and GAME metrics.

	MAE = GAME(0)	GAME(1)	GAME(2)	GAME(3)
[8] + RGB Norm	20.25	22.57	26.78	29.54
[8] + LBP	19.98	23.15	28.04	31.19
[8] + RGB Norm + LBP	20.15	22.66	27.04	29.97
[8] + Filters	17.77	20.14	23.65	25.99
[8] + RGB Norm + Filters	17.68	19.97	23.54	25.84
[7] + SIFT	13.76	**16.72**	**20.72**	**24.36**
HOG-2	**13.29**	18.05	23.65	28.41

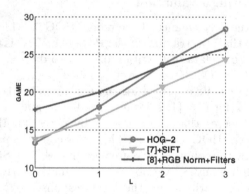

Fig. 4. GAME metric evolution with respect to L.

5 Conclusions

We conclude that the TRANCOS dataset introduces a very challenging and novel problem. The experimental evaluation proposed sets a new benchmark. With the novel GAME metric proposed, we overcome some of the limitations of the traditional MAE for object counting solutions, and provide a more precise evaluation where both the localization and the count are taken into account simultaneously.

Acknowledgements. This work is supported by projects SPIP2014-1468, CCG2013/EXP-047, CCG2014/EXP-054, TEC2013-45183-R and IPT-2012-0808-370000.

References

1. Everingham, M., Van Gool, L., Williams, C.K.I., Winn, J., Zisserman, A.: The PASCAL visual object classes (VOC) challenge. IJCV **88**(2), 303–338 (2010)
2. Guerrero-Gómez-Olmedo, R., López-Sastre, R.J., Maldonado-Bascón, S., Fernández-Caballero, A.: Vehicle tracking by simultaneous detection and viewpoint estimation. In: Ferrández Vicente, J.M., Álvarez Sánchez, J.R., de la Paz López, F., Toledo Moreo, F.J. (eds.) IWINAC 2013, Part II. LNCS, vol. 7931, pp. 306–316. Springer, Heidelberg (2013)
3. Geiger, A., Lenz, P., Stiller, C., Urtasun, R.: Vision meets robotics: the KITTI dataset. IJRR **32**(11), 1231–1237 (2013)
4. Caraffi, C., Vojir, T., Trefny, J., Sochman, J., Matas, J.: A system for real-time detection and tracking of vehicles from a single car-mounted camera. In: ITS Conference (2012)
5. Dalal, N., Triggs, B.: Histograms of oriented gradients for human detection. In: CVPR (2005)
6. Sudowe, P., Leibe, B.: Efficient use of geometric constraints for sliding-window object detection in video. In: Crowley, J.L., Draper, B.A., Thonnat, M. (eds.) ICVS 2011. LNCS, vol. 6962, pp. 11–20. Springer, Heidelberg (2011)
7. Lempitsky, V., Zisserman, A.: Learning to count objects in images. In: NIPS (2010)
8. Fiaschi, L., Köthe, U., Nair, R., Hamprecht, F.A.: Learning to count with regression forest and structured labels. In: ICPR (2012)
9. Chan, A.B., Liang, Z.S.J., Vasconcelos, N.: Privacy preserving crowd monitoring: counting people without people models or tracking. In: CVPR (2008)
10. Lu, W., Wang, S., Ding, X.: Vehicle detection and tracking in relatively crowded conditions. In: IEEE International Conference on Systems, Man, and Cybernetics (2009)
11. Jun, G., Aggarwal, J.K., Gökmen, M.: Tracking and segmentation of highway vehicles in cluttered and crowded scenes. In: IEEE Workshops on Applications of Computer Vision (2008)
12. Tamersoy, B., Aggarwal, J.K.: Robust vehicle detection for tracking in highway surveillance videos using unsupervised learning. In: AVSS (2009)
13. Chen, K., Loy, C.C., Gong, S., Xiang, T.: Feature mining for localised crowd counting. In: BMVC (2012)
14. Arteta, C., Lempitsky, V., Noble, J., Zisserman, A.: Learning to detect partially overlapping instances. In: CVPR (2013)
15. Selinummi, J., Seppala, J., Yli-Harja, O., Puhakka, J.A.: Software for quantification of labeled bacteria from digital microscope images by automated image analysis. Biotechniques **39**(6), 859–863 (2005)
16. Lowe, D.G.: Distinctive image features from scale-invariant keypoints. IJCV **60**(2), 91–110 (2004)
17. Vedaldi, A., Fulkerson, B.: VLFeat: An open and portable library of computer vision algorithms (2008). http://www.vlfeat.org/

Sentence Clustering Using Continuous Vector Space Representation

Mara Chinea-Rios[(⊠)], Germán Sanchis-Trilles,
and Francisco Casacuberta

Pattern Recognition and Human Language Technologies Center,
Universitat Politècnica de València, Valencia, Spain
{machirio,gersantr,fcn}@prhlt.upv.es

Abstract. In this paper, we present a clustering approach based on the combined use of a continuous vector space representation of sentences and the k-means algorithm. The principal motivation of this proposal is to split a big heterogeneous corpus into clusters of similar sentences. We use the word2vec toolkit for obtaining the representation of a given word as a continuous vector space. We provide empirical evidence for proving that the use of our technique can lead to better clusters, in terms of intra-cluster perplexity and $F1$ score.

Keywords: Clustering · k-means · Continuous vector spaces

1 Introduction

With the rapid growth of online information, huge corpora are available, e.g. the wikipedia corpus, the common crawl corpus and others. These corpora may contain text from a variety of domains, especially if they are built from heterogeneous resources such as crawled web pages. The goal of *text categorization* [11] is the classification of documents into a fixed number of predefined categories. Several approaches have been applied to text categorisation, ranging from naive Bayes classifiers [11] to *Support Vector Machines* (SVM) [6,9].

Text clustering is entailed as a more difficult task than text categorisation. In text clustering we do not know the classes into which the documents should be classified, which means that the only data available is a database of documents without class information. Several attempts have been made in text clustering. For instance, in [7] several kernel-based, text categorisation techniques are adapted to text clustering by using the k-means algorithm.

An especially appealing problem in text categorisation is sentence clustering, in which a document is made up of only one single sentence. This problem has been receiving special attention in the natural language processing (NLP) community since it allows for training specific models for each of the obtained clusters, leading to more task-focused models [1,8]. Moreover, sentence clustering can also be of interest in other NLP tasks, such as done for text recognition [4] or statistical machine translation [15,16].

© Springer International Publishing Switzerland 2015
R. Paredes et al. (Eds.): IbPRIA 2015, LNCS 9117, pp. 432–440, 2015.
DOI: 10.1007/978-3-319-19390-8_49

In this paper, we present an approach for sentence clustering based in the k-means algorithm and a continuous vector representation of sentences. This new approach is evaluated in practise under the scope of sentence clustering.

This paper is structured as follows. Section 2, reviews the k-means algorithm. In Sect. 3, we explain word representation in vector space and extend it to vector representation of sentences. The empirical results are gathered in Sect. 4, and concluding remarks are discussed in Sect. 5.

2 k-means Methods

The k-means [10] is one of the simplest unsupervised learning algorithms that solve the well known clustering problem. The procedure follows a simple and easy way to classify a given data set through a certain number of clusters K fixed a priori. The main idea is to define K centroids, one for each cluster. These centroids should be placed in a cunning way because of different location causes different result. However, it is common practise to initialise them randomly [5]. The algorithm finds a local optimum for the following minimisation:

$$S = \operatorname*{argmin}_{S} \sum_{k=1}^{K} \sum_{\mathbf{x} \in S_k} \| \mathbf{x} - m_k \|^2 \tag{1}$$

where $S = \{S_1, S_2, \ldots, S_K\}$, $\| \mathbf{x} - m_k \|^2$ is a distance function between the sample $\mathbf{x}$ and m_k being the centroid of the cluster k, usually the euclidean distance.

$$d(\mathbf{x}_j, m_k) = (\mathbf{x}_j - m_k)^T (\mathbf{x}_j - m_k)$$

Even though the euclidean distance is very well studied in the literature, its application in the context of sentence clustering is not direct. For this reason, other authors [1] propose different alternatives. Here, we resort to a continuous vector space representation of sentences (explained in next section), and compare it with the approach of [1] in Sect. 4.

3   Continuous Vector Space Representations of Sentences

Representation of words as continuous vectors are very used [2]. Deriving from this work, word vectors were used in many natural languages processing applications [3,19].

In the present paper, we used the *word2vec* [12] toolkit for continuous vector space representation of words. Word2vec is a recently developed technique for building a neural network that maps words to real-number vectors, with the purpose that words with similar meanings will map to similar vectors. Word2vec takes a text corpus as input and produces the word vectors as output. It first constructs a vocabulary from the training corpus and then learns vector representation of words. The representation of word *distance* would be:

$$v(distance) = (0.18094 \ -1.56289 \ -0.73434 \ -0.02778 \ 0.41745)^T$$

Word vectors generated by the neural net have nice semantic and syntactic behaviours. Semantically, "iOS" is close to "Android" and their vector representation is also close. Similarly, but in a more syntactic sense, "boys" minus "boy" is close to "girls" minus "girl".

However, a problem that arises when using continuous vector space representations of words is how to represent a whole sentence with a continuous vector. Following the idiosyncrasy described in the previous paragraph (i.e., semantically close words are also close in their vector representation), we propose to represent a given sentence by adding the vectors of each one of the words within that specific sentence:

$$F(\mathbf{x}) = \sum_{w \in \mathbf{x}} f(w) \tag{2}$$

where w is a word that appears in sentence $\mathbf{x}$ and $f(w)$ is the vector representation of w according to [12].

4   Experiments

In this section, we describe the experimental framework employed to evaluate the proposed model. Then, we show the results for our method in terms of two automatic evaluation metrics, followed by a comparative with a state-of-the-art sentence clustering method based on bilingual word-sequence kernels. This method was presented in [1], alongside with monolingual word-sequence method. The best results were obtained with bilingual word-sequence kernels, so we decided to use this method in this paper so as to compare with the best performing word-sequence kernel clustering method available.

4.1   Experimental Set-Up

To assess our clustering method, we propose to use labelled data and evaluate to which extent our clustering method is able to recover such labels whenever they are not available. For this purpose, we need a set of data comprised of sentences which can be grouped according to some common characteristic. In the experiments we conducted, such common characteristic was chosen to be the domain the sentence has been produced in. Hence, the training corpus was composed artificially from four different corpora belonging to different domains readily available in the literature. Even though our method can be applied to monolingual text, bilingual word-sequence kernels clustering requires a bilingual corpus. Hence, we considered English-French bilingual corpora. Table 1 shows the main features of the four corpora used. The News Comentary (NC) corpus[1] [18] is composed of translations of news articles. The EMEA[2] corpus [17] contains documents from the European Medicines Agency. The PatTr[3] [20] is a parallel corpus extracted from the

---

[1] Available at http://www.statmt.org/wmt13.

[2] Available at http://www.statmt.org/wmt14/medical-task/.

[3] Available at http://www.cl.uni-heidelberg.de/statnlpgroup/pattr/.

Table 1. Corpora main figures. M denotes millions of elements and k thousands of elements, $|S|$ stands for number of sentences, $|W|$ for number of words (tokens) and $|V|$ for vocabulary size (types).

	EMEA		PatTr		NC		Subs	
	FR	EN	FR	EN	FR	EN	FR	EN
$|S|$	1.0M		8.0M		117k		19.1M	
$|W|$	12.3M	10.5M	207.0M	189.0M	2.8M	2.4M	177.5M	186.5k
$|V|$	45.8k	39.3k	349.3k	356.0k	33.7k	27.6k	228.9k	182.1k

MAREC patent collection. The Subtitles (Subs) corpus[4] [17] is composed of subtitles translations in 30 languages.

We selected 2500 random sentence from each corpus. With these sentences, we performed all the experiments, named corpus-train. The corpus-test was created with 51 random sentence from each corpus.

Since the k-means algorithm needs a random initialisation, each experiment was repeated 10 times, reporting average 95 % confidence intervals.

We used two different measures for automatically measuring the quality of the produced clusters, intra-cluster perplexity and $F1$ score, defined as follows:

- Intra-cluster perplexity (IC-PPL) [1] is defined as the average perplexity of each one of the clusters, formally

$$ppl_{avg} = 2^{\sum_{k=1}^{K} \frac{1}{K} \frac{1}{W_k} log_2 p(k)} \tag{3}$$

where $p(k)$ is the probability of the samples of cluster k according to the language model estimated on that same cluster; W_k is the total number of words in the sentences belonging to the cluster k; and K is the total number of clusters. Lower values of IC-PPL are desirable. We decided to compute IC-PPL based on a 5-gram language model.

We compare the IC-PPL improvement with the IC-PPL oracle, which is computed using as clusters the real labels, i.e., Subs, NC, PatTr or EMEA.

- $F1$ score is a measure of the accuracy achieved by the system. It considers both the precision and the recall of the test to compute the score. The $F1$ score can be interpreted as a weighted average of precision and recall, where an $F1$ score reaches its best value at 1 and worst score at 0.

Word2vec has different parameters that affect the experimental results. We conducted experiments with different vector dimensions, i.e., $v\_size = \{1, 5, 10, 50, 100, 500\}$. In addition, a given word is only considered for building its vector when it appears a given number of times within the training data. If a given word appears nc times in the corpus it is considered an important word and the toolkit computes its vector. We analysed the effect of considering different values $nc = \{1, 3, 5, 10\}$.

---

[4] Available at http://opus.lingfil.uu.se/.

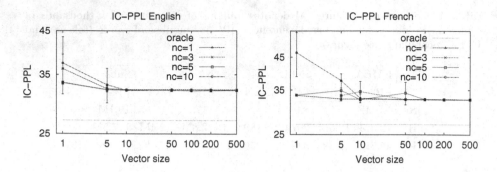

Fig. 1. Effect in average IC-PPL. Horizontal lines represent IC-PPL oracle.

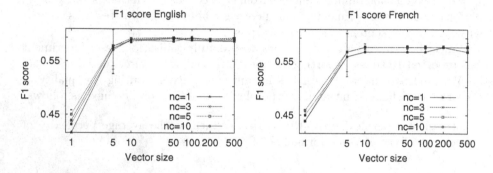

Fig. 2. Effect in average $F1$ score.

4.2   Experimental Results

In this section, we present the results using different parameters (i.e., v_size and nc, see above) for obtaining the continuous vector representation of the sentences that is later used within the k-means clustering. Several conclusions can be drawn:

- In terms of IC-PPL, we compared the results with the IC-PPL oracle, which is 26.99. Results are not equal than the oracle, but the difference is less 5 point.
- The results are very similar in both languages, although results were slightly better when considering the English data.
- Above 50 or 100, vector size does not have any effect on the results. However, considering a vector size of 5 or 10 yields do very unstable results (even with high confidence intervals, 0.05 in $F1$ in the worst cases).
- nc does not seem to have a significant impact on the results obtained. We assume that this is due to the fact that the more discriminant words (i.e., those that are important for each domain) appear frequently enough so that they are never left out when computing their vector representation.

4.3   Considering Different Amount of Domains

In this section we analyse the behaviour of our clustering strategy when considering increasing amount of domains. Different conclusions can be drawn:

- $F1$ value decreases with increasing domains significantly. 2-domain= 0.82 and 4-domain=0.58. This result was expected, since the more the domains, the harder it is to classify the sentences according to the original clusters, but in an unsupervised manner.
- All the experiments with our method do not achieve similar results to the oracle. We obtained the lower difference respect to the oracle with 4 domains.

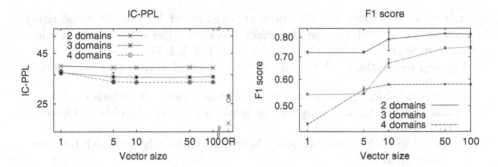

Fig. 3. IC-PPL and $F1$ score when considering increasing amount of domains. OR represent the IC-PPL oracle results and nc=1

4.4   Comparative with Bilingual Word-Sequence Kernels

We compared our method with the method based on bilingual word-sequence kernels presented in [1]. The authors proposed the direct use of kernels as similarity measure, and applied it to the specific case of sentence clustering via k-means algorithm. This technique has also been used in posterior works [13,14] and may be hence considered state-of-the-art. The authors assumed that a sentence-aligned bilingual corpus is available, and they clustered the data taking into account such bilingual information. A bilingual word-sequence kernels is defined taking into account two different vocabularies, namely Σ for the source language and Δ for the target language. Let be $\mathbf{s} = \{\mathbf{x}, \mathbf{y}\}$ a bilingual sentence pair, where $\mathbf{x}$ is the sentence belonging to the source language and $\mathbf{y}$ is the sentence belonging to the target language. Then, a bilingual word-sequence kernel can be defined as

$$B_n(\mathbf{s}, \mathbf{s}') = C_n(\mathbf{x}, \mathbf{x}') + C_n(\mathbf{y}, \mathbf{y}') = \sum_{u \in \Sigma^n} |\mathbf{x}|_u |\mathbf{x}'|_u + \sum_{v \in \Delta^n} |\mathbf{y}|_v |\mathbf{y}'|_v \qquad (4)$$

where $|\mathbf{x}|_u$ stands for the number of occurrences of u in sentence $\mathbf{x}$ and $|\mathbf{y}|_v$ for the number of occurrences of v in sentence $\mathbf{y}$. Note that this method depends

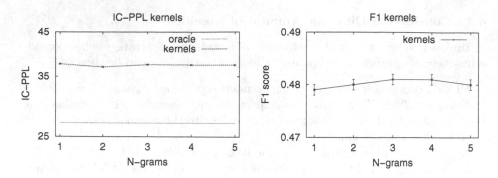

Fig. 4. Word sequence kernel clustering experiments, with $n = \{1, 2, 3, 4, 5\}$.

on strings of fixed-size n, since u and v are elements of Σ^n and Δ^n, respectively. In this work, we will analyse the effect of varying the order of the n-grams considered. Specifically, we will consider $n = \{1, 2, 3, 4, 5\}$.

Figure 4 shows the results obtained with bilingual word-sequence kernels.

- In terms of IC-PPL, results are not equal than the oracle, which is 26.99.
- n does not seem to have a significant impact on the results obtained in terms IC-PPL score.
- $F1$ score results have an increasing behaviour when n is increased, this trend is broken when $n = 5$.

Table 2 shows the best results in terms of $F1$ score and IC-PPL achieved by the two methods, i.e., continuous vector representation clustering (`Continuous`) and word-sequence kernel clustering (`Kernels`). Our method obtained the best $F1$ results, with a significant difference of 0.12. Comparing the two methods, `Continuous` obtained better results in terms of IC-PPL than `Kernels`. However, the both methods were even able to improve the IC-PPL of the real labels which were present in the data.

Table 2. Summary of the best results obtained with each set-up.

Methods	$F1$ score	IC-PPL
Oracle	N/A	26.99
Continuous	0.60	31.92
Kernels	0.48	36.93

5   Conclusions and Future Works

The main objective in this paper is to group sentences into similar clusters. For this work, we used the k-means algorithm for obtaining the clusters and represented the sentences by means of a novel technique, i.e., continuous vector space representation. The quality of clusters obtained was measured with two metrics, $F1$ score and IC-PPL. The results obtained in terms of $F1$ score were encouraging. In terms of IC-PPL, the clusters obtained by our method were not even able to improve the IC-PPL oracle, but the results are positive. In addition, we compared our clustering strategy with a state-of-the-art strategy, i.e., bilingual word-sequence kernel clustering. In terms of $F1$ score and IC-PPL, our method was able to yield better results.

In future work, we will carry out new experiments with larger amounts of data, and we also plan to perform statistical machine translation experiments that will validate whether the proposed approach is useful in a statistical machine translation domain adaptation task. In addition, we also intend to propose other more sophisticated ways of representing sentences using the continuous vector space representation of the words each sentence is composed of.

References

1. Andrés-Ferrer, J., Sanchis-Trilles, G., Casacuberta, F.: Similarity word-sequence kernels for sentence clustering. In: Hancock, E.R., Wilson, R.C., Windeatt, T., Ulusoy, I., Escolano, F. (eds.) SSPR & SPR 2010. LNCS, vol. 6218, pp. 610–619. Springer, Heidelberg (2010)
2. Bengio, Y., Schwenk, H., Senécal, J. and Morin, F.: Neural probabilistic language models. In: Innovations in Machine Learning, pp. 137–186 (2006)
3. Collobert, R., Weston, J., Bottou, L., Karlen, M., Kavukcuoglu, K., Kuksa, P.: Natural language processing (almost) from scratch. JMLR **12**, 2493–2537 (2011)
4. Cortes, C., Mohri, M., Weston, J.: A general regression technique for learning transductions. In: Proceedings of conference on ML, pp. 153–160 (2005)
5. Hamerly, G., Elkan, C.: Alternatives to the k-means algorithm that find better clusterings. In: Proceedings of Conference on Information and Knowledge Management, pp. 600–607 (2002)
6. Joachims, T.: Text categorisation with support vector machines: learning with many relevant features. In: Proceedings of ECML, pp. 137–142 (1998)
7. Karatzoglou, A., Feinerer, I.: Text clustering with string kernels in R. JSS **15**, 1–28 (2006)
8. Lagarda, A., Juan, A.: Topic detection and classification techniques. WP4 deliverable, TransType2 (2003)
9. Lodhi, H., Saunders, C., Shawe-Taylor, J., Cristianini, N., Watkins, C.J.C.H.: Text classification using string kernels. JMLR **2**, 419–444 (2002)
10. MacQueen, J., and others: Some methods for classification and analysis of multivariate observations. In: Berkeley Symposium on Mathematical Statistics and Probability, pp. 281–297 (1967)
11. McCallum, A., Nigam, K.: A comparison of event models for naive bayes text classification. In: Proceedings of ICML, pp. 41–48 (1998)
12. Mikolov, T., Chen, K., Corrado, G., Dean, J.: Efficient estimation of word representations in vector space (2013). arXiv preprint arXiv:1301.3781
13. Sanchis, G.: Building task-oriented machine translation systems (Doctoral dissertation, Universitat Politcnica de Valncia) (2012)

14. Sennrich, R.: Mixture-modeling with unsupervised clusters for domain adaptation in statistical machine translation. In: Proceedings of EAMT, pp. 185–192 (2012)
15. Serrano, N., Andrés-Ferrer, J., Casacuberta, F.: On a kernel regression approach to machine translation. In: Araujo, H., Mendonça, A.M., Pinho, A.J., Torres, M.I. (eds.) IbPRIA 2009. LNCS, vol. 5524, pp. 394–401. Springer, Heidelberg (2009)
16. Szedmak, Z.W.S.T.: Kernel regression based machine translation. In: Proceedings of ACL, pp. 185–188 (2007)
17. Tiedemann, J.: News from OPUS - a collection of multilingual parallel corpora with tools and interfaces. In: Proceedings of RANLP, pp. 237–248 (2009)
18. Tiedemann, J.: Parallel data, tools and interfaces in OPUS. In: Proceedings of LREC, pp. 2214–2218 (2012)
19. Turian, J., Ratinov, L., Bengio, Y.: Word representations: a simple and general method for semi-supervised learning. In: Proceedings of ACL, pp. 384–394 (2010)
20. Wäschle, K., Riezler, S.: Structural and topical dimensions in multi-task patent translation. In: Proceedings of EACL, pp. 818–828 (2012)

Online Learning of Stochastic Bi-automaton to Model Dialogues

Odei Rey Orozko[✉] and M. Inés Torres

Dpto. Electricidad Y Electrónica., Universidad Del País Vasco., Leioa, Spain
{orey002,manes.torres}@ehu.es
http://www.ehu.es/en/web/speech-interactive/about-us

Abstract. The Interactive Pattern Recognition framework has been proposed to deal with Spoken Dialog Systems. In this framework the joint probability distribution over some semantic language provided by the speech understanding system and the language of actions provided by the Dialog Manager have been modeled by stochastic regular bi-languages. In this work we propose an algorithm to estimate the parameters of the corresponding Probabilistic Finite State Bi-Automaton. Moreover an on line learning methodology aimed at updating the model parameters at each interaction step is also proposed. The experimental evaluation carried out with different simulated users over LetsGo task shows the learning and adaptation capabilities of the proposal.

Keywords: Spoken dialogue · Pattern recognition · Online learning

1 Introduction

The design of a Spoken Dialog System (SDS) is a very complex task that involves many other problems to be solved like Automatic Speech Recognition (ASR) or Speech Understanding (SU). The Dialog Manager (DM) is the main component of a SDS. It is devoted to manage the state of the dialog as well as the dialog strategy. Due to its complexity the design of DM has been traditionally based on hand-crafted rules, sometimes combined with some statistical knowledge [5,9]. However, over the last few years some proposal based on classical pattern recognition methodologies can be found in the literature [2,5,10,13,19]. These include Bayesian networks [14], Stochastic Finite-State models [7,15] and the state-of-the-art Partially Observable Markov Decision Process [8,12]. The interactive pattern recognition framework [18] has also been proposed to represent SDS [16]. This formulation needs to estimate the joint probability distribution over the semantic language provided by the SU system and the language of actions provided by the DM. In [15] this joint probability distribution has been modeled by stochastic regular *bi-languages*. To this end a deterministic and Probabilistic Finite State Bi-Automata (PFSBA) was defined in that work. Our goal now is to present an algorithm to estimate the parameters of this PFSBA from a sample of dialogs. As another contribution we propose an on line learning

© Springer International Publishing Switzerland 2015
R. Paredes et al. (Eds.): IbPRIA 2015, LNCS 9117, pp. 441–451, 2015.
DOI: 10.1007/978-3-319-19390-8_50

methodology aimed at updating the model parameters at each interaction step. The algorithm is aimed at adapting the DM behavior to an specific task or speaker. The methodology was evaluated through a dialog generation task over the known LetsGo domain. Additional contributions include the definition and evaluation of different simulated user strategies employed to asses the learning and adaptation capabilities of the proposed methodology.

Section 2 summarizes the definition of the PFSBA and its application to model SDS. In Sect. 3 the learning algorithm is presented and in Sect. 4 it is extended to deal with online adaptation. In Sect. 5 the simulated user strategies are presented. Section 6 shows the experimental evaluation and in Sect. 7 some concluding remarks and future work are presented.

2   Finite State Bi-automata to Model Dialogs

In SDS we assume that the system interacts with the user providing a first hypothesis h through a greeting turn that acts as unique stimulus. Under the IPR framework [18] the user provides some feedback signals, f, which may iteratively help the system to improve its hypothesis. Ignoring the user feedback except for the last interaction or hypothesis h' and assuming a classical minimum-error criterion, the Bayes decision rule is simplified to maximize the posterior $Pr(h|h', f)$ [18]. In a SDS the interpretation of the decoding d of the user feedback f cannot be considered as a deterministic process. In fact the space of decoded feedback signals is the output of an ASR system. Thus, a best hypothesis $\hat{h}$ is obtained as follows [16]:

$$\hat{h} = arg\ max_{h \in H} P(h|h', f) = arg\ max_{h \in H} \sum_d P(h, d|h', f) \qquad (1)$$

being H the space of all possible hypotheses.

A suboptimal approach can be considered through a two step decoding: find first an optimal user feedback $\hat{d}$ and then, use $\hat{d}$ to decode system hypothesis $\hat{h}$ as follows:

$$\hat{d} = arg\ max_d P(f|d) P(d|h') \qquad (2)$$

$$\hat{h} \approx arg\ max_{h \in H} P(h|\hat{d}, h') \qquad (3)$$

In the same way the user feedback f depends on its previous feedback f' and system previous act h through some unknown distribution $P(f|f', h)$. However, the feedback f' produced by the user in the previous interaction is not corrupted by any noisy channel, such as an ASR system, before arriving to the user again. Thus, a deterministic decoding $d : F \rightarrow D$ maps each user turn signal into its corresponding unique decoding $d' = d(f')$. Let us now define a PFSBA to deal with both $P(h|h', d)$ and $P(f|d', h)$. A Dialog Model (M) is defined as a Deterministic PFSBA. A more detailed definition of the model could be found in the bibliography related to Deterministic PFSBA [15,17].

Table 1. An example of a dialog of the Lets Go corpus. Machine turns are labelled as sequences $\hat{h}_i \in \Delta^{\leq n}$ and User turns as sequences of decoding units $\hat{d}_i \in \Sigma^{\leq m}$.

state labelled $(\tilde{d}_i : \tilde{h}_i)$	System hypotheses and user feedbacks
$q_0 \in Q_{\mathcal{M}}$ ($\epsilon : \epsilon$)	S: *Welcome to the CMU Let's Go bus information system. To get help at any time, just say Help pr press zero. Where do you like to leave from?* $\tilde{h}_1 =$ inform_welcome,inform_get_help, request_query_departure_place
$q_1 \in Q_{\mathcal{U}}$ ($\tilde{h}_1 : \epsilon$)	U:*I'm leaving from Johnston* $\tilde{d}_1 =$ inform_departure_place, PlaceInformation_registered_stop
$q_2 \in Q_{\mathcal{M}}$ ($\tilde{h}_1 : \tilde{d}_1$)	S: *Departing from Johnston. Did I get that right?* $\tilde{h}_2 =$ Explicit_confirm, request_query_departure_place
$q_3 \in Q_{\mathcal{U}}$ ($\tilde{h}_2 : \tilde{d}_1$)	U: ...

3   Learning the Model

Let S be a sample consisting of dialogues. Each dialogue is a bi-string $\mathbf{z}$ over the extended alphabet Γ such as z: $z = z_1 \ldots z_{|z|}, z_i = (\tilde{d}_i : \tilde{h}_i)$. $\mathbf{z}$ represents a dialog when z_i is of the form $z_{2i} = (\tilde{d}_i : \varepsilon)$ for user turns and of the form $z_{2i+1} = (\varepsilon : \tilde{h}_{i+1})$ for system turns where $i = 1, 2, \ldots$. Table 1 shows an example of a dialog representation. . Our goal is to find the *PFSBA* $\hat{M}$ that maximizes the probability distribution function as follows:

$$\hat{M} = arg\ max_M\ \mathbb{P}_M(S) = arg\ max_M \prod_{\mathbf{z} \in S} \mathbb{P}_M(\mathbf{z}) \tag{4}$$

The *PFSBA* $\hat{M} = (\Sigma, \Delta, \Gamma, Q, q_0, \delta, \mathbb{P}_{\mathbb{F}}, \mathbb{P})$ can be defined as follows:

- Σ is the finite set of all the decoded feedbacks in the sample S.
- Δ is the finite set of all the dialog acts in the sample S.
- Γ is an extended alphabet such that $\Gamma \subseteq (\Sigma^{\leq m} \cup \Delta^{\leq n})$. ε represents the empty symbol for both alphabets.
- $Q = Q_M \cup Q_U$ labelled by the finite set of pairs of a user turn and a system turn in the sample S. Note that, when a state $q_i' \in Q_U$ is reached only $\tilde{h}_i$ has varied from the previous system state $q_{i-1} \in Q_M$. In the same way when a state $q_i \in Q_M$ is reached only $\tilde{d}_i$ has varied from the previous user state $q_{i-1}' \in Q_U$. See Fig.1.
- Let $q_0 = (\varepsilon : \varepsilon)$ be the initial state.
- The unambiguity of the automaton allows to obtain a maximum likelihood estimation of both, the probability $\mathbb{P} : \delta \longrightarrow [0, 1]$ of each transition (q, z, q') : $q, q' \in Q, z \in \Gamma$ and the probability $\mathbb{P}_{\mathbb{F}} : Q \longrightarrow [0, 1]$ that each state $q \in Q$ is a final state, as follows:

$$\mathbb{P}_{\mathbb{F}}(q) = \frac{c_s(\downarrow q)}{c_s(\looparrowright q)} \tag{5}$$

where $c_s(\downarrow q)$ represents the number of times that a state $q \in Q$ is a final state in the dialogs in S and $c_s(\looparrowright q)$ represents the number of times that q appears when decoding all $\mathbf{z} \in S$. And,

$$\mathbb{P}(q, z, q') = \frac{c_s(\leadsto q, z, q')}{c_s(\looparrowright q)} \tag{6}$$

where $c_s(\leadsto q, z, q')$ represents the number of times that the transition from state q to state q' appears when decoding all $\mathbf{z} \in S$. $\mathbb{P}_{\mathbb{F}}$ and $\mathbb{P}$ fulfill the normalization condition described in [15,17].

4   Online Learning

Let us get an initial estimation of the $PFSBA$ parameters as shown in Sect. 3. Let now put the DM to work with users. Each time the DM produces an hypothesis according to Eq. 3 the user provides a feedback that not always leads to one of the already defined model states, i.e. $q \notin Q$. So, the model has to deal with unforeseen situations, i.e. unseen events. To this end, smoothing strategies allowing the model to deal with any user feedback have to be defined [16]. Our goal in this work is to adapt the model to each new event appearing in each new dialog. For such purpose the model parameters are continuously updated each time a new dialogue $\mathbf{z}$ is created by a DM-user interaction through the following Online Learning procedure.

Let $\Delta_q^{\leq n} \subseteq \Delta^{\leq n}$ be the set of hypothesis associated to state $q \in Q_S$, i.e.:

$$\tilde{h} \in \Delta_q^{\leq n} \Leftrightarrow \exists q' \in Q_U \; : \; \mathbb{P}(q, (\varepsilon : \tilde{h}), q') \neq 0 \tag{7}$$

Let $\Sigma_{q'}^{\leq m} \subseteq \Sigma^{\leq m}$ be the set of decoded feedbacks associated to state $q' \in Q_U$:

$$\tilde{d} \in \Sigma_{q'}^{\leq m} \Leftrightarrow \exists q \in Q_M \; : \; \mathbb{P}(q', (\tilde{d} : \varepsilon), q) \neq 0 \tag{8}$$

The procedure explained in the next paragraphs is illustrated in Fig. 1.

User Turn. Let $q_i' \in Q_U$ be the current user state and $z_{i+1} = (\tilde{d}_i : \varepsilon)$ be the element that represents the decoding of an user feedback. Three possible situations have been identified and thus three parameter online-update are defined:

1. If $\tilde{d}_i \in \Sigma_{q_i'}^{\leq m}$ then the transition count is updated, i.e. $c_s(\leadsto q_i', z_{i+1}, q_{i+1}) \leftarrow c_s(\leadsto q_i', z_{i+1}, q_{i+1}) + 1$ and thus the state count $c_s(\looparrowright q_{i+1}) \leftarrow c_s(\looparrowright q_{i+1}) + 1$
2. Else, if $\tilde{d}_i \notin \Sigma_{q_i'}^{\leq m}$ but $q_{i+1} \in Q_M$ then a new transition $\delta(q_i', z_{i+1}, q_{i+1})$ is added to the model, i.e. $\Sigma_{q_i'}^{\leq m} = \Sigma_{q_i'}^{\leq m} \cup \tilde{d}_i$. Then the transition and state counts are also updated as before.
3. And conversely, if $\tilde{d}_i \notin \Sigma_{q_i'}^{\leq m}$ and $q_{i+1} \notin Q_M$ then a new state q_{i+1} is added to the DM model, i.e. $Q_M = q_{i+1} \cup Q_M$. Then the new transition $\delta(q_i', z_{i+1}, q_{i+1})$ is added to the model, i.e. $\Sigma_{q_i'}^{\leq m} = \Sigma_{q_i'}^{\leq m} \cup \tilde{d}_i$ Then the new transition and the state counts are also updated.

DM Turn. Let $q_{i+1} \in Q_S$ be the current DM state.

1. If $\Delta_{q_{i+1}}^{\leq n} \neq \emptyset$ and assuming a classical minimum-error criterion a best hypothesis $\hat{z}_{i+2} = (\varepsilon : \hat{\tilde{h}}_{i+1})$ is proposed by the DM to the user, which can be estimated as follows:

$$\hat{\tilde{h}}_{i+1} = arg\ max_{\tilde{h} \in \Delta_{q_{i+1}}^{\leq n}}\ \mathbb{P}(q_{i+1}, (\varepsilon : \tilde{h}), (\tilde{h} : \tilde{d}_i)) \qquad (9)$$

This maximization procedure defines the way the DM of an SDS chooses the best hypothesis in the space of hypotheses $\Delta_{q_{i+1}}^{\leq n}$, i.e. the best action at each interaction step, given the previous state q_{i+1} labelled by the previous hypothesis and the user decoded feedback. However, different criteria could also be considered [4,16]. In fact, in SDS the Dialog Manager strategy is usually based on maximizing the probability of achieving the unknown user goals while minimizing the cost of getting them [3,6,19]. The best action defines a new transition from the previous state to the new one, q'_{i+2} labelled $(\tilde{h}_{i+1} : \tilde{d}_i)$. As $\tilde{h}_{i+1} \in \Delta_{q_{i+1}}^{\leq n}$ the transition count is updated $c_s(\leadsto q_{i+1}, z_{i+2}, q'_{i+2}) \leftarrow c_s(\leadsto q_{i+1}, z_{i+2}, q'_{i+2}) + 1$ and thus the state count $c_s(\looparrowright q'_{i+2}) \leftarrow c_s(\looparrowright q'_{i+2}) + 1$

2. If $\Delta_{q_{i+1}}^{\leq n} = \emptyset$, i.e. if the user provides a feedback that does not lead to one of the states in the model then search for the most similar state $\hat{q}_{i+1}$ to state q_{i+1}. Then get the best action $\hat{z}_{i\mid 2} = (\varepsilon : \hat{\tilde{h}}_{i+1})$ according to Eq. 9 but choosing $\hat{\tilde{h}}_{i+1}$ in the space of hypotheses $\Delta_{\hat{q}_{i+1}}^{\leq n}$ of the estimated most similar state $\hat{q}_{i+1}$ instead of in the empty space $\Delta_{q_{i+1}}^{\leq n}$. Thus, a new state q'_{i+2} is added to the model, i.e. $Q_U = q'_{i+2} \cup Q_U$. Also a new transition $\delta(q_{i+1}, \hat{z}_{i+2}, q'_{i+2})$ is now added to the model, i.e. $\Sigma_{q_{i+1}}^{\leq n} = \Sigma_{q_{i+1}}^{\leq n} \cup \tilde{h}_{i+1}$. As a consequence the transition count $c_s(\leadsto q_{i+1}, \hat{z}_{i+2}, q'_{i+2})$ and the state count $c_s(\looparrowright q'_{i+2})$ are also updated.

Searching for the most similar state. We have identified two different situations where the user provides a feedback that does not lead to an state in the model. Two strategies are then defined:

1. Select a state in the model labelled with the same user feedback. If more than one state can be found then choose the nearest state to a final state.
2. Else choose the most similar state to the given one according to a similarity metric between two states that has to be defined. The user perception about the system is strongly related to the similarity metric between the two states. When it is not very accurate the user may notice an incongruence in the system response.

The Online Learning procedure defined in this section allows to add new states and transitions to the model while the system is running. The DM is continuously adapting to new user feedbacks and learns from them (See Fig. 1). However, models found in the literature are usually learned through a batch procedure and they remain static while they are running.

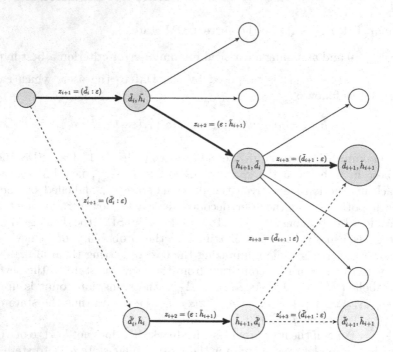

Fig. 1. Graphical representation of the Online learning procedure. If the user provides a feedback, $\tilde{d}'_i$, that does not lead to an state in the model, let $(\tilde{d}_i, \tilde{h}_i)$ be the most similar state to $(\tilde{d}_i{}', \tilde{h}_i)$. From $(\tilde{d}_i, \tilde{h}_i)$ a best action z_{i+2} is obtained by Eq. 9. Thus, two new transitions and two new states are added to the model (green states). If in the next user turn the user feedback $\tilde{d}_i$ leads to an state in the model $(\tilde{d}_{i+1}, \tilde{h}_{i+1})$, then only a new transition is added to the model. If not, a new state $(\tilde{d}'_{i+1}, \tilde{h}_{i+1})$ and a new transition are added to the model.

5   Simulated User

Due to the difficulties of the SDS evaluation with real users, a previous testing and adaptation procedure with simulated users (SU) is usually carried out. To this end the probability distribution $P(f|d', h)$ can be approached by some user model whose parameters have also to be estimated from data through a learning procedure. Such a model can be defined under the IPR framework considering now the user point of view [16]. We only need to define the way the user chooses the *best* feedback $\hat{f}$ to be provided to the DM. In this work we propose two strategies to approach a user random behavior.

Strategy 1: Fully Random. Let $q'_i \in Q_U$ be the current user state. The SU has to provide a feedback f_i such that $z_{i+1} = (\tilde{d}_i : \varepsilon)$ represents the decoding of f_i by some ASR system.

- If $\Sigma^{\leq m}_{q'_i} \neq \emptyset$ then $\tilde{d}_i$ is randomly estimated in the space of decodings $\Sigma^{\leq m}_{q'_i}$ i.e.
  $$\tilde{d}_i = random(\tilde{d})_{\tilde{d} \in \Sigma^{\leq m}_{q'_i}}$$

– When $\Sigma_{\hat{q}'_i}^{\leq m} = \emptyset$ the system has provided an hypothesis that did not lead to one of the states in the model. We then search for the state $\hat{q}'_i \in Q_U$ most similar to $q'_i \notin Q_U$ according to the procedure defined in Sect. 4. Then $\tilde{d}_i$ is randomly estimated in the space of decodings $\Sigma_{\hat{q}'_i}^{\leq m}$ of the estimated state.

A random selection of the SU feedback could lead to loops when generating dialogues if SU feedbacks are repeated. To prevent this, the SU ignores feedbacks already proposed in the two previous user turns.

Strategy 2: Avoiding Closings. The fully random SU strategy tends to close dialogues before retrieving results or completing a certain number of turns. To avoid a high number of user final states, i.e. closing turns, we propose to learn the final state distribution from the training corpus. We found that the 50 % of closed dialogues in the training corpus did not provided any result or provided uncovered as system answer.

To this end we implemented two strategies to avoid closing turns before a minimum number of turns:

– Strategy 2.1: Count the number of dialogues already closed with and without results. If the number of closed dialogs without results is higher than the number with results then avoid the transition to the user closing state.
– Strategy 2.2: Use the probabilistic distribution of closing dialogues in the training corpus.

6 Experiments

For these experiments the DM and SU model parameters were estimated from Let's Go corpus [11]. The Olympus SDS architecture including Ravenclaw DM [1] was used by Carnegie Mellon University (CMU) to develop a SDS that provides schedules and route information about the city of Pittsburgh bus service to the general public. In this work we use the set of dialogues collected in about two months in 2005. The main features of this corpus are summarized in Table 2.

A first DM and SU models were obtained through the batch learning procedure defined in Sect. 3. To this end the corpus was split into two subsets to train the DM and the SU respectively, performing a first maximum likelihood

Table 2. Main features of the set of Lets Go dialogues used in this work

Dialogues	1840
Speakers	1840
System Turns	28141
User Turns	28071
System Dialogue Acts	49
User Dialogue Acts	138
Attributes	14

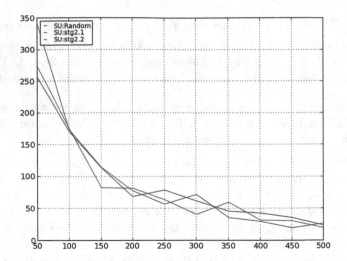

Fig. 2. Number of new states added to the DM while learning from 500 DM-SU interactions according to the updating procedure defined in Sect. 4 when the three SU strategies defined in Sect. 5 were considered. The evaluation is carried out each 50 dialogues.

estimation of both models (initial models). Then the Initial DM was used to interact 500 times with each of the three SU strategies defined in Sect. 5 while updating the model parameters through the online learning procedure defined in Sect. 4 and thus generate 500 dialogs. Due to the random component of the SU these online learning procedures were repeated three times.

Table 3 shows the number of nodes and edges of the initial DM and SU models as well as the average sizes of the ones obtained after the three series of 500 interactions and dialog generation while the model parameters were updated online. This table shows a high increase of the DM model size both in terms of the number of nodes, between 12,72 % to 13,24 % depending of the SU strategies, and also in terms of the number of edges, ranking between 10,48 % and 11,45 %. when the online procedure was applied and 500 new dialogs were generated. These results demonstrate the learning effort carried out by the DM to adapt its behavior to the random SUs. Figure 2 shows the number of new states added to the DM evaluated in steps of 50 dialogues. According to Fig. 2 the number of new states added to the DM model decreases after a learning procedure of about 150 dialogs for this task.

For each of the three repetitions of the 500 DM-SU interactions updating the model parameters two new series of experiments were carried out:

1. **100-OFF** Use the initial DM and SU models and generate 100 dialogues. Repeat 100 times. Repeat for each SU strategy.
2. **100-ON** Use the DM model learned through the 500 dialogs online learning procedure and generate 100 dialogues. Repeat 100 times. Repeat for each SU strategy.

Table 3. Sizes of the Initial and Learned Models (DM and SU)for each SU behavior

	Initial model		Learned Model SU-Random		Learned Model SU-Stg 2.1		Learned Model SU-Stg 2.2	
	Nodes	Edges	Nodes	Edges	Nodes	Edges	Nodes	Edges
System	5300	3064	5974	3401	6002	3415	5942	3385
User	6273	4604	6499	4724	6520	4736	6493	4718

Table 4. Mean of TC and ADL of the dialogues generated at each series of experiments using the initial models (100-OFF) and using the online learned model (100-ON). The mean of the percentage of smoothed turns used is also provided for each SU behavior.

	SU-Random			SU-Strategy 2.1			SU-Strategy 2.2		
	TC	ADL	Smoothed turns (%)	TC	ADL	Smoothed turns(%)	TC	ADL	Smoothed turns (%)
100-ON	33,6	28,6	0,79	43,3	36,9	0,52	34,1	28,76	0,86
100-OFF	33,9	28,4	12,47	43,45	36,49	12,8	34,3	28,5	12,5

For these experiments two evaluation metrics were computed:

Task Completion(TC). Measures the success of the system in providing the user with the information requested. We compute it by checking if the dialogue ends with a system goodbye turn or if the DM makes one of more queries to the backend to get the information required by the user.

Averague Dialogue Lenght(ADL). The average number of turns in a dialogue.

Table 4 shows the mean of the TC and ADL values of the 50.000 dialogues generated at each series of experiments using the initial models (100-OFF) and using the online learned model (100-ON) for each SU behavior. The mean of the percentage of smoothed turns used is also provided. The difference in the percentage of smoothed turns used in 100-OFF and 100-ON experiments is significant and measures, to some extend, the capacity for learning of the proposed algorithm for this task and SU models. Table 4 also shows a higher ability of SU-strategy2.1 to complete tasks at the cost of consuming a higher number of turns. However similar TC and ADL values were obtained in 100-OFF and 100-ON experiments for every SU, probably due to the random component of SU strategies.

7 Conclusions and Future Work

We have presented an algorithm to estimate the parameters of a Deterministic and Probabilistic Finite State Bi-Automata from a sample of dialogs. An on line learning methodology aimed at updating the model parameters at each interaction step has also been proposed. The experimental evaluation carried out with different simulated users over the well known LetsGo task has showed the learning capabilities of the proposed methodology. However simulated user behaviors without a random component have to be defined to assess the ability for adaptation of the proposed online learning algorithm. Future work also includes task adaptation where open vocabularies have to be considered.

Acknowledgements. This work has been partially supported by the Spanish Ministry of Science under grant TIN2011-28169-C05-04, and by the Basque Government under grants PRE_2013_1_1249 and IT685-13.

References

1. Bohus, D., Rudnicky, A.I.: The RavenClaw dialog management framework: architecture and systems. Comput. Speech Lang. **23**, 332–361 (2009)
2. Cuayáhuitl, H., Renals, S., Lemon, O., Shimodaira, H.: Evaluation of a hierarchical reinforcement learning spoken dialogue system. Comput. Speech Lang. **25**, 395–429 (2010)
3. Ghigi, F., Torres, M.I., Justo, R., Benedí, J.M.: Evaluating spoken dialogue models under the interactive pattern recognition framework. In: INTERSPEECH. pp. 480–484 (2013)
4. Ghigir, F., Torres, M.: Decision making strategies for finite-state bi-automaton in dialog management. In: Proceedings of International Workshop on Spoken Dialog Systems Technology (2015)
5. Griol, D., Hurtado, L.F., Segarra, E., Sanchis, E.: A statistical approach to spoken dialog systems design and evaluation. Speech Commun. **50**, 666–682 (2008)
6. Hajdinjak, M., Mihleič, F.: The paradise evaluation framework: issues and findings. Comput. Linguist. **32**(2), 263–272 (2006)
7. Hurtado, L.F., Planells, J., Segarra, E., Sanchis, E., Griol, D.: A stochastic finite-state transducer approach to spoken dialog management. In: INTERSPEECH, pp. 3002–3005 (2010)
8. Jurčíček, F., Thomson, B., Young, S.: Reinforcement learning for parameter estimation in statistical spoken dialogue systems. Comput. Speech Lang. **26**(3), 168–192 (2012)
9. Lemon, O., Pietquin, O.: Machine learning for spoken dialogue systems. In: Proceedings of the 10th European Conference on Speech Communication and Technology. Interspeech. pp. 2685–2688. Antwerp, Belgium, 27–31 August 2007
10. Meng, H., Wai, C., Picraccini, R.: The use of belief networks for mixed-initiative dialog modeling. IEEE Trans. Speech Audio Process. **11**(6), 757–773 (2003)
11. Raux, A., Langner, B., Bohus, D., Black, A.W., Eskenazi, M.: Let's go public! taking a spoken dialog system to the real world. In: Proceeding of Interspeech (2005)
12. S. Young, M. Gasic, B.T., Williams, J.: Pomdp-based statistical spoken dialogue systems: a review. In: Proceedings of the IEEE (2013, to appear)
13. Sarigaya, R., Gao, Y., Picheney, M.: A comparison of rule-based and statistical methods for semantic language modeling and confidence measurement. In: Proceedings of the Human Language Technology conference. North American chapter of the Association for Computational Linguistics annual meeting. HLT-NAACL, pp. 65–68. Boston (2007)

14. Thomson, B., Yu, K., Keizer, S., Gasic, M., Jurcicek, F., Mairesse, F., Young, S.: Bayesian dialogue system for the let's go spoken dialogue challenge. In: 2010 IEEE Spoken Language Technology Workshop (SLT), pp. 460–465. IEEE (2010)
15. Torres, M.I.: Stochastic bi-languages to model dialogs. In: Finite State Methods and Natural Language Processing p. 9 (2013)
16. Inés Torres, M., Benedí, J.M., Justo, R., Ghigi, F.: Modeling spoken dialog systems under the interactive pattern recognition framework. In: Gimel'farb, G., et al. (eds.) SSPR&SPR 2012. LNCS, pp. 519–528. Springer, Heidelberg (2012)
17. Torres, M.I., Casacuberta, F.: Stochastic K-TSS bi-languages for machine translation. In: Proceedings of the 9th International Workshop on Finite State Models for Natural Language Processing (FSMNLP). pp. 98–106. Association for Computational Linguistics, Blois (France) (2011)
18. Toselli, A.H., Vidal, E., Casacuberta, F. (eds.): Multimodal Interactive Pattern Recognition and Applications. Springer-Verlag, London (2011)
19. Williams, J.D., Young, S.: Partially observable markov decision processes for spoken dialog systems. Comput. Speech Lang. **21**, 393–422 (2007)

Single-Channel Separation Between Stationary and Non-stationary Signals Using Relevant Information

J.D. Martínez-Vargas[1]([⊠]), C. Castro-Hoyos[1], J.J. Espinosa-Oviedo[2],
A.M. Álvarez-Mesa[1], and G. Castellanos-Dominguez[1]

[1] Signal Processing and Recognition Group,
Universidad Nacional de Colombia, Bogotá, Colombia
{jmartinezv,ccastroh,amalvarezme,cgcastellanosd}@unal.edu.co
[2] Grupo de Automática, Universidad Nacional de Colombia, Bogotá, Colombia
jairo.espinosa@ieee.org

Abstract. We propose a novel unsupervised single-channel approach to separate between stationary and non-stationary signals. To this, we enhance data representation through its *time-frequency* space, where stationarity is defined based on information theory. Then, we search for the projection of the time-frequency representation that is as stationarity as possible, but preserving most of the data information. The proposed approach validated on synthetic data. As performance measure, we use the correlation coefficient and the mean squared error between the original and the estimated stationary composing signals. Obtained results are compared against the baseline non-negative matrix factorization that separates dynamics from the *time-frequency* representation. As a result, our approach gets better performance even if assuming low power ratios, i.e., non-stationary signal power is higher or even equal than the stationary signal power.

Keywords: Stationary signal separation · Information theoretic learning · Time frequency analysis

1 Introduction

In practice, the number of applications requiring for separation between non-stationary and stationary signals continues to expand. The cornerstone of this filtering task is the separation model holding those stochastic constraints that must be imposed to make the composing signals statistically disjoint. Identifying signals of the apparent variability in non-stationary scenarios is a fundamental problem in many biological data analysis settings. The origin and functional role of this observed variability is one of the fundamental questions in neuroscience. To this end, signal separation methods should have as desired properties the following: (i) to highlight stochastic behavior of an underlying random process during estimation [1], (ii) to ensure established stochastic constraints dealing with non-stationary signal structure within the projection framework.

© Springer International Publishing Switzerland 2015
R. Paredes et al. (Eds.): IbPRIA 2015, LNCS 9117, pp. 452–459, 2015.
DOI: 10.1007/978-3-319-19390-8_51

This work concerns the challenging case of separation between non-stationary and stationary composing signals when a single observation signal is available (known as *unsupervised single-channel* composing signal separation) that is the case as in monitoring of machine operating conditions, seismic analysis, climatic and economic time series prediction, etc. Specifically for this situation, solutions based on adaptive filters are commonly employed [2,3]. However, to improve representation of single observations, a solution is suggested involving two main steps [4]: (*i*) calculation of a suitable enhanced representation of input data, and (*ii*) composing signal separation over estimated enhanced space. Nevertheless, these algorithms impose strong assumptions about local stationarity and the composing signal nature to ensure their convergence. In order to face this issue, a bi-dimensional non-negative matrix factorization over a Time-Frequency Representation (TFR) of the observed (mixed) signal is proposed in [5], where several mixed non-stationary signals are separated. However, as no formal stationary definitions are formulated, the source separation task becomes highly dependent on the parameter set that are heuristically tuned based on prior knowledge of non-stationary dynamics. However, this knowledge is not always feasible in practice.

In this paper, we propose a less restrictive separating approach that can be developed grounded in conventional subspace analysis to overcome the aforementioned problems. This approach consists of searching the projection maximally bearing input information, at the same time, retaining only those data contributing the most to data stationarity representation. Also, our approach uses an enhancement of the observed time-series into a TFR that provides, besides the local stationarity assumption, a suitable stationarity definition over the *t-f* space. Afterwards, we seek, based on information theory, a projected space where the stationarity definition is fulfill but preserving as much as possible the information provided in the original *t-f* space. As a result, projection provides TFRs that are as stationary as possible.

2 Stationary Source Separation Based on Relevant Information

Let $x_s \in \mathbb{R}^T$ denote a stationary signal of length T that is assumed to be corrupted by a non-stationary signal $x_n \in \mathbb{R}^T$, so that any measured observation of the linearly mixing signal, $x \in \mathbb{R}^T$, is given by $x = x_s + x_n$. The problem of source separation (between stationary and non-stationary sources) is to determine conditions on x_s and x_n such that an estimate of the desired signal $\hat{x}_s$ can be obtained, from filtered x, to a given degree of accuracy [2].

Solutions to this problem are commonly based on suitable time-frequency representations (TFRs) of the mixture signal x, that is: $\mathcal{F}:\mathbb{R}^T \to \mathbb{R}^{F \times T}:x \mapsto S$, where $\mathcal{F}$ is the time-frequency transform operator mapping a real input signal from the time domain to the time-frequency domain. Consequently, it can be assumed that a linear relation between the time-varying spectrum of stationary and non-stationary sources exists in the form: $S = S_s + S_n$, where S,

$S_s, S_n \in \mathbb{R}^{F \times T}$ are the magnitude of the mixture, stationary, and non-stationary signal TFRs, respectively. Besides, $F, T \in \mathbb{R}^+$ are the number of frequency bins and time samples, respectively.

The aim of stationary source estimation in the t-f domain is to find a projection matrix, $W \in \mathbb{R}^{F \times \tilde{F}}$, where sources fulfill an *a priori* provided stationary constraint, that is, $S_s = W^\top S$. As described in [6], as a suitable stationary restriction on the t-f domain, the uncertainty of the frequency bands along the time can be used. Consequently, we want to find that projection of S where the entropy of its frequency bands along the time is minimized, but maximally preserving the relevant stationary content. This problem can be solved by using the Principle of relevant information that minimizes the following objective function [7]:

$$J = \sum_{\forall f \in F} \mathbb{H}\{s_s^f\} + \lambda \sum_{\forall f \in F} d_{cs}(p(s_s^f)\|p(s^f)) \tag{1}$$

where $s_s^f \in \mathbb{R}^{1 \times T}$ is the f-th frequency band of S_s, and $\lambda \in \mathbb{R}^+$ is the regularization parameter ruling the weight of both terms in Eq. (1).

We formulate the task in Eq. (1) in terms of minimizing the sum over all the frequency bands of the f-th frequency band entropy in the projected space, namely $\mathbb{H}\{s_s^f\}$, tha is constrained by the divergence between the probability density (pdf) of the original and the pdf of projected f-th frequency band. The former quantity can be seen as the stationary constraint, while the latter one – as an information preservation term [8]. For simplicity, we use the Cauchy Schwartz divergence defined as:

$$d_{cs}(p(s_s^f)\|p(s^f)) = 2\mathbb{H}\{p(s_s^f); p(s^f)\} - \mathbb{H}\{p(s_s^f)\} - \mathbb{H}\{p(s^f)\}, \tag{2}$$

Grounded on the introduced measure in Eq. (2), the optimization task in Eq. (1) can be rewritten in the form:

$$J = (1 - \lambda) \sum_{\forall f \in F} \mathbb{H}\{s_s^f\} + 2\lambda \sum_{\forall f \in F} \mathbb{H}\{(p(s_s^f); p(s^f))\}. \tag{3}$$

On the other hand, we can employ the Parzen estimate of $p(s_f^s)$ and $p(s_f)$, in particular, we make use of Gaussian kernels. As a result, we obtain the following non-parametric estimator of the Renyi's quadratic entropy:

$$\widehat{\mathbb{H}}\{s_f^s\} = -\log\left(\mathbb{E}\{G_\sigma(s_f^s(t) - s_f^s(l)) : \forall t, l \in 1, \dots T\}\right)$$
$$= -\log\left(\mathbb{E}\{G_\sigma(w_f^\top s_t - w_f^\top s_l) : \forall t, l\}\right) \tag{4}$$

where notation $\mathbb{E}\{\cdot\}$ stands for the expectation operator, $s_t \in \mathbb{R}^{F \times 1}$ is the t-th column vector of S, $w_f \in \mathbb{R}^{F \times 1}$ is the f-th column vector of W, and the Gaussian kernel is defined as: $G_\sigma(w_f^\top s_t - w_f^\top s_l) = (\sqrt{2\pi}\sigma^2)^{-1} \exp\left((w_f^\top s_t - w_f^\top s_l)^2/(2\sigma^2)\right)$.

Thus, the second term of Eq. (3) is estimated by the Renyi's cross entropy as:

$$\widehat{\mathbb{H}}\{p(s_s^f); p(s^f)\} = -\log\left(\mathbb{E}\{G_\sigma(w_f^\top s_t - s(f, l)) : \forall t, l\}\right) \tag{5}$$

where $s(f,l) \in \mathbb{R}^+$ is the value of the TFR evaluated at $f \in F, l \in T$.

By replacing Eqs. (4) and (5) in Eq. (3), the problem is solved by searching for the projection matrix W that minimizes the following objective function:

$$W^* = \underset{W}{\operatorname{argmin}} \left\{ -(1-\lambda) \sum_{f \in F} \log \left(\mathbb{E} \left\{ G_\sigma(w_f^\top s_t - w_f^\top s_l) : \forall t, l \right\} \right) \right.$$
$$\left. -2\lambda \sum_{f \in F} \log \left(\mathbb{E} \left\{ G_\sigma(w_f^\top s_t - s(f,l)) : \forall t, l \right\} \right) \right\} \quad (6)$$

Here, we carry out the optimization problem by using the Gradient descendant method until a convergence threshold, i.e.: $W^{k+1} = W^k - \eta \partial J / \partial W$, where $\eta \in \mathbb{R}^+$ is the step size and the f-th derivative column is computed as follows:

$$(T/\sigma)^{-2} \frac{\partial J}{\partial w_f} = (1-\lambda) \mathbb{E} \left\{ \left(w_f^\top s_l - w_f^\top s_t \right) \left(s_l - s_t \right) : \forall t, l \right\}$$
$$+ 2\lambda \mathbb{E} \left\{ \left(w_f^\top s_l - s(f,t) \right) s_l : \forall t, l \right\}. \quad (7)$$

Thus, we obtain the stationary and sources in the t-f domain, $S_s = W^\top S$, and $S_n = S - S_s$. respectively. So, we compute the stationary and non-stationary signals through the inverse TFR by using the obtained TFR magnitude and phase information.

3 Experimental Set-Up

3.1 Testing Dataset and Performance Measure

All observed time-series are generated as a linear superposition of simulated stationary and non-stationary signals. Thus, given the stationarity constraint in the t-f domain, stationary sources are generated so that the time-varying spectrum S^s is as stationary as possible. For this, two types of stationary sources are considered: (i) a cosine signal with normalized central frequency randomly sampled within the interval $[0, 0.5]$, (ii) an autoregressive moving average model (particularly an ARMA(3,3) model is used) with parameters randomly sampled from the Normal distribution $\mathcal{N}(0, 1)$. To illustrate simulated processes, an example of stationary sources can be seen in Fig. 1a and b. Additionally, the non-stationary sources are formed by one of the following models: a cosine signal fading or intensifying its amplitude by a modulating envelope (exponential or linear, respectively), a chaotic Lorenz attractor, a linear chirp sinusoid or a cosine signal modulated by a Gaussian pulse at a random instant (wavelet). All involved parameters are randomly sampled from normal distributions within the appropriate intervals. Examples of simulated non-stationary signals are shown in Fig. 1e-g.

As performance measures, mean squared error (MSE), $\epsilon^2 \in \mathbb{R}^+$, and correlation coefficient, $\rho \in \mathbb{R}[0, 1]$ (between true and estimated stationary components) are used; both defined respectively as:

$$\epsilon^2 = \mathbb{E} \left\{ (\hat{x}_i^s - x_i^s)^2 : \forall i \in T \right\} \quad (8a)$$

$$\rho = \operatorname{cov}(x^s, \hat{x}^s) / (\sigma_x \sigma_{\hat{x}^s}) \quad (8b)$$

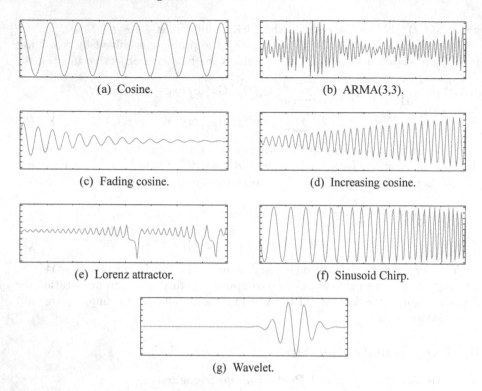

(a) Cosine.

(b) ARMA(3,3).

(c) Fading cosine.

(d) Increasing cosine.

(e) Lorenz attractor.

(f) Sinusoid Chirp.

(g) Wavelet.

Fig. 1. Examples of simulated stationary and non-stationary real-valued time series.

Table 1. Separation performance for SVD-based initialization

(a) Mean Squared Error ε^2.

Snr	NMF2D	TF-PRISS				
	N/A	λ				
		0.001	0.25	0.5	0.75	0.999
-3	0.607	**0.337**	0.451	0.472	0.483	0.495
0	0.227	0.339	0.168	0.163	0.163	**0.163**
3	0.149	0.339	0.077	0.077	0.077	**0.076**
6	0.115	0.326	0.058	**0.057**	0.057	0.057
12	0.096	0.335	0.071	0.071	0.071	**0.071**
-3	**0.345**	0.452	0.401	0.407	0.401	0.404
0	0.174	0.468	0.165	0.154	0.152	**0.145**
3	0.124	0.441	0.073	0.074	**0.073**	0.073
6	0.107	0.452	0.057	**0.057**	0.057	0.057
12	0.087	0.445	0.056	0.056	**0.055**	0.055

(b) Correlation Coefficient ρ.

Snr	NMF2D	TF-PRISS				
	N/A	λ				
		0.001	0.25	0.5	0.75	0.999
-3	**0.386**	0.254	0.356	0.357	0.358	0.359
0	0.616	0.126	0.653	0.658	**0.659**	0.658
3	0.773	0.308	0.828	0.828	**0.828**	0.828
6	0.871	0.470	0.870	0.870	0.870	**0.871**
12	0.943	0.505	0.878	0.878	0.878	**0.878**
-3	0.397	0.246	0.412	0.406	**0.430**	0.407
0	0.623	0.126	0.730	0.732	**0.735**	0.733
3	0.795	0.273	**0.884**	0.883	0.878	0.882
6	0.877	0.524	0.922	**0.926**	0.926	0.925
12	**0.964**	0.364	0.940	0.941	0.940	0.941

where cov is the covariance function and σ_x is the standard deviation of the signal x.

Experiments of the proposed separation method are carried out under 5 different power ratios between stationary and non–stationary sources, namely, the signal to noise-ratio (SNR) values of $-3, 0, 3, 6, 12\ dB$ are used. The sample

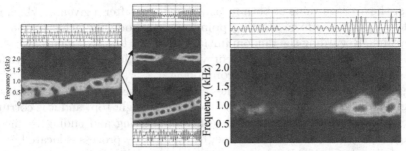

(a) TFR of a stationary signal (right top), (b) Stationary component estimation by contaminated by a non–stationary com-NMF2D.
ponent (right bottom).

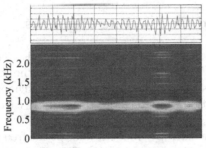

(c) Stationary component estimation by TF-PRISS.

Fig. 2. Example of stationary component separation in time and t-f.

size of simulated time series is set to 200 samples, whereas the sampling frequency f_s is set to $5\,kHz$. The separation task is carried out 30 times, where only one stationary component is assumed to be affected by a random number of non–stationary sources. For the TFR, the short time Fourier transform is employed, with a window parameter of 0.315 times the signal duration, that is, $L_w = 63$.

To carry out the gradient search, we consider two initializations for the projection matrix $\boldsymbol{W}$, the eigenvectors of the covariance matrix $\boldsymbol{SS}^\top$ and a random orthonormal matrix with rank F. The step size η is set empirically.

For the sake of comparison, we use a non-negative matrix two dimensional factorization, called NMF2D [5], that separates several dynamics from a time-varying spectrum. We set the frequency window length as $L_f = 1$ to obtain a direct comparison with our approach, while the time window length is set as $L_t = L_w = 63$ to search for stationary components.

Table 1 shows the average results for the baseline NMF2D and the proposed TF-PRISS (Time-Frequency and Principal Relevant Information based Stationary Separation), under different configurations of the regularization parameter λ. As seen, the proposed approach yields lower MSE values when using SVD based initialization. Our approach also achieves values of the correlation coefficient either better or comparable to the results reached by the approach NMF2D.

Besides, the average value of both measures remains after a given λ, which indicates that, given the fixed starting point, the methodology achieves the same local optima. Regarding the random initialization, for low SNR values, we obtain better MSE and correlation coefficient values with higher values of λ, yielding better estimation of the stationary component.

Figure 2a–c show an example of the separation procedure. The stationary signal is given by an ARMA (3,3) process (see Fig. 2a, right top) and it is corrupted by two different chirp sinusoids with different starting and ending frequencies (see Fig. 2a, right bottom). In this case, the stationary process is located around the $1\,kHz$ band, specifically the highest energy concentration exist at $859\,Hz$. It can be seen that TF-PRISS Fig. 2c shows a better approximation of the stationary ARMA process than the NMF2D methodology (see Fig. 2b).

4   Discussion and Concluding Remarks

In the present paper, a novel approach for unsupervised stationary component separation is presented. The methodology is based on the principal relevant information theory and aims to separate stationary single channel time-series, which is corrupted by non–stationary signals. To this end, we carry out minimization of an introduced stationary restriction in the t-f domain. As stationary constraint, we propose the use of the entropy since its value of the frequency bands along the time must tend to zero, as suggested in [6]. Therefore, we seek for a projection matrix that makes each frequency band as stationary as possible. Additionally, we include a term guaranteeing that the information available in the original space is preserved as much as possible.

Regarding the solution of the non–linear optimization problem, we employ the conventional gradient descendant search that requires for the tuning of the step size and the regularization parameters in order to get suitable solutions. The former parameter is empirically set, while several values for the regularization parameter are considered. Thus, fixing the λ value equals to 0 leads to have no constraints about how much information must be preserved, though the entropy is minimized. In contrast, fixing $\lambda \to \infty$, we only optimize over the preserved information. As result, both the projected and input data match (since W tends to be an identity matrix), yielding no separated sources. Lastly, making values of λ close to 0.5 equally weights both terms in Eq. 6, resulting in acceptable separation sources.

We carry out validation of the proposed methodology over synthetic time-series for different values of the power ratio between the stationary and non-stationary signals (see Table 1). Obtained result show that TF-PRISS is able to properly separate stationary sources even in cases when their powers are equivalent, providing values of the correlation coefficient as high as 0.735.

It is important to remark that we are providing with a unsupervised stationary component separation methodology based on information theoretic learning and stationarity definitions given in a time-frequency space, yet another stationarity definitions may be also be included into the model to improve the achieved results. Additionally, we assume independence among the stationary frequency bands, which may entail a limitation of the proposed approach.

As future work, it would of benefit to include conditional and joint probability estimation terms into the optimization problem, such that relationships among frequencies should be considered in the projection matrix. Also, Authors plan to extend the methodology for multi-channel environments where entropy based stationarity is further analyzed in a joint time-frequency and time–space representation. Besides, further optimization methods will be studied aiming to reduce the computational burden. Finally, the methodology will be tested in real problems, as EEG artifact rejection.

Acknowledgments. This research is carried out under the grant project *22056 - DESARROLLO DE UN SISTEMA AUTOMÁTICO DE MAPEO CEREBRAL PARA EL MONITOREO Y TRATAMIENTO DE ENFERMEDADES NEURODEGENER- ATIVAS* sponsored by DIMA from Universidad Nacional de Colombia - Manizales. It is also supported by the scholarship Programa Nacional de Formacion de Investigadores GENERACION DEL BICENTENARIO, 2011 and project *Evaluación asistida de potenciales evocados cognitivos como marcador del transtorno por déficit de atensión e hiperactividad (TDAH)* founded by COLCIENCIAS.

References

1. Martínez-Vargas, J., Sepulveda-Cano, L., Travieso-Gonzalez, C., Castellanos-Dominguez, G.: Detection of obstructive sleep apnoea using dynamic filter-banked features. Expert Syst. Appl. **39**(10), 9118–9128 (2012)
2. Hopgood, J., Rayner, P.J.W.: Single channel nonstationary stochastic signal separation using linear time-varying filters. IEEE Trans. Signal Process. **51**(7), 1739–1752 (2003)
3. Gu, F., Zhang, H., Tan, X., Zhu, D.: Rls algorithm for blind source separation in non-stationary environments. In: Symposium on ICT and Energy Efficiency and Workshop on Information Theory and Security (CIICT 2012), pp. 162–165, July 2012
4. Mijovic, B., De Vos, M., Gligorijevic, I., Taelman, J., Van Huffel, S.: Source separation from single-channel recordings by combining empirical-mode decomposition and independent component analysis. IEEE Trans. Biomed. Eng. **57**(9), 2188–2196 (2010)
5. Gao, B., Woo, W., Dlay, S.: Unsupervised single-channel separation of nonstationary signals using gammatone filterbank and itakura-saito nonnegative matrix two-dimensional factorizations. IEEE Trans. Circ. Syst. I Regul. Pap. **60**(3), 662–675 (2013)
6. Tong, S., Li, Z., Zhu, Y., Thakor, N.V.: Describing the nonstationarity level of neurological signals based on quantifications of time-frequency representation. IEEE Trans. Biomed. Eng. **54**(10), 1780–1785 (2007)
7. Principe, J.C.: Information Theoretic Learning: Renyi's Entropy and Kernel Perspectives, 1st edn. Springer Publishing Company, Incorporated, Berlin (2010)
8. Rao, S.M.: Unsupervised learning: an information theoretic framework. Ph.D. dissertation, Gainesville, FL, USA (2008). aAI3367034

Computer Vision

A New Trajectory Based Motion Segmentation Benchmark Dataset (UdG-MS15)

Muhammad Habib Mahmood[1]([✉]), Luca Zappella[2], Yago Díez[1], Joaquim Salvi[1], and Xavier Lladó[1]

[1] Computer Vision and Robotics Group (ViCOROB),
University of Girona, Girona, Spain
{mhabib,yago,qsalvi,llado}@eia.udg.edu
[2] Metaio GmbH, Munich, Germany
luca.zappella@metaio.com

Abstract. Motion segmentation (MS) is an essential step in video analysis. Its quantitative and qualitative evaluation is largely dependent on the dataset used for testing. Although there are publicly available datasets such as Hopkins and FBMS, they have limitations in terms of number of motions, partial/complete occlusion, stopping motion, sequence length, and real life natural sequences. Due to these limitations, many recent proposals have reached nearly zero misclassification, especially for Hopkins, which leaves no room for quantitatively differentiating among proposals. In this paper, we present a new challenging trajectory based MS dataset of 15 sequences, where number of motions and sequence length have been largely increased as compared to the state of the art. An effort has been made to include all forms of distortions that are present in real life scenes. As a starting point, a preliminary benchmark evaluation using a recent and well known state of the art algorithm has been provided for this dataset.

Keywords: Motion segmentation · Tracking · Trajectory · Benchmark · Dataset

1 Introduction

Motion Segmentation (MS) is a preprocessing step for many computer vision applications (e.g. surveillance, semantic analysis, etc.), and comprises the classification of regions or trajectories in videos into sets according to motion cues.

MS has been of particular interest to researchers in recent years. For instance, the problem has been approached by subspace clustering methods in [1–5]. With a different view point, *Rao et al.* [6] and *Vidal et al.* [7] addressed the issue of corrupted trajectories and missing data in a mathematical framework. MS has also been approached by statistical [8] and layer techniques [9]. Moreover, Optical flow based long term analysis of point trajectories has been performed for moving object segmentation [10,11].

© Springer International Publishing Switzerland 2015
R. Paredes et al. (Eds.): IbPRIA 2015, LNCS 9117, pp. 463–470, 2015.
DOI: 10.1007/978-3-319-19390-8_52

Since 2007, *Hopkins155* [12] is considered as the reference benchmark for MS. This trajectory based database was widely accepted in the community because it provided a unique opportunity for researchers to easily compare their algorithms. However, misclassification rates started to drop, and now have become insignificant: 0.8 % [1], mostly due to overfitting, but partly because the dataset is limited for recent algorithms. It is composed of 155 short sequences of almost 1 to 2 s at 30 fps, with more than 100 having synthetic motions e.g. checkerboard and books. Nowadays, it can not be considered a challenging MS dataset as all trajectories are complete without real noise i.e. occlusion, stopping motion, perspective distortions. In 'Hopkins Additional' 12 sequences were added with 8 % missing data to include real noise but the need for more challenging sequences still stands.

In [10] and [13] two region based datasets *BMS29* and *FBMS59*, respectively were presented, with the later being the extension of the first. The sequences have partial occlusion resulting in missing data. The average length of videos is relatively small around 8 s at 30 fps. The ground truth is provided as segmented regions of moving objects on a small subset of images of the dataset (one every 20 frames). Although, *FBMS59* tries to address the limitations present in *Hopkins155*, still the number of motions captured per sequence are less, on average around 3, the length of videos is small, and annotation is available only on few frames per sequence.

The existing datasets, due to their limitations, fail to analyze performance of algorithms in the presence of multiple occlusions, stopping motion, perspective distortion, and real life noise of camera motion. With this work, we aim to tackle all these shortcomings by creating a new benchmark dataset, focusing on long sequences with real objects, increased number of motions per sequence, and real distortions.

In this paper, we present a dataset of 15 challenging sequences, with up to 17 motions per sequence, more than double the state of the art. The length of the sequences is large, ranging from 15 to around 40 s, captured at 30 fps, with each frame analyzed at 640 x 480 pixels. We provide ground truth as a true label on all trajectories of all frames, which results in almost 0.32 million labeled trajectories on over 12400 frames. We also use a state of the art well-known MS algorithm [11] to provide an initial evaluation on the new database, establishing a starting point for the research community in this field.

2   Motion Segmentation Benchmark

The two MS datasets *Hopkins155* [12] and *FBMS59* [13] have their limitations. Hopkins contains mostly synthetic motions without occlusion, stopping motion and perspective distortion. The ground truth is provided on all trajectories but there is no label on background. FBMS improves on Hopkins a bit, but still the average length of videos is small, the number of motions captured per sequence are low, and ground truth is provided only on 5 % of the whole set of frames.

The proposal of this new benchmark dataset is made with the aim to overcome the limitations posed by the state of the art datasets for MS. The database was created in three steps: *Acquisition*, *Tracking* and *Annotation*.

2.1 Acquisition

The acquisition of all sequences is performed at 1920×1080 pixels per frame at 30 fps. For processing purpose, the frame size was reduced to 640×480.

All sequences are real life videos containing cars, motorbikes, bicycles and people. The database contains a diverse collection of rigid and non-rigid motions. The total number of sequences is 15, where 11 were captured while standing or walking, and 4 were captured with the camera inside a moving car. The videos are of variable length ranging from 460 frames (15 s) to 1160 frames (39 s). The number of captured motions per sequence including the camera motion are, minimum 5 and maximum 17. The maximum number of moving objects per frame reaches 6 in some sequences.

2.2 Tracking

The choice of a tracker is dependent on the kind of motions to be captured. The acquired sequences include diverse motion types including small and large rigid and non-rigid objects e.g. cars, bikes, people individually or in groups. Moving objects have partial or complete occlusion, perspective distortion, stopping motion, and some appear-disappear and appear again in the field of view.

Many recent tracking approaches have shown promising results. For instance, Wang *et al.* [14], presented an optical flow based tracking algorithm which enables robust extraction of densely sampled trajectories. These trajectories are then used to define descriptors for action recognition by limiting the frame length of trajectories to 15. This means that there is always an upper bound on the length of each trajectory. If used for longer frame lengths, the algorithm results in sparse trajectories on homogeneous regions of moving objects.

Recently, Brox *et al.* [15] proposed a promising Large Displacement Optical Flow (LDOF) based tracking algorithm whose GPU-accelerated implementation was made publicly available by Sundaram *et al.* [16]. The algorithm tracks robust point trajectories over densely sampled regions using LDOF. The trajectories on rigid and non-rigid objects are consistent. It stops sampling in homogeneous regions of background, while retaining densely sampled trajectories on homogeneous regions of moving objects.

We used this algorithm for tracking in our dataset. The computational cost of LDOF calculation is high but once LDOF is known, dense point sampling and tracking is fast. Tracking can be carried out for samples of variable size, depending on the required density of image coverage. If the sample size is kept small e.g. 4, a sample every four pixels, the total number of trajectories and the overall computation cost of MS increases. If the sample size is kept high, e.g. 16, small objects are missed and there are less number of trajectories per moving object. A sample size of 8 is chosen in our database as a trade off between

(a) seq07:139   (b) seq09:108   (c) seq10:190

(d) seq13:478   (e) seq14:693   (f) seq15:30

Fig. 1. Example of one frame each of 6 sequences with ground truth labels overlay. 'seqXX:YYY' means, XX is the sequence number and YYY is the frame number.

overall computational cost and dense coverage of small objects. The tracker code used by *Ochs et al.* [11] in their binary *'mosegOB'* is used. Its output is a post processed result in which outlying bad trajectories are filtered. This results in almost 0.32 million trajectories, capturing all major motions in all sequences.

Some tracking results with ground truth overlay can be seen in Fig. 1. Motion of rigid non-degenerate objects is captured with long densely populated points per frame, as compared to non-rigid degenerate objects whose population per frame is relatively sparse, representative nonetheless. There is also a subset of noisy trajectories, outliers, that capture motion of more than one object in the sequence. Consistent shadow of moving objects is also tracked with the object.

2.3   Annotation

Annotating 0.32 million trajectories is cumbersome. This annotation problem is a topic of research under label propagation, in which manually assigned region labels in a few frames are propagated to the rest of the video. It is a very challenging task, yet some recent work has been presented in [17] and [18]. For instance, Vijayanarasimhan *et al.* [19], proposed an active frame selection method to best utilize human effort. They minimize an error cost for any set of k manually labeled frames. However, due to pixel based annotation, there are multiple steps of pixel label propagation over multiple frames and then re-propagation of these labels to trajectory labels, which results in accumulation of error.

A close to ideal solution is to acquire an approximation of labels on all trajectories and then perform manual correction to obtain an accurate ground truth (GT). The first step of approximation on all trajectories is acquired by a recent MS algorithm proposed by Ochs *et al.* [11,13]. Afterwards, the wrongly estimated

Table 1. UdG-MS15 Benchmark attributes and the evaluation results. Acronyms are **OB:** Ochs *et al.* binary in [11], **GT:** # ground truth motion labels, **OC:** Occlusion (**N**:none, **P**:partial, **C**:complete), **SL:** # classified labels, **OM:** overall misclassification, **SM:** separation of motion from background, **ML:** misclassification of motion labels w/o background.

UdG-MS15 dataset attributes					OB algorithm results					
Name	GT	Frames	Time	Trajectories	OC	SL	OM(%)	SM(%)	ML(%)	F-measure(%)	$F \geq 75\%$
seq01	5	621	20.70	7423	P	3	25.45	66.39	66.39	37.03	2/5
seq02	6	800	26.67	6107	P	5	0.93	13.48	15.36	64.09	4/6
seq03	7	786	26.20	33657	N	1	0.99	100.00	100.00	14.21	1/7
seq04	8	706	23.53	53492	N	1	2.56	100.00	100.00	12.34	1/8
seq05	8	1000	33.33	8081	P/C	5	45.42	2.06	66.47	39.82	2/8
seq06	8	460	15.33	41441	N	8	27.62	64.41	68.56	13.90	1/9
seq07	9	700	23.33	6727	P	9	3.81	8.54	30.57	73.60	5/10
seq08	10	780	26.00	7571	P/C	6	6.16	8.85	26.85	45.99	4/9
seq09	10	900	30.00	14544	P	8	5.26	14.17	28.61	66.04	6/10
seq10	10	1160	38.67	9676	P	10	14.14	11.03	19.01	74.99	7/10
seq11	11	996	33.20	68322	C	8	15.15	81.38	81.57	11.64	1/10
seq12	14	681	22.70	13827	C	12	8.13	24.93	49.27	43.59	4/14
seq13	15	795	26.50	14463	P/C	9	5.38	8.14	30.66	53.79	7/15
seq14	15	1050	35.00	9821	P/C	6	7.24	36.20	63.62	28.79	4/15
seq15	17	980	32.67	26499	P/C	10	9.45	40.05	47.25	48.74	8/17
Overall statistics											
Total	153	12415	413.83	321651	–	101	11.53	38.50	50.96	42.72	57/153
Avg/seq	10.2	827.67	27.59	21443.40	–	6.73	11.84	38.64	52.95	41.91	3.8/10.2
Max	17	1160	38.67	68322	–	12	45.42	100.00	100.00	74.99	8
Min	5	460	15.33	6107	–	1	0.93	2.06	15.36	11.64	1

labels are manually corrected by a user with a ground truth annotation software. The amount of time taken by manual effort is proportional to the number of wrongly labeled trajectories.

All tracks on a moving object are given a unique label. There are two distinct possibilities which have been catered for: *(a)* two separate objects with similar kind of motion are labeled uniquely, if at any point in the sequence the object boundaries are visually separable. *(b)* the noisy subset of trajectories, outliers as mentioned in Sect. 2.2, are assigned a label of the moving object which they are most representative of. The main features of the UdG-MS15 benchmark dataset are listed in Table. 1. All sequences, dataset attributes, evaluation source code and annotation software are available for download at www.UdG-MS15.udg.edu.

3   Experiments

Many well known algorithms for MS rely on the assumption of no real noise, like complete occlusion, stopping motion, perspective distortion. The computational cost of some who have the capability to tackle distortions is enormous. Considering this limitation, the most recent MS algorithm presented by *Ochs et al.* [11] is chosen to provide an initial benchmark evaluation. Though computationally extensive, still it provides promising results in relatively challenging situations.

Evaluation: The choice of an evaluation criteria in such a dataset is difficult. *Ochs et al.* in *FBMS59* [13] proposed the use of Hungarian method, with *precision* and *recall* measures to weigh each group of ground truth and classified labels. They use *Recall* as a fraction of ground truth region covered by a cluster, because in *FBMS59* region based annotations were provided. This is not applicable in our situation as instead of region annotation, we provide labels on trajectories like in Hopkins database, as most MS methods are evaluated using trajectories [1–4,6–8,12]. Therefore, we propose a similar approach based on trajectory matching with extended performance evaluation measures.

Trajectory Matching (TM): A one to one correspondence of each annotated trajectory is resolved with each evaluated labeled trajectory. With *TM* known, the determination of correct corresponding labels is performed with probabilistic measures.

Considering N ground truth labels (GT) and M segmentation labels (SL), a label correspondence matrix, LC_{NXM} is computed. The evaluation measures true positives (TP), false positives (FP) and false negatives (FN) are computed to estimate *Sensitivity* $S = TP/(TP+FN)$, and *Precision* $P = TP/(TP+FP)$. With S and P known, we compute the F-measure (F score), using Hungarian method as done in [13],

$$F_{i,j} = \frac{2 * S_{i,j} * P_{i,j}}{S_{i,j} + P_{i,j}} \tag{1}$$

The F-score is computed for each pair of GT_i, $i = 1..N$ and SL_j, $j = 1..M$. The best assignment of SL with GT is found by maximum F-score, and is stored in the label correspondence matrix, LC. If N>M, there remain unassigned GT labels, and if N<M, there are unassigned SLs.

Table 1 shows all performance measures for all the sequences. There are three measures of misclassifications *(Overall misclassification, Motion separation and Misclassified motion labels)* whose ideal value is 0 %. One F-measure, whose ideal value is 100 % and a threshold based estimation of number of motions.

The *Overall Misclassification (OM)* is the total number of misclassified trajectories in the sequence computed based on the best correspondences found in *LC*. It is the standard measure used in *Hopkins155* benchmark [12]. OM is misleading in our case because it is highly biased, as a large percentage of trajectories belong to the background. So, if the algorithm undersegments and classifies everything as background, it can have very low OM, as in the case of some sequences shown in Table 1, especially *seqs {02, 03, 04, 07}*. Therefore, two different measures which ignore all background trajectories by using *TM* matrix, are also computed.

Motion Separation (SM) is the percentage of motion that was wrongly assigned to the background by the MS algorithm. This measure specifically gives an insight on the MS algorithm's ability to separate motion from background, without getting into the correctness of the assigned motion label. The lower it is the better motion separation is done.

Misclassified Motion Labels (ML) is the percentage of wrongly assigned motion labels computed based on the best correspondences found in *LC*. This measure gives an insight on the actual performance of motion segmentation.

In Table 1, *seq05* is a unique case with SM 2 % and ML 66 %, this means that motion was successfully separated from the background but due to incorrect label assignment ML is high. The *seqs* {*02, 10*} have less ML because in partial occlusion the algorithm successfully recovers the label.

F-measure: It is the average F-measure which refers to the harmonic mean of *Sensitivity* and *Precision*. It is the measure proposed in *FBMS59* [13] for performance evaluation. It gives an overall view of segmentation of motion by the algorithm. A high percentage signifies a good segmentation. When compared with ML, both measures give a coherent result on the performance. Here again *seqs* {*02, 10*} have better results but *seqs* {*03, 04, 06, 11*}, which were captured from inside a moving car, have very low results meaning that the algorithm fails to detect relative motions.

The number of extracted motions are reported by the same criteria, F-measure $F \geq 75\,\%$, as used in [13] to maintain continuity. Based on this criterion, all extracted object labels, including background label, are listed in the last column of Table 1.

The overall average, ML is 52 % and F-measure is 42 %, and the average number of estimated moving objects is 4 out of 10. This performance from *Ochs et al.* [11] illustrates the difficulty of the challenge. Note that the algorithm [11] tends to undersegment all sequences. The difficulties embedded in our database can yield improved results if MS algorithms estimate the number of motions better, recover the labels after complete occlusion, are able to detect relative motion and can perceive small slow moving objects.

4 Conclusions

Currently motion segmentation research is experiencing a difficult time, as most forthcoming algorithms still adopt the same set of assumptions, (known and limited number of motions, complete trajectories, no perspective distortions, etc.), and mostly assess their performances on an old dataset where a 0.5 % reduced error rate is used as a proof of improvement. Therefore, we provide a new dataset comprising 15 long sequences of real life scenes with distortions to fill the void of a challenging benchmark, where critical performance of algorithms can be better evaluated. The proposed database has increased number of motions, up to 17, and sequence length around 40 s. As a starting benchmark, an initial evaluation using a recent well known state of the art algorithm has been provided. The average misclassification performance measure, ML 53 % goes to show the difficulty level of our challenging dataset. We hope that our new dataset will provide the opportunity for a deeper understanding of the motion segmentation problem and will push researchers towards new challenges.

Acknowledgement. This work has been supported by the FP7-ICT-2011-7 project PANDORA-Persistent Autonomy through Learning, Adaptation, Observation and Replanning (Ref 288273) funded by the European Commission and the project RAIMON-Autonomous Underwater Robot for Marine Fish Farms Inspection and Monitoring (Ref

CTM2011-29691-C02-02) funded by the Ministry of Economy and Competitiveness of the Spanish Government. Muhammad Habib Mahmood is supported by an FI grant associated with the RAIMON project.

References

1. Liu, G., Yan, S.: Latent low-rank representation for subspace segmentation and feature extraction. In: ICCV, pp. 1615–1622 (2011)
2. Zappella, L., Lladó, X., Provenzi, E., Salvi, J.: Enhanced local subspace affinity for feature-based motion segmentation. PR **44**, 454–470 (2011)
3. Zappella, L., Provenzi, E., Lladó, X., Salvi, J.: Adaptive motion segmentation algorithm based on the principal angles configuration. In: Kimmel, R., Klette, R., Sugimoto, A. (eds.) ACCV 2010, Part III. LNCS, vol. 6494, pp. 15–26. Springer, Heidelberg (2011)
4. Elhamifar, E., Vidal, R.: Sparse subspace clustering: algorithm, theory, and applications. PAMI **35**, 2765–2781 (2013)
5. Zappella, L., Del Bue, A., Lladó, X., Salvi, J.: Joint estimation of segmentation and structure from motion. CVIU **117**, 113–129 (2013)
6. Rao, S., Tron, R., Vidal, R., Ma, Y.: Motion segmentation in the presence of outlying, incomplete, or corrupted trajectories. PAMI **32**, 1832–1845 (2010)
7. Vidal, R., Ma, Y., Sastry, S.: Generalized principal component analysis (GPCA). PAMI **27**, 1945–1959 (2005)
8. Thakoor, N., Gao, J., Devarajan, V.: Multibody structure-and-motion segmentation by branch-and-bound model selection. ITIP **19**, 1393–1402 (2010)
9. Wang, Y., Gong, J., Zhang, D., Gao, C., Tian, J., Zeng, H.: Large disparity motion layer extraction via topological clustering. ITIP **20**, 43–52 (2011)
10. Brox, T., Malik, J.: Object segmentation by long term analysis of point trajectories. In: Daniilidis, K., Maragos, P., Paragios, N. (eds.) ECCV 2010, Part V. LNCS, vol. 6315, pp. 282–295. Springer, Heidelberg (2010)
11. Ochs, P., Brox, T.: Higher order motion models and spectral clustering. In: CVPR, pp. 614–621 (2012)
12. Tron, R., Vidal, R.: A benchmark for the comparison of 3-D motion segmentation algorithms. In: CVPR, pp. 1–8 (2007)
13. Ochs, P., Malik, J., Brox, T.: Segmentation of moving objects by long term video analysis. PAMI **36**, 1187–1200 (2014)
14. Wang, H., Kläser, A., Schmid, C., Liu, C.: Dense trajectories and motion boundary descriptors for action recognition. IJCV **103**, 1–20 (2013)
15. Brox, T., Malik, J.: Large displacement optical flow: descriptor matching in variational motion estimation. PAMI **33**, 500–513 (2011)
16. Sundaram, N., Brox, T., Keutzer, K.: Dense point trajectories by GPU-accelerated large displacement optical flow. In: Daniilidis, K., Maragos, P., Paragios, N. (eds.) ECCV 2010, Part I. LNCS, vol. 6311, pp. 438–451. Springer, Heidelberg (2010)
17. Badrinarayanan, V., Galasso, F., Cipolla, R.: Label propagation in video sequences. In: CVPR, pp. 3265–3272 (2010)
18. Budvytis, I., Badrinarayanan, V., Cipolla, R.: Label propagation in complex video sequences using semi-supervised learning. BMVC **2257**, 2258–2259 (2010)
19. Vijayanarasimhan, S., Grauman, K.: Active frame selection for label propagation in videos. In: Fitzgibbon, A., Lazebnik, S., Perona, P., Sato, Y., Schmid, C. (eds.) ECCV 2012, Part V. LNCS, vol. 7576, pp. 496–509. Springer, Heidelberg (2012)

Escritoire: A Multi-touch Desk with e-Pen Input for Capture, Management and Multimodal Interactive Transcription of Handwritten Documents

Daniel Martín-Albo[✉], Verónica Romero, and Enrique Vidal

Pattern Recognition and Human Language Technology Research Center,
Camí de Vera, 46022 Valencia, Spain
{damarsi1,vromero,evidal}@prhlt.upv.es

Abstract. A large quantity of documents used every day are still hand-written. However, it is interesting to transform each of these documents into its digital version for managing, archiving and sharing. Here we present Escritoire, a multi-touch desk that allows the user to capture, transcribe and work with handwritten documents. The desktop is continuously monitored using two cameras. Whenever the user makes a specific hand gesture over a paper, Escritoire proceeds to take an image. Then, the capture is automatically preprocesses, obtaining as a result an improved representation. Finally, the text image is transcribed using automatic techniques and finally the transcription is displayed on Escritoire.

Keywords: Multimodal interaction · Handwritten text recognition · Multi-touch desk · User gestures

1 Introduction

Although digital data are increasingly more widely used, many documents are still on paper. Ideally, those documents should become accessible as a machine-readable text for searching, browsing, and editing. To bridge the gap between the *analog* and the digital, paper handwritten documents need to be captured [9] and transcribed.

This paper presents Escritoire, a system that takes a step into this direction. The user works in a digital desk environment that combines the advantages of paper documents and the digital world, allowing an intuitive, natural and comfortable way to annotate, modify and work with both paper and digital documents in a seamless manner.

This desk is continuously monitored using two cameras. The first one allows Escritoire to perform high-resolution scans. The second one is used by the built-in gesture recognizer. Escritoire automatically preprocesses the captured images, obtaining an adequate representation for the subsequent steps. Finally, if the

© Springer International Publishing Switzerland 2015
R. Paredes et al. (Eds.): IbPRIA 2015, LNCS 9117, pp. 471–478, 2015.
DOI: 10.1007/978-3-319-19390-8_53

document is handwritten, a multimodal interactive transcription is carried out using a tablet where the user interacts with the comfort provided by a high-resolution e-pen.

The major challenges in designing and implementing such system are: real-time performance, accurate detection of documents, reliable detection and interpretation of the user gestures, preprocessing and layout analysis of camera-based captured handwritten documents, interactive transcription and customized interfaces design.

Below we comment on prior works that bear direct relevance with the different research areas involved in the digital desk presented here.

2   Related Work

There is a huge body of research on capture of paper documents. In [9] a survey regarding the state-of-the-art on the document capture and detection is presented. In [8] a prototype where a capture is triggered by some pointing gestures and performed using a consumer camera is presented. Unfortunately, this system can only deal with printed documents, for which transcriptions can be carried out using OCR.

User interface design is not an easy task, mainly because designers do not tend to follow any strict rule-based procedure. Several studies on user-friendly interfaces, have been carried out. In [15] a set of shortcomings in current user interfaces along with some guidelines are presented. Given that design involves personal stylistic preferences, a system that applies an adaptive algorithm to interface design is described in [3].

Some important work has been carried out [10] on detecting and interpreting user gestures. The applications of gesture recognition are manifold: sign language, medical rehabilitation, virtual reality, etc. In [14] a survey on gesture recognition is provided with particular emphasis in hand gestures and facial expressions. Applications involving Hidden Markov models, particle filtering and condensation, finite-state machines, optical flow and skin color are discussed in detail. Existing challenges and future research possibilities are also highlighted. In [19], the requirements of hand-gesture interfaces and the challenges in meeting the needs of various application types are described. Moreover, in [20] ideas for extracting user behavior and intentions from objects and gestures are presented.

With respect to handwritten text recognition, the results provided by automatic text recognition technologies have improved dramatically in recent years, although results are still far from being perfect. In [17], a multimodal interactive scenario where the user and the system collaborate to generate a better solution was presented for handwritten text recognition (HTR). The situation in layout analysis and text line segmentation is rather similar. The segmentation quality does not reach the acceptable levels needed by end-user applications [6,11].

3   Interacting with Escritoire

Here the system is presented by following Alice while she uses it. Alice wants to transcribe a handwritten document. So she places the sheet in the capture zone

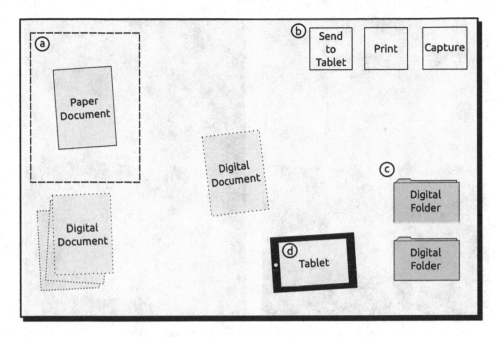

Fig. 1. Escritoire user interface mock-up. (a) Capture zone where a *real* document is placed to be digitized. (b) Action buttons: The first button, labeled on the real interface with a tablet icon, allows the user to transfer a transcribed document to the tablet to improve the transcription. The second one, tagged with a printer icon, allows the user to print a copy of a digitized document. Finally, by pressing the button tagged with a camera and after a five-seconds countdown, any document located in the capture zone will be digitized. (c) Similarly to traditional desktops, documents can be stacked or arranged into folders in Escritoire. (d) The tablet used for interactive transcription.

(Fig. 1a) and points with her index finger the *capture* button (Fig. 1b). Escritoire captures and preprocesses the document, generating a better representation. Escritoire automatically detects that the document is handwritten and proceeds to transcribe it. After this, Alice decides to save the document for now. She aims with her index finger at the digital document and moves it into one of the available folders (Fig. 1c).

Sometime later, Alice realizes that the system proposed transcription was not entirely correct. So she aims with her index finger at the folder to open it and extracts the saved transcribed document. Alice points at the Tablet button (Fig. 1b) to send the document to the (physical) interactive transcription tablet (Fig. 1d). When she is happy with the result, she clicks the *Return to Escritoire* button at the tablet interface and the document returns modified to the digital desktop.

4   System Implementation

A system comprising a digital desktop can be designed in many different ways: it can be composed by a real physical desk, with a conventional screen and an

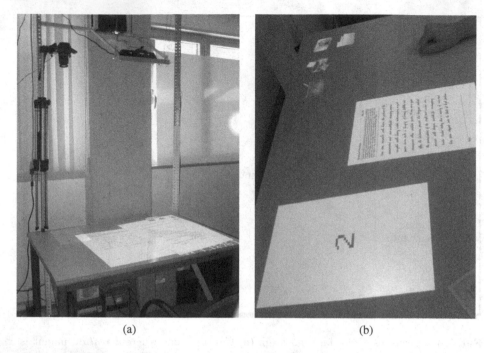

(a)   (b)

Fig. 2. (a) Escritoire prototype showing two digitized documents. (b) A sheet of paper near the capture zone, showing the five-seconds countdown.

e-pen or digital tablet; projecting the display onto the desktop and interacting using a digital pen or touch screen; or directly work in a large desktop-sized multi-touch screen.

Figure 2a shows the prototype that we have built. We decided to use a physical desk where the screen was projected. In our opinion, this was the simplest and cheapest way to create a prototype. Due to the distance between the desktop and the projector, a short throw projector (*InFocus IN1503*) was chosen, allowing us to display the proper image size.

Two cameras were used: a fixed-location high-resolution camera (*Canon EOS 1100D*) is responsible for capturing documents. This camera is zoomed and focused on the *capture zone* (Figure 1a). This type of set-up provides us with a more robust configuration (same light conditions, less geometric distortions due to perspective, etc.), therefore simplifying the subsequent steps. A camera with a depth sensor (*Microsoft Kinect*) was used to detect the finger gestures.

Finally, the interactive transcription is carried out using a *Lenovo Thinkpad Tablet 2* instead of directly on the desktop. This decision is based on previous experience. We realized that, due to the minimum font size and the projector resolution, trying to write directly on the desktop is cumbersome and inaccurate.

4.1   Gesture Monitoring and Detection

As we said before, Escritoire is a desktop on top of which a Kinect device has been mounted. This monitors the work area searching for possible user gestures.

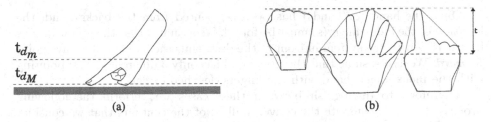

Fig. 3. (a) Maximum and minimum threshold for defining a pixel of interest. t_{d_m} and t_{d_M} were empirically tunned. (b) Example (with $n = 4$) of convex hull for different hand positions.

To date, we use a simple set of gestures that are performed using one or the two index fingers. The current set of gestures includes:

Select: the system will select the item shown on Escritoire under the finger.
Move: after selecting an item, the user can translate it by just moving the hand around.
Rotate: pointing both index fingers to a document and rotating hands.
Zoom: pointing both index fingers to a document and pinch open or close.

Since the set of gestures is performed with the index fingers, our system must be able to detect them. The first step in order to achieve this is to be able to differentiate the hands from the background. As the virtual desktop is displayed over the desk surface, we could not use any color-based technique (e.g., skin detection) to segment the hands.

Here we used the depth map provided by the Kinect, which captures depth information under any ambient light condition. From this depth image we need to isolate the pixels of interest (Fig. 3a). We will calculate for every pixel contained in the depth image if they are a pixel of interest. Figure 1 provides the formal definition of pixel of interest ($\mathcal{S}_{ij}$). We compute the depth median value for every pixel ($\eta_{d_{ij}}$) during a period of 2 s. This way we can obtain a more stable value, minimizing the influence of out-layers derived from the sensor. Then, we calculate the difference between $\eta_{d_{ij}}$ with respect to the current depth value ($c_{d_{ij}}$). If this difference is within a minimum (t_{d_m}) and a maximum (t_{d_M}) threshold we can say that the current pixel is a pixel of interest.

$$\mathcal{S}_{ij} = \begin{cases} \text{True} & \text{if } t_{d_m} \leq \eta_{d_{ij}} - c_{d_{ij}} \leq t_{d_M} \\ \text{False} & \text{otherwise} \end{cases} \tag{1}$$

After segmenting the pixels of interest from the depth image, we want to know whether a group of pixels of interest are a hand. Previous to this, we apply a *closing* to the image, to remove any possible internal small hole and an *opening*, to remove any small noise object. As a simplification, we will assume that the biggest volumes, with a maximum of two, exceeding a certain area threshold, will be considered hands. This area threshold was empirically tunned to distinguish between noise and actually hands.

Once the hand (or hands) has been segmented from the background, the location of the index finger(s) must be found. We assumed that the user is always interacting with the system in front of the desk, thus the hands will always point *forward*. We also assume that the user hand has only 3 different states: pointing with the index finger, hand with the fingers clenched or flat.

Therefore, to distinguish between these cases we perform the following process. First, we compute the convex hull [1] of the contours that we consider hands. Then we apply the following technique: if the distance between the higher y-value vertex of the convex hull contour and the next n y-value vertex is for any case greater than a threshold d_t, we will say that the highest y-value point of this contour is the tip of an index finger (where n and d_t are parameters to be optimized). Otherwise, we assume that the user has the hand flat or with the fingers clenched. Figure 3b illustrates this process. Once we have found the tip of the index finger(s), a simple Nearest Neighbor tracking algorithm was applied to track their consecutive positions. After this, a Kalman filter [5] is applied to the tracked path(s) in order to reduce the noise.

Finally, depending on the number of fingers that the system has recognized and their position with respect to the desktop (located over a document, a button, etc.), we can clearly identify the user gesture and react with the corresponding action.

4.2   Document Capture and Management

The document capture is carried out using a *Canon EF-S 18-55mm f/3.5-5.6 IS II* objective. The capture is performed when Alice selects the camera button. The system automatically will show the capture area, where the sheet must be placed in order to be captured. Figure 2b shows a captured document and the countdown.

Alice can work with the document on Escritoire once it has been captured. As previously explained, there are several options: the document can be moved, rotated and zoomed. In addition the document can be archived in a folder.

4.3   Handwritten Text Recognition

Once the document has been captured, it is automatically transcribed. The handwritten text recognition (HTR) system employed here follows the classical architecture composed of: preprocessing, feature extraction and recognition. Each captured image is preprocessed in order to remove margins, noise and geometric distortions [16]. After these steps, each line is detected and extracted [2]. Each preprocessed line image is repr esented as a sequence of feature vectors [7]. The recognition module accepts a sequence of feature vectors and is based on Hidden Markov Models (HMMs), n-gram language models. The search (or decoding) is optimally carried out by using the Viterbi algorithm [4]. After this, the transcript will be shown on Escritoire and Alice will be visually notified.

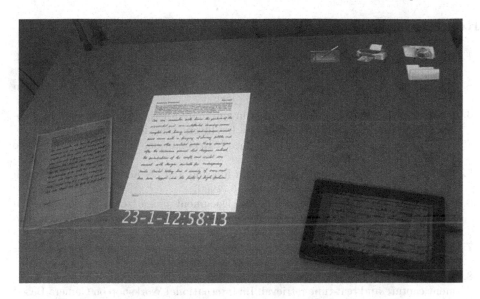

Fig. 4. From left to right: a paper document, its digital version shown on Escritoire and tablet.

4.4   Multimodal Interactive Handwritten Text Transcription

Finally, as we commented before, the edition of the transcribed document is by means of a tablet (see Fig. 4), giving the process greater comfort. When Alice wants to edit the transcription, she moves the document to the tablet icon on the desktop and the document is transfered.

Here we will follow a multimodal interactive approach [12,13,18], in which an automatic HTR system and the user cooperate to generate a better transcript. At each interaction step, the system proposes its best transcript. If Alice finds the proposal correct, she can accept it and the process goes on. Otherwise, Alice can correct the first erroneous element and the system reacts with a revised output where this error is fixed and other related errors are potentially fixed.

5   Summary and Future Work

We have presented Escritoire, a document management system in which digital and paper documents coexist. We have integrated well-known computer vision and handwriting recognition techniques. We plan to carry out experiments with real users in order to test the gesture recognizer performance or the computer assisted transcription. Additionally, we intend to include more input modalities, for example, allowing the user to perform certain actions by voice.

Acknowledgment. This work was partially supported by the Spanish MEC under FPU scholarship (AP2010-0575), STraDA research project (TIN2012-37475-C02-01) and MITTRAL research project (TIN2009-14633-C03-01); the EU's 7th Framework Programme under tranScriptorium grant agreement (FP7/2007-2013/600707).

References

1. Andrew, A.: Another efficient algorithm for convex hulls in two dimensions. Inf. Process. Lett. **9**(5), 216–219 (1979)
2. Bosch, V., Toselli, A.H., Vidal, E.: Statistical text line analysis in handwritten documents. In: Proceedings of ICFHR (2012)
3. Eisenstein, J., Puerta, A.: Adaptation in automated user-interface design. In: Proceedings of International Conference on Intelligent User Interfaces (2000)
4. Jelinek, F.: Statistical Methods for Speech Recognition. MIT Press, Cambridge (1998)
5. Kalman, R.E.: A new approach to linear filtering and prediction problems. Trans. ASME-J. Basic Eng. **82**(Series D), 35–45 (1960)
6. Keysers, D., Shafait, F., Breuel, T.M.: Document image zone classification - a simple high-performance approach. In: Proceedings of International Conference on Computer Vision Theory (2007)
7. Kozielski, M., Forster, J., Ney, H.: Moment-based image normalization for handwritten text recognition. In: Proceedings of ICFHR (2012)
8. Lampert, C.H., Braun, T., Ulges, A., Keysers, D., Breuel, T.M.: Oblivious document capture and real-time retrieval. In: International Workshop on Camera Based Document Analysis and Recognition (2005)
9. Liang, J., Doermann, D., Li, H.: Camera based analysis of text and documents a survey. Int. J. Doc. Anal. Recogn. **7**(2–3), 84–104 (2005)
10. Liwicki, M., Rostanin, O., El-Neklawy, S.M., Dengel, A.: Touch & write: a multi-touch table with pen-input. In: Proceedings of International Workshop on Document Analysis Systems (2010)
11. Marti, U.V., Bunke, H.: Text line segmentation and word recognition in a system for general writer independent handwriting recognition. In: Proceedings of ICDAR (2001)
12. Martín-Albo, D., Romero, V., Toselli, A.H., Vidal, E.: Multimodal computer-assisted transcription of text images at character-level interaction. Int. J. Pattern Recogn. Artif. Intell. **26**(5), 19 (2012)
13. Martín-Albo, D., Romero, V., Vidal, E.: Interactive off-line handwritten text transcription using on-line handwritten text as feedback. In: Proceedings of ICDAR (2013)
14. Mitra, S., Acharya, T.: Gesture recognition: a survey. IEEE Trans. Syst. Man Cybern. B Cybern. **37**(3), 311–324 (2007)
15. Terry, M., Mynatt, E.D.: Recognizing creative needs in user interface design. In: Proceedings of C&C (2002)
16. Toselli, A.H., Juan, A., Keysers, D., González, J., Salvador, I., Ney, H., Vidal, E., Casacuberta, F.: Integrated handwriting recognition and interpretation using finite-state models. Int. J. Pattern Recognit. Artif. Intell. **18**(4), 519–539 (2004)
17. Toselli, A.H., Romero, V., Pastor, M., Vidal, E.: Multimodal interactive transcription of text images. Pattern Recognit. **43**(5), 1814–1825 (2010)
18. Toselli, A.H., Romero, V., Vidal, E.: Computer assisted transcription of text images and multimodal interaction. In: Popescu-Belis, A., Stiefelhagen, R. (eds.) MLMI 2008. LNCS, vol. 5237, pp. 296–308. Springer, Heidelberg (2008)
19. Wachs, J.P., Kolsch, M., Stern, H., Edan, Y.: Vision-based hand-gesture applications. Commun. ACM. **54**(2), 60–71 (2011)
20. Wobbrock, J.O., Morris, M.R., Wilson, A.D.: User-defined gestures for surface computing. In: Proceedings of CHI (2009)

Person Enrollment by Face-Gait Fusion

Javier Ortells[✉] and Ramón A. Mollineda

Institute of New Imaging Technologies, University Jaume I, Castelló, Spain
{jortells,mollined}@uji.es

Abstract. This paper studies the problem of automatic person enrollment based on face-gait fusion within a context of anonymous identification. Enrollment should determine whether an observed subject has been seen before or not. Traditionally, this process has been embedded into a major identification system and its potential has been undervalued. This work claims that enrollment can be considered as a task in itself, and that there are real applications that can benefit from exclusively managing it. To this end, it is shown that the enrollment error model is different from that of anonymous identification. Enrollment experiments, conducted over three types of random permutations of probe samples, showed the benefits of face-gait fusion over single biometrics.

Keywords: Enrollment · Face-gait fusion · Anonymous identification

1 Introduction

The anonymous biometric identification problem, as defined in [1], consists in assigning a synthetic identity label to a given (*probe*) biometric sample, after comparing it against a number of samples previously collected in a (*gallery*) set. In a conventional approach, a scoring engine computes similarity scores between the probe sample and all gallery samples, and the maximum score is compared with a decision threshold. If this score is above the threshold, a *matching* decision is made and the identity linked to the matched gallery sample is assigned to the probe sample. Otherwise, a *non-matching* occurs, and the probe sample is enrolled in the gallery set under a new synthetic identity dynamically created. Anonymous identification is similar to people re-identification, although the latter is expected also to manage multiple sensors and poses [2,3].

Automatic enrollment has mostly been considered as an indivisible piece of the anonymous identification workflow. That is, both the matching and non-matching events seem to lead to a monolithic response, where the enrollment decision is embedded. However, by closely examining this process, enrollment can be understood as a more primary decision level than identification. In addition, it is easy to find real applications than can benefit from an enrollment function.

This work has been supported by the grants P1-1B2012-22 and PREDOC/2012/05 from Universitat Jaume I, PROMETEOII/2014/062 from Generalitat Valenciana, and TIN2013-46522-P from the Spanish Ministerio de Economía y Competitividad.

© Springer International Publishing Switzerland 2015
R. Paredes et al. (Eds.): IbPRIA 2015, LNCS 9117, pp. 479–486, 2015.
DOI: 10.1007/978-3-319-19390-8_54

The most straightforward one could be to count unique people or, in other words, to strictly address the question "Has this person been encountered before?" [1].

Given a probe sample as input, a basic on-line enrollment approach should determine whether that sample is sufficiently similar to any gallery sample. If so, it is accepted as belonging to a previously *enrolled subject* (no matter who). Otherwise, it is labeled as a *new subject*. In both cases the probe can be added to the gallery set, which could be empty at the very beginning. Note that these class labels will depend on the position of the samples in a given sequence: the first sample of someone should be considered as *new subject*, while the rest should be labeled as *enrolled subject* samples. Thus, as in anonymous identification, enrollment efficacy relies heavily on the sequential order of probe samples.

The main difference of plain enrollment with respect to anonymous identification is that no identities (nor clusters) are required. That is, the gallery can be viewed as a general repository comprising all previously enrolled samples together, without any labeling. Thus, while the number of classes in the anonymous identification problem is a dynamic number that is expected to grow continuously, the enrollment model is based on only two classes. This structural difference may induce different decision rules and error counts, as well as distinct impacts of errors in the future system behavior. In view of the above discussion, this paper is first intended to state that enrollment can be considered as an independent process able to solve interesting problems by itself.

In this paper, enrollment experiments have been carried out by fusing face and gait scores, which is a popular multi-biometric approach [4,5]. A recent and comprehensive survey can be found in [6]. To the best of our knowledge, no automatic enrollment results based on face-gait fusion have been reported in the literature so far. The advantages of combining face and gait rely on the expected complementarity of their properties. While face analysis requires the subject to be close to the sensor, gait can be properly measured in low resolution videos captured at a distance. In addition, frontal faces generally provide more discriminant information than side faces, while the opposite is expected for gait.

Summarizing, the main contributions of this work are: (1) to state automatic enrollment as a task of interest in itself, by stressing its operational singularities and identifying real applications that capitalize it; and (2) to present, possibly, the first automatic enrollment results from face-gait fusion.

2   The Enrollment Problem

A pure on-line enrollment strategy is intended to determine whether a new probe sample belongs to any known (*enrolled*) subject or it is the first occurrence of a *new* subject. A simple operational scope can be defined by the following elements:

- **Scoring function** $s(\cdot)$. Given a probe sample p and a gallery sample g, it computes a match score $s(p, g)$, thus generating a matching hypothesis $h(p, g)$. The function $s(\cdot)$ is usually normalized in $[0, 1]$. From now on, it will be assumed that $s(\cdot)$ measures dissimilarity or distance between two samples.

- **Numerical threshold** γ. A match score $s(p, g)$ is compared with γ to make a decision on the acceptance or rejection of $h(p, g)$.
- **Gallery set** G. It accommodates the samples from the enrollment process.

Given a (probe) sample p, the enrollment method searches for the gallery sample $\hat{g}$ most similar to p, and the associated match score $\hat{s}(p) = s(p, \hat{g})$ is used to make a decision. A *matching* takes place if $\hat{s}(p) \le \gamma$, while a *non-matching* occurs when $\hat{s}(p) > \gamma$[1]. The fact that $\hat{s}(p)$ omits $\hat{g}$ means that only the minimum score is required. When the gallery set is empty, p is directly added to G.

Two types of errors are intrinsic to this process:

- **False Match** (FM): A matching decision is made, $\hat{s}(p) \le \gamma$, with p being the first occurrence of a subject, i.e., a sample from the New subject class is misclassified. This FM event also holds in anonymous identification (AI).
- **False Non-Match** (FNM): A non-matching decision is made, $\hat{s}(p) > \gamma$, with p being *not* the first occurrence of a subject, i.e., a sample from the Enrolled subject class is misclassified. This FNM event also holds in AI.

Complementarily, two types of hits may occur:

- **True Match** (TM): A matching decision is correctly made, $\hat{s}(p) \le \gamma$, with p being a sample of any previously enrolled subject (no matter who). Note that no condition is imposed on the gallery sample $\hat{g}$ that supports the decision. That is, p and $\hat{g}$ could belong to different identities. This TM event does *not* hold in AI, where $\hat{s}(p)$ is also required to be a genuine score (p and $\hat{g}$ come from a same identity). Otherwise ($\hat{s}(p)$ is an impostor score and there exists at least one genuine score), AI designates the event as a FM.
- **True Non-Match** (TNM): A non-matching decision is correctly made, $\hat{s}(p) > \gamma$, with p being the first sample of a subject. It also holds in AI.

While anonymous identification assesses a matching decision depending on whether the minimum score is genuine or impostor, plain enrollment analysis is based only on the overall minimum score (disregarding its origin). These two different criteria to judge enrollment hits and misses might lead to distinct true or false event rates, as well as to different optimal threshold values.

These conjectures were experimentally validated through a simple study. Two enrollment experiments were simulated using the genuine minimum scores (identity-based) and the overall minimum scores (plain), respectively. In the first case, when no genuine score was available, the overall minimum score was used. Optimal thresholds were found as those that lead to the highest geometric mean of enrollment class rates. Average results of optimal thresholds and geometric means, computed over 500 repetitions, are shown in Table 1. This number of trials comes from 100 random permutations of samples of each of 5 independent subsets of people. Face and gait data were extracted from synchronous videos in frontal and side viewpoints[2]. Results prove that the use of the overall minimum score can lead to different enrollment results, even being slightly better than those obtained by using the genuine minimum score for both biometrics.

---

[1] Note that the converse holds when scores encode similarities (rather than distances).
[2] The reader will find more details on methods and datasets in next sections.

Table 1. Identity-based enrollment versus plain enrollment. The second strategy, a much simpler approach, succeeded in solving enrollment without loss of performance.

	Identity-based enrollment		Plain enrollment	
	Face	Gait	Face	Gait
Optimal threshold	41,69	13,47	41,91	13,52
Geometric mean	0,946	0,974	0,948	0,975

3   Methodology

Figure 1 depicts a methodology overview. Two classifiers were used as scoring engines: RankSVM [7] and 1-NN. The former has proven to be able to learn from training subjects different to those in the test subset under appearance changes. Meanwhile, 1-NN performs template matching between a probe sample and all gallery samples using the Euclidean distance. Next sections provide details of three other key areas: Face methods, Gait methods and Score fusion.

3.1   Data Usage

Given a dataset containing biometric samples of a number of people, this study randomly separates people into two subsets for training and testing purposes, so that each subject is fully assigned to one of them through all their samples. The Training partition is used to learn some transferable knowledge from subjects different to those who will be enrolled. The Test subset is entirely used as the Probe set, whose samples are gradually added to the Gallery as they occur.

Three types of random permutations were generated as in [1], which are intended to simulate three complexity levels. After randomizing probe people, *Increment Probe* (IP) consists in alternating their samples strictly following the order given to the people. *Random Probe* (RP) arranges probe samples in a purely random order. Finally, after a random permutation of probe people, *Increment Subject* (IS) arranges all probe samples such that all samples corresponding to each particular identity occur in a row. IP (IS) implements the quickest (slowest) way to enroll all people, so it should recreate the easiest (hardest) scenario. RP is expected to lead to in-between situations.

3.2   Gait Methods

Given a probe video, binary silhouettes from all video frames were extracted, normalized to 44×64 px., and averaged to build a Gait Energy Image (GEI) [8]. It is a simple but effective model-free characterization method, widely used in gait recognition, which condenses the shape and the dynamics of the body parts.

3.3   Face Methods

Given a video frame, the face was extracted from the upper $1/7$ of the body silhouette area (ROI), as in [4]. Let w and h be the width and the height in

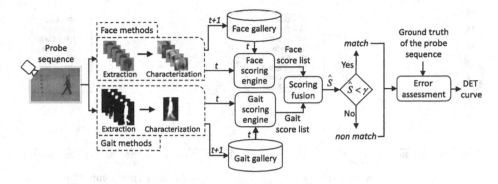

Fig. 1. Methodology overview.

pixels of the ROI. ROIs with $h \notin [w/4, 3w/4]$ were discarded. Given a suitable ROI, the largest blob contained therein, which is expected to be the face area, was cropped by an $h \times h$ region horizontally centered on the blob's x-centroid. Face regions were then converted to gray-scale, histogram equalized and resized to a same resolution (18×18 px. due to database constraints). All pre-processed faces drawn from the frames of a particular video were projected onto the space defined by a Fisherface matrix [9] computed from all available faces in the Training subset. Finally, the projected face images were averaged to build a single face representation of the video under analysis.

3.4 Face-Gait Fusion

The two biometric scores of a subject are obtained, normalized and combined into a joint score which feeds a threshold-based rule. Given a particular biometric, raw scores are normalized by the pth percentile of the distribution of all *minimum* scores obtained when enrolling an independent subset of training people (one minimum score per sample). Normalized scores above 1 are truncated at 1. As each enrollment decision is made solely using the minimum distance, this process is intended to expand differences between minimum genuine scores and impostor ones, so that a suitable threshold can be stated (avoiding the effect of outliers). In this work, p^{th} was set to 90th. Training people were further divided into two independent subsets, one for learning the RankSVM model and one for estimating the 90th score. Given a probe sequence p, let $\hat{s}_f(p)$ and $\hat{s}_g(p)$ be the minimum face and gait normalized scores, respectively. The fused score is computed as $s(p) = \alpha \cdot \hat{s}_f(p) + (1-\alpha) \cdot \hat{s}_g(p)$, where α takes value in $\{0, 0.25, 0.75, 1\}$. Note that $\alpha = 0$ and $\alpha = 1$ represent single-biometric approaches.

4   Experiments

The *Dataset B* of the CASIA gait Database [10] was chosen to assess the proposed methodology, due to its high number of people (124), videos per person (10), and different view angles (11). However, only sequences recorded from

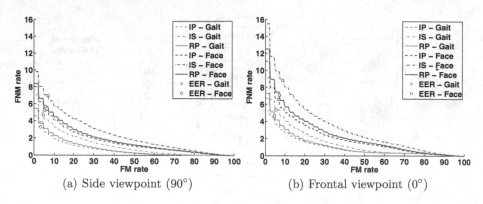

(a) Side viewpoint (90°)   (b) Frontal viewpoint (0°)

Fig. 2. Average DET curves from using 1-NN over *neutral* gait and face samples (without fusion) as regards the three permutation types, both from 0° and 90° view angles (Color figure online).

0° and 90° subject-to-camera angles were considered, as they are supposed to be the most discriminant viewpoints for face and gait description, respectively. The 10 videos per person and angle comprise 6 events under neutral appearance, 2 with changes in clothing and 2 with changes in load carrying. Since all video frames contain the entire body, gait and face data were extracted from them. As a gait database, the resolution was sufficient to build the gait model, but it showed poor to face description. Two experimental studies have been designed:

Study I: Impact of sample arrangement. It is intended to probe that enrollment performance strongly depends on sample permutation. To reduce analysis to essentials, face and gait models from *neutral* sequences were separately computed and arranged following the three types of permutations. Results using 1-NN for 0° and 90° view angles are discussed.

Study II: Impact of face-gait fusion. It aims at showing that face-gait fusion leads to better enrollment results than face and gait on their own. RankSVM and 1-NN results based on fusion and on single biometrics were compared using *all* sequences under the RP setting and both viewpoints.

From each database view regarding angle and appearance filters, 5 independent partitions of people were built as explained in Sects. 3.1 and 3.4 (67 % Training + 33 % Test). Given any of the 5 test subset, 100 sample arrangements were created by chance for each of the three types of permutation. It yielded 500 *Detection Error Tradeoff* (DET) curves [11] by experiment, which were finally graphed as a vertically averaged DET curve [12]. Unlike ROC curves, DET plots FNM rate on the Y axis, focusing on the trade-off between both errors.

4.1 Study I: Impact of Sample Arrangement on Enrollment

From the analysis of the Fig. 2(a) and (b), two important issues should be discussed. Firstly, gait leads to better enrollment results than those derived from face data for both viewpoints and the three types of permutation. In the case

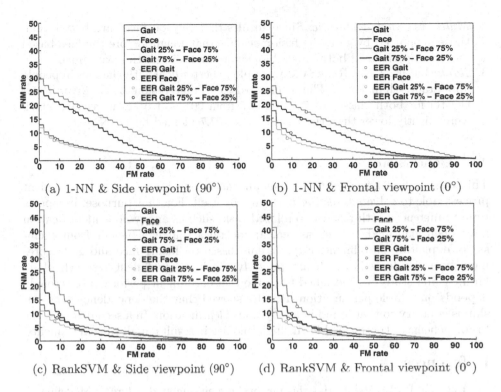

(a) 1-NN & Side viewpoint (90°)   (b) 1-NN & Frontal viewpoint (0°)

(c) RankSVM & Side viewpoint (90°)   (d) RankSVM & Frontal viewpoint (0°)

Fig. 3. Average DET curves showing 1-NN and RankSVM performances over *all* samples arranged following the RP permutation, both from 0° and 90° view angles (Color figure online).

of 90° angle, it can be explained by the expected superiority of the side gait over the side face. In the case of the 0° angle, the video resolution might be the answer: it seems appropriate for gait description, but poor for face modeling. Secondly, it has been empirically proved that sample arrangement has a strong impact on enrollment performance. In this regard, the permutation types IP and IS clearly represent the easiest and the hardest scenarios, respectively. This evidence confirms the singularity of pure enrollment, because the effect of both types of arrangement on anonymous identification is just the opposite [1].

4.2 Study II: Impact of Face-Gait Fusion on Enrollment

In this study, three levels of analysis are worth pointing out:

1. *Face vs. gait.* Unlike the Study I, samples comprise changes in clothing and load carrying. This affects gait appearance more than faces, as shown in Fig. 3(a) and (b). The red and blue solid lines, which depict the gait- and face-based 1-NN behavior on the RP setting (as in Study I), have moved away from the coordinate center as compared to their positions in the Fig. 2(a) and (b), with the gait-based (red) curve being more affected.

2. *Multi- vs. single-biometric.* Since results that rely on faces are better than those supported by gait, the fusion scheme that weights more the face-based scores outperformed both single-biometric results in all the experiments.
3. *RankSVM vs. 1-NN.* RankSVM was able to better deal with changes in people appearance than 1-NN. The former led to average fusion *Equal Error Rates* (EER) for both classes of 7.3 and 6.7 from 90° and 0° respectively, which were slightly lower than the EERs 7.4 and 7.7 yielded by 1-NN.

4.3   Conclusions

This work is first intended to present automatic enrollment as an independent process able to solve interesting problems by itself. For that purpose, its operational differences with respect to related tasks such as anonymous identification have been identified, as well as real applications that can benefit from exclusively exploiting enrollment. Experiments based on fusing face and gait scores have been conducted, which are possibly the first enrollment research of its kind. A first study was designed to probe that enrollment performance strongly depends on sample permutation. Results showed that the dependency relationship is contrary to that found in anonymous identification. In a second study, the fusion scheme outperformed both single-biometric results in all the experiments.

References

1. DeCann, B., Ross, A.: "Has this person been encountered before?": Modeling an anonymous identification system. In: CVPRW, pp. 89–96 (2012)
2. Zheng, W.S., Gong, S., Xiang, T.: Person re-identification by probabilistic relative distance comparison. In: CVPR, pp. 649–656 (2011)
3. Roy, A., Sural, S., Mukherjee, J.: A hierarchical method combining gait and phase of motion with spatiotemporal model for person re-identification. Pattern Recogn. Lett. **33**(14), 1891–1901 (2012)
4. Geng, X., Smith-Miles, K., Wang, L., Li, M., Wu, Q.: Context-aware fusion: a case of study on fusion of gait and face for human identification in video. Pattern Recogn. **43**, 3660–3673 (2010)
5. Hossain, E., Chetty, G.: Person identity verification based on multimodal face-gait fusion. Int. J. Comput. Sci. Netw. Secur. **11**(6), 77–86 (2011)
6. Almohammad, M.S., Salama, G.I., Mahmoud, T.A.: Face and gait fusion methods: a survey. Int. J. Comput. Sci. Telecommun. **4**(4), 19–28 (2013)
7. Martín-Félez, R., Xiang, T.: Gait recognition by ranking. In: Fitzgibbon, A., Lazebnik, S., Perona, P., Sato, Y., Schmid, C. (eds.) ECCV 2012, Part I. LNCS, vol. 7572, pp. 328–341. Springer, Heidelberg (2012)
8. Han, J., Bhanu, B.: Individual recognition using Gait Energy Image. PAMI **28**(2), 316–322 (2006)
9. Belhumeur, P.N., Hespanha, J.P., Kriegman, D.J.: Eigenfaces vs. fisherfaces: recognition using class specific linear projection. PAMI **19**(7), 711–720 (1997)
10. Yu, S., et al.: A framework for evaluating the effect of view angle, clothing and carrying condition on gait recognition. In: 18th ICPR, pp. 441–444 (2006)
11. Martin, A., et al.: The DET curve in assessment of detection task performance. In: EuroSpeech, pp. 1895–1898 (1997)
12. Fawcett, T.: An introduction to ROC analysis. Pattern Recogn. Lett. **27**(8), 861–874 (2006)

Homographic Class Template for Logo Localization and Recognition

Raluca Boia[✉] and Corneliu Florea

University Politehnica of Bucharest, Bucharest, Romania
rboia@imag.pub.ro, corneliu.florea@upb.ro

Abstract. We propose a method for localizing and recognizing brand logos in natural images. The task is extremely challenging, due to the various changes in the appearance of the logos. We construct class templates by matching features between examples of the same class to build homographies. An interconnections graph is developed for each class and the representative points are added to the class model. Finally, each class is depicted by the reunion of the suitable keypoints and descriptors, thus leading to a high precision of the proposed logo recognition system. Results show that we outperform the state of the art systems on the challenging Flickr-32 database.

Keywords: Logo · Localization · Recognition · Class model

1 Introduction

A logo is a graphic entity containing colors, shapes, textures, and perhaps text as well, organized in some spatial layout format. Logo localization and recognition is a subproblem of object detection and recognition and a challenging pattern recognition task. Being of interest for the marketing industry (e.g. to measure the impact of an advertising campaign), trademark registration or vehicle tracking, logo recognition has gained consistent attention in the last few years. Yet, the problem of integrated recognition (i.e. detection/localization + recognition) still remains unresolved. As the number of brands having personalized logos increases every day, such recognition systems require robust processing capabilities to support high numbers of classes.

The challenges of a logo detection system are due to perspective deformations, varying background, possible occlusions, scaling variability (from high resolutions of 1000×1000 to 20×20). Furthermore, although the objects are almost planar, there are situations when the pattern suffers from warping. Finally, the main difference to near-duplicate retrieval approaches is the high intra-class variability, as a certain brand logo can have variations in the used colors or even in shape. Examples that illustrate some of the mentioned issues are in Fig. 1.

R. Boia—This work was supported by the Romanian Sectoral Operational Programme Human Resources Development 2007-2013 through the European Social Fund Financial Agreements POSDRU/159/1.5/S/132395 and POSDRU/159/1.5/S/134398.

© Springer International Publishing Switzerland 2015
R. Paredes et al. (Eds.): IbPRIA 2015, LNCS 9117, pp. 487–495, 2015.
DOI: 10.1007/978-3-319-19390-8_55

Fig. 1. Sample images from FlickrLogos-32 containing logos from the classes Coca Cola, FedEx, Ferrari and Paulaner. Note the variability in logo appearance or due to shadowing, color balance, warping, etc.

State of the Art. The algorithms from the generic class of object recognition can be divided in two categories: generative [1,2]. and discriminative [3,4]. Discriminative techniques use the information concerning all the existing classes and train classifiers to distinguish between them. They are distressed by missing data and prior knowledge. Generative algorithms create object class models using, separately, the data of each class, being more suitable to high intra-class variation as is the case of logo recognition. The proposed method falls in the generative category.

To deal with extreme viewpoint changes, Schneiderman et al. [2] or Bernstein and Amit [5] used the aspect graphs for simulating the perspective point variation in mixture models, idea which is developed in the current work. Yet, they construct multiple models per class, while we use a single model.

Next, into the specific problem of the logo recognition, we note two main directions: general logo recognition and specific domain recognition such as vehicle logo. The first approaches [6–8] concerning generic logo recognition were limited in handling large image collections. Later methods [9] did recognize logos by performing frequent item-set mining to discover association rules in spatial pyramids of visual words. Revaud et al. [10] use a bag-of-words (BoW) based approach coupled with learned weights to penalize inter-class appearances, while Romberg et al. [11] enhanced the BoW system by embedding spatial knowledge into the cascaded index. Romberg and Lienhart, [12], extended the BoW by bundling on the min-hashing of SIFT-based visual words. However, most work done in this direction has the purpose of image retrieval, which is more permissive as compared to localization (aimed here), since the actual location is not reported. For vehicle logo detection, the problem of localization is handled [13], but on small databases with few classes.

Database. For a realistic evaluation of the proposed method, we chose the Flickr Logos-32 database [11], which was formed by careful selecting images from collections of photos in a real word environment, depicting brand logos. The testing/training scheme is the same as in the case of Romberg et al. [11]: 30 images per class for training and 30 images per class for testing phase for a total of 32 classes. For the training phase, we used only the crops of the logos in the images, while for the test part, we scan the entire images.

We chose FlickrLogos-32 over the BelgaLogos dataset [7], as the latter was originally used for logo retrieval rather than for classification and it only defines a small number of images per class with limited variability. Taking into account the average object size, when compared to other databases for object detection, FlickrLogos-32 can be considered a small-object dataset.

2   Class Description by Class Model

The proposed method builds a class model by starting with SIFT features extraction from the training logo crops. The features are then matched and, using random sample consensus, a homography transform is found to stitch each 2 images of the same class in the training set. This pairing in fact builds a graph of the interconnections of images. The image with most links will represent its class and the entire model will be built on top of it. Using the graph and the homopraphies found, all the images are projected on the plane of the central one. Using a quality map for each matching, the suitable keypoints and features are chosen to be part of the model that is further used in detection and recognition.

Feature Extraction. To learn the logo classes, the most relevant features are extracted using the Scale-invariant feature transform (SIFT) [14] algorithm: the Difference-of-Gausssians (DoG) locator of keypoints and the description of the keypoints' vicinity by the SIFT local features. We used the following adaptation: the edge threshold that eliminates peaks of the DoG scale space was increased (from 10 to 100 - value empirically found) to enforce a high number of features from the logo area.

To thwart the very small size of some logos, we increased the number of features extracted, by upscaling the small images at 200 pixels while keeping the aspect ratio. A similar idea is in [10], but we differ by the fact we did not enlarge all the images, to keep the running time low.

Image Matching. In this stage we develop the process of image stitching for finding correspondences between the features of each two training images from every class. The basic image stitching algorithm uses the VLFeat open source code. Given the features from two input images, we match them with the algorithm from [15], which rejects the correspondences that are too ambiguous.

Once the features are matched, the correspondences of their locations should indicate the transform that projects the second image onto the plane of the first one. This transform, called the *homography* transform and denoted by H, has the role of moving a point (a, b) from the plane of the first image to the coordinates (x, y) on the plane of the second image:

$$\begin{bmatrix} a \\ b \\ 1 \end{bmatrix} H = \begin{bmatrix} x \\ y \\ 1 \end{bmatrix}, where \quad H = \begin{bmatrix} h_{11} & h_{12} & h_{13} \\ h_{21} & h_{22} & h_{23} \\ h_{31} & h_{32} & h_{33} \end{bmatrix} \tag{1}$$

Since each point correspondence provides 2 equations, 4 correspondences suffice in solving the 8 degrees of freedom of H. Often, more than 4 correspondences are available for a more robust solution.

To address the problem of outliers, the RANSAC (random sample consensus) algorithm is employed to estimate H [15]. For each 4 feature correspondences, the homography H between them is found with the direct linear transformation (DLT) [16]. This is repeated n times and the solution with most inliers is selected: the winner is the case when the projections are consistent with H within a tolerance of ϵ pixels. Our experiments proved that at least 20 pairs of points should be matched in order to obtain a correct homography.

The algorithm should iterate enough to maximize the chance to find the best match. Given the probability p_i that a feature match is correct between a pair of matching images (the inlier probability), the probability of finding the correct transformation $p(H^{Correct})$ after n trials is:

$$p(H^{Correct}) = 1 - (1 - (p_i)^r)^n \qquad (2)$$

We modify the algorithm by significantly augmenting the number of trials to 200,000 iterations, compared to 500 used in [15] as logos are smaller, possibly occluded and with fewer keypoints than panoramas. If the number of inliers is high, then the homography is quickly found and, to limit the calculus, we introduced a stopping criteria based on obtaining a score above a threshold for the homography.

In the test phase, this same algorithm is used to match the test images to the class models and often no matches are found. Here, also to limit the time, if the initial number of matching pairs is below 20, then the algorithm decides that there is no chance of finding a suitable homography and exits.

The Interconnections Graph. To sum up, the training process consists in estimating the homography between each 2 training crops of logos of the same class with RANSAC. Thus for n crops images per class, $n(n-1)/2$ image pairs are matched. Due to occlusions, inverted colors, or large variations or distortions in shape, not all the pairs of images have enough matching points to output an appropriate homography. In the end, the output of the matching procedure is a graph if only some nodes (images) are connected, similar to the idea in [11].

Each class will finally have a graph expressing the doable connections between its training images and most likely a core image (i.e. the one most connected to the others). The model of the class will be built on it, since it is clearly the most representative image in the class. We illustrate this in Fig. 2 by showing an example with a high number of image connections.

The Class Model. Each link between two images indicates different keypoints that are being used in the matching, since each image in particular has its own representative features. For example Fig. 3 proves that in the first case some keypoints are selected, while in the second, others are highlighted in the matching process. The consequence is that if only one of the images in the training set is used to represent the class, many important features can be lost.

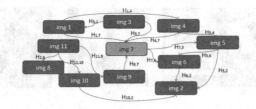

Fig. 2. Small part of a class graph. H_{ij} projects image j onto image i while the inverse of H_{ij} projects i onto j. The image most connected to the others is highlighted, and is the *central image*.

Fig. 3. The merging onto the central image of the representative keypoints coming from 2 images. (a) the matching pairs of descriptors between first image and central one, (b) the important keypoints of the first image, (c) the matching pairs of descriptors between second image and central one, (d) the important keypoints of the second image, (e) the reunion of the important keypoints on the central image

The main idea of the training stage is to conglomerate all the representative keypoints and their corresponding descriptors. We choose the central image to be the one on which this aggregation takes place, since it is obviously the best to represent the class. Using the homographies found, all the images are projected on the plane of the central image. The projected locations of the important keypoints from these images are computed and, in the end, the model of the class will be the central image described by the reunion of all the suitable points and descriptors in the class. Figure 3 shows the result of the aggregation of the keypoints from the two images, proving that each matching process reveals different pairs of keypoints that must be merged in order to obtain the best representation of the logo.

The merging is an easy task if the images are directly connected to the core image. This part of the training stage resembles [13], with the difference that there, the most representative image is manually selected. Moreover, they consider a smaller database where all the images connect to the chosen one. Contrary, we take into account also the case of the images that have no direct link to the central image by considering the path from that image to the central one. For example, in Fig. 2 images 1 and n are connected through images $2, 3, \ldots n-1$. The homography between image 1 and n is the composition of the homographies of the images connecting them:

$$H_{1,n} = H_{1,2} \circ H_{2,3} \circ \cdots \circ H_{n-1,n} \tag{3}$$

Fig. 4. Building the quality map. (a) The matching pairs of points. (b) The mosaic of images after applying the found homography. (c) The quality map. The darker areas show good quality of matching.

To select the shortest path (as it introduces fewest errors), from the many possible ones existing between two images, we use the Djikstra algorithm on the image connections graph. Given the corresponding coordinates of the points between any training image to the core image, we select the most representative keypoints for further use by computing the quality of match.

The Quality Map. The quality of matching is retrieved by means of quality map, which is built for each pair of images stitched. The map values are directly related to the correctness of the matching in that area. This procedure is similar to shape matching score from [17]: given a training set of shapes the joint distribution is computed; given an actual pair, the score is retrieved by back projecting the joint distribution.

A pixel having a good quality value is a point that represents a suitable connection between the images and is not an occlusion or distortion of the shape. Figure 4 describes the matching process and the overlaid images after applying the homography. Figure 4(c) shows the quality map created for this matching, where the darker regions in the map show the areas where the matching is correct. The areas of occlusion or difference in the shape of the logo are indicated by the lighter values in the map showing a poor quality of the matching.

Quantization of Descriptors. To keep the descriptor invariant to perspective transform, the original SIFT descriptor is stored. The final descriptor is formed by the merged keypoint vector and the merged descriptor vector of the core image, as it is more robust to perspective and more comprehensive than the central image as a model. This fact is illustrated by Fig. 5.

Some of the positions found originate from the same interest points of the logo and, thus, become adjacent on the model image. Evidently, their descriptors are extremely similar. This requires a quantization step that keeps the unique keypoints and features describing the image. The quantization has the purpose of reducing the testing computation time.

3 Implementation and Results

3.1 Testing

The purpose of testing is to locate logos and classify them. Given a model for each class, the testing phase tries to match the current image to be tested against all

Fig. 5. (a) Matching fails when using only the keypoints and descriptors of the central image. (b) Successful detection when using the model of the class.

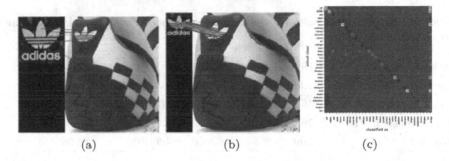

Fig. 6. (a) The failed detection of the very small logo. (b) The successful detection after resizing the test image. (c) The confusion matrix of the proposed method.

the class models. The matching is done just as in the training phase, using SIFT feature matching and RANSAC search for the correct homography. Since now the logos are part of natural images, with large areas of non-uniform background yielding a considerable number of keypoints, the ratio of outliers versus inliers is higher than in training phase, where we used only the logo crops. This motivates the use of a high number of iterations in the RANSAC stage.

The same type of quality map is built for each matching result and its average is used as an indicator of the quality of the image stitching. If the score is high enough, the decision is taken that the logo is present. The system will indicate its position and the corresponding homography that stitches the model of the logo class to the test image. An example of detection after matching a high number of keypoints is in Fig. 7 (a). If after being confronted to all the class models, no score is large enough, then the test image will be classified as "no-logo".

The training phase has taught us that small sized logos do not present enough features to be correctly represented and then classified. Thus, the test images might contain also very small logos. Since there is no information about their sizes or locations, we doubled the size of test images before trying the matching. Figure 6 shows a case when the detection fails as the logo in the test image is extremely small. (b) presents the solution of the problem by enlarging the test image.

(a)   (b)   (c)

Fig. 7. Examples of detections: (a) with blurry and shadowed logo, (b) with occluded over the logo or (c) for a very small logo (30×30).

Table 1. Classification results for the compared methods for 5 example classes and respectively entire set.

Method	Detection rate [%]					
Classes	Aldi	Coca cola	DHL	Esso	Paulaner	All classes
Romberg et al. [11]	56.66	60	16.6	76.6	60	61.14
Central image model [13]	76.66	66.66	70	63.3	90	60.1
Proposed method	*100*	*86.6*	*96.6*	*96.6*	*100*	*84.06*

3.2   Results. Comparison with State of the Art

We have obtained 100 % classification rate for 13 classes and over 90 % for 20 classes and respectively 84,06 % for the entire dataset. A true detection is if the found logo is present in that image. The localization is correct if the intersection-over-union, (i.e. Jaccard index), is above 50 % [18]. The results are better described by the confusion matrix presented in Fig. 6 (c). Again we have used the same scenario as Romberg et al. [11]. Comparative results may be seen in Table 1. To show the benefits of the proposed homography based construction, we considered the central image as class model as discussed in [13] for vehicle logo recognition. Examples of the method detecting logos in extreme situations, such as small sizes, highly occluded or very blurred are in Fig. 7.

4   Discussion and Continuations

The proposed method falls short for symmetric and circular logos with too few keypoints, and which do not represent well the area, leading to an inability to compute homographies. While normally we find over 300 pairs of images that match, for "Pepsi" and "Apple" only ≈ 5 connections are in the class describing graph, thus, leading to wrong class model and low classification performance.

Yet, overall, the method is effective in detecting the majority of classes, surpassing many challenges of logo detection in natural images. Continuation envisages the cases of failure by changing the matching process so to take into account the vicinity of the points, thus improving the homography building.

References

1. Lowe, D.: Object recognition from local scale-invariant features. In: ICCV, pp. 1150–1157 (1999)
2. Schneiderman, H., Kanade, T.: A statistical method for 3d object detection applied to faces and cars. In: CVPR, pp. 746–751 (2003)
3. Torralba, A., Murphy, K., Freeman, W.: Sharing visual features for multiclass and multiview object detection. In: CVPR, pp. 762–769 (2004)
4. Opelt, A., Fusseneger, M., Pinz, A., Auer, P.: Generic object recognition with boosting. IEEE Trans. PAMI 28(3), 416–431 (2006)
5. Bernstein, E., Amit, Y.: Part-based statistical models for object classification and detection. In: CVPR, pp. 734–740 (2005)
6. Bagdanov, A., Ballan, L., Bertini, M., Del Bimbo, A.: Trademark matching and retrieval in sports video databases. In: ACM MIR, pp. 79–86 (2007)
7. Joly, A., Buisson, O.: Logo retrieval with a contrario visual query expansion. In: ACM MM, pp. 581–584 (2009)
8. Sivic, J., Zisserman, A.: Video google: a text retrieval approach to object matching in videos. In: ICCV, pp. 1470–1477 (2003)
9. Kleban, J., Xie, X., Ma, W.Y.: Spatial pyramid mining for logo detection in natural scenes. In: IEEE ICME, pp. 1470–1477 (2008)
10. Revaud, J., Douze, M., Schmid, C.: Correlation-based burstiness for logo retrieval. In: ACM MM, pp. 965–968 (2012)
11. Romberg, S., Garcia Pueyo, L., Lienhart, R., van Zwol, R.: Scalable logo recognition in real-world images. In: ACM ICMR, pp. 965–968 (2011)
12. Romberg, S., Lienhart, R.: Bundle min-hashing for logo recognition. In: ACM ICMR (2013)
13. Psyllos, A.P., Anagnostopoulos, C.N.E., Kayafas, E.: Vehicle logo recognition using a sift-based enhanced matching scheme. IEEE TITS 11(2), 322–328 (2010)
14. Lowe, D.: Distinctive image features from scale-invariant keypoints. IJCV 62(2), 91–110 (2004)
15. Brown, M., Lowe, D.: Automatic panoramic image stitching using invariant features. IJCV 74(1), 59–73 (2006)
16. Hartley, R., Zisserman, A.: Multiple View Geometry in Computer Vision. Cambridge University Press, New York (2004)
17. Florea, L., Florea, C., Vranceanu, R., Vertan, C.: Can your eyes tell me how you think? a gaze directed estimation of the mental activity. In: BMVC (2013)
18. Everingham, M., Van Gool, L., Williams, C., Winn, J., Zisserman, A.: The pascal visual object classes (voc) challenge. IJCV. 1, 303–338 (2010)

Multimodal Object Recognition Using Random Clustering Trees

M. Villamizar[✉], A. Garrell, A. Sanfeliu, and F. Moreno-Noguer

Institut de Robotica i Informatica Industrial CSIC-UPC, Barcelona, Spain
{mvillami,agarrell,sanfeliu,fmoreno}@iri.upc.edu

Abstract. In this paper, we present an object recognition approach that in addition allows to discover intra-class modalities exhibiting high-correlated visual information. Unlike to more conventional approaches based on computing multiple specialized classifiers, the proposed approach combines a single classifier, Boosted Random Ferns (BRFs), with probabilistic Latent Semantic Analysis (pLSA) in order to recognize an object class and to find automatically the most prominent intra-class appearance modalities (clusters) through tree-structured visual words.

The proposed approach has been validated in synthetic and real experiments where we show that the method is able to recognize objects with multiple appearances.

Keywords: Object recognition · Random trees · Clustering · Boosting

1 Introduction

Computer vision is nowadays a very active research field where it has made great strides in recent years, especially in the recognition of objects in images and videos. Currently, there exist methods that can detect and identify objects with outstanding results despite the large difficulties present in this problem such as intra-class variations, 3D rotations, scaling, illumination changes [2,4,8,14].

However, most of these methods are based on complex algorithms that depend of a rigorous training and large object databases. Usually, these methods compute object detectors using a supervised and offline learning where time constraints and computational cost are not a big issue.

In order to compute efficient and robust object detectors, approaches based on randomized trees have been proposed in the past with outstanding results, especially in terms of efficiency and reliability [7,9]. Particularly, these methods have been focused mainly on the fast matching of binary descriptors. Subsequently, a robust and efficient classifier for the detection of object classes was proposed in [16]. This method, called Boosted Random Ferns (BRFs), combines multiple extremely randomized trees (e.g. Random Ferns [9]) using AdaBoost so as to select automatically the most relevant trees in one single classifier.

Although this classifier has shown remarkable results to detect objects with multiple intra-class modalities (e.g. multiple object's views), this method is

© Springer International Publishing Switzerland 2015
R. Paredes et al. (Eds.): IbPRIA 2015, LNCS 9117, pp. 496–504, 2015.
DOI: 10.1007/978-3-319-19390-8_56

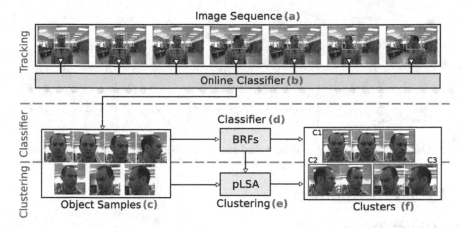

Fig. 1. Overall scheme of the proposed approach to compute object classifiers using weakly supervised learning. In this approach only the first frame is annotated manually. For clarity, this figure does not include background (negative) samples.

unable to distinguish these modes automatically. For this purpose, methods based on the computation of multiple specialized classifiers have been proposed, where each one is devoted to a particular appearance cluster [6, 13]. However, these methods increase the complexity and computational cost of the detector since various classifiers are considered during run time. Additionally, computing these classifiers in a supervised learning require annotating all training samples with their corresponding appearance cluster. This task is cumbersome and tedious since it is usually carried out manually.

In this work, we present a more straightforward approach to recognize object appearance clusters (i.e., intra-class modalities) using weakly human supervision during the training phase. More precisely, the proposed method consists of three main stages, observe Fig. 1. In the initial stage (*object tracking*), an online classifier is computed in order to detect and track the object through a sequence of images (Fig. 1-a,b). This process is automatic and requires only the assignment of the object in the first frame using a bounding box (yellow box). The result of this step is a set of training samples (images) of the object with different appearance (Fig. 1-c). In the second stage (*classifier*), a more robust classifier (BRFs) is computed using the training samples (Fig. 1-d). Finally, in the third step (*clustering*), the training samples are clustered using probabilistic Latent Semantic Analysis (pLSA) [1,5,11] and the responses of the BRFs classifier on the samples (Fig. 1-e). Figure 1-f shows as example three clusters of training samples grouped according their visual similarity.

The method we present is a further step of the approach proposed in [3, 12] for learning and detecting objects using human-robot interactions. Actually, this method corresponds to the *tracking* stage in Fig. 1. In this work, we combine this method with BRFs and pLSA in order to detect and distinguish multiple object appearances. This is particular useful for robotics applications where knowing a specific object view allows to take actions. For example, for human-robot interaction is important to determine whether people look at the robot (see Fig. 1).

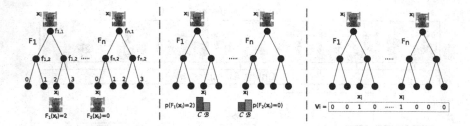

Fig. 2. Online classifier used to detect and track the object trough an image sequence.

2 Proposed Approach

2.1 Object Tracking

The first stage of the proposed method corresponds to perform object detection and tracking over an input image sequence, observe Fig. 1. The goal of this stage is to extract automatically a set of training samples which are used later to compute the object classifier.

To track the object in every frame, we compute an online classifier based on extremely randomized trees [9,12]. This classifier is initialized using an object annotation provided by the user in the first frame (Fig. 1-a). Subsequently, the classifier is computed and updated incrementally using their own detection hypotheses on new input images. This self-learning approach allows computing and adapting an object detector while discovers object instances in images.

More formally, the classifier is comprised of a series of N random ferns where each fern F_k computes a set of M signed comparisons between pairs of intensity pixel values $\{f_{k,m}\}_{m=1}^{M}$, known commonly as binary features. Figure 2-left shows for example the output of two fern instances over an input sample $\mathbf{x}_i$. We observe that the fern output $F_k(\mathbf{x}_i)$ depends of the responses of the binary features. The co-occurrence of these features determines the tree leaf where the sample falls.

Once the response of each fern k is computed $F_k(\mathbf{x}_i)$, the classifier updates its class-conditional probabilities in each tree, $p(F_k(\mathbf{x}_i)|\mathcal{C})$ and $p(F_k(\mathbf{x}_i)|\mathcal{B})$, according whether the sample $\mathbf{x}_i$ belongs to either the object $\mathcal{C}$ or background $\mathcal{B}$ class. This is illustrated in Fig. 2-middle, where the input sample is used to update the fern distributions. For further information about this online classifier and its computation see [12,15].

2.2 The Object Classifier

The object classifier is computed using Boosted Random Ferns (BRFs) since they have demonstrated to be an efficient and robust classifier for object recognition [16]. Further in detail, the object classifier $H(\mathbf{x})$ is built using a boosting combination of weak classifiers h_t where each is a random fern F_t computed to particular object location (u_t, v_t). The classifier is computed in order to find the ferns and locations that most discriminate the object (positive) class from the

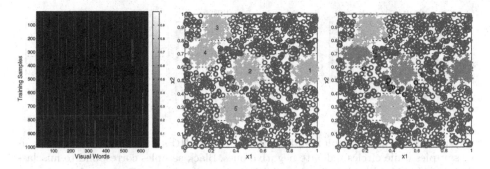

Fig. 3. Computation of object class clusters using pLSA. Left: table including the co-occurrence between training samples and visual words. Middle: two-class classification problem in 2D feature space. The positive class (crosses) has five intra-class modalities. Right: output of the clustering stage to find latent topics (sample clusters).

background (negative) one. The computation of the classifier is done using real AdaBoost, that iteratively assembles weak classifiers and adapts their weighting values to focus all its effort on the misclassified samples from previous weak classifiers [10].

The object classifier with T weak classifiers is then defined as:

$$H(\mathbf{x}) = \sum_{t=1}^{T} h_t(\mathbf{x}) > \beta,$$

(1)

where $\mathbf{x}$ is a test sample, β is the classifier threshold and h_t is a weak classifier computed by

$$h_t(\mathbf{x}) = \frac{1}{2} \log \frac{p(F_t(\mathbf{x}) = r|\mathcal{C}) + \epsilon}{p(F_t(\mathbf{x}) = r|\mathcal{B}) + \epsilon},$$

(2)

where r is the output of the fern F_t on the sample $\mathbf{x}$, ϵ is a smoothing parameter, and $\mathcal{B}$ and $\mathcal{C}$ are the background and object class labels, respectively. In order to extract the most discriminative weak classifier at each iteration, the AdaBoost algorithm seeks for the fern that minimizes the distance between class-conditional probabilities, $p(F_t(\mathbf{x})|\mathcal{C})$ and $p(F_t(\mathbf{x})|\mathcal{B})$. For more information refer to [16].

2.3 Clustering

With the aim of finding important internal structures of the object class without human supervision, we propose to use pLSA to discretize the overall appearance of the object in multiple clusters of samples with a strong feature similarity. More specifically, pLSA is a generative model from the statistical text literature that allows discovering latent variables (topics) from a corpus containing co-occurrences between documents and words [1,5,11].

In this work, we use image samples and tree-structured visual words instead of text documents and words in order to find the most relevant clusters of the

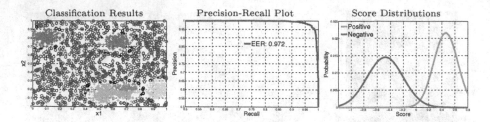

Fig. 4. Left: 2D classification results provided by the BRFs classifier. Crosses are positive samples while circles indicate negative ones. Black samples correspond to misclassified samples. Middle: classification plots using recall-precision curves and equal error rate (EER). Right: class score distributions for the positive and negative classes.

object appearance (topics). The pLSA algorithm is suitable for this problem because it provides a statistical model that allows represent an object sample $\mathbf{x}_i$ as a mixture of K topics,

$$p(w_j|\mathbf{x}_i) = \sum_{k=1}^{K} p(z_k|\mathbf{x}_i)p(w_j|z_k), \tag{3}$$

where $p(z_k|\mathbf{x}_i)$ is the probability of topic z_k occurring in the sample $\mathbf{x}_i$ whereas $p(w_j|z_k)$ is the probability of the visual word w_j occurring in the topic z_k [11].

The pLSA computation is done using the EM algorithm and an input table containing the co-occurrence of training samples and the bag of visual words. Figure 3-left shows this table where the object samples have been ordered by cluster in order to distinguish visually the strong patterns in the corpus. For our case, we use the object samples extracted by the online classifier, and define that each fern leaf j corresponds to a particular visual word w_j since it represents a specific configuration of binary features. This is shown in Fig. 2-right. For this simple example, the activated visual words (i.e., ones) co-occur with the input sample $\mathbf{x}_i$ since this sample falls in the corresponding fern leaves.

Finally, in Fig. 3-right we show the output of the clustering stage over a set of training samples using a 2D feature space with complex and multimodal class distributions (see Fig. 3-middle). In this figure, crosses are object or positive samples whereas circles make reference to background or negative samples. As a result, we can see that the positive samples are clustered in $K=5$ different clusters, indicated through different colors, and that each one keeps strong feature correlation in the 2D space.

3   Experiments

3.1   Synthetic Experiments - 2D Classification Problem

The proposed approach has been evaluated in synthetic experiments in order to observe more clearly the performance of the method. Figure 4 shows, for

Table 1. 2D classification results of the BRFs and RFs classifiers.

	Classification Performance													
	RFs			BRFs										
	# Clusters (K)			# Clusters (K)			# Ferns (R)				# Features (S)			
	3	5	10	3	5	10	5	10	20	50	1	3	5	7
EER(%)	90.6	92.4	84.4	96.9	97.4	96.0	95.4	96.6	96.9	97.2	83.1	96.1	96.9	97.2
Distance(%)	59.0	68.8	46.5	83.1	90.6	73.2	77.2	80.4	83.1	88.8	41.2	73.0	83.1	88.4

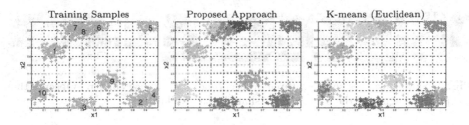

Fig. 5. 2D clustering results.

example, the output of the proposed method on a scenario generated at random in which two class distributions (positive and negative) with high complexity are considered. For this experiment, the method was computed using $K = 5$ clusters.

We see in Fig. 4-left that the proposed approach achieves correctly classify most samples while discovers multiple intra-class modalities (indicated through clusters with different colors). The method only produces a small number of misclassified samples (black ones). This result is also shown in the precision-recall curve (Fig. 4-middle) where the method obtains a high equal error rate (EER). Moreover, the approach also increases the separability between classes and reduces the risk of misclassification.This is observed in Fig. 4-right where the class score distributions are shown.

The Table 1 shows the average classification results of the BRFs classifier over 10 runs in order to consider the randomness of the classifier and the 2D scenario. Each scenario is generated at random with multiple sample clusters (K). We see that BRFs obtain high classification rates (EER) and large distances between classes when the amount of features (F) and ferns (R) gets larger. Here, we use the Hellinger distance to measure the separability between Gaussian distributions. The default parameters for this experiment are $K = 5$, $R = 20$ and $S = 5$. The table also shows a comparison, in terms of the number of clusters, of BRFs against its counterpart without using boosting (RFs). Observe that the BRFs classifier attains the best performance rates.

Figure 5 shows the clustering results of the presented approach in comparison with the K-means algorithm. The left figure corresponds to the positive training samples belonging to 20-dimensional feature space. In this figure, we only plot the first two feature dimensions $(x1,x2)$. Figure 5-middle plots the clustering

Table 2. Clustering results.

	Clustering Results											
	BRFs+pLSA				K-means (Euclidean)				BRFs+K-means			
D	2	5	10	20	2	5	10	20	2	5	10	20
$K=3$	0.097	0.001	0.033	0.000	0.147	0.100	0.133	0.067	0.177	0.036	0.086	0.113
$K=5$	0.240	0.022	0.019	0.020	0.180	0.139	0.163	0.201	0.304	0.127	0.114	0.173
$K=10$	0.514	0.144	0.092	0.096	0.367	0.143	0.159	0.116	0.548	0.251	0.207	0.102

Fig. 6. Sample images showing three different face appearance clusters. Observe that samples belonging to the same cluster share visual similarities.

output of the proposed approach (BRFs+pLSA), whereas the right figure shows the results of K-means using Euclidean distance in the sample feature space. We can see that our approach yields good clustering results, in contrast to the K-means algorithm which produces some incorrect clustering labels (observed through the confusion of colors in clusters). Finally, Table 2 shows the average confusion values in the clustering labels for varying numbers of clusters and feature space dimensions (D). Here, we use as measure of confusion the entropy function over the confusion matrix (using ground truth labels). The table also includes a BRFs+K-means approach using the Hamming distance. As a result, we observe that the proposed approach (BRFs+pLSA) produces low confusion values, especially for large feature spaces.

3.2   Real Experiments - Multi-view Face and Object Detection

The proposed approach has also been tested to detect faces under multiple views, see Fig. 7. This corresponds to a classification problem involving multiple intra-classes where each one is associated to a particular view. For this experiment, we have used two face sequences of the dataset proposed in [12], where each sequence contains more than 200 images. For training, we have used the first sequence, whereas the second one is used for validation.

Figure 6 shows some samples images corresponding to $K = 3$ different intra-class appearances modalities found by the proposed method during the training phase. We see that these samples share similar visual features and that the proposed method is able to cluster these samples using the output of a tree-structured classifier. In Fig. 7 are shown some detection results on the test images. Note that the method is capable of detecting most faces at the same time that it can estimate the face pose. This is indicated in the images through colored boxes. This experiment reveals that the proposed method using a single classifier can be used for pose estimation using the co-occurrence of visual words.

Similar to the previous experiment, our method has been tested for object recognition. In this case, for detecting a toy car from multiple viewpoints using $K = 5$ appearance clusters. Figure 8 shows some example images where the response of the classifier is indicated by the bounding boxes and the color represents the object cluster. We can see that the proposed method is able to discretize automatically the overall object appearance in diverse modalities, each one corresponding to a particular object view.

Fig. 7. Face detection results provided by the proposed approach. The output of the classifier is indicated by boxes whereas the face pose is shown through different colors (Color figure online).

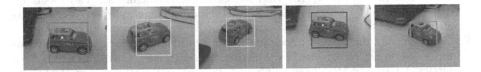

Fig. 8. Object recognition results.

4   Conclusions

In this paper, a weakly supervised learning approach has been proposed in order to compute an object classifier that is able to identify multiple intra-class modalities. The proposed approach combines a tree-structured classifier with a text document analysis algorithm so as to cluster the output of the classifier. The approach has been validated in synthetic and real experiments.

Acknowledgments. Work partially supported by the Spanish Ministry of Science and Innovation under project DPI2013-42458-P, ERA-Net Chistera project ViSen PCIN-2013-047, and by the EU project ARCAS FP7-ICT-2011-28761.

References

1. Bosch, A., Zisserman, A., Muñoz, X.: Scene classification via pLSA. In: Leonardis, A., Bischof, H., Pinz, A. (eds.) ECCV 2006. LNCS, vol. 3954, pp. 517–530. Springer, Heidelberg (2006)
2. Felzenszwalb, P.F., Girshick, R.B., McAllester, D., Ramanan, D.: Object detection with discriminatively trained part-based models. PAMI **32**(9), 1627–1645 (2010)
3. Garrell, A., Villamizar, M., Moreno-Noguer, F., Sanfeliu, A.: Proactive behavior of an autonomous mobile robot for human-assisted learning. In: RO-MAN (2013)
4. Hinterstoisser, S., Lepetit, V., Fua, P., Navab, N.: Dominant orientation templates for real-time detection of texture-less objects. In: CVPR (2010)
5. Hofmann, T.: Unsupervised learning by probabilistic latent semantic analysis. Mach. Learn. **42**(1–2), 177–196 (2001)
6. Kim, T.K., Cipolla, R.: Mcboost: multiple classifier boosting for perceptual co-clustering of images and visual features. In: NIPS, pp. 841–848 (2009)
7. Lepetit, V., Fua, P.: Keypoint recognition using randomized trees. PAMI **28**(9), 1465–1479 (2006)
8. Lowe, D.G.: Distinctive image features from scale-invariant keypoints. IJCV **60**(2), 91–110 (2004)
9. Ozuysal, M., Calonder, M., Lepetit, V., Fua, P.: Fast keypoint recognition using random ferns. PAMI **32**(3), 448–461 (2010)
10. Schapire, R.E., Singer, Y.: Improved boosting algorithms using confidence-rated predictions. Mach. Learn. **37**(3), 297–336 (1999)
11. Sivic, J., Russell, B., Efros, A., Zisserman, A., Freeman, W.T.: Discovering objects and their location in images. In: ICCV (2005)
12. Villamizar, M., Garrell, A., Sanfeliu, A., Moreno-Noguer, F.: Online human-assisted learning using random ferns. In: ICPR (2012)
13. Villamizar, M., Grabner, H., Andrade-Cetto, J., Sanfeliu, A., Van Gool, L., Moreno-Noguer, F.: Efficient 3D object detection using multiple pose-specific classifiers. In: BMVC (2011)
14. Villamizar, M., Sanfeliu, A., Andrade-Cetto, J.: Orientation invariant features for multiclass object recognition. In: Martínez-Trinidad, J.F., Carrasco Ochoa, J.A., Kittler, J. (eds.) CIARP 2006. LNCS, vol. 4225, pp. 655–664. Springer, Heidelberg (2006)
15. Villamizar, M., Sanfeliu, A., Moreno-Noguer, F.: Fast online learning and detection of natural landmarks for autonomous aerial robots. In: ICRA (2014)
16. Villamizar, M., Andrade-Cetto, J., Sanfeliu, A., Moreno-Noguer, F.: Bootstrapping boosted random ferns for discriminative and efficient object classification. Pattern Recognit. **45**(9), 3141–3153 (2012)

Videogrammetry System for Wind Turbine Vibration Monitoring

Germán Rodríguez[✉], Maria Fuciños, Xosé M. Pardo,
and Xosé R. Fdez-Vidal

Centro de Investigación en Tecnoloxías da Información (CITIUS),
Universidade de Santiago de Compostela,
15782 A Coruña, Spain
german.rodriquez.garcia.usc@gmail.com

Abstract. Early detection of component failure in wind turbines produces a great value in savings. We present an external method for obtaining the tower vibrations using videogrammetry. We use a multi-view image acquisition system and a set of fiducial markers set on the surface of the tower. Targets are identified using a radial symmetry measure, their centre is located through elliptical model fitting, and they are recognized through a standard segmentation and decoding method. Finally targets are tracked and displacements processed. We have obtained good results in the tests performed and we intend to continue gathering data to build a classification system for identifying abnormal vibrations.

Keywords: Videogrammetry · Wind turbine monitoring · Vibrations

1 Introduction

A key factor within the wind power industry is to guarantee the structural integrity of wind turbine components. Exposed continuously to the forces of the wind, adverse weather, and ageing, blades and rotor mechanics can get damaged and cause balance asymmetries which can result in further damage in the components themselves and over the nacelle, tower and foundations. Periodic inspections are performed, being usually intrusive and requiring scheduled downtime. Maintenance and downtime costs caused by structural fatigue and failure are estimated to be around 25 % of the operation cost for kWh produced. In addition, wind turbine condition between checks remains unknown [1].

The Structural Health Monitoring (SHM) is the process of implementing a damage detection and characterization strategy for engineer structures. Vibration based condition monitoring has been used extensively since 1970 in aerospace and offshore oil industries [2]. The time history response of a structure can be measured using different sensors as accelerometers, strain gauges, velocity sensors, etc. These sensors present some disadvantages. They are subject to failure and therefore maintenance is required, they are expensive and require a complex installation for which experts are needed.

© Springer International Publishing Switzerland 2015
R. Paredes et al. (Eds.): IbPRIA 2015, LNCS 9117, pp. 505–513, 2015.
DOI: 10.1007/978-3-319-19390-8_57

Videogrammetry presents some advantages over the prior described sensors. Markers are usually just stickers. They are cheaper and for their installation it is not required specific training. If a wider frequency range is needed, markers are still valid, changing the cameras is enough. Being an external method it can be easily used for identifying vibrations on the tower and rotation of the blades.

Usual videogrammetric approaches involve expensive stereoscopic calibrated systems for acquiring 3D, real world, coordinates of the markers. This data is then used within computer models for estimating and analysing their behaviour [3]. In these systems physical characteristics of the lenses and camera sensors must be equal, and require complex processes of calibration. Calibration is also dependant of the distances, marker sizes, etc.

We present a SHM method for monitoring the wind turbine condition using videogrammetry which potentially can be applied to identify tower and blades problems. We count with a set of fiducial markers located on the surface of the tower in orthogonal positions at different heights. A multi-view video system aiming to these markers is set to obtain their displacement through different stages of the wind turbine's operation. Analysing this data and comparing it with the historical records of previous vibrations we intend to stablish a classification system for identifying anomalous behaviours. This would allow to take action on preventing further damage, by repairing the problematic components or modifying the wind turbine operation adapting it to the current circumstances.

We use circular coded markers, similar to markers used in commercial systems like AICON 3D® or Photomodeler Scanner®. They are white circles over a black background surrounded by an outer ring with black and white sections or bits. We do not use a calibrated system as our approach does not involve obtaining the 3D coordinates of the markers. We acquire the orthogonal vibration components instead, which for the structural health monitoring should be enough.

2   Videogrammetry Health Monitoring System

2.1   System Architecture

In this section we describe the global architecture of the system. Figure 1 summarizes all the process. Data is acquired from a multi-view video system with synchronized cameras located around the tower. Each one of them is installed pointing to a fiducial marker. There will be at least two pairs of markers located orthogonally and at different heights each. This will allow us to obtain the vibration component of each axe. The system is structured in two main subsystems. One for vibration acquisition and the second one for vibration analysis.

The **Vibration Acquisition Subsystem** includes the following steps. First the video sequences are processed as described in Sect. 2.2, for detecting and identifying the markers in the initial frames. The initial location of the marker is calculated with subpixel precision using elliptical model fitting. Tracking of the markers from frame to frame is achieved by local thresholding within a region of interest defined around the position of the markers in the previous frame and

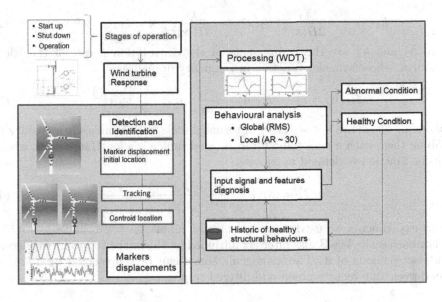

Fig. 1. System architecture

using elliptical model fitting again for locating the centroid. The sequence of positions identified through all the frames form the observed displacement. If there are missing values caused by blades occlusion, interpolation is applied. Apparent accelerations are estimated through double differentiation and smoothing.

The first step in the **Vibration Analysis Subsystem** involves processing the signal acquired. Accelerations are decomposed using the discrete wavelet transform (DWT). For each wavelet level the Root Mean Squared vibration magnitude is estimated among an autoregressive model. These coefficients are used as descriptors in addition of the data gathered from the SCADA. This data is used for diagnosis by comparing them with previous records as seen in [4]. If a signal is found to be normal, it is added to the database of known behaviours for future comparisons, otherwise an alarm is triggered.

In this paper we focus on the stages of detection, recognition and tracking.

2.2   Target Detection and Recognition

In this section, we introduce a more computationally efficient measure aimed at reducing time and memory requirements while keeping or improving performance. We chose a monogenic scale space because it allows access to local phase. As these filters are not selective in orientation, a further step to reject non-elliptical regions was added.

Monogenic signal [5] allows the decomposition f_m of an image I to provide information of local energy, phase and orientation:

$$f_m(\mathbf{x}) = (I(\mathbf{x}), (h_1 * I)(\mathbf{x}), (h_2 * I)(\mathbf{x})), \tag{1}$$

$$h_1(\mathbf{x}) = -\frac{x_1}{2\Pi|\mathbf{x}|^3} \quad h_2(\mathbf{x}) = -\frac{x_2}{2\Pi|\mathbf{x}|^3}, \quad \mathbf{x} = (x_1, x_2)\epsilon\mathbb{R}^2. \tag{2}$$

where h_1 and h_2 are the components of the convolution kernel of the Riesz transform, whose transfer function in frequency domain is:

$$H_1(\mathbf{u}) = i\frac{u_1}{|\mathbf{u}|} \quad H_2(\mathbf{u}) = i\frac{u_2}{|\mathbf{u}|}, \quad \mathbf{u} = (u_1, u_2)\epsilon\mathbb{R}^2. \tag{3}$$

Monogenic filters are not selective in terms of scale, which makes it necessary to combine them with a pass-band filter. A good choice is a log-Gauss filter, whose transfer function is defined as follows:

$$T_i = \exp\left(-\frac{\log(\rho/\rho_i)^2}{2\log(\sigma_{\rho i}/\rho_i)^2}\right). \tag{4}$$

In our experiments we used $N_s = 4$, $\lambda_{min} = 5$ pixels, $M = 2.1$, and $\sigma_{\rho i} = 0.55$.

For each scale, log-Gauss filter is multiplied by the image to produce different bandpass versions of it. The monogenic signal can be represented by a scalar-valued even and vector-valued odd filtered responses:

$$\mathbf{M} = (f_i, fh_{1,i}, fh_{2,i}) = (\mathcal{F}^{-1}(\mathcal{F}(I)\cdot T_i), \mathcal{F}^{-1}((\mathcal{F}(I)\cdot T_i)\cdot H_1), \mathcal{F}^{-1}((\mathcal{F}(I)\cdot T_i)\cdot H_2)). \tag{5}$$

From them, we compute a symmetry measure for each scale:

$$Sym = \sum_i f_i - \sqrt{(fh_{1,i})^2 + (fh_{2,i})^2}. \tag{6}$$

Finally, assuming Gaussian noise, a threshold T is applied and the result is half wave rectifying:

$$RS_M = \max(0, Sym - T). \tag{7}$$

We do not apply a divisive normalization as Kovesi (1997) did [6], in order to avoid enhancing regions with weak phase symmetry.

An iterative normalization operation is performed on RS_M to reduce the number of symmetry regions by minimizing the weakest symmetry maxima and to maximize the strongest ones [7]. This step increases the execution time during the detection stage, however, it reduces the number of candidates to be markers centres and consequently execution time in the precise location of markers.

Since monogenic filters are not selective to orientation, we add a last step to reject non-elliptical regions around local maxima, via elliptical model fitting.

Once available the elliptical model targets are decoded. The elliptical ring is mapped into a circular region of unit radius by means of an inverse affine transformation, and then mapped to polar coordinates. Finally, intensity is normalized to the range [0, 1]. The normalized rectangular image of the ring is decoded to get the corresponding binary sequence using standard segmentation techniques.The procedure adopted here involves taking the intensity maximum in the radial dimension to get a one-dimensional profile [8]. The one-dimensional profile is thresholded to get the binary sequence. The threshold level is computed as the average of the maximum and minimum intensity levels of the profile.

2.3   Target Tracking

Once we have successfully identified the targets and their location in the initial frames, we can adopt a simpler approach for the tracking. The previously described methods for detection and recognition have been proved very effective, but they have the disadvantage of being computationally expensive. That is not a problem since we know already the sizes and positions of the targets in the initial frames. Knowing also that the displacement of the targets from frame to frame will not be big, we can define a region of interest (ROI) for each frame based on the data gathered from the previous one, and look for the new position of the ellipse there. From this ROI a local threshold is established and used for segmentation. The centre of the ellipse with subpixel precision is again obtained by fitting the segmented ROI to an elliptical model. In this case it is not needed to obtain again the target code as it will be only one target for each ROI.

The procedure is repeated for each frame updating the centre of the ROI with the centre of the ellipse detected in the previous frame.

Finally a check for missing values is performed. If the targets are high in the tower the passing blades can occlude them for a couple of frames. Interpolation is applied if needed, followed by a simple moving average smoothing.

2.4   Analysis and Diagnosis

Displacements are recorded among other data as wind direction, mean wind speed, temperature, etc. A Supervisory Control And Data Acquisition (SCADA) system integrated in the wind turbine provides this data. SCADA systems are computer based systems that monitor and control large scale industrial processes.

Once the displacements are obtained, apparent accelerations are estimated through double differentiation followed by smoothing. These accelerations are decomposed using the discrete wavelet transform (DWT). Wavelet analysis has been accepted as a key signal processing tool for wind turbine monitoring [1,9], as it provides a representation of the signals both in time and frequency domain.

For each signal and its wavelet levels the Root Mean Squared (RMS) vibration magnitude is estimated among an autoregressive model (AR). These coefficients are used as descriptors in addition of the data gathered from the SCADA. This data is then used in the diagnosis subsystem for classifying the input signal as normal or abnormal by comparing them with previous records as seen in [4]. When a signal is obtained the closest signal to it is recovered from the database of healthy behaviours. Then the Euclidean distance between the features of both signals is calculated and if it is under a threshold is accepted as healthy and added to the database for future comparisons.

3   Results

3.1   Target Detection and Recognition

The detection and recognition algorithm was evaluated against a database of images taken in different perspective conditions with more than 1000 targets.

The efficiency of our methods was measured by using the F_1 score statistical parameter that represents the trade off between sensitivity and precision [10].

Table 1 shows the performances and efficiencies of this method. The targets were divided into two different groups depending on their perspective distortion. If the eccentricity of the ellipse that describes the center of each marker was higher than 0.8, it was labelled to have a strong perspective distortion, otherwise it was labelled to have a weak perspective distortion.

Table 1. Results obtained in the detection and location stage for AICON targets under weak and strong perspective distortions.

	Weak perspective distortions			Strong perspective distortions		
	Sensitivity	Precision	F_1^{-1}score	Sensitivity	Precision	F_1^{-1}score
RS_M	0.895	0.998	0.944	0.777	0.991	0.871

Results obtained with the recognition methods are summarized in Table 2. It shows a comparison for 12-bit and 14-bit codes under weak perspective distortion (WPD) and strong perspective distortion (SPD). The selected images are the same that in the detection stage.

Table 2. Results obtained in the recognition stage for 12-bit and 14-bit AICON targets under weak (WPD) and strong perspective distortions (SPD).

	12-bit markers			14-bit markers		
	Sensitivity	Precision	F_1^{-1}score	Sensitivity	Precision	F_1^{-1}score
WPD	0.768	0.970	0.857	0.889	1	0.941
SPD	0.609	0.980	0.751	0.665	0.963	0.787

Robustness to illumination changes was tested by modifying images taken from realistic scenarios. These images were modified using GIMP (GNU Image Manipulation Program) for casting shadows with opacities from 10 % to 90 %. Figure 2 shows the results of the comparisons of the detected targets using our method and the radial symmetry blob detector RS proposed in [11] .

3.2 Field Testing

We tested our videogrammetry system on different wind turbines and weather conditions. Two pairs of fiducial markers were set on the surface of each tower. Each pair was set orthogonally at different heights. For recording the markers we counted with a multi view image acquisition system with each camera synchrony recording a marker from ground level. Cameras recorded at 20 frames per second. We also counted with the data provided by a SCADA system.

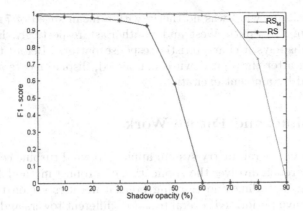

Fig. 2. Efficiency for different illumination conditions

Three kinds of sequences were recorded corresponding to different stages of the wind turbine operation: start up, normal operation and shut down. For the start up three minutes were recorded since the start up order was send, one for the normal operation and two for the shut down.

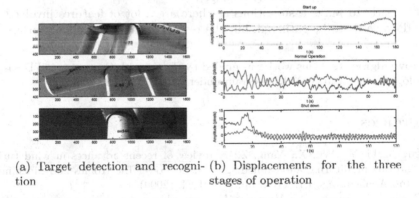

(a) Target detection and recogni- (b) Displacements for the three
tion   stages of operation

Fig. 3. This figure shows three examples of the displacements obtained from targets under different perspectives and lighting conditions for the three stages of the operation

Figure 3(a) shows three targets successfully detected and decoded under different lighting conditions and perspectives. The first one shows an image in colour when the target is under direct sunlight. The second and third one are black and white images, being the target in the second one in shadows and the third under direct sunlight. The system is efficient detecting and decoding targets as long as the information in the images is not excessively dim or saturated.

Figure 3(b) shows the typical displacements of a pair of orthogonal markers obtained through the different stages of operation in a healthy tower. In this test the predominant wind was northerly with a mean speed of 7 m/s. Markers were set pointing to South West and South East respectively. Each stage of the operation displays a characteristic response pattern. Before the operation has started and after the shut down is completed, displacements are still being obtained caused by ambient excitation.

4   Conclusions and Future Work

We presented a videogrammetry system applied to wind turbine condition monitoring. Our approach involves the application of a robust methodology for identifying, locating, decoding and tracking fiducial markers set on the surface of the tower. We have performed several test over different towers and recognizable patterns of displacement were obtained for the different stages of operation.

We intend to build a classification system able to identify anomalous vibrations of the tower which could be related to component malfunction or failure.For that we are using the discrete wavelet decomposition over the obtained accelerations. From each decomposition level descriptors will be acquired and compared with historical records. This will allow us to identify not only if a signal behaves abnormally, but also to know in which frequency band the problem is produced. Knowing the abnormal frequencies will be easy to correlate them with components which could be potentially damaged [4].

It is early to make assumptions as there are a lot of features involved and more data needs to be gathered, but the results of the first tests are promising.

Acknowledgments. This work was funded by the Spanish Centro para el Desarrollo Tecnológico Industrial (CDTI), program under Grant ITC_20133096.

References

1. Lu, B., Li, Y., Wu, X., Yang, Z.: A review of recent advances in wind turbine condition monitoring and fault diagnosis. In: Power Electronics and Machines in Wind Applications, PEMWA, pp. 1–7. IEEE (2009)
2. Carden, P., Fanning, P.: Vibration based condition monitoring: a review. Struct. Health Monit. **3**, 355–377 (2004)
3. Sabel, J.C.: Optical 3D motion measurement. In: IEEE Instrumentation and Measurement Technology Conference. Brussels, Belgium (1996)
4. Bassett, K.: Vibration based structural health monitoring for utility scale wind turbines. Electronic Theses and Dissertations, Paper 173 (2010)
5. Felsberg, M., Sommer, G.: A new extension of linear signal processing for estimating local properties and detecting features. In: 22 DAGM Symposium Mustererkennung. Springer-Verlag (2000)
6. Kovesi, P.: Invariant measures of image features from phase information. Ph.D. Thesis, University of Western Australia (1996)
7. Itti, L., Koch, C.: A saliency-based search mechanism for overt and covert shifts of visual attention. Vis. Res. **40**, 1489–1506 (2000)

8. Chen, Z., Ye, Z., Chan, D.T.W., Peng, G.: Target recognition based on mathematical morphology. In: CAD/Graphics 2007, pp 457–460 (2007)
9. Yang, W., Tavner, P.J., Wilkinson, M.R.: Condition monitoring and fault diagnosis of a wind turbine synchronous generator drive train. IET Renew. Power Gener. **3**(1), 1–11 (2009)
10. Rijsbergen, C.J.V.: Information Retrieval, 2nd edn. Butterworth-Heinemann, Newton (1979)
11. Dosil, R., Pardo, X., Fdez-Vidal, X., Garca-Daz, A., Leboran, V.: A new radial symmetry measure applied to photogrammetry. Pattern Anal. Appl. **16**, 637–646 (2013)

Canonical Views for Scene Recognition
in Mobile Robotics

D. Santos-Saavedra$^{(\boxtimes)}$, X.M. Pardo, and R. Iglesias

CITIUS, University of Santiago de Compostela, Santiago de Compostela, Spain
{david.santos,xose.pardo,roberto.iglesias.rodriguez}@usc.es

Abstract. Scene understanding is still an important challenge in robotics. Nevertheless scene recognition involves determining when an image is good enough to represent the scene and therefore it can be used for classification. Most research on scene recognition involves working with sets of images which have been acquired using a predefined sampling rate, nevertheless, this means working with very noisy and redundant sets of images. In this paper we analyse different alternatives to automatically select images according to amount of information they provide and how representative they are.

Keywords: Scene recognition · Sampling · Canonical views

1 Introduction

Scene understanding is still an important challenge in robotics. Robots must be aware of the kind of environment where they move. We have already carried out research to get a robot being able to recognize the scene [1,2]. In our case we assumed that the robot would take an observation at some location and it would use a classifier (SVM in our case) to identify this observation. Nevertheless, to get the training data set the most common solution is to move the robot around the environment acquiring images from the camera on the robot using a fixed frame rate: for example 1 frame per second in the experiments we describe in this paper, or five frames per second in the public data base, *KTH_IDOL1*, commonly used for benchmark (Image Database for rObot localization [4], etc.). The problem in this case lies on the fact that working with a fixed frame rate provides many images that are either too noisy or too redundant (there are many images that are too similar amongst them, or images that only show characteristics of the environment that are hardly recognizable such as an empty wall, a door, etc.). Something similar happens when it comes to classifying an image, i.e. depending on the visual content of the image the recognition of the scene might be easy or almost impossible (it is not the same trying to recognize a room by just seeing an empty wall than from a full perspective of the whole room). Therefore, we need an strategy to be able to determine automatically which images are suitable either to train a classifier or to recognize the scene, avoiding the use of fixed frame rate. The strategy we will describe in this paper, based in what is called

© Springer International Publishing Switzerland 2015
R. Paredes et al. (Eds.): IbPRIA 2015, LNCS 9117, pp. 514–521, 2015.
DOI: 10.1007/978-3-319-19390-8_58

canonical views, will determine when an image is significant and therefore should be taken to recognize the scene.

2   Canonical Views

As it is described in [5], although people can recognize familiar objects in any orientation, there seem to be preferred or standard views form recognizing these objects. These preferred views are the "canonical" views. Therefore, in general, a canonical view of an object is a view which maximizes the amount of visible object surface. This can be somehow extrapolated to scenes, i.e., scenes and places, like objects, are three-dimensional entities that can be recognized from a variety of angles.

Inspired in the works [6,7], the criteria for choosing views as canonical or relevant for scene recognition will be:

- Coverage: An image should be included if it covers an large number of visual features in the scene.
- Likelihood: An image should be included if it is similar to many other images in the input set.
- Orthogonality: Two images should not both be included as canonical if they are similar to each other.

Obviously, the problem is how to translate the previous characteristics to a formal procedure that can be automatized into the robot.

Our robot is equipped with a Kinect, a increasingly common sensor in robotics which provides RGBD images. Therefore, we assume that we have both visual and depth information in every acquisition. In this article we will describe a procedure to select canonical views based on (i) only visual information, (ii) only depth information, and finally (iii) a combination of both visual and depth information. Through the experimental results we will validate these strategies.

2.1   Selection of Canonical Views Based on Visual Features

Selection of representative or canonical views based on the amount of information in each image is one of the most logic solutions to this problem. Obviously the first decision is the determination of the image descriptor. In our case we have decided to work with local features, i.e., the discovering of salient points in the image. The usual approach consists on selecting some salient points in the image, and then building a description from this unstructured set of points. We have used SURF [8] to detect the interest points and their description. In fact, SURF provides a set of salient points in the image together with a description (64 values) for each one of them. On a second stage, we carried out a quantization of the descriptors into a codebook, in particular we used the k-means to project all the descriptors (64 dimensional vectors) into K clusters. This clusters are often called *Visual Words*, and the whole set of clusters is often referred to as the *Bag of Words* [3]. It is important to realize that to build this dictionary of words (*Bag of Words*), it is necessary to compute all the salient points and their description in all the images acquired by the robot in the environment where it moves. Finally, once the *Bag of words* has been built, any image can be represented by the histogram of the visual words, i.e., a k-dimensional vector that contains for every dimension i the relative frequency with which the visual word i appears in the image. Next we will describe how we will used these histograms to select canonical views.

Likelihood. According to the previous section, an image should be considered as canonical if it is similar to many other images in the input set. Hence, in our case, given a set of N images taken from the environment where the robot moves, we can get their corresponding histograms $h_1, ..., h_N$ (following the approach of visual words described before). Once again, using a clustering algorithm (like K-means) we can project the N histograms into a set of L clusters. This means that after this procedure we get N images labeled with a cluster (the closest cluster center considering the euclidean distances amongst the histograms of the images and the centers of the clusters). Once this is done, we sort the images within each cluster, using again the Euclidean distances from the histogram of each image to the cluster center.

Coverage. An image should be included if it covers an large number of visual features in the scene. In our case, we will sort the L clusters computed before, considering the number of non-null components of the centers of the clusters. To understand this, it is necessary to realize that the images are described by their histograms (which represent the relative frequency with which each visual word appear in the image). Therefore, the center of a cluster is a vector that reflects which visual words appear in the images that are within that cluster. Hence, counting the non-null components of the cluster center is equivalent to determine the number of visual words that appear in the cluster, and obviously, the clusters with the highest number of visual words are the most preferable for being considered as canonical.

Orthogonality. After applying likelihood and coverage, we end up with a set of L ordered clusters (considering their coverage), and we have a set of M images labeled by their cluster, and ordered according to their distance to the center of the cluster (likelihood).

The orthogonality property means that two images should not both be included as canonical if they are similar to each other. To implement this characteristic, starting from the set of N ordered images and their histograms obtained before, we apply a simple computation to remove part of those N images and select a subset of images that are orthogonal amongst them. In particular the procedure can be summarized in the following steps:

1. Initialize the set of canonical views: *canonical_views* $= \emptyset$.

2. For every cluster C (from the set of L sorted clusters) search for an image within that cluster that is orthogonal with all the canonical views:
   (a) We compute the orthogonality of each image in the cluster with the rest of canonical images already selected:

   $$orthogonality_i = min_{\forall j \in canonical\_views} acos\{\frac{h_i.h_j}{|h_i|.|h_j|}\}$$

   where image i belongs to cluster C, h_i and h_j are the histograms corresponding to the images i and j respectively. $acos$ is the arc_cosine.
   (b) Select the candidate image as canonical if it is orthogonal with the rest of the images already selected:

   if $orthogonality\_i > T$ then $canonical\_views - canonical\_views \bigcup\{i\}$ discard the image i otherwise, and check the next image in the cluster

   T a threshold that needs to be determined.

2.2 Selection of Canonical Views Based on Depth Features: Shape of the Environment

Some authors argue the use of the shape of the environment can be another good way of selecting canonical views [5], because of this we have analysed the possibility of using the depth information provided by the Kinect camera to determine the canonical views. Kinect provides depth information in each pixel with a range which goes from 0.8 m up to 8 m. In this case, to describe each image we build a histogram that reflects, for every bin, the relative frequency with which an interval of distances appear in the image. The last bin of the histogram reflect the number of pixels whose depth information is *out of range*, in our case those pixels that reflect parts of the environment which are further from 3.5 m.

Taking the histograms as image descriptors we followed the same procedure as the one described in the previous section (visual descriptors using bags of words). This means that we used K-means to cluster the images into groups, and therefore label each image as belonging to a cluster and sort the images within each cluster. We then used the coverage characteristic to prioritize the clusters. In this case, we considered two different criteria: (i) in one case we considered the number of non-null components of the center of the cluster. This is equivalent to say that we prefer those clusters whose images contain all ranges of distances, in this case we are prioritizing those images that are a perspective view of the environment. (ii) On the other hand we also considered the histogram bin that reflects the "out-of-range", therefore, we prioritize those images that are taken far from the obstacles/walls of the environment. In the experimental results we provided the results achieved with each one of these criteria. Finally, the orthogonality property is applied in the same way as described before.

2.3   Selection of Canonical Views Based on Both, Depth and Visual Characteristics

So far we have described the procedure we have followed to select canonical images considering either visual appearance (discovery of salient points), or depth information. Nevertheless, we also have carried out a preliminary analysis trying to merge both kinds of information to determine when an image can be considered as canonical. We now describe the different merging strategies we have explored.

Direct Combination. One of the easiest ways of integrating both sources of information is by a simple concatenation of the visual and depth histograms. To understand this we must only remember that in the combination of SURF and the Bag of words approach, every image is described by a histogram that reflects the frequency with which each visual word appears in the image. Something similar happens with the depth information, in this case the histogram reflects the relative frequency with which each possible range of distances appear in the scene. Therefore, the concatenation of the two normalized histograms provides a new vector that can be used to detect canonical images. Following the same procedure as described in the two previous sections, a clustering algorithm will allow the achievement of different groups of images. We then have to sort out these clusters considering the number of not null components of center of each of them (coverage property). Finally, an image will be selected as canonical if it is close enough to the center of the cluster (likelihood property) and it belongs to a cluster from which there are no other images already selected as canonical (orthogonal property).

Combination by Pairs. The previous strategy is very simple to implement and test. Nevertheless, we suspect that there might be a problem derived from the different dimensions of the visual and depth histograms that are being concatenated (the number of dimensions is much higher in the visual histogram than in the histogram obtained using depth information). Because of this we have decided to test a more complex way of merging both sources. In this case we perform two clustering processes: in the first one, the images are divided into groups considering only the visual histograms. On the second clustering process, we split the images into a new set of groups considering only depth histograms. Once we have obtained the visual and depth clusters, we sort all the possible pairs of clusters (one visual and the other obtained from the depth information), considering the number of non-null components of centers of both clusters:

$$value(C_i(visual), C_k(depth)) = \frac{\frac{number\_of\_non\_null\_components center\_of\_C_i}{dimension\_visual\_histograms} + \frac{number\_of\_non\_null\_components center\_of\_C_k}{dimension\_depth\_histograms}}{2}$$

The previous equation allows the arrangement of the clusters in a prioritized list. Like we did before, once the pairs of clusters have been sorted out, an image will be selected as canonical if it is orthogonal to the rest of images that have been already selected as canonical, and if it belongs to a pair of clusters from which no image has been selected as canonical before.

Combination of Sets. Another very easy way of combining both sources of information is by simply putting together the set of images that have been selected considering only visual information, *and* the set of images that have been selected using only depth information. Hence, in this case an image is selected as canonical if it is relevant from the visual point of view *or* from the point of view of the depth information. This option guarantees the best from each individual strategy but increases the size of the final set of canonical images.

Combination of Sets and Re-evaluation. To avoid the increase in the size of the final set of canonical images mentioned before, we have also tested a different way of putting together the images selected as canonical either by the visual or the depth characteristics of the image. In this case, and like we described before, the images that have been selected as canonical considering only visual information, *and* the set of images that have been selected using only depth information, are put together in the same set. Nevertheless, this augmented set of images is sorted once again considering an evaluation function that prioritizes the images considering the number of pixels that reflect a part of the environment out-of-range (last bin of the depth histograms).

3   Experimental Setup and Results

We have carried out several preliminary experiments to analyse the performance of a SVM classifier using different sets of canonical images. To carry out the experiments described in this section we used an image data set obtained at the Centro Singular de Investigacion en Tecnologias de la Informacion (CITIUS), at the University of Santiago de Compostela. To build this dataset we used a sequence of RGBD images taken from a kinect sensor located on our robot Pioneer P3DX. The sequence of images were taken at 1 sample per second while the robot was being moved in the research center. We have defined 11 different classes (according to the type of room shown in the images): Office, Entrepreneurship Laboratory, Staircase, Common staff areas (first and second floors), Assembly Hall, Common staff areas (S1 floor), Kitchen, laboratories 1, 2 and 3, Common staff areas (ground floor), instrumentation laboratory, robotics laboratory. The number of images taken for each one of these classes are: 417 for Entrepreneurship Laboratory, 172 for Kitchen, 167 for Staircase, 129 for Instrumentation laboratory, 296 for Laboratories, 465 for Ground floor, 496 for First and Second floor, 395 for S1 floor, 154 for Robotics laboratory, 171 for Assembly Hall and 216 for Office.

As we pointed out in the introduction we want to use canonical images to reduce the size of the training data, or even to determine when an image is representative enough to identify the scene. The problem so far, is that there are many alternatives to determine when an image can be considering as canonical. We only know the general characteristics that all the canonical images should meet, nevertheless, so far we do not know the best way of achieving these characteristics. Because of this, in this article we show the performance of an SVM classifier which has been trained using the different sets of canonical images that have been obtained applying the strategies described in the previous sections. In order to be able to compare the results and thus achieve some conclusions, we limited the number of canonical images per class, so that we can determine which set of canonical images seem to be better to build the classifier. Thus, using the image dataset obtained at the CITIUS research center, we applied each one of the strategies described in the previous sections to get a training set with 4 or 8 canonical images per class. This set of canonical images was used to train the Support Vector Machine and the rest of the images were used for testing purposes (Table 1).

In all the strategies described for the selection of canonical images, there is a clustering procedure to identify similar images. In our experiments we have applied k-means to identify 15 clusters. On the other hand, all methods check whether an image is orthogonal to the rest of images that have been already selected. In the experiments we have carried out the angle which was established as threshold to determine whether the orthogonality is held or not is 50 (parameter T that appears in Sect. 2.1).

Table 1. Performance of a SVM classifier that has been trained using either 4 or 8 canonical views per class.

	Strategy	4 canoni./class	8 canoni./class
Individual	SURF/Bags of words	53.73	65.95
	Depth info. and non-zero values	43.24	51.85
	Depth info. and out-of-range value	**54.90**	62.57
Combination	Direct combination	45.32	57.66
	Combination of sets $(4+4)$	-	65.95
	Pair combination	52.66	62.24
	Combination of sets and re-evaluation	53.70	**68.74**

The results show that the performance obtained using only visual characteristics or depth information is hardly improved by their combination. On the other hand, the use of visual characteristics seem to be better than using depth information. The combination of both visual and depth information, using the strategy: *combination of sets with re-evaluation* seems to be the best option. Finally, regarding the use of depth information, the results show a higher performance when the coverage property is built considering the relative number of out-of-range pixels, than using the non-negative components of the distance histograms.

4 Conclusions and Future Work

This paper describes the use of *canonical images* to determine when an image is meaningful to identify the scene. This is relevant in the field of robotics, due to the real-time restrictions, or even the need of automatizing this task, i.e., robots must be able to categorize and recognize the scenes in a largely unsupervised way. The experiments we have carried out and that are described in this paper, although preliminary, allow a comparison of different alternatives developed to achieve sets of canonical images. In this sense, we also plan to use a new dataset [9] to validate the usefulness of the canonical views.

Acknowledgment. This work was supported by grants: GPC2013/040 (FEDER), TIN2012-32262.

References

1. Santos-Saavedra, D., Pardo, X.M., Iglesias, R., lvarez-Santos, V., Canedo-Rodrguez, A., Regueiro, C.V.: Global image features for scene recognition invariant to symmetrical reflections in robotics. In: XV Workshop of Physical Agents, pp. 29–37 (2014)
2. Santos-Saavedra, D., Pardo, X. M., Iglesias, R., Canedo-Rodrguez, A., lvarez-Santos, V.: Scene recognition invariant to symmetrical reflections and illumination conditions in robotics (Submitted to ibPRIA 2015)
3. Lazebnik, S., Schmid, C., Ponce, J. : Beyond bags of features: spatial pyramid matching for recognizing natural scene categories. In: 2006 IEEE Computer Society Conference on Computer Vision and Pattern Recognition, vol. 2, pp. 2169–2178. IEEE (2006)
4. Luo, J., Pronobis, A., Caputo, B., Jensfelt, P.: The KTH-IDOL2 database. Technical report CVAP304, Kungliga Tekniska Hgskolan, CVAP/CAS, October 2006. http://cogvis.nada.kth.se/IDOL/
5. Ehinger, K. A., Oliva, A.: Canonical views of scenes depend on the shape of the space. In: Proceedings of the 33rd Annual Cognitive Science Conference, COGSCI 2011, Boston, Massachusetts, USA, 20–23 July 2011
6. Simon, I., Snavely, N., Seitz, S.M.: Scene summarization for online image collections. In: ICCV, vol. 7, pp. 1–8 (2007)
7. Hall, P.M., Owen, M.: Simple canonical views. In: BMVC (2005)
8. Bay, H., Ess, A., Tuytelaars, T., Van Gool, L.: Speeded-up robust features (SURF). Comput. Vis. Image Underst. **110**(3), 346–359 (2008)
9. Martinez-Gomez, J., Garcia-Varea, I., Caputo, B.: Overview of the ImageCLEF 2012 Robot Vision Task. In: CLEF 2012 Evaluation Labs and Workshop, Online Working Notes, Rome, Italy, 17–20 September 2012. ISBN: 978-88-904810-3-1

Crater Detection in Multi-ring Basins
of Mercury

Miriam M. Pedrosa[1]([⊠]), Pedro Pina[2], Marlene Machado[2],
Lourenço Bandeira[2], and Erivaldo A. da Silva[1]

[1] Universidade Estadual Paulista – UNESP, Presidente Prudente, Brazil
miriammmp@hotmail.com, erivaldo@fct.unesp.br
[2] CERENA-IST, University of Lisbon, Lisbon, Portugal
{ppina,marlene.machado,lpcbandeira}@tecnico.ulisboa.pt

Abstract. This paper presents the automated detection of impact craters on large regions of Mercury. The processing sequence is composed by three main phases: the first consists on creating the image mosaics of the large areas of interest, the second by finding crater candidates on these mosaics, and finally by extracting a set of features that are used in the classification by SVM-Support Vector Machine in the third phase. The detections are performed on images acquired by the MDIS-NAC camera of MESSENGER probe covering three large basins on Mercury (Rachmaninoff, Mozart and Raditladi).

Keywords: Automatic detection · Mercury · Image processing · Pattern recognition

1 Introduction

In the last decade, the number of works that used remotely sensed images for expanding our knowledge about the surfaces of the bodies that form the solar system have greatly increased, since probes in orbit are capturing each time more detailed data. Among them, the images are particularly important since they can quickly show signs of the geological history of each surface. The huge amount of data already available in the archives and the rhythm that new imagery is daily obtained require the use of automatic methods to identify widespread features of interest. The structures that assume a great importance are impact craters that are formed from the collisions of meteorites with a planetary body. They exist in large number in all rocky surfaces and at all scales so that a detailed analysis of size and morphology makes them a key feature for chronological analysis. In particular, impact craters represent the single tool available to estimate, remotely, the age of planetary geological formations [17]. For instance, on the Moon, Mercury and Mars they show a higher accumulation over time, due to the lower rate of surface erosion [16]. There are several approaches that deal with the automated detection of impact craters [1, 2, 7, 19, 20] and that are used for the construction of crater catalogues [13–15]. However, the large majority of them only deal with the surfaces of Mars and the Moon. This is directly related to the huge amount of imagery available for these two bodies, in comparison to other surfaces. For instance, for Mercury this number is only becoming relevant in the last couple of years

R. Paredes et al. (Eds.): IbPRIA 2015, LNCS 9117, pp. 522–529, 2015.
DOI: 10.1007/978-3-319-19390-8_59

after the insertion in orbit of the probe MESSENGER. Thus, the catalogues available for Mercury are recent, were generated manually and only contain craters larger than 10 km [5] and 20 km [6]. Since few attempts have been done to make automated crater detections on Mercury [12], we decided to deepen the preliminary investigations [10, 11] we have been developing on this planet. For that, we selected 3 large basins with few hundreds of kilometers in diameter (Rachmaninoff, Mozart and Raditladi), shown in Fig. 1, which are currently a focus of interest for discovering the origin of their floor plains and other features of interest [4].

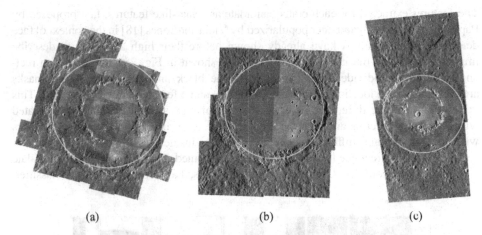

(a)   (b)   (c)

Fig. 1. Mosaic of images of MDIS-NAC camera from MESSENGER probe covering the multi-ring impact basins of interest: (a) Rachmaninoff (diameter of 290 km with images at a resolution of 125 m/pixel), (b) Mozart (225 km at 206 m/pixel), and (c) Raditladi (263 km at 261 m/pixel). The circles are delimitating the rims of the basins. [Image credits: MESSENGER MDIS NAC]

2   Methodology

The automated detection of craters on the selected sites of Mercury is based on an approach inspired by two works [8, 17], which was successfully applied on Mars [3] and Phobos [15]. We remind briefly the three main phases of this methodology: first, a set of crater candidates are selected from the images; second, a set of features describing them are extracted; third, the features are used to train a classifier that delivers a binary decision for each candidate analysed into crater and non-crater. Some adjustments are required in the training of the algorithm due to the intrinsic differences between planetary surfaces and the distinct erosion processes involved.

2.1   Crater Candidate Selection

The candidate selection is based on connected operators from mathematical morphology. It consists of finding typical pairs of crescent-like shapes (one highlighted, the other shaded), that are formed by the solar illumination around the rim of each crater.

This procedure is done with openings by reconstruction for detecting the dark crescent shapes and with closings by reconstruction for the light crescent shapes. A region is considered for a crater candidate only when a pair of similar dark and bright crescent shapes is found at a given distance. A multi-scale procedure is performed by increasing the dimension of the structuring element in openings/closings in order to cover the complete range of crater dimensions.

2.2 Feature Extraction

The features extracted for each crater candidate are Haar-like features, first proposed by Papageorgiou et al. [9] and later popularized by Viola and Jones [18] in the context of face detection. These features have already shown before their high adequacy to describe impact craters. The masks or blocks we use are shown in Fig. 2. Each block is a rectangular region subdivided into two sectors, one black and one white. These masks are centered on the location of the each candidate, and a feature value is calculated. This value represents the difference between the sum of gray scale values in pixels located within the white sectors and the black sectors. The set of blocks is composed by masks with several size and different positions of sectors inside the blocks. For each crater candidate the feature value for all set of masks is computed. Thus, for each crater candidate we have an over completed representation which is used as information for the classifier.

Fig. 2. The different types of masks used for the extraction of texture features.

2.3 Classification

The classification is performed with a supervised classifier, selecting positive (crater) and negative feature examples (non-crater) in a proportion equal to 1:3. We have previously tested Adaboost and SVM classifiers, achieving very similar (high) performances. Thus, we have opted now for using only SVM, due to its higher computational performance.

3 Experimental Results

3.1 Mosaics Construction

The Mercury Dual Imaging System (MDIS) onboard MESSENGER probe consists of a pair of imagers: Narrow Angle Camera (NAC) and Wide Angle Camera (WAC). For identifying as much craters as possible we are using the images from MDIS-NAC. Nevertheless, the resolutions of the images currently available that completely cover the 3 basins still are of medium resolution: 100–125 m/pixel for Rachmaninoff, 206–236 m/pixel for Mozart and 261 m/pixel for Raditladi. Although images with much better resolution (up to 15 m/pixel) are already available for those basins, at the moment of writing of this paper they only cover parts of them. We started building the mosaics for each basin, using overlapping raw images acquired along different orbits to make the registering and geometric corrections. Using the geographic information provided for each image we were able to produce mosaics for Rachmaninoff basin using 39 images, for Mozart with 6 images and for Raditladi with 2 images. For each mosaic, we fixed the spatial resolution to the worst one in each dataset. The resulting mosaics are those already shown in Fig. 1.

3.2   Parameters Selection and Performance Evaluation

As in [3] we use only square mask-features in order to reduce its total amount. The 9 masks used are shown in Fig. 2 and have four different sizes (12×12, 24×24, 36×36 or 48×48 pixels). It means that each crater candidate is represented by 1089 features. The features are linearly normalized to the interval $[-1, 1]$ to become independent from size of the mask.

The training set consists of 315 candidates; 105 of them are true craters (positive) and 210 are non-crater samples (negative). The negative examples were randomly selected from parts of the image that are not overlaying any crater.

The dimensional range of detection was fixed between a minimum diameter of 10 pixels and the maximum crater diameter present in the images. Below 10 pixels in diameter the number of false positives increases a lot due to the strong decrease of discriminative power of the images. This means that, for instance, craters as small as 1250 m in diameter can be detected in Rachmaninoff crater.

To evaluate the performance of our methodology we computed the three quantities that are commonly used in the evaluation of crater detection algorithms: the detection percentage (D), the quality percentage (Q), the branching factor (B). They are based are based on the comparison of the output of the algorithm with a ground-truth manually built. They are obtained through the following equations:

$$D = \frac{TP}{(TP + FN)} * 100 \tag{1}$$

$$Q = \frac{TP}{(TP + FP + FN)} * 100 \tag{2}$$

$$B = \frac{FP}{TP} \tag{3}$$

where TP refers to true positives, FP to false positives and FN to false negatives.

3.3   Results

We consider that the results obtained are good, although the individual performances obtained per basin are a bit different (see statistics in Table 1 and detection examples in

Fig. 3). The amount of true detections is particularly high in all sites (D from 95 % to 82 %), as well as the amount of non-detected craters is low (relatively low values of FN). This means that most of the existing craters are correctly detected with a very low amount of misses.

Table 1. Crater detection performances per basin

	D (%)	Q (%)	B
Rachmaninoff	95	74	0.29
Mozart	82	62	0.39
Raditladi	85	56	0.60

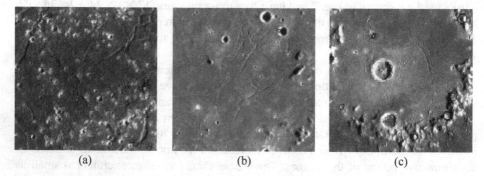

(a)   (b)   (c)

Fig. 3. Examples of crater detection in Rachmaninoff, Mozart and Raditladi, respectively in images: (a) EN0219562953 M (b) EN0213239986 M and (c) EN0108826792 M. TP are represented in green, FP in red and FN in blue. Note that craters not marked are below the detection limit of 10 pixels (Color figure online).

On the contrary, we faced a main drawback in the high number of false-positive detections, which heavily contributed to reduce the overall performances. They are mainly related to the interior rings located inside each basin where the false detections are plotted along the circular peaks; this is particularly evident in Fig. 3. We have trained the classifier with many negative examples from these locations but the improvements are still not very evident. In addition, the spatial resolution of the mosaics seems to play an important role in this procedure, since the FP values diminish directly with the increase of the resolution (check the values of B from Raditladi to Rachmaninoff).

We also tested this same methodology in the highest resolution images available (16 m/pixel) inside Raditladi basin. This permitted us to evaluate the detections on craters smaller than 3 km and until 160 m (or 10 pixels) in diameter. The coverage of the basin at his resolution is still very incomplete, thus we used only a set of images from two regions in relation to the internal ring (one interior (B1–B5 images), the other exterior (A1–A5 images)) that were acquired sequentially in two distinct orbits for the testing (Fig. 4a).

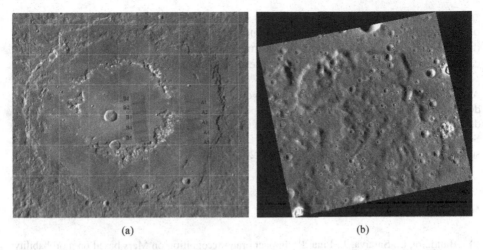

(a)   (b)

Fig. 4. Crater detections on higher resolution images: (a) Footprints of the 10 MDIS-NAC images used inside Raditladi basin; (b) Automated detections on the image EN0221023202 M with a spatial resolution of 16 m/pixel (area of 17×17 km^2). TP are green, FP are red and FN are blue circles (Color figure online).

The performances obtained were, in terms of the quality value (Q), very similar to the ones at lower resolution (equal to 65 and 70 %). The detection rate (D) is lower and also the FP values (reflected in lower B). The complexity of the surface at this scale is much higher than expected (see its irregularity in Fig. 4b) but, although some difficulties faced the algorithm performs globally well (Table 2).

Table 2. Crater detection performances inside Raditladi basin

	D (%)	Q (%)	B
A1-A5 images	78	70	0.15
B1-B5 images	75	65	0.20

4   Conclusions and Future Work

The purpose of testing in Mercury at several scales a methodology designed, implemented and enhanced for detecting craters on Mars and the Moon surfaces can be considered successful. The performances are consistent from location to location (craters within three different multi-ring basins were analysed) and at several resolutions or scales (125–261 m/pixel and 16 m/pixel) and with crater dimensions down to 10 pixels in diameter. Nevertheless, although good, we know that the performances should be improved, reaching the figures already obtained for Mars and Phobos. We think that a finer analysis of the features extracted should be investigated, by testing if there is any redundancy in the set used or if any particular feature of interest should be added to deal with the Mercurian types of surfaces.

We also intend to greatly enlarge the dataset of images from Mercury to improve our algorithms and the performances, encompassing all types of terrains and crater dimensions. This will be particularly important for expanding the available crater catalogues of Mercury, namely to include detections below 10 km in diameter.

Acknowledgments. The authors acknowledge the financial support provided by Coordenação de Aperfeiçoamento de Pessoal de Ensino Superior (CAPES – Grant: 9022/13-9), the Fundação de Amparo à Pesquisa do Estado de São Paulo (FAPESP – Grant: 2014/08822-2), the Portuguese Science Foundation (FCT) through project ANIMAR (PTDC/CTE-SPA/110909/2009) and support for MM and LB (SFRH/BPD/79546/2011).

References

1. Bandeira, L., Saraiva, J., Pina, P.: Impact crater recognition on Mars based on a probability volume created by template matching. IEEE Trans. Geosci. Remote Sens. **45**(12), 4008–4015 (2007)
2. Bandeira, L.P.C., Saraiva, J., Pina, P.: Development of a methodology for automated crater detection on planetary images. In: Martí, J., Benedí, J.M., Mendonça, A.M., Serrat, J. (eds.) IbPRIA 2007. LNCS, vol. 4477, pp. 193–200. Springer, Heidelberg (2007)
3. Bandeira, L., Ding, W., Stepinski, T.F.: Detection of sub-kilometer craters in high resolution planetary images using shape and texture features. Adv. Space Res. **49**, 64–74 (2012)
4. Blair, D.M., Freed, A.M., Byrne, P.K., Klimczak, C., Prockter, L.M., Ernst, C.M., Solomon, S.C., Melosh, H.J., Zuber, M.T.: The origin of graben and ridges in Rachmaninoff, Raditladi, and Mozart basins, Mercury. J. Geophys. Res.-Planets **118**, 47–58 (2013)
5. Fasset, C.I., Kadish, S.J., Head, J.W., Solomon, S.C., Strom, R.G.: The global population of large craters on Mercury and comparison with the Moon. Geophys. Res. Lett. **38**, L10202 (2011)
6. Herrick, R.R., Curran, L.L., Baer, A.T.: A Mariner/MESSENGER global catalog of mercurian craters. Icarus **215**, 452–454 (2011)
7. Jin, S., Zhang, T.: Automatic detection of impact craters on Mars using a modified adaboosting method. Planet. Space Sci. **99**, 112–117 (2014)
8. Martins, R., Pina, P., Marques, J.S., Silveira, M.: Crater detection by a boosting approach. IEEE Geosci. Remote Sens. Lett. **6**, 127–131 (2009)
9. Papageorgiou, C.P., Oren, M., Poggio, T.: A general framework for object detection. In: ICCV VI, pp. 555–562 (1998)
10. Pedrosa, M.M., Pina, P., Machado, M., Bandeira, L., Silva, E.A.: Automated crater detection in the surface of Mercury in MDIS-NAC imagery. In: Lunar and Planetary Science Conference XLV, Abs. #2475, The Woodlands, TX (2014)
11. Pedrosa, M.M., Pina, P., Machado, M., Bandeira, L., Silva, E.A.: Automated crater detection in Rachmaninoff basin. In: European Planetary Science Conference, vol. 9, Abs. #546, Cascais, Portugal (2014)
12. Salamuniccar, G., Crater detection from Mercurian digital topography and comparison with Lunar and Martian craters. In: Lunar and Planetary Science Conference XLIV, Abs. #1866, The Woodlands, TX (2013)
13. Salamuniccar, G., Loncaric, S., Mazarico, E.: LU60645GT and MA132843GT catalogues of Lunar and Martian impact craters developed using a Crater shape-based interpolation crater detection algorithm for topography data. Planet. Space Sci. **60**, 236–247 (2012)

14. Salamuniccar, G., Loncaric, S., Pina, P., Bandeira, L., Saraiva, J.: MA130301GT catalogue of Martian impact craters and advanced evaluation of crater detection algorithms using diverse topography and image datasets. Planet. Space Sci. **59**, 111–131 (2011)
15. Salamuniccar, G., Loncaric, S., Pina, P., Bandeira, L., Saraiva, J.: Integrated method for crater detection from topography and optical images and the new PH9224GT catalogue of Phobos impact craters. Adv. Space Res. **53**, 1798–1809 (2014)
16. Stepinski, T., Ding, W., Vilalta, R.: Detecting impact craters in planetary images using machine learning. In: Magdalena-Benedito, R., Martinez-Sober, M., Martinez-Martinez, J. M., Vila-Frances, J., Escandell-Monter, P. (eds.) Handbook of Intelligent Data Analysis of Real-Life: Theory and Practice 149–159. IGI Global, Hershey (2012)
17. Urbach, E.R., Stepinski, T.F.: Automatic detection of sub-km craters in high resolution planetary images. Planet. Space Sci. **57**, 880–887 (2009)
18. Viola, P., Jones, M.: Robust real-time face detection. Int. J. Comput. Vis. **57**, 137–154 (2004)
19. Vijayan, S., Vani, K., Sanjeevi, S.: Crater detection, classification and contextual information extraction in lunar images using a novel algorithm. Icarus **226**, 798–815 (2013)
20. Yin, J., Li, H., Jia, X.: Crater detection based on Gist features. IEEE Sel. Top. Appl. Earth Obs. Remote Sens. **8**, 23–29 (2015)

Iterative Versus Voting Method to Reach Consensus Given Multiple Correspondences of Two Sets

Carlos Francisco Moreno-García, Xavier Cortés,
and Francesc Serratosa[(✉)]

Departament d'Enginyeria Informàtica i Matemàtiques,
Universitat Rovira i Virgili, Tarragona, Spain
carlosfrancisco.moreno@estudiants.urv.cat,
{xavier.cortes,francesc.serratosa}@urv.cat

Abstract. Point Set Registration is the process of finding the correspondence between points of two sets. There are some Point Set Registration applications in which given two sets of points, several correspondences between these points may be deduced. However, the use of different parameters or optimisation strategies makes these correspondences differ from each other. In this paper, we present two different methods to obtain a consensus correspondence given several correspondences between two sets of points. The first one is based on the classical voting strategy. The second one iteratively updates the consensus correspondence given two correspondences: a non-previously explored correspondence and the current consensus. In this last method, the computation of the consensus given two correspondences is done through a method recently published. We compare the voting and iterative methods using an image dataset and validate the runtime and the quality of the consensus correspondence using an existing homography between the considered images.

Keywords: Point set registration · Two sets correspondence · Consensus correspondence · Cost matrix · Correspondence matrix · Inlier · Outlier · Voting method · Iterative method

1 Introduction

Some classical image registration methods [1] are based on two main steps. In the first one, two sets of salient points are extracted from the involved images. Each point is composed of a position and some local features. In the second one, the correspondence between points of both sets is computed through a Point Set Registration process. Since there are several features' extractors [2, 3], between others, and also there are several Point Set Registration processes [4, 5], given two images, multiple correspondences may be considered correct. For instance, suppose we intend to use SIFT [2] and SURF [3] to extract the salient points in the first step, and in the second step we intend to use Iterative Closest Point [6], Coherent Point Drift [7] or Smooth Point-set Registration [8] to obtain the correspondence. If we combine these options, different correspondences between both sets may occur. The aim of this paper is to define a method to

© Springer International Publishing Switzerland 2015
R. Paredes et al. (Eds.): IbPRIA 2015, LNCS 9117, pp. 530–540, 2015.
DOI: 10.1007/978-3-319-19390-8_60

obtain a consensus correspondence given several correspondences that represent the pairing of two images or sets of points. The consensus method has to be independent of the feature extractors and the Point Set Registration processes.

Besides the aforementioned Point Set Registration methods, other methods exist, which represent the points' set as a graph [9, 10]. Also, the ones that are explicitly defined to map a tiny point set to a larger set [11] have been presented. Finally, interactive methods have been defined to improve the automatically found correspondences [12, 13]. Interesting surveys on this matter are [4, 5]. As general correspondence methods, we can select the Hungarian method [14], the Jonker-Volgenant [15] or the graph-based methods [16, 18–21].

One of the crucial aspects in image registration or Point Set Registration is the ability to deal with outliers. An outlier is a point in the image or in the points' set such that is has been created due to the noise and so, the method does not have to map them to a point of the other image or points set. Most of the current Point Set Registration methods take into consideration the presence of outliers, but the simplest ones, which are based on a linear solver (Hungarian method [14] or the Jonker-Volgenant solver [15]) do not consider it.

In [22], a consensus method that returns a consensus correspondence given two points' correspondences was presented. In this paper, we propose to extend this idea and define a consensus correspondence given several points' correspondences. We present two solutions. The first one is based on a voting process [23, 24] and the second one is based on an iterative method that updates the current consensus correspondence through iteratively calling the method presented in [22]. The input and output sets of the involved correspondences do not have to be exactly the same, although a certain degree of intersection seems to be logical.

This paper is organised as follows. In Sect. 2, we set the basic definitions and briefly describe the method presented in [22]. In Sect. 3, we introduce the voting and iterative methods to find the consensus of multiple correspondences. In Sect. 4, we empirically validate and compare both methods. Finally, Sect. 5 is reserved for conclusions and further work.

2 Basic Definitions

In Subsect. 2.1, we introduce the Point Set Mapping methodology and in Subsect. 2.2, we summarise the consensus correspondence given a pair of correspondences published in [22].

2.1 Point Set Mapping

Given two sets of elements $G = \{g_1, g_2, \ldots, g_n,\}$ and $G' = \{g'_1, g'_2, \ldots, g'_n,\}$, where elements are defined in some domain $T \cup \{\emptyset\}$, $g_a \in T \cup \{\emptyset\}$ and $g'_i \in T \cup \{\emptyset\}$, a correspondence or bijection f can be established between these sets G and G', $f : g_a \to g'_i$. Note this bijection can be defined through a so called Correspondence Matrix F, where $F[k, t] = 1$ if $f(g_k) = g'_t$ and $F[k, t] = 0$ otherwise. Elements defined as $\emptyset$ are called null elements and do not belong to the original domain T, but they have been introduced to deal with outlier points in the application.

Moreover, we define the cost of this correspondence as the addition of the individual elements' costs,

$$Cost(G, G', f) = \sum_{k=1}^{n} c(g_k, f(g_k)) \tag{1}$$

where c is defined as a distance function over the domain of attributes $T \cup \{\emptyset\}$. Distance c is application dependent and it has to consider the case that two original elements are mapped and the case that one of them is an outlier [18]. It is always considered that $c(\emptyset, \emptyset) = 0$. Without restricting the general definition of the method, we suppose $c \in [0, 1]$ to make further definitions simpler.

The distance between sets is defined as the minimum cost for all possible bijections between elements of both sets,

$$Dist(G, G') = \min\{Cost(G, G', f)\} \forall f : G \times G' \tag{2}$$

The correspondence f that obtains a minimum distance is known as the optimal correspondence f^*, and it is defined as

$$f^* = argmin_{\forall f : G \times G'}\{Cost(G, G', f)\} \tag{3}$$

This linear assignation problem is usually solved through methods such as the Hungarian method [14] or the Jonker-Volgenant solver [15]. The input of these algorithms is a cost matrix C defined such that $C[k, t] = c(g_k, g'_t)$. Thus, they obtain,

$$f^* = argmin_{\forall f : G \times G'}\{C_f\} \quad \text{where} \quad C_f = \sum_{k=1}^{n} C[k, f(k)] \tag{4}$$

Given two correspondences $f^a : G \times G'$ and $f^b : G \times G'$ defined exactly on the same domain G and codomain G', the Hamming Distance is defined as follows,

$$d_H(f^a, f^b) = \sum_{k=1}^{n} (1 - \mu(f^a(g_k), f^b(g_k))) \tag{5}$$

where $\mu(g'_t, g'_s) = 1$ if both elements are close enough and $\mu(g'_t, g'_s) = 0$ otherwise. Being close enough means having a distance between parts of the element's features within a radius. For instance, in Image Registration applications, the elements are points composed of a location and other local features. In this case, μ is only applied to the location of the point. It can be seen as a more general expression of the Kronecker delta.

Suppose M correspondences $f^1, \ldots, f^M$ are participants in a consensus scenario. We propose an algorithmic function called *Extend* which, by using the respective correspondences' sets of elements $G^1, \ldots, G^M$ and $G'^1, \ldots, G'^M$, is able to create a new set of correspondences $\hat{f}^1, \ldots, \hat{f}^M$ along with a common sets of elements $G^{1, \ldots M}$ and $G'^{1, \ldots M}$. The new $\hat{f}^1, \ldots, \hat{f}^M$ are created by translating the indicated correspondences

$G^1, \ldots, G^M \to G'^1, \ldots, G'^M$ to $G^{1,..M} \to G'^{1,..M}$, locating the feature that corresponds to such translation, in other words, the closest feature from the original set to the ones stored in $G^{1,..M}$ or $G'^{1,..M}$ respectively. Notice that once again, the definition of being close enough is given by function μ. From the algorithmic point of view, we describe this method through the following function,

$$(\{\hat{f}^1, \ldots, \hat{f}^M\}, G^{1,..M}, G'^{1,..M}) = Extend(\{f^1, \ldots, f^M\}, \{G^1, \ldots, G^M\}, \{G'^1, \ldots, G'^M\})$$
(6)

2.2   Consensus Correspondence of a Pair of Correspondences of Two Sets

Assume $f^a : G^a x G'^a$ and $f^b : G^b x G'^b$ are two correspondence functions between the two output sets $G^a = \{g_1^a, g_2^a, \ldots, g_{n^a}^a\}$ and $G^b = \{g_1^b, g_2^b, \ldots, g_{n^b}^b\}$ and the two input sets $G'^a = \{g_1'^a, g_2'^a, \ldots, g_{n^a}'^a\}$ and $G^b = \{g_1'^b, g_2'^b, \ldots, g_{n^b}'^b\}$. The order of G^a and G'^a is n^a, and the order of G^b and G'^b is n^b, since the correspondences f^a and f^b are defined to be bijective. Note that we assume there is some level of intersection between both input sets and also both output sets, therefore $G^a \cap G^b$ and $G'^a \cap G'^b$ are non null sets, although it is not strictly necessary and also it may happen that $n^a \neq n^b$. The problem at hand is to define a consensus correspondence $f^{a,b}$ given, $f^a : G^a x G'^a$ and $f^b : G^b x G'^b$. As commented before, correspondences have to be defined as bijective functions, for this reason, the obtained consensus is defined in the following domain and codomain: $f^{a,b} : G^{a,b} x G'^{a,b}$. The domain set is defined as $G^{a,b} = G^a \cup G^b \cup \{\phi, \ldots \phi\}$ and the codomain set is defined as $G'^{a,b} = G'^a \cup G'^b \cup \{\phi, \ldots \phi\}$. The number of inserted null elements $\emptyset$ depends on the initial correspondences and sets. This is because, in the definition of the method, it is needed to extend bijections f^a and f^b to be defined in the same domain and codomain. These extended functions are $\hat{f}^a : G^{a,b} x G'^{a,b}$ and $\hat{f}^b : G^{a,b} x G'^{a,b}$ and they have been obtained through $(\{\hat{f}^a, \hat{f}^b\}, G^{a,b}, G'^{a,b}) = Extend(\{f^a, f^b\}, \{G^a, G^b\}, \{G'^a, G'^b\})$ (Eq. 6).

Figure 1 shows an example of this method. In Fig. 1(a), one extractor algorithm has selected the squared points (G^a and G'^a) and another extractor algorithm has selected circular points (G^b and G'^b). Afterwards, a Point Set Registration algorithm has been applied to the square points, and another Point Set Registration algorithm (or the same one) has been applied to the circle points (Fig. 1b). These algorithms have found the blue correspondences for the square points (f^a) and the red correspondences for the circle points (f^b). Some new elements have appeared, which are marked as null ($\emptyset$), to allocate the original elements that the Point Set Registration algorithm considers as outliers. Between the blue and red correspondences, there are some discrepancies not only in the selected points, but also in the elements mappings. Moreover, $n^a = 3$ and $n^b = 4$. In Fig. 1(c), we show the obtained consensus $f^{a,b}$. Notice $G^{a,b}$ has one extended point and $G'^{a,b}$ has two extended points and so, $n^{a,b} = 6$.

(a): Two feature extractors on two images   (b): f^a and f^b correspondences   (c): $f^{a,b}$ correspondence

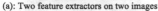

Fig. 1. The process of obtaining a consensus correspondence from the original extracted salient points to the final consensus correspondence.

The method published in [22] obtains a consensus correspondence $f^{a,b*}$ through a minimisation process composed of two terms. The first one is the cost of the obtained correspondence (Eq. 1) and the second term is the sum of the Hamming Distances (Eq. 4) between the obtained correspondence and the original correspondences. There is a weighting parameter λ [24] to gauge the importance of both terms.

$$f^{a,b*} = \min_{\forall f^{a,b}:G^{a,b} \times G'^{a,b}} \left\{ (1 - \lambda) \cdot Cost\left(G^{a,b}, G'^{a,b}, f^{a,b}\right) + \lambda \cdot \left(d_H\left(\hat{f}^a, f^{a,b}\right) + d_H\left(f^{a,b}, \hat{f}^b\right)\right) \right\}$$

(7)

Moreover, [22] computes correspondence $f^{a,b*}$ in a sub-optimal way, defining a Cost Matrix C through $Cost\left(G^{a,b}, G'^{a,b}, f^{a,b}\right)$ and a Correspondence Matrix through the addition of Correspondence matrices $\hat{F}^a$ and $\hat{F}^b$. Thus, a linear assignation method such as [14] or [15] is applied to the following matrix H if outliers are not considered, and an algorithm like the one presented in [14, 17] if outliers are considered.

$$H = (1 - \lambda) \cdot C + \lambda \cdot \left[\mathbf{1} - \left(\hat{F}^a + \hat{F}^b\right)\right]$$

(8)

where $\mathbf{1}$ represents an all ones matrix and expression $[\cdot]_f$ is the cost of the labelling f applied on matrix $[\cdot]$ (Eq. 4). See [22] for more details.

From the algorithmic point of view, we describe this method through the following function,

$$\left\{f^{a,b}, G^{a,b}, G'^{a,b}\right\} = PairConsensus\left(\lambda, f^a, G^a, G'^a, f^b, G^b, G'^b\right)$$

(9)

3   Consensus Correspondence of Multiple Correspondences of Two Sets

In this section, we explain an iterative and a voting method to compute a consensus correspondence given several correspondences of two points' sets. We assume that we have M correspondences defined on different domains and codomains: $f^i : G^i x G'^i$; $1 \leq i \leq M$. Note that it is assumed there is some level of intersection between sets

G^i; $1 \le i \le M$ and also between sets G'^i; $1 \le i \le M$. Besides, the order of sets n^i; $1 \le i \le M$ may be different. The aim of both methods is to obtain a consensus correspondence $f^{1,..M} : G^{1,..M} x\, G'^{1,..M}$ defined on the domain set $G^{1,..M}$ and the codomain set $G'^{1,..M}$.

3.1   Iterative Method

The order in which correspondences are chosen affects on the final result, as it is usual in the learning iterative methods. To select the proper order, some usual strategies are to order the initial correspondences with respect to a certain criteria, such as accuracy in previous experiments, cost, or number of delivered mappings.

Algorithm 1. Iterative consensus

Input: $\lambda, f^i,\, G^i, G'^i$; $1 \le i \le M$

Output: $f^{1,..M}$, $G^{1,..M}$, $G'^{1,..M}$

Begin

    $f^{1,..M} = f^1$

    $G^{1,..M} = G^1$

    $G'^{1,..M} = G'^1$

    For i=2..M

        $(f^{1,..M}, G^{1,..M}, G'^{1,..M})$ $= PairConsensus(\lambda, f^{1,..M}, G^{1,..M}, G'^{1,..M}, f^i, G^i, G'^i)$

    End for

End algorithm

3.2   Voting Method

Clustering or classification methods based on a voting process [24] select as a final result the one that most of the contributions decide it is the best one. Nevertheless, in some frameworks, different parties only partially contribute on the final result. In these cases, a minimisation process is needed to arrive at the solution. In example of Fig. 1, both Feature Extractors obtain some different points and so both correspondences do not contribute on a complete solution. When there are several feature extractors, the number of discrepancies increases and so the initial correspondences tend to be less complete. Algorithm 2 shows how to obtain the consensus correspondence based on a voting process. It has three main steps. In the first one, a set of extended correspondences is obtained together with their common domains and codomains (Sect. 2.1). In the second step, the Correspondence Matrices are defined (Sect. 2.1). Finally in the third step, the final consensus correspondence is computed through minimising matrix $M - \sum_{i=1}^{M} \hat{F}^i$ where M is a matrix with all cells with the value M. This minimisation can be done through algorithms [14, 15] or [14], among others.

Algorithm 2. Voting consensus

Input: f^i, G^i, G'^i; $1 \leq i \leq M$

Output: $f^{1..M}$, $G^{1..M}$, $G'^{1..M}$

Begin

$$(\{\hat{f}^1, \dots, \hat{f}^M\}, G^{1..M}, G'^{1..M}) = Extend(\{f^1, \dots, f^M\}, \{G^1, \dots, G^M\}, \{G'^1, \dots, G'^M\})$$

$$(\hat{F}^1, \dots, \hat{F}^M) = CorrespondenceMatrix(\hat{f}^1, \dots, \hat{f}^M)$$

$$f^{1..M} = LinearSolver\left(M - \sum_{i=1}^{M} \hat{F}^i\right)$$

End algorithm

---

4 Experimentation

4.1 Dataset Used

We show the validity of both consensus correspondence methods through the correspondence found given two images and five Feature Extractors (FAST, HARRIS, MINEIGEN, SURF and SIFT). We used the *Tarragona Exteriors* database [25]. Better the correspondence is, lower the cost is and more properly mapped elements it has. The cost of a correspondence is defined in Eq. 1 and a mapping between two points of two different images is considered correct if the ground truth homography projects the first point to a position close to the second point.

The "Tarragona Exteriors" database was defined through five public image databases called "BOAT", "EAST_PARK", "EAST_SOUTH", "RESIDENCE" and "ENSIMAG". These databases are composed of a sequence of images taken from the same object, but from different points of views and scales. Together with the images, the homography estimations that convert the first image (img00) of the set into the other ones (img01 through img10) is provided. From each of the images, the 50 most reliable salient points were extracted using 5 methodologies: FAST, HARRIS, MINEIGEN, SURF (native Matlab 2013b libraries) and SIFT (own library). Moreover, they computed 5correspondences between the first image of the sequence and the other ten ones using the Matlab function *MatchFeatures*. This function was applied with the parameter *MaxRatio* set to 1 to include as many matches as possible, but discarding the non-bijective correspondences. Finally, they deducted the oracle correspondence using the homography provided by the original image databases. Thus, the database has a total of 5 sequences × 5 extractor methods × 10 pairs of images = 250 quartets $\{G^i, G'^i, f^i, h^i\}$ composed of two sets of features G^i and G'^i the correspondencef^i extracted by *MatchFeatures* and the ground truth homography h^i extracted through the given homography. In Fig. 2, we can appreciate an example of the first two images of the "BOAT" sequence. Lines show the correspondence f^i. Correct mappings are marked in green and incorrect ones in red. The correct ones are distinguished from the incorrect ones through homography h^i.

Fig. 2. The first two images of sequence BOAT and the correct (green) and incorrect (red) correspondences (Color figure online).

4.2 Results and Interpretation

On these tests, we compared seven different outputs (5 single methods, the Iterative method and the Voting method) expecting to reduce the correspondence's cost while increasing the correspondence's accuracy (number of correct mappings). Figure 3 shows the average cost of the obtained consensus correspondences together with the average cost of the correspondences generated using a single set (FAST, HARRIS, MINEIGEN, SURF and SIFT) in the *Tarragona Exteriors* database, using the *MatchFeatures* function built in Matlab. For the Iterative method, there is the weighting parameter λ that ranges from $[0, 1]$. Additionally, since the obtained consensus depends on the order of presentation of the input correspondences, we tested all the 5! combinations and only show the best result. For the two consensus methods, we used the Fast Bipartite Matching algorithm [16] as the linear minimisation solver (Outlier Costs; Iterative: $k_v = 0.1$, Voting: $k_v = 4$). We selected this solver since it is a fast and reliable form to obtain correspondences with outliers. We have presented previous work [26, 27] in which we show that this method outperforms other state of the art methods which are compatible with our experimental dataset, thus the implementation of only one minimisation solver. The Iterative method obtains lower costs than the original correspondences if the weighting parameter λ is properly set (between 0.2 and 0.8), while the cost of the correspondence generated by the Voting method is always higher than any of the original correspondences. Nevertheless, a high cost may also mean a high number of inliers found and thus, the Voting method's high cost is not necessarily a negative aspect.

Figure 4 shows the average number of correct mappings. In this case, the Voting method obtains a higher amount of correct mappings than the Iterative method or than any of the individual methods. Notice that as mentioned before, although in Fig. 3 the Voting method denoted a high average cost, this happened because the number of inliers found by the method is higher than the others and thus, the Voting method's labelling cost increased. In counterpart, the Iterative method only obtains better results than the individual methods as λ is low. When λ is set between 0.2 and 0.8 the worse results are obtained, this confirming that the low cost was due to the poor accuracy. If $\lambda \langle 0.2$, this means that the method is only considering the Cost Matrix, and no real consensus is taking place.

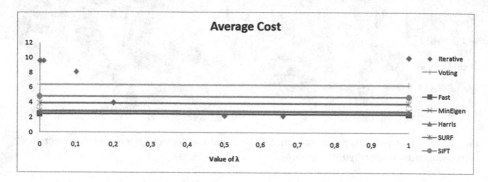

Fig. 3. Average cost of the consensus and the original correspondences.

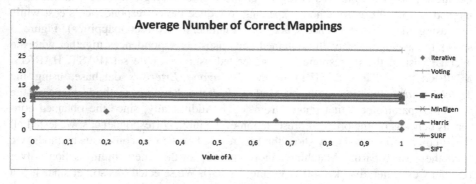

Fig. 4. Average number of correct mappings of the consensus and the original correspondences.

Table 1 shows the runtime in seconds of both consensus methods in the five datasets. The runtime of the Voting method is almost independent of the number of correspondences but the Iterative method is linearly dependent on them. In these experiments, the Voting method is clearly faster than the Iterative method. Table 2 shows the runtime of Matlab function called *MatchFeatures* that obtains a correspondence given two sets of points using any extractor. The computational cost of the Iterative method is linearly dependent on this cost.

Table 1. Average time in seconds of Matlab function *MatchFeatures*.

	BOAT	EAST_PARK	EAST_SOUTH	ENSIMAG	RESIDENCE
Iterative method	1288,6	904,2	902,8	597,2	927,8
Voting method	40,6	34,2	36,1	29,9	36,9

Table 2. Average time in seconds of the Iterative and Voting methods.

	BOAT	EAST_PARK	EAST_SOUTH	ENSIMAG	RESIDENCE
MatchFeatures	17,4	3,3	20,2	9,6	2,2

5 Conclusions and Further Work

As multiple parties intend to solve a similar problem, differences in their decisions may occur. In this paper, we present two different methods to obtain a consensus correspondence given several correspondences between two sets of points. The first solution is an adaptation of a previously presented method, and the second solution is a strategy based on voting methods. Experiments using a public image dataset show that the two methods have contrasting characteristics that make them suitable for two different purposes. If the purpose of calculating a consensus correspondence is to find one with a minimum cost, then we must not discard using the iterative method. Nevertheless, a higher amount of correct mappings for this particular dataset indicates that the voting method is a more suitable option to use. Additionally, a much lower computational runtime is spent by the voting method. Our current work is devoted to find a new solution in which the methodology presented in [22] can be directly adapted into a multiple consensus solution without the need of an iterative implementation, since our aim is to present a method that still considers a gauging parameter.

Acknowledgements.. This research is supported by the Spanish projects DPI2013-42458-P and TIN2013-47245-C2-2-R, and by Consejo Nacional de Ciencia y Tecnologías (CONACyT Mexico).

References

1. Simonson, K., Drescher, S., Tanner, F.: A statistics based approach to binary image registration with uncertainty analysis. IEEE Pattern Anal. Mach. Intell. **29**(1), 112–125 (2007)
2. Lowe, D.G.: Distinctive image features from scale-invariant keypoints. IJCV **60**(2), 91–110 (2004)
3. Bay, H., Ess, A., Tuytelaars, T., Van Gool, L.: SURF: speeded up robust features. Comput. Vis. Image Underst. (CVIU) **110**(3), 346–359 (2008)
4. Van Kaick, O., Zhang, H., Hamarneh, G., Cohen-Or, D.: A survey on shape correspondence. Comput. Graph. Forum **30**, 1681–1707 (2011)
5. Tam, G., Cheng, Z.Q., Lai, Y.K., Langbein, F., Liu, Y., Marshall, D., Martin, R., Sun, X.F., Rosin, P.: Registration of 3D point clouds and meshes: a survey from rigid to non rigid. IEEE Trans. Vis. Comput. Graph. **19**, 1199–1217 (2013)
6. Besl, P.J., McKay, N.D.: A Method for Registration of 3-D Shapes. IEEE Trans. Pattern Anal. Mach. Intell. **14**(2), 239–256 (1992)
7. Myronenko, A., Song, X.: Point set registration: coherent point drift. IEEE Trans. Pattern Anal. Mach. Intell. **32**(2), 2262–2275 (2010)

8. Sanromà, G., Alquézar, R., Serratosa, F., Herrera, B.: Smooth point-set registration using neighbouring constraints. Pattern Recogn. Lett. **33**, 2029–2037 (2012)
9. Sanromà, G., Alquézar, R., Serratosa, F.: A new graph matching method for point-set correspondence using the EM algorithm and softassign. Comput. Vis. Image Underst. **116** (2), 292–304 (2012)
10. Serratosa, F., Alquézar, R., Sanfeliu, A.: Estimating the joint probability distribution of random vertices and arcs by means of second-order random graphs. In: Caelli, T.M., Amin, A., Duin, R.P., Kamel, M.S., de Ridder, D. (eds.) SPR 2002 and SSPR 2002. LNCS, vol. 2396, pp. 252–262. Springer, Heidelberg (2002)
11. Moreno-García, C.F., Cortés, X., Serratosa, F.: Partial to full image registration based on candidate positions and multiple correspondences. In: Bayro-Corrochano, E., Hancock, E. (eds.) CIARP 2014. LNCS, vol. 8827, pp. 745–753. Springer, Heidelberg (2014)
12. Cortés, X., Serratosa, F.: An interactive method for the image alignment problem based on partially supervised correspondence. Expert Syst. Appl. **42**(1), 179–192 (2015)
13. Serratosa, F., Cortés, X.: Interactive graph-matching using active query strategies. Pattern Recogn. **48**, 1360–1369 (2015)
14. Kuhn, H.W.: The Hungarian method for the assignment problem export. Naval Res. Logist. Q. **2**(1–2), 83–97 (1955)
15. Jonker, R., Volgenant, T.: Improving the Hungarian assignment algorithm. Oper. Res. Lett. **5**(4), 171–175 (1986)
16. Serratosa, F.: Fast computation of Bipartite graph matching. Pattern Recogn. Lett. **45**, 244–250 (2014)
17. Serratosa, F.: Speeding up fast Bipartite graph matching through a new cost matrix. Int. J. Pattern Recognit Artif. Intell. **29**(2), 1–17 (2015)
18. Solé, A., Serratosa, F., Sanfeliu, A.: On the graph edit distance cost: properties and applications. Int. J. Pattern Recognit. Artif. Intell. **26**(5), 1–21 (2012)
19. Cortés, X., Serratosa, F.: Learning graph-matching edit-costs based on the optimality of the Oracle's node correspondences. Pattern Recognit. Lett. **56**, 22–29 (2015)
20. Serratosa, F., Cortés, X., Solé, A.: component retrieval based on a database of graphs for hand-written electronic-scheme digitalisation. Expert Syst. Appl. **40**, 2493–2502 (2013)
21. Solé, A., Serratosa, F.: Models and algorithms for computing the common labelling of a set of attributed graphs. Comput. Vis. Image Underst. **115**(7), 929–945 (2011)
22. Moreno-García, C.F., Serratosa, F.: Weighted mean assignment of a pair of correspondences using optimisation functions. In: Fränti, P., Brown, G., Loog, M., Escolano, F., Pelillo, M. (eds.) S+SSPR 2014. LNCS, vol. 8621, pp. 301–311. Springer, Heidelberg (2014)
23. Bauer, E., Kohavi, R.: An empirical comparison of voting classification algorithms: bagging, boosting and variants. Mach. Learn. **36**, 105–139 (1999)
24. Saha, S., Ekbal, A.: Combining multiple classifiers using vote based classifier Ensemble technique for named entity recognition. Data Knowl. Eng. **85**, 15–39 (2013)
25. http://deim.urv.cat/ ∼ francesc.serratosa/databases/
26. Moreno-García, C.F., Serratosa, F.: Fast and efficient Palmprint identification of a small sample within a full image. Computación y Sistemas **18**(4), 683–691 (2014)
27. Moreno-García, C.F., Cortés, X., Serratosa, F.: Partial to full image registration based on candidate positions and multiple correspondences. In: Bayro-Corrochano, E., Hancock, E. (eds.) CIARP 2014. LNCS, vol. 8827, pp. 745–753. Springer, Heidelberg (2014)

Extracting Categories by Hierarchical Clustering Using Global Relational Features

Wail Mustafa[⊠], Dirk Kraft, and Norbert Krüger

The Mærsk Mc-Kinney Møller Institute, University of Southern Denmark,
Campusvej 55, 5230 Odense M, Denmark
wail@mmmi.sdu.dk

Abstract. We introduce an object categorization system which uses hierarchical clustering to extract categories. The system is able to assign multiple, nested categories for unseen objects. In our system, objects are represented with global pair-wise relations computed from 3D features extracted by three RGB-D sensors. We show that our system outperforms a state-of-the-art approach particularly when only a few number of training samples is used.

1 Introduction

Object categorization is important for a variety of tasks especially when systems are expected to deal with novel objects based on prior knowledge. For instance in robotic applications, categories can be linked to manipulation actions allowing for performing predefined actions on novel objects (see e.g., [1]). Categorizing novel objects is also useful in other applications such as driver assistance [2] and video surveillance [3]. The prior knowledge is built from previous observations by identifying common structures in the visual data. In this paper, we introduce an object categorization method based on unsupervised clustering of 3D relational features. Clustering [4] is a powerful tool to automatically find structures in the data that can be, in this context, translated into categories.

In our system, visual data are provided in terms of view-point invariant representations of objects extracted from 3D sensors. These representations code the properties of objects by computing global, pair-wise relations from 3D features (i.e., 3D texlets [5]). This space of feature relations is then expressed in histograms, providing unique and specific object descriptors. Moreover, such descriptors provide a fixed-length feature space, which can be directly fed into the clustering algorithm. The representations used here have been found to achieve high performance on object instance recognition [6].

In this paper, we apply hierarchical agglomerative clustering [7]. In contrast to flat clustering algorithms such as k-means, hierarchical clustering allows for overlapping of categories (see Fig. 1a for an illustration). This means that very similar categories are nested within larger clusters forming a structure in which more generic categories are found on top of less generic ones. This provides flexibility in selecting the abstraction level.

R. Paredes et al. (Eds.): IbPRIA 2015, LNCS 9117, pp. 541–551, 2015.
DOI: 10.1007/978-3-319-19390-8_61

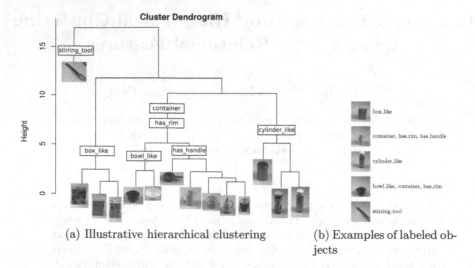

(a) Illustrative hierarchical clustering   (b) Examples of labeled objects

Fig. 1. Examples of hierarchical clustering and object labeling. The thumbnails are resized for better visualization and they don't necessarily reflect their actual relative sizes.

Existing object categorization methods assume that objects belong to mutually-exclusive (single) categories [8]. In this paper, we consider scenarios where objects can have multiple, nested categories (see Fig. 1b). Such scenarios are very common when dealing with everyday objects. One important aspect of this approach is that it is inherently capable of providing multiple categories. In contrary, other approaches will not only require learning multiple classifiers (see e.g., [8]) but also—as we show in this paper—perform poorly on nested categories.

To evaluate the system, we hand-labeled our benchmark object set with a number of visual categories. We use the labeled categories from the training subset to find the best matching ones in the hierarchy. Then, we evaluate the performance of the system on the test subset. Note that although the hierarchy is built unsupervised, finding the corresponding categories is done in a supervised way. This is, however, necessary for evaluation. This procedure is repeated using different parameterizations of the visual representations in order to empirically find the best set of parameters for each category.

We compare this approach to a supervised approach using Random Forests [9] using the same visual features. In addition, we make a comparison with a state-of-the-art method (Hierarchical Matching Pursuit, HMP [8]) that works on RGB-D data and extracts distinct visual features. The main achievements of this work can be summarized as follows:

– We introduce an object categorization method that is capable of predicting multiple, nested categories.
– We show that—using hierarchical clustering for finding categories—we perform better than classification with Random Forests. Our method also outperforms a state-of-the-art method on our dataset.

– We demonstrate that the use of our visual features, compared to features extracted a state-of-the-art method, allow the system to have high performance with fewer training samples.

2 Related Work

Early research on object categorization focused on generic object representations that capture shape at high levels of abstraction (such as generalized cylinders [10], superquadrics [11], or geons [12]). The difficulty involved in reconstructing such abstractions from real objects has led to the development of solutions that could recognize only exemplar objects [13] (i.e., object recognition), which require little or no abstraction. Over the years, the gap between the low-level and the high-level abstractions has been narrowed by introducing representations that are invariant to a number of geometrical properties such as view-point, rotation, and scaling. Such representations often make use of local descriptors such the popular SIFT [14] features and various recently developed 3D features [15].

Belongie et al. [16] proposed representing objects using 'shape contexts', which uses relative shape information within a local neighborhood. The shape contexts were later extended to 3D in [17]. In this paper, we use shape relations of 3D features presented in [6], which are similar to shape context but are defined in a global context. Additionally, we go beyond the work in [6] by addressing the scale invariance to obtain a more abstract representation that is important for object categorization.

Recently, hierarchical approaches for object representation have shown high performance on large dataset [18]. Notably, Bo et al. [8] introduced a multi-layer network that builds feature hierarchies layer by layer with an increasing receptive field size to capture abstract representations. They shows that their method achieves state-of-the-art performance in a large-scale RGB-D dataset of objects [19]. It is worth noting that these results are based on very large training data with significant computational cost.

Existing object categorization systems typically apply supervised learning to recognize object classes that correspond to labeled categories and associate only one category per object (single-label) [1,8]. In our approach, to summarizing the novelty, categories are learned in an unsupervised way using hierarchical agglomerative clustering [7]. Based on that, we built a method capable of associating more than one category per object (multi-label). Building such a hierarchy can be seen as a way to obtain higher levels of abstraction (from the visual features) where more generic categories are formed at the top of the hierarchy.

3 System Description

The components of the object categorization system introduced in this paper are shown Fig. 2. The system operates in a set-up in which three views are captured by three Kinect sensors, which are mounted in a close to equilateral triangular configuration. The process starts with scene preprocessing for table removal and

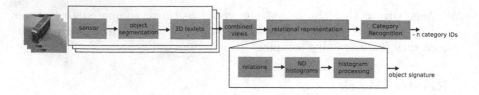

Fig. 2. System Overview: block diagram of the different components.

object segmentation in the 3D point cloud data. In following, we describe in detail the other components.

3.1 Object Representation Using Histogram of Relational Features

For the approach we introduce in this paper, object shapes are described as distributions of *relations* between pairs of 3D features. The relations we use are intrinsically pose-invariant.

From RGB-D data (Kinect sensor), we extract our 3D features—*3D texlets* [5]. The 3D texlet has both position and orientation, and provides absolute informations (relative to an external reference frame) of objects in the 3D space. In our system, we combine 3D texlets from three view resulting in a rather complete object information (see Fig. 3a). To describe an object, we compute a set of pair-wise relations from all pairs of texlets belonging to the object.

Shape relations are similar to the 3D shape context introduced as local descriptors by [17], however, they are used here as global descriptors of objects. Having combined multiple 3D views of objects allows such global descriptors to become robust and rich representations for fast learning.

In [6], we defined in detail three shape relations used for object instance recognition, namely, Angle Relation $R_a(\Pi_i^T, \Pi_j^T)$, Distance (Euclidean) Relation $R_d(\Pi_i^T, \Pi_j^T)$, and Normal Distance Relation $R_{nd}(\Pi_i^T, \Pi_j^T)$—they are also depicted in Fig. 3b. Note that the relations transform an absolute pose-dependent representation into a relative pose-independent one. For instance, the distance relation $\mathcal{R}_d$ transforms texlets' positions into inter-texlet distances.

The two distance relations are scale-variant, which is suitable for object instance recognition where object size matters and shall be encoded. However, for object categorization, because what defines a category is usually independent of scale, scale-invariance is crucial. Therefore, we introduce a new scale-invariant distance relation referred to as *Scaled Distance Relation*, $R_{sd}(\Pi_i^T, \Pi_j^T)$. The scaled distance is computed by dividing the Distance Relation by the maximum distance within an object. For robustness against outliers, the maximum distance is calculated as the median value of the highest 10 % distance relation values. Figure 3c shows an example of two objects with different sizes (belong to the same category), comparing using distance and scaled distance when representing objects. One aspect we investigate in the experiment section is the performance of the system on each category when combinations of different relations are used.

The final object representation is obtained by binning the selected relations in *multi-dimensional histograms*, which model the distributions of the relations

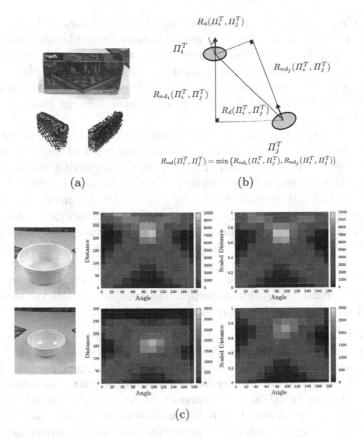

Fig. 3. Texlet's shape relations. (a) extracted 3D texlets of an object. (b) definition of three shape relations. (c) 2D histograms of two objects belonging to the same categorize. In the right column the distance is scaled

in fixed-sized feature vectors fed to the learning algorithm. Examples of 2D histograms are shown in Fig. 3c. Different values of binning size are also investigated in the experiments. Another process that is optionally performed on our histograms is *smoothing* using ND Gaussian filters to reduce the noise.

3.2   Finding Categories Using Hierarchical Clustering

Hierarchical Clustering. The quality and the invariance properties of the object representation presented in the previous section make it attractive for object categorization. We propose using unsupervised category learning through clustering using agglomerative hierarchical clustering [7] (R implementation [20]). By doing so, we build a hierarchy of clusters from unlabeled data where each cluster (branching point in the hierarchy) is considered as a potential category that can be linked (by an autonomous process) to an actual category. Note that we use the Euclidean distance as a dissimilarity measure (between all pairs of data samples or object instances in our case) whereas as a linkage metric, we use Ward's criterion, which aims at minimizing the total within-cluster variance [7].

Finding Categories From Human-Labeled Categories. Particularly for this paper, to validate our approach, we use human-defined labels from the training samples (Fig. 1b shows some examples) and then we find the corresponding categories in the hierarchy. Those definitions of categories are rather subjective and might not correspond to real ones. Therefore, we also compare our approach with other approaches—one of which even extracts different features from the raw RGB-D data.

To find a category in the hierarchy that correspond to a labeled one, we search for the cluster that contains the most similar set of object instances to the set of objects labeled as such. To compute the similarity, we use Jaccard's index [21], which measures the similarity between finite sample sets and is defined as the size of the intersection divided by the size of the union. The Jaccard's index rewards the existence of the object in the prospective cluster and also punishes for the absence thereof. This prohibits assigning categories to very specific (at the bottom of the hierarchy) or very generic clusters (at the top of the hierarchy).

Note that, although building the structure is done in an unsupervised way, finding the learned categories corresponding best to the labeled categories is performed in a supervised fashion (based on labeled data).

Predicting Categories for Novel Objects. To allow the system to categorize objects, the proposed method should provide a prediction mechanism. Traditionally for supervised learning, the learned model is used to make predictions for the novel object. Such a model usually forms a map of the feature space allowing for making predictions based on the features of the novel object. In our method, the principle concept we propose for prediction is to identify where the novel object falls in the learned (previously-built) hierarchy. This requires involving the training samples because the hierarchy is built directly from the training data. This seems computationally inefficient especially for large set of training samples. However, we show in this paper that our method requires few training samples.

To implement this, in the prediction phase, we first add the novel object to the objects previously used for training. Once the hierarchy is built again, we identify the closest sibling of the novel object. The novel object will then inherit all the branching points—including the ones associated with the labeled categories—from the sibling object. Finally, the predicted categories for the novel object will be all the inherited categories.

4   Dataset and Experiments

Dataset. To benchmark our approach, we use a dataset of 100 objects with 30 different samples (random poses) for each object[1]. The dataset was originally created to test the performance of the object instance recognition present in [6]. The selection of objects covers a wide range including industrial and household objects, some of them taken from the KIT dataset [22].

---

[1] http://caro.sdu.dk/index.php/sdu-dataset.

To validate our approach, we hand-labeled the objects in the dataset with purely visual as well action-related categories (see Fig. 1b). Note that a single object can have multiple (nested) categories. This allows us to study the performances of the different approaches on such cases.

Comparison Methods. The approach we introduce in this paper is compared with two different methods that use classical supervised learning. We apply those methods in N-classifier mode where N refers to the number of categories. This allows the methods to provide multiple categories per object and hence make them comparable with our approach. The first method we compare with is *a Random Forest classifier*, which uses the same features as the introduced approach (see Sect. 3).

The second method is HMP [8], which is a state-of-the-art method. HMP is a multi-layer sparse coding network that builds feature hierarchies layer by layer with an increasing receptive field size to capture abstract representations from raw RGB-D data. Note that HMP was not designed to combine features from different views in the 3D space. Therefore, to make it comparable to our multiview system, we provide all the three views in the training phase. Additionally, we compare all methods when only one view is used.

The comparison also includes a 'dummy' classifier that generates uniformly-distributed random category predictions. Comparing the different methods with this classifier may indicate whether a particular method has failed to achieve reasonably good performance on the category in question.

Histogram Variations. In the experiments below, we vary the parametrization of our object representation. The objective is to find out the set of parameters that yields the best performance on each category. Note that those variations are applied to the methods in which our object representation is used (namely, the proposed approach and the Random Forest approach). The object representation was discussed in detail in Sect. 3. The exact list of parameters we vary are the following:

- Set of relations: We vary what relations to use for representing objects from the ones defined in Sect. 3: Angle Relation, Distance Relation, Normal Distance Relation, and Scaled Distance Relation.
- Relational dimensionality: We vary how we combine relations in ND histograms. The combinations we apply are: 1D histograms of the individual relations and 2D histograms of Angle Relation with one of distance relations.
- Histogram binning: Here, we vary the ND histogram bin size among the following values: 10, 20, 50 and 100. For simplicity, the bin size is fixed across dimensions in the 2D case.
- Filtering: We analyze the impact of applying filtering with Gaussian kernel.

In addition to the above-mentioned parameters, we also experiment with the impact of performing vector normalization on the final object representation.

Experimental Procedure. In the following experiments, we study the performance of each method for categorizing novel objects. Therefore, in each experiment, the object dataset is divided into training and test subsets where sampling

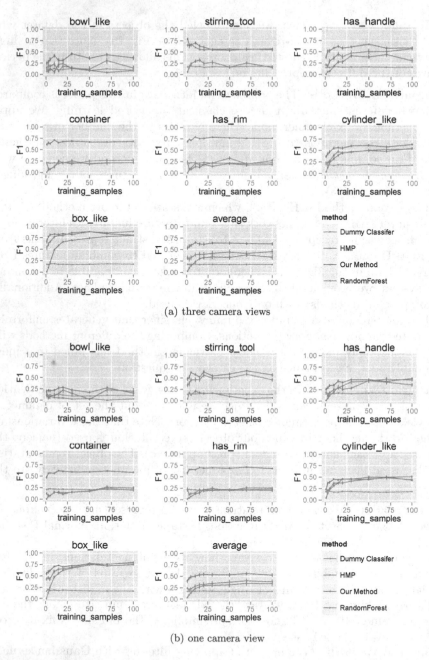

(a) three camera views

(b) one camera view

Fig. 4. The performance of object categorization on 7 categories. In (a) three camera views are used whereas in (b) one camera view is used. Using a 2D histogram of angle and scaled distance (with 10 bins at each dimension) yields the best performance in all categories except for 'bowl_like' (in this case, combining two 1D histograms of angle and scaled distance with 12 bins). Also, applying filtering and vector normalization helps achieving the best performance in all cases.

is performed in a way that prohibits the presence of samples from the same object in both subsets. Allowing otherwise, results in performing recognition of object instances rather than object categories in which in our tests we obtained significantly higher performance. The size of the test subset is set to 100 samples per category whereas the size of the training subset is allowed to vary—all samples are randomly chosen. Each experiment is executed 20 times from which the average F1 score and the standard deviation are computed. Note that the same training and test subsets are passed to each method.

In the result shown in Fig. 4b, the size of the training set varies among certain values: 1, 3, 5, 10, 15, 20, 30, 50, 70 and 100 per category. By doing this, we are able to study the performance of each method when only a small number of training samples are available and how that changes when the number increases.

Results. Figure 4 shows the performance of object categorization on 7 categories. Each sub-figure shows the average F1 score and the standard deviation for a varying number of training samples. The average performance on all categories is also shown in a separate sub-figure. The results show that the method introduced in this paper generally achieves the highest performance in identifying the categories particularly when a few training samples are used. This means that our method is able to learn faster and also generalize better when the training samples are limited.

Conclusion. Both the proposed method and the Random Forest approach use the same extracted visual representations of objects. This indicates that finding categories in clusters formed hierarchically in unsupervised way has a better generalization than the supervised learning of categories. Additionally, because both approaches outperform the HMP method, which extracts different visual representations, the results suggest that our visual representation provides strong features for describing object categories. This is particularly clear in the three-view case where our representation allows for combing the three views in 3D resulting in a rather complete object description.

For some categories (namely, 'container' and 'has_rim'), our method achieves relatively good performance in identifying the categories whereas the other methods fail (perform comparatively the same as the dummy classifier). Those categories are nested categories (i.e., in this case, any container also has a rim). This indicates that our approach is able to identify the relation between the two categories. The supervised approaches, on the other hand, try to learn discriminatively the two categories, which for most samples have very similar representations. This may explain their failure in identifying the nested categories.

Acknowledgment. This work has been funded by the EU project Xperience (FP7-ICT-270273).

References

1. Marton, Z.C., Pangercic, D., Rusu, R.B., Holzbach, A., Beetz, M.: Hierarchical object geometric categorization and appearance classification for mobile manipulation. In: 2010 10th IEEE-RAS International Conference on Humanoid Robots (Humanoids), pp. 365–370. IEEE (2010)
2. Laika, A., Stechele, W.: A review of different object recognition methods for the application in driver assistance systems. In: Eighth International Workshop on Image Analysis for Multimedia Interactive Services, p. 10. IEEE (2007)
3. Graham, S., Wood, D.: Digitizing surveillance: categorization, space, inequality. Crit. Soc. Policy 23(2), 227–248 (2003)
4. Xu, R., Wunsch, D., et al.: Survey of clustering algorithms. IEEE Trans. Neural Netw. 16(3), 645–678 (2005)
5. Olesen, S.M., Lyder, S., Kraft, D., Krüger, N., Jessen, J.B.: Real-time extraction of surface patches with associated uncertainties by means of kinect cameras. J. Real-Time Image Process. 10(1), 105–118 (2015)
6. Mustafa, W., Pugeault, N., Buch, A., Krüger, N.: Multi-view object instance recognition in an industrial context. Robotica (accepted)
7. Ward, J.H.: Hierarchical grouping to optimize an objective function. J. Am. Stat. Assoc. 58(301), 236–244 (1963)
8. Bo, Liefeng, Ren, Xiaofeng, Fox, Dieter: Unsupervised feature learning for RGB-D based object recognition. In: Desai, Jaydev P., Dudek, Gregory, Khatib, Oussama, Kumar, Vijay (eds.) Experimental Robotics. STAR, vol. 88, pp. 387–402. Springer, Heidelberg (2013)
9. Breiman, L.: Random forests. Mach. Learn. 45(1), 5–32 (2001)
10. Binford, T.O.: Visual perception by computer. In: IEEE Conference on Systems and Control, vol. 261, p. 262 (1971)
11. Pentland, A.P.: Perceptual organization and the representation of natural form. Artif. Intell. 28(3), 293–331 (1986)
12. Biederman, I.: Recognition by components: a theory of human image understanding. Psychol. Rev. 94(2), 115–147 (1987)
13. Campbell, R., Flynn, P.: A survey of free-form object representation and recognition techniques. Comput. Vis. Image Underst. 81(2), 166–210 (2001)
14. Lowe, D.: Object recognition from local scale-invariant features. In: The Proceedings of the Seventh IEEE International Conference on Computer Vision, vol. 2, pp. 1150–1157 (1999)
15. Alexandre, L.A.: 3d descriptors for object and category recognition: a comparative evaluation. In: Workshop on Color-Depth Camera Fusion in Robotics, IROS (2012)
16. Belongie, S., Malik, J., Puzicha, J.: Shape matching and object recognition using shape contexts. IEEE Trans. Pattern Anal. Mach. Intell. 24(4), 509–522 (2002)
17. Frome, A., Huber, D., Kolluri, R., Bülow, T., Malik, J.: Recognizing objects in range data using regional point descriptors. In: Pajdla, T., Matas, J.G. (eds.) ECCV 2004. LNCS, vol. 3023, pp. 224–237. Springer, Heidelberg (2004)
18. Bengio, Y., Courville, A.C., Vincent, P.: Unsupervised feature learning and deep learning: a review and new perspectives. CoRR, abs/1206.5538 1 (2012)
19. Lai, K., Bo, L., Ren, X., Fox, D.: A large-scale hierarchical multi-view RGB-D object dataset. In: IEEE International Conference on Robotics and Automation (2011)
20. R Core Team: R: A Language and Environment for Statistical Computing. R Foundation for Statistical Computing, Vienna, Austria (2013). ISBN: 3-900051-07

21. Levandowsky, M., Winter, D.: Distance between sets. Nature **234**(5323), 34–35 (1971)
22. Kasper, A., Xue, Z., Dillmann, R.: The kit object models database: an object model database for object recognition, localization and manipulation in service robotics. Int. J. Robot. Res. (IJRR) **31**(8), 927–934 (2012)

A Calibration Algorithm for Multi-camera Visual Surveillance Systems Based on Single-View Metrology

J.C. Neves[1]($\boxtimes$), J.C. Moreno[1], S. Barra[2], and H. Proença[1]

[1] IT - Instituto de Telecomunicações, Department of Computer Science,
University of Beira Interior, 6201-001 Covilhã, Portugal
jcneves@penhas.di.ubi.pt
[2] Department of Mathematics and Computer Science, University of Cagliari,
Via Ospedale 40, 09124 Cagliari, Italy

Abstract. The growing concerns about persons security and the increasing popularity of pan-tilt-zoom (PTZ) cameras, have been raising the interest on automated master-slave surveillance systems. Such systems are typically composed by (1) a fixed wide-angle camera that covers a large area, detects and tracks moving objects in the scene; and (2) a PTZ camera, that provides a close-up view of an object of interest. Previously published approaches attempted to establish 2D correspondences between the video streams of both cameras, which is a ill-posed formulation due to the absence of depth information. On the other side, 3D-based approaches are more accurate but require more than one fixed camera to estimate depth information. In this paper, we describe a novel method for easy and precise calibration of a master-slave surveillance system, composed by a single fixed wide-angle camera. Our method exploits single view metrology to infer 3D data of the tracked humans and to self-perform the transformation between camera views. Experimental results in both simulated and realistic scenes point for the effectiveness of the proposed model in comparison with the state-of-the-art.

1 Introduction

Video surveillance has been mainly used for traffic monitoring and security systems in both public and private places. Many current surveillance systems need a human operator to record the video and store the data for later analysis. Also, the number of cameras and the area under surveillance are limited by the personal availability. In order to overcome the limitations of traditional video surveillance systems, the development of new methods is a current effort in the computer vision and artificial intelligence community.

A satisfactory surveillance system must be capable of monitoring larger areas as well as presenting high resolution images of an event of interest [1,2]. Systems based on wide-angle cameras are able to monitor an area that covers 180° but have limited scale of range due to the relatively reduced resolution. PTZ cameras are currently used in several surveillance environments due to their capabilities of monitoring large areas of interest providing details of moving objects by

© Springer International Publishing Switzerland 2015
R. Paredes et al. (Eds.): IbPRIA 2015, LNCS 9117, pp. 552–559, 2015.
DOI: 10.1007/978-3-319-19390-8_62

(a) Wide-angle camera   (b) PTZ camera

(c) The surveillance system monitors a large area and zooms-up over a object of interest, i.e. a subject head.

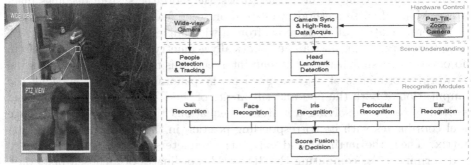

Fig. 1. Dual surveillance system. (a) Wide-angle camera. (b) PTZ camera. (c) The wide-angle camera gives a panoramic view of the scene, while the PTZ camera takes a snapshot of the full body of the tracked subject,in order to provide both physical and behavioural features for an a posteriori biometric recognition.

decreasing or increasing the focal length. A dual camera system can be defined by combining a wide-angle camera and a PTZ camera. The wide-angle camera provides a large resolution coverage of the scene as well as a global tracking of a human activity [3,4], while the PTZ camera is responsible of acquiring close-up views at high resolution [5,6]. The cooperation of both relies on a calibration method where an accurate interaction between the cameras is needed. Further challenges can be found in controlling and scheduling the desired pan and tilt angles of the PTZ camera, in order to better satisfy the competing request. The precision of the pan and tilt estimation mainly depends on the accuracy of the spatial calibrations, determined by mapping onto a common space the pixels of both the cameras [7].

Several methods have been proposed in the past, in order to perform a dual camera calibration system: Hampapur et al. [8] controlled a PTZ camera by triangulating 3D positions computed from two calibrated wide-angle cameras. Chen et al. [9] connected multiple 3D position camera models by fitting the best polynomial, to better describe the camera projection model and the spatial relations. Senior et al. [10] mapped wide-angle camera coordinates to PTZ camera coordinates by estimating the homography between cameras. Zhou et al. [11] triangulated the target position between cameras at pixel level (2D geometry) using different pixel locations of the image given by the wide-angle camera and then mapping the pixels by linear interpolation over the pan-tilt angles. You et al. [12] estimated the relationship between wide-angle and PTZ cameras using a mosaic of images created by snapshots derived from the slave camera, in order to define a linear interpolation for describing the calibration of the dual surveillance system. Liu et al. [13] presented a calibration approach that interpolates two camera models by matching feature points. Even if many of these methods are accurate enough, they heavily depend on the precision of the spatial mappings based either on 3D or 2D geometry. In the former, target position is based on stereo vision, while in the latter, because of the lack of informations about depth, the more the distance between camera and target grows, the more the system becomes inaccurate. Many of these methods are based on scene features which, by defining a fundamental matrix, allow to move from a wide-angle to PTZ camera [14].

In this work, we propose an automatically geometry-based calibration system (no particular system setup or human intervention is needed) that estimates the 3D world coordinates of a given pixel in the panoramic view by allowing the computation of both the pan and tilt angles of the PTZ camera. The proposed method is based on solving a system of equations that directly relates image pixel coordinates with its corresponding position in the space, via a projection matrix. Then, the intrinsic and extrinsic parameters of each camera need to be determined. For computing the 3D world-coordinates of a chosen pixel on a human head, we first need to fix a Euclidean structure on the image scene, such that the vanishing lines, as well as the related vanishing points can be identified from a single view image. Once the height of the detected human is computed, a 3×3 system of equation is solved to determine the 3D position of the human head. Figure 1(c) shows the final iteration of the calibration module which is followed by the recognition module.

The remainder of the paper is organized as follows. Section 2 introduces the calibration method between wide-angle and PTZ cameras. In Sect. 3, experiments are implemented and the experimental results are shown. Finally, Sect. 4 concludes the paper.

2   Dual Surveillance System Description

The proposed dual surveillance system is based on a wide-angle camera, responsible of pointing to a target on a large panoramic scene, and a PTZ camera focusing at the same position and taking a close-up snapshot of the head of the tracked person. The image coordinate system is the usual xy affine image frame. A point $\mathbf{X}$ with homogeneous coordinates in space is projected to the image point $\mathbf{x}$ using the following 3×4 projection matrix $\mathbf{P}_1$ [15]:

$$\begin{pmatrix} x \\ y \\ 1 \end{pmatrix} = \underbrace{\mathbf{K}_1[\mathbf{R}_1 \, \mathbf{T}_1]}_{:=\mathbf{P}_1} \begin{pmatrix} X \\ Y \\ Z \\ 1 \end{pmatrix}, \tag{1}$$

where $\mathbf{T}_1$ is a 3×1 vector that represents the camera location, $\mathbf{R}_1$ is a 3×3 rotation matrix that represents the orientation of the camera, with respect to an absolute coordinate frame, and $\mathbf{K}_1$ is a 3×3 upper triangular matrix encompassing the parameters of the camera.

Our aim is to compute the height of an object relative to a reference. To this aim we use minimal calibration information as well as a perspective approach for mensuration. The minimal calibration condition is based on the vanishing line of a ground plane, the vertical point and a reference height [16,17]. The vanishing line (or line at infinite) is the line through two or more vanishing points of the plane. A vanishing point is the intersection point of a set of parallel lines in the image plane [18]. If $\mathbf{v}$ is the vanishing point for the vertical direction, $\mathbf{l}$ is the vanishing line of the ground plane, $\mathbf{t}_r$ and $\mathbf{b}_r$ are the top and base point of a reference with height equal to Z_r and $\mathbf{t}_x$ and $\mathbf{b}_x$ are the top and the base point of the tracked human, we compute the height using the following equations:

$$Z_x = -\frac{\|\mathbf{b}_x \times \mathbf{t}_x\|}{\alpha(\mathbf{l}.\mathbf{b}_x)\|\mathbf{v} \times \mathbf{t}_x\|}, \tag{2}$$

with

$$\alpha = -\frac{\|\mathbf{b}_r \times \mathbf{t}_r\|}{Z_r(\mathbf{l}.\mathbf{b}_r)\|\mathbf{v} \times \mathbf{t}_r\|}. \tag{3}$$

It can be noticed that the success of the height computation of the tracked human depends on the accurate estimation of the vertical vanishing point $\mathbf{v}$ and the vanishing line $\mathbf{l}$ of the reference plane.

The final 3D position $\mathbf{X} = (X, Y, Z_x)$ of the main object in the scene is then computed by solving the wide-angle camera system (1) at the pixel point $\mathbf{t}_x$. By including the computed height, Z_x the equation systems (1) is reduced to the 3×3 equation systems

$$\begin{pmatrix} \mathbf{t}_x \\ w \end{pmatrix} = [\mathbf{p}_1 \quad \mathbf{p}_2 \quad Z_x\mathbf{p}_3 + \mathbf{p}_4] \begin{pmatrix} X \\ Y \\ W \end{pmatrix}, \tag{4}$$

with w, W representing the homogenous coordinate of the extended points $\mathbf{t}_x$, (X, Y) in the projective space, and $\mathbf{p}_i$ (i=1,2,3,4) are the column vectors of the projection matrix $\mathbf{P}_1$. From (4) an unique solution is computed. Therefore the final 3D position of the main object in the scene is $\mathbf{X} = (X/W, Y/W, Z_x)$.

Without loss of generality, we start the PTZ camera with pan angle $\theta = 0$ and some tilt angle ϕ. By panning with respect to the $Y-$axis, the point $\mathbf{X}$ changes with respect to the PTZ camera coordinate system by first translating the opposite of the center of projection C and the rotation matrix R:

$$C = \begin{pmatrix} 0 \\ \rho\sin\theta \\ \rho\cos\theta \end{pmatrix}, \quad R = \begin{pmatrix} \cos\phi & 0 & -\sin\phi & 0 \\ 0 & 1 & 0 & 0 \\ \sin\phi & 0 & \cos\phi & 0 \\ 0 & 0 & 0 & 1 \end{pmatrix}, \tag{5}$$

where ρ is the focal length of the PTZ camera. According to (5), the point $\mathbf{X}$, with respect to the PTZ camera, is given by

$$\begin{pmatrix} X_{PTZcam} \\ Y_{PTZcam} \\ Z_{PTZcam} \end{pmatrix} = \begin{pmatrix} X\cos\phi + Z\sin\phi \\ Y + \rho\cos\theta \\ -X\sin\phi + Z\cos\phi - \rho\sin\theta \end{pmatrix}. \tag{6}$$

The final pan and tilt angles for the PTZ camera are

$$\theta = \arccos\left(\frac{Z_{PTZcam}}{\sqrt{X_{PTZcam}^2 + Y_{PTZcam}^2 + Z_{PTZcam}^2}}\right), \quad \phi = \arctan\left(\frac{Y_{PTZcam}}{X_{PTZcam}}\right). \quad (7)$$

3   Experimental Results

In order to validate our dual calibration system, we designed the following experiment: 1) A pixel (x_1, y_1) from the panoramic image using the wide-angle camera is selected; then we compute its corresponding position in the space $\mathbf{X}_1 = (X_1, Y_1, Z_1)$ using the Eqs. (2) and (4). 2) With respect to the PTZ camera we select the same pixel used in the wide-angle view (x_2, y_2) in order to compute the ray $\mathbf{r}$ of projection of (x_2, y_2). $\mathbf{r}$ is determined by the system of equations

$$\begin{pmatrix} x_2 \\ y_2 \\ 1 \end{pmatrix} = \mathbf{P}_2 \begin{pmatrix} X_2 \\ Y_2 \\ Z_2 \\ 1 \end{pmatrix}, \quad (8)$$

with $\mathbf{P}_2$ the projection matrix associated to the PTZ camera. Then, we calculate the distance $d(\mathbf{r}, \mathbf{X}_1)$ between the line $\mathbf{r}$ and the point $\mathbf{X}_1$.

For the initial testing, we validate the interaction between the cameras in our dual surveillance system. For this purpose, we manually selected 60 points on the floor, as shown in Fig. 2(a) (*green* points). The Euclidean structure on the fixed scene is determined by $Z = 0$ millimetres (mm) in the space. The performance of the distance $d(\mathbf{r}, \mathbf{X}_1)$ over all the points in the proposed experiment are measured in millimeters with results visible in terms of the histogram displayed in Fig. 2(b). From the histogram graph, we can appreciate that the biggest and the lowest distance measure 390.1 mm and 58.3 mm, respectively. Comparisons with previous methods based on homography mappings also validate the improvements of our results. Figure 2(c) and (d) display the results according to the works due to Hartley et al. [14] and Liu et a.l [13] respectively. By implementing our model we have 37 points such that the distance measure is between 91.5 and 125.3 mm, while in the Hartley et al. [14] approach there are 31 points with distance measure between 66.2 and 219.7 mm; moreover the biggest distance measure is equal to 1520.4 mm; Liu et al. [13] method presents 12 points with distance measure between 662.3 and 775.7 mm and highest and lowest distance measure equal to 1865.4 mm and 308.5 mm, respectively.

For the next experiment, we validate the complete dual surveillance system by applying the single view metrology techniques in order to compute height of people in the scene and use the information to focus the PTZ camera in the selected pixel over the human head. In this case we have $Z \neq 0$, then we need to compute the heights by implementing Eqs. (2) and (3) using the scene display in Fig. 3(a). The reference height Z_r is taken from the door with pixels $\mathbf{b}_r$ and $\mathbf{t}_r$

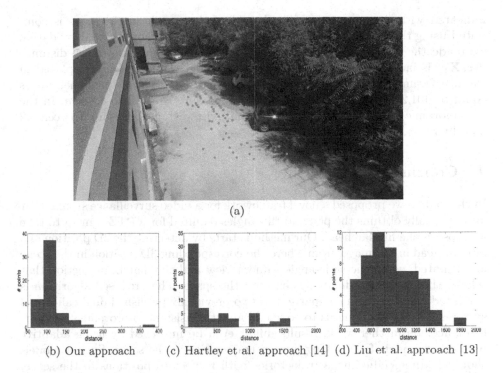

(a)

(b) Our approach   (c) Hartley et al. approach [14]   (d) Liu et al. approach [13]

Fig. 2. Validation of the proposed dual surveillance system calibration. (a) Panoramic view given by the wide angle camera. (b), (c) and (d) show the histograms validating our approach and the models [14] and [13] . In particular, they display the number of points (y axis) lying at several distances (in mm, x axis), according to the manually selected points (*green* dots in (a)) (Color figure online).

Fig. 3. Validation of the complete dual surveillance system calibration. The image on the left shows a panoramic view together with the lines defining the vanishing line (*green* line) and vanishing point (*red* lines intersection) as well as the reference height given by the distance between the two points in *magenta* color. On the right, the histogram shows the performance of the proposed method, when the distance $d(\mathbf{r}, \mathbf{X}_1)$ is calculated with respect to the points selected on the heads of the people in the scene(Color figure online).

indicated with *magenta* color. The height of the people in the scene is computed using the head and foots marked with *cyan* color. For the final validation we made the people fill seven different positions. Computation of the distance $d(\mathbf{r}, \mathbf{X}_1)$ is implemented over the people head and the results are displayed in the histogram (2), where it is appreciable that the biggest distance measure is equal to 401.2 mm and the lowest distance measure is equal to 8.2 mm. In the 32 panoramic view points, we have 16 points with distance measure between 8.2 and 49.5 mm.

4   Conclusion

In this paper, we proposed a novel framework for a video surveillance system that automatically obtains the pan and tilt angles required for a PTZ camera to take a snapshot of a human head. Our method starts by detecting the 2D position of a human head in an image, from where the corresponding 3D position in the scene is estimated, using the wide-angle camera view and the matrix projection that relates the image coordinate system and the space. The proposed algorithm is validated empirically in comparison to two previously published dual calibrated systems [13,14], enabling us to conclude about consistent improvements in performance. As further work, results might even be improved by using adaptive prediction models for tracking human trajectories in the scene. Such a models should learn specific image trajectories with respect to positions in the scene, improving the calibration dual system and therefore the accurate interaction between surveillance cameras.

Acknowledgements. This work is supported by '*FCT - Fundação para a Ciência e Tecnologia*' (Portugal) through the research grant 'SFRH/BD/92520/2013', and the funding from 'FEDER - QREN - Type 4.1 - *Formação Avançada*', co-founded by the European Social Fund and by national funds through Portuguese 'MEC - *Ministério da Educação e Ciência*'. It is also supported by the *IT - Instituto de Telecomunicações* through 'PEst-OE/EEI/LA0008/2013'.

References

1. Valera, M., Valestin, S.A.: Intelligence distributed surveillance systems: a review. IEE Proc. Vis. Image Sig. Proc. **152**(2), 192–204 (2005)
2. Xu, Y., Song, D.: Systems and algorithms for autonomous and scalable crowd surveillance using robotic ptz cameras assisted by a wide-angle camera. Auton. Robots **29**(1), 53–66 (2010)
3. Kannala, J., Brandt, S.S.: A generic camera model and calibration method for conventional wide-angle, and fish-eye lenses. IEEE Trans. Pattern Anal. Mach. Intell. **28**(8), 1335–1340 (2006)
4. Wang, J., Shi, F., Zhang, J., Liu, Y.: A new calibration model of camera lens distortion. Pattern Recogn. **41**(2), 607–615 (2008)
5. Sinha, S.N., Pollefeys, M.: Pan-tilt-zoom camera calibration and high-resolution mosaic generation. Comput. Vis. Image Underst. **103**(3), 170–183 (2006)

6. Wu, Z., Radke, R.J.: Keeping a pan-tilt-zoom camera calibrated. Image Vis. Comput. **35**(8), 1994–2007 (2013)
7. Del Bimbo, A., Dini, F., Lisanti, G., Percini, F.: Exploiting distinctive visual landmark maps in pan-tilt-zoom camera networks. Comput. Vis. Image Underst. **114**(6), 611–623 (2010)
8. Hampapur, A., Pankanti, S., Senior, A., Tian, Y.-L., Brown, L., Bolle, R.: Face cataloger: multi-scale imaging for relating identity to location. In: Proceedings of the IEEE Conference on Advance Video and Signal Based Surveillance, pp. 13–20, Miami, USA (2003)
9. Chen, C.-H., Yao, Y., Page, D., Abidi, B., Koschan, A., Abidi, M.: Heterogeneous fusion of omnidirectional and ptz cameras for multiple object tracking. IEEE Trans. Circuits Syst. Video Technol. **18**(8), 1052–1063 (2008)
10. Senior, A.W., Hampapur, A., Lu, M.: Acquiring multiscale images by pan-titl-zoom control and automatic multicamera calibration. In: Proceedings of the 7th IEEE Workshop on Application ofComputer Vision, vol.1, pp. 433–438, Breckenridge, USA (2005)
11. Zhou, X., Collins, R., Kanade, T., Metes, P.: A master-slave system to acquire biometric imagery of human at distance. In: Proceedings of the 1st ACM International Workshop on Video Surveillance, pp. 113–120, Berkeley, USA (2003)
12. You, L., Li, S., Jia, W.: Automatic weak calibration of master-slave surveillance system based on mosaic images. In: Proceedings of the 20th International Conference on Pattern Recognition, pp. 1824–1827, Istanbul, Turkey (2010)
13. Liu, Y., Lai, S., Zuo, S., Shi, H., Zhang, M.: A master-slave surveillance system to acquire panoramic and multiscale videos. Sci. World J. **2014**, 11 (2014). Article ID 491549
14. Hartley, R., Zisserman, A.: Multiple View Geometry in Computer Vision. Cambridge University Press, New York, USA (2004)
15. Zhang, Z.: A flexible new technique for camera calibration. IEEE Trans. Pattern Anal. Mach. Intell. **22**(11), 1330–1334 (2000)
16. Criminisi, A., Reid, I., Zisserman, A.: Single view metrology. Int. J. Comput. Vision **40**(2), 123–148 (2000)
17. Wang, G., Hu, Z., Wu, F., Tsui, H.-T.: Single view metrology from scene constraints. Image Vis. Comput. **23**(9), 831–840 (2005)
18. Schaffalitzky, F., Zisserman, A.: Planar grouping for automatic detection of vanishing lines and points. Image Vis. Comput. **18**(9), 647–658 (2000)

3D-Guided Multiscale Sliding Window
for Pedestrian Detection

Alejandro González[✉], Gabriel Villalonga, German Ros,
David Vázquez, and Antonio M. López

Computer Vision Center and Universitat Autònoma de Barcelona,
Bellaterra, Barcelona, Spain
{agalzate,gvillalonga,gros,dvazquez,antonio}@cvc.uab.es

Abstract. The most relevant modules of a pedestrian detector are the
candidate generation and the candidate classification. The former aims
at presenting image windows to the latter so that they are classified as
containing a pedestrian or not. Much attention has being paid to the
classification module, while candidate generation has mainly relied on
(multiscale) sliding window pyramid. However, candidate generation is
critical for achieving real-time. In this paper we assume a context of
autonomous driving based on stereo vision. Accordingly, we evaluate the
effect of taking into account the 3D information (derived from the stereo)
in order to prune the hundred of thousands windows per image generated
by classical pyramidal sliding window. For our study we use a multimodal (RGB, disparity) and multi-descriptor (HOG, LBP, HOG+LBP)
holistic ensemble based on linear SVM. Evaluation on data from the
challenging KITTI benchmark suite shows the effectiveness of using 3D
information to dramatically reduce the number of candidate windows,
even improving the overall pedestrian detection accuracy.

1 Introduction

Pedestrian detection is a key technology for many applications related to safety
(e.g., autonomous driving) and security (e.g., video-surveillance). In this paper
we focus on the context of autonomous driving, relying on stereo vision. Thus,
we want to detect pedestrians using 2D image information as well as the 3D
information provided by processing the stereo images, here assuming still images.

The most relevant modules of a *pedestrian detector* are *candidate generation*
and *candidate classification*. The former presents image windows to the latter so
that they are classified as containing a *pedestrian* or *background*. In the pedestrian
detection literature much attention has being paid to the classification module in
terms of image descriptors, classifiers, and models. As a result different concepts
are nowadays of common use. For instance, descriptors such as Haar, EOH,
HOG, and LBP; classifiers such as SVM, AdaBoost, Random Forest , CNNs; and
models such as holistic, deformable part-based, and patch-based ensembles [11].
All these concepts can be applied to different image modalities such as RGB, far
infrared, and 3D-based stereo. For an in deep review the reader can check [6].

© Springer International Publishing Switzerland 2015
R. Paredes et al. (Eds.): IbPRIA 2015, LNCS 9117, pp. 560–568, 2015.
DOI: 10.1007/978-3-319-19390-8_63

In comparison, candidate generation has mainly relied on a dominant approach, namely, the popular (multiscale) sliding window pyramid, which normally generates hundred of thousands candidates (image windows) even for images with VGA resolution. Therefore, candidate generation is critical for achieving real-time, a mandatory requirement to fulfil in driver assistance and autonomous driving. Of course, a faster computation of the particular descriptors is also a proper direction towards real-time (e.g., see [2] for HOG or [3] for Integral Channels). However, each new descriptor will require its own optimization. Therefore, an orthogonal approach (yet complementary) is to design a candidate generation scheme able to generate a relatively small number of candidates, without harming the detection accuracy and even improving such accuracy by directly discarding tricky candidates that may confuse the classifier.

In this line, here we evaluate the effect of taking into account 3D information (derived from stereo) in order to dramatically prune the hundred of thousands windows per image generated by classical sliding window pyramid. We remark that, in our application context, such information is not used in exclusive for pedestrian detection but also for other tasks such as the navigation of an autonomous vehicle [12]. Thus, it does not involves an extra cost. In addition, it allows to have an accurate distance estimation for the detected pedestrians.

For our study we use a multi-modal (RGB, disparity map) and multi-descriptor (HOG, LBP, HOG+LBP) holistic ensemble based on linear SVM. Evaluation on data from the challenging KITTI benchmark suite [5] shows how, in deed, our proposal (based on 3D information) dramatically reduces the number of candidate windows, and even significantly improves the overall detection accuracy.

2   Related Work

Beyond the sliding window pyramid there are other methods for 2D candidate selection [9]. They can provide accurate object detectors depending on the number of classes under consideration and the typical sizes covered. However, these methods tend to be very time consuming since they normally rely on some sort of segmentation or classification procedure (e.g., see the selective search [14] and edge boxes [16], two of the best methods according to [9]). In a way, candidate generation and classification rely on the same kind of information, i.e. visual appearance.

When 3D information is available geometric constraints can be applied [1,7]. In short, pedestrians must be standing at the ground plane. In [7] candidate generation is based on detecting the road plane from the 3D information, and then uniformly distribute candidate windows sitting on the road and projecting them to the image plane (e.g. to the left image of the stereo pair). We call this approach *Linear-To-Road* (LtR) strategy. Moreover, after classifying the candidate windows, for those passing the pedestrian-test, a further post-processing is performer to remove *incoherent* detections. Here, incoherent refers to the fact that the 3D data corresponding to the image pixels contained in a 2D candidate window (considered a *detection*) should be consistent with the 3D window position and that the window content fulfils the pedestrian size constraints. In [1], candidates are generated according to a clustering based on 3D point density. Then, starting from the 2D window corresponding to each 3D cluster, a set of neighbour windows are generated to have 15 windows for each cluster.

In this paper, we investigate LtR strategy and also an alternative called *Linear-to-Image* (LtI). LtI is based on the combination of sliding window pyramid and the effective use of depth. In short, each candidate window is back-projected to 3D and accepted as a candidate if it *hits* the road surface and agrees with pedestrian size. Therefore, we work densely in 2D and more sparsely in 3D, but with respect to [1] we are more robust to 3D clustering errors, and with respect to [7] we avoid the post-processing step for rejecting false positives. Our results, show better performance for LtI with respect to LtR regarding processing time without losing detection accuracy. In addition, both LtR and LtI show better detection accuracy than the sliding window pyramid.

3   Candidate Proposal via Structural Constraints

One of the biggest bottle necks on detection strategies is the generation of a set of candidates to be classified. A classical way is to evaluate all possibilities in an exhaustive fashion (sliding window). However, due to the inefficiency of sliding window, more sophisticated techniques for object proposal have gained popularity. These techniques propose candidates showing certain degree of "objectness", and can be seen as a more basic detection system, using low-level features. Some example of this trend are SelectiveSearch [13] and the work by Gu et al. [8] (see [9] for a complete survey on the topic). However, using candidate proposal based on "objectness" involves an extra level of computation, since a new (soft) classifier needs to be run over the entire image.

As an alternative, we propose to improve candidate generation by using structural information —that anyhow will be available— for the detector, i.e., the image disparity. Since 3D information has to be computed for other tasks involved in autonomous navigation, we can assume that image disparities are available at no extra cost. Then, we can exploit this information to establish constraints on the location of the candidate windows, i.e., pedestrians have to be touching the ground and meet clear size constraints. This process is explained in Sects. 3.1 and 3.2.

3.1   Ground Plane Estimation

The estimation of the ground plane is a fundamental step that allows for fast candidate rejection. The ground plane $\Pi_G = (\mathbf{n}^T, h)^T$ is here defined by its normal vector $\mathbf{n}$ and its height h with respect to the camera center. This magnitudes can be easily computed through the V-disparity map. Given a disparity map $D_{i,j} \in \{0, 255\}^{m \times n}$, its V-disparity V_D is an $m \times n$ matrix representing the normalized distribution of disparities per row. This can be formally expressed as follows:

$$V_D = \begin{bmatrix} H(D_{m,*})/\max(H(D_{m,*})) \\ \vdots \\ H(D_{1,*})/\max(H(D_{1,*})) \end{bmatrix} \in [0,1]^{m \times 256}, \tag{1}$$

where $H(\cdot) : \{0, 255\}^n \to \mathbb{R}^{256}$, is a function computing a histogram and $D_{i,*}$ is a n-vector with the information of the i-th row. From V_D one can estimate $(\mathbf{n}^T, h)^T$ by following Labayrade's proposal [10]. To achieve this, a Hough transform is applied to V_D to estimate the dominant line, $\mathfrak{l}$. Then, the estimation of $(\mathbf{n}^T, h)^T$ is given by

$$\theta = \arctan{(c_v - v_{r_0}/f)} \tag{2}$$

$$h = B\cos{(\theta)}/\bar{\theta} \tag{3}$$

$$\mathbf{n} = [X, Y, Y\cos(\theta)/h\sin(\theta)]^T, \quad \text{for arbitrary X, Y,} \tag{4}$$

assuming that the intrinsic parameters of the camera, c_v (v-coordinate of the principal point), f (camera focal length) and the baseline B of the stereo rig are known; and that $\bar{\theta}$ is the slope of $\mathfrak{l}$ and v_{r_0} is the row for which $\mathfrak{l}$ has zero disparity in V_D.

3.2 Fast Candidate Rejection

As mentioned before, it is critical to reduce the number of candidates for classification, in order to achieve real-time capabilities. Here we propose two alternative strategies that make use of the plane Π_C to reject unlikely candidates.

Linear-to-Road Strategy. The *Linear-to-Road* (LtR) policy, consists of positioning candidate windows directly in the 3D scene. To this end, we establish

Fig. 1. Example of candidate generation for *Linear-to-Road* (top) and *Linear-to-Image* (bottom). Notice how in the case of the Linear-to-Road strategy, windows are uniformly distributed in 3D, while for Linear-to-Image candidates are not uniformly distributed due to perspective distortion.

a practical operation range for $X = \pm 20$ meters, $Y = -h$ meters (i.e., on the ground) and $Z = 1, \ldots, 50$ meters with an increment of 3.5 meters. At each specific location $(X, -h, Z)$, we set three candidate windows with respective heights of 1.50, 1.75 and 2.00 meters (see Fig. 1-Top). These parameters give us an effective and practical coverage of the scene, while still producing good results as show in Sect. 5. However, it is possible to increase the efficiency of the LtR candidate search at the cost of a minimal accuracy loss, by using a second strategy called Linear-to-Image (LtI).

Linear-to-Image Strategy. This second strategy is based on the combination of a classical sliding window pyramid (SWP) and the effective use of depth to generate candidates at multiple scales. First, SWP generates a large amount of candidates across all the scales. Each candidate is back-projected to 3D by using the available disparity information and the known calibration parameters. However, this step requires special care due to the presence of noise on the stereo data. In order to be robust to noise we select N_p random points $\{(u, v)^{(i)}\}_{i=1}^{N_p}$ within the given bounding box. The depth of each point $(u, v)^{(i)}$ is independently computed as $Z_i = Bd_i/f$, where $d_i = D_{v,u}$ is the disparity of that point. Then, each of the depths $\{Z_i\}_{i=1}^{N_p}$ is used to back-project the four corners defining the bounding box $\{(u', v')^{(t,l)}, (u', v')^{(t,r)}, (u', v')^{(b,l)}, (u', v')^{(b,r)}\}$, as follows

$$Y_i^{(j)} = Z_i(v'^{(j)} + c_v)/f \tag{5}$$
$$X_i^{(j)} = Z_i(u'^{(j)} + c_u)/f, \quad \text{for } j = (t,l),\ (t,r),\ (b,l),\ (b,r).$$

Then, for each of the N_p hypotheses we check if the bottom of the back-projected bounding box is touching the ground, i.e., $\frac{1}{2}(|Y_i^{(b,l)}| + |Y_i^{(b,r)}|) < \epsilon$; otherwise, the candidate is rejected. If the size of the bounding box exceeds a given maximum size, i.e., $||Y_i^{(t,l)} - Y_i^{(b,r)}||_{\ell_2} > \max_S$ the candidate is also reject. These two criteria are able to reduce the amount of candidates dramatically, while maintaining a good recall and being highly efficient (see Fig. 1-Bottom).

4   Ensemble of Multi-modal Features

The proposed classification stage is inspired on one of the most accepted pipelines of the literature [15], i.e., a holistic detector based on the combination of HOG and LBP as input features and linear SVM as the learning method. Such an approach has shown to be both efficient and accurate, and it is the starting point for more modern and sophisticated detectors [4].

Here, we propose to boost the accuracy of this basic classifier by performing an ensemble over multiple image modalities, which in our case are the standard RGB space and the space of disparities. The idea is as follows. We consider the candidates proposed by one of the strategies introduced in Sect. 3.2. These candidates guide the process of features extraction for HOG and LBP on both modalities, originating four different set of features. Such features are just extracted there where candidates are present, avoiding to perform dense feature extraction. This process can be run in parallel —since the image modalities and the features are assumed to be independent— speeding up the process four times.

Then, for each type of feature (i.e., HOG, LBP and HOG-LBP) and a given modality (i.e., RGB and Disparity), a linear SVM, $\mathcal{W}_{\text{feat}}^{\text{mod}}$, is trained. During testing time, the ensemble is performed by applying all the classifiers to a given sample S_i and then combining their outputs via the direct application of the max function,

$$\max(\mathcal{W}_{\text{HOG}}^{\text{RGB}}S_i, \mathcal{W}_{\text{LBP}}^{\text{RGB}}S_i, \mathcal{W}_{\text{HOG-LBP}}^{\text{RGB}}S_i, \mathcal{W}_{HOG}^{\text{Disp}}S_i, \mathcal{W}_{LBP}^{\text{Disp}}S_i, \mathcal{W}_{\text{HOG-LBP}}^{\text{Disp}}S_i). \quad (6)$$

We would like to highlight that, this simple way of performing the ensemble on the raw output of linear SVMs, although rough at first sight fulfil all our goals. It is very fast and turns out to increase the final accuracy as we will show in next section.

5   Experimental Evaluation

In this section we assess the benefits of the proposed approach, analysing the impact that each of the ingredients has in both, the accuracy and the computational performance of the final detector. For comparison, we have chosen a consolidated baseline consisting in HOG-LBP linear-SVM [15] in combination with a spatial window pyramid, which is one of the most popular techniques for holistic pedestrian detection. To this purpose we make use of the object detection dataset of the challenging KITTI benchmark suite [5], using 3738 samples for training and 3740 for testing through all our experiments.

5.1   Candidate Proposal Assessment

For evaluating the different candidate proposal techniques we have considered a metric based on the number of false positives per image (FPPI) and the miss rate of the final detector. For ease of comparison we run all the techniques, i.e., *Linear-to-Road* (LtR), *Linear-to-Image* (LtI) and the classic sliding sindow pyramid, for training detectors on just the RGB data modality and HOG features, using a linear-SVM. We also evaluate the number of candidates generated by each method in order to have a clear indicator of the computational efficiency of the resulting detector. This comparison is shown in Fig. 2.

Notice that both proposed strategies, LtR and LtI, reduce the miss rate of the final detector in more than 7 points when compared against the standard SWP. For this experiment SWP has been set up to use 6 scales with factors $f_s = \{1, 1.14, 2, 2.8, 4, 5.6\}$, generating 673×10^3 candidates (on average). LtR can drastically reduce this number to an average of 246×10^3 candidates (36 % of candidates w.r.t. SWP) to produce the most accurate results. However, it seems very convenient to select the LtI strategy instead, since for the price of a small sacrifice in accuracy (less than one point) we just need to examine 75×10^3 windows on average (11 % of candidates w.r.t. SWP).

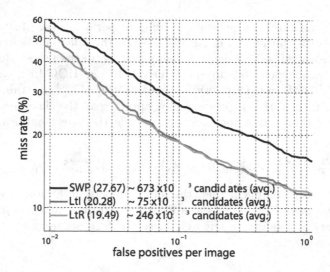

Fig. 2. Comparison of candidate proposal strategies: *Linear-to-Road* (LtR), *Linear-to-Image* (LtI) and the classic sliding window pyramid (SWP), with respect to the number of false positives per image (FPPI) and the detection miss rate, for a HOG linear-SVM detector applied on the RGB modality of the KITTI benchmark suite.

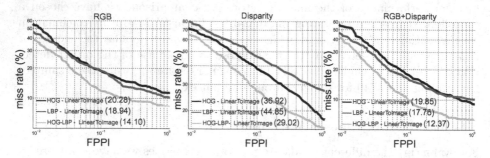

Fig. 3. Feature comparison (HOG, LBP and HOG-LBP) at the level of FPPI and miss rate for three image modalities: RGB (left), Disparity (middle) and RGB-Disparity (right).

5.2 Features Assessment

Our second experiment measures how the use of different types of features and image modalities affects detection accuracy. In this case all the candidates are generated by following the *Linear-to-Image* strategy. Figure 3 shows detection results with respect to FPPI and miss rate for the different modalities (RGB, Disparity and RGB+Disparity). As one can observe, the ensemble of HOG-LBP features over multiple modalities (**12.37 %** of miss rate) leads to better results than using single modalities. This represents an improvement of almost 2 points with respect to the baseline (HOG-LBP linear-SVM on RGB), which obtained a miss rate of 14.10 %.

6   Conclusion

We have presented an approach that exploits 3D structure to dramatically reduce the number of candidate windows for pedestrian detection, making use of the *Linear-to-Image* strategy. Furthermore, 3D structure also served to improve the overall pedestrian detection accuracy. This is due to the LtI strategy itself, as it discards tricky samples, but also due to a proposed multi-modal (RGB, disparity) and multi-descriptor (HOG, LBP, HOG+LBP) holistic ensemble based on linear SVM. We showed the superiority of our technique by comparing it against one of the most accepted baselines, i.e., the HOG-LBP SVM detector, in the challenging KITTI benchmark suite.

Acknowledgments. This work is supported by the Spanish MICINN projects TRA2011-29454-C03-01 and TIN2011-29494-C03-02.

References

1. Alonso, I.P., Llorca, D.F., Sotelo, M.A., Bergasa, L.M., de Toro, P.R., Nuevo, J., Ocana, M., Garrido, M.A.: Combination of feature extraction methods for svm pedestrian detection. Trans. Intell. Transport. Sys. **8**(2), 292–307 (2007)
2. Benenson, R., Mathias, M., Timofte, R., Van Gool, L.: Pedestrian detection at 100 frames per second. In: Proceedings of the IEEE Conference on Computer Vision and Pattern Recognition, Providence, RI, USA (2012)
3. Dollár, P., Tu, Z., Perona, P., Belongie, S.: Integral channel features. In: Proceedings of the British Machine Vision Conference, London, UK (2009)
4. Felzenszwalb, P., Girshick, R., McAllester, D., Ramanan, D.: Object detection with discriminatively trained part based models. IEEE Trans. Pattern Anal. Mach. Intell. **32**(9), 1627–1645 (2010)
5. Geiger, A., Lenz, P., Urtasun, R.: Are we ready for autonomous driving? the kitti vision benchmark suite. In: CVPR 2012 (2012)
6. Gerónimo, D., López, A.: Vision-based Pedestrian Protection Systems for Intelligent Vehicles. Springer Briefs in Computer Science. Springer, New York (2013)
7. Gerónimo, D., Sappa, A., Ponsa, D., López, A.: 2D–3D based on-board pedestrian detection system. J. Comput. Vis. Image Underst. **114**(5), 583–595 (2010)
8. Gu, C., Lim, J.J., Arbelez, P., Malik, J.: Recognition using regions. In: Proceedings of the IEEE Conference on Computer Vision and Pattern Recognition (2009)
9. Hosang, J., Benenson, R., Schiele, B.: How good are detection proposals, really? In: Proceedings of the British Machine Vision Conference (2014)
10. Labayrade, R., Aubert, D., Tarel, J.P.: Real time obstacle detection in stereovision on non flat road geometry through "v-disparity" representation. In: IEEE Intelligent Vehicle Symposium (2002)
11. Marin, J., Vázquez, D., López, A., Amores, J., Leibe, B.: Random forests of local experts for pedestrian detection. In: Proceedings of the IEEE International Conference on Computer Vision (2013)
12. Ros, G., Ramos, S., Granados, M., Bakhtiary, A., Vazquez, D., Lopez, A.: Vision-based offline-online paradigm for autonomous driving. In: Winter Conference on Applications of Computer Vision (WACV) (2015)

13. Uijlings, J.R.R., van de Sande, K.E.A., Gevers, T., Smeulders, A.W.M.: Selective search for object recognition. Int. J. Comput. Vision **104**(2), 154–171 (2013)
14. van de Sande, K.E.A., Uijlings, J.R.R., Gevers, T., Smeulders, A.W.M.: Segmentation as selective search for object recognition. In: Proceedings of the IEEE International Conference on Computer Vision (2011)
15. Wang, X., Han, T.X., Yan, S.: An HOG-LBP human detector with partial occlusion handling. In: Proceedings of the IEEE International Conference on Computer Vision, Kyoto, Japan (2009)
16. Zitnick, C.L., Dollár, P.: Edge boxes: locating object proposals from edges. In: Fleet, D., Pajdla, T., Schiele, B., Tuytelaars, T. (eds.) ECCV 2014, Part V. LNCS, vol. 8693, pp. 391–405. Springer, Heidelberg (2014)

A Feature-Based Gaze Estimation Algorithm for Natural Light Scenarios

Onur Ferhat[1,2]([⊠]), Arcadi Llanza[1,2], and Fernando Vilariño[1,2]

[1] Universitat Autònoma de Barcelona, Bellaterra, Spain
oferhat@cvc.uab.es
http://mv.cvc.uab.es/projects/eye-tracker
[2] Computer Vision Center, Bellaterra, Spain

Abstract. We present an eye tracking system that works with regular webcams. We base our work on open source CVC Eye Tracker [7] and we propose a number of improvements and a novel gaze estimation method. The new method uses features extracted from iris segmentation and it does not fall into the traditional categorization of appearance–based/model–based methods. Our experiments show that our approach reduces the gaze estimation errors by 34 % in the horizontal direction and by 12 % in the vertical direction compared to the baseline system.

Keywords: Eye tracking · Gaze estimation · Natural light · Webcam

1 Introduction

Gaze estimation is the task of guessing where a person is looking at, outputting either the position of the gaze point on a 2D/3D surface (e.g. pixel coordinates on a display) or just the gaze angle as a vector. The systems with gaze estimation capability are called eye trackers and are used in a variety of scenarios such as visual behavior assessment, marketing and human-computer interaction (HCI) [6].

Traditionally, eye trackers have been expensive and thus, not accesible to the common users. However, over the last years several affordable commercial models have been introduced in the market [1,2]. The most common gaze estimation technique in eye trackers is the use of infrared (IR) light sources and IR cameras to assess the 3D pose of the eyeballs, making use of the light sources' reflections on the cornea as cues. However, the alternative of using natural light also received attention as it requires a simpler hardware setup and it provides a larger scalability to laptops and mobile devices.

Natural light techniques, in turn, can be grouped in two: model–based techniques and appearance–based techniques [9]. Model–based techniques try to fit a geometric model to the subject's face or eyes, in order to calculate the gaze geometrically. In the simpler case, the iris boundary is modeled as a circle in 3D and its normal vector is taken as the gaze vector [19,20]. Other methods try to model the entire face, by either using a fixed 3D face model [4], or by using a model that adapts to subject's face [5,11,22].

© Springer International Publishing Switzerland 2015
R. Paredes et al. (Eds.): IbPRIA 2015, LNCS 9117, pp. 569–576, 2015.
DOI: 10.1007/978-3-319-19390-8_64

Appearance–based methods try to calculate the gaze by mapping the eye appearance (i.e. image pixels corresponding to eye area) directly to the gaze estimations. Neural networks [3,10,21] and Gaussian Process (GP) interpolators [8,15] are two of the most popular mapping algorithms used. Adaptive linear regression (ALR) is another alternative used for this step [13]. The main weakness of appearance–based methods occurs when head movement is involved, since these techniques cannot combine head pose information with the appearance in a robust way. Some works tried to tackle this problem by clustering the training samples according to head pose [16], or by applying a geometric transformation to the eye region in the image [17]. Adding another step of calibrating for different head poses is yet another proposed line of work [12].

Our work relies on the open source CVC Eye Tracker [7], which in turn is derived from Opengazer [23]. The structure of proposed system, and its comparison to the base system can be observed in Fig. 1. The base system works by initializing facial feature points, tracking them over time and training a GP interpolator with grayscale eye images as the input. We start our contributions by introducing a totally automatized initialization technique, and a novel method to stabilize the tracking of points. Finally, we apply iris segmentation and convert the segmentation results to histogram features that feed the GP.

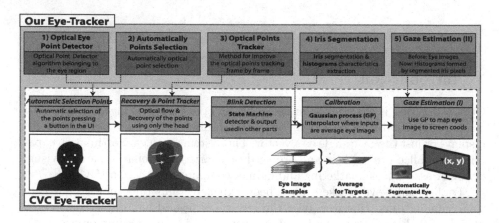

Fig. 1. Structure of the proposed system and its comparison to the base system. The top row of modules denote our contributions, and the arrowheads specify in which step they are connected to the base pipeline.

In the rest of the paper, we detail our methods and provide qualitative results for the performance of the newly designed eye tracker. We also explain a functional prototype for an interaction that makes use of the eye tracker. We finish by drawing our conclusions and pointing some directions in which this work may be extended in the future.

2 Methodology

2.1 Eye Corner Detection and Iris Segmentation

The first module is the eye corner detector, which allows make a good initialization of these anchor points. Next, we add iris segmentation functionality to this module and use it in each frame to extract our histogram features as explained later.

As the first step, we detect the subject's face using a Viola–Jones detector [14,18] (larger rectangle in Fig. 2), and then we use another detector to search for the region containing the two eyes inside the face detection rectangle (smaller rectangle around eyes in Fig. 2).

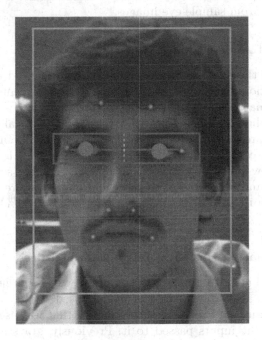

Fig. 2. Outer eye corner detection algorithm steps. Outer rectangle shows the face detection, whereas the inner rectangle is the detection for eye region. The two filled circles inside the eyes mark the iris detections and the line passing through iris centers is shown in green. Outer eye corners (yellow dots) are selected on this line (Color figure online).

After the region containing both eyes is detected, we divide it into two horizontally and search for the centers of the left and the right iris. For each side, we apply an iris template detector to calculate the likelihoods for iris center location. As we expect to find the iris mostly around the center, we multiply the detection likelihoods with a Gaussian centered at the midpoint of the rectangle.

We repeat the search with templates of different sizes (radius between 15–25 pixels), and combine their results; prioritizing bigger templates so that the system does not fall into the trap of choosing a small square inside the iris as the detection. For prioritization, detection likelihoods for different disk sizes are multiplied by the disk areas.

When there are prominent shadows near the nose, this system may output a detection inside this shadow. In order to avoid it, we apply an ellipsoidal mask around the eye in order not to consider this area for the detection.

After we have the final estimations for the iris locations, we choose the outer eye corners on the line that passes through the centers of iris detections, at a fixed distance proportional to the distance between iris centers.

Finally, we focus on the part of the eye that has given us the best likelihood for the iris and perform the segmentation process (Fig. 3). To segment the iris area, we use the grayscale eye image and apply binarization based on a threshold chosen empirically from sample eye images.

2.2 Tracking of Anchor Points

Once we initialize the facial feature points with the method explained above, these points' positions must be kept stable across subsequent video frames so that the gaze estimation components work better.

In the base application, the points are tracked using optical flow between the video frames. We propose an additional layer of processing, and extract square eye corner templates when these points are initialized. In later frames, after calculating the new point positions using optical flow, we search around the eye corner points and apply template matching using the previously extracted templates. If there is a good match (with *likelihood* > 60 %), we update the point positions.

2.3 Gaze Estimation Based on Histogram Features

We propose a novel algorithm for gaze estimation, which can neither be categorized as completely appearance based or model based.

We keep the Gaussian Process (GP) estimator that was used in the original work, but replace the inputs passed to it. Previously, grayscale images of the eyes were used directly as 64×32 dimensional features. In our application, after we segment the iris area; we project the segmented pixel positions to the vertical axis and the horizontal axis, to come up with features that are detached from the pixel intensities (appearances).

To generate these histograms, we take the iris segmentation as seen in Fig. 3, and then we calculate histogram features where each histogram bin accumulates the number of segmented pixels corresponding to that row (for the vertical histogram) or column (for the horizontal histogram) of the image. Considering that the eye image is 128×64 pixels in size, the vertical and horizontal histograms have 64 and 128 dimensions, consecutively. These histograms are then joined together to have the 192-dimensional input.

After obtaining average histogram features for each calibration target on the display, we train the GP estimator with these as inputs. This component needs

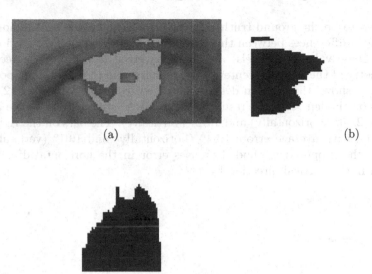

Fig. 3. (a) Iris segmentation (b) Vertical histogram features calculated by projecting iris pixels to vertical axis (c) Horizontal histogram features

a kernel function to evaluate the similarity between two inputs, for which we use the standard squared exponential kernel which is calculated as:

$$K_{SE}(x, x') = \sigma^2 exp(-\frac{(x - x')^2}{2lscale^2})$$ (1)

Here, x and x' are the feature histograms to compare, and the squared difference $((x - x')^2)$ is calculated as the sum of the squared differences between the two histogram bins. The kernel parameters are set to $lscale = 125$ and $\sigma = 80$ after a numerical analysis of its effects on a cross validation set.

3   Results

In order to test the effects of our contributions on the eye-tracker performance, we designed an experimental setup and recorded 12 videos from 6 subjects. Next, we evaluated the performance of the baseline system and our approach, calculating the errors for each video and for two versions of the system.

The experiments were carried out on a laptop computer with a 13" monitor. The subjects were asked to sit $60\,cm$ away from the monitor, facing its center point. In each session, first the subject went through the process of eye tracker calibration, which consisted of following a target point as it moved to 15 different positions on the monitor. These 15 positions cover the whole monitor area in a 3×5 grid structure. After the system was calibrated, the same process was repeated to gather the data for testing. For each subject, these steps were repeated twice and in total 12 videos were recorded. The target point position is assumed to be the ground truth and the error is calculated as the horizontal and vertical differences between the ground truth and the gaze estimation coordinates. These values (in pixels) are then converted to errors in degrees using the geometry of the face, the center of the monitor and the two points' positions.

Figure 4 shows the error in degrees obtained from the dataset of 12 videos. The bars on the left show the results for the base system [7], where the average errors are 2.35° (horizontally) and 1.82° (vertically). The bars on the right show our results, with average errors 1.54° (horizontally) and 1.61° (vertically). As observed, the proposed method decreases error in the horizontal direction by 34 % and in the vertical direction by 12 %.

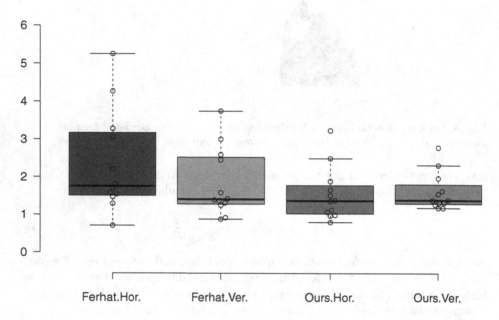

Fig. 4. Horizontal and vertical errors in degrees for the baseline system and our system. Center lines show the medians; box limits indicate the 25th and 75th percentiles, whiskers extend 1.5 times the interquartile range from the 25th and 75th percentiles; data points are plotted as open circles.

To convert these numbers into pixel units and assess the significance on a monitor of 1280 × 800 resolution, the errors in degrees can be multiplied by a conversion factor of $47 \frac{pixels}{degrees}$.

These results are comparable those of other works referenced in the Introduction, which vary between 1–5°.

4   Conclusion

In this work, we proposed a novel algorithm for gaze estimation, which brings together the advantages of appearance based and model based estimation algorithms to create a hybrid approach. As in appearance based techniques, our algorithm is as direct as possible, neither requiring personalized 2D/3D models nor using too much computational power. It eliminates the effects of change in appearance (lighting conditions, small instabilities, etc.) just like model based algorithms, and the features it extracts can be invariant to small changes in head pose without much effort. Therefore it will be possible to incorporate head pose correction algorithms as a future work. Traditionally, this has been the main problem with appearance based models (neural networks, etc.) and we believe our approach is the first step towards solving it. Our final results show significant improvement compared to previously used appearance based estimation method.

The rest of the described work has the aim of making the eye tracker easier to use and more robust. We believe these features will be the deciding factor for the application to be used outside research laboratories and to be included in real life scenarios.

Acknowledgements. This work was supported in part by Universitat Autònoma de Barcelona PIF grants and Google Research Awards.

References

1. NUIA eyeCharm (2014). https://www.kickstarter.com/projects/4tiitoo/nuia-eyecharm-kinect-to-eye-tracking
2. The Eye Tribe (2014). http://theeyetribe.com/
3. Baluja, S., Pomerleau, D.: Non-intrusive gaze tracking using artificial neural networks. In: Cowan, J.D., Tesauro, G., Alspector, J. (eds.) NIPS, pp. 753–760. Morgan Kaufmann (1993)
4. Chen, J., Ji, Q.: 3D gaze estimation with a single camera without IR illumination. In: ICPR, pp. 1–4. IEEE (2008)
5. Cootes, T.F., Edwards, G.J., Taylor, C.J.: Active appearance models. IEEE Trans. Pattern Anal. Mach. Intell. **23**(6), 681–685 (2001)
6. Duchowski, A.T.: Eye Tracking Methodology - Theory And Practice. Springer, London (2003)
7. Ferhat, O., Vilariño, F., Sánchez, F.J.: A cheap portable eye-tracker solution for common setups. J. Eye Mov. Res. **7**(3), 1–10 (2014)
8. Hansen, D.W., Hansen, J.P., Nielsen, M., Johansen, A.S., Stegmann, M.B.: Eye typing using Markov and active appearance models. In: WACV, pp. 132–136. IEEE Computer Society (2002)
9. Hansen, D.W., Ji, Q.: In the eye of the beholder: a survey of models for eyes and gaze. IEEE Trans. Pattern Anal. Mach. Intell. **32**(3), 478–500 (2010)
10. Holland, C., Komogortsev, O.V.: Eye tracking on unmodified common tablets: challenges and solutions. In: Morimoto, C.H., Istance, H.O., Spencer, S.N., Mulligan, J.B., Qvarfordt, P. (eds.) ETRA, pp. 277–280. ACM, New York (2012)
11. Ishikawa, T., Baker, S., Matthews, I., Kanade, T.: Passive driver gaze tracking with active appearance models. In: Proceedings of the 11th World Congress on Intelligent Transportation Systems, vol. 3 (2004)

12. Lu, F., Okabe, T., Sugano, Y., Sato, Y.: A head pose-free approach for appearance-based gaze estimation. In: Proceedings of the British Machine Vision Conference, pp. 126.1–126.11. BMVA Press (2011). doi:10.5244/C.25.126

13. Lu, F., Sugano, Y., Okabe, T., Sato, Y.: Inferring human gaze from appearance via adaptive linear regression. In: Metaxas, D.N., Quan, L., Sanfeliu, A., Gool, L.J.V. (eds.) ICCV, pp. 153–160. IEEE (2011)

14. Santana, M.C., Dniz-Surez, O., Hernndez-Sosa, D., Lorenzo, J.: A comparison of face and facial feature detectors based on the viola-jones general object detection framework. Mach. Vis. Appl. **22**(3), 481–494 (2011)

15. Sugano, Y., Matsushita, Y., Sato, Y.: Appearance-based gaze estimation using visual saliency. IEEE Trans. Pattern Anal. Mach. Intell. **35**(2), 329–341 (2013)

16. Sugano, Y., Matsushita, Y., Sato, Y., Koike, H.: An incremental learning method for unconstrained gaze estimation. In: Forsyth, D., Torr, P., Zisserman, A. (eds.) ECCV 2008, Part III. LNCS, vol. 5304, pp. 656–667. Springer, Heidelberg (2008)

17. Valenti, R., Sebe, N., Gevers, T.: Combining head pose and eye location information for gaze estimation. IEEE Trans. Image Process. **21**(2), 802–815 (2012)

18. Viola, P., Jones, M.: Rapid object detection using a boosted cascade of simple features. In: Proceedings of the IEEE Conference on Computer Vision and Pattern Recognition. Hawaii (2001)

19. Wang, J.G., Sung, E.: Gaze determination via images of irises. In: Mirmehdi, M., Thomas, B.T. (eds.) BMVC: British Machine Vision Association (2000)

20. Wu, H., Chen, Q., Wada, T.: Conic-based algorithm for visual line estimation from one image. In: FGR, pp. 260–265. IEEE Computer Society (2004)

21. Xu, L.Q., Machin, D., Sheppard, P.: A novel approach to real-time non-intrusive gaze finding. In: Carter, J.N., Nixon, M.S. (eds.) BMVC: British Machine Vision Association (1998)

22. Yamazoe, H., Utsumi, A., Yonezawa, T., Abe, S.: Remote gaze estimation with a single camera based on facial-feature tracking without special calibration actions. In: ETRA, pp. 245–250. ACM (2008)

23. Zielinski, P.: Opengazer: open-source gaze tracker for ordinary webcams (software) (2013). http://www.inference.phy.cam.ac.uk/opengazer/

Image and Signal Processing

Fast Simple Linear Iterative Clustering by Early Candidate Cluster Elimination

Kang-Sun Choi$^{(\boxtimes)}$ and Ki-Won Oh

KOREATECH, Cheonan, Chungnam 330-708, Republic of Korea
ks.choi@koreatech.ac.kr
http://cv3vpl.koreatech.ac.kr

Abstract. For superpixel segmentation, simple linear iterative clustering (SLIC) has attracted much attention due to its outstanding performance in terms of speed and accuracy. However, computational-efficiency challenge still remains for applying it to real-time applications. In this paper, by applying the Cauchy-Schwarz inequality, we derive a simple condition to get rid of unnecessary operations from the cluster inspection procedure. Candidate clusters can be early eliminated without cluster inspection requiring high computation. In the experimental results, it is confirmed that the proposed superpixel segmentation algorithm improves efficiency of SLIC by 21 % on average without any degradation in segmentation performance.

Keywords: Superpixels · Segmentation · Clustering · Fast implementation

1 Introduction

The superpixel concept was originally presented by Ren and Malik [1] as defining perceptually homogeneous regions using the normalized cuts (NCuts) algorithm. Although superpixel segmentation yields over-segmented results rather than image object segments, it reduces the number of image primitives effectively and the efficiency of subsequent processing steps can increase drastically.

In addition, since superpixel segmentation provides a more natural and perceptually meaningful representation of the input image, it is more convenient and effective to extract the region-based visual features using superpixels [2]. This is why superpixel segmentation is widely used as a preprocessing step for various computer vision applications such as foreground object detection [3], segmentation, motion segmentation [4], object recognition [5], and saliency object detection [2].

Among the various superpixel segmentation algorithms, SLIC, proposed by Achanta et al., has attracted great attention. As summarized in the literature [3], SLIC outperforms the other algorithms in several desirable properties for superpixel segmentation; SLIC is capable of fast creating compact and uniform superpixels, offers an explicit control over the amount of superpixels and their compactness, and is accurate in aligning superpixels well with object boundaries.

© Springer International Publishing Switzerland 2015
R. Paredes et al. (Eds.): IbPRIA 2015, LNCS 9117, pp. 579–586, 2015.
DOI: 10.1007/978-3-319-19390-8_65

Although SLIC is an iterative algorithm based on k-means clustering, a high speed-up is achieved in a way that the best cluster for each pixel is chosen among only a few spatially neighboring clusters rather than all clusters as in k-means clustering. Nevertheless, computational challenges still remain for real-time computer vision applications, since superpixel segmentation is usually used as a preprocessing step in the applications.

Kim et al. attempted to improve segmentation accuracy with respect to boundary adherence by updating cluster representatives with only the pixels having similar luminance [6]. In [7], a GPU-based parallel implementation of SLIC was presented to speed up its execution time. In [8], Borovec and Kybic presented an implementation of SLIC where repetitive distance calculation is simplified by using pre-computed Look-Up Tables (LUTs). However, LUTs usually increase huge amount of memory usage.

In this paper, the speed of the tedious cluster search process of SLIC is improved by removing unnecessary calculation. To do this, we derive a robust inequality condition by applying the Cauchy-Schwarz inequality similarly as in [9], which involves simpler operations than actual cluster inspection. By employing the inequality condition adaptively according to characteristics of SLIC, candidate clusters are inspected with simple operations and a respectable number of them is early eliminated without additional operations. As a result, this acceleration approach reduces the computational complexity of the cluster search without compromising segmentation accuracy.

The paper is organized as follows: In the following section, we review the conventional SLIC algorithm. In Sect. 3, both the proposed acceleration approaches are explicated in detail. Performance evaluation and comparison of the proposed algorithms is presented in Sect. 4. Finally, conclusion is given in Sect. 4.

2   Simple Linear Iterative Clustering

Before describing the proposed acceleration algorithms in detail, we review the conventional SLIC algorithm [3] after defining some notations.

A pixel i in an input image $\mathbf{I}$ of size $L \times M = N$ is represented as a feature vector of its color in the CIELAB color space and position, $\mathbf{f}_i = [l_i, a_i, b_i, x_i, y_i]^T$. Similarly, a cluster center C_k is represented with mean color and center of mass of the cluster, $\mathbf{f}_{C_k} = [l_{C_k}, a_{C_k}, b_{C_k}, x_{C_k}, y_{C_k}]^T$. In SLIC, cluster centers are initially sampled from $\mathbf{I}$ and S-pixel apart from each other.

Let $\mathcal{D}(i, C_k)$ denote a distance metric between i and C_k, which is defined as

$$\mathcal{D}(i, C_k) = \sqrt{\mathcal{D}_c(i, C_k)^2 + \lambda^2 \cdot \mathcal{D}_s(i, C_k)^2}, \tag{1}$$

where $\lambda = r/S$ and r represents a regularization factor controlling compactness. In [3], the default value of 10 was used for r.

$$\mathcal{D}_c(i, C_k) = \sqrt{(l_i - l_{C_k})^2 + (a_i - a_{C_k})^2 + (b_i - b_{C_k})^2} \tag{2}$$

$$\mathcal{D}_s(i, C_k) = \sqrt{(x_i - x_{C_k})^2 + (y_i - y_{C_k})^2} \tag{3}$$

indicate Euclidean distances in color and spatial domains, respectively.

The distance metric in (1) can be also expressed in vector form. A weighted L^2-norm of a vector $\mathbf{f}$ on $\mathbb{C}^p$ can be written as

$$\|\mathbf{f}\|_{\mathbf{W}} \triangleq \|\mathbf{W}\mathbf{f}\| = \left(\sum_i^p |w_{ii} f_i|^2 \right)^{\frac{1}{2}}, \tag{4}$$

where $\mathbf{W}$ is a diagonal matrix in which the ith diagonal entry is the weight $w_{ii} \neq 0$.

Given $\mathbf{W} = \operatorname{diag}(1, 1, 1, \lambda, \lambda)$, the weighted L^2-norm of the feature vector representation of the original pixel i, $\mathbf{f}_i = [l_i, a_i, b_i, x_i, y_i]^T$, is obtained by

$$\|\mathbf{f}_i\|_{\mathbf{W}} = \sqrt{l_i^2 + a_i^2 + b_i^2 + \lambda^2(x_i^2 + y_i^2)}. \tag{5}$$

In the same way, the weighted L^2-norm of the cluster center C_k is expressed as

$$\|\mathbf{f}_{C_k}\|_{\mathbf{W}} = \sqrt{l_{C_k}^2 + a_{C_k}^2 + b_{C_k}^2 + \lambda^2(x_{C_k}^2 + y_{C_k}^2)}. \tag{6}$$

Therefore, the vector form of the distance metric can be expressed as

$$\mathcal{D}(i, C_k) = \|\mathbf{f}_i\|_{\mathbf{W}}^2 + \|\mathbf{f}_{C_k}\|_{\mathbf{W}}^2 - 2\mathbf{f}_i^T \mathbf{W}^T \mathbf{W} \mathbf{f}_{C_k}, \tag{7}$$

which will be used later in deriving the second acceleration approach with concise representation.

The procedure of the conventional SLIC algorithm is described below. SLIC consists of three steps; initialization, cluster assignment, and update.

For color images in the CIELAB color space, K cluster centers are initially sampled on $\mathcal{L}_S$. To prevent the initial cluster centers from being located on object boundaries, the initial cluster centers are re-located to the lowest gradient position within their 3×3 neighborhood.

In the cluster assignment step, each pixel i is associated with the nearest cluster center in terms of (1) by inspecting neighboring cluster centers whose search regions overlap the position of i. Here, the cluster inspection includes distance calculation in (1) and comparison. In [3], the size of the search region is set to $2S \times 2S$ around the cluster center. Let $\mathfrak{C}_i$, $R(i)$, and $\mathfrak{R}_{C_k}$, respectively, denote a set of cluster centers whose search regions contain i, a label associated with i, and a superpixel corresponding to C_k, i.e. $\{i | R(i) = C_k\}$.

In the update step, each $\mathbf{f}_{C_k}$ is updated in accordance with $\mathfrak{R}_{C_k}$ that is determined in the cluster assignment step. The cluster assignment and update steps are repeated until the segmentation converges, specifically a residual error E between the new cluster center locations and previous cluster center locations becomes smaller than a threshold T_E for termination. The entire algorithm is summarized in Algorithm 1.

Algorithm 1. The Conventional SLIC Algorithm

Input: the input image $\mathbf{I}$, the initial cluster sampling interval S, the regularization factor r

/* *Initialization* */

1. Sample cluster centers C_k initially on $\mathfrak{L}_S$ of interval S
2. Move cluster centers to the lowest gradient position within their 3×3 neighborhood

/* *Cluster Assignment* */

3. Compute $R(i) = C_{k^*} = \underset{C_k \in \mathfrak{C}_i}{\operatorname{argmin}} \mathcal{D}(i, C_k)$ to obtain the labels by assigning label $R(i)$ to each pixel i

/* *Update* */

4. Compute $\mathbf{f}_{C_k}$ with all the pixels in $\mathfrak{R}_{C_k} = \{i | R(i) = C_k\}$, where $k = 1, \cdots, K$
5. Compute residual error E
6. Repeat Steps 3 to 5 until $E < T_E$

Output: superpixel results $\mathfrak{R}_{C_k}$, where $k = 1, \cdots, K$

In SLIC, limiting the size of the search region reduces the number of candidate cluster centers to be inspected, $|\mathfrak{C}_i|$, and thus, leads to a significant speed advantage over conventional k-means clustering where each pixel is compared with all K cluster centers, i.e. $K \gg |\mathfrak{C}_i|$.

3   Proposed Fast Simple Linear Iterative Clustering

As seen in Algorithm 1, SLIC modified from the k-means algorithm is inherently an iterative algorithm. Through iterations, superpixels gradually deform to hold homogeneous regions. At the first iteration, the deformation of superpixels can be severe, but the deformation becomes gradually smaller after a certain iteration and finally the segmentation converges.

Therefore, after the certain iteration, most of pixels generally tend to belong to an identical cluster repeatedly. That implies that a huge amount of unnecessary cluster search consisting of distance computation and comparison is performed redundantly. In the proposed algorithm, we reduce the redundant computation by using a robust inequality condition based on weighted L^2-norm of pixel and cluster center representation.

The cluster search finding the closest cluster center C_{k^*} for i is expressed as

$$
\begin{aligned}
C_{k^*} &= \underset{C_k \in \mathfrak{C}_i}{\operatorname{argmin}} \mathcal{D}(i, C_k) \\
&= \underset{C_k \in \mathfrak{C}_i}{\operatorname{argmin}} \left(\|\mathbf{f}_i\|_{\mathbf{W}}^2 + \|\mathbf{f}_{C_k}\|_{\mathbf{W}}^2 - 2\mathbf{f}_i^T \mathbf{W}^T \mathbf{W} \mathbf{f}_{C_k} \right).
\end{aligned}
\tag{8}
$$

The cluster search problem can be recast into a simpler one by getting rid of a common term in (8)

$$
\mathcal{D}'(i, C_{k^*}) = \underset{C_k \in \mathfrak{C}_i}{\min} \mathcal{D}'(i, C_k),
\tag{9}
$$

where

$$\mathcal{D}'(i, C_k) \triangleq \mathcal{D}(i, C_k) - \|\mathbf{f}_i\|_{\mathbf{W}}^2$$
$$= \|\mathbf{f}_{C_k}\|_{\mathbf{W}}^2 - 2\mathbf{f}_i^T \mathbf{W}^T \mathbf{W} \mathbf{f}_{C_k}. \tag{10}$$

The following inequality can be derived from (10) by using the Cauchy-Schwarz inequality

$$\mathcal{D}'(i, C_k) = \|\mathbf{f}_{C_k}\|_{\mathbf{W}}^2 - 2\mathbf{f}_i^T \mathbf{W}^T \mathbf{W} \mathbf{f}_{C_k}$$
$$\geq \|\mathbf{f}_{C_k}\|_{\mathbf{W}}^2 - 2\|\mathbf{f}_{C_k}\|_{\mathbf{W}} \cdot \|\mathbf{f}_i\|_{\mathbf{W}}$$
$$= \|\mathbf{f}_{C_k}\|_{\mathbf{W}} \cdot (\|\mathbf{f}_{C_k}\|_{\mathbf{W}} - 2\|\mathbf{f}_i\|_{\mathbf{W}})$$
$$\triangleq \mathcal{D}''(i, C_k). \tag{11}$$

Let us assume that some of candidate cluster centers have been inspected and $d'_{\min}$ denote the "so far" minimum distance obtained using (10).

Then, if another candidate C_k satisfies

$$\mathcal{D}''(i, C_k) \geq d'_{\min}, \tag{12}$$

$\mathcal{D}'(i, C_k) \geq d'_{\min}$ is always guaranteed. Hence, C_k can be eliminated without calculating $\mathcal{D}'(i, C_k)$ since it cannot be closer to i than the "so far" nearest cluster center. We refer to the inequality in (12) as early candidate cluster elimination (ECCE) condition. It is notable that the ECCE using the Cauchy-Schwarz inequality achieves computation reduction producing exactly same clustering results as compared to that without the early elimination.

The distance calculation in (1) requires 9 additions, 6 multiplications, and 1 square-root operation with λ^2 pre-calculated, while, given $\|\mathbf{f}_{C_k}\|_{\mathbf{W}}$ and $\|\mathbf{f}_i\|_{\mathbf{W}}$, the left part in (12) needs much lesser operations, i.e. 1 addition(subtraction) and 2 multiplications. Even these operations can become 2 additions and 1 multiplication by replacing the doubling $\|\mathbf{f}_i\|_{\mathbf{W}}$ with one more subtraction of $\|\mathbf{f}_i\|_{\mathbf{W}}$. Another distance in (10) needs 6 additions and 7 multiplications given $\|\mathbf{f}_{C_k}\|_{\mathbf{W}}$.

The weighted L^2-norm of all the pixels, $\{\|\mathbf{f}_i\|_{\mathbf{W}} \mid 1 \leq i \leq N\}$, can be computed in advance in the preprocessing procedure because they do not change once obtained, while $\{\|\mathbf{f}_{C_k}\|_{\mathbf{W}} \mid 1 \leq k \leq K\}$ should be re-calculated at every iteration due to the update of $\mathbf{f}_{C_k}$. Fortunately, the number of cluster centers is sufficiently small, i.e. $K \approx \frac{N}{S^2} \ll N$.

However, if $\mathbf{f}_{C_k}$ does not satisfy the ECCE condition, the exact distance $\mathcal{D}'(i, C_k)$ is calculated additionally and compared with $d'_{\min}$. As a result, in that case, more computational operations are performed to inspect the candidate cluster center C_k.

Therefore, effective prediction for the best candidate cluster is crucial to maximize computational efficiency of this acceleration approach. This is because the smaller $d'_{\min}$ is initially obtained, the more frequently the ECCE occurs and computational efficiency increases.

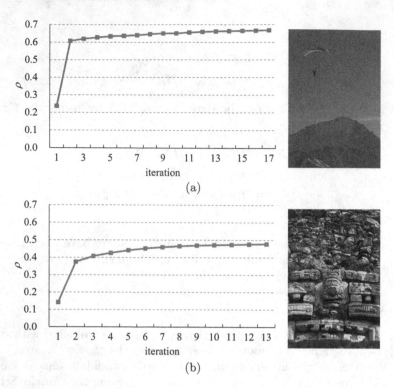

Fig. 1. Graphs of the success rates of the early candidate cluster elimination, ρ. (a) For a smooth and homogenous image. (b) For a complex image.

Algorithm 2. The Proposed Cluster Search applying the Early Candidate Cluster Elimination

---

If 1st iteration **Then**

$\quad R(i) \leftarrow C_{k^*} \leftarrow \underset{C_k \in \mathfrak{C}_i}{\operatorname{argmin}} \mathcal{D}(i,\ C_k)$

$\quad e(i) \leftarrow \mathcal{D}(i,\ R(i))$

Else

$\quad d'_{\min} \leftarrow \mathcal{D}'(i,\ R(i))$

$\quad C_{k^*} \leftarrow R(i)$

$\quad$**For** $C_k \in \mathfrak{C}_i \backslash \{R(i)\}$,

$\quad\quad$**If** $\mathcal{D}''(i,\ C_k) < d'_{\min}$ **Then**

$\quad\quad\quad d_k \leftarrow \mathcal{D}'(i,\ C_k)$

$\quad\quad\quad$**If** $d_k < d'_{\min}$ **Then**

$\quad\quad\quad\quad d'_{\min} \leftarrow d_k$

$\quad\quad\quad\quad C_{k^*} \leftarrow C_k$

$\quad\quad\quad$**EndIf**

$\quad\quad$**EndIf**

$\quad$**EndFor**

$\quad R(i) \leftarrow C_{k^*}$

$\quad e(i) \leftarrow d'_{\min} + \|\mathbf{f}_i\|_{\mathbf{W}}^2$

EndIf

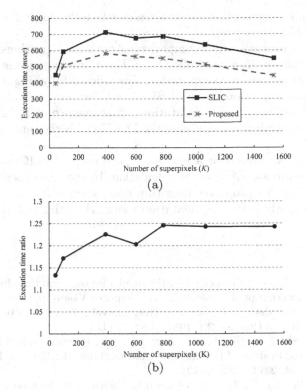

Fig. 2. Comparison of computational performance of SLIC and the proposed algorithm. (a) Comparison in terms of execution time (ms). (b) Execution time ratio.

Based on the observation that labels will not change after a certain iteration (usually from the second iteration), in the proposed acceleration algorithm, the cluster associated with each pixel at the previous iteration is inspected firstly and its distance is set to d'_{min} initially.

The proposed fast SLIC algorithm is obtained by substituting the cluster search in Algorithm 2 for the line 3 in Algorithm 1.

4 Experimental Results and Conclusions

In order to demonstrate performance of the proposed algorithm, we tested the conventional SLIC and our proposed algorithm with the Berkeley database [10] containing three-hundred 321×481 images with ground truth segmentation data. The algorithms were implemented in C based on VLFeat library [11] and tested on a Quad-core 3.50GHz processor with 16GB of RAM.

Figure 1 depicts the success rate of the ECCE, ρ. From the second iteration, ρ rises rapidly because the best cluster for each pixel can be predicted with the one associated with the pixel at the previous iteration. The tendency of ρ depends on image characteristics. For the smooth and homogeneous input image as in

Fig. 1(a), ρ rapidly increases, while ρ increases relatively slowly for the complex image in Fig. 1(b).

Figure 2 shows execution time comparison of both the algorithms in which the number of superpixels, K, is controlled by S. For all the parameter settings, the proposed algorithm reduces computation time successfully. Figure 2(b) shows the ratio between execution times of SLIC and the proposed algorithm. The proposed algorithm improves computational performance of SLIC by 21 % on average. It is noteworthy that applying the ECCE yields the same segmentation results as SLIC.

In this paper, we presented a fast implementation of SLIC which successfully reduces the number of distance calculation. In the experimental results, it was confirmed that the proposed algorithm runs twice as fast as SLIC while it produces even slightly better segmentation results than those of SLIC.

References

1. Ren X., Malik, J.: Learning a classification model for segmentation. In: Proceedings of the IEEE International Conference on Computer Vision, pp. 10–17 (2003)
2. Liu, Z., Zou, W., Meur, O.L.: Saliency tree: a novel saliency detection framework. IEEE Trans. Image Process. **23**, 1937–1952 (2014)
3. Achanta, R., Shaji, A., Smith, K., Lucchi, A., Fua, P., Süsstrunk, S.: SLIC superpixels compared to state-of-the-art superpixel methods. IEEE Trans. Pattern Anal. Mach. Intell. **34**, 2274–2282 (2012)
4. Ayvaci, A., Soatto, S.: Motion segmentation with occlusions on the superpixel graph. In: Proceedings of the IEEE International Conference on Computer Vision Workshops, pp. 727–734 (2009)
5. Mori, G., Ren, X., Efros, A.A., Malik, J.: Recovering human body configurations: Combining segmentation and recognition. In: Proceedings of the IEEE International Conference on Computer Vision, Pattern Recognition, pp. 326–333 (2004)
6. Kim, K.-S., Zhang, D., Kang, M.-C., Ko, S.-J.: Improved simple linear iterative clustering superpixels. In: Proceedings of the IEEE International Symposium Consumer Electron, pp. 259–260 (2013)
7. Ren, C.Y., Reid, I.: gSLIC: a real-time implementation of slic superpixel segmentation. Technical report, University of Oxford (2011)
8. Robovec, J., Kybic, J.: jSLIC: superpixels in ImageJ. Computer Vision Winter Workshop (2014)
9. Wu, K.-S., Lin, J.-C.: Fast VQ encoding by an efficient kick-out condition. IEEE Trans. Circuits Syst. Video Technol. **10**, 59–62 (2000)
10. Martin, D., Fowlkes, C., Tal, D., Malik, J.: A database of human segmented natural images and its application to evaluating segmentation algorithm and measuring ecological statistics. In: Proceedings of the IEEE International Conference on Computer Vision, pp. 416–423 (2001)
11. VLFeat.org, VLFeat: http://www.vlfeat.org. Accessed November 2014
12. Veksler, O., Boykov, Y., Mehrani, P.: Superpixels and supervoxels in an energy optimization framework. In: Proceedings of the European Conference on Computer Vision, pp. 211–224 (2010)

Pectoral Muscle Segmentation in Mammograms Based on Cartoon-Texture Decomposition

Adrian Galdran[1,2]([⊠]), Artzai Picón[1], Estibaliz Garrote[1], and David Pardo[2,3]

[1] TECNALIA, Computer Vision Group, Parque Científico y Tecnológico,
Edificio 700, 48160 Derio, Spain
{adrian.galdran,artzai.picon,estibaliz.garrote}@tecnalia.com
http://www.computervisionbytecnalia.com/
[2] Department of Applied Mathematics, Statistics, and Operational Research,
University of the Basque Country, Barrio Sarriena S/N,
Campus de Leioa, 48940 Leioa, Spain
[3] IKERBASQUE, Basque Foundation for Science,
University of the Basque Country, Barrio Sarriena S/N,
Campus de Leioa, 48940 Leioa, Spain
dzubiaur@gmail.com
https://sites.google.com/site/m2sigroup/

Abstract. Pectoral muscle segmentation on medio-lateral oblique views of mammograms represents an important preprocessing step in many mammographic image analysis tasks. Although its location can be perceptually obvious for a human observer, the variability in shape, size, and intensities of the pectoral muscle boundary turns its automatic segmentation into a challenging problem. In this work we propose to decompose the input mammogram into its textural and structural components at different scales prior to dynamically thresholding it into several levels. The resulting segmentations are refined with an active contour model and merged together by means of a simple voting scheme to remove possible outliers. Our method performs well compared to several other state-of-the-art techniques. An average DICE similarity coefficient of 0.91 and mean Hausdorff distance of 3.66 ± 3.23 mm. validate our approach.

Keywords: Pectoral muscle segmentation · Mammographic image analysis · Breast cancer detection · Computer-aided diagnosis

1 Introduction

Breast cancer is ranked as one of the most prevalent cancers worldwide [1], and prevention remains the most useful method to reduce its impact. In this sense, it is widely accepted that computer vision and image processing techniques can assist radiologists in mammographic image analysis tasks such as detection and characterization of breast lesions or estimation of breast density, which is often used for prediction of breast cancer risk.

A typical preprocessing step applied to a mammogram before any other image analysis method is the location of three representative landmarks, namely the

© Springer International Publishing Switzerland 2015
R. Paredes et al. (Eds.): IbPRIA 2015, LNCS 9117, pp. 587–594, 2015.
DOI: 10.1007/978-3-319-19390-8_66

breast border, the nipple, and the pectoral muscle [2]. From these, automatic pectoral muscle detection and segmentation from medio-lateral oblique view of mammographies is particularly interesting due to several factors. For example, an internal analysis of the pectoral muscle region may reveal the presence of axillary lymph nodes. Moreover, its presence can bias lesion detection algorithms, since its characteristics may be similar to those of abnormal tissues. Furthermore, the pectoral muscle can be useful in breast density estimation tasks: if the pectoral muscle is not properly removed, the residual pectoral region may be considered as dense tissue, producing an overestimation of the breast density.

In a mammogram, the pectoral muscle always appears as a roughly triangular region in one side of the image. Still, due to the intrinsic irregularity in anatomy and patient positions in the acquisition moment its location is highly variable, as well as its size, which may range from a few percentage of the image to half of the breast region. Besides, curvature of the pectoral muscle contour can appear as convex, concave or even a combination of both. Moreover, although humans perceive the muscle boundary as a visually continuous curve, variations in edge contrast are substantial along it. Often, the upper section of the boundary contains high contrast and is well delineated, but the lower part appears faded and blurred with fibro-glandular tissue.

Due to these and other implicit difficulties, pectoral muscle segmentation in mammograms is considered a demanding image analysis problem. As a result, a significant amount of research has been devoted to it in the last years. Based on the approximately triangular structure of the pectoral muscle, earlier algorithms relied on the Hough transform to identify its contour [3]. However, pectoral muscles may possess a considerably curved boundary, making the linearity assumption inadequate. Nevertheless, straight line fitting has been the basis for many methods that make an effort to refine initial linear approximations with different strategies. For example Kwok et al. [2] suggested Hough transform followed by cliff detection to progressively refine the obtained line into a curve that better fits the pectoral muscle boundary. In [4], the authors also detect the pectoral muscle initially as a straight line and then they look for local gradient maxima within a band enclosing it. Likewise, Kinoshita et al. [5] approximated the pectoral muscle by the longest straight line in the Radon domain.

There exist other strategies aiming to overcome the limitations related to general shape and position assumptions. To take into account texture as well as intensity cues, filtering approaches have been designed, such as the method proposed in [6], where a Gabor wavelets filter bank is applied to emphasize the pectoral muscle edge. Region growing and merging techniques have also been explored, such as in [7], where the watershed segmentation method is applied to obtain an initial over-segmentation that is refined afterwards by means of an specialized region merging algorithm.

Machine Learning techniques have also been suggested to effectively identify pixels belonging to the pectoral muscle. For instance in [8] the endpoints of the muscle contour in the vertical and horizontal directions are learnt with SVMs, and the shortest path joining both endpoints is selected as a candidate for the pectoral muscle boundary. Although these methods obtain good results, it must be taken into account that this class of techniques requires a set of segmented mammograms to train the classifiers before they can proceed to obtain a segmentation.

In this work we depart from previous approaches by building a method to segment the pectoral muscle that relies on an initial decomposition of the input mammogram into its cartoon and texture components. We apply the recently developed Rolling Guidance Filter [9] to remove the textural component of the mammography while retaining its underlying high-scale structure, including the pectoral muscle boundary. Simple connected component analysis and dynamic thresholding allow us to produce a reliable estimate of the location and contour of the pectoral muscle. These estimates are obtained pixelwise, and this generates ragged boundaries that are further processed with a generic active contour model in order to regularize them. To the best of our knowledge, this is the first time the cartoon-texture decomposition is proposed as a way to handle the variability in texture and intensity present within the pectoral muscle.

The rest of this work is structured as follows. In Sect. 2, we give the details of our approach. First, we provide an overview of the cartoon-texture decomposition problem and the Rolling Guidance Filter, the method we selected to remove textural information while preserving and emphasizing the edges of the pectoral muscle. Next we explain the dynamic thresholding and connected component analysis we perform to obtain the initial estimates of the pectoral muscle and we describe the active contour model we employ to post-process them. We then detail the obtained experimental results and comparison with other methods. We end up with a discussion on the results and some possible directions of improvement of our technique.

2 Pectoral Muscle Detection Method

The proposed method for pectoral muscle detection involves a multi-stage algorithm. First, a cartoon-texture decomposition is computed, followed by a simple dynamic thresholding that generates a rough segmentation feeding an active contours model to refine and regularize it. After running this process for different scale parameters, the method automatically extracts an optimal segmentation by merging the produced candidate regions. Full details about the main components of this process are provided in the remainder of the section.

2.1 Initial Segmentation by Cartoon-Texture Decomposition

Separating texture from geometry in natural images is a well-studied problem. Since the pioneering work of Yves Meyer [10], many researchers have proposed different methods to obtain a decomposition of an image I into the sum of a cartoon part u, a simplified piecewise constant version of I where only the image shapes and edges appear, and a textural part v where the oscillating patterns lie. To obtain such a decomposition $I = u + v$, the predominant approach is to minimize a variational formulation that tries to express I as a combination of functions lying in different functional spaces representing texture and structure.

In [11] a comprehensive analysis of the existing variational algorithms that have been developed from the work of Meyer can be found.

Apart from the variational point of view, other approaches are possible to solve the cartoon-texture decomposition problem. If a denoising filtering process is able to keep or even enhance the edges of objects while removing noise, it can also be used to separate texture from structure. In this paper, we use such an scale-aware filtering procedure, namely, the recently developed Rolling Guidance filter [9]. This technique consists of an iterated non-linear filter that is able to effectively remove the texture component of an image at different scales while preserving edges and other general structures. The enderlying idea is to remove first the small structures of the input image, followed by an iterative edge recovery step. The first of these steps is achieved by simple Gaussian filtering:

$$G(p) = \frac{1}{K_p} \sum_{q \in N(p)} \exp\left(-\frac{|p - q|^2}{2\sigma_s^2}\right) I(q), \tag{1}$$

where p and q are pixels in the image, σ_s denotes standard deviation, $N(p)$ is a neighborhood around pixel p and K_p is a normalization factor.

Then, a joint bilateral filtering is iteratively applied to the initial image. This procedure generates a series of iterations according to the following formula:

$$J^{t+1} = \frac{1}{K_p} \sum_{q \in N(p)} \exp\left(-\frac{|p - q|^2}{2\sigma_s^2} - \frac{|J^t(p) - J^t(q)|^2}{2\sigma_r^2}\right) I(q), \tag{2}$$

where σ_s, σ_r are parameters controlling the spatial and intensity range of the filter. Along these iterations, the guidance image remains the input I. The initial J is the smoothed version of I obtained with Eq. (1). To obtain the subsequent iterations, we perform a smoothing of the input image I guided by the structure present at the previous iteration J^t. Equation (2) smoothes the original image guided by the structure underlying in the J^t iteration, yielding a new iteration J^{t+1} in which small structures are not present, but a part of the original large scale structure is retrieved. This process has the ability to enhance the so-called virtual edges. These are edges that do not come from large gradients, but rather from different large scale image information. An example of the ability of the Rolling Guidance Filter to emphasize this kind of information is shown in Fig. 1.

2.2 Dynamic Thresholding and Connected Component Analysis

After extracting the structural part from the input mammogram, we threshold it at multiple values supplied by a dynamic thresholding procedure. Quantization of the cartoon part of the mammogram at these values provides a piecewise constant image in which the upper leftmost connected component roughly represents the pectoral muscle, see Fig. 2. To ensure a correct segmentation, we employ several number of quantization levels, specifically 3 to 5 levels. In each quantized image, we pick the largest upper leftmost connected component that passes a simple triangularity test. This test is an easy verification of the triangular arrangement

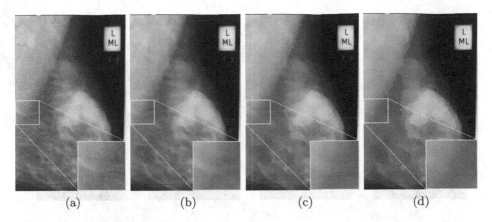

(a)   (b)   (c)   (d)

Fig. 1. (a) Original mammogram, (b)-(d) Mammogram filtered at different scales $\sigma_s \in \{6, 10, 20\}$. Notice how the border of the muscle is hardly distinguishable by its intensity in a close look, although its presence is intuitively obvious. As the scale of the removed structures increases that virtual edge is emphasized, while vessels and other structures lying within the pectoral muscle are blended together and eventually disappear.

of pixels: sample lines of the segmentation are scanned from the top to the bottom of the image. If a sample line contains more pectoral muscle pixels than the next one we reject that candidate segmentation. Equivalently, the number of pectoral muscle pixel per line must be a decreasing function for the segmentation to be accepted. Finally, we select the output with the largest area.

2.3 Active Contours Segmentation Refinement

The segmentations produced so far already supply a good approximation of the pectoral muscle. However, we have experimentally observed a general tendency to underestimate the real pectoral muscle area. Moreover, the contours of the regions appear ragged, due to the pixel-wise cartoon-texture decomposition. To regularize the border of the segmentation, as well as to recover part of the missed region, we perform an active contours-based refinement process. This is carried out by means of the popular Chan-Vese model for image segmentation [12]. The energy this model aims to minimize is given by:

$$F(c_1, c_2) = \mu \cdot \text{length}(C) + \lambda_1 \iint_{in(C)} |I(x, y) - c_1|^2 dxdy$$

$$+ \lambda_2 \iint_{out(C)} |I(x, y) - c_2|^2 dxdy, \tag{3}$$

where $\mu, \lambda_1, \lambda_2$ are fixed parameters and C is a closed curve that evolves over the image $I : \Omega \rightarrow [0, 255]$, being Ω the domain of the image. This curve encloses an inner region, denoted by $in(C)$, and the outer region is defined as $out(C) = \Omega - in(C)$. The constants c_1, c_2 represent the average of the image intensity inside and outside C respectively. Thus, they depend on C and change

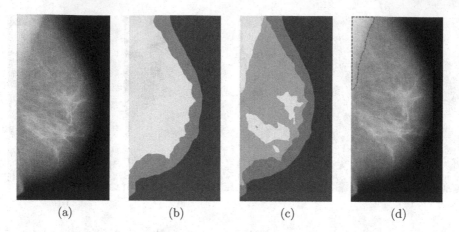

(a)   (b)   (c)   (d)

Fig. 2. (a) Original mammogram (b) Result after filtering at scale $\sigma_s = 6$, dynamic thresholding with 3 levels and quantization (c) Result after filtering at scale $\sigma_s = 6$, dynamic thresholding with 4 levels and quantization (e) Final output of our method.

as the curve evolves. This functional is minimized when these average intensities are as different as possible, while respecting the constraint on keeping the length of C relatively low, imposed by the first term in Eq. (3). The initial contour is given in our case by the border of the segmentation generated in the previous subsection. This segmentation is iteratively grown in the directions that minimize Eq. (3). The low length constraint on the boundary of the segmentation implies that the border will remain simple, solving this way the issue about the ragged high-curvature contours remarked above. Let us underline that the evolution of the active contour takes place on the correspondent cartoon part of the decomposition of the input mammography, rather than on the latter.

2.4   Multi-scale Decomposition and Merged Segmentation

Since texture is a scale-dependent concept, there is no unique possible cartoon-texture decomposition of an image. A texture seen at a close inspection is a group of well-contrasted objects, such as leaves or bricks. This structure can be considered as cartoon in a low-scale processing and texture from a large-scale point of view. Thus, the scale at which an image must be processed to suppress every texture from the cartoon part comes with some subjectivity. To make our approach robust, we run the Rolling Guidance Filter for different realizations of the scale parameter σ_s to remove texture at different scales. This generates a set of segmentations that we merge by means of a simple voting scheme in which a pixel is considered to be part of the pectoral muscle if more than one of the produced segmentations contains it. This allows us to get rid of spurious outliers that may appear when removing texture with only one scale parameter. The full computational procedure of the proposed method is outlined below.

Algorithm 1. Full algorithm for Pectoral Muscle Segmentation

1: Set range of scales for processing, in our case $\sigma_s \in S = [6, 15, 20, 50, 100]$
2: **for** σ_s in S **do**
3:     Obtain cartoon-texture decomposition of the mammography at scale σ.
4:     Compute dynamic thresholding on the cartoon part at $3 - 6$ levels.
5:     **for** each quantized image **do**
6:         Keep the leftmost connected component, if it passes the triangularity test.
7:         Run Active Contour Minimization to refine and regularize the segmentation.
8:     **end for**
9:     Keep the largest of the refined segmentations for this scale.
10: **end for**
11: Merge candidate segmentations obtained for each σ_s with a voting scheme.
12: Return the merged segmentation.

---

3   Experimental Results and Discussion

We have tested our method on a subset of the mini-MIAS database consisting of 84 mammographies. Ground-truth supplied by expert radiologists was provided in [6] and has been widely used in the literature for performance comparison.

In terms of general behavior, our method seems to be effective and robust, obtaining an average DICE coefficient of similarity 0.91 between the generated segmentations and the available ground-truth. Another popular index to compare pectoral muscle segmentation methods is the Hausdorff distance, that reflects the geometric distance between two sets A, B, given by:

$$h(A, B) = \max_{a \in A} \min_{b \in B} \text{dist}(a, b),$$

where $\text{dist}(a, b)$ is the Euclidean distance between two points a, b. Another common performance measure pectoral muscle segmentation is the average rate of false positives (FP) and false negatives (FN) found in a segmentation. Both of these coefficients, as well as the average Hausdorff distance, for our method and the techniques suggested in [4–8] are displayed in Table 1.

Table 1. Error analysis - Hausdorff distance, mean FP and mean FN

Methods	[6]	[7]	[4]	[8]	[5]	Ours
Hausdorff distance - Mean	3.84	3.85	3.84	2.49	12.45	**3.66**
Hausdorff distance - StDev	1.73	1.07	3.85	0.99	22.96	**3.23**
Mean FP	0.58	0.85	0.42	–	0.89	**0.27**
Mean FN	5.77	4.88	6.71	–	9.13	**5.75**

We see that our method slightly outperforms the other techniques. Only [8] reports better performance. Yet, this method relies on the availability of a training set. Also, classifiers running over mammographies acquired with a given system may produce errors if applied to mammograms coming from another one.

4   Conclusions and Future Research

We have presented a new pectoral muscle segmentation method that employs cartoon-texture decomposition to overcome the variability in texture and intensity that hinders the performance of other techniques. Experimental results support our approach, showing a good comparison against other recent methods. Furthermore, our method implements a generic active contour method to refine the produced segmentation. Further improvements can be achieved by designing a specialized active contour model accounting for the specificities of the problem.

The cartoon-texture decomposition may also be an effective tool to handle other mammographic image analysis problems, such as breast-skin line detection. We are currently exploring this an other applications.

References

1. Bray, F., Ren, J.S., Masuyer, E., Ferlay, J.: Global estimates of cancer prevalence for 27 sites in the adult population in 2008. Int. J. Cancer **132**(5), 1133–1145 (2013)
2. Kwok, S.M., Chandrasekhar, R., Attikiouzel, Y., Rickard, M.: Automatic pectoral muscle segmentation on mediolateral oblique view mammograms. IEEE Trans. Med. Imaging **23**(9), 1129–1140 (2004)
3. Karssemeijer, N.: Automated classification of parenchymal patterns in mammograms. Phys. Med. Biol. **43**(2), 365 (1998)
4. Chakraborty, J., Mukhopadhyay, S., Singla, V., Khandelwal, N., Bhattacharyya, P.: Automatic detection of pectoral muscle using average gradient and shape based feature. J. Digit. Imaging **25**(3), 387–399 (2012)
5. Kinoshita, S.K., Azevedo-Marques, P.M., Pereira, R.R., Rodrigues, J.A.H., Rangayyan, R.M.: Radon-domain detection of the nipple and the pectoral muscle in mammograms. J. Digit. Imaging **21**(1), 37–49 (2008)
6. Ferrari, R., Rangayyan, R., Desautels, J., Borges, R., Frere, A.: Automatic identification of the pectoral muscle in mammograms. IEEE Trans. Med. Imaging **23**(2), 232–245 (2004)
7. Camilus, K.S., Govindan, V.K., Sathidevi, P.S.: Pectoral muscle identification in mammograms. J. Appl. Clin. Med. Phys. **12**(3), 3285 (2011)
8. Domingues, I., Cardoso, J.S., Passarinho, P., Cardoso, M.J.: Pectoral muscle detection in mammograms based on the shortest path with endpoints learnt by SVMs. Conf. Proc. IEEE Eng. Med. Biol. Soc. **2010**, 3158–3161 (2010)
9. Zhang, Q., Shen, X., Xu, L., Jia, J.: Rolling guidance filter. In: Fleet, D., Pajdla, T., Schiele, B., Tuytelaars, T. (eds.) ECCV 2014, Part III. LNCS, vol. 8691, pp. 815–830. Springer, Heidelberg (2014)
10. Meyer, Y.: Oscillating Patterns in Image Processing and Nonlinear Evolution Equations: The Fifteenth Dean Jacqueline B. Lewis Memorial Lectures. American Mathematical Society, Boston (2001)
11. Buades, A., Le, T., Morel, J.M., Vese, L.: Fast cartoon + texture image filters. IEEE Trans. Image Process. **19**(8), 1978–1986 (2010)
12. Chan, T.F., Vese, L.A.: Active contours without edges. IEEE Trans. Image Process. **10**(2), 266–277 (2001)

PPG Beat Reconstruction Based on Shape Models and Probabilistic Templates for Signals Acquired with Conventional Smartphones

Diego Martín-Martínez[1,2], Alexandre Domingues[2],
Pablo Casaseca-de-la-Higuera[1,3], Carlos Alberola-López[1],
and J. Miguel Sanches[2(✉)]

[1] Laboratorio de Procesado de Imagen, Universidad de Valladolid, Valladolid, Spain
dmarmar@lpi.tel.uva.es
[2] Institute for Systems and Robotics (ISR/IST), LARSyS,
Instituto Superior Técnico, Universidade de Lisboa, Lisboa, Portugal
jmrs@tecnico.ulisboa.pt
[3] Centre for Artificial Intelligence, Visual Communications, and Networking,
University of the West of Scotland, Paisley, UK

Abstract. Ubiquitous monitoring has become a useful tool for the prevention and early diagnosis of some disorders. This kind of monitoring is nowadays very common thanks to the irruption of smartphones, which make easier the collection and delivery of the patient's data. However, some problems arise due to the occasional low quality of the acquired data. This paper presents a novel methodology in which the shape of PPG beats is recovered through a multistage fully-automatic pipeline featuring a shape modeling stage as well as a template-based shape recovery through a level-set approach; the template is not assumed or derived from previously acquired data but it is estimated from the surrounding beats. To validate the proposal, a registry acquired using the camera of a *Motorola MotoG* has been used. Results can be qualified as promising, since the shape of damaged beats is recovered, although a comprehensive validation should be addressed.

Keywords: Ubiquitous monitoring · Smartphone · Photopletysmography · Shape model · Probabilistic template · Level-set

1 Introduction

In the last decades, the clinical community has promoted several initiatives for diseases prevention, specially those affecting the cardiovascular system, such as stroke, myocardial infarction, etc. The major part of these initiatives are based on the assessment of the patient condition (e.g. cardiovascular state) through biochemical analysis and some tests (measurement of the arterial pressure, electrocardiographic studies, etc.) that patients undergo periodically [1]; however, these procedures present mainly two issues that prevent from performing them as

© Springer International Publishing Switzerland 2015
R. Paredes et al. (Eds.): IbPRIA 2015, LNCS 9117, pp. 595–602, 2015.
DOI: 10.1007/978-3-319-19390-8_67

frequently as might be wished: the economic impact and the time requirements, both for patients and for physicians. To overcome these drawbacks, ubiquitous monitoring has arisen as a promising tool during last years, since that kind of monitoring can be performed everyday at home by the patient itself just for a few minutes thanks to the use of inexpensive devices connected to any data network. In this sense, the wide usage of smartphones has contributed to make swifter the deployment of that technology as they can both cope with collecting the information and uploading it to the network. Currently, some companies are taking the step towards ubiquitous monitoring through smartphones by embedding the acquisition devices into them, so one can find some plug- and -play devices able to provide an accurate ECG as well as several contributions on how to acquire PPG signals by means of the smartphone camera. Since almost all the smartphones have a camera, and PPG can provide information about some relevant aspects of the cardiovascular system (heart rate, arterial stiffness, cardiac output, etc.) [2,3], this seems a reasonable branch of the ubiquitous monitoring to explore first. However, so far, the quality of these signals is not good enough to use them for clinical purposes.

There are several methods in the literature aiming at improving the quality of PPG signals, however to the best of our knowledge, none of them is aimed at correcting the shape of pulses, but just at removing some mild artifacts (trend, low amplitude noise, etc.) and replacing the corrupted pieces (manually identified) by means of statistically equivalent strings of synthetic pulses ([4], for instance). In this paper, we propose a novel methodology that strives for recovering the shape of damaged pulses according to the shape of the surrounding ones. So, the current proposal differs from the so far proposed ones in the following aspects: (1) the method is fully automatic, and (2) the reconstructed shape is obtained, through a level-set based approach, taking into account the shape of the corrupted pulse and a template consisting on a cumulative density function estimated from the surrounding pulses. The assessment of the proposal has been performed only with one signal, so this work must be qualified as a first approach; nevertheless, results are promising enough to suggest following this research line.

This paper is structured as follows: a broad description of the proposal is presented in Sect. 2, whereas the validation is addressed in Sect. 3; to conclude, a summary of the most relevant conclusions is brought in Sect. 4.

2   Methods

As stated in Sect. 1, this work presents a methodology aimed at recovering the original shape of pulses that have been degraded to a large extent. To this end, we have developed a three-stage methodology, namely, preprocessing, shape modeling and shape recovery. The main contribution of this work lies on the third stage, since both the first and the second stages have been described in elsewhere.

2.1   Preprocessing

This stage aims at properly conditioning the signal and consists of three stages: resampling, statistical detrending and pulse delineation; all of them are described below.

Resampling.– Registries resulting from the camera consist of a set of pairs representing the timestamps and the corresponding amplitude values , i.e., $[t_n, x_n]$. The exact sampling time of the camera acquisitions cannot be easily controlled by developers at API level, so, signal conditioning needs to be done to ensure uniform sampling times. This stage thus aims at resampling the signal so that the condition $t_{n+1} - t_n = t_n - t_{n-1}$ could be satisfied all over the registry. To this end, a L'Hêrmite piecewise interpolation [5] is carried out using the minimum value of $t_n - t_{n-1}$ (for each signal) as the sampling period.

Statistical Detrending.– The nature of the acquisition system makes these signals prone to artifacts that may alter both the baseline and the amplitude. These artifacts, however, can be easily overcome by removing the mean and the variance trends as follows:

$$y(t) = \frac{x(t) - \eta_x(t)}{\sigma_x(t)}, \qquad \text{with} \qquad \begin{matrix} x(t) \sim \mathcal{N}(\eta_x(t), \sigma_x(t)) \\ \\ y(t) \sim \mathcal{N}(0, 1) \end{matrix} \qquad (1)$$

where $x(t)$ and $y(t)$ are the input and the output signals, and $\eta_x(t)$ and $\sigma_x(t)$ are the instantaneous mean and variance estimated through a 20-s sliding window[1]. One might argue that the underlying information of the PPG is distorted by altering the mean and, specially, the standard deviation, however, that information is coded mainly on the pulse-rate as well as on the shape of the pulse, which are not altered when the above mentioned statistics are modified.

Pulse Delineation.– By means of the pulse delineation, the signal $y(t)$ is split into a set of K pulses: $\{\mathcal{B}(k; \tau)\}_{k=1}^{K}$. For this purpose, quite a few off the shelf methods ([6], for instance) are available; however, if signals are only moderately corrupted, simpler methods based on low-pass filtering and valley (local minimum) detection can be used instead. Using that methodology, we have achieved a 99 % of correctly delineated pulses.

2.2   Shape Modeling

To improve the quality of the shape of the pulses, we have used the shape-model proposed in [4] in which each pulse is modeled through a parametric curve formed by two Gaussian curves and a linear trend:

---

[1] The χ^2 goodness of fit test has been used to assess the distribution of the data. The choice of the window length is an open issue to be tackled in future works. This case, we have chosen 20 s since major part of artifacts usually last 5–15 s.

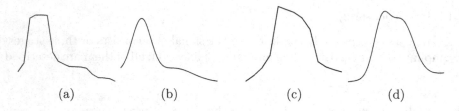

(a)   (b)   (c)   (d)

Fig. 1. Shape of two pulses before —(a) and (c)— and after —(b) and (d)—the shape modeling stage.

$$\mathcal{B}(\tau; k) \simeq \sum_{\ell=1}^{2} a_\ell[k] \exp\left[-\frac{(\tau - b_\ell[k])^2}{c_\ell[k]^2}\right] + m_0[k] + m_1[k] \cdot \tau, \qquad (2)$$

where $a_1, b_1, c_1, a_2, b_2, c_2, m_0$ and m_1 are the parameters characterizing the model, whose values have been estimated by means of the non-linear least squares minimization method. For the sake of simplicity, these parameters are compiled in a vector series that summarizes all the information provided by the PPG registry:

$$\mathbf{w}[k] = [a_1[k], b_1[k], c_1[k], a_2[k], b_2[k], c_2[k], m_0[k], m_1[k]], \quad k = 1, \cdots, K. \quad (3)$$

Once the parameters are estimated, each beat is substituted by the parametric curve $\Gamma(\tau, \mathbf{w}[k])$. In Fig. 1, the shape of two pulses before —$\mathcal{B}(\tau; k)$— and after —$\Gamma(\tau, \mathbf{w}[k])$— the modeling stage is depicted; it can be observed that shape of pulses derived from the model looks more natural and less artifacted.

2.3   Shape Recovery

To the best of our knowledge, published methods that aim at recovering the pulse shape focus on this specific issue but leave the problem of identifying abnormal pulses to the visual inspection of an specialist; however, our procedure is fully automatic and, therefore, that step is performed without user intervention. To this end, we propose the following procedure:

Substage 1: In this substage, we propose to use the likelihood of each pulse to determine how intense the recovery process should be; the pulse probability density function is estimated out of pulses surrounding the one under study. So, the $m = 20$ surrounding pulses[2] have been synchronized (see [4] for more details on the synchronization process) and overlapped to estimate a probability density function from them: being $\{\Gamma(\tau, \mathbf{w}[\ell])\}_{\ell \in \mathcal{M}}$ the set of 20 pulses, the marginal density function is constructed as

$$f_\Gamma(\gamma; \tau) \sim \mathcal{N}\left(\eta_\Gamma(\tau), \sigma_\Gamma(\tau)\right), \qquad (4)$$

---

[2] The rationale of that choice is the same as for the footnote 1.

where $\eta_{\mathbf{\Gamma}}(\tau)$ and $\sigma_{\mathbf{\Gamma}}(\tau)$ are the sample estimations of the mean and the standard deviation of the amplitude for each time instant τ using the $\{\Gamma(\tau, \mathbf{w}[\ell])\}_{\ell \in \mathcal{M}}$ dataset. The joint density function is built by assuming independence in time. Therefore, an α_k parameter defined as

$$\alpha_k = 1 - \frac{2}{\pi} \arctan\left(\mathcal{L}\left(\Gamma(\tau, \mathbf{w}[k]), f_{\mathbf{\Gamma}}(\gamma; \tau)\right)\right) \tag{5}$$

with $\mathcal{L}$ the likelihood function, is used to weigh one of the terms of the functional to be optimized. It must be noted that the $\arctan(\cdot)$ function is included to limit the dynamic range of the parameter so that $0 \le \alpha_k \le 1$.

Substage 2: Once the α_k parameter is obtained, we propose the usage of a level set approach to modify the shape of pulses using the surrounding beats as a template. For that purpose, we have defined the level-set surface as (for clarity, time dependence is hereafter not explicitly written since the procedure takes place for each beat):

$$\phi(x, y) = \begin{cases} 0 & \text{if } (x, y) \in \{(x_0, y_0) : y_0 = \Gamma(x_0), \ x_0 = \tau, \forall \tau\} \\ d\left((x, y), (x_0, y_0)\right) & \text{if } (x, y) \notin \{(x_0, y_0)\} \end{cases}, \tag{6}$$

where

$$d\left((x, y), (x_0, y_0)\right) = \min\{\|(x - x_0, y - y_0)\|\} \cdot \text{sign}(y_0 - y). \tag{7}$$

As for the template, we have defined it as

$$T(x, y) = 1 - F_{\mathbf{\Gamma}}(x; y), \qquad x = \tau, \quad y = \gamma, \tag{8}$$

where $F_{\mathbf{\Gamma}}(\gamma; \tau)$ is the cumulative density function associated to $f_{\mathbf{\Gamma}}(\gamma; \tau)$. So, the evolution of the pulse shape, i.e., the evolution of the surface $\phi(x, y)$, is governed by the iterative equation

$$\phi(x, y)_{(n)} - \phi(x, y)_{(n-1)} = F_0 \cdot |\nabla\phi(x, y)| + \underbrace{\beta \cdot \nabla \cdot \left(\frac{\nabla\phi(x, y)}{|\nabla\phi(x, y)|}\right)}_{\text{Curvature}} + \underbrace{\alpha \cdot T(x, y)}_{\text{Template}}.$$
$$\tag{9}$$

The choice of F_0 and β has not been addressed in this work, so, after trying several values, we have set them *ad hoc* for each registry. That equation should be applied to update $\phi(x, y)$ until the convergence criterion is achieved, i.e., when the amount of points satisfying $\phi(x, y)_{(n)} \cdot p\phi(x, y)_{(n-1)} < 0$ is less than the 1% of the points. Both the initial level-set, $\phi(x, y)_{(0)}$, and the template estimated for a pair of pulses are depicted in Fig. 2.

3   Experiments and Results

The performance assessment of the method above is carried out by reconstructing a 5-min long signal acquired from a healthy subject with a Motorola MotoG Smartphone.

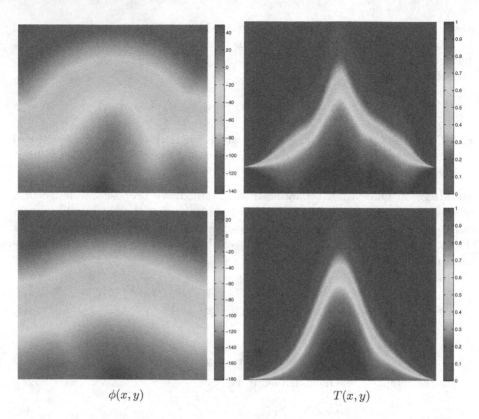

$$\phi(x,y) \qquad\qquad\qquad T(x,y)$$

Fig. 2. Level-set —$\phi(x,y)$— and template —$T(x,y)$— estimated for two pulses.

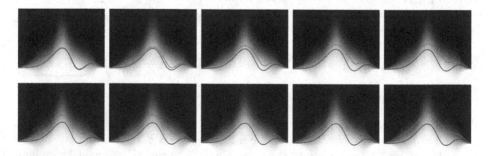

Fig. 3. Evolution of the shape of an abnormally-shaped pulse. White shadow represents the template, whereas blue and red lines represent the initial and the current shape of the pulse (Color figure online).

As for the shape modeling stage, the performance of our proposal can be seen in Fig. 1. Regarding shape recovery, we have summarized the process for one pulse in Fig. 3. There, one can see that the abnormal gap of the pulse (blue line) disappears and the shape progressively becomes more natural. It must be

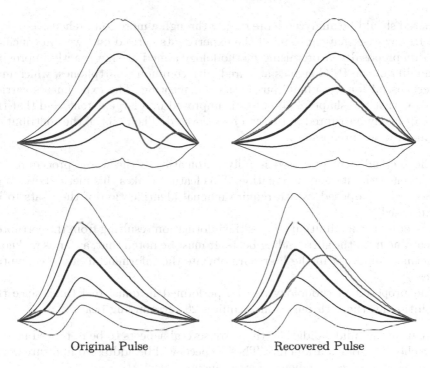

Original Pulse   Recovered Pulse

Fig. 4. Shape of pulses before (blue colored line) and after (red line) applying the proposed methodology for shape–recovery. Black lines represent the mean, the mean ± the standard deviation and the mean ± two times the standard deviation of the distribution of pulses created with the method proposed in [4] (Color figure online).

remarked that the final pulse is a mixture of the raw pulse and the template, i.e., it gathers information of both contributions. Regarding the goodness of the proposal, we have compared with the method proposed in [4]. Thanks to the stochastic nature of that method, we can generate several synthetic pulses that are statistically equivalent to the one to be replaced. Therefore, we have synthesized 100 pulses to analyze whether the solution provided by the current proposal may be also considered statistically equivalent. In Fig. 4, we have plotted the statistics of the pulses synthesized through the method in [4] together with the solution provided by the current proposal. We can see from the figure that the solution provided by the method here proposed "falls" within the bell of the distribution given by the synthetic pulses and looks natural. Hence, we can assert that our method is able to provide solutions within the range provided by [4] but in a fully-automatic manner, i.e., without any sort of user intervention.

4   Conclusion

In this work we have presented a novel contribution aimed at improving the quality of PPG signals acquired with the camera of a conventional smartphone. First of all, we should stress the preliminary nature of this work; therefore conclusions extracted should be analyzed more deeply through a more comprehensive validation. In any case, having in mind the experiments carried out, we can conclude that our proposal is a promising methodology aimed at significantly improving the quality of the PPG signals acquired with common smartphones, which may be very useful for the ubiquitous patient monitoring. The experiments carried out show that the shape of all pulses is improved in a large extent, and that the shape of highly corrupted pulses can be recovered. The point of the contribution lies, mainly, on three issues:

1. The method here proposed is fully automatic, so the whole procedure can be done without user intervention. This feature makes this method overcome the so far proposed, which require manual identification of the beats to be processed.
2. The current contribution merges the information resulting from the corrupted beat and from the surrounding beats. It must be noted that, as far as we know, methods reported in the literature obviate the information of the corrupted beat.
3. The proposed methodology can be performed in quasi real time, since the solution for the k-th pulse only requires 20 surrounding beats.

Apart from the mild validation, there are several aspects to be improved related to the choice of some parameters. These aspects will be addressed in future works by means of more comprehensive experiments.

References

1. World Health Statistics. World Health Organization, Geneva, Switzerland (2011)
2. Murthy, V.S., Ramamoorthy, S., Srinivasan, N., Rajagopal, S., Rao, M.M.: Analysis of photoplethysmographic signals of cardiovascular patients. In: Proceedings of the 23rd Annual International Conference Engineering Medicine Biology Society, pp. 2204–2207 (2001)
3. Sornmo, L., Laguna, P.: Bioelectrical Signal Processing in Cardiac and Neurological Applications. Elsevier Academic Press, Cambridge (2005)
4. Martín-Martínez, D., Casaseca-de-la-Higuera, P., Martín-Fernández, M., Alberola-López, C.: Stochastic modeling of the PPG signal: a synthesis-by-analysis approach with applications. IEEE Trans. Biomed. Eng. **60**, 2432–2441 (2013)
5. Birkhoff, G., Schulz, M.H., Varga, R.S.: Piecewise Hermite interpolation in one and two variables with applications to partial differential equations. Numer. Math. **11**, 232–256 (1968)
6. Aboy, M., McNames, J., Thong, T., Tsunami, D., Ellenby, M., Goldstein, B.: An automatic beat detection algorithm for pressure signals. IEEE Trans. Biomed. Eng. **52**, 1662–1670 (2005)

Peripheral Nerves Segmentation in Ultrasound Images Using Non-linear Wavelets and Gaussian Processes

Julián Gil González$^{(\boxtimes)}$, Mauricio A. Álvarez, and Álvaro A. Orozco

Faculty of Engineering, Universidad Tecnológica de Pereira,
Pereira 660003, Colombia
{jugil,malvarez,aaog}@utp.edu.co

Abstract. Regional anesthesia is carried out using a technique called peripheral nerve blocking (PNB), which involves the administration of an anesthetic nearby the nerve. Ultrasound images have been widely used for PNB procedure due to their low cost and because they are non-invasive. However, the segmentation of nerve structures in ultrasound images is a challenging task for the specialists since the images are affected by echo perturbations and speckle noise. Automatic or semi-automatic segmentation systems can be developed in order to aid the specialist for locating nerves structures accurately. In this paper we propose a methodology for the semi-automatic segmentation of nerve structures in ultrasound images. We use non-linear Wavelets transform in the feature extraction step and for the classification stage we use a Gaussian Processes classifier. Experimental results show that the implemented methodology can segment nerve structures accurately.

Keywords: Machine learning · Non-linear wavelets · Ultrasound image segmentation

1 Introduction

Regional anesthesia is carried out using the peripheral nerve blocking (PNB) technique, which consists of the administration of an anesthetic near to a nerve structure. The anesthetic diffusion throughout the nerve inhibits its electrical conduction by blocking sodium channels, and thus the transmission of nociceptive information to the central nervous system. Localization of peripheral nerves is a very important step when a regional anesthesia procedure is performed [1]. Four methods have been used in the clinical practice for the achievement of PNB: Application of anatomical surface landmarks, elicitation of paresthesia, electrical stimulation and ultrasound imaging [1]. The use of anatomical landmarks enables the specialist to find the place where the needle has to be inserted, this approach is not very common in clinical practice due to anatomical differences from a patient to another [1]. Paresthesia elicited during the exploration with a needle indicates that the needle is located in the proximity of a nerve

© Springer International Publishing Switzerland 2015
R. Paredes et al. (Eds.): IbPRIA 2015, LNCS 9117, pp. 603–611, 2015.
DOI: 10.1007/978-3-319-19390-8_68

structure [1], however its use imposes inconvenience on the patient [2]. The electrical stimulation of nerves is carried out applying an electrical impulse with a neuron-stimulation needle in the proximity of a peripheral nerve [3]. The stimulated nerve produces a muscle contraction in the area innervated by the nerve. This approach has been established as the standard for several years [1].

Unlike the aforementioned techniques, the ultrasound imaging gives a non-invasive visualization of the peripheral nerve, the nearby tissues and the injected anesthetic to ensure optimal distribution [1]. However, the ultrasound images are affected by echo-perturbations and Speckle noise [4,5], which makes difficult the nerve structures location process, this is one reason why anesthesiologists have to take long trainings in order to acquire the necessary experience in recognizing nerves with ultrasound images. This problem can be minimized through the development of automatic or semi-automatic segmentation systems in order to help the specialist in location of nerves structures in ultrasound images and thus improve the accuracy in PNB procedures.

Different methods have been proposed for segmenting anatomical structures in ultrasound images. Such structures include: the thyroid gland [4,6], the prostate [7], and breast tumors [8]. Among the methods employed, we can found: region growing methods [9], active contour models [5] and methods based on machine learning techniques [4]. The latter has gained great attention for segmentation in ultrasound images, because it deals with inhomogeneity in the target regions with good performance [10]. In the literature no information was found about segmentation methods for blocking peripheral nerves, so the development of this work provides important information to the study of segmentation techniques for this type of organic structures (nerves).

In this paper we propose a methodology for the semi-automatic segmentation of peripheral nerves based on machine learning techniques for assisting in regional anesthesia procedures. This methodology includes: non-linear wavelets for the features extraction step and a model based on Gaussian processes for the classification stage The performance of this methodology is measured in terms of accuracy, sensibility and specificity.

2   Materials and Methods

2.1   Dataset

The dataset was collected at the Confamiliar Clinic located in Pereira, Colombia. It is formed by 31 images, where 18 correspond to the cubital nerve and 13 images correspond to the median nerve (both nerves are located in the forearm). The anesthesiologist obtains each nerve image using a Sonosite Nano-Maxx device, with a maximum resolution of 640×480. The images were obtained with informed consent from the patients. Figure 1 shows two images belonging to the dataset.

2.2   Non-linear Wavelet Transform

Originally, the wavelet transform is a linear tool. However it is possible to build a non-linear Wavelet using the lifting schemes proposed in [11]. The discrete

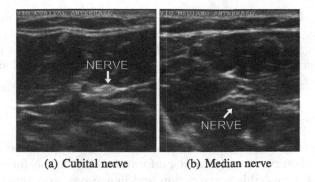

(a) Cubital nerve   (b) Median nerve

Fig. 1. Image from cubital nerve and median nerve contained in the dataset

Wavelet transform represents a signal in terms of shifts and dilations of a scaling function $\varphi(t)$ and a Wavelet function $\psi(t)$ [12]. As the scaling function and the Wavelet function are related with filters, the Wavelet transform is usually implemented using a low-pass and high-pass filter banks ($\hat{h}$ and $\hat{g}$).

The lifting schemes are simple modifications made on the filters $\hat{h}$ and $\hat{g}$, in order to improve the Wavelet properties related with the filters [11]. A typical lifting scheme begins with the decomposition of the input signal X into its even X_e and odd X_o components. Then successive updates are used to gradually build a variable resolution analysis with particular properties. The lifting on the even component X_e is known as Primar lifting. Whereas, the lifting on the odd component X_o is called Dual lifting.

The lifting schemes allows to include adaptive stages for selecting the primar lifting filter U and the dual lifting filter P based on some decision criterion D, which depends of local characteristics of the signal X. The adaptive lifting schemes can be applied for the Non-linear Wavelet transform in images, according to the scheme proposed by [12].

2.3 Gaussian Processes for Classification

Let $\mathcal{D} = \{\mathbf{X}, \mathbf{y}\}$ be a training set with N samples, where $\mathbf{X}$ corresponds to the input matrix $\mathbf{X} = [\mathbf{x}_1, \mathbf{x}_2, \ldots, \mathbf{x}_N]^\top$ and $\mathbf{y}$ is the target vector. Each feature vector $\mathbf{x}_i$ with dimensionality d, is associated a target value $y_i \in \{-1, 1\}$. The probability of a sample $\mathbf{x}_i$ belonging to a class $y_i = 1$, $p(\mathbf{y}_i = 1|\mathbf{x}_i)$ is monotonically related to a value of some latent function f_i. This relationship between $p(y_i = 1|\mathbf{x}_i)$ and f_i is defined according to a squashing function $\sigma(\cdot)$ [14]. There are several functions that can be adopted as squashing function, but in this work we use the logistic function. The Gaussian processes prior over the latent values $\mathbf{f}$ is given by $p(\mathbf{f}|\mathbf{X}) = \mathcal{N}(\mathbf{f}|\mathbf{0}, \mathbf{K})$, where $\mathbf{K}$ is the covariance matrix computed using an specific kernel function. It can be shown that the probabilistic prediction for the new sample $\mathbf{x}_\star$ is given by [15].

$$p(y_\star = 1|\mathcal{D}, \mathbf{x}_\star) = \int p(y_\star|f_\star)p(f_\star|\mathcal{D}, \mathbf{x}_\star)df_\star \tag{1}$$

The predictive distribution given by (1), has no analytic solution and should be computed using analytic approximations [15]. In this case we use the Laplace approximation. The covariance matrix $\mathbf{K}$ is computed using an squared exponential function kernel. The unspecified parameters in the model are estimated by minimizing the negative log of the marginal likelihood.

2.4   Procedure

We follow a methodology similar to the one proposed in [4]. The semi-automatic segmentation of nerve structures is performed through the following stages: (1) Location of a probable nerve region and image pre-processing; (2) Feature extraction; (3) Classification; and (4) Post-processing.

1. **Location of a Probable Nerve Region and Image Pre-processing.** The acquisition of medical images from ultrasound devices introduces noise and artifacts that affect the segmentation results and therefore they have to be minimized without removing or altering the anatomical details of the structures in the image. For that reason, a pre-processing step is necessary for enhancing the location of a probable nerve region. The location of a probable nerve region and image pre-processing are carried out following the next steps:
   (a) **Locating the Probable Nerve Region.** Commonly, nerve structures occupy a very small region of the ultrasound image (see Fig. 1), for that reason it is not necessary to analyze all the regions for segmenting the nerve. A location of a probable nerve region is thus required in order to define a region of interest (ROI) that allows to reduce computational times. For this work, the location of a probable nerve region is performed manually by an anesthesiologist who has to indicate two values of rows (R_1 and R_2) among which the nerve is probably located. So the generated ROI will have the same number of columns as the original image and a number of rows given by ($R_2 - R_1$).
   (b) **Filtering.** A median filter is performed on the ROI with the purpose of minimizing the speckle noise. Two morphological opening and closing operators are applied in order to improve the result from filtering. For this procedure we configure a rectangular mask with size 3×3.
2. **Feature Extraction.** For the feature extraction step, the ROI is divided in grids with size $M \times M$ without overlapping (several experiments are necessary in order to define the appropriate value for the size of the grid M), then a set of texture features are extracted from each grid. For this work we extract a set of features based on the first level non-linear Wavelet transform. This set is formed by the mean μ_B, the standard deviation σ_B and the entropy E_B, computed from each band obtained with the non-linear Wavelet transform ($X_{LL}, X_{LH}, X_{HL}, X_{HH}$), thus forming a set of features with dimensionality 12. We use three different feature sets: set 1 is based on the dual adaptive lifting scheme; for the set 2 we use the primar adaptive lifting scheme and set 3 is formed from the primar-dual adaptive lifting scheme.

3. **Classification.** The classifier based on Gaussian Processes[1] is trained using the set of features extracted from each block on the ROI; where each block has been labeled by a specialist as a nerve structure or not. Usually there are more grids labeled as non-nerve than grids labeled as nerve, hence it is necessary to ensure the balance of number of grids labeled as nerve structures and grids labeled as non-nerves. Now for the test stage, the ROI, is split into grids of size $M \times M$, with overlapping equal to 50 %. Then the features extracted from each grid are considered as input for the trained classifier. The Classifier based on Gaussian process classifies each grid as nerve or non-nerve. Now for each grid classified as nerve, we analyze its 8 nearest neighbors, and if at least 4 of those neighbors are non-nerves then the grid is re-assigned to the class non-nerve. Finally the largest connected component is considered as part of the nerve structure [4].
4. **Post-processing.** Using the procedure described above, a region with a pure nerve structure is extracted. However, the shape of the nerve extracted is serrated. Hence, it is necessary to implement a methodology that allows to recover the complete nerve region. In this paper we implement a methodology based on a specific-region-growing proposed in [4]

2.5 Validation

The classifier performance is evaluated using the leave-one-out scheme due to the small number of images in the dataset. Each experiment is repeated 20 times, in each repetition we choose randomly the set for training the classifiers, ensuring the balance between the number of samples labeled as nerves and samples labeled as non-nerves. For measuring the performance of the implemented methodology we proposed three metrics: accuracy, sensitivity and specificity.

3 Results and Discussion

In this work two experiments were performed. The first experiment was carried out in order to estimate the appropriate values for the parameter M (size of the grid) and the parameter T (corresponding the threshold for the specific-region-growing used in the post-processing step). For this experiment, we use different values for M and T and we use the methodology mentioned in Sect. 2.4. For the feature extraction step, we use the parametrization proposed in [4] and for the classification step, we use a model based on support vector machine (SVM) which was implemented using the radial basis function kernel. Table 1 shows the results for the first experiment configured.

From the results reported in the Table 1, we see that in this implemented methodology there were not significant differences between the values of accuracy and specificity when the parameters M and T were changed; but this does

---

[1] For the Gaussian Processes classifier, we use the software available on http://www.gaussianprocess.org/gpml/code/matlab/doc/.

Table 1. Results from the first experiment configured. We use four values for M (4, 8, 16, 32) and six values for the parameter T (5, 10, 15, 20, 25, 30). Columns "Accuracy (%)", "Sensitivity (%)" and "Specificity (%)" report mean and standard deviation.

		Accuracy(%)	Sensitivity (%)	Specificity (%)
$M = 4$	T=5	90,62±0,24	81,47±1,67	91,36±0,22
	T=10	90,49±0,27	81,78±1,49	91,19±0,23
	T=15	90,44±0,26	82,18±1,52	91,11±0,25
	T=20	90,38±0,28	82,05±1,32	91,06±0,29
	T=25	90,30±0,24	82,46±1,32	90,93±0,28
	T=30	**90,28±0,22**	**82,94±1,45**	**90,87±0,23**
$M = 8$	T=5	93,99±0,32	65,58±2,36	96,28±0,25
	T=10	93,92±0,24	66,07±1,95	96,16±0,19
	T=15	93,83±0,31	66,27±2,43	96,05±0,24
	T=20	93,88±0,26	66,65±1,25	96,07±0,23
	T=25	93,80±0,36	66,39±2,08	96,01±0,32
	T=30	93,72±0,31	66,73±2,39	95,90±0,23
$M = 16$	T=5	93,87±0,21	34,50±2,33	98,66±0,24
	T=10	93,88±0,23	34,83±2,63	98,64±0,15
	T=15	93,86±0,31	34,45±2,98	98,65±0,22
	T=20	93,76±0,22	34,75±3,13	98,55±0,21
	T=25	93,73±0,27	34,33±2,93	98,52±0,24
	T=30	93,84±0,38	35,34±3,95	98,55±0,23
$M = 32$	T=5	86,49±2,27	15,14±5,01	92,24±2,67
	T=10	88,07±1,80	13,45±5,38	94,09+2,25
	T=15	88,39±2,07	11,84±3,64	94,56±2,38
	T=20	87,72±1,87	14,42±4,38	93,62±2,23
	T=25	87,51±2,03	13,87±4,22	93,45±2,38
	T=30	87,66±1,80	14,75±4,42	93,53±2,22

not occur with the sensitivity which significantly decreases when the grid size M becomes larger. These results can be explained in the sense that the nerve structures have tiny sizes (see Fig. 1), so when the grid size becomes greater, the methodology can not segment the entire nerve region and hence reason the performance decreases. From this analysis it is possible to determine the appropriate value for the size of the grid M is four. Whereas, it was observed that the threshold value T does not generate significants changes in the performance, so it is possible to assume any value in the range [5, 30].

A second experiment was configured in order to compare the methodology performance using four different feature sets, the first three sets were obtained with the non-linear Wavelet transform (see Sect. 2.4) and the last one, is the proposed in [4]. In the classification step we used two classifier models: One of

Table 2. Results from the second experiment. We compare the methodology performance using two different classifiers: Gaussian Process for Classification (GPC) and Support Vector Machine (SVM). We use three sets of features the first three sets are based in non-linear Wavelet transform (see Sect. 2.4). Finally, we use the parametrization proposed by [4] for the set 4. Columns "Accuracy (%)", "Sensitivity (%)" and "Specificity (%)" report the means and standard deviation

		Accuracy(%)	Sensitivity (%)	Specificity (%)
SVM	Set 1	90,14±0,23	84,58±1,63	90,59±0,18
	Set 2	89,74±0,39	82,19±2,14	90,35±0,37
	Set 3	88,74±0,36	**86,88±2,46**	88,89±0,37
	Set 4	90,30±0,24	82,46±1,32	90,93±0,28
GPC	Set 1	92,52±0,43	51,57±6,45	95,82±0,58
	Set 2	89,14±0,15	**85,22±0,97**	89,45±0,17
	Set 3	89,52±0,15	80,81±1,43	90,22±0,16
	Set 4	92,64±0,42	32,85±6,52	97,46±0,58

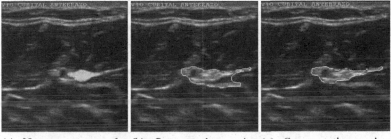

(a) Nerve structure labeled by the anethesiologist (b) Segmentation using GPC (c) Segmentation using SVM

Fig. 2. Segmentation results using the implemented methodology in comparison to the manual segmentation carried out by the anesthesiologist

them based on Gaussian Processes for Classification (GPC) and the other one based on SVM. For this experiment we grids with size 4×4 and a value of threshold $T = 25$. Table 2 shows the results for the second experiment. Figure 2 shows the segmentation for a cubital nerve using the implemented methodology.

From the results reported in Table 2, it is possible to analyze that there are not major differences between the performance of the two classifiers, with the exception of set 1 and set 4 in which the classifier based on SVM shows clearly a major level of sensitivity. However it is important to note that the result for the classifier based on Gaussian processes has lower level of standard deviation than the one based on SVM. In this sense we can deduce the Gaussian processes classifier offer more reliable results. Moreover, we can see the methodology performs better when it uses a parameterization based on non-linear Wavelet transform than when it uses the characterization implemented in [4]. These results can be explained in the sense that non-linear Wavelet transform can obtain a better representation of textures present in the nerve structures.

4   Conclusions

We have presented a semi-automatic methodology for the segmentation of nerve structures based on supervised machine learning techniques. The experimental results shows this methodology can be used for segmenting nerves structures accurately, having as the best average performance 85,22 % in terms of sensitivity. This methodology can be used in order to assist the specialist in locating nerve structures in ultrasound images when a regional anesthesia procedure is performed. Future work can be focused on development of an automatic segmentation methodology in order to avoid the manual search of the possible nerve region.

Acknowledgment. This work was developed under the project "Desarrollo de una metodología para la segmentación automática de regiones objetivo en imágenes ultrasónicas a partir de modelos estadísticos. Aplicación a los procedimientos de anestesia regional", with financial support of the Universidad Tecnológica de Pereira. Furthermore we want to thank the Dr. Diego Salazar from Confamiliar Clinic, who labeled the nerve structures and helped us to acquire the ultrasound images.

References

1. Shi, J., Schwaiger, J., Lueth, T.C.: Nerve block using a navigation system and ultrasound imaging for regional anesthesia. In: 2011 Annual International Conference of the IEEE Engineering in Medicine and Biology Society, EMBC, pp. 1153–1156. IEEE (2011)
2. Karaca, P., Hadzic, A., Yufa, M., Vloka, J.D., Brown, A.R., Visan, A., Santos, A.C.: Painful paresthesiae are infrequent during brachial plexus localization using low-current peripheral nerve stimulation. Reg. Anesth. Pain Med. **28**(5), 380–383 (2003)
3. Marhofer, P., Chan, V.W.: Ultrasound-guided regional anesthesia: current concepts and future trends. Anesth. Analg. **104**(5), 1265–1269 (2007)
4. Chang, C.Y., Lei, Y.F., Tseng, C.H., Shih, S.R.: Thyroid segmentation and volume estimation in ultrasound images. IEEE Trans. Biomed. Eng. **57**(6), 1348–1357 (2010)
5. Maroulis, D.E., Savelonas, M.A., Iakovidis, D.K., Karkanis, S.A., Dimitropoulos, N.: Variable background active contour model for computer-aided delineation of nodules in thyroid ultrasound images. IEEE Trans. Inf. Tech. Biomed. **11**(5), 537–543 (2007)
6. Selvathi, D., Sharnitha, V.S.: Thyroid classification and segmentation in ultrasound images using machine learning algorithms. In: 2011 International Conference on Signal Processing, Communication, Computing and Networking Technologies (ICSCCN), pp. 836–841. IEEE (2011)

7. Xie, J., Jiang, Y., Tsui, H.T.: Segmentation of kidney from ultrasound images based on texture and shape priors. IEEE Trans. Med. Imaging **24**(1), 45–57 (2005)
8. Liu, B., Cheng, H.D., Huang, J., Tian, J., Tang, X., Liu, J.: Fully automatic and segmentation-robust classification of breast tumors based on local texture analysis of ultrasound images. Pattern Recogn. **43**(1), 280–298 (2010)
9. Oghli, M.G., Fallahi, A., Pooyan, M.: Automatic region growing method using GSmap and spatial information on ultrasound images. In: 2010 18th Iranian Conference on Electrical Engineering (ICEE), pp. 35–38. IEEE (2010)
10. Qian, X., Yoon, B.J.: Contour-based hidden Markov model to segment 2D ultrasound images. In: 2011 IEEE International Conference on Acoustics, Speech and Signal Processing (ICASSP), pp. 705–708. IEEE May 2011
11. Sweldens, W.: The lifting scheme: A construction of second generation wavelets. SIAM J. Math. Anal. **29**(2), 511–546 (1998)
12. Mallat, S.: A Wavelet Tour of Signal Processing. Academic press, Chicago (1999)
13. Claypoole, R.L., Davis, G.M., Sweldens, W., Baraniuk, R.G.: Nonlinear wavelet transforms for image coding via lifting. IEEE Trans. Image Process. **12**(12), 1449–1459 (2003)
14. Bazi, Y., Melgani, F.: Classification of hyperspectral remote sensing images using Gaussian processes. In: IEEE International Geoscience and Remote Sensing Symposium. IGARSS 2008 vol. 2, pp. II-1013. IEEE July 2008
15. Rasmussen, C.E.: Gaussian processes for machine learning (2006)

Improving Diffusion Tensor Estimation Using Adaptive and Optimized Filtering Based on Local Similarity

Andrés F. López-Lopera(✉), Mauricio A. Álvarez, and Álvaro Á. Orozco

Electrical Engineering Program, Universidad Tecnológica de Pereira,
Pereira, Colombia
{anfelopera,malvarez,aaog}@utp.edu.co

Abstract. The diffusion-weighted magnetic resonance imaging (DW-MRI) has been used to diagnose anomalies in human brain by describing the magnitude and directionality of water diffusion per voxel. Such information can be represented alternatively in diffusion tensor imaging (DT-MRI), yielding images of normal and abnormal white matter fiber structures, and maps of brain connectivity through fiber tracking. A DW-MRI study is usually characterized by a low signal to noise ratio, which may reflect in the poor estimation of DT-MRI. Filters based on local similarity have been receiving increasing attention, but they have been barely studied for DT-MRI. In this proposal we introduce adaptive and optimized filtering techniques based on local similarity for MRI to remove the biasing in both DW-MRI filtering and DT-MRI estimation, evidencing a better performance respect to classical filters and robust DT estimation algorithms. We estimate the DT-MRI extracting metrics computed from the DT to evaluate the filtering performance.

Keywords: Adaptive and optimized filtering · Diffusion tensor imaging · Diffusion-weighted magnetic resonance imaging

1 Introduction

The diffusion-weighted magnetic resonance imaging (DW-MRI or DWI) studies 4D diffusion images, and widely used to diagnose several pathological anomalies in human brain [1]. The DW-MRI describes the neuronal pathways which are used for communication among several centers of brain activity. In the last decades, different clinical communities have focused on DW-MRI for studying the microscopic water particles' motion within brain tissue for the diagnosis of pathologies. This information can be represented alternatively in diffusion tensor imaging (DT-MRI or DTI), where the diffusion tensor (DT) describes the magnitude and the directionality of water diffusion in a specific voxel, producing images of normal and abnormal white matter fiber structure. Also, DT-MRI yields maps of brain connectivity through fiber tracking [2]. Therefore, the studies of DW-MRI and DT-MRI are promising in pre-operative planning of neurodegenerative diseases [3].

© Springer International Publishing Switzerland 2015
R. Paredes et al. (Eds.): IbPRIA 2015, LNCS 9117, pp. 612–620, 2015.
DOI: 10.1007/978-3-319-19390-8_69

The DW-MRI has an inherent low signal to noise ratio (SNR) due to a low signal amplitude and a pronounced thermal noise, complicating and biasing the estimation of diffusion tensors [1]. A common practice for increasing the SNR in DW-MRI is averaging several DW-MRI studies in order to reduce noise variance [2]. This practice does not remove noise bias and consume a long acquisition time, therefore it is not adequate for typical clinical settings [1]. A potential alternative to the averaging of several DW-MRI studies, is to include an additional denoising stage in DWI that helps to improve the DTI estimation. Different filtering methods have been applied in the preprocessing stages, aiming to achieve denoised images that help to improve the DT-MRI estimation [1]. Classic denoising techniques in DW-MRI filtering such as Gaussian filters [4] and the algorithm proposed by Perona and Malik in [5], assume an equal noise distribution across the image, modifying important information (e.g. edges, structures and type of matter), leading to suboptimal filtering results. Methods based on local similarity have been receiving increasing attention due their local filtering adaptation, having the potential to improve qualitatively and quantitatively the estimation of diffusion information with respect to another filtering techniques [1,2,6]. Moreover, adaptive and optimized filters based on local similarity can mitigate the drawbacks of having to deal with tuning the filter parameters, but they have been barely studied for DW-MRI data. In this proposal, we introduce some adaptive and optimized methods grounded in non-local means (NLM) similarity, and principal component analysis decomposition (PCA) in order to achieve better results in both denoising DW-MRI and DT-MRI estimation. We experimentally show that by using filters that take into account local similarity in the DWI, it is possible to outperform classical filters previously used in this literature.

In this paper, we compare the DTI estimation results using different adaptive and optimized filtering techniques based on local similarity to remove Rician noise, smoothing images and enhancing the edges of the brain structures. We use several metrics computed from the diffusion tensors to evaluate the performance for each filter. This paper is organized as follows. The materials and methods are described in Sect. 2. In Sect. 3, we discuss and compare the final results obtained by using the different filtering techniques, evaluating the performance for each one using the DT estimated. Finally, conclusions are given in Sect. 4.

2   Materials and Methods

In order to introduce the solution for a better DW-MRI filtering, ensuring a reliable diffusion information, in this section we will describe the advantages and disadvantages for the different filters that were used in this paper. We will describe three classic filters used to denoising DW-MRI, evidencing the tuning problem of the filtering parameters. Second, we introduce a series of adaptive and optimized filtering techniques based on local similarity used in brain imaging preprocessing, aiming to achieve a better DW-MRI filtering. Third, we introduce the concept of DT estimation to evaluate the performance of the above filters.

Finally, we describe the procedure and the experimental background used to obtain the results in Sect. 3.

2.1 Gaussian Filter (GF)

GF is the first of the most common filters used in DW-MRI. This filter can be applied in brain image preprocessing, aiming to achieve an isotropic or anisotropic smoothing by the convolution between a multivariate Gaussian kernel with the corrupted image. This filter can remove noise from images, but a poor tuning of the scale parameter tends to blur the edges from brain structures [4].

2.2 Perona-Malik Algorithm

Perona and Malik in [5], proved that the problem of denoising DW-MRI can be based on the diffusion equation expressed in (1), if we assume that the images are both spatial and temporal functions. The diffusion equation over the intensities $\mathbf{u}(x)$ per voxel x is given by

$$\frac{\partial \mathbf{u}(x,t)}{\partial t} = \mathrm{div}\left\{g(\|\nabla \mathbf{u}(x,t)\|)\nabla \mathbf{u}(x,t)\right\}, \tag{1}$$

where $\mathrm{div}\{\cdot\}$ is the divergence operator, $g(\cdot)$ is a monotonically decreasing function, and the initial condition from (1) is the noisy image. The performance of this filter depends of the type and monotonic trend of $g(\cdot)$ [5].

2.3 Non-local Means Filter (NLM)

Filters based on NLM, originally proposed by Baudes et al. in [7], have become an attractive way to remove noise preserving original structures. NLM considers the high level of pattern redundancy from images, aiming to achieve high-quality image denoising by averaging similar realizations of the noisy signals [6]. In a 2D set of parallel images $\mathbf{u}$, the restored intensities $\hat{\mathbf{u}}(x_i)$ of the position or voxel x_i, is a weighted average of the surrounding voxels intensities $\mathbf{u}(x_i)$ in a sliding volume V_i [1], given by Eq. (2)

$$\hat{\mathbf{u}}(x_i) = \sum_{x_j \in V_i} w(x_i, x_j)\mathbf{u}(x_j), \tag{2}$$

where $w(x_i, x_j) \in [0, 1]$ is the weight assigned to $\mathbf{u}(x_j)$ to restore the intensity $\mathbf{u}(x_i)$, based on the square of the Euclidean distance given as

$$w(x_i, x_j) = \frac{1}{Z_i} \exp\left\{\frac{\|\mathbf{u}(x_i) - \mathbf{u}(x_j)\|_2^2}{h^2}\right\}, \tag{3}$$

with Z_i a normalization constant and h controls the contributed information of the surrounding voxels in V_i. Once again, the performance of this filter depends on the parameters h and V_i.

The performance of the above filters heavily depends on how well we tune the parameter for each one. To avoid this problem, several researches have proposed a series of adaptive and optimized filter techniques based on local similarity for brain imaging preprocessing (e.g. NLM, DCT and PCA). Next, we briefly review some optimized variants of filters based on NLM, DCT and PCA decomposition.

2.4   Adaptive and Optimized NLM Filter (AONLM)

The AONLM filter was proposed by Majón et al. in [1], designed for spatially varying noise typically presented in MRI. This filter includes a noise estimation module (e.g. Gaussian or Rician noise), making it an automatic and robust to outliers. This method deals with the non stationary noise with the introduction of the local noise estimation proposed by Wiest Daessl [8], removing the bias intensity using the properties of the second-order moment of the Rician law. In practice, AONLM is more robust than an optimized NLM but it does not achieve the intensity bias correction. Results in [1], have showed a better performance with respect to NLM for different image types and noise levels.

2.5   Oracle-Based 3D Discrete Cosine Transform Filter (ODCT)

In [6], the authors propose an extension of the original method proposed by Guleryuz in [9]. ODCT is based on a discrete cosine transform (DCT) that takes advantages of the sparseness information from images. In contrast to DCT, ODCT assumes that the previous well known null coefficients of the denoised image can be applied to improve the denoising. This method minimizes the mean squared error with respect to a pre-filtered image obtained by DCT. In [10], the authors propose the Rician median absolute deviation method (RMAD) in order to estimate a slanted the noise variance making the filter to be fully automatic. Results in [6] evidence a successful filtering of MRI in a few time [6].

2.6   Prefiltered Rotationally Invariant NLM Filter (PRINLM)

Coupé et al. propose an approach that uses the extended ODCT preprocessing results for a new filtering stage based on a rotationally invariant version of the NLM filtering to compute patch similarities. It is known as PRINLM [6]. This filter takes advantage of both sparseness and self-similarity properties between voxel intensities and the corresponding local patch mean using a Gaussian kernel. The authors propose the RMAD method in order to estimate the noise variance. Whereas ODCT tends to slightly oversmooth edges and some fine details, the PRINLM seems to retain more details in the denoised image because of its voxelwise processing. Experimental works in [6] have shown a high compressibility of MRI data, allowing a more efficient noise reduction and benefiting visual diagnostics in MRI brain tissue segmentation.

2.7   Local PCA Filter (LPCA)

Recently, Majón et al. have proposed an efficient denoising filter that takes into account the nature of 4D images structures (e.g. DWI) in [2], integrating a noise estimation module making it an automatic and a robust filter. This filter computes the PCA decomposition over a 4D sliding window at each image position in order to locally find a reduced representation of diffusion information, promoting sparser representation in contrast to related PCA methods [11]. In [2], the authors have proposed an automatic method for estimate and provide the local noise variance prior for the LPCA filter. In DW-MRI preprocessing, the LPCA filter takes advantages of the locality to reduces the bias induced by the Rician noise in DWI, producing a better diffusion parameter estimations that reflect the real characteristics of tissues, rather than noise-biased measurements. Results in clinical datasets [2], evidence high degree of confidence, potentially improving any quantitative measure derived from them.

2.8   Diffusion Tensors (DT)

As previously stated, the DWI contains information of the neuronal pathways used for communication in the brain [3], and it is possible to embed this information in symmetric 3×3 matrices known as diffusion tensors (DT) per voxel [12]. Stejskal-Tanner in [13], relates the DWI and DTI fields by the Eq. (4)

$$S_k = S_0 \exp\left\{-b\hat{\mathbf{g}}_k^\top \mathbf{D}\hat{\mathbf{g}}_k\right\}, \tag{4}$$

where S_k is the DW-MRI associated to the k-th diffusion direction with $k = 1, 2 \cdots, \mathcal{K}$ and $\mathcal{K}$ is the number of directions. S_0 is the baseline image, $\hat{\mathbf{g}}$ is a normalized gradient vector, b is a diffusion parameter and $\mathbf{D}$ is the tensor matrix per voxel. Also it is possible to visualize the diffusion information from the DT calculating metrics based on diffusion information such as the fractional anisotropy (FA) and the mean diffusivity (MD). Several researches have proposed different methods for DTI estimation such as linear systems with non-negative constraints [14] and methods based on least-squares criterion (e.g. RESTORE)[1] [15]. Recently, clinical studies have proved that there is a relationship between some diseases and the changes in the connectivity of certain brain areas. Therefore, the DW-MRI potential and the use of DT-MRI are promising in terms of diagnosis and pre-operative planning of neurodegenerative diseases [3].

2.9   Procedure

Experimental Background: In this proposal, we worked with a complete set of DWI images in the Nifti format[2] (dti30.nii), with both the direction and

---

[1] The robust estimation of tensors by outlier rejection (RESTORE), uses iteratively reweighted least-squares regression to identify potential outliers and exclude them. Available on http://nipy.org/dipy/examples_built/restore_dti.html.

[2] Dataset used by Leigh Morrow et al. from a 3-Tesla Siemens Trio. Available at http://www.cabiatl.com/CABI/resources/dti-analysis/.

header information (`dti30.bvec`,`dti30.bval`). This dataset contains 60 slices (102 × 102 each one) and 62 gradient directions per slice. We applied the LPCA filter over the dataset in order to remove the intrinsic noise. We refer to this pre-processed dataset as the `DTI30-DWI.nii` dataset. We use the new dataset as the goal standard to compare the preprocessing methods listed above in Sect. 2. Subsequently, we introduce a Rician noise with $\sigma = 25$ for evaluating the filtering performance.

Filtering techniques and DT estimation method: The parameters for GF and PM were tuned by cross-validation, aiming to achieve the best performance. For PM implementation, we chose a monotonic function privileging wide regions over smaller ones proposed in [5]. For the optimized filters described in Sect. 2, we

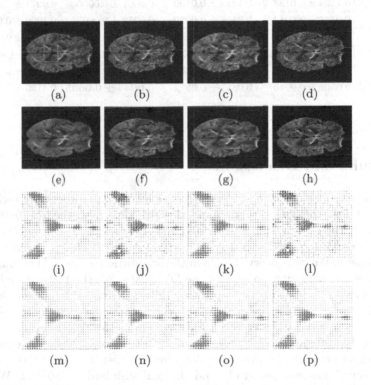

Fig. 1. DWI and DTI results for the proposed filtering methods using the 38th direction and the 30th slide from the `DTI30-DWI.nii`. In (a) and (i) both DWI and DTI estimated from `DTI30-DWI` are showed, respectively. In (b) and (j) we show the corrupted DWI with Rician noise and its estimated DTI. In (c), (d), (e), (f), (g) and (h) we show the filtering results using GF, PM, AONLM, ODCT, PRINLM and LPCA, respectively. Finally in (k), (l), (m), (n), (o) and (p) we show the estimated DTI from the yellow square window drawn in (a) in the same order of the filtering techniques listed above (Color figure online).

used the package dedicated for 4D MRI proposed by Coupé[3]. Finally, we rely on the DT estimation method proposed by Barmpoutis in [14]. Also, we use RESTORE algorithm to evaluate the filtering performance.

Table 1. Frobenius norm from the difference of metrics computed from the DTI between the case under study and `DTI30-DWI.nii`. MD: mean diffusivity error. RA: relative anisotropy error. FA: fractional anisotropy error. Frob: Frobenius error norm. The mean performance and standard deviation are drawn using all the slices ($\mu \pm \sigma$).

Scheme	MD ($\times 10^{-4}$)	RA ($\times 10^{-3}$)	FA	Frob ($\times 10^{-3}$)
Noisy	0.1234 ± 0.0131	0.1912 ± 0.0190	0.0061 ± 0.0006	0.9274 ± 0.0974
GF	0.0679 ± 0.0078	0.1366 ± 0.0149	0.0060 ± 0.0006	0.5371 ± 0.0449
PM	0.1234 ± 0.0131	0.1912 ± 0.0190	0.0061 ± 0.0006	0.9274 ± 0.0974
AONLM	0.0145 ± 0.0014	0.0558 ± 0.0070	0.0058 ± 0.0007	0.1960 ± 0.0237
ODCT	0.0112 ± 0.0017	0.0448 ± 0.0059	0.0059 ± 0.0006	0.1453 ± 0.0198
PRINLM	$\mathbf{0.0090 \pm 0.0019}$	$\mathbf{0.0300 \pm 0.0040}$	0.0059 ± 0.0006	$\mathbf{0.1148 \pm 0.0239}$
LPCA	0.0104 ± 0.0017	0.0437 ± 0.0057	0.0058 ± 0.0006	0.1296 ± 0.0161
RESTORE	0.0508 ± 0.0046	0.0857 ± 0.0072	$\mathbf{0.0044 \pm 0.0005}$	0.4130 ± 0.0077

3   Results and Discussions

In order to visualize the filtering performance for each preprocessing technique, in Fig. 1 we show the 38th direction and the 30th slide from the `DTI30-DWI.nii` dataset with their both respective noisy and filtered images using the above filters mentioned in Sect. 2. Also, we show the estimated DTI for each previous DW-MRI cases. We can observe a bias in the orientation of the DTI estimated by the introduction of Rician noise over the DWI data. All the filtering techniques tend to remove this bias, but the optimized filters denoise the image in a better way with respect to the classical filters, concluding that the methods based on local similarity have a better performance in both DWI filtering and DTI estimating. Finally, in Table 1 we evaluate quantitatively the filters computing the Frobenius error norm from the difference of metrics computed from the DTI between the case under study and the goal standard `DTI30-DWI`. We draw the mean performance and standard deviation using all the slices from each dataset. Also, we extract this error metrics for the results using RESTORE. This robust algorithm obtains a better FA performance due it was designed to recover the trace and the FA from the DT by using Monte Carlo simulations [15]. However, the optimized filters have better behaviour among the other metric errors. Finally, we can conclude that PRINLM and LPCA filters show the best performances among the optimized filters including the RESTORE algorithm.

---

[3] https://sites.google.com/site/pierrickcoupe.

4   Conclusions

The DW-MRI study has an inherently low signal to noise ratio, biasing the estimation of diffusion parameters. Classic denoising techniques that assume an equal noise distribution across the image modifying important information, produce suboptimal filtering results. Moreover, methods based on local similarity improves the performance of diffusion information. However, the performance of the above filters depend on how well we tune the filtering parameters.

Adaptive and optimized filter techniques based on local similarity for brain images, tend to remove the bias in both DWI filtering and DTI estimation by local information, showing a better performance respect to the classical filters and the robust RESTORE algorithm. According to our results, the PRINLM and LPCA filters show the best performances among the optimized filters, making them the most suitable for DWI.

Acknowledgment. This work was funded by COLCIENCIAS under the project 1110-569-34461. Authors were also supported by the 617 agreement, "Jóvenes Investigadores e Innovadores", funded by COLCIENCIAS. Finally, the authors are thankful to the research group in Automática ascribed to the engineering program at the Universidad Tecnológica de Pereira, and M.Sc. H.F. García for technical support.

References

1. Manjón, J.V., Coupé, P., Martí-Bonmatí, L., Collins, D.L., Robles, M.: Adaptive non-local means denoising of MR images with spatially varying noise levels. J. Magn. Reson. Imaging **31**(1), 192–203 (2010)
2. Manjón, J.V., Coupé, P., Concha, L., Buades, A., Collins, D.L., Robles, M.: Diffusion weighted image denoising using overcomplete local PCA. PLoS ONE **8**(9), 1–12 (2013)
3. Butson, C.R., Cooper, S.E., Henderson, J.M., Wolgamuth, B., McIntyre, C.C.: Probabilistic analysis of activation volumes generated during deep brain stimulation. NeuroImage **54**(3), 2096–2104 (2011)
4. Lee, J.E., Chung, M.K., Alexander, A.L.: Evaluation of anisotropic filters for diffusion tensor imaging. In: ISBI, pp. 77–78. IEEE (2006)
5. Perona, P., Malik, J.: Scale-space and edge detection using anisotropic diffusion. IEEE Trans. Pattern Anal. Mach. Intell. **12**(7), 629–639 (1990)
6. Manjón, J.V., Coupé, P., Buades, A., Louis Collins, D., Robles, M.: New methods for MRI denoising based on sparseness and self-similarity. Med. Image Anal. **16**(1), 18–27 (2012)
7. Buades, A., Coll, B., Morel, J.M.: A non-local algorithm for image denoising. In: IEEE Computer Society Conference on Computer Vision and Pattern Recognition. In: CVPR 2005, vol. 2, pp. 60–65, June 2005
8. Wiest-Daesslé, N., Prima, S., Coupé, P., Morrissey, S.P., Barillot, C.: Rician noise removal by non-local means filtering for low signal-to-noise ratio MRI: applications to DT-MRI. In: Metaxas, D., Axel, L., Fichtinger, G., Székely, G. (eds.) MICCAI 2008, Part II. LNCS, vol. 5242, pp. 171–179. Springer, Heidelberg (2008)
9. Guleryuz, O.: Weighted averaging for denoising with overcomplete dictionaries. IEEE Trans. Image Process. **16**(12), 3020–3034 (2007)

10. Coupé, P., Manjón, J.V., Gedamu, E., Arnold, D., Robles, M., Collins, D.L.: Robust rician noise estimation for MR images. Med. Image Anal. **14**(4), 483–493 (2010)
11. Phillip, K.P., Wei-Ren, Ng., Varun, S.: Image denoising with singular value decomposition and principal component analysis. The University of Arizona, pp. 1–29 (2009). http://www.u.arizona.edu/~ppoon/ImageDenoisingWithSVD.pdf
12. Niethammer, M., Estepar, R., Bouix, S., Shenton, M., Westin, C.F.: On diffusion tensor estimation. In: EMBS 2006, pp. 2622–2625, August 2006
13. Stejskal, E.O., Tanner, J.E.: Spin diffusion measurements: spin echoes in the presence of a time-dependent field gradient. J. Chem. Phys. **42**(1), 288–292 (1965)
14. Barmpoutis, A.: Tutorial on Diffusion Tensor MRI using Matlab. University of Florida (2010)
15. Chang, L.C., Jones, D.K., Pierpaoli, C.: Restore: Robust estimation of tensors by outlier rejection. Magn. Reson. Med. **53**, 1088–1095 (2005)

Dimension Reduction of Hyperspectral Image with Rare Event Preserving

Jihan Khoder[1(✉)], Rafic Younes[1,2], Hussein Obeid[2], and Mohamad Khalil[2]

[1] LISV Laboratory, University of Versailles Saint-Quentin En-Yvelines, Versailles, France
jihan.khoder@hotmail.com
[2] Faculty of Engineering, Lebanese University, Beirut, Lebanon

Abstract. Rare events can potentially occur in many applications, particularly in hyperspectral image analysis. In this work, we focus on the rare event preservation rate of the different dimension reduction approaches. The objective is to test whether the rare event is preserved after dimension reduction, or not. This paper introduced an improvement on the principal component analysis method (PCA) with added constraint related based on the Chi2 density function to rare event preservation, it was shown that the performance of the new method is better on the reduced image tested on natural hyperspectral images. Then we must use the constrained dimension reduction method for the rare event to be preserved. Given these results, we believe that it is very important to integrate this constraint to all the other dimension reduction methods, and then compare the potential contributions of information losses.

Keywords: PCA · Rare event · Hyperspectral · Reduction

1 Introduction

In Hyperspectral imaging, the acquired data volumes often reach the gigabyte for a single observed scene. Therefore, the analysis of these data, which have a complex physical content, must pass through a preliminary step of dimension reduction [22]. In fact, this reduction has a final objective to facilitate subsequent processing (information extraction, object classification and Pattern Recognition) while preserving the richness of information provided by this type of data, especially rare events [21]. A rare event is by definition, an event with a low probability of occurrence [17]. The development of methods to estimate the rare event probability is still a little in the shade, but nowadays we can find several researches in this domain.

Generally, rare events can potentially occur in many applications: Physically, to determine the expected amount of radiation that passes through a given shield; this amount is a rare event [1]. In the area of insurance companies [2], or construction companies, if a major project accomplishment time exceeds a certain deadline [1], this is a rare event. In telecommunications, a rare event can be as the probability of overflow of a buffer memory, or the mean time of overflow in a queue system [1], or the proportion of packets lost in a communication system [3]. In the electronic devices field or in factories,

© Springer International Publishing Switzerland 2015
R. Paredes et al. (Eds.): IbPRIA 2015, LNCS 9117, pp. 621–629, 2015.
DOI: 10.1007/978-3-319-19390-8_70

if the average failure time of an electronic device is smaller than the defined threshold [1], this is a rare event. In image analysis, hiding information in a digital file (typically audio or video), in a way that the change is not noticed, and is very difficult to remove (robust to any type of processing, coding, compression …) [4], can be considered as a rare event. Also, rare events may occur in mine research [5] and in pattern recognition [6].

A certain number of approaches have been proposed in the literature [7, 8] to estimate a signal subspace and rank, under the assumption that the data are independent, fixed, zero mean, and Gaussian. It is shown in [9], that the principal components analysis (PCA) is optimal, in the sense of maximum likelihood, for estimating a signal subspace. The author determines the signal space by minimizing the residues norm l_2 that belongs to the complementary subspace, which can be obtained by singular value decomposition (SVD). Nascimento and Dias [10] propose an approach called HySime, designed to determine both the signal subspace and rank in the hyperspectral imaging. The method involves three steps: (1) Signal definition and calculation of the noise covariance matrices, (2) Signal rank estimation, to find the subset of eigenvalues that best represents the subspace, in the sense of the data average, (3) Finding the signal subspace by applying SVD with reduced noise, on the data covariance matrix.

Oleg Kuybeda [11] addressed the redundancy minimization of large dimension data problem, by preserving rare vectors. He proposed an algorithm called Maximum Orthogonal-Complements (MOCA) to determine the signal subspace and rank, keeping both abundant and rare vectors, by using a standard $L_{2,\infty}$. This standard has two objectives: L_2 to minimize the abundant vectors and L_∞ to minimize rare vectors.

In [12], the authors proved that the standard $l_{2,\infty}$ can be used effectively for anomalies detection. However, the algorithm developed in [12], named Min-Max-SVD (MX-SVD), used for signal subspace estimation, only minimizes the standard $l_{2,\infty}$ for misrepresentation residues. A new optimal approach, that aims to minimize the standard $l_{2,\infty}$, called Maximum Orthogonal Subspace Optimal Estimation (MOOSE), is developed in [13]. The optimization is performed via learning gradient method, performed on all the subspaces of dimension n in R^m, where m > n. The results of MOOSE application, MX-SVD, and the approach based on the standard $l_{2,\infty}$, have been proven on real hyperspectral data.

Other approaches, related to the detection literature, have been used by the authors in [14, 15]. The aim of the research is to identify one or more rare events among all n events given by the data set. The authors have developed an optimal information criterion process that maximizes the reliability decision, preserving the rare information. Also, the sequential detection aims to identify all rare events or only one rare event, with probability ratio test (SPRT) [14] and the cumulative sum (CUMSUM) [16]. In [23], visual saliency is a bottom-up process that identifies those regions in an image that stand out from their surroundings. Oversegment an image as a collection of "super pixels" (SPs). Each SP is salient if it is different in color from all other SPs and if it's most similar SPs are nearby.

In this paper, we focus on the rare event preservation rate of the different dimension reduction approaches. Different approaches exist, such as those based on high dimension data projection (linear or nonlinear) on well-chosen representation subspaces or spectral band selection techniques [21]. We introduced an improvement on the principal component analysis method (PCA) to preserve the rare event in dimension reduction.

In this work, the rare event is defined as a set of neighbor pixels, which their values differs from its neighbors. This means that rare event pixels have a low occurrence probability in their neighborhood. In hyperspectral image analysis, we often find rare events. These rare events, or those rare vectors, can sometimes carry important data. We can consider the hyperspectral image as a combination of rare vectors and not rare vectors. The objective is to test whether the rare event is preserved after dimension reduction, or not. To achieve this, we need a method that detects rare events in a hyperspectral image, and then we must calculate the amount of the rare event preserved after the dimension reduction. A method to detect rare events in hyperspectral images is presented in [17].

This paper is composed of 4 parts. The first part seeks a statistical definition of a rare event and its rate of preservation. In the second part, we propose an improvement on principal component analysis that improves the rare event preservation. The third section presents a comparative study on the loss of information with the developed PCA, tested on natural hyperspectral images. The final section presents the conclusions of this research and the future work.

2 Statistical Definition of a Rare Event

Users of data reduction techniques are very interested in rare events studies. However, the scientific literature on this subject is very rare. Our initiation in this area could provide a quantitative measure of this phenomenon. A statistical proposal is made in [17] to estimate the relevance of a variable, defined by a ratio of local similarity between a variable and its neighbors. Let us consider a dataset $\{v_i\}_{i=1}^{k-1}$, which are independent realizations of the same hyperspectral image. The element x_i ($i = 1, \ldots,$ $n \ll k$) is a rare event in realization. We define $V(x_i)$ as the neighbor of order $m < n$ of this element, $\bar{\mu} = \mu - \{x_i\}$ the representative average of $V(x_i)$ not included x_i, and σ its standard deviation. This measure is defined by:

$$\text{Relevance}(x_i) = \frac{\|x_i - \bar{\mu}\|^2}{\mu^2 + \sigma^2} \forall i = 1, \ldots, n$$

$$\text{Relevance } (x_i) = \begin{cases} 0 < P(x_i) < \varepsilon = 0.5 : x_i \text{ is not rare event} \\ P(x_i) \geq \varepsilon = 0.5 : x_i \text{ is rare event} \end{cases}$$

A quantitative measure based on the relevance of x_i would be used to estimate the preservation rate of the rare event x_i. This measure, denoted $T(x_i)$ is calculated as the ratio of the relevance after the reduction $P(x_i)_{\text{after}}$, and the relevance before reduction P $(x_i)_{\text{before}}$ [8]. This conservation ratio is defined as follows by:

$$T(x_i) = \frac{P(x_i)_{\text{after}}}{P(x_i)_{\text{before}}}$$

$$T(x_i) = \begin{cases} 0 < T(x_i) < 0.5 : & \text{the rare event } x_i \text{ is not preserved} \\ 0.5 \le T(x_i) \le 1 : & \text{the rare event } x_i \text{ is preserved} \end{cases}$$

However, after defining the preservation rate of the rare event based on local similarity, it is necessary to compare it with other criteria that are specially adapted to the field of hyperspectral imaging, and can also be used to measure the local similarity. We present here the loss of information related criteria (Fidelity F, Average Absolute Error EMA Mean Square Error MSE) [18, 19], stability related criteria.

(Normalized Cross Correlation NCC) [20] and the similarity related criteria (Relevance) [17]. These criteria are applied on the original image and on the reduced image. Following this test, it can be concluded if the rare event in the original image is preserved or not. The problem is to determine a best performing local criterion for the rare event. We apply different criteria on 2 matrices (image before reduction and image after reduction) and the ratio is determined between the original image and the reduced image. As the rare event is not preserved, then the most powerful test is the one that gives the smallest ratio. Applying these criteria to the following example formed of two matrices. We adjusted a pixel of the original image to make it a rare event (different pixel of its neighbors). This pixel takes a value as its neighbors in the reduced image. We assume in this example that the rare event is not preserved.

Table 1. Original image.

	0.40	2.41	1.69	0.14	1.18	
	0.42	7	1.83	1.10	0.91	
	1.48	1.19	0.75	1.72	0.93	
	0.82	2.58	1.21	3.58	0.56	
	0.80	0.19	0.16	0.33	0.79	

Table 2. Reduced image.

	0.40	2.41	1.69	0.14	1.18	
	0.42	1.29	1.83	1.10	0.91	
	1.48	1.19	0.75	1.72	0.93	
	0.82	2.58	1.21	3.5	0.56	
	0.80	0.19	0.16	0.33	0.79	

The first matrix is the original image (Table 1), containing a rare event. The second matrix is the reduced image (Table 2) after the application of a dimension reduction technique on the original image. The rare event is not preserved. These results (Tables 3 and 4) represent the average of 10 random trials, obtained for Delta = 3. Delta refers to the difference between the pixel assumed rare event, and its neighbors. In all these tests, delta remains constant. The results show that the relevance method is the most efficient method compared with other criteria to preserve the rare event.

Table 3. Comparison table presenting 10 random trials.

Criteria	Original image	Reduced image	Ratio	Comments
Variance	3.52	1.41	0.4	Bad criterion
MAD	132	35.3	0.26	Good criterion
EMA	4.69	0.7	0.14	Good criterion
EQM	23.3	1.5	0.06	Very good criterion
NCC	2.7	0.6	0.25	Good criterion
Relevance	7.03	0.4	0.05	Very good criterion

Table 4. Comparison table for Delta = 3 presenting 10 random trials.

Criteria	Original image	Reduced image	Ratio	Comments
EQM	8.37	1.29	0.15	Good criterion
Relevance	3.19	0.16	0.05	Very good criterion

3 New Proposed PCA with Event Preservation

In the literature, there are many different dimension reduction methods, most of them are optimization problems [21]. We propose to carry on a simple method such as Principal Component Analysis. This method is defined by the projection of data V into a new unit vector space u by maximizing the variance. The mathematical formulation is as follows:

$$\begin{cases} \max_u (u^t V u) \\ u^t u = 1 \end{cases}$$

The objective of this work is to study the influence of adding a constraint on the principal component analysis to test the preservation of rare event. We propose to incorporate a new inequality constraint related to the rare event. This constraint is obtained from the definition of the rare event. In order to maintain the rare event, Chi Squre law χ^2 is used to verify the presence of the rare event. We have a rare event if this equation is verified

$$\sum_{i=1}^{N} \left[u^T Z_i - u^T r\right]^2 \le \left[1 - \chi^2(\text{N})\right] \text{Max} \quad \sum_{i=1}^{N} \left[Z_i - r\right]^2$$

Consider a pixel which is a rare event and all its neighbors are normal (N elements for example) we can write:

$$S = \left[1 - \chi^2(\text{N})\right] \text{Max} \sum_{i=1}^{N} \left[Z_i - r\right]^2$$

If a rare event exists in the original image, then this equation is satisfied. For this, a constraint is added that this equation remains true in the reduced image. We must find the unit vector u, solution of the optimization problem with the following constraints:

$$\begin{cases} \max_u \left(u^t V u\right) \\ u^t u = 1 \\ \sum_{i=1}^{N} \left[u^T Z_i - u^T r\right]^2 < S \end{cases}$$

Z is a matrix (N * n). It has N lines which are the rare event and its neighbors, and n columns representing the number of pixels. This is the first principal axis; we must then search for the other axes in the same way. The resolution requires the construction of the Lagrangian in the form:

$$\mathcal{L} = u^T \cdot \cos(\text{M}) \cdot u - \lambda\left(u^T \cdot u - 1\right) - \beta\left\{\sum_{i=1}^{N} \left[u^T \cdot Z_i^t - u^T r\right]^2 - S\right\}$$

The solution is given by the Euler-Lagrange under the conditions of Kuhn-Tucker

$$\text{cov}(\text{M}) \cdot u - \lambda \cdot u - 2\beta \cdot Z u \cdot \sum_{i=1}^{N} \left[u^T Z_i - u^T r\right]^2 = 0$$

$$\beta\left\{\sum_{i=1}^{N} \left[u^T \cdot Z_i^t - u^T r\right]^2 - S\right\} = 0$$

4   Application and Results

To validate our approach, we propose in this paragraph to perform a test for the PCA with the added constraint on a real image. This image is retrieved from the David Foster site: http://personalpages.manchester.ac.uk/staff/david.foster/. It represents a green scene in which is embedded a flower considered rare in the general context (Fig. 1). This scene of 820 × 820 × 31 consists of 31 bands each with a size of 820 × 820 pixels.

We proceed by applying two projection methods. One is a method known linear reduction method, known by its powerful potentials, which is the PCA method, and the other is the PCA with constraints. We scanned all possible reductions for this image starting from 30 bands until a single band. The following figure (Fig. 2) illustrates the efficiency of each of these two methods to preserve the rare event. It is clear that the

Fig. 1. Green image with rare event.

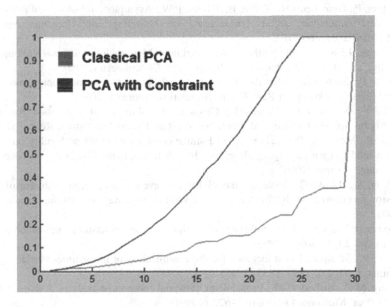

Fig. 2. Preservation rate for rare event.

PCA method loses its potential on a "challenging" image (challenging image: image containing a rare event). The difficulty came from the fact that a boundless and monotonous green in the image becomes very difficult to detect during the projection. If we choose the number of reduced bands to 3, the two methods do not preserve the rare event. In the other hand, the new definition of PCA has significant performance gain. It is thus important to note the positive role of the new constraint related to rare event preservation on the overall behavior of the PCA method.

5 Conclusion

In this article, we have demonstrated the performance of the new method based on the Chi2 density function to detect rare event, as in the real hyperspectral images, the difference between rare event and its neighbors is very low. Then, after the application of two dimension reduction methods, the PCA and PCA with added constraint related to rare event preservation, it was shown that the performance of the new method is better on the reduced image. Then we must use the constrained dimension reduction method for the rare event to be preserved. Given these results, we believe that it is very important to integrate this constraint to all the other dimension reduction methods, and then compare the potential contributions of information losses.

References

1. L'ecuyer, P., Blanchet, J.H., Tuffin, B., Glynn, P.W.: Asymptotic robustness of estimators in rare-event simulation. ACM Transactions on Modeling and Computer Simulation (TOMACS) 20(1), 6 (2010)
2. Collamore, J.: Rare event simulation for the ruin problem with investments via importance sampling and duality. Master thesis, University of Copenhagen (2010)
3. Dupuis, P.: Subsolutions for the design and analysis of rare event monte carlo. In: 7th International Workshop on Rare Events Simulation, Rennes (2008)
4. Cérou, F., Moral, P.D., Furon, T., Guyader, A.: Rare event simulation for a static distribution. In: 7th International Workshop on Rare Events Simulation, Rennes (2008)
5. Pastel, R., Morio, J., Piet-Lahanier, H.: Estimation of a rare event probability on complex system modeled with a kriging algorithm. In: 7th International Workshop on Rare Events Simulation, Rennes (2008)
6. Berikov, V., Lbov, G.: Bayesian model for rare events recognition with use of logical decision functions class. In: 7th International Workshop on Rare Events Simulation, Rennes (2008)
7. Overshee, P.V., Moor, B.D.: Subspace algorithms for the stochastic identification problem. Automatica 29, 649–660 (1993)
8. Viberg, V.: Subspace-based methods for the identification of linear time-invariant systems. Automatica 31(12), 1835–1853 (1995)
9. Tipping, M.E., Bishop, C.M.: Probabilistic principal component analysis. J. Roy. Stat. Soc.: Ser. B (Stat. Methodol.) 61(3), 611–622 (1999)
10. Nascimento, J.M.P., Dias, J.M.B.: Signal subspace identification in hyperspectral linear mixtures. In: Marques, J.S., Pérez de la Blanca, N., Pina, P. (eds.) Second Iberian Conference, IbPRIA 2005. LNCS, vol. 3523, pp. 207–214. Springer, Heidelberg (2005)
11. Kuybeda, O., Malah, D., Barzohar, M.: Rank estimation and redundancy reduction of high-dimensional noisy signals with preservation of rare vectors. IEEE Trans. Signal Process. 55 (12), 5579–5592 (2007)

12. Kuybeda, O., Malah, D., Barzohar, M.: Global unsupervised anomaly extraction and discrimination in hyperspectral images via maximum-orthogonal complement analysis. In: European Signal Processing Conference (EUSIPCO), Lausanne, Switzerland, August 2008
13. Chen, H.F., Jiang, G.F., Yoshihira, K.: Robust nonlinear dimensionality reduction for manifold learning. In: Proceeding of 18th International Conference on Pattern Recognition, pp. 447–450 (2006)
14. Marcus, M., Swerling, P.: Sequential detection in radar with multiple resolution elements. IEEE Trans. Inf. Theory 8(3), 237–245 (1962)
15. Thottan, M., Ji, C.: Anomaly detection in ip networks. IEEE Trans. Signal Process. 51(8), 2191–2204 (2003)
16. Lai, L., Poor, H.V., Xin, Y., Georgiadis, G.: Quickest search over multiple sequences. IEEE Trans. Inf. Theory 57(8), 5375–5386 (2011)
17. Khoder, J., Younes, R.: Proposal for preservation criteria to rare event. Application on multispectral / hyperspectral images. In: International Conference on Microelectronics. IEEE, Lebanon (2013)
18. He, X., Cai, D., Yan, S., Zhang, H.: Neighborhood preserving embedding. In: IEEE International Conference on Computer Vision, pp. 1208–1213. Vancouver, Canada (2005)
19. Teh, Y.W., Roweis, S.: Automatic alignment of local representations. In: Becker, S., Thrun, S., Obermayer, K. (eds.) Advances in Neural Information Processing Systems, pp. 841–848. MIT Press, Cambridge (2003)
20. Wang, Z., Sheikh, H.R., Bovik, A.: Objective video quality assessment. In: Furht, B., Marques, O. (eds.) The Handbook of Video Databases: Design and Applications. CRC Press, New York (2003)
21. Khoder, J.: Nouvel algorithme pour la réduction de la dimensionnalité en imagerie hyperspectrale. Ph.D. thesis. Versailles University (2013)
22. Khoder, J., Younes, R.: Dimensionality reduction on hyperspectral images: a comparative review based on artificial datas. In: 4th International Congress on Image and Signal Processing (CISP-IEEE), vol. 4, pp. 1875–1883, October 2011
23. Singh, A., Pratt, M.A., Chu, C-H.H, et al.: Visual saliency approach to anomaly detection in an image ensemble. In : SPIE Defense, Security, and Sensing. International Society for Optics and Photonics, pp. 87500T-87500T-7 (2013)

Applications

Clustering of Strokes from Pen-Based Music Notation: An Experimental Study

Jorge Calvo-Zaragoza$^{(\boxtimes)}$ and Jose Oncina

Departamento de Lenguajes y Sistemas Informáticos,
Universidad de Alicante, Alicante, Spain
{jcalvo,oncina}@dlsi.ua.es

Abstract. A comfortable way of digitizing a new music composition is by using a pen-based recognition system, in which the digital score is created with the sole effort of the composition itself. In this kind of systems, the input consist of a set of pen strokes. However, it is hitherto unclear the different types of strokes that must be considered for this task. This paper presents an experimental study on automatic labeling of these strokes using the well-known *k-medoids* algorithm. Since recognition of pen-based music scores is highly related to stroke recognition, it may be profitable to repeat the process when new data is received through user interaction. Therefore, our intention is not to propose some stroke labeling but to show which stroke dissimilarities perform better within the clustering process. Results show that there can be found good methods in the trade-off between cluster complexity and classification accuracy, whereas others offer a very poor performance.

1 Introduction

Still nowadays many musicians consider pen and paper as the natural tools for expressing a new music composition. The ease and ubiquity of this method, as well as the fact of avoiding tedious music score editors, favor this consideration. Nevertheless, after composition is finished, it may be appropriate to have the score digitized to take advantage of many benefits such as storage, reproduction or distribution. To provide a profitable way of performing the whole process, pen-based music notation recognition systems can be developed. This way, musicians are provided with a friendly interface to work with and save the effort of digitizing the score afterwards. Although offline music score recognition systems (also known as Optical Music Recognition) could be used, it is widely known that the additional data provided by the time collection sampling of a pen-based system can lead to a better performance since more information is captured. The process of recognizing handwritten music notation is very related to other pattern recognition fields, especially that of Optical Character Recognition (OCR). Despite similarities between text and music recognition processes, this latter presents several features that make it be considered a harder task [3]. Therefore, new recognition algorithms must be developed to deal with music scores. In the case of online recognition, the natural segmentation of the input

© Springer International Publishing Switzerland 2015
R. Paredes et al. (Eds.): IbPRIA 2015, LNCS 9117, pp. 633–640, 2015.
DOI: 10.1007/978-3-319-19390-8_71

is the set of strokes. Each stroke is defined as the data collected between pen-up and pen-down events over the digital surface. Nevertheless, given both the high variability in handwritten musical notation and differences among writer styles (see [4]), as well as the immaturity of the field itself, it is still unclear the classes of strokes that must be considered or which are the most accurate techniques to recognize them.

This paper presents an experimental study on automatic clustering of the strokes found in pen-based music notation. From the interactive system point of view, it is specially interesting to know which algorithms provide the best results since this clustering might be repeated in order to adapt the recognition to the style of the actual user. Therefore, this work does not intend to provide just a proposal of stroke labeling, but to find which techniques would be the most appropriate within this scenario. The paper is structured as follows: Sect. 2 addresses the intrinsics of the clustering problem described; techniques for measuring dissimilarity between strokes from pen-based music notation are presented in Sect. 3; Sect. 4 describes the experimental setup, results and analysis; finally, Sect. 5 concludes.

2   The Clustering Problem

When dealing with a pen-based music recognition task, raw input consists of a series of strokes. This is the natural segmentation of such systems since the beginning and ending of a stroke are easily detected by pen-down and pen-up events. From a labeled set of isolated handwritten musical symbol we can obtain definitions of these symbols in terms of strokes. If we considered a stroke labeling, we would reduce this set by assigning the same label to similar strokes. Then, the first step would be to classify each stroke within a set of labels. A label would represent a part of a musical symbol, *i.e.*, a white note head or a stem (Fig. 1(b)), or even a whole symbol (Fig. 1(a)).

(a) Two strokes   (b) One stroke

Fig. 1. *Half Note* symbol written with different set of primitives.

At this point, we have to deal with the open problem of the set of primitives to be considered. Some *ad-hoc* labeling could be used but it might not be appropriate for this task due to several reasons: the data would be clustered considering human similarity perception instead of computer-based similarity, which is what it is applied in the final system; labels would be created from the data available at that moment, thus generalization could be poor; clustering may need to be repeated after user interaction, in which new data would be received and, therefore, the system must be adapted to actual user writing style. All these reasons lead us to perform an algorithmic-based clustering of the strokes found in pen-based music notation. As aforementioned, the main goal of this paper is not to give a good proposal of stroke labeling, but to measure the goodness and generalization of each possible clustering considered.

One of the key questions in any clustering problem is to choose the number of labels that must be considered (referred here as parameter k). Note that if music notation can be defined by a formal language, in which the alphabet is the primitives set, the lower the size of this set the less complex the language. Therefore, we are interested in lowering k as much as possible. On the other hand, low values of k can lead to ambiguous definitions, that is, more than one musical symbol defined by the same sequence of primitives. Considering that we should avoid these ambiguous definitions, our problem can be modeled as a constrained clustering problem.

Constrained clustering is the task of clustering data in which some conditions over the cluster assignments must be fulfilled. In the literature, several works on constrained clustering can be found [1,17]. The two considered cases are those of *must-link* and *cannot-link* conditions. The first defines pairs of data points that must be in the same cluster while the latter defines pairs of data points that must be in different clusters. The constraint in our case is to avoid more than one musical symbol defined by the same primitives. Let us consider just two musical symbols (*Whole Note* and *Half Note*). Let us assume that we have some definitions in which these symbols are described in terms of strokes. That is,

$$\text{Whole Note} \to s_1$$
$$\text{Whole Note} \to s_2\ s_3$$
$$\text{Half Note} \to s_4$$
$$\text{Half Note} \to s_5\ s_6$$

in which $s_1, s_2, \ldots, s_6$ denote strokes.

Let $\zeta(s)$ stands for the label assigned to stroke s. Then, we are looking for a labeling such that $\zeta(s_1) \neq \zeta(s_4)$ as well as $\zeta(s_2) \neq \zeta(s_5) \vee \zeta(s_3) \neq \zeta(s_6)$. This way, none but one symbol could be defined by the same sequence of primitives. Note that, although we are stating *cannot-link* conditions, we are not interested in just pairwise constraints but to *n-to-n* as shown above.

To our best knowledge, this kind of conditions is not approached in previous works on constrained clustering. Since developing such algorithm is out of the scope of the present work, we are going to follow a straightforward approach: unconstrained clustering will be performed and conditions will be checked afterwards. The lowest value of k that achieves a valid clustering will be considered. The problem with this approach is that it may lead to a very high number of k. Thus, some rate of ambiguous symbols will be allowed. We assume that some disambiguation can be solved by means of semantic music language models, as typically happens in offline Optical Music Recognition [11].

The unconstrained clustering process will be guided by a *k-medoids* algorithm [16], one of the most common and successful algorithms for data clustering [14]. This algorithm is very related to *k-means* but instead of taking the mean point at the expectation step, it searches the point of the cluster that minimizes the actual cost (set mean). In order to provide a more robust clustering, the initialization of the method is performed as described for *k-means++* algorithm [2]. This algorithm proposes a initialization (first centroids) that is expected to provide better results and faster convergence. It starts with a random centroid and the rest of the centroids are chosen randomly following a decreasing probability with respect to the distance to the nearest centroid already selected.

To perform the clustering we need to define some function that measures the distance or dissimilarity between two strokes. Next section will describe the techniques considered for such task.

3   Dissimilarity Functions for Pen-Based Music Notation Strokes

The data points of our clustering problem are handwritten strokes. Each stroke is composed of a sequence of consecutive two dimensional points defining the path that the pen follows. For the clustering algorithm we need to define some techniques to measure the dissimilarity between two given strokes. Below we present some functions that can be applied directly to the stroke data. Moreover, we also describe some ways of mapping the strokes onto feature vectors, for which other several dissimilarity measures can be applied.

Before computing these dissimilarities, a smoothing process will also be considered. Smoothing is a common preprocessing step in pen-based recognition to remove some noise and jitters [7]. It consists in replacing each point of the stroke by the mean of their neighbors points. Some values of neighborhood size will be considered at the experimentation stage.

3.1   Raw Stroke Distance

The digital surface collects the strokes at a fixed sampling rate so that each one may contain a variable number of points. However, some dissimilarity functions can be applied to this kind of data. Those considered in this work are the following:

- Dynamic Time Warping (DTW) [15]: a technique for measuring the dissimilarity between two time signals which may be of different duration.
- Edit Distance with Freeman Chain Code (FCC): the sequence of points representing a stroke is converted into a string using a codification based on Freeman Chain Code [5]. Then, the common Edit Distance [9] is applied.
- Edit Distance for Ordered Set of Points (OSP) [13]: an extension of the Edit Distance for its use over ordered sequences of points.

3.2   Feature Extraction

On the other hand, if a set of features is extracted from the stroke path, a fixed-sized vector is obtained. Then, other common distances can be applied. In this work we are going to consider the following feature extraction and distances:

- Normalized stroke (Norm): the whole set of points of the stroke is normalized to a sequence of n points by an equally resampling technique. Therefore, a stroke can be characterized by $2n$-dimensional real-valued feature vector. Given vectors x and y, two different distances are going to be considered:
  - Average Euclidean Distance (Norm+Euc) between the points of the sequences: $\frac{1}{n}\sum_{i=1}^{n} d(x_i, y_i)$
  - Average Turning Angle (Norm+Ang) between segments of the two sequences: $\frac{1}{n}\sum_{i=2}^{n} d_{\Theta}(x_{i-1}x_i, y_{i-1}y_i)$, where $x_{i-1}x_i$ represents the segment connecting points x_{i-1} and x_i, and d_{Θ} is the angular difference in radians. It has been chosen due to its good results in [8].
- Squared Image: an image of the stroke can be obtained by reconstructing the drawing made. Preliminary experimentation showed that the best results are obtained by simulating a pen thickness of 3. Images are then resized to 20×20 as done in the work of Rebelo et al. [10]. A 400-dimensional feature vector is obtained, for which the Euclidean distance is applied.
- Image Features: the image is partitioned into sub-regions, from which background, foreground and contour local features are extracted [12]. Then, similarity is measured using Euclidean distance.

4   Experimentation

This section contains the experimentation performed with the musical symbols of the Handwritten Online Musical Symbols (HOMUS) dataset [4]. HOMUS is a freely available dataset which contains 15200 samples from 100 musicians of pen-based isolated musical symbols. Within this set of symbols, 39219 strokes can be found. Taking advantage of the features of the HOMUS, two experiments will be carried out: user-dependent and user-independent scenarios. In the first, the clustering is performed separately for the samples of each writer since it is interesting to see how clustering behaves for small and similar data. In the latter, the whole dataset is used at the same time. However, since this can lead to an unfeasible computation in terms of time, only a subset of samples is selected at the beginning of the task. This subset selection is performed so that each symbol of any musician appears at least once. Clustering will be performed on this subset and the rest of the strokes will be assigned to their nearest cluster afterwards. In both experiments, some values of neighborhood parameter of the smoothing will be tested: 0 (no filtering), 1 and 2. Our experiments start with a low k that is increased iteratively until reaching a valid assignment (see Sect. 2), with a maximum established to 150. In both cases, we allow an ambiguity rate of 0.1 of the total number of symbols considered. When an acceptable clustering is obtained, we measure the classification accuracy using a *leaving-one-out* scheme.

For the classification step we are going to restrict ourselves to the use of the Nearest Neighbor (NN) rule with the same similarity used for the clustering. The obvious reason is to measure the goodness of the stroke dissimilarity utilized for both clustering and classification. Nevertheless, considering the interactive nature of the task (the system may be continuously receiving new labeled sample through user interaction), other reasons also justify this choice: distance-based classification methods such as NN (or k-NN) are easily adaptable to new data; Data Reduction techniques based on dissimilarity functions could be applied to not overflow the system [6]; in addition, fast similarity search techniques could also be used in order to provide fast response. It is clear, however, that once strokes are labeled conveniently, other advanced techniques can be applied to classify this data but that experimentation will be placed as future work.

4.1   Results

Results of the user-dependent experiment described above is shown in Table 1. Since dataset contains 100 different writers, average results are reported. For the user-independent experiment, average results from 10 different initial random subsets are shown in Table 2.

Table 1. Average results (**k**: number of clusters; **acc**: classification accuracy) of a 100-fold cross-validation with each writer subset. Several values of neighborhood for smoothing are considered (0, 1, 2).

Dissimilarity	Smoothing (0)		Smoothing (1)		Smoothing (2)	
	k	acc	k	acc	k	acc
DTW	18.1	88.9	18.4	89.4	19.1	88.8
FCC	14.9	87.6	15.7	88.0	15.4	87.8
OSP	15.4	87.7	15.4	88.3	15.1	89.1
Norm+Euclidean	17.5	89.1	17.6	89.0	17.8	88.9
Norm+Angular	18.7	78.7	19.1	79.0	21.0	79.2
Squared Image	30.6	79.0	30.2	78.7	30.5	80.5
Image Features	22.6	89.4	22.5	89.0	24.8	86.7

An initial remark to begin with is that smoothing demonstrates small relevance in the process since results hardly vary among the different values considered. Moreover, dissimilarities that make use of the image representation of the stroke obtain very poor results in both experiments. In fact, they obtain the worst results in the user-dependent experiment and none of them reach a low enough clustering value in the writer-independent experiment. Although variability is low when using small and similar data, differences in performance among methods are increased in the writer-independent experiment. Thorough the experimentation, OSP and FCC dissimilarities have reported the best results in terms of number of clusters, in spite of showing a lower accuracy rate than

Table 2. Average results (**k**: number of clusters; **acc**: classification accuracy) of a 10-fold cross-validation experiment with the whole dataset. Several values of neighborhood for smoothing are considered (0, 1, 2).

Dissimilarity	Smoothing (0)		Smoothing (1)		Smoothing (2)	
	k	acc	k	acc	k	acc
DTW	72.0	81.8	77.0	81.3	86.8	80.0
FCC	52.8	79.3	53.4	80.3	52.4	80.2
OSP	47.9	77.1	49.8	80.7	46.8	81.3
Norm+Euclidean	68.8	83.8	76.1	83.4	86.3	83.4
Norm+Angular	141.4	71.5	143.5	70.7	146.3	70.5
Squared Image	>150	-	>150	-	>150	-
Image Features	>150	-	>150	-	>150	-

DTW or Normalized strokes with Euclidean distance. Nevertheless, it is expected that both OSP and FCC methods may improve their accuracy performance by allowing them to use a high number of clusters. Results have reported that the dissimilarity applied has a big impact in the clustering process, especially when dealing with a high number of samples. Thus, if the process has to be performed when new data is available, it is profitable to use methods such as OSP or FCC that have shown a better ability to group the strokes.

5 Conclusions

This work presents an experimental study on clustering of strokes from pen-based music notation. The main goal is to show which dissimilarity measure between strokes performs better since we are interested in repeating the process when new data is received. Experimentation showed that, although the clustering process is robust in a user-dependent experiment, much attention should be devoted to the user-independent scenario. In this last, some techniques like OSP and FCC achieved good results whereas others, especially image-based techniques, were reported less suitable for grouping these strokes. As future work, there are several promising lines that should be explored with respect to clustering. These lines include approaching the unconstrained clustering problem when n-to-n constraints are required or developing an efficient clustering that repeats the process when new data is received taking advantage of the previous assignment. In addition, once a valid clustering is achieved, some advanced classification techniques could be considered instead of resorting to the NN rule.

Acknowledgements. This work was partially supported by the Spanish Ministerio de Educación, Cultura y Deporte through a FPU Fellowship (AP2012–0939), the Spanish Ministerio de Economía y Competitividad through Project TIMuL (No. TIN2013-48152-C2-1-R supported by EU FEDER funds) and Consejería de Educación de la Comunidad Valenciana through Project PROMETEO/2012/017.

References

1. de Amorim, R.: Constrained clustering with minkowski weighted k-means. In: 2012 IEEE 13th International Symposium on Computational Intelligence and Informatics (CINTI), pp. 13–17, November 2012
2. Arthur, D., Vassilvitskii, S.: K-means++: the advantages of careful seeding. In: Proceedings of the Eighteenth Annual ACM-SIAM Symposium on Discrete Algorithms, SODA 2007, pp. 1027–1035. Society for Industrial and Applied Mathematics, Philadelphia (2007)
3. Bainbridge, D., Bell, T.: The challenge of optical music recognition. Lang. Resour. Eval. **35**, 95–121 (2001)
4. Calvo-Zaragoza, J., Oncina, J.: Recognition of pen-based music notation: the HOMUS dataset. In: Proceedings of the 22nd International Conference on Pattern Recognition, Stockholm, Sweden, pp. 3038–3043 (2014)
5. Freeman, H.: On the encoding of arbitrary geometric configurations. IRE Trans. Electron. Comput. **10**(2), 260–268 (1961)
6. García, S., Luengo, J., Herrera, F.: Data Preprocessing in Data Mining. Intelligent Systems Reference Library, vol. 72. Springer, Switzerland (2015)
7. Kim, J., Sin, B.K.: Online handwriting recognition. In: Doermann, D., Tombre, K. (eds.) Handbook of Document Image Processing and Recognition, pp. 887–915. Springer, London (2014)
8. Kristensson, P.O., Denby, L.C.: Continuous recognition and visualization of pen strokes and touch-screen gestures. In: Proceedings of the 8th Eurographics Symposium on Sketch-Based Interfaces and Modeling, SBIM 2011, pp. 95–102. ACM, New York (2011)
9. Levenshtein, V.I.: Binary codes capable of correcting deletions, insertions, and reversals. Technical report 8 (1966)
10. Rebelo, A., Capela, G., Cardoso, J.: Optical recognition of music symbols. Int. J. Doc. Anal. Recogn. **13**(1), 19–31 (2010)
11. Rebelo, A., Fujinaga, I., Paszkiewicz, F., Marçal, A.R.S., Guedes, C., Cardoso, J.S.: Optical music recognition: state-of-the-art and open issues. IJMIR **1**(3), 173–190 (2012)
12. Rico-Juan, J.R., Iñesta, J.M.: Confidence voting method ensemble applied to off-line signature verification. Pattern Anal. Appl. **15**(2), 113–120 (2012)
13. Rico-Juan, J.R., Iñesta, J.M.: Edit distance for ordered vector sets: a case of study. In: Yeung, D.-Y., Kwok, J.T., Fred, A., Roli, F., de Ridder, D. (eds.) SSPR 2006 and SPR 2006. LNCS, vol. 4109, pp. 200–207. Springer, Heidelberg (2006)
14. Rokach, L.: A survey of clustering algorithms. In: Maimon, O., Rokach, L. (eds.) Data Mining and Knowledge Discovery Handbook, 2nd edn, pp. 269–298. Springer, New York (2010)
15. Sakoe, H., Chiba, S.: Readings in speech recognition. In: Waibel, A., Lee, K.-F. (eds.) Dynamic Programming Algorithm Optimization for Spoken Word Recognition, pp. 159–165. Morgan Kaufmann Publishers Inc., San Francisco (1990)
16. Theodoridis, S., Koutroumbas, K.: Pattern Recognition, 3rd edn. Academic Press Inc., Orlando (2006)
17. Wagstaff, K., Cardie, C., Rogers, S., Schrödl, S.: Constrained k-means clustering with background knowledge. In: Proceedings of the Eighteenth International Conference on Machine Learning, pp. 577–584. Morgan Kaufmann Publishers Inc., San Francisco (2001)

Image Analysis-Based Automatic Detection of Transmission Towers Using Aerial Imagery

Tanima Dutta, Hrishikesh Sharma$^{(\boxtimes)}$, Adithya Vellaiappan,
and P. Balamuralidhar

Innovation Labs, Tata Consultancy Services, Bengaluru, India
{tanima.dutta,hrishikesh.sharma,adithya.v,balamurali.p}@tcs.com

Abstract. Uninterrupted electricity transmission is a critical utility service for any nation. A major component of nation-wide infrastructure carrying electricity are the transmission towers. To give uninterrupted supply, timely maintenance of towers is a must. Due to vastness of power grid, fault detection via aerial inspection and imaging is emerging as a popular method. In this paper, we attend to the problem of *automatic* detection of towers in specific images. We present a four-stage algorithm for such detection. For a porous, cage like object structure that of a tower, we use gradient density and a novel feature called cluster density to detect pylon blocks. The algorithm was tested against image data captured for many towers along two different power grid corridors. The algorithm demonstrated missed detection of $< 1\%$ and complete absence of false positives, which is very encouraging. We believe that our result is far more useful in tower detection, than available previous works.

Keywords: Object detection · Image analysis · Aerial imaging

1 Introduction

In any nation, maintenance of critical infrastructures is an important and costly legal responsibility, mainly for public safety, of any distribution/service provider company. Such infrastructures include power grid, oil/gas pipelines, railway corridor etc. These outdoor systems are **vast** in the sense that their installation area runs into hundreds of kilometers, which may run through inhospitable terrain e.g. dense forests. Faults can occur due to aging of components, severe weather, overloading and overstraining, natural calamities etc. Periodic inspections and subsequent maintenance acts help to minimize the number and duration of service/supply outages in daily life.

The use of Unmanned Aerial Vehicles (UAVs) for inspections, especially for power grid infrastructures, is rapidly emerging as a popular option [1]. Detailed motivation for employment of UAVs can be found in [2]. In vision based surveillance, the amount of video or image data acquired is typically huge, due to vastness of infrastructures. Hence **automated analysis** of so much data is generally sought, especially when it comes to locate possible faults.

© Springer International Publishing Switzerland 2015
R. Paredes et al. (Eds.): IbPRIA 2015, LNCS 9117, pp. 641–651, 2015.
DOI: 10.1007/978-3-319-19390-8_72

Only a handful of research works exist in literature, for transmission tower identification from aerial images using machine vision. In [3], electricity towers are detected using straight lines in each video frame 2-D IIR filter, and Hough transformation. However, **discrete** set of image blocks onto which tower projection is expected the exact threshold criterion for choosing "confidence windows"is not defined. In [4], a supervised learning approach is used for classification of towers. However, the authors, for reasons not provided, have merged the class of **utility poles** with **pylons**. This has led to poor classification results for type-3 and type-4 towers (essentially poles), as they themselves claim. No other work, to the best of authors' knowledge, does such mix up: in fact, much more research work is available on automatic detection of just the electricity utility poles. To summarize, to the best of authors' knowledge, there is no holistic and practically useful vision-based or learning-based approach known publicly till date, that targets automatic detection of electricity towers in aerial images.

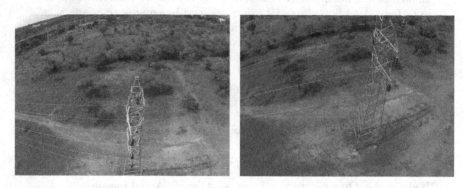

Fig. 1. Sample transmission towers captured using UAV in outskirts of Bangalore

At this stage of research, we are interested in enabling semi-automated processing of fault detection. For a flight along long power grid corridor, a video is captured of the grid. Our priority is to locate and highlight the regions that snugly contain towers, in key frames from the grid image sequence. An expert later analyzes such frames, and the corresponding regions, for any fault, manually. For detection under such circumstances, we propose a four-stage detection algorithm, which has following properties.

- As a novelty, at the core stage of color- and gradient-based segmentation, we mark key image blocks from where we "grow" the desired tower region. More specifically, candidate clusters along the pylon within key blocks are shortlisted, which are then extended along the boundary on either side, using total covered area and boundary considerations.
- The gradient density (defined later) and cluster density of image blocks, total covered area and boundary size of clusters play an important role for detection of pylon. Therefore, we select these features as key parameters in our

detection algorithm. It is expected that gradient will always be a common feature for detection of *any* linear infrastructure and similarly, cluster density for *all* standardized classes of pylons, since they have metallic surface and cage like structure, respectively. These claims hold good even when the pylon is damaged/bent for some reasons.

The proposed algorithm is able to minimize full as well as partial false negatives, as shown in Sect. 4. In former case, no tower region is detected, while in latter case, some pylon area is missed during region detection. We also minimize any mis-classification of pylon *i.e.* a false positive, since a combination of cage like feature and linearity feature are unique to pylons.

The rest of the paper is organized as follows. We first describe our detection algorithm in Sect. 2. We then describe the nature of our experiments in Sect. 3, which is followed by the main Sect. 4 on results and analysis. We conclude the paper finally in Sect. 5.

2   Proposed Detection Algorithm

The algorithm consists of four stages, as shown in Fig. 2. To minimize clutter related to heterogeneous background, an optimized mean shift-based segmentation is used as filter at **first** stage. It also helps in preserving the dominant pylon edges while aiding better clustering of the background. The image is then divided into a grid of rectangular patches called *granules*. The **second** stage uses gradient density, as well as cluster density based thresholding for each granule, to shortlist the candidate granules. Such thresholding isolates the granules corresponding to pylon projection, in varying light/photometric conditions. The **third** stage picks up clusters corresponding to pylon region within key granules, and merges them via shared boundary criterion discussed later. The **fourth** stage uses the context information that pylon is the closest imaged object of interest in an inspection, to discard false positives. Careful design of second and third stage are key to performance of our algorithm. The algorithm for detection of electricity pylons in aerial images is facilitated in Algorithm 1.

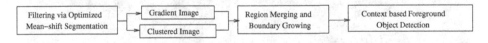

Fig. 2. Block diagram of the proposed pylon detection framework.

2.1   Filtering via Optimized Mean Shift Segmentation

Due to complex outdoor surroundings, various edge detection algorithms give far more edges in the background. At the same time, due to presence of numerous beams in its truss, a striking feature of a pylon is presence of multiple linear features in its corresponding image. Distinguishing the subset of linear features of pylon, from those of the background, is a complex task. Therefore, to reduce background clutter and simultaneously accentuate the foreground, we first filter the images. The mean shift based image segmentation is a straightforward extension of the discontinuity preserving smoothing algorithm. A comparison of various segmentation algorithms using objective evaluation measure is described in [5,6]. The authors found that foreground clustering arising from mean shift outperforms other popular segmentation schemes. We use the optimized mean shift scheme proposed in [7], which has the following features (a) mean shift in the spatial and color dimensions, (b) anisotropic diffusion for edge preserving and smoothing, and (c) joined bilateral filtering for both the intensity and position of each pixel by replacing with the weighted average of its neighbors. The **typical** output of such segmentation for Fig. 1 is shown in Fig. 3.

Algorithm 1. Detection of Transmission Tower/Pylon in Aerial Images

---

Optimized mean shift segmentation to
　　Find the peak of a confidence map using the color histogram of the image.
　　Cluster the image into mean color based clusters.
Gradient magnitude density estimation for all image granules.
Cluster density estimation for all granules.
Select all granules which have higher value in the 2D vector of gradient magnitude and cluster density.
For Each Key granule in descending order of vector values
　　Pick a cluster in that granule, which has maximum area within that granule.
　　Merge the selected cluster with neighboring clusters which has maximum boundary sharing with
　　the selected cluster, and maximum area within that granule in a iterative manner.
　　Detection of foreground cluster as Pylon based on context knowledge.
EndFor

Fig. 3. Output of background suppression using optimized mean-shift

2.2   Generating Search Space of Key Granules

To narrow down on probable pylon region, we consider 128×96 sized granules organized as a grid within 1280×960 pixel-sized images. The granule size is configurable, and is decided based on estimation of height of pylon projection. This in turn depends on the distance the pylon is imaged from, UAV flight orientation, as well as pylon size. Too small granules give many false candidate regions. Too big granules might not contain enough chunks of pylon projection, in order to arrive at a meaningful conclusion.

To shortlist the granules from the granule grid, we consider **two** specific, **granule-level** distinguishing features. Intuitively, we expect the granules overlapping with pylon projection to exhibit both high gradient density, as well as high cluster density, when compared to background in the smoothened image. The former is an effect of dominant amount of pylon beams as edges, while the latter is an effect of cage-like structure of the pylon. The perspective view of the pylon from the down-looking camera during sideways tracking results in lines of varying thickness *across* the projection. In addition, since aerial cameras are wide lens camera, the images have fish eye effect. Due to non-parallel and jittery trajectory of the UAV with respect to the pylon, the pylon can have any orientation in the image plane, though. Also, imaging distance can limit the height of pylon that is captured within camera's field of view. Irrespective of these variabilities, the cage-like structure is always present in pylon projection. Consequently, the high linearity and cluster density features remain consistent in all kind of pylon projections in all imaging scenarios.

We estimate the gradient using Sobel function [8] on the filtered image, while clustering is done by imposing similar color and boundary-sharing conditions on the filter image. The **gradient density** GD_i of a granule i is then calculated as the average gradient magnitude within that granule as shown in Fig. 4. Similarly, the **cluster density** CD_i of a granule i is the number of clusters in that granule subject to condition that they have more than 80 % area within that granule, as shown in Fig. 5.

Fig. 4. Typical gradient profile image (Color figure online)

Fig. 5. Typical clustered profile image (Color figure online)

The shortlisting of key granules is done by arranging the density values in descending order, and omitting the tail of such sorted distribution. More specifically, it is done by dropping out granules that have densities less than 30 % of the peak density values in **both** distributions.

$$KG = \left\{ \exists i : (GD_i > (0.3 \cdot GD_{max})) \bigwedge (CD_i > (0.3 \cdot CD_{max})) \right\} \quad (1)$$

The union of these granules comprises of our search space. The **typical** granules selected for a background-suppressed frame of Fig. 1 is shown in Fig. 6.

2.3 Boundary Growing and Region Merging

After the previous stage, we are left with granules that contain pylon and similar object regions in the image. To get a snug fit pylon region, we need to merge the contiguous clusters in these connected granules. Cluster merging must simultaneously entail extracting the prominent pylon structure in the foreground.

For merging, first a granule **set of sets** G, comprising of two or more *connected* granules is defined. Next, for each granule set G_i, a set of **member**

Fig. 6. Typical output of key image granules selection (Color figure online)

clusters C_{ij} is identified. Member clusters are those having 80 % or more area within the granules of the set G_i. A *seed cluster* C_{is}, which is the largest cluster in set of member clusters C_{ij}, is also identified.

$$C_{is} = \text{Max}(C_{ij}) \qquad (2)$$

Once the seed cluster is identified, the region is grown by **iteratively** by combining member clusters that share boundaries. The order of combining them is based on maximum boundary sharing with current merged cluster. This is repeated for all the granule sets G_i for i = 1, 2, 3... The output of this iterative process is a "forest" of a few merged segments as shown in Fig. 7.

$$\text{Iteration Step: } \{MC_{next} \in C_i\} = \{MC_{current} \cup$$
$$\{\exists k : (C_k \in C_{ij}) \wedge (C_k \cap MC_{current} \neq \varnothing)\}\} \qquad (3)$$

Fig. 7. Typical output of region merging and boundary growing

2.4   Context Based Pylon Detection

In practice, for all inspections, the UAV path planning for inspection is always done so that pylon and all other components of the power grid are the physically closest objects to be imaged. Such context-based sensory information is assumed to be fed as a prior knowledge to the detection framework. We use this information to select one out of many blobs, whose bottom-left corner of bounding box is closest to the bottom-left corner of the image frame, i.e. closest during projection. The output of this stage is shown in Fig. 8.

3   Experiments and Data Collection

The image data was captured using a 11 MP f/2.8 wide lens RGB camera, GoPro Hero3, which was mounted on a mini-UAV. The image size captured was 3000×2250, which was resized to 1280×960 for testing purposes. Two test

Fig. 8. Typical output of foreground object detection

sites provided by *Hot Line Training Center*, outside Bangalore, were used for imaging two power grids. A quadcopter provided by our collaborators was flown so as to have a sideways view of the power grids. For such view, the pitch of the camera mount was fixed to around 60°, while yaw was azimuth-facing and roll angle towards horizon. Enough length of power grids was imaged, giving us around **115** different pylon frames within the video. The background of the power lines was varying, typically consisting of vegetation, sky, unpaved roads and houses.

4   Results and Performance Analysis

While the testing and analysis has been carried out on all **115** pylon frames, we have only shown results for two sample images for sake of brevity. The two images have been chosen with different angle of view, for different sized pylons. The configurable thresholds e.g. 80 % area overlap, 30 % tail discarding etc., while making intuitive sense, were hand-tuned so as to minimize what we call as **partial false positive** as well as **partial false negative**. A *partial false positive* occurs when a neighboring region other than the actual pylon region is present in the final detected pylon region (c.f. Fig. 9). Similarly, a *partial false negative* occurs when a part of actual pylon region is not present within the boundary of the detected pylon region (c.f. Fig. 10). We also consider standard (full) false positive i.e. detection of a non-pylon region as pylon region, and standard (full) false negative, i.e. complete non-detection of a pylon region, though present.

The accuracy of pylon detection is measured based on the ground truth results, where pylons are detected manually using GIMP toolbox as shown in Fig. 11. Overlap analysis of ground truth region and detected region, as shown for two example images in Figs. 9 and 10 reveals that the *partial false positives* are mostly limited to co-detection of small length of power lines, insulators and vegetation whose boundary intersects with pylon boundary in the projection. Due to target of semi-automated processing, presence of these minor protrusions in desired region is not a serious problem, though. *Partial false negatives* were

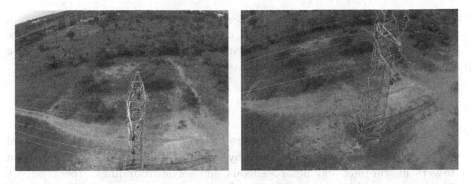

Fig. 9. Typical output of pylon detection. Few prominent partial false positive are visible on left boundary of detected region in left image (Color figure online).

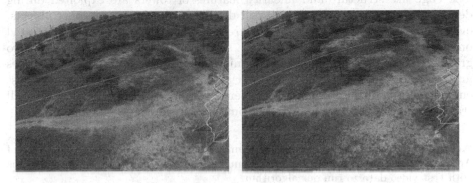

Fig. 10. Typical output of partial pylon detection, and depiction of partial false negatives (Color figure online).

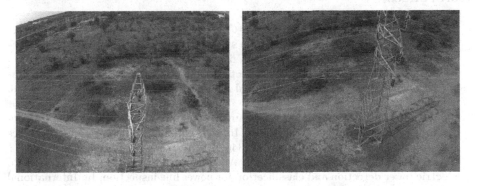

Fig. 11. Ground truth images (Color figure online)

present in 8 % of the frames, due to the fact that pylon projection is slant at times, thus resulting in some granules having a limited part of pylon getting discarded as non-key granules. Such losses are limited to upto 2 out of maximum of 10 key granules being considered per frame i.e. $< 20\%$, so such "dent" is not widespread. Full false negative is limited to just 1 frame, since a very small part of pylon ($< 10\%$) is all that got captured in image. Full false positives are typically restricted to presence of truss-like structures in background, e.g. a power station. However, the final stage of our algorithm removes them all.

5   Conclusion

Automatic detection of electricity towers in aerial images is a practically useful research problem. In this paper, we have proposed an algorithm of detection of towers in complex and heterogeneous outdoor surroundings. To do so, we first suppress the background clutter. Then we select the candidate granules and finally a novel region merging approach is used to detect the tower region. The cage like structure and linearity features of towers are exploited during detection. Both these features will still discriminate pylons from other objects, even when it is damaged/bent for some reasons. The entire algorithm was tested on 100+ tower images collected using a small quad copter mini-UAV, over two grid corridors. It was found to exhibit minimum presence of both false positives and false negatives. We believe that our algorithm for tower detection is robust enough with good performance, and hence can be applicable for detecting all standard types of towers in any other outdoor surroundings as well.

Acknowledgements. We thank Prof. Omkar and his research group from Dept. of Aerospace, Indian Institute of Science, Bangalore for collaborating and providing us with test video data to run our algorithm.

References

1. Li, Z., Liu, Y., Hayward, R., Zhang, J., Cai, J.: Knowledge-based power line detection for UAV surveillance and inspection systems. In: IEEE International Conference on Image and Vision Computing, pp. 1–6 (2008)
2. Sharma, H., et al. : Vision-based Detection of Power Distribution Lines in Complex Remote Surroundings. In: National Conference on Communications, pp. 1–6, February 2014
3. Tilawat, J., Theera-Umpon, N., Auephanwiriyakul, S.: Automatic detection of electricity pylons in aerial video sequences. In: International Conference on Electronics and Information Engineering, pp. 342–346 (2010)
4. Sampedro, C., Martinez, C., Chauhan, A., Campoy, P.: A supervised approach to electric tower detection and classification for power line inspection. In: International Joint Conference on Neural Networks, pp. 1970–1977 (2014)
5. Unnikrishnan, R., Pantofaru, C., Hebert, M.: Toward objective evaluation of image segmentation algorithms. IEEE Trans. Pattern Anal. Mach. Intell. **29**(6), 929–944 (2007)
6. Dutta, T., Dogra, D., Jana, B.: Object extraction using novel region merging and multidimensional features. In: Fourth Pacific-Rim Symposium on Image and Video Technology (2010)

7. Bing, C., Nanning, Z., Ying, W., Yongping, Z., Zhihua, Z.: Color image segmentation based on edge-preservation smoothing and soft C-means clustering. MG & V **11**(2/3), 183–194 (2002)
8. Sonka, M., Hlavac, V., Boyle, R.: Image Processing, Analysis, and Machine Vision. Thomson-Engineering, Toronto (2007)

A Sliding Window Framework for Word Spotting Based on Word Attributes

Suman K. Ghosh[✉] and Ernest Valveny

Dept. Ciències de la Computació, Computer Vision Center,
Universitat Autònoma de Barcelona, 08193 Bellaterra, Barcelona, Spain
sghosh@cvc.uab.es

Abstract. In this paper we propose a segmentation-free approach to word spotting. Word images are first encoded into feature vectors using Fisher Vector. Then, these feature vectors are used together with pyramidal histogram of characters labels (PHOC) to learn SVM-based attribute models. Documents are represented by these PHOC based word attributes. To efficiently compute the word attributes over a sliding window, we propose to use an integral image representation of the document using a simplified version of the attribute model. Finally we re-rank the top word candidates using the more discriminative full version of the word attributes. We show state-of-the-art results for segmentation-free query-by-example word spotting in single-writer and multi-writer standard datasets.

Keywords: Word spotting · Sliding window · Word attributes

1 Introduction

Due to recent development of image databases of handwritten and historic manuscripts, the demand for algorithms to make these databases accessible for browsing and indexing are in rise. The state of the art OCR technologies are not directly applicable to these type of documents due to challenges like the diversity of the handwriting style, the presence of noise and distortions in historical manuscripts, etc.

To overcome this one can perform an image based search in the form of query by example. The goal of query by example word spotting can be defined as identifying and retrieving all those regions in a dataset of document images that contain an instance of a query word image. In a multi-writer collections, where handwriting can differ significantly from document to document, this task can be quite challenging. In the literature, word spotting appears under two distinct trends wherein the fundamental difference concerns the search space which could be either a set of segmented word images (segmentation-based approaches) or the complete document image (segmentation-free approaches). In this work, we address the query by example word spotting problem in a segmentation-free multi-writer scenario.

© Springer International Publishing Switzerland 2015
R. Paredes et al. (Eds.): IbPRIA 2015, LNCS 9117, pp. 652–661, 2015.
DOI: 10.1007/978-3-319-19390-8_73

Initial works in word spotting followed a traditional path of OCR technologies, starting with a binarization followed by layout analysis to perform a word level segmentation. Popular matching techniques like Hidden Markov Model (HMM) and Dynamic Time Warping (DTW) were used to match query words with these extracted word candidates by representing both query and word candidates as sequence of features. Example of this type of framework are the works of [1–3]. The main drawbacks of these methods come from the dependence on the segmentation step, which can be very sensible to handwriting distortions, and the computational cost of the sequence-based comparison.

More recently, word spotting methods which do not use a precise segmentation step have been reported [4–8]. Some of these methods [4–6] are based on the extraction of local keypoints that are encoded using descriptors based on gradient information [4,5] or Heat Kernel Signature [6]. Word spotting is then performed by locating zones of the document images with similar interest points and, in some cases with the same spatial configuration as the query model [4]. In general, they use a costly distance computation, which is not scalable to large datasets. The work of Rusiñol et al. [7] avoids segmentation by representing regions with a fixed-length descriptor based on the well-known bag of visual words (BoW) framework [9]. In this case, comparison of regions is much faster since a dot-product or Euclidean distance can be used, making a sliding window over the whole image feasible. In addition, Latent Semantic Indexing (LSI) is used to learn a latent space where the distance between word representations is more meaningful than in the original space. Rothacker et al. [8] also makes use of the BoW representation to feed a HMM obtaining a robust representation of the query and avoiding segmentation using a patch-based framework. Comparison of regions is slower than in the BoW-based approach of [7], so it could not be directly applied in a large-scale scenario. In [10] Almazán et al. proposed to use a HOG based framework in combination with an exemplar-SVM framework to learn a better representation of the query from a single example. Compression of the descriptors by means of product quantization permits a very efficient computation over a large dataset in combination with a sliding window-based search. In [10] the authors also proposed to use a reranking step to further improve the accuracy using a more costly Fisher Vector based representation over the top results retrieved using HOG descriptors.

Though all these methods perform well in the case of single writer documents, the representations used are not capable of handling the variation imposed by documents written by multiple writers. More powerful representation and learning techniques are needed to deal with this problem. In this sense, in [11], Almazán et al. used a fixed length attribute representation which gives an efficient way of performing word spotting in both QBE (Query By Example) and QBS (Query By String) scenarios using the same framework. They achieved good results in a segmentation-based framework in both single and multi-writer datasets. The attribute representation encodes the spatial position of characters in the word image through a Pyramidal Histogram of Characters (PHOC) and is learned using the more powerful Fisher Vector representation of the images.

Once word images are represented in this attribute space spotting is reduced to a Nearest Neighbour problem. Though this framework has achieved high accuracy in case of segmented words it can not be applied directly in a segmentation-free approach as it involves computation of costly Fisher Vector representation, which is unfeasible at query time.

In this work we propose to use a similar representation over a sliding window protocol for segmentation-free word spotting. As the computation of such a costly representation at query time is not feasible, we propose to pre-compute an integral image representation of the attributes. However, it is not possible to encode exactly the same original attribute representation in an integral image. Some simplifications have to be done which makes the attribute representation a bit less discriminative. To overcome this we propose an additional re-ranking step at the end of the pipeline which uses the same attribute representation as of [11] for final ranking of the top candidate windows. Our main contributions can be summarized as: (i) We propose an efficient computation of the attribute word representation over a whole document using an integral image (ii) We combine an initial ranking based on a sliding window search with a re-ranking step on the top candidate windows using a more powerful attribute representation (iii) With this combined approach we are able to perform segmentation-free query by example in the challenging multi-writer scenario, where we are not aware of any previous reported results.

The rest of the paper is organised as follows: in Sect. 2 we briefly describe the computation of the attribute model and its extension in the sliding window protocol followed by the explanation of re-ranking step. In Sect. 3, we discuss about the various experiments carried out to compare our method with other state of the art methods. Finally we conclude the paper with possible extensions and improvements.

2   Method Description

The approach proposed is illustrated in Fig. 1, the query and document images are first converted to its PHOC representation. Then, the retrieval step is simplified to a nearest neighbour problem, computing cosine distance of the query image to all of the candidates given by the sliding window and ranking them in order of similarity. Finally, we compute the more discriminative attributes for the top $N\%$ candidates and re-rank these to give final ranked list as result. In the following subsections we first give a summary of the attribute word representation proposed by Almazán et al. in [11], next we describe how it can be adapted to compute the integral image. Finally we explain the combination of both representations to obtain the final spotting pipeline.

2.1   Attribute-Based Word Representation

The main idea of the approach proposed by Almazán et al. [11] is to learn a common low dimensional representation for word images and text strings, that

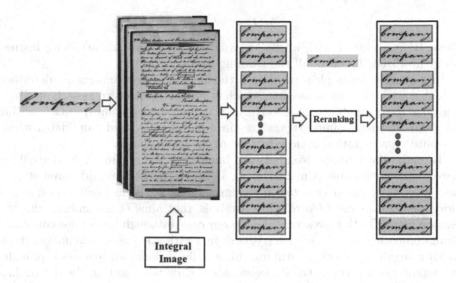

Fig. 1. General overview of the proposed pipeline

permits to address retrieval as a simple nearest neighbor problem. Though this representation can be utilized to accomplish both QBE and QBS, here our focus is on QBE word spotting.

To learn the attribute representation first, text strings are embedded into a d−dimensional binary space, in a way similar to the bag of characters string kernels [14,15]. This embedding – called Pyramidal Histogram Of Characters (PHOC) – encodes if a particular character appears in a particular spatial region of the string. The basic representation is just a binary histogram of characters, encoding which characters appear in the string. In order to add more discriminative power new levels are added to this histogram in a pyramidal way. At each level of the pyramid the word is further split and a new histogram of characters is added for each new division to account for characters at different parts of the word. At the end, 5 levels are used leading to a word representation of 604 dimensions.

Then, this embedding is used as a source for learning character attributes from word images. Each word image is projected into a d−dimensional space (same dimension as the PHOC representation) where each dimension is an attribute encoding the probability of appearance of a given character in a particular region of the image, using the same pyramidal decomposition as in the PHOC representation. Each attribute is independently learned using an SVM classifier on a Fisher Vector description of the word image, enriched with the x and y coordinates and the scale of the SIFT descriptor.

More formally, given a training image I, we can compute its Fisher Vector representation [18] $f(I)$, where $f(I)$ is a function of the form $f : I \to R^D$, being D the dimension of the Fisher Vector representation. Now, to project Fisher Vector representations into the PHOC attribute space, we learn an embedding function ϕ_I of the form $\phi_I : I \to R^d$ such that

$$\phi_I(I) = W^T f(I) \tag{1}$$

where W is a matrix with an SVM-based classifier for each attribute learned using the PHOC labels of all the training words.

In a query by example setting both the query and word images are described with this attribute representation, which is very discriminative as each attribute is giving the probability of a certain character in a specific position within the word. Retrieval simply translates into finding the word candidates whose attribute representation is close to that of the query image.

To make direct comparison between binary PHOCs and real valued attribute representations feasible Almazán *et al.* in [11], proposed an additional step to learn a common subspace between strings and images. A final calibration step is added, using Canonical Correlation Analysis, that aims at maximizing the correlation among both representations. In our case, although we are not concerned about comparing the PHOCs from text strings with attributes from images (typical for recognition tasks), we still use this low dimensional subspace as it provides an elegant way to reduce the dimensionality while not affecting the discriminativeness of the representations.

This final calibration and dimensionality reduction step can be represented with an additional embedding function ψ represented as $\psi_I : I \rightarrow R^{d'}$ and can be given as:

$$\psi_I(I) = U^T \phi_I(I) \tag{2}$$

being U the transformation matrix obtained with Canonical Correlation Analysis.

2.2   Representation of Word Attributes and Ranking

The main bottleneck of using word attributes as basic representation over a sliding window protocol is that it involves the costly computation of SIFT descriptors and Fisher Vector representation at run time – it takes around 110 ms for a single candidate window –. Moreover, note that to compute attributes for every window given by a sliding window protocol, one have to compute SIFT descriptors and the Fisher Vector for a large number of overlapping windows redundantly over the same image. To alleviate these problems we propose to pre-compute off-line the attribute representation for every pixel of the image and store it in an efficient integral image [19] that can be used to compute very fast the representation of any candidate window at query time.

To describe the computation of the integral image of the attribute representation, let us denote the document images of the dataset as $I^k, k = 1...n$ where n is the total number of images. For a given image I^k, we first compute the set of dense SIFT descriptors $d_{i,j}^k$ at every location (i, j). Then, we can define the embedding function into the attribute space ϕ_I for every pixel location as:

$$\phi_I(i,j) = W^T f(d_{i,j}) \tag{3}$$

where $f(d_{i,j})$ is the Fisher Vector representation for the (i, j) pixel of image I^k and W is a matrix encoding the attribute classifiers as in previous section.

Finally this attribute representation for every pixel is projected to the lower dimensional subspace obtained through Canonical Correlation Analysis using the same transformation matrix U introduced in previous section:

$$\psi_I(i,j) = \mathbf{U}^{\mathrm{T}}\phi_I(i,j) \tag{4}$$

Once we have the final attribute representation for every pixel, it can be easily aggregated into an integral image $\Psi_{i,j}$:

$$\Psi_{i,j} = \sum_{i' <= i, j' <= j} \psi_{i,j} \tag{5}$$

The time and memory requirements for computing the attribute representation can be further reduced if we arrange the image into $N \times N$ dimensional blocks and instead of computing Fisher Vector representation for every pixel, we only compute one Fisher Vector for each block.

Finally, given a query image and the integral image representation we have to generate candidate windows using a sliding window and rank the list of candidate windows according to the similarity with the query image. We first compute the attribute representation for the query and compute the attribute representation for all the candidate windows. Given a window $w = (X_1, Y_1, X_2, Y_2)$, where (X_1, Y_1) are the co-ordinates of the top left corner and (X_2, Y_2) are the co-ordinates of the bottom right corner of the w, we can compute the attribute representation Ψ_w in a very simple way with just 4 vector additions as:

$$\Psi_w = \Psi(X_2, Y_2) + \Psi(X_1, Y_1) - \Psi(X_1, Y_2) - \Psi(X_2, Y_1) \tag{6}$$

Now to compute the similarity between the query and the candidates we use cosine similarity by taking dot products.

2.3 Reranking

The integral image of attributes while being fast can not exploit the full discriminative power of the original attribute representation due to certain simplifications that are required to be able to compute the integral image offline before the query time. In particular: (i) as we are computing Fisher Vector on a per pixel basis, we can not have, at the time of computing the integral image, the relative position of the key-points inside a given candidate box. Therefore, SIFT descriptors cannot be enriched using the relative positional information x, y coordinates, as explained in Sect. 2.1. (ii) Also, as we cannot know the size of the underlying window, we can not apply the window size normalization performed in the original approach.

These limitations result in a significant loss of accuracy that can be partially alleviated by introducing a re-ranking step, as it is usual in other applications of image retrieval [16,17]. Basically it consists of applying more discriminative and costly features to the best windows retrieved by the first ranking step in order to obtain the final ranking list. In the context of word spotting example of re-ranking can be seen in [10], where they re-rank top windows by Fisher Vector after selecting them using a HOG based representation.

In this work we use the same strategy: the top $N\%$ candidates from the ranked list given by the initial ranking obtained with the sliding window search are re-ranked using the more discriminative original attribute representation described in Sect. 2.1.

3   Experimental Results

To evaluate our method and compare with other state of the art methods we use three different datasets. First, we briefly describe each of these datasets before moving to the results section.

3.1   Datasets

The George Washington (GW) dataset [12] contains 5000 words annotated at word level. The dataset comprises 20 handwritten letters written by George Washington and his associates in 18th century. The writing styles present only small variations and it can be considered a single-writer dataset.

The Lord Byron (LB) dataset similar to the GW dataset it also contains approximately 5000 words spread over 20 pages annotated at word level. However the nature of the data is completely different as it consists of typewritten text.

To evaluate our method in a multi-writer setting we used the **IAM Offline Dataset** [13]. It is a large dataset comprised of 1539 pages of modern handwritten English text written by 657 different writers. The document images are annotated at word and line level and contain the transcriptions of more than 13000 lines and 115000 words. We follow the official partition for writer independent text line recognition task.

3.2   Results

To evaluate and compare to state-of-the-art approaches, we follow standard protocols as in [7,10] in case of GW and LB datasets. Every word in the dataset is considered as a query and after ranking, a candidate window is considered as a true positive if it overlaps by more then 50% with any of the ground truth annotated boxes. We measure accuracy in terms of Mean Average Precision. In case of IAM dataset, however, we follow a different strategy as in line spotting instead of word spotting, *i.e.* the whole lines are retrieved if they contain the query word. Each query word is searched inside all annotated text lines using sliding window approach. The distance between query and text line is defined as the distance between query and the closest candidate word of that line. A similar strategy has been followed by Almazán *et al.* in [11].

Table 1 summarizes the results of our method, compared to other state-of-the-art methods. We provide results for three settings of our method: the first one without reranking, and then reranking with two different choices of N. From the results it can be observed that our base line system without any reranking can give better results than [10] without reranking in the GW dataset and only a bit lower in the LB dataset. Using reranking we obtain the best results among all systems in the GW dataset and very close to the best system in the LB dataset. For the IAM dataset none of the existing approaches reporting results for word spotting can be directly compared to our approach as they either work in a segmentation based framework [11] or in Query By String [4, 21]. Up to our knowledge our results are the first ones reported for IAM dataset in a segmentation-free query by example framework. Results, specially with the reranking step, compare pretty well with the 52.61 MAP reported in [11] in the much easier task of segmentation-based word spotting.

Table 1. Result of our word spotting method in comparison with state-of-the-art. (1) Proposed method without the reranking step. (2) Re-ranking with top 80 % of candidates. (3) Re-ranking with top 60 % of the candidates from first step.

	GW	LB	IAM
Almazán et al. [10]	51.88	84.34	-
Almazán et al. [10] (with RR)	57.46	84.51	-
Russiñol et al. [7]	30.42	42.83	-
Kovalchuk et al. [20]	50.1	90.7	-
Proposed (1)	56.27	84.45	35.68
Proposed (2) with RR (80 %)	67.7	90.45	42.08
Proposed (3) with RR (60 %)	63.87	87.85	39.94

We also show the average computational time to evaluate each query in Table 2. In this table we kept only one variant of re-ranking with top 80 % of the candidates. It can be observed that the proposed method without the re-ranking step is quite fast to be used in a real time environment. In comparison with Almazán et al. [10] it is marginally slow while achieving a higher accuracy. The re-ranking step significantly increases the computational time as it must compute SIFT and Fisher Vector for each candidate window.

Table 2. Result with respect to the computation time in per query basis

	GW	LB
Almazán et al. [10]	1.04 s	0.83 s
Kovalchuk et al. [20]	0.033	0.009
Proposed	3.45 s	2.87 s
Proposed with RR	15.6 s	11.7 s

4   Conclusion

This paper proposes a segmentation-free approach to word spotting in document images. We have shown an efficient way to represent PHOC based word attributes in an integral image format, which can be computed offline and used efficiently in query time. The results of our method shows significant improvements over the current state-of-the-art. In addition we are able to apply our method to the multi-write IAM dataset where we are not aware of other published results in the context of segmentation-free word spotting. Computational time could be further improved integrating our approach with a compression technique such as product quantization as done in [10].

The proposed method is based on a simplification of the original attribute word representation. Context information around a pixel can be exploited in the future in order to compensate for the poorer Fisher Vector representation that we use in our method.

References

1. Marti, U.V., Bunke, H.: Using a statistical language model to improve the performance of an HMM-based cursive handwriting recognition systems. IJPRAI **15**, 65–90 (2001)
2. Vinciarelli, A., Bengio, S., Bunke, H.: Offline recognition of unconstrained handwritten texts using HMMs and statistical language models. IEEE Trans. PAMI **26**, 709–720 (2004)
3. Rodríguez-Serrano, J., Perronnin, F.: Local gradient histogram features for word spotting in unconstrained hand-written documents. In: International Conference on Frontiers in Handwriting Recognition (2008)
4. Frinken, V., Fischer, A., Manmatha, R., Bunke, H.: A novel word spotting method based on recurrent neural networks. IEEE Trans. PAMI **34**, 211–224 (2012)
5. Leydier, Y., Ouji, A., Lebourgeois, F., Emptoz, H.: Towards an omnilingual word retrieval system for ancient manuscripts. Pattern Recogn. **42**, 2089–2105 (2009)
6. Zhang, X., Tan, C.L.: Segmentation-free keyword spotting for handwritten documents based on heat kernel signature. In: International Conference on Document Analysis and Recognition, pp. 827–831 (2013)
7. Rusiñol, M., Aldavert, D., Toledo, R., Lladós, J.: Browsing heterogeneous document collections by a segmentation-free word spotting method. In: International Conference on Document Analysis and Recognition, pp. 63–67 (2011)
8. Rothacker, L., Rusiñol, M., Fink, G.A.: Bag-of-features HMMs for segmentation-free word spotting in handwritten documents. In: International Conference on Document Analysis and Recognition, pp. 1305–1309 (2013)
9. Csurka, G., Dance, C.R., Fan, L., Willamowski, J., Bray, C.: Visual categorization with bags of keypoints. In: Workshop on Statistical Learning in Computer Vision, European Conference on Computer Vision, pp. 1–22 (2004)
10. Almazán, J., Gordo, A., Fornés, A., Valveny, E.: Segmentation-free word spotting with exemplar SVMs. Pattern Recogn. **47**, 3967–3978 (2014)
11. Almazán, J., Gordo, A., Fornés, A., Valveny, E.: Word spotting and recognition with embedded attributes. IEEE Trans. PAMI **36**, 2552–2566 (2014)

12. Rath, T., Manmatha, R.: Word spotting for historical documents. IJDAR **9**, 139–152 (2007)
13. Marti, U.V., Bunke, H.: The IAM-database: an english sentence database for off-line handwriting recognition. IJDAR **5**, 39–46 (2002)
14. Leslie, C., Eskin, E., Noble, W.: The spectrum kernel: a string kernel for SVM protein classification. In: Pacific Symposium on Biocomputing (2002)
15. Lodhi, H., Saunders, C., Shawe-Taylor, J., Cristianini, N., Watkins, C.: Text classification using string kernels. JMLR **2**, 419–444 (2002)
16. Chum, O., Philbin, J., Sivic, J., Isard, M., Zisserman, A.: Total recall: automatic query expansion with a generative feature model for object retrieval. In: International Conference on Computer Vision, pp. 1–8 (2007)
17. Arandjelović, R., Zisserman, A.: Three things everyone should know to improve object retrieval. In: IEEE Conference on Computer Vision and Pattern Recognition, pp. 2911–2918 (2012)
18. Perronnin, F., Sánchez, J., Mensink, T.: Improving the Fisher kernel for large-scale image classification. In: Daniilidis, K., Maragos, P., Paragios, N. (eds.) ECCV 2010, Part IV. LNCS, vol. 6314, pp. 143–156. Springer, Heidelberg (2010)
19. Dalal, N., Triggs, B.: Histograms of oriented gradients for human detection. In: IEEE Conference on Computer Vision and Pattern Recognition (2005)
20. Kovalchuk, A., Wolf, L., Dershowitz, N.: A simple and fast word spotting method. In: International Conference on Frontiers in Handwriting Recognition (2014)
21. Fischer, A., Keller, A., Frinken, V., Bunke, H.: HMM-based word spotting in handwritten documents using subword models. In: International Conference on Pattern Recognition (2010)

Combining Statistical and Semantic Knowledge for Sarcasm Detection in Online Dialogues

José María Alcaide$^{(\boxtimes)}$, Raquel Justo, and María Inés Torres

Universidad del País Vasco (UPV/EHU), Leioa, Spain
josemaria.alcaide@ehu.es

Abstract. The detection of secondary emotions, like sarcasm, in online dialogues is a difficult task that has rarely been treated in the literature. In this work (This work has been partially supported by the Spanish Ministry of Science under grant TIN2011-28169-C05-04, and by the Basque Government under grant IT685-13.), we tackle this problem as an affective pattern recognition problem. Specifically, we consider different kind of information sources (statistical and semantic) and propose alternative ways of combining them. We also provide a comparison of a Support Vector Machine (SVM) classification method with a simpler Naive Bayes parametric classifier. The experimental results show that combining statistical and semantic feature sets comparable performances can be achieved with Naive Bayes and SVM classifiers.

Keywords: Affective pattern recognition · Sarcasm detection · Online dialogues · Combining information sources

1 Introduction

Affective computing was first introduced in [12] as computing that relates to, arises from, or influence emotions. Research on emotion involves psychology, neuroscience, sociology, computer science and affect pattern recognition in particular. One of the research frameworks involving affect computing is human machine interaction, where the machine should interpret the emotional state of users and adapt its behavior when responding to them. In this context spoken dialogues have been analyzed to detect emotions [8]. To this end emotional features were extracted from facial expression, speech, gestures, biosignals and language [1]. Primary emotions like fear, anger, sadness, disgust or joy, are the ones that we feel first as a reaction to external events. They are very important in decision making and have a direct impact in facial expression, speech or biosignals [2]. Secondary emotions, in contrast, come from reasoning about events being then influenced by personal experiences and expectations as well as by the environment and cultural frameworks. Therefore, language as a conceptual process is very important in perception of secondary emotions. In fact, it seems that language cues are the only valid ones to detect emotions like irony and sarcasm, even if in spoken language sarcasm might be manifested partly in vocal inflections [8].

© Springer International Publishing Switzerland 2015
R. Paredes et al. (Eds.): IbPRIA 2015, LNCS 9117, pp. 662–671, 2015.
DOI: 10.1007/978-3-319-19390-8_74

The understanding process of natural language requires computational models that can decode the semantic meaning of utterances as well as the sentics [5]. According to [4] the most relevant text features for sentiment classification include term and n-gram frequencies and presence, certain adjectives as indicators, phrases chosen by Part-Of-Speech (POS) patterns and sentiment lexicons. Keyword spotting, lexical affinity, and concept-based approaches as well as Bayesian inference are also frequently employed, being Support Vector Machines (SVMs) the most used statistical classifiers.

In this paper the sarcasm detection is addressed as an affect pattern recognition problem that was tackled trough some supervised learning experiments. In particular we are aimed at detecting sarcasm in social web where language is very different from the one employed in newspaper articles or task-oriented dialogues typically studied [15]. Information is informal and unstructured so the detection of relevant cues and its classification are challenge topics. Previous work on sarcasm detection has primarily focused on product reviews and tweets rather than online dialogues. Reference [16] proposes a semi-supervised algorithm based on k-nearest neighbors to detect sarcasm in online product reviews using pattern and punctuation based features. Subsequently the same algorithm was applied to millions of tweets [6] producing significantly better results. Reference [9] uses n-gram features to build a Winnow classifier to identify sarcastic tweets in Dutch. Reference [13] presents a method to detect a common form of sarcasm consisting of contrasting a positive sentiment with a negative situation in tweets.

In [7] it was investigated whether it is possible to automatically obtain a set of features valuable for identifying different forms of sarcasm in online conversations regardless of the topic, style, speaker, or affordances of the online forum. To do so, a range of features such as n-grams, Part-of-Speech (POS) tags, Semantic or Concept Information as well as some cues identified by human annotators were compared to each other. These feature sets were used to establish a baseline for both a rule-based and a Naive Bayes classifiers. In that context statistical and semantic features seemed to be the best ones for sarcasm detection. In this work, we are presenting an in depth and extensive experimental analysis of several combination of statistical and semantic knowledge for sarcasm detection in online dialogues. Another contribution of this work is the use of the state-of-the-art Support Vector Machines (SVM) for classification purposes. In this manner a comparison between a parametric Bayes classifier and a non-parametric SVM classifier is also presented for this task.

In Sect. 2 the task and corpus used in this work are presented. Section 3 deals with the way in which the relevant statistical and semantic information was extracted as well as with the way in which we combined those information sources for classification purposes. Section 4 presents the employed classification methods and Sect. 5 shows the experiments carried out. Finally Sect. 6 discuss some conclusions and further work.

2   Internet Argument Corpus

Our work draws on the recently released Internet Argument Corpus (IAC), a publicly available corpus of online forum conversations on a range of social

Category	Post or Post Pair
Sarcastic	**P1**: That's it? That was your post? To attack a source without anything backing you up? Bravo!
Sarcastic	**P2**: But...but...I just swallowed 56 zygotes so that they could vote by proxy through me for the Ripofflican(tm) party this upcoming election so they can win. Now I'm going to have all that indigestion for nothin'
Sarcastic	**P3**: OK, I get it! It's not being gay that is a sin; it's the gay sex that is a sin. You are such an expert on gay people! How about this EZ, what if two gay men live together, love each other, sleep in separate beds, never have sex but maybe give each other a little French kiss now and then? Is that OK, EZ? Here let me answer that question for you since your famous for avoiding the issue. Why yes Mr. Monster that is perfectly fine and a totally realistic thing to ask people to do! I know why you're avoiding answering the topic question directly. Believe me I am going to rip you a new one regardless (figuratively speaking.) You may as well let it all out. You know you want to. So go ahead, make my day.
Sarcastic	**P4-1**: "God" Does NOT play dice with Sexual Orientation. It is this way, because it was made this way before there was even the notion of a Bible, or Society. It is this way throughout the Animal Kingdom and remains so with us. **P4-2**: You need to experiment with the notion that you will be sexually attracted to your own sex. After youfe done, come back and report your findings!
Sarcastic	**P5-1**: I simply mean a member of the species of "human." If something is a member of that species, it is a human being. **P5-2** If that is a human being, then is my kidney a human being too?

Fig. 1. Sarcastic Posts and Post Pairs from 4forums.com. Sarcastic examples were all reliably rated sarcastic (by more than 50 % of Turkers).

and political topics [17]. The IAC includes a large set of conversations from *4forums.com*, a website for political debate and discourse. This site is a fairly typical internet forum where people post a discussion topic, other people post responses, and a treelike conversation structure is created. The corpus comes with annotations of different types of social language categories including sarcastic vs. not sarcastic, nasty vs. not nasty, rational vs. emotional and respectful vs. insulting. In this work, we only consider the detection of sarcasm and the corresponding annotation labels. These labels were collected with Mechanical Turk procedure and 5-7 Turkers answered the binary annotation question "Is the respondent using sarcasm?" $(0, 1)$. Some related examples of posts and post pairs labeled as sarcastic from the IAC are shown in Fig. 1.

3 Combining Statistical and Semantic Knowledge

This section is devoted to the extraction of relevant information from the text for the correct classification of the posts into sarcastic and not-sarcastic. Thus, different aspects related to the ways in which the sarcasm is expressed were considered in Sect. 3.1 leading to the definition of different feature sets. Additionally, a feature selection procedure described in Sect. 3.2 was considered. Finally, alternative ways of combining different information sources were considered in Sect. 3.3.

3.1 Definition of Feature Sets

Statistical and semantic information seemed to provide better results than other choices based on linguistic features for online dialogues, according to [7]. This might be because different forms of sarcasm can be found in the mentioned task:

sarcastic utterances that can be identified due to the use of a specific vocabulary, like words or sequences of words: "Bravo", "Really? Well",... and sarcastic forms that do not contain any surface sarcastic indicators but the semantic interpretation of the sentence is needed to identify them. In this sense the two sets of features associated to that kind of information were considered in this work:

Statistical Cues: Finding the cues that are good indicators of sarcasm is very laborious and requires human annotation. Moreover, it is difficult to get a set of cues big enough to warranty the needed coverage [7]. Thus, sets of features made up of word n-grams have also been used to identify sarcasm [4,9]. In this work, a set of features consisting of the unigrams, bigrams and trigrams extracted from each utterance was automatically extracted from the training set. Thus, we obtain a d−dimensional vector $\mathbf{x}_{stat}$ of the following form for each post:

$$\mathbf{x}_{stat} = [x_1, \ldots, x_d] = [\, c_{1gram_1}, c_{1gram_2}, \ldots, c_{1gram_N},$$
$$c_{2gram_1}, c_{2gram_2}, \ldots, c_{2gram_M}, \qquad (1)$$
$$c_{3gram_1}, c_{3gram_2}, \ldots, c_{3gram_P}]$$

where c_{ngram_i} is a counter with the number of times the ngram i appears in the corresponding post. N is the number of $1\,g$ in the post and M and P the number of $2\,g$ and $3\,g$ respectively. Thus, $d = N + M + P$.

Semantic information: Here, we consider *Linguistic Inquiry and Word Count* (LIWC) semantic classes [11] to get a new feature set. The LIWC dictionary includes 64 different lexical categories including sets of words related to *anger, affect, feelings, social, number, health,...* but also more general categories such as *pronoun, verb* or *future*. In order to make more meaningful feature patterns, we associate each word in a post with its corresponding LIWC semantic category or categories. For example, the word "address" is associated with the LIWC category "home" while "adult" is associated with LIWC categories "social" and "humans". Then, a vector of the following form is built for each post:

$$\mathbf{x}_{sem} = [x_1, x_2, \ldots, x_{64}] = [c_{LIWC_1}, c_{LIWC_2}, \ldots, c_{LIWC_{64}}] \qquad (2)$$

where c_{LIWC_i} is the number of times a word in the post has been associated to LIWC category i.

3.2   Feature Selection

When the number of features is very high, a previous selection procedure is usually employed in order to extract the most significant features. This might be useful to remove noise and hence obtain better classification results and also to reduce execution time. In this work, the chosen feature selection procedure was based on the χ^2 distribution, which determines whether there is a significant association between two variables.

In this work, the set of features with the highest values for the χ^2 statistic was selected. This selection was carried out in a tuning step where the classifier was run over the training data set. The appropriate number of features was selected as follows: Different sets with increasing number of features were obtained according to the χ^2 criterion. The number of features added to each step was the total number divided by 25. Then, the training set was classified, and the F-measure computed, using each of the 25 sets. The feature set that maximized F was selected, and the test set, which was not seen during feature selection and tuning, was evaluated using the selected features.

3.3 Alternative Ways of Combining Information

In this Section we propose alternative approaches to merge statistical and semantic knowledge in an only one set according to the following criteria:

Weighted combination of features: According to the description given in Sect. 3.1 each post can be represented by a very high and variable dimensional vector $\mathbf{x}_{stat}$ and a low dimensional (64) vector $\mathbf{x}_{sem}$. Since the number of statistical features is much higher than the number of semantic ones a T weight was assigned to semantic features in this approach in order explore the impact of their relevance in the final results. However, this weighted combination was carried out in two different ways:

Stat_Sem_1. All the features were combined in an only one vector consisting of a copy of the statistical vector and T replications of the semantic one. Then the feature selection procedure described in Sect. 3.2 was carried out leading to the following vector: $\chi^2(\mathbf{x}_{stat\_sem} = [\mathbf{x}_{stat}, \underbrace{\mathbf{x}_{sem}, \mathbf{x}_{sem}, \ldots, \mathbf{x}_{sem}}_{T \text{ times}}])$

Stat_Sem_2. In this case, the feature selection was carried out over the statistical vector to reduce dimensionality there, and all the semantic features were kept to provide more relevance to this set. The resulting vector is as follows: $\mathbf{x}_{stat\_sem2} = [\chi^2(\mathbf{x}_{stat}), \underbrace{\mathbf{x}_{sem}, \mathbf{x}_{sem}, \ldots, \mathbf{x}_{sem}}_{T \text{ times}}]$.

Score combination of classifiers (**Score_Comb**): Finally, two different classifiers were trained over the training set, one of them considering statistical features and the other one considering semantic ones. In this way, the test set is evaluated with each of the classifiers that provide a probability of being sarcastic for each post of the test set ($P_{C_{stat}}(post), P_{C_{sem}}(post)$). The probability used to carry out the final classification is obtained according to the linear combination $P(post) = \lambda \cdot P_{C_{stat}}(post) + (1 - \lambda) \cdot P_{C_{sem}}(post)$.

4   Classification

In this Section the description of the two different classification methods that were employed and compared to each other (Naive Bayes vs. SVM) is given.

4.1   Naive Bayes Classifier

A Naive Bayes Classifier implements Bayes' theorem under the assumption of independence between pairs of features. Given a class ω and a feature vector $\mathbf{x} = [x_1, \ldots x_d]$ the Bayes' formula states:

$$P(\omega|x_1,\ldots,x_d) = \frac{p(x_1,\ldots,x_d|\omega)P(\omega)}{\sum_{j=1}^{c} p(x_1,\ldots,x_d|\omega_j)P(\omega_j)} \tag{3}$$

Using the naive independence assumption $p(x_1,\ldots,x_d|\omega) = \prod_{i=1}^{d} p(x_i|\omega)$ the naive Bayes classification rule is set as:

$$\hat{\omega} = \arg\max_{\omega} P(\omega|x_1,\ldots,x_d) \approx \arg\max_{\omega}(P(\omega)\prod_{i=1}^{d} p(x_i|\omega)) \tag{4}$$

Usually Naive Bayes classifiers assume classic forms for the distribution $p(x_i|\omega)$ such as Gaussian, multinomial or Bernouilli. In this work, we assume our data to be multinomially distributed, Naive Bayes Multinomial (NBM). The distribution is parametrized by vectors $\theta_\omega = (\theta_{\omega_1},\ldots,\theta_{\omega_d})$ for each class ω, where d is the number of features and $\theta_{\omega_i} = p(x_i|\omega)$ is the probability of feature i appearing in a sample in class ω. Parameters θ_ω are estimated as:

$$\hat{\theta}_{\omega_i} = \frac{N_{\omega_i} + \alpha}{N_\omega + \alpha d} \tag{5}$$

where $N_{\omega_i} = \sum_{\mathbf{x}\in\mathcal{H}} x_i$ is the number of times feature i appears in a sample of class ω in the training set $\mathcal{H}$, $N_\omega = \sum_{i=1}^{|\mathcal{H}|} N_{\omega_i}$ is the total count of all features for class ω, and $\alpha \geq 0$ implements a smoothed maximum likelihood estimation that prevents zero probabilities.

4.2 Support Vector Machines

The Support Vector Machine is a state-of-the-art classification method introduced by [3]. Given a set of m d-dimensional vectors $X = \{\mathbf{x}_1,\ldots,\mathbf{x}_m\}$ where $X \subset \mathcal{R}^d$ and $\mathbf{x}_i = [x_{i1}, x_{i2},\ldots, x_{id}]$, representing the training samples, we assume that they can be assigned to one of two classes, ω_1 and ω_2. Then, the problem consists of building a hyperplane ($H : \mathbf{v}^T\mathbf{x}_i + b$, where $\mathbf{v}$ is a vector normal to H) that separates $\mathcal{R}^d$ in two regions. That is, the linear discriminant function $g(x) = \mathbf{v}^T\mathbf{x}_i + b$ will be considered with decision rule:

$$\begin{aligned} g(x) > 0 &\rightarrow x \in \omega_1 \text{ with corresponding numeric value } y_i = +1 \\ g(x) < 0 &\rightarrow x \in \omega_2 \text{ with corresponding numeric value } y_i = -1 \end{aligned} \tag{6}$$

When the training data are separable the goal of a SVM is to obtain the hyperplane, that leaves the samples closest to it, at maximum distance. This problem can be solved by using Lagrange formalism that leads to the dual form of the Lagrangian

$$L_D = \sum_{i=1}^{m} \alpha_i - \frac{1}{2}\sum_{i=1}^{m}\sum_{j=1}^{m} \alpha_i\alpha_j y_i y_j \mathbf{x}_i^T\mathbf{x}_j \tag{7}$$

which is maximised with respect to α_i subject to:

$$\alpha_i \geq 0 \qquad \sum_{i=1}^{m} \alpha_i y_i = 0 \tag{8}$$

Those vectors in the training set which provide a positive Lagrange multiplier α_i are called support vectors and they are crucial because the main problem can be simplified to consider only those samples.

In many real-world practical problems there will be no linear boundary separating the classes. However, those data that are not linearly separable in a specific d-dimensional feature space might be separable in a higher d'-dimensional space by using a $\Phi(\mathbf{x}) : \mathcal{R}^d \rightarrow R^{d'}$ function to transform the data. In this case, Optimisation of L_D and the subsequent classification of a sample relies only on scalar products between transformed feature vectors, which can be replaced by a kernel function $K(\mathbf{x_i}, \mathbf{x_j}) = \Phi(\mathbf{x})^\mathbf{T}\Phi(\mathbf{y})$. Thus, we can avoid computing the transformation $\Phi(\mathbf{x})$ explicitly and replace the scalar product with $K(\mathbf{x_i}, \mathbf{x_j})$.

There are many different kernel functions that can be used (polynomial, sigmoid,...) but in this work we used Radial Basis Function (RBF) kernel function (a gaussian kernel) shown in eq (9) where γ is an adjustable parameter.

$$K(\mathbf{x_i}, \mathbf{x_j}) = exp\left(-\gamma||\mathbf{x_i} - \mathbf{x_j}||^2\right) \tag{9}$$

Sometimes a training sample labeled as a specific class falls into the region associated to the other class. In such a case it does not exist a hyperplane that separates the samples into two classes and we say that the set is non-separable. The problem in this case is solved by relaxing the constraints for the specific samples that do not fulfil the requirement and a margin error is introduced. Thus, we employed the ν-SVM realisation [14] where $\nu \in [0, 1]$ is the lower and upper bound on the number of examples that are support vectors and that lie on the wrong side of the hyperplane, respectively.

5   Experimental Results

Our experimentation drew on the Internet Argument Corpus (Sect. 2). This corpus is comprised of 6,458 posts extracted from the website *4forums.com* with annotations of several types of social language categories, of which we only considered sarcasm and its corresponding labels. A k-fold cross-validation procedure (where $k = 10$) was applied and the results were derived as the averages for the resulting 10 different combinations of the subsets.

Feature extraction was carried out as described in Sect. 3.1. The total number of statistical features (word n-grams with $n = 1, 2, 3$) extracted was 569,275. On the other hand, there are only 64 semantic features, which correspond to the LIWC categories. Two different kinds of classifiers were used: multinomial Naive Bayes (MNB) and $\nu-$Support Vector Machine (ν-SVM). We employed the implementations provided in the Scikit-learn Python package [10] for these algorithms.

We carried out five types of experiments, each of them employing both MNB and ν-SVM classifiers. For those employing ν-SVM, we tested values of the ν parameter between 0.2 and 0.8 (step=0.1) in order to evaluate the effect of establishing an upper bound to the fraction of training errors:

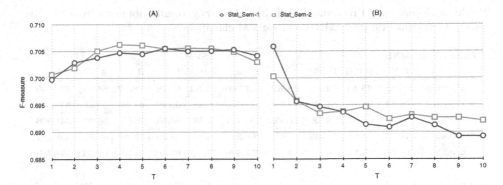

Fig. 2. Comparative results of F-measure obtained from combination methods **Stat_Sem_1** and **Stat_Sem_2** using (A) MNB and (B) ν-SVM classifiers respectively.

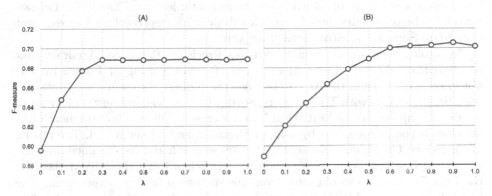

Fig. 3. F-measure obtained from **Score_Comb** using (A) MNB and (B) ν-SVM classifiers respectively.

Experiment 1 (baseline): Only the statistical features (with feature selection).

Experiment 2 (baseline): Only the semantic features.

Experiment 3: Feature combination method **Stat_Sem_1**, with $T \in [1, 10]$ in steps of 1

Experiment 4: Feature combination method **Stat_Sem_2**, with $T \in [1, 10]$ in steps of 1

Experiment 5: Score combination method **Score_Comb**, with $\lambda \in [0, 1]$ in 0.1 steps

The results of the experiments (**Stat_Sem_1**) and (**Stat_Sem_2**) are shown in the Fig. 2. With the MNB classifier a slightly better F-measure was obtained using $T = 6$ replications of the vectors of semantic features; on the other hand, with the ν-SVM classifier the best F-measure was obtained using $T = 1$. Also, there are only slight differences between the results obtained from the combination methods **Stat_Sem_1** and **Stat_Sem_2**.

Table 1. F-measure, Precision, Recall and Accuracy results obtained from the five types of experiments, using MNB and ν-SVM classifiers.

Experiment	MNB					ν-SVM				
	F (%)	P (%)	R (%)	A (%)	#feat	F (%)	P (%)	R (%)	A (%)	#feat
Statistical	68.88	**68.51**	70.82	**68.62**	357,506	**71.32**	65.78	**78.97**	68.89	378,000
Semantic	59.53	58.85	61.20	59.10	64	60.91	60.49	61.98	60.87	64
Stat_Sem_1	70.55	64.66	78.58	67.85	346,151	70.58	66.56	76.07	68.90	341,596
Stat_Sem_2	**70.62**	64.83	**78.69**	67.91	200,386	70.03	66.09	75.46	68.33	398,494
Score_Comb	68.83	68.42	70.82	68.55	357,506	70.54	**67.94**	74.34	**69.51**	334,735

The results of the experiment (**Score_Comb**) are shown in the Fig. 3. Independently of the classifier employed, the F-measure improves rapidly as more weight λ is given to the classification score obtained using the statistical features against the score obtained from the semantic features. The ν-SVM classifier yields better results, but **Score_Comb** does not represent an improvement over **Stat_Sem_1** and **Stat_Sem_2** anyway.

In Table 1 we summarize the F-measure, Precision, Recall and Accuracy that resulted from the experiment of each type for which a higher F-measure was obtained. When using the MNB classifier the highest F-measure was obtained with **Stat_Sem_2** (with $T = 6$); **Stat_Sem_1** ($T = 6$) yielded very slightly lower results. Compared to the Statistical baseline experiment, the improvement of F-measure is counterweighted by a lower Precision and higher Recall. The results of the **Score_Comb** experiment were always worse than those obtained from the statistical baseline, being closer when $\lambda \to 1$. When using the ν-SVM classifier the best F-measure was obtained from the statistical baseline experiment. The highest Accuracy and Precision were obtained from **Score_Comb** using $\lambda = 0.9$. With respect to the effect of the ν parameter of the ν-SVM classifier, the best results were obtained using $\nu = 0.6$, except for the semantic baseline experiment, which yielded the best results using $\nu = 0.4$.

6   Concluding Remarks and Future Work

In this work, different information sources (statistical and semantic) were combined using alternative methods in a sarcasm detection task for online dialogues. Additionally, two different classifiers (MNB and SVM) were compared to each other. The experimental evaluation show that the best results are achieved with the SVM classifier without considering semantic information. However, when considering MNB classifier the combination of feature sets provides results comparable to those obtained with SVM, that although more modest, can be useful in many practical applications due to the simplicity of the classifier. For further work we propose to study different choices of SVM configuration (different kernels,...) in order to conclude whether the inclusion of semantic information might also be useful with this classifier. Additionally, we propose to consider alternative learning paradigms like semisupervised or online learning within the affective pattern recognition framework.

References

1. Barrett, L.F., Lindquist, K.A., Gendron, M.: Language as context for the perception of emotion. Trends Cogn. Sci. **11**, 327–332 (2007)
2. Becker-Asano, C., Wachsmuth, I.: Affective computing with primary and secondary emotions in a virtual human. Auton. Agent. Multi-Agent Syst. **20**(1), 32–49 (2010)
3. Boser, B.E., Guyon, I.M., Vapnik, V.N.: A training algorithm for optimal margin classifiers. In: Haussler, D. (ed.) Proceedings of COLT 1992, pp. 144–152. ACM Press, Pittsburgh, PA, USA (1992)
4. Cambria, E., Schuller, B., Xia, Y., Havasi, C.: New avenues in opinion mining and sentiment analysis. IEEE Intell. Syst. **28**, 15–21 (2013)
5. Cambria, E., White, B.: Jumping NLP curves: a review of natural language processing research. IEEE Comput. Intell. Mag. **9**, 48–57 (2014)
6. González-Ibáñez, R., Muresan, S., Wacholder, N.: Identifying sarcasm in twitter: a closer look. In: Proceedings of the 49th ACL: Human Language Technologies HLT 2011, vol. 2, pp. 581–586. ACL, Stroudsburg, PA, USA (2011)
7. Justo, R., Corcoran, T., Lukin, S., Walker, M., Torres, M.I.: Extracting relevant knowledge for the detection of sarcasm and nastiness in the social web. Knowl.-Based Syst. **69**, 124–133 (2014)
8. Lee, C.M., Narayanan, S.S.: Toward detecting emotions in spoken dialogs. IEEE Trans. Speech Audio Process. **13**(2), 293–303 (2005). [IEEE Signal Processing Society Best Paper Award 2009]
9. Liebrecht, C., Kunneman, F., Van den Bosch, A.: The perfect solution for detecting sarcasm in tweets #not. In: Proceedings of the 4th WASSA, pp. 29–37. ACL, Atlanta, Georgia June 2013
10. Pedregosa, F., Varoquaux, G., Gramfort, A., Michel, V., Thirion, B., Grisel, O., Blondel, M., Prettenhofer, P., Weiss, R., Dubourg, V., Vanderplas, J., Passos, A., Cournapeau, D., Brucher, M., Perrot, M., Duchesnay, E.: Scikit-learn: machine learning in python. J. Mach. Learn. Res. **12**, 2825–2830 (2011)
11. Pennebaker, J.W., Booth, R.J., Francis, M.E.: Linguistic inquiry and word count: LIWC 2007 (2007)
12. Picard, R.: Affective computing. Technical report. 321, Media Laboratory, perceptual Computing Section, Massachusetts Institute of Technology, 20 Ames St., Cambridge, MA 02139 (1995)
13. Riloff, E., Qadir, A., Surve, P., De Silva, L., Gilbert, N., Huang, R.: Sarcasm as contrast between a positive sentiment and negative situation. In: Proceedings of the 2013 EMNLP, pp. 704–714. ACL, Seattle, Washington, USA (October 2013)
14. Schölkopf, B., Smola, A.J., Williamson, R.C., Bartlett, P.L.: New support vector algorithms. Neural Comput. **12**(5), 1207–1245 (2000)
15. Subba, R., Di Eugenio, B.: An effective discourse parser that uses rich linguistic information. In: Proceedings of NAACL HLT 2009, pp. 566–574. ACL (2009)
16. Tsur, O., Davidov, D., Rappoport, A.: Icwsm - a great catchy name: semi-supervised recognition of sarcastic sentences in online product reviews. In: Cohen, W.W., Gosling, S. (eds.) ICWSM. The AAAI Press (2010)
17. Walker, M., Tree, J.F., Anand, P., Abbott, R., King, J.: A corpus for research on deliberation and debate. In: Proceedings of LREC 2012, pp. 23–25. ELRA (2012)

Estimating Fuel Consumption from GPS Data

Afonso Vilaça[1]([✉]), Ana Aguiar[1,2], and Carlos Soares[1,3]

[1] Faculty of Engineering of University of Porto, Porto, Portugal
meinf12005@fe.up.pt
[2] Instituto de Telecomunicações, Porto, Portugal
[3] Instituto de Engenharia de Sistemas E Computadores Do Porto, Porto, Portugal

Abstract. The road transportation sector is responsible for 87 % of the human CO_2 emissions. The estimation and prediction of fuel consumption plays a key role in the development of systems that foster the reduction of those emissions through trip planing. In this paper, we present a predictive regression model of instantaneous fuel consumption for diesel and gasoline light-duty vehicles, based on their instantaneous speed and acceleration and on road inclination. The parameters are extracted from GPS data, thus the models do not require data from dedicated vehicle sensors. We use data collected by 17 drivers during their daily commutes using the SenseMyCity crowdsensor.

We perform an empyrical comparison of several regression algorithms for prediction across trips of the same vehicle and for prediction across vehicles. The results show that models trained for a vehicle show similar RMSE when are applied to other vehicles with similar characteristics. Relying on these results, we propose fuel type specific models that provide an accurate prediction for vehicles with similar characteristics to those on which the models were trained.

Keywords: Fuel consumption · Regression · Prediction

1 Introduction

Private car is the most used transport mode worldwide, with 2700 passenger km per capita [2]. The transportation sector is responsible for 22 % of the CO_2 emissions from fossil fuel consumption (FC), which in turn occupies 87 % of the human sources of CO_2 [3]. To encourage people to save FC on their trips, they should know how much fuel their vehicles consume on alternative routes. The possibility of predicting the instantaneous FC for any vehicle according to its movement (e.g. instantaneous speed and acceleration) and road inclination, is a key component of mobility support systems for route and trip management that aim at reducing FC and CO_2 emissions.

Using the dataset collected during daily commutes, we present the design of a predictive model of instantaneous FC. We followed a novel approach, empirically comparing several regression algorithms initially for prediction within the same trip, then to predict across trips of a same vehicle and, finally, to predict FC of a different vehicle. Finally, we present a fuel-specific generic model for instantaneous FC.

© Springer International Publishing Switzerland 2015
R. Paredes et al. (Eds.): IbPRIA 2015, LNCS 9117, pp. 672–682, 2015.
DOI: 10.1007/978-3-319-19390-8_75

The rest of the article is organized as follows: In Sect. 2 we review related work; in Sect. 3 we explain the dataset, including data collection and processing; in Sect. 4 we expose the exploratory data analysis; Sect. 5 presents the approach on the regression, the different experiments, and the used algorithms; Sect. 6 presents the results and Sect. 7 discuss them; finally, we conclude the article in Sect. 8.

2 Related Work

Table 1 presents previous work on FC estimation. For each model, we focus on its granularity and on the used variables. Fine granularity means that the model is for instantaneous FC estimation (typically with a frequency of 1 Hz), while coarse means it is an aggregated model that estimates the total or average FC on a specific road or route.

Table 1. Fuel consumption estimation models

Authors	Granularity	Vehicle	Variables
Bowyer et al. [5]	fine	light	S, A, I
Joumard et al. [6]	fine	light	S, A
Jimenez-Palacios [7]	fine	light and heavy	S, A, I, S_w, veh. char.
Cappiello et al. [8]	fine	light	S, A, weight
Rakha et al. [9]	fine	light and heavy	S, A
Lei et al. [10]	fine	light	S, A
Ribeiro et al. [4]	fine	light	S, A, I
Pelkmans et al. [11]	coarse	light and heavy	S, I, road class
Ericsson et al. [12]	coarse	light	veh. char.
Song et al. [13]	coarse	light	A, S
Tavares et al. [14]	coarse	heavy	S, I, load
André et al. [15]	coarse	light and heavy	S, A, veh. char., road class, hour

There are three types of variables: related to the route (e.g. car movement and road characteristics), vehicle specifications and the time of the trip. The most used variables are the speed and the acceleration, as they are straightforward to obtain. The use of road inclination is also frequent. Besides the inclination, some models consider road characteristics [11,15], like the type (arterial road, motorway, street, etc.), traffic intensity or number of traffic lights. Vehicles are often characterized according to their dimension, weight and engine specifications, doing different fitting for each type of vehicle [12,15]. One of the aggregated models add the time of trip, considering different traffic intensities for each hour [15].

In terms of the regression methods used, a multivariate linear regression is commonly used, though in some cases the techniques are not explicit. The effort is focused more on the reliability of the variables than on the regression.

We follow the data collection process of Ribeiro et al. [4] and we use a extended version of the same database, with larger quantity and variety of vehicles. They built two models using the multivariate least squares regression algorithm.

3   Dataset

The gathering process carried out by Ribeiro et al. [4] was extended to more volunteers and their vehicles. The data collection is done using the SenseMyCity crowdsensing platform[1][1], using an OBD device. We successfully collected data from 13 additional vehicles. This data was merged with the data from the previous 5 vehicles with larger number of points. From the 17 vehicles, 8 have gasoline engine and 9 have diesel engine. Table 2 shows their models and main

Table 2. Vehicles specifications and number of collected points after filtering

User	Model	Fuel	Disp. (cm^3)	Weight (Kg)	Power	Points (KW)	Avg FC $(L/100\,Km)$	SD FC $(L/100\,Km)$
205	Fiat Punto	d	1248	1205	66	43293	6.35	6.40
204	Renault Clio	d	1461	1515	49	128688	7.69	5.14
57	Nissan Qashqai	d	1461	2170	76	35873	3.72	6.01
202	Peugeot 207	d	1560	1500	66	31966	5.65	6.12
206	VW Golf	d	1598	1314	77	23240	5.11	6.60
60	BMW S1	d	1600	1475	172	23620	8.87	11.01
11	Audi A4	d	1896	1450	96	84514	8.85	6.71
76	VW Passat	d	1968	1585	158	12947	8.50	12.04
59	Mercedes C200	d	2143	2175	100	18722	6.97	9.35
78	Dacia Sandero	g	898	1520	66	85589	21.38	11.87
25	VW Polo	g	1198	1550	51	11161	11.49	12.95
23	Opel Corsa	g	1199	1430	55	41798	9.62	9.15
108	Renault Clio	g	1200	990	54	17997	7.90	9.40
56	Opel Corsa	g	1229	1455	59	21227	9.94	10.91
107	Mazda 2	g	1349	955	63	18026	7.73	8.12
84	Citroen X Picasso	g	1587	1790	70	5773	7.72	5.77
109	Audi A4	g	1600	1520	60	17236	23.55	13.66

[1] http://futurecities.up.pt/site/crowdsensor-sensemycity-prototype-and-testbed/.

specifications: engine displacement and power and vehicle's weight. The same table includes the number of data points for each vehicle after filtering and the average and standard deviation of the ground truth FC. That filtering consisted on the removal of points with missing values, with low GPS accuracy and with rare values, representing improbable situations in the physical world. To ensure more accuracy of the points, those with GPS accuracy less than 50 m and with a difference on S given by GPS and by OBD higher than 3 m/s were excluded. Other filtered points were those with $|I|$ larger than 15°, $|A|$ larger than $4\,\mathrm{m/s^2}$ and FC larger than 100 L/100 Km.

4 Exploratory Data Analysis

In order to have a notion of the data distribution, histograms of each individual variable were made, and also plots representing relations between every two variables. We could observe the most typical values and tendencies on the relations between variables.

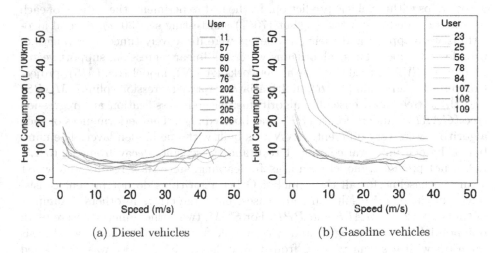

(a) Diesel vehicles   (b) Gasoline vehicles

Fig. 1. Average fuel consumption vs speed (Color figure online)

To better understand the behaviour of the FC with each independent variable, distributions of the FC for several bins of S, A and I were studied. Here, we present the evolution of the average FC with the S (Fig. 1^2). We see a high similarity on the shape of the different curves. The stranger phenomenon is the large vertical shift for users 78 and 109. Those vehicles have total mean FC of 21.4 and 23.6 L/100 Km, respectively. We suspect that the cause for these improbable values lies on a data collection of processing error. These results also happen for

---

^{2} Available at https://drive.google.com/open?id=0B2ORPNQ5UJHefjBRSTE2UmR hZ0ZFd0hBelRDbXlKMUVicHhQdHZwbEVtNVJ1SHZkdXN6QkE&authuser=0.

the plots of average FC versus A and I. The two vehicles were not included in the across vehicles FC prediction. Some differences exist between diesel and gasoline curves. Although the trips from gasoline vehicles do not present many points with large S, above 25 m/s, we note that the change on the average FC is larger for diesel vehicles than for gasoline vehicles. Another remark is the fact of the total mean FC being mostly higher for gasoline vehicles than for diesel vehicles. This analysis leads us to conclude that the fuel type is an important attribute for the regression of FC.

5   Regression

To evaluate the results, we used the root mean squared error ($RMSE$) because it is a metric with the same dimensions of the target variable, allowing a better performance analyses. The mean of the FC on the training set was chosen as baseline. All experiments were performed using the *caret* package[3] in R^4.

This article has a greater focus on the across vehicles FC prediction. Before we explore that approach we did two experiments: within trip prediction and across trips within vehicle prediction. In the first experiment, the dataset of each trip was divided into a training set (70 %) and testing set (30 %). Several algorithms were applied and their parameters were iteratively tuned over ranges of preselected values. Those algorithms were [16]: linear regression, support vector machines (SVM), artificial neural networks (ANN), model tree ($M5$), projection pursuit regression (PPR), multivariate adaptive regression splines ($MARS$) and three tree-based ensemble algorithms: bagged classification and regression tree ($CART$), random forest (RF) and boosted tree. The performances of each algorithm were very different. ANN was built with one hidden layer. The number of hidden units varied from 1 to 6 and the weights decay from 0.1 to 1.5. It did not provide a model with a useful learning, since their results were worst than the baseline for all the vehicles. Other algorithms do not present consistency, having good results on some cases, but large errors in others. Examples of that are SVM, $MARS$ and PPR. For SVM, two kernel functions were used: polynomial up to 6th degree and with a scale from 0.5 to 2; and a radial basis function with a sigma varying from 0.1 to 3. The SVM cost was also tuned between the values of 0.1, 1 and 10. In $MARS$ the tuned parameters were the number of terms (from 5 to 20) and the degree (up to 4). Several PPR models were tested, from varying the degree from 1 to 6. Tree based algorithms produced the best results, having large progression in comparison with the baseline in most cases, and without a large variance on the $RMSE$. Bagged $CART$ was applied using 10 bootstrap iterations. Three RF were used: with 1 to 3 randomly selected variables. Boosted trees were applied with a number of boosting iterations going from 500 to 5000 (with a step of 500) and a maximum tree depth varying from 1 to 5. Finally, the $M5$ algorithm were used with and without pruning and smoothing. Three of those tree-based algorithms were selected

---

[3] http://cran.r-project.org/web/packages/caret/index.html.
[4] http://www.r-project.org/.

to be used in the second experiment: $M5$ with smoothing process and without pruning, RF with 1 randomly selected predictor on each node and boosted tree with 500 trees and a maximum tree depth equal to 5. The separation of each vehicle data into training and testing sets was identical to what was done with the individual trips. For each vehicle, the models were trained and tested on points from multiple trips. Training sets always have data that was collected before testing data, conserving the sense of prediction. The performances of the three models were very similar, as it can be observed in the next section.

This fact motivated the used of those three models on the across-vehicles prediction. Their performances were evaluated on data from different vehicles. Part of the data from a vehicle was used for training and all the data from another was used on testing. Again, as it is shown in Sect. 6, the results do not significantly differ from model to model.

A further step was done. The performances of the models on vehicles with same fuel type and the similarity of the curves of average FC for vehicles with that same characteristic motivated the generation of a more generic model, specific for each fuel type. For this last experiment, we chose the algorithm with best results until then: the boosted tree. The parameters used were the same and the training and testing processes were similar.

6   Results

Figure 2[5] shows the results of the application of models from all vehicles on trips from users 76, 204, 25 and 107. We present the results for the cases with largest baseline error: users 76 (diesel) and 25 (gasoline); and smallest baseline error: users 204 (diesel) and 107 (gasoline). The improvements regarding the baseline can be analysed in those graphics by the distance between the top of the bars and the horizontal line. It is also possible to compare the results with the performance of the within vehicle prediction, since the RMSE of those models are also presented (in each graphic, the errors for the same user represent the values tested on the testing set of that user).

The results of the application of the fuel-specific generic models on each vehicle are presented in Fig. 3[6]. Users 78 and 109 were excluded, due to their extremely large FC values, assumed to be caused by errors on the data gathering or processing. The values for the baseline, for the vehicle-specific models, and for the models from the previous work (FC_1 and FC_2) are also shown. To support the analysis of these results, Table 3 contains the values of the RMSE for three cases.

---

[5] Available at https://drive.google.com/open?id=0B2ORPNQ5UJHefjVNU081MnpU MlZRTm5pZHNMc2VzQVY1QndzVFZ4aXR0RWdGWU9Nd05kTTg&authuser=0.

[6] Available at https://drive.google.com/open?id=0B2ORPNQ5UJHefmU5Z3VSdk1H dXdiZl9lekh4RnpMWXQybFJJQ0l0b1dvb25sb2U0Mk1uTG8&authuser=0.

7 Discussion

From Fig. 2, we can see that in many cases the performance of a model applied to a different vehicle is very similar to the performance when it is applied to the same vehicle, sometimes even better. We noticed that 3 very similar vehicles in terms of their specifications from Table 2, those from users 23, 25 and 56, are able to model each other with very similar performance and low RMSE, as can be observed on Fig. 2c. There is no other group of vehicles so similar to each other, and from the other results is not possible to say that this observation generalises to other cases. However, it indicates that the prediction of FC in a new vehicle using a model from a similar vehicle should lead to good results. Again, the three algorithms have similar performances. Even so, boosted tree shows better performances in most cases.

Trips from users 78 and 109 can not be modelled by the other vehicles because of their huge FC values. A user hardly to be modelled by any of the others is user 57. Although it does not present very different vehicle characteristics, it has the lowest total average FC (3.72 L/100 Km) (Table 2). Models trained in vehicles with larger mean FC are not adaptable to this vehicle. There is no

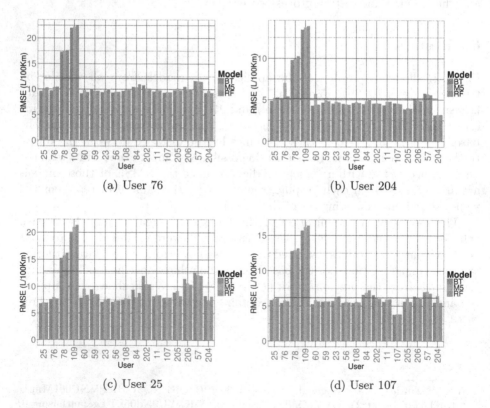

(a) User 76   (b) User 204

(c) User 25   (d) User 107

Fig. 2. RMSE of the models from each vehicle tested on trips from four users. The red horizontal line represents the baseline error (Color figure online).

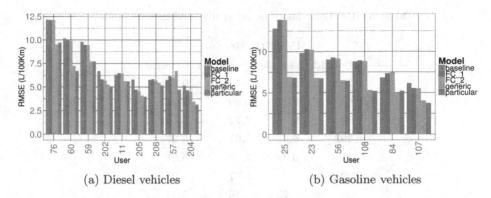

(a) Diesel vehicles   (b) Gasoline vehicles

Fig. 3. RMSE for vehicle specific and fuel-specific models. $FC1$ and $FC2$ are the models proposed by [4].

similar vehicle, so it is not possible to conclude if the cause lies on the vehicle specifications.

From Fig. 3, we can see that the differences between the RMSE from the vehicle-specific model and the fuel-specific model are small. An exception is the user 57, where the fuel-specific model fails, having a higher error than the baseline. The reason is the same as explained in the previous paragraph, since the generic fuel-specific model is based on users which, in majority, have a much higher average FC. The RMSE of these fuel-specific models are smaller when the baseline error is small. FC prediction is very imprecise for vehicles with large baseline error. For these vehicles, the variance of the ground truth FC is high. The explanation for a high baseline error may lie on the fact that the points responsible for the large variance show larger variance in the relations with the independent variables. In these conditions, it is more difficult for an algorithm to model the data. However, for users 25, 23 and 108 the improvement with respect to the baseline is large, decreasing the RMSE in more than $3\,L/100\,Km$. We also observe that these models are more accurate than polynomial models proposed by Ribeiro et al. [4], in the previous work. Although the error for the generic and particular models are similar in most cases, the generic model may fail for vehicles with a deviant behaviour or for vehicles with a much higher or much lower total average fuel consumption.

Thus, the choice of the model to apply should depend on the information about the vehicle in consideration. We propose the following rationale:

- if information about engine displacement, power and vehicle weight is provided, and there is on our database at least one vehicle with the same fuel type at a distance less than δ in the $d'p'w'$ volume, then the boosted tree model from the closest vehicle should be used;
- otherwise, the generic boosted tree model corresponding to the vehicle fuel type is applied.

Table 3. RMSE for baseline, particular and generic models

User Id	RMSE (L/100 Km)		
	Baseline	Particular	Generic
76	12.16	9.72	9.53
60	10.17	6.69	7.22
59	9.78	7.72	7.70
202	6.69	5.07	5.27
11	6.32	5.58	5.61
205	5.79	3.97	4.09
206	5.75	5.16	5.44
57	5.74	4.73	6.72
204	5.15	3.14	3.46
25	12.82	6.84	6.91
23	9.83	6.76	6.81
56	8.99	6.42	6.47
108	8.78	5.21	5.31
84	6.82	5.22	4.98
107	6.16	3.76	4.05

The $d'p'w'$ volume is the volume obtained by the displacement, power and weight, after the transformation:

$$x_i' = 1 - \frac{max(x) - x_i}{max(x) - min(x)} \tag{1}$$

where $max(x)$ and $min(x)$ are the maximum and the minimum of each parameter in our dataset. They will change if it expands. After analysing the vehicle proximity for our dataset and the results from the across vehicle prediction, we propose a δ equal to 0.35, considering it as the maximum distance between vehicles for model sharing. This value is indicative, our database is to small to take conclusions about a reliable value.

8   Conclusions

We extended a previous dataset of with 13 new vehicles. After the exploratory analysis, we mined a dataset of GPS points and OBD fuel consumption estimations for 17 vehicles using several regression algorithms with parameter tuning. From a dataset that represents real driving patterns, we showed that it is possible to predict fuel consumption with models trained on trips from different vehicles with similar characteristics. We also showed the importance of vehicle specifications in the choice of the best model. The models proposed in this paper can be applied in route management, traffic control, urban planning, etc., with the purpose of reducing CO_2 emission and contribute to a cleaner environment in urban areas.

For future work, a new collection campaign should be carried out to increase the quantity and variety of vehicles. That will provide the grounds for more precise generalized fuel-specific models and also a deeper understanding of the influence of vehicles specifications.

References

1. Rodrigues, J.G.P., Aguiar, A., Barros, J.: SenseMyCity: Crowdsourcing an Urban Sensor. ArXiv e-prints (2014)
2. EU Transport in Figures - Statistical Pocket Book. European Commission, Directorate-General for Energy and Transport, in co-operation with Eurostat (2000)
3. CO2 Emissions from Fuel Combustion 2012. International Energy Agency. Paris: Organisation for Economic Co-operation and Development (2012)
4. Ribeiro, V., Rodrigues, J., Aguiar, A.: Mining geographic data for fuel consumption estimation. In: 16th International IEEE Annual Conference on Intelligent Transportation Systems (2013)
5. Bowyer, D.P., Akçelik, R., Biggs, D.C.: Guide to fuel consumption analysis for urban traffic management. Special Report SR No. 32. ARRB Transport Research Ltd, Vermont South, Australia (1985)
6. Joumard, R., Jost, P., Hassel, D.: Hot passenger car emissions modelling as a function of instantaneous speed and acceleration. Sci. Total Environ. 169, 129–139 (1995)
7. Jimenez-Palacios, J.L.: Understanding and Quantifying Motor Vehicle Emissions with Vehicle Specific Power and TILDAS Remote Sensing. Massachusetts Institute of Technology, Cambridge (1999)
8. Cappiello, A., Chabini, I., Nam, E.K., Luè, A., Zeid, M.A.: A statistical model of vehicle emissions and fuel consumption. In: IEEE 5th International Conference on Intelligent Transportation Systems (2002)
9. Rakha, H., Ahn, K., Trani, A.: Development of VT-Micro model for estimating hot stabilized light duty vehicle and truck emissions. Transp. Res. Part D: Transp. Environ. 9(1), 4974 (2004)
10. Lei, W., Chen, H., Lu, L.: Microscopic emission and fuel consumption modeling for light-duty vehicles using portable emission measurement system data. World Acad. Sci. Eng. Technol. 42, 918–925 (2010)
11. Pelkmans, L., Debal, P., Hood, T., Hauser, G., Delgado, M.R.: Development of a simulation tool to calculate fuel consumption and emissions of vehicles operating in dynamic conditions. SAE Technical Paper (2004)
12. Ericsson, E., Larsson, H., Brundell-Freij, K.: Optimizing route choice for lowest fuel consumption Potential effects of a new driver support tool. Transp. Res. Part C 14, 369–383 (2006)
13. Song, G., Yu, L., Wang, W.: Aggregate fuel consumption model of light-duty vehicles for evaluating effectiveness of traffic management strategies on fuels. J. Transp. Eng. 135, 611–618 (2009)

14. Tavares, G., Zsigraiova, Z., Semiao, V., Carvalho, M.G.: Optimisation of MSW collection routes for minimum fuel consumption using 3D GIS modelling. Waste Manage. **29**, 1176–1185 (2009)
15. André, M., Keller, M., Sjödin, A., Gadrat, M., Mc Crae, I., Dilara, P.: The ARTEMIS European tools for estimating the transport pollutant emissions. In: 18th International Emission Inventories Conference, pp. 1–10 (2009)
16. Han, J., Kamber, M., Pei, J.: Data Mining: Concepts and Techniques, 3rd edn. Morgan Kaufmann Publishers, San Francisco (2011)

A Bag-of-phonemes Model for Homeplace Classification of Mandarin Speakers

Hanqing Zhao[1,2]($\boxtimes$), Zengchang Qin[1], Yiyu Wang[2], and Yuxiao Wang[3]

[1] Intelligent Computing and Machine Learning Lab School of ASEE,
Beihang University, Beijing, People's Republic of China
zhq@gmx.com
[2] École d'Ingénieur Généraliste École Centrale de Pékin,
Beihang University, Beijing, People's Republic of China
[3] Department of Chinese Literature College of Liberal Arts,
Fu Jen Catholic University, New Taipei City, Republic of China

Abstract. Mandarin, also known as Standard Chinese is the official language of China and Singapore, there are certain differences when mandarin is spoken by people from different homeplaces. The homeplace classification is important in speech recognition and machine translation. In this paper, we proposed a novel model named Bag-of-phonemes (BOP) for homeplace classification of mandarin speakers, which follows the conceptually similar idea of the Bag-of-words (BOW) model in text processing. The low-level Mel-frequency cepstral coefficients (MFCC) speech features of each homeplace are clustered into a set of codewords referred to as phonemes. With this codebook, each speech signal can be represented by a feature vector of distribution on phonemes. Classical classifiers such as support vector machine (SVM) can be applied for classification. This model is tested by RASC863 database, empirical studies show that the new model has a better performance on the RASC863 database comparing to previous works [1].

Keywords: Bag-of-words · Bag-of-phonemes · Mandarin accents

1 Introduction

The homeplace recognition and classification is for identifying speaker's homeplace by detecting characteristics of their voice (voice biometrics). The elements which decide the characteristics of the speakers' voices include acoustic features (cepstrum), lexical features, prosodic features, languages, channel information, and accents information. According to one's accent, we can judge where he comes from, which means his homeplace. With the rapid growth and development of the society, the needs for homeplace identification spread to several areas. For example, in expert testimony and even in military field, the homeplace identification technology helps change "manpower" into "intelligence". However, existing homeplace identification technology mainly concentrates on the machines which recognize the homeplace mainly by dialects in China. As the popularization of

© Springer International Publishing Switzerland 2015
R. Paredes et al. (Eds.): IbPRIA 2015, LNCS 9117, pp. 683–690, 2015.
DOI: 10.1007/978-3-319-19390-8_76

Mandarin, which is the official language of China and Singapore, accents of Mandarin becomes another way to judge one's original place.

For the subject of the identification of homeplace Gu *et al.* [1] used Gaussian mixture models (GMM) and n-gram language models to produce a global language feature, and makes decision using clustered support vector machine. Hou *et al.* [2] proposed an approach for homeplace identification using both cepstral and prosodic features with gender-dependent model. The identification of homeplace plays an important role not only in China. Malhotra and Khosla [3] discussed text independent and identifies accent among four regional Indian groups spoken Hindi. Teixeira *et al.* [4] proposed an approach using a parallel set of ergodic nets with context independent HMM units to identify six English-spoken countries in Europe. There was also the recognition of hometown based on the prosody of accents. In Gholipour *et al.* [5], prosodic features are used for recognition that including rhythm-related features, global statistics on pitch contour, energy contour and their derivatives.

In this paper, we proposed a novel model named Bag-of-phonemes (BOP) for homeplace identification of mandarin speakers. We deal with sound files in .wav format which is well used in the real-world. The structure of the remainder of the paper is as follows: in Sect. 2, we introduced the basic feature for homeplace identification. In Sect. 3, we fully described the Bag-of-phonemes in details. In Sect. 4, we designed experiments and tested the model. Finally, the conclusions were given in Sect. 5.

2   Voice Features Extraction

In sound processing, the Mel-frequency cepstrum (MFC) is a representation of the short-term power spectrum of a sound, based on a linear cosine transform of a log power spectrum on a nonlinear Mel scale of frequency. Mel Frequency Cepstrum Coefficients (MFCC) are coefficients that collectively make up an MFC and such features have been widely used in speaker recognition [11]. The following are the main steps to extract the coefficients from voice or sound.

2.1   Pre-emphasis

The first step of MFCC extracting is to enhance the energy in high frequencies which has been suppressed by certain parts of the human vocal system, such as lips. This step makes the voice signal more smoothly, and improve the accuracy of the model. A high-pass filter is used in this step:

$$S_2(n) = S(n) - \alpha \times S(n-1) \tag{1}$$

where $S(n)$ is the input signal in time domain. And α is a coefficient, in general, we have $\alpha = 0.95$.

2.2   Fast Fourier Transform (FFT)

The voice spectrum changes rapidly in time domain. In order to obtain stable voice features, we extract features from a small window. Each window is determined by three following parameters: the width of window, the offset between successive windows and the shape of window. The piece extracted from a window is called a frame. The frame size β is a number of milliseconds, generally between 10 ms to 30 ms. And the number of milliseconds between the left edge of successive windows is called frame shift, in our experiment, we use $\beta/4$ to avoid information losses.

In order to calculate the energy contains by the signal in different frequency bands, We use FFT to extract the spectral information. The FFT is a improved algorithm of Discrete Fourier Transform (DFT). For each sequence of N complex numbers $x_0, x_1, ..., x_{N-1}$, we transform them into an N-periodic sequence of complex numbers $X_0, X_1, ..., X_{N-1}$, by using this following DFT formula:

$$X_k = \sum_{n=0}^{N-1} x_n \exp\left(-\frac{2\pi i}{N} nk\right) \qquad k = 1, 2, ..., N-1 \tag{2}$$

where x_n is a windowed signal as the input of DFT, and the output X_K is a complex number representing the magnitude and phase of that frequency component in the input signal. N is the sample length of analysis window, and the sinusoid's frequency is k cycles per N samples, and i is the imaginary unit of complex number.

2.3   Mel Filter Bank

The mapping between frequency in Hertz and Mel scale is linear in low-frequency and logarithmic in high frequency. The Mel scale can be computed from sound frequency by using this following formula:

$$Mel = 2595 \log_{10}(1 + \frac{f}{700}) \tag{3}$$

During MFCC computation, a bank of filter is created to collect energy from each frequency band. The filter bank contains 12 filters which spread linearly in low-frequency and spread logarithmically in high-frequency. As shown in Fig. 1. Finally, we calculate the log of each Mel spectrum value.

2.4   Cepstrum

The last step of extracting the coefficients is to calculate the cepstrum of the log of the Mel spectrum values. We can use Discrete Cosine Transform (DCT) to get the following:

$$Mel_k = \sum_{n=0}^{N-1} x_n \cos[k(n+0.5)\frac{\pi}{N}]; \quad (0 \le k \le N-1) \tag{4}$$

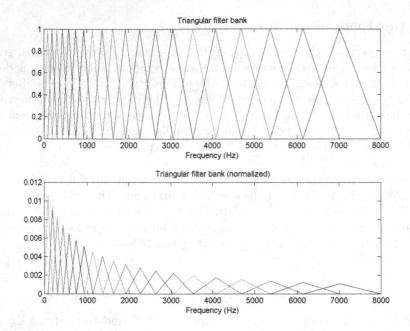

Fig. 1. An example of Mel filter bank.

where N is the number of filters in the filter bank, k is the number of cesptral coefficients. and x_n is formulated as the "log-energy"output of the n-th filter.

3   Bag-of-phonemes Model

The Bag-of-words (BOW) model is a simplified assumption which is well-used in statistical natural language processing and information retrieval (IR) [6]. In this model, a text is regarded as a bag of unordered words, disregarding grammar. The Bag-of-words model is commonly used in document classification, where the (frequency of) occurrence of each word is used as a feature for training a classifier [7,8]. In computer vision, the BOW model is also borrowed and re-invented as the Bag-of-features model, it can be applied to image classification [9,10] by treating image features as "visual words". In document classification, a bag of words is a sparse vector of occurrence counts of words; that is, a sparse histogram over the vocabulary. In computer vision, a bag of visual words is a sparse vector of occurrence counts of a vocabulary of local image features. Some other variants of BOW model were also proposed in music genre classification which named Bag-of tones [11].

Following the similar idea, we propose the Bag-of-phonemes model, in which we treat voice as a document, and the term "words" need to be defined. To achieve this, all files of voice are transformed into a high dimensional space of low-level features (i.e., MFCC in this paper) of each type are respectively clustered to obtain some significant basic units such as topics in text processing and visual words in image processing, in this paper, we call them the phonemes. Each voice file is then can be represented as a distribution of the phonemes. The details are described as the following.

3.1 Feature Description

MFCC feature has been widely used in voice recognition. Because of the good performance of MFCC in speaker recognition, it is employed to transform each voice file into a 12-dimensional matrix. It is like to have 12 channels where the length is related to the original voice file L_v, the sliding window frame length L_f and the window frame increment n. In all, each voice file can be transformed into a $12 \times \frac{L_v}{L_f \times n}$ dimensions matrix.

3.2 Codebook Generation

Each vector represented voice files is named codewords in Bag-of-phonemes (BOP) model, and listed"codewords" is named codebook. In our experiment the codebook is constituted by eight types which are the male and female speakers with homeplaces from four chinese cities: Chongqing, Shanghai, Xiamen and Guangzhou.

In clustering, all the voice files in the training set are mapped into a 12-dimensional space, where each voice is represented as a point in this space. Given the size of the codebook (number of clusters), K-means is used to cluster codewords of 8 types respectively, training codewords of each type is clustered into $k/8$ clusters, where k is the size of codebook and each clusters can be regarded as a codeword or phoneme. Given a voice file in the .wav format, each voice is classified to either of these basic phonemes based on nearest Euclidean distance in this space. The distribution of a voice file on phonemes can be simply calculated using frequency counting. As shown in Fig. 2.

3.3 Classification

Once descriptors has been assigned to cluster to form the feature vectors, we reduce the problem to a multi-classes supervised learning. The classifier performs two separate steps to predict the class of the unlabeled speakers: training and testing. During the training operation, labeled spoken clips are sent to classifier and used to adapt a statistical division procedure to distinguishing categories. In this paper, we chose the SVM classifier to test the Bag-of-phonemes model, and made a comparison of performance with pervious work [1]. The complete process of the Bag-of-phoneme model is shown in Fig. 2.

4   Experimental Studies

In order to verify the performance of the novel model, we use a speaker database named RASC863[1], including 800 speech clips of 800 speakers (400 male speakers, 400 female speakers) with homeplace of four Chinese cities: Chongqing,

---

[1] http://www.chineseldc.org/doc/CLDC-SPC-2004-003/intro.htm

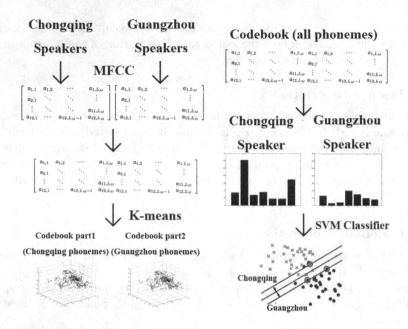

Fig. 2. A illustrative process of the codebook generation (left-hand side) and classification of Mandarin speakers from Chongqing and Guangzhou (right-hand side) by using the BOP model.

Shanghai, Xiamen and Guangzhou, each city has 100 speakers (50 male and 50 female). All the speech clips are mono channel. During the pre-emphasis process, the parameter $\alpha = 0.95$. The window length $\beta = 1024$ points, and the framing shift is 256 points. Each sound clip is transformed into a 12-dimensional matrix.

4.1 Influence of the Size of Codebook

In this paper, the BASC863 database including 800 speech clips in 8 types is used for testing. A 50 % cross-validation is used to validate this model, precisely, we use 400 speech clips as the training and other 400 clips for testing, then we exchange the testing and training sets and run the test again. As a result, the average accuracy with 2 times calculation is regarded as the final result.

In order to study the influence of the length of Codebook, the BOP model tested with the size of Codebook of 800, 720, 696, 680, 640, 600, 560, 504, for a 8-types codebook, its size should be a multiple of 8. And we have also calculated the accuracy with SVM classifier in different kernel functions (linear and polynomial), where k is the number of clusters. When $k = 696$, the SVM classifier with linear function reaches a hit rate of homeplace classification of 63.67 %. The accuracy in different sizes of codebook as shown in Table 1:

Table 1. Accuracy of BOP model with SVM classifier.

k	504	560	600	640	680	696	720	800
Polynomial	57.13 %	56.88 %	56.25 %	56.38 %	56.38 %	55.67 %	55.38 %	55.00 %
Linear	60.50 %	60.75 %	61.50 %	62.63 %	62.13 %	**63.67 %**	61.88 %	61.25 %

4.2 Comparisons to Pervious Works

Given the RASC863 database, the Bag-of-phonemes model is compared to Gu et al. [1], which uses the GMM symbolization method for dimensionality reduction and SVM classifier for classification. In this comparison, we used the same testing and training sets and the same calculation method. With 384 Gaussian models, the SVM classifier with polynomial function reaches a hit rate of homeplace classification in 61.75 % (see Table 2). It is obviously lower that the best results we obtained by using the BOP model in Table 1.

Table 2. Accuracy of GMM symbolization model with SVM classifier.

GMM	32	64	96	128	256	384	512
Polynomial	58.88 %	59.88 %	59.75 %	59.88 %	61.00 %	**61.75 %**	61.25 %
Linear	58.75 %	59.88 %	59.25 %	59.63 %	60.00 %	61.50 %	61.00 %

5 Conclusion and Future Work

In this paper, we have presented a simple but novel model named the Bag-of-phonemes for homeplace classification of mandarin speakers. The codebook is built up by clustering the MFCC features of training data. Following the similar idea of Bag-of-words model in natural language processing, each input of voice information is classified according to these basic phonemes (codewords) representations. Classical classifier SVM was used to testify this model. Empirical evidence showed that the new model outperforms GMM on the BASC863 database. In order to testify the effectiveness of the new proposed model, more comprehensive experimental studies on different datasets and more comparisons to other speech recognition models should be considered as the future work.

Acknowledgments. This work is supported by the National Science Foundation of China No. 61305047 and the Chinese National Undergraduate Training Programs for Innovation and Entrepreneurship No. 201410006113.

References

1. Gu, M., Xia, Y., Zhang, C.: Chinese dialect identification using clustered support vector machine. In: Signal and Image Processing, pp. 396–399 (2008)

2. Hou, J., Liu, Y., Zheng, T.F., Olsen, J., Tian, J.: Using cepstral and prosodic features for chinese accent identification. In: Chinese Spoken Language Processing, pp. 177–181 (2010)
3. Malhotra, K., Khosla, A.: Automatic identification of gender and accent in spoken hindi utterances with regional indian accents. In: IEEE Workshop on Spoken Language Technology, pp. 309–312 (2008)
4. Teixeira, C., Trancoso, I., Serralheiro, A.J.: Accent identification. In: International Conference on Spoken Language Proceedings, vol. 3, pp. 1784–1787 (1996)
5. Gholipour, A., Sedaaghi, M.H., Shamsi, M.: The contribution of prosody to the identification of persian regional accents. In: IEEE Symposium on Industrial Electronics and Applications, pp. 346–350 (2012)
6. De Santo, M., Napoletano, P., Pietrosanto, A., Liguori, C., Paciello, V., Polese, F.: Mixed graph of terms: beyond the bags of words representation of a text. In: Hawaii International Conference on System Sciences, pp. 1070–1079 (2012)
7. Zhao, Q., Qin, Z., Wan, T.: What is the basic semantic unit of chinese language? a computational approach based on topic models. In: Kanazawa, M., Kornai, A., Kracht, M., Seki, H. (eds.) MOL 12. LNCS, vol. 6878, pp. 143–157. Springer, Heidelberg (2011)
8. Zhao, Q., Qin, Z., Wan, T.: Topic modeling of chinese language using character-word relations. In: Lu, B.-L., Zhang, L., Kwok, J. (eds.) ICONIP 2011, Part III. LNCS, vol. 7064, pp. 139–147. Springer, Heidelberg (2011)
9. Yuan, X., Yu, J., Qin, Z., Wan, T.: A SIFT-LBP image retrieval model based on bag of features. In: IEEE International Conference on Image Processing (2011)
10. Yu, J., Qin, Z., Wan, T., Zhang, X.: Feature integration analysis of bag-of-features model for image retrieval. Neurocomput. **120**, 355–364 (2013)
11. Qin, Z., Liu, W., Wan, T.: A bag-of-tones model with MFCC features for musical genre classification. In: Motoda, H., Wu, Z., Cao, L., Zaiane, O., Yao, M., Wang, W. (eds.) ADMA 2013, Part I. LNCS, vol. 8346, pp. 564–575. Springer, Heidelberg (2013)

A Gaussian Process Emulator for Estimating the Volume of Tissue Activated During Deep Brain Stimulation

Iván De La Pava[1]([⊠]), Viviana Gómez[1], Mauricio A. Álvarez[1],
Óscar A. Henao[1], Genaro Daza-Santacoloma[2], and Álvaro A. Orozco[1]

[1] Automatic Research Group, Faculty of Engineerings,
Universidad Tecnológica de Pereira, Pereira, Colombia
{ide,vigomez,malvarez,oscarhe,aaog}@utp.edu.co
[2] Instituto de Epilepsia Y Parkinson Del Eje Cafetero - Neurocentro,
Pereira, Colombia
research@neurocentro.com.co

Abstract. The volume of tissue activated (VTA) is a well established approach to model the effects of deep brain stimulation (DBS), and previous studies have pointed to its potential benefits in clinical applications. However, the elevated computational cost of the standard technique for VTA estimation limits its suitability for practical use. In this study we developed a novel methodology to reduce the cost of VTA estimation. Our approach combines multicompartment axon models coupled to the stimulating electric field with a Gaussian emulator. We achieved a remarkable reduction in the average time required for VTA estimation, without the loss of accuracy and other limitations entailed by alternative methods used to attain similar benefits, such as activation threshold curves.

Keywords: Deep brain stimulation · Volume of tissue activated · Multicompartment axon model · Emulation · Gaussian process classification

1 Introduction

Deep brain stimulation (DBS) is a surgical technique used mainly to treat movement disorders, such as Parkinson's disease, essential tremor, and dystonia, in patients whose symptoms cannot be appropriately controlled with drugs. It involves the placement of an electrode in the basal ganglia, the thalamus, or other subcortical structures. The electrode is used to apply high frequency electric pulses to the target regions, which results in symptom improvement. Although DBS is widely practiced the mechanisms by which it works are still not completely clear, and most of the insight gained in recent years has come from computer simulations [10,11]. A common approach to assess the impact of DBS computationally is to estimate the volume of tissue activated (VTA), that is, the spatial spread of direct neural activation in response to the electrical stimulation [4].

© Springer International Publishing Switzerland 2015
R. Paredes et al. (Eds.): IbPRIA 2015, LNCS 9117, pp. 691–699, 2015.
DOI: 10.1007/978-3-319-19390-8_77

The gold standard for VTA estimation is to couple the electric potential generated by the DBS electrode with a model of multicompartment axons arranged in a field around the electrode shaft, in order to compute the changes in the transmembrane potential induced by the stimulation [4]. Axons that fire action potentials in a one to one ratio with the stimulation pulses are considered active, and their spatial distribution defines the VTA. The downside of this approach is its elevated computational cost, relative to its potential clinical applications [1,7,8]. This hindrance has led to the development of simplified methods that try to minimize the use of such models by exploiting the relationship between the spatial location of the axons and the electrical stimulation. This relationship is captured in the form of activation threshold curves, that are then used to estimate the VTA [1,5]. However, these curves do not reproduce the results of multicompartment models accurately and cannot be applied successfully to non-monopolar stimulation. A possible solution to these problems, based on artificial neural networks, is described in [7], but it only works under the assumption of isotropic tissue conductivity.

We propose an alternative approach that could reduce the computational cost of VTA estimation and overcome the limitations of threshold-curve based methods: determining the volume of tissue activated from a field of axons can be treated as a binary classification problem, that is, active and inactive axons can be thought of as belonging to two different classes. Under this premise, the output of the standard VTA model can be represented statistically, it can be emulated. The emulation of computer simulations circumvents the problems posed by complex and computationally intensive models by building statistical representations of them, that once obtained are used to address the issue under study without additional runs of the original simulation. The main approach to developing emulators uses Gaussian processes [2,13]. Thus, our aim was to train a Gaussian process based classifier to determine whether an axon at a given position in space was or was not active due to DBS, and by doing so, to estimate the VTA.

2   Materials and Methods

2.1   Electric Propagation in the Brain Tissue

The calculation of the electric potential generated by the DBS electrode was carried out in the finite element method (FEM) software COMSOL Multiphysics 4.2. A simplified 3D model of a clinical electrode (Medtronic DBS 3389 electrode) positioned in the middle of a conductive extracellular medium was built. The simplified electrode model consisted of four conductive contacts (4×10^6 Sm^{-1}) 1.27 mm in width and 1.5 mm in height separated by insulating bands (1×10^{-10} Sm^{-1}) 0.5 mm in height, and of an insulating semicircular tip with radius 0.635 mm (Fig. 1a)[16]. The conductive extracellular medium, the bulk of brain tissue, was modeled as a sphere of diameter 10 cm with an isotropic conductivity of 0.3 Sm^{-1}. A representation of a 0.5 mm encapsulation layer around the electrode was also included, and its conductivity was set to three different values (0.680 Sm^{-1}, 0.18 Sm^{-1}, 0.066 Sm^{-1}) to represent low ($\sim$ 500 Ω), medium ($\sim$ 900 Ω), and high ($\sim$ 1500 Ω) impedance conditions [6,7]. The model also integrated the voltage drop at the electrode-tissue interface and the electrode capacitance (3.3 μF). The boundary conditions used were the same as in [5]. Finally, Poisson's equation was solved to obtain the voltage propagation in the brain tissue generated by the DBS electrode.

2.2   Axonal Distribution and VTA Estimation

To estimate the volume of tissue activated a population of 8112 straight axons of 5.7 μm diameter was built around the electrode shaft. The axonal model used in this work corresponds to the multicompartment myelinated axon model detailed in [12]. Briefly, each axon includes 21 nodes of Ranvier, 2 myelin attachment segments, 2 paranode main segments, and 3 internode segments between each node. The nodes are modeled by a parallel combination of the membrane capacitance with nonlinear conductances (fast Na$^+$, persistent Na$^+$, and slow K$^+$) and a linear leakage conductance. The paranodal and internodal compartments include two concentric layers, each including a linear conductance in parallel with the membrane capacitance, to represent the myelin sheath and the axolemma.

The axonal fibers were oriented in four different directions, perpendicular to the axis of the electrode (Fig. 1b), and with a distance between axons of 0.5 mm in both the vertical and horizontal directions. Despite the fact that in this study only isotropic tissue properties were considered, this axonal field setup is also intended to work in case anisotropic properties were used.

(a)   (b)

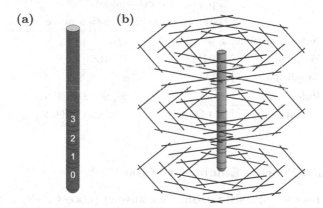

Fig. 1. (a) DBS electrode model. The electrode contacts were numbered from 0 to 3. (b) Orientation of the axons around the electrode shaft (for visualization purposes only a small fraction of the total axonal population is shown).

To simulate the neurostimulation the values of the electric potential were linearly interpolated from the nodes of the FEM solution onto each of the axonal model compartments. An axon was considered active if it would fire in a one to one ratio with the DBS pulses. The VTA was defined as the volume enclosed by the locations of the central nodes of Ranvier of the activated axons [15]. The simulations of the axonal response to the electric stimulation were implemented in NEURON 7.3[1] configured as a Python module [4,9]. NEURON is a widely used tool to simulate the electrical behaviour of biological neurons, and its compatibility with Python allowed us to implement most of the VTA estimation model without the hurdles of changing programming platforms.

The methodology described here and in Sect. 2.1 corresponds to the gold standard for VTA estimation. A full implementation of it was used to compute volumes of tissue activated, for a range of stimulation parameter settings (Table 1), that would serve as reference data sets to evaluate the performance of the proposed emulator.

Table 1. Realistic stimulation parameter settings used in this study (Medtronic ACTIVA-RC stimulator). The base parameters were varied, one at a time, in a range of possible values for the monopolar and bipolar cases.

	Monopolar	
	Base parameters	Variation range
Active contacts	3	3
Frequency	130 Hz	130 Hz
Amplitude	-3 V	-1, -2, -3, -4, -5 V
Pulse-width	90 μs	60, 90, 210, 450 μs
Impedance	900 Ω	500, 900, 1500 Ω
	Bipolar (cathode-anode)	
	Base parameters	Variation range
Active contacts	2, 3	2, 3
Frequency	130 Hz	130 Hz
Amplitude	$\pm$3 V	$\pm$1, $\pm$2, $\pm$3, $\pm$4, $\pm$5 V
Pulse-width	90 μs	60, 90, 210, 450 μs
Impedance	900 Ω	500, 900, 1500 Ω

2.3   Gaussian Process Emulation of the VTA

Gaussian Process Classification. A Gaussian process (GP) is defined as a probability distribution over functions such that the values of said functions evaluated at an arbitrary set of points jointly have a Gaussian distribution [3], and it is completely specified by second order statistics, that is, by its mean vector and its covariance matrix. In a Bayesian framework GPs offer the advantage of analytical tractability: a Gaussian prior and a Gaussian likelihood will result

---

[1] www.neuron.yale.edu/neuron/download

in a Gaussian posterior, and even though the discrete nature of the classification problem gives rise to a non-Gaussian likelihood, a posterior distribution can still be approximated by methods such as Lapace approximation or Expectation Propagation. In general, the idea behind binary GP classification is to define a Gaussian process over the implicit or latent function that describes the labeled data {−1,1} and to map that to the unit interval through a response function, so that when given an input vector, the trained classifier returns for that entry a probability between 0 and 1 of belonging to the positive class [14].

Procedure. A random sample of 400 axons was taken from the total axonal population. The axons were sampled from a uniform distribution with respect to the euclidean distance between their central nodes of Ranvier and the midpoint of the active contacts. Next, a multicompartment simulation was executed to determine which of the sampled neural fibers were active during the stimulation. The data provided by the multicompartment axon model was used to train a Gaussian process-based classifier. The perpendicular distance from each central node of Ranvier to the axis of the DBS electrode, their distance to the plane containing the electrode tip and that is perpendicular to the electrode axis, the values of the electric potential at each central node of Ranvier, and the labels that identified them as belonging to either an active or an inactive axon served as inputs to the classification algorithm (pyGPs library[2] for Python 2.7). The inputs were selected so that the relationship between activation, the position of each axon with respect to the electrode shaft, and the electric potential was represented in the classification outcome.

The classifier was trained using the 70 % of the data obtained from the multicompartment axon model, prescribing a general purpose kernel (squared exponential covariance function with automatic relevance determination), and executing successive runs of an optimization algorithm to minimize the Laplace approximation of the negative log marginal likelihood. Since the classifier assigns class probabilities instead of labels, a cut off probability was determined with a receiver-operating characteristic (ROC) analysis performed on all available data from the axonal model. Then the VTA was estimated by predicting which of the 8112 central nodes of Ranvier of the entire axonal population, and therefore the axonal fibers they belong to, would be activated by the applied stimulus. Finally, the spreads of activation predicted by the classifier were compared against those obtained with activation threshold curves customized to our data [5] in terms of the total error, defined as the sum of the prediction errors with respect to the reference data set (false positives and false negatives) divided by the reference number of active axons, for each of the stimulation parameters (Table 1).

3   Results and Discussion

In this study we explored an alternative approach to VTA estimation: active and inactive axons can be viewed as belonging to two different classes. Based on this

---

[2] github.com/marionmari/pyGPs

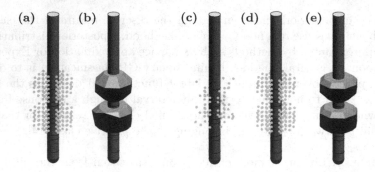

Fig. 2. (a) Distribution of active axons, obtained from multicompartment axon models (Bipolar stimulation: ± 3 V, $90\,\mu s$, $900\,\Omega$). **(b)** The VTA is defined as the volume enclosed by this distribution. **(c)** The computational cost demanded by models large enough, that is, with enough axons, to describe accurately the region of interest around the electrode shaft is very high. Our method uses a comparatively small number of axons. The locations of active and inactive axons provided by this reduced model (only active locations shown) are used to train a Gaussian process based classifier. **(d)** The classifier takes information of the stimulating electric field to predict the positions of all active axons. **(e)** The VTA is obtained from the predictions of the classifier.

assumption we aimed to develop a classification system that could reduce the computational cost of VTA estimation, without the shortcomings of activation threshold curves. Figure 2 summarizes our approach. Instead of a large model with enough axons to describe the entire region of interest around the electrode shaft, we used a small number of axons to obtain labeled data to train a Gaussian process based classifier. Then, we used the classifier to predict which elements of the total axonal population would be active, estimating the VTA.

The reduction in computational cost comes from the use of fewer axons in the multicompartment axon model. The average time to obtain a solution with the proposed method was cut down by 90 % to 3 min, compared with the 30 min required to solve the model described in Sect. 2.2 (parallelized implementation of the model running in a HP Compaq Pro 6300 computer with an Intel Core i5-3470 processor, and 8 GB RAM). Prediction threshold curves, however, can be faster, much more so if they are not fitted every time the stimulation parameters vary, but they are prone to error. Figure 3 shows the total errors generated by the classifier and by threshold curves with respect to the reference data set, for several combinations of stimulation parameters. The Gaussian process-based classifier always outperformed the threshold curves, and unlike them, it also allowed for the estimation of the VTA for non-monopolar stimulation. The error for bipolar stimulation was larger than the error of the classifier for the monopolar case, due to the higher complexity of the shape of the VTA for the former configuration, but it is worth noting that even in that scenario the classifier performed better than the threshold curves did for the simpler monopolar case.

Despite the results described above, we must note that the use of a classification algorithm to estimate the VTA lacks the direct connection to the biophysical

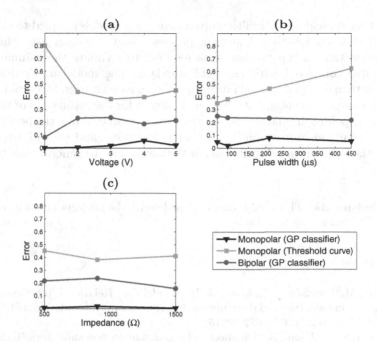

Fig. 3. Prediction errors for the range of stimulation parameters settings used in this study: amplitude **(a)**, pulse width **(b)**, and impedance **(c)** variations. The error for monopolar stimulation obtained with the Gaussian process based classifier (black) was smaller than the obtained with the activation threshold curves (light gray) for all the configurations studied. The classifier produced larger errors for the bipolar case (dark gray), but it still outperformed the activation threshold curve predictions for the simpler monopolar case.

interpretation of neural activation that threshold curves can have [7]. Our approach also assumes idealized brain tissue properties and axonal orientations and trajectories. Nonetheless, models based on these simplifications have yielded positive results in studies that compared their predictions of the extent of neurostimulation with experimental data from Parkinson's disease patients implanted with DBS systems [8]. Furthermore, the integration of realistic anisotropic tissue properties to our model would be straightforward, since the distribution of the axonal population is not based on any assumptions about the isotropy of the brain tissue medium. Only minor modifications to the electric propagation model would be necessary to that end. Finally, the classification procedure itself could be improved. The number and distribution of the axons used to generate the training data set were not systematically selected. A more systematic treatment of these variables could perhaps enhance the performance of our model.

4   Conclusions

In this study we implemented a new methodology to reduce the computational cost of VTA estimation, avoiding the faults of alternative methods. Our approach combined the typical use of multicompartment axon models coupled to the stimulating electric field with a Gaussian process based classifier. We achieved a ten-fold reduction in the average time required to estimate the volume of tissue activated compared with the gold standard. The model also exhibited a lower error than commonly used alternatives, such as activation threshold curves, for all the parameter settings studied, and allowed for the estimation of the VTA for non-monopolar stimulation. As future work, we will evaluate the performance of the model under anisotropic brain tissue conditions, and we will attempt to optimize the number and distribution of the axons used to generate the training data sets.

Acknowledgments. This study was developed under the projects 111056934461 and 499153530997 funded by Colciencias.

References

1. Astrom, M., Diczfalusy, E., Martens, H., Wardell, K.: Relationship between neural activation and electric field distribution during deep brain stimulation. IEEE Trans. Biomed. Eng. **62**(2), 664–672 (2015)
2. Bastos, L.S., O'Hagan, A.: Diagnostics for gaussian process emulators. Technometrics **51**(4), 425–438 (2009)
3. Bishop, C.M., et al.: Pattern Recognition and Machine Learning. Springer, New York (2006)
4. Butson, C.R., McIntyre, C.C.: Tissue and electrode capacitance reduce neural activation volumes during deep brain stimulation. Clin. Neurophysiol. **116**(10), 2490–2500 (2005)
5. Butson, C.R., McIntyre, C.C.: Role of electrode design on the volume of tissue activated during deep brain stimulation. J. Neural Eng. **3**(1), 1 (2006)
6. Chaturvedi, A., Butson, C.R., Lempka, S.F., Cooper, S.E., McIntyre, C.C.: Patient-specific models of deep brain stimulation: influence of field model complexity on neural activation predictions. Brain Stimul. **3**(2), 65–77 (2010)
7. Chaturvedi, A., Luján, J.L., McIntyre, C.C.: Artificial neural network based characterization of the volume of tissue activated during deep brain stimulation. J. Neural Eng. **10**(5), 056023 (2013)
8. Frankemolle, A.M., Wu, J., Noecker, A.M., Voelcker-Rehage, C., Ho, J.C., Vitek, J.L., McIntyre, C.C., Alberts, J.L.: Reversing cognitive-motor impairments in parkinson's disease patients using a computational modelling approach to deep brain stimulation programming. Brain **133**(3), 746–761 (2010)
9. Hines, M.L., Davison, A.P., Muller, E.: Neuron and python. Front. Neuroinf. **3**, 1–12 (2009)
10. McIntyre, C.C., Grill, W.M., Sherman, D.L., Thakor, N.V.: Cellular effects of deep brain stimulation: model-based analysis of activation and inhibition. J. Neurophysiol. **91**(4), 1457–1469 (2004)
11. McIntyre, C.C., Hahn, P.J.: Network perspectives on the mechanisms of deep brain stimulation. Neurobiol. Dis. **38**(3), 329–337 (2010)
12. McIntyre, C.C., Richardson, A.G., Grill, W.M.: Modeling the excitability of mammalian nerve fibers: influence of afterpotentials on the recovery cycle. J. Neurophysiol. **87**(2), 995–1006 (2002)

13. O'Hagan, A.: Bayesian analysis of computer code outputs: a tutorial. Reliab. Eng. Syst. Saf. **91**(10), 1290–1300 (2006)
14. Rasmussen, C.E., Williams, C.K.I.: Gaussian Processes for Machine Learning. The MIT Press, Cambridge (2006)
15. Walckiers, G.: Bio-electromagnetic model of deep brain stimulation. École polytechnique fëdërale de Lausanne EPFL (2009). doi:10.5075/epfl-thesis-4369
16. Zhang, T.C., Grill, W.M.: Modeling deep brain stimulation: point source approximation versus realistic representation of the electrode. J. Neural Eng. **7**(6), 066009 (2010)

Genetic Seam Carving: A Genetic Algorithm Approach for Content-Aware Image Retargeting

Saulo A.F. Oliveira$^{(\boxtimes)}$, Francisco N. Bezerra, and Ajalmar R. Rocha Neto

Federal Institute of Ceará, IFCE, Fortaleza, Brazil
{sauloa,nivando,ajalmar}@ifce.edu.br

Abstract. Seam Carving is a method to retarget images by removal of pixels paths with minimal visual impact. The method acts by exhaustive searching of minimal cost paths according to a pixel relevance function. In the present paper, we explore optimal or suboptimal paths obtained by a new Genetic Algorithm method called Genetic Seam Carving. Besides the suboptimal character of this approach, we show in the experiments that, we achieve quality results similar to the original Seam Carving method, and in some cases we even obtain less degradation.

Keywords: Genetic Algorithms · Content-aware retargeting · Seam Carving · SSIM · SIFT

1   Introduction

Image retargeting is a technique that adjusts input images into arbitrary dimensions (rows and columns) and simultaneously preserves regions of interest in the input images. The basic idea of the retargeting process is to find less important regions of interest (ROIs) in the image and then to expand or to reduce surround these regions in order to generate an output image with few noticeable changes. Several content-aware image retargeting methods have been proposed last years, where some of them are focused on the content preservation while other ones on how to obtain these less important ROIs [12]. As an example, we highlight the Seam Carving (SC) method which is a technique to find connected pixels path named seam [1]. For reducing dimensions, Seam Carving method finds and then removes seams located in less important ROIs. A very interesting survey of retargeting and Seam Carving is found in [15].

In a new formulation of retargeting for video [9], the dynamic programming method is replaced by graph cuts that are suitable for 3D volumes. So, instead of removing 1D seams from 2D images, 2D seams are removed from 3D space-time volumes. The usage of streams (wider seams) introduced a new retargeting method based on SC named Stream Carving [5]. The difference between a seam and a stream is the number of pixel width, which in a stream is greater than a conventional seam. This choice is motivated by the usual locations of the seams in an image so that they are usually in easily reproducible areas and may be enlarged without causing any visual distortion. In addition to the presented

© Springer International Publishing Switzerland 2015
R. Paredes et al. (Eds.): IbPRIA 2015, LNCS 9117, pp. 700–707, 2015.
DOI: 10.1007/978-3-319-19390-8_78

works, another improvement is concerned with finding multiple seams simultaneously by extending the seamlet transform [4] in order to carve a few seams at each step of retargeting. These multi-seam carving approaches were explored in [3,4]. Moreover, a merging approach - Seam Merging - with structure preservation was proposed in [8], where the structural distortion is minimized by merging a two-pixel-width seam into a single-pixel-width one.

Besides aforementioned techniques, Computational Intelligence methods have been applied on image processing, in particular Genetic Algorithms (GAs) [6,11]. GAs are optimization methods and therefore they can be used to generate useful solutions to search problems. Due to the underlying features of GAs some optimization problems can be solved without the assumption of linearity, differentiability, continuity or convexity of the objective function. Unfortunately, these desired characteristics are not found in several mathematical methods when applied to the same kind of problems. We have not found, for the best of our knowledge, any work dealing with Genetic Algorithms and Seam Carving for retargeting.

Thus, in this work, we propose a new method called Genetic Seam Carving (GSC) that aims at retargeting images by using Genetic Algorithms. The main idea of our proposal is to use GAs for searching seams by minimizing an energy function was defined as a fitness function. In our proposal, we are also taking into account the area close to the solution to obtain other seams in a multi-seam carving sense. To do so, we analyze these feasible solutions and according to their quality a few seams (related to the optimal or suboptimal one) are selected to be carved. In fact, working with suboptimal seams to be carved, expanded (or so on) leads to similar quality results allowing to propose efficient multi-seam removal as one can see in [3,5]. In our proposal we are able to highlight two different contributions. The first one is a new formulation of the seam search problem in the GAs paradigm and a the second one is a multi-seam carving-driven approach.

The remaining part of this paper is organized as follows. In Sect. 2.1, we recall the Seam Carving method. So, we present our proposal in Sect. 3. After that, We describe the experiments carried out in Sect. 4. Finally, we present some conclusion remarks in Sect. 5.

2 Background

2.1 Seam Carving

Seam Carving [1] searches and evaluates feasible seams and chooses the one with the lowest cost of processing. For sake of simplicity, consider vertical seams in the following description and notation, since a similar description and notation for a horizontal seam can be done straightforward. Moreover, consider the system coordinate as having the first pixel located at the upper left corner. Let I be an image of size $m \times n$, as well as let a vertical seam be defined as $s = \{(i, x(i))\}_{i=1}^{m}$ s.t. , $\forall i, |x(i) - x(i - 1)| \leq 1$, where x is a mapping $x : [1, \ldots, m] \to [1, \ldots, n]$. The seam cost is assigned through an energy function

$e(i, j)$, which gives a pixel certain value indicating the significance of that particularly point in the image. The energy function is based on two terms. The first one penalizes solutions that are inconsistent with the observed data and the second one enforces some kind of spatial coherence [10]. The optimal vertical seam search is computed by an exhaustive algorithm that keeps a cumulative cost for each seam computed. The search starts in the first row ($i = 1$) and continues to the neighbor pixels in the next row that have the lowest additional cost until the last row ($i = m$). The cost of a vertical seam that begins at the pixel (i, j) in the image I is computed by the cumulative minimum energy M as

$$M(i, j) = e(i, j) + \min \left\{ M(i + 1, j - 1), M(i + 1, j), M(i + 1, j + 1) \right\}, \quad (1)$$

where $e(i, j)$ is the value obtained by the energy function. The optimal vertical seam is given by $s^* = arg\ min\{M(1, j)\}_{j=1}^n$. More details can be found in [1]. Figure 1 illustrates an ideal retargeting process.

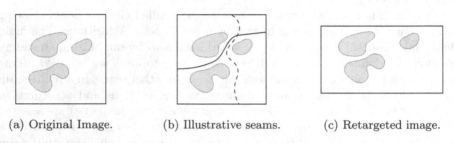

(a) Original Image.   (b) Illustrative seams.   (c) Retargeted image.

Fig. 1. Retargeting process. Vertical and horizontal seams computed from image (a) are shown in (b). Image (c) depicts a retargeted output, where vertical seams were inserted and horizontal ones were carved (removed).

2.2   Genetic Algorithms

Genetic Algorithms (GAs) [14] are a search meta-heuristic method inspired by natural evolution, such as inheritance, mutation, natural selections and crossover. This meta-heuristic can be used to generate useful solutions to optimization problems. Due to the characteristics of GAs methods, it is easier to solve few kind of problems by GAs than other mathematical methods which do have to rely on the assumption of linearity, differentiability, continuity, or convexity of the objective function. In a genetic algorithm, a population of candidate individuals (or solutions) to an optimization problem is evolved toward better solutions by natural selection, i.e., a fitness function. In this population, each individual has a set of genes (gene vector), named chromosome, which can be changed by mutation or combined generation-by-generation with other one to build new individuals by reproduction processes which use crossover. Standard implementation of genetic algorithm for natural selection is the roulette wheel. After the selection process, the selected individuals are used as input to other genetic operators: crossover and mutation. Crossover operator combines two strings of chromosomes, but mutation modifies a few bits in a single chromosome.

3 Genetic Seam Carving

In this section, we present our proposal called Genetic Seam Carving (GSC). The idea behind our proposal is to put Genetic Algorithms and Seam Carving to work together according to an energy function as fitness for guiding our approach into useful solutions. In the following subsections more details are presented.

3.1 Individuals or Chromosomes

Our individual is composed only by a single chromosome and it is defined as $C = [g_1, \ldots, g_{i-1}, g_{i=p}, g_{i+1} \ldots, g_m]$, where m is the image width (also the individual) and p is the pivot position. Each gene has an integer value bounded as follows.

$$g_i \in \begin{cases} [1, m], & \text{if } i = p; \\ [-1, 1], & \text{otherwise.} \end{cases}$$

The pivot indicates the seam construction starting point. The function $f_v(.)$ maps a gene to its corresponding coordinate in the image and is defined as

$$f_v(i) = \begin{cases} g_i, & \text{if } i = p; \\ g_i + f_v(i-1), & \text{if } i > p; \\ g_i + f_v(i+1), & \text{if } i < p. \end{cases} \tag{2}$$

The transformation of an individual into a seam is given by converting its genes into coordinates. The definition of a vertical seam is now $s = \{(i, f_v(i))\}_{i=1}^m$. This notation is adopted because it must be guaranteed that an individual maps a 8-connected path, $|f_v(i) - f_v(i+1)| \leq 1, \forall i \text{ s.t. } 1 \geq i \geq m$, so the $f_v(.)$ function complies with this domain restriction. To illustrate the transformation, let $C_1 = [0, -1, 2^*, 0]$ and $C_2 = [3^*, 1, -1, 0]$ be two individuals, where the $*$ indicates the pivot location. The corresponding seams are, $s_1 = \{(1, 1), (2, 1), (3, 2), (4, 2)\}$ and $s_2 = \{(1, 3), (2, 4), (3, 3), (4, 3)\}$, respectively. We recall that our approach uses a single point crossover operator and an uniform mutation operator. These operators are quite suitable, once our pivot position is fixed at each GAs process.

3.2 Fitness Function

The main idea of our fitness function is to give seams with lower energy higher fitness values. We used edge detection through the Sobel operator as image energy function, as suggested in [1]. Formally, let $e(.)$ be an energy function that yields the importance of a pixel at the coordinate (i, j), the *sobel* function yields the information about the contour, where $0 \leq sobel(i, j) \leq 1$. Now we define the seam cost function E as the sum of its pixels energy

$E(s) = \sum sobel(i,j), \forall (i,j) \in s$. Thus, we define the *fitness*, as the objective function, by

$$fitness(s) = \begin{cases} 0 & \text{, if } s - I = \varnothing; \\ \dfrac{m - E(s)}{m} & \text{, otherwise.} \end{cases} \qquad (3)$$

A seam during the crossover or mutation may produce any coordinate out of the image bounds $(s - I = \varnothing)$, such as $C_3 = [2^*, -1, -1, 0]$ which produces an invalid seam $s_3 = \{(1,2), (2,1), (3,0), (4,-1)\}$. These kind of seams will be given low fitness value to reduce the probability of mutation and crossover. In fact, their genetic material will be left out of next population.

3.3   Multi-seam Carving

As stated before, we desire to obtain a set of feasible solutions and solutions surround that one with best fitness for improve our proposal in a multi-seam carving way. To do so, we first discard individuals with fitness values under the fitness mean μ_{fit} for non-zero fitness individuals. This set of such individuals is stood for $\mathbb{S}^*$. The idea of Multi-seam carving in our approach is to search in the neighborhood of the individuals that belong to $\mathbb{S}^*$ in order to obtain other seams as good as those ones in $\mathbb{S}^*$. For each $s_i \in \mathbb{S}^*$, we generate k-valid neighbor seams $\{s_\alpha\}_{\alpha=1}^k$ by changing the pivot gene value, where $1 \le |f_v(p_i) - f_v(p_\alpha)| \le k, \forall \alpha \in [1, k]$. We highlight that changing the pivot also results in changing the other gene values besides pivot for a certain seam.

3.4   Algorithm for Genetic Seam Carving

The Algorithm for Genetic Seam Carving is presented below. Take into account that t is the current generation and t_{max} is the max generation number.

1. **while** image is not retargeted **do**
2.   generate randomly the pivot position p;
3.   generate initial population $P(0)$ with the previously pivot generated;
4.   **for** $t = 1$ **to** t_{max};
5.   select chromosomes from $P(t-1)$ to apply genetic operators;
6.   apply crossover and mutation on selected chromosomes;
7.   compute fitness value for each chromosome;
8.   add 1 to t;
9.   **end for**
10.   remove invalid individuals (with fitness equals zero);
11.   compute μ_{fit};
12.   remove individuals under μ_{fit} to get $\mathbb{S}^*$;
13.   generate k-valid seams $\{s_\alpha\}_{\alpha=1}^k$ where $1 \le |f_v(p_i) - f_v(p_\alpha)| \le k, \forall \alpha \in [1, k]$
14.   carve image with the resulting set $\mathbb{S}^* \cup \{s_\alpha\}_{\alpha=1}^k$.
15. **end while**

4   Experiments and Discussion

Initially, we adjust some parameters that guide the GA behavior, namely the chromosome size, the population size P_S and the number of generations G_N to evolve. Each of these parameters directly affects memory space or computational time requirements, or both. We choose to keep the population size constant along all generations. We developed an application experiment to assess the GSC performance. For each image in the IVC database [7], we reduced their height and width by 20 %. For the GSC, we carried out this experiment for 10 times because, according to the GA convergence, the results may vary at each experiment. The results can be seen in Fig. 2.

(a) Input.   (b) SC.   (c) GSC.   (d) Input.   (b) SC.   (c) GSC.

Fig. 2. Worse and best cases of SC and GSC (see Table 1). Columns (a)–(d) show the input images and the interest points found. Columns (b)–(e) show the outputs from SC and the matched points, respectively. The outputs from SC and the matched points are showed in columns (c)–(f).

We express the visual impact caused by carving seams as the result of similarity obtained by the SSIM (Structural SIMilarity) index [13]. Since we have images with different sizes, it is not possible to compute SSIM directly. In this case a technique SIFT-based SSIM [2] is applicable. SIFT (Scale-invariant feature transform) is used to match corresponding interest points between the images before and after carving. Then, for each matched interest point we center a window w, 50×50, and then, compute the SSIM index between both. So now, we define the Q index as the mean of the SSIM index between each matched windows of the original (w) image and the retargeted one (w'), as: $Q_{I'} = \frac{1}{k} \sum_{j=1}^{k} SSIM(w_j, w'_j)$, where k is the number of matched points $\in I'$. As the SSIM index has the maximal bound equals to 1, we assume that a value close to 1 for a given pair of images indicates high similarity. As the carving proceeds removing several seams, high energy pixels are inevitably removed. So, in real case applications, the Q index decreases as more seams are removed, as is illustrated in Fig. 3. Table 1 summarizes the results obtained by the experiments. Q_{SC} and Q_{GSC}: the Q index from the original and the retargeted image

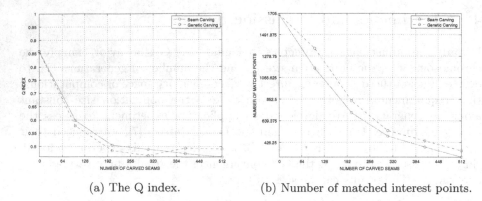

(a) The Q index.   (b) Number of matched interest points.

Fig. 3. This metrics are from Lena image, by retargeting 50 % of its width and height. Image (a) shows the quality index Q and image (b) is the number of matched interest points using SC (solid) and GSC (dashed).

by SC and GSC, respectively; $\sigma_{Q_{GSC}}$: the standard deviation for the 10 retargeted images by GSC; $\#P_{SC}$ and $\#P_{GSC}$: the percentages of preserved interest points matched between the original and the retargeted by SC and GSC, respectively. In the case of GSC, we have the average quality index of 10 retargeted images, $Q_{GSC} = \frac{1}{10}\sum_{i=1}^{10} Q(I, I_{GSC_i})$. During our tests, we noted that all 10 carved images generally have similar quality. This observation is confirmed by the very low standard deviation σ_{GSC} shown in the Table 1. Most of Q_{GSC} results showed values close to the Q_{SC}. But, when we consider only the number of matched interest points as a quality metric, GSC outperforms SC in most results. We assume that the optimal and non-optimal seams found helped at the preservation of the interest points during the retargeting.

Table 1. The quality index Q from the images in the IVC database.

Metric	Avion	Barba	Boats	Clown	Fruit	House	Isbabe	Lena	Mandr	Pimen
$Q_{SC}(\%)$	72.91	50.96	65.69	64.98	61.09	56.43	61.93	65.49	52.80	66.04
$Q_{GSC}(\%)$	65.42	**51.67**	**68.55**	**69.45**	**62.69**	52.61	58.18	63.11	47.80	**69.48**
$\sigma_{Q_{GSC}}$	0.0023	0.0002	0.0001	0.0009	0.0002	0.0000	0.0002	0.0000	0.0002	0.0001
$\#P_{SC}$ (%)	61.91	45.22	51.47	38.66	49.71	50.09	37.75	48.86	26.56	55.67
$\#P_{GSC}$ (%)	60.18	**64.38**	50.16	**45.76**	**50.66**	**56.32**	**46.00**	**64.16**	**31.13**	46.81

A present limitation is that GSC not always achieve the optimal seam as in SC, but the seams computed are still valid. At glance we can highlight the fixed population size and number of generations restricting the search. The population size and the number of generations impact directly on the result quality.

5   Conclusion

We proposed a new formulation for the image retargeting problem in the framework of genetic algorithms. Our experiments show that this new formulation can produce image quality similar to the traditional Seam Carving. In some cases, Genetic Seam Carving outperforms Seam Carving according to the number of matched interest points preserved. Our current research seeks out distinct energy functions from which the Genetic Algorithms can benefit. Also, we intend to explore different strategies to choose chromosomes to eliminate at each iteration. In particular, the constant population size and the numbers of generations seems to be very restrictive.

References

1. Avidan, S., Shamir, A.: Seam carving for content-aware image resizing. ACM Trans. Graph. **22**(3), 277–286 (2007)
2. Azuma, D., Tanaka, Y., Hasegawa, M., Kato, S.: Ssim based image quality assessment applicable to resized images. IEICE Technical report (2011)
3. Conger, D.D., Kumar, M., Radha, H.: Multi-seam carving via seamlets. In: IS&T/SPIE Electronic Imaging, p. 78700H. International Society for Optics and Photonics (2011)
4. Conger, D.D., Radha, H., Kumar, M.: Seamlets: content-aware nonlinear wavelet transform. In: 2010 IEEE International Conference on Acoustics Speech and Signal Processing (ICASSP), pp. 1450–1453. IEEE (2010)
5. Domingues, D., Alahi, A., Vandergheynst, P.: Stream carving: an adaptive seam carving algorithm. In: 2010 17th IEEE International Conference on Image Processing (ICIP), pp. 901–904, September 2010
6. Hashemi, S., Kiani, S., Noroozi, N., Moghaddam, M.E.: An image contrast enhancement method based on genetic algorithm. Pattern Recogn. Lett. **31**(13), 1816–1824 (2010). Meta-heuristic Intelligence Based image Processing
7. Le Callet, P., Autrusseau, F.: Subjective quality assessment irccyn/ivc database (2005). http://www.irccyn.ec-nantes.fr/ivcdb/
8. Mishiba, K., Ikehara, M.: Seam merging for image resizing with structure preservation. In: 2011 IEEE International Conference on Acoustics Speech and Signal Processing (ICASSP), pp. 1001–1004. IEEE (2011)
9. Rubinstein, M., Shamir, A., Avidan, S.: Improved seam carving for video retargeting. ACM Trans. Graph. **27**(3), 16:1–16:9 (2008)
10. Szeliski, R., Zabih, R., Scharstein, D., Veksler, O., Kolmogorov, V., Agarwala, A., Tappen, M., Rother, M.: A comparative study of energy minimization methods for markov random fields with smoothness-based priors. IEEE Trans. Pattern Anal. Mach. Intell. **30**(6), 1068–1080 (2008)
11. Tao, W.-B.: Image segmentation by three-level thresholding based on maximum fuzzy entropy and genetic algorithm. Pattern Recogn. Lett. **24**(16), 3069–3078 (2003)
12. Vaquero, D., Turk, M., Pulli, K., Tico, M., Gelfand, N.: A survey of image retargeting techniques. In: SPIE Optical Engineering+ Applications, p. 779814. International Society for Optics and Photonics (2010)
13. Wang, Z., Bovik, A.C., Sheikh, H.R., Simoncelli, E.P.: Image quality assessment: from error visibility to structural similarity. IEEE Trans. Image Process. **13**(4), 600–612 (2004)
14. Whitley, D.: A genetic algorithm tutorial. Stat. Comput. **4**, 65–85 (1994)
15. Yan, Z., Chen, H.: A study of image retargeting based on seam carving. In: 2014 Sixth International Conference on Measuring Technology and Mechatronics Automation (ICMTMA), pp. 60–63. IEEE (2014)

Analysis of Expressiveness of Portuguese Sign Language Speakers

Inês V. Rodrigues[1], Eduardo M. Pereira[1,2]([⊠]), and Luis F. Teixeira[1]

[1] Faculty of Engineering of the University of Porto,
Rua Dr. Roberto Frias, 378, 4200-465 Porto, Portugal
[2] INESC TEC, Porto, Portugal
ejmp@inescporto.pt

Abstract. Nowadays, there are several communication gaps that isolate deaf people in several social activities. This work studies the expressiveness of gestures in Portuguese Sign Language (PSL) speakers and their differences between deaf and hearing people. It is a first effort towards the ultimate goal of understanding emotional and behaviour patterns among such populations. In particular, our work designs solutions for the following problems: (i) differentiation between deaf and hearing people, (ii) identification of different conversational topics based on body expressiveness, (iii) identification of different levels of mastery of PSL speakers through feature analysis. With these aims, we build up a complete and novel dataset that reveals the duo-interaction between deaf and hearing people under several conversational topics. Results show high recognition and classification rates.

1 Introduction

The research on emotion, behaviour and expressiveness analysis was leveraged on 1962 by the important work on facial expression by Tomkins [1] and continued by Ekman [2] on 1975. The power of nonverbal behaviour in emotions became a central issue in most psychology textbooks as these started to be invaded by photos with prototypical expressions and simple emotions [3]. Nowadays, the panorama regarding the nonverbal emotional experiences has changed drastically. Every year, more than 50 books and papers are published featuring nonverbal channels of expressive communication. The channels considered are mainly facial expression, gestures, gaze, vocal quality, paralinguistic features, posture and body position, head nods, among others [3]. The focus of this work will be in body gestures which serve as main communicative function and contain substantial affective and cognitive information that help us emphasise certain parts of our speech and pass on expressive content.

Concerning the computer vision field, using automatic tools to extract body features allows a better understanding of the human behaviour so that it is possible to detect and interpret nonverbal temporal patterns. The fusion of several elements such as motion, appearance, shape, among others, is the key for solving the analysis of expressiveness that has driven the efforts of many researchers [4].

© Springer International Publishing Switzerland 2015
R. Paredes et al. (Eds.): IbPRIA 2015, LNCS 9117, pp. 708–717, 2015.
DOI: 10.1007/978-3-319-19390-8_79

Sign language speakers experience their languages very passionately. This may be explained by the fact that language plays a crucial role in the construction of a community and that it is a clear mark of belonging [5]. Emotion recognition from body language and its implications to the social adjustment of a sign language speaker are, therefore, very important issues. This study brings, in a novel way, this thematic to the field of computer vision, and presents important contributions: (i) creation of a novel video dataset that presents dialogues between deaf and hearing people (it will be release publicly for research purposes), (ii) proof of the differences in motion expressiveness between deaf and hearing people speaking PSL, (iii) the ability to distinguish different conversational moments that reveals behaviour differences based on context.

2   Related Work

Computer vision research on human behaviour analysis includes a broad range of studies to understand nonverbal sensitivity in different contexts and through different channels. Whole-body expressions provide information about the emotional state of the producer, but also signal his action intentions. The work in body expression was initiated in 1872 by Darwin who described the body expressions of many different emotions [6]. More recent studies showed that even in the absence of facial and vocal cues, it is possible to identify basic emotions signalled by static body postures [7], arm movement [8] and whole body movement [7–9]. Therefore, gestures serve an important communicative function in face-to-face communication since they often occur in conjunction with speech. According to Cassell [10], the fact that gestural errors are extremely rare demonstrates how essential their nature is for accurate communication.

For the particular case of the proposed work it is important to assimilate that gestures and the way they are performed work as an identity of a subject. The same action may be executed in several different ways depending on the executant. It is not rare that we are able to recognise a person by gait analysis, and it is also possible to infer emotional states by the way that person is moving [11]. This perspective enables us to classify walking as an expressive gesture [12]. Indeed, several everyday actions may constitute expressive gesture. For instance, Pollick et al. [13] investigated expressive content of actions such as knocking or drinking, and Heloir and Gibet [14] worked on the identification and representation of the variations induced by style for the synthesis of realistic and convincing expressive gesture sequences in sign language speakers. We bring this new topic to the field of expressiveness analysis in computer vision.

3   Methodology

As stated previously, emotion recognition from body language and its implications to the social adjustment of a sign language speaker are very important issues. Therefore, this study focused on evaluating the differences between deaf and hearing people, in terms of expressive patterns through body motion analysis in several conversational topics. It is a preliminary work that intends to point out directions for future research that help to reduce the gaps that nowadays prevent deaf people from interacting easily with other people in society.

3.1 PSL Database

There was the need to create a database that could accomplish the requirements needed to accurately study differences of sign language speakers and measure their levels of nonverbal expressiveness according to the context. Indeed, the aim of the dataset was to enable the possibility of performing studies that analyse dialogue relationships between two individuals.

Table 1. Volunteer population for the creation of the database. All subjects are females between the ages of 27 and 39.

Deaf people	Gender	Age	Hearing people	Gender	Age
D1	Female	38	H1	Female	38
D2	Female	35	H2	Female	27
D3	Female	36	H3	Female	30
D4	Female	39	H4	Female	29
D5	Female	31	H5	Female	30
D6	Female	39	H6	Female	37
–	–	–	H7	Female	37

We were advised by experts in the fields of social-psychology and sign-language. The conversational scenarios designed by the team of the Faculdade de Psicologia e Ciências da Educação da Universidade do Porto were: (i) conversation between two hearing people, (ii) conversation between two deaf people, (iii) conversation between a deaf and a hearing person. They also defined some requirements regarding the type of population and the recording scenario, for instance participants should have some kind of a priori knowledge between them, they should have the same gender, and the acquisition should take place in a venue that was familiar to all subjects. The contact with the volunteers was obtained by a partnership with the Agrupamento de Escolas Eugenio de Andrade, Escola EB2/3 de Paranhos. Table 1 displays the population that volunteered for the creation of this database.

Since our aim is the analysis of expressiveness, a set of conversational topics, that would awaken certain positive and negative emotions in the individuals, was defined. Those topics follow a staggered way so that the discussion would generate emotions of increasing intensity in the actors. The topics were chosen assuming that a dialogue would occur between a pair of subjects and that both would intervene actively. The conversation topics as well as the whole database structure is detailed on Fig. 1. Each conversational pair of subjects is called a session. Since this work is oriented to the study of sign language speakers, the recording sessions in which two hearing people were having a conversation were not considered since they did not use sign language. We also discarded one session (between subjects D3 and D2) since they kept a standing position, which does not allow a fair comparison. Under this constraints, we base our experiences on 9 sessions.

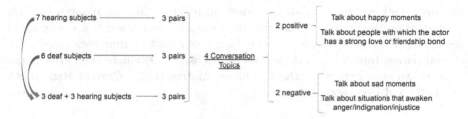

Fig. 1. Diagram of the database structure.

3.2   Dataset Preparation and Feature Construction

Each session is represented by a video and on each one a region of interest (ROI) was defined so that only the area bounding the subject was considered. Before building the feature vector for each video the following statistics were measured for each one: frames per second (fps), total number of frames and duration. Each one was subdivided into miniclips with the same number of frames (120) and the same fps (25) in order to be used as samples for the learning and classification tasks. Depending on each video's fps, some videos underwent a downsampling and others an up-sampling process. For each video, a region of interest (ROI) was defined so that only the area bounding the subject was considered.

We explored several trajectory and pixel based features to capture and represent body expressiveness regarding our aims. Some of those features were motion history image (MHI), motion gradients, several body part trackers, and other kinematic features. However, for the sake of simplicity and lack of space we just present here the results and conclusions obtained considering motiongrams feature [15]. Indeed, we performed some feature selection techniques that clearly highlight their discriminative power over the remaining features. Therefore, we use histogram representations for both vertical and horizontal motiongrams and concatenate them to be used as the final feature vector. Special care was taken in order to allow all feature vectors for each miniclip to have the same dimension. In this way, we considered the minimum values for width and height of all miniclips to reduce bin widths, obtaining a 114 and 162 dimensional bin size for both vertical and horizontal motiongrams, respectively.

3.3   Distinguishing Deaf from Hearing People

For this problem the two classes were known a priori for each miniclip, namely if the performer was a deaf or a hearing person. For classification purposes, the miniclips were grouped by topic so that it was possible to compare the classification performance for the different groups. We considered two classification methods: k-Nearest Neighbours (k-NN), which is simple and widely used as a first approach for classification problems, and Support Vector Machine (SVM), which is a more complex algorithm but usually more accurate. Both algorithms were used under a cross-validation mechanism and different number of folds (dependent on the number of samples per grouping) were used in order to avoid over-fitting. For the SVM we performed a grid search to automatically infer the optimal parameters. The statistical measures used to evaluate the performance of these two classifiers were the Confusion Matrix (CM), Correct Rate (CR), Recall (R) and Precision (P).

3.4   Distinguishing Different Conversation Topics

Regarding the differentiation of the conversational topics (two with positive connotation and two with negative) spotting the differences in terms of expressiveness among the four topics was the primary reason why these moments were included on the database. In this case, the miniclips were grouped by subject.

The same classifiers, k-NN and SVM, were used to approach this problem. However, we use a multi-class SVM for ordinal data, since we want to inspect if the topics could follow a natural order of expressiveness, and analyse the intra-class and inter-class boundary decision between the topics that belong to the same positive or negative connotation. We used the approach generalised in [16]. The same metrics were used for evaluation performance.

3.5   Identifying Levels of Mastery in PSL

For the purpose of distinguishing different levels of expertise in PSL, an agglomerative hierarchical clustering method was used. In order to identify groups of similar feature values, clustering procedures use distance measures to group data points in a way that provides minimal inner-cluster distances and maximal inter-cluster distances [17]. The possibility of our miniclips containing information regarding this question was not known a priori, this means that we were not aware if it would be possible to obtain a reliable answer. This problem is very abstract but also a valuable addition to the overall framework of this study.

One of the drawbacks of the agglomerative approach is the requirement for the number of clusters to be specified before the algorithm is applied. In order to overcome this issue, using the questionnaires that all subjects filled, it was decided to define 3 and 4 levels of expertise in PSL based on the score of each subject's answers to the following questions: number of years familiarised with sign language and the current profession. The combined score of the two answers was also used. Table 2 shows the organisation of the subjects in levels regarding their answers to the two mentioned questions. The weighted combination of the scores of each answer (0.5 for each) originated 4 different levels.

Table 2. Division of our population regarding the number of years in contact with the PSL and current job for classification purposes.

Level	Year range	Subjects	Level	Current profession	Subjects
1	7–15	D1 / H2 / H7	1	Non Related to PSL	D4
2	16–25	H6 / D5 / D6	2	Speech Therapist	H7
3	26–35	D4	3	PSL Interpretation	H2
–	–	–	4	PSL Teaching	D1 / D5 / D6 / H6

4 Results and Discussion

4.1 Distinguishing Deaf from Hearing People

Distinguishing deaf from hearing people when using PSL is the main enquiry to be answered by this work. Table 3 shows the results of the two classifiers used for the different data groupings.

Table 3. k-NN and SVM classification results obtained for the task of distinguishing between deaf and hearing people.

	Correct rate		Recall		Precision	
	k-NN	SVM	k-NN	SVM	k-NN	SVM
Topic 1	0.98	0.98	0.98	0.98	**0.99**	0.97
Topic 2	0.95	**0.98**	0.97	**0.98**	0.94	**0.98**
Topic 3	0.97	**0.98**	0.97	**0.99**	0.98	**0.99**
Topic 4	0.97	**0.98**	0.98	0.98	0.97	**0.98**
All topics	0.96	**0.97**	**0.97**	0.96	0.96	0.96

The results obtained for both classifiers are in concordance with each, although the performance is slightly improved for the SVM. For the SVM the best performance is observed for Topic 3. Inspecting Table 4, we observe a balance in the misclassification rates of the classes which leads to conclude that both classifiers perform well, and that our feature vector is highly discriminative for all classes. Accumulated CM are more a less equivalent for all the miniclip groupings, being the highest misclassification rates observed for the grouping of all topics, where more samples may confuse the classifier.

It is reasonable to say that the information contained in the videos of our database is rich and the feature approach made to extract that information was

Table 4. Accumulated confusion matrix (CM) for both k-NN and SVM methods.

	k-NN	CM	SVM	CM
Topic 1	0.97	0.03	0.97	0.03
	0.05	0.95	0.01	0.99
Topic 2	0.95	0.05	0.98	0.02
	0.04	0.96	0.00	1.00
Topic 3	0.98	0.02	0.99	0.01
	0.04	0.96	0.01	0.99
Topic 4	0.98	0.02	1.00	0.00
	0.03	0.97	0.03	0.97
All topics	0.97	0.03	0.98	0.02
	0.05	0.95	0.04	0.96

appropriate. The consulted PSL experts stated that in order to distinguish if a subject using LGP is deaf or hearing we should focus mainly on evaluating facial features. With this result we prove that the body features are also very descriptive.

4.2 Distinguishing Different Conversation Topics

When the database was created, the definition of four different moments had the goal of making it more robust and complete. Only PSL speakers are able to evaluate the contents of the videos and verify if the four distinct moments were in fact present. Therefore, this supervised evaluation was done for some of the videos confirming that the subjects were demonstrating different levels of expressiveness and emotion accordingly to the current discussion topic.

The remaining videos were also analysed without expert supervision in order to extract some conclusions based on the queues given previously by the experts. It was possible to deduce that, regarding the presence of four different conversational moments, the framework being developed is accurate and valuable. Table 5 shows the results of the two classifiers used for the different data groupings.

4.3 Identifying Levels of Mastery in PSL

In this task we used a non-supervised agglomerative hierarchical tree to build a hierarchy of clusters. Considering the process explained in Sect. 3.5, we get different configurations for the number of clusters to be used: (i) 3 in the case that we wanted to group our subjects by the number of years familiarised with PSL, (ii) 4 for the current profession, (iii) 4 for the combined score of the answer of the two questions. Tables 6, 7 and 8 show the evaluation statistics of the clusterings performed on each configuration, respectively, where *cid* indicates the id of the cluster, *Size* the number of samples that belong to each cluster, *ISim* and *ISdev* represent both the average and standard deviation in terms of

Table 5. *k*-NN and SVM classification results obtained for the task of distinguishing the different conversational topics.

	Correct rate		Recall		Precision	
	k-NN	SVM	k-NN	SVM	k-NN	SVM
Subject D1	0.91	0.91	0.85	**0.92**	0.90	0.90
Subject D4	0.96	**0.98**	0.94	**0.98**	0.91	**0.97**
Subject D5	**0.93**	0.91	0.86	**0.90**	**0.93**	0.89
Subject D6	**0.93**	0.90	**0.95**	0.89	**0.96**	0.89
Subject H2	**0.91**	0.86	**0.93**	0.86	**0.98**	0.85
Subject H6	0.89	**0.98**	0.83	**0.98**	0.89	**0.97**
Subject H7	0.96	**0.97**	0.94	**0.98**	**0.99**	0.98
All subjects	**0.92**	0.78	**0.91**	0.82	**0.93**	0.77

similarity between each cluster, whereas *ESim* and *ESdev* represent the same statistics but for similarity of the objects of each cluster and the rest of the objects.

Table 6. Clustering statistics: the class considered is the number of years in contact with PSL.

cid	Size	ISim	ISdev	ESim	ESdev	Entpy	Purty	1	2	3
1	70	0.669	0.075	0.332	0.079	0.625	0.557	0.44	0.56	0.00
2	167	0.606	0.105	0.477	0.117	0.596	0.707	0.71	0.28	0.01
3	1029	0.597	0.112	0.437	0.12	0.75	0.646	0.28	0.65	0.07

According to the opinion of the PSL experts, the number of years alone might not be a clear indicator of how experienced a subject is in terms of PSL, since several factors may influence it. In fact, the overall entropy and purity of this clustering are 0.723 and 0.649 respectively. These values reveal that the clustering was performed poorly. Purity is quite low which indicates us that the samples in each cluster are not as homogeneous as desired.

Table 7. Clustering statistics: the class considered is the current profession of the subject.

cid	Size	ISim	ISdev	ESim	ESdev	Entpy	Purty	4	3	1	2
1	70	0.669	0.075	0.332	0.079	0.584	0.6	0.60	0.36	0.00	0.04
2	167	0.606	0.105	0.477	0.117	0.529	0.695	0.69	0.28	0.01	0.02
3	144	0.709	0.078	0.559	0.087	0.669	0.674	0.67	0.12	0.18	0.03
4	885	0.602	0.111	0.481	0.127	0.536	0.739	0.74	0.01	0.05	0.20

When performing the clustering in relation to the levels in terms of professional occupation, the overall entropy and purity of the solution were the best of the three analysis performed (0.553 and 0.718). From the questions featured on the questionnaires, this one regarding the current professional occupation of the subjects was the one considered by PSL experts to possibly be more discriminative when it comes to the expertise on this language. This is confirmed by an improvement on entropy and purity values.

Table 8. Clustering statistics: the class are the number of years in contact with PSL combined with the current profession.

cid	Size	ISim	ISdev	ESim	ESdev	Entpy	Purty	3	4	2	1
1	70	0.669	0.075	0.332	0.079	0.695	0.557	0.04	0.56	0.36	0.04
2	167	0.606	0.105	0.477	0.117	0.831	0.413	0.41	0.28	0.29	0.02
3	144	0.709	0.078	0.559	0.087	0.845	0.424	0.25	0.42	0.30	0.03
4	885	0.602	0.111	0.481	0.127	0.66	0.682	0.06	0.68	0.06	0.20

The combination of previous classes into a weighted distribution was done with the intention of obtaining classes that could concatenate more information about the expertise of each subject. The less promising results of entropy and purity tell us this fusion impair the performance of the clustering solution. To overcome this issue a different type of combination of the information could help.

5   Conclusions

This study was focused on automated visual analysis of expressiveness of PSL speakers using computer vision techniques. We achieve important breakthroughs under this topic: (i) we provide a novel and rich dataset for the study of expressiveness and emotion states on a duo-interaction between deaf and hearing people, (ii) we achieve a high discriminative feature vector capable of distinguishing deaf from hearing people and also different conversational topics, (iii) we point out directions about the stratification of levels of expertise in PSL, and their recognition through the correlation of video with social data. The future work intends to go in the direction of finding emotional and behaviour patterns through face and body expressions analysis, of deaf and hearing people. New techniques and approaches need to be reviewed and tested since this is a very ambitious goal.

Acknowledgment. The authors would like to thank to the PSL experts, Ana and Paula, who helped to find the volunteer population, to the socio-psychologist team from the Faculdade de Psicologia e Ciências da Educação da Universidade do Porto who helped to define the sociological constraints of the database, to the Agrupamento de Escolas Eugenio de Andrade, Escola EB2/3 de Paranhos for providing the venue for acquisition of the videos of the database, and finally to Stephano Piana for his help with the EyesWeb platform.

References

1. Tomkins, S.: Affect Imagery Consciousness: Volume:II: The Negative Affects. Springer Series. Springer Publishing Company, New York (1963)
2. Ekman, P., Friesen, W.V.: Facial Action Coding System: A Technique for the Measurement of Facial Movement. Consulting Psychologists Press, Palo Alto (1978)
3. Harrigan, J., Rosenthal, R., Scherer, K.: New Handbook of Methods in Nonverbal Behavior Research. Series in affective science. OUP, Oxford (2008)
4. Metaxas, D., Zhang, S.: A review of motion analysis methods for human nonverbal communication computing. Image Vis. Comput. **31**(6–7), 421–433 (2013). Machine learning in motion analysis: New advances
5. Nadal, J.M., Monreal, P., Perera, S.: Emotion and linguistic diversity. Procedia Soc. Behav. Sci. **82**, 614–620 (2013). World Conference on Psychology and Sociology 2012
6. Darwin, C.: The Expression of the Emotions in Man and Animals. John Murray, London (1872)
7. Nakajima, C., Pontil, M., Heisele, B., Poggio, T.: Full-body person recognition system. Pattern Recogn. **36**(9), 1997–2006 (2003)
8. Piana, S., Staglianó, A., Odone, A.C.A.: A set of full-body movement features for emotion recognition to help children affected by autism spectrum condition. In: IDGEI International Workshop (2013)
9. Atkinson, A., Dittrich, W., Gemmell, A., Young, A.: Emotion perception from dynamic and static body expressions in point-light and full-light displays. Perception **33**, 717–746 (2004)
10. Cassell, J.: A framework for gesture generation and interpretation. In: Cipolla, R., Pentland, A. (eds.) Computer Vision in Human-Machine Interaction, pp. 191–215. Cambridge University Press, Cambridge (2000)
11. Kobayashi, Y.: The emotion sign: human motion analysis classifying specific emotion. JCP **3**(9), 20–28 (2008)
12. Hwang, B.-W., Kim, S.-M., Lee, S.-W.: 2D and 3D full-body gesture database for analyzing daily human gestures. In: Huang, D.-S., Zhang, X.-P., Huang, G.-B. (eds.) ICIC 2005. LNCS, vol. 3644, pp. 611–620. Springer, Heidelberg (2005)
13. Pollick, F., Paterson, H., Bruderlin, A., Sanford, A.: Perceiving affect from arm movement. Cognition **82**(2), B51–61 (2001)
14. Heloir, A., Gibet, S.: A qualitative and quantitative characterisation of style in sign language gestures. In: Sales Dias, M., Gibet, S., Wanderley, M.M., Bastos, R. (eds.) GW 2007. LNCS (LNAI), vol. 5085, pp. 122–133. Springer, Heidelberg (2009)
15. Jensenius, A.R.: Using motiongrams in the study of musical gestures. In: Proceedings of the International Computer Music Conference, pp. 499–502. Tulane University, New Orleans (2006)
16. Pinto da Costa, J., Sousa, R., Cardoso, J.: An all-at-once unimodal svm approach for ordinal classification. In: Ninth International Conference on Machine Learning and Applications (ICMLA 2010), pp. 59–64, December 2010
17. Zhao, Y., Karypis, G.: Evaluation of hierarchical clustering algorithms for document datasets. In: Proceedings of the Eleventh International Conference on Information and Knowledge Management, CIKM 2002, pp. 515–524. ACM, New York (2002)

Automatic Eye Localization; Multi-block LBP vs. Pyramidal LBP Three-Levels Image Decomposition for Eye Visual Appearance Description

Djamel Eddine Benrachou[1], Filipe Neves dos Santos[2](✉),
Brahim Boulebtateche[1], and Salah Bensaoula[1]

[1] Laboratory of Automatic and Signals- Annaba (LASA),
Department of Electronics, University Badji Mokhtar Annaba,
BP 12, 23000 Annaba, Algeria
djamelben.univ@gmail.com, brahim.boulebtateche@univ-annaba.dz,
bensaoula_salah@yahoo.fr
[2] INESC TEC(formerly INESC Porto) and Faculty of Engineering,
University of Porto,
Campus da FEUP, Rua Dr.Roberto Frias, 378, Porto, Portugal
fbnsantos@fe.up.pt

Abstract. This manuscript presents the performance evaluation of our algorithm that precisely finds human eyes in still gray-scale images and describes the state of the founded eye. This algorithm has been evaluated considering two descriptors - Pyramid transform domain (PLBP) and Multi-Block Histogram LBP (BHLBP), which are extended versions of the Local Binary Pattern descriptor (LBP). For the classification stage, two types of supervised learning techniques have also been evaluated, Support Vector Machine (SVM) and Multilayer Perceptron (MLP). The proposed method is assessed on the Face Recognition Grand Challenge (BioID) and (CAS-PEAL-R1) databases, and experimental results demonstrate improved performance than some state-of-the-art eye detection approaches.

Keywords: Eye localization · Block histogram LBP · Pyramidal LBP · Supervised machine learning

1 Introduction and Related Works

Individual's affective state and focus attention are one of the most important information sources to analyze the human's face. Understanding the eye states by artificial vision system is essential to a wide range of face related research efforts. The eye localization and state detection are two complementary challenging topics, which have shown expanding interest this last decade and gained a large attention from the academic and industrial communities for real world applications. Eye state characteristics are increasingly used in safety applications to detect situations such as somnolence or lack of attention while driving.

© Springer International Publishing Switzerland 2015
R. Paredes et al. (Eds.): IbPRIA 2015, LNCS 9117, pp. 718–726, 2015.
DOI: 10.1007/978-3-319-19390-8_80

This significant index is considered in the Advanced Driver Assistance System (ADAS) for automatic driver drowsiness detection based on visual information [1,2]. Some facial expressions are clearly distinguished through the eye state, since it has been proven that the driver's fatigue has a high correlation with the **PERCLOS** [3]. In fact, there exist commercial eye localization systems, which perform well under relatively controlled environmental conditions, but tend to fail when the variation appears from different factors such as, **facial expressions, the partial occlusion, the pose variation** and **lighting conditions**. Several eye localization techniques have been emerged, and are broadly categorized into three main types; *Methods based on the measurement of the eye characteristics* [4], others *Exploiting structural information* [5], [6] and those using *Learning statistical appearance model* [7,8]. In this paper, the proposed algorithm is based on conventional appearance approaches, which involves ; i) the feature description processing of the ocular region and ii) the model prediction for classifying extracted eye features. However, the employed descriptors, must have some essential proprieties such as, identifiability of the interesting object, rotation and scale invariance, noise resistance, robust against environmental illumination conditions and lighting changes. In agreement with these conditions, the adopted pyramidal representation of LBP (**PLBP**) is suitable to describe the eye patterns. SVM and Multilayer Perception (MLP) classifiers are utilized as classification rules, to handle residual variability and learn effective models. We extensively evaluate our algorithm on the very challenging BioID [9] and CAS-PEAL-R1 [10] databases. Discriminative PLBP performances are compared with a multi-blocks LBP histogram sequence (**BHLBP**). The remainder of this paper is organized as follows, Sect. 2 devotes to the details of the proposed approach, in Sect. 3 the pyramid transform descriptor modeling is presented in detail and the conventional Multi-blocks LBP is briefly introduced. Section 4 presents the implementation of our experiments and finally Sect. 5 contains conclusion, remarks and future work.

2   Proposed Approach

In this research, the conventional LBP has been extended to pyramid transform domain PLBP. We firstly prepare two sets of images (eye/ not eye) and LBP code is computed in each picture of the 3-levels of the image pyramid with LBP^{u2}, LBP^{ri} and LBP^{riu2} patterns, then all the LBP pyramid's histograms are concatenated to form a feature vector representing the eye. The performance of PLBP is compared against BHLBP, to encode micro and macro structure of the eye image. For the decision issue on eye detection, two well established classifiers were used, *SVM* and *MLP* for binary classification between eye/not-eye classes.

For more accuracy in eye detection, a small bench of eye images with size (24×24) is selected with both eye states (open/closed), to calculate the $LBP^{ri}_{8,1}$ histogram templates by averaging all histograms extracted from the neighborhoods of the eye center. Based on the LBP template, (χ^2) distance is considered

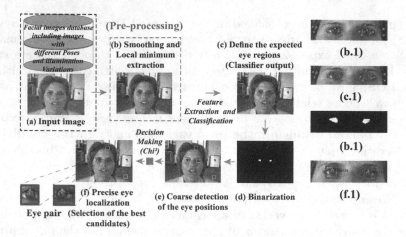

Fig. 1. Overview of the employed process to localize the eye position: (b.1) Local minimum extraction, (c.1) Exception of the ocular regions, (d.1) Image Mask (binarization of the pre-processed input image); the output of the classifier is used to create a binary image map with the same size as the input image and highlight the regions of interest within the image (white region), while omitting the non-interesting regions (black regions), (f.1) Precise eye localization results.

to measure the similarity between the present eye candidates and the designed templates. This post-classification phase increases the possibility to localize the eye for whatever state. To reduce the noise effect, the gray scale input image is blurred using 2-D Gaussian filter; the LBP descriptor has the disadvantage of being sensitive to noise in near uniform image regions. Therefore, we extract the local minimum from the pre-processed image, which correspond to the low gray scale regions and should contain the true position of the eye within the image Fig. 1(b.1). An overview of the precise eye detection process is illustrated in Fig. 1.

3   Feature Extraction

3.1   Pyramidal Pre-processed Local Binary Pattern Representation

Local binary pattern in spatial pyramid domain (PLBP), is an effective multi-resolution analysis approach, where each pixel in the low spatial resolution layer of the pyramid is obtained by down-sampling the low-pass filtered high resolution image at the pyramidal level just bellow. PLBP is the combination of the LBP histogram of N-spatial pyramid images, $PLBP_{P,R} = <LBP_{P,R,1}; \ldots; LBP_{P,R,N}>$. According to Ojala *et al.*'s rules, *Uniform* ($LBP_{P,R}^{u2}$), *Rotation-Invariant* ($LBP_{P,R}^{ri}$) and *Rotation-Invariant Uniform* ($LBP_{P,R}^{riu2}$) patterns can be constructed. $LBP_{P,R}^{*}$, where $*$ stands for $\{u2, ri, riu2\}$, is the LBP descriptor in a neighborhood of P sampling points on a circle of radius R for the spatial pyramid. The histogram dimensions of $LBP_{P,R}^{u2}$, $LBP_{P,R}^{ri}$ and $LBP_{P,R}^{riu2}$ patterns, for $P = 8$ and $R = 1$ are generated with 59, 36 and 10 different outputs, respectively. In our implementation, the eye pattern is down-sampled twice, generating a three levels pyramid I_0, I_1 and I_2, the size of the nth level image has the half size of the $(n-1)^{th}$ level image. The original image, represents the 0th level image I_0 of the pyramid, The $LBP_{P,R}^{u2}$ is directly computed in the 0th image of the pyramid with size 24×24, the use of only *'uniform'* patterns is motivated, by the reasoning that they tolerate rotation better because they contain fewer spatial transitions exposed to unwanted changes upon image rotation. Besides, being highly descriptive, LBP^{u2} is statistically stable and less sensitive to noise [11], which is favorable in our case, because I_0 is the highest resolution image in our pyramid, which contains more details about the eye appearance. At the 1st level of the image pyramid with size 12×12, $LBP_{P,R}^{ri}$ code is generated, to handle the invariance to texture rotation. The 0th image of the pyramid, is equally divided into 4 non-overlapped sub-regions, and the global spatial histogram is computed by concatenating the LBP^{u2} histograms of each subregion, the obtained histogram is denoted as H_0^{u2} with $(59 \times 4)bins$. The same process is applied to the 1st pyramid level and the LBP^{ri} histogram obtained is denoted as H_1^{ri} with $(36 \times 4)bins$. l_1 is smoothed and the extracted information is not very discriminant, the subregion-division and histogram concatenating strategy, is employed to improve the discriminative power of the descriptor. In the highest level of the image pyramid, the $LBP_{P,R}^{riu2}$ histogram is computed directly from the full image of size 6×6, the obtained histogram is denoted as H_2^{riu2} with $10bins$. At last, all histograms H_0^{u2}, H_1^{ri} and H_2^{riu2} are concatenated, to form a $300((59bins \times 4) + (36bins \times 4) + 10bins)$ dimensional feature vector $\mathbf{F}$, $F = \{H_0^{u2}, H_1^{ri}, H_2^{riu2}\}$.

3.2 Multi-block Histogram Local Binary Pattern

Multi-block histogram LBP (BHLBP) is formed on the basis of the eye image of size 24×24, which is divided into 4 non-overlapped sub-blocks of size 12×12 pixels; and then the 59-label $LBP_{8,1}^{u2}$ operator is adopted to extract the LBP features. Hence, the local histogram is computed over the sub-regions and the global spatial histogram of $236bins$ (i.e. $59bins \times 4$) is obtained, by concatenating all sub-regional histograms. These parameter settings for eye representation were suggested in [12].

4 Results and Discussion

We investigate the performance of an extended LBPs for eye localization by conducting experiments on the two following public databases:

- BioID Face database, that consists about 1521 images (384×286 pixels, gray level), recorded for face detection, through large variety of human face, captured in real world conditions, a **large range of illumination, background** and **face sizes with/without accessories**.

- CAS-PEAL-R1 database, which contains about 30900 images (360×480 pixels, gray level) of 1040 subjects. 1521 frontal face images have been selected, with open eyes including 464 **frontal** face in **normal state** and with some **expressions** involved, 330 faces with **accessories (myopia glasses, hat, cap. . . etc.)**, 101 individual's face in different **background**, 302 persons with **eye closed** and 324 face images took with a certain **distance** from the camera.

The search of eye location is carried out by applying the proposed approach on sliding window on low-gray scale regions, with local minimum of the input image. For the training phase, we used 3042 eye images and 3419 non-eye images, The collected eye/non-eye samples are randomly divided, with 70% used for training, and the remaining images are randomly divided with 15% for validation and 15% for testing. The discriminative performance of PLBP has been compared against BHLBPs image descriptor. In this work, PLBP and BHLBP are trained and validated with SVMs and MLP classifiers. We used the open source SVM implementation, Libsvm version 3.18 [13], and RBF kernel's hyper-parameters (C and σ) optimization is done by the grid search technique.

Table 1. Statistical results on BioID database

Approach	TP %	FP %	TN %	FN %	Precision	Recall	$F_1 Score$	Acc (%)
PLBP+SVM(Linear)	45, 49	2, 62	50, 28	1, 59	0.945	0.966	0.955	95.778
PLBP+SVM(Poly)	27, 39	1, 45	51, 40	19, 74	0.949	0.581	0.720	78.799
PLBP+SVM(RBF)	45, 59	1, 78	51, 12	1, 5	0.962	0.968	0.965	96.716
PLBP+*MLP*	46, 38	1, 12	51, 73	0, 75	0.976	0.984	0.980	**98.123**
BHLBP+SVM(Linear)	45, 73	3, 79	49, 10	1, 36	0.923	0.971	0.946	94.840
BHLBP+SVM(Poly)	7, 17	0, 42	52, 53	39, 86	0.944	0.152	0.262	59.709
BHLBP+SVM(RBF)	46, 15	1, 59	51, 31	0, 93	0.966	0.980	0.973	97.467
BHLBP+*MLP*	45, 87	1, 17	51, 78	1, 17	0.975	0.975	0.975	*97.654*

PLBP+SVM(RBF $C \simeq 2.0\ \sigma \simeq 1.23114$), PLBP+*MLP* ($\xi = 6 \times 10^{-2}, \alpha = 0.6$).
BHLBP+SVM(RBF $C \simeq 3.369\ \sigma \simeq 1.23114$), BHLBP+*MLP*($\xi = 6 \times 10^{-2}, \alpha = 0.6$).

The *MLPs* are fully connected and designed with a number of input neurones equal to the length of the descriptors (i.e. PLBP and BHLBP are 390 and 236, respectively). The output vector for positive samples is $\mathbf{Y}_i = (1,0)^T$ and output vector for negative samples is $\mathbf{Y}_i = (0,1)^T$, one hidden layer of 50 neurons for PLBP and one hidden layer of 22 neurons for the BHLBP, have been selected with sigmoid activation function. The *Softmax* function is used in the output layer and the number of output units is equal to the number of classes, which is two for our case. During our experiments, we have tested several neural configuration, varying the number of neurons in the hidden layer. The exposed configurations were found to be a good compromise between classification error minimization and architecture complexity. Regularization terms are used; momentum α and learning rate ξ, in order to improve the convergence velocity and avoid the over-fitting

Table 2. Statistical results on CAS-PEAL database

Approach	TP %	FP %	TN %	FN %	Precision	Recall	$F_1 Score$	Acc (%)
PLBP+SVM(Linear)	45, 26	2, 20	50, 70	1, 82	0.953	0.961	0.957	95.966
PLBP+SVM(Poly)	17, 68	1, 82	51, 07	29, 31	0.906	0.376	0.531	68.761
PLBP+SVM(RBF)	46, 06	1, 17	51, 73	1, 03	0.975	0.978	0.976	**97.795**
PLBP+MLP	45, 77	1, 31	51, 64	1, 26	0.972	0.973	0.972	97.420
BHLBP+SVM(Linear)	44, 55	5, 15	47, 74	2, 53	0.896	0.946	0.920	92.307
BHLBP+SVM(Ploy)	0, 93	0, 79	52, 11	46, 15	0.540	0.019	0.036	53.048
BHLBP+SVM(RBF)	45, 82	2, 48	50, 42	1, 26	0.948	0.973	0.960	*96.247*
BHLBP+MLP	44, 93	2, 48	50, 46	2, 11	0.947	0.955	0.951	95.403

PLBP+SVM(RBF $C \simeq 2.0 \; \sigma \simeq 1.23114$), PLBP+$MLP$ ($\xi = 6 \times 10^{-2}, \alpha = 0.6$).
BHLBP+SVM(RBF $C \simeq 3.369 \; \sigma \sim 1.23114$), BHLBP+$MLP$($\zeta = 6 \times 10^{-2}, \alpha = 0.6$).

problem. The connecting weights are randomly initialized with a very small values, in the range of $(-0.1, 0.1)$. Tables 1 and 2 display the statistical evaluation of our approach on the public BioID and CAS-PEAL-R1 datasets. In the second row of Table 1, the performance assessment of BHLBP with three SVM's kernels (linear, polynomial, RBF) yields a scores of 95.77 %, 78, 79 %, 97.46 % respectively and the score of 97.65 % for the MLP. In the first row of this table, the performance gained by adopting the pyramid transform LBP (PLBP) descriptor are 0.938 %, 19.09 % for the SVM's (linear, polynomial) kernels respectively and 0.469 % with MLP. Table 2 shows the performance of PLBP, BHLBP on the CAS-PEAL-R1 test image set. In the second row of Table 2, the performance of BHLBP evaluated with the SVM(linear, Polynomial, RBF) kernels are 92.3 %, 53.04 %, 96.24 %, respectively. BHLBP/MLP generates an accuracy of 95.403 %. The PLBPs improvements are 3.659 %, 15.713 %, 1.548 % and 2.017 %, corresponding to the evaluation with the SVMs (linear, polynomial, RBF) kernels and the MLP classifiers respectively. The eye localization results are illustrated in Fig. 2, the ground-truth of the real eye location is presented as a red circle, within the pupil radius, different colors correspond to different matching objects, detection results cover the missed positives and false alarms. **The blue rectangle** represents the eye position according to the eye open state and **the red rectangle** corresponds to the eye closed state, both result from the χ^2 measure. The similarity distance is employed to verify the presence of the eye, not its state. **The yellow rectangle** corresponds to false positive resulting from the classification stage and rejected once the similarity is measured, this is considered as an insignificant information by the system. A comparison between our method and the most recent published methods which focus on eyes region detection is listed in Table 3, and it has been demonstrated that proposed approach outperforms the published eye detection methods especially on BioID database.

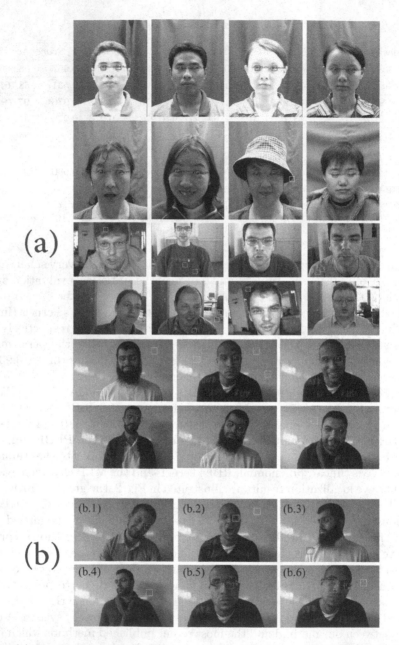

Fig. 2. (a) Snapshots illustrate some successful detection on CAS-PEAL-R1, BioID databases and some pictures captured within the laboratory, (b) Snapshots from captured pictures illustrating some typical failures of our method: In some pictures eyes are completely occulted by strong highlights reflecting into the glasses (b.5, b.6), in some cases our system fails under these circumstance. The eye state could not be reached, due to the missed eye region localization, this is due to occulted eye region (b.4), (b.3) or the failure of the similarity measure (b.2), which is generally caused by the intensity changing, or the output of the classifier. Hence, one eye is not detected at all (b.1).

Table 3. Comparison of the proposed method with existing methods

Eye detection method	Face database	Average detection rate %
Proposed approach	BioID	**98.123**
	1521 images from CAS-PEAL-R1	97.795
Hassaballah et al.[14]	XM2VTS	98.4
	BioID	**97.1**
	1500 images from FERET	97.3
Guan [15]	CVL	96.2
Wang and Yin [16]	JAFFE	95.8
Campadelli et al. [17]	750 images of XM2VTS	95.7
Qiong and Yang [18]	BioID	**95.6**
Peng et al. [19]	ORL	95.2
Wang and Ji [20]	5600 frontal images of FRGC V1.0 database	94.5
Wu and Trivedi [21]	317 images from FERET	94.1

5   Conclusion and Future Works

Eye localization is a crucial step in face recognition and many other applications. However, due to the high degree of appearance variability of the eye, this task is challenging. In this study, we have described an eye localization framework essentially based on appearance statistical approach. The main interest is to evaluate the usefulness of our method in relevant applications such as eye localization for state detection in still monochrome images. Different local binary pattern extensions with pyramidal pre-processing (PLBP) approach are proposed. Textured eye pattern information in spatial pyramid domain can improve the discriminative capability of LBP descriptors. Compared to the conventional block division-based LBP descriptor strategy, PLBP shows its effectiveness for eye appearance description despite arbitrary resolution changes within the image. The PLBP model gives a recognition rate of **98.12** % and **97.79** % on BioID and CAS-PEAL databases, respectively. In the future, the discriminative power of PLBP descriptors can be further improved by a combination with a pre-processed variance LBP pyramid to characterize the local contrast information and to prevent the information loss caused by LBPs. This process does not need quantization step. Furthermore, this work could be extended to track the eye state information, within a video stream to monitor the driver's vigilance while he is conducting a car.

References

1. Benrachou, D.E., Boulebtateche, B., Bensaoula, S.: Gabor/pca/svm-based face detection for drivers monitoring. J. Autom. Control Eng. **1**, 115–118 (2013)
2. González-Ortega, D., Díaz-Pernas, F., Antón-Rodríguez, M., Martínez-Zarzuela, M., Díez-Higuera, J.: Real-time vision-based eye state detection for driver alertness monitoring. Pattern Anal. Appl. **16**(3), 285–306 (2013)

3. Dinges, D.F., Grace, R.: Perclos: a valid psychophysiological measure of alertness as assessed by psychomotor vigilance. Federal Highway Administration. Office of motor carriers. Technical report. MCRT-98-006 (1998)
4. Bourlai, T., Whitelam, C., Kakadiaris, I.: Pupil detection under lighting and pose variations in the visible and active infrared bands. In: 2011 IEEE International Workshop on Information Forensics and Security (WIFS), pp. 1–6. IEEE (2011)
5. Wu, J., Mei, L.: A face recognition algorithm based on asm and gabor features of key points. In: 2012 International Conference on Graphic and Image Processing, pp. 87686L–87686L. International Society for Optics and Photonics (2013)
6. Hollingsworth, K., Clark, S., Thompson, J., Flynn, P.J., Bowyer, K.W.: Eyebrow segmentation using active shape models. In: SPIE Defense, Security, and Sensing, pp. 871208–871208. International Society for Optics and Photonics (2013)
7. Zheng, Y., Wang, Z.: Robust and precise eye detection based on locally selective projection. In: ICPR, pp. 1–4 (2008)
8. Sun, R., Ma, Z.: Robust and efficient eye location and its state detection. In: Cai, Z., Li, Z., Kang, Z., Liu, Y. (eds.) ISICA 2009. LNCS, vol. 5821, pp. 318–326. Springer, Heidelberg (2009)
9. : http://www.bioid.com/downloads/software/bioid-face-database.html
10. Gao, W., Cao, B., Shan, S., Chen, X., Zhou, D., Zhang, X., Zhao, D.: The cas-peal large-scale chinese face database and baseline evaluations. IEEE Trans. Syst. Man Cybern. Part A Syst. Hum. **38**(1), 149–169 (2008)
11. Jian, W., Honglian, Z.: Eye detection based on multi-angle template matching. In: International Conference on Image Analysis and Signal Processing. IASP 2009, pp. 241–244. IEEE (2009)
12. Benrachou, D.E., dos Santos, F.N., Boulebtateche, B., Bensaoula, S.: Online vision-based eye detection: LBP/SVM vs LBP/LSTM-RNN. In: Moreira, A.P., Matos, A., Veiga, G. (eds.) CONTROLO 2014. LNEE, vol. 321, pp. 659–668. Springer, Switzerland (2015)
13. Chang, C.-C., Lin, C.-J.: LIBSVM: a library for support vector machines. ACM Trans. Intell. Syst. Technol. (TIST) **2**(3) (2011)
14. Hassaballah, M., Kanazawa, T., Ido, S.: Efficient eye detection method based on grey intensity variance and independent components analysis. Comput. Vis., IET **4**(4), 261–271 (2010)
15. Guan, Y.: Robust eye detection from facial image based on multi-cue facial information. In: IEEE International Conference on Control and Automation, ICCA 2007, pp. 1775–1778. IEEE (2007)
16. Wang, J., Yin, L.: Eye detection under unconstrained background by the terrain feature. In: IEEE International Conference on Multimedia and Expo ICME 2005, pp. 1528–1531. IEEE (2005)
17. Campadelli, P., Lanzarotti, R.: Fiducial point localization in color images of face foregrounds. Image Vis. Comput. **22**(11), 863–872 (2004)
18. Wang, Q., Yang, J.: Eye detection in facial images with unconstrained background. J. Pattern Recogn. Res. **1**(1), 55–62 (2006)
19. Peng, K., Chen, L., Ruan, S., Kukharev, G.: A robust agorithm for eye detection on gray intensity face without spectacles. J. Comput. Sci. Technol. **5**, 127–132 (2005)
20. Wang, P., Ji, Q.: Multi-view face and eye detection using discriminant features. Comput. Vis. Image Underst. **105**(2), 99–111 (2007)
21. Wu, J., Trivedi, M.M.: A binary tree for probability learning in eye detection. In: IEEE Computer Society Conference on Computer Vision and Pattern Recognition-Workshops. CVPR Workshops, pp. 170–170. IEEE (2005)

Clinical Evaluation of an Automatic Method for Segmentation and Characterization of the Thoracic Aorta with and Without Aneurysm Patients

Juan Antonio Martínez-Mera[1(✉)], Pablo G. Tahoces[1], R. Varela-Ponte[2], Jorge Juan Suárez-Cuenca[2], Miguel Souto[2], and José M. Carreira[2]

[1] CITIUS (Centro de Investigación en Tecnoloxías da Información), Universidad de Santiago de Compostela, Santiago, Spain
juanantonio.martinez@usc.es
[2] Departamento de Radiología, Complejo Hospitalario Universitario de Santiago (CHUS), Santiago de Compostela, Spain

Abstract. The aim of this study was to clinically evaluate a fully automatic method for segmentation and characterizing the thoracic aorta. From 2010 to 2013, a total of 27 patients were randomly selected for the study. The automatic method was compared with two segmentations manually performed by two independent radiologists amd a commercial software for gauging calibres.

The results of the segmentation measurements showed a Dice Similarity Coefficient of 93.98 ± 0.27, a correlation coefficient of 0.875 ± 0.013, and an intraclass correlation coefficient of 0.909 ± 0.011 for both experts. For the diameter measurements, the values were a Pearson's Correlation Coefficient of 0.933, and an intraclass correlation of 0.913. The Bland-Altman plots showed no statistically significant differences between the commercial method and the proposed method.

In conclusion, the method developed is capable of automatically calculating the diameters, and the segmentation of the thoracic aorta.

Keywords: TAA · MDCT · Aneurysm · Diameter · Segmentation · Characterization

1 Introduction

Aneurisms of the thoracic aorta (TAA) occur at an estimated incidence of around $6/100.000$ persons-year. The risk of rupture for untreated large-sized aneurysms is around 74 % with a 90 % mortality rate [1]. The diameter of the aorta on its normal plane must be measured in order to establish a reliable diagnosis.

The diameter can be calculated manually on the basis of the inner lumen [2]. Notwithstanding, the manual process entails several factors that introduce a series of errors that contaminate the measurement process leading to discrepancies between the measured size of the aneurysm and its true size [3], which have

© Springer International Publishing Switzerland 2015
R. Paredes et al. (Eds.): IbPRIA 2015, LNCS 9117, pp. 727–734, 2015.
DOI: 10.1007/978-3-319-19390-8_81

been estimated to be around 5 mm, approximately equivalent to 10 % of total vessel diameter [4].

In order to measure the vessel diameter on the basis of the segmentation performed, it is assumed that the shape of the aorta is circular or elliptic [5]. The manner in which the diameter of the aorta should be calculated is widely agreed upon by the clinical community [6]. That is, the mean value between the maximum and the minimum diameters must be calculated. In this model, maximum refers to the length of the maximum diameter of the aorta, and minimum to the length of the diameter that is perpendicular to this maximum diameter. The methods described in the literature for calculating the maximum diameters on the normal planes are conventionally calculated by undertaking a multi-directional analysis of each plane [7].

The aim of this study was to clinically evaluate an automatic method [8,9] for the segmentation, and characterization of the thoracic aorta.

2   Material

The sample consisted of 17 patients with thoracic aortic aneurisms and 10 without aortic aneurisms (11,583 images) who were examined using a 64-detector row MDCT scanner (Lightspeed VCT; GE Medical Systems, Milwaukee, Wisconsin). To carry out the study an intravenous radiopaque contrast medium was administered prior to image acquisition to enhance lumen visibility.

3   Method

The method developed in this study involved eight basic steps subdivided into two stages: segmentation and characterization.

3.1   Segmentation

Automatic segmentation has been described in detail [8], and consists of the following steps: (1) Image segmentation begins with the most caudal slice in each case using Hough transformation method. To calculate the image in the parameter space (H), we used the convolution of the image of the baseline slice (G) with a circular mask (K) having a radius r, where:

$$H = G \otimes K \tag{1}$$

The radius of the circular mask (r) ranges from a minimum to a maximum radius pre-set for all images.

(2) The previously calculated coordinates are then used as volume growth seed points to segment the descending aorta, aortic arch and a part of the ascending aorta. This volumetric region growing consists of the use of the 17 pixel neighbors corresponding to the previous and current slices for the calculation of the mean and variance. This 17-connectivity restricts region growing in one

direction in the z-axis. **(3)** This segmentation is then used to begin the segmentation of the remaining region of the aorta ascending. To avoid any overlapping in this region, ascending aorta is extracted with the level set algorithm proposed by Malladi [10], where, for segmenting the 2D closed curve corresponding to the aorta in each axial plane, we use a 3D function intersected by a plane at a specific height:

$$\psi_t + F \mid \nabla\psi \mid = 0 \tag{2}$$

where F is the velocity function and it describes the evolution of the curve $\gamma(t)$ along the time:

$$F(x,y) = \{F_0 \nabla \psi_{x,y} + F_c(x',y') \nabla \psi_{x',y'}\}e^{I_i'(x',y')} \tag{3}$$

F_c that lends greater or lesser rigidity to the curve; a translation term F_0 that allows for the curve's displacement across the plane in which it lies; and an energy term that contains the image obtained in the previous process, $I_0(x,y)$.

Manual segmentation was performed by two expert radiologists with 20 years (expert A), and 6 years (expert B) experience in vascular imaging. Manual segmentation was performed on the inner wall of the aorta, and in axial slices. Only 20 % of the slices that correspond to the descending region, and 30 % to the region of the aortic arch were selected. For the ascending region which is the most difficult section to segment as the borders of this section of the aorta are not well defined, 40 % of the whole set of slices where chosen.

3.2 Characterization

The characterization of previous segmentation automatically calculated the diameters of the normal planes. This type of calculus has been previously described by [9], and consisted of the following **(4)**: The centreline was extracted from the previous segmentation. **(5)** The calculated set of centreline datapoints were interpolated with B-Spline curves.

$$s(u) = \sum_{i=0}^{m-n-2} P_i N_i^n(u) \quad u \in [u_{n-1}, u_{m-n}] \tag{4}$$

where m is the number of real values u, n is the degree of *B-Spline*, P_i denotes the selected control points coinciding with the skeleton of the aorta, and N_i^n denotes the piecewise polynomial functions defined by the *Cox-de Bor* recursion formula:

$$N_i^0(u) = \begin{cases} 1 & u_j \leq u \leq u_{j+1} \\ 0 & otherwise \end{cases} \tag{5}$$

$$N_i^n(u) = \frac{u - u_j}{u_{j+n} - uj} \cdot N_j^{n-1}(u) + \frac{u_{j+n+1} - u}{u_{j+n+1} - u_{j+1}} \cdot N_{j+1}^{n-1}(u) \tag{6}$$

(6) Then the slope of the angles on the normal planes were calculated.

$$\alpha_x = \arcsin \frac{|u_x \cdot N_x|}{\sqrt{N_x^2 + N_y^2 + N_z^2}} \tag{7}$$

$$\alpha_y = \arcsin \frac{|u_y \cdot N_y|}{\sqrt{N_x^2 + N_y^2 + N_z^2}} \tag{8}$$

where $u = (u_x, u_y, u_z)$ is the unitary vector in the direction of the axis, and $N = (N_x, N_y, N_z)$ is the normal vector.

Once the angles are obtained, we used rotation matrices to calculate the positions of the planes normal to the container.

$$\begin{bmatrix} x' \\ y' \\ z' \end{bmatrix} = R_x \cdot R_y \cdot R_z \begin{bmatrix} x_0 \\ y_0 \\ z_0 \end{bmatrix} \tag{9}$$

where R_x, R_y and R_z are the rotation matrices about the X, Y and Z axes. As the Z axis is rotation invariant $\alpha_z = 0$, $sin(\alpha_z) = 0$ and $cos(\alpha_z) = 1$.

(7) Finally, the maximum and minimum diameters were calculated using principal component analysis. **(8)** A scale factor that based on spatial orientation was used.

The manual method of measuring the diameter of the aorta was undertaken by the most experienced radiologist using commercial software at the Complejo Clínico Hospitalario de Santiago de Compostela, Spain.

4   Results

4.1   Segmentation Results

All of the cases in this study were manually and automatically segmented. A Bland-Altman plot was used to show the results for the full and partial series of cases (Fig. 1).

The results for the segmentations have undergone several types of comparative analysis. The DSC factor indicates the degree of overlap of the volumes and was defined as:

$$DSC = 2\frac{A \cap B}{A \cup B} \quad DSC_{error} = \frac{2((V(A) - V(B)))}{V(B)} \tag{10}$$

where A and B were the manual and automatic segmentation masks. The DSC factor for the segmentation of radiologist A was: $94.76 \pm 0.43\,\%$ in the descending region, $94.62 \pm 0.60\,\%$ in the aortic arch, and $95.93 \pm 0.40\,\%$ in the ascending region, with a $95.10 \pm 0.28\,\%$ mean coefficient value for the entire thoracic aorta. The mean values for expert B were: $91.52 \pm 0.81\,\%$ in the descending region, $92.72 \pm 0.65\,\%$ in the aortic arch, $94.35 \pm 0.62\,\%$ in the ascending region, with a mean coefficient value of $92.87 \pm 0.41\,\%$ for the entire thoracic aorta.

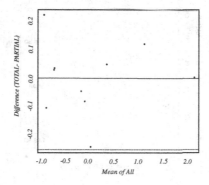

Fig. 1. Bland-Altman graph showing the data comparing the full segmentation of ten cases with the partial random segmentation of expert radiologist A.

For the twenty seven patients analysed, Bland-Altman plots were used to compare the two segmentation methods, in order to ascertain whether they were interchangeable. Bland-Altman plots showed the results obtained when the limit of concordance was set at 95 %, that is, when the concordance-limit values were set by the mean difference ± 1.96 times the standard deviation of the differences (Figs. 2 and 3).

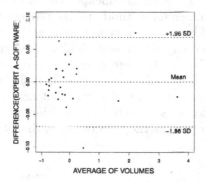

Fig. 2. Bland-Altman graph showing the data obtained from the partial segmentation of 27 cases performed by expert A and the automatic method.

A Pearson's Correlation Coefficient was calculated for each of the aortic regions in each patient: the ascending and descending aorta, and arch. The mean values obtained for each of the regions were: 0.908 ± 0.043 in the descending region, 0.987 ± 0.037 in the aortic arch, and 0.886 ± 0.048 in the ascending region for expert A with a mean value of 0.927 ± 0.015. The values for expert B were 0.870 ± 0.040 for the descending region, 0.974 ± 0.037 for the aortic arch, and 0.831 ± 0.046 for the ascending region with a mean value for the entire aorta of 0.892 ± 0.015.

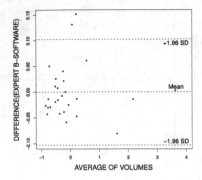

Fig. 3. Bland-Altman graph showing the data obtained from the partial segmentation of 27 cases performed by expert B and the automatic method

Intraclass Correlation Coefficient (ICC) for the descending, arch, and ascending aorta was: 0.844 ± 0.037, 0.971 ± 0.006, and 0.896 ± 0.026, respectively for expert A with a mean value of 0.903 ± 0.016, and 0.793 ± 0.035, 0.918 ± 0.022, 0.827 ± 0.031, respectively for expert B with a mean value of 0.846 ± 0.018.

4.2   Characterization Results

In order to determine statistically significant differences between the diameters calculated using the commercial method and the proposed automatically calculated method, a Bland-Altman plot was used to show the results obtained for the 27 cases assessed in this study. The result obtained with the Bland-Altman plot is shown in the graph (Fig. 4). The agreement limit on the plot was set at 95 %. The standard deviation of the differences was SD=0.37. We have analysed the value of the differences and we have observed that they were normally distributed, so 95 % of the differences expected to lie within the interval. This implied that differences between both methods were within the interval [-0.72, 0.72] mm.

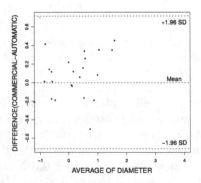

Fig. 4. Bland-Altman graph showing the data obtained from the diameter of 27 cases performed by commercial and automatic method

The value for Pearson's Correlation Coefficient for the diameters was 0.933. This result show a strong correlation between both methods.

The value obtained for the ICC for maximum diameters was 0.913, which illustrates an almost perfect correlation between both measurement methods for the maximum diameters, and a moderate correlation for the minimum diameters.

For Pearson coefficient values and ICC stated as follows: values of 0.40 or below indicating a positive but poor agreement, 0.41-0.60 good agreement; 0.61-0.80 very good agreement, and above 0.80 excellent agreement.

5   Discussion and Results

The aim of this study was to evaluate a previously developed automatic segmentation and characterization algorithm. One of the main characteristics of the method is that it is a fully automatic method. The advantages are threefold: it saves time, the process can be run online without human intervention, and reproducibility is guaranteed.

The Bland Altman plot for 10 cases of full manual random segmentation (Fig. 1), revealed no statistically significant differences, therefore the feasibility of the study using partial manual segmentation was confirmed. As the Bland-Altman graph shows (Figs. 2 and 3), the differences were randomly distributed on both sides of the horizontal axis, the randomness did not vary with sample size; consequently, it neither depended on the size of the aorta, nor on whether it is a normal or a pathological case. The most of the data on the Bland-Altman plot was within the confidence limits, Therefore there were no statistically significant differences between both measurement methods. In terms of linear correlation, the proposed method exhibited a high degree of similarity, given that the mean Pearson's Correlation Coefficient for each of the regions was higher than 0.9 for each region segmented by radiologist A, and almost 0.8 for radiologist B. Moreover, intraclass correlation coefficients ranged from 0.85 to 0.8 in all of the aortic regions for each of the two segmentation methods, these values underscored a strong linear correlation between both segmentation methods. The high degree of linearity was paralleled by a high degree of overlapping (DSC), observed in each of the regions under study. The results showed a very strong similarity among all of the thoracic aortic regions, regardless of the radiologist.

As for the validity of the automatic method for measuring the diameters on the basis of segmentation, the Bland-Altman plot revealed that very few of the measurements obtained with the commercial method overlapped with the measurements of the automatic method. The differences were randomly distributed on either side of the horizontal axis, randomness did not vary with sample size; thus, it neither depended on the size of the diameter nor on whether it was a normal or pathological case. In terms of the linear correlation, the proposed method obtained a high degree of similarity given that the Pearson's Correlation Coefficient was higher than 0.9. Notwithstanding, one should not overlook that the Pearson Correlation Coefficient does not provide information on the agreement observed, since it only measures the linear association of two variables.

Thus, to measure the degree of agreement between two measurements, the ICC were calculated. The ICC average value for the measurement of maximum diameter was 0.913, indicating a strong linear correlation between both segmentation methods.

In conclusion, the method developed in this study was capable of automatically calculating the diameters and segments of the ascending thoracic aorta, the descending aorta, and arch.

References

1. Matsumura, J.S., Cambria, R.P., Dake, M.D., Moore, R.D., Svensson, L.G., Snyder, S.: International controlled clinical trial of thoracic endovascular aneurysm repair with the Zenith TX2 endovascular graft: 1-year results. J. Vasc. Surg. **47**, 247–257 (2008)
2. Garzón, G., Velilla, M.F., Marti, M., Acitores, I., Ybaez, F., Riera, L.: Endovascular stent-graft treatment of thoracic aortic disease. Radiogr. **25**, S229–S244 (2005)
3. Sensier, Y., Akil, Y., Khodabakhsh, P., Naylor, M., Sharpe, R., Walker, J., Hartshorne, T.: The impact of using inner-to-inner wall diameter measurement of abdominal aortic aneurysm. Ultrasound **21**(1), 8–11 (2013)
4. Cayne, N.S., Veith, F.J., Lipsitz, E.C., Ohki, T., Mehta, M., Gargiulo, N., Suggs, W.D., Rozenblit, A., Ricci, Z., Timaran, C.H.: Variability of maximal aortic aneurysm diameter measurements on CT scan: significance and methods to minimize. J. Vasc. Surg. **39**(4), 811–815 (2004)
5. Broeders, I.A.J.M., Blankensteijn, J.D., Olree, M., Mali, W., Eikelboom, B.C.: Preoperative sizing of grafts for transfemoral endovascular aneurysm management: a prospective comparative study of spiral CT angiography, arteriography, and conventional CT images. J. Endovasc. Surg. **4**, 252–261 (1997)
6. Rousseau, H., Chabberta, V., Marachera, M.A., El Aassar, O., Auriol, J., Massabuau, P., Morenoa, R.: The importance of imaging assessment before endovascular repair of thoracic aorta. Eur. J. Vasc. Endovasc. Surg. **38**, 408–421 (2009)
7. Boskamp, T., Math, D., Rinck, D., Link, F., Kummerler, D.B., Phys, D., Stamm, F., Mildenberger, P.: New vessel analysis tool for morphometric quantification and visualization of vessels in CT and MR imaging data sets. Radiogr. **24**, 287–297 (2004)
8. Martínez-Mera, J.A., Tahoces, P.G., Carreira, J.M., Suárez-Cuenca, J.J., Souto, M.: A hybrid method based on level set and 3D region growing for segmentation of thoracic aorta. Comput. Aided Surg. **18**, 109–117 (2013)
9. Martínez-Mera, J.A., Tahoces, P.G., Carreira, J.M., Suárez-Cuenca, J.J., Souto, M.: Automatic characterization of thoracic aortic aneurysms from CT images. Comput. Biol. Med. **57**, 74–83 (2014)
10. Malladi, R., Sethian, J.A., Vemury, B.R.: Shape modeling with front propagation: a level set approach. IEEE Trans. Pattern Anal. Mach. Intell. **17**, 158–175 (1995)

Combined MPEG7 Color Descriptors for Image Classification: Bypassing the Training Phase

Salma Kammoun Jarraya[1](✉), Emna Fendri[2], Mohamed Hammami[2], and Hanêne Ben-Abdallah[1]

[1] FCIT, King Abdulaziz University, Jeddah, Saudi Arabia
{Smohamad1,hbenabdallah}@kau.edu.sa
[2] MIRACL Laboratory, FSS, Sfax University, Sfax, Tunisia
fendri.msf@gnet.tn, Mohamed.Hammami@fss.rnu.tn

Abstract. Although several image classification methods have been proposed in the literature, most of them require an offline training phase to generate appropriate classifiers. In this paper, we show how combining MPEG-7 color descriptors can achieve an accurately image classification while bypassing the training phase. More specifically, we illustrate how the combination of Compact Color, Dominant Color and Color Layout was used to extract Global Similarity feature for input into ascending hierarchical classification. We introduce a weighting process to compute the global similarity from descriptors. Our experimental evaluation of the proposed classification method shows its significant effectiveness and high reliability.

Keywords: Image classification · MPEG-7 color descriptors · Ascending Hierarchical Classification

1 Introduction

Image classification is an important task within the field of content-based image retrieval [1]. It is also a challenging task in various applications, including biomedical imaging, biometry, video surveillance, vehicle navigation, robot navigation, and remote sensing [2]. Furthermore, image classification can be exploited as part of a preprocessing step for many complex computer vision systems like autonomous navigation of blind or vision impaired people [3].

Within this variety of applications, the goal of automatic image classification is to assign a given input image to a category that is most similar. In order to determine the level of similarity, highly discriminative and invariant descriptors must be used to characterize the images. Thus, performance of the image classification process is tightly related to the chosen descriptors. The MPEG-7 standard [4,5] defines multiple visual descriptors (color, texture and shape)among which a few independent descriptors is sufficient to achieve efficient image classification. In [6], the authors have shown that the best descriptors for image classification are Color Layout, Dominant Color, Edge Histogram and Texture Browsing Descriptors.

© Springer International Publishing Switzerland 2015
R. Paredes et al. (Eds.): IbPRIA 2015, LNCS 9117, pp. 735–742, 2015.
DOI: 10.1007/978-3-319-19390-8_82

Once the descriptors have been computed, an automatic image classification method must be applied. The classification methods proposed in the literature can be divided in two categories: The first category uses a supervised learning [7] process such as decisions trees, SVM, etc.; the second category relies on an unsupervised learning technique [8] to determine the image class according to some similarity criteria. This latter category includes k-Nearest Neighbors (K-NN), Ascending Hierarchical Classification (AHC), etc. The method presented in [9] applies SVM on merged Color Layout and Edge Histogram descriptors. Although this method presents a high discriminative process, it suffers from the SVM high processing time.

Focussing on image classification for real-time applications, we impose two requirements on the method: high accuracy and fast computation time. These requirements led us to choose color descriptors (Compact Color, Dominant Color and Color Layout) as input for an unsupervised learning technique for an optimal classification. In fact, unsupervised learning techniques require no learning steps and are able to naturally handle a large number of classes. Among the unsupervised learning techniques, Ascending Hierarchical Classification (AHC) is proven efficient. The herein presented contribution shows how global similarity feature, computed by combining MPEG-7 color descriptors, can achieve an accurate image classification without a training phase.

The rest of this paper is organized as follow: Sect. 2, first, presents the MPEG-7 color descriptors extraction, secondly, it introduces the weighting process to compute global similarity feature and, finishes up by presenting the image classification method. The efficiency and accuracy of the proposed method are illustrated through an experimental evaluation in Sect. 3. Finally, a summary and ongoing works are presented in Sect. 4.

2   Proposed method

The proposed method operates in three steps : the first step extracts the descriptors; the second step computes the Global similarity; and the third step classifies the image. In the following subsections, we describe these steps.

2.1   MPEG-7 Color Descriptor Extraction

MPEG-7 provides seven color descriptors: Compact Color (**CC**), Dominant Color (**DC**) and Color Layout (**CL**) are the most important descriptors for describing the visual content. In the following paragraphs, we present processes to extract these three descriptors.

Extraction of the Compact Color Descriptor. This is a histogram derived descriptor and can provide the global color features when measured over an entire image. It is encoded by the Haar transform and uses the RGB color space uniformly quantified to 255 bins [10,11]. Figure 1 shows the process to generate the CC descriptor vector (64 bits) from a JPEG image.

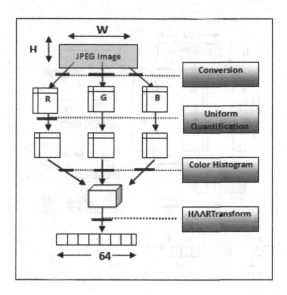

Fig. 1. Process to extract the Compact Color descriptor.

Extraction of the Dominant Color Descriptor. This descriptor gives a description of the representative colors in an image. It consists of the number of dominant colors (N), and a vector of color components(C_i) for each dominant color as well as the percentage of pixels (P_i) in the image in the cluster corresponding to C_i. A more precise characterization of the color distribution can be obtained with color variance and the spatial coherence. The color variance describes the variance of color of the pixels in a cluster around the corresponding representative color. In addition the spatial coherence describes the spatial distribution of pixels associated with each representative color where, in a high value indicates that pixels of similar color are co-located [10–12]. Figure 2 shows the process to generate the DC descriptor vectors from a JPEG image

Extraction of Color Layout Descriptor. The CL descriptor is a very compact and resolution invariant representation of color. It captures the spatial layout of the representative colors on a grid super imposed on an image based on the Discrete Cosine Transform (DCT). It is expressed in the YCbCr color space. The size of the array is fixed to 8 × 8 elements to ensure scale invariance. It is then transformed using DCT followed by zig-zag re-oredering [11,13]. This process is shown in Fig. 3.

2.2 Global Similarity Computation

Combining MPEG-7 color descriptors is achieved through the computation of the Global similarity feature. To compute this feature, we define a weighting process for distance measurement between two images. In fact, we start by computing

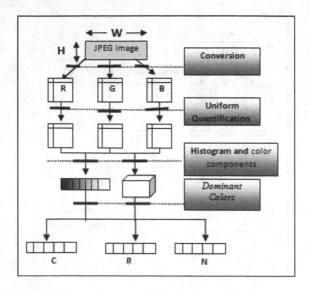

Fig. 2. Process to extract Dominant Color descriptor.

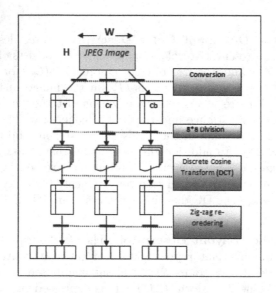

Fig. 3. Process to extract Color Layout descriptor.

images similarities according to each descriptor separately. Afterward, the weighting process is used to combine the output of the last step.

Similarity Measure Based on the Compact Color Descriptor. This descriptor has a vector form of 64 bits. Given two images I_1 and I_2, the distance used to calculate the similarity between them is given by the following equation:

$$dc(I_1, I_2) = \sqrt{\sum_{i=1}^{64} (I_{1i} - I_{2i})^2} \qquad (1)$$

Similarity Measure Based on the Dominant Color Descriptor. The Dominant Color descriptor has the form of eight vectors representing eight dominant colors in an image. It also contains a scalar which corresponds to the spatial coherence (SP) of the color point of view. Given two images I_1 and I_2, the distance used to calculate the similarity between them is the sum of the two distances given by Eq. 2.

$$D(I_1, I_2) = DM\_DIFF(I_1, I_2) + DC\_DIFF(I_1, I_2) \qquad (2)$$

- $DM\_DIFF(I_1, I_2) = |spatial\_coherence(I_2) - spatial\_coherence(I_1)|$
- $DC\_DIFF(I_1, I_2) = \sum_{i=1}^{N_1} \sum_{j=1}^{N_2} a_{1i,2j} P_{1i} P_{2j}$

where: $a_{k,l} = \|c_k - c_l\|$ is the distance between two color components, P_1 percentage vector of I_1, P_2 percentage vector of I_2, and $N_1 = N_2 = 8$.

This distance accounts for all color pairs. For each color pair, the measured distance is weighted by the product of the percentages of its components. These percentages represent the importance of color in each image.

Similarity Measure Based on the Color Layout Descriptor. This descriptor has a three vector forms of 64 values. Let (Y, Cr, Cb) and (Y ', Cr', Cb') be, respectively, pixels' values of two images in YCrCb color. The similarity between these two images is obtained by the sum of three distances given by Eq. 3.

$$dL(I_1, I_2) = dY + dCr + dCb \qquad (3)$$

where: $dY = \sqrt{\sum_{i=1}^{64} (Y_i - Y_i')^2}$,

$dCr = \sqrt{\sum_{i=1}^{64} (Cr_i - Cr_i')^2}$,

$dCb = \sqrt{\sum_{i=1}^{64} (Cb_i - Cb_i')^2}$

Global Similarity Computation Based on CC, DC and CL. Each of the descriptors described above provides information in the form of a digital quantity characterizing each color in the image, independently from the others. Indeed, the compact color descriptor provides comprehensive information regardless of the spatial distribution and unlike the color Layout descriptor which takes into account this feature in the major regions of the image. The dominant color descriptor provides only eight dominant colors in an image.

To quantify these informational variety of descriptions, we propose to compute a weighted sum to provide a single measure of consolidated similarity: Global similarity. The weighting process standardizes the components' distances. Experimental studies on a large database of images allowed us to adjust these weights. Figure 4 illustrates our process to compute a Global similarity based on the MPEG7 color descriptors.

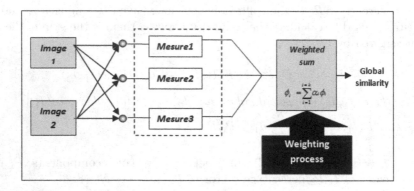

Fig. 4. Flowchart of weighting process.

2.3   Image Classification

Our image classification is based on unsupervised learning called clustering process by Ascending Hierarchical procedures. Let Ω is a set of N Global similarities (W) of N images $(\Omega = W_1, W_2, ..., W_i, ..., W_N)$, the ascending hierarchical clustering procedures start with N distinct clusters of a single image. Theses clusters are the objects of Ω and the dissimilarity distances (W_i^*, W_j^*) (Eq. 4) between all pairs of clusters (W_i, W_j) are the elements of the initial intercluster dissimilarity matrix (M) (Table 1). At each level of the clustering process, the two nearest clusters are joined together A$=(W_i^* \cup W_j^*)$. Thus, the number of clusters decreases by 1 and the dissimilarity between the new cluster (A) and the remaining clusters (B) is calculated according to Eq. 5.

$$d(w_i^*, w_j^*) \leq \min_{w_i, w_j \in M} \{d(w_i, w_j)\} \tag{4}$$

$$\forall (A, B) \in (M)^2; d_2(A, B) = \max_{\substack{\in A \\ \in B}} \{d(x, y)\} \tag{5}$$

Table 1. Distances matrix

$d(W_i,W_j)$	W_1	W_2	W_3	W_4
W_1	0	$d(W_1,W_2)$	$d(W_1,W_3)$	$d(W_1,W_4)$
W_2	$d(W_2,W_1)$	0	$d(W_2,W_3)$	$d(W_2,W_4)$
W_3	$d(W_3,W_1)$	$d(W_3,W_2)$	0	$d(W_3,W_4)$
W_4	$d(W_4,W_1)$	$d(W_4,W_2)$	$d(W_4,W_3)$	0

3   Experimental Results

In order to validate our contributions, we experimentally evaluated the proposed
method to classify images. We used a well-known dataset called COREL1000,
which is frequently applied for the evaluation of image classification methods.
It contains a total of 1000 images classified into 10 classes. The qualitative classification results for significant images are given in Fig. 5 (from 1 to 5). These
results show the robustness of our method. In fact, our method works independently of the variety of images. Quantitatively, our method records a high correct
classification rate of 89 percent. The robustness is shown not only by the correct
classification rate but also by the speed accuracy.

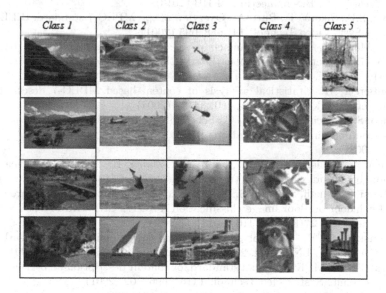

Fig. 5. Classification results : classes from 1 to 5.

4   Conclusion

In this paper, we presented a method for image classification based on the combination of MPEG-7 Compact Color, Dominant Color and Color Layout. From these color descriptors, we defined a weighted process to computed a Global Similarity feature. This feature is used to classify image by ascending hierarchical classification technique.

The proposed method was evaluated by a series of experiments with various images against different classes. We obtained a good compromise between classification and speed accuracy. Future works will focus on evaluating our method for computer vision applications; our method will be used part of the preprocessing step for an autonomous navigation of visually impaired people.

References

1. Datta, R., Joshi, D., Li, J., Wang, J.Z.: Image retrieval: ideas, influences, and trends of the new age. ACM Comput. Surv. **40**(2), 1–60 (2008)
2. Kantorov, V., Laptev, I.: Efficient feature extraction, encoding and classification for action recognition. In: CVPR Conference (2014)
3. Tapu, R., Mocanu, B., Zaharia, T.: A computer vision system that ensure the autonomous navigation of blind people. In: The 4th IEEE International Conference on E-Health and Bioengineering - EHB (2013)
4. Chang, S.F., Sikora, T., Puri, A.: Overview of the MPEG-7 standard. IEEE trans. Circuits Syst. Video Technol. **11**, 688–695 (2001)
5. Abdel-Mottaleb, M., Krishnamachari, S.: Multimedia descriptions based on MPEG-7: extraction and applications. IEEE Trans. Multimed. **6**(3), 459–468 (2004)
6. Eidenberger, H.: Statistical analysis of content-based MPEG-7 descriptors for image retrieval. Multimed. Syst. **10**, 84–97 (2004)
7. Bianco, S., Ciocca, G., Cusano, C., Schettini, R.: Improving color constancy using indoor-outdoor image classification. IEEE Trans. Image Process. **17**(12), 2381–2392 (2008)
8. Vailaya, A., Figueiredo, M.A.T., Jain, A.K., Zhang, H.-J.: Image classification for content-based indexing. IEEE Trans. Image Process. **10**(1), 117–130 (2001)
9. Cvetkovi, S., Nikoli, S.V., Ili, S.: Effective combining of color and texture descriptors for indoor-outdoor image classification. FACTA UNIVERSITATIS Ser. Electron. Energetics **27**(3), 399–410 (2014)
10. Cieplinski, L.: MPEG-7 color descriptors and their applications. In: Skarbek, W. (ed.) CAIP 2001. LNCS, vol. 2124, pp. 11–20. Springer, Heidelberg (2001)
11. Sikora, T.: The MPEG-7 visual standard for content description-an overview. IEEE Trans. Circuits Syst. Video Technol. **11**(6), 696–702 (2001)
12. Tremeau, A., Tominaga, S., Plataniotis, K.N.: Color in image and videoprocessing: most recent trends and future research directions. EURASIP J. Image Video-Process. 2008, (Article ID 581371), 26p (2008)
13. Sripan, T., El-Sharkawy, M., Rizkalla, M.: Fast multiplierless approximation of the DCT for MPEG-7 color layout descriptor. In: Proceedings of the 46th IEEE International Midwest Symposium on Circuits and Systems. MWSCAS 2003, vol. 2, pp. 708–713, 27 January 2004

A Multi-platform Graphical Software for Determining Reproductive Parameters in Fishes Using Histological Image Analysis

J.M. Pintor[1], P. Carrión[1], E. González-Rufino[1], A. Formella[1],
M. Fernández-Delgado[2], E. Cernadas[2](✉), R. Domínguez-Petit[3],
and S. Rábade-Uberos[3]

[1] Universidade de Vigo, Centro de Investigación, Transferencia e Innovación, Parque
Tecnolóxico de Galicia, 32900 Ourense, Spain
[2] CITIUS: Centro de Investigación en Tecnoloxías da Información da USC,
Campus Vida, 15872 Santiago de Compostela, Spain
eva.cernadas@usc.es
[3] Department of Fisheries Ecology, Instituto de Investigacións Mariñas–CSIC, 36208
Vigo, Spain

Abstract. Govocitos is a multi-platform application designed to integrate all processes to estimate the fecundity of fish, a fundamental issue for the management of sustainable fisheries. Govocitos incorporates supervised and unsupervised algorithms to extract oocytes and their features in digitized histological images. Oocytes are classified automatically into the classes used traditionally in studies of reproductive ecology. A database gives support to allow for reproducible data management and to share results among different laboratories. The output of Govocitos has been evaluated through extensive validation procedures and found to be precise and accurate. Govocitos is open source software running on Linux and Windows platforms.

Keywords: Histological image · Fish fecundity · Edge detection · Object recognition · Texture analysis · Classification

1 Introduction

The assessment of fecundity is a fundamental issue in the study of population dynamics of fish species. Fecundity is also important as an indicator of stock production and a reference point for the management of sustainable fisheries [1]. The importance of fecundity for studying reproductive ecology of fish has led to many research efforts to provide simple, fast, and low-cost methods [2]. The main goal is to estimate the number and the size of oocytes in different development stages in the gonad of a female fish. Stereometry [3] is one of the most precise and accurate methods for the task of analyzing histological images. However, it is a very time-consuming procedure and it needs specialized technicians (biologists), which makes difficult its routinely usage. It is based on

© Springer International Publishing Switzerland 2015
R. Paredes et al. (Eds.): IbPRIA 2015, LNCS 9117, pp. 743–750, 2015.
DOI: 10.1007/978-3-319-19390-8_83

the stereological method, which relates tridimensional parameters of a structure with bidimensional measures obtained from sections of the structure.

In the current paper we describe a software proposed by us called Govocitos, which is a multi-platform application that both automatically and semi-automatically recognizes, counts, classifies and measures matured oocytes, and eventually estimates the fecundity from histological images. The use of Govocitos significantly reduces the time a technician needs to employ for the image analysis, makes the results reproducible, and allows not so experienced users to gather statistically relevant fecundity data. To the best of our knowledge, there are no other software tools available that—based on the stereological principle—provide a similar functionality. Govocitos is already installed at the *Instituto de Investigacións Mariñas* (IIM) of the Spanish *Consejo Superior de Investigaciones Científicas* (CSIC) since 2012 with the aim to evaluate the software operating in a real environment.

Section 2 describes the principle software functionality and Sect. 3 shows the results achieved by the software compared to the traditional workflow. The last section provides the main conclusions.

2   Software Description

Govocitos is a multi-platform software written in C++ running on Windows and Linux platforms. Its main purpose is to provide an application to researchers so they can analyze histological images of fish ovarian and estimate the fish fecundity. The input and output data are handled either in a local or in a web-based database.

The software provides a friendly graphical user interface to interactively work with histological images. It uses sophisticated algorithms to automatically recognize and classify the matured oocytes in histological images. The oocytes diameter and their distribution are estimated automatically, facilitating the study of fish reproductive biology (even for less experienced technicians). The underlying database provides the means to share data among researchers from different laboratories and allows to review the results. The use of Govocitos allows for faster and more precise works, overcoming manual or semi-automatic traditional methods. Govocitos has been validated in a real working environment, it is accurate and trustworthy.

The oocyte recognition step segments the histological images automatically into matured oocytes and background. We have tested different segmentation methods: region-based, edge-based, and mixture method [4–6]. This research concluded that histological images are textured and very complex, and that the conventional methods are not robust and general enough to work satisfactory with different fish species and variations in the illumination conditions. In order to overcome these drawbacks, Govocitos uses a multi-scalar Canny filter for the detection of oocyte outlines. The unsupervised edge detection algorithm has two steps: (1) the image is processed by a multi-scalar Canny filter, and (2) an edge analysis step determines which edges are candidates to represent a true oocyte, discarding those outlines which are considered as erroneously detections. In the algorithm for the supervised detection of oocytes, a point inside the true oocyte is provided by the technician to help the edge analysis algorithm.

Once the outlines of matured oocytes are recognized in the histological image, the software can automatically classify the oocytes into classes according to the presence or absence of the nucleus, and into classes according to their development stages, i.e., *cortical alveoli*, *hydrated*, *vitelline*, and *atretic*. Govocitos uses a combination of a Support Vector Machine classifier with First Order Statistics of the color RGB image and the uniform rotation invariant Local Binary Patterns of a grey scale version, because we found in [7] that it provides the best trade-off between computation time and efficiency for both types of classifications. The texture feature vector has only 15 elements. Govocitos provides a functionality to train the classifiers in order to operate with different fish species or sample processing conditions.

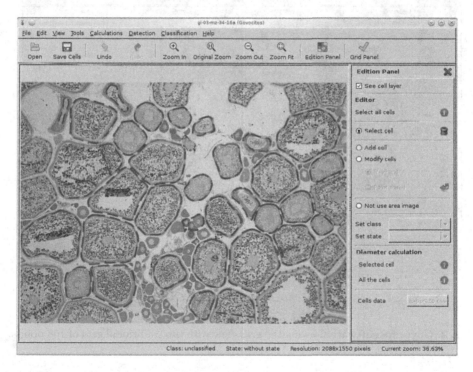

Fig. 1. Screenshot of Govocitos showing the editing view after having performed the automatic recognition and classification steps.

A typical working session for a user employing Govocitos might be as follows. First, the histological images together with other relevant information must be inserted into the database. This step can be performed either with Govocitos or with a web-based interface designed to insert data into the database, which is outside the scope of this paper. The user must configure the colors and line styles for the classes and development stages of each species under study. Then the user opens a histological image and starts the unsupervised detection algorithm to detect the contours of the matured cells. These contours can be edited in the graphical user interface deleting or modifying entirely or partly detected contours. Then, the user can mark with the mouse those oocytes that have not been recognized by the automatic detection algorithm, and re-start this process using the marked points as clues to detect the cell outlines and to discard false outlines. The supervised version of the algorithm will try to provide the outlines of the annotated oocytes as well. After this, the user can edit again the results using the editing view (Fig. 1).

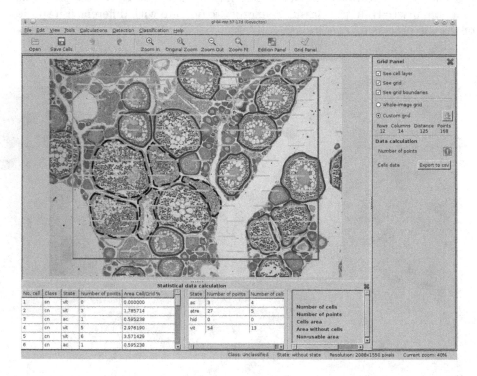

Fig. 2. Govocitos software showing the grid view with the traditional grid of 168 points.

This process is repeated for all images belonging the same fish. The access to the database supports the user in this task. Once the technician considers that the outlines of all mature oocytes are correctly outlined, either by the automatic detection alone or by the user supervision (marking points inside undetected cells and running again the automatic detection, or marking the outline of undetected cells in the editing panel), Govocitos automatically classifies them according to the presence/absence of nucleus, and to the corresponding development stage. Here as well, the classes and stages can be manually modified or re-assigned in the edition panel if necessary. Govocitos computes and displays the mean diameters and areas for the selected classes and stages, and it stores the data in files or in the database for further analysis, including the outlines and classifications of the matured oocytes in the histological image. This last feature is specially important to develop a reliable fecundity estimation and to make the entire process reproducible.

To estimate fecundity, the user opens all the processed images of an individual fish, just by clicking in the specimen identification code. The estimation is either based on the traditional 168 points hexagonal grid covering only the central area of the image (see Fig. 2) or with a custom grid configured with Govocitos, e.g., by specifying the number of points and their in between distance. Moreover, Govocitos allows to estimate the fecundity based on the entire image, i.e., considering all pixels as the Weibel grid area. Govocitos estimates the partial areas of each oocyte in all maturity stages counting all pixels occupied by each of them. Unlike the traditional method, which uses a fixed-size grid, Govocitos allows to use other grid sizes, providing more precise fecundity estimations almost instantaneously (about 2 s). Figure 3 shows the fecundity view, which computes and visualizes histograms of the diameter distribution by class and stage. All data are stored in the database and reports are easily generated.

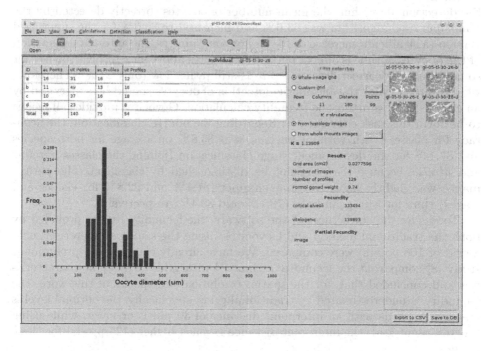

Fig. 3. Fecundity view of the Govocitos graphical user interface.

3   Software Validation

The validation of Govocitos took place in the *Instituto de Investigacións Mariñas* (IIM), a real environment where a network version of Govocitos was installed and evaluated comparing its results and the results generated manually using the traditional method. The biologists of the IIM used Govocitos in their daily work to calculate the fecundity, for which they need to recognize and classify all matured oocytes in quite a large set of histological images. Their operations in the Govocitos graphical user interface were logged in files for a later statistical evaluation. The samples were prepared using standard histological procedures to section the ovaries. The sections had been stained with haematoxylin–eosin and captured using a LEICA equipment at a spatial resolution of $1.09\,\mu m$ with automatically set exposure time and color balance. The fish species handled were the European hake (*Merluccius merluccius*) and lane snapper (*Lutjanus synagris*). A total of 61 images belonging to 8 fishes of European hake (31 images) and 8 to lane snapper (30 images) were analyzed. A total of 2405 oocytes were detected and classified (1186 for European hake and 1219 for lane snapper).

Assuming that the manually generated data were correct, the following results have been obtained for the automatic process in Govocitos. In relation to the detection algorithm, the mean number of oocytes correctly detected by the non-supervised algorithm was 63.6 % and increased to 80.0 % for the supervised version (a significant increase of 16 %). For some images, the automatic detection of the oocytes outline is almost perfect (with rates above 95 %). Nevertheless, for some others the correct detection rate is still rather low (only 27 %). Therefore, we recommend that the automatic detection of oocytes should be supervised by an expert before starting the fecundity calculation. Govocitos provides all means to perform this task conveniently. Regarding the oocyte classification, the accuracy for classes (with/without nucleus) was 83.8 % on average for both species and 87.1 % for the development stage classification (joining the classes *vitteline* and *atretic*, because they can not be distinguished by classifier). The performance was slightly higher for lane snapper (81.4 % and 92.8 % for classes and stages) than for European hake (78.1 % and 89.4 %, respectively).

To ensure the correctness of the software, the fecundity results provided by both the traditional method and Govocitos (using the same parameter set, e.g., a grid of 168 points) were compared. We have already elaborated a preliminary study [8] comparing the fecundity estimated with grids of different characteristics and concluded that, for the spatial resolution and species of this work, the fecundity is underestimated by traditional grids: specifically, the optimal level is reached for grids with an interpoint distance of 30 pixels or lower, while using the 168-point grid, the interpoint distance is much higher (125 pixels) for these images.

The time needed by the technicians to analyze each fish is difficult to determine in general, due to the performance variability of the automatic recognition algorithm among samples and the necessary supervision by the expert. The automatic recognition of oocytes takes less than one minute on a common personal computer for an image with 1550×2088 pixels. The automatic classification step takes about 1 s. So, the overall processing time is dominated by the time needed to modify and/or add the miss-detected and miss classified oocytes in the sample. Once the oocytes are detected and classified in the image, the diameters, areas and fecundity estimations are obtained almost instantaneously (about 2 s). As well, Govocitos integrates other laboratory tasks into a single program and it allows to review the intermediate results each time. Hence, it avoids repetitions of a complete analysis whenever the results appear not to be adequate and suspected to be incorrect. Anyway, for most of the images the automatic computation of diameter, profile histograms and fecundity is precise enough, alleviating the expert's daily work and making it easy to carry out studies of fish reproductivity by non-expert technicians.

4   Conclusions

Govocitos offers an easy and automatic way to estimate fish fecundity based on the traditional stereological method: use of a grid of points defined by the user, counting of points and objects inside the grid, estimation of stereological parameters, partial areas and volumes and estimation of potential fecundity and partial fecundity (for each development stage). Besides, Govocitos autamatically detect the outlines of oocytes in the histological images, classifies oocytes based on the presence/absence of nucleus as well as its development stage, calculates ooll diameters, areas and roundness, builds diameter frequency histograms, and exports data for later analysis, integrating all these tasks in a single application. In addition, Govocitos provides the possibility of varying the grid characteristics; even more, it allows using all pixels of the image as grid points increasing the accuracy of the calculation of partial areas of different objects within the image. Further, it allows checking and reviewing the calculations whenever convenient. Automatic recognition and classification of oocytes can be interactive supervised by experts using the Govocitos GUI. While the automatic oocyte detection is accurate enough for most images, for some others it may require further supervision of a technician (semi-automatic detection).

Govocitos works automatically, manually, or semi-automatic, as well as in local or networked way. In summary, Govocitos is an easy-to-use software (even for less experienced personnel) that facilitates laboratory routines for studying fish reproductive ecology. It can be trained for working with different fish species. It is free software available from http://lia.ei.uvigo.es/daeira that can be easily used after a short training period offering the same or even better performance than other expensive and complex image analysis software tools.

Acknowledgments. This investigation was partly supported by the Xunta de Galicia (regional government) project PGIDIT08MMA010402PR and partly executed at the *Centro de Investigación, Transferencia e Innovación (CITI)* in Ourense, Spain.

References

1. Hunter, J.R., Macewicz, J., Lo, N.C.H., Kimbrell, C.A.: Fecundity, spawning, and maturity of female Dover sole, Microstomus pacificus, with an evaluation of assumptions and precision. Fish. Bull. **90**, 101–128 (1992)
2. Murua, H., Kraus, G., Saborido-Rey, F., Witthames, P., Thorsen, A., Junquera, S.: Procedures to estimate fecundity of marine fish species in relation to their reproductive strategy. J. Northwest Atlantic Fish. Sci. **33**, 33–54 (2003)
3. Emerson, L.S., Greer-Walker, M., Witthames, P.R.: A stereological method for estimating fish fecundity. J. Fish Biol. **36**, 721–730 (1990)
4. Alén, S., Cernadas, E., Formella, A., Domínguez, R., Saborido-Rey, F.: Comparison of region and edge segmentation approaches to recognize fish oocytes in histological images. In: Campilho, A., Kamel, M.S. (eds.) ICIAR 2006. LNCS, vol. 4142, pp. 853–864. Springer, Heidelberg (2006)
5. Anta, P., Carrión, P., Formella, A., Cernadas, E., Domínguez, R., Saborido-Rey, F.: Combining region and edge information to extract fish oocytes in histological images. In: 7th IASTED International Conference on Visualization, Imaging and Image Processing, pp. 82–87 (2007)
6. Cernadas, E., Carrión, P., Formella, A., Domínguez, R., Saborido-Rey, F.: Recognize and classify fish oocytes in histological images. In: 8th IASTED International Conference on Visualization, Imaging and Image Processing, pp. 180–186 (2008)
7. González-Rufino, E., Carrión, P., Cernadas, E., Fernández-Delgado, M., Domínguez-Petit, R.: Exhaustive comparison of colour texture features and classification methods to discriminate cells categories in histological images of fish ovary. Pattern Recogn. **46**, 2391–2407 (2013)
8. Dominguez-Petit, R., Pintor Freire, J.M., Rábade, S., Fabeiro, M., Dacal Nieto, A., Carrión, P., Rufino, N., Cernadas, E., Fernández-Delgado, M., Dominguez-Vázquez, D., Saborido-Rey, F., Formella, A.: New automatic software tool to estimate fish fecundity based on image analysis. In: Fish Reproduction and Fisheries (2011)

Author Index

Printed in the United States
By Bookmasters